monitoring the future

questionnaire responses from the nation's high school seniors

1983

Lloyd D. Johnston, Jerald G. Bachman, and
Patrick M. O'Malley

Survey Research Center • Institute for Social Research
The University of Michigan
Ann Arbor, Michigan

ISR Code Number 4653
ISSN 0190-9185
ISBN 0-87944-300-6
Library of Congress Catalog Card Number 79-640937

Published in 1984 by:
Institute for Social Research,
The University of Michigan, Ann Arbor, Michigan

6 5 4 3 2 1

Printed in the United States of America

Table of Contents

Preface

This volume is the latest in a series which presents descriptive statistical results from a national survey of young people entitled Monitoring the Future: A continuing Study of the Lifestyles and Values of Youth. Each year the study surveys a large sample of high school seniors, located in approximately 125 schools nationwide, and drawn to be representative of all seniors in the coterminous United States.

The first four volumes in this series, dealing with the high school classes of 1975, 1976, 1977, and 1978 were published simultaneously early in 1980. Additional volumes appear on an annual basis. The most important contribution of this series is likely to be the opportunity it provides for the exploration of trends, a process that obviously involves the use of several different volumes. With that in mind, we have kept the format highly consistent from one volume to another, and we have developed an index (described below) which should facilitate the process of matching data across years. It should be noted that the volume presenting 1975 data is different from the others in several respects.*

Although we designed the volumes to fit together as a series, we also saw distinct advantages in having each volume able to stand alone — to be usable without reference to any of the others. For that reason, the introductory material on research design and questionnaire content, the instructions for accessing the data tables, and the appendices on sampling errors are all included in each volume. Thus, the small price we pay for making each volume self-contained is that much of the text portion is repeated each year.

Purposes of this Series of Publications

Monitoring the Future, which is conducted by the University of Michigan's Institute for Social Research and receives its core funding from the National Institute on Drug Abuse, is an unusually comprehensive research project in several respects: surveys are conducted annually on an ongoing basis; the samples are large and nationally representative; and the subject matter is very broad, encompassing some 1,300 variables per year. Many people — scholars, policy makers, educators, and so on — will have an interest in the results.

The principal investigators are already writing for a number of these audiences and will continue to do so. Because of the limitations in our own time, interests, and expertise, however, there is an enormous amount of valuable information which may never be utilized if the initiative to digest and disseminate all of it must come from us alone. Further, since the project is in part a social indicator series, its value rests to a considerable degree on *timely* dissemination of the results. For these reasons, we wish to share the study's results with others in a number of fields on a rapid and regular basis. We have chosen to provide two major and complementary vehicles for doing this: (a) these annual reference volumes of descriptive results, and (b) machine-readable data archives for direct analysis by others.

We believe that many potential users who would not mount the effort required to conduct computer analyses of archived data will be able to get most of

---

*The 1975 volume does not include comparison data for black and white subgroups, nor does it include data for the subgroups who did and did not plan to complete four years of college. Also, somewhat fewer questionnaire items appear than in the other volumes. These restrictions are the result primarily of missing data problems that occurred only in the 1975 survey. In most respects, however, those seeking to compare different classes of high school seniors will find the 1975 data useful.

what they want from these volumes of descriptive results. The user of any one of these volumes can estimate — usually with considerable accuracy — a wide variety of characteristics of the high school class described in that volume. To take just one example, the user of the 1978 volume can ascertain that 50.2 percent of seniors in the high school class of 1978 reported using marijuana at least once during the preceding year. Further, by utilizing two or more of these volumes the reader can describe recent trends in any such characteristic. To continue with the same example, the volume describing the high school class of 1975 indicates that 40.0 percent of these seniors reported marijuana use during the preceding year; and when that is combined with the data from the 1978 volume the reader is able to discern a shift of 10.2 percent over the three years between the classes of 1975 and 1978. And if all of the first four volumes in the series are used, one can observe a steady increase in the proportion of high school seniors who report having used marijuana at least once during the twelve months preceding the survey:

> 40.0 percent of seniors in 1975
> 44.5 percent of seniors in 1976
> 47.6 percent of seniors in 1977
> 50.2 percent of seniors in 1978

A similar examination of trends can be carried out for over 1,300 different variables dealing with a wide variety of subject areas (listed in Table 2 of the Introduction). A simple indexing system (described below) has been developed which makes it quite straightforward for the reader wishing to do trend analyses to locate the results for a given question for any year of the study. The index in the present volume lists the location of all items included in the surveys from 1976 onward, as well as most items included in 1975.

Analyses such as those illustrated above need not be limited to the total sample. The data provided in these volumes also permit examination of a variety of subgroups (e.g., males, females, those from different regions, those with different levels of drug use experience).

We recognize that providing ready access to essentially undigested data carries certain risks, particularly the risk of mistaken interpretations based on inadequate controls, lack of awareness of sample limitations, etc. More than offsetting the risks, in our view, are the advantages of prompt and widespread dissemination of these nationally representative survey indicator data. Although we are unable to eliminate the risks, we hope to reduce them by providing the reader with an extensive list of caveats presented at the end of the Introduction section. We ask all who use the data to read these caveats carefully and take them seriously.

A Guide for the Reader

This volume is divided into three main parts: (1) the introductory section, (2) the section giving the descriptive results from the current year's survey, and (3) the cross-time item reference index.

Introductory Section. The introduction contains a description of the study — its purposes, major content areas, design, field procedures, response rates, and methods of publication and data dissemination. Since most of this material remains unchanged from year to year, anyone having read another of the volumes may wish to skim this section. We do, however, suggest reviewing the caveats, located at the end of the introductory section, which deal with interpreting and extrapolating from these data.

Descriptive Results Section. In this section all questions contained in this year's survey are presented along with percentagized frequency distributions of answers for the entire sample and for selected subgroups. The questions in this section are organized according to the number of the questionnaire form in which they were contained (forms one through five) and according to the order in which the questions occurred. There is one important exception, however. A major segment of questions common to all five forms of the questionnaire (dealing with drug use, background characteristics, and some other subjects) is presented only once, at the beginning of the Descriptive Results section, using the data from respondents on all five forms.

The first portion of the descriptive results section contains detailed definitions of all subgroups for whom data are presented. It also describes the statistical conventions used in generating the tables.

Cross-Time Index of Questionnaire Items. Beginning with the 1982 volume, this index is ordered by subject area. (It was ordered by item reference number prior to 1982.) The index is intended to serve two purposes.

First, it should be useful in locating items dealing with a subject area of interest. The subject area key at the beginning of the cross-time item index shows the alphabetical code assigned to various subject areas (e.g., "politics" or "work and leisure"). Having selected a subject area of interest, one can then go to that section of the index to locate all questions in any of the surveys which deal with that subject. (The procedure is slightly different in volumes prior to 1982, as described in those volumes.) To locate the results for any given question in this volume, simply look in column two of the item index for its page location.

The cross-time index can also be used to determine in which other years an item was used and where to locate it. If, in reviewing the Descriptive Results section, one locates an interesting item and would like to know in which of the other annual surveys of seniors it has appeared, it may be found in the cross-time index by the unique "item reference number" within the relevant subject area. The index will indicate all years in which that same item appeared and show the questionnaire form, section, and item number for each year. This information thus can be used to decide which other volumes in this series might be of relevance; and the same item may be readily located by its reference number in the index of any other volume prior to the 1982 volume, and by its subject area and reference number in any volume from 1982 on.

Sampling Appendices. Appendix A is provided for those wishing to determine the confidence limits around a percentage estimate, or to test the statistical significance of an observed difference between two groups, or to test the significance of a change from one year to another. It gives the necessary procedures and tables for such tests and provides the appropriate factors by which to correct for the fact that the study makes use of a multi-stage probability sample clustered in a limited number of schools (usually about 125). Appendix B provides further detail on sample design effects and the procedures which were used to derive the sampling error estimates.

Availability of Archived Data

As was mentioned earlier, this series of volumes is complemented by an archiving of the raw data set for direct analysis by others not associated with the project. The present volumes should be a considerable help to those wishing to access the archived data since they provide a verbatim statement of items and answer categories, and also because they include basic univariate and bivariate frequency distributions for all items, as well as the missing data rates. The cross-time index of items contained in each of these volumes also provides an efficient way to identify the relevant variables in various content areas, as well as to determine when they were measured and their questionnaire locations. In fact, we hope that the availability of this series will not only facilitate the use of the archived data but actually stimulate interest in their use.

The individual level data which are summarized in this and previous volumes are available from:

The Interuniversity Consortium for Political
and Social Research (ICPSR)
Institute for Social Research
P.O. Box 1248
Ann Arbor, Michigan 48106

The ICPSR archive makes individual-level data available to interested investigators for analysis. A few variables have been modified or deleted to ensure that the answers of an individual respondent cannot be located through pattern recognition (i.e., using various descriptor variables in combination to make a unique identification). The changed or deleted variables include month of birth, race, and the sampling weight, which adjusts for selection probability.

Other Publications from the Study

A number of different forms of publications based on Monitoring the Future data have been developed or are being planned. One series of reports, dealing with trends in drug use and drug-related attitudes and beliefs, is being published by the National Institute on Drug Abuse. The first report in that series, *Drug Use Among American High School Students 1975-1977* (Johnston, Bachman, and O'Malley), was published in late 1977. Subsequent reports have been issued annually.

An Occasional Paper series has been launched by the project. It includes papers on design and methodological issues as well as special substantive analyses and early, and sometimes more detailed, drafts of articles planned for journal publication. The first occasional paper, "The Monitoring the Future Project Design and Procedures" (Bachman and Johnston, 1978), provides a detailed description of the study and its underlying rationale.

The present series of reference volumes is being published by the Institute for Social Research. A new volume will be added to this series each year.

To request particular papers, reprints, or periodic notification of publications available from the study, write to Monitoring the Future, Room 2030, Institute for Social Research, The University of Michigan, Box 1248, Ann Arbor, Michigan 48106.

---

*Single copies of these reports may be ordered without cost from the National Clearinghouse for Drug Abuse Information, National Institute on Drug Abuse, 5600 Fishers Lane, Rockville, Maryland 20857. See References for a complete list of reports.

Acknowledgements

A great many people have contributed to the launching and development of this research effort. We are indebted to a number of officials of the National Institute on Drug Abuse and the Special Action Office for Drug Abuse Prevention for their encouragement and advice at the outset — in particular, Richard Bucher, Robert DuPont, William Pollin, and Louise Richards.

Our colleagues at the Institute for Social Research and elsewhere who shared their insights, and often their most cherished instrumentation, are too numerous to mention; but their contributions are greatly appreciated. To the former director of the Survey Research Center's Sampling Section, Irene Hess, and to her colleagues we owe a particular debt for the creativity of the sampling design for the study. The contributions of the SRC Field Section also have been very valuable.

Major contributions to the production of this particular volume were made by staff members Jerome Hiniker, Dawn Bare, and Deborah Poinier. We would also like to thank the staff of the Publishing Division of the Institute for Social Reserch for their work in arranging publication.

The present and former members of the project staff (listed below) have, of course, contributed greatly to the building of this large and complex research series.

Finally, we would like to acknowledge the tens of thousands of high school seniors, their teachers, and their principals, whose cooperation and generous contributions of time make the Monitoring the Future project possible.

Lloyd D. Johnston
Jerald G. Bachman
Patrick M. O'Malley

Present and Former Members of the Project Staff

Donna Ando	Michael Fisher	Marion Morse
Margaret Bailey	Henry Freeman	Jim Neveaux
Dawn Bare	Walter Gruhn	Dorothy Paulette
Ellen Berger	James Hersey	Susan Pauls
Mary Lou Bewley	A. Regula Herzog	Sharon Pietila
Katherine Blatt	Jerome Hiniker	Joseph Pleck
Mary Lea Bonucchi	Pamela Kittel	Deborah Poinier
Marcy Breslow	Mark Krell	Judith Redmond
Susan Burek	Sally Lawson	Barbara Renaud
Mary Danneffel-Mashruwala	Ludmilla Litus	Don Rubinstein
Mary Lou Davis	A. Kathryn Loker	Maria Sanchez
Mary Dempsy	Regina Lumbard	Tina Smith
William Diedrich	Mary Lutz	Ann Taylor
Karen Donahue	Oksana Malanchuk	Richard Taylor
Leslie Eveland	Wayne McCulloch	Lynda Tolen
Halford Fairchild	Joan McGraw	Sandra Wronski
Marjorie Fisher	John Miller	Thelma Wurzelbacher

Introduction

The Monitoring the Future project is designed to explore changes in many important values, behaviors, and lifestyle orientations of contemporary American youth. Two general types of tasks may be distinguished. The first is to provide a systematic and accurate *description* of the youth population of interest in a given year, and to quantify the direction and rate of the changes taking place among them over time. The second task, more analytic than descriptive, involves the *explanation* of the relationships and trends observed to exist.

The task of description may be subdivided into three parts: (1) the description of static conditions (which may be accomplished through a single cross-sectional study); (2) the description of cross-cohort or, in longer time-spans, generational changes (usually accomplished using repeated cross sections of the same age groups); and (3) the description of changes with aging (usually accomplished by means of longitudinal studies). The Monitoring the Future project has the capacity to provide each of these three types of description, since it incorporates all three types of research design into a single study. (This complex design, in which multiple cohorts are followed longitudinally, has been referred to as a cohort-sequential design.)

The content of this volume exemplifies the first of these types of description in that it contains cross-sectional data on a single high school class. When the data in this volume are used in combination with data from other such volumes in the series, the nature, direction, and rates of change from one cohort of seniors to another also may be described — the type of reporting which is often labeled as the social indicator approach. The third class of description — dealing with the maturational changes which occur during the years after high school — will not be dealt with in this series of volumes but will be reported in other publications from the study.*

The accurate characterization of American young people and the description of important changes occurring among them is but one class of objectives for the study. The second class of objectives involves the development of a greater understanding of what causes these young people to be as they are, and why the changes being documented are occurring. Explanation will be sought through both the analysis of change at the aggregate level and at the individual level. The results of these explorations will be disseminated via the various publications discussed in the Preface.

The merging of the social indicator approach and the analysis of relationships (particularly longitudinal relations) into a single cohort-sequential design is, in our view, synergistic: the effectiveness of the two approaches combined is greater than if the two were undertaken separately. Because the present series of volumes deals with senior year data only, our remarks here focus primarily on the project's social indicator contributions — the accurate description of high

---

* Panels of students from each graduating class are being randomly selected and followed longitudinally for up to ten years. Thus it soon will be possible to characterize the changes which seem to take place consistently with aging during the early adult years. Not only will longitudinal development in the years after high school be studied, but once enough of these longitudinal panels have accumulated, it will also be possible to characterize cross-sectionally most American young people aged 18 to 28, (at least the major segment of the population who completed high school — roughly 80-85 percent), and to describe the changing characteristics of that age group each year.

school seniors and the documentation of trends over time. It is worth noting, however, that even the limited amount of bivariate data included in the present volumes will suggest promising directions for relational analyses, many of which can be carried out using the archived data tapes from the project.

The Need for Social Indicators

The fundamental argument for developing social indicators is that there are considerable scientific and practical benefits derived from having accurate information about current social realities and the way those realities have been changing. For the scientific community such indicators provide a rich set of information against which existing theory may be tested and from which new theory may be suggested. For the community at large, social indicators permit the "reality testing" of common perceptions and beliefs about the nation and its people. Past experience has demonstrated that widely held conceptions, which themselves may serve to create or exacerbate problems, can be most inaccurate. One example is the exaggerated popular conception of the size and nature of the "gap" between generations (see Adelson, 1970, 1979); another is the mistaken assumption that most young people condone the use of a variety of illegal drugs (Johnston, 1973; Johnston, Bachman, and O'Malley, 1977; 1979 a, b; 1981).

While deflating exaggerated perceptions, a continual monitoring of indicators on youth also can reveal the beginning of new problems and thus give rise to corrective efforts at a relatively early stage. For instance, most would view with concern the emergence of new types of drug use. Monitoring the Future has already documented and reported a sharp increase in regular marijuana use among high school seniors, and as a result more attention has been paid to the issue by policy makers, the media, and the general public. The discovery of such trends may trigger more intense efforts to discover the causes, consequences, and (when appropriate) preventatives of such behaviors.

Although social indicators seldom translate directly into specific policy decisions, the availability of descriptive information can substantially enhance the decision-making capabilities of policy makers. These data provide considerable insight into the size and nature of problems, the rate of change occurring nationally and in subgroups, and in some instances information about related factors and even the likely impacts of major social interventions (such as changed drug laws, or new incentives for recruitment into the military, to name but two). They also provide the possibility of feedback on the consequences of some social interventions as well as major historical events.

The particular topics included in our monitoring system are summarized later in this introduction and, of course, they are presented fully in the complete set of data tables. For present purposes, it is enough to indicate that the range of topics is very broad. This breadth is partly due to the wide interests of the principal investigators; but it also reflects our conviction that the concurrent examination of trends in a variety of areas is not only much more cost efficient but also more scientifically productive.

Research Design and Procedures*

The basic research design involves annual data collections from high school seniors during the spring of each year, beginning with the class of 1975. Each data collection takes place in approximately 125 public and private high schools selected to provide an accurate cross section of high school seniors throughout the coterminous United States. The design also provides for the longitudinal study of a subsample from each class of participating seniors; but since the focus of this series of volumes is exclusively on the data collected annually from seniors, the follow-up procedures will not be discussed here.

Reasons for Focusing on High School Seniors. There are several reasons for choosing the senior year of high school as an optimal point for monitoring the behaviors and attitudes of youth. One is that the completion of high school represents the end of an important developmental stage in this society, since it demarcates both the end of universal public education and, for many, the end of living in the parental home. Therefore, it is a logical point at which to take stock of the accumulated influences of these two environments on American youth.

Further, the completion of high school represents the jumping off point from which young people diverge into widely differing social environments, including college, business firms, military service, and homemaking. But these environmental transitions are not the only important changes which coincide with the end of high school. Most young men and women now reach the formal age of adulthood shortly before or after graduation; more significantly, they begin to assume adult roles, including financial self-support, marriage, and parenthood.

Finally, there are some important practical advantages to building a system of data collections around samples of high school seniors. The last year of high school constitutes the final point at which a reasonably good national sample of an age-specific cohort can be drawn and studied economically. The need for systematically repeated, large-scale samples from which to make reliable estimates of change requires

*A more extensive description of the research design and procedures may be found in Bachman and Johnston (1978).

that considerable stress be laid on efficiency and feasibility; the present design meets those requirements.

One limitation in the design is that it does not include in the target population those young men and women who drop out of high school before graduation (or before the last few months of the senior year, to be more precise). This excludes a relatively small proportion of each age cohort — between 15 and 20 percent (Dearman and Plisko, 1982) — though not an unimportant segment, since we know that certain behaviors such as illicit drug use (Johnston, 1973) and delinquency (Bachman, O'Malley, and Johnston, 1978) tend to be higher than average in this group. However, the addition of a representative sample of dropouts would increase the cost of the present research enormously, because of their dispersion and generally higher level of resistance to being located and interviewed.

For the purposes of estimating characteristics of the entire age group, the omission of high school dropouts does introduce certain biases; however, their small proportion sets outer limits on the bias (Johnston, O'Malley, and Eveland, 1975, Appendix B). For the purposes of estimating *changes* from one cohort of high school seniors to another, the omission of dropouts represents a problem only if different cohorts have considerably different proportions who drop out. We have no reason to expect dramatic changes in those rates for the foreseeable future, and recently published government statistics indicate a great deal of stability in dropout rates since 1970 (Dearman and Plisko, 1982, p. 4).

Some may use our high school data to draw conclusions about changes for the entire age group. While we do not encourage such extrapolation, we suspect that the conclusions reached often would be valid, since over 80 percent of the age group is in the surveyed segment of the population *and* we expect that change among those not in school are very likely to parallel the changes among those who are. Nevertheless, for purposes of characterizing the entire age group we would urge the user to check the results emanating from the present monitoring system against those emerging from other data collection systems using different methods, such as household interviews. (It is encouraging to note that when we have compared drug use data for this age group from the present study with those from interview studies, the findings have shown a high degree of similarity.)

Sampling Procedures. The procedure for securing a nationwide sample of high school seniors is a multistage one. Stage 1 is the selection of particular geographic areas, Stage 2 is the selection of one or more high schools in each area, and Stage 3 is the selection of seniors within each high school.

Stage 1: Geographic Areas. The geographic areas used in this study are the primary sampling units (PSUs) developed by the Sampling Section of the Survey Research Center for use in the Center's nationwide interview studies. These consist of 74 primary areas throughout the coterminous United States — including the 12 largest metropolitan areas, which contain about 30 percent of the nation's population. Of the 62 other primary areas, 10 are in the Northeast, 18 in the North Central area, 24 in the South, and 10 in the West. Because these same PSUs are used for personal interview studies by the Survey Research Center (SRC), local field representatives can be assigned to administer the data collections in practically all schools.

Stage 2: Schools. In the major metropolitan areas more than one high school is often included in the sampling design; in most other sampling areas a single high school is sampled. In all cases, the selections of high schools are made such that the probability of drawing a school is proportionate to the size of its senior class. The larger the senior class (according to recent records), the higher the selection probability assigned to the high school. When a sampled school is unwilling to participate, a replacement school as similar to it as possible is selected from the same geographic area.

Stage 3: Students. Within each selected school, up to about 400 seniors may be included in the data collection. In schools with fewer than 400 seniors, the usual procedure is to include all of them in the data collection. In larger schools, a subset of seniors is selected either by randomly sampling classrooms or by some other random method that is convenient for the school and judged to be unbiased. Sample weights are assigned to each respondent so as to take account of variations in the sizes of samples from one school to another, as well as the (smaller) variations in selection probabilities occurring at the earlier stages of sampling.

The three-stage sampling procedure described above yielded the number of participating schools and students indicated in Table 1.

One other important feature of the base-year sampling procedure should be noted here. All schools (except for half of the initial 1975 sample) are asked to participate in two data collections, thereby permitting replacement of half of the total sample of schools each year. One motivation for requesting that schools participate for two years is administrative efficiency; it is a costly and time-consuming procedure to secure the cooperation of schools, and a two-year period of participation cuts down that effort substantially. Another important advantage is that whenever an appreciable shift in scores from one graduating class to the next is observed, it is possible to check whether the shift might be attributable to some differences in the newly sampled schools. This is done simply by repeating the analysis using only the 60 or so schools which participated both years. Thus far, the half-sample approach

Table 1

Sample Sizes and Student Response Rates

	1975	1976	1977	1978	1979	1980	1981	1982	1983
Number of Public Schools	111	108	108	111	111	107	109	116	112
Number of Private Schools	14	15	16	20	20	20	19	21	22
Total Number of Schools	125	123	124	131	131	127	128	137	134
Actual Number of Participating Students	15792	16678	18438	18924	16662	16524	18267	18348	16947
Number of Weighted Cases (Total)*	15104	15299	15839	18924	16662	16524	18267	18348	16947
Student Response Rate**	78%	77%	79%	83%	82%	82%	81%	83%	84%

* Sample weights are assigned to each respondent to correct for unequal probabilities of selection which arise in the multi-stage sampling procedure.

** The student response rate is derived by dividing the attained sample by the target sample (both based on weighted numbers of cases). The target sample is based upon listings provided by schools. Since such listings may fail to take account of recent student attrition, the actual response rate may be slightly underestimated.

has worked quite well; and examination of drug prevalance data from the "matched half-samples" showed that the half samples of repeat schools yielded drug prevalence trends which were virtually identical to trends based on all schools.

School Recruiting Procedures. Early during the fall semester an initial contact is made with each sampled school. First a letter is sent to the principal describing the study and requesting permission to survey seniors. The letter is followed by a telephone call from a project staff member, who attempts to deal with any questions or problems and (when necessary) makes arrangements to contact and seek permission from other school district officials. Basically the same procedures are followed for schools asked to participate for the second year.

Once the school's agreement to participate is obtained, arrangements are made by phone for administering the questionnaires. A specific date for the survey is mutually agreed upon and a local SRC representative is assigned to carry out the administration.

Advance Contact with Teachers and Students. The local SRC representative is instructed to visit the school two weeks ahead of the actual date of administration. This visit serves as an occasion to meet the teachers whose classes will be affected and to provide them with a brochure describing the study, a brief set of guidelines about the questionnaire administration, and a supply of flyers to be distributed to the students a week to 10 days in advance of the questionnaire administration. The guidelines to the teachers include a suggested announcement to students at the time the flyers are distributed.

From the students' standpoint, the first information about the study usually consists of the teacher's announcement and the short descriptive flyer. In announcing the study, the teachers are asked to stress that the questionnaires used in the survey are not tests, and that there are no right or wrong answers. The flyer tells students that they will be invited to participate in the study, points out that their participation is strictly voluntary, and stresses confidentiality (including a reference to the fact that the Monitoring the Future project has a special government grant of confidentiality which allows their answers to be protected). The flyer also serves as an informative document which the students can show to their parents.

Questionnaire Administrations. The questionnaire administration in each school is carried out by the local SRC representatives and their assistants, following standardized procedures detailed in a project instruction manual. The questionnaires are administered in classrooms during normal class periods whenever possible, although circumstances in some schools require the use of larger group administrations. Teachers are not asked to do anything more than introduce the SRC staff members and (in most cases) remain in the classroom to help guarantee an orderly atmosphere for the survey. Teachers are urged to avoid walking around the room, so that students may feel free to write their answers without fear of being observed.

The actual process of completing the questionnaires is quite straightforward. Respondents are given sharpened pencils and asked to use them because the questionnaires are designed for automatic scanning. Most respondents can finish within a 45-minute class period; for those who cannot, an effort is made to provide a few minutes of additional time.

Procedures for Protecting Confidentiality. In any study that relies on voluntary reporting of drug use or other illegal acts, it is essential to develop procedures which guarantee the confidentiality of such reports. It is also desirable that these procedures be described adequately to respondents so that they are comfortable about providing honest answers.

We noted that the first information given to students about the survey consists of a descriptive flyer stressing confidentiality and voluntary participation. This theme is repeated at the start of the questionnaire administration. Each participating student is instructed to read the message on the cover of the questionnaire, which stresses the importance and value of the study, notes that answers will be kept strictly confidential, states that the study is completely voluntary, and tells the student "If there is any question you or your parents would find objectionable for any reason, just leave it blank." The instructions then point out that in a few months a summary of nationwide results will be mailed to all participants and also that a follow-up questionnaire will be sent to some students after a year. The cover message explains that these are the reasons for asking that name and address be written on a special form which will be removed from the questionnaire and handed in separately. The message also points out that the two different code numbers (one on the questionnaire and one on the tear-out form) cannot be matched except by a special computer tape at The University of Michigan. (The content of the inside and outside of the standard questionnaire cover, including the tear-out form, may be found in Appendix C.)

Content Areas and Questionnaire Design

Drug use and related attitudes are the topics which receive the most extensive coverage in the Monitoring the Future project; but the questionnaires also deal with a wide range of other subject areas, including attitudes about government, social institutions, race relations, changing roles for women, educational aspirations, occupational aims, and marital and family plans, as well as a variety of background and demographic factors.* (Table 2 provides an outline of the 19 general subject areas into which all items are categorized in the Question Index toward the end of this volume.) Given this breadth of content, the study is not presented to respondents as a "drug use study," nor do they tend to view it as such.

Because many questions are needed to cover all of these topic areas, much of the questionnaire content is divided into five different questionnaire forms which are distributed to participants in an ordered sequence that produces five virtually identical subsamples. About one-third of each questionnaire form consists of key or "core" variables which are common to all forms. All demographic variables and some measures of drug use are included in this "core" set of measures. This use of the full sample for drug and demographic measures provides a more accurate estimation on these dimensions and also makes it possible to link them statistically to all of the other measures which are included in a single form only.**

Representativeness and Validity

The samples for this study are intended to be representative of high school seniors throughout the 48 coterminous states. We have already discussed the fact that this definition of the sample excludes one important portion of the age cohort: those who have dropped out of high school before nearing the end of the senior year. But given the aim of representing high school seniors, it will now be useful to consider the extent to which the obtained samples of schools and students are likely to be representative of all seniors and the degree to which the data obtained are likely to be valid.

We can distinguish at least four ways in which survey data of this sort might fall short of being fully accurate. First, some sampled schools refuse to participate, which could introduce some bias. Second, the failure to obtain questionnaire data from 100 percent of the students sampled in participating schools would also introduce bias. Third, the answers provided by participating students are open to both conscious and unconscious distortions which could reduce validity. Finally, limitations in sample size and/or design could place limits on the accuracy of estimates. Each of these issues is treated extensively elsewhere (Johnston, Bachman, and O'Malley, 1979a, especially Appendices A and B), so in this section we will present only the highlights of each of those discussions.

School Participation. As noted in the description of the sampling design, schools are invited to participate

---

*An example of analyses relating background, demographic, and lifestyle factors to drug use is Bachman, Johnston, and O'Malley (1981); a much broader array of other subject areas included in the study is treated by Bachman and Johnston (1979).

**These core variables are the first ones on which data are presented in the Descriptive Results Section.

Table 2

Measurement Content Areas

A. **Drugs.** Drug use and related attitudes and beliefs, drug availability and exposure, surrounding conditions and social meanings of drug use. Views of significant others regarding drugs.

B. **Education.** Educational lifestyle, values, experiences, and environments.

C. **Work and Lesisure.** Vocational values, meaning of work and leisure, work and leisure activities, preferences regarding occupational characteristics and type of work setting.

D. **Sex Roles and Family.** Values, attitudes, and expectations about marriage, family structure, sex roles, and sex discrimination.

E. **Population Concerns.** Values and attitudes about overpopulation and birth control.

F. **Conservation, Materialism, Equity, etc.** Values, attitudes, and expectations related to conservation, pollution, materialism, equity, and the sharing of resources. Preferences regarding type of dwelling and urbanicity.

G. **Religion.** Religious affiliation, practices, and views.

H. **Politics.** Political affiliation, activities, and views.

I. **Social Change.** Values, attitudes, and expectations about social change.

J. **Social Problems.** Concern with various social problems facing the nation and the world.

K. **Major Social Institutions.** Confidence in and commitment to various major social institutions (business, unions, branches of government, press, organized religion, military, etc.).

L. **Military.** Views about the armed services and the use of military force. Personal plans for military service.

M. **Interpersonal Relationships.** Qualitative and quantitative characteristics of cross-age and peer relationships. Interpersonal conflict.

N. **Race Relations.** Attitudes toward and experiences with other racial groups.

O. **Concern for Others.** Concern for others; voluntary and charitable activities.

P. **Happiness.** Happiness and life satisfaction, overall and in specific life domains.

Q. **Other Personality Variables.** Attitudes about self (including self-esteem), locus of control, loneliness, risk-taking, trust in others, health habits and symptoms, importance placed on various life goals, counter-culture orientation, hostility.

R. **Background.** Demographic and family background characteristics, living arrangements.

S. **Deviant Behavior and Victimization.** Delinquent behaviors, driving violations and accidents (including those under the influence of drugs), victimization experiences.

in the study for a two-year period. With very few exceptions, each school which has participated for one data collection has agreed to participate for a second. Thus far, from 66 percent to 80 percent of the schools initially invited to participate have agreed to do so each year; for each school refusal, a similar school (in terms of size, geographic area, urbanicity, etc.) was recruited as a replacement. The selection of replacement schools almost entirely removes problems of bias in region, urbanicity, and the like that might result from certain schools refusing to participate. Other potential biases are more subtle, however. For example, if it turned out that most schools with "drug problems" refused to participate, that could seriously bias the drug estimates derived from the sample. And if any other single factor were dominant in most refusals, that also might suggest a source of serious bias. In fact, however, the reasons for schools' refusals to participate are varied and largely a function of happenstance events of the particular year. Thus, we feel fairly confident that school refusals have not seriously biased the surveys.

Student Participation. Completed questionnaires are obtained from three-fourths to four-fifths of all students sampled. The single most important reason that students are missed is that they are absent from class at the time of data collection, and in most cases it is not workable to schedule a special follow-up data collection for them. Students with fairly high rates of absenteeism also report above-average rates of drug use; therefore, there is some degree of bias introduced by missing the absentees. That bias could be largely corrected through the use of special weighting; however, this course was not chosen because the bias in estimates (for drug use, where the potential effect was hypothesized to be largest) was determined to be quite small and because the necessary weighting procedures would have introduced undesirable complications (see Johnston et al., 1977).

In addition to absenteeism, student nonparticipation occurs because of schedule conflicts with school trips and other activities which tend to be more frequent than usual during the final months of the senior year. Of course, some students refuse to complete or turn in a questionnaire. However, the SRC representatives in the field estimate this proportion to be only about one percent.

Validity of Self-Report Data. Survey measures of delinquency and of drug use depend upon respondents reporting what are, in many cases, illegal acts. Thus, a critical question is whether such self-reports are likely to be valid. Like most studies dealing with

these areas, we have no direct, objective validation of the present measures; however, the considerable amount of inferential evidence which exists strongly suggests that the self-report questions produce largely valid data. A number of factors have given us reasonable confidence about the validity of the responses to what are presumably among the most sensitive questions in the study: a low nonresponse on the drug questions; a large proportion admitting to some illicit drug use; the consistency of findings across several years of the present study; strong evidence of construct validity (based on relationships observed between variables); a close match between our data and the findings from other studies using other methods; and the findings from several methodological studies which have used objective validation methods.*

As for others of the measures, a few have a long and venerable history — as scholars of the relevant literatures will recognize — though some of these measures have been modified to fit the present questionnaire format. Many (probably most) questions, however, have been developed specifically for this project through a careful process of question writing, pilot testing, pretesting, and question revision or elimination. Some already have been included in other publications from the study, but many have not; therefore, there currently exists little *empirical* evidence of their validity and reliability. On the other hand, the fact that virtually all results presented in this volume are based on individual items, rather than indexes or abstract concepts, should make it easy for the reader to judge the degree to which each item has "face validity" and also the degree to which there is some evidence of construct validity in the bivariate results.

Accuracy of the Sample. A sample survey never can provide the same level of accuracy as would be obtained if the entire target population were to participate in the survey — in the case of the present study, about three million seniors per year. But perfect accuracy of this sort would be extremely expensive and certainly not worthwhile considering the fact that a high level of accuracy can be provided by a carefully designed probability sample. The accuracy of the sample in this study is affected both by the size of the student sample and by the number of schools in which they are clustered. Appendix B presents a discussion of the ways in which this clustering and other aspects of the sampling design are taken into account in computing the precision or accuracy of the samples. For the purposes of this introduction, it is sufficient to note that virtually all estimates based on the total sample have confidence intervals of ± 1.5 percentage points or smaller — sometimes considerably smaller.

---

* A more detailed discussion of the evidence for validity of the measures of illicit drug use may be found in Johnston et al. (1977; 1979a), Appendix A. An analysis of inconsistencies in students' reports of monthly versus yearly drug use is provided by Bachman and O'Malley (1981).

This means that, had we been able to invite all schools and all seniors in the 48 coterminous states to participate, the results from such a massive survey would be within an estimated 1.5 percentage points of our present sample findings at least 95 times out of 100. We consider this to be a quite high level of accuracy, and one that permits the detection of fairly small trends from one year to the next.

Consistency and the Measurement of Trends. One other point is worth noting in a discussion of the validity of our findings. The Monitoring the Future project is, by intention, a study designed to be sensitive to changes from one time to another. Accordingly, the measures and procedures have been standardized and applied consistently across each data collection. To the extent that any biases remain because of limits in school and/or student participation, and to the extent that there are distortions (lack of validity) in the responses of some students, it seems very likely that such problems will exist in much the same way from one year to the next. In other words, biases in the survey estimates should tend to be consistent from one year to another, which means that the measurement of *trends* should be affected very little by any such biases.

Caveats to Users of the Data

In attempting to understand and interpret the statistical results contained in this volume, the reader should keep in mind the several considerations discussed below.

Estimation of Sampling Errors. Appendix A provides figures which allow the reader to determine the 95 percent confidence interval around any observed percentage for both the total sample and the several subgroups for which statistics are given. Appendix A also provides tables and guidelines for testing the statistical significance of observed differences between subgroups (e.g., males vs. females) and the significance of year-to-year changes for the entire sample and for the various subgroups on any given variable. Estimates based on subgroups containing relatively few cases (e.g., those who have used heroin) will have substantially larger margins of error than those subgroups with large numbers of cases.

Subgroup Definitions. At the beginning of the Descriptive Results section there is a careful definition of each of the subgroups analyzed in this series of volumes. It is important for the reader to read these definitions so as not to be misled by the necessarily abbreviated descriptions given in the column headings of the data tables. For example, the column labeled "4-year college plans" includes data only for seniors who

expect to be graduated from a four-year college, which is only a subset of all who expect to receive some college training. To take another example, several column headings in the lifetime illicit drug use index use the term "pills"; however, these categories contain people who indicate that they used any of a number of drugs — including some which usually are not taken in pill form (e.g., cocaine and narcotics other than heroin).

Missing Data Notes. Each column of percentages for a given variable adds to 100 percent (with slight variations due to rounding), whether based on the entire sample or any one of the subgroups being described. Missing data were not included in computing these percentages, so it is up to the reader to determine whether an exceptional level of missing data exists on any given question. This can be done by comparing the weighted number of cases on which those percentages were based (given in italics under each percentage distribution) with the total number of weighted cases who took the questionnaire (given at the top of the same column). As would be expected, the missing data rate tends to rise modestly toward the end of each questionnaire. Occasionally there is an exceptional level of nonresponse for some other reason, the most common being that the respondent has been branched around a question or set of questions which are inappropriate for him or her. In this case the percentages are based only on those for whom the question was appropriate *and* who answered. A footnote has been entered to help call attention to the fact that completing a particular question is contingent upon the answer on a prior question. Most such cases are contained in Form 1 of the questionnaire, which has several sets of detailed questions about drug use which are answered only by those respondents who have used a particular class of drug during the past year.

Characterizing Heroin Users. Because this project places a special emphasis on the study of drug use, one set of columns distinguishes respondents according to the extent to which they have been involved with illicit drugs. The five drug use categories are based on an index of seriousness of involvement. The index has Guttman-like properties — that is, anyone classified at a given level is also very likely to have exhibited any drug-using behaviors which are associated with the lower levels in the index.

The most extreme category in the index is defined in terms of the respondent's ever having used heroin during his or her lifetime. However, any interpretations made about heroin users from these data must be tempered with extreme caution, not only because the small number of cases makes estimation in a given year relatively unreliable, but also because heroin users are probably the most selectively represented of all of the subgroups presented here. Heroin users — especially continuing users — are among those most likely to drop out of high school (Johnston, 1973). Therefore, we feel that heroin users are particularly underrepresented in a sample of high school seniors. Furthermore, most of those included in the study report only very occasional heroin use. Frequent users — addicts, if you will — are not well represented in these data.

Given these problems with the representation of heroin users, the readers may wonder why it was decided to present them as a separate category of drug users. There are two reasons for doing so. First, because even occasional heroin use represents such an extreme point on the continuum of drug involvement, it seems preferable that the heroin users not be mixed in with the next highest category of use (the "more pills" category). It remains quite possible, of course, for anyone to combine any two or more categories in the drug use continuum (by computing means of percentages weighted by the number of cases in each category); therefore, those wishing to incorporate heroin users with the next category can do so whenever they wish. The second reason for keeping them separate is that we suspect the data based on high school seniors provide some indication of the characteristics which might be found among heavier heroin users who dropped out of school. Some variables in the study are strongly correlated with the drug use continuum, and the present heroin user category provides both an end point for that continuum and an indication of the direction (further out on the continuum) in which heavier heroin users are likely to lie.

In sum, the reporting of separate percentages for heroin users among high school seniors permits greater clarity in analyzing other levels of drug use and provides data which may be suggestive about the larger population of young heroin users. But the particular data are clearly limited and should be interpreted with these cautions in mind.

Interpreting Racial Differences. Data are given for the two largest racial/ethnic subgroups in the population — those who identify themselves as white or Caucasian and those who identify themselves as black or Afro-American. Data are not given for the other ethnic categories (American Indians, Asian Americans, Mexican Americans, Puerto Ricans, or other Latin Americans) since each of these groups comprises less than three percent of the sample in any given year, which means that their small Ns (in combination with their clustered groupings in a limited number of schools) would yield estimates which would be too unreliable. In fact, even blacks — who constitute approximately 12 percent of each year's sample — are represented by only 350 to 425 respondents per year on any single questionnaire form. Further, because our sample is a stratified clustered sample, it yields less accuracy than would be yielded by a pure random sample of equal size (see Appendix B for details). Therefore, because of the limited number of cases, the margin of sampling error around any statistic describing blacks is larger than for most other subgroups described in this volume.

There exists, however, a quick way to determine the replicability of any finding involving racial comparisons. Since most questions are repeated from year to year, one can readily establish the degree to which a finding is replicated by looking at the results for the same question in prior or subsequent years. Given the relatively small Ns for blacks, the reader is urged to seek such replication before putting much faith in the reliability of any particular racial comparison.

There are factors in addition to unreliability, however, which could be misleading in the interpretation of racial differences. Given the social importance which has been placed on various racial differences reported in the social science literature, we would like to caution the reader to consider the various factors which could account for differences. These factors fall into three categories: differential representation in the sample, differential response tendencies, and the confounding of race with a number of other background and demographic characteristics.

Differential Representation. Census data characterizing American young people in the approximate age range of those in our sample show that somewhat lower proportions of blacks than whites remain in school through the end of twelfth grade (Dearman and Plisko, 1979, p. 185). Therefore, a slightly different segment of the black population than of the white population resides in our target population of high school seniors. Further, our samples appear to underrepresent slightly those black males who, according to census figures, are in high school at the twelfth grade level. Identified black males comprise about 6 percent of our sample, whereas census data suggest that they should comprise around 7 percent (U.S. Bureau of the Census, 1978). Therefore, it appears that we are losing more black males from our target population than white males or females of either race. This may be due to generally poorer attendance rates on the part of some black males and/or an unwillingness on the part of some to participate in data collections of this sort.

In sum, a smaller segment of the black population than of the white population of high school age is represented by the data contained here. Insofar as any characteristic is associated with being a school dropout or absentee, it is likely to be somewhat disproportionately underrepresented among blacks in our sample.

Differential Response Tendencies. In examining our full range of variables, we have noted certain racial differences in response tendencies. First, the tendency to state agreement in response to agree-disagree questions is generally somewhat greater among blacks than among whites. For example, blacks tend to agree more with the positively worded items in our index of self-esteem, but they also tend to agree more with the negatively worded items. As it happens, that particular index has an equal number of positively and negatively worded items, so that any overall "agreement bias" should be self-cancelling when the index score is computed. Since all data in this volume are based on single items, however, group differences in agreement bias are likely to affect results on questions employing the agree-disagree format. Fortunately, most of our questions are not of that type.

We have also observed a somewhat greater than average tendency for black respondents to select extreme answer categories on attitudinal scales. For example, even if the same proportion of blacks as whites felt positively (or negatively) about some subject, fewer of the whites are likely to say they feel **very** positively (or *very* negatively). We do not have any ready explanations for these differences in response styles, but what seems important for our present purposes is that, in the process of interpreting racial differences, the reader should be aware that differences in responses to particular questions may be related to these more general tendencies.

A somewhat separate issue in response tendency is a respondent's willingness to answer particular questions. The missing data rate, which can be determined by dividing the number responding to a question by the number taking the questionnaire (given at the top of each page), may reflect willingness to answer particular questions. If a particular question or set of questions has a missing data rate higher than is true for the prior or subsequent questions, then presumably more respondents than usual were unwilling (or perhaps unable) to answer it. We have observed such an exaggerated missing data rate for black males on the set of questions dealing with the respondent's own use of illicit drugs. Clearly a respondent's willingness to be candid on such questions depends on his or her trust of the research process and of the researchers themselves. We interpret the exaggerated missing data rates for black males in these sections as possibly reflecting, at least in part, less trust. The reader is advised to check for exceptional levels of missing data when making comparisons on any variable in which candor is likely to be reduced by lower system trust. One bit of additional evidence related to trust in the research process is that higher proportions of blacks than whites indicated that if they had used marijuana or heroin they would not have been willing to report it in the survey.

Covariance with Other Factors. Some characteristics such as race are highly confounded (correlated) with other variables — variables which may in fact explain some observed racial differences. Put another way, at the aggregate level we might observe a consid-

erable racial difference on some characteristic, but once we control for some background characteristics such as socio-economic level or region of the country — that is, once we compare the black respondents with whites who come from similar backgrounds — there may be no racial difference at all.

Race happens to be correlated with important background and demographic variables much more than some of the other variables dealt with here (like the respondent's sex). When we compare males and females in this sample we know that observed differences between them are not likely to be explained by differences in their family background (such as the socioeconomic level of their families, the region of the country, or the size of the cities in which they grew up) because males and females on the average come from extremely similar backgrounds. A perusal of Section C of Questionnaire Forms 1 through 5, however, will illustrate that on the average the black subgroup in this sample is quite different from the white subgroup in a number of such respects. A higher proportion of blacks live in the South and a higher proportion grew up in families with the father and/or mother absent, and more had mothers who worked while they were growing up. A substantially higher proportion of blacks are Baptists, and blacks tend to attribute more importance to religion in their lives than do whites. Fewer are enrolled in a college-preparatory curriculum (though a higher proportion say they plan to attend some type of college). A slightly higher proportion of black respondents are married and have children, and on the average they are slightly older than the white sample. As was mentioned earlier, black males are more underrepresented in our sample than black females, with the result that each year roughly 58 percent of our black sample is female versus roughly 51 percent of the white sample.

We note these differences in demographic, background, and ascriptive characteristics because, in any attempt to understand *why* a racial difference exists, one would want to be able to examine the role of these covarying characteristics. It is not possible, given the amount of data contained in this volume, to "factor out" the contribution of most of these covarying characteristics when interpreting racial differences. Therefore, while the data here may provide a relatively accurate *description* of racial differences (keeping in mind our earlier cautions about representativeness and response style), they do not by themselves yield a great deal by way of explanation.

However, since the full data sets now reside in an archive, described in the Preface, it is possible for the reader to conduct a more in depth exploration of observed differences—or nondifferences, for that matter. We particularly encourage readers interested in racial comparisons to make further explorations in the data in order to determine the possible role of the other variables discussed here.

Users of the data are also encouraged to contact the principal investigators for information on the most recent analyses of racial differences, some of which are already underway.

Given the long list of caveats about interpreting racial differences, one might ask why we chose to publish the statistics for racial subgroups at all. After considerable deliberation among ourselves as well as with colleagues more knowledgeable in the field of race relations, we concluded that the expected benefits of making these data available (along with this cautionary discussion) outweigh the potential costs of having them misused. Unfortunately, because blacks constitute a relatively small proportion of the American population, they constitute too small a number in most surveys to be characterized separately. Because the sample sizes in the present survey are large in comparison to most, we have at least sufficient numbers of cases to consider publishing data on blacks separately. Further, given the iterative nature of the series, we are also able to provide checks for replication of findings on different samples each year. While there may be some risk that findings will be taken out of context or used carelessly in ways that might tend to increase racial misunderstandings, there is substantially greater risk that valuable information concerning the races (and relative to their well-being) will be lost if it were not included here.

A note on the questions about amphetamine use. Prior to the 1982 survey, we discovered that some respondents' answers to questions on amphetamine use erroneously included use of over-the-counter stay-awake and diet pills, as well as some "look-alike" pills. In the 1982 survey, we introduced some new questions on the use of amphetamines in order to make more clear to the respondents that "look-alike" pills and over-the-counter products should be excluded. We also kept the old version of the questions in two questionnaire forms in the 1982 and 1983 surveys so that it would be possible to "splice" the trend lines resulting from the old and new questions.

As a result of these changes, the reader who uses these volumes to examine trends in amphetamine use must be careful not to make inappropriate comparisons. The response distributions shown in the combined Forms 1 to 5 section (pages 28–29) from 1975 to 1981 contain the responses for Forms 1 through 5. In 1982 and 1983, that section contains two sets of responses. The first set is for Forms 1, 2, and 4 (with Form 1 double-weighted); these provide what we believe to be the best estimates of current amphetamine use and of trends from 1982 on. The second set of responses are based on Forms 3 and 5, the old versions of the questions; thus, these questions provide the best comparisons for looking at trends over time from 1975 to 1983 (although there is reason to be cautious about these trends because of the erroneous inclusion of non-amphetamines,, as described above). Beginning with 1984, all forms use the new versions of the questions.

---

* An exended analysis and discussion of black-white differences in response styles may be found in Bachman and O'Malley (1984).

Descriptive Results

Introduction to the Table Format and Conventions

Univariate and selected bivariate percentage distributions are given in this section for all questions asked of this year's senior class. The definitions of column headings and the source of the standard contents for each table are given below under the numbers indicated in Figure 1.

Definitions of Column Headings

① **Questionnaire Form.** The form from which all data on the page were derived is given here. When the designation "Forms 1-5" is used, it indicates that responses from students completing all five questionnaires have been combined; accordingly, the numbers of respondents in each column are five times as large for questions contained in a single form only.

② **Total Sample.** Univariate percentage distributions based on the total sample of respondents are given in this column.

③ **Sex.** Percentage distributions are given separately for males (M) and females (F). Respondents with missing data on the question asking the respondent's sex (Question C03) are omitted from both groupings.

④ **Race.** Percentage distributions are given separately for those describing themselves as "White or Caucasian" (W) and "Black or Afro-American" (B) in answer to Question C04. Comparable columns for the other racial or ethnic groups (Mexican Americans, Asian Americans, American Indians, etc.) are not shown because of the low number of cases in each group. *Note:* See the caveats regarding the interpretation of racial differences in the introduction section of this volume.

⑤ **Region.** Percentage distributions are given separately for respondents living in each of four mutually exclusive regions of the country. The regional classifications are based on Census categories and are defined as follows:

Northeast (NE): Census classifications of New England and Middle Atlantic states; includes Maine, New Hampshire, Vermont, Massachusetts, Rhode Island, Connecticut, New York, New Jersey, and Pennsylvania.

North Central (NC): Census classifications of East North Central and West North Central states; includes Ohio, Indiana, Illinois, Michigan, Wisconsin, Minnesota, Iowa, Missouri, North Dakota, South Dakota, Nebraska, and Kansas.

South (S): Census classifications of South Atlantic, East South Central, and West South Central states; includes Delaware, Maryland, District of Columbia, Virginia, West Virginia, North Carolina, South Carolina, Georgia, Florida, Kentucky, Tennessee, Alabama, Mississippi, Arkansas, Louisiana, Oklahoma, and Texas.

West (W): Census classifications of Mountain and Pacific states; includes Montana, Idaho, Wyoming, Colorado, New Mexico, Arizona, Utah, Nevada, Washington, Oregon, and California.

⑥ **Four-Year College Plans.** Percentage distributions are given separately for (1) respondents who indicate that they "definitely will" or "probably will" graduate from a four-year college program and (2) those who say that they "definitely won't" or "probably won't" graduate from a four-year college program, based on responses to Question C21d. Respondents not answering question C21d are omitted from both columns. (A number of those who do not expect to complete a four-year college program *do* expect to get some post-secondary education, as may be seen in

13

the tables for questions C21a and c.)

⑦ Illicit Drug Use: Lifetime. Percentage distributions are given separately for five mutually exclusive subgroups differentiated by their degree of involvement with illicit drugs. Eligibility for each category is defined below.

None. This column contains data from those respondents who indicated that they had not used marijuana at any time and did not report use of any of the following illicit drugs in their lifetime: LSD, other psychedelics, cocaine, amphetamines, tranquilizers, methaqualone, barbiturates, heroin, or other narcotics.*

Marijuana Only. This column contains data from other respondents who indicated that they had used marijuana (or hashish) but had never used any of the other illicit drugs just listed.

Few Pills. This column contains data from those respondents who indicated having used one or more of the above listed drugs (other than marijuana) but who had not used any one class of them on three or more occasions *and* who had not used heroin at all.

More Pills. This column contains data from respondents who had used any of the above listed drugs (other than marijuana) on three or more occasions but who had never used heroin.

Any Heroin. This column contains data from those respondents who indicated having used heroin on one or more occasions in their lifetime.

⑧ N(Weighted Number of Cases). This row contains the number of students who turned in questionnaires in each of the categories indicated by the column headings. The number of cases is stated in terms of the weighted number of respondents rather than the actual number, since all percentages in the tables have been calculated using weighted cases. The actual number of respondents generally is about 15 percent higher than the weighted number for data collected in 1975, 1976, and 1977. (A comparison of weighted and unweighted numbers is provided in Tables B-1 and B-2 in Appendix B.) For data collected in 1978 or later, the actual number of respondents is roughly equal to the weighted number. Weighting is used to improve the accuracy of estimates by correcting for unequal probabilities of selection which arise in the multi-stage sampling procedures.

⑨ Percentage of Weighted Total. This row indicates the percentage of the total number of respondents who fall into the category indicated by each column heading. Unlike all other percentages on the page, which can be summed vertically, these percentages sum horizontally. To the extent that the subcate-

gories in a column (e.g., Males and Females) fail to sum to 100 percent, cases have been eliminated because of missing data on the variable in question (e.g., Sex), or, in the case of Race, because several subcategories have been omitted intentionally.

Table Contents

⑩ Questions and Answers. Each question along with its accompanying answer alternatives is presented verbatim. The alphanumeric prefix to the question indicates the section of the questionnaire in which it is located and its sequence within that section. So, for example, a prefix of B12c indicates that the item was question 12c in the B Section of the questionnaire.

⑪ Item Reference Number. This is a unique identification number permanently assigned to each question. Any question may be located in the Question Index of the 1975–1981 volumes by using this number, and in the Question Index of all subsequent volumes by using this number in conjunction with the subject area code.

⑫ Subject Area Code. Every question has been classified into one or more subject areas; the alphanumeric code indicates the subject area (or areas) applicable to the question shown. The complete listing of subject areas is presented in Table 3 (at the beginning of the Question Index near the end of this volume). Starting with the 1982 volume, the Question Index is ordered first by subject area, and then (within areas) by item reference number.

⑬ Percentage Distribution. Each column of numbers beside a question gives the percentage of each group (defined by the column heading) who chose each answer alternative, rounded to the nearest tenth of a percent. These figures add vertically to 100 percent (with some rounding error). Nonrespondents to the question are excluded from the percentage calculations.

⑭ Number of Weighted Cases Answering (N). The number of students in the relevant group (defined by the column heading) who answered the question is given just below the percentage distribution. The number of nonrespondents may be determined by subtracting this weighted number answering from the weighted number taking the questionnaire, shown at the top of the same column. Nonresponse may be due to the subject not answering the question, even though it pertains to him or her, or to the subject skipping inappropriate questions as instructed on a prior item.

*Inhalants (including the amyl and butyl nitrites) are not included in this list of illicit drugs because the relevant questions are not contained in all questionnaire forms nor in all years of the study. Similarly, the use of PCP is counted only if it was reported under "other psychedelics" use, because specific questions about PCP are not included in all forms or years. This results in a few apparent inconsistencies in the tables relating the drug use index to specific questions about these drugs.

Figure 1
Guide to Table Format

(1) (2) (3) (4) (5) (6) (7)

QUESTIONNAIRE FORM 1-5 1982	TOTAL	SEX		RACE		REGION				4YR COLLEGE PLANS		ILLICIT DRUG USE: LIFETIME				
		M	F	White	Black	NE	NC	S	W	Yes	No	None	Marijuana Only	Few Pills	More Pills	Any Heroin
(8) N (Weighted No. of Cases):	18348	8828	8788	13887	2080	4741	5383	5551	2672	9360	7507	6328	4040	2439	4839	210
(9) % of Weighted Total:	100.0	48.1	47.9	75.7	11.3	25.8	29.3	30.3	14.6	51.0	40.9	34.5	22.0	13.3	26.4	1.1

These next questions ask for some background information about yourself.

C01: In what year were you born?

	TOTAL	M	F	White	Black	NE	NC	S	W	Yes	No	None	Mari-juana Only	Few Pills	More Pills	Any Heroin
1. Before '62	.3	.3	.3	.1	.6	.2	.3	.4	.2	.2	.4	.4	.1	.3	.2	1.1
2. 1962	2.0	2.6	1.4	1.3	3.9	1.5	2.0	2.7	1.5	1.0	2.9	2.0	1.9	2.2	1.4	5.3
3. 1963	23.3	26.6	19.6	21.8	26.1	15.2	27.2	25.6	24.4	19.4	27.1	23.4	23.9	23.4	22.0	25.4
4. 1964	72.8	69.3	76.6	75.6	66.3	80.5	69.5	69.9	72.2	77.3	68.6	72.2	72.2	72.7	75.2	67.9
5. 1965	1.6	1.1	2.1	1.2	3.0	2.5	1.0	1.4	1.6	2.1	1.0	1.8	1.9	1.3	1.2	.2
6. 1966	*	*	*	*	*	*	*	*	*	*	*	.1	-	-	-	-
7. 1967	*	*	*	*	*	*	*	*	*	*	*	-	-	-	-	-
8. After 1967	*	*	*	*	*	*	*	*	*	*	*	-	-	-	-	-
(11) Item 10 Subject R01 N	17899	8816	8787	13882	2079	4572	5306	5428	2593	9324	7466	6259	3986	2408	4718	207

C02: In what month were you born?

	TOTAL	M	F	White	Black	NE	NC	S	W	Yes	No	None	Mari-juana Only	Few Pills	More Pills	Any Heroin
01. January	8.0	8.0	8.3	7.7	10.0	8.4	8.0	8.4	6.9	8.2	7.9	8.2	7.3	9.1	7.5	11.6
02. February	7.3	7.3	7.5	7.2	7.8	7.4	7.2	7.8	6.6	7.4	7.4	7.4	7.6	7.1	7.2	7.0
03. March	7.8	8.2	7.5	7.8	7.7	8.4	7.6	7.0	8.8	8.0	7.6	7.2	8.3	7.2	8.7	4.3
04. April	7.7	7.7	7.7	7.8	7.3	8.1	7.5	7.4	8.1	7.8	7.7	7.5	7.8	7.7	7.6	12.1
05. May	8.2	8.2	8.1	8.4	7.2	8.6	8.5	7.4	8.9	8.4	8.0	8.3	8.2	7.8	8.6	8.4
06. June	8.2	8.7	7.9	8.6	7.4	7.3	8.9	8.2	8.5	7.9	8.8	7.8	8.0	8.1	9.0	6.1
07. July	9.0	9.1	8.9	9.1	9.2	8.6	9.2	8.9	9.3	9.1	8.8	8.9	9.1	9.2	8.7	13.4
08. August	9.1	9.5	8.6	9.1	9.1	9.3	8.9	9.4	8.9	8.9	9.5	9.7	9.4	8.9	8.5	8.4
09. September	9.2	8.7	9.8	9.2	10.0	9.3	9.2	9.5	8.3	8.9	9.5	9.5	8.4	9.8	9.4	4.9
10. October	8.9	8.6	9.0	8.9	8.0	8.6	8.8	9.6	8.5	9.0	8.8	9.2	9.0	9.0	8.5	7.4
11. November	8.1	8.0	7.9	8.2	7.3	7.8	8.0	8.4	8.2	8.0	8.4	8.0	8.2	8.4	8.2	5.4
12. December	8.3	8.0	8.7	8.0	8.8	8.1	8.3	8.0	9.0	8.6	7.8	8.4	8.5	7.8	8.1	11.0
Item 20 Subject R01 N	17871	8802	8779	13863	2079	4566	5294	5420	2591	9312	7455	6253	3986	2398	4706	207

C03: What is your sex?

	TOTAL	M	F	White	Black	NE	NC	S	W	Yes	No	None	Mari-juana Only	Few Pills	More Pills	Any Heroin
1. Male	50.1	100.0	-	50.9	43.2	49.8	50.6	50.0	49.9	50.0	48.7	47.8	55.3	48.7	48.7	62.6
2. Female	49.9	-	100.0	49.1	56.8	50.2	49.4	50.0	50.1	50.0	51.3	52.2	44.7	51.3	51.3	37.4
(14) Item 30 Subject R01 N	17616	8828	8788	13676	2047	4511	5214	5339	2552	9216	7324	6177	3913	2370	4650	202

C04: How do you describe yourself?

	TOTAL	M	F	White	Black	NE	NC	S	W	Yes	No	None	Mari-juana Only	Few Pills	More Pills	Any Heroin
1. American Indian	1.4	1.5	1.2	-	-	.8	1.2	1.6	2.4	.6	2.2	.8	1.5	1.4	1.7	3.2
2. Black or Afro-American	11.7	10.1	13.3	-	100.0	10.2	5.1	21.9	6.3	11.3	10.5	13.7	16.1	11.4	4.3	13.1
3. Mexican American or Chicano	2.2	2.3	2.1	-	-	.2	1.0	.9	10.9	1.7	2.4	2.2	2.1	2.4	1.9	2.5
4. Puerto Rican or other Latin American	1.9	1.8	2.0	-	-	4.1	.5	1.4	1.6	2.1	1.3	2.2	2.0	1.3	1.6	1.5
5. Oriental or Asian American	1.8	1.9	1.7	-	-	2.4	1.3	.3	5.1	3.0	.4	3.4	1.0	.8	.8	1.6
6. White or Caucasian	78.1	79.4	76.9	100.0	-	78.9	87.7	72.4	69.3	78.7	80.0	74.7	74.3	79.8	87.3	68.5
7. Other	2.9	3.1	2.7	-	-	3.4	3.3	1.5	4.4	2.6	3.1	3.0	3.0	2.9	2.4	9.6
Item 40 Subject R01 N	17775	8763	8729	13887	2080	4534	5272	5406	2562	9286	7412	6215	3961	2392	4688	203

C05: Where did you grow up mostly?

	TOTAL	M	F	White	Black	NE	NC	S	W	Yes	No	None	Mari-juana Only	Few Pills	More Pills	Any Heroin
1. On a farm	7.9	8.3	7.4	8.9	4.0	2.7	9.7	11.7	5.2	5.3	11.3	10.1	6.7	7.2	6.1	4.1
2. In the country, not on a farm		15.4	13.7	14.8	17.0	12.3	13.1	19.5	11.5	11.1	19.2	16.0	14.2	14.6	12.8	14.0
3. In a small ci...					20.8	34.5	31.4	26.4	24.4	29.0	31.0	30.3	28.4	29.4	30.2	30.1

(left-margin guide markers: (8), (9), (10), (11), (12), (13), (14))

QUESTIONNAIRE FORM 1-5 1983	TOTAL	SEX		RACE		REGION				4YR COLLEGE PLANS		ILLICIT DRUG USE: LIFETIME				
		M	F	White	Black	NE	NC	S	W	Yes	No	None	Marijuana Only	Few Pills	More Pills	Any Heroin
N (Weighted No. of Cases):	16947	8074	8227	12806	2066	4056	4784	5434	2673	9061	6555	6082	3598	2315	4306	206
% of Weighted Total:	100.0	47.6	48.5	75.6	12.2	23.9	28.2	32.1	15.8	53.5	38.7	35.9	21.2	13.7	25.4	1.2

These next questions ask for some background information about yourself.

C01: In what year were you born?

	TOTAL	M	F	White	Black	NE	NC	S	W	Yes	No	None	Marijuana Only	Few Pills	More Pills	Any Heroin
1. Before '62	-	-	-	-	-	-	-	-	-	-	-	-	-	-	-	-
2. 1962	0.2	0.2	0.2	*	0.6	0.3	0.1	0.3	0.1	0.1	0.3	0.2	0.2	-	0.2	0.4
3. 1963	2.2	2.4	1.9	1.4	5.1	1.8	2.1	2.9	1.8	1.3	3.2	2.3	2.1	1.9	2.0	2.0
4. 1964	23.8	27.7	19.5	22.9	23.8	16.4	27.9	25.2	24.4	20.7	27.6	23.4	23.5	24.9	23.2	38.4
5. 1965	72.0	68.4	76.0	74.6	65.8	78.6	68.9	70.1	71.4	75.7	67.7	71.9	72.4	71.8	73.4	56.3
6. 1966	1.7	1.0	2.3	1.0	4.3	2.7	0.9	1.4	2.0	2.0	1.1	2.0	1.6	1.4	1.1	0.8
7. 1967	0.1	0.1	0.1	*	0.2	*	*	0.1	0.2	0.1	*	0.1	0.1	*	-	0.7
8. After 1967	*	0.1	*	*	*	*	0.1	*	0.1	0.1	-	0.1	*	-	*	-
Item 10 Subject R01 N	16578	8065	8223	12794	2065	3921	4725	5312	2620	9035	6509	6038	3540	2290	4210	204

C02: In what month were you born?

	TOTAL	M	F	White	Black	NE	NC	S	W	Yes	No	None	Marijuana Only	Few Pills	More Pills	Any Heroin
01. January	8.4	8.1	8.8	8.2	9.1	8.5	8.5	8.8	7.4	8.3	8.5	8.0	9.0	8.5	8.4	6.1
02. February	7.6	7.8	7.3	7.8	6.8	7.8	7.6	7.5	7.4	7.6	7.6	7.2	7.1	7.8	8.2	8.8
03. March	8.0	8.2	7.9	7.9	7.8	8.0	8.2	8.0	7.6	8.3	7.4	7.7	7.8	8.9	8.1	7.1
04. April	7.6	7.6	7.5	7.7	7.8	7.6	7.7	7.5	8.0	7.6	7.7	8.2	6.7	7.5	7.6	12.0
05. May	7.8	8.0	7.6	8.0	7.4	8.4	8.1	7.4	7.4	7.5	8.3	7.9	8.6	7.5	7.5	7.5
06. June	8.5	7.9	9.3	8.6	8.0	8.6	9.1	7.8	8.6	7.9	9.2	8.0	7.9	8.2	9.9	8.4
07. July	8.8	9.2	8.3	8.8	8.9	9.0	8.4	8.9	9.1	9.1	8.6	9.3	8.3	9.3	8.4	9.2
08. August	8.9	8.6	9.2	8.8	10.3	7.5	9.1	9.6	9.4	8.8	9.0	9.1	9.3	8.3	8.6	8.4
09. September	8.9	9.0	9.0	8.9	8.3	9.5	8.4	8.8	9.1	9.0	8.8	8.6	8.9	9.3	9.1	6.4
10. October	9.3	9.1	9.2	9.1	9.3	9.9	9.0	9.2	8.9	9.5	9.0	9.5	8.7	9.7	8.9	10.6
11. November	7.8	8.1	7.3	7.7	8.1	7.7	7.7	7.8	8.4	7.8	7.7	7.8	8.1	8.0	7.8	6.4
12. December	8.3	8.3	8.6	8.5	8.3	7.6	8.3	8.8	8.7	8.4	8.3	8.7	9.6	7.0	7.4	9.2
Item 20 Subject R01 N	16532	8046	8211	12762	2063	3902	4715	5301	2614	9012	6496	6028	3535	2283	4191	202

C03: What is your sex?

	TOTAL	M	F	White	Black	NE	NC	S	W	Yes	No	None	Marijuana Only	Few Pills	More Pills	Any Heroin
1. Male	49.5	100.0	-	50.1	43.3	46.9	52.9	48.6	49.3	49.2	48.7	47.1	54.4	48.4	48.8	64.3
2. Female	50.5	-	100.0	49.9	56.7	53.1	47.1	51.4	50.7	50.8	51.3	52.9	45.6	51.6	51.2	35.7
Item 30 Subject R01 N	16301	8074	8227	12612	2024	3862	4661	5200	2578	8905	6399	5950	3486	2243	4145	191

C04: How do you describe yourself?

	TOTAL	M	F	White	Black	NE	NC	S	W	Yes	No	None	Marijuana Only	Few Pills	More Pills	Any Heroin
1. American Indian	1.5	1.7	1.2	-	-	1.1	1.6	1.3	2.1	0.7	2.4	1.0	1.4	1.4	2.0	6.2
2. Black or Afro-American	12.5	10.9	14.0	-	100.0	15.2	4.2	23.4	1.6	12.5	11.4	13.1	19.6	11.0	5.0	10.0
3. Mexican American or Chicano	2.4	2.6	2.1	-	-	0.1	0.8	1.1	11.2	2.0	2.7	2.1	2.5	2.9	2.0	3.7
4. Puerto Rican or other Latin American	1.7	1.7	1.8	-	-	4.0	0.4	1.3	1.7	1.8	1.5	2.1	1.7	1.9	1.0	1.6
5. Oriental or Asian American	1.5	1.6	1.5	-	-	1.3	0.7	0.8	5.0	2.3	0.5	2.2	1.1	1.6	0.8	1.7
6. White or Caucasian	77.7	78.8	76.9	100.0	-	75.4	89.6	70.9	73.6	78.7	78.5	76.9	71.7	78.8	86.5	71.8
7. Other	2.6	2.6	2.4	-	-	2.9	2.7	1.2	4.8	2.0	3.0	2.6	2.1	2.4	2.6	5.1
Item 40 Subject R01 N	16473	8020	8178	12806	2067	3888	4706	5288	2591	8991	6463	6008	3512	2270	4191	198

C05: Where did you grow up mostly?

	TOTAL	M	F	White	Black	NE	NC	S	W	Yes	No	None	Marijuana Only	Few Pills	More Pills	Any Heroin
1. On a farm	7.1	7.9	6.2	7.8	2.5	2.6	11.6	6.8	5.8	5.2	9.9	10.1	4.6	6.2	4.9	12.1
2. In the country, not on a farm	12.3	12.9	11.8	12.8	11.9	13.1	14.0	12.9	6.9	9.4	16.2	13.6	10.8	12.0	12.2	8.6
3. In a small city or town (under 50,000 people)	31.2	30.0	32.2	33.2	22.3	34.6	30.2	28.4	33.7	30.1	33.3	30.7	32.8	31.5	31.0	23.7
4. In a medium-sized city (50,000 - 100,000)	16.0	15.3	16.8	16.1	17.2	13.9	14.5	16.8	20.5	16.2	15.8	14.3	16.5	18.4	17.1	16.4
5. In a suburb of a medium-sized city	9.1	8.5	9.8	9.9	6.4	10.9	8.1	9.3	8.1	10.3	7.3	7.7	10.1	8.3	10.6	9.0
6. In a large city (100,000 - 500,000)	9.0	8.4	9.6	6.4	20.2	9.3	4.8	11.6	11.1	9.8	7.6	9.2	8.8	9.7	8.4	9.9
7. In a suburb of a large city	6.6	7.4	5.9	7.2	4.2	6.1	7.7	6.5	5.8	8.3	4.3	6.0	7.1	6.1	7.6	8.4
8. In a very large city (over 500,000)	4.6	4.6	4.5	2.3	13.0	5.9	3.8	4.1	5.1	5.4	3.3	4.5	5.6	3.8	3.8	6.1
9. In a suburb of a very large city	4.0	4.9	3.2	4.2	2.3	3.5	5.4	3.5	3.0	5.3	2.4	3.9	3.7	3.9	4.3	5.9
Item 50 Subject R03 N	15353	7487	7562	11885	1906	3627	4467	4878	2381	8432	6004	5610	3282	2130	3885	176

C06: What is your present marital status?

	TOTAL	M	F	White	Black	NE	NC	S	W	Yes	No	None	Marijuana Only	Few Pills	More Pills	Any Heroin
1. Married	2.1	1.9	2.2	1.7	2.2	1.5	1.9	2.5	2.6	1.4	2.9	2.2	1.9	1.8	1.9	5.8
2. Engaged	6.8	3.8	9.6	6.8	5.8	5.4	6.8	8.1	6.1	3.8	10.8	4.8	6.2	8.0	9.1	12.9
3. Separated/divorced	0.6	0.7	0.4	0.4	1.1	0.6	0.3	0.6	0.8	0.5	0.6	0.5	0.4	0.6	0.6	2.4
4. Single	90.6	93.6	87.8	91.1	90.9	92.4	91.1	88.8	90.4	94.3	85.8	92.6	91.4	89.7	88.4	78.8
Item 60 Subject D01,R01 N	16547	8004	8209	12753	2048	3897	4714	5315	2621	9028	6518	6023	3532	2294	4204	200

*=less than .05 per cent.

QUESTIONNAIRE FORM 1-5 1983	TOTAL	SEX		RACE		REGION				4YR COLLEGE PLANS		ILLICIT DRUG USE: LIFETIME				
		M	F	White	Black	NE	NC	S	W	Yes	No	None	Marijuana Only	Few Pills	More Pills	Any Heroin
N (Weighted No. of Cases):	16947	8074	8227	12806	2066	4056	4784	5434	2673	9061	6555	6082	3598	2315	4306	206
% of Weighted Total:	100.0	47.6	48.5	75.6	12.2	23.9	28.2	32.1	15.8	53.5	38.7	35.9	21.2	13.7	25.4	1.2

C07: Which of the following people live in the same household with you? (Mark ALL that apply.)

	TOTAL	M	F	White	Black	NE	NC	S	W	Yes	No	None	Marijuana Only	Few Pills	More Pills	Any Heroin
A. I live alone	0.6	0.9	0.3	0.5	0.7	0.5	0.5	0.7	0.8	0.3	0.9	0.3	0.5	0.4	0.9	5.1
B. Father (or male guardian)	77.5	79.5	76.0	83.0	49.0	75.5	82.7	73.6	79.1	79.9	75.4	82.2	75.1	74.9	75.7	68.3
C. Mother (or female guardian)	91.5	91.2	92.2	93.1	85.8	92.7	91.9	90.2	91.6	93.9	89.1	93.9	91.4	91.9	89.1	79.1
D. Brother(s) and/or sister(s)	75.4	75.5	75.9	75.7	72.6	79.0	77.0	72.0	74.1	76.7	74.1	78.3	76.7	74.6	71.1	69.2
E. Grandparent(s)	4.7	4.7	4.7	4.0	7.9	5.9	3.9	4.8	4.2	4.5	5.0	4.5	4.6	5.2	4.7	8.7
F. My husband/wife	0.9	0.5	1.3	0.8	0.5	0.7	0.9	1.2	0.7	0.4	1.6	0.7	0.8	0.8	1.1	3.4
G. My children	0.9	0.3	1.5	0.6	2.9	0.8	1.1	1.2	0.5	0.4	1.6	0.6	1.0	1.0	1.1	5.2
H. Other relative(s)	5.3	4.8	5.7	3.5	13.7	5.1	4.2	6.6	4.6	4.7	5.9	4.4	6.0	5.3	5.6	8.1
I. Non-relative(s)	3.4	2.7	4.0	3.4	2.2	3.1	3.3	2.8	5.1	2.7	4.3	2.3	3.1	3.2	5.1	7.0
Item 80-160 Subject R03 N	16525	7988	8201	12752	2042	3898	4709	5307	2611	9021	6510	6015	3520	2295	4200	200

The next three questions ask about your parents. If you were raised mostly by foster parents, step-parents, or others, answer for them. For example, if you have both a step-father and a natural father, answer for the one that was most important in raising you.

C08: What is the highest level of schooling your father completed?

	TOTAL	M	F	White	Black	NE	NC	S	W	Yes	No	None	Marijuana Only	Few Pills	More Pills	Any Heroin
1. Completed grade school or less	6.4	5.7	7.2	4.9	9.2	5.8	6.1	7.4	6.2	4.5	9.1	7.2	5.7	6.4	5.7	7.3
2. Some high school	14.9	14.5	15.1	13.6	19.9	15.0	15.7	15.9	11.2	10.0	21.4	13.2	15.6	15.5	15.7	16.3
3. Completed high school	31.3	31.2	31.3	32.3	31.1	33.2	34.6	30.6	24.3	26.9	37.0	32.0	31.0	30.4	31.5	32.9
4. Some college	14.4	14.9	14.0	15.5	10.7	11.3	14.1	14.6	19.3	17.3	10.9	14.1	13.4	15.4	15.5	12.2
5. Completed college	17.0	18.0	16.1	18.8	9.7	16.1	16.9	16.2	19.9	21.6	10.7	17.3	17.0	16.4	17.0	14.6
6. Graduate or professional school after college	10.5	11.1	10.0	11.5	4.7	12.5	8.5	9.2	13.6	15.7	3.7	10.4	11.4	10.4	10.2	11.9
7. Don't know, or does not apply	5.5	4.6	6.3	3.3	14.7	6.1	4.1	6.2	5.7	4.0	7.3	5.8	5.8	5.5	4.3	4.9
Item 310 Subject R02 N	16436	7958	8149	12703	2001	3856	4698	5271	2611	9006	6503	5995	3509	2281	4170	201

C09: What is the highest level of schooling your mother completed?

	TOTAL	M	F	White	Black	NE	NC	S	W	Yes	No	None	Marijuana Only	Few Pills	More Pills	Any Heroin
1. Completed grade school or less	3.8	3.3	4.3	2.1	6.0	3.6	3.1	4.1	4.9	2.8	5.2	4.4	3.7	3.6	2.5	4.7
2. Some high school	15.0	13.4	16.3	13.1	21.8	14.2	14.2	17.7	12.1	10.1	21.2	14.2	14.7	15.2	15.7	21.2
3. Completed high school	41.6	42.8	40.6	44.6	34.4	43.0	45.7	41.1	33.5	38.0	47.0	42.8	39.4	40.5	43.5	37.7
4. Some college	15.7	16.0	15.5	16.4	13.9	13.1	14.5	15.6	21.7	19.4	10.8	14.7	16.9	17.2	15.3	14.0
5. Completed college	14.6	15.2	14.0	15.6	11.9	15.3	14.3	13.3	16.9	19.0	9.0	14.4	15.7	14.3	14.6	14.7
6. Graduate or professional school after college	6.3	6.2	6.5	6.3	5.9	7.5	5.5	5.6	7.3	8.5	3.1	6.1	6.2	6.1	6.7	6.7
7. Don't know, or does not apply	3.0	3.1	2.9	1.8	6.0	3.4	2.7	2.6	3.6	2.3	3.8	3.4	3.4	3.0	1.6	1.0
Item 320 Subject R02 N	16462	7965	8169	12707	2017	3870	4696	5280	2615	9017	6517	6003	3517	2285	4173	201

C10: Did your mother have a paid job (half-time or more) during the time you were growing up?

	TOTAL	M	F	White	Black	NE	NC	S	W	Yes	No	None	Marijuana Only	Few Pills	More Pills	Any Heroin
1. No	27.9	29.3	26.8	30.7	11.0	29.5	31.5	22.3	30.5	28.7	27.3	32.1	25.8	26.2	24.8	26.7
2. Yes, some of the time when I was growing up	29.2	30.5	28.0	30.7	20.7	29.1	30.7	28.2	29.0	29.5	29.3	29.3	28.1	29.4	29.7	31.6
3. Yes, most of the time	18.4	18.3	18.4	17.8	21.2	18.2	17.3	19.4	18.8	17.5	19.6	16.6	19.0	18.9	20.7	17.8
4. Yes, all or nearly all of the time	24.4	21.9	26.8	20.7	47.1	23.2	20.5	30.1	21.7	24.3	23.8	22.0	27.1	25.5	24.8	23.9
Item 330 Subject R02 N	16405	7943	8140	12684	1997	3848	4685	5258	2614	9004	6506	5989	3498	2281	4161	198

C11: How would you describe your political preference?

	TOTAL	M	F	White	Black	NE	NC	S	W	Yes	No	None	Marijuana Only	Few Pills	More Pills	Any Heroin
1. Strongly Republican	6.5	8.4	4.4	7.2	3.2	4.6	6.9	6.9	7.6	7.6	4.9	7.7	6.1	5.5	5.3	10.0
2. Mildly Republican	13.4	14.7	12.2	15.6	4.0	11.3	14.5	12.8	15.7	16.1	10.1	14.9	13.4	12.8	12.3	6.1
3. Mildly Democrat	13.6	13.4	13.8	13.2	16.1	12.7	12.5	15.0	14.0	14.4	12.4	12.6	14.8	15.3	13.1	14.4
4. Strongly Democrat	10.7	10.3	11.0	7.1	33.0	8.8	8.9	15.0	7.7	10.7	10.4	10.6	12.3	10.2	9.3	13.0
5. American Independent Party	1.3	1.5	1.1	1.1	1.7	1.8	0.8	1.4	1.2	1.2	1.3	1.2	1.1	1.2	1.4	3.5
6. No preference, independent	23.7	25.3	22.0	25.6	11.8	25.4	26.0	21.6	21.1	23.3	24.5	23.0	21.3	23.8	27.1	24.3
7. Other	1.5	2.0	1.0	1.3	1.3	1.6	1.4	1.2	2.2	1.3	1.5	1.4	0.9	1.6	1.7	5.1
8. Don't know, haven't decided	29.4	24.4	34.5	28.9	28.9	33.6	28.9	26.2	30.5	25.4	34.9	28.6	30.1	29.6	29.8	23.7
Item 340 Subject H01 N	16320	7901	8102	12627	2000	3822	4663	5234	2602	8988	6467	5950	3489	2261	4140	196

QUESTIONNAIRE FORM 1-5 1983	TOTAL	SEX		RACE		REGION				4YR COLLEGE PLANS		ILLICIT DRUG USE: LIFETIME				
		M	F	White	Black	NE	NC	S	W	Yes	No	None	Marijuana Only	Few Pills	More Pills	Any Heroin
N (Weighted No. of Cases):	16947	8074	8227	12806	2066	4056	4784	5434	2673	9061	6555	6082	3598	2315	4306	206
% of Weighted Total:	100.0	47.6	48.5	75.6	12.2	23.9	28.2	32.1	15.8	53.5	38.7	35.9	21.2	13.7	25.4	1.2
C12: How would you describe your political beliefs?																
1. Very conservative	2.9	3.7	2.1	2.6	4.1	2.3	2.3	3.5	4.0	3.0	2.8	3.8	2.5	2.4	2.2	4.0
2. Conservative	12.5	14.1	11.0	13.0	10.5	10.3	13.3	13.1	13.3	14.1	10.4	14.4	12.3	12.3	10.1	12.7
3. Moderate	31.7	31.7	31.6	33.0	29.1	29.7	31.7	34.1	29.4	34.2	28.5	33.1	31.4	33.2	29.6	24.4
4. Liberal	14.2	14.0	14.4	14.2	13.3	14.7	14.6	13.2	15.0	16.5	11.0	11.6	14.6	14.5	17.6	15.9
5. Very liberal	3.0	3.2	2.8	2.7	4.3	2.9	2.7	2.8	4.2	3.5	2.3	2.3	2.9	3.3	3.9	3.2
6. Radical	2.9	4.5	1.3	2.8	3.4	3.4	2.9	2.6	2.9	2.9	3.0	1.6	2.4	3.0	4.7	12.7
8. None of the above, or don't know	32.7	28.8	36.9	31.7	35.4	36.8	32.5	30.7	31.1	25.8	42.0	33.3	33.9	31.3	32.0	27.1
Item 350 Subject H01 N	16284	7885	8084	12599	1980	3810	4667	5213	2594	8977	6459	5937	3472	2261	4141	197
C13: The next three questions are about religion.																
C13A: What is your religious preference?																
01. Baptist	21.8	20.2	23.0	17.2	58.8	10.8	12.0	44.4	9.9	19.1	25.4	23.5	22.7	23.5	16.7	24.0
02. Churches of Christ	5.6	5.9	5.4	5.1	7.1	4.7	5.0	5.9	7.6	4.5	7.1	5.8	5.8	5.1	5.4	6.2
03. Disciples of Christ	0.4	0.4	0.4	0.4	0.5	0.6	0.2	0.5	0.3	0.5	0.4	0.5	0.3	0.4	0.4	0.6
04. Episcopal	1.5	1.4	1.7	1.6	1.4	1.4	0.9	2.1	1.6	1.9	0.9	1.0	2.1	1.9	1.7	1.3
05. Lutheran	6.2	6.0	6.6	7.7	0.3	2.6	14.8	2.2	4.2	6.4	6.6	6.2	6.5	6.0	6.6	4.2
06. Methodist	7.4	7.1	7.7	8.0	6.7	6.3	7.5	10.3	3.0	7.5	7.3	8.0	6.1	7.3	7.8	5.4
07. Presbyterian	3.8	3.7	3.9	4.2	1.8	3.4	4.2	2.9	5.5	4.3	3.1	3.8	3.8	3.5	4.0	1.4
08. United Church of Christ	0.8	0.9	0.8	0.9	0.7	1.2	1.5	0.3	0.3	0.8	1.0	0.9	0.8	0.9	0.9	0.7
09. Other Protestant	3.9	3.4	4.3	4.3	2.1	4.9	4.1	2.5	4.7	3.7	4.1	4.4	3.3	3.5	3.9	4.7
10. Unitarian	0.1	0.1	0.2	0.2	-	0.2	0.1	0.2	0.1	0.2	0.1	0.2	-	0.1	0.2	-
11. Roman Catholic	30.2	31.3	29.3	32.7	4.9	46.1	34.6	16.1	27.3	33.7	25.4	28.8	31.9	30.7	31.2	24.1
12. Eastern Orthodox	0.3	0.3	0.3	0.3	-	0.5	0.3	0.1	0.2	0.4	0.1	0.2	0.4	0.3	0.2	-
13. Jewish	1.2	1.2	1.2	1.4	0.1	3.9	0.3	0.2	0.7	1.8	0.3	0.9	1.6	1.2	1.3	1.5
16. Latter Day Saints	1.8	1.6	1.9	2.1	0.1	*	0.4	0.5	9.3	2.0	1.4	2.7	1.1	1.7	1.1	1.4
14. Other religion	5.6	5.2	6.0	4.3	8.8	4.5	5.3	5.4	8.1	4.7	6.6	6.1	4.4	4.8	5.9	9.0
15. None	9.3	11.4	7.3	9.4	6.6	8.7	8.8	6.3	17.2	8.6	10.2	7.0	9.2	8.9	12.8	15.6
Item 360 Subject G N	16231	7826	8086	12564	1975	3792	4643	5219	2576	8955	6440	5927	3466	2250	4111	198
C13B: How often do you attend religious services?																
1. Never	9.3	11.3	7.3	9.4	6.0	10.4	9.0	6.2	15.0	7.4	11.9	6.6	10.1	7.9	13.0	20.1
2. Rarely	34.6	36.3	32.9	34.4	34.0	37.3	32.3	33.2	37.5	30.2	39.9	25.8	35.6	37.1	44.9	34.1
3. Once or twice a month	17.0	16.7	17.3	16.2	23.8	16.8	15.9	19.5	14.1	16.9	16.9	14.8	19.6	19.2	16.8	18.5
4. About once a week or more	39.1	35.7	42.5	40.0	36.2	35.5	42.8	41.1	33.5	45.5	31.2	52.8	34.7	35.8	25.2	27.2
Item 370 Subject G N	16386	7916	8150	12671	2003	3837	4679	5260	2610	9030	6509	5981	3490	2278	4159	198
C13C: How important is religion in your life?																
1. Not important	10.6	13.6	7.6	11.4	4.3	12.5	10.8	6.4	15.9	10.1	11.3	7.2	11.4	9.6	15.1	18.8
2. A little important	26.9	29.5	24.4	28.3	18.5	30.5	28.1	22.3	28.9	23.3	31.7	19.4	28.0	30.2	35.4	30.9
3. Pretty important	34.2	33.0	35.3	34.7	34.7	35.2	36.6	35.6	25.2	35.1	33.2	33.5	35.7	36.0	32.5	32.3
4. Very important	28.3	23.8	32.6	25.6	42.6	21.7	24.5	35.7	30.0	31.5	23.9	39.8	24.8	24.2	17.0	17.9
Item 380 Subject G N	16365	7909	8137	12653	2004	3832	4671	5253	2609	9030	6499	5980	3490	2268	4146	199
C14: When are you most likely to graduate from high school?																
1. By this June	98.0	97.3	98.8	98.6	96.5	98.6	98.4	97.6	97.0	98.9	96.9	98.8	98.2	98.2	97.1	89.3
2. July to January	1.7	2.3	1.0	1.2	3.3	1.0	1.2	2.2	2.6	0.9	2.6	1.0	1.7	1.6	2.4	8.0
3. After next January	-	-	-	-	-	-	-	-	-	-	-	-	-	-	-	-
6. Don't expect to graduate	0.3	0.4	0.2	0.2	0.3	0.4	0.3	0.2	0.3	0.1	0.5	0.2	0.1	0.3	0.5	2.7
Item 390 Subject B01 N	16376	7905	8133	12655	2001	3835	4676	5260	2606	9043	6539	5985	3487	2273	4155	198
C15: Which of the following best describes your present high school program?																
1. Academic or college prep	45.9	44.6	47.8	49.0	39.5	51.4	43.1	46.2	42.0	67.7	17.5	52.9	46.8	45.1	37.4	31.7
2. General	31.8	31.0	32.4	31.2	32.6	26.7	33.2	31.5	37.8	22.3	44.3	27.4	32.2	31.7	36.8	40.7
3. Vocational, technical, or commercial	14.5	16.7	12.1	13.7	16.4	13.9	15.9	15.4	11.1	6.1	25.4	12.2	13.4	14.7	18.3	17.9
4. Other, or don't know	7.8	7.8	7.8	6.2	11.5	8.1	7.8	6.9	9.1	3.9	12.8	7.4	7.6	8.5	7.6	9.7
Item 400 Subject B01 N	16281	7855	8094	12595	1992	3801	4655	5239	2586	9026	6504	5956	3468	2255	4133	195

*=less than .05 per cent.

QUESTIONNAIRE FORM 1-5 1983	TOTAL	SEX		RACE		REGION				4YR COLLEGE PLANS		ILLICIT DRUG USE: LIFETIME				
		M	F	White	Black	NE	NC	S	W	Yes	No	None	Mari- juana Only	Few Pills	More Pills	Any Her- oin
N (Weighted No. of Cases):	16947	8074	8227	12806	2066	4056	4784	5434	2673	9061	6555	6082	3598	2315	4306	206
% of Weighted Total:	100.0	47.6	48.5	75.6	12.2	23.9	28.2	32.1	15.8	53.5	38.7	35.9	21.2	13.7	25.4	1.2

C16: Compared with others your age throughout the country, how do you rate yourself on school ability?

	TOTAL	M	F	White	Black	NE	NC	S	W	Yes	No	None	Mari- juana Only	Few Pills	More Pills	Any Her- oin
1. Far below average	0.6	0.6	0.4	0.3	1.0	0.5	0.6	0.5	0.6	0.3	0.8	0.6	0.4	0.7	0.5	1.5
2. Below average	1.6	1.9	1.3	1.5	1.7	1.8	1.8	1.2	1.7	1.0	2.4	1.2	1.5	1.5	2.1	3.5
3. Slightly below average	5.3	6.6	4.1	4.8	5.8	5.4	5.9	4.7	5.7	3.0	8.4	4.0	5.5	5.7	6.6	11.0
4. Average	38.0	36.4	39.2	35.1	49.9	38.8	35.0	42.3	33.5	26.8	52.3	32.5	39.1	40.3	42.4	49.5
5. Slightly above average	23.4	22.9	24.1	24.1	22.0	23.4	23.4	22.9	24.6	25.1	21.1	23.1	23.7	24.9	23.7	15.1
6. Above average	25.8	25.1	26.8	28.3	16.5	25.0	27.9	23.4	27.9	35.7	13.4	31.7	24.5	22.9	21.0	15.5
7. Far above average	5.3	6.5	4.1	5.8	3.0	5.0	5.4	4.9	6.0	8.1	1.6	6.9	5.3	4.0	3.8	4.0
Item 410 Subject B01 N	15979	7747	7907	12395	1927	3714	4579	5138	2548	8877	6398	5861	3400	2217	4051	188

C17: How intelligent do you think you are compared with others your age?

	TOTAL	M	F	White	Black	NE	NC	S	W	Yes	No	None	Mari- juana Only	Few Pills	More Pills	Any Her- oin
1. Far below average	0.5	0.6	0.4	0.4	0.8	0.5	0.4	0.6	0.4	0.3	0.7	0.6	0.3	0.5	0.4	1.6
2. Below average	1.2	1.3	1.1	1.1	1.0	1.2	1.4	1.0	1.5	0.7	2.0	1.0	1.2	0.9	1.6	4.6
3. Slightly below average	4.2	4.2	4.2	4.0	3.7	4.0	4.8	3.9	4.0	2.2	6.7	3.4	4.1	5.4	4.5	8.2
4. Average	36.2	32.8	39.2	34.6	40.2	36.6	34.8	39.3	31.9	25.5	50.2	32.3	36.9	39.4	38.6	39.0
5. Slightly above average	23.9	24.1	23.8	24.4	23.0	24.7	23.5	23.4	24.7	25.0	22.6	23.5	24.4	23.1	25.1	18.9
6. Above average	27.5	28.7	26.7	29.1	23.7	26.6	29.2	25.1	30.2	37.2	14.8	31.7	26.8	25.0	24.2	20.3
7. Far above average	6.5	8.3	4.6	6.4	7.5	6.5	5.8	6.7	7.3	9.1	2.9	7.4	6.3	5.7	5.6	7.4
Item 420 Subject B01 N	16058	7740	7997	12461	1930	3746	4618	5158	2537	8952	6418	5895	3411	2235	4063	192

C18:   During the LAST FOUR WEEKS, how many whole days of school have you missed . . .

C18A: Because of illness

	TOTAL	M	F	White	Black	NE	NC	S	W	Yes	No	None	Mari- juana Only	Few Pills	More Pills	Any Her- oin
1. None	57.7	63.5	52.6	58.5	56.6	53.9	60.6	59.0	55.4	60.3	54.8	65.8	57.6	54.0	49.0	48.1
2. 1 day	17.7	16.2	19.2	18.2	14.9	18.1	16.9	17.6	19.0	18.0	17.5	15.8	18.2	19.5	19.3	15.1
3. 2 days	11.1	9.8	12.3	10.8	11.5	13.1	9.7	10.4	12.0	10.2	11.9	8.5	10.9	13.0	13.8	11.1
4. 3 days	6.4	5.1	7.4	6.1	7.4	6.7	6.3	6.3	6.2	5.6	7.2	4.8	6.2	6.6	8.2	13.3
5. 4-5 days	4.4	3.2	5.4	4.1	5.3	5.2	4.1	4.0	4.7	3.8	5.2	3.4	4.1	4.6	5.7	7.6
6. 6-10 days	1.8	1.4	2.0	1.6	2.4	1.9	1.8	1.7	1.5	1.3	2.3	1.1	2.0	1.8	2.4	2.5
7. 11 or more	0.9	0.8	1.0	0.8	1.9	1.2	0.6	1.0	1.1	0.7	1.1	0.6	1.0	0.6	1.5	2.4
Item 430 Subject B06 N	15857	7632	7905	12282	1937	3698	4570	5094	2496	8833	6374	5819	3390	2195	4009	184

C18B: Because you skipped or "cut"

	TOTAL	M	F	White	Black	NE	NC	S	W	Yes	No	None	Mari- juana Only	Few Pills	More Pills	Any Her- oin
1. None	71.8	70.1	73.8	71.5	78.4	70.5	75.9	74.6	60.3	75.3	67.6	84.7	73.6	69.1	54.6	44.5
2. 1 day	12.7	12.9	12.3	13.1	10.9	14.3	11.2	12.6	13.2	12.4	13.0	9.2	12.4	14.9	16.8	13.9
3. 2 days	6.3	6.5	5.9	6.3	4.8	6.2	5.6	5.5	9.2	5.4	7.1	3.0	6.3	7.4	9.9	14.6
4. 3 days	3.7	4.3	3.2	3.7	3.1	4.0	2.8	3.5	5.6	3.0	4.7	1.7	3.4	3.4	6.9	7.6
5. 4-5 days	3.1	3.5	2.7	3.0	1.3	2.9	2.4	2.2	6.3	2.2	4.1	0.9	2.2	3.1	6.6	8.9
6. 6-10 days	1.6	1.7	1.4	1.6	0.6	1.2	1.4	1.1	3.3	1.1	2.2	0.3	1.3	1.3	3.4	6.5
7. 11 or more	0.9	1.0	0.7	0.8	0.7	1.0	0.5	0.5	2.0	0.6	1.2	0.3	0.7	0.8	1.8	4.0
Item 440 Subject B06 N	15398	7451	7643	11961	1854	3583	4468	4910	2437	8584	6209	5609	3280	2141	3944	183

C18C: For other reasons

	TOTAL	M	F	White	Black	NE	NC	S	W	Yes	No	None	Mari- juana Only	Few Pills	More Pills	Any Her- oin
1. None	59.2	60.9	57.6	58.7	62.8	58.7	60.1	60.8	54.8	58.0	60.8	63.0	60.1	57.5	53.9	52.9
2. 1 day	19.4	18.1	20.7	20.4	15.5	19.8	20.0	18.9	18.7	20.3	18.4	18.7	18.6	21.1	20.7	14.3
3. 2 days	10.3	9.9	10.7	10.1	10.7	11.0	9.3	10.1	11.5	10.7	9.7	9.5	10.3	10.1	11.5	11.2
4. 3 days	5.2	5.1	5.2	4.9	5.6	5.0	4.7	4.7	7.1	5.2	5.0	4.5	4.9	5.3	6.0	10.8
5. 4-5 days	3.9	3.9	3.9	3.9	3.2	3.5	3.6	3.8	5.4	3.9	3.8	2.9	4.0	4.2	5.1	4.5
6. 6-10 days	1.3	1.3	1.2	1.3	1.2	1.4	1.4	1.1	1.5	1.3	1.3	1.0	1.3	1.2	1.7	3.5
7. 11 or more	0.7	0.6	0.8	0.7	1.0	0.6	0.8	0.6	1.0	0.5	1.0	0.4	0.8	0.5	1.1	2.8
Item 450 Subject B06 N	15547	7490	7747	12082	1863	3608	4529	4958	2452	8698	6242	5725	3300	2173	3915	185

C19: During the last four weeks, how often have you gone to school, but skipped a class when you weren't supposed to?

	TOTAL	M	F	White	Black	NE	NC	S	W	Yes	No	None	Mari- juana Only	Few Pills	More Pills	Any Her- oin
1. Not at all	66.2	62.7	69.7	66.8	69.7	63.4	70.1	74.5	46.6	67.0	65.5	78.9	64.4	62.8	52.5	41.7
2. 1 or 2 times	20.1	21.6	18.7	19.7	19.8	21.3	19.1	16.3	27.9	20.3	19.7	15.1	22.3	23.6	23.4	21.8
3. 3-5 times	8.5	9.8	7.4	8.6	6.0	9.0	7.4	5.8	15.2	7.9	9.2	3.6	8.7	9.4	14.5	22.7
4. 6-10 times	2.9	3.5	2.2	3.0	2.2	3.5	1.9	1.7	5.9	2.7	3.0	1.0	3.0	2.5	5.6	6.9
5. 11-20 times	1.2	1.4	1.0	1.2	0.8	1.4	0.8	0.8	2.4	1.2	1.2	0.5	0.8	0.9	2.6	2.3
6. More than 20 times	1.1	1.1	1.0	0.7	1.5	1.2	0.7	0.9	1.9	0.9	1.4	1.0	0.8	0.9	1.4	4.6
Item 460 Subject B06 N	16241	7828	8080	12576	1971	3779	4665	5218	2579	9039	6539	5963	3456	2249	4106	194

QUESTIONNAIRE FORM 1-5 1983	TOTAL	SEX		RACE		REGION				4YR COLLEGE PLANS		ILLICIT DRUG USE: LIFETIME				
		M	F	White	Black	NE	NC	S	W	Yes	No	None	Marijuana Only	Few Pills	More Pills	Any Heroin
N (Weighted No. of Cases):	16947	8074	8227	12806	2066	4056	4784	5434	2673	9061	6555	6082	3598	2315	4306	206
% of Weighted Total:	100.0	47.6	48.5	75.6	12.2	23.9	28.2	32.1	15.8	53.5	38.7	35.9	21.2	13.7	25.4	1.2

C20: Which of the following best describes your average grade so far in high school?

	TOTAL	M	F	White	Black	NE	NC	S	W	Yes	No	None	Marijuana Only	Few Pills	More Pills	Any Heroin
9. A (93-100)	8.1	6.5	9.8	9.3	2.9	8.0	7.6	8.5	8.6	11.9	3.3	12.8	6.7	6.1	4.1	6.2
8. A- (90-92)	10.3	8.0	12.9	11.4	5.2	10.3	9.9	10.2	11.5	14.1	5.5	14.1	9.3	8.6	7.4	4.8
7. B+ (87-89)	16.5	14.1	19.0	17.4	13.5	17.5	15.8	16.1	17.1	19.8	12.8	18.9	16.3	16.7	13.6	9.2
6. B (83-86)	19.9	18.8	21.2	20.7	17.2	20.9	20.4	18.8	19.8	20.8	18.9	19.9	20.3	19.5	20.5	15.0
5. B- (80-82)	15.3	16.9	13.6	14.7	17.8	15.9	15.2	15.4	14.4	14.4	16.1	12.8	16.8	16.9	16.2	14.1
4. C+ (77-79)	14.3	16.4	12.1	12.6	22.3	14.1	14.0	14.9	13.7	11.0	18.2	11.5	14.3	16.4	16.5	20.2
3. C (73-76)	10.1	12.3	7.8	9.2	13.5	8.6	11.0	10.5	10.1	5.8	15.9	6.7	10.7	10.3	14.0	18.4
2. C- (70-72)	4.3	5.6	2.9	3.8	6.1	3.5	5.0	4.7	3.6	1.8	7.4	2.7	4.5	4.3	6.3	8.8
1. D (69 or below)	1.1	1.5	0.7	0.8	1.6	1.1	1.2	0.9	1.1	0.3	2.0	0.6	1.1	1.2	1.5	3.3
Item 470 Subject B01 N	16162	7786	8048	12524	1964	3755	4636	5203	2568	9017	6501	5934	3451	2234	4080	191

C21: How likely is it that you will do each of the following things after high school?

C21A: Attend a technical or vocational school

	TOTAL	M	F	White	Black	NE	NC	S	W	Yes	No	None	Marijuana Only	Few Pills	More Pills	Any Heroin
1. Definitely won't	42.0	37.5	46.7	43.6	39.0	54.4	38.8	41.3	31.6	55.9	24.3	45.9	43.3	40.2	37.0	33.9
2. Probably won't	29.3	31.6	27.0	30.0	24.1	23.6	31.9	28.4	34.5	29.4	29.8	29.1	28.8	30.3	29.8	29.8
3. Probably will	19.1	20.8	17.4	17.2	25.6	13.8	18.8	21.2	23.1	10.4	30.2	16.7	18.7	19.9	21.9	25.0
4. Definitely will	9.6	10.1	8.9	9.2	11.3	8.2	10.4	9.1	10.7	4.4	15.7	8.2	9.3	9.6	11.4	11.3
Item 480 Subject B09,C03 N	15456	7404	7737	12022	1835	3530	4493	4968	2464	8698	6526	5729	3277	2141	3895	179

C21B: Serve in the armed forces

	TOTAL	M	F	White	Black	NE	NC	S	W	Yes	No	None	Marijuana Only	Few Pills	More Pills	Any Heroin
1. Definitely won't	56.4	39.2	73.3	59.1	43.1	60.4	56.6	52.1	58.9	60.6	51.5	58.5	54.1	55.5	57.3	43.3
2. Probably won't	25.9	33.6	18.4	26.7	19.4	22.8	28.7	25.6	25.6	26.4	25.4	26.3	25.9	25.3	25.3	29.7
3. Probably will	10.6	15.1	6.0	8.4	21.9	10.1	8.3	13.2	10.5	8.4	13.3	8.7	12.1	12.2	10.8	11.0
4. Definitely will	7.1	12.1	2.3	5.8	15.6	6.7	6.4	9.2	4.9	4.5	9.8	6.5	7.9	7.0	6.6	16.0
Item 490 Subject B09,L01 N	15015	7200	7525	11787	1726	3426	4373	4827	2389	8536	6272	5578	3181	2090	3788	158

C21C: Graduate from a two-year college program

	TOTAL	M	F	White	Black	NE	NC	S	W	Yes	No	None	Marijuana Only	Few Pills	More Pills	Any Heroin
1. Definitely won't	34.4	34.9	33.9	35.6	31.4	41.6	37.4	32.7	21.8	39.0	29.4	36.7	36.2	31.1	31.5	40.1
2. Probably won't	28.9	32.2	25.8	30.1	25.7	23.3	32.2	30.6	27.6	29.8	28.6	29.8	27.5	31.7	27.6	30.6
3. Probably will	23.6	22.3	24.9	21.7	29.8	19.6	20.8	24.7	31.9	18.8	29.0	20.7	24.5	24.7	26.1	19.5
4. Definitely will	13.1	10.6	15.4	12.7	13.1	15.4	9.6	12.0	18.7	12.4	13.1	12.8	11.8	12.5	14.8	9.8
Item 500 Subject B09 N	15395	7331	7756	11978	1820	3523	4473	4946	2452	8622	6514	5696	3278	2131	3884	176

C21D: Graduate from college (four-year program)

	TOTAL	M	F	White	Black	NE	NC	S	W	Yes	No	None	Marijuana Only	Few Pills	More Pills	Any Heroin
1. Definitely won't	22.6	21.6	23.4	22.6	20.6	23.3	24.8	22.2	18.2	-	53.8	19.0	21.2	23.3	27.5	41.1
2. Probably won't	19.4	20.0	18.7	19.1	19.1	16.4	19.9	20.1	21.4	-	46.2	17.3	18.2	20.0	23.2	18.1
3. Probably will	22.4	23.4	21.5	21.9	24.9	19.8	21.3	23.0	27.1	38.6	-	22.0	23.2	23.4	22.1	16.5
4. Definitely will	35.6	35.0	36.5	36.3	35.4	40.5	34.0	34.7	33.4	61.4	-	41.7	37.4	33.4	27.2	24.2
Item 510 Subject B09 N	15617	7501	7803	12150	1863	3593	4517	5018	2488	9062	6555	5802	3305	2151	3928	186

C21E: Attend graduate or professional school after college

	TOTAL	M	F	White	Black	NE	NC	S	W	Yes	No	None	Marijuana Only	Few Pills	More Pills	Any Heroin
1. Definitely won't	31.0	30.3	31.5	31.4	29.1	30.2	34.6	31.6	24.4	11.2	57.6	26.5	30.6	30.5	37.0	44.7
2. Probably won't	34.9	36.5	33.3	36.2	30.3	31.5	35.9	35.7	36.7	36.1	33.7	35.8	34.3	35.7	34.6	25.8
3. Probably will	23.4	22.9	24.1	22.8	26.7	26.0	20.8	22.4	26.3	36.3	6.0	25.8	24.8	23.1	19.3	18.0
4. Definitely will	10.7	10.4	11.1	9.6	14.0	12.3	8.7	10.4	12.6	16.5	2.6	11.8	10.3	10.7	9.1	11.5
Item 520 Subject B09 N	15328	7310	7708	11923	1815	3494	4459	4934	2441	8674	6515	5696	3249	2106	3858	182

QUESTIONNAIRE FORM 1-5 1983	TOTAL	SEX		RACE		REGION				4YR COLLEGE PLANS		ILLICIT DRUG USE: LIFETIME				
		M	F	White	Black	NE	NC	S	W	Yes	No	None	Mari-juana Only	Few Pills	More Pills	Any Her-oin
N (Weighted No. of Cases):	16947	8074	8227	12806	2066	4056	4784	5434	2673	9061	6555	6082	3598	2315	4306	206
% of Weighted Total:	100.0	47.6	48.5	75.6	12.2	23.9	28.2	32.1	15.8	53.5	38.7	35.9	21.2	13.7	25.4	1.2

C22: Suppose you could do just what you'd like and nothing stood in your way. How many of the following things would you WANT to do? (Mark ALL that apply)

	TOTAL	M	F	White	Black	NE	NC	S	W	Yes	No	None	Mari-juana Only	Few Pills	More Pills	Any Her-oin
A. Attend a technical or vocational school	27.2	30.6	23.6	26.3	27.9	21.6	30.5	27.2	29.2	13.2	46.4	24.3	25.8	26.9	31.8	39.8
B. Serve in the armed forces	17.9	24.3	11.6	15.6	30.6	16.5	16.6	21.6	14.6	14.4	22.4	16.9	19.4	19.2	16.8	20.4
C. Graduate from a two-year college program	27.2	21.7	32.4	26.3	25.9	25.7	25.0	25.7	36.4	18.6	38.5	25.4	26.1	26.5	31.1	21.2
D. Graduate from college (four year program)	61.8	61.2	62.8	62.5	63.7	61.0	61.0	62.1	63.7	88.7	26.2	66.8	63.9	60.1	55.6	37.0
E. Attend graduate or professional school after college	39.5	38.1	41.2	39.8	38.1	40.7	38.9	38.0	41.7	56.0	17.7	42.1	40.3	38.6	36.6	32.7
F. None of the above	7.7	8.0	7.4	8.0	4.7	8.7	7.9	7.5	6.4	2.7	14.8	6.7	6.5	8.7	9.3	14.1
Item 530-580 Subject B09,C03 N	15884	7614	7947	12339	1915	3660	4572	5120	2531	8957	6426	5872	3381	2197	3989	183

C23: On the average over the school year, how many hours per week do you work in a paid or unpaid job?

	TOTAL	M	F	White	Black	NE	NC	S	W	Yes	No	None	Mari-juana Only	Few Pills	More Pills	Any Her-oin
1. None	24.8	22.4	27.1	21.4	42.7	24.6	21.8	28.5	22.9	25.4	23.8	28.2	25.1	24.0	19.2	27.3
2. 5 or less hours	10.9	10.5	11.3	11.1	9.9	9.7	12.9	9.4	12.0	12.1	9.4	12.9	11.3	10.9	8.0	3.5
3. 6 to 10 hours	10.2	10.3	10.1	10.4	8.1	10.2	10.9	8.0	13.5	10.9	9.3	11.5	9.2	11.1	8.9	6.7
4. 11 to 15 hours	10.8	10.2	11.3	11.6	7.5	11.3	11.5	9.8	10.5	12.0	9.3	10.2	11.6	9.6	11.6	12.1
5. 16 to 20 hours	15.8	15.4	16.2	17.0	10.7	18.4	15.7	14.3	15.3	16.4	14.9	14.2	16.2	16.3	17.8	14.5
6. 21 to 25 hours	11.8	12.2	11.4	12.5	9.1	12.9	11.7	11.6	10.7	11.4	12.3	9.8	12.0	11.9	14.7	10.8
7. 26 to 30 hours	6.9	7.8	5.9	7.2	4.3	5.8	6.7	8.0	6.5	5.6	8.6	5.5	6.7	7.2	8.9	8.8
8. More than 30 hours	8.9	11.1	6.8	8.9	7.8	7.2	8.8	10.3	8.6	6.3	12.4	7.7	8.0	9.0	11.0	16.3
Item 590 Subject C01,Q07 N	15976	7665	7984	12419	1908	3685	4602	5141	2547	8984	6482	5870	3402	2219	4032	191

C24: During an average week, how much money do you get from . . .

C24A: A job or other work

	TOTAL	M	F	White	Black	NE	NC	S	W	Yes	No	None	Mari-juana Only	Few Pills	More Pills	Any Her-oin
1. None	28.2	25.5	31.0	25.6	41.8	26.5	28.1	30.2	26.8	29.2	27.1	33.4	27.6	25.6	22.4	24.8
2. $1-5	4.5	4.1	4.8	4.8	3.1	3.7	5.9	3.3	5.2	4.6	4.3	5.2	4.0	5.3	3.3	2.8
3. $6-10	4.6	4.0	5.2	4.8	3.7	4.0	5.6	4.0	5.1	4.6	4.8	5.2	4.2	4.7	4.2	4.1
4. $11-20	6.1	6.2	6.0	6.4	4.5	5.7	7.7	4.9	6.1	6.2	5.8	6.6	5.3	6.7	5.5	8.0
5. $21-35	8.8	8.7	8.9	9.5	5.8	8.7	10.3	7.1	9.5	9.3	8.1	8.6	9.2	9.2	8.6	6.7
6. $36-50	11.7	11.3	12.3	12.8	7.4	13.8	11.8	10.2	11.7	12.3	10.8	11.1	12.1	12.0	12.5	6.7
7. $51-75	16.5	16.3	16.4	17.5	11.7	18.3	15.5	16.2	16.3	16.7	16.3	13.5	17.8	18.3	18.8	16.9
8. $76-125	14.5	16.9	12.3	14.1	15.5	15.6	11.5	17.0	13.3	13.1	16.1	12.2	14.7	13.0	18.3	18.2
9. $126+	5.1	7.0	3.2	4.5	6.6	3.6	3.7	7.0	6.0	3.9	6.7	4.2	4.9	5.1	6.3	11.7
Item 600 Subject C02 N	15297	7356	7635	11970	1777	3506	4451	4918	2422	8610	6230	5633	3285	2122	3853	174

C24B: Other sources (allowances, etc.)

	TOTAL	M	F	White	Black	NE	NC	S	W	Yes	No	None	Mari-juana Only	Few Pills	More Pills	Any Her-oin
1. None	34.9	34.1	35.7	36.2	25.0	37.2	35.3	31.9	37.0	33.4	37.3	36.4	35.2	33.5	33.8	27.5
2. $1-5	19.4	18.1	20.7	20.8	13.5	19.9	22.8	15.5	20.2	19.8	18.9	21.4	18.2	19.6	17.6	15.1
3. $6-10	18.3	18.2	18.5	18.6	17.1	18.3	18.4	18.4	17.6	19.1	17.1	18.4	18.2	18.7	18.0	18.2
4. $11-20	14.3	14.9	13.5	13.1	21.5	13.0	13.0	16.9	13.1	14.6	13.7	12.9	15.0	14.6	15.4	11.4
5. $21-35	6.1	6.7	5.5	5.6	9.9	5.3	4.8	8.2	5.4	6.6	5.4	4.9	6.6	6.4	7.2	9.8
6. $36-50	2.7	2.9	2.4	2.2	4.7	2.3	2.3	3.4	2.8	2.6	2.8	2.3	2.7	3.2	2.7	5.5
7. $51-75	1.5	1.5	1.4	1.3	2.3	1.2	1.3	1.9	1.4	1.5	1.4	1.3	1.4	1.4	1.7	2.9
8. $76-125	1.1	1.3	1.0	0.8	2.5	0.9	1.0	1.6	1.0	1.1	1.2	1.1	1.2	1.1	1.1	4.6
9. $126+	1.7	2.1	1.3	1.3	3.5	1.8	1.2	2.1	1.5	1.2	2.2	1.3	1.4	1.6	2.4	5.0
Item 610 Subject C02 N	14964	7167	7504	11690	1758	3435	4344	4818	2367	8466	6058	5509	3189	2091	3775	169

C25: During a typical week, on how many evenings do you go out for fun and recreation?

	TOTAL	M	F	White	Black	NE	NC	S	W	Yes	No	None	Mari-juana Only	Few Pills	More Pills	Any Her-oin
1. Less than one	7.8	6.1	9.3	6.3	13.3	8.0	7.1	7.4	9.2	7.3	8.5	11.7	6.2	5.7	4.3	5.6
2. One	14.2	12.4	16.0	13.3	16.7	12.6	13.5	14.7	16.9	15.3	12.8	19.9	13.0	12.7	8.0	8.9
3. Two	29.9	29.6	30.3	30.5	27.9	29.0	30.6	29.5	30.8	31.8	27.3	32.5	32.1	30.6	24.6	17.6
4. Three	25.2	25.3	25.2	26.4	22.1	26.0	25.2	25.7	23.2	26.1	24.1	21.4	26.6	28.5	28.0	24.7
5. Four or five	16.4	18.1	14.7	17.5	11.0	16.8	17.1	16.2	14.7	14.8	18.5	10.9	16.1	17.5	23.9	23.5
6. Six or seven	6.5	8.6	4.5	6.0	9.0	7.6	6.5	6.5	5.2	4.7	8.8	3.6	6.0	5.1	11.2	19.7
Item 620 Subject C07,M01 N	15928	7636	7967	12385	1903	3663	4595	5132	2538	8960	6458	5859	3394	2210	4018	189

QUESTIONNAIRE FORM 1-5 1983	TOTAL	SEX M	SEX F	RACE White	RACE Black	REGION NE	REGION NC	REGION S	REGION W	4YR COLLEGE PLANS Yes	No	None	Marijuana Only	Few Pills	More Pills	Any Heroin
N (Weighted No. of Cases):	16947	8074	8227	12806	2066	4056	4784	5434	2673	9061	6555	6082	3598	2315	4306	206
% of Weighted Total:	100.0	47.6	48.5	75.6	12.2	23.9	28.2	32.1	15.8	53.5	38.7	35.9	21.2	13.7	25.4	1.2
C26: On the average, how often do you go out with a date (or your spouse, if you are married)?																
1. Never	12.9	12.9	12.9	11.3	17.0	13.4	12.9	11.1	16.3	12.9	13.2	19.4	10.0	10.8	7.1	7.4
2. Once a month or less	19.0	20.3	17.8	19.0	18.9	18.7	20.3	17.2	20.8	21.4	15.9	22.7	19.6	17.7	14.4	11.8
3. 2 or 3 times a month	18.6	20.6	16.7	18.4	21.5	16.7	18.7	19.8	18.5	19.7	16.7	17.0	19.1	20.5	19.6	17.7
4. Once a week	16.2	18.0	14.5	16.2	16.5	16.0	15.5	17.2	15.8	16.7	15.7	15.4	16.3	16.6	16.5	19.6
5. 2 or 3 times a week	21.8	20.0	23.6	22.9	18.5	20.6	21.5	23.6	20.7	20.8	23.2	18.5	24.5	21.9	24.5	27.2
6. Over 3 times a week	11.5	8.3	14.5	12.2	7.6	14.7	11.1	11.2	8.0	8.6	15.3	7.0	10.6	12.5	18.0	16.3
Item 630 Subject C07,M01 N	15735	7520	7894	12262	1872	3602	4557	5080	2496	8837	6368	5791	3349	2178	3982	188
C27: During an average week, how much do you usually drive a car, truck, or motorcycle?																
1. Not at all	14.6	8.9	19.8	9.5	37.9	24.6	9.9	12.2	13.5	13.0	16.5	15.7	15.0	14.4	11.7	16.9
2. 1 to 10 miles	13.5	10.5	16.3	11.7	22.2	15.3	13.1	12.4	13.7	12.8	14.3	15.3	13.7	12.5	11.2	7.7
3. 11 to 50 miles	31.8	29.2	34.6	33.8	24.0	31.6	35.4	28.8	31.9	34.5	28.5	34.3	32.4	32.3	28.7	21.9
4. 51 to 100 miles	20.4	24.6	16.5	22.8	9.8	15.5	22.1	21.9	21.3	21.2	19.4	21.0	21.0	19.8	22.8	21.2
5. 100 to 200 miles	13.0	17.4	8.7	14.8	3.3	8.7	13.2	15.9	12.9	13.0	13.1	10.4	12.8	14.5	15.9	16.9
6. More than 200 miles	6.7	9.4	4.0	7.4	2.7	4.3	6.3	8.7	6.6	5.6	8.2	5.2	5.1	6.5	9.6	15.5
Item 640 Subject F07 N	15881	7598	7956	12372	1879	3642	4600	5107	2532	8922	6417	5839	3379	2205	4010	187
C28: Within the LAST 12 MONTHS, how many times, if any, have you received a ticket (OR been stopped and warned) for moving violations such as speeding, running a stop light, or improper passing?																
0. None–GO TO Q.C30	72.8	63.0	82.3	70.0	87.8	82.1	69.5	70.9	69.4	73.2	72.3	81.3	72.9	69.2	62.7	58.0
1. Once	17.3	21.4	13.5	19.1	8.8	12.3	19.5	17.7	19.4	17.7	16.8	13.3	17.8	20.5	20.9	19.3
2. Twice	5.8	8.7	3.0	6.4	2.3	3.6	6.4	6.5	6.6	5.7	6.0	3.4	5.8	6.9	8.6	12.8
3. Three times	2.3	3.6	0.9	2.5	0.9	1.1	2.3	3.0	2.6	2.1	2.6	1.2	1.9	2.2	4.2	5.4
4. Four or more times	1.8	3.2	0.4	2.0	0.2	0.9	2.3	1.8	2.0	1.3	2.3	0.8	1.6	1.2	3.5	4.5
Item 650 Subject A07a,S02 N	15514	7411	7792	12159	1774	3536	4523	4974	2480	8766	6222	5751	3293	2158	3903	175
C29: How many of these tickets or warnings occurred after you were . . .																
C29A: Drinking alcoholic beverages?																
0. None	81.1	79.0	85.8	80.4	93.1	83.7	76.0	83.4	83.9	83.2	78.3	91.6	83.9	84.5	70.6	62.0
1. One	14.7	15.9	12.5	15.4	4.6	12.6	18.4	12.9	13.1	13.6	16.3	7.2	12.2	12.7	22.2	29.8
2. Two	2.5	3.0	1.3	2.6	1.8	2.5	3.1	2.3	2.0	2.0	3.2	0.9	2.3	1.5	4.4	5.1
3. Three	1.0	1.2	0.5	1.0	0.6	0.5	1.5	1.0	0.7	0.8	1.3	0.2	0.7	1.0	1.8	1.6
4. Four or more	0.6	0.8	0.1	0.6	-	0.6	1.0	0.5	0.3	0.4	0.9	*	1.0	0.3	1.0	1.5
Item 660 Subject A07a,S02 N★	4193	2723	1380	3630	219	629	1371	1439	754	2348	1708	1076	888	664	1446	73
C29B: Smoking marijuana or hashish?																
0. None	93.5	92.6	95.5	93.3	95.0	92.5	92.9	94.2	94.1	94.9	91.4	100.0	98.2	98.6	84.5	70.3
1. One	4.8	5.1	3.9	4.9	3.6	5.6	4.7	4.8	4.2	4.0	6.2	-	1.4	1.2	11.3	20.5
2. Two	1.2	1.5	0.6	1.2	1.4	1.0	1.7	0.6	1.5	0.8	1.5	-	0.3	-	2.9	6.1
3. Three	0.3	0.5	-	0.3	-	0.4	0.4	0.2	0.2	0.2	0.5	-	-	0.2	0.7	2.3
4. Four or more	0.3	0.3	0.1	0.3	-	0.6	0.3	0.2	0.1	0.1	0.4	-	0.1	-	0.7	0.8
Item 670 Subject A07a,S02 N★	4127	2673	1364	3575	216	621	1336	1426	744	2319	1679	1063	860	655	1432	72
C29C: Using other illegal drugs?																
0. None	98.0	97.4	99.1	97.9	98.0	98.4	97.7	97.8	98.4	98.9	96.7	100.0	99.9	99.6	95.2	85.5
1. One	1.4	1.8	0.6	1.4	1.4	1.2	1.5	1.7	1.0	0.8	2.4	-	-	0.4	3.4	9.7
2. Two	0.4	0.5	0.3	0.5	-	0.2	0.6	0.4	0.4	0.3	0.6	-	0.1	-	1.0	4.8
3. Three	0.1	0.1	-	*	0.6	-	0.1	*	0.2	-	0.2	-	-	-	0.2	-
4. Four or more	0.1	0.1	-	0.1	-	0.2	0.1	0.1	0.1	-	0.2	-	0.1	-	0.3	-
Item 680 Subject A07a,S02 N★	4103	2658	1356	3553	214	614	1331	1415	743	2314	1662	1062	855	655	1417	70

*=less than .05 per cent.   ★=excludes respondents for whom question was inappropriate.

QUESTIONNAIRE FORM 1-5 1983	TOTAL	SEX		RACE		REGION				4YR COLLEGE PLANS		ILLICIT DRUG USE: LIFETIME				
		M	F	White	Black	NE	NC	S	W	Yes	No	None	Marijuana Only	Few Pills	More Pills	Any Heroin
N (Weighted No. of Cases):	16947	8074	8227	12806	2066	4056	4784	5434	2673	9061	6555	6082	3598	2315	4306	206
% of Weighted Total:	100.0	47.6	48.5	75.6	12.2	23.9	28.2	32.1	15.8	53.5	38.7	35.9	21.2	13.7	25.4	1.2

C30: We are interested in any accidents which occurred while you were driving a car, truck, or motorcycle. ("Accidents" means a collision involving property damage or personal injury– not bumps or scratches in parking lots.)

During the LAST 12 MONTHS, how many accidents have you had while you were driving (whether or not you were responsible)?

	TOTAL	M	F	White	Black	NE	NC	S	W	Yes	No	None	Mari juana Only	Few Pills	More Pills	Any Heroin
0. None–GO TO Q.C32	77.8	73.2	82.2	75.5	90.5	81.0	76.6	76.4	78.3	77.8	77.4	83.8	78.3	75.4	70.5	59.9
1. One	17.3	20.1	14.8	19.0	8.0	15.4	17.7	18.2	17.8	17.6	17.2	13.7	16.5	20.5	21.9	23.6
2. Two	3.7	5.0	2.4	4.1	1.1	2.5	4.3	4.2	3.0	3.5	4.1	2.1	4.0	3.1	5.7	11.0
3. Three	0.9	1.3	0.5	1.0	0.2	0.8	1.1	0.8	0.7	0.8	1.0	0.4	0.9	0.7	1.6	1.7
4. Four or more	0.3	0.5	0.1	0.3	0.1	0.3	0.2	0.4	0.2	0.3	0.3	0.1	0.2	0.4	0.4	3.8
Item 690 Subject A07a,S02 N	15314	7317	7698	12029	1733	3476	4488	4904	2445	8685	6123	5718	3246	2125	3831	170

C31: How many of these accidents occurred after you were . . .

C31A: Drinking alcoholic beverages?

	TOTAL	M	F	White	Black	NE	NC	S	W	Yes	No	None	Mari juana Only	Few Pills	More Pills	Any Heroin
0. None	86.2	83.4	90.6	86.1	95.3	88.7	81.9	87.8	88.3	87.9	84.0	94.8	89.0	86.7	78.2	62.9
1. One	12.1	14.2	9.0	12.2	4.2	10.2	15.2	10.9	11.1	10.6	14.2	4.6	9.9	12.5	18.8	29.2
2. Two	1.3	1.9	0.4	1.3	0.5	0.9	1.9	1.1	0.6	1.0	1.5	0.6	0.5	0.3	2.6	3.6
3. Three	0.3	0.4	*	0.3	–	0.1	0.7	0.2	–	0.4	0.2	–	0.5	0.2	0.2	4.4
4. Four or more	0.1	0.2	*	0.1	–	0.2	0.3	–	–	0.1	0.1	–	0.1	0.3	0.1	–
Item 700 Subject A07a,S02 N★	3396	1954	1376	2936	178	659	1047	1161	529	1931	1376	939	698	524	1124	68

C31B: Smoking marijuana or hashish?

	TOTAL	M	F	White	Black	NE	NC	S	W	Yes	No	None	Mari juana Only	Few Pills	More Pills	Any Heroin
0. None	94.8	93.2	96.9	94.9	96.5	94.8	92.9	96.1	96.0	96.1	92.9	100.0	98.0	97.7	88.6	69.1
1. One	4.3	5.5	2.8	4.3	2.2	4.5	5.9	3.1	3.6	3.2	6.2	–	1.7	1.7	9.8	21.0
2. Two	0.6	0.9	0.2	0.6	1.3	0.5	0.7	0.8	0.2	0.4	0.8	–	0.1	0.5	1.2	5.6
3. Three	0.1	0.2	0.1	0.2	–	0.1	0.3	–	0.1	0.2	0.1	–	–	–	0.2	4.3
4. Four or more	0.1	0.1	*	0.1	–	0.1	0.2	–	–	0.1	0.1	–	0.1	–	0.2	–
Item 710 Subject A07a,S02 N★	3325	1906	1359	2884	172	641	1029	1139	515	1888	1350	926	677	508	1106	64

C31C: Using other illegal drugs?

	TOTAL	M	F	White	Black	NE	NC	S	W	Yes	No	None	Mari juana Only	Few Pills	More Pills	Any Heroin
0. None	98.5	98.3	98.8	98.5	98.6	98.7	97.9	98.6	99.3	98.8	98.2	100.0	99.7	99.2	97.1	82.4
1. One	1.2	1.3	1.2	1.2	1.4	1.0	1.7	1.2	0.4	0.9	1.5	–	0.2	0.8	2.3	14.1
2. Two	0.2	0.2	–	0.2	–	0.1	0.1	0.2	0.3	0.2	0.1	–	–	–	0.3	3.5
3. Three	*	0.1	–	*	–	–	0.1	–	–	0.1	–	–	–	–	0.1	–
4. Four or more	0.1	0.1	*	0.1	–	0.2	0.2	–	–	0.1	0.1	–	0.1	–	0.2	–
Item 720 Subject A07a,S02 N★	3304	1891	1355	2866	171	638	1022	1132	512	1877	1341	926	673	505	1093	63

C32: If you have not entered military service, and do not expect to enter, GO TO PART D.

What is, or will be, your branch of service?

	TOTAL	M	F	White	Black	NE	NC	S	W	Yes	No	None	Mari juana Only	Few Pills	More Pills	Any Heroin
1. Army	25.8	26.3	25.4	25.5	29.3	24.4	28.8	26.9	19.6	23.6	27.6	25.6	26.5	27.1	24.2	36.7
2. Navy	15.7	16.6	13.5	17.3	12.8	17.5	15.3	14.3	17.8	15.1	16.2	14.4	15.6	15.6	16.9	16.6
3. Marine Corps	12.6	15.4	4.9	12.2	10.1	10.7	14.9	12.4	11.8	10.5	13.7	12.2	13.6	12.3	12.3	16.3
4. Air Force	32.3	29.0	41.5	31.3	36.6	32.0	28.4	33.7	36.0	38.0	28.1	33.3	32.4	34.6	30.9	19.3
5. Coast Guard	2.1	2.3	1.5	2.2	1.4	2.6	1.5	2.4	1.9	1.9	2.6	2.0	1.5	2.1	2.6	4.2
6. Uncertain	11.4	10.4	13.1	11.4	9.7	12.7	11.2	10.3	12.8	10.9	11.8	12.5	10.3	8.3	13.1	7.0
Item 730 Subject L01 N★	2994	2154	741	1963	654	636	769	1179	410	1288	1531	956	698	441	757	57

C33: Do you expect to be an officer?

	TOTAL	M	F	White	Black	NE	NC	S	W	Yes	No	None	Mari juana Only	Few Pills	More Pills	Any Heroin
1. No	13.8	13.4	14.2	13.9	9.9	15.2	17.1	10.0	16.4	8.5	17.4	13.9	14.2	8.9	14.7	16.1
2. Uncertain	46.2	44.7	50.5	46.4	47.3	44.1	50.2	44.8	45.8	34.0	56.2	42.7	47.2	50.3	49.3	36.7
3. Yes	40.0	41.9	35.3	39.7	42.7	40.7	32.6	45.2	37.8	57.5	26.4	43.4	38.6	40.8	36.0	47.1
Item 740 Subject L01 N★	3033	2185	750	1977	665	656	770	1187	420	1313	1547	968	704	446	770	58

*=less than .05 per cent.   ★=excludes respondents for whom question was inappropriate.

QUESTIONNAIRE FORM 1-5 1983	TOTAL	SEX		RACE		REGION				4YR COLLEGE PLANS		ILLICIT DRUG USE: LIFETIME				
		M	F	White	Black	NE	NC	S	W	Yes	No	None	Mari-juana Only	Few Pills	More Pills	Any Her-oin
N (Weighted No. of Cases):	16947	8074	8227	12806	2066	4056	4784	5434	2673	9061	6555	6082	3598	2315	4306	206
% of Weighted Total:	100.0	47.6	48.5	75.6	12.2	23.9	28.2	32.1	15.8	53.5	38.7	35.9	21.2	13.7	25.4	1.2
C34: Do you expect to have a career in the Armed Forces?																
1. No	25.0	25.9	22.7	26.9	19.4	26.0	27.3	21.4	29.1	27.9	21.7	22.7	25.6	22.0	28.5	33.8
2. Uncertain	50.5	50.9	48.9	52.3	44.5	48.4	50.9	50.5	52.8	48.7	52.6	49.8	48.0	55.2	53.1	37.7
3. Yes	24.5	23.2	28.4	20.8	36.1	25.6	21.8	28.1	18.0	23.3	25.6	27.5	26.4	22.8	18.4	28.5
Item 750 Subject L01 N★	3025	2175	751	1972	668	651	767	1188	418	1311	1540	961	703	448	766	58

★=excludes respondents for whom question was inappropriate.

QUESTIONNAIRE FORM 1-5 1983	TOTAL	SEX		RACE		REGION				4YR COLLEGE PLANS		ILLICIT DRUG USE: LIFETIME				
		M	F	White	Black	NE	NC	S	W	Yes	No	None	Mari-juana Only	Few Pills	More Pills	Any Her-oin
N (Weighted No. of Cases):	16947	8074	8227	12806	2066	4056	4784	5434	2673	9061	6555	6082	3598	2315	4306	206
% of Weighted Total:	100.0	47.6	48.5	75.6	12.2	23.9	28.2	32.1	15.8	53.5	38.7	35.9	21.2	13.7	25.4	1.2

The following questions are about CIGARETTE SMOKING.

B01: Have you ever smoked cigarettes?

	TOTAL	M	F	White	Black	NE	NC	S	W	Yes	No	None	Mari-juana Only	Few Pills	More Pills	Any Her-oin
1. Never	29.4	31.0	28.4	28.9	33.7	27.1	25.7	30.8	36.4	34.2	24.0	55.6	16.2	17.9	10.4	8.9
2. Once or twice	30.1	32.7	27.8	28.8	39.0	27.5	29.4	31.2	33.0	32.6	27.4	30.4	41.6	33.3	19.3	16.5
3. Occasionally but not regularly	16.3	14.9	17.7	16.7	15.0	16.5	17.4	16.2	14.4	16.3	16.0	9.1	20.5	21.2	20.3	16.8
4. Regularly in the past	7.2	6.6	7.9	7.8	3.9	7.7	7.6	6.8	6.6	6.2	8.4	2.2	7.7	10.0	12.1	13.0
5. Regularly now	17.0	14.8	18.3	17.8	8.4	21.1	19.8	15.0	9.7	10.7	24.2	2.7	13.9	17.5	37.9	44.8
Item 760 Subject A01a N	16553	7925	8087	12643	1984	3952	4703	5295	2604	8933	6413	5973	3546	2277	4244	202

B02: How frequently have you smoked cigarettes during the past 30 days?

	TOTAL	M	F	White	Black	NE	NC	S	W	Yes	No	None	Mari-juana Only	Few Pills	More Pills	Any Her-oin
1. Not at all - incl. (1) in B01	69.7	72.0	68.4	68.7	78.8	65.4	66.8	71.3	78.2	76.7	62.0	91.0	70.4	66.0	42.9	34.1
2. Less than one cigarette per day	9.2	8.8	9.5	9.4	8.6	8.6	9.7	9.3	8.7	9.5	8.7	5.0	10.7	10.8	12.7	9.4
3. One to five cigarettes per day	7.4	6.1	8.5	7.1	8.0	9.5	6.3	7.0	6.6	6.2	8.4	2.0	8.6	10.6	11.9	13.4
4. About one-half pack per day	6.4	5.7	6.7	6.6	3.4	8.3	7.4	5.4	3.7	3.8	9.6	1.1	5.8	6.9	13.7	13.9
5. About one pack per day	5.8	5.8	5.5	6.6	0.8	6.5	7.5	5.7	2.1	3.2	8.7	0.6	3.6	5.2	14.8	19.9
6. About one and one-half packs per day	1.2	1.2	1.2	1.4	0.2	1.4	1.9	1.0	0.4	0.5	2.1	0.1	0.7	0.6	3.3	7.0
7. Two packs or more per day	0.3	0.3	0.3	0.3	0.2	0.4	0.3	0.3	0.2	0.1	0.5	0.1	0.2	0.1	0.7	2.3
Item 780 Subject A01c N	16546	7924	8085	12627	1988	3952	4703	5290	2601	8923	6415	5969	3549	2275	4241	201

B03: Next we want to ask you about drinking alcoholic beverages, including beer, wine, and liquor.

Have you ever had any beer, wine, or liquor to drink?

	TOTAL	M	F	White	Black	NE	NC	S	W	Yes	No	None	Mari-juana Only	Few Pills	More Pills	Any Her-oin
1. No	7.2	6.4	8.1	5.7	12.1	4.4	5.1	8.9	11.6	7.6	6.5	17.1	1.3	2.3	0.8	2.2
2. Yes	92.8	93.6	91.9	94.3	87.9	95.6	94.9	91.1	88.4	92.4	93.5	82.9	98.7	97.7	99.2	97.8
Item 790 Subject A01a N	12896	6210	6345	9984	1484	3069	3671	4110	2046	7034	5088	4637	2662	1827	3438	164

B04: On how many occasions have you had alcoholic beverages to drink . . .

B04A: . . . in your lifetime?

	TOTAL	M	F	White	Black	NE	NC	S	W	Yes	No	None	Mari-juana Only	Few Pills	More Pills	Any Her-oin
1. 0 occasions - incl. (1) in B03	7.4	6.5	8.4	5.8	14.2	4.6	5.2	9.5	11.6	8.0	6.7	17.5	1.4	2.2	0.8	2.5
2. 1-2	6.3	5.2	7.2	5.0	13.7	4.3	4.9	8.6	7.1	6.3	6.3	12.5	4.5	3.0	0.8	3.1
3. 3-5	8.4	6.6	10.3	7.1	16.2	7.3	7.4	9.9	8.7	9.1	7.7	14.7	7.1	7.5	1.5	1.4
4. 6-9	7.7	6.3	9.2	6.9	12.0	8.0	6.9	8.7	7.0	8.2	7.2	11.1	8.1	7.9	3.0	2.2
5. 10-19	11.9	10.4	13.5	12.0	13.1	11.9	11.5	11.9	12.7	12.3	11.8	13.8	15.2	13.3	6.5	2.6
6. 20-39	13.9	12.8	15.4	14.8	10.5	15.6	14.2	12.8	13.3	14.2	14.1	12.1	17.3	17.4	12.4	8.7
7. 40 or more	44.3	52.1	36.0	48.5	20.3	48.3	49.8	38.6	39.5	42.0	46.2	18.4	46.4	48.7	75.1	79.5
Item 810 Subject A01a N	16005	7695	7816	12388	1800	3817	4592	5057	2540	8718	6172	5798	3427	2211	4144	188

B04B: . . . during the last 12 months?

	TOTAL	M	F	White	Black	NE	NC	S	W	Yes	No	None	Mari-juana Only	Few Pills	More Pills	Any Her-oin
1. 0 occasions - incl. (1) in B03	12.7	11.1	14.5	10.0	26.1	8.4	9.8	16.5	17.1	13.2	12.5	27.3	6.0	4.9	2.2	4.8
2. 1-2	13.6	10.6	16.4	11.7	23.6	11.6	11.7	16.3	14.6	13.9	13.1	22.0	12.4	11.9	3.9	4.9
3. 3-5	12.6	10.8	14.5	11.8	16.9	13.2	12.3	12.4	12.9	13.0	12.1	15.8	14.5	13.7	6.8	3.7
4. 6-9	11.1	10.4	11.8	11.5	9.4	11.9	10.9	10.6	11.5	11.1	11.3	10.9	13.6	13.3	8.8	4.4
5. 10-19	15.7	15.7	16.1	17.1	11.4	17.1	16.8	13.9	15.3	15.8	16.1	11.4	18.7	20.3	17.1	11.3
6. 20-39	13.7	14.1	13.6	15.4	5.0	14.7	15.4	11.9	12.9	14.1	13.5	7.0	15.2	16.5	20.6	14.5
7. 40 or more	20.4	27.2	13.0	22.6	7.5	23.1	23.0	18.4	15.8	18.9	21.3	5.6	19.6	19.4	40.6	56.3
Item 820 Subject A01b N	15943	7640	7810	12338	1797	3809	4562	5041	2532	8671	6156	5743	3425	2210	4145	187

B04C: . . . during the last 30 days?

	TOTAL	M	F	White	Black	NE	NC	S	W	Yes	No	None	Mari-juana Only	Few Pills	More Pills	Any Her-oin
1. 0 occasions - incl. (1) in B03	30.6	25.6	35.7	26.5	50.7	25.6	25.6	35.7	37.1	31.9	29.5	53.4	23.8	21.5	10.1	12.4
2. 1-2	23.0	21.4	24.8	22.8	25.2	23.7	22.6	22.3	24.1	23.3	22.7	24.6	26.9	27.3	16.3	11.1
3. 3-5	18.1	19.1	17.3	20.0	11.8	19.7	19.8	16.3	16.6	18.6	17.7	11.9	22.3	21.7	22.0	11.0
4. 6-9	12.8	14.0	11.6	14.2	5.9	14.1	14.3	11.3	10.9	13.2	12.2	5.3	13.6	15.8	20.4	17.9
5. 10-19	10.0	12.2	7.7	10.9	4.1	11.0	11.4	9.0	7.7	8.9	11.2	3.3	8.8	9.2	20.1	22.0
6. 20-39	3.1	4.0	2.0	3.2	1.1	3.5	3.6	2.7	2.3	2.4	3.8	0.8	2.6	2.8	6.3	13.8
7. 40 or more	2.4	3.7	0.8	2.4	1.1	2.4	2.6	2.6	1.4	1.6	3.0	0.6	1.9	1.7	4.9	11.7
Item 830 Subject A01c N	15980	7673	7815	12381	1790	3809	4586	5052	2533	8685	6174	5738	3427	2222	4172	188

QUESTIONNAIRE FORM 1-5 1983	TOTAL	SEX		RACE		REGION				4YR COLLEGE PLANS		ILLICIT DRUG USE: LIFETIME				
		M	F	White	Black	NE	NC	S	W	Yes	No	None	Mari-juana Only	Few Pills	More Pills	Any Her-oin
N (Weighted No. of Cases):	16947	8074	8227	12806	2066	4056	4784	5434	2673	9061	6555	6082	3598	2315	4306	206
% of Weighted Total:	100.0	47.6	48.5	75.6	12.2	23.9	28.2	32.1	15.8	53.5	38.7	35.9	21.2	13.7	25.4	1.2

B05: On the occasions that you drink alcoholic beverages, how often do you drink enough to feel pretty high?

1. On none of the occasions	22.6	18.1	27.4	19.6	39.5	21.3	20.0	26.8	21.1	24.9	20.1	47.5	16.5	13.8	5.1	3.7
2. On few of the occasions	32.2	29.3	35.0	31.6	35.9	35.0	29.7	32.5	31.7	32.3	31.6	32.4	39.0	36.0	25.3	16.1
3. On about half of the occasions	17.3	18.6	16.0	18.6	10.3	17.5	18.6	16.3	16.5	17.3	17.5	8.9	18.7	21.2	23.4	21.6
4. On most of the occasions	18.6	22.0	15.0	20.3	8.8	18.2	21.0	15.9	20.2	17.9	19.5	7.9	17.4	20.3	30.1	33.1
5. On nearly all of the occasions	9.3	12.0	6.6	9.9	5.6	7.9	10.7	8.6	10.5	7.5	11.3	3.3	8.4	8.7	16.2	25.5
Item 840 Subject A01e N ★	12173	5924	5917	9560	1334	3000	3547	3802	1822	6585	4856	3895	2682	1811	3483	167

B06: Think back over the LAST TWO WEEKS. How many times have you had five or more drinks in a row? (A "drink" is a glass of wine, a bottle of beer, a shot glass of liquor, or a mixed drink.)

1. None - incl. (1) in B03	59.2	49.6	69.0	55.6	80.2	57.8	52.8	62.4	66.7	62.8	55.1	82.0	57.9	53.5	32.7	23.8
2. Once	12.5	13.2	12.0	13.7	6.9	12.2	13.3	12.1	11.8	12.6	12.7	8.4	14.9	16.1	14.7	7.6
3. Twice	10.2	12.5	7.8	11.0	5.9	10.9	11.5	9.3	8.5	9.5	10.9	4.7	11.5	12.3	15.6	14.3
4. Three to five times	12.4	16.5	8.2	13.7	4.9	13.2	15.6	10.3	9.5	11.1	13.8	3.4	11.5	13.7	24.6	21.0
5. Six to nine times	3.5	4.9	1.9	3.8	1.4	3.5	4.2	3.6	2.1	2.6	4.5	1.0	2.6	3.1	7.3	20.5
6. Ten or more times	2.2	3.3	1.0	2.2	0.7	2.4	2.5	2.1	1.3	1.4	3.1	0.5	1.6	1.3	5.0	12.9
Item 850 Subject A01d N	15834	7576	7791	12291	1773	3766	4525	5032	2510	8666	6069	5768	3390	2171	4108	180

The next major section of this questionnaire deals with various other drugs. There is a lot of talk these days about this subject, but very little accurate information. Therefore, we still have a lot to learn about the actual experiences and attitudes of people your age.

We hope that you can answer all questions; but if you find one which you feel you cannot answer honestly, we would prefer that you leave it blank.

Remember that your answers will be kept strictly confidential: they are never connected with your name or your class.

B07: On how many occasions (if any) have you used marijuana (grass, pot) or hashish (hash, hash oil) . . .

B07A: . . . in your lifetime?

1. 0 occasions	43.0	40.1	46.6	42.8	44.6	36.3	43.0	49.2	40.8	47.8	38.8	100.0	-	26.8	7.6	4.8
2. 1-2	11.9	11.9	11.9	11.1	16.0	11.8	11.4	12.7	11.1	11.4	12.1	-	37.8	15.8	5.0	6.2
3. 3-5	7.9	7.6	7.9	8.1	7.6	8.4	7.5	7.3	8.7	8.3	7.4	-	20.7	12.1	6.2	2.0
4. 6-9	5.7	5.4	6.0	5.6	6.6	6.1	6.4	5.0	5.2	5.9	5.6	-	12.6	9.8	5.8	6.8
5. 10-19	6.8	6.6	7.0	7.0	6.3	8.0	6.4	5.9	7.4	6.7	6.7	-	12.1	10.5	10.2	2.5
6. 20-39	6.0	5.5	6.5	6.2	4.9	7.6	5.5	5.1	6.3	5.6	6.5	-	7.7	9.2	11.4	9.2
7. 40 or more	18.8	22.9	14.2	19.2	14.0	21.8	19.8	14.8	20.5	14.5	22.9	-	9.1	15.9	53.7	68.4
Item 860 Subject A01a N	16297	7828	7980	12567	1905	3871	4651	5197	2577	8862	6324	6082	3573	2240	4181	196

B07B: . . . during the last 12 months?

1. 0 occasions	57.7	54.3	61.6	57.0	61.3	50.7	58.0	63.9	55.2	61.7	54.0	100.0	40.3	47.3	18.4	12.1
2. 1-2	11.5	11.1	11.9	11.5	12.7	12.4	11.2	10.6	12.8	11.6	11.5	-	28.0	16.9	11.9	7.3
3. 3-5	7.2	7.2	7.2	7.5	6.8	8.8	7.3	5.8	7.3	7.1	7.2	-	12.7	11.8	10.4	8.1
4. 6-9	4.6	4.6	4.7	4.8	3.8	5.3	4.7	4.2	4.5	4.5	4.7	-	7.5	7.0	7.5	7.4
5. 10-19	5.3	5.7	4.8	5.4	4.5	6.1	5.2	4.3	6.1	4.7	5.8	-	5.7	7.3	11.3	9.3
6. 20-39	4.1	4.2	3.9	4.1	4.1	4.9	3.9	3.6	4.2	3.4	4.8	-	3.2	4.1	10.5	8.5
7. 40 or more	9.6	12.9	5.8	9.6	6.9	11.8	9.8	7.7	9.9	7.0	11.9	-	2.7	5.5	29.9	47.3
Item 870 Subject A01b N	16234	7788	7966	12541	1885	3862	4626	5172	2574	8835	6304	6082	3525	2233	4170	194

★=excludes respondents for whom question was inappropriate.

QUESTIONNAIRE FORM 1-5 1983	TOTAL	SEX		RACE		REGION				4YR COLLEGE PLANS		ILLICIT DRUG USE: LIFETIME				
		M	F	White	Black	NE	NC	S	W	Yes	No	None	Marijuana Only	Few Pills	More Pills	Any Heroin
N (Weighted No. of Cases):	16947	8074	8227	12806	2066	4056	4784	5434	2673	9061	6555	6082	3598	2315	4306	206
% of Weighted Total:	100.0	47.6	48.5	75.6	12.2	23.9	28.2	32.1	15.8	53.5	38.7	35.9	21.2	13.7	25.4	1.2
B07C: . . . during the last 30 days?																
1. 0 occasions	73.0	69.0	77.8	73.4	73.1	68.0	72.8	77.1	72.9	77.1	69.3	100.0	71.4	70.0	39.0	27.2
2. 1-2	9.3	9.6	9.0	9.3	10.4	10.8	9.8	7.8	9.4	9.2	9.3	-	17.1	14.4	13.7	7.7
3. 3-5	4.7	5.1	4.3	4.7	4.4	5.5	4.5	4.2	5.2	4.3	5.2	-	5.6	5.4	10.4	8.9
4. 6-9	3.3	3.8	2.7	3.3	3.4	3.6	3.6	2.9	3.1	2.7	3.8	-	2.4	4.0	8.1	8.6
5. 10-19	4.2	5.1	3.0	4.0	4.6	5.2	3.9	3.6	4.3	3.3	5.1	-	2.1	3.5	11.8	14.3
6. 20-39	2.8	3.5	2.1	2.7	2.5	3.8	2.6	2.3	2.8	1.8	3.8	-	0.9	1.7	8.6	14.8
7. 40 or more	2.6	3.8	1.1	2.5	1.7	3.1	2.8	2.2	2.3	1.5	3.5	-	0.5	1.0	8.3	18.5
Item 880 Subject A01c N	16238	7800	7959	12557	1881	3861	4631	5177	2569	8836	6305	6082	3522	2232	4179	195
B08: On how many occasions (if any) have you used LSD ("acid") . . .																
B08A: . . . in your lifetime?																
1. 0 occasions	91.1	89.6	93.1	90.3	98.1	91.3	88.3	93.3	91.6	93.5	89.0	100.0	100.0	95.0	71.4	29.4
2. 1-2	4.1	4.7	3.4	4.6	1.1	4.3	4.9	3.2	4.5	3.4	4.8	-	-	5.0	12.4	21.7
3. 3-5	1.9	2.3	1.4	2.0	0.4	1.8	2.7	1.1	1.9	1.4	2.3	-	-	-	6.8	9.0
4. 6-9	1.1	1.3	0.9	1.2	0.2	1.0	1.6	0.9	0.8	0.7	1.6	-	-	-	3.7	12.6
5. 10-19	0.9	1.1	0.7	1.1	0.1	0.8	1.3	0.7	0.8	0.5	1.3	-	-	-	3.2	7.2
6. 20-39	0.6	0.7	0.5	0.6	0.1	0.5	0.8	0.7	0.2	0.4	0.7	-	-	-	1.7	13.4
7. 40 or more	0.3	0.4	*	0.2	*	0.4	0.3	0.1	0.1	0.2	0.3	-	-	-	0.7	6.7
Item 890 Subject A01a N	16499	7920	8095	12658	1985	3934	4686	5278	2600	8938	6435	6046	3571	2286	4237	197
B08B: . . . during the last 12 months?																
1. 0 occasions	94.6	93.3	96.2	94.2	99.2	94.4	93.0	95.6	95.8	96.2	93.1	100.0	100.0	98.6	82.1	46.1
2. 1-2	3.3	4.0	2.4	3.6	0.5	3.3	4.1	2.7	2.8	2.4	4.1	-	-	1.4	10.9	24.4
3. 3-5	1.1	1.4	0.8	1.2	0.1	1.3	1.5	0.9	0.7	0.8	1.4	-	-	-	4.0	9.3
4. 6-9	0.5	0.7	0.4	0.5	0.1	0.4	0.8	0.5	0.4	0.3	0.8	-	-	-	1.8	7.4
5. 10-19	0.3	0.5	0.2	0.4	-	0.4	0.5	0.2	0.2	0.2	0.5	-	-	-	0.9	10.5
6. 20-39	*	*	*	*	-	*	*	*	*	*	*	-	-	-	0.1	1.2
7. 40 or more	0.1	0.1	*	0.1	*	0.1	0.1	*	*	0.1	*	-	-	-	0.3	1.1
Item 900 Subject A01b N	16479	7905	8093	12643	1983	3930	4681	5270	2598	8933	6424	6046	3572	2285	4222	193
B08C: . . . during the last 30 days?																
1. 0 occasions	98.1	97.6	98.8	98.0	99.8	97.8	97.8	98.3	98.8	98.9	97.3	100.0	100.0	99.6	94.3	68.2
2. 1-2	1.4	1.8	0.9	1.5	0.1	1.7	1.6	1.1	0.9	0.8	1.9	-	-	0.4	4.3	17.9
3. 3-5	0.4	0.4	0.3	0.4	*	0.2	0.5	0.4	0.2	0.1	0.6	-	-	-	0.9	10.7
4. 6-9	0.1	0.1	*	0.1	-	0.1	0.1	0.1	*	*	0.1	-	-	-	0.3	1.7
5. 10-19	*	*	*	*	-	*	*	*	-	*	*	-	-	-	-	1.5
6. 20-39	-	-	-	-	-	-	-	-	-	-	-	-	-	-	-	-
7. 40 or more	*	0.1	-	*	*	0.1	*	-	*	*	*	-	-	-	0.2	-
Item 910 Subject A01c N	16487	7911	8094	12650	1983	3931	4685	5273	2599	8936	6427	6046	3576	2286	4226	192
B09: On how many occasions (if any) have you used psychedelics other than LSD (like mescaline, peyote, psilocybin, PCP) . . .																
B09A: . . . in your lifetime?																
1. 0 occasions	92.7	91.6	94.0	92.2	97.1	89.7	91.6	95.7	93.0	94.4	91.4	100.0	100.0	94.8	77.4	34.7
2. 1-2	3.7	4.2	3.1	3.9	1.5	5.2	4.0	2.5	3.6	3.1	4.1	-	-	5.2	10.7	22.4
3. 3-5	1.4	1.5	1.2	1.5	0.8	2.2	1.4	0.7	1.6	1.1	1.6	-	-	-	4.9	11.7
4. 6-9	0.8	0.9	0.6	0.9	0.2	1.1	0.9	0.4	0.8	0.5	0.9	-	-	-	2.5	10.6
5. 10-19	0.7	0.9	0.5	0.8	0.4	0.9	1.1	0.3	0.7	0.5	1.0	-	-	-	2.3	9.9
6. 20-39	0.3	0.4	0.3	0.4	-	0.6	0.5	0.2	0.1	0.2	0.5	-	-	-	1.1	3.6
7. 40 or more	0.3	0.4	0.2	0.4	-	0.4	0.5	0.3	0.1	0.2	0.4	-	-	-	1.0	7.1
Item 920 Subject A01a N	16470	7908	8085	12646	1978	3922	4687	5262	2598	8919	6434	6031	3562	2277	4236	202
B09B: . . . during the last 12 months?																
1. 0 occasions	95.9	95.1	96.9	95.7	98.1	93.9	95.6	97.6	95.9	96.9	95.2	100.0	100.0	98.4	86.9	55.4
2. 1-2	2.4	2.8	1.9	2.5	1.5	3.6	2.4	1.5	2.4	2.1	2.5	-	-	1.6	7.6	19.0
3. 3-5	0.9	1.1	0.6	0.9	0.3	1.4	0.8	0.5	1.0	0.5	1.2	-	-	-	3.0	10.4
4. 6-9	0.4	0.4	0.4	0.4	-	0.5	0.5	0.2	0.5	0.3	0.5	-	-	-	1.3	7.5
5. 10-19	0.2	0.3	0.2	0.3	0.1	0.3	0.3	0.2	0.1	0.1	0.4	-	-	-	0.6	6.1
6. 20-39	0.1	0.1	0.1	0.1	-	0.2	0.2	0.1	*	0.1	0.2	-	-	-	0.4	0.8
7. 40 or more	*	0.1	*	*	-	*	0.1	-	0.1	*	*	-	-	-	0.1	0.8
Item 930 Subject A01b N	16450	7898	8075	12626	1975	3918	4678	5256	2598	8913	6423	6031	3562	2275	4221	198

*=less than .05 per cent.

QUESTIONNAIRE FORM 1-5 1983	TOTAL	SEX		RACE		REGION				4YR COLLEGE PLANS		ILLICIT DRUG USE: LIFETIME				
		M	F	White	Black	NE	NC	S	W	Yes	No	None	Mari-juana Only	Few Pills	More Pills	Any Her-oin
N (Weighted No. of Cases):	16947	8074	8227	12806	2066	4056	4784	5434	2673	9061	6555	6082	3598	2315	4306	206
% of Weighted Total:	100.0	47.6	48.5	75.6	12.2	23.9	28.2	32.1	15.8	53.5	38.7	35.9	21.2	13.7	25.4	1.2

B09C: . . . during the last 30 days?

1. 0 occasions	98.5	98.2	99.0	98.5	99.4	97.8	98.3	99.1	98.7	99.0	98.2	100.0	100.0	99.7	95.3	77.8
2. 1-2	1.0	1.2	0.8	1.0	0.6	1.7	1.1	0.5	0.9	0.8	1.1	-	-	0.3	3.3	11.1
3. 3-5	0.3	0.4	0.2	0.3	0.1	0.3	0.4	0.2	0.3	0.2	0.4	-	-	-	0.8	7.0
4. 6-9	0.1	0.1	0.1	0.1	-	0.1	0.1	0.1	*	*	0.2	-	-	-	0.2	3.0
5. 10-19	0.1	*	*	*	-	0.1	0.1	*	-	*	0.1	-	-	-	0.2	1.2
6. 20-39	*	*	*	*	-	-	-	*	*	-	*	-	-	-	-	-
7. 40 or more	*	*	-	-	-	*	*	-	*	-	*	-	-	-	0.1	-
Item 940 Subject A01c N	16448	7897	8074	12627	1975	3918	4677	5255	2599	8912	6420	6031	3562	2276	4220	197

B10: On how many occasions (if any) have you use cocaine (sometimes called "coke") . . .

B10A: . . . in your lifetime?

1. 0 occasions	83.8	81.4	86.6	83.8	87.1	79.5	87.5	88.0	74.9	86.4	81.7	100.0	100.0	79.4	51.9	18.2
2. 1-2	7.5	8.7	6.1	7.5	7.1	8.6	6.6	6.4	9.6	6.5	8.5	-	-	20.6	17.1	18.4
3. 3-5	3.0	3.9	2.0	2.9	2.8	3.9	2.4	2.2	4.1	2.7	3.1	-	-	-	10.8	16.1
4. 6-9	1.8	1.8	1.8	2.0	0.8	2.8	1.0	1.0	3.4	1.6	2.0	-	-	-	6.6	9.9
5. 10-19	1.7	1.7	1.6	1.7	1.2	2.3	1.0	1.2	3.0	1.2	2.1	-	-	-	5.7	17.1
6. 20-39	1.1	1.1	1.1	1.1	0.5	1.4	0.7	0.5	2.5	0.7	1.4	-	-	-	3.9	9.4
7. 40 or more	1.2	1.4	0.8	1.1	0.6	1.4	0.7	0.6	2.5	0.8	1.3	-	-	-	4.0	11.0
Item 950 Subject A01a N	16464	7925	8092	12664	1980	3913	4691	5260	2599	8935	6445	6032	3550	2291	4229	202

B10B: . . . during the last 12 months?

1. 0 occasions	88.6	86.8	90.7	88.5	92.1	84.8	92.0	92.3	80.8	90.1	87.8	100.0	100.0	90.1	64.1	35.5
2. 1-2	5.8	7.1	4.6	5.9	5.2	7.2	4.8	4.5	8.3	5.4	6.1	-	-	9.9	16.3	22.7
3. 3-5	2.4	2.7	1.9	2.5	1.1	3.6	1.3	1.6	4.1	2.1	2.4	-	-	-	8.5	15.5
4. 6-9	1.2	1.3	1.1	1.2	0.7	1.9	0.7	0.6	2.4	1.1	1.3	-	-	-	4.2	10.6
5. 10-19	1.1	1.1	1.0	1.0	0.6	1.5	0.7	0.5	2.2	0.8	1.3	-	-	-	3.8	6.4
6. 20-39	0.5	0.5	0.5	0.5	0.1	0.5	0.2	0.2	1.6	0.3	0.6	-	-	-	1.8	4.5
7. 40 or more	0.4	0.5	0.2	0.4	0.3	0.6	0.3	0.2	0.6	0.3	0.4	-	-	-	1.2	4.9
Item 960 Subject A01b N	16437	7907	8083	12647	1975	3909	4685	5250	2593	8925	6430	6032	3551	2284	4213	199

B10C: . . . during the last 30 days?

1. 0 occasions	95.1	94.3	95.9	95.1	97.0	93.1	97.2	97.2	90.0	96.0	94.5	100.0	100.0	97.6	83.8	64.5
2. 1-2	3.2	3.6	2.8	3.2	2.1	4.3	1.9	2.0	6.6	2.8	3.5	-	-	2.4	10.5	17.4
3. 3-5	0.9	1.0	0.8	0.9	0.4	1.7	0.3	0.5	1.5	0.6	1.3	-	-	-	3.1	8.0
4. 6-9	0.4	0.5	0.3	0.4	0.2	0.5	0.3	0.2	0.9	0.3	0.4	-	-	-	1.4	4.4
5. 10-19	0.2	0.2	0.1	0.2	-	0.3	0.1	0.1	0.6	0.1	0.2	-	-	-	0.7	3.4
6. 20-39	0.1	0.1	*	0.1	0.1	0.1	0.1	*	0.3	0.1	0.1	-	-	-	0.2	1.6
7. 40 or more	0.1	0.2	*	0.1	0.1	0.1	0.1	*	0.1	0.1	0.1	-	-	-	0.3	0.7
Item 970 Subject A01c N	16438	7905	8086	12649	1974	3908	4687	5250	2592	8922	6433	6033	3551	2282	4214	200

B11: Amphetamines can be prescribed by doctors to help people lose weight or to give people more energy. They are sometimes called uppers, ups, speed, bennies, dexies, pep pills, and diet pills. Drugstores are not supposed to sell them without a prescription from a doctor. Amphetamines do NOT include any non-prescription drugs, such as over-the-counter diet pills (like Dexatrim) or stay-awake pills (like No-Doz), or any mail-order drugs. On how many occasions (if any) have you taken amphetamines on your own–that is, without a doctor telling you to take them...

B11A: . . . in your lifetime? *

1. 0 occasions	73.1	74.0	72.7	70.1	90.5	73.1	70.2	76.6	71.6	78.2	68.3	100.0	100.0	50.8	16.9	25.5
2. 1-2	8.3	8.2	8.7	9.2	4.0	8.4	7.7	8.3	9.3	7.6	9.1	-	-	49.2	7.2	6.1
3. 3-5	4.0	4.1	3.8	4.3	2.4	4.3	3.8	3.6	4.9	3.3	4.7	-	-	-	17.0	4.0
4. 6-9	3.4	3.2	3.4	3.7	0.7	3.0	4.2	2.4	4.3	2.5	4.3	-	-	-	13.9	9.1
5. 10-19	3.4	3.4	3.3	3.9	1.3	3.7	3.8	2.9	3.1	2.8	3.8	-	-	-	13.9	9.3
6. 20-39	2.7	2.6	2.6	2.9	0.8	3.0	2.9	2.1	2.9	2.2	3.1	-	-	-	11.3	5.0
7. 40 or more	5.1	4.4	5.5	5.9	0.3	4.5	7.5	4.1	4.0	3.4	6.6	-	-	-	19.9	41.1
Item 980 Subject A01a N	13145	6292	6469	10088	1596	3093	3774	4199	2079	7024	5042	4975	3016	1753	3072	154

*=less than .05 per cent.   ** Two sets of amphetamine questions are shown here; see page 11 for explanation.

QUESTIONNAIRE FORM 1-5 1983	TOTAL	SEX		RACE		REGION				4YR COLLEGE PLANS		ILLICIT DRUG USE: LIFETIME				
		M	F	White	Black	NE	NC	S	W	Yes	No	None	Mari- juana Only	Few Pills	More Pills	Any Her- oin
N (Weighted No. of Cases):	16947	8074	8227	12806	2066	4056	4784	5434	2673	9061	6555	6082	3598	2315	4306	206
% of Weighted Total:	100.0	47.6	48.5	75.6	12.2	23.9	28.2	32.1	15.8	53.5	38.7	35.9	21.2	13.7	25.4	1.2
B11B: . . . during the last 12 months? **																
1. 0 occasions	82.1	82.8	82.1	79.9	95.0	82.1	79.6	84.6	81.8	85.5	79.1	100.0	100.0	80.7	37.2	39.7
2. 1-2	6.3	6.2	6.3	7.1	2.7	6.7	5.9	5.9	7.5	5.7	7.0	-	-	19.3	15.7	9.0
3. 3-5	3.4	3.7	3.1	3.9	0.8	3.3	3.9	3.0	3.5	2.6	4.2	-	-	-	14.5	3.0
4. 6-9	2.4	2.4	2.4	2.6	0.8	2.3	3.0	2.0	2.2	2.0	2.8	-	-	-	9.7	12.3
5. 10-19	2.3	1.9	2.7	2.7	0.4	2.5	2.8	1.9	2.0	1.7	2.8	-	-	-	9.3	12.1
6. 20-39	1.8	1.6	1.9	2.1	*	1.8	2.4	1.4	1.6	1.4	2.1	-	-	-	7.2	12.5
7. 40 or more	1.6	1.4	1.7	1.8	0.3	1.3	2.4	1.2	1.4	1.2	1.9	-	-	-	6.4	11.5
Item 990 Subject A01b　　　　N	13110	6279	6453	10069	1588	3093	3768	4173	2076	7009	5033	4977	3018	1732	3055	152
B11C: . . . during the last 30 days? **																
1. 0 occasions	91.1	91.8	90.9	90.0	97.6	91.1	88.7	92.8	92.0	93.6	88.7	100.0	100.0	95.7	66.5	55.0
2. 1-2	4.1	4.4	3.7	4.6	1.5	4.2	4.8	3.3	4.4	2.9	5.2	-	-	4.3	14.5	14.5
3. 3-5	1.8	1.5	2.0	2.0	0.4	2.2	2.0	1.6	1.0	1.4	2.2	-	-	-	7.2	8.9
4. 6-9	1.2	1.0	1.3	1.3	0.2	0.9	1.8	0.9	1.3	1.0	1.4	-	-	-	4.8	9.6
5. 10-19	1.0	0.7	1.3	1.2	0.2	0.7	1.4	1.1	0.8	0.6	1.5	-	-	-	3.9	8.4
6. 20-39	0.6	0.4	0.6	0.6	-	0.6	1.0	0.2	0.3	0.3	0.8	-	-	-	2.3	0.9
7. 40 or more	0.2	0.2	0.2	0.2	0.1	0.3	0.2	0.2	*	0.1	0.2	-	-	-	0.8	2.7
Item 1000 Subject A01c　　　N	13108	6275	6455	10066	1592	3094	3767	4173	2075	7007	5028	4977	3021	1734	3049	152
B11: Amphetamines can be prescribed by doctors to help people lose weight or to give people more energy. They are sometimes called uppers, ups, speed, bennies, dexies, pep pills, and diet pills. On how many occasions (if any) have you taken amphetamines on your own– that is, without a doctor telling you to take them...																
B11A: . . . in your lifetime? **																
1. 0 occasions	64.6	68.3	61.5	60.3	88.2	66.7	58.5	68.9	63.8	69.1	58.5	100.0	100.0	37.8	10.7	16.6
2. 1-2	10.6	9.3	11.7	11.4	6.4	10.3	10.9	10.7	10.3	10.2	11.0	-	-	62.2	5.4	9.0
3. 3-5	5.7	5.4	6.0	6.4	2.5	5.8	6.2	4.8	6.9	5.3	6.5	-	-	-	19.8	8.1
4. 6-9	4.1	3.4	4.7	4.5	1.2	4.7	4.6	3.0	4.4	3.5	4.7	-	-	-	14.0	7.9
5. 10-19	4.5	4.1	4.7	5.2	1.2	3.4	6.2	4.1	3.7	3.6	5.7	-	-	-	15.2	9.7
6. 20-39	3.8	3.3	4.4	4.4	0.3	3.3	4.9	3.1	4.3	3.4	4.5	-	-	-	13.2	8.0
7. 40 or more	6.6	6.2	6.9	7.6	0.2	5.9	8.8	5.4	6.6	4.8	9.0	-	-	-	21.6	40.7
Item 980 Subject A01a　　　　N	6574	3146	3253	5044	795	1586	1846	2110	1032	3645	2580	2283	1334	945	1872	78
B11B: . . . during the last 12 months? **																
1. 0 occasions	75.4	77.4	73.6	72.1	93.3	77.5	69.1	79.6	74.6	78.7	70.7	100.0	100.0	76.0	28.4	24.8
2. 1-2	8.3	7.8	8.6	9.1	4.2	8.5	10.1	6.8	8.1	7.5	9.7	-	-	24.0	16.6	15.9
3. 3-5	5.1	5.2	5.0	5.9	1.2	4.3	6.7	4.2	5.1	4.5	5.7	-	-	-	17.5	8.7
4. 6-9	3.1	2.4	3.7	3.6	0.7	2.8	4.2	2.2	3.3	2.8	3.5	-	-	-	10.5	8.6
5. 10-19	3.4	2.9	3.9	3.9	0.3	3.1	3.5	3.0	4.3	3.0	3.9	-	-	-	11.6	7.8
6. 20-39	2.3	2.1	2.5	2.5	0.3	1.5	3.1	1.8	2.9	1.6	3.3	-	-	-	7.7	9.2
7. 40 or more	2.5	2.1	2.7	2.9	0.1	2.3	3.2	2.3	1.6	2.0	3.2	-	-	-	7.6	24.9
Item 990 Subject A01b　　　　N	6560	3135	3249	5033	790	1585	1841	2101	1033	3636	2574	2284	1334	942	1864	75
B11C: . . . during the last 30 days? **																
1. 0 occasions	87.6	89.1	86.2	85.9	97.3	89.8	84.1	89.1	87.3	90.1	84.2	100.0	100.0	94.3	61.6	43.7
2. 1-2	5.1	4.5	5.6	5.7	2.0	4.2	6.3	4.5	5.6	4.2	6.3	-	-	5.7	14.3	16.7
3. 3-5	2.7	2.5	2.8	3.1	0.3	2.1	3.1	2.6	2.8	1.9	3.7	-	-	-	9.1	7.4
4. 6-9	2.1	1.9	2.2	2.3	0.4	1.7	2.6	2.0	1.8	1.8	2.2	-	-	-	7.0	8.0
5. 10-19	1.5	1.4	1.5	1.7	0.1	1.0	2.4	0.9	1.8	1.0	2.2	-	-	-	4.7	13.5
6. 20-39	0.8	0.4	1.2	1.0	-	1.0	1.1	0.7	0.5	0.7	1.1	-	-	-	2.6	9.7
7. 40 or more	0.3	0.2	0.4	0.3	-	0.2	0.4	0.2	0.2	0.3	0.3	-	-	-	0.9	1.1
Item 1000 Subject A01c　　　N	6560	3135	3251	5037	790	1583	1841	2107	1030	3636	2576	2284	1334	940	1866	75
B12: On how many occasions (if any) have you used quaaludes (quads, soapers, methaqualone) on your own–that is, without a doctor telling you to take them . . .																

*=less than .05 per cent.　　　　** Two sets of amphetamine questions are shown here; see page 11 for explanation.

QUESTIONNAIRE FORM 1-5 1983	TOTAL	SEX		RACE		REGION				4YR COLLEGE PLANS		ILLICIT DRUG USE: LIFETIME				
		M	F	White	Black	NE	NC	S	W	Yes	No	None	Mari-juana Only	Few Pills	More Pills	Any Her-oin
N (Weighted No. of Cases):	16947	8074	8227	12806	2066	4056	4784	5434	2673	9061	6555	6082	3598	2315	4306	206
% of Weighted Total:	100.0	47.6	48.5	75.6	12.2	23.9	28.2	32.1	15.8	53.5	38.7	35.9	21.2	13.7	25.4	1.2

B12A: . . . in your lifetime?

	TOTAL	M	F	White	Black	NE	NC	S	W	Yes	No	None	Mari-juana Only	Few Pills	More Pills	Any Her-oin
1. 0 occasions	89.9	88.4	91.5	88.6	97.6	91.3	89.2	88.2	92.7	92.3	87.2	100.0	100.0	91.8	68.3	34.9
2. 1-2	4.6	5.1	4.1	5.2	1.5	4.7	4.1	5.4	3.5	3.8	5.6	-	-	8.2	12.6	14.8
3. 3-5	1.9	2.3	1.5	2.2	0.3	1.7	1.9	1.9	1.8	1.4	2.5	-	-	-	6.9	6.6
4. 6-9	1.1	1.2	0.9	1.3	0.1	0.8	1.4	1.3	0.7	0.9	1.2	-	-	-	4.0	7.0
5. 10-19	1.1	1.4	0.8	1.3	0.2	0.6	1.5	1.3	0.7	0.7	1.7	-	-	-	3.7	12.0
6. 20-39	0.7	0.7	0.6	0.7	0.2	0.5	0.8	0.8	0.3	0.4	0.8	-	-	-	2.1	10.3
7. 40 or more	0.8	0.9	0.6	0.9	0.1	0.4	1.1	1.1	0.3	0.5	1.0	-	-	-	2.4	14.4
Item 1010　Subject A01a　N	16481	7942	8119	12681	1998	3916	4697	5272	2596	8944	6459	6028	3536	2296	4232	203

B12B: . . . during the last 12 months?

	TOTAL	M	F	White	Black	NE	NC	S	W	Yes	No	None	Mari-juana Only	Few Pills	More Pills	Any Her-oin
1. 0 occasions	94.6	93.7	95.7	93.9	98.7	95.2	94.0	93.6	96.9	96.1	93.1	100.0	100.0	98.5	82.1	53.1
2. 1-2	2.7	3.1	2.3	3.0	0.8	2.8	2.6	3.2	2.0	2.2	3.1	-	-	1.5	9.2	12.0
3. 3-5	1.0	1.4	0.7	1.2	0.2	0.9	1.3	1.1	0.5	0.7	1.5	-	-	-	3.6	9.0
4. 6-9	0.8	0.9	0.6	0.9	0.1	0.6	1.1	1.0	0.2	0.4	1.1	-	-	-	2.7	9.0
5. 10-19	0.5	0.6	0.4	0.6	0.1	0.3	0.7	0.6	0.3	0.3	0.7	-	-	-	1.4	10.5
6. 20-39	0.2	0.2	0.1	0.2	0.1	0.2	0.1	0.3	*	0.1	0.2	-	-	-	0.5	2.7
7. 40 or more	0.2	0.2	0.1	0.2	-	*	0.3	0.2	*	0.1	0.2	-	-	-	0.5	3.7
Item 1020　Subject A01b　N	16461	7933	8110	12665	1998	3914	4686	5265	2595	8935	6448	6028	3537	2291	4219	200

B12C: . . . during the last 30 days?

	TOTAL	M	F	White	Black	NE	NC	S	W	Yes	No	None	Mari-juana Only	Few Pills	More Pills	Any Her-oin
1. 0 occasions	98.2	97.8	98.7	98.0	99.6	98.6	97.8	97.6	99.5	98.8	97.6	100.0	100.0	99.8	94.3	72.2
2. 1-2	1.1	1.4	0.7	1.2	0.2	0.9	1.5	1.3	0.4	0.8	1.4	-	-	0.2	3.5	13.8
3. 3-5	0.4	0.4	0.3	0.4	*	0.3	0.4	0.6	*	0.2	0.5	-	-	-	1.2	7.2
4. 6-9	0.2	0.2	0.2	0.2	*	0.1	0.2	0.2	*	0.1	0.3	-	-	-	0.5	4.9
5. 10-19	0.1	0.1	0.1	0.1	*	0.1	0.2	0.1	*	0.1	0.2	-	-	-	0.4	1.4
6. 20-39	*	*	*	*	*	-	*	*	*	*	*	-	-	-	0.1	-
7. 40 or more	*	*	-	*	*	*	-	-	*	*	-	-	-	-	-	0.5
Item 1030　Subject A01c　N	16458	7932	8109	12664	1998	3913	4684	5265	2596	8936	6445	6030	3537	2290	4218	198

B13: Barbiturates are sometimes prescribed by doctors to help people relax or get to sleep. They are sometimes called downs, downers, goofballs, yellows, reds, blues, rainbows. On how many occasions (if any) have you taken barbiturates on your own–that is, without a doctor telling you to take them...

B13A: . . . in your lifetime?

	TOTAL	M	F	White	Black	NE	NC	S	W	Yes	No	None	Mari-juana Only	Few Pills	More Pills	Any Her-oin
1. 0 occasions	90.1	89.3	91.2	89.3	96.3	91.6	88.1	90.1	91.3	92.6	87.1	100.0	100.0	90.7	69.4	33.2
2. 1-2	4.4	4.5	4.3	4.8	2.1	3.9	5.2	4.3	4.2	3.7	5.5	-	-	9.3	11.8	11.3
3. 3-5	1.8	2.1	1.4	1.9	0.4	1.6	2.3	1.6	1.5	1.2	2.5	-	-	-	6.5	10.6
4. 6-9	1.0	1.1	0.9	1.1	0.4	0.8	1.1	1.0	1.3	0.8	1.3	-	-	-	3.6	8.9
5. 10-19	1.1	1.3	0.8	1.2	0.4	1.0	1.1	1.3	0.8	0.7	1.5	-	-	-	3.8	9.8
6. 20-39	0.6	0.6	0.7	0.8	0.1	0.5	1.0	0.7	0.2	0.5	0.7	-	-	-	2.3	5.6
7. 40 or more	0.9	1.1	0.7	1.0	0.3	0.6	1.3	1.0	0.7	0.6	1.3	-	-	-	2.6	20.6
Item 1040　Subject A01a　N	16359	7886	8068	12600	1983	3883	4662	5240	2574	8918	6407	6003	3516	2272	4179	203

B13B: . . . during the last 12 months?

	TOTAL	M	F	White	Black	NE	NC	S	W	Yes	No	None	Mari-juana Only	Few Pills	More Pills	Any Her-oin
1. 0 occasions	94.8	94.1	95.8	94.3	98.4	95.3	93.9	94.8	96.0	96.2	93.3	100.0	100.0	97.8	83.3	50.0
2. 1-2	2.5	2.9	2.1	2.8	0.8	2.5	3.0	2.3	2.1	1.9	3.2	-	-	2.2	8.1	13.7
3. 3-5	1.0	1.2	0.8	1.1	0.1	1.1	1.1	1.0	0.7	0.7	1.4	-	-	-	3.5	9.2
4. 6-9	0.6	0.7	0.5	0.7	0.2	0.4	0.8	0.7	0.5	0.5	0.7	-	-	-	2.0	8.7
5. 10-19	0.6	0.6	0.6	0.6	0.4	0.5	0.6	0.7	0.4	0.4	0.8	-	-	-	1.9	6.5
6. 20-39	0.2	0.3	0.2	0.3	0.1	0.1	0.3	0.3	0.1	0.1	0.3	-	-	-	0.6	5.4
7. 40 or more	0.2	0.3	0.1	0.2	0.1	0.1	0.4	0.2	0.1	0.1	0.3	-	-	-	0.5	6.5
Item 1050　Subject A01b　N	16334	7871	8059	12582	1981	3879	4654	5230	2570	8905	6394	6003	3516	2260	4167	200

B13C: . . . during the last 30 days?

	TOTAL	M	F	White	Black	NE	NC	S	W	Yes	No	None	Mari-juana Only	Few Pills	More Pills	Any Her-oin
1. 0 occasions	97.9	97.8	98.2	97.7	99.3	98.6	97.6	97.4	98.7	98.6	97.2	100.0	100.0	99.3	93.7	69.6
2. 1-2	1.2	1.2	1.1	1.3	0.4	0.9	1.3	1.5	0.8	0.9	1.5	-	-	0.7	3.6	15.3
3. 3-5	0.4	0.4	0.4	0.4	0.1	0.2	0.4	0.7	0.2	0.3	0.5	-	-	-	1.4	4.2
4. 6-9	0.2	0.2	0.1	0.2	0.1	0.2	0.2	0.1	0.1	0.1	0.3	-	-	-	0.5	2.9
5. 10-19	0.2	0.3	0.2	0.2	0.1	0.2	0.3	0.3	0.1	0.1	0.3	-	-	-	0.6	4.8
6. 20-39	*	0.1	*	0.1	-	-	0.1	*	*	*	0.1	-	-	-	0.1	1.7
7. 40 or more	*	0.1	-	0.1	-	*	0.1	*	*	*	0.1	-	-	-	0.1	1.4
Item 1060　Subject A01c　N	16343	7879	8061	12592	1981	3880	4658	5234	2571	8909	6401	6003	3519	2260	4175	199

*=less than .05 per cent.

QUESTIONNAIRE FORM 1-5 1983	TOTAL	SEX		RACE		REGION				4YR COLLEGE PLANS		ILLICIT DRUG USE: LIFETIME				
		M	F	White	Black	NE	NC	S	W	Yes	No	None	Mari- juana Only	Few Pills	More Pills	Any Her- oin
N (Weighted No. of Cases):	16947	8074	8227	12806	2066	4056	4784	5434	2673	9061	6555	6082	3598	2315	4306	206
% of Weighted Total:	100.0	47.6	48.5	75.6	12.2	23.9	28.2	32.1	15.8	53.5	38.7	35.9	21.2	13.7	25.4	1.2

B14: Tranquilizers are sometimes prescribed by doctors to calm people down, quiet their nerves, or relax their muscles. Librium, Valium, and Miltown are all tranquilizers. On how many occasions (if any) have you taken tranquilizers on your own–that is, without a doctor telling you to take them...

B14A: ... in your lifetime?

1. 0 occasions	86.7	86.3	87.3	85.5	94.5	87.7	86.6	86.1	86.8	88.7	84.7	100.0	100.0	78.6	62.8	37.1
2. 1-2	6.6	6.4	6.7	7.0	3.5	5.8	6.5	6.6	7.7	6.0	6.9	-	-	21.4	13.3	14.7
3. 3-5	2.7	2.8	2.5	3.0	0.7	2.9	2.5	2.9	2.2	2.3	3.2	-	-	-	10.1	9.0
4. 6-9	1.3	1.3	1.2	1.5	0.5	1.4	1.1	1.4	1.5	1.1	1.6	-	-	-	4.7	9.2
5. 10-19	1.2	1.3	1.1	1.4	0.4	1.0	1.3	1.4	0.9	0.9	1.4	-	-	-	4.2	9.8
6. 20-39	0.7	0.7	0.7	0.8	0.1	0.6	0.9	0.7	0.5	0.5	1.0	-	-	-	2.6	4.2
7. 40 or more	0.8	1.1	0.5	0.8	0.3	0.7	1.1	0.8	0.4	0.5	1.2	-	-	-	2.3	16.0
Item 1070 Subject A01a N	16401	7912	8094	12644	1984	3895	4669	5250	2587	8927	6434	6010	3525	2290	4192	199

B14B: ... during the last 12 months?

1. 0 occasions	93.1	93.0	93.3	92.4	97.4	93.2	93.2	92.6	93.8	94.2	92.0	100.0	100.0	93.9	78.4	53.9
2. 1-2	3.8	3.7	3.8	4.1	1.6	3.7	3.4	4.0	4.1	3.5	4.0	-	-	6.1	10.7	16.3
3. 3-5	1.4	1.4	1.4	1.6	0.5	1.9	1.4	1.4	0.9	1.1	1.7	-	-	-	5.2	8.7
4. 6-9	0.7	0.7	0.7	0.8	0.1	0.4	0.8	1.0	0.6	0.6	0.9	-	-	-	2.5	5.7
5. 10-19	0.5	0.5	0.5	0.5	0.2	0.5	0.6	0.5	0.4	0.4	0.6	-	-	-	1.7	6.9
6. 20-39	0.3	0.4	0.2	0.3	0.1	0.2	0.4	0.3	0.1	0.2	0.4	-	-	-	0.8	5.9
7. 40 or more	0.2	0.3	0.1	0.2	0.1	0.1	0.3	0.2	0.1	0.1	0.3	-	-	-	0.6	2.6
Item 1080 Subject A01b N	16383	7902	8088	12626	1983	3888	4663	5246	2586	8917	6427	6012	3526	2279	4182	198

B14C: ... during the last 30 days?

1. 0 occasions	97.5	97.4	97.6	97.2	99.2	97.7	97.3	97.1	98.1	98.1	96.6	100.0	100.0	98.8	91.8	76.2
2. 1-2	1.5	1.5	1.5	1.8	0.4	1.5	1.3	1.8	1.5	1.3	1.8	-	-	1.2	4.9	10.8
3. 3-5	0.5	0.5	0.4	0.5	0.2	0.3	0.6	0.6	0.2	0.3	0.7	-	-	-	1.7	3.4
4. 6-9	0.3	0.2	0.3	0.3	0.1	0.3	0.3	0.3	0.2	0.2	0.3	-	-	-	0.8	4.7
5. 10-19	0.2	0.1	0.2	0.2	0.1	0.1	0.2	0.2	*	0.1	0.2	-	-	-	0.5	3.0
6. 20-39	0.1	0.1	*	0.1	*	*	0.1	*	*	*	0.1	-	-	-	0.2	0.8
7. 40 or more	0.1	0.1	-	0.1	*	*	0.1	*	*	*	0.1	-	-	-	0.2	1.1
Item 1090 Subject A01c N	16382	7901	8088	12628	1982	3892	4665	5241	2584	8914	6431	6012	3526	2279	4182	198

B15: On how many occasions (if any) have you used heroin (smack, horse, skag) . . .

B15A: . . . in your lifetime?

1. 0 occasions	98.8	98.5	99.2	98.9	99.1	98.9	98.7	98.6	99.1	99.2	98.3	100.0	100.0	100.0	100.0	-
2. 1-2	0.8	0.9	0.5	0.7	0.6	0.6	0.9	0.8	0.7	0.6	1.0	-	-	-	-	61.1
3. 3-5	0.2	0.2	0.1	0.2	0.1	0.2	0.2	0.1	0.1	0.1	0.2	-	-	-	-	12.7
4. 6-9	0.1	0.1	0.1	0.1	0.1	0.1	0.1	0.2	0.1	*	0.2	-	-	-	-	9.5
5. 10-19	0.1	0.1	*	*	0.1	*	0.1	0.1	-	*	0.1	-	-	-	-	4.6
6. 20-39	*	*	*	*	0.1	*	*	0.1	-	*	0.1	-	-	-	-	3.6
7. 40 or more	0.1	0.2	*	0.1	-	0.2	*	0.1	0.1	0.1	0.2	-	-	-	-	8.6
Item 1100 Subject A01a N	16378	7899	8108	12637	1985	3873	4681	5241	2583	8927	6427	5993	3524	2279	4197	203

B15B: . . . during the last 12 months?

1. 0 occasions	99.4	99.3	99.6	99.5	99.5	99.4	99.6	99.3	99.5	99.7	99.1	100.0	100.0	100.0	100.0	53.3
2. 1-2	0.3	0.4	0.2	0.3	0.3	0.3	0.3	0.2	0.4	0.2	0.5	-	-	-	-	26.2
3. 3-5	0.1	0.1	*	0.1	0.1	0.1	*	0.2	-	*	0.1	-	-	-	-	6.3
4. 6-9	0.1	0.1	*	*	*	0.1	-	0.1	-	*	0.1	-	-	-	-	4.4
5. 10-19	*	*	*	*	0.1	*	-	*	-	*	*	-	-	-	-	1.6
6. 20-39	*	*	*	*	-	*	*	0.1	-	*	0.1	-	-	-	-	2.3
7. 40 or more	0.1	0.1	-	0.1	-	0.1	*	*	0.1	*	0.1	-	-	-	-	5.9
Item 1110 Subject A01b N	16376	7895	8109	12636	1984	3872	4680	5240	2584	8926	6426	5994	3525	2279	4198	198

*=less than .05 per cent.

QUESTIONNAIRE FORM 1-5 1983	TOTAL	SEX		RACE		REGION				4YR COLLEGE PLANS		ILLICIT DRUG USE: LIFETIME				
		M	F	White	Black	NE	NC	S	W	Yes	No	None	Marijuana Only	Few Pills	More Pills	Any Heroin
N (Weighted No. of Cases):	16947	8074	8227	12806	2066	4056	4784	5434	2673	9061	6555	6082	3598	2315	4306	206
% of Weighted Total:	100.0	47.6	48.5	75.6	12.2	23.9	28.2	32.1	15.8	53.5	38.7	35.9	21.2	13.7	25.4	1.2

B15C: ... during the last 30 days?

	TOTAL	M	F	White	Black	NE	NC	S	W	Yes	No	None	Marijuana Only	Few Pills	More Pills	Any Heroin
1. 0 occasions	99.8	99.6	99.9	99.8	99.8	99.7	99.8	99.7	99.8	99.9	99.6	100.0	100.0	100.0	100.0	80.3
2. 1-2	0.1	0.2	*	0.1	0.1	0.1	0.1	0.1	0.1	*	0.2	-	-	-	-	8.8
3. 3-5	*	*	*	*	*	*	-	*	-	*	*	-	-	-	-	1.4
4. 6-9	*	*	*	*	0.1	-	*	0.1	-	*	0.1	-	-	-	-	2.1
5. 10-19	*	*	*	*	-	0.1	*	*	-	*	*	-	-	-	-	2.6
6. 20-39	*	*	-	*	0.1	0.1	-	*	-	*	*	-	-	-	-	1.7
7. 40 or more	*	0.1	-	*	-	0.1	*	*	0.1	*	0.1	-	-	-	-	3.2
Item 1120 Subject A01c N	16377	7897	8109	12637	1986	3872	4680	5242	2584	8925	6426	5993	3525	2280	4198	199

B16: There are a number of narcotics other than heroin, such as methadone, opium, morphine, codeine, demerol, paregoric, talwin, and laudanum. These are sometimes prescribed by doctors. On how many occasions (if any) have you taken narcotics other than heroin on your own–that is, without a doctor telling you to take them...

B16A: ... in your lifetime?

	TOTAL	M	F	White	Black	NE	NC	S	W	Yes	No	None	Marijuana Only	Few Pills	More Pills	Any Heroin
1. 0 occasions	90.6	89.3	91.9	89.6	96.1	91.0	90.0	91.5	89.2	92.0	88.8	100.0	100.0	90.8	71.2	35.8
2. 1-2	4.6	4.9	4.3	5.0	2.4	4.5	4.5	4.2	5.8	4.2	5.0	-	-	9.2	12.1	18.9
3. 3-5	1.8	2.1	1.5	2.1	0.5	1.8	2.3	1.5	1.7	1.6	2.0	-	-	-	6.7	10.0
4. 6-9	1.1	1.2	1.0	1.3	0.4	1.1	1.2	0.9	1.4	1.0	1.2	-	-	-	3.8	12.6
5. 10-19	0.8	1.0	0.6	0.9	0.2	0.8	0.8	0.8	1.1	0.6	1.1	-	-	-	3.0	5.2
6. 20-39	0.5	0.7	0.2	0.5	0.2	0.2	0.6	0.6	0.3	0.3	0.7	-	-	-	1.6	4.9
7. 40 or more	0.6	0.8	0.4	0.6	0.3	0.6	0.6	0.6	0.5	0.3	1.0	-	-	-	1.7	12.5
Item 1130 Subject A01a N	16299	7884	8082	12619	1971	3855	4663	5212	2568	8915	6376	5983	3505	2277	4155	195

B16B: ... during the last 12 months?

	TOTAL	M	F	White	Black	NE	NC	S	W	Yes	No	None	Marijuana Only	Few Pills	More Pills	Any Heroin
1. 0 occasions	94.9	94.0	95.8	94.4	98.3	94.4	94.7	95.6	94.8	95.7	93.9	100.0	100.0	97.0	83.7	55.9
2. 1-2	2.9	3.2	2.5	3.2	1.0	3.5	2.9	2.2	3.2	2.6	3.1	-	-	3.0	8.8	18.3
3. 3-5	0.9	1.0	0.7	1.0	0.2	1.0	0.9	0.8	0.9	0.8	0.9	-	-	-	3.2	5.7
4. 6-9	0.6	0.8	0.5	0.7	0.2	0.5	0.8	0.7	0.4	0.4	1.0	-	-	-	2.2	6.5
5. 10-19	0.4	0.6	0.3	0.5	0.2	0.3	0.5	0.5	0.3	0.3	0.6	-	-	-	1.4	5.2
6. 20-39	0.1	0.2	0.1	0.1	-	0.1	0.1	0.2	0.2	0.1	0.2	-	-	-	0.4	3.9
7. 40 or more	0.1	0.2	0.1	0.1	-	0.2	0.2	*	0.2	0.1	0.2	-	-	-	0.4	4.4
Item 1140 Subject A01b N	16282	7874	8076	12607	1972	3856	4658	5205	2563	8908	6371	5985	3505	2273	4145	192

B16C: ... during the last 30 days?

	TOTAL	M	F	White	Black	NE	NC	S	W	Yes	No	None	Marijuana Only	Few Pills	More Pills	Any Heroin
1. 0 occasions	98.2	97.6	98.7	98.0	99.5	98.3	97.9	98.3	98.3	98.6	97.6	100.0	100.0	99.5	94.2	76.5
2. 1-2	1.0	1.4	0.7	1.2	0.3	1.0	1.3	0.9	0.9	0.9	1.2	-	-	0.5	3.3	9.4
3. 3-5	0.4	0.5	0.4	0.4	0.1	0.4	0.4	0.5	0.3	0.3	0.7	-	-	-	1.5	3.9
4. 6-9	0.1	0.2	0.1	0.2	0.1	0.1	0.2	0.2	0.1	0.1	0.2	-	-	-	0.5	1.4
5. 10-19	0.1	0.2	0.1	0.1	0.1	*	0.1	0.2	0.1	0.1	0.1	-	-	-	0.2	5.2
6. 20-39	0.1	0.1	*	0.1	-	0.1	0.1	*	0.2	*	0.1	-	-	-	0.2	2.9
7. 40 or more	*	0.1	-	*	-	*	0.1	-	*	-	0.1	-	-	-	0.1	0.7
Item 1150 Subject A01c N	16281	7870	8078	12599	1974	3853	4657	5205	2566	8911	6365	5984	3505	2272	4144	193

B17: On how many occasions (if any) have you sniffed glue, or breathed the contents of aerosol spray cans, or inhaled any other gases or sprays in order to get high . . .

B17A: ... in your lifetime?

	TOTAL	M	F	White	Black	NE	NC	S	W	Yes	No	None	Marijuana Only	Few Pills	More Pills	Any Heroin
1. 0 occasions	86.4	83.4	89.6	85.5	92.8	87.0	85.6	87.6	84.7	87.7	85.1	96.8	89.7	82.7	72.8	59.6
2. 1-2	8.6	10.3	6.8	9.1	5.3	7.3	8.9	8.3	10.3	7.9	9.2	2.5	7.6	11.7	15.8	13.5
3. 3-5	2.3	2.8	1.8	2.6	0.7	2.7	2.4	1.9	2.3	2.1	2.6	0.3	1.4	3.4	5.0	5.9
4. 6-9	1.1	1.2	0.8	1.1	0.4	1.0	1.2	0.9	1.2	1.1	1.1	*	0.5	1.4	2.5	5.0
5. 10-19	0.7	1.0	0.5	0.8	0.3	0.7	0.9	0.6	0.7	0.7	0.8	0.2	0.3	0.5	1.7	7.9
6. 20-39	0.4	0.5	0.3	0.4	0.1	0.5	0.3	0.3	0.5	0.3	0.5	*	0.2	0.3	1.0	3.0
7. 40 or more	0.5	0.8	0.2	0.5	0.3	0.8	0.6	0.4	0.3	0.3	0.8	0.1	0.3	0.2	1.2	5.1
Item 1160 Subject A01a N	13153	6390	6506	10192	1597	3152	3736	4196	2069	7205	5220	4771	2707	1865	3508	170

*=less than .05 per cent.

QUESTIONNAIRE FORM 1-5 1983	TOTAL	SEX		RACE		REGION				4YR COLLEGE PLANS		ILLICIT DRUG USE: LIFETIME				
		M	F	White	Black	NE	NC	S	W	Yes	No	None	Mari- juana Only	Few Pills	More Pills	Any Her- oin
N (Weighted No. of Cases):	16947	8074	8227	12806	2066	4056	4784	5434	2673	9061	6555	6082	3598	2315	4306	206
% of Weighted Total:	100.0	47.6	48.5	75.6	12.2	23.9	28.2	32.1	15.8	53.5	38.7	35.9	21.2	13.7	25.4	1.2
B17B: . . . during the last 12 months?																
1.　0 occasions	95.7	94.2	97.2	95.3	98.0	95.0	95.5	96.2	95.7	96.1	95.3	99.1	97.4	95.6	90.4	79.4
2.　1-2	2.6	3.4	1.6	2.9	1.2	2.8	2.7	2.4	2.4	2.3	2.8	0.7	1.8	2.7	5.5	5.2
3.　3-5	0.6	0.7	0.5	0.7	0.1	1.0	0.5	0.5	0.8	0.6	0.6	0.1	0.3	0.7	1.4	6.0
4.　6-9	0.5	0.8	0.3	0.5	0.3	0.6	0.4	0.5	0.8	0.5	0.4	0.1	0.2	0.6	1.3	4.0
5.　10-19	0.3	0.4	0.2	0.3	0.2	0.4	0.4	0.2	0.2	0.2	0.4	0.1	0.1	0.1	0.8	2.7
6.　20-39	0.1	0.1	0.1	0.1	0.2	0.1	0.2	0.1	0.1	0.1	0.1	-	*	0.2	0.3	0.8
7.　40 or more	0.2	0.3	*	0.2	*	0.2	0.3	0.1	0.2	0.2	0.3	*	0.3	0.1	0.3	1.8
Item 1170　Subject A01b　　N	13135	6386	6492	10179	1595	3145	3734	4192	2063	7196	5211	4768	2702	1861	3502	168
B17C: . . . during the last 30 days?																
1.　0 occasions	98.3	97.6	99.1	98.2	99.0	98.2	98.1	98.6	98.4	98.6	98.1	99.6	98.9	98.3	96.8	86.7
2.　1-2	1.0	1.5	0.5	1.1	0.7	1.3	0.9	1.0	0.8	1.0	0.9	0.3	0.7	1.0	1.9	5.9
3.　3-5	0.3	0.3	0.2	0.3	0.1	0.1	0.3	0.2	0.4	0.2	0.4	*	*	0.4	0.5	3.0
4.　6-9	0.2	0.3	0.1	0.2	0.2	0.2	0.4	0.1	0.2	0.1	0.3	0.1	*	0.1	0.5	1.9
5.　10-19	0.1	0.1	0.1	0.1	0.1	0.1	0.2	0.1	*	*	0.2	*	*	*	0.2	1.7
6.　20-39	0.1	0.1	*	*	*	0.1	0.1	*	-	*	0.1	-	0.2	0.1	*	-
7.　40 or more	*	0.1	-	*	-	*	*	*	0.1	*	0.1	-	0.1	-	*	0.8
Item 1180　Subject A01c　　N	13127	6379	6492	10174	1593	3144	3736	4186	2061	7193	5208	4768	2702	1861	3496	167

*＝less than .05 per cent.

QUESTIONNAIRE FORM 1 1983	TOTAL	SEX		RACE		REGION				4YR COLLEGE PLANS		ILLICIT DRUG USE: LIFETIME				
		M	F	White	Black	NE	NC	S	W	Yes	No	None	Mari-juana Only	Few Pills	More Pills	Any Her-oin
N (Weighted No. of Cases):	3448	1611	1667	2555	435	814	974	1118	541	1798	1246	1269	848	428	746	30
% of Weighted Total:	100.0	46.7	48.3	74.1	12.6	23.6	28.3	32.4	15.7	52.2	36.1	36.8	24.6	12.4	21.6	.9

A001: Taking all things together, how would you say things are these days–would you say you're very happy, pretty happy, or not too happy these days?

3. Very happy	17.6	15.8	19.5	19.0	12.9	17.8	15.2	17.4	22.4	20.5	14.6	21.3	15.7	12.8	17.0	16.2
2. Pretty happy	68.4	70.4	67.4	69.9	64.2	67.8	72.3	67.5	64.6	68.5	68.9	66.0	68.4	73.9	69.9	56.1
1. Not too happy	13.9	13.8	13.1	11.2	22.9	14.4	12.6	15.1	13.1	11.0	16.5	12.7	15.9	13.3	13.1	27.7
Item 1190 Subject P01,Q01 N	3435	1605	1664	2550	434	810	971	1115	538	1796	1241	1265	845	426	743	30

A002: How much do you agree or disagree with each of the following statements?

A002A: The nation needs much more long-range planning and coordination to be prepared for the future

1. Disagree	1.7	1.9	1.4	1.6	2.2	2.0	1.4	1.8	1.7	1.3	1.7	1.5	1.5	1.8	1.9	9.2
2. Mostly disagree	3.8	3.7	3.4	3.5	2.8	4.5	3.5	3.7	3.3	3.5	3.3	3.6	3.0	4.2	4.1	-
3. Neither	9.3	9.1	9.5	9.6	6.9	9.7	9.0	9.4	9.2	8.7	9.7	8.8	9.3	8.1	10.8	12.4
4. Mostly agree	44.0	41.5	47.0	47.0	34.8	43.0	48.5	40.0	45.4	46.1	44.0	44.5	42.5	48.1	43.3	45.2
5. Agree	41.2	43.8	38.6	38.4	53.4	40.8	37.6	45.1	40.5	40.4	41.3	41.6	43.6	37.7	39.9	33.2
Item 1200 Subject I01 N	3397	1592	1641	2526	426	801	967	1095	535	1782	1224	1249	841	426	734	29

A002B: I enjoy the fast pace and changes of today's world

1. Disagree	14.9	14.2	15.0	12.2	26.7	17.1	13.1	16.5	11.5	10.4	19.2	15.1	14.7	14.8	12.2	27.9
2. Mostly disagree	16.1	15.7	17.3	16.3	17.4	14.7	14.8	17.2	17.8	15.3	18.6	17.5	17.0	12.5	15.6	12.3
3. Neither	18.3	19.3	17.6	19.6	10.2	16.9	20.3	16.5	20.7	19.0	18.0	20.3	15.6	22.1	17.2	5.7
4. Mostly agree	33.4	32.3	34.9	35.3	26.0	30.3	36.8	32.4	34.0	36.8	29.2	31.0	36.2	33.4	35.2	19.7
5. Agree	17.3	18.4	15.2	16.6	19.8	20.9	15.0	17.3	16.0	18.5	15.0	16.2	16.5	17.2	19.9	34.4
Item 1210 Subject I03,Q02 N	3412	1596	1651	2536	429	802	968	1106	537	1789	1228	1257	843	425	738	29

A002C: Things change too quickly in today's world

1. Disagree	12.1	13.6	9.9	11.9	14.2	12.9	10.5	13.3	11.1	12.7	10.5	11.8	11.7	9.6	13.6	22.8
2. Mostly disagree	21.2	21.6	21.1	24.0	11.6	22.0	23.3	19.1	20.7	24.9	16.9	19.8	22.6	19.4	24.3	11.0
3. Neither	19.2	19.7	19.0	20.9	10.8	16.5	21.9	18.1	20.8	21.6	16.4	19.9	18.1	21.6	19.5	19.9
4. Mostly agree	24.1	21.9	26.5	24.3	22.0	23.2	23.7	24.8	24.5	23.0	26.1	25.3	22.7	27.6	23.2	12.0
5. Agree	23.4	23.1	23.6	18.9	41.3	25.4	20.6	24.7	22.9	17.8	30.1	23.2	24.9	21.8	19.4	34.2
Item 1220 Subject I03,Q02 N	3405	1590	1650	2529	428	800	965	1103	537	1782	1228	1255	842	425	736	28

A002D: I think the times ahead for me will be tougher and less fun than things are now

1. Disagree	17.9	17.3	18.4	19.0	13.9	18.2	16.8	18.4	18.6	20.0	14.8	18.3	17.6	15.1	18.3	38.2
2. Mostly disagree	18.1	15.4	21.4	19.6	12.2	17.1	19.7	16.0	21.2	21.1	14.7	18.5	17.8	22.9	17.2	16.9
3. Neither	13.6	15.1	12.1	14.5	9.0	14.7	14.5	12.1	13.5	14.3	13.0	13.3	13.7	11.8	15.9	7.7
4. Mostly agree	22.5	24.6	20.3	21.9	23.9	22.2	25.3	20.7	21.5	22.6	23.0	22.8	22.4	21.4	22.1	16.1
5. Agree	27.8	27.6	27.8	25.0	41.1	27.9	23.6	32.8	25.1	22.0	34.6	27.1	28.3	28.8	26.4	21.1
Item 1230 Subject I01,J N	3407	1590	1652	2532	426	799	970	1100	538	1786	1228	1257	843	424	733	30

A003: Of all the time you spend with other people, about how much is spent with people over 30?

1. Very little	22.1	22.9	20.8	19.0	33.2	27.3	20.2	22.7	16.5	19.4	24.7	18.2	26.0	22.3	23.4	17.9
2. Some	39.5	43.8	35.7	42.5	30.2	38.5	42.3	37.2	40.5	43.3	35.7	38.9	39.7	37.8	41.8	60.6
3. About half	30.7	26.7	34.5	31.4	25.2	27.3	30.0	31.2	35.9	30.7	30.1	33.5	28.1	33.0	27.4	17.4
4. Most	6.4	5.7	7.3	6.1	8.1	5.7	6.3	7.2	6.1	5.7	7.5	7.6	5.1	5.9	6.5	4.1
5. Nearly all	1.3	0.9	1.7	0.9	3.3	1.2	1.1	1.6	0.9	0.9	2.0	1.7	1.1	1.0	0.9	-
Item 1240 Subject M02 N	3442	1609	1666	2555	435	813	973	1115	541	1797	1244	1268	848	426	744	30

QUESTIONNAIRE FORM 1 1983	TOTAL	SEX		RACE		REGION				4YR COLLEGE PLANS		ILLICIT DRUG USE: LIFETIME				
		M	F	White	Black	NE	NC	S	W	Yes	No	None	Marijuana Only	Few Pills	More Pills	Any Heroin
N (Weighted No. of Cases):	3448	1611	1667	2555	435	814	974	1118	541	1798	1246	1269	848	428	746	30
% of Weighted Total:	100.0	46.7	48.3	74.1	12.6	23.6	28.3	32.4	15.7	52.2	36.1	36.8	24.6	12.4	21.6	.9

A004: Would you like to spend more time, or less time, with people over 30 if you could?

	TOTAL	M	F	White	Black	NE	NC	S	W	Yes	No	None	Mari- juana Only	Few Pills	More Pills	Any Her- oin
1. Much less time	3.1	3.3	2.4	2.9	3.4	4.5	2.5	3.0	2.4	2.0	3.7	2.7	2.5	2.4	4.1	6.1
2. Somewhat less time	7.0	8.0	6.1	6.9	6.9	6.8	5.7	7.7	8.1	5.6	8.9	5.5	7.9	8.5	8.0	4.2
3. About the same as now	68.2	68.5	68.4	70.2	60.9	69.0	68.4	68.0	66.9	70.3	67.4	69.1	66.7	70.7	68.8	54.4
4. Somewhat more time	18.3	17.3	19.6	17.8	21.9	16.8	20.4	18.4	16.9	19.4	16.5	18.4	21.0	15.4	16.4	17.7
5. Much more time	3.3	2.9	3.6	2.2	6.9	2.8	2.9	2.9	5.7	2.8	3.5	4.4	1.8	2.9	2.8	17.6
Item 1250 Subject M02 N	3435	1606	1663	2551	435	811	970	1115	540	1795	1241	1266	848	422	744	30

A005: Would you like to spend more time, or less time, working with or helping younger children?

	TOTAL	M	F	White	Black	NE	NC	S	W	Yes	No	None	Mari- juana Only	Few Pills	More Pills	Any Her- oin
1. Much less time	5.6	8.5	2.3	5.5	3.1	7.5	5.0	4.5	6.0	4.6	5.6	3.8	4.3	5.5	8.6	19.0
2. Somewhat less time	6.3	10.1	2.7	6.7	3.4	5.4	7.0	6.3	6.5	6.1	6.3	5.6	5.9	6.2	7.2	11.9
3. About the same as now	33.4	41.3	25.2	34.8	26.8	32.7	35.4	32.7	32.2	33.5	32.5	32.8	34.5	33.1	35.0	27.0
4. Somewhat more time	35.0	29.3	41.8	36.4	31.9	33.3	36.4	33.4	38.5	36.1	35.6	36.1	35.3	36.7	33.8	24.2
5. Much more time	19.7	10.8	28.1	16.5	34.8	21.1	16.3	23.0	16.8	19.7	19.9	21.7	20.0	18.6	15.5	17.8
Item 1260 Subject M02 N	3431	1601	1663	2550	434	812	968	1114	538	1792	1240	1264	846	423	744	30

A006: The next questions ask how satisfied or dissatisfied you are with several aspects of your life. For each question, mark the circle that shows best how you feel. If you are neutral about something, or are just as satisfied as you are dissatisfied, mark the middle answer.

How satisfied are you with...

A006A: Your job? (If you have no job, leave blank)

	TOTAL	M	F	White	Black	NE	NC	S	W	Yes	No	None	Mari- juana Only	Few Pills	More Pills	Any Her- oin
7. Completely satisfied	22.8	22.0	23.1	22.5	22.6	20.8	22.3	24.4	23.4	20.9	23.3	27.9	21.7	16.8	19.2	20.4
6.	17.9	20.7	15.7	19.9	9.0	14.7	23.4	14.4	20.3	20.1	16.0	19.1	19.0	16.4	16.1	8.3
5.	12.4	12.0	12.5	14.4	1.7	10.7	13.0	11.6	15.7	14.1	10.8	11.3	12.2	15.0	14.1	-
4. Neutral	30.2	28.3	32.3	26.7	49.4	37.7	24.0	32.8	24.0	28.1	32.1	28.6	29.1	30.3	32.0	36.2
3.	6.7	6.5	6.9	7.1	3.5	6.4	7.2	6.0	7.4	8.0	5.8	5.6	7.0	9.3	7.3	11.2
2.	4.1	4.7	3.6	4.6	3.2	3.7	4.9	4.6	2.4	4.1	4.8	2.8	4.5	5.3	5.0	3.8
1. Completely dissatisfied	6.0	5.9	5.9	4.9	10.6	6.0	5.1	6.2	6.8	4.6	7.3	4.6	6.5	6.9	6.2	20.2
Item 1270 Subject C01,P02 N	2116	1070	949	1631	200	537	593	664	323	1095	777	746	502	262	508	21

A006B: The neighborhood where you live?

	TOTAL	M	F	White	Black	NE	NC	S	W	Yes	No	None	Mari- juana Only	Few Pills	More Pills	Any Her- oin
7. Completely satisfied	34.9	33.9	36.1	35.3	34.6	30.2	35.4	37.5	35.4	34.5	36.2	38.7	35.8	26.3	31.9	22.6
6.	18.4	20.1	17.2	20.6	9.5	17.0	20.4	17.1	19.4	21.5	14.9	19.2	17.3	19.9	18.5	23.0
5.	8.9	10.8	7.3	10.3	4.6	9.8	10.0	7.2	9.1	10.6	7.6	9.1	8.9	8.9	10.0	10.4
4. Neutral	23.0	20.8	24.2	19.6	33.4	26.3	20.8	23.2	21.4	19.4	25.8	21.8	22.3	23.2	24.5	25.0
3.	4.8	5.1	4.6	5.5	2.2	3.9	5.3	4.9	4.9	4.9	4.6	3.8	4.5	9.9	4.0	7.2
2.	3.7	3.9	3.7	3.8	3.3	3.8	3.0	3.9	4.7	3.7	3.8	2.8	4.1	4.4	5.0	2.0
1. Completely dissatisfied	6.4	5.4	7.0	4.9	12.5	8.9	5.1	6.3	5.0	5.3	7.0	4.7	7.1	7.4	6.3	9.9
Item 1280 Subject P02 N	3432	1609	1658	2549	434	809	969	1114	539	1793	1240	1268	844	428	739	30

A006C: Your personal safety in your neighborhood, on your job, and in your school—safety from being attacked and injured in some way?

	TOTAL	M	F	White	Black	NE	NC	S	W	Yes	No	None	Mari- juana Only	Few Pills	More Pills	Any Her- oin
7. Completely satisfied	41.4	47.7	35.4	43.7	32.3	39.4	44.2	42.1	37.8	41.0	40.8	41.7	40.1	42.4	41.1	60.1
6.	20.2	21.7	19.4	23.2	9.7	17.9	23.2	18.1	22.4	22.7	18.2	21.6	19.5	20.0	20.2	6.6
5.	7.8	7.4	8.4	7.7	8.4	7.1	7.7	7.3	10.3	8.5	8.0	7.4	7.9	8.9	8.1	5.7
4. Neutral	19.3	14.9	23.1	15.9	32.5	23.3	15.6	21.0	16.6	16.3	22.2	19.3	19.7	17.4	19.2	14.8
3.	4.3	2.5	5.9	4.4	2.8	3.7	3.7	4.1	6.6	5.0	3.4	3.8	4.6	4.9	5.0	-
2.	2.2	2.0	2.3	2.3	2.1	1.8	2.8	2.0	2.1	2.0	2.4	1.9	2.6	2.0	2.7	-
1. Completely dissatisfied	4.8	3.8	5.6	2.8	12.2	6.8	2.9	5.4	4.3	4.4	5.0	4.2	5.5	4.4	3.7	12.9
Item 1290 Subject P02 N	3428	1603	1660	2549	429	811	968	1109	541	1792	1239	1267	841	427	743	30

QUESTIONNAIRE FORM 1 1983	TOTAL	SEX		RACE		REGION				4YR COLLEGE PLANS		ILLICIT DRUG USE: LIFETIME				
		M	F	White	Black	NE	NC	S	W	Yes	No	None	Marijuana Only	Few Pills	More Pills	Any Heroin
N (Weighted No. of Cases):	3448	1611	1667	2555	435	814	974	1118	541	1798	1246	1269	848	428	746	30
% of Weighted Total:	100.0	46.7	48.3	74.1	12.6	23.6	28.3	32.4	15.7	52.2	36.1	36.8	24.6	12.4	21.6	.9

A006D: The safety of things you own from being stolen or destroyed in your neighborhood, on your job, and in your school?

7. Completely satisfied	20.6	20.5	20.7	20.6	21.1	17.9	21.8	22.9	18.0	18.9	23.1	21.6	22.0	18.3	19.3	22.0
6.	18.3	19.3	17.8	21.4	4.8	18.0	20.5	15.2	21.2	21.4	14.9	19.9	17.8	16.5	18.2	8.7
5.	12.9	13.4	12.9	14.7	8.0	11.2	14.3	11.8	15.0	15.8	9.9	12.1	12.6	14.7	13.0	10.4
4. Neutral	21.9	21.3	22.0	19.0	32.5	25.9	19.2	22.4	19.5	18.9	24.3	23.1	22.2	18.7	20.7	34.5
3.	9.8	9.8	9.8	10.6	4.7	8.6	10.8	9.1	11.3	10.6	9.2	8.4	8.8	13.2	11.8	4.3
2.	5.5	5.2	5.6	5.2	6.1	5.7	5.6	4.9	5.9	5.2	5.7	4.9	5.5	5.8	6.6	3.1
1. Completely dissatisfied	11.0	10.4	11.3	8.5	22.7	12.7	7.8	13.6	9.1	9.2	12.9	10.0	11.1	12.8	10.3	17.0
Item 1300 Subject P02 N	3414	1599	1652	2538	432	804	967	1107	535	1782	1238	1257	844	425	739	30

A006E: Your educational experiences?

7. Completely satisfied	22.0	20.2	23.8	19.5	35.5	21.7	17.6	27.1	20.1	22.3	21.4	26.0	22.8	19.3	14.1	27.2
6.	22.7	23.0	23.7	25.7	11.6	19.9	25.4	21.3	24.6	27.7	18.3	26.2	22.2	22.6	19.3	6.6
5.	15.6	17.1	14.5	18.2	7.1	12.2	17.2	14.9	19.3	17.0	14.7	14.3	16.9	16.3	16.9	12.1
4. Neutral	25.2	24.8	24.2	22.5	30.6	30.2	25.3	23.0	21.9	19.4	30.1	21.7	25.1	25.6	30.8	20.7
3.	6.2	6.3	6.4	7.0	3.2	6.6	7.0	5.2	6.3	6.9	6.0	4.9	5.6	7.5	8.4	15.4
2.	3.0	3.3	2.6	2.8	3.3	2.6	3.0	2.7	3.9	2.6	3.4	2.6	2.6	4.1	3.1	1.8
1. Completely dissatisfied	5.4	5.4	4.8	4.4	8.7	6.8	4.5	5.7	4.0	4.1	6.1	4.3	4.7	4.5	7.4	16.3
Item 1310 Subject B01,P02 N	3402	1593	1647	2528	429	796	971	1104	531	1777	1231	1258	837	419	738	28

A006F: Your friends and other people you spend time with?

7. Completely satisfied	48.1	44.6	51.3	47.3	51.9	49.0	43.0	55.1	41.2	43.1	54.2	48.3	51.0	46.9	44.8	42.4
6.	26.9	30.3	24.7	30.5	14.9	22.3	33.6	22.9	30.0	32.0	22.0	27.4	25.4	28.7	29.3	7.5
5.	8.7	10.4	7.2	9.1	6.0	8.2	10.2	7.7	8.9	9.6	7.8	7.9	8.8	10.9	9.1	11.3
4. Neutral	11.8	10.3	12.4	8.8	23.4	15.6	9.1	10.6	13.4	11.3	11.2	12.4	10.5	8.5	12.0	17.0
3.	2.3	2.0	2.2	2.4	1.3	1.8	2.3	1.9	3.5	1.9	2.4	1.7	2.5	2.1	2.7	10.0
2.	0.9	0.7	1.1	0.8	0.2	1.3	0.9	0.5	1.1	1.1	0.6	0.7	1.1	0.8	1.1	-
1. Completely dissatisfied	1.4	1.7	1.1	1.2	2.2	1.8	0.9	1.3	1.9	1.0	1.8	1.5	0.7	2.0	1.0	11.8
Item 1320 Subject M04,P02 N	3430	1603	1663	2547	433	809	970	1111	540	1794	1242	1265	842	428	743	30

A006G: The way you get along with your parents?

7. Completely satisfied	37.4	36.7	38.2	34.6	51.6	37.5	31.5	43.1	36.0	36.3	38.7	42.3	36.9	34.9	29.4	29.1
6.	20.1	21.8	19.2	22.7	12.4	18.2	22.8	18.4	21.9	23.1	17.4	22.8	20.4	19.9	17.7	4.5
5.	11.2	13.2	9.3	12.6	4.6	11.5	13.9	8.9	10.8	12.6	10.3	9.9	10.9	14.1	13.0	8.6
4. Neutral	17.3	17.0	16.9	16.0	20.5	20.3	16.8	16.5	15.3	14.6	19.5	14.6	17.3	16.3	21.2	30.3
3.	5.6	5.1	6.4	6.4	2.0	5.8	6.4	3.5	8.2	6.7	4.5	4.3	6.4	6.5	7.4	1.4
2.	3.2	2.6	3.6	3.3	1.7	2.7	4.2	2.9	2.7	2.7	3.7	2.3	3.3	2.7	5.0	3.7
1. Completely dissatisfied	5.2	3.7	6.4	4.5	7.3	4.0	4.4	6.7	5.1	4.1	5.9	4.0	4.8	5.5	6.2	22.3
Item 1330 Subject M03,P02 N	3424	1602	1658	2546	435	806	968	1113	537	1786	1243	1262	844	426	741	30

A006H: Yourself?

7. Completely satisfied	33.2	34.1	31.5	27.6	60.4	35.4	27.5	40.0	25.7	29.1	36.1	35.2	34.5	32.7	25.5	43.7
6.	26.1	28.1	25.1	30.0	12.9	23.5	29.6	23.5	29.2	29.8	22.6	26.9	26.2	25.7	26.2	23.7
5.	12.9	13.9	12.5	14.8	4.7	12.8	14.8	11.0	13.8	15.7	11.0	11.5	14.1	16.3	13.8	-
4. Neutral	20.0	17.0	22.5	19.5	15.9	20.4	20.2	19.0	20.9	17.7	22.3	19.6	17.9	16.6	25.4	17.3
3.	4.0	3.4	4.2	4.4	2.0	3.7	5.2	2.6	5.1	4.2	3.7	2.9	4.1	4.8	5.1	3.8
2.	1.5	1.2	1.7	1.4	1.4	1.3	1.4	1.1	2.5	1.8	1.2	1.5	1.5	1.6	1.0	4.3
1. Completely dissatisfied	2.3	2.3	2.4	2.2	2.8	2.9	1.2	2.7	2.8	1.8	3.3	2.3	1.7	2.2	3.0	7.3
Item 1340 Subject P01,Q01 N	3409	1592	1657	2540	426	804	962	1105	538	1783	1236	1257	842	426	738	30

A006I: Your standard of living–the things you have like housing, car, furniture, recreation, and the like?

7. Completely satisfied	34.4	33.7	35.0	34.0	36.8	35.7	32.2	36.5	31.8	34.2	33.8	38.4	34.6	31.1	28.4	31.6
6.	24.6	25.5	24.2	28.3	10.5	23.0	27.9	22.3	26.1	27.9	21.0	25.2	25.0	23.2	25.6	19.3
5.	13.2	14.2	12.4	14.3	9.3	11.5	13.5	12.6	16.1	14.7	12.1	11.0	13.4	18.0	14.9	4.7
4. Neutral	17.2	16.1	17.6	13.7	28.9	19.4	14.7	18.8	15.4	13.7	21.2	16.5	16.6	14.4	19.6	17.9
3.	4.5	4.2	4.8	4.6	3.9	4.5	5.5	3.7	4.2	4.2	4.4	3.3	4.4	6.1	5.9	-
2.	2.5	2.7	2.5	2.4	3.0	2.0	3.3	2.1	2.6	2.6	2.8	2.1	2.5	4.2	2.2	1.3
1. Completely dissatisfied	3.6	3.5	3.5	2.7	7.6	3.8	3.0	4.0	3.6	2.7	4.7	3.5	3.5	2.9	3.5	25.3
Item 1350 Subject F01,P02 N	3429	1603	1662	2546	432	808	970	1112	539	1789	1243	1265	844	428	740	30

QUESTIONNAIRE FORM 1 1983	TOTAL	SEX		RACE		REGION				4YR COLLEGE PLANS		ILLICIT DRUG USE: LIFETIME				
		M	F	White	Black	NE	NC	S	W	Yes	No	None	Marijuana Only	Few Pills	More Pills	Any Heroin
N (Weighted No. of Cases):	3448	1611	1667	2555	435	814	974	1118	541	1798	1246	1269	848	428	746	30
% of Weighted Total:	100.0	46.7	48.3	74.1	12.6	23.6	28.3	32.4	15.7	52.2	36.1	36.8	24.6	12.4	21.6	.9
A006J: The amount of time you have for doing things you want to do?																
7. Completely satisfied	18.1	18.1	18.0	16.9	21.6	17.5	17.6	19.3	17.6	16.0	20.5	19.0	20.5	16.5	14.8	18.0
6.	16.7	17.5	16.1	18.7	10.1	16.7	20.2	13.9	15.9	17.4	16.1	17.1	15.8	19.3	16.0	9.6
5.	15.5	16.3	14.9	17.2	9.9	13.7	16.9	14.2	18.4	17.8	13.6	15.9	15.5	15.5	15.6	7.7
4. Neutral	19.5	18.8	19.9	17.9	29.7	22.5	16.8	21.9	14.6	18.6	20.0	19.9	18.4	19.7	19.1	24.3
3.	10.6	10.9	10.5	11.6	5.1	10.6	11.5	9.2	12.2	12.0	9.2	11.1	10.1	9.3	12.0	10.5
2.	6.7	6.3	6.9	7.4	2.9	6.6	7.1	6.0	7.3	7.8	5.4	6.5	6.9	4.6	7.8	2.9
1. Completely dissatisfied	12.9	12.0	13.6	10.5	20.7	12.3	9.9	15.4	14.0	10.4	15.2	10.4	12.8	15.1	14.6	27.1
Item 1360 Subject P02 N	3426	1602	1663	2547	434	808	969	1111	538	1793	1240	1266	844	426	742	30
A006K: The way you spend your leisure time—recreation, relaxation, and so on?																
7. Completely satisfied	31.8	32.2	31.1	30.8	38.7	32.4	29.9	35.0	27.6	28.6	35.3	31.7	31.3	33.4	30.6	44.6
6.	20.8	22.5	19.7	23.4	11.6	19.5	24.0	19.0	20.7	22.7	19.4	22.4	19.2	18.4	22.7	7.6
5.	13.9	15.1	13.1	15.8	6.5	12.1	16.9	11.0	16.8	17.2	9.8	13.7	14.9	14.4	13.2	11.7
4. Neutral	19.5	16.7	21.6	17.4	26.6	21.8	16.8	20.7	18.8	17.6	21.3	18.8	19.3	20.6	19.6	9.2
3.	6.0	6.8	5.6	6.3	3.4	5.8	6.1	5.3	7.6	6.8	5.1	6.4	6.5	5.3	5.9	3.8
2.	3.2	3.0	3.3	2.8	4.0	3.8	2.9	2.9	3.4	2.6	4.1	2.8	3.5	3.5	3.3	6.1
1. Completely dissatisfied	4.8	3.8	5.7	3.5	9.1	4.6	3.4	6.0	5.2	4.5	4.9	4.3	5.3	4.4	4.6	17.1
Item 1370 Subject C08,P02 N	3433	1607	1661	2549	433	811	968	1114	541	1793	1242	1268	843	426	743	30
A006L: Your life as a whole these days?																
7. Completely satisfied	20.2	18.5	21.7	18.7	28.4	21.4	17.6	22.4	18.9	19.3	21.6	22.9	21.0	19.1	15.2	15.3
6.	27.3	29.7	25.9	31.4	14.5	23.0	30.6	26.0	30.4	32.3	22.1	29.5	26.4	26.4	26.1	22.6
5.	16.2	17.9	15.1	18.0	10.9	15.7	17.5	16.3	14.6	17.7	15.5	15.5	15.5	20.1	17.9	7.5
4. Neutral	25.7	23.9	26.8	22.0	35.0	28.9	23.0	26.9	23.3	20.8	30.6	22.8	27.6	24.6	27.7	32.2
3.	4.8	4.6	4.7	5.1	2.5	5.1	6.1	2.6	6.2	5.2	3.9	4.5	4.3	5.2	5.8	-
2.	2.1	2.2	2.0	2.0	1.0	1.6	2.9	1.6	2.5	1.9	2.3	1.8	2.2	1.4	2.8	-
1. Completely dissatisfied	3.7	3.3	3.8	2.7	7.7	4.3	2.2	4.2	4.1	2.8	3.9	3.0	3.0	3.1	4.4	22.5
Item 1380 Subject P01 N	3426	1602	1660	2545	433	810	968	1109	539	1791	1239	1263	842	426	741	30
A006M: The way our national government is operating?																
7. Completely satisfied	2.4	2.7	1.9	2.1	2.7	1.6	2.4	3.0	2.5	2.8	1.8	3.0	2.0	1.5	1.7	4.0
6.	3.8	4.3	3.3	4.4	1.5	2.3	4.3	4.0	4.7	4.4	2.5	5.0	3.1	2.9	3.0	-
5.	11.0	13.0	9.7	12.9	4.5	10.0	12.6	9.6	12.6	13.8	8.8	12.3	10.2	11.8	10.2	4.4
4. Neutral	36.8	32.4	41.0	37.5	32.4	35.9	34.3	39.7	36.9	35.8	37.1	37.1	36.2	37.8	37.7	22.1
3.	13.4	13.7	13.2	15.2	7.7	13.8	15.1	11.2	14.6	16.0	11.8	13.2	16.3	11.8	13.2	11.7
2.	11.4	11.9	11.0	11.5	10.9	12.3	11.9	10.4	10.9	11.6	11.1	10.2	10.8	12.5	13.2	18.8
1. Completely dissatisfied	21.1	22.0	19.4	16.4	40.3	24.2	19.4	22.0	17.8	15.6	26.9	19.1	21.5	21.7	21.1	39.0
Item 1390 Subject H02,K02 N	3422	1601	1658	2544	431	808	968	1107	539	1793	1235	1263	840	425	743	30
A006N: The amount of fun you are having?																
7. Completely satisfied	26.3	24.7	27.9	24.8	33.4	27.7	22.9	30.8	20.7	23.6	30.0	25.0	28.0	25.1	25.9	34.4
6.	24.2	25.6	23.3	27.8	12.2	21.3	28.5	21.6	26.3	28.8	19.5	26.5	22.4	25.5	22.9	10.6
5.	16.8	19.1	15.1	18.7	10.5	16.3	17.8	15.5	18.4	19.6	14.1	17.0	17.5	16.6	16.7	8.6
4. Neutral	19.8	18.3	20.4	16.8	27.4	22.1	18.1	19.8	19.7	16.7	22.2	19.3	20.4	19.6	19.5	18.4
3.	5.5	5.6	5.5	5.9	2.7	5.3	6.5	3.9	7.4	6.1	4.4	5.7	4.8	6.9	5.5	9.3
2.	2.8	2.6	2.9	2.6	2.9	2.7	2.7	2.5	3.8	2.3	3.7	2.3	2.3	2.0	4.3	-
1. Completely dissatisfied	4.6	4.0	4.9	3.4	10.9	4.7	3.5	6.0	3.6	2.9	6.1	3.8	4.7	4.2	5.3	18.7
Item 1400 Subject P02,Q01 N	3437	1608	1664	2551	435	810	971	1115	541	1796	1243	1268	845	428	744	30
A007: How important is each of the following to you in your life?																
A007A: Being successful in my line of work																
1. Not important	1.3	1.7	0.8	1.2	1.4	1.9	1.1	1.1	1.0	0.6	2.1	0.9	1.1	1.5	1.7	8.1
2. Somewhat important	8.8	8.6	9.0	9.3	5.9	10.9	8.4	7.9	8.5	6.2	12.5	9.0	7.6	10.0	9.0	19.0
3. Quite important	29.4	29.7	29.7	31.1	21.6	29.1	32.9	25.4	31.8	28.6	31.0	29.3	28.2	32.2	29.3	17.9
4. Extremely important	60.5	60.1	60.5	58.4	71.2	58.1	57.6	65.5	58.8	64.5	54.4	60.9	63.1	56.4	60.0	55.0
Item 1410 Subject C06,Q07 N	3409	1593	1653	2536	424	805	965	1100	539	1785	1228	1257	842	425	736	29

MONITORING THE FUTURE

QUESTIONNAIRE FORM 1 1983	TOTAL	SEX		RACE		REGION				4YR COLLEGE PLANS		ILLICIT DRUG USE: LIFETIME				
		M	F	White	Black	NE	NC	S	W	Yes	No	None	Mari-juana Only	Few Pills	More Pills	Any Her-oin
N (Weighted No. of Cases):	3448	1611	1667	2555	435	814	974	1118	541	1798	1246	1269	848	428	746	30
% of Weighted Total:	100.0	46.7	48.3	74.1	12.6	23.6	28.3	32.4	15.7	52.2	36.1	36.8	24.6	12.4	21.6	.9

A007B: Having a good marriage and family life

1. Not important	3.4	5.2	1.3	3.0	3.1	3.9	3.6	3.3	2.6	2.5	4.2	2.8	2.5	2.9	5.0	8.6
2. Somewhat important	6.9	8.8	4.9	6.9	6.2	7.2	6.2	6.6	8.4	6.1	7.8	4.9	6.6	7.2	10.1	10.4
3. Quite important	14.5	16.8	11.7	14.1	13.8	18.5	14.8	11.7	13.5	14.4	14.3	12.4	13.5	15.5	18.1	24.7
4. Extremely important	75.2	69.2	82.2	76.1	76.8	70.4	75.4	78.4	75.6	77.0	73.7	79.9	77.4	74.4	66.7	56.4
Item 1420 Subject D03,Q07 N	3401	1587	1652	2529	427	800	960	1102	540	1786	1224	1258	840	425	728	29

A007C: Having lots of money

1. Not important	6.4	5.4	7.6	7.0	3.8	5.7	6.6	6.4	7.0	6.4	7.1	7.9	5.1	5.7	5.5	4.1
2. Somewhat important	34.3	28.5	40.7	36.5	28.1	30.3	37.3	32.7	38.1	34.7	36.1	38.5	33.3	34.9	30.7	16.7
3. Quite important	36.4	37.4	35.8	36.6	34.7	38.7	36.3	36.3	33.3	39.4	32.5	35.1	38.9	38.6	34.5	34.3
4. Extremely important	22.9	28.7	16.0	20.0	33.4	25.3	19.8	24.6	21.6	19.5	24.3	18.4	22.7	20.8	29.2	44.9
Item 1430 Subject F01,Q07 N	3412	1592	1656	2535	428	796	969	1109	537	1787	1232	1258	842	425	736	29

A007D: Having plenty of time for recreation and hobbies

1. Not important	2.7	2.6	2.6	1.9	6.0	2.9	2.0	3.6	1.5	1.8	3.8	3.0	3.0	1.7	2.4	-
2. Somewhat important	31.1	24.5	37.5	29.1	40.9	29.4	33.8	30.5	29.7	28.4	34.8	32.5	29.3	36.9	27.1	27.8
3. Quite important	41.8	42.4	41.8	43.8	33.2	41.9	39.9	42.7	43.3	44.0	39.6	43.1	43.0	38.0	41.8	36.4
4. Extremely important	24.5	30.5	18.1	25.2	20.0	25.8	24.3	23.1	25.5	25.7	21.8	21.4	24.7	23.4	28.7	35.7
Item 1440 Subject C08,Q07 N	3425	1601	1659	2543	432	805	969	1111	540	1790	1239	1262	845	428	741	29

A007E: Having strong friendships

1. Not important	1.4	1.5	1.2	0.7	4.7	1.2	0.6	2.8	0.5	0.9	2.1	1.5	1.3	1.8	1.1	-
2. Somewhat important	7.5	7.6	6.9	4.7	20.6	9.1	5.8	8.9	5.2	5.7	8.3	5.6	9.2	8.6	6.3	17.1
3. Quite important	29.0	31.3	26.5	27.6	32.3	25.6	31.2	30.3	27.6	26.6	32.6	31.4	28.3	29.5	24.5	26.3
4. Extremely important	62.0	59.5	65.4	67.0	42.5	64.2	62.4	58.0	66.6	66.8	57.1	61.5	61.2	60.1	68.1	56.6
Item 1450 Subject M04,Q07 N	3421	1599	1660	2540	433	801	967	1112	540	1790	1236	1262	845	428	739	29

A007F: Being able to find steady work

1. Not important	0.8	1.1	0.4	0.7	0.9	1.3	0.4	1.1	0.4	0.6	0.9	0.9	0.1	1.1	1.3	2.1
2. Somewhat important	4.5	4.4	4.6	4.5	3.1	3.7	5.2	3.4	6.4	5.4	3.3	4.8	3.1	4.4	4.5	13.9
3. Quite important	21.4	20.8	22.5	22.6	12.7	21.4	22.5	18.4	25.9	21.1	21.6	21.9	20.1	23.5	21.3	5.4
4. Extremely important	73.3	73.7	72.5	72.2	83.3	73.7	72.0	77.1	67.3	72.8	74.3	72.4	76.7	71.1	72.9	78.6
Item 1460 Subject C04,Q07 N	3420	1600	1658	2538	432	803	969	1109	539	1787	1240	1259	845	428	740	29

A007G: Making a contribution to society

1. Not important	8.0	8.6	7.4	8.2	6.5	8.4	8.7	7.9	6.4	5.8	11.3	7.8	5.7	8.9	9.2	28.7
2. Somewhat important	40.2	39.5	40.0	40.4	36.4	42.8	41.8	36.7	40.5	35.1	46.3	35.0	42.8	47.2	42.0	37.2
3. Quite important	34.6	34.8	35.1	35.1	35.7	31.6	34.0	36.9	35.4	36.6	31.7	37.1	34.5	31.1	33.3	23.7
4. Extremely important	17.2	17.1	17.5	16.3	21.4	17.2	15.5	18.5	17.7	22.5	10.8	20.1	17.0	12.8	15.5	10.4
Item 1470 Subject O01,Q07 N	3405	1593	1650	2528	429	803	960	1103	539	1780	1233	1255	842	425	736	29

A007H: Being a leader in my community

1. Not important	35.4	33.0	37.0	36.7	27.6	39.2	36.9	31.6	34.7	28.1	45.5	32.1	34.9	42.2	36.4	54.1
2. Somewhat important	39.9	39.4	41.1	39.9	41.1	41.5	40.0	39.3	38.9	41.7	37.6	39.8	39.2	37.5	43.9	30.6
3. Quite important	17.3	19.1	15.5	17.0	19.0	13.0	16.9	20.1	18.4	20.6	12.4	19.7	18.2	14.8	13.8	1.8
4. Extremely important	7.4	8.4	6.4	6.4	12.3	6.3	6.2	9.0	8.0	9.5	4.5	8.4	7.7	5.6	5.9	13.5
Item 1480 Subject M05,Q07 N	3415	1598	1655	2536	431	800	968	1109	538	1784	1238	1257	842	428	740	29

A007I: Being able to give my children better opportunities than I've had

1. Not important	2.5	3.3	1.7	2.4	2.2	3.0	2.4	1.9	3.0	2.5	2.5	2.0	1.7	2.0	3.6	4.0
2. Somewhat important	10.2	10.2	10.5	12.1	2.3	11.0	12.8	6.5	11.7	12.0	8.4	10.1	9.6	10.4	11.7	10.3
3. Quite important	28.6	29.3	28.5	32.2	13.7	28.3	33.8	23.9	29.0	29.9	27.5	29.3	27.4	31.2	29.2	21.6
4. Extremely important	58.8	57.3	59.3	53.3	81.8	57.7	51.0	67.7	56.3	55.6	61.5	58.6	61.3	56.4	55.5	64.1
Item 1490 Subject Q07 N	3396	1585	1650	2525	428	801	958	1103	534	1781	1226	1254	844	423	729	29

QUESTIONNAIRE FORM 1 1983	TOTAL	SEX M	SEX F	RACE White	RACE Black	REGION NE	REGION NC	REGION S	REGION W	4YR COLLEGE PLANS Yes	4YR COLLEGE PLANS No	ILLICIT DRUG USE: LIFETIME None	Marijuana Only	Few Pills	More Pills	Any Heroin
N (Weighted No. of Cases):	3448	1611	1667	2555	435	814	974	1118	541	1798	1246	1269	848	428	746	30
% of Weighted Total:	100.0	46.7	48.3	74.1	12.6	23.6	28.3	32.4	15.7	52.2	36.1	36.8	24.6	12.4	21.6	.9

A007J: Living close to parents and relatives

	TOTAL	M	F	White	Black	NE	NC	S	W	Yes	No	None	Mari.	Few	More	Any
1. Not important	21.5	23.2	19.7	21.8	23.1	18.8	24.1	22.0	20.0	21.8	20.8	17.6	20.8	25.6	25.7	48.7
2. Somewhat important	44.3	44.6	44.0	44.9	44.2	45.6	43.4	43.8	45.3	45.1	43.3	46.4	44.1	42.0	44.7	31.1
3. Quite important	22.5	22.4	23.2	23.3	18.2	23.5	23.3	21.0	22.5	22.0	23.4	22.8	24.2	21.1	21.1	7.0
4. Extremely important	11.7	9.9	13.1	10.0	14.4	12.1	9.2	13.2	12.2	11.1	12.5	13.2	11.0	11.3	8.5	13.2
Item 1500 Subject M03,Q07 N	3409	1596	1654	2535	430	797	963	1109	540	1784	1235	1259	844	425	733	29

A007K: Getting away from this area of the country

	TOTAL	M	F	White	Black	NE	NC	S	W	Yes	No	None	Mari.	Few	More	Any
1. Not important	53.8	54.0	54.3	57.8	39.3	50.6	53.2	53.8	59.6	55.1	54.0	62.6	51.3	53.0	44.9	31.7
2. Somewhat important	22.8	22.8	22.6	21.8	26.6	23.5	22.0	23.6	21.6	22.3	22.7	19.8	21.3	25.4	26.4	22.1
3. Quite important	11.4	11.6	10.9	10.1	15.5	14.0	11.2	10.7	9.6	11.3	10.6	9.2	13.6	10.6	12.9	26.7
4. Extremely important	12.0	11.5	12.1	10.3	18.6	11.8	13.5	12.0	9.3	11.2	12.7	8.5	13.8	11.0	15.7	19.4
Item 1510 Subject Q07 N	3418	1597	1658	2537	433	803	967	1113	535	1791	1234	1262	841	427	739	29

A007L: Working to correct social and economic inequalities

	TOTAL	M	F	White	Black	NE	NC	S	W	Yes	No	None	Mari.	Few	More	Any
1. Not important	21.0	24.3	18.7	23.3	12.0	22.9	23.3	18.1	20.1	20.3	23.9	19.3	20.0	23.4	23.5	29.5
2. Somewhat important	46.2	45.4	46.6	47.9	40.9	44.1	47.1	45.8	48.3	45.1	47.6	45.0	45.3	49.1	47.7	43.4
3. Quite important	24.1	22.1	25.7	22.3	28.1	23.9	22.8	25.7	23.6	24.8	21.4	25.1	24.8	22.2	22.8	18.0
4. Extremely important	8.7	8.2	9.1	6.5	19.0	9.1	6.8	10.4	8.0	9.8	7.1	10.6	9.9	5.3	5.9	9.1
Item 1520 Subject N02,O01,Q07 N	3406	1594	1652	2533	429	797	964	1107	538	1781	1236	1260	842	424	733	29

A007M: Discovering new ways to experience things

	TOTAL	M	F	White	Black	NE	NC	S	W	Yes	No	None	Mari.	Few	More	Any
1. Not important	8.4	8.7	8.4	8.5	9.5	7.8	10.0	9.0	5.1	8.2	9.4	9.6	7.0	10.2	6.8	8.6
2. Somewhat important	36.6	37.3	36.6	38.2	32.7	35.0	39.1	37.2	33.3	36.4	38.2	39.7	38.7	37.8	29.7	31.3
3. Quite important	36.7	36.4	36.8	37.4	32.4	37.9	36.3	33.8	41.5	35.8	37.4	34.9	35.0	35.2	42.8	20.3
4. Extremely important	18.3	17.6	18.2	16.0	25.5	19.3	14.6	20.0	20.0	19.5	15.0	15.8	19.3	16.8	20.7	39.7
Item 1530 Subject Q07 N	3414	1594	1658	2533	433	799	964	1111	540	1787	1235	1260	845	425	735	29

A007N: Finding purpose and meaning in my life

	TOTAL	M	F	White	Black	NE	NC	S	W	Yes	No	None	Mari.	Few	More	Any
1. Not important	2.0	3.1	0.9	2.2	0.6	1.3	2.4	2.3	1.4	1.8	2.1	1.9	0.9	2.3	2.8	7.6
2. Somewhat important	9.7	14.0	5.6	10.4	6.9	12.3	10.3	7.1	10.3	9.3	9.9	8.5	10.2	10.9	10.0	12.6
3. Quite important	26.3	30.8	21.9	28.1	15.0	26.5	28.9	23.2	27.6	24.8	29.9	28.6	24.7	25.4	26.6	18.1
4. Extremely important	62.0	52.0	71.7	59.2	77.5	59.9	58.4	67.4	60.7	64.1	58.1	61.1	64.1	61.4	60.6	61.7
Item 1540 Subject Q07 N	3420	1596	1662	2539	434	802	965	1114	539	1789	1238	1263	844	425	739	29

A008: Generally speaking, would you say that most people can be trusted or that you can't be too careful in dealing with people?

	TOTAL	M	F	White	Black	NE	NC	S	W	Yes	No	None	Mari.	Few	More	Any
3. Most people can be trusted	27.7	28.9	27.4	31.3	14.2	24.3	33.7	23.0	32.0	32.2	23.2	32.7	25.2	26.8	24.4	21.7
2. Don't know, undecided	28.6	29.3	27.7	28.8	21.1	29.2	29.5	27.6	27.9	27.1	30.0	26.1	30.6	33.9	27.9	21.2
1. Can't be too careful	43.7	41.8	44.9	39.9	64.7	46.5	36.8	49.5	40.0	40.7	46.8	41.2	44.2	39.3	47.7	57.1
Item 1550 Subject Q05 N	3344	1559	1634	2503	421	786	958	1078	523	1764	1205	1234	825	415	730	29

A009: Would you say that most of the time people try to be helpful or that they are mostly just looking out for themselves?

	TOTAL	M	F	White	Black	NE	NC	S	W	Yes	No	None	Mari.	Few	More	Any
3. Try to be helpful	34.0	31.9	36.4	36.5	25.5	28.9	39.6	32.7	34.2	36.4	32.5	39.1	30.3	36.0	29.3	25.4
2. Don't know, undecided	31.1	33.4	28.6	31.3	29.8	35.3	29.7	29.0	31.6	29.9	31.6	28.9	33.7	28.1	33.3	24.8
1. Just looking out for themselves	34.9	34.7	35.0	32.2	44.6	35.9	30.7	38.3	34.1	33.7	36.0	32.0	36.0	35.9	37.4	49.8
Item 1560 Subject Q05 N	3414	1593	1658	2531	434	802	965	1109	537	1783	1236	1256	846	426	737	29

A010: Do you think most people would try to take advantage of you if they got a chance or would they try to be fair?

	TOTAL	M	F	White	Black	NE	NC	S	W	Yes	No	None	Mari.	Few	More	Any
3. Would try to be fair	26.6	26.2	27.7	29.9	13.7	25.2	30.1	23.1	29.4	29.8	24.6	30.0	24.4	27.2	23.8	28.8
2. Don't know, undecided	35.5	36.7	34.3	37.4	23.5	39.2	35.1	32.9	36.3	34.7	35.8	34.2	36.5	37.8	36.6	23.5
1. Would try to take advantage of you	37.9	37.2	38.0	32.7	62.8	35.6	34.8	44.0	34.3	35.5	39.6	35.8	39.0	35.1	39.6	47.7
Item 1570 Subject Q05 N	3409	1591	1656	2531	433	802	965	1107	535	1780	1236	1254	846	425	736	29

QUESTIONNAIRE FORM 1 1983	TOTAL	SEX		RACE		REGION				4YR COLLEGE PLANS		ILLICIT DRUG USE: LIFETIME				
		M	F	White	Black	NE	NC	S	W	Yes	No	None	Marijuana Only	Few Pills	More Pills	Any Heroin
N (Weighted No. of Cases):	3448	1611	1667	2555	435	814	974	1118	541	1798	1246	1269	848	428	746	30
% of Weighted Total:	100.0	46.7	48.3	74.1	12.6	23.6	28.3	32.4	15.7	52.2	36.1	36.8	24.6	12.4	21.6	.9

A011: These next questions ask your opinions about a number of different topics. How much do you agree or disagree with each statement below?

A011A: I feel that you can't be a good citizen unless you always obey the law

1. Disagree	19.0	22.9	14.8	17.3	24.4	22.5	19.4	17.2	17.1	17.3	19.0	12.9	19.8	20.9	26.1	39.3
2. Mostly disagree	16.1	15.6	17.4	17.3	11.2	16.1	18.8	13.5	16.7	17.2	15.7	12.7	17.6	19.2	18.1	23.6
3. Neither	19.2	18.8	19.5	20.4	11.7	21.6	18.4	19.3	16.8	19.3	18.6	18.0	17.7	22.4	22.2	15.2
4. Mostly agree	33.3	31.1	35.8	35.2	29.1	28.0	34.5	34.5	36.3	36.5	31.9	40.0	32.9	28.4	26.7	10.4
5. Agree	12.4	11.6	12.6	9.8	23.5	11.8	8.9	15.6	13.0	9.7	14.8	16.4	12.0	9.1	7.0	11.4
Item 1580 Subject H03　　N	3419	1602	1655	2541	432	802	968	1109	540	1788	1236	1257	846	428	739	29

A011B: I feel a good citizen should go along with whatever the government does even if he disagrees with it

1. Disagree	38.9	38.0	39.4	36.4	48.1	44.1	36.5	37.0	39.2	37.8	38.8	34.2	42.4	39.6	41.8	54.6
2. Mostly disagree	24.8	24.2	25.7	26.2	20.8	26.2	26.7	23.3	22.4	25.5	23.4	25.1	23.9	25.7	25.5	22.7
3. Neither	17.9	18.2	17.7	19.5	10.7	15.5	20.1	17.6	17.7	17.7	19.5	17.8	16.6	18.3	19.1	14.4
4. Mostly agree	13.0	14.0	12.0	13.5	10.9	11.2	12.4	14.3	14.0	13.6	12.9	15.3	12.2	12.4	10.7	4.0
5. Agree	5.4	5.7	5.2	4.3	9.4	3.0	4.2	7.7	6.6	5.4	5.4	7.7	5.0	4.0	3.0	4.3
Item 1590 Subject H03　　N	3419	1600	1656	2539	432	802	969	1109	538	1788	1236	1260	845	426	739	29

A011C: I feel a good citizen tries to change the government policies he disagrees with

1. Disagree	6.6	5.7	7.2	5.8	10.2	7.9	5.1	7.5	5.7	5.2	8.0	7.2	6.2	3.7	7.0	8.1
2. Mostly disagree	9.1	7.8	9.7	8.3	11.3	7.7	9.1	10.4	8.3	8.7	10.3	9.4	9.9	10.3	7.3	7.9
3. Neither	26.4	24.8	28.1	25.9	24.4	23.4	28.3	27.0	26.2	24.2	28.9	26.5	24.4	27.6	28.4	20.3
4. Mostly agree	32.4	33.3	32.3	34.7	28.0	37.2	31.7	29.2	32.9	34.6	30.0	32.4	34.1	33.1	30.7	23.5
5. Agree	25.6	28.4	22.8	25.4	26.1	23.8	25.8	26.0	26.8	27.3	22.7	24.6	25.4	25.3	26.6	40.2
Item 1600 Subject H03　　N	3410	1592	1656	2534	431	799	967	1107	537	1785	1232	1258	845	426	734	29

A011D: The way people vote has a major impact on how things are run in this country

1. Disagree	5.4	6.3	4.2	5.1	5.7	6.8	5.5	5.0	3.8	4.9	5.4	3.8	5.7	5.6	6.6	7.9
2. Mostly disagree	9.2	10.5	8.2	10.2	5.1	11.1	9.0	8.6	8.3	10.0	7.6	8.3	7.8	10.2	11.8	9.6
3. Neither	12.7	12.9	12.5	13.9	6.8	13.9	15.1	9.9	12.2	12.5	12.6	12.3	10.3	11.6	15.4	26.1
4. Mostly agree	33.9	33.6	34.4	35.1	30.3	32.2	34.8	33.5	35.6	34.2	34.9	34.4	34.0	34.6	33.8	26.4
5. Agree	38.8	36.7	40.8	35.7	52.1	36.1	35.6	43.0	40.1	38.4	39.6	41.2	42.1	38.0	32.4	30.0
Item 1610 Subject H05,I02　　N	3408	1595	1655	2537	432	799	964	1107	537	1789	1229	1255	842	428	735	29

A011E: People who get together in citizen action groups to influence government policies can have a real effect

1. Disagree	4.0	4.4	3.2	3.4	6.3	4.4	3.6	4.2	3.5	3.3	4.0	3.0	2.8	3.1	6.9	4.4
2. Mostly disagree	9.5	10.8	8.0	10.0	4.0	10.3	9.3	9.2	9.0	9.5	8.6	8.7	8.3	8.5	11.8	6.0
3. Neither	23.9	24.9	23.6	26.0	16.7	23.4	25.3	23.0	23.6	22.8	26.5	22.7	23.5	25.2	25.9	35.8
4. Mostly agree	37.7	36.3	39.8	38.9	38.7	37.6	37.8	37.6	37.8	41.3	34.6	39.5	37.3	42.1	34.4	26.6
5. Agree	25.0	23.6	25.5	21.8	34.2	24.3	23.9	26.0	26.2	23.1	26.3	26.0	28.1	21.0	21.1	27.2
Item 1620 Subject H03,I02　　N	3411	1595	1654	2534	432	799	965	1109	538	1785	1235	1258	842	428	736	29

A011F: Despite its many faults, our system of doing things is still the best in the world

1. Disagree	5.2	4.4	5.9	3.5	12.4	6.3	4.3	5.7	4.3	3.6	6.9	4.1	5.3	6.2	5.7	11.4
2. Mostly disagree	7.2	6.6	7.3	5.8	10.5	7.0	7.8	7.2	6.5	6.2	8.2	5.9	6.8	8.0	8.5	10.4
3. Neither	20.7	17.8	23.5	20.2	21.4	24.1	21.0	18.6	19.4	18.6	23.9	20.4	20.8	21.8	20.7	27.7
4. Mostly agree	32.7	32.4	33.2	33.6	28.9	33.3	33.1	31.3	33.8	33.4	32.7	32.6	34.4	33.3	32.3	22.4
5. Agree	34.2	38.9	30.1	36.8	26.7	29.4	33.8	37.2	35.9	38.3	28.3	37.1	32.7	30.7	32.8	28.1
Item 1630 Subject H04　　N	3397	1588	1650	2528	428	796	964	1102	535	1780	1228	1257	840	426	732	29

QUESTIONNAIRE FORM 1 1983	TOTAL	SEX		RACE		REGION				4YR COLLEGE PLANS		ILLICIT DRUG USE: LIFETIME				
		M	F	White	Black	NE	NC	S	W	Yes	No	None	Mari-juana Only	Few Pills	More Pills	Any Her-oin
N (Weighted No. of Cases):	3448	1611	1667	2555	435	814	974	1118	541	1798	1246	1269	848	428	746	30
% of Weighted Total:	100.0	46.7	48.3	74.1	12.6	23.6	28.3	32.4	15.7	52.2	36.1	36.8	24.6	12.4	21.6	.9
A011G: America needs growth to survive, and that is going to require some increase in pollution																
1. Disagree	34.5	34.7	35.2	35.6	31.1	36.3	35.6	33.9	31.3	35.8	33.1	33.0	35.1	30.5	38.5	47.5
2. Mostly disagree	21.4	21.4	21.8	23.6	13.6	19.2	23.4	17.7	28.6	24.5	18.9	23.5	19.2	24.5	20.7	10.4
3. Neither	22.6	21.2	23.5	22.6	21.1	23.2	22.5	24.0	19.2	22.2	23.2	23.2	23.3	24.8	19.1	20.2
4. Mostly agree	13.8	15.0	12.2	12.4	18.0	13.1	12.3	16.0	12.9	11.2	16.0	12.7	13.9	14.7	14.6	2.1
5. Agree	7.7	7.7	7.4	5.8	16.1	8.2	6.2	8.5	8.0	6.3	8.8	7.5	8.5	5.5	7.2	19.7
Item 1640 Subject F04 N	3399	1595	1647	2529	429	798	959	1106	537	1778	1233	1253	845	425	734	29
A011H: If we just leave things to God, they will turn out for the best																
1. Disagree	17.8	20.5	15.3	18.8	8.8	22.6	17.5	11.5	23.8	21.2	13.1	13.2	20.2	17.7	24.0	17.9
2. Mostly disagree	13.6	14.2	13.3	14.8	5.6	14.1	15.0	10.1	17.5	14.7	11.7	13.0	13.6	14.4	14.7	6.3
3. Neither	26.9	28.5	24.7	29.1	14.5	30.8	29.8	23.2	23.4	24.3	30.8	25.5	27.7	27.2	28.7	26.2
4. Mostly agree	18.7	17.6	20.2	18.5	22.6	15.0	19.4	21.6	16.8	18.8	18.4	19.0	18.2	18.4	17.3	29.7
5. Agree	23.1	19.2	26.5	18.9	48.5	17.5	18.2	33.6	18.4	21.0	26.0	29.3	20.2	22.2	15.3	19.9
Item 1650 Subject I02 N	3389	1583	1649	2523	426	796	959	1099	536	1776	1229	1254	837	424	729	29
A011I: Going to school has been an enjoyable experience for me																
1. Disagree	5.6	6.5	4.3	5.7	4.3	5.4	7.1	4.5	5.3	3.8	7.4	4.3	4.9	4.9	7.6	23.9
2. Mostly disagree	7.0	7.9	6.0	7.5	3.8	9.3	7.7	5.9	4.4	5.1	8.7	4.6	5.7	7.9	11.8	10.4
3. Neither	14.7	16.5	12.2	15.0	7.6	17.4	13.7	13.2	15.5	13.3	15.3	11.4	15.4	15.0	18.3	13.2
4. Mostly agree	40.0	39.7	41.2	41.9	36.3	39.3	42.2	37.9	41.3	41.9	39.0	40.7	41.6	43.1	36.7	34.7
5. Agree	32.8	29.5	36.3	29.9	48.1	28.7	29.3	38.5	33.4	35.9	29.5	38.9	32.3	29.1	25.5	17.8
Item 1660 Subject B01 N	3413	1600	1655	2541	431	799	969	1109	537	1787	1239	1262	846	426	735	29
A011J: Doing well in school is important for getting a good job																
1. Disagree	2.0	2.7	1.2	2.0	1.3	2.4	2.1	1.7	1.9	1.6	2.6	0.9	1.5	2.6	3.7	12.2
2. Mostly disagree	3.0	4.2	1.7	2.9	2.4	2.6	2.7	2.8	4.2	2.8	2.8	2.2	2.9	3.2	4.3	2.1
3. Neither	7.4	8.9	5.7	7.9	2.4	8.1	7.2	7.2	7.3	5.2	10.1	4.8	6.0	9.0	11.6	26.0
4. Mostly agree	30.4	31.7	29.3	30.7	29.2	31.6	30.5	29.4	30.9	28.9	32.0	28.2	32.6	34.6	30.4	15.2
5. Agree	57.2	52.5	62.1	56.5	64.8	55.3	57.5	59.0	55.7	61.5	52.6	63.9	57.1	50.5	50.0	44.5
Item 1670 Subject B01 N	3417	1601	1656	2538	434	800	967	1112	538	1789	1239	1260	846	427	738	29
The following questions are about CIGARETTE SMOKING.																
B001: Have you ever smoked cigarettes?																
1. Never–GO TO Q.B006	29.6	30.5	29.8	29.8	32.9	26.3	27.7	31.0	35.5	35.6	24.8	56.1	14.7	16.7	9.5	-
2. Once or twice	29.9	32.6	27.6	27.9	43.4	29.2	28.1	29.5	34.9	32.7	26.7	29.6	41.8	31.8	17.5	12.9
3. Occasionally but not regularly	17.4	15.8	19.2	18.0	14.3	17.4	19.2	17.8	13.4	18.0	16.8	10.1	22.0	21.9	21.4	24.9
4. Regularly in the past	6.8	6.3	7.6	7.7	2.9	6.8	6.6	6.8	7.4	5.2	9.1	2.2	7.6	8.4	12.9	15.7
5. Regularly now	16.2	14.7	15.8	16.5	6.5	20.3	18.4	14.9	8.8	8.4	22.5	2.0	13.9	21.2	38.7	46.5
Item 760 Subject A01a N	3379	1580	1639	2522	421	800	963	1092	524	1772	1225	1241	835	424	735	29
B002: When did you first smoke cigarettes on a daily basis?																
0. Never smoked daily	50.4	52.9	49.3	51.1	58.9	46.7	50.4	49.3	59.2	61.8	41.8	69.5	59.4	49.1	28.6	21.3
1. Grade 6 or earlier	6.5	8.5	4.2	6.7	5.7	6.2	7.6	6.7	4.3	4.4	8.2	6.6	3.3	5.7	9.9	22.1
2. Grade 7 or 8	12.4	11.0	13.1	12.8	8.3	12.8	14.3	11.5	9.5	8.9	15.4	6.6	10.4	19.1	19.1	20.1
3. Grade 9 (Freshman)	10.7	10.0	11.1	10.6	6.8	12.3	10.3	10.5	9.1	7.6	12.9	5.5	8.5	12.3	16.2	12.2
4. Grade 10 (Sophomore)	8.1	6.8	9.3	7.7	7.6	8.2	7.9	9.3	6.0	5.8	9.8	4.5	8.6	8.6	9.5	16.5
5. Grade 11 (Junior)	8.3	7.1	9.2	7.5	9.5	9.7	7.0	8.0	9.0	7.8	8.4	5.2	7.1	8.9	11.6	-
6. Grade 12 (Senior)	3.6	3.7	3.8	3.6	3.3	4.0	2.5	4.6	2.9	3.8	3.5	2.1	2.7	3.5	5.1	7.8
Item 1680 Subject A01g N★	2362	1089	1143	1753	281	586	693	748	335	1125	920	539	708	353	660	29

★=excludes respondents for whom question was inappropriate.

QUESTIONNAIRE FORM 1 1983	TOTAL	SEX		RACE		REGION				4YR COLLEGE PLANS		ILLICIT DRUG USE: LIFETIME				
		M	F	White	Black	NE	NC	S	W	Yes	No	None	Mari-juana Only	Few Pills	More Pills	Any Her-oin
N (Weighted No. of Cases):	3448	1611	1667	2555	435	814	974	1118	541	1798	1246	1269	848	428	746	30
% of Weighted Total:	100.0	46.7	48.3	74.1	12.6	23.6	28.3	32.4	15.7	52.2	36.1	36.8	24.6	12.4	21.6	.9
B003: How frequently have you smoked cigarettes during the past 30 days?																
1. Not at all	59.4	60.9	59.7	58.8	73.7	53.1	57.9	61.3	69.5	67.7	54.3	80.3	68.1	56.9	37.4	19.7
2. Less than one cigarette per day	12.6	12.4	13.1	12.8	12.7	12.3	12.6	12.7	12.8	14.8	11.2	12.1	11.3	13.8	12.8	17.8
3. One to five cigarettes per day	8.7	7.9	9.6	8.2	8.9	13.4	6.3	7.5	8.3	7.9	8.4	3.7	8.9	11.6	11.0	14.1
4. About one-half pack per day	9.3	8.5	9.3	9.5	3.8	10.3	11.1	8.0	7.2	4.8	13.3	1.7	7.0	8.3	17.7	20.7
5. About one pack per day	7.6	8.4	5.7	8.1	0.9	7.9	9.3	8.6	1.4	4.1	9.2	1.4	3.8	8.2	15.9	13.3
6. About one and one-half packs per day	1.7	1.2	2.2	1.9	-	2.3	2.3	1.4	0.6	0.7	2.5	0.3	0.6	1.1	4.2	14.4
7. Two packs or more per day	0.6	0.7	0.4	0.6	-	0.8	0.5	0.6	0.3	0.1	1.1	0.4	0.4	-	1.0	-
Item 780 Subject A01c N★	2366	1091	1145	1758	281	589	691	749	336	1128	921	541	709	350	663	29
B004: Have you ever tried to stop smoking and found that you could not?																
1. Yes	17.6	16.9	16.6	16.3	13.8	20.2	18.7	14.9	16.9	11.7	21.2	10.3	12.3	17.5	26.6	51.4
2. No	82.4	83.1	83.4	83.7	86.2	79.8	81.3	85.1	83.1	88.3	78.8	89.7	87.7	82.5	73.4	48.6
Item 1690 Subject A01i N★	2247	1045	1082	1679	265	557	661	711	317	1070	879	497	664	342	650	29
B005: Do you want to stop smoking now?																
1. Yes	11.4	11.5	10.2	10.9	8.4	15.2	12.0	9.3	8.7	6.7	15.4	3.2	11.5	13.8	22.6	36.4
2. No	11.8	11.0	11.6	12.1	4.9	13.5	13.4	11.7	6.5	8.3	14.4	2.4	11.1	13.3	26.4	35.2
8. Don't smoke now	46.7	46.4	47.9	46.7	53.2	44.6	46.5	47.4	48.7	48.7	45.1	37.6	62.3	55.9	41.4	28.4
Item 1700 Subject A01i N★	3318	1552	1615	2481	414	786	947	1070	516	1743	1208	1225	816	417	723	29
B006: Do you think you will be smoking cigarettes five years from now?																
1. I definitely will	1.4	1.1	1.6	1.1	0.9	1.4	1.1	1.4	2.2	1.2	1.6	1.1	1.6	0.6	1.8	-
2. I probably will	12.1	10.5	12.5	11.9	6.7	14.1	13.8	11.7	7.1	7.8	16.0	3.6	10.8	10.7	27.6	42.7
3. I probably will not	26.3	25.9	25.9	25.6	28.4	30.1	25.9	26.3	21.2	23.3	28.3	18.0	29.6	35.0	30.7	36.8
4. I definitely will not	60.2	62.4	60.0	61.4	64.0	54.4	59.2	60.6	69.6	67.8	54.1	77.4	57.9	53.8	39.9	20.5
Item 1710 Subject A04a N	3390	1581	1647	2519	428	798	958	1099	535	1772	1231	1248	836	425	732	29

The different questionnaire forms used in this study tend to emphasize somewhat different topics. The next major section in this form deals with alcohol and various other drugs. There is a lot of talk these days about these subjects, but very little accurate information. Therefore, we still have a lot to learn about the actual experiences and attitudes of people your age.

We hope that you can answer all questions; but if you find one which you feel you cannot answer honestly, we would prefer that you leave it blank.

Remember that your answers will be strictly confidential. We never connect them with your name or your class.

The next questions are about ALCOHOLIC BEVERAGES, including beer, wine, and liquor.

B007: On how many occasions (if any) have you had alcohol to drink . . .

B007A: . . . in your lifetime?

	TOTAL	M	F	White	Black	NE	NC	S	W	Yes	No	None	Mari-juana Only	Few Pills	More Pills	Any Her-oin
1. 0 occasions	7.9	6.7	9.1	5.7	19.2	5.0	5.2	10.8	11.1	9.1	7.4	18.0	1.9	1.8	0.4	-
2. 1-2	7.3	6.1	8.5	5.5	15.8	4.9	5.4	10.0	8.9	7.4	7.9	14.1	4.4	3.0	1.1	7.4
3. 3-5	8.7	6.2	11.6	8.1	13.7	8.1	7.0	8.5	13.3	9.7	8.1	15.0	6.9	7.3	1.2	-
4. 6-9	8.2	6.4	9.8	7.3	11.2	9.3	7.5	8.9	6.2	8.5	7.5	11.0	8.4	6.4	4.3	4.5
5. 10-19	12.0	11.4	12.9	12.0	12.6	11.5	12.4	12.6	11.0	12.7	11.6	12.9	15.7	12.6	6.3	7.7
6. 20-39	14.1	12.6	16.3	15.2	11.8	15.5	14.8	13.3	12.2	14.1	14.7	11.5	18.7	16.3	12.5	-
7. 40 or more	41.9	50.7	31.8	46.1	15.7	45.7	47.7	36.0	37.2	38.6	42.9	17.6	44.0	52.7	74.3	80.3
Item 810 Subject A01a N	3257	1538	1567	2458	394	774	926	1044	514	1723	1173	1221	798	410	709	29

★=excludes respondents for whom question was inappropriate.

QUESTIONNAIRE FORM 1 1983	TOTAL	SEX		RACE		REGION				4YR COLLEGE PLANS		ILLICIT DRUG USE: LIFETIME				
		M	F	White	Black	NE	NC	S	W	Yes	No	None	Mari-juana Only	Few Pills	More Pills	Any Her-oin
N (Weighted No. of Cases):	3448	1611	1667	2555	435	814	974	1118	541	1798	1246	1269	848	428	746	30
% of Weighted Total:	100.0	46.7	48.3	74.1	12.6	23.6	28.3	32.4	15.7	52.2	36.1	36.8	24.6	12.4	21.6	.9

B007B: ... during the last 12 months?

	TOTAL	M	F	White	Black	NE	NC	S	W	Yes	No	None	Mari-juana Only	Few Pills	More Pills	Any Her-oin
1. 0 occasions	14.2	12.3	16.2	10.8	31.9	10.1	11.6	17.7	17.7	15.1	14.8	30.0	6.4	4.6	1.1	7.6
2. 1-2	14.2	10.2	17.9	12.3	25.1	11.7	11.2	16.9	18.1	15.1	13.4	21.2	12.4	12.5	5.2	9.1
3. 3-5	12.9	11.1	15.0	12.7	12.6	14.0	13.7	11.6	12.8	13.4	12.8	16.0	15.6	11.6	5.9	7.9
4. 6-9	11.0	10.7	11.5	11.6	7.5	12.3	9.9	11.4	10.4	10.8	11.0	9.8	13.5	15.0	8.7	6.2
5. 10-19	15.4	15.5	15.9	16.5	12.7	16.2	16.5	14.6	13.9	14.2	17.9	10.7	18.4	19.4	18.1	10.6
6. 20-39	13.6	14.8	12.9	15.8	5.0	13.4	15.4	12.3	13.2	15.1	11.6	6.8	15.8	18.9	20.1	4.4
7. 40 or more	18.7	25.4	10.5	20.5	5.1	22.4	21.6	15.7	13.8	16.3	18.5	5.6	18.0	18.0	40.9	54.3
Item 820 Subject A01b N	3249	1523	1573	2452	390	769	925	1041	514	1716	1171	1211	808	406	706	29

B007C: ... during the last 30 days?

	TOTAL	M	F	White	Black	NE	NC	S	W	Yes	No	None	Mari-juana Only	Few Pills	More Pills	Any Her-oin
1. 0 occasions	32.3	26.9	37.7	27.9	52.7	27.6	26.4	36.3	41.7	34.6	31.6	55.3	23.8	19.5	9.7	23.3
2. 1-2	23.9	21.7	26.5	23.8	25.5	23.1	23.6	25.1	22.8	22.3	26.2	23.6	28.1	30.7	16.4	23.1
3. 3-5	17.4	18.6	16.7	19.6	10.7	19.3	20.3	14.0	16.2	18.7	15.8	10.1	22.8	20.1	23.0	4.6
4. 6-9	12.3	14.4	9.9	13.6	5.6	14.5	13.4	11.2	9.2	12.7	11.2	5.3	12.6	14.5	21.7	19.7
5. 10-19	9.1	11.2	6.8	9.9	3.4	9.3	10.4	8.7	7.2	8.2	9.4	3.7	8.8	10.8	16.8	14.9
6. 20-39	3.3	4.3	1.9	3.3	1.4	3.2	4.4	2.6	2.6	2.6	3.6	1.4	2.6	2.8	7.5	11.6
7. 40 or more	1.9	2.9	0.5	1.9	0.7	2.9	1.6	2.1	0.2	0.9	2.2	0.6	1.3	1.6	4.8	2.9
Item 830 Subject A01c N	3277	1541	1584	2478	394	777	935	1049	515	1732	1180	1215	808	413	721	29

IF YOU HAVE NOT HAD ANY BEER, WINE, OR LIQUOR IN THE LAST TWELVE MONTHS, GO TO Q.B017.

B008: When you used alcohol during the last year, how often did you use it in each of the following situations?

B008A: When you were alone

	TOTAL	M	F	White	Black	NE	NC	S	W	Yes	No	None	Mari-juana Only	Few Pills	More Pills	Any Her-oin
1. Not at all	69.0	61.7	77.9	69.5	72.4	69.8	66.7	65.8	78.7	74.8	64.6	81.7	73.7	68.9	52.6	19.6
2. A few of the times	23.6	28.2	18.3	24.0	19.4	23.6	26.2	24.4	17.2	20.5	25.5	14.2	21.1	24.8	35.3	46.5
3. Some of the times	5.7	8.1	2.9	5.3	4.6	5.0	5.9	7.5	2.6	3.5	8.0	3.0	3.4	5.6	9.5	29.6
4. Most of the times	1.3	1.6	0.8	0.9	2.4	0.9	1.0	1.9	1.0	1.0	1.4	0.5	1.4	0.6	2.3	4.3
5. Every time	0.4	0.4	0.1	0.2	1.2	0.6	0.2	0.4	0.4	0.1	0.5	0.6	0.3	0.1	0.3	-
Item 1720 Subject A05a N★	2826	1357	1330	2218	270	699	830	870	427	1467	1012	844	760	395	720	28

B008B: With just 1 or 2 other people

	TOTAL	M	F	White	Black	NE	NC	S	W	Yes	No	None	Mari-juana Only	Few Pills	More Pills	Any Her-oin
1. Not at all	12.6	9.6	15.9	11.4	18.9	15.1	10.9	11.0	15.2	16.0	8.3	23.3	11.1	9.9	3.8	-
2. A few of the times	31.2	29.4	34.1	31.1	32.8	31.5	29.1	31.2	34.8	32.5	31.6	36.4	32.7	34.5	22.7	20.9
3. Some of the times	25.1	28.3	21.6	25.9	19.3	24.4	28.1	24.2	22.4	24.3	25.9	15.3	26.0	26.8	35.8	14.5
4. Most of the times	24.3	27.1	20.7	25.3	18.1	22.8	25.6	24.7	23.6	21.4	26.5	17.6	23.8	24.4	30.9	36.9
5. Every time	6.7	5.6	7.7	6.4	10.9	6.1	6.3	8.9	4.0	5.7	7.7	7.3	6.5	4.4	6.8	27.7
Item 1730 Subject A05b N★	2825	1356	1329	2218	267	698	830	872	425	1468	1010	840	765	394	719	28

B008C: At a party

	TOTAL	M	F	White	Black	NE	NC	S	W	Yes	No	None	Mari-juana Only	Few Pills	More Pills	Any Her-oin
1. Not at all	13.5	11.7	16.1	12.8	24.0	9.4	10.8	17.0	18.6	13.7	14.9	24.1	10.1	11.1	6.3	3.4
2. A few of the times	18.7	15.8	21.9	17.6	26.3	18.2	15.2	21.4	20.6	18.4	18.5	24.8	18.7	18.8	11.2	17.8
3. Some of the times	16.5	18.3	14.1	16.3	17.5	16.1	18.9	14.6	16.0	17.0	16.4	14.5	18.9	19.0	14.8	14.7
4. Most of the times	30.4	31.6	29.1	32.1	19.5	32.6	33.0	27.7	27.1	31.5	28.9	21.6	33.7	32.9	36.7	19.2
5. Every time	21.0	22.6	18.8	21.2	12.7	23.6	22.0	19.4	17.7	19.4	21.4	15.1	18.6	18.2	31.0	44.8
Item 1740 Subject A05c N★	2820	1352	1328	2214	270	695	830	871	423	1466	1007	838	763	395	717	28

B008D: When your date or spouse was present

	TOTAL	M	F	White	Black	NE	NC	S	W	Yes	No	None	Mari-juana Only	Few Pills	More Pills	Any Her-oin
1. Not at all	32.3	37.0	28.0	29.3	53.0	31.6	30.4	33.4	34.9	35.9	29.1	51.5	30.4	25.9	15.4	15.2
2. A few of the times	27.9	27.6	28.3	27.8	32.2	26.3	29.4	28.2	26.9	29.0	27.4	24.8	32.1	34.2	24.7	20.9
3. Some of the times	19.0	20.6	17.0	20.2	7.6	23.6	20.0	15.6	16.7	18.2	19.7	10.6	18.6	21.7	27.7	22.7
4. Most of the times	13.8	10.3	17.2	15.2	4.7	12.0	14.4	14.3	14.7	11.8	15.7	8.2	13.3	12.4	21.6	17.8
5. Every time	7.0	4.5	9.6	7.6	2.6	6.5	5.8	8.6	6.7	5.1	8.1	4.9	5.7	5.8	10.6	23.3
Item 1750 Subject A05b N★	2801	1344	1317	2197	269	688	822	871	420	1454	1003	829	758	388	718	28

★=excludes respondents for whom question was inappropriate.

QUESTIONNAIRE FORM 1 1983	TOTAL	SEX		RACE		REGION				4YR COLLEGE PLANS		ILLICIT DRUG USE: LIFETIME				
		M	F	White	Black	NE	NC	S	W	Yes	No	None	Mari-juana Only	Few Pills	More Pills	Any Her-oin
N (Weighted No. of Cases):	3448	1611	1667	2555	435	814	974	1118	541	1798	1246	1269	848	428	746	30
% of Weighted Total:	100.0	46.7	48.3	74.1	12.6	23.6	28.3	32.4	15.7	52.2	36.1	36.8	24.6	12.4	21.6	.9
B008E: When people over age 30 were present																
1. Not at all	28.9	28.3	29.7	26.9	46.7	27.0	26.1	32.8	29.7	29.7	29.2	34.3	33.1	30.0	18.0	12.4
2. A few of the times	38.9	40.0	38.2	39.2	38.5	38.9	40.1	37.9	39.0	40.0	38.7	36.2	42.6	38.2	39.1	31.3
3. Some of the times	18.5	19.9	16.3	19.5	8.0	20.7	19.0	17.3	16.4	17.2	18.3	12.4	17.0	18.0	27.3	16.4
4. Most of the times	8.7	7.9	9.4	9.2	3.6	8.9	9.6	7.9	8.4	7.9	9.0	7.8	5.4	11.2	11.0	33.7
5. Every time	5.0	3.9	6.3	5.2	3.1	4.6	5.2	4.2	6.5	5.1	4.8	9.3	2.0	2.7	4.5	6.2
Item 1760 Subject A05b N★	2829	1361	1330	2219	271	700	831	871	428	1469	1013	843	766	393	720	28
B008F: During the daytime (before 4:00 p.m.)																
1. Not at all	55.2	44.7	67.2	53.4	73.6	53.0	53.5	58.9	54.7	58.9	53.8	73.9	60.5	49.2	33.3	29.4
2. A few of the times	32.2	38.9	25.2	34.0	19.7	33.8	34.4	29.4	31.3	30.8	32.5	19.1	32.1	38.9	43.9	26.7
3. Some of the times	9.4	13.0	4.9	9.7	4.6	10.8	9.2	8.8	8.7	7.8	9.9	4.0	6.0	8.4	18.8	29.3
4. Most of the times	2.1	2.3	1.7	1.9	1.5	1.9	2.1	1.6	3.1	1.7	2.2	1.2	0.9	3.1	2.9	8.1
5. Every time	1.1	1.2	1.0	1.1	0.7	0.4	0.8	1.2	2.2	0.8	1.6	1.9	0.5	0.3	1.1	6.5
Item 1770 Subject A05c N★	2819	1357	1325	2214	271	694	829	874	423	1465	1010	836	764	395	718	28
B008G: At your home (or apartment or dorm)																
1. Not at all	35.8	34.4	38.6	35.4	40.3	31.0	31.6	41.1	40.9	38.3	36.3	49.3	36.8	32.5	21.9	18.6
2. A few of the times	33.4	33.3	32.7	33.8	32.2	36.6	37.3	29.6	28.1	33.2	32.4	27.1	37.5	38.1	33.1	16.7
3. Some of the times	17.9	19.1	16.4	18.2	13.4	19.9	19.8	14.8	17.1	16.6	17.8	9.6	16.1	16.5	30.5	33.3
4. Most of the times	9.3	10.1	8.1	9.0	9.2	9.2	8.0	10.2	10.2	7.9	10.4	8.1	8.0	10.3	10.9	20.3
5. Every time	3.6	3.2	4.2	3.6	4.9	3.3	3.2	4.2	3.7	3.9	3.1	5.9	1.6	2.5	3.6	11.1
Item 1780 Subject A05c N★	2819	1357	1327	2212	271	694	826	871	427	1469	1009	836	763	395	720	28
B008H: At school																
1. Not at all	85.3	81.1	90.8	86.1	88.5	84.5	84.1	87.7	84.0	88.2	83.4	94.6	87.7	85.4	74.9	38.9
2. A few of the times	10.8	13.8	7.0	10.4	10.2	10.6	11.9	9.9	11.0	9.3	11.4	4.0	9.6	12.4	17.2	34.3
3. Some of the times	2.6	2.9	1.7	2.4	0.8	3.8	2.5	1.5	3.0	1.7	3.2	1.0	2.0	1.1	5.4	14.0
4. Most of the times	0.9	1.5	0.4	0.8	0.5	0.6	1.0	1.0	1.1	0.5	1.6	0.3	0.3	1.0	1.8	9.9
5. Every time	0.4	0.7	0.1	0.3	-	0.4	0.5	0.1	0.9	0.3	0.5	0.1	0.4	0.1	0.7	2.9
Item 1790 Subject A05c N★	2822	1357	1328	2215	269	695	828	870	428	1470	1007	837	764	395	721	28
B008I: In a car																
1. Not at all	32.6	26.4	39.5	30.5	44.2	34.1	28.8	31.0	40.7	36.1	30.1	54.9	28.1	24.9	16.6	15.8
2. A few of the times	26.9	26.7	26.5	26.6	30.2	28.1	26.1	27.9	24.5	26.8	26.1	21.5	30.8	32.9	25.8	12.5
3. Some of the times	22.6	25.8	20.0	24.2	16.7	23.2	26.5	21.4	16.6	23.6	22.2	13.8	21.8	26.7	32.5	17.0
4. Most of the times	15.1	18.2	11.4	15.9	8.5	12.4	15.4	16.6	15.9	12.1	17.5	7.8	17.8	14.2	20.2	27.6
5. Every time	2.8	2.9	2.6	2.9	0.4	2.2	3.1	3.1	2.3	1.4	4.0	1.9	1.6	1.3	4.9	27.2
Item 1810 Subject A05c N★	2823	1359	1327	2215	271	696	828	873	426	1470	1008	838	766	395	719	28
B009: What have been the most important reasons for your drinking alcoholic beverages? (Mark all that apply.)																
A. To experiment–to see what it's like	39.4	36.1	43.5	36.5	55.4	36.9	34.7	44.6	42.1	41.2	38.3	47.6	39.2	39.4	29.9	41.6
B. To relax or relieve tension	40.3	38.7	41.5	41.7	31.5	44.7	41.5	37.1	37.5	40.0	38.8	30.3	39.1	41.9	52.0	60.0
C. To feel good or get high	50.4	52.1	46.9	50.9	42.1	51.5	52.2	45.1	56.0	48.3	50.7	24.9	52.1	53.6	74.3	77.9
D. To seek deeper insights and understanding	3.5	5.1	1.7	3.1	4.7	4.1	3.3	3.3	3.6	2.8	4.1	1.6	3.7	4.0	4.7	7.7
E. To have a good time with my friends	72.1	76.7	67.1	74.1	58.1	73.1	77.4	66.3	72.3	72.1	72.9	59.9	76.4	73.3	80.4	81.6
F. To fit in with a group I like	11.0	12.0	10.4	11.2	9.4	9.2	13.3	10.5	10.6	13.0	9.2	13.4	10.7	12.4	8.3	10.2
G. To get away from my problems or troubles	19.7	18.2	20.7	20.4	12.7	18.5	21.7	19.3	18.7	16.6	22.6	11.3	19.3	22.0	27.6	50.6
H. Because of boredom, nothing else to do	21.7	22.6	19.9	21.1	24.7	21.6	21.2	22.7	20.7	18.7	25.7	12.1	23.5	19.1	31.6	41.5
I. Because of anger or frustration	16.0	14.2	17.8	16.3	12.7	15.0	17.2	16.5	14.6	13.6	18.9	8.7	17.9	15.5	22.5	37.6
J. To get through the day	2.3	2.5	1.8	1.7	3.3	2.0	1.8	2.8	2.5	1.7	2.6	0.9	1.9	1.5	4.1	11.6
K. To increase the effects of some other drug(s)	6.0	6.2	4.3	5.0	7.1	8.5	4.0	6.2	5.3	3.5	7.3	0.1	2.1	2.3	16.4	48.0
L. To decrease (offset) the effects of some other drug(s)	1.1	1.6	0.4	1.0	1.2	0.8	1.5	1.1	1.0	1.1	0.9	0.2	0.6	0.8	2.4	7.3
M. To get to sleep	6.7	7.6	5.0	6.2	6.6	8.4	5.7	5.9	7.6	6.6	5.8	5.1	4.8	7.7	9.2	22.9
N. Because it tastes good	48.8	50.0	47.8	51.6	30.1	50.6	51.5	46.2	46.2	50.3	46.9	40.6	47.7	53.4	57.1	54.2
O. Because I am "hooked"–I feel I have to drink	1.4	1.8	0.8	1.4	0.2	2.3	1.4	1.3	0.5	1.1	1.7	0.5	1.3	0.6	3.0	8.8
Item 1820-1960 Subject A06a N★	2746	1330	1285	2161	261	671	811	853	411	1420	993	783	759	391	710	28

★=excludes respondents for whom question was inappropriate.

QUESTIONNAIRE FORM 1 1983	TOTAL	SEX		RACE		REGION				4YR COLLEGE PLANS		ILLICIT DRUG USE: LIFETIME				
		M	F	White	Black	NE	NC	S	W	Yes	No	None	Mari-juana Only	Few Pills	More Pills	Any Her-oin
N (Weighted No. of Cases):	3448	1611	1667	2555	435	814	974	1118	541	1798	1246	1269	848	428	746	30
% of Weighted Total:	100.0	46.7	48.3	74.1	12.6	23.6	28.3	32.4	15.7	52.2	36.1	36.8	24.6	12.4	21.6	.9
B010: When you drink alcoholic beverages, how high do you usually get?																
1. Not at all high	18.8	15.7	22.6	17.9	27.1	15.6	17.5	22.0	19.9	21.7	16.9	42.5	10.8	11.7	4.0	7.7
2. A little high	35.8	34.1	38.5	34.8	46.1	35.7	34.6	39.7	30.0	33.9	38.0	37.5	42.8	37.2	25.7	12.1
3. Moderately high	38.8	42.7	34.1	40.9	23.0	42.0	40.0	33.1	42.7	39.0	38.5	18.6	41.0	46.0	56.1	51.9
4. Very high	6.7	7.5	4.8	6.5	3.8	6.7	7.9	5.1	7.5	5.4	6.6	1.4	5.5	5.2	14.3	28.4
Item 1970 Subject A01e N★	2808	1349	1328	2208	272	695	821	871	420	1460	1014	841	763	392	710	28
B011: When you drink alcoholic beverages, how long do you usually stay high?																
1. Usually don't get high	21.4	17.9	25.8	20.0	32.0	19.2	18.4	25.8	21.6	24.3	18.5	45.8	13.9	15.3	5.4	4.8
2. One to two hours	40.8	40.0	42.6	40.9	42.7	40.7	39.0	44.2	37.5	40.9	42.0	37.9	48.2	43.9	36.0	18.4
3. Three to six hours	33.7	38.0	28.3	35.5	22.3	34.9	37.2	27.4	37.9	31.8	35.2	14.7	35.4	39.6	49.0	60.5
4. Seven to 24 hours	3.9	3.9	3.2	3.3	3.0	4.9	5.2	2.5	2.6	2.8	4.0	1.6	2.4	1.2	8.9	16.4
5. More than 24 hours	0.3	0.2	0.1	0.2	-	0.3	0.3	0.2	0.5	0.2	0.3	-	0.1	-	0.8	-
Item 1980 Subject A01f N★	2792	1348	1314	2195	269	690	822	866	414	1447	1011	823	764	390	713	28

The following questions ask about how much you have to drink on the occasions when you drink alcoholic beverages. For these questions, a "drink" means any of the following: A 12-ounce can (or bottle) of beer, a 4-ounce glass of wine, a mixed drink or shot glass of liquor.

	TOTAL	M	F	White	Black	NE	NC	S	W	Yes	No	None	Mari-juana Only	Few Pills	More Pills	Any Her-oin
B012: Think back over the LAST TWO WEEKS. How many times have you had five or more drinks in a row?																
1. None	58.6	46.6	71.9	55.6	79.1	57.8	51.1	62.4	67.2	62.5	55.9	78.1	59.9	58.2	34.9	45.0
2. Once	12.9	13.9	12.3	14.1	9.1	11.4	15.1	12.8	11.4	13.2	13.4	9.3	14.7	14.6	15.0	8.9
3. Twice	10.5	13.7	7.0	11.1	6.1	11.1	11.5	10.0	8.7	9.8	10.5	6.6	10.6	10.7	14.8	17.9
4. 3 to 5 times	12.2	18.2	5.8	13.2	4.0	12.3	15.5	9.8	10.2	10.5	13.3	3.9	10.7	12.6	22.6	12.8
5. 6 to 9 times	4.0	5.1	2.1	4.3	0.8	4.9	4.7	3.3	2.3	2.7	5.1	1.8	2.9	2.3	8.1	12.4
6. 10 or more times	1.8	2.5	0.9	1.7	1.0	2.4	2.1	1.7	0.3	1.3	1.8	0.3	1.1	1.5	4.6	3.0
Item 850 Subject A01d N★	2782	1332	1324	2195	267	688	824	851	419	1455	1003	843	754	383	705	27
B013: During the last two weeks, how many times have you had 3 or 4 drinks in a row (but no more than that)?																
1. None	55.8	48.5	63.8	53.5	74.6	55.1	51.9	56.7	62.8	59.2	54.1	73.8	56.2	53.5	35.9	37.5
2. Once	19.5	20.6	18.8	20.4	14.9	19.9	19.9	18.7	19.9	18.4	19.9	14.5	20.7	24.4	22.0	11.8
3. Twice	12.9	15.4	10.1	13.8	6.8	12.6	15.0	13.6	8.1	12.5	12.8	7.3	13.0	12.2	20.3	10.8
4. 3 to 5 times	8.9	12.2	5.5	9.6	2.5	8.7	10.3	8.7	7.0	8.2	9.8	3.8	8.2	8.9	14.7	25.3
5. 6 to 9 times	2.0	2.3	1.3	2.0	0.9	2.9	1.8	1.8	1.5	1.1	2.4	0.4	1.5	0.8	5.0	7.9
6. 10 or more times	0.8	0.9	0.6	0.7	0.3	0.8	1.1	0.5	0.6	0.6	1.0	0.1	0.5	0.2	2.1	6.7
Item 1990 Subject A01d N★	2790	1340	1325	2200	270	682	825	862	421	1458	1009	841	763	385	706	27
B014: During the last two weeks, how many times have you had two drinks in a row (but no more than that)?																
1. None	57.5	54.9	60.8	56.9	63.8	54.1	58.6	55.2	65.8	60.2	57.1	71.5	56.5	51.4	46.1	47.1
2. Once	20.9	22.1	20.3	22.0	19.3	21.7	22.2	21.8	15.4	20.2	21.7	17.9	23.4	25.3	20.1	8.1
3. Twice	10.6	10.5	10.3	9.9	10.8	13.1	8.6	10.9	9.6	10.3	9.4	6.5	10.4	13.6	13.4	10.3
4. 3 to 5 times	7.2	7.9	6.5	7.7	3.4	6.8	6.6	8.0	7.7	6.9	7.0	3.2	6.9	7.7	12.0	7.7
5. 6 to 9 times	2.3	3.0	1.3	2.3	1.1	2.6	2.6	2.4	1.1	1.6	2.8	0.8	1.7	1.0	5.2	19.7
6. 10 to 19 times	1.1	1.4	0.6	1.0	1.5	1.2	1.1	1.4	0.4	0.7	1.4	0.1	0.7	1.1	2.6	7.1
7. 20 or more times	0.3	0.3	0.2	0.2	-	0.4	0.3	0.2	-	0.1	0.5	0.1	0.3	-	0.7	-
Item 2000 Subject A01d N★	2749	1317	1307	2174	264	673	813	848	414	1438	987	826	742	391	699	26

★=excludes respondents for whom question was inappropriate.

QUESTIONNAIRE FORM 1 1983	TOTAL	SEX		RACE		REGION				4YR COLLEGE PLANS		ILLICIT DRUG USE: LIFETIME				
		M	F	White	Black	NE	NC	S	W	Yes	No	None	Mari-juana Only	Few Pills	More Pills	Any Her-oin
N (Weighted No. of Cases):	3448	1611	1667	2555	435	814	974	1118	541	1798	1246	1269	848	428	746	30
% of Weighted Total:	100.0	46.7	48.3	74.1	12.6	23.6	28.3	32.4	15.7	52.2	36.1	36.8	24.6	12.4	21.6	.9

B015: During the last two weeks, how many times have you had just one drink?

1. None	55.8	55.9	56.4	56.1	56.5	53.2	57.0	54.5	60.0	55.7	58.0	64.4	53.6	52.4	50.7	45.6
2. Once	25.6	23.9	27.6	25.5	27.1	26.0	25.4	26.1	24.7	26.7	24.0	22.9	27.8	31.4	23.4	10.2
3. Twice	9.8	10.1	9.4	10.1	10.0	11.4	9.8	10.1	6.8	9.6	9.3	8.1	9.7	10.5	11.2	20.6
4. 3 to 5 times	6.2	7.2	4.8	6.0	5.2	7.1	4.7	6.5	6.8	6.3	5.4	3.9	6.0	5.0	9.6	13.8
5. 6 to 9 times	1.5	1.5	1.3	1.6	0.3	1.1	2.1	1.4	1.3	1.1	2.0	0.4	1.7	0.7	3.0	6.7
6. 10 to 19 times	0.7	0.9	0.3	0.5	1.0	0.5	0.7	0.8	0.5	0.5	0.8	0.3	0.7	-	1.2	3.1
7. 20 or more times	0.4	0.4	0.2	0.3	-	0.7	0.3	0.5	-	0.1	0.6	-	0.5	0.1	1.0	-
Item 2010 Subject A01d N★	2681	1287	1271	2124	253	648	797	833	402	1407	955	803	724	376	687	26

B016: Have you ever tried to stop using alcoholic beverages and found that you couldn't stop?

1. Yes	3.4	4.1	2.5	2.8	6.7	2.4	3.8	4.2	2.4	2.9	3.6	2.3	2.9	4.5	3.9	6.2
2. No	96.6	95.9	97.5	97.2	93.3	97.6	96.2	95.8	97.6	97.1	96.4	97.7	97.1	95.5	96.1	93.8
Item 2020 Subject A01i N★	2773	1344	1304	2196	266	678	824	860	411	1449	997	812	755	390	717	28

B017: Do you think you will be drinking alcoholic beverages five years from now?

1. I definitely will	17.0	21.1	12.4	19.2	5.6	25.2	19.4	11.0	12.7	17.1	16.0	9.4	18.0	15.0	30.1	24.4
2. I probably will	54.7	54.7	55.3	57.5	42.6	54.9	58.7	52.0	52.7	54.7	53.7	44.2	60.2	67.3	61.1	40.9
3. I probably will not	13.8	12.3	15.3	12.4	20.9	10.6	11.3	17.9	14.7	12.7	16.4	21.0	12.4	10.5	4.9	15.5
4. I definitely will not	14.6	11.9	17.1	10.9	30.9	9.4	10.7	19.1	19.9	15.4	13.9	25.4	9.5	7.2	4.0	19.2
Item 2030 Subject A04a N	3380	1588	1644	2529	426	788	963	1097	531	1774	1232	1246	842	426	732	30

The next questions are about MARIJUANA and HASHISH.

Marijuana is sometimes called: grass, pot, dope.

Hashish is sometimes called: hash, hash oil.

B018: On how many occasions (if any) have you used hashish . . .

B018A: . . . in your lifetime?

1. 0 occasions	71.1	65.9	78.4	69.8	85.2	64.1	71.6	77.4	67.9	77.0	68.7	100.0	73.7	61.3	25.7	15.4
2. 1-2	10.6	11.7	9.4	11.3	8.0	13.2	11.3	8.2	10.5	10.0	10.3	-	17.4	19.7	16.1	4.4
3. 3-5	5.1	5.6	4.4	5.3	3.1	6.1	3.4	5.7	5.7	4.2	5.6	-	4.5	7.6	13.5	4.6
4. 6-9	3.4	4.0	2.9	3.6	1.6	3.5	3.3	2.9	4.6	2.4	4.5	-	1.6	5.0	10.1	10.5
5. 10-19	2.9	3.8	2.0	3.2	1.0	4.1	2.8	1.9	3.4	2.3	3.6	-	1.1	2.9	9.9	9.1
6. 20-39	2.6	3.2	1.5	2.8	0.2	3.7	3.1	1.0	3.3	1.6	3.3	-	0.6	1.2	10.1	7.2
7. 40 or more	4.2	5.7	1.5	4.1	0.9	5.3	4.4	2.9	4.7	2.5	4.0	-	1.0	2.3	14.6	48.7
Item 2040 Subject A01a N	3341	1570	1631	2518	413	782	955	1078	525	1768	1216	1269	846	418	731	30

B018B: . . . during the last 12 months?

1. 0 occasions	81.9	77.9	88.0	81.2	93.2	76.2	82.2	86.6	79.9	86.5	80.9	100.0	86.8	80.8	47.5	24.0
2. 1-2	8.0	8.8	6.9	8.6	4.0	11.0	7.5	5.8	9.2	6.4	8.2	-	9.4	12.4	17.3	16.8
3. 3-5	3.7	4.6	2.5	3.7	1.6	3.7	3.1	3.2	6.0	3.1	4.3	-	1.7	2.7	12.9	12.0
4. 6-9	2.2	3.2	0.8	2.1	0.5	3.2	2.3	1.6	2.1	1.5	2.5	-	0.6	1.9	8.2	4.7
5. 10-19	2.3	2.9	1.4	2.7	0.6	3.4	3.1	1.4	1.3	1.5	2.4	-	1.0	1.9	7.8	12.1
6. 20-39	0.7	1.0	0.2	0.7	-	0.8	0.8	0.5	0.4	0.3	0.7	-	0.1	-	2.7	6.3
7. 40 or more	1.1	1.6	0.2	1.0	0.3	1.8	0.9	0.8	1.0	0.6	0.9	-	0.3	0.2	3.6	24.2
Item 2050 Subject A01b N	3333	1565	1631	2513	413	781	955	1075	523	1766	1213	1269	844	419	727	29

B018C: . . . during the last 30 days?

1. 0 occasions	93.5	91.3	97.0	93.7	97.4	91.8	93.6	94.2	94.3	95.8	93.8	100.0	97.0	95.1	79.0	53.3
2. 1-2	3.4	4.7	1.5	3.2	1.0	4.1	3.2	3.2	2.9	2.3	3.3	-	2.1	3.2	10.3	7.6
3. 3-5	1.6	1.8	1.0	1.5	1.3	2.2	1.8	1.2	1.3	1.2	1.5	-	0.5	1.5	5.3	13.6
4. 6-9	0.7	0.9	0.3	0.7	-	0.7	1.1	0.3	0.8	0.4	0.8	-	0.1	-	2.6	8.3
5. 10-19	0.3	0.5	-	0.3	-	0.4	-	0.4	0.3	0.1	0.3	-	-	-	1.2	-
6. 20-39	0.1	0.1	0.1	0.1	0.3	0.2	-	0.2	0.1	0.1	0.1	-	-	-	0.5	3.6
7. 40 or more	0.4	0.7	0.1	0.4	-	0.5	0.3	0.6	0.3	0.2	0.3	-	0.2	0.2	1.1	13.6
Item 2060 Subject A01c N	3333	1565	1630	2512	413	779	954	1077	523	1767	1210	1269	842	419	727	29

★=excludes respondents for whom question was inappropriate.

QUESTIONNAIRE FORM 1 1983	TOTAL	SEX		RACE		REGION				4YR COLLEGE PLANS		ILLICIT DRUG USE: LIFETIME				
		M	F	White	Black	NE	NC	S	W	Yes	No	None	Mari-juana Only	Few Pills	More Pills	Any Her-oin
N (Weighted No. of Cases):	3448	1611	1667	2555	435	814	974	1118	541	1798	1246	1269	848	428	746	30
% of Weighted Total:	100.0	46.7	48.3	74.1	12.6	23.6	28.3	32.4	15.7	52.2	36.1	36.8	24.6	12.4	21.6	.9

B019: On how many occasions (if any) have you used marijuana . . .

B019A: . . . in your lifetime?

	TOTAL	M	F	White	Black	NE	NC	S	W	Yes	No	None	Mari Only	Few Pills	More Pills	Heroin
1. 0 occasions	43.5	42.3	46.5	44.3	42.4	33.0	46.5	49.2	42.0	49.8	40.8	100.0	0.6	26.4	6.5	5.5
2. 1-2	12.1	11.5	12.9	11.6	17.3	14.4	10.7	12.1	11.2	11.8	12.2	-	37.0	11.4	4.4	3.8
3. 3-5	7.0	6.3	7.7	7.2	7.9	6.6	8.0	6.8	6.1	7.5	6.2	-	19.0	9.4	4.1	-
4. 6-9	6.3	6.6	6.0	5.7	9.7	5.5	6.4	6.7	6.2	6.3	6.8	-	14.1	11.1	5.2	3.8
5. 10-19	6.3	5.8	7.2	6.5	6.2	9.2	5.0	6.3	4.6	6.1	5.8	-	11.6	9.7	9.2	4.4
6. 20-39	6.1	5.7	6.3	5.9	5.5	8.6	4.8	4.7	7.3	5.9	5.7	-	9.0	8.6	11.6	12.4
7. 40 or more	18.8	21.9	13.4	18.6	11.0	22.7	18.6	14.3	22.6	12.5	22.5	-	8.8	23.3	59.0	70.1
Item 2070 Subject A01a N	3301	1558	1603	2500	399	768	955	1058	520	1748	1204	1269	843	413	720	30

B019B: . . . during the last 12 months?

	TOTAL	M	F	White	Black	NE	NC	S	W	Yes	No	None	Mari Only	Few Pills	More Pills	Heroin
1. 0 occasions	58.4	56.2	62.5	58.5	60.3	49.0	61.5	63.9	55.7	62.8	57.0	100.0	39.8	43.2	17.8	11.4
2. 1-2	11.5	10.6	12.9	11.6	15.5	12.3	11.6	11.2	10.9	12.4	10.6	-	28.9	15.3	9.5	11.7
3. 3-5	6.3	6.5	6.2	6.2	7.3	8.9	5.6	4.9	6.3	6.6	6.1	-	11.4	9.6	9.5	4.6
4. 6-9	5.3	5.1	5.1	5.6	4.1	6.4	4.5	4.9	5.8	5.0	4.9	-	8.8	8.4	8.0	12.2
5. 10-19	4.7	5.4	4.1	5.0	2.7	6.9	4.1	3.9	4.3	4.0	5.2	-	5.1	9.2	10.0	2.9
6. 20-39	4.3	4.4	4.2	4.2	3.5	4.5	4.8	3.6	5.0	3.1	5.6	-	3.0	5.6	12.9	2.9
7. 40 or more	9.5	11.8	5.1	9.0	6.5	12.0	7.9	7.8	12.0	6.2	10.5	-	3.0	8.6	32.2	54.3
Item 2080 Subject A01b N	3285	1554	1593	2492	394	769	948	1051	516	1743	1197	1269	829	414	719	29

B019C: . . . during the last 30 days?

	TOTAL	M	F	White	Black	NE	NC	S	W	Yes	No	None	Mari Only	Few Pills	More Pills	Heroin
1. 0 occasions	72.9	69.4	78.8	73.8	74.3	65.9	75.0	77.0	71.2	77.6	71.3	100.0	70.7	64.0	34.9	36.8
2. 1-2	9.5	10.3	8.7	9.1	11.7	11.6	9.1	8.2	9.6	10.4	8.4	-	18.6	13.8	13.0	8.0
3. 3-5	4.5	4.8	4.0	4.7	3.4	5.5	4.1	4.1	4.4	3.8	4.7	-	4.8	6.5	10.9	-
4. 6-9	3.5	3.9	2.8	3.6	2.2	3.8	4.1	2.6	4.1	2.5	3.7	-	1.6	6.7	9.8	2.9
5. 10-19	3.6	4.5	2.6	3.3	4.5	4.0	2.8	3.6	4.5	2.4	5.0	-	2.4	5.4	10.3	5.1
6. 20-39	2.9	2.9	2.0	2.7	2.2	4.3	2.5	2.3	2.8	1.6	3.5	-	1.1	2.3	9.9	14.4
7. 40 or more	3.1	4.2	1.1	2.9	1.6	4.9	2.4	2.4	3.5	1.6	3.4	-	0.8	1.2	11.2	32.8
Item 2090 Subject A01c N	3281	1554	1590	2493	391	769	947	1049	516	1740	1198	1269	827	414	717	29

IF YOU HAVE NOT USED MARIJUANA OR HASHISH IN THE LAST TWELVE MONTHS, GO TO Q.B028.

B020: When you used marijuana or hashish during the last year, how often did you use it in each of the following situations?

B020A: When you were alone

	TOTAL	M	F	White	Black	NE	NC	S	W	Yes	No	None	Mari Only	Few Pills	More Pills	Heroin
1. Not at all	65.1	58.0	76.8	69.0	60.0	63.4	66.3	64.9	66.1	74.2	60.4	-	83.0	73.3	48.6	10.6
2. A few of the times	20.9	24.6	16.3	18.5	28.1	22.3	20.2	21.0	19.4	16.7	25.4	-	13.1	18.8	27.8	33.8
3. Some of the times	10.7	13.0	5.5	9.7	8.0	11.9	10.6	10.1	9.8	6.4	11.1	-	2.5	6.3	18.3	40.4
4. Most of the times	2.4	2.7	1.4	1.9	4.0	2.0	2.4	2.8	2.2	2.2	2.0	-	0.9	0.7	4.2	5.1
5. Every time	1.0	1.7	0.1	0.9	-	0.4	0.5	1.2	2.6	0.6	1.0	-	0.6	0.8	1.1	10.2
Item 2100 Subject A05a N★	1364	678	598	1035	155	387	369	379	229	642	519	-	497	235	588	25

B020B: With just 1 or 2 other people

	TOTAL	M	F	White	Black	NE	NC	S	W	Yes	No	None	Mari Only	Few Pills	More Pills	Heroin
1. Not at all	7.6	8.0	7.5	7.8	8.2	7.3	7.6	7.8	7.9	10.1	5.1	-	11.5	9.9	3.3	6.4
2. A few of the times	30.5	26.6	36.2	30.2	40.3	32.0	31.3	32.5	23.4	31.0	32.9	-	44.8	37.1	17.2	5.4
3. Some of the times	19.1	20.0	16.6	17.4	22.1	22.4	14.3	20.9	18.1	17.2	20.3	-	12.4	15.5	26.5	19.9
4. Most of the times	31.2	33.9	27.4	32.7	18.5	30.1	33.9	26.3	36.7	30.2	28.7	-	19.1	25.9	42.7	53.4
5. Every time	11.6	11.5	12.4	11.9	10.8	8.2	12.8	12.5	13.9	11.5	13.2	-	12.3	11.6	10.4	15.0
Item 2110 Subject A05b N★	1374	682	604	1042	157	387	370	386	231	644	522	-	503	235	591	27

B020C: At a party

	TOTAL	M	F	White	Black	NE	NC	S	W	Yes	No	None	Mari Only	Few Pills	More Pills	Heroin
1. Not at all	25.9	24.5	29.9	25.9	37.0	22.2	24.5	31.1	26.0	27.3	29.1	-	39.7	27.5	14.2	14.7
2. A few of the times	23.8	22.6	27.3	24.7	28.4	27.9	20.2	23.5	23.3	28.7	20.7	-	31.2	24.6	17.9	20.3
3. Some of the times	19.6	21.0	17.9	20.1	16.9	19.6	21.4	17.7	20.0	19.0	18.8	-	11.0	26.2	25.4	4.6
4. Most of the times	17.5	17.7	14.9	16.8	7.0	16.7	17.6	15.4	22.3	16.1	17.5	-	10.4	15.5	24.1	15.9
5. Every time	13.1	14.1	10.1	12.5	10.7	13.6	16.3	12.3	8.5	8.9	13.9	-	7.7	6.3	18.4	44.4
Item 2120 Subject A05c N★	1365	677	601	1034	155	388	368	379	229	639	520	-	499	234	588	26

★=excludes respondents for whom question was inappropriate.

QUESTIONNAIRE FORM 1 1983	TOTAL	SEX		RACE		REGION				4YR COLLEGE PLANS		ILLICIT DRUG USE: LIFETIME				
		M	F	White	Black	NE	NC	S	W	Yes	No	None	Mari-juana Only	Few Pills	More Pills	Any Her-oin
N (Weighted No. of Cases):	3448	1611	1667	2555	435	814	974	1118	541	1798	1246	1269	848	428	746	30
% of Weighted Total:	100.0	46.7	48.3	74.1	12.6	23.6	28.3	32.4	15.7	52.2	36.1	36.8	24.6	12.4	21.6	.9

B020D: When your date or spouse was present

1. Not at all	47.9	57.8	39.6	48.4	56.5	44.8	50.1	45.5	53.6	57.2	43.1	-	66.1	47.3	34.2	10.9
2. A few of the times	21.3	19.0	23.4	21.3	21.3	22.3	20.2	23.2	18.3	19.2	23.1	-	18.3	27.1	22.2	13.3
3. Some of the times	14.2	13.7	13.5	13.5	11.5	18.4	12.9	12.0	12.7	11.6	13.9	-	8.0	10.6	19.8	25.9
4. Most of the times	10.3	6.8	13.5	10.4	5.5	7.9	10.9	12.1	10.1	8.0	11.5	-	4.0	9.3	15.4	28.9
5. Every time	6.4	2.7	10.0	6.3	5.3	6.6	6.0	7.1	5.3	4.0	8.5	-	3.6	5.7	8.5	21.0
Item 2130 Subject A05b N★	1367	676	601	1034	154	388	369	381	229	641	517	-	500	233	589	27

B020E: When people over age 30 were present

1. Not at all	66.2	63.8	73.3	66.8	80.8	71.3	67.8	64.6	57.6	73.5	63.5	-	84.9	68.8	50.2	35.6
2. A few of the times	19.5	20.6	16.0	18.4	11.6	16.7	17.8	18.6	28.7	17.1	19.7	-	9.3	22.2	27.6	12.6
3. Some of the times	10.3	11.7	7.4	10.8	6.5	9.7	9.9	12.1	9.3	6.6	13.0	-	3.4	7.9	16.4	36.7
4. Most of the times	2.4	2.8	1.6	2.6	1.1	0.9	2.4	3.8	2.5	1.3	3.1	-	1.0	0.8	4.2	3.1
5. Every time	1.6	1.1	1.7	1.5	-	1.4	2.1	0.9	1.9	1.5	0.7	-	1.5	0.4	1.6	12.0
Item 2140 Subject A05b N★	1373	680	604	1039	156	389	370	385	230	642	522	-	503	236	590	26

B020F: During the daytime (before 4:00 p.m.)

1. Not at all	39.8	35.4	47.5	39.1	53.0	36.5	43.2	42.4	35.9	49.0	35.3	-	61.9	43.0	20.8	16.3
2. A few of the times	26.5	28.0	26.0	27.6	24.5	31.1	24.8	26.3	21.7	27.1	26.3	-	24.4	32.4	26.4	15.1
3. Some of the times	20.3	22.4	16.4	20.7	15.6	19.3	18.9	20.4	24.2	16.8	21.6	-	8.2	18.0	31.6	24.1
4. Most of the times	10.1	11.1	7.6	9.7	6.1	10.5	9.8	9.3	11.4	5.1	14.2	-	4.0	5.5	15.9	35.1
5. Every time	3.2	3.0	2.6	3.0	0.8	2.7	3.2	1.6	6.8	2.0	2.6	-	1.5	1.1	5.4	9.4
Item 2150 Subject A05c N★	1371	679	602	1039	156	389	369	382	231	644	520	-	502	235	590	27

B020G: At your home (or apartment or dorm)

1. Not at all	54.6	53.6	59.2	56.9	57.5	55.0	58.2	54.6	48.1	62.9	50.9	-	76.4	57.7	35.6	24.1
2. A few of the times	20.6	19.0	23.0	20.6	25.3	20.9	18.3	21.8	22.1	19.2	22.6	-	14.4	25.2	24.8	13.9
3. Some of the times	13.3	14.9	9.6	12.1	9.0	13.2	12.5	11.8	17.0	8.4	15.6	-	3.6	8.8	22.8	26.4
4. Most of the times	8.1	8.1	6.2	7.3	4.8	8.2	7.5	7.6	9.9	7.2	7.4	-	2.7	7.3	12.3	24.3
5. Every time	3.4	4.4	2.0	3.2	3.4	2.7	3.5	4.1	3.0	2.3	3.4	-	2.9	1.0	4.5	11.3
Item 2160 Subject A05c N★	1374	681	603	1041	156	388	370	385	231	644	521	-	503	235	591	27

B020H: At school

1. Not at all	66.3	63.4	73.3	68.0	69.4	61.0	69.3	72.0	60.5	74.9	62.1	-	83.1	75.4	50.6	16.5
2. A few of the times	16.5	16.8	16.0	16.4	19.8	18.3	15.3	15.0	17.8	13.9	18.9	-	12.1	14.4	21.0	21.5
3. Some of the times	10.3	12.4	6.6	10.1	4.9	13.0	8.2	8.0	13.3	6.8	12.3	-	2.8	8.1	16.5	27.1
4. Most of the times	4.8	5.2	2.9	3.8	3.8	5.6	5.1	3.4	5.2	3.3	4.9	-	1.6	1.3	7.9	30.3
5. Every time	2.1	2.3	1.2	1.8	2.1	2.0	2.1	1.6	3.2	1.1	1.9	-	0.4	0.7	4.0	4.6
Item 2170 Subject A05c N★	1372	681	603	1039	155	386	371	384	231	643	522	-	503	234	591	27

B020I: In a car

1. Not at all	20.6	17.5	25.1	19.9	33.0	20.0	22.9	19.1	20.7	26.3	17.1	-	34.0	20.0	9.7	7.9
2. A few of the times	26.7	26.0	29.1	26.3	35.1	33.2	18.4	31.5	21.3	26.8	27.6	-	34.1	29.3	20.8	-
3. Some of the times	24.1	25.3	22.0	25.0	16.0	23.2	24.0	19.9	32.6	22.7	23.7	-	15.4	27.0	30.9	13.0
4. Most of the times	21.2	23.4	17.1	20.9	13.0	18.0	27.0	20.0	19.4	18.5	23.3	-	11.2	19.3	29.1	54.1
5. Every time	7.4	7.8	6.6	8.0	2.8	5.7	7.8	9.5	6.0	5.6	8.4	-	5.4	4.5	9.4	25.0
Item 2190 Subject A05c N★	1374	682	604	1041	155	388	371	384	231	643	524	-	503	235	592	27

B021: How many of the times when you used marijuana or hashish during the last year did you use it along with alcohol–that is, so that their effects overlapped?

1. Not at all	29.5	26.9	34.1	28.6	43.8	31.1	25.4	31.8	29.7	30.6	30.1	-	48.1	30.4	13.9	4.7
2. A few of the times	29.2	27.8	30.8	27.0	38.2	33.7	24.6	27.5	31.5	31.2	28.2	-	30.5	35.1	25.8	21.3
3. Some of the times	20.4	24.3	15.6	22.1	9.9	18.1	21.0	20.7	22.7	18.5	21.3	-	10.0	18.7	29.8	30.6
4. Most of the times	15.2	15.4	13.8	15.8	6.9	12.8	21.1	14.8	10.2	12.2	16.3	-	5.2	11.5	24.8	29.4
5. Every time	5.8	5.6	5.6	6.6	1.3	4.3	7.9	5.2	5.9	7.5	4.1	-	6.2	4.3	5.7	14.0
Item 2200 Subject A06a N★	1347	663	597	1028	149	382	363	374	228	634	511	-	491	231	580	27

★=excludes respondents for whom question was inappropriate.

QUESTIONNAIRE FORM 1 1983	TOTAL	SEX		RACE		REGION				4YR COLLEGE PLANS		ILLICIT DRUG USE: LIFETIME				
		M	F	White	Black	NE	NC	S	W	Yes	No	None	Mari-juana Only	Few Pills	More Pills	Any Her-oin
N (Weighted No. of Cases):	3448	1611	1667	2555	435	814	974	1118	541	1798	1246	1269	848	428	746	30
% of Weighted Total:	100.0	46.7	48.3	74.1	12.6	23.6	28.3	32.4	15.7	52.2	36.1	36.8	24.6	12.4	21.6	.9

B022: What have been the most important reasons for your using marijuana or hashish? (Mark all that apply.)

	TOTAL	M	F	White	Black	NE	NC	S	W	Yes	No	None	Mari-juana Only	Few Pills	More Pills	Any Her-oin
A. To experiment–to see what it's like	64.6	61.3	70.3	66.8	61.7	61.9	66.7	68.7	59.1	71.0	62.4	-	79.2	65.7	52.7	54.7
B. To relax or relieve tension	41.8	42.8	38.6	40.8	36.2	44.1	39.2	40.8	43.7	37.0	42.3	-	26.5	43.5	52.8	73.9
C. To feel good or get high	72.8	72.5	71.4	72.7	69.2	72.0	69.6	74.4	76.4	70.7	73.3	-	57.0	70.0	86.8	100.0
D. To seek deeper insights and understanding	10.7	13.2	7.1	10.6	8.5	13.0	8.0	10.8	11.4	10.2	9.8	-	4.8	7.0	16.5	27.4
E. To have a good time with my friends	64.5	64.6	62.3	64.9	55.6	64.1	65.1	59.3	73.2	62.0	65.0	-	53.6	64.8	73.0	77.2
F. To fit in with a group I like	13.1	13.8	11.9	12.7	10.5	13.6	15.4	10.7	12.4	15.5	9.8	-	13.4	16.9	10.4	20.7
G. To get away from my problems or troubles	19.3	17.2	19.8	18.5	17.4	18.4	20.8	20.4	16.7	16.6	19.8	-	15.0	15.0	22.6	68.6
H. Because of boredom, nothing else to do	27.5	27.5	25.7	25.7	29.9	26.9	28.8	25.4	29.8	23.8	31.7	-	18.6	21.8	36.3	55.3
I. Because of anger or frustration	12.4	9.4	14.1	10.9	14.5	12.2	10.8	14.4	11.8	9.5	13.3	-	8.6	9.9	14.4	60.5
J. To get through the day	7.1	7.5	5.1	5.7	6.2	7.6	7.8	5.6	7.4	4.0	8.3	-	2.3	2.6	11.2	45.5
K. To increase the effects of some other drug(s)	11.8	13.1	8.0	11.3	7.7	12.5	11.5	13.1	8.8	8.6	13.1	-	4.1	2.9	19.3	67.7
L. To decrease (offset) the effects of some other drug(s)	1.8	1.7	1.6	1.8	0.7	1.8	1.1	2.0	2.8	2.1	1.3	-	0.5	0.8	2.9	14.7
M. Because I am "hooked"–I have to have it	2.8	3.4	1.0	2.5	1.4	2.9	2.4	3.3	2.3	1.6	2.4	-	1.3	-	4.0	29.9
Item 2210-2330 Subject A06a N★	1371	675	607	1038	156	388	370	384	229	642	519	-	501	236	589	27

B023: When you use marijuana or hashish how high do you usually get?

	TOTAL	M	F	White	Black	NE	NC	S	W	Yes	No	None	Mari-juana Only	Few Pills	More Pills	Any Her-oin
1. Not at all high	6.6	6.3	7.6	6.6	8.0	7.6	7.7	5.9	4.5	8.2	6.5	-	13.1	6.2	0.9	-
2. A little high	29.4	27.7	33.0	29.0	41.3	30.7	30.9	30.3	23.6	32.0	28.6	-	42.7	32.5	18.2	10.2
3. Moderately high	41.9	44.5	40.0	43.4	32.2	37.4	41.9	42.6	48.5	40.8	42.7	-	32.3	43.9	49.2	45.3
4. Very high	22.0	21.5	19.4	21.0	18.5	24.4	19.5	21.3	23.4	19.0	22.2	-	11.9	17.4	31.6	44.5
Item 2340 Subject A01e N★	1366	672	607	1033	157	385	370	384	226	638	521	-	500	233	588	26

B024: When you use marijuana or hashish, how long do you usually stay high?

	TOTAL	M	F	White	Black	NE	NC	S	W	Yes	No	None	Mari-juana Only	Few Pills	More Pills	Any Her-oin
1. Usually don't get high	9.9	9.5	10.4	9.4	13.8	10.2	11.1	10.0	7.1	12.4	9.3	-	19.2	8.2	1.9	2.6
2. One to two hours	55.6	54.8	58.3	57.8	48.9	55.3	55.0	53.3	61.0	55.6	57.2	-	55.7	62.8	53.9	41.8
3. Three to six hours	30.4	31.4	27.7	29.5	31.9	30.0	30.9	33.0	26.1	27.6	29.8	-	22.1	27.4	38.9	35.7
4. Seven to 24 hours	3.5	3.9	2.9	3.0	3.9	3.9	3.0	2.8	4.7	3.7	3.5	-	2.7	1.6	4.6	7.9
5. More than 24 hours	0.6	0.5	0.6	0.3	1.5	0.6	-	1.0	1.2	0.6	0.3	-	0.3	-	0.7	12.0
Item 2350 Subject A01f N★	1357	673	599	1030	155	379	368	382	228	636	518	-	499	232	581	27

B025: During the LAST MONTH, about how many marijuana cigarettes (joints, reefers), or the equivalent, did you smoke a day, on the average? (If you shared them with other people, count only the amount YOU smoked.)

	TOTAL	M	F	White	Black	NE	NC	S	W	Yes	No	None	Mari-juana Only	Few Pills	More Pills	Any Her-oin
1. None	41.5	36.9	50.9	43.7	41.9	41.2	42.0	39.4	44.4	49.3	38.2	-	61.9	41.0	25.5	18.0
2. Less than 1 a day	34.2	36.2	31.8	35.4	27.2	32.6	35.1	35.9	32.5	36.4	32.4	-	30.5	39.4	36.1	16.9
3. 1 a day	7.7	7.8	6.8	7.3	7.0	5.7	8.4	9.7	6.9	4.7	9.7	-	1.6	6.0	13.7	3.6
4. 2 - 3 a day	10.0	11.6	7.0	9.0	12.1	12.6	8.9	8.0	10.6	6.5	11.9	-	2.9	7.1	16.4	27.8
5. 4 - 6 a day	4.7	5.1	2.7	3.1	9.5	6.3	3.7	5.3	2.4	2.4	5.2	-	2.5	5.2	5.3	22.1
6. 7 - 10 a day	1.3	2.0	0.3	1.2	0.4	1.0	1.9	0.5	2.0	0.3	2.0	-	-	0.9	2.1	9.7
7. 11 or more a day	0.7	0.5	0.5	0.4	1.9	0.6	-	1.2	1.1	0.4	0.6	-	0.6	0.4	0.9	1.9
Item 2360 Subject A01d N★	1284	636	563	978	141	363	346	358	218	598	490	-	466	215	563	23

B026: Do you know how much marijuana you have used (in ounces) during the LAST MONTH?

	TOTAL	M	F	White	Black	NE	NC	S	W	Yes	No	None	Mari-juana Only	Few Pills	More Pills	Any Her-oin
8. Don't know	20.5	16.8	23.7	18.6	25.6	19.5	20.0	23.4	18.0	20.1	20.5	-	17.6	20.7	22.7	7.0
1. None	37.4	32.8	45.8	38.4	41.2	37.6	36.8	37.2	38.5	42.2	35.5	-	55.5	39.2	22.1	18.0
2. Less than 1/2 ounce	21.8	25.1	18.7	23.1	17.9	19.2	23.9	19.7	26.3	22.7	22.1	-	21.5	25.1	22.4	-
3. About 1/2 ounce	7.2	9.3	4.8	7.2	8.3	8.5	6.4	6.4	7.6	6.6	7.4	-	2.1	7.0	11.3	12.8
4. About 1 ounce	6.3	7.9	3.6	6.5	2.0	7.1	5.4	5.9	7.0	4.8	7.4	-	1.6	5.2	10.3	14.9
5. About 2 ounces	4.0	4.0	2.8	3.7	2.2	5.0	4.9	3.6	1.8	2.0	4.2	-	0.4	1.6	7.3	25.3
6. 3 to 5 ounces	1.8	2.3	0.4	1.5	1.1	2.7	1.6	1.6	0.5	0.7	1.5	-	0.5	1.3	2.5	12.7
7. 6 or more ounces	1.0	1.8	0.2	1.0	1.7	0.3	0.9	2.1	0.3	0.9	1.4	-	0.7	-	1.3	9.3
Item 2370 Subject A01d N★	1285	636	564	978	141	365	346	358	215	598	488	-	468	215	562	23

★=excludes respondents for whom question was inappropriate.

QUESTIONNAIRE FORM 1 1983	TOTAL	SEX		RACE		REGION				4YR COLLEGE PLANS		ILLICIT DRUG USE: LIFETIME				
		M	F	White	Black	NE	NC	S	W	Yes	No	None	Mari-juana Only	Few Pills	More Pills	Any Her-oin
N (Weighted No. of Cases):	3448	1611	1667	2555	435	814	974	1118	541	1798	1246	1269	848	428	746	30
% of Weighted Total:	100.0	46.7	48.3	74.1	12.6	23.6	28.3	32.4	15.7	52.2	36.1	36.8	24.6	12.4	21.6	.9
B027: Have you ever tried to stop using mar-ijuana or hashish and found that you couldn't stop?																
1. Yes	6.8	7.5	4.6	4.6	13.2	8.5	6.3	6.6	5.3	6.1	5.4	-	5.5	5.2	7.8	22.0
2. No	93.2	92.5	95.4	95.4	86.8	91.5	93.7	93.4	94.7	93.9	94.6	-	94.5	94.8	92.2	78.0
Item 2380 Subject A01i N★	1355	669	601	1033	154	378	368	385	225	635	515	-	493	233	586	26
B028: Thinking back over your whole life, has there ever been a period when you used mar-ijuana or hashish on a daily, or almost daily, basis for at least a month?																
1. No–GO TO QUESTION B032.	83.4	82.0	86.7	83.9	91.1	79.9	84.2	87.4	79.2	89.7	80.1	100.0	93.5	80.2	48.7	18.6
2. Yes	16.6	18.0	13.3	16.1	8.9	20.1	15.8	12.6	20.8	10.3	19.9	-	6.5	19.8	51.3	81.4
Item 21180 Subject A01a N	3238	1530	1579	2450	395	748	933	1041	516	1713	1179	1181	811	412	726	28
B029: How old were you when you first smoked marijuana or hashish that frequently?																
1. Grade 6 or earlier	8.9	10.4	4.9	8.3	2.1	7.2	7.2	9.9	12.5	9.2	6.8	-	8.0	3.7	9.0	24.2
2. Grade 7 or 8	30.6	34.4	23.6	29.6	33.5	28.8	36.7	26.1	31.1	31.7	29.4	-	26.5	25.3	33.9	37.5
3. Grade 9(Freshman)	22.2	18.1	29.7	23.3	28.9	19.1	25.4	21.7	22.9	20.7	24.9	-	17.6	30.7	22.8	24.3
4. Grade 10(Sophomore)	19.1	18.5	22.1	20.1	20.1	18.7	15.5	23.7	18.7	13.5	23.4	-	16.1	14.8	21.5	10.5
5. Grade 11(Junior)	15.3	12.9	18.2	15.6	12.8	22.6	13.1	12.2	11.4	18.2	14.0	-	24.9	18.8	11.4	3.5
6. Grade 12(Senior)	3.9	5.7	1.5	3.1	2.7	3.6	2.1	6.5	3.5	6.7	1.5	-	7.0	6.8	1.4	-
Item 21190 Subject A01g N★	682	344	268	464	80	195	181	175	131	226	296	-	120	109	399	24
B030: How recently did you use marijuana or hashish on a daily, or almost daily, basis for at least a month?																
1. During the past month	28.0	31.8	21.2	23.9	51.9	28.4	24.7	33.4	24.7	19.2	32.3	-	24.7	21.1	28.5	34.2
2. 2 months ago	8.0	8.5	7.4	7.8	7.4	10.4	7.4	5.9	8.0	11.6	4.8	-	12.7	11.6	6.3	1.9
3. 3 to 9 months ago	12.8	13.8	11.8	14.3	2.8	8.7	15.7	15.8	10.8	10.5	15.0	-	10.4	10.4	13.1	25.3
4. About 1 year ago	15.4	12.7	19.6	16.1	7.2	16.3	14.8	16.8	13.1	17.3	14.8	-	10.0	18.2	16.7	14.7
5. About 2 years ago	19.3	17.1	23.7	21.4	5.8	18.2	20.0	14.2	27.0	19.6	19.6	-	15.0	13.9	23.1	8.6
6. 3 or more years ago	16.4	16.0	18.6	16.5	24.9	17.9	17.3	13.9	16.5	21.7	13.5	-	27.2	24.7	12.3	15.2
Item 21200 Subject A01g N★	614	310	239	434	58	175	164	161	115	193	276	-	89	99	382	23
B031: Over your whole lifetime, during how many months have you used marijuana or hashish on a daily or near-daily basis?																
1. Less than 3 months	34.3	29.3	44.0	32.8	51.2	37.7	35.0	28.8	35.8	39.5	31.4	-	59.6	47.4	25.8	7.2
2. 3 to 9 months	18.7	20.3	16.5	17.8	17.5	20.5	13.6	18.9	22.7	19.5	19.8	-	14.3	18.7	20.3	19.6
3. About 1 year	10.4	10.0	11.1	10.2	10.7	9.8	11.8	13.3	5.4	10.8	11.6	-	5.6	10.1	11.4	11.8
4. About 1 and 1/2 years	5.3	5.9	4.3	6.2	1.9	2.3	5.0	7.2	7.6	5.0	5.3	-	2.7	2.0	6.9	-
5. About 2 years	12.5	14.9	8.4	14.0	4.8	11.2	15.5	11.2	11.9	11.8	13.8	-	5.8	10.2	15.1	6.1
6. About 3 to 5 years	15.5	16.4	12.4	16.0	10.9	16.3	17.1	16.4	11.0	11.3	14.5	-	8.7	11.0	16.8	53.4
7. 6 to 9 years	1.5	0.9	2.3	1.2	-	1.3	0.7	-	4.8	1.3	1.3	-	2.2	-	1.7	1.8
8. 10 or more years	1.8	2.3	1.1	1.8	2.9	0.8	1.4	4.2	0.6	0.7	2.3	-	1.3	0.6	2.0	-
Item 21210 Subject A01d N★	616	304	246	425	64	175	164	160	118	190	277	-	88	96	385	24
B032: Do you think you will be using marijuana or hashish five years from now?																
1. I definitely will	3.1	3.9	1.8	2.7	2.8	4.4	2.8	2.8	2.3	1.8	2.5	0.5	2.0	2.3	8.0	28.1
2. I probably will	14.6	15.7	12.8	13.9	15.9	18.3	12.8	12.4	17.3	11.2	17.8	0.3	14.0	18.8	36.7	33.6
3. I probably will not	22.2	22.4	21.2	22.2	20.4	25.8	22.4	19.9	21.5	22.5	20.6	7.4	32.4	29.2	31.9	19.3
4. I definitely will not	60.0	58.0	64.2	61.1	60.9	51.5	62.0	64.9	58.9	64.6	59.1	91.8	51.5	49.8	23.4	18.9
Item 2390 Subject A04a N	3306	1551	1620	2477	424	769	942	1077	518	1737	1214	1223	828	415	724	30
The next questions are about LSD, the psychedelic drug which is sometimes called "acid".																
B033: On how many occasions (if any) have you taken LSD . . .																

★=excludes respondents for whom question was inappropriate.

QUESTIONNAIRE FORM 1 1983	TOTAL	SEX		RACE		REGION				4YR COLLEGE PLANS		ILLICIT DRUG USE: LIFETIME				
		M	F	White	Black	NE	NC	S	W	Yes	No	None	Mari-juana Only	Few Pills	More Pills	Any Her-oin
N (Weighted No. of Cases):	3448	1611	1667	2555	435	814	974	1118	541	1798	1246	1269	848	428	746	30
% of Weighted Total:	100.0	46.7	48.3	74.1	12.6	23.6	28.3	32.4	15.7	52.2	36.1	36.8	24.6	12.4	21.6	.9
B033A: . . . in your lifetime?																
1. 0 occasions	91.3	90.3	93.7	91.1	99.0	91.9	88.7	93.3	91.2	94.5	89.7	100.0	100.0	92.4	67.5	19.2
2. 1-2	3.6	3.9	2.8	3.8	0.2	3.0	5.0	2.6	4.2	2.8	4.0	-	-	7.6	11.4	23.1
3. 3-5	1.9	1.7	1.8	1.9	0.5	2.1	1.8	1.6	2.3	1.2	2.5	-	-	-	8.2	10.8
4. 6-9	1.4	1.8	0.7	1.3	-	1.2	2.2	1.1	0.6	0.5	2.0	-	-	-	5.9	11.0
5. 10-19	0.9	0.8	0.7	0.9	-	0.9	1.2	0.7	0.7	0.4	1.2	-	-	-	3.6	12.6
6. 20-39	0.7	1.0	0.2	0.7	0.3	0.6	0.7	0.7	0.6	0.4	0.4	-	-	-	2.3	18.4
7. 40 or more	0.3	0.5	0.1	0.3	-	0.2	0.5	*	0.4	0.2	0.3	-	-	-	1.0	4.8
Item 890 Subject A01a N	3278	1531	1616	2481	400	762	951	1057	509	1741	1200	1245	830	412	714	28
B033B: . . . during the last 12 months?																
1. 0 occasions	94.0	92.9	96.1	93.9	99.4	94.1	92.3	95.1	94.6	96.4	93.2	100.0	100.0	97.3	76.4	34.2
2. 1-2	3.6	4.1	2.5	3.6	0.2	3.2	4.7	2.7	3.7	2.1	4.3	-	-	2.7	13.6	32.6
3. 3-5	1.2	1.4	0.7	1.1	0.5	1.9	1.2	0.9	0.9	0.7	1.2	-	-	-	5.5	3.8
4. 6-9	0.6	0.7	0.4	0.6	-	0.1	0.9	0.8	0.2	0.2	0.7	-	-	-	2.0	15.1
5. 10-19	0.5	0.7	0.2	0.6	-	0.4	0.8	0.5	0.5	0.3	0.6	-	-	-	2.0	12.8
6. 20-39	*	0.1	-	*	-	0.1	-	*	-	*	-	-	-	-	*	1.5
7. 40 or more	0.1	0.3	-	0.1	-	0.2	0.2	-	0.1	0.2	*	-	-	-	0.6	-
Item 900 Subject A01b N	3274	1531	1616	2480	400	762	950	1055	507	1741	1199	1245	830	412	710	28
B033C: . . . during the last 30 days?																
1. 0 occasions	97.8	97.0	98.8	97.6	99.5	97.8	97.1	98.1	98.3	98.7	97.7	100.0	100.0	99.1	91.8	60.9
2. 1-2	1.6	2.3	0.8	1.8	0.3	1.8	2.1	1.2	1.4	0.9	1.8	-	-	0.9	6.0	25.6
3. 3-5	0.4	0.3	0.4	0.3	0.2	0.1	0.5	0.7	0.2	0.2	0.4	-	-	-	1.4	11.9
4. 6-9	0.1	0.1	-	0.1	-	0.1	0.2	-	-	-	0.1	-	-	-	0.2	1.5
5. 10-19	-	-	-	-	-	-	-	-	-	-	-	-	-	-	-	-
6. 20-39	-	-	-	-	-	-	-	-	-	-	-	-	-	-	-	-
7. 40 or more	0.1	0.3	-	0.1	-	0.2	0.2	-	0.1	0.2	*	-	-	-	0.6	-
Item 910 Subject A01c N	3278	1533	1616	2482	400	762	950	1057	508	1741	1200	1245	830	412	713	28

IF YOU HAVE NOT TAKEN LSD IN THE LAST TWELVE MONTHS, GO TO Q.B041.

B034: When you used LSD during the last year, how often did you use it in each of the following situations?

B034A: When you were alone	TOTAL	M	F	White	Black	NE	NC	S	W	Yes	No	None	Mari-juana Only	Few Pills	More Pills	Any Her-oin
1. Not at all	84.9	82.7	90.9	85.8	50.2	85.8	85.3	83.1	85.9	81.7	91.8	-	-	100.0	86.6	56.5
2. A few of the times	8.7	8.6	5.6	7.2	38.4	7.6	8.6	9.3	10.0	11.6	3.9	-	-	-	7.5	26.7
3. Some of the times	2.0	1.7	3.5	2.8	-	1.6	2.5	2.8	-	-	1.6	-	-	-	2.0	5.0
4. Most of the times	1.8	3.2	-	2.4	-	0.8	1.5	3.7	-	2.3	2.0	-	-	-	0.9	11.8
5. Every time	2.6	3.7	-	1.9	11.5	4.2	2.0	1.1	4.0	4.4	0.8	-	-	-	3.1	-
Item 2400 Subject A05a N★	209	114	66	155	6	50	75	55	28	65	87	-	-	10	171	18
B034B: With just 1 or 2 other people																
1. Not at all	22.2	22.5	19.4	21.0	67.8	31.4	27.0	16.6	3.5	25.8	17.7	-	-	46.2	17.6	15.0
2. A few of the times	39.3	40.5	44.3	43.2	18.6	35.9	37.9	38.1	51.5	32.6	52.3	-	-	42.3	42.6	24.8
3. Some of the times	7.7	9.9	1.7	6.7	-	10.5	6.4	9.3	2.7	5.6	7.6	-	-	2.1	8.6	5.6
4. Most of the times	12.2	11.5	15.5	13.5	-	9.6	16.6	9.0	11.4	12.4	11.9	-	-	-	11.2	34.6
5. Every time	18.6	15.6	19.1	15.7	13.6	12.6	12.1	27.0	30.8	23.5	10.5	-	-	9.5	20.0	20.0
Item 2410 Subject A05b N★	209	114	67	156	6	51	75	55	28	65	86	-	-	10	172	18
B034C: At a party																
1. Not at all	33.8	31.4	41.7	30.7	74.0	32.8	25.1	32.5	61.3	43.0	32.7	-	-	45.4	31.5	18.4
2. A few of the times	27.3	28.5	29.4	30.4	26.0	32.1	28.2	22.4	25.6	27.6	33.3	-	-	37.7	28.1	24.3
3. Some of the times	15.9	16.5	7.9	13.4	-	11.5	22.7	16.1	5.2	14.7	12.0	-	-	-	17.3	19.8
4. Most of the times	13.0	14.0	10.0	15.1	-	12.0	13.4	19.0	1.9	10.7	14.5	-	-	-	13.6	21.1
5. Every time	10.1	9.6	10.9	10.4	-	11.5	10.6	10.0	6.0	4.1	7.5	-	-	16.9	9.5	16.4
Item 2420 Subject A05c N★	208	113	66	153	6	50	74	55	28	63	87	-	-	10	170	18

*=less than .05 per cent.   ★=excludes respondents for whom question was inappropriate.

QUESTIONNAIRE FORM 1 1983	TOTAL	SEX		RACE		REGION				4YR COLLEGE PLANS		ILLICIT DRUG USE: LIFETIME				
		M	F	White	Black	NE	NC	S	W	Yes	No	None	Mari-juana Only	Few Pills	More Pills	Any Her-oin
N (Weighted No. of Cases):	3448	1611	1667	2555	435	814	974	1118	541	1798	1246	1269	848	428	746	30
% of Weighted Total:	100.0	46.7	48.3	74.1	12.6	23.6	28.3	32.4	15.7	52.2	36.1	36.8	24.6	12.4	21.6	.9
B034D: When your date or spouse was present																
1. Not at all	56.7	67.8	39.0	54.6	90.9	60.9	55.4	44.6	76.2	66.2	52.4	-	-	84.1	55.3	34.9
2. A few of the times	24.5	20.6	33.0	26.6	9.1	21.2	27.3	29.1	14.4	20.2	29.1	-	-	6.8	26.6	24.6
3. Some of the times	4.9	3.0	5.3	4.2	-	3.8	5.8	5.2	4.0	2.6	4.3	-	-	-	5.7	2.9
4. Most of the times	7.0	6.3	8.8	8.0	-	8.1	6.9	9.6	-	4.8	7.0	-	-	-	6.1	23.2
5. Every time	6.9	2.3	13.8	6.7	-	6.0	4.6	11.5	5.4	6.3	7.2	-	-	9.1	6.3	14.4
Item 2430 Subject A05b N★	209	113	66	153	6	52	74	55	28	63	87	-	-	10	171	18
B034E: When people over age 30 were present																
1. Not at all	72.1	71.3	78.7	73.2	90.9	66.7	69.6	72.2	88.4	73.7	76.3	-	-	81.5	72.3	53.6
2. A few of the times	12.4	12.1	8.9	10.4	9.1	14.3	14.2	12.9	3.4	7.6	14.6	-	-	9.5	13.2	10.3
3. Some of the times	8.7	8.5	8.5	9.5	-	14.3	5.2	9.8	6.2	6.9	7.0	-	-	9.1	8.2	17.4
4. Most of the times	0.8	1.5	-	1.1	-	1.9	1.1	-	-	2.7	-	-	-	-	0.6	4.4
5. Every time	5.9	6.5	4.0	5.7	-	2.9	10.0	5.2	1.9	9.2	2.2	-	-	-	5.7	14.4
Item 2440 Subject A05b N★	209	114	66	155	6	50	75	55	28	65	87	-	-	10	171	18
B034F: During the daytime (before 4:00 p.m.)																
1. Not at all	54.5	50.2	69.2	55.9	76.2	51.2	51.1	67.0	44.8	62.2	55.9	-	-	72.6	53.0	35.7
2. A few of the times	26.5	31.9	14.9	25.1	23.8	29.7	28.9	14.0	39.2	20.6	32.0	-	-	17.9	29.4	17.2
3. Some of the times	9.2	6.9	9.5	9.1	-	4.7	11.6	12.2	4.9	6.2	8.3	-	-	9.5	9.3	13.2
4. Most of the times	5.1	6.3	1.0	4.6	-	9.8	5.3	1.9	1.9	4.0	1.6	-	-	-	3.8	22.2
5. Every time	4.7	4.7	5.4	5.4	-	4.7	3.1	4.8	9.3	7.0	2.2	-	-	-	4.5	11.7
Item 2450 Subject A05c N★	209	114	66	156	6	51	75	55	27	65	87	-	-	10	171	18
B034G: At your home (or apartment or dorm)																
1. Not at all	61.1	58.4	69.1	62.3	78.6	64.6	62.3	61.8	50.0	71.2	59.6	-	-	100.0	58.4	46.8
2. A few of the times	20.4	17.6	22.0	20.0	21.4	15.9	22.6	20.3	23.0	13.5	24.9	-	-	-	22.7	18.4
3. Some of the times	9.5	11.8	7.8	9.5	-	11.0	9.1	8.1	10.8	4.4	13.5	-	-	-	9.4	21.0
4. Most of the times	6.7	9.2	0.7	6.2	-	7.0	1.6	9.2	14.6	5.2	2.0	-	-	-	7.2	9.4
5. Every time	2.3	3.0	0.3	2.0	-	1.5	4.4	0.6	1.6	5.7	-	-	-	-	2.4	4.4
Item 2460 Subject A05c N★	206	111	66	153	6	49	74	55	28	63	85	-	-	10	168	18
B034H: At school																
1. Not at all	69.8	67.1	72.0	67.2	70.7	74.8	58.3	76.7	77.6	70.2	70.6	-	-	82.1	72.0	27.2
2. A few of the times	18.5	19.0	19.4	19.4	29.3	12.0	28.7	10.1	19.8	20.1	22.4	-	-	17.9	19.1	22.5
3. Some of the times	8.5	9.1	8.6	9.8	-	8.4	10.5	10.1	0.8	6.4	5.0	-	-	-	7.5	27.1
4. Most of the times	1.1	1.5	-	1.1	-	3.4	-	-	1.8	-	-	-	-	-	0.3	9.4
5. Every time	2.1	3.4	-	2.5	-	1.4	2.6	3.1	-	3.3	2.0	-	-	-	1.1	13.8
Item 2470 Subject A05c N★	208	113	66	153	6	50	74	55	28	63	87	-	-	10	170	18
B034I: In a car																
1. Not at all	42.6	43.7	45.2	42.9	61.6	49.3	36.5	42.5	46.8	57.9	34.7	-	-	53.2	42.6	10.4
2. A few of the times	23.8	21.5	25.5	23.4	9.1	30.4	28.8	12.7	20.2	17.7	28.3	-	-	46.8	24.1	17.2
3. Some of the times	17.8	21.2	12.6	17.2	16.9	10.6	17.5	27.0	13.6	11.9	20.4	-	-	-	17.7	38.4
4. Most of the times	4.9	5.5	5.9	6.1	12.4	-	6.0	8.0	4.6	5.3	7.2	-	-	-	4.2	16.4
5. Every time	10.9	8.1	10.8	10.4	-	9.8	11.1	9.7	14.7	7.2	9.4	-	-	-	11.4	17.6
Item 2490 Subject A05c N★	210	114	66	155	6	51	75	55	28	65	87	-	-	10	172	18
B035: How many of the times when you used LSD during the last year did you use it along with each of the following drugs–that is, so that their effects overlapped?																
B035A: With alcohol																
1. Not at all	24.5	24.2	30.3	25.0	63.9	22.2	21.2	30.7	25.7	31.8	20.6	-	-	33.1	19.8	26.5
2. A few of the times	25.3	23.4	30.8	27.1	-	18.2	28.0	24.9	32.1	33.5	26.7	-	-	40.6	26.5	17.6
3. Some of the times	12.6	13.4	10.7	13.0	-	8.7	16.9	11.0	11.0	6.1	17.7	-	-	-	14.3	10.0
4. Most of the times	14.1	13.9	8.8	11.5	21.5	17.8	12.9	19.6	-	6.1	12.7	-	-	-	14.5	25.9
5. Every time	23.5	25.1	19.4	23.5	14.6	33.1	21.1	13.7	31.2	22.4	22.2	-	-	26.3	24.9	20.1
Item 2500 Subject A01h N★	205	111	65	151	5	51	75	52	27	64	85	-	-	10	168	18

★=excludes respondents for whom question was inappropriate.

QUESTIONNAIRE FORM 1 1983	TOTAL	SEX		RACE		REGION				4YR COLLEGE PLANS		ILLICIT DRUG USE: LIFETIME				
		M	F	White	Black	NE	NC	S	W	Yes	No	None	Marijuana Only	Few Pills	More Pills	Any Heroin
N (Weighted No. of Cases):	3448	1611	1667	2555	435	814	974	1118	541	1798	1246	1269	848	428	746	30
% of Weighted Total:	100.0	46.7	48.3	74.1	12.6	23.6	28.3	32.4	15.7	52.2	36.1	36.8	24.6	12.4	21.6	.9
B035B: With marijuana																
1. Not at all	19.2	18.1	23.4	17.8	55.2	20.2	20.2	20.3	12.5	24.2	19.0	-	-	44.6	14.5	10.9
2. A few of the times	19.0	17.9	20.6	19.0	-	17.2	20.0	16.4	24.2	28.4	16.2	-	-	32.7	20.5	5.6
3. Some of the times	12.1	9.9	19.0	14.7	-	6.1	17.3	13.6	6.2	10.8	14.6	-	-	-	13.9	7.0
4. Most of the times	20.4	23.4	12.4	18.4	32.2	20.8	15.3	28.3	18.1	9.2	21.0	-	-	-	21.7	29.0
5. Every time	29.4	30.6	24.7	30.1	12.6	35.6	27.2	21.4	39.0	27.3	29.1	-	-	22.7	29.3	47.5
Item 2510 Subject A01h N★	207	112	66	154	6	51	74	54	28	63	86	-	-	10	170	18
B036: What have been the most important reasons for your taking LSD? (Mark all that apply.)																
A. To experiment-to see what's like	85.8	87.4	81.9	85.7	77.0	80.2	86.5	87.3	90.0	93.0	83.2	-	-	91.5	87.2	68.9
B. To relax or relieve tension	13.9	14.7	12.5	14.3	-	6.0	13.8	14.5	25.7	5.2	20.2	-	-	9.5	13.5	20.3
C. To feel good or get high	70.5	70.6	75.9	74.2	24.9	61.3	72.1	79.0	65.1	73.1	70.3	-	-	66.0	69.7	82.6
D. To seek deeper insights and understanding	26.2	27.6	21.1	26.3	23.0	26.6	17.5	36.0	29.8	20.8	29.9	-	-	11.2	25.4	42.7
E. To have a good time with my friends	48.4	43.3	56.7	51.1	-	46.2	62.3	37.1	36.4	51.1	47.7	-	-	27.4	49.3	53.3
F. To fit in with a group I like	6.7	7.5	7.2	8.3	-	3.1	10.7	6.8	1.6	2.5	10.5	-	-	14.3	4.0	27.3
G. To get away from my problems or troubles	13.4	11.6	15.5	14.5	34.0	9.1	14.9	21.3	1.8	7.3	15.2	-	-	-	10.7	47.5
H. Because of boredom, nothing else to do	19.7	19.4	13.4	18.2	-	20.3	25.0	16.5	10.4	11.8	20.3	-	-	-	19.5	33.4
I. Because of anger or frustration	5.2	3.3	10.1	6.0	-	1.6	7.1	8.4	-	3.3	8.5	-	-	-	2.4	34.3
J. To get through the day	4.2	4.6	1.7	3.4	34.0	-	5.4	5.2	5.8	4.9	3.9	-	-	-	3.3	15.2
K. To increase the effects of some other drug(s)	14.0	17.3	9.8	15.2	-	19.6	16.1	13.5	-	9.6	14.1	-	-	-	12.2	38.6
L. To decrease (offset) the effects of some other drug(s)	1.8	1.5	2.1	2.0	-	-	2.5	3.2	-	-	3.5	-	-	-	0.3	16.4
M. Because I am "hooked"-I have to have it	3.7	3.6	-	3.0	-	1.6	2.9	5.5	5.8	-	5.3	-	-	-	3.3	9.4
Item 2520-2640 Subject A06a N★	201	112	61	152	3	46	74	53	28	60	85	-	-	10	171	18
B037: When you take LSD how high do you usually get?																
1. Not at all high	-	-	-	-	-	-	-	-	-	-	-	-	-	-	-	-
2. A little high	4.2	3.6	6.2	3.8	-	1.9	1.6	4.3	14.5	8.7	1.8	-	-	18.1	3.8	-
3. Moderately high	26.9	21.3	32.4	26.4	-	27.0	33.7	23.2	15.7	26.0	28.7	-	-	27.0	28.0	10.3
4. Very high	68.9	75.1	61.5	69.8	100.0	71.1	64.7	72.6	69.8	65.3	69.5	-	-	54.9	68.2	89.7
Item 2650 Subject A01e N★	200	111	61	152	3	46	74	52	28	60	84	-	-	10	170	18
B038: When you take LSD how long do you usually stay high?																
1. Usually don't get high	-	-	-	-	-	-	-	-	-	-	-	-	-	-	-	-
2. One to two hours	2.6	1.4	3.1	2.0	-	4.6	0.9	3.7	1.6	1.5	1.4	-	-	2.1	1.5	4.1
3. Three to six hours	43.6	46.3	42.2	45.9	-	45.1	43.9	45.3	37.3	45.8	41.9	-	-	51.0	43.6	43.0
4. Seven to 24 hours	49.3	47.3	50.6	48.5	100.0	47.4	51.8	47.8	48.2	51.6	50.2	-	-	42.2	49.8	52.9
5. More than 24 hours	4.6	4.9	4.2	3.6	-	3.0	3.4	3.3	12.8	1.1	6.5	-	-	4.7	5.1	-
Item 2660 Subject A01f N★	199	111	61	152	3	46	74	51	28	60	84	-	-	10	170	17
B039: Have you ever had a "bad trip" on LSD?																
1. No	76.7	80.6	72.4	77.1	58.5	68.9	79.4	73.6	88.7	81.4	75.9	-	-	93.2	80.8	25.1
2. Yes, once	19.5	16.5	23.3	19.8	-	29.3	17.9	20.6	5.5	16.2	19.3	-	-	6.8	17.6	48.2
3. Yes, more than once	3.7	2.8	4.3	3.1	41.5	1.7	2.6	5.8	5.8	2.3	4.8	-	-	-	1.6	26.6
Item 2670 Subject A01k N★	202	111	63	153	3	47	74	54	28	60	84	-	-	10	171	18
B040: Have you ever tried to stop using LSD and found that you couldn't stop?																
1. Yes	5.0	7.6	-	5.0	-	6.5	4.1	7.3	-	2.5	4.7	-	-	-	3.4	13.8
2. No	95.0	92.4	100.0	95.0	100.0	93.5	95.9	92.7	00.0	97.5	95.3	-	-	-	96.6	86.2
Item 2680 Subject A01i N★	201	110	63	153	3	47	72	55	28	60	82	-	-	9	171	18

★=excludes respondents for whom question was inappropriate.

QUESTIONNAIRE FORM 1 1983	TOTAL	SEX		RACE		REGION				4YR COLLEGE PLANS		ILLICIT DRUG USE: LIFETIME				
		M	F	White	Black	NE	NC	S	W	Yes	No	None	Mari-juana Only	Few Pills	More Pills	Any Her-oin
N (Weighted No. of Cases):	3448	1611	1667	2555	435	814	974	1118	541	1798	1246	1269	848	428	746	30
% of Weighted Total:	100.0	46.7	48.3	74.1	12.6	23.6	28.3	32.4	15.7	52.2	36.1	36.8	24.6	12.4	21.6	.9

B041: Do you think you will be using LSD five years from now?

1. I definitely will	0.8	0.9	0.8	0.7	0.7	0.9	0.5	0.9	1.2	0.5	1.0	0.5	0.8	0.7	1.0	9.6
2. I probably will	1.6	1.9	1.1	1.6	-	2.3	1.6	1.2	1.2	0.8	1.7	-	0.1	0.5	6.6	12.1
3. I probably will not	8.6	9.5	7.0	8.7	5.7	8.2	10.0	7.4	9.3	7.0	9.9	2.8	5.1	6.5	23.3	43.3
4. I definitely will not	88.9	87.7	91.2	89.0	93.7	88.6	87.8	90.4	88.4	91.8	87.4	96.7	94.0	92.3	69.1	34.9
Item 2690 Subject A04a N	3246	1505	1618	2444	412	733	945	1063	505	1714	1192	1227	809	405	686	29

The next questions are about PSYCHEDELICS OTHER THAN LSD.

his group would include the following drugs: Mescaline, Peyote, Psilocybin, PCP.

B042: On how many occasions (if any) have you taken psychedelics other than LSD . . .

B042A: . . . in your lifetime?

1. 0 occasions	92.0	91.1	94.2	92.0	97.5	88.8	92.5	94.4	90.9	94.9	91.0	100.0	100.0	92.6	70.7	28.3
2. 1-2	3.1	3.0	2.8	2.7	1.6	3.7	2.8	2.6	3.9	2.3	3.0	-	-	7.4	9.4	18.7
3. 3-5	1.8	2.1	1.1	2.0	0.4	3.0	1.6	0.6	2.5	1.4	1.6	-	-	-	7.5	14.4
4. 6-9	0.9	1.1	0.6	0.9	0.5	1.0	0.6	1.1	1.2	0.5	1.2	-	-	-	3.8	12.9
5. 10-19	0.8	1.1	0.5	1.0	-	1.0	0.9	0.5	1.1	0.5	1.1	-	-	-	3.3	9.6
6. 20-39	0.6	0.7	0.5	0.7	-	1.4	0.6	0.3	0.1	0.1	1.3	-	-	-	2.5	6.1
7. 40 or more	0.7	0.9	0.3	0.7	-	1.0	1.0	0.5	0.1	0.3	0.8	-	-	-	2.8	9.9
Item 920 Subject A01a N	3239	1519	1596	2459	389	750	943	1039	508	1721	1190	1231	814	407	709	28

B042B: . . . during the last 12 months?

1. 0 occasions	94.7	93.4	96.9	94.6	98.1	92.0	95.1	96.4	94.7	96.8	93.9	100.0	100.0	96.7	80.0	46.0
2. 1-2	2.5	3.1	1.6	2.5	1.7	3.8	2.6	1.6	2.6	2.0	2.4	-	-	3.3	9.0	19.3
3. 3-5	1.4	2.0	0.5	1.5	0.2	2.6	0.7	1.2	1.4	0.5	1.8	-	-	-	5.9	17.1
4. 6-9	0.5	0.5	0.5	0.5	-	0.4	0.6	0.3	0.7	0.4	0.5	-	-	-	1.9	7.5
5. 10-19	0.4	0.5	0.3	0.5	-	0.7	0.3	0.3	0.4	0.1	0.7	-	-	-	1.5	10.2
6. 20-39	0.3	0.3	0.2	0.3	-	0.4	0.3	0.2	-	0.1	0.4	-	-	-	1.2	-
7. 40 or more	0.1	0.2	0.1	0.1	-	0.1	0.3	-	0.1	0.1	0.2	-	-	-	0.6	-
Item 930 Subject A01b N	3234	1518	1592	2454	390	748	941	1038	508	1718	1188	1231	815	406	705	28

B042C: . . . during the last 30 days?

1. 0 occasions	97.6	97.4	98.4	97.6	99.4	96.5	97.6	98.1	98.3	98.7	97.3	100.0	100.0	99.8	90.2	72.3
2. 1-2	1.6	1.6	1.1	1.6	0.6	2.9	1.5	0.9	1.0	1.0	1.6	-	-	0.2	6.3	17.4
3. 3-5	0.3	0.5	0.2	0.4	-	0.2	0.4	0.3	0.4	0.3	0.4	-	-	-	1.4	3.4
4. 6-9	0.3	0.3	0.2	0.3	-	0.1	0.3	0.5	-	*	0.4	-	-	-	0.9	6.9
5. 10-19	0.1	0.1	-	0.1	-	0.2	0.2	0.1	-	-	0.1	-	-	-	0.5	-
6. 20-39	0.1	*	0.1	0.1	-	-	-	0.1	0.1	*	0.1	-	-	-	0.3	-
7. 40 or more	0.1	*	-	-	-	0.1	0.1	-	0.2	-	0.1	-	-	-	0.3	-
Item 940 Subject A01c N	3236	1520	1591	2455	389	748	941	1039	508	1719	1186	1231	814	406	708	28

IF YOU HAVE NOT TAKEN ANY PSYCHEDELICS OTHER THAN LSD IN THE LAST TWELVE MONTHS, GO TO Q.B046.

B043: When you take psychedelics other than LSD how high do you usually get?

1. Not at all high	4.0	1.2	8.1	1.2	33.8	8.2	3.3	-	1.6	3.6	3.3	-	-	16.3	2.0	-
2. A little high	8.2	9.2	6.7	9.5	-	8.8	6.8	10.4	6.1	6.1	8.8	-	-	-	9.8	2.5
3. Moderately high	36.6	38.0	37.3	40.8	-	29.8	49.1	28.7	41.4	38.1	39.4	-	-	42.0	37.4	28.1
4. Very high	51.2	51.6	48.0	48.6	66.2	53.2	40.8	60.9	50.8	52.3	48.5	-	-	41.6	50.9	69.5
Item 2700 Subject A01e N★	170	100	50	132	7	59	46	39	27	55	72	-	-	14	139	15

*=less than .05 per cent.   ★=excludes respondents for whom question was inappropriate.

QUESTIONNAIRE FORM 1 1983	TOTAL	SEX		RACE		REGION				4YR COLLEGE PLANS		ILLICIT DRUG USE: LIFETIME				
		M	F	White	Black	NE	NC	S	W	Yes	No	None	Marijuana Only	Few Pills	More Pills	Any Heroin
N (Weighted No. of Cases):	3448	1611	1667	2555	435	814	974	1118	541	1798	1246	1269	848	428	746	30
% of Weighted Total:	100.0	46.7	48.3	74.1	12.6	23.6	28.3	32.4	15.7	52.2	36.1	36.8	24.6	12.4	21.6	.9

B044: When you take psychedelics other than LSD how long do you usually stay high?

	TOTAL	M	F	White	Black	NE	NC	S	W	Yes	No	None	Marijuana Only	Few Pills	More Pills	Any Heroin
1. Usually don't get high	4.8	2.6	8.1	2.4	33.8	8.0	6.9	-	0.8	3.2	5.5	-	-	17.6	2.9	-
2. One to two hours	7.9	10.2	5.9	8.2	-	1.8	8.2	13.1	13.8	11.8	4.9	-	-	5.3	8.4	6.5
3. Three to six hours	54.1	55.1	53.9	57.8	22.5	49.9	59.3	56.4	51.4	56.0	57.5	-	-	39.1	55.5	60.7
4. Seven to 24 hours	30.5	32.1	27.4	31.6	11.5	40.3	24.4	22.7	29.9	27.2	30.3	-	-	38.0	30.7	25.4
5. More than 24 hours	2.7	-	4.8	-	32.3	-	1.2	7.8	4.0	1.9	1.8	-	-	-	2.5	7.4
Item 2710 Subject A01f N★	171	99	50	132	7	60	45	38	28	55	72	-	-	13	142	14

B045: What psychedelics other than LSD have you taken during the last year? (Mark all that apply.)

	TOTAL	M	F	White	Black	NE	NC	S	W	Yes	No	None	Marijuana Only	Few Pills	More Pills	Any Heroin
A. Mescaline	50.3	47.0	53.6	48.9	82.0	72.1	59.5	34.5	10.4	33.1	56.5	-	-	46.0	48.7	77.2
B. Peyote	10.9	9.4	11.8	10.4	-	6.9	15.7	13.8	8.4	5.8	9.0	-	-	-	12.0	10.9
C. Psilocybin	14.0	20.6	4.0	17.2	-	8.2	8.5	8.2	42.7	22.3	10.4	-	-	-	14.4	23.7
D. PCP	28.2	25.1	35.8	27.4	54.7	19.9	24.2	47.9	24.8	30.9	22.0	-	-	15.3	26.2	62.1
E. Concentrated THC	27.0	29.6	21.6	29.6	14.3	17.0	26.9	46.0	23.1	23.7	30.4	-	-	11.7	25.7	57.1
F. Other	28.2	29.1	18.7	26.7	-	20.6	26.7	34.9	38.1	33.2	23.1	-	-	24.1	24.4	55.2
G. Don't know the names of some I have used	23.2	21.8	23.8	21.4	32.3	20.3	25.2	35.4	9.6	16.7	28.6	-	-	14.6	22.5	40.3
Item 2720-2780 Subject A01l N★	172	100	48	132	7	63	41	40	28	55	72	-	-	13	141	15

The next questions are about some non-prescription drugs.

B046: Some types of diet pills (also called appetite suppressants) can be sold legally without a doctor's prescription by drugstores, through the mail, etc. These "over-the-counter" drugs include Dexatrim, Dietac, Prolamine, and others.

On how many occasions (if any) have you taken such non-prescription diet pills ...

B046A: ... in your lifetime?

	TOTAL	M	F	White	Black	NE	NC	S	W	Yes	No	None	Marijuana Only	Few Pills	More Pills	Any Heroin
1. 0 occasions	68.6	82.6	55.2	65.4	83.7	70.9	65.4	71.4	65.2	71.9	65.6	86.1	72.6	57.3	40.3	40.8
2. 1-2	11.5	6.5	16.7	12.6	6.8	9.5	11.0	10.4	17.5	10.3	11.7	8.1	10.9	21.4	12.6	12.4
3. 3-5	4.9	3.0	6.5	5.3	3.1	5.2	4.8	5.7	3.1	4.4	5.9	1.6	4.7	9.3	8.4	7.0
4. 6-9	3.5	1.8	5.1	3.9	1.9	4.3	3.4	3.1	3.4	3.5	3.5	1.1	3.3	3.6	8.1	-
5. 10-19	4.2	2.3	5.9	4.5	2.6	4.5	5.6	2.5	4.4	4.5	4.2	1.8	3.5	3.5	9.5	8.8
6. 20-39	2.7	1.5	3.9	3.2	-	2.8	3.1	2.3	2.4	2.1	3.5	0.5	1.9	2.0	7.6	4.7
7. 40 or more	4.7	2.2	6.8	5.2	1.9	2.8	6.6	4.7	3.9	3.3	5.7	0.9	3.1	3.1	13.5	26.3
Item 21220 Subject A01a N	3301	1553	1619	2496	406	759	958	1067	517	1753	1205	1243	833	419	715	29

B046B: ... during the last 12 months?

	TOTAL	M	F	White	Black	NE	NC	S	W	Yes	No	None	Marijuana Only	Few Pills	More Pills	Any Heroin
1. 0 occasions	79.5	89.4	70.0	76.6	91.8	81.5	76.7	80.8	79.0	81.0	78.6	91.8	83.4	74.0	56.7	56.0
2. 1-2	8.4	4.2	12.8	9.7	3.6	8.0	7.9	7.9	11.2	8.4	7.8	4.8	6.9	15.5	13.3	4.2
3. 3-5	3.3	2.2	4.4	3.6	2.3	2.8	3.6	4.1	2.1	3.1	3.7	0.9	2.9	3.5	7.6	9.6
4. 6-9	2.5	1.9	3.1	3.0	0.4	2.4	2.9	2.3	2.5	1.7	3.4	0.7	1.4	2.3	7.2	4.4
5. 10-19	2.5	0.8	4.0	2.9	0.6	2.9	3.5	1.3	2.6	3.0	2.2	1.0	2.6	2.1	5.2	8.3
6. 20-39	1.6	0.4	2.7	1.9	0.3	0.8	2.6	1.6	1.1	1.2	1.7	0.3	1.1	1.3	4.4	3.5
7. 40 or more	2.1	1.2	3.1	2.4	1.0	1.6	3.0	2.0	1.7	1.7	2.6	0.5	1.7	1.3	5.5	13.9
Item 21230 Subject A01b N	3284	1550	1607	2485	404	759	955	1059	511	1748	1200	1241	824	414	715	29

B046C: ... during the last 30 days?

	TOTAL	M	F	White	Black	NE	NC	S	W	Yes	No	None	Marijuana Only	Few Pills	More Pills	Any Heroin
1. 0 occasions	90.5	95.1	86.3	89.2	96.5	92.7	86.8	91.8	91.3	91.9	89.0	96.2	92.9	89.8	78.4	76.4
2. 1-2	4.2	2.9	5.5	4.9	1.6	3.2	5.5	3.8	4.1	3.9	4.9	2.2	3.2	5.5	8.5	-
3. 3-5	1.6	0.7	2.3	1.7	0.6	1.7	2.8	0.8	0.9	1.5	1.6	0.4	1.5	1.9	3.5	10.4
4. 6-9	1.2	0.5	1.8	1.3	0.4	1.0	1.9	0.6	1.8	0.9	1.6	0.3	1.0	0.5	3.4	3.5
5. 10-19	1.4	0.3	2.5	1.7	0.6	0.7	1.6	2.0	0.9	1.1	1.5	0.3	0.7	1.4	3.9	9.6
6. 20-39	0.9	0.3	1.4	1.0	0.3	0.6	0.9	0.9	1.0	0.6	1.2	0.4	0.7	1.0	1.8	-
7. 40 or more	0.1	0.2	0.1	0.2	-	0.1	0.4	-	-	0.1	0.2	0.1	-	-	0.5	-
Item 21240 Subject A01c N	3277	1549	1602	2477	405	758	951	1059	509	1742	1197	1240	825	413	709	29

★=excludes respondents for whom question was inappropriate.

QUESTIONNAIRE FORM 1 1983	TOTAL	SEX		RACE		REGION				4YR COLLEGE PLANS		ILLICIT DRUG USE: LIFETIME				
		M	F	White	Black	NE	NC	S	W	Yes	No	None	Mari-juana Only	Few Pills	More Pills	Any Her-oin
N (Weighted No. of Cases):	3448	1611	1667	2555	435	814	974	1118	541	1798	1246	1269	848	428	746	30
% of Weighted Total:	100.0	46.7	48.3	74.1	12.6	23.6	28.3	32.4	15.7	52.2	36.1	36.8	24.6	12.4	21.6	.9

B047: Some stay-awake pills can be sold legally without a doctor's prescription by drugstores, through the mail, etc. These non-prescription or "over-the-counter" drugs include No-Doz, Vivarin, Wake, Caffedrine, and others.

On how many occasions (if any) have you taken such non-prescription stay-awake pills...

B047A: . . . in your lifetime?

1. 0 occasions	79.6	77.7	81.8	77.3	93.0	83.6	75.3	82.0	76.4	81.1	79.6	93.7	83.5	74.0	54.0	41.7
2. 1-2	9.5	10.4	8.8	10.8	3.3	8.1	9.9	8.5	12.7	8.9	9.7	4.5	9.9	14.1	15.5	4.6
3. 3-5	3.7	4.2	3.0	4.0	2.1	3.2	4.8	3.1	3.3	4.1	2.7	1.1	2.4	5.3	8.9	7.0
4. 6-9	2.2	2.3	2.0	2.5	0.2	1.5	2.5	2.2	2.7	1.5	2.9	-	1.8	2.8	6.5	-
5. 10-19	1.7	2.3	1.2	1.7	0.7	1.6	2.1	1.5	1.4	1.5	1.7	0.4	1.6	1.7	3.7	9.3
6. 20-39	1.7	1.8	1.5	2.0	0.4	1.2	2.7	1.0	2.2	1.8	1.5	0.2	0.4	1.5	6.0	9.1
7. 40 or more	1.7	1.4	1.7	1.7	0.4	0.8	2.6	1.7	1.3	1.1	1.9	0.1	0.5	0.6	5.5	28.3
Item 21250 Subject A01a N	3297	1542	1628	2495	403	761	949	1068	519	1743	1212	1243	828	419	718	29

B047B: . . . during the last 12 months?

1. 0 occasions	87.7	86.2	89.5	86.1	97.4	90.5	83.2	89.3	88.5	87.4	89.2	95.9	91.2	85.4	70.9	56.9
2. 1-2	6.0	6.5	5.5	6.9	1.1	5.4	7.4	5.4	5.6	6.7	5.0	2.9	4.8	9.1	11.7	2.1
3. 3-5	2.1	2.9	1.4	2.5	0.6	2.2	2.4	2.1	1.6	2.0	1.8	0.6	1.7	2.7	4.9	8.0
4. 6-9	1.4	1.8	1.1	1.4	0.4	0.7	2.1	0.9	1.9	1.2	1.6	-	1.0	1.0	4.4	4.4
5. 10-19	1.5	1.5	1.3	1.6	0.6	0.5	2.8	1.2	1.1	1.5	1.1	0.3	0.7	0.8	4.5	16.0
6. 20-39	0.7	0.6	0.8	0.8	-	0.5	1.1	0.5	0.9	0.7	0.7	0.1	0.5	1.1	2.0	-
7. 40 or more	0.5	0.6	0.4	0.6	-	0.2	1.0	0.5	0.3	0.4	0.5	0.1	0.1	-	1.6	12.5
Item 21260 Subject A01b N	3288	1542	1620	2487	403	761	949	1062	516	1744	1206	1244	823	417	714	29

B047C: . . . during the last 30 days?

1. 0 occasions	94.7	94.5	95.5	94.4	98.6	95.4	92.2	96.2	95.4	95.0	95.9	98.8	96.1	95.1	86.7	65.9
2. 1-2	2.9	3.1	2.8	3.3	1.1	3.5	3.7	1.8	3.1	3.2	1.9	1.0	2.7	3.5	6.2	11.7
3. 3-5	1.1	1.3	0.6	1.1	0.2	0.3	2.0	1.1	0.8	0.8	1.1	0.1	0.8	1.0	3.0	13.7
4. 6-9	0.6	0.4	0.6	0.5	0.1	0.4	1.2	0.3	0.3	0.8	0.3	-	0.4	0.1	1.9	2.8
5. 10-19	0.4	0.3	0.4	0.4	-	0.2	0.7	0.2	0.3	0.2	0.4	-	-	0.3	1.5	-
6. 20-39	0.1	0.1	0.1	0.1	-	-	0.1	0.3	0.2	0.1	0.2	0.1	-	-	0.5	-
7. 40 or more	0.1	0.2	*	0.2	-	0.1	0.2	0.2	-	-	0.2	-	-	-	0.3	6.0
Item 21270 Subject A01c N	3286	1540	1620	2484	404	761	948	1061	516	1742	1206	1243	824	417	713	29

B048: In addition to non-prescription diet and stay-awake pills, there are other stimulants and pep pills which can be sold legally in most states without a prescription--usually by mail. These are sometimes called "fake pep pills," "imitation speed," or "look-alikes," because they look like prescription amphetamines and sometimes have similar names.

Other than diet pills and stay-awake pills you have already told us about, on how many occasions (if any) have you taken other non-prescription stimulants or pep pills ...

B048A: . . . in your lifetime?

1. 0 occasions	85.2	85.8	85.6	83.8	96.3	84.8	81.4	88.4	86.1	90.1	80.8	99.1	95.0	81.5	52.3	38.0
2. 1-2	5.2	4.9	5.3	5.8	1.4	6.5	5.3	3.6	6.4	3.7	6.8	0.4	3.1	13.9	11.2	6.5
3. 3-5	2.2	2.4	1.9	2.5	0.6	1.7	2.5	1.9	2.9	1.6	2.4	0.2	0.5	2.0	8.1	-
4. 6-9	1.8	2.0	1.5	1.9	0.8	1.9	2.5	1.1	1.8	1.3	2.5	-	0.5	1.4	6.7	4.4
5. 10-19	1.6	1.6	1.7	1.8	0.4	1.7	2.2	1.4	1.0	0.9	2.3	0.2	0.6	0.6	5.9	5.4
6. 20-39	1.7	2.0	1.3	1.8	0.3	1.2	2.7	1.5	1.1	1.3	1.9	-	0.1	0.3	7.0	10.4
7. 40 or more	2.3	1.4	2.6	2.5	0.2	2.3	3.5	2.2	0.8	1.0	3.3	0.1	0.2	0.3	8.8	35.2
Item 21280 Subject A01a N	3297	1544	1630	2497	406	764	947	1068	518	1745	1214	1243	829	422	713	30

*=less than .05 per cent.

QUESTIONNAIRE FORM 1 1983	TOTAL	SEX		RACE		REGION				4YR COLLEGE PLANS		ILLICIT DRUG USE: LIFETIME				
		M	F	White	Black	NE	NC	S	W	Yes	No	None	Mari-juana Only	Few Pills	More Pills	Any Her-oin
N (Weighted No. of Cases):	3448	1611	1667	2555	435	814	974	1118	541	1798	1246	1269	848	428	746	30
% of Weighted Total:	100.0	46.7	48.3	74.1	12.6	23.6	28.3	32.4	15.7	52.2	36.1	36.8	24.6	12.4	21.6	.9
B048B: . . . during the last 12 months?																
1. 0 occasions	90.6	90.8	91.4	89.9	98.3	91.0	87.7	92.3	92.1	93.9	88.2	99.7	98.0	91.4	66.8	47.4
2. 1-2	3.1	3.3	2.6	3.3	0.8	4.2	2.9	1.9	4.2	1.9	4.0	0.1	0.9	6.2	9.3	2.1
3. 3-5	2.0	2.6	1.4	2.3	0.2	1.6	2.6	1.8	2.2	1.6	2.6	0.1	0.5	1.6	7.7	-
4. 6-9	1.3	1.2	1.5	1.4	0.6	0.6	2.1	1.4	0.7	0.7	1.8	-	0.1	0.6	4.9	18.6
5. 10-19	1.0	0.6	1.2	1.1	-	1.0	1.4	1.1	0.1	0.7	1.1	-	0.3	-	3.7	16.3
6. 20-39	1.1	0.7	1.2	1.2	-	0.7	2.1	1.0	0.4	0.7	1.4	0.1	0.2	0.3	4.5	3.4
7. 40 or more	0.8	0.7	0.7	0.8	0.2	0.9	1.2	0.6	0.3	0.5	0.9	-	-	-	3.2	12.2
Item 21290 Subject A01b N	3293	1542	1630	2493	406	763	947	1065	517	1744	1212	1244	828	420	710	30
B048C: . . . during the last 30 days?																
1. 0 occasions	94.8	95.5	94.6	94.4	98.8	95.4	92.3	95.6	97.1	96.7	92.9	99.7	98.8	96.4	81.4	64.2
2. 1-2	2.4	2.8	2.1	2.6	0.9	2.6	3.2	1.8	2.2	1.7	3.2	0.2	0.8	3.2	7.8	8.5
3. 3-5	0.9	0.7	1.1	1.0	0.3	0.6	1.7	0.9	0.1	0.7	1.2	-	-	0.1	3.7	15.4
4. 6-9	0.5	0.1	0.7	0.4	-	0.4	1.0	0.3	*	0.3	0.6	-	-	-	2.1	2.7
5. 10-19	0.9	0.4	1.1	1.0	-	0.7	1.3	1.0	0.2	0.2	1.6	0.1	0.3	0.3	3.2	3.4
6. 20-39	0.3	0.2	0.3	0.3	-	0.3	0.3	0.1	0.3	0.2	0.2	-	-	-	1.2	-
7. 40 or more	0.2	0.3	0.1	0.2	-	0.1	0.2	0.3	-	*	0.3	-	-	-	0.6	5.8
Item 21300 Subject A01c N	3291	1541	1629	2491	406	763	947	1065	517	1743	1211	1244	828	420	709	30

The next questions are about AMPHETA-MINES, which doctors can prescribe to help people lose weight or to give people more en-ergy. Drugstores are not supposed to sell them without a prescription from a doctor.

Amphetamines are sometimes called: uppers, ups, speed, bennies, dexies, pep pills, diet pills. They include the following drugs: Ben-zedrine, Dexedrine, Methedrine, Ritalin, Pre-ludin, Dexamyl, Methamphetamine.

IN YOUR ANSWERS ABOUT AMPHETA-MINES, DO NOT INCLUDE ANY NON-PRESCRIPTION OR OVER-THE-COUNTER DRUGS.

	TOTAL	M	F	White	Black	NE	NC	S	W	Yes	No	None	Mari-juana Only	Few Pills	More Pills	Any Her-oin
B049: Have you ever taken amphetamines because a doctor told you to use them?																
1. No	92.6	91.4	94.0	92.3	95.9	93.9	92.8	92.0	91.8	93.7	91.9	96.4	95.1	89.5	85.9	79.1
2. Yes, but I had already tried them on my own	2.3	2.3	1.9	2.2	1.4	2.0	2.2	2.3	2.7	1.4	2.6	-	-	1.3	8.3	20.9
3. Yes, and it was the first time I took any	5.1	6.3	4.1	5.5	2.7	4.1	5.0	5.7	5.5	4.9	5.6	3.6	4.9	9.3	5.9	-
Item 2790 Subject A01j N	3292	1542	1632	2492	408	767	944	1061	520	1739	1215	1233	821	423	725	29
B050: On how many occasions (if any) have you taken amphetamines on your own–that is, without a doctor telling you to take them . . .																
B050A: . . . in your lifetime?																
1. 0 occasions	76.4	77.4	76.6	73.8	93.0	75.9	74.2	80.2	73.1	82.1	72.5	100.0	100.0	58.0	19.6	23.6
2. 1-2	7.0	7.5	6.7	8.2	2.0	6.8	6.7	6.3	8.9	5.7	8.2	-	-	42.0	7.3	-
3. 3-5	3.6	3.5	3.4	3.7	1.9	3.7	2.8	3.3	5.6	2.7	4.1	-	-	-	16.4	2.1
4. 6-9	3.4	3.0	3.5	3.6	0.4	3.1	4.1	2.2	4.9	2.3	4.2	-	-	-	14.8	15.2
5. 10-19	2.8	3.0	2.7	3.2	1.6	3.5	3.4	2.2	2.0	2.4	2.9	-	-	-	12.7	4.4
6. 20-39	2.2	2.3	1.7	2.1	0.6	3.1	2.1	1.8	1.5	1.5	2.5	-	-	-	9.7	3.6
7. 40 or more	4.7	3.3	5.3	5.4	0.4	3.9	6.8	3.9	4.0	3.2	5.5	-	-	-	19.5	51.1
Item 980 Subject A01a N	3273	1531	1620	2484	400	761	941	1054	516	1740	1201	1237	820	417	716	29
B050B: . . . during the last 12 months?																
1. 0 occasions	84.3	85.2	84.8	82.6	96.2	84.2	82.1	86.6	84.0	87.8	83.0	100.0	100.0	82.9	40.6	31.7
2. 1-2	5.1	5.1	4.9	5.8	1.6	5.4	4.7	4.7	6.4	4.1	5.5	-	-	17.1	13.4	6.1
3. 3-5	3.2	3.3	3.0	3.6	0.9	3.1	3.5	2.9	3.3	2.4	3.6	-	-	-	14.5	-
4. 6-9	2.1	2.4	1.7	2.3	0.6	2.4	2.7	1.6	1.9	1.7	2.5	-	-	-	8.9	21.2
5. 10-19	1.8	1.0	2.4	2.0	0.4	1.8	2.1	1.8	1.4	1.5	1.8	-	-	-	7.8	13.4
6. 20-39	1.9	1.7	1.7	2.1	-	1.7	2.9	1.5	1.0	1.5	2.0	-	-	-	8.1	15.2
7. 40 or more	1.6	1.3	1.5	1.7	0.3	1.4	2.1	1.0	1.9	1.0	1.6	-	-	-	6.7	12.3
Item 990 Subject A01b N	3261	1528	1614	2477	397	761	939	1045	516	1736	1197	1237	820	410	710	29

*=less than .05 per cent.

QUESTIONNAIRE FORM 1 1983	TOTAL	SEX		RACE		REGION				4YR COLLEGE PLANS		ILLICIT DRUG USE: LIFETIME				
		M	F	White	Black	NE	NC	S	W	Yes	No	None	Mari- juana Only	Few Pills	More Pills	Any Her- oin
N (Weighted No. of Cases):	3448	1611	1667	2555	435	814	974	1118	541	1798	1246	1269	848	428	746	30
% of Weighted Total:	100.0	46.7	48.3	74.1	12.6	23.6	28.3	32.4	15.7	52.2	36.1	36.8	24.6	12.4	21.6	.9

B050C: . . . during the last 30 days?

	TOTAL	M	F	White	Black	NE	NC	S	W	Yes	No	None	Mari. Only	Few Pills	More Pills	Any Heroin
1. 0 occasions	92.2	93.2	92.2	91.3	97.9	92.5	89.4	93.9	93.6	94.7	90.9	100.0	100.0	96.8	68.2	49.5
2. 1-2	3.5	3.8	3.0	3.9	1.3	3.7	4.8	2.5	3.0	2.2	4.3	-	-	3.2	13.7	17.3
3. 3-5	1.4	0.9	1.8	1.6	0.4	1.8	1.5	1.4	0.7	1.3	1.3	-	-	-	6.2	5.9
4. 6-9	1.2	1.0	1.1	1.2	0.3	0.5	1.8	0.8	1.6	0.8	1.4	-	-	-	4.8	14.0
5. 10-19	0.8	0.4	1.2	1.0	0.1	0.4	1.3	0.9	0.5	0.6	1.0	-	-	-	3.5	7.4
6. 20-39	0.6	0.4	0.6	0.7	-	0.7	0.9	0.2	0.6	0.4	0.9	-	-	-	2.7	-
7. 40 or more	0.2	0.3	0.1	0.3	-	0.3	0.3	0.3	-	0.1	0.3	-	-	-	0.9	5.9
Item 1000 Subject A01c N	3259	1526	1615	2477	399	761	937	1045	516	1734	1195	1237	820	411	707	29

IF YOU HAVE NOT TAKEN AMPHETAMINES IN THE LAST TWELVE MONTHS, GO TO Q.B059.

THE FOLLOWING QUESTIONS REFER ONLY TO TAKING AMPHETAMINES WITHOUT A DOCTOR'S ORDERS. IF YOU HAVE NOT DONE THIS IN THE LAST TWELVE MONTHS, GO TO Q.B059

B051: When you used amphetamines during the last year, how often did you use them in each of the following situations?

B051A: When you were alone

	TOTAL	M	F	White	Black	NE	NC	S	W	Yes	No	None	Mari. Only	Few Pills	More Pills	Any Heroin
1. Not at all	43.3	50.8	36.9	43.3	51.7	39.7	37.3	47.2	55.6	41.8	44.8	-	-	77.5	38.5	16.3
2. A few of the times	26.9	27.6	25.4	26.1	13.4	31.6	28.4	23.8	21.7	26.7	27.5	-	-	12.6	29.1	34.9
3. Some of the times	12.5	7.6	15.7	12.6	-	11.9	14.6	12.7	8.4	10.1	13.3	-	-	1.5	13.5	29.5
4. Most of the times	10.1	7.7	12.5	10.1	30.6	8.7	13.1	10.4	4.6	10.8	9.1	-	-	-	12.0	6.9
5. Every time	7.2	6.3	9.3	7.9	4.2	8.0	6.6	5.9	9.8	10.6	5.2	-	-	8.4	6.9	12.4
Item 2800 Subject A05a N★	482	213	229	403	16	113	164	136	68	195	192	-	-	60	396	20

B051B: With just 1 or 2 other people

	TOTAL	M	F	White	Black	NE	NC	S	W	Yes	No	None	Mari. Only	Few Pills	More Pills	Any Heroin
1. Not at all	18.0	19.0	16.7	17.1	34.1	23.2	12.8	14.0	29.4	20.5	17.8	-	-	37.6	13.9	13.4
2. A few of the times	39.8	36.7	43.8	39.8	45.4	44.7	38.9	41.8	29.3	34.4	46.8	-	-	42.4	41.1	16.1
3. Some of the times	21.2	22.4	20.4	21.9	9.6	16.8	25.6	20.3	20.0	22.8	19.3	-	-	1.9	23.2	48.3
4. Most of the times	14.4	17.1	10.4	14.2	3.5	11.1	14.3	16.8	15.4	14.0	12.3	-	-	2.2	16.3	19.3
5. Every time	6.7	4.9	8.7	7.0	7.4	4.2	8.5	7.1	6.0	8.3	3.7	-	-	15.9	5.5	2.9
Item 2810 Subject A05b N★	479	212	227	399	15	115	160	136	68	194	191	-	-	62	392	20

B051C: At a party

	TOTAL	M	F	White	Black	NE	NC	S	W	Yes	No	None	Mari. Only	Few Pills	More Pills	Any Heroin
1. Not at all	39.5	38.9	43.4	40.5	82.5	39.1	36.6	43.1	39.9	45.5	38.5	-	-	72.0	34.6	26.1
2. A few of the times	19.2	16.2	22.2	19.4	11.7	23.0	15.9	15.3	27.9	21.5	16.7	-	-	8.7	22.0	-
3. Some of the times	18.4	17.2	17.6	18.1	-	6.4	26.7	20.3	14.7	16.5	20.8	-	-	3.5	20.8	20.0
4. Most of the times	15.4	19.7	10.6	15.3	-	21.4	15.1	13.0	11.3	9.8	17.7	-	-	3.3	15.6	52.1
5. Every time	7.5	8.1	6.2	6.7	5.8	10.0	5.7	8.3	6.1	6.7	6.3	-	-	12.5	7.1	1.9
Item 2820 Subject A05c N★	473	209	223	394	14	112	158	135	68	191	188	-	-	59	389	20

B051D: When your date or spouse was present

	TOTAL	M	F	White	Black	NE	NC	S	W	Yes	No	None	Mari. Only	Few Pills	More Pills	Any Heroin
1. Not at all	56.2	64.5	49.7	56.6	78.4	60.6	57.6	45.1	67.8	65.5	52.8	-	-	80.0	53.1	33.5
2. A few of the times	20.5	17.6	23.1	19.6	9.6	17.6	19.6	26.1	16.3	17.4	23.1	-	-	10.6	22.3	21.3
3. Some of the times	13.4	11.8	14.6	14.2	3.5	10.8	12.9	19.7	6.5	10.9	14.1	-	-	1.5	14.5	32.4
4. Most of the times	5.3	3.8	6.5	5.2	8.5	7.1	5.7	4.1	3.6	2.3	7.0	-	-	-	6.0	8.1
5. Every time	4.6	2.3	6.1	4.3	-	3.9	4.2	5.0	5.8	4.0	3.0	-	-	7.9	4.2	4.8
Item 2830 Subject A05b N★	473	208	225	393	15	111	157	138	68	192	190	-	-	58	389	20

B051E: When people over age 30 were present

	TOTAL	M	F	White	Black	NE	NC	S	W	Yes	No	None	Mari. Only	Few Pills	More Pills	Any Heroin
1. Not at all	59.8	58.8	63.0	59.6	89.2	63.8	51.0	64.7	63.7	64.1	58.8	-	-	89.6	56.8	12.6
2. A few of the times	21.8	23.6	19.5	21.6	10.8	23.4	24.3	18.6	19.4	18.5	24.4	-	-	5.5	23.4	47.4
3. Some of the times	12.0	12.3	12.1	13.3	-	8.5	18.7	9.1	8.1	11.5	12.5	-	-	3.5	13.4	14.2
4. Most of the times	3.5	3.2	2.4	2.9	-	3.5	3.0	3.0	6.0	1.9	3.3	-	-	-	3.7	11.8
5. Every time	2.9	2.2	3.1	2.6	-	0.7	3.0	4.5	2.8	4.0	0.9	-	-	1.4	2.6	14.0
Item 2840 Subject A05b N★	474	211	224	395	15	111	159	136	68	193	189	-	-	60	390	19

★=excludes respondents for whom question was inappropriate.

QUESTIONNAIRE FORM 1 1983	TOTAL	SEX		RACE		REGION				4YR COLLEGE PLANS		ILLICIT DRUG USE: LIFETIME				
		M	F	White	Black	NE	NC	S	W	Yes	No	None	Mari-juana Only	Few Pills	More Pills	Any Her-oin
N (Weighted No. of Cases):	3448	1611	1667	2555	435	814	974	1118	541	1798	1246	1269	848	428	746	30
% of Weighted Total:	100.0	46.7	48.3	74.1	12.6	23.6	28.3	32.4	15.7	52.2	36.1	36.8	24.6	12.4	21.6	.9
B051F: During the daytime (before 4:00 p.m.)																
1. Not at all	20.4	28.6	12.8	18.9	52.1	21.1	17.5	21.1	24.5	22.6	17.6	-	-	50.4	15.0	12.2
2. A few of the times	26.4	29.0	25.2	27.3	22.0	27.5	17.8	33.8	30.1	24.1	28.5	-	-	29.6	26.1	31.6
3. Some of the times	18.4	17.8	18.7	19.8	-	19.6	24.6	10.9	16.4	21.7	19.2	-	-	3.4	21.0	17.5
4. Most of the times	21.3	15.9	24.3	20.0	14.1	20.0	23.7	22.1	16.1	16.7	20.8	-	-	3.3	24.6	15.2
5. Every time	13.6	8.7	19.0	14.1	11.8	11.7	16.4	12.1	12.9	14.9	13.8	-	-	13.2	13.4	23.6
Item 2850 Subject A05c N★	476	212	224	397	15	111	160	135	69	194	189	-	-	60	392	19
B051G: At your home (or apartment or dorm)																
1. Not at all	36.5	45.4	30.0	37.5	36.0	36.3	29.2	38.5	50.7	35.7	38.3	-	-	67.9	31.7	22.3
2. A few of the times	26.4	28.1	25.1	25.8	25.5	32.1	22.3	28.3	23.1	24.6	28.2	-	-	20.1	28.4	12.6
3. Some of the times	19.1	14.3	21.7	19.6	12.6	13.2	29.4	15.9	10.8	21.0	18.6	-	-	3.6	21.7	19.8
4. Most of the times	11.6	7.3	15.3	10.7	17.4	14.1	12.7	9.6	8.8	9.2	11.5	-	-	-	12.5	30.1
5. Every time	6.4	5.0	7.9	6.4	8.5	4.3	6.5	7.7	6.7	9.6	3.4	-	-	8.4	5.7	15.2
Item 2860 Subject A05c N★	477	213	225	398	15	111	162	135	68	191	193	-	-	58	393	20
B051H: At school																
1. Not at all	33.0	37.7	30.8	33.6	59.9	41.6	27.9	31.8	33.5	38.1	30.4	-	-	78.7	26.1	11.4
2. A few of the times	22.6	25.5	21.2	22.9	4.4	28.6	15.6	24.4	25.4	20.9	26.6	-	-	18.7	23.9	13.4
3. Some of the times	19.6	18.4	19.6	20.6	14.8	14.8	22.1	21.6	17.8	20.0	18.4	-	-	1.5	22.2	30.2
4. Most of the times	17.3	12.0	19.7	15.2	13.5	10.3	25.6	15.7	12.2	14.4	16.3	-	-	-	20.5	11.2
5. Every time	7.5	6.4	8.8	7.8	7.4	4.7	8.7	6.5	11.1	6.6	8.2	-	-	1.1	7.3	33.8
Item 2880 Subject A05c N★	481	215	227	402	15	111	163	138	69	195	193	-	-	60	396	20
B051I: In a car																
1. Not at all	44.2	41.7	49.2	44.3	85.4	47.5	39.1	48.8	41.6	50.9	40.3	-	-	84.1	39.1	7.7
2. A few of the times	26.9	30.7	22.6	27.1	11.1	26.7	27.9	22.3	33.8	28.5	27.7	-	-	8.3	30.5	19.4
3. Some of the times	15.6	15.2	14.9	16.0	3.5	15.8	15.0	18.4	11.1	11.8	18.9	-	-	1.5	16.7	43.1
4. Most of the times	9.8	10.0	9.2	9.1	-	7.3	14.2	7.2	8.9	5.3	10.4	-	-	-	11.1	16.7
5. Every time	3.5	2.4	4.1	3.6	-	2.7	3.7	3.3	4.6	3.5	2.6	-	-	6.2	2.6	13.2
Item 2890 Subject A05c N★	478	214	224	398	15	113	161	138	67	193	190	-	-	61	392	20
B052: How many of the times when you used amphetamines during the last year did you use them along with each of the following drugs– that is, so that their effects overlapped?																
B052A: With alcohol																
1. Not at all	33.2	34.0	36.1	34.1	65.1	32.1	32.5	31.0	40.8	37.7	32.1	-	-	55.3	29.5	22.7
2. A few of the times	25.8	22.5	26.7	24.9	21.3	24.6	21.9	30.6	27.7	26.5	25.6	-	-	20.3	26.7	31.4
3. Some of the times	17.8	16.2	19.6	18.2	13.6	16.9	20.3	16.8	15.2	20.7	15.9	-	-	1.4	16.9	18.5
4. Most of the times	14.7	16.3	11.6	13.8	-	17.9	18.7	9.0	11.0	7.1	18.2	-	-	-	16.9	18.8
5. Every time	8.5	11.0	6.0	9.1	-	8.4	6.6	12.6	5.3	8.1	8.3	-	-	23.0	6.3	8.6
Item 2900 Subject A01h N★	485	216	230	406	16	115	163	137	69	197	193	-	-	63	398	20
B052B: With marijuana																
1. Not at all	43.4	41.2	49.1	45.9	42.2	41.4	43.0	41.9	50.9	52.9	40.8	-	-	89.9	37.3	10.2
2. A few of the times	20.9	20.5	20.9	21.4	22.5	26.0	18.1	19.8	21.2	22.1	20.7	-	-	5.5	23.5	20.6
3. Some of the times	14.8	16.4	13.3	14.1	14.1	15.5	16.6	11.1	16.6	10.4	16.1	-	-	1.5	17.4	6.0
4. Most of the times	15.3	16.2	13.0	14.3	9.6	8.9	19.1	18.5	10.4	12.0	17.3	-	-	-	16.9	33.7
5. Every time	5.6	5.7	3.7	4.4	14.0	8.2	3.2	8.7	0.9	2.5	5.0	-	-	3.1	4.9	29.6
Item 2910 Subject A01h N★	470	211	224	399	15	111	157	136	66	196	187	-	-	61	386	20
B052C: With LSD																
1. Not at all	93.6	91.1	96.9	94.3	100.0	93.3	95.4	90.9	95.0	96.9	95.1	-	-	100.0	94.3	56.7
2. A few of the times	4.0	6.2	1.4	3.7	-	6.3	2.2	5.7	1.6	0.6	3.8	-	-	-	3.5	28.7
3. Some of the times	1.1	1.2	0.8	1.1	-	-	2.0	1.4	-	1.3	0.3	-	-	-	0.8	10.3
4. Most of the times	0.3	0.4	-	0.2	-	0.5	0.5	-	-	0.4	-	-	-	-	0.1	4.2
5. Every time	1.1	1.1	1.0	0.7	-	-	-	2.0	3.4	0.7	0.8	-	-	-	1.3	-
Item 2920 Subject A01h N★	463	207	223	396	14	104	160	133	66	193	186	-	-	60	380	19

★=excludes respondents for whom question was inappropriate.

QUESTIONNAIRE FORM 1 1983	TOTAL	SEX		RACE		REGION				4YR COLLEGE PLANS		ILLICIT DRUG USE: LIFETIME				
		M	F	White	Black	NE	NC	S	W	Yes	No	None	Mari- juana Only	Few Pills	More Pills	Any Her- oin
N (Weighted No. of Cases):	3448	1611	1667	2555	435	814	974	1118	541	1798	1246	1269	848	428	746	30
% of Weighted Total:	100.0	46.7	48.3	74.1	12.6	23.6	28.3	32.4	15.7	52.2	36.1	36.8	24.6	12.4	21.6	.9
B052D: With psychedelics other than LSD																
1. Not at all	93.0	90.0	95.6	93.1	100.0	95.6	93.6	90.1	93.5	94.8	92.2	-	-	100.0	93.7	57.4
2. A few of the times	4.9	7.1	3.3	4.7	-	4.0	4.7	5.7	5.4	3.0	7.1	-	-	-	4.7	25.5
3. Some of the times	1.3	1.7	1.1	1.5	-	-	1.2	2.9	-	0.7	0.6	-	-	-	1.2	7.1
4. Most of the times	0.7	1.3	-	0.7	-	0.5	0.5	0.9	1.1	1.4	-	-	-	-	0.3	10.0
5. Every time	0.1	-	-	-	-	-	-	0.4	-	-	-	-	-	-	0.1	-
Item 2930 Subject A01h N★	463	209	221	395	13	104	159	133	68	191	188	-	-	60	380	20
B053: What have been the most important reasons for your taking amphetamines without a doctor's orders? (Mark all that apply.)																
A. To experiment–to see what it's like	51.2	54.7	47.6	50.4	64.9	55.4	48.5	53.6	46.1	50.3	53.2	-	-	66.4	48.8	51.9
B. To relax or relieve tension	14.2	17.1	12.2	14.1	41.6	7.1	16.9	19.0	10.1	15.2	13.7	-	-	9.2	14.4	26.1
C. To feel good or get high	44.0	51.6	36.2	43.5	41.6	37.6	42.3	49.4	47.9	37.2	48.1	-	-	25.1	46.0	61.8
D. To seek deeper insights and understanding	2.1	3.1	1.3	1.4	17.4	0.4	1.8	3.9	2.0	2.6	1.9	-	-	-	1.8	13.9
E. To have a good time with my friends	25.6	27.1	22.5	24.9	33.9	25.0	21.8	31.6	24.0	27.1	25.3	-	-	21.0	26.3	27.5
F. To fit in with a group I like	4.3	5.0	3.6	3.8	-	0.6	4.1	9.0	1.8	2.4	5.6	-	-	8.2	3.0	18.6
G. To get away from my problems or troubles	8.8	9.6	8.0	8.0	17.4	9.9	4.4	14.3	6.9	4.9	10.8	-	-	3.3	8.4	33.9
H. Because of boredom, nothing else to do	14.6	16.1	12.0	13.1	37.3	10.5	13.1	21.2	11.6	12.8	16.1	-	-	12.8	13.3	44.5
I. Because of anger or frustration	6.7	6.3	6.7	6.2	17.4	2.8	5.1	13.4	3.7	5.0	8.8	-	-	4.9	5.4	36.4
J. To get through the day	36.9	38.2	36.7	37.7	26.9	33.7	40.9	40.1	25.9	30.5	44.1	-	-	10.3	40.7	44.7
K. To increase the effects of some other drug(s)	10.9	15.5	7.1	11.4	27.4	10.3	7.3	16.7	9.1	10.4	11.0	-	-	3.3	10.1	50.7
L. To decrease (offset) the effects of some other drug(s)	3.3	5.2	1.5	2.8	17.4	2.9	3.6	4.2	1.1	5.0	2.1	-	-	1.7	2.8	17.5
M. To stay awake	60.5	56.6	64.7	59.1	73.6	63.3	62.9	57.8	55.5	55.7	63.1	-	-	32.0	63.7	87.9
N. To get more energy	69.5	65.4	75.4	70.3	79.0	68.7	73.9	65.7	67.7	68.3	73.9	-	-	33.1	74.8	77.8
O. To help me lose weight	39.5	12.1	66.1	39.8	73.5	37.3	42.5	43.5	27.8	42.7	39.9	-	-	20.5	42.0	49.4
P. Because I am "hooked"–I feel I have to have them	2.9	1.3	2.8	1.8	9.1	4.1	2.9	2.4	1.7	1.5	2.7	-	-	-	2.7	15.6
Item 2940-3090 Subject A06a N★	475	212	228	404	13	113	162	133	66	194	191	-	-	62	392	20
B054: When you take amphetamines, how high do you usually get?																
1. Not at all high	11.9	13.5	10.3	10.8	34.5	14.3	9.6	12.2	12.3	15.5	8.4	-	-	35.5	7.6	-
2. A little high	33.0	34.6	33.4	35.8	2.9	33.7	31.7	29.7	41.5	30.2	35.3	-	-	38.3	33.0	22.5
3. Moderately high	27.0	30.6	22.2	26.4	24.2	24.1	23.9	34.5	23.5	22.8	31.9	-	-	7.5	29.7	44.3
4. Very high	3.9	3.4	3.6	2.8	13.4	4.0	3.3	4.0	4.9	3.0	4.3	-	-	2.8	3.5	16.4
5. I don't take them to get high	24.2	17.9	30.4	24.1	25.0	23.8	31.5	19.5	17.8	28.4	20.0	-	-	15.8	26.1	16.7
Item 3100 Subject A01e N★	463	211	216	391	15	110	151	135	66	190	185	-	-	63	377	18
B055: When you take amphetamines how long do you usually stay high?																
1. Usually don't get high	22.7	20.2	25.3	22.0	50.0	26.5	21.7	22.4	19.2	30.9	15.4	-	-	44.7	19.0	12.6
2. One to two hours	23.2	30.5	17.0	23.8	2.9	26.2	23.4	17.7	29.0	20.1	23.9	-	-	32.2	22.1	22.8
3. Three to six hours	42.6	40.2	42.5	42.6	26.7	41.1	43.8	45.4	36.4	37.4	46.5	-	-	17.8	46.4	50.7
4. Seven to 24 hours	9.7	6.8	13.5	10.3	13.4	5.5	9.6	12.3	11.8	10.2	11.2	-	-	3.9	10.8	8.6
5. More than 24 hours	1.8	2.3	1.7	1.3	7.0	0.8	1.5	2.2	3.7	1.3	3.0	-	-	1.4	1.7	5.3
Item 3110 Subject A01f N★	478	214	226	403	15	112	163	136	67	194	192	-	-	61	393	20
B056: What amphetamines have you taken during the last year without a doctor's orders? (Mark all that apply.)																
A. Benzedrine	10.9	14.9	6.5	10.2	26.5	9.5	12.0	11.3	10.2	10.2	11.1	-	-	3.1	10.4	45.2
B. Dexedrine	10.2	12.4	8.3	10.0	17.9	8.0	12.8	8.6	10.7	9.1	9.8	-	-	-	10.4	36.8
C. Methedrine	22.8	26.6	18.8	23.4	3.1	22.5	24.6	19.1	26.5	18.6	26.0	-	-	25.0	21.7	39.2
D. Ritalin	1.9	3.7	-	2.0	-	2.2	0.9	2.8	2.0	2.4	0.4	-	-	-	2.0	4.9
E. Preludin	4.5	4.7	2.9	4.1	-	1.3	6.1	6.4	2.0	3.1	3.6	-	-	1.6	4.7	9.3
F. Dexamyl	4.1	4.3	3.7	4.3	-	3.6	5.8	2.8	3.3	4.1	4.3	-	-	-	4.0	17.0
G. Methamphetamine	12.7	10.3	14.5	13.2	7.6	20.1	12.2	9.5	7.7	11.0	14.8	-	-	3.9	13.2	28.7
H. Other	29.7	30.8	26.0	28.6	32.6	23.2	35.0	29.9	27.1	27.5	33.5	-	-	22.5	30.9	22.9
I. Don't know the names of some amphetamines I have used	59.6	53.5	65.9	59.0	70.6	51.6	62.8	64.0	56.2	65.5	56.3	-	-	53.9	60.1	69.8
Item 3120-3200 Subject A01l N★	454	206	216	389	14	107	154	131	62	185	185	-	-	57	376	19

★=excludes respondents for whom question was inappropriate.

QUESTIONNAIRE FORM 1 1983	TOTAL	SEX		RACE		REGION				4YR COLLEGE PLANS		ILLICIT DRUG USE: LIFETIME				
		M	F	White	Black	NE	NC	S	W	Yes	No	None	Mari- juana Only	Few Pills	More Pills	Any Her- oin
N (Weighted No. of Cases):	3448	1611	1667	2555	435	814	974	1118	541	1798	1246	1269	848	428	746	30
% of Weighted Total:	100.0	46.7	48.3	74.1	12.6	23.6	28.3	32.4	15.7	52.2	36.1	36.8	24.6	12.4	21.6	.9
B057: What methods have you used for taking amphetamines? (Mark all that apply.)																
A. By mouth	98.8	97.8	100.0	98.9	100.0	97.4	99.0	99.1	00.0	99.4	98.2	-	-	100.0	98.8	93.9
B. Injection	2.3	2.7	1.4	1.8	8.3	2.2	1.7	3.8	1.1	2.4	1.7	-	-	-	1.3	30.0
C. Other	13.0	15.2	9.0	13.1	-	17.8	9.9	14.2	9.8	10.2	11.9	-	-	1.4	13.2	46.9
Item 3210-3230 Subject A05d N★	_476_	_212_	_227_	_403_	_13_	_114_	_160_	_136_	_67_	_194_	_191_	-	-	_63_	_392_	_19_
B058: Have you ever tried to stop using am- phetamines and found that you couldn't stop?																
1. Yes	4.2	2.2	4.7	3.7	-	6.5	2.0	4.6	4.5	2.5	3.1	-	-	-	4.3	7.0
2. No	95.8	97.8	95.3	96.3	100.0	93.5	98.0	95.4	95.5	97.5	96.9	-	-	100.0	95.7	93.0
Item 3240 Subject A01i N★	_477_	_212_	_228_	_402_	_15_	_113_	_161_	_136_	_67_	_197_	_189_	-	-	_61_	_393_	_20_
B059: Do you think you will be using am- phetamines without a doctor's orders five years from now?																
1. I definitely will	0.9	0.9	0.6	0.7	0.7	0.6	1.1	0.8	1.1	0.6	0.8	0.5	0.5	0.4	2.2	-
2. I probably will	6.7	6.1	6.5	7.0	3.7	8.0	8.1	4.7	6.1	4.5	8.3	1.0	2.1	3.9	23.2	30.9
3. I probably will not	21.3	21.0	21.4	22.0	17.4	21.3	22.0	19.1	24.6	20.8	21.3	12.0	16.2	27.4	39.7	32.8
4. I definitely will not	71.1	72.0	71.4	70.3	78.2	70.1	68.8	75.4	68.2	74.2	69.5	86.6	81.2	68.4	34.9	36.3
Item 3250 Subject A04a N	_3303_	_1550_	_1642_	_2498_	_419_	_760_	_953_	_1064_	_525_	_1758_	_1209_	_1235_	_821_	_418_	_714_	_30_

The next questions are about QUAALUDES (Methaqualone), which are sometimes pre- scribed by doctors. Drugstores are not sup- posed to sell them without a prescription.

Quaaludes are sometimes called: soapers, quads.

B060: On how many occasions (if any) have you taken quaaludes on your own–that is, without a doctor telling you to take them . . .

B060A: . . . in your lifetime?

	TOTAL	M	F	White	Black	NE	NC	S	W	Yes	No	None	Mari- juana Only	Few Pills	More Pills	Any Her- oin
1. 0 occasions	90.6	89.3	92.8	89.5	99.0	91.7	90.0	88.4	94.8	94.1	88.2	100.0	100.0	90.1	66.0	22.5
2. 1-2	4.3	4.9	3.6	5.1	0.3	4.2	3.8	5.7	2.5	2.7	6.0	-	-	9.9	13.3	16.3
3. 3-5	1.5	1.8	1.2	1.8	-	1.6	1.2	1.6	1.7	1.4	1.3	-	-	-	6.8	3.8
4. 6-9	1.2	1.3	0.8	1.3	-	1.0	1.3	1.5	0.6	0.8	0.9	-	-	-	5.1	6.8
5. 10-19	0.8	1.0	0.5	0.9	-	0.4	1.1	1.1	-	0.4	1.4	-	-	-	3.4	5.7
6. 20-39	0.7	0.7	0.6	0.7	0.4	0.5	0.9	0.9	0.1	0.3	0.9	-	-	-	2.4	20.5
7. 40 or more	0.9	1.0	0.5	0.8	0.2	0.6	1.7	0.7	0.2	0.4	1.2	-	-	-	3.0	24.3
Item 1010 Subject A01a N	_3262_	_1538_	_1615_	_2485_	_398_	_752_	_948_	_1050_	_512_	_1736_	_1206_	_1237_	_816_	_422_	_707_	_30_

B060B: . . . during the last 12 months?

	TOTAL	M	F	White	Black	NE	NC	S	W	Yes	No	None	Mari- juana Only	Few Pills	More Pills	Any Her- oin
1. 0 occasions	95.5	94.6	97.1	95.2	99.2	95.5	94.3	94.8	99.1	97.4	94.5	100.0	100.0	97.7	83.2	36.3
2. 1-2	2.0	2.6	1.2	2.2	0.4	2.0	2.2	2.5	0.6	1.2	2.2	-	-	2.3	7.4	13.0
3. 3-5	0.8	1.0	0.4	0.8	-	1.4	0.6	0.8	0.1	0.3	1.0	-	-	-	3.4	5.7
4. 6-9	1.0	1.1	0.6	1.0	-	0.8	1.7	0.9	0.1	0.5	1.4	-	-	-	3.5	24.4
5. 10-19	0.5	0.3	0.6	0.6	-	0.1	0.7	0.8	0.1	0.4	0.6	-	-	-	1.7	11.5
6. 20-39	0.1	0.1	*	-	0.4	0.2	-	0.2	-	-	0.1	-	-	-	0.4	3.4
7. 40 or more	0.1	0.2	0.1	0.2	-	0.1	0.5	-	-	0.2	0.1	-	-	-	0.4	5.7
Item 1020 Subject A01b N	_3252_	_1534_	_1611_	_2476_	_398_	_752_	_944_	_1044_	_512_	_1733_	_1201_	_1237_	_816_	_418_	_701_	_30_

B060C: . . . during the last 30 days?

	TOTAL	M	F	White	Black	NE	NC	S	W	Yes	No	None	Mari- juana Only	Few Pills	More Pills	Any Her- oin
1. 0 occasions	98.6	98.6	98.9	98.6	99.6	98.9	98.3	98.0	99.8	99.3	98.4	100.0	100.0	100.0	94.8	64.3
2. 1-2	0.8	0.9	0.4	0.7	-	0.7	0.9	1.0	0.2	0.3	1.0	-	-	-	2.9	15.9
3. 3-5	0.3	0.3	0.1	0.2	-	0.2	0.5	0.3	-	0.2	-	-	-	-	1.0	7.4
4. 6-9	0.2	*	0.4	0.3	-	0.1	0.2	0.5	-	0.1	0.5	-	-	-	0.7	6.8
5. 10-19	0.1	0.2	0.1	0.1	0.2	0.1	0.1	0.1	-	0.1	0.1	-	-	-	0.4	4.3
6. 20-39	*	-	*	-	0.1	-	-	0.1	-	-	*	-	-	-	0.2	-
7. 40 or more	*	*	-	*	-	0.1	-	-	-	-	-	-	-	-	-	1.4
Item 1030 Subject A01c N	_3254_	_1536_	_1611_	_2477_	_398_	_752_	_944_	_1045_	_512_	_1733_	_1201_	_1237_	_816_	_418_	_703_	_30_

*=less than .05 per cent.   ★=excludes respondents for whom question was inappropriate.

QUESTIONNAIRE FORM 1 1983	TOTAL	SEX		RACE		REGION				4YR COLLEGE PLANS		ILLICIT DRUG USE: LIFETIME				
		M	F	White	Black	NE	NC	S	W	Yes	No	None	Mari-juana Only	Few Pills	More Pills	Any Her-oin
N (Weighted No. of Cases):	3448	1611	1667	2555	435	814	974	1118	541	1798	1246	1269	848	428	746	30
% of Weighted Total:	100.0	46.7	48.3	74.1	12.6	23.6	28.3	32.4	15.7	52.2	36.1	36.8	24.6	12.4	21.6	.9

IF YOU HAVE NOT TAKEN QUAALUDES IN THE LAST TWELVE MONTHS, GO TO Q.B063.

THE FOLLOWING QUESTIONS REFER ONLY TO TAKING QUAALUDES WITHOUT A DOCTOR'S ORDERS. IF YOU HAVE NOT DONE THIS IN THE LAST TWELVE MONTHS, GO TO Q.B063.

B061: When you take quaaludes how high do you usually get?

	TOTAL	M	F	White	Black	NE	NC	S	W	Yes	No	None	Mari-juana Only	Few Pills	More Pills	Any Her-oin
1. Not at all high	4.6	5.1	3.0	4.2	23.4	7.3	5.1	3.1	-	3.1	6.2	-	-	4.3	5.3	-
2. A little high	12.4	11.6	15.9	12.3	-	6.2	12.3	15.6	15.6	16.3	7.8	-	-	23.7	9.3	29.6
3. Moderately high	38.6	32.0	48.8	38.0	76.6	31.8	43.5	39.7	15.6	37.2	40.0	-	-	31.9	40.6	27.4
4. Very high	43.3	50.4	31.1	44.9	-	52.4	39.1	41.7	51.8	42.0	44.9	-	-	40.1	43.6	43.1
5. I don't take them to get high	1.0	0.9	1.2	0.6	-	2.3	-	-	17.0	1.4	1.0	-	-	-	1.3	-
Item 3260 Subject A01e N★	145	80	48	119	2	31	54	55	5	42	68	-	-	9	121	15

B062: When you take quaaludes how long do you usually stay high?

	TOTAL	M	F	White	Black	NE	NC	S	W	Yes	No	None	Mari-juana Only	Few Pills	More Pills	Any Her-oin
1. Usually don't get high	3.9	4.4	1.9	2.9	-	7.0	2.2	4.1	-	3.1	4.8	-	-	4.5	4.4	-
2. One to two hours	14.0	10.9	21.8	15.4	-	4.4	13.9	19.5	15.6	27.3	4.5	-	-	55.9	11.2	12.7
3. Three to six hours	61.8	56.4	63.8	62.4	29.9	79.4	59.3	53.2	72.1	45.4	67.8	-	-	23.8	64.4	62.6
4. Seven to 24 hours	18.2	26.3	9.3	18.0	21.3	9.2	21.7	20.5	12.3	21.9	19.8	-	-	15.8	18.2	18.9
5. More than 24 hours	2.1	2.0	3.1	1.3	48.8	-	2.9	2.8	-	2.4	3.1	-	-	-	1.7	5.8
Item 3270 Subject A01f N★	147	81	49	121	3	32	54	56	5	43	68	-	-	8	121	18

B063: The next questions are about BARBITURATES, which doctors sometimes prescribe to help people relax or get to sleep. Drugstores are not supposed to sell them without a prescription.

Barbiturates are sometimes called: downs, downers, goofballs, yellows, reds, blues, rainbows.

They include the following drugs: Phenobarbital, Seconal, Tuinal, Nembutal, Luminal, Desbutal, Amytal.

Have you ever taken barbiturates because a doctor told you to use them?

	TOTAL	M	F	White	Black	NE	NC	S	W	Yes	No	None	Mari-juana Only	Few Pills	More Pills	Any Her-oin
1. No	92.5	91.4	93.9	91.8	97.4	94.3	91.2	92.0	93.3	92.0	94.0	96.8	95.6	89.7	83.6	73.4
2. Yes, but I had already tried them on my own.	2.1	2.4	1.5	2.1	0.3	0.9	2.8	2.3	2.0	1.1	2.9	-	-	1.5	7.3	24.9
3. Yes, and it was the first time I took any	5.4	6.2	4.7	6.1	2.3	4.8	6.0	5.7	4.7	6.9	3.2	3.2	4.4	8.9	9.1	1.6
Item 3280 Subject A01j N	3179	1486	1591	2422	393	736	925	1024	494	1708	1173	1213	792	408	677	30

B064: On how many occasions (if any) have you taken barbiturates on your own–that is, without a doctor telling you to take them . . .

B064A: . . . in your lifetime?

	TOTAL	M	F	White	Black	NE	NC	S	W	Yes	No	None	Mari-juana Only	Few Pills	More Pills	Any Her-oin
1. 0 occasions	92.2	92.0	93.4	91.9	97.0	93.2	90.8	92.5	92.7	94.9	90.6	100.0	100.0	93.3	70.4	25.6
2. 1-2	3.0	3.1	2.6	3.0	1.4	3.2	4.0	1.9	3.0	2.2	3.3	-	-	6.7	9.9	2.0
3. 3-5	1.4	1.4	1.2	1.6	0.3	1.2	1.6	1.5	1.4	0.9	1.8	-	-	6.3	10.7	-
4. 6-9	0.8	0.8	0.7	0.9	0.2	0.8	0.4	0.7	1.5	0.4	0.8	-	-	3.1	11.6	-
5. 10-19	0.8	0.8	0.7	0.7	0.3	0.6	0.6	1.3	0.3	0.7	0.7	-	-	3.4	4.0	-
6. 20-39	0.5	0.7	0.1	0.5	0.2	0.7	0.8	0.3	0.1	0.3	0.7	-	-	2.3	2.4	-
7. 40 or more	1.4	1.3	1.2	1.4	0.6	0.4	1.7	1.9	1.0	0.6	2.1	-	-	4.5	43.7	-
Item 1040 Subject A01a N	3169	1492	1576	2420	382	730	925	1019	495	1710	1170	1218	795	405	671	30

★=excludes respondents for whom question was inappropriate.

QUESTIONNAIRE FORM 1 1983	TOTAL	SEX		RACE		REGION				4YR COLLEGE PLANS		ILLICIT DRUG USE: LIFETIME				
		M	F	White	Black	NE	NC	S	W	Yes	No	None	Mari- juana Only	Few Pills	More Pills	Any Her- oin
N (Weighted No. of Cases):	3448	1611	1667	2555	435	814	974	1118	541	1798	1246	1269	848	428	746	30
% of Weighted Total:	100.0	46.7	48.3	74.1	12.6	23.6	28.3	32.4	15.7	52.2	36.1	36.8	24.6	12.4	21.6	.9

B064B: . . . during the last 12 months?

1. 0 occasions	96.0	95.9	96.7	95.8	98.7	96.7	95.3	95.6	97.1	97.6	94.9	100.0	100.0	98.7	84.3	43.2
2. 1-2	1.5	1.7	1.2	1.6	0.6	1.4	2.0	1.3	1.4	0.9	1.8	-	-	1.3	6.4	4.3
3. 3-5	0.7	0.7	0.7	0.8	-	1.0	0.3	1.0	0.3	0.3	1.1	-	-	-	2.9	9.7
4. 6-9	0.6	0.3	0.5	0.4	-	0.5	0.6	0.4	1.0	0.3	0.4	-	-	-	2.6	2.7
5. 10-19	0.6	0.8	0.4	0.6	0.7	0.3	1.0	0.5	0.3	0.5	0.8	-	-	-	2.4	7.7
6. 20-39	0.3	0.2	0.3	0.4	-	-	0.5	0.4	*	0.2	0.3	-	-	-	0.7	12.3
7. 40 or more	0.4	0.5	0.2	0.4	-	0.1	0.3	0.8	-	0.1	0.7	-	-	-	0.8	20.2
Item 1050 Subject A01b N	3162	1487	1575	2414	382	730	921	1017	494	1706	1167	1218	795	403	666	30

B064C: . . . during the last 30 days?

1. 0 occasions	97.8	98.1	98.0	97.7	99.3	98.7	97.9	96.7	98.7	98.9	97.0	100.0	100.0	99.4	91.7	61.4
2. 1-2	1.0	0.8	1.0	1.1	0.4	0.8	0.7	1.4	1.1	0.7	1.0	-	-	0.6	4.0	9.9
3. 3-5	0.5	0.4	0.4	0.4	-	0.2	0.6	1.0	-	0.2	0.7	-	-	-	2.2	6.1
4. 6-9	0.2	0.2	0.2	0.3	-	0.1	0.5	*	0.1	0.1	0.3	-	-	-	0.9	3.2
5. 10-19	0.3	0.2	0.3	0.3	0.2	0.1	0.1	0.6	*	0.1	0.5	-	-	-	0.9	9.2
6. 20-39	*	-	0.1	0.1	-	-	-	0.1	-	-	0.1	-	-	-	-	4.5
7. 40 or more	0.1	0.3	-	0.2	-	0.1	0.2	0.2	-	-	0.3	-	-	-	0.3	5.7
Item 1060 Subject A01c N	3164	1489	1575	2416	382	730	921	1019	494	1706	1168	1218	795	403	668	30

IF YOU HAVE NOT TAKEN BARBITURATES IN THE LAST TWELVE MONTHS, GO TO Q.B072.

THE FOLLOWING QUESTIONS REFER ONLY TO TAKING BARBITURATES WITHOUT A DOCTOR'S ORDERS. IF YOU HAVE NOT DONE THIS IN THE LAST TWELVE MONTHS, GO TO Q.B072.

B065: When you used barbiturates during the last year, how often did you use them in each of the following situations?

B065A: When you were alone

1. Not at all	37.7	44.3	38.1	39.0	60.3	41.2	45.5	33.6	18.4	39.7	37.4	-	-	56.0	38.0	9.2
2. A few of the times	30.8	28.5	33.1	28.7	39.7	27.4	29.5	38.3	15.8	22.0	38.0	-	-	8.8	35.3	20.8
3. Some of the times	18.6	17.4	16.7	19.8	-	24.7	15.5	22.0	4.7	20.2	16.1	-	-	14.8	56.4	
4. Most of the times	4.1	7.9	0.7	5.5	-	5.0	3.5	4.7	1.8	1.6	7.4	-	-	-	3.0	13.6
5. Every time	8.8	2.0	11.5	7.0	-	1.7	6.1	1.4	59.2	16.4	1.0	-	-	35.3	8.9	
Item 3290 Subject A05a N ★	124	59	51	92	8	25	42	44	12	36	60	-	-	6	98	15

B065B: With just 1 or 2 other people

1. Not at all	30.5	29.8	34.8	28.9	62.4	30.1	34.1	20.6	58.0	51.0	25.2	-	-	73.7	28.9	7.7
2. A few of the times	30.2	38.0	20.9	28.3	37.6	49.2	29.6	22.1	21.8	15.2	41.5	-	-	26.3	31.5	30.4
3. Some of the times	23.6	17.6	27.2	24.2	-	15.0	20.3	36.1	5.3	13.3	25.0	-	-	-	21.4	52.6
4. Most of the times	8.5	9.4	7.6	10.1	-	5.7	11.6	8.1	4.6	13.9	5.7	-	-	-	9.2	9.2
5. Every time	7.2	5.2	9.5	8.5	-	-	4.4	13.1	10.3	6.6	2.5	-	-	-	9.0	-
Item 3300 Subject A05b N ★	125	60	50	93	7	25	44	45	11	36	59	-	-	6	100	15

B065C: At a party

1. Not at all	41.1	40.6	47.4	43.2	46.4	36.2	40.8	35.5	76.3	56.5	34.9	-	-	100.0	41.1	7.2
2. A few of the times	16.2	15.0	15.9	15.9	14.6	23.4	22.1	9.9	2.0	11.6	19.4	-	-	-	18.2	13.4
3. Some of the times	18.6	20.4	15.4	16.5	23.0	19.6	12.5	25.9	11.4	9.7	24.6	-	-	-	20.1	20.7
4. Most of the times	17.2	17.3	14.5	17.5	-	20.8	12.9	23.7	-	4.2	19.5	-	-	-	14.6	42.6
5. Every time	6.8	6.7	6.8	6.8	16.0	-	11.7	5.0	10.3	18.0	1.6	-	-	-	5.9	16.2
Item 3310 Subject A05c N ★	126	61	50	94	7	25	45	45	11	36	61	-	-	6	100	17

B065D: When your date or spouse was present

1. Not at all	60.1	66.5	55.2	55.4	100.0	56.8	65.2	50.9	85.1	75.7	54.8	-	-	85.8	65.0	12.9
2. A few of the times	12.5	11.4	11.9	12.6	-	21.6	14.6	8.5	-	6.3	15.6	-	-	14.2	10.4	27.1
3. Some of the times	12.9	12.1	13.3	15.0	-	15.3	11.3	15.1	4.6	6.6	16.3	-	-	-	13.9	14.5
4. Most of the times	7.8	5.1	10.9	9.2	-	6.3	4.2	14.0	-	7.8	5.4	-	-	-	6.6	19.3
5. Every time	6.7	4.8	8.7	7.8	-	-	4.8	11.5	10.3	3.6	7.9	-	-	-	4.1	26.1
Item 3320 Subject A05b N ★	125	60	50	93	7	25	44	45	11	35	61	-	-	6	99	17

*=less than .05 per cent.   ★=excludes respondents for whom question was inappropriate.

QUESTIONNAIRE FORM 1 1983	TOTAL	SEX		RACE		REGION				4YR COLLEGE PLANS		ILLICIT DRUG USE: LIFETIME				
		M	F	White	Black	NE	NC	S	W	Yes	No	None	Mari-juana Only	Few Pills	More Pills	Any Her-oin
N (Weighted No. of Cases):	3448	1611	1667	2555	435	814	974	1118	541	1798	1246	1269	848	428	746	30
% of Weighted Total:	100.0	46.7	48.3	74.1	12.6	23.6	28.3	32.4	15.7	52.2	36.1	36.8	24.6	12.4	21.6	.9
B065E: When people over age 30 were present																
1. Not at all	65.0	64.9	67.3	61.2	86.9	65.0	70.9	54.3	84.5	74.5	66.1	-	-	92.7	68.6	23.0
2. A few of the times	12.1	14.2	5.1	11.9	-	13.4	11.4	15.1	-	7.9	9.7	-	-	-	10.3	31.2
3. Some of the times	14.7	15.4	15.8	18.6	-	16.2	14.4	17.8	-	10.6	19.2	-	-	-	12.6	37.2
4. Most of the times	4.7	4.2	6.8	4.7	13.1	3.8	3.4	6.5	5.3	6.0	3.8	-	-	-	4.6	8.7
5. Every time	3.5	1.3	4.9	3.5	-	1.7	-	6.3	10.3	1.0	1.2	-	-	7.3	4.0	-
Item 3330 Subject A05b N★	124	59	50	92	7	25	44	44	11	34	61	-	-	6	99	15
B065F: During the daytime (before 4:00 p.m.)																
1. Not at all	43.5	46.7	47.6	42.0	88.7	51.1	43.2	43.8	26.5	56.8	36.8	-	-	79.3	42.4	24.8
2. A few of the times	22.5	27.6	17.0	24.2	11.3	25.8	31.3	10.8	28.2	17.4	28.1	-	-	-	27.2	7.7
3. Some of the times	18.2	12.4	24.3	19.1	-	8.0	11.9	31.8	9.9	9.4	27.0	-	-	-	17.7	31.6
4. Most of the times	5.2	5.5	1.9	4.5	-	15.0	1.8	4.4	-	2.3	2.8	-	-	-	2.2	25.6
5. Every time	10.6	7.8	9.3	10.2	-	-	11.8	9.2	35.3	14.1	5.3	-	-	20.7	10.5	10.3
Item 3340 Subject A05c N★	124	59	50	93	6	24	44	45	11	35	60	-	-	6	98	17
B065G: At your home (or apartment or dorm)																
1. Not at all	35.6	36.7	42.4	36.3	69.7	35.1	42.3	33.7	18.5	42.9	36.9	-	-	58.3	34.6	19.1
2. A few of the times	20.6	24.2	14.4	17.2	30.3	31.9	23.2	16.1	4.4	9.9	26.9	-	-	23.8	21.6	18.2
3. Some of the times	19.9	19.3	15.2	20.6	-	9.6	14.8	32.7	11.3	13.8	21.6	-	-	-	21.1	24.2
4. Most of the times	7.2	10.5	5.5	9.1	-	4.8	6.0	7.2	17.2	12.4	5.1	-	-	-	4.4	28.3
5. Every time	16.7	9.3	22.6	16.7	-	18.6	13.7	10.3	48.7	21.0	9.4	-	-	18.0	18.3	10.3
Item 3350 Subject A05c N★	126	60	51	94	7	25	44	45	12	36	61	-	-	6	100	17
B065H: At school																
1. Not at all	50.7	44.4	60.2	48.2	75.6	52.3	53.0	43.4	67.4	65.2	48.5	-	-	79.3	55.6	-
2. A few of the times	24.1	33.8	11.4	25.5	9.9	33.6	26.9	20.2	6.7	11.1	30.5	-	-	-	24.8	33.2
3. Some of the times	16.0	13.4	20.4	17.8	14.6	10.6	10.9	26.6	4.6	14.0	16.3	-	-	-	11.4	52.6
4. Most of the times	3.6	3.9	3.4	3.1	-	3.4	3.1	5.2	-	3.3	4.7	-	-	-	3.2	8.0
5. Every time	5.7	4.4	4.6	5.4	-	-	6.1	4.7	21.2	6.5	-	-	-	20.7	4.9	6.1
Item 3360 Subject A05c N★	125	60	50	93	7	25	44	45	11	35	61	-	-	6	99	17
B065I: In a car																
1. Not at all	50.2	47.2	59.2	48.5	86.9	51.6	58.3	34.6	78.8	65.1	44.5	-	-	79.3	53.6	8.6
2. A few of the times	20.0	20.6	16.5	19.8	13.1	33.9	19.9	17.1	-	21.5	21.6	-	-	-	21.5	22.5
3. Some of the times	19.2	19.4	15.0	20.7	-	11.6	13.0	33.9	-	7.8	22.3	-	-	-	15.2	53.8
4. Most of the times	8.0	12.7	4.9	8.6	-	2.9	8.7	12.2	-	2.3	10.0	-	-	-	7.6	15.1
5. Every time	2.6	-	4.3	2.3	-	-	-	2.1	21.2	3.4	1.6	-	-	20.7	2.1	-
Item 3380 Subject A05c N★	125	60	50	93	7	25	44	45	11	35	61	-	-	6	99	17
B066: How many of the times when you used barbiturates during the last year did you use them along with each of the following drugs– that is, so that their effects overlapped?																
B066A: With alcohol																
1. Not at all	35.6	39.4	33.5	33.1	53.1	31.5	41.4	25.6	62.2	44.1	31.3	-	-	79.3	34.6	11.9
2. A few of the times	20.4	15.0	28.2	19.3	33.8	33.6	21.2	14.0	11.8	7.5	29.5	-	-	-	23.4	14.4
3. Some of the times	17.4	18.0	14.2	18.2	13.1	13.8	14.7	23.5	12.5	14.4	19.2	-	-	-	19.2	16.5
4. Most of the times	13.3	12.3	15.6	14.9	-	8.2	19.2	12.8	2.1	20.4	13.0	-	-	-	10.6	36.6
5. Every time	13.3	15.3	8.6	14.5	-	13.0	3.6	24.1	11.4	13.7	7.0	-	-	20.7	12.2	20.6
Item 3390 Subject A01h N★	124	61	51	95	7	25	45	43	11	37	61	-	-	6	98	17
B066B: With marijuana																
1. Not at all	35.0	32.5	38.3	31.5	64.8	42.9	37.4	20.4	67.2	42.5	30.5	-	-	100.0	33.4	11.4
2. A few of the times	17.2	18.8	16.5	17.6	-	24.9	20.4	11.8	6.3	8.8	25.8	-	-	-	20.0	10.0
3. Some of the times	12.7	9.8	14.4	12.8	18.4	8.2	19.7	10.4	-	6.8	16.4	-	-	-	15.0	6.1
4. Most of the times	23.4	26.7	20.8	25.8	16.8	10.4	19.2	34.7	26.5	32.2	19.4	-	-	-	22.4	40.6
5. Every time	11.8	12.2	10.0	12.4	-	13.6	3.3	22.7	-	9.7	7.9	-	-	-	9.2	31.9
Item 3400 Subject A01h N★	118	59	48	91	6	23	45	41	9	36	57	-	-	6	93	17

★=excludes respondents for whom question was inappropriate.

QUESTIONNAIRE FORM 1 1983	TOTAL	SEX		RACE		REGION				4YR COLLEGE PLANS		ILLICIT DRUG USE: LIFETIME				
		M	F	White	Black	NE	NC	S	W	Yes	No	None	Marijuana Only	Few Pills	More Pills	Any Heroin
N (Weighted No. of Cases):	3448	1611	1667	2555	435	814	974	1118	541	1798	1246	1269	848	428	746	30
% of Weighted Total:	100.0	46.7	48.3	74.1	12.6	23.6	28.3	32.4	15.7	52.2	36.1	36.8	24.6	12.4	21.6	.9

B066C: With LSD

1. Not at all	87.0	83.8	91.3	86.2	81.6	96.3	84.6	82.7	94.5	82.7	91.5	-	-	100.0	90.5	62.0
2. A few of the times	5.7	6.7	5.6	6.0	18.4	1.6	6.5	8.3	-	10.2	3.1	-	-	-	4.3	15.7
3. Some of the times	3.9	3.7	3.2	4.0	-	-	5.2	4.5	5.5	6.2	2.6	-	-	-	0.9	22.3
4. Most of the times	1.7	3.3	-	2.1	-	-	3.7	0.9	-	1.0	2.8	-	-	-	2.1	-
5. Every time	1.7	2.6	-	1.7	-	2.1	-	3.7	-	-	-	-	-	-	2.2	-
Item 3410 Subject A01h N★	117	60	47	92	6	23	43	41	9	36	57	-	-	5	92	17

B066D: With psychedelics other than LSD

1. Not at all	86.6	83.2	91.5	86.6	81.6	93.2	94.8	74.7	86.2	84.2	91.4	-	-	100.0	91.0	55.8
2. A few of the times	8.5	9.7	5.4	8.0	18.4	3.7	3.3	15.3	13.8	10.2	6.1	-	-	-	6.5	23.2
3. Some of the times	2.0	1.3	3.1	2.5	-	-	1.9	3.5	-	2.2	2.5	-	-	-	-	13.8
4. Most of the times	1.0	2.0	-	1.3	-	-	-	2.8	-	3.3	-	-	-	-	-	7.2
5. Every time	1.9	3.8	-	1.7	-	3.1	-	3.6	-	-	-	-	-	-	2.4	-
Item 3420 Subject A01h N★	117	60	48	92	6	23	43	42	9	36	59	-	-	5	93	17

B066E: With amphetamines

1. Not at all	77.9	80.1	76.7	77.1	84.2	87.9	89.6	56.5	94.0	75.3	81.9	-	-	100.0	82.4	41.8
2. A few of the times	13.5	10.7	16.9	13.4	15.8	1.6	8.6	27.0	6.0	18.1	10.1	-	-	-	11.7	29.9
3. Some of the times	6.1	4.1	6.4	6.1	-	10.5	1.8	9.3	-	2.3	8.0	-	-	-	2.7	28.3
4. Most of the times	-	-	-	-	-	-	-	-	-	-	-	-	-	-	-	-
5. Every time	2.6	5.0	-	3.3	-	-	-	7.3	-	4.4	-	-	-	-	3.2	-
Item 3430 Subject A01h N★	119	61	47	91	7	24	44	42	9	35	59	-	-	5	95	17

B066F: With quaaludes

1. Not at all	76.6	73.7	79.8	75.1	70.0	80.9	83.3	62.9	94.5	77.9	78.8	-	-	100.0	84.5	21.1
2. A few of the times	13.8	18.5	8.6	14.5	30.0	14.1	9.7	21.2	-	11.6	14.0	-	-	-	9.7	43.8
3. Some of the times	5.1	2.0	9.0	6.0	-	-	1.2	12.2	5.5	3.3	7.3	-	-	-	1.6	27.4
4. Most of the times	1.1	2.1	-	1.4	-	-	2.9	-	-	3.6	-	-	-	-	1.4	-
5. Every time	3.4	3.7	2.7	3.0	-	5.0	2.9	3.7	-	3.6	-	-	-	-	2.9	7.7
Item 3440 Subject A01h N★	119	61	48	92	7	24	44	41	9	36	59	-	-	5	94	17

B067: What are the most important reasons for your taking barbiturates without a doctor's orders? (Mark all that apply.)

A. To experiment–to see what it's like	40.9	44.9	32.0	38.6	31.7	25.5	34.3	57.1	36.4	35.4	46.6	-	-	12.9	40.9	48.0
B. To relax or relieve tension	69.0	64.0	76.3	68.5	77.4	61.1	78.8	65.4	59.3	69.4	79.6	-	-	46.2	70.3	67.3
C. To feel good or get high	58.0	59.1	57.1	59.8	41.2	37.1	63.3	65.8	49.3	38.2	67.2	-	-	-	56.9	79.9
D. To seek deeper insights and understanding	7.3	9.2	-	4.6	18.6	18.0	2.9	6.9	4.8	-	6.2	-	-	-	5.4	20.6
E. To have a good time with my friends	32.9	38.0	30.6	33.3	41.2	27.5	29.9	45.8	4.8	22.4	40.7	-	-	-	31.0	52.7
F. To fit in with a group I like	5.8	8.8	3.8	5.2	-	3.2	2.9	11.7	-	-	8.8	-	-	-	3.3	22.2
G. To get away from my problems or troubles	34.2	32.4	38.0	36.6	18.6	34.3	24.2	43.1	39.9	21.9	47.4	-	-	58.3	28.2	63.6
H. Because of boredom, nothing else to do	16.1	13.7	15.0	16.4	-	9.5	13.7	21.6	18.1	8.9	21.1	-	-	-	14.1	32.0
I. Because of anger or frustration	18.7	20.9	17.2	18.7	18.6	10.8	5.8	32.2	35.7	10.1	28.3	-	-	-	14.7	47.7
J. To get through the day	13.0	7.8	17.2	10.9	20.6	3.4	4.1	29.3	5.5	12.3	14.9	-	-	-	4.9	64.3
K. To increase the effects of some other drug(s)	20.6	22.6	16.8	20.6	39.2	13.3	16.5	29.6	17.3	13.7	23.8	-	-	-	16.6	49.7
L. To decrease (offset) the effects of some other drug(s)	9.0	12.7	5.3	8.7	20.6	12.4	3.2	15.5	-	14.3	7.0	-	-	-	6.6	25.2
M. To get to sleep	54.6	51.4	60.3	55.8	58.8	51.2	45.1	64.0	63.6	48.8	59.2	-	-	37.0	51.5	77.7
N. To relieve physical pain	45.5	41.8	50.6	46.9	53.1	37.3	53.1	46.2	28.5	39.8	55.0	-	-	9.8	40.8	83.0
O. Because I am "hooked"–I have to have them	5.7	4.6	5.3	4.6	18.6	6.4	2.9	9.6	-	3.5	7.0	-	-	-	1.5	32.2
Item 3450-3580 Subject A06a N★	119	57	49	93	5	22	44	42	11	36	57	-	-	4	98	17

B068: When you take barbiturates how high do you usually get?

1. Not at all high	13.5	9.7	12.3	10.6	-	23.0	12.9	7.7	17.7	5.7	12.9	-	-	28.8	13.1	4.2
2. A little high	20.3	23.3	15.5	20.5	34.5	15.9	26.1	21.4	-	36.5	7.9	-	-	-	20.5	28.6
3. Moderately high	38.7	44.3	35.6	41.7	41.2	24.9	48.4	39.2	26.7	27.1	48.4	-	-	-	41.6	31.3
4. Very high	16.8	15.4	20.3	16.0	-	23.3	4.1	25.8	19.9	9.9	23.8	-	-	-	15.2	33.6
5. I don't take them to get high	10.6	7.2	16.3	11.3	24.3	12.9	8.5	5.8	35.8	20.8	7.0	-	-	71.2	9.6	2.3
Item 3590 Subject A01e N★	120	57	50	94	5	24	44	42	10	36	58	-	-	4	96	17

★=excludes respondents for whom question was inappropriate.

QUESTIONNAIRE FORM 1 1983	TOTAL	SEX		RACE		REGION				4YR COLLEGE PLANS		ILLICIT DRUG USE: LIFETIME				
		M	F	White	Black	NE	NC	S	W	Yes	No	None	Mari- juana Only	Few Pills	More Pills	Any Her- oin
N (Weighted No. of Cases):	3448	1611	1667	2555	435	814	974	1118	541	1798	1246	1269	848	428	746	30
% of Weighted Total:	100.0	46.7	48.3	74.1	12.6	23.6	28.3	32.4	15.7	52.2	36.1	36.8	24.6	12.4	21.6	.9
B069: When you take barbiturates how long do you usually stay high?																
1. Usually don't get high	21.9	16.5	26.6	20.6	24.3	29.5	19.5	13.5	48.6	27.2	18.5	-	-	83.7	21.2	4.2
2. One to two hours	20.5	19.7	19.2	19.1	55.1	20.6	25.3	18.8	7.0	23.5	13.7	-	-	16.3	20.9	22.4
3. Three to six hours	40.4	48.9	35.4	46.8	-	37.1	45.8	40.3	26.4	31.4	52.7	-	-	-	40.9	55.7
4. Seven to 24 hours	15.2	14.9	14.2	12.2	-	12.8	9.4	22.0	18.1	15.0	12.9	-	-	-	17.0	11.3
5. More than 24 hours	1.9	-	4.6	1.3	20.6	-	-	5.5	-	2.8	2.2	-	-	-	-	6.3
Item 3600 Subject A01f N★	121	57	51	95	5	24	44	42	11	37	58	-	-	4	97	17
B070: What barbiturates have you taken during the last year without a doctor's orders? (Mark all that apply.)																
A. Phenobarbital	25.2	30.0	24.4	27.5	39.2	23.0	25.1	27.7	20.6	15.9	34.1	-	-	-	21.0	58.7
B. Seconal	20.6	13.9	25.3	21.8	-	24.3	19.1	19.0	25.5	20.1	17.9	-	-	-	16.0	54.6
C. Tuinal	9.3	6.2	9.8	8.9	-	5.4	11.4	10.3	4.9	8.5	9.3	-	-	-	7.7	22.2
D. Nembutal	8.5	12.2	6.5	7.7	20.6	8.9	5.3	12.3	5.6	4.4	14.9	-	-	-	5.2	30.9
E. Luminal	11.9	8.7	11.7	9.3	41.2	24.3	13.3	7.1	-	4.1	13.2	-	-	-	10.3	25.6
F. Desbutal	7.8	10.3	4.7	7.6	20.6	7.6	5.5	12.2	-	6.0	7.4	-	-	-	1.2	49.8
G. Amytal	10.6	12.5	9.3	10.9	18.6	8.2	17.6	4.7	10.5	6.3	16.4	-	-	-	10.3	15.7
H. Adrenocal	6.3	6.7	6.4	5.3	39.2	6.4	2.2	11.8	-	2.8	8.3	-	-	-	4.9	16.6
I. Other	39.8	46.1	36.5	40.1	52.4	39.1	39.8	41.4	34.7	28.5	48.2	-	-	9.8	42.8	32.8
J. Don't know the names of some that I have used	58.5	55.7	67.0	61.2	77.4	48.4	51.6	68.0	70.2	69.4	57.9	-	-	90.2	55.5	64.6
Item 3610-3700 Subject A01l N★	120	57	51	95	5	22	44	44	10	37	58	-	-	4	98	17
B071: Have you ever tried to stop using barbiturates and found that you couldn't stop?																
1. Yes	8.9	8.6	4.9	3.9	18.6	17.6	-	14.1	4.8	3.2	10.8	-	-	-	6.8	15.2
2. No	91.1	91.4	95.1	96.1	81.4	82.4	00.0	85.9	95.2	96.8	89.2	-	-	100.0	93.2	84.8
Item 3710 Subject A01i N★	122	57	51	95	5	24	44	43	11	37	58	-	-	4	98	17
B072: Do you think you will be using barbiturates without a doctor's prescription five years from now?																
1. I definitely will	1.0	1.1	0.8	0.8	1.0	0.5	1.0	1.2	1.5	0.8	1.0	0.5	0.4	0.4	2.3	8.9
2. I probably will	2.0	2.0	1.6	1.9	1.7	2.4	2.5	1.4	2.0	1.1	2.6	0.6	0.4	0.2	7.5	11.1
3. I probably will not	17.5	18.2	16.9	18.2	12.8	17.6	19.7	14.6	19.3	16.4	18.5	9.1	13.0	22.4	35.3	41.8
4. I definitely will not	79.4	78.8	80.7	79.0	84.6	79.5	76.8	82.8	77.2	81.7	77.9	89.8	86.2	77.0	55.0	38.2
Item 3720 Subject A04a N	3272	1535	1637	2487	412	746	950	1055	521	1763	1198	1238	815	414	692	30

The next questions are about TRANQUILIZERS, which doctors sometimes prescribe to calm people down, quiet their nerves, or relax their muscles.

They include the following drugs: Librium, Valium, Miltown, Equanil, Meprobamate, Serax, Atarax, Tranxene, Vistaril.

	TOTAL	M	F	White	Black	NE	NC	S	W	Yes	No	None	Mari- juana Only	Few Pills	More Pills	Any Her- oin
B073: Have you ever taken tranquilizers because a doctor told you to use them?																
1. No	87.1	87.6	86.8	85.6	92.6	89.2	88.2	84.9	86.6	87.3	88.1	93.2	90.8	79.2	77.1	58.7
2. Yes, but I had already tried them on my own.	1.9	1.6	1.9	2.0	0.5	1.5	2.0	2.2	1.6	1.6	1.7	-	-	1.5	6.4	32.1
3. Yes, and it was the first time I took any	11.0	10.8	11.3	12.4	6.9	9.4	9.8	12.9	11.8	11.2	10.3	6.8	9.2	19.4	16.5	9.2
Item 3730 Subject A01j N	3243	1526	1623	2472	408	750	938	1050	505	1742	1197	1235	811	417	690	30

B074: On how many occasions (if any) have you taken tranquilizers on your own—that is, without a doctor telling you to take them . . .

★=excludes respondents for whom question was inappropriate.

QUESTIONNAIRE FORM 1 1983	TOTAL	SEX		RACE		REGION				4YR COLLEGE PLANS		ILLICIT DRUG USE: LIFETIME				
		M	F	White	Black	NE	NC	S	W	Yes	No	None	Mari-juana Only	Few Pills	More Pills	Any Her-oin
N (Weighted No. of Cases):	3448	1611	1667	2555	435	814	974	1118	541	1798	1246	1269	848	428	746	30
% of Weighted Total:	100.0	46.7	48.3	74.1	12.6	23.6	28.3	32.4	15.7	52.2	36.1	36.8	24.6	12.4	21.6	.9

B074A: . . . in your lifetime?

	TOTAL	M	F	White	Black	NE	NC	S	W	Yes	No	None	Mari-juana Only	Few Pills	More Pills	Any Her-oin
1. 0 occasions	89.7	89.5	90.4	88.6	95.7	89.7	89.3	90.3	89.0	92.0	88.8	100.0	100.0	79.1	67.1	28.4
2. 1-2	5.3	5.4	5.1	5.8	2.7	5.1	5.1	5.1	6.4	4.4	5.4	-	-	20.9	11.8	11.0
3. 3-5	1.9	2.0	1.6	2.2	0.2	2.4	1.7	1.8	1.7	1.2	2.4	-	-	-	8.7	6.3
4. 6-9	0.9	0.9	0.8	1.1	0.6	0.9	0.9	0.7	1.7	1.0	0.8	-	-	-	4.2	5.7
5. 10-19	0.9	0.6	1.1	0.9	0.3	0.8	1.1	1.0	0.6	0.8	0.6	-	-	-	3.8	14.5
6. 20-39	0.6	0.6	0.6	0.7	0.3	0.5	0.9	0.5	0.4	0.3	0.9	-	-	-	2.1	15.4
7. 40 or more	0.7	1.0	0.4	0.7	0.2	0.6	1.0	0.6	0.2	0.4	1.0	-	-	-	2.3	18.7
Item 1070 Subject A01a N	3216	1518	1603	2464	388	742	933	1034	507	1734	1185	1233	805	416	682	30

B074B: . . . during the last 12 months?

	TOTAL	M	F	White	Black	NE	NC	S	W	Yes	No	None	Mari-juana Only	Few Pills	More Pills	Any Her-oin
1. 0 occasions	95.3	95.8	95.3	94.8	98.8	94.5	95.0	95.7	95.8	96.5	95.1	100.0	100.0	94.6	83.2	45.7
2. 1-2	2.5	2.3	2.4	2.7	0.4	3.5	2.2	2.0	2.6	1.8	2.5	-	-	5.4	7.9	12.3
3. 3-5	0.9	0.5	1.1	1.0	0.1	1.3	0.9	0.9	0.5	0.6	0.8	-	-	-	4.0	7.9
4. 6-9	0.3	0.4	0.3	0.4	0.1	-	0.4	0.5	0.4	0.3	0.5	-	-	-	1.2	6.6
5. 10-19	0.4	0.3	0.5	0.5	0.3	0.3	0.5	0.3	0.5	0.4	0.2	-	-	-	1.6	9.2
6. 20-39	0.4	0.5	0.3	0.5	-	0.1	0.9	0.3	-	0.1	0.7	-	-	-	1.2	17.1
7. 40 or more	0.2	0.3	0.1	0.1	0.2	0.2	0.1	0.2	0.2	0.1	0.3	-	-	-	0.8	1.3
Item 1080 Subject A01b N	3211	1514	1601	2459	387	741	931	1031	507	1730	1183	1233	805	414	678	30

B074C: . . . during the last 30 days?

	TOTAL	M	F	White	Black	NE	NC	S	W	Yes	No	None	Mari-juana Only	Few Pills	More Pills	Any Her-oin
1. 0 occasions	98.1	98.4	98.1	98.0	99.5	98.2	97.7	98.2	98.9	98.8	97.6	100.0	100.0	99.2	93.0	71.7
2. 1-2	0.8	0.5	0.9	0.9	-	1.1	0.6	0.8	0.5	0.5	0.8	-	-	0.8	2.9	5.9
3. 3-5	0.7	0.8	0.6	0.8	0.3	0.4	1.1	0.6	0.5	0.5	1.0	-	-	-	2.7	11.4
4. 6-9	0.2	0.1	0.2	0.2	-	0.2	0.4	*	0.2	0.1	0.2	-	-	-	0.6	6.1
5. 10-19	0.2	*	0.3	0.1	-	0.1	0.2	0.3	-	0.1	0.3	-	-	-	0.5	5.0
6. 20-39	0.1	0.2	-	0.1	0.2	0.1	-	0.2	-	-	0.2	-	-	-	0.4	-
7. 40 or more	-	-	-	-	-	-	-	-	-	-	-	-	-	-	-	-
Item 1090 Subject A01c N	3211	1514	1601	2459	387	741	931	1031	507	1730	1183	1233	805	414	678	30

IF YOU HAVE NOT TAKEN TRANQUILIZERS IN THE LAST TWELVE MONTHS, GO TO Q.B082.

THE FOLLOWING QUESTIONS REFER ONLY TO TAKING TRANQUILIZERS WITHOUT A DOCTOR'S ORDERS. IF YOU HAVE NOT DONE THIS IN THE LAST TWELVE MONTHS, GO TO Q.B082.

B075: When you used tranquilizers during the last year, how often did you use them in each of the following situations?

B075A: When you were alone

	TOTAL	M	F	White	Black	NE	NC	S	W	Yes	No	None	Mari-juana Only	Few Pills	More Pills	Any Her-oin
1. Not at all	41.5	47.4	36.7	41.0	36.0	34.7	48.0	43.6	34.5	37.6	39.3	-	-	69.5	38.9	31.6
2. A few of the times	33.7	33.1	33.1	34.0	25.7	34.2	34.1	40.6	15.5	28.6	41.0	-	-	19.0	35.6	32.6
3. Some of the times	8.3	5.2	11.9	8.0	21.9	6.8	8.6	6.6	15.3	8.9	6.9	-	-	-	6.6	30.0
4. Most of the times	6.3	8.4	5.4	7.3	-	6.8	3.5	5.3	14.8	7.2	7.7	-	-	-	7.3	5.7
5. Every time	10.1	5.9	12.9	9.8	16.4	17.5	5.8	4.0	20.0	17.8	5.2	-	-	11.5	11.6	-
Item 3740 Subject A05a N★	134	57	66	112	6	36	43	39	16	50	56	-	-	12	104	14

B075B: With just 1 or 2 other people

	TOTAL	M	F	White	Black	NE	NC	S	W	Yes	No	None	Mari-juana Only	Few Pills	More Pills	Any Her-oin
1. Not at all	28.6	28.8	27.8	26.0	70.6	35.3	22.9	22.5	45.0	47.1	19.1	-	-	58.6	27.0	7.4
2. A few of the times	31.4	34.3	32.5	34.6	7.5	36.7	30.5	29.5	27.2	23.9	44.7	-	-	20.0	33.5	32.9
3. Some of the times	18.1	22.3	12.4	16.1	21.9	17.7	13.2	26.4	11.0	9.3	20.3	-	-	-	17.7	32.1
4. Most of the times	12.2	7.9	15.1	12.8	-	10.3	21.6	3.4	12.8	13.8	11.3	-	-	-	11.8	27.6
5. Every time	9.7	6.7	12.2	10.6	-	-	11.8	18.3	4.0	5.9	4.6	-	-	21.4	10.0	-
Item 3750 Subject A05b N★	132	58	64	111	6	34	43	39	15	48	56	-	-	12	103	14

*=less than .05 per cent.   ★=excludes respondents for whom question was inappropriate.

QUESTIONNAIRE FORM 1 1983	TOTAL	SEX		RACE		REGION				4YR COLLEGE PLANS		ILLICIT DRUG USE: LIFETIME				
		M	F	White	Black	NE	NC	S	W	Yes	No	None	Marijuana Only	Few Pills	More Pills	Any Heroin
N (Weighted No. of Cases):	3448	1611	1667	2555	435	814	974	1118	541	1798	1246	1269	848	428	746	30
% of Weighted Total:	100.0	46.7	48.3	74.1	12.6	23.6	28.3	32.4	15.7	52.2	36.1	36.8	24.6	12.4	21.6	.9

B075C: At a party

	TOTAL	M	F	White	Black	NE	NC	S	W	Yes	No	None	Mar. Only	Few Pills	More Pills	Any Heroin
1. Not at all	57.1	45.3	72.1	56.6	80.3	54.6	51.4	53.4	87.7	62.4	56.7	-	-	100.0	58.9	5.0
2. A few of the times	15.5	14.9	11.5	13.5	19.7	15.7	20.6	11.0	12.3	17.5	12.7	-	-	-	15.8	27.8
3. Some of the times	16.5	23.5	10.1	17.9	-	19.7	18.4	18.0	-	8.1	23.1	-	-	-	15.6	37.2
4. Most of the times	9.2	13.0	6.3	10.3	-	8.9	6.4	16.4	-	8.2	7.5	-	-	-	8.9	20.0
5. Every time	1.7	3.3	-	1.7	-	1.1	3.3	1.1	-	3.8	-	-	-	-	0.8	10.0
Item 3760 Subject A05c N★	129	55	64	109	5	34	42	37	15	48	55	-	-	11	103	14

B075D: When your date or spouse was present

	TOTAL	M	F	White	Black	NE	NC	S	W	Yes	No	None	Mar. Only	Few Pills	More Pills	Any Heroin
1. Not at all	66.4	70.1	64.5	64.8	100.0	67.0	64.8	54.0	00.0	82.4	57.9	-	-	93.8	69.5	18.2
2. A few of the times	15.8	17.5	12.3	15.1	-	12.5	17.4	23.6	-	6.2	19.6	-	-	-	15.0	35.9
3. Some of the times	8.1	11.1	6.9	9.7	-	9.0	11.2	7.1	-	8.1	8.9	-	-	-	6.6	25.9
4. Most of the times	4.7	0.7	6.9	4.5	-	9.4	3.1	4.0	-	0.8	8.0	-	-	-	4.4	10.5
5. Every time	5.0	0.6	9.5	6.0	-	2.1	3.6	11.3	-	2.5	5.6	-	-	6.2	4.3	9.5
Item 3770 Subject A05b N★	129	54	64	107	6	34	41	37	15	47	55	-	-	11	102	14

B075E: When people over age 30 were present

	TOTAL	M	F	White	Black	NE	NC	S	W	Yes	No	None	Mar. Only	Few Pills	More Pills	Any Heroin
1. Not at all	55.4	61.0	48.7	52.2	73.2	69.8	62.0	38.5	46.5	44.2	57.3	-	-	64.4	56.2	36.3
2. A few of the times	14.5	13.0	16.1	14.6	18.2	10.0	13.4	14.0	28.9	22.9	13.6	-	-	17.8	12.6	27.8
3. Some of the times	12.9	12.4	14.1	14.7	-	13.2	9.0	18.5	8.8	6.2	18.7	-	-	-	14.1	15.9
4. Most of the times	4.8	2.8	7.2	4.7	8.6	2.1	-	12.9	3.8	4.5	7.3	-	-	-	3.3	20.0
5. Every time	12.4	10.8	13.9	13.8	-	4.8	15.6	16.0	12.0	22.1	3.1	-	-	17.8	13.8	-
Item 3780 Subject A05b N★	129	54	64	107	6	34	41	37	15	47	55	-	-	11	102	14

B075F: During the daytime (before 4:00 p.m.)

	TOTAL	M	F	White	Black	NE	NC	S	W	Yes	No	None	Mar. Only	Few Pills	More Pills	Any Heroin
1. Not at all	46.3	45.4	46.5	46.8	61.7	37.8	55.2	46.4	41.9	53.7	41.7	-	-	38.9	47.2	38.6
2. A few of the times	30.5	29.6	32.5	31.9	-	30.9	25.9	32.2	37.6	20.9	44.3	-	-	41.8	29.5	32.0
3. Some of the times	10.3	14.1	6.3	10.0	16.4	20.9	8.9	5.4	1.5	7.1	9.9	-	-	-	10.3	21.0
4. Most of the times	6.4	5.5	6.3	3.6	21.9	4.4	5.8	7.4	10.3	6.7	2.8	-	-	-	7.0	8.3
5. Every time	6.5	5.4	8.4	7.7	-	5.9	4.2	8.6	8.7	11.6	1.3	-	-	19.3	6.0	-
Item 3790 Subject A05c N★	130	54	65	109	6	36	41	37	15	48	55	-	-	12	102	14

B075G: At your home (or apartment or dorm)

	TOTAL	M	F	White	Black	NE	NC	S	W	Yes	No	None	Mar. Only	Few Pills	More Pills	Any Heroin
1. Not at all	28.0	29.9	28.2	27.4	45.7	30.2	25.0	37.7	8.3	18.8	33.2	-	-	33.0	25.6	30.9
2. A few of the times	23.1	18.9	24.9	24.5	-	29.1	23.9	21.3	12.0	19.6	30.5	-	-	19.0	24.1	22.6
3. Some of the times	13.5	21.4	7.7	15.2	-	15.4	16.0	11.2	8.3	8.6	13.1	-	-	-	13.0	31.0
4. Most of the times	10.4	9.7	9.1	8.7	16.1	6.9	13.0	5.9	22.2	12.7	9.2	-	-	-	11.2	15.5
5. Every time	24.9	20.0	30.1	24.1	38.3	18.5	22.1	23.9	49.2	40.3	14.0	-	-	48.0	26.1	-
Item 3800 Subject A05c N★	130	54	66	109	6	35	41	37	16	49	55	-	-	12	101	14

B075H: At school

	TOTAL	M	F	White	Black	NE	NC	S	W	Yes	No	None	Mar. Only	Few Pills	More Pills	Any Heroin
1. Not at all	65.9	50.0	78.4	63.5	81.8	55.3	71.3	59.0	91.4	80.3	57.5	-	-	79.6	71.6	14.0
2. A few of the times	21.7	34.2	11.7	23.5	18.2	28.7	16.0	29.0	3.6	10.9	32.0	-	-	20.4	19.6	42.3
3. Some of the times	6.3	8.5	5.2	7.4	-	12.4	3.8	6.1	-	3.4	8.5	-	-	-	3.1	28.0
4. Most of the times	5.3	7.4	3.0	4.5	-	3.6	8.9	3.0	5.0	5.4	2.0	-	-	-	4.6	15.7
5. Every time	0.8	-	1.7	1.0	-	-	-	2.8	-	-	-	-	-	-	1.1	-
Item 3810 Subject A05c N★	130	57	64	110	6	34	43	38	15	48	56	-	-	11	102	14

B075I: In a car

	TOTAL	M	F	White	Black	NE	NC	S	W	Yes	No	None	Mar. Only	Few Pills	More Pills	Any Heroin
1. Not at all	66.0	50.3	76.3	61.7	100.0	65.1	60.9	62.2	91.4	81.9	56.5	-	-	92.0	67.1	31.3
2. A few of the times	15.7	24.4	10.5	17.6	-	12.1	19.2	17.8	8.6	5.7	24.5	-	-	-	16.1	28.2
3. Some of the times	9.6	14.9	6.5	11.4	-	12.1	14.0	6.6	-	9.1	11.7	-	-	-	6.6	40.5
4. Most of the times	6.8	8.7	4.4	7.0	-	10.7	5.9	7.1	-	3.3	7.4	-	-	-	8.7	-
5. Every time	1.9	1.7	2.3	2.2	:	-	-	6.3	-	-	-	-	-	8.0	1.5	-
Item 3830 Subject A05c N★	129	55	64	108	6	34	41	38	15	47	55	-	-	12	101	14

B076: How many of the times when you used tranquilizers during the last year did you use them along with each of the following drugs– that is, so that their effects overlapped?

★=excludes respondents for whom question was inappropriate.

QUESTIONNAIRE FORM 1 1983	TOTAL	SEX M	F	RACE White	Black	REGION NE	NC	S	W	4YR COLLEGE PLANS Yes	No	None	Mari-juana Only	Few Pills	More Pills	Any Her-oin
N (Weighted No. of Cases):	3448	1611	1667	2555	435	814	974	1118	541	1798	1246	1269	848	428	746	30
% of Weighted Total:	100.0	46.7	48.3	74.1	12.6	23.6	28.3	32.4	15.7	52.2	36.1	36.8	24.6	12.4	21.6	.9

B076A: With alcohol

1. Not at all	51.9	53.5	54.3	49.6	92.5	47.1	47.5	53.5	70.3	65.7	44.1	-	-	96.5	47.2	40.7
2. A few of the times	21.5	19.9	22.0	24.0	7.5	34.4	21.8	11.2	16.6	11.5	30.5	-	-	3.5	23.1	28.6
3. Some of the times	12.3	10.3	14.0	12.5	-	1.1	15.2	19.8	11.7	9.9	16.2	-	-	-	14.8	6.5
4. Most of the times	9.4	15.5	3.7	10.0	-	11.5	12.5	7.2	1.4	9.6	9.3	-	-	-	9.9	15.1
5. Every time	4.9	0.8	6.0	4.0	-	5.8	3.0	8.3	-	3.4	-	-	-	-	5.0	9.0
Item 3840 Subject A01h N★	131	56	66	111	6	35	43	37	16	50	55	-	-	12	103	14

B076B: With marijuana

1. Not at all	52.0	41.7	59.9	49.1	81.8	47.9	44.6	47.0	96.0	66.4	41.3	-	-	100.0	50.8	12.2
2. A few of the times	18.9	26.0	15.4	20.4	18.2	34.9	13.7	17.2	-	14.2	27.4	-	-	-	17.9	44.8
3. Some of the times	11.2	16.0	7.9	12.3	-	1.3	14.3	19.8	4.0	7.2	14.8	-	-	-	13.6	5.7
4. Most of the times	10.7	15.6	4.3	10.5	-	13.6	18.0	4.1	-	4.4	13.1	-	-	-	11.6	15.1
5. Every time	7.2	0.8	12.5	7.7	-	2.4	9.4	11.8	-	7.8	3.4	-	-	-	6.0	22.3
Item 3850 Subject A01h N★	128	56	63	108	6	35	42	37	15	49	55	-	-	12	100	14

B076C: With LSD

1. Not at all	96.5	94.6	97.7	95.9	100.0	98.8	94.8	95.1	00.0	94.7	97.3	-	-	100.0	99.7	70.8
2. A few of the times	3.2	4.7	2.3	3.8	-	1.2	5.2	4.0	-	4.5	2.7	-	-	-	-	29.2
3. Some of the times	-	-	-	-	-	-	-	-	-	-	-	-	-	-	-	-
4. Most of the times	0.3	0.6	-	0.3	-	-	-	0.9	-	0.7	-	-	-	-	0.3	-
5. Every time	-	-	-	-	-	-	-	-	-	-	-	-	-	-	-	-
Item 3860 Subject A01h N★	130	56	65	110	6	35	43	37	15	49	55	-	-	12	101	14

B076D: With psychedelics other than LSD

1. Not at all	96.0	92.6	98.4	96.2	81.8	98.8	94.8	93.2	00.0	93.2	97.3	-	-	100.0	98.5	73.9
2. A few of the times	2.9	4.7	1.6	2.4	18.2	1.2	5.2	2.8	-	6.8	-	-	-	-	-	26.1
3. Some of the times	1.2	2.7	-	1.4	-	-	-	4.0	-	-	2.7	-	-	-	1.5	-
4. Most of the times	-	-	-	-	-	-	-	-	-	-	-	-	-	-	-	-
5. Every time	-	-	-	-	-	-	-	-	-	-	-	-	-	-	-	-
Item 3870 Subject A01h N★	129	56	64	109	6	35	43	37	14	48	55	-	-	12	101	14

B076E: With amphetamines

1. Not at all	91.8	90.5	95.0	93.2	100.0	90.5	94.4	87.0	00.0	93.9	90.7	-	-	100.0	91.0	89.3
2. A few of the times	3.5	3.5	2.7	3.4	-	3.7	2.3	6.0	-	3.2	3.1	-	-	-	3.4	8.0
3. Some of the times	4.7	6.0	2.4	3.4	-	5.8	3.3	7.0	-	2.9	6.3	-	-	-	5.7	2.7
4. Most of the times	-	-	-	-	-	-	-	-	-	-	-	-	-	-	-	-
5. Every time	-	-	-	-	-	-	-	-	-	-	-	-	-	-	-	-
Item 3880 Subject A01h N★	129	56	64	109	6	35	43	37	14	48	55	-	-	12	101	14

B076F: With quaaludes

1. Not at all	87.2	86.0	88.3	86.9	81.8	96.6	83.7	77.5	00.0	88.4	83.2	-	-	100.0	91.5	44.1
2. A few of the times	7.5	8.1	6.3	6.9	18.2	1.2	8.7	14.9	-	5.3	10.1	-	-	-	6.7	20.9
3. Some of the times	4.3	5.9	3.5	5.1	-	2.2	4.6	7.5	-	3.7	6.8	-	-	-	1.8	26.0
4. Most of the times	-	-	-	-	-	-	-	-	-	-	-	-	-	-	-	-
5. Every time	1.0	-	2.0	1.2	-	-	3.0	-	-	2.6	-	-	-	-	-	9.0
Item 3890 Subject A01h N★	130	56	65	110	6	35	43	37	15	49	55	-	-	12	101	14

B076G: With barbiturates

1. Not at all	89.3	86.7	90.0	88.4	100.0	91.7	88.2	86.1	95.0	90.5	87.2	-	-	100.0	94.1	44.3
2. A few of the times	4.1	4.3	4.5	3.8	-	1.2	4.2	6.3	5.0	3.2	6.0	-	-	-	4.0	8.7
3. Some of the times	3.2	5.9	1.4	3.8	-	2.2	4.6	4.0	-	3.7	4.3	-	-	-	1.8	16.5
4. Most of the times	-	-	-	-	-	-	-	-	-	-	-	-	-	-	-	-
5. Every time	3.3	3.1	4.1	4.0	-	4.9	3.0	3.6	-	2.6	2.4	-	-	-	-	30.6
Item 3900 Subject A01h N★	129	56	64	109	6	35	43	37	15	48	55	-	-	12	101	14

★=excludes respondents for whom question was inappropriate.

QUESTIONNAIRE FORM 1 1983	TOTAL	SEX		RACE		REGION				4YR COLLEGE PLANS		ILLICIT DRUG USE: LIFETIME				
		M	F	White	Black	NE	NC	S	W	Yes	No	None	Marijuana Only	Few Pills	More Pills	Any Heroin
N (Weighted No. of Cases):	3448	1611	1667	2555	435	814	974	1118	541	1798	1246	1269	848	428	746	30
% of Weighted Total:	100.0	46.7	48.3	74.1	12.6	23.6	28.3	32.4	15.7	52.2	36.1	36.8	24.6	12.4	21.6	.9

B077: What have been the most important reasons for taking tranquilizers without a doctor's orders? (Mark all that apply.)

	TOTAL	M	F	White	Black	NE	NC	S	W	Yes	No	None	Marijuana Only	Few Pills	More Pills	Any Heroin
A. To experiment–to see what it's like	32.4	50.3	17.0	32.1	25.1	42.6	33.8	34.4	3.4	24.8	38.5	-	-	21.0	31.0	52.2
B. To relax or relieve tension	72.7	67.9	75.7	71.8	63.1	49.2	81.3	81.7	76.5	71.2	78.1	-	-	51.9	76.4	64.0
C. To feel good or get high	40.7	53.0	33.7	44.4	-	35.0	54.0	42.9	12.9	24.6	52.0	-	-	-	40.2	79.7
D. To seek deeper insights and understanding	5.2	5.0	6.0	6.0	-	8.1	2.8	4.0	8.3	5.0	1.7	-	-	-	4.8	12.1
E. To have a good time with my friends	22.9	32.1	15.1	24.5	-	12.4	31.7	28.6	8.3	12.2	37.2	-	-	-	24.2	33.5
F. To fit in with a group I like	3.4	2.5	4.6	4.0	-	-	5.9	5.0	-	-	3.8	-	-	-	2.3	14.0
G. To get away from my problems or troubles	28.5	23.0	33.3	28.8	30.2	20.7	26.5	38.4	26.3	23.7	39.3	-	-	2.9	29.1	46.7
H. Because of boredom, nothing else to do	13.3	16.0	11.3	14.4	-	14.3	16.2	9.9	12.0	12.0	18.8	-	-	-	13.8	21.4
I. Because of anger or frustration	20.5	14.1	28.5	23.9	-	11.9	18.3	28.0	26.3	15.3	33.3	-	-	2.9	20.4	36.7
J. To get through the day	9.4	10.0	8.5	7.4	22.6	10.3	6.8	8.4	16.7	7.2	10.2	-	-	-	11.3	3.8
K. To increase the effects of some other drug(s)	17.3	20.3	14.4	18.3	-	13.8	19.8	21.5	8.3	16.2	16.9	-	-	-	17.1	33.8
L. To decrease (offset) the effects of some other drug(s)	1.5	3.6	-	1.7	-	1.4	3.4	-	-	2.9	0.9	-	-	-	1.8	-
M. To get to sleep	50.9	45.1	57.2	52.3	58.0	50.5	41.9	61.0	50.7	56.0	52.3	-	-	26.8	52.1	63.3
N. To relieve physical pain	37.0	28.5	42.2	35.8	36.9	38.9	38.4	41.5	18.7	42.7	35.2	-	-	23.8	39.6	29.6
O. Because I am "hooked"–I have to have them	0.9	-	1.7	-	-	-	-	3.1	-	-	2.2	-	-	-	1.1	-
Item 3910-4040 Subject A06a N★	127	52	66	109	4	32	41	37	16	49	52	-	-	12	100	14

B078: When you take tranquilizers how high do you usually get?

	TOTAL	M	F	White	Black	NE	NC	S	W	Yes	No	None	Marijuana Only	Few Pills	More Pills	Any Heroin
1. Not at all high	17.1	19.6	15.3	13.4	57.7	18.5	8.4	15.9	41.4	19.9	11.1	-	-	43.2	13.5	19.5
2. A little high	27.7	32.7	24.3	30.7	-	38.2	42.9	10.7	5.2	17.7	33.6	-	-	23.9	29.0	21.1
3. Moderately high	26.0	27.9	24.1	29.4	-	19.0	27.0	27.8	35.0	29.2	30.8	-	-	-	27.3	45.7
4. Very high	9.0	7.9	9.5	8.4	-	9.6	3.9	17.2	-	3.4	10.3	-	-	-	11.1	3.8
5. I don't take them to get high	20.2	11.8	26.8	18.1	42.3	14.7	17.7	28.5	18.4	29.8	14.3	-	-	32.9	19.1	9.9
Item 4050 Subject A01e N★	128	55	62	107	5	34	41	38	15	46	54	-	-	12	98	14

B079: When you take tranquilizers how long do you usually stay high?

	TOTAL	M	F	White	Black	NE	NC	S	W	Yes	No	None	Marijuana Only	Few Pills	More Pills	Any Heroin
1. Usually don't get high	38.8	28.0	48.1	34.0	91.7	31.1	37.4	40.6	55.0	55.2	26.9	-	-	72.6	37.2	14.6
2. One to two hours	21.6	33.0	15.5	25.4	-	38.7	17.1	16.4	8.0	17.0	20.6	-	-	5.8	22.6	25.4
3. Three to six hours	32.5	34.2	29.8	35.7	-	26.8	38.8	29.1	37.0	27.8	41.9	-	-	18.1	32.0	56.2
4. Seven to 24 hours	6.3	4.8	5.0	3.9	8.3	3.4	4.1	13.9	-	-	8.6	-	-	3.5	7.2	3.8
5. More than 24 hours	0.8	-	1.6	1.0	-	-	2.6	-	-	-	1.9	-	-	-	1.0	-
Item 4060 Subject A01f N★	132	55	66	112	5	35	42	39	16	49	55	-	-	12	103	14

B080: What tranquilizers have you taken during the last year without a doctor's orders? (Mark all that apply.)

	TOTAL	M	F	White	Black	NE	NC	S	W	Yes	No	None	Marijuana Only	Few Pills	More Pills	Any Heroin
A. Librium	29.6	32.5	28.3	29.8	28.5	28.6	36.1	29.1	15.8	32.6	26.9	-	-	-	25.1	84.8
B. Valium	80.6	88.8	73.2	81.8	65.8	85.4	82.4	76.7	74.6	76.0	81.2	-	-	58.5	81.5	92.0
C. Miltown	2.7	3.3	0.8	2.1	-	5.1	4.3	-	-	-	1.0	-	-	-	1.2	15.9
D. Equanil	4.1	3.2	3.6	2.7	28.5	5.3	4.3	3.8	1.5	6.4	1.7	-	-	-	3.2	13.9
E. Meprobamate	2.4	5.8	-	2.8	-	-	-	8.2	-	0.7	5.0	-	-	-	3.0	-
F. Serax	2.8	4.7	1.6	1.4	54.1	2.8	3.7	2.9	-	2.2	4.5	-	-	-	2.4	7.4
G. Atarax	1.2	2.8	-	1.3	-	-	1.7	2.1	-	3.1	-	-	-	-	1.5	-
H. Tranxene	6.6	2.9	7.4	4.8	28.5	12.2	-	11.5	-	2.9	9.1	-	-	-	5.6	19.6
I. Vistaril	2.6	4.5	1.5	3.0	-	1.1	4.9	1.0	3.9	2.2	4.2	-	-	-	1.6	11.7
J. Don't know the names of some tranquilizers I have used	41.9	38.6	46.2	40.2	88.3	28.3	50.6	49.9	29.7	40.0	53.1	-	-	41.5	37.9	70.5
Item 4070-4160 Subject A01l N★	125	52	64	109	4	33	40	37	15	48	54	-	-	11	100	14

B081: Have you ever tried to stop using tranquilizers and found that you couldn't stop?

	TOTAL	M	F	White	Black	NE	NC	S	W	Yes	No	None	Marijuana Only	Few Pills	More Pills	Any Heroin
1. Yes	1.9	2.5	1.7	0.4	19.9	3.9	-	2.9	-	-	4.6	-	-	-	2.5	-
2. No	98.1	97.5	98.3	99.6	80.1	96.1	00.0	97.1	00.0	100.0	95.4	-	-	100.0	97.5	100.0
Item 4170 Subject A01i N★	131	54	66	112	5	35	41	39	15	49	55	-	-	12	102	14

★=excludes respondents for whom question was inappropriate.

QUESTIONNAIRE FORM 1 1983	TOTAL	SEX		RACE		REGION				4YR COLLEGE PLANS		ILLICIT DRUG USE: LIFETIME				
		M	F	White	Black	NE	NC	S	W	Yes	No	None	Marijuana Only	Few Pills	More Pills	Any Heroin
N (Weighted No. of Cases):	3448	1611	1667	2555	435	814	974	1118	541	1798	1246	1269	848	428	746	30
% of Weighted Total:	100.0	46.7	48.3	74.1	12.6	23.6	28.3	32.4	15.7	52.2	36.1	36.8	24.6	12.4	21.6	.9

B082: Do you think you will be using tranquilizers without a doctor's orders five years from now?

	TOTAL	M	F	White	Black	NE	NC	S	W	Yes	No	None	Mar. Only	Few Pills	More Pills	Any Her.
1. I definitely will	0.8	0.8	0.6	0.7	0.3	1.0	0.5	0.5	1.4	0.7	0.7	0.6	0.5	0.2	1.3	1.5
2. I probably will	3.5	3.4	3.4	3.3	2.4	4.6	2.9	3.3	3.5	2.5	3.9	1.5	0.8	2.6	10.2	25.6
3. I probably will not	24.3	24.2	24.4	25.2	19.8	25.9	26.8	20.8	24.5	23.3	25.4	15.2	21.0	31.7	41.0	42.6
4. I definitely will not	71.4	71.6	71.5	70.8	77.5	68.6	69.7	75.3	70.6	73.5	70.0	82.8	77.6	65.5	47.5	30.3
Item 4180 Subject A04a N	3248	1527	1629	2469	414	745	939	1047	517	1742	1199	1232	808	414	682	30

The next questions are about COCAINE, which is sometimes called "coke".

B083: On how many occasions (if any) have you taken cocaine ...

B083A: ... in your lifetime?

	TOTAL	M	F	White	Black	NE	NC	S	W	Yes	No	None	Mar. Only	Few Pills	More Pills	Any Her.
1. 0 occasions	84.9	82.9	88.4	85.1	89.1	81.5	89.7	87.5	75.8	88.7	83.9	100.0	100.0	74.4	49.0	19.3
2. 1-2	6.6	7.7	5.3	6.7	6.2	8.2	5.0	6.1	7.9	5.2	7.1	-	-	25.6	14.3	19.5
3. 3-5	3.1	3.7	2.2	3.0	2.8	3.3	2.3	2.6	5.4	2.3	3.4	-	-	-	14.3	-
4. 6-9	1.7	1.7	1.5	1.7	0.9	1.8	1.3	1.3	3.1	1.4	1.7	-	-	-	7.5	10.3
5. 10-19	1.4	1.3	1.1	1.1	0.6	2.2	0.5	1.1	2.4	0.8	1.6	-	-	-	5.8	14.3
6. 20-39	1.1	1.1	0.8	1.0	0.3	1.5	0.4	0.5	2.9	0.8	1.1	-	-	-	4.6	9.1
7. 40 or more	1.2	1.6	0.6	1.3	-	1.5	0.7	0.8	2.5	0.7	1.1	-	-	-	4.4	27.6
Item 950 Subject A01a N	3256	1541	1616	2486	401	753	947	1042	512	1745	1202	1233	815	421	706	29

B083B: ... during the last 12 months?

	TOTAL	M	F	White	Black	NE	NC	S	W	Yes	No	None	Mar. Only	Few Pills	More Pills	Any Her.
1. 0 occasions	88.9	87.7	91.3	88.7	94.0	85.3	93.6	91.5	80.2	91.6	88.5	100.0	100.0	86.7	59.2	41.2
2. 1-2	5.9	6.8	4.9	6.2	4.3	7.8	4.1	5.3	8.0	4.7	6.6	-	-	13.3	19.1	9.1
3. 3-5	2.4	2.5	1.7	2.3	1.4	3.1	1.2	1.8	5.0	2.0	2.2	-	-	-	10.3	17.7
4. 6-9	1.0	0.9	0.8	0.8	-	1.0	0.2	0.5	3.1	0.7	1.0	-	-	-	4.4	-
5. 10-19	0.8	0.7	0.8	0.8	0.3	1.6	0.3	0.4	1.2	0.6	0.8	-	-	-	3.2	9.3
6. 20-39	0.7	0.9	0.4	0.7	-	0.6	0.5	0.5	1.6	0.2	0.8	-	-	-	2.2	21.2
7. 40 or more	0.3	0.5	0.1	0.4	-	0.7	0.1	-	0.9	0.3	0.1	-	-	-	1.5	1.5
Item 960 Subject A01b N	3253	1539	1615	2484	399	752	949	1040	512	1743	1202	1233	815	417	707	29

B083C: ... during the last 30 days?

	TOTAL	M	F	White	Black	NE	NC	S	W	Yes	No	None	Mar. Only	Few Pills	More Pills	Any Her.
1. 0 occasions	95.5	94.5	96.8	95.3	98.2	94.4	97.6	96.7	90.8	96.5	95.7	100.0	100.0	97.1	82.2	70.1
2. 1-2	3.0	3.4	2.2	3.0	1.6	3.2	1.9	2.4	5.7	2.5	2.8	-	-	2.9	11.5	10.4
3. 3-5	0.9	1.0	0.8	1.0	0.3	1.3	0.2	0.6	2.2	0.6	1.0	-	-	-	3.9	3.6
4. 6-9	0.3	0.6	-	0.3	-	0.7	0.2	0.1	0.3	0.1	-	-	-	-	0.9	10.8
5. 10-19	0.2	0.3	0.2	0.3	-	0.3	-	0.3	0.5	0.1	0.4	-	-	-	0.9	5.1
6. 20-39	*	-	-	0.1	-	-	-	-	0.3	0.1	-	-	-	-	0.2	-
7. 40 or more	0.1	0.2	-	0.1	-	0.1	0.1	-	0.3	0.1	-	-	-	-	0.4	-
Item 970 Subject A01c N	3249	1537	1614	2481	399	750	947	1041	512	1740	1201	1233	815	414	707	29

IF YOU HAVE NOT TAKEN COCAINE IN THE LAST TWELVE MONTHS, GO TO Q.B091.

B084: When you used cocaine during the last year, how often did you use it in each of the following situations?

B084A: When you were alone

	TOTAL	M	F	White	Black	NE	NC	S	W	Yes	No	None	Mar. Only	Few Pills	More Pills	Any Her.
1. Not at all	84.8	80.0	91.2	86.8	78.3	79.3	91.6	87.4	84.5	85.9	87.0	-	-	97.7	83.9	53.3
2. A few of the times	10.6	11.8	8.6	9.4	19.8	12.7	4.2	9.8	13.0	10.6	10.1	-	-	1.2	11.6	28.4
3. Some of the times	2.7	4.6	0.3	2.7	1.9	3.7	2.1	2.0	2.5	1.6	1.6	-	-	1.1	2.4	15.4
4. Most of the times	0.8	1.5	-	0.2	-	1.9	-	0.7	-	0.4	1.2	-	-	-	1.0	-
5. Every time	1.1	2.1	-	0.9	-	2.5	2.0	-	-	1.4	-	-	-	-	1.2	2.9
Item 4190 Subject A05a N★	342	180	134	266	22	106	58	84	93	138	137	-	-	51	272	15

*=less than .05 per cent.   ★=excludes respondents for whom question was inappropriate.

QUESTIONNAIRE FORM 1 1983	TOTAL	SEX		RACE		REGION				4YR COLLEGE PLANS		ILLICIT DRUG USE: LIFETIME				
		M	F	White	Black	NE	NC	S	W	Yes	No	None	Mari-juana Only	Few Pills	More Pills	Any Her-oin
N (Weighted No. of Cases):	3448	1611	1667	2555	435	814	974	1118	541	1798	1246	1269	848	428	746	30
% of Weighted Total:	100.0	46.7	48.3	74.1	12.6	23.6	28.3	32.4	15.7	52.2	36.1	36.8	24.6	12.4	21.6	.9

B084B: With just 1 or 2 other people

1. Not at all	12.7	11.6	15.5	12.8	26.0	9.4	14.1	18.3	10.3	16.1	11.6	-	-	27.0	9.7	-
2. A few of the times	31.1	28.8	33.7	29.3	35.5	35.6	27.9	32.9	26.3	28.4	36.6	-	-	23.6	33.1	26.6
3. Some of the times	10.0	12.2	7.6	12.1	1.9	6.5	7.7	7.0	17.8	10.5	9.5	-	-	1.1	12.0	5.4
4. Most of the times	19.9	20.1	18.1	20.6	7.1	21.4	27.8	10.7	21.9	16.2	21.4	-	-	2.5	22.1	41.0
5. Every time	26.3	27.3	25.1	25.1	29.5	27.0	22.5	31.1	23.6	28.8	20.9	-	-	45.8	23.1	27.0
Item 4200 Subject A05b N★	357	187	140	277	23	109	59	89	100	147	139	-	-	52	285	16

B084C: At a party

1. Not at all	42.8	42.0	49.7	41.4	75.0	40.3	35.6	51.0	42.6	40.0	49.3	-	-	56.2	40.4	28.5
2. A few of the times	19.4	18.4	19.3	20.4	8.2	17.0	21.3	21.8	18.9	19.8	19.1	-	-	26.9	19.4	-
3. Some of the times	14.1	13.1	13.1	13.8	10.0	15.0	17.9	10.4	14.0	17.3	9.6	-	-	1.9	16.2	18.8
4. Most of the times	9.5	9.6	10.0	11.0	-	6.0	8.0	7.5	16.1	8.8	12.4	-	-	-	10.4	26.7
5. Every time	14.2	16.9	7.9	13.4	6.9	21.6	17.2	9.4	8.4	14.2	9.5	-	-	14.9	13.6	26.0
Item 4210 Subject A05c N★	351	184	137	272	23	108	58	86	99	143	138	-	-	51	280	16

B084D: When your date or spouse was present

1. Not at all	55.4	73.1	36.6	56.4	67.7	56.8	55.4	52.2	56.6	61.6	56.6	-	-	79.1	50.7	52.7
2. A few of the times	14.8	9.5	19.1	11.7	19.2	13.1	12.8	16.2	16.5	13.1	14.5	-	-	8.7	15.6	22.6
3. Some of the times	6.9	7.5	3.9	6.3	-	11.0	4.4	2.6	7.5	9.2	2.8	-	-	-	8.6	-
4. Most of the times	8.3	4.1	14.3	8.9	10.2	7.1	7.4	9.7	8.8	3.1	14.0	-	-	-	9.5	16.4
5. Every time	14.7	5.7	26.0	16.6	2.9	11.9	20.1	19.4	10.7	12.9	12.1	-	-	12.2	15.7	8.4
Item 4220 Subject A05b N★	351	183	139	272	23	110	58	84	99	142	138	-	-	53	279	16

B084E: When people over age 30 were present

1. Not at all	67.1	62.1	73.6	66.8	83.0	75.5	63.9	64.6	61.7	72.5	63.9	-	-	95.0	63.3	37.7
2. A few of the times	13.7	15.8	11.2	13.6	5.8	6.8	10.0	15.3	22.3	11.3	18.1	-	-	1.9	16.7	3.0
3. Some of the times	9.4	9.2	8.9	8.7	11.2	7.2	12.6	7.7	11.5	8.4	9.2	-	-	1.9	10.3	19.2
4. Most of the times	3.6	3.1	3.8	3.5	-	6.8	1.5	4.2	0.6	1.8	5.2	-	-	-	2.9	26.4
5. Every time	6.2	9.8	2.5	7.4	-	3.8	12.0	8.1	3.8	6.1	3.5	-	-	1.2	6.7	13.7
Item 4230 Subject A05b N★	345	182	135	268	22	108	58	82	97	142	134	-	-	51	275	16

B084F: During the daytime (before 4:00 p.m.)

1. Not at all	62.1	63.1	63.7	63.9	69.6	57.5	75.7	70.1	52.3	73.8	55.4	-	-	70.9	61.7	32.1
2. A few of the times	21.2	19.9	20.1	20.9	10.9	21.6	7.6	19.4	30.2	19.3	23.9	-	-	13.1	22.8	23.1
3. Some of the times	7.9	7.7	8.0	7.2	7.7	7.8	11.2	6.2	7.5	3.2	10.0	-	-	-	7.9	34.5
4. Most of the times	3.4	3.8	3.6	3.4	11.8	6.4	-	1.2	4.2	0.7	6.4	-	-	3.9	3.6	-
5. Every time	5.4	5.6	4.6	4.6	-	6.7	5.4	3.1	5.8	3.0	4.3	-	-	12.2	3.9	10.3
Item 4240 Subject A05c N★	349	182	138	272	22	107	58	85	99	143	137	-	-	50	279	16

B084G: At your home (or apartment or dorm)

1. Not at all	60.6	57.7	64.9	63.7	55.6	56.9	68.6	67.6	54.0	63.8	62.5	-	-	78.9	58.3	29.2
2. A few of the times	18.7	16.6	20.9	16.5	35.5	20.8	14.3	17.2	20.3	18.3	20.0	-	-	13.2	19.3	31.7
3. Some of the times	7.7	8.3	5.3	6.7	8.9	7.8	12.9	3.4	8.2	7.7	5.9	-	-	-	8.5	20.0
4. Most of the times	6.0	7.2	4.6	5.7	-	5.6	2.2	5.5	8.9	4.2	7.7	-	-	-	6.9	10.7
5. Every time	7.1	10.3	4.3	7.5	-	9.0	2.0	6.4	8.5	6.0	3.9	-	-	8.0	7.0	8.3
Item 4250 Subject A05c N★	351	184	141	273	25	110	58	85	100	144	138	-	-	53	278	16

B084H: At school

1. Not at all	90.6	91.7	90.9	91.4	86.4	89.3	87.9	94.1	90.6	93.9	90.9	-	-	100.0	90.5	59.3
2. A few of the times	5.5	4.3	5.9	5.0	11.1	5.4	10.0	1.2	6.6	4.9	4.8	-	-	-	6.6	5.8
3. Some of the times	2.6	3.4	1.5	2.5	-	5.3	-	2.0	1.7	-	3.0	-	-	-	1.9	24.1
4. Most of the times	1.0	-	1.7	0.7	2.4	-	-	2.7	1.1	0.4	1.3	-	-	-	0.6	10.8
5. Every time	0.3	0.6	-	0.4	-	-	2.0	-	-	0.8	-	-	-	-	0.4	-
Item 4260 Subject A05c N★	346	181	138	271	23	105	58	84	99	143	137	-	-	51	275	16

★=excludes respondents for whom question was inappropriate.

QUESTIONNAIRE FORM 1 1983	TOTAL	SEX		RACE		REGION				4YR COLLEGE PLANS		ILLICIT DRUG USE: LIFETIME				
		M	F	White	Black	NE	NC	S	W	Yes	No	None	Mari-juana Only	Few Pills	More Pills	Any Her-oin
N (Weighted No. of Cases):	3448	1611	1667	2555	435	814	974	1118	541	1798	1246	1269	848	428	746	30
% of Weighted Total:	100.0	46.7	48.3	74.1	12.6	23.6	28.3	32.4	15.7	52.2	36.1	36.8	24.6	12.4	21.6	.9

B084I: In a car

1. Not at all	61.5	63.4	61.1	62.6	75.9	59.1	66.4	76.6	48.3	63.4	60.0	-	-	84.1	56.8	61.2
2. A few of the times	17.9	18.6	17.3	18.8	10.5	14.4	19.1	11.7	26.1	20.3	17.9	-	-	7.1	21.0	2.4
3. Some of the times	8.4	8.1	8.6	8.0	6.1	9.6	5.4	4.9	11.9	7.3	7.8	-	-	-	10.2	6.1
4. Most of the times	7.4	7.5	7.6	6.9	5.0	12.2	2.0	3.3	9.0	3.5	11.3	-	-	-	7.6	30.4
5. Every time	4.8	2.4	5.5	3.6	2.4	4.7	7.1	3.5	4.7	5.5	2.9	-	-	8.8	4.4	-
Item 4280 Subject A05c N★	349	184	138	273	23	108	58	85	99	144	138	-	-	51	278	16

B085: How many of the times when you used cocaine during the last year did you use it along with each of the following drugs–that is, so that their effects overlapped?

B085A: With alcohol

1. Not at all	31.6	34.4	29.7	29.7	65.0	33.7	16.7	43.4	27.7	28.9	31.6	-	-	51.6	26.7	36.5
2. A few of the times	26.5	25.3	30.9	28.9	20.6	25.4	32.0	23.8	27.1	31.5	30.5	-	-	24.2	27.7	19.2
3. Some of the times	12.3	10.3	12.5	11.6	11.6	13.7	14.8	9.6	11.7	8.2	13.3	-	-	1.8	14.6	9.9
4. Most of the times	14.8	14.0	13.9	14.4	2.8	14.7	22.0	7.6	17.0	14.0	16.4	-	-	0.7	17.6	17.2
5. Every time	14.7	16.0	13.0	15.5	-	12.4	14.5	15.7	16.4	17.3	8.1	-	-	21.7	13.4	17.2
Item 4290 Subject A01h N★	353	187	138	274	24	108	58	88	99	145	138	-	-	54	281	15

B085B: With marijuana

1. Not at all	35.0	32.0	39.3	33.3	43.3	30.1	26.8	41.7	38.9	34.9	33.3	-	-	63.3	28.8	29.9
2. A few of the times	26.5	24.0	31.5	27.7	28.5	35.3	24.9	22.5	21.7	27.1	32.2	-	-	19.5	29.2	8.9
3. Some of the times	12.4	13.7	10.1	11.9	5.0	9.2	13.7	9.5	17.6	9.2	16.0	-	-	4.1	14.8	2.7
4. Most of the times	10.5	12.2	8.1	10.5	16.1	11.6	15.8	8.8	7.7	11.8	10.4	-	-	-	12.0	22.7
5. Every time	15.6	18.2	11.0	16.6	7.1	13.8	18.8	17.4	14.1	17.0	8.1	-	-	13.0	15.2	35.8
Item 4300 Subject A01h N★	346	184	137	270	23	102	58	88	98	141	139	-	-	54	273	16

B085C: With LSD

1. Not at all	95.8	95.2	97.2	96.2	97.6	92.6	00.0	94.5	98.0	99.1	96.6	-	-	100.0	95.6	84.2
2. A few of the times	1.9	1.6	1.3	1.1	-	5.3	-	-	1.2	-	2.5	-	-	-	2.3	2.4
3. Some of the times	1.1	1.8	0.4	1.2	2.4	0.4	-	3.8	-	0.4	0.9	-	-	-	1.2	2.7
4. Most of the times	-	-	-	-	-	-	-	-	-	-	-	-	-	-	-	-
5. Every time	1.2	1.4	1.1	1.5	-	1.7	-	1.7	0.8	0.5	-	-	-	-	0.8	10.7
Item 4310 Subject A01h N★	339	177	135	264	23	102	57	87	93	139	132	-	-	53	266	16

B085D: With psychedelics other than LSD

1. Not at all	96.4	96.7	97.4	98.2	100.0	94.2	98.6	97.5	96.7	99.5	94.0	-	-	100.0	96.0	91.2
2. A few of the times	2.3	2.3	0.9	0.4	-	3.5	1.4	1.2	2.6	-	3.9	-	-	-	2.4	8.8
3. Some of the times	1.0	0.7	1.7	1.1	-	2.2	-	1.4	-	-	2.1	-	-	-	1.3	-
4. Most of the times	-	-	-	-	-	-	-	-	-	-	-	-	-	-	-	-
5. Every time	0.2	0.4	-	0.3	-	-	-	-	0.8	0.5	-	-	-	-	0.3	-
Item 4320 Subject A01h N★	344	181	135	267	22	104	57	87	97	139	136	-	-	53	270	16

B085E: With amphetamines

1. Not at all	90.6	94.2	89.7	91.1	93.3	87.5	91.3	93.2	91.2	91.6	90.9	-	-	100.0	89.7	74.0
2. A few of the times	6.3	3.3	9.1	6.5	6.7	8.6	4.4	5.2	6.0	5.2	7.9	-	-	-	7.6	6.4
3. Some of the times	1.6	1.1	0.3	0.9	-	2.7	-	-	2.8	1.4	0.3	-	-	-	1.9	2.4
4. Most of the times	0.8	0.8	-	0.5	-	1.2	2.4	-	-	1.0	-	-	-	-	0.5	8.9
5. Every time	0.7	0.6	1.0	0.9	-	-	1.9	1.6	-	0.8	1.0	-	-	-	0.4	8.4
Item 4330 Subject A01h N★	339	177	137	264	25	101	58	86	94	137	135	-	-	51	268	16

B085F: With quaaludes

1. Not at all	96.1	95.7	97.4	95.8	100.0	98.5	86.4	96.3	99.5	97.1	95.0	-	-	100.0	95.8	88.6
2. A few of the times	2.6	2.3	2.3	2.7	-	-	11.6	2.3	-	2.1	3.2	-	-	-	2.9	6.4
3. Some of the times	0.9	1.3	0.3	1.0	-	1.5	-	1.4	0.5	-	1.7	-	-	-	0.9	5.0
4. Most of the times	0.3	0.7	-	0.4	-	-	2.0	-	-	0.8	-	-	-	-	0.4	-
5. Every time	-	-	-	-	-	-	-	-	-	-	-	-	-	-	-	-
Item 4340 Subject A01h N★	339	179	134	266	22	101	58	85	94	139	132	-	-	53	267	16

★=excludes respondents for whom question was inappropriate.

QUESTIONNAIRE FORM 1 1983	TOTAL	SEX		RACE		REGION				4YR COLLEGE PLANS		ILLICIT DRUG USE: LIFETIME				
		M	F	White	Black	NE	NC	S	W	Yes	No	None	Mari- juana Only	Few Pills	More Pills	Any Her- oin
N (Weighted No. of Cases):	3448	1611	1667	2555	435	814	974	1118	541	1798	1246	1269	848	428	746	30
% of Weighted Total:	100.0	46.7	48.3	74.1	12.6	23.6	28.3	32.4	15.7	52.2	36.1	36.8	24.6	12.4	21.6	.9
B085G: With barbiturates																
1. Not at all	97.2	98.1	96.7	97.1	100.0	97.5	00.0	92.6	99.5	100.0	95.3	-	-	100.0	98.3	69.4
2. A few of the times	1.6	1.0	2.1	1.7	-	1.6	-	4.5	-	-	2.5	-	-	-	1.1	17.1
3. Some of the times	0.7	0.9	0.3	0.7	-	0.8	-	1.4	0.5	-	1.2	-	-	-	0.6	5.0
4. Most of the times	-	-	-	-	-	-	-	-	-	-	-	-	-	-	-	-
5. Every time	0.4	-	1.0	0.5	-	-	-	1.5	-	-	1.0	-	-	-	-	8.4
Item 4350 Subject A01h N★	338	179	136	267	23	100	58	87	94	141	133	-	-	53	265	16
B085H: With tranquilizers																
1. Not at all	98.8	99.1	99.0	99.3	95.4	99.2	00.0	96.3	00.0	99.3	98.8	-	-	100.0	99.6	82.0
2. A few of the times	1.0	0.7	0.8	0.4	4.6	-	-	3.7	-	0.7	0.9	-	-	-	0.4	13.0
3. Some of the times	0.2	0.2	0.3	0.3	-	0.8	-	-	-	-	0.3	-	-	-	-	5.0
4. Most of the times	-	-	-	-	-	-	-	-	-	-	-	-	-	-	-	-
5. Every time	-	-	-	-	-	-	-	-	-	-	-	-	-	-	-	-
Item 4360 Subject A01h N★	338	177	136	267	23	100	58	87	94	141	132	-	-	53	265	16
B086: What have been the most important reasons for your taking cocaine? (Mark all that apply.)																
A. To experiment–to see what it's like	79.3	76.7	83.3	79.0	86.5	80.5	81.9	74.3	80.9	83.7	79.6	-	-	90.2	79.4	58.9
B. To relax or relieve tension	22.5	22.6	20.8	22.1	2.0	20.1	26.5	26.7	19.2	19.8	21.6	-	-	12.9	23.9	33.2
C. To feel good or get high	70.8	70.0	71.2	71.8	35.4	71.5	68.2	66.3	75.6	64.6	78.0	-	-	34.1	77.0	90.8
D. To seek deeper insights and understanding	8.1	9.3	5.6	7.0	12.0	9.6	2.0	10.3	8.2	8.4	5.3	-	-	-	8.0	36.1
E. To have a good time with my friends	49.8	50.6	47.0	50.8	26.7	45.4	55.1	33.4	66.2	50.8	55.8	-	-	29.1	54.5	42.8
F. To fit in with a group I like	5.0	5.1	2.7	3.9	-	6.8	8.9	2.8	2.7	3.7	4.4	-	-	7.4	4.1	4.4
G. To get away from my problems or troubles	4.5	5.4	3.7	4.4	2.6	5.7	3.7	5.0	3.2	3.9	4.4	-	-	2.0	3.8	25.9
H. Because of boredom, nothing else to do	9.8	9.8	9.9	10.1	15.6	10.8	14.6	8.0	7.2	7.2	12.7	-	-	1.2	10.2	30.4
I. Because of anger or frustration	1.7	1.8	1.0	1.7	-	1.0	2.0	4.1	-	0.8	2.3	-	-	-	0.8	21.5
J. To get through the day	4.4	5.2	3.4	2.7	13.5	5.5	2.0	6.8	2.6	2.6	7.0	-	-	3.9	3.5	23.7
K. To increase the effects of some other drug(s)	9.9	12.7	6.8	10.7	13.8	8.5	14.7	14.8	4.0	10.0	7.3	-	-	-	10.3	34.6
L. To decrease (offset) the effects of some other drug(s)	2.8	2.7	3.4	2.9	4.8	0.6	6.0	5.6	0.8	3.4	3.0	-	-	0.7	1.9	17.3
M. To stay awake	16.5	12.4	21.9	16.2	10.8	12.0	10.0	15.7	26.4	9.9	26.0	-	-	10.4	16.6	36.5
N. To get more energy	29.7	25.5	36.2	31.1	18.4	22.1	31.0	23.3	43.3	25.5	40.1	-	-	13.6	32.0	46.4
O. Because I am "hooked"–I have to have it	1.3	0.7	1.6	0.4	10.2	1.5	2.0	1.9	-	1.2	-	-	-	3.3	0.6	6.4
Item 4370-4510 Subject A06a N★	344	180	139	272	22	107	59	84	94	142	134	-	-	50	275	16
B087: When you take cocaine how high do you usually get?																
1. Not at all high	10.1	5.7	14.9	8.2	33.9	9.1	4.9	11.8	12.7	7.3	9.7	-	-	31.3	5.8	-
2. A little high	25.7	28.2	22.8	24.7	34.4	33.4	20.6	11.1	32.8	27.1	29.7	-	-	34.2	25.5	5.4
3. Moderately high	37.0	33.8	41.7	37.3	26.4	34.4	44.5	37.5	35.1	36.8	38.2	-	-	15.6	41.0	43.1
4. Very high	25.3	30.2	19.7	28.3	5.2	19.7	28.3	39.7	17.5	26.7	22.4	-	-	15.4	25.9	51.6
5. I don't take it to get high	1.9	2.0	0.9	1.5	-	3.4	1.7	-	2.0	2.0	-	-	-	3.5	1.7	-
Item 4520 Subject A01e N★	343	182	137	271	21	107	57	82	97	141	135	-	-	52	274	15
B088: When you take cocaine how long do you usually stay high?																
1. Usually don't get high	14.5	12.0	16.8	11.8	36.1	16.9	8.6	11.3	17.9	12.6	12.6	-	-	40.6	9.8	-
2. One to two hours	41.3	46.2	35.9	42.1	23.8	39.7	46.0	33.0	47.2	40.3	45.8	-	-	29.5	43.8	40.7
3. Three to six hours	34.1	28.6	41.0	36.1	23.4	32.0	35.6	38.5	31.9	37.4	31.7	-	-	23.6	36.6	28.4
4. Seven to 24 hours	8.7	11.4	5.2	8.6	11.9	11.0	7.7	13.8	2.4	8.1	8.6	-	-	6.3	9.0	11.9
5. More than 24 hours	1.4	1.8	1.2	1.4	4.7	0.4	2.0	3.4	0.6	1.6	1.3	-	-	-	0.8	18.9
Item 4530 Subject A01f N★	344	181	138	270	22	109	57	81	97	142	133	-	-	52	275	15
B089: Have you ever tried to stop using cocaine and found that you couldn't stop?																
1. Yes	3.8	4.4	1.7	2.8	2.5	4.2	4.2	6.1	1.1	1.6	3.1	-	-	1.0	3.6	6.4
2. No	96.2	95.6	98.3	97.2	97.5	95.8	95.8	93.9	98.9	98.4	96.9	-	-	99.0	96.4	93.6
Item 4540 Subject A01i N★	346	182	139	272	22	108	58	83	97	145	134	-	-	52	275	16

★=excludes respondents for whom question was inappropriate.

QUESTIONNAIRE FORM 1 1983	TOTAL	SEX		RACE		REGION				4YR COLLEGE PLANS		ILLICIT DRUG USE: LIFETIME				
		M	F	White	Black	NE	NC	S	W	Yes	No	None	Marijuana Only	Few Pills	More Pills	Any Heroin
N (Weighted No. of Cases):	3448	1611	1667	2555	435	814	974	1118	541	1798	1246	1269	848	428	746	30
% of Weighted Total:	100.0	46.7	48.3	74.1	12.6	23.6	28.3	32.4	15.7	52.2	36.1	36.8	24.6	12.4	21.6	.9

B090: What methods have you used for taking cocaine? (Mark all that apply.)

	TOTAL	M	F	White	Black	NE	NC	S	W	Yes	No	None	Mari Only	Few Pills	More Pills	Any Heroin
A. Sniffing or "snorting"	96.7	97.0	95.7	96.9	88.2	95.6	98.9	96.9	96.3	95.4	98.0	-	-	89.5	97.8	100.0
B. Smoking	23.6	24.3	18.8	20.2	41.6	24.3	14.6	21.3	30.2	19.9	23.4	-	-	2.6	26.1	52.6
C. Injection	4.3	3.9	4.9	4.4	2.5	1.8	4.4	8.6	3.3	4.7	3.8	-	-	-	4.3	18.4
D. By mouth	30.7	31.6	30.7	31.2	29.2	31.8	31.8	25.3	33.7	33.8	25.9	-	-	18.9	31.7	56.6
E. Other	2.7	4.1	0.4	1.8	7.5	3.6	2.4	2.6	2.0	2.5	2.6	-	-	-	3.2	2.7
Item 4550-4590 Subject A05d N★	346	181	139	272	22	108	58	83	97	143	135	-	-	52	276	16

B091: Do you think you will be using cocaine five years from now?

	TOTAL	M	F	White	Black	NE	NC	S	W	Yes	No	None	Mari Only	Few Pills	More Pills	Any Heroin
1. I definitely will	1.3	1.6	0.8	1.0	0.8	2.6	0.9	0.8	0.9	0.8	1.3	0.5	0.6	0.3	3.7	3.0
2. I probably will	6.2	6.7	4.9	6.2	3.1	7.0	4.1	5.0	11.4	4.6	6.9	0.1	1.6	2.0	23.9	41.3
3. I probably will not	15.0	16.7	13.4	15.7	10.5	18.8	15.2	11.4	16.2	14.2	15.3	4.6	12.4	23.6	31.4	28.0
4. I definitely will not	77.5	75.1	80.8	77.1	85.5	71.5	79.8	82.8	71.4	80.4	76.6	94.8	85.4	74.1	41.0	27.8
Item 4600 Subject A04a N	3235	1529	1623	2479	405	745	946	1035	508	1741	1197	1219	806	411	691	29

The next questions are about HEROIN, which is sometimes called smack, horse, skag.

B092: On how many occasions (if any) have you taken heroin . . .

B092A: . . . in your lifetime?

	TOTAL	M	F	White	Black	NE	NC	S	W	Yes	No	None	Mari Only	Few Pills	More Pills	Any Heroin
1. 0 occasions	99.1	99.0	99.3	99.1	99.4	99.1	99.2	98.7	99.6	99.3	99.1	100.0	100.0	100.0	100.0	-
2. 1-2	0.6	0.7	0.5	0.7	0.3	0.4	0.6	0.9	0.4	0.5	0.7	-	-	-	-	69.0
3. 3-5	0.1	0.2	0.1	0.1	0.3	0.2	-	0.2	-	0.1	-	-	-	-	-	13.5
4. 6-9	0.1	-	0.1	0.1	-	-	0.1	0.1	-	-	0.2	-	-	-	-	6.8
5. 10-19	*	-	-	-	-	-	-	0.1	-	-	-	-	-	-	-	3.5
6. 20-39	-	-	-	-	-	-	-	-	-	-	-	-	-	-	-	-
7. 40 or more	0.1	0.1	-	*	-	0.3	-	-	-	0.1	-	-	-	-	-	7.2
Item 1100 Subject A01a N	3183	1506	1602	2448	391	723	933	1024	504	1721	1180	1219	806	408	673	29

B092B: . . . during the last 12 months?

	TOTAL	M	F	White	Black	NE	NC	S	W	Yes	No	None	Mari Only	Few Pills	More Pills	Any Heroin
1. 0 occasions	99.7	99.6	99.7	99.7	99.7	99.4	99.8	99.6	00.0	99.8	99.7	100.0	100.0	100.0	100.0	59.3
2. 1-2	0.3	0.3	0.2	0.3	0.3	0.6	0.2	0.3	-	0.2	0.2	-	-	-	-	32.8
3. 3-5	*	-	-	-	-	-	-	0.1	-	-	-	-	-	-	-	3.7
4. 6-9	*	-	-	*	-	-	-	0.1	-	-	0.1	-	-	-	-	2.6
5. 10-19	-	-	-	-	-	-	-	-	-	-	-	-	-	-	-	-
6. 20-39	-	-	-	-	-	-	-	-	-	-	-	-	-	-	-	-
7. 40 or more	*	*	-	*	-	0.1	-	-	-	-	-	-	-	-	-	1.6
Item 1110 Subject A01b N	3182	1505	1602	2448	391	723	933	1024	504	1721	1181	1219	806	408	674	27

B092C: . . . during the last 30 days?

	TOTAL	M	F	White	Black	NE	NC	S	W	Yes	No	None	Mari Only	Few Pills	More Pills	Any Heroin
1. 0 occasions	99.9	99.9	99.9	100.0	100.0	99.8	00.0	00.0	00.0	100.0	100.0	100.0	100.0	100.0	100.0	94.0
2. 1-2	*	*	0.1	*	-	0.2	-	-	-	*	-	-	-	-	-	4.5
3. 3-5	-	-	-	-	-	-	-	-	-	-	-	-	-	-	-	-
4. 6-9	-	-	-	-	-	-	-	-	-	-	-	-	-	-	-	-
5. 10-19	-	-	-	-	-	-	-	-	-	-	-	-	-	-	-	-
6. 20-39	-	-	-	-	-	-	-	-	-	-	-	-	-	-	-	-
7. 40 or more	*	*	-	*	-	0.1	-	-	-	-	-	-	-	-	-	1.5
Item 1120 Subject A01c N	3183	1505	1603	2449	391	722	933	1024	505	1721	1181	1219	806	408	674	28

The next questions are about NARCOTICS OTHER THAN HEROIN, which are sometimes prescribed by doctors. Drugstores are not supposed to sell them without a prescription. These include:

Methadone, Codeine, Talwin, Morphine, Opium, Demerol, Laudanum, Paregoric.

*=less than .05 per cent.   ★=excludes respondents for whom question was inappropriate.

QUESTIONNAIRE FORM 1 1983	TOTAL	SEX		RACE		REGION				4YR COLLEGE PLANS		ILLICIT DRUG USE: LIFETIME				
		M	F	White	Black	NE	NC	S	W	Yes	No	None	Mari-juana Only	Few Pills	More Pills	Any Her-oin
N (Weighted No. of Cases):	3448	1611	1667	2555	435	814	974	1118	541	1798	1246	1269	848	428	746	30
% of Weighted Total:	100.0	46.7	48.3	74.1	12.6	23.6	28.3	32.4	15.7	52.2	36.1	36.8	24.6	12.4	21.6	.9
B093: Have you ever taken any narcotics other than heroin because a doctor told you to use them?																
1. No	82.8	84.6	81.1	80.0	94.9	81.2	85.5	83.9	78.1	79.5	87.8	89.6	86.1	73.1	72.7	54.6
2. Yes, but I had already tried them on my own.	1.7	2.0	1.5	1.9	0.4	1.8	1.6	1.5	2.4	1.5	1.7	-	-	0.5	6.2	39.2
3. Yes, and it was the first time I took any	15.5	13.4	17.4	18.2	4.6	16.9	13.0	14.7	19.5	19.0	10.6	10.4	13.9	26.4	21.0	6.2
Item 5020 Subject A01j N	3135	1481	1585	2425	383	712	914	1011	498	1710	1156	1205	786	411	650	29
B094: On how many occasions (if any) have you taken narcotics other than heroin on your own–that is, without a doctor telling you to take them . . .																
B094A: . . . in your lifetime?																
1. 0 occasions	91.7	91.3	92.3	90.8	97.2	92.8	90.8	92.6	90.2	91.9	92.3	100.0	100.0	88.4	70.8	21.0
2. 1-2	4.1	4.7	3.5	4.5	1.8	3.1	4.0	4.4	5.2	4.5	3.3	-	-	11.6	11.4	28.3
3. 3-5	1.7	1.5	1.7	1.9	0.7	1.2	2.6	1.0	1.9	1.8	1.4	-	-	-	7.9	2.2
4. 6-9	1.0	0.8	1.2	1.1	-	1.4	0.7	0.5	1.7	0.7	1.1	-	-	-	3.9	17.0
5. 10-19	0.8	0.7	0.7	0.8	0.3	0.8	0.9	0.5	1.1	0.6	1.1	-	-	-	3.3	8.6
6. 20-39	0.4	0.7	0.2	0.6	-	0.2	0.7	0.5	-	0.3	0.6	-	-	-	1.7	10.2
7. 40 or more	0.3	0.3	0.3	0.4	-	0.4	0.3	0.5	-	0.3	0.2	-	-	-	1.1	12.8
Item 1130 Subject A01a N	3149	1498	1583	2435	382	707	925	1020	497	1721	1157	1215	793	415	650	28
B094B: . . . during the last 12 months?																
1. 0 occasions	96.0	95.9	96.3	95.6	98.7	95.3	95.2	97.2	96.3	96.0	96.3	100.0	100.0	95.6	85.6	53.9
2. 1-2	2.3	2.6	2.0	2.4	1.3	3.0	2.7	1.4	2.4	2.5	1.7	-	-	4.4	7.4	21.5
3. 3-5	0.7	0.5	0.7	0.8	-	0.7	0.7	0.6	0.7	0.8	0.5	-	-	-	3.0	3.6
4. 6-9	0.5	0.6	0.5	0.6	-	0.5	0.7	0.4	0.6	0.3	1.0	-	-	-	2.3	7.0
5. 10-19	0.4	0.4	0.4	0.5	-	0.3	0.6	0.3	-	0.3	0.4	-	-	-	1.5	7.3
6. 20-39	0.1	*	0.2	0.1	-	0.1	0.1	0.1	-	0.1	0.1	-	-	-	0.2	5.2
7. 40 or more	*	*	-	*	-	0.1	-	-	-	-	-	-	-	-	-	1.5
Item 1140 Subject A01b N	3147	1498	1580	2435	382	708	924	1017	497	1722	1156	1216	793	413	650	28
B094C: . . . during the last 30 days?																
1. 0 occasions	98.2	98.3	98.1	98.0	99.9	97.5	98.0	98.6	98.5	98.3	98.3	100.0	100.0	98.3	93.2	74.5
2. 1-2	1.2	1.1	1.3	1.3	0.1	1.7	1.2	0.8	1.4	1.3	0.9	-	-	1.7	4.3	12.4
3. 3-5	0.4	0.5	0.4	0.5	-	0.4	0.5	0.5	0.2	0.3	0.6	-	-	-	2.0	-
4. 6-9	0.1	-	0.2	0.1	-	-	0.3	-	-	0.1	0.1	-	-	-	0.4	-
5. 10-19	0.1	0.1	0.1	0.1	-	0.2	-	0.1	-	-	0.1	-	-	-	-	11.5
6. 20-39	-	-	-	-	-	-	-	-	-	-	-	-	-	-	-	-
7. 40 or more	*	*	-	*	-	0.1	-	-	-	-	-	-	-	-	-	1.6
Item 1150 Subject A01c N	3147	1498	1581	2433	383	706	924	1020	497	1722	1155	1215	793	413	651	28
IF YOU HAVE NOT TAKEN NARCOTICS OTHER THAN HEROIN IN THE LAST TWELVE MONTHS, GO TO Q.B103.																
THE FOLLOWING QUESTIONS REFER ONLY TO TAKING NARCOTICS OTHER THAN HEROIN WITHOUT A DOCTOR'S ORDERS. IF YOU HAVE NOT DONE THIS IN THE LAST TWELVE MONTHS, GO TO Q.B103.																
B095: When you used narcotics other than heroin during the last year, how often did you use them in each of the following situations?																
B095A: When you were alone																
1. Not at all	51.1	53.1	46.2	46.7	70.9	53.3	56.5	53.9	31.0	44.8	57.7	-	-	41.5	51.2	54.4
2. A few of the times	25.3	30.6	22.1	26.5	17.7	27.8	22.7	28.5	21.0	24.8	24.3	-	-	27.7	27.0	11.7
3. Some of the times	8.3	5.9	11.3	9.9	-	11.9	11.2	5.8	-	6.0	13.6	-	-	15.0	5.5	24.7
4. Most of the times	9.1	2.6	15.1	9.5	11.4	3.0	5.1	10.5	25.9	13.0	4.4	-	-	15.8	8.8	4.2
5. Every time	6.2	7.9	5.3	7.4	-	4.1	4.4	1.4	22.1	11.4	-	-	-	-	7.5	4.9
Item 5030 Subject A05a N★	100	46	50	84	6	27	32	26	15	51	39	-	-	12	78	9

*=less than .05 per cent.　★=excludes respondents for whom question was inappropriate.

QUESTIONNAIRE FORM 1 1983	TOTAL	SEX		RACE		REGION				4YR COLLEGE PLANS		ILLICIT DRUG USE: LIFETIME				
		M	F	White	Black	NE	NC	S	W	Yes	No	None	Marijuana Only	Few Pills	More Pills	Any Heroin
N (Weighted No. of Cases):	3448	1611	1667	2555	435	814	974	1118	541	1798	1246	1269	848	428	746	30
% of Weighted Total:	100.0	46.7	48.3	74.1	12.6	23.6	28.3	32.4	15.7	52.2	36.1	36.8	24.6	12.4	21.6	.9
B095B: With just 1 or 2 other people																
1. Not at all	27.6	24.0	29.5	23.0	86.2	25.5	21.4	29.0	43.8	31.1	24.7	-	-	64.7	22.1	19.8
2. A few of the times	33.5	31.9	34.4	35.5	13.8	34.7	37.2	30.5	27.8	29.3	29.6	-	-	12.8	39.0	15.6
3. Some of the times	12.0	13.1	12.1	12.8	-	18.0	5.7	21.2	-	9.1	18.2	-	-	17.3	10.1	24.5
4. Most of the times	16.7	17.8	16.0	18.4	-	12.0	24.2	11.0	17.4	16.8	20.3	-	-	5.2	20.5	-
5. Every time	10.2	13.2	8.0	10.3	-	9.8	11.5	8.3	10.9	13.7	7.2	-	-	-	8.3	40.0
Item 5040 Subject A05b N★	97	47	46	82	5	25	33	25	14	48	40	-	-	10	76	9
B095C: At a party																
1. Not at all	57.7	48.2	70.2	55.5	100.0	50.0	54.2	49.6	94.5	73.9	39.2	-	-	75.6	57.7	27.7
2. A few of the times	17.3	18.6	14.0	17.2	-	28.6	17.1	15.0	1.6	12.4	20.0	-	-	8.7	19.5	12.3
3. Some of the times	14.5	17.3	10.8	16.0	-	16.4	16.4	18.2	-	6.0	25.6	-	-	15.7	12.1	35.9
4. Most of the times	6.1	7.7	5.0	6.6	-	1.5	8.1	9.2	3.9	3.2	11.0	-	-	-	7.8	-
5. Every time	4.4	8.2	-	4.7	-	3.5	4.2	8.0	-	4.5	4.3	-	-	-	2.9	24.1
Item 5050 Subject A05c N★	98	47	47	82	6	25	33	26	14	49	40	-	-	11	76	9
B095D: When your date or spouse was present																
1. Not at all	73.1	78.3	70.1	72.2	100.0	60.5	82.4	62.9	92.3	83.3	59.7	-	-	89.3	72.9	51.4
2. A few of the times	12.5	12.2	13.9	13.3	-	21.4	8.2	14.0	3.6	11.7	16.2	-	-	10.7	14.3	-
3. Some of the times	3.2	3.2	2.6	3.3	-	1.8	2.0	5.9	4.0	0.9	6.8	-	-	-	4.1	-
4. Most of the times	5.0	1.7	8.8	5.9	-	8.0	7.4	1.7	-	4.1	7.4	-	-	-	6.4	-
5. Every time	6.2	4.6	4.7	5.3	-	8.3	-	15.5	-	-	9.9	-	-	-	2.2	48.6
Item 5060 Subject A05b N★	97	47	47	82	5	25	33	25	14	49	40	-	-	11	76	9
B095E: When people over age 30 were present																
1. Not at all	59.1	65.2	49.0	55.0	100.0	58.7	52.8	69.7	56.4	66.1	49.0	-	-	62.3	59.2	49.9
2. A few of the times	18.3	17.0	21.4	20.5	-	27.7	21.5	11.2	6.0	13.8	28.5	-	-	21.1	18.3	16.6
3. Some of the times	11.0	14.0	8.8	12.7	-	-	12.5	15.2	20.2	6.2	17.7	-	-	6.7	10.8	19.2
4. Most of the times	8.1	2.8	14.3	8.8	-	8.6	13.2	-	9.4	7.8	4.8	-	-	-	10.4	-
5. Every time	3.5	0.9	6.4	3.0	-	5.0	-	3.9	8.0	6.0	-	-	-	9.9	1.3	14.3
Item 5070 Subject A05b N★	96	47	45	83	3	26	32	24	14	48	38	-	-	11	75	9
B095F: During the daytime (before 4:00 p.m.)																
1. Not at all	33.7	32.8	29.3	28.7	71.9	41.1	31.0	39.3	17.4	33.5	29.6	-	-	32.4	34.3	23.1
2. A few of the times	41.3	46.9	39.3	46.4	-	33.3	49.0	40.4	39.5	36.9	53.9	-	-	55.0	39.6	43.9
3. Some of the times	9.2	6.4	13.1	10.6	-	3.0	3.9	13.7	25.7	6.0	13.5	-	-	7.4	9.3	12.1
4. Most of the times	11.2	6.4	16.4	10.1	28.1	10.3	14.2	6.6	13.5	15.5	3.0	-	-	-	14.3	-
5. Every time	4.5	7.4	1.9	4.2	-	12.3	1.8	-	3.8	8.2	-	-	-	5.2	2.5	20.8
Item 5080 Subject A05c N★	95	47	44	83	2	26	32	23	14	47	38	-	-	10	75	9
B095G: At your home (or apartment or dorm)																
1. Not at all	37.5	45.7	26.9	33.9	60.9	39.5	42.5	42.0	16.0	33.0	41.4	-	-	27.0	36.3	55.1
2. A few of the times	25.3	27.1	23.5	25.8	19.5	35.1	30.0	20.0	6.5	23.6	29.1	-	-	44.8	23.7	16.6
3. Some of the times	10.5	5.6	16.4	12.2	-	11.6	11.2	6.2	14.0	2.3	15.8	-	-	-	13.0	4.2
4. Most of the times	9.5	11.6	8.3	9.6	19.5	1.5	12.0	13.6	11.5	14.2	5.9	-	-	-	9.9	19.2
5. Every time	17.1	10.0	24.9	18.6	-	12.3	4.3	18.2	51.9	26.8	7.8	-	-	28.2	17.1	4.9
Item 5090 Subject A05c N★	97	47	46	83	3	26	32	24	15	49	38	-	-	11	75	9
B095H: At school																
1. Not at all	62.1	50.8	71.8	57.8	100.0	70.0	62.6	52.1	64.8	74.0	46.4	-	-	76.8	58.8	68.1
2. A few of the times	18.7	21.6	17.2	21.8	-	14.6	19.2	21.6	19.1	7.0	33.5	-	-	10.5	22.3	-
3. Some of the times	9.8	13.8	6.3	11.4	-	10.1	7.8	14.3	6.0	12.2	6.8	-	-	-	11.6	7.9
4. Most of the times	7.9	11.7	4.6	7.8	-	1.6	10.3	12.0	6.0	4.8	13.3	-	-	7.5	6.7	19.2
5. Every time	1.5	2.1	-	1.2	-	3.8	-	-	4.2	2.1	-	-	-	5.2	0.6	4.9
Item 5100 Subject A05c N★	93	47	42	79	3	23	32	24	13	47	38	-	-	10	73	9

★=excludes respondents for whom question was inappropriate.

QUESTIONNAIRE FORM 1 1983	TOTAL	SEX		RACE		REGION				4YR COLLEGE PLANS		ILLICIT DRUG USE: LIFETIME				
		M	F	White	Black	NE	NC	S	W	Yes	No	None	Marijuana Only	Few Pills	More Pills	Any Heroin
N (Weighted No. of Cases):	3448	1611	1667	2555	435	814	974	1118	541	1798	1246	1269	848	428	746	30
% of Weighted Total:	100.0	46.7	48.3	74.1	12.6	23.6	28.3	32.4	15.7	52.2	36.1	36.8	24.6	12.4	21.6	.9

B095I: In a car

	TOTAL	M	F	White	Black	NE	NC	S	W	Yes	No	None	Mari. Only	Few Pills	More Pills	Any Heroin
1. Not at all	72.1	62.1	82.2	69.3	100.0	74.3	67.0	67.5	87.7	83.0	58.6	-	-	87.1	72.3	47.2
2. A few of the times	12.8	15.8	9.6	13.8	-	22.4	12.9	6.2	6.9	10.2	15.5	-	-	6.2	13.5	17.5
3. Some of the times	6.6	8.1	5.6	7.6	-	1.5	9.1	9.2	5.5	4.7	10.5	-	-	6.7	6.4	8.3
4. Most of the times	7.4	12.8	2.6	8.6	-	-	9.2	17.1	-	-	15.4	-	-	-	7.2	20.2
5. Every time	1.1	1.3	-	0.7	-	1.8	1.8	-	-	2.1	-	-	-	-	0.6	6.9
Item 5120　Subject A05c　N★	96	46	45	82	3	25	32	24	14	48	38	-	-	11	75	8

B096: How many of the times when you used narcotics other than heroin during the last year did you use them along with each of the following drugs–that is, so that their effects overlapped?

B096A: With alcohol

	TOTAL	M	F	White	Black	NE	NC	S	W	Yes	No	None	Mari. Only	Few Pills	More Pills	Any Heroin
1. Not at all	54.8	45.6	61.7	51.3	100.0	45.3	54.6	49.2	81.3	67.2	36.3	-	-	75.6	54.2	37.5
2. A few of the times	21.5	21.7	21.8	22.8	-	28.9	11.2	34.5	10.0	12.1	34.5	-	-	15.7	21.3	35.8
3. Some of the times	9.5	10.6	9.3	11.1	-	5.8	21.6	-	5.0	13.1	7.6	-	-	8.7	10.6	4.2
4. Most of the times	7.9	13.6	2.8	9.2	-	15.0	8.5	4.8	-	-	20.2	-	-	-	9.3	8.1
5. Every time	6.2	8.5	4.4	5.6	-	5.1	4.2	11.5	3.7	7.7	1.4	-	-	-	4.6	14.3
Item 5130　Subject A01h　N★	98	47	46	84	4	25	33	25	15	49	38	-	-	11	75	9

B096B: With marijuana

	TOTAL	M	F	White	Black	NE	NC	S	W	Yes	No	None	Mari. Only	Few Pills	More Pills	Any Heroin
1. Not at all	52.8	43.7	61.2	50.2	73.7	45.3	51.4	42.8	84.8	60.5	40.4	-	-	91.3	50.4	19.3
2. A few of the times	14.7	13.5	17.3	15.6	26.3	13.9	11.3	28.7	1.5	9.1	22.3	-	-	8.7	14.2	28.4
3. Some of the times	10.4	14.4	7.3	12.1	-	8.0	16.7	7.3	5.0	8.1	15.7	-	-	-	10.5	23.4
4. Most of the times	9.2	16.4	2.8	10.7	-	16.5	8.5	5.0	5.0	2.3	20.2	-	-	-	10.8	8.1
5. Every time	12.9	12.1	11.4	11.4	-	16.4	12.1	16.2	3.7	20.0	1.4	-	-	-	14.1	20.8
Item 5140　Subject A01h　N★	96	46	46	83	4	25	33	24	15	49	38	-	-	11	75	9

B096C: With LSD

	TOTAL	M	F	White	Black	NE	NC	S	W	Yes	No	None	Mari. Only	Few Pills	More Pills	Any Heroin
1. Not at all	99.6	99.2	100.0	99.6	100.0	100.0	00.0	98.4	00.0	99.3	100.0	-	-	100.0	99.5	100.0
2. A few of the times	-	-	-	-	-	-	-	-	-	-	-	-	-	-	-	-
3. Some of the times	-	-	-	-	-	-	-	-	-	-	-	-	-	-	-	-
4. Most of the times	-	-	-	-	-	-	-	-	-	-	-	-	-	-	-	-
5. Every time	0.4	0.8	-	0.4	-	-	-	1.6	-	0.7	-	-	-	-	0.5	-
Item 5150　Subject A01h　N★	94	45	46	81	4	24	33	22	15	49	37	-	-	11	74	8

B096D: With psychedelics other than LSD

	TOTAL	M	F	White	Black	NE	NC	S	W	Yes	No	None	Mari. Only	Few Pills	More Pills	Any Heroin
1. Not at all	95.4	90.2	100.0	94.6	100.0	100.0	91.2	93.3	00.0	100.0	88.2	-	-	100.0	94.0	100.0
2. A few of the times	4.6	9.8	-	5.4	-	-	8.8	6.7	-	-	11.8	-	-	-	6.0	-
3. Some of the times	-	-	-	-	-	-	-	-	-	-	-	-	-	-	-	-
4. Most of the times	-	-	-	-	-	-	-	-	-	-	-	-	-	-	-	-
5. Every time	-	-	-	-	-	-	-	-	-	-	-	-	-	-	-	-
Item 5160　Subject A01h　N★	94	45	46	81	4	24	33	22	15	49	37	-	-	11	74	8

B096E: With amphetamines

	TOTAL	M	F	White	Black	NE	NC	S	W	Yes	No	None	Mari. Only	Few Pills	More Pills	Any Heroin
1. Not at all	92.4	89.3	96.4	92.0	100.0	95.6	88.5	93.3	94.7	92.1	93.0	-	-	100.0	90.8	95.5
2. A few of the times	3.7	3.3	2.8	3.4	-	2.8	1.6	6.7	5.3	1.1	6.0	-	-	-	4.7	-
3. Some of the times	2.4	4.2	0.8	2.8	-	1.6	5.7	-	-	3.9	1.0	-	-	-	2.6	4.5
4. Most of the times	-	-	-	-	-	-	-	-	-	-	-	-	-	-	-	-
5. Every time	1.5	3.1	-	1.7	-	-	4.2	-	-	2.9	-	-	-	-	1.9	-
Item 5170　Subject A01h　N★	94	45	45	80	4	24	33	22	14	48	37	-	-	11	73	8

B096F: With quaaludes

	TOTAL	M	F	White	Black	NE	NC	S	W	Yes	No	None	Mari. Only	Few Pills	More Pills	Any Heroin
1. Not at all	90.2	87.7	91.7	89.8	73.7	95.6	87.3	82.0	00.0	97.1	78.8	-	-	100.0	90.9	70.2
2. A few of the times	7.6	7.6	8.3	7.6	26.3	1.5	8.5	18.0	-	2.9	15.5	-	-	-	6.3	29.8
3. Some of the times	2.2	4.7	-	2.6	-	2.9	4.2	-	-	-	5.6	-	-	-	2.8	-
4. Most of the times	-	-	-	-	-	-	-	-	-	-	-	-	-	-	-	-
5. Every time	-	-	-	-	-	-	-	-	-	-	-	-	-	-	-	-
Item 5180　Subject A01h　N★	95	45	46	81	4	25	33	22	15	49	37	-	-	11	74	8

★=excludes respondents for whom question was inappropriate.

QUESTIONNAIRE FORM 1 1983	TOTAL	SEX		RACE		REGION				4YR COLLEGE PLANS		ILLICIT DRUG USE: LIFETIME				
		M	F	White	Black	NE	NC	S	W	Yes	No	None	Mari-juana Only	Few Pills	More Pills	Any Her-oin
N (Weighted No. of Cases):	3448	1611	1667	2555	435	814	974	1118	541	1798	1246	1269	848	428	746	30
% of Weighted Total:	100.0	46.7	48.3	74.1	12.6	23.6	28.3	32.4	15.7	52.2	36.1	36.8	24.6	12.4	21.6	.9
B096G: With barbiturates																
1. Not at all	91.0	92.3	89.0	91.0	100.0	96.5	92.1	81.5	95.0	97.6	79.7	-	-	100.0	91.3	78.0
2. A few of the times	8.5	7.7	10.1	8.5	-	1.7	7.9	18.5	5.0	2.4	19.2	-	-	-	8.7	17.5
3. Some of the times	0.4	-	0.9	0.5	-	1.7	-	-	-	-	1.1	-	-	-	-	4.5
4. Most of the times	-	-	-	-	-	-	-	-	-	-	-	-	-	-	-	-
5. Every time	-	-	-	-	-	-	-	-	-	-	-	-	-	-	-	-
Item 5190 Subject A01h N★	91	44	43	77	4	22	32	22	15	48	35	-	-	10	72	8
B096H: With tranquilizers																
1. Not at all	92.4	95.7	88.7	93.9	73.7	95.0	00.0	76.8	95.0	95.6	87.6	-	-	100.0	94.3	65.7
2. A few of the times	5.5	4.3	7.0	5.1	26.3	1.6	-	18.0	5.0	4.4	8.2	-	-	-	3.6	29.8
3. Some of the times	2.1	-	4.2	1.0	-	3.4	-	5.2	-	-	4.2	-	-	-	2.2	4.5
4. Most of the times	-	-	-	-	-	-	-	-	-	-	-	-	-	-	-	-
5. Every time	-	-	-	-	-	-	-	-	-	-	-	-	-	-	-	-
Item 5200 Subject A01h N★	94	44	47	81	4	24	33	22	15	49	36	-	-	11	73	8
B096I: With cocaine																
1. Not at all	90.8	90.5	94.0	92.0	100.0	90.5	93.1	84.3	96.3	98.0	84.0	-	-	91.3	92.9	70.5
2. A few of the times	7.4	5.8	6.0	6.6	-	9.5	6.9	10.7	-	2.0	11.5	-	-	8.7	4.8	29.5
3. Some of the times	1.8	3.8	-	1.4	-	-	-	5.0	3.7	-	4.5	-	-	-	2.3	-
4. Most of the times	-	-	-	-	-	-	-	-	-	-	-	-	-	-	-	-
5. Every time	-	-	-	-	-	-	-	-	-	-	-	-	-	-	-	-
Item 5210 Subject A01h N★	96	46	46	82	4	24	33	24	15	49	38	-	-	11	75	8
B096J: With heroin																
1. Not at all	98.5	99.0	100.0	99.5	100.0	98.2	00.0	95.4	00.0	100.0	100.0	-	-	100.0	100.0	83.7
2. A few of the times	1.1	-	-	-	-	-	-	4.6	-	-	-	-	-	-	-	11.4
3. Some of the times	-	-	-	-	-	-	-	-	-	-	-	-	-	-	-	-
4. Most of the times	-	-	-	-	-	-	-	-	-	-	-	-	-	-	-	-
5. Every time	0.5	1.0	-	0.5	-	1.8	-	-	-	-	-	-	-	-	-	4.9
Item 5220 Subject A01h N★	95	45	46	82	4	25	33	22	15	49	37	-	-	11	74	9
B097: What have been the most important reasons for your using narcotics other than heroin without a doctor's orders? (Mark all that apply.)																
A. To experiment–to see what it's like	50.9	59.4	39.2	50.8	-	54.8	59.4	38.7	45.2	48.5	52.6	-	-	28.2	51.9	73.9
B. To relax or relieve tension	53.6	66.7	42.8	56.3	26.3	52.4	50.3	66.2	42.3	42.1	66.4	-	-	45.0	52.7	73.9
C. To feel good or get high	46.8	66.9	26.8	48.8	-	43.7	50.0	60.3	22.6	38.6	59.8	-	-	28.2	46.9	72.4
D. To seek deeper insights and understanding	5.3	11.1	-	5.5	-	5.4	4.4	7.3	3.8	2.8	8.7	-	-	-	3.8	26.1
E. To have a good time with my friends	30.8	38.2	21.7	31.1	-	23.3	47.8	20.6	22.7	25.2	38.5	-	-	19.0	34.2	17.7
F. To fit in with a group I like	3.0	6.3	-	3.5	-	7.5	3.1	-	-	2.0	3.9	-	-	8.4	1.9	5.3
G. To get away from my problems or troubles	6.9	8.6	5.0	6.1	-	7.7	3.1	15.2	-	3.5	9.0	-	-	14.4	3.0	30.7
H. Because of boredom, nothing else to do	16.3	20.9	13.4	18.3	-	18.9	6.1	18.7	30.7	13.2	20.3	-	-	-	17.8	26.1
I. Because of anger or frustration	6.4	5.6	7.8	7.5	-	11.5	-	13.6	-	0.8	14.4	-	-	-	2.7	48.8
J. To get through the day	11.6	17.7	6.7	12.1	-	10.5	11.0	18.5	3.8	9.0	17.0	-	-	4.5	8.7	48.8
K. To increase the effects of some other drug(s)	12.2	16.4	9.3	14.0	-	6.4	15.8	19.9	1.6	3.8	25.6	-	-	-	10.6	44.2
L. To decrease (offset) the effects of some other drug(s)	4.5	9.4	-	5.2	-	4.6	4.4	7.3	-	2.8	6.7	-	-	-	2.8	26.1
M. To get to sleep	23.7	30.0	18.3	24.6	43.3	14.1	11.6	45.6	31.6	26.1	23.6	-	-	10.8	24.1	38.9
N. As a substitute for heroin	3.4	4.8	2.3	2.7	26.3	1.8	-	11.7	-	2.2	4.7	-	-	-	-	38.9
O. To relieve physical pain	52.2	47.8	59.6	53.9	83.1	33.9	51.5	55.3	80.6	54.3	47.4	-	-	56.8	51.0	56.9
P. To control coughing	19.5	18.1	20.5	20.1	26.3	8.4	22.7	26.2	20.3	12.3	24.7	-	-	3.2	18.5	51.2
Q. Because I am "hooked"–I have to have it	-	-	-	-	-	-	-	-	-	-	-	-	-	-	-	-
Item 5230-5370 Subject A06a N★	94	45	45	81	4	25	32	24	14	49	36	-	-	12	74	8

★=excludes respondents for whom question was inappropriate.

QUESTIONNAIRE FORM 1 1983	TOTAL	SEX		RACE		REGION				4YR COLLEGE PLANS		ILLICIT DRUG USE: LIFETIME				
		M	F	White	Black	NE	NC	S	W	Yes	No	None	Marijuana Only	Few Pills	More Pills	Any Heroin
N (Weighted No. of Cases):	3448	1611	1667	2555	435	814	974	1118	541	1798	1246	1269	848	428	746	30
% of Weighted Total:	100.0	46.7	48.3	74.1	12.6	23.6	28.3	32.4	15.7	52.2	36.1	36.8	24.6	12.4	21.6	.9

B098: When you take narcotics other than heroin how high do you usually get?

1. Not at all high	9.9	8.3	9.0	8.2	31.7	8.4	8.8	4.5	23.4	13.1	3.9	-	-	12.1	8.6	-
2. A little high	17.9	21.0	15.0	19.1	-	25.7	12.2	11.8	26.8	19.5	7.1	-	-	13.0	20.9	-
3. Moderately high	34.3	35.7	32.9	35.3	-	41.2	40.0	32.3	13.9	28.3	44.0	-	-	34.2	35.4	31.9
4. Very high	16.0	20.4	11.4	15.8	16.2	19.0	11.9	28.5	-	12.4	23.5	-	-	-	15.0	54.0
5. I don't take them to get high	21.9	14.6	31.7	21.6	52.1	5.8	27.0	22.9	36.0	26.6	21.4	-	-	40.8	20.2	14.0
Item 5380 Subject A01e N★	94	45	44	81	3	24	32	23	15	47	37	-	-	12	73	7

B099: When you take narcotics other than heroin how long do you usually stay high?

1. Usually don't get high	23.9	15.3	31.7	22.0	43.3	12.8	24.3	16.5	52.9	26.2	22.5	-	-	51.3	20.4	-
2. One to two hours	26.7	23.3	29.4	28.2	-	35.8	32.0	15.7	18.1	32.1	16.2	-	-	20.4	29.3	17.2
3. Three to six hours	38.6	44.3	34.6	40.1	30.4	37.7	39.5	44.4	29.1	33.0	45.3	-	-	28.3	41.5	34.6
4. Seven to 24 hours	8.4	14.5	1.9	8.1	-	13.7	4.3	13.8	-	6.4	12.8	-	-	-	7.2	34.2
5. More than 24 hours	2.4	2.6	2.4	1.5	26.3	-	-	9.6	-	2.2	3.2	-	-	-	1.6	14.0
Item 5390 Subject A01f N★	94	45	44	81	4	24	32	23	15	47	37	-	-	11	73	7

B100: What narcotics other than heroin have you taken during the last year without a doctor's orders? (Mark all that apply.)

A. Methadone	18.3	27.8	7.7	18.2	19.5	11.0	20.2	29.0	10.2	14.4	24.3	-	-	-	18.7	39.7
B. Opium	39.1	39.6	35.4	37.7	30.5	33.5	47.7	55.6	5.2	32.5	48.5	-	-	8.4	37.6	92.1
C. Morphine	28.2	26.5	32.0	30.5	30.5	31.5	24.4	48.6	-	18.8	41.3	-	-	8.4	31.0	32.6
D. Codeine	82.9	84.0	82.5	83.1	100.0	86.8	79.1	78.2	91.8	78.6	88.8	-	-	77.9	88.7	43.0
E. Demerol	30.1	25.1	32.1	28.3	50.0	23.1	16.9	57.2	28.2	23.5	35.9	-	-	9.2	33.2	32.6
F. Paregoric	8.4	3.3	14.5	8.7	19.5	-	6.6	21.0	6.7	12.9	4.2	-	-	-	10.8	-
G. Talwin	5.7	6.6	5.3	6.5	-	-	-	23.6	-	5.4	7.6	-	-	-	7.4	-
H. Laudanum	5.8	7.0	5.0	5.8	19.5	-	2.2	20.9	-	1.4	13.4	-	-	-	3.0	35.8
I. Other	19.9	29.2	12.1	20.3	-	21.0	24.7	25.3	-	18.2	27.4	-	-	4.6	21.7	26.1
J. Don't know the names of some I have used	9.4	10.2	9.5	10.7	-	4.5	2.1	27.8	5.2	3.9	17.2	-	-	-	7.7	35.8
Item 5400-5490 Subject A01l N★	93	45	43	81	3	24	31	22	15	49	35	-	-	12	72	9

B101: Have you ever tried to stop using narcotics other than heroin and found that you couldn't stop?

1. Yes	4.4	0.9	4.9	2.3	-	8.0	-	9.3	-	-	6.0	-	-	-	1.0	21.5
2. No	95.6	99.1	95.1	97.7	100.0	92.0	00.0	90.7	00.0	100.0	94.0	-	-	100.0	99.0	78.5
Item 5500 Subject A01i N★	97	46	45	83	4	26	32	24	15	49	37	-	-	12	75	9

B102: What methods have you used for taking any of these narcotics other than heroin? (Mark all that apply.)

A. Sniffing or "snorting"	23.2	28.5	13.1	20.6	30.5	35.1	16.4	34.2	-	13.0	34.4	-	-	-	20.7	64.7
B. Smoking	31.5	37.5	24.0	31.7	-	38.6	37.2	32.6	5.2	23.7	44.5	-	-	23.6	29.6	68.0
C. Injection	3.4	3.7	3.4	3.9	-	-	-	14.3	-	-	8.7	-	-	-	-	40.4
D. By mouth	85.7	82.6	91.9	86.2	100.0	77.4	83.2	90.2	98.5	84.5	90.1	-	-	91.6	89.5	59.2
E. Other	1.8	3.7	-	2.1	-	-	-	7.6	-	-	4.7	-	-	-	-	21.6
Item 5510-5550 Subject A05d N★	95	46	44	83	3	26	32	22	15	49	37	-	-	12	74	8

B103: Do you think you will be using any narcotics other than heroin without a doctor's orders five years from now?

1. I definitely will	0.7	0.9	0.5	0.7	0.5	0.7	0.6	0.6	1.2	0.5	0.9	0.5	0.4	0.1	1.3	12.5
2. I probably will	2.0	2.5	1.5	2.1	0.9	2.6	2.1	1.1	2.9	1.3	2.5	0.3	0.2	0.8	7.7	13.5
3. I probably will not	14.6	15.2	14.1	15.4	10.0	15.6	14.9	13.3	15.6	13.7	15.3	7.0	10.2	18.1	31.4	38.1
4. I definitely will not	82.6	81.4	84.0	81.8	88.6	81.1	82.4	85.0	80.3	84.5	81.3	92.2	89.2	81.0	59.6	36.0
Item 5560 Subject A04a N	3247	1538	1640	2491	414	735	943	1053	517	1757	1205	1230	815	417	675	28

B104: When (if ever) did you FIRST do each of the following things? Don't count anything you took because a doctor told you to.

★=excludes respondents for whom question was inappropriate.

QUESTIONNAIRE FORM 1 1983	TOTAL	SEX		RACE		REGION				4YR COLLEGE PLANS		ILLICIT DRUG USE: LIFETIME				
		M	F	White	Black	NE	NC	S	W	Yes	No	None	Marijuana Only	Few Pills	More Pills	Any Heroin
N (Weighted No. of Cases):	3448	1611	1667	2555	435	814	974	1118	541	1798	1246	1269	848	428	746	30
% of Weighted Total:	100.0	46.7	48.3	74.1	12.6	23.6	28.3	32.4	15.7	52.2	36.1	36.8	24.6	12.4	21.6	.9

B104A: Smoke cigarettes on a daily basis

	TOTAL	M	F	White	Black	NE	NC	S	W	Yes	No	None	Marijuana Only	Few Pills	More Pills	Any Heroin
8. Never	64.6	66.2	63.1	63.7	75.9	59.1	64.5	64.9	71.9	73.6	55.0	87.1	63.8	54.7	33.2	11.0
1. Grade 6 or below	6.0	7.6	4.6	6.6	4.2	6.4	6.2	6.1	5.0	4.6	8.0	3.1	4.7	7.0	11.6	35.0
2. Grade 7 or 8	8.6	8.3	9.0	9.5	4.1	8.5	10.7	7.7	6.9	6.1	11.7	2.9	10.0	9.4	16.0	24.5
3. Grade 9 (Freshman)	7.6	6.6	8.2	7.6	4.8	10.2	6.7	7.2	6.3	5.1	9.6	2.5	7.9	9.6	14.7	14.4
4. Grade 10 (Sophomore)	5.1	4.2	5.9	5.0	4.1	5.5	5.5	5.6	3.1	3.3	7.1	1.2	5.7	7.3	10.0	9.0
5. Grade 11 (Junior)	5.6	4.6	6.6	5.3	4.9	6.8	5.2	5.5	4.9	4.8	6.4	2.0	5.9	8.9	10.4	-
6. Grade 12 (Senior)	2.5	2.4	2.6	2.3	2.0	3.6	1.2	3.0	1.9	2.5	2.2	1.2	2.1	3.1	4.1	6.1
Item 5570 Subject A01g N	3092	1478	1557	2409	369	705	894	997	495	1687	1158	1177	766	404	652	27

B104B: Try an alcoholic beverage–more than just a few sips

	TOTAL	M	F	White	Black	NE	NC	S	W	Yes	No	None	Marijuana Only	Few Pills	More Pills	Any Heroin
8. Never	8.2	7.4	9.0	5.9	19.9	5.3	5.8	10.7	12.2	9.7	7.2	19.8	1.2	1.4	0.7	-
1. Grade 6 or below	9.8	13.2	6.8	10.3	7.9	9.8	11.7	8.3	9.3	9.3	10.7	6.4	8.2	10.4	16.3	28.3
2. Grade 7 or 8	22.2	26.2	18.3	24.0	10.6	21.8	25.9	18.2	24.2	20.2	24.1	10.9	23.9	25.5	37.2	33.2
3. Grade 9 (Freshman)	24.0	23.5	24.5	24.9	17.2	26.9	24.6	23.1	20.3	22.5	25.2	17.8	28.5	28.0	27.7	28.4
4. Grade 10 (Sophomore)	18.6	16.0	20.8	19.0	18.1	18.1	18.6	19.8	16.7	19.8	17.3	18.7	22.7	21.6	12.0	5.3
5. Grade 11 (Junior)	12.0	9.9	14.2	11.4	18.7	13.8	9.8	14.0	9.4	12.6	11.2	16.9	11.4	10.1	5.1	4.8
6. Grade 12 (Senior)	5.2	3.7	6.5	4.5	7.7	4.3	3.6	6.1	7.9	5.9	4.4	9.6	4.0	3.1	1.0	-
Item 5580 Subject A01g N	3019	1450	1517	2370	356	702	892	951	474	1641	1127	1098	765	404	665	24

B104C: Try marijuana or hashish

	TOTAL	M	F	White	Black	NE	NC	S	W	Yes	No	None	Marijuana Only	Few Pills	More Pills	Any Heroin
8. Never	45.2	43.5	46.9	45.0	45.7	34.3	47.6	51.4	43.7	51.2	41.1	100.0	-	26.0	7.3	6.4
1. Grade 6 or below	2.7	4.3	1.2	2.9	1.5	3.1	2.2	2.1	4.5	2.1	3.2	-	2.3	2.3	7.9	19.7
2. Grade 7 or 8	15.1	18.6	12.1	15.4	13.0	18.2	16.3	11.1	18.4	13.1	17.3	-	19.1	20.1	35.2	30.2
3. Grade 9 (Freshman)	13.5	13.8	13.4	13.5	13.4	18.2	12.4	12.3	11.8	11.6	14.2	-	22.3	19.2	25.2	24.4
4. Grade 10 (Sophomore)	11.6	9.7	12.9	11.5	12.3	12.7	11.8	11.4	10.2	10.4	12.1	-	24.3	15.4	16.4	11.6
5. Grade 11 (Junior)	8.3	6.8	9.6	8.0	11.3	11.5	7.0	8.0	7.1	8.3	8.1	-	22.4	12.6	5.6	7.7
6. Grade 12 (Senior)	3.5	3.2	3.9	3.8	2.8	3.3	2.9	3.8	4.4	3.3	3.9	-	9.7	4.4	2.3	-
Item 5590 Subject A01g N	3089	1473	1565	2408	377	688	922	991	489	1683	1159	1209	736	400	660	26

B104D: Try LSD

	TOTAL	M	F	White	Black	NE	NC	S	W	Yes	No	None	Marijuana Only	Few Pills	More Pills	Any Heroin
8. Never	92.9	91.3	94.5	91.9	99.2	94.4	91.1	93.7	92.3	94.8	91.2	100.0	100.0	94.9	71.4	17.0
1. Grade 6 or below	0.1	0.1	-	0.1	-	0.2	-	-	0.1	*	0.1	-	-	-	0.3	-
2. Grade 7 or 8	0.3	0.4	0.2	0.3	-	0.5	0.2	*	0.6	0.3	0.3	-	-	-	1.2	4.1
3. Grade 9 (Freshman)	1.7	2.3	1.2	1.9	0.2	1.3	2.0	1.5	2.3	1.2	2.4	-	-	0.5	7.1	28.5
4. Grade 10 (Sophomore)	2.4	2.7	2.0	2.8	0.3	1.7	3.3	2.4	1.9	1.4	3.1	-	-	1.2	10.0	26.5
5. Grade 11 (Junior)	1.3	1.7	1.0	1.6	0.2	0.9	1.7	1.3	1.3	1.1	1.5	-	-	1.0	5.4	12.3
6. Grade 12 (Senior)	1.3	1.5	1.1	1.4	0.2	1.0	1.8	1.1	1.5	1.1	1.4	-	-	2.4	4.6	11.6
Item 5600 Subject A01g N	3148	1498	1599	2441	393	707	918	1024	499	1720	1171	1218	790	401	647	23

B104E: Try any psychedelic other than LSD

	TOTAL	M	F	White	Black	NE	NC	S	W	Yes	No	None	Marijuana Only	Few Pills	More Pills	Any Heroin
8. Never	94.7	93.2	96.3	94.0	99.1	92.9	95.2	96.2	93.3	96.6	93.2	100.0	100.0	96.0	78.4	24.9
1. Grade 6 or below	0.1	0.2	-	0.1	-	0.2	0.2	-	0.1	0.1	0.2	-	-	-	0.5	2.0
2. Grade 7 or 8	0.4	0.5	0.3	0.5	-	0.9	0.3	0.1	0.5	0.2	0.7	-	-	-	2.0	1.8
3. Grade 9 (Freshman)	1.3	1.5	1.0	1.7	-	1.9	1.2	1.2	0.8	0.7	1.7	-	-	0.6	5.2	26.2
4. Grade 10 (Sophomore)	1.8	2.2	1.2	1.9	0.3	1.9	1.6	1.2	3.0	1.1	2.3	-	-	1.0	7.5	22.0
5. Grade 11 (Junior)	1.1	1.6	0.7	1.2	0.7	0.8	1.3	0.7	1.8	0.8	1.5	-	-	0.9	4.3	19.6
6. Grade 12 (Senior)	0.6	0.7	0.5	0.6	-	1.4	0.2	0.5	0.4	0.6	0.3	-	-	1.5	2.0	3.5
Item 5610 Subject A01g N	3113	1482	1580	2401	398	701	904	1014	494	1703	1161	1221	800	391	606	24

B104F: Try amphetamines

	TOTAL	M	F	White	Black	NE	NC	S	W	Yes	No	None	Marijuana Only	Few Pills	More Pills	Any Heroin
8. Never	81.8	82.4	81.4	78.6	96.8	81.9	78.9	84.8	80.9	85.8	77.7	100.0	100.0	70.2	24.0	23.5
1. Grade 6 or below	0.1	0.2	-	0.1	-	-	0.2	-	0.3	*	0.1	-	-	-	0.5	-
2. Grade 7 or 8	1.8	2.2	1.5	2.3	0.2	2.2	1.7	1.8	1.5	1.3	2.5	-	-	0.5	9.0	11.5
3. Grade 9 (Freshman)	5.1	5.0	5.3	6.0	0.7	4.5	7.0	3.5	5.6	2.9	7.5	-	-	5.9	22.2	32.0
4. Grade 10 (Sophomore)	5.2	5.0	5.3	6.2	1.0	5.7	5.7	4.3	5.7	4.5	6.1	-	-	5.6	23.7	27.6
5. Grade 11 (Junior)	3.6	3.2	3.8	4.1	0.9	3.4	4.1	3.6	2.9	3.3	3.8	-	-	8.1	14.4	5.3
6. Grade 12 (Senior)	2.4	2.1	2.7	2.8	0.5	2.2	2.5	2.0	3.1	2.2	2.2	-	-	9.7	6.2	-
Item 5620 Subject A01g N	2985	1428	1505	2300	391	672	879	980	454	1651	1108	1218	794	330	549	25

*=less than .05 per cent.

QUESTIONNAIRE FORM 1 1983	TOTAL	SEX		RACE		REGION				4YR COLLEGE PLANS		ILLICIT DRUG USE: LIFETIME				
		M	F	White	Black	NE	NC	S	W	Yes	No	None	Mari-juana Only	Few Pills	More Pills	Any Her-oin
N (Weighted No. of Cases):	3448	1611	1667	2555	435	814	974	1118	541	1798	1246	1269	848	428	746	30
% of Weighted Total:	100.0	46.7	48.3	74.1	12.6	23.6	28.3	32.4	15.7	52.2	36.1	36.8	24.6	12.4	21.6	.9

B104G: Try quaaludes

	TOTAL	M	F	White	Black	NE	NC	S	W	Yes	No	None	Mari-juana Only	Few Pills	More Pills	Any Her-oin
8. Never	92.0	90.8	93.4	90.6	99.2	93.8	92.5	89.0	95.1	95.1	89.0	100.0	100.0	92.1	68.7	22.8
1. Grade 6 or below	0.1	0.2	0.1	0.1	-	0.3	-	0.2	-	0.1	-	-	-	0.6	0.3	-
2. Grade 7 or 8	0.7	0.9	0.6	0.8	-	0.4	1.0	0.7	1.0	0.5	1.1	-	-	-	3.3	10.0
3. Grade 9 (Freshman)	2.3	2.7	1.9	2.8	0.4	1.7	2.5	3.3	0.7	1.0	3.9	-	-	2.4	8.5	35.3
4. Grade 10 (Sophomore)	2.4	2.8	1.9	2.9	-	1.4	2.8	2.9	2.2	1.5	3.0	-	-	1.6	10.1	21.1
5. Grade 11 (Junior)	1.8	2.2	1.4	2.1	0.4	1.7	1.3	3.1	0.5	1.2	2.5	-	-	2.3	7.1	7.9
6. Grade 12 (Senior)	0.6	0.4	0.7	0.6	-	0.7	0.1	1.0	0.5	0.5	.5	-	-	1.0	2.1	2.9
Item 5630 Subject A01g N	3151	1498	1604	2438	401	703	914	1032	501	1722	1180	1221	800	401	635	24

B104H: Try barbiturates

	TOTAL	M	F	White	Black	NE	NC	S	W	Yes	No	None	Mari-juana Only	Few Pills	More Pills	Any Her-oin
8. Never	94.6	94.0	95.1	93.9	98.3	95.1	93.6	95.2	94.5	96.3	93.2	100.0	100.0	96.7	77.1	25.7
1. Grade 6 or below	*	*	-	-	-	0.1	-	-	-	-	-	-	-	-	0.1	-
2. Grade 7 or 8	1.0	0.8	1.3	1.2	0.2	0.7	1.2	0.6	1.8	0.9	1.1	-	-	0.2	4.7	8.3
3. Grade 9 (Freshman)	1.7	2.2	1.2	2.1	-	1.4	2.4	1.6	1.0	0.6	2.4	-	-	0.3	7.4	31.4
4. Grade 10 (Sophomore)	1.4	1.7	1.1	1.6	0.6	1.4	2.0	1.2	0.6	1.2	1.7	-	-	1.1	5.5	26.0
5. Grade 11 (Junior)	1.0	1.1	1.0	1.0	0.5	0.8	0.8	1.0	1.8	0.8	1.3	-	-	0.5	4.5	8.6
6. Grade 12 (Senior)	0.3	0.2	0.4	0.2	0.5	0.5	*	0.4	0.2	0.3	0.3	-	-	1.1	0.8	-
Item 5640 Subject A01g N	3104	1485	1576	2403	397	702	897	1014	491	1703	1157	1222	800	394	595	24

B104I: Try tranquilizers

	TOTAL	M	F	White	Black	NE	NC	S	W	Yes	No	None	Mari-juana Only	Few Pills	More Pills	Any Her-oin
8. Never	93.5	93.2	93.7	92.5	97.0	93.0	93.0	93.8	94.2	94.8	93.1	100.0	100.0	90.8	74.8	31.0
1. Grade 6 or below	0.3	0.2	0.3	0.3	-	0.2	0.2	0.4	0.2	0.2	0.4	-	-	0.7	0.8	5.6
2. Grade 7 or 8	1.0	1.1	1.1	1.2	0.3	1.2	1.0	0.8	1.3	0.8	1.4	-	-	0.5	4.4	16.9
3. Grade 9 (Freshman)	1.8	2.7	1.1	2.1	0.6	1.8	1.6	2.2	1.6	1.0	1.9	-	-	1.1	7.5	33.8
4. Grade 10 (Sophomore)	1.6	1.6	1.6	1.8	1.3	1.4	2.4	1.2	1.0	1.5	1.5	-	-	2.4	6.5	4.6
5. Grade 11 (Junior)	1.2	0.8	1.5	1.4	0.6	1.9	1.1	1.0	0.8	1.1	1.1	-	-	2.4	4.1	8.2
6. Grade 12 (Senior)	0.7	0.4	0.9	0.7	0.2	0.5	0.5	0.7	0.9	0.6	0.6	-	-	2.2	1.9	-
Item 5650 Subject A01g N	3040	1454	1540	2348	392	685	899	985	471	1677	1124	1218	793	351	583	24

B104J: Try cocaine

	TOTAL	M	F	White	Black	NE	NC	S	W	Yes	No	None	Mari-juana Only	Few Pills	More Pills	Any Her-oin
8. Never	86.6	84.0	89.4	85.9	91.8	83.6	91.2	88.9	77.9	89.7	85.1	100.0	100.0	77.5	52.1	16.7
1. Grade 6 or below	0.1	0.2	*	0.1	-	0.1	0.2	-	0.3	0.1	0.2	-	-	-	0.5	2.0
2. Grade 7 or 8	0.3	0.5	0.1	0.3	-	-	0.3	*	1.0	0.3	0.1	-	-	0.4	1.0	2.1
3. Grade 9 (Freshman)	2.0	2.7	1.3	2.2	0.4	2.1	1.0	1.9	4.0	1.3	2.3	-	-	0.2	7.9	46.0
4. Grade 10 (Sophomore)	2.8	3.1	2.6	3.1	1.7	4.0	2.3	2.3	3.3	2.1	4.0	-	-	2.6	11.6	12.9
5. Grade 11 (Junior)	4.4	5.8	2.8	4.6	3.8	5.3	3.0	3.5	7.8	3.2	5.3	-	-	9.1	15.7	5.1
6. Grade 12 (Senior)	3.7	3.6	3.8	3.8	2.3	5.0	2.0	3.4	5.8	3.3	3.1	-	-	10.1	11.1	15.1
Item 5660 Subject A01g N	3170	1514	1607	2456	398	714	924	1030	502	1733	1184	1223	799	401	653	24

B104K: Try heroin

	TOTAL	M	F	White	Black	NE	NC	S	W	Yes	No	None	Mari-juana Only	Few Pills	More Pills	Any Her-oin
8. Never	99.3	99.2	99.5	99.2	99.7	99.5	99.4	99.1	99.6	99.5	99.3	100.0	100.0	100.0	100.0	4.3
1. Grade 6 or below	-	-	-	-	-	-	-	-	-	-	-	-	-	-	-	-
2. Grade 7 or 8	*	*	-	*	-	0.1	-	-	-	-	-	-	-	-	-	2.3
3. Grade 9 (Freshman)	0.2	0.4	0.1	0.2	0.3	0.1	0.2	0.4	0.1	0.2	0.3	-	-	-	-	30.5
4. Grade 10 (Sophomore)	0.2	0.2	0.2	0.3	-	-	0.2	0.3	0.2	0.2	0.2	-	-	-	-	24.7
5. Grade 11 (Junior)	0.2	0.2	0.1	0.2	-	0.3	0.2	0.1	0.1	0.1	0.1	-	-	-	-	28.6
6. Grade 12 (Senior)	0.1	-	0.1	0.1	-	0.1	-	0.1	-	-	0.2	-	-	-	-	9.6
Item 5670 Subject A01g N	3160	1510	1604	2449	400	709	926	1028	498	1726	1184	1223	797	408	642	19

B104L: Try any narcotic other than heroin

	TOTAL	M	F	White	Black	NE	NC	S	W	Yes	No	None	Mari-juana Only	Few Pills	More Pills	Any Her-oin
8. Never	94.2	93.6	94.6	93.1	98.5	94.7	93.6	95.1	92.5	94.4	94.1	100.0	100.0	94.4	76.4	23.8
1. Grade 6 or below	0.3	0.2	0.3	0.3	0.2	0.1	0.2	0.3	0.5	0.3	0.2	-	-	0.8	0.9	-
2. Grade 7 or 8	0.6	0.7	0.5	0.7	0.2	1.1	0.4	0.6	0.3	0.4	0.8	-	-	0.3	2.3	15.8
3. Grade 9 (Freshman)	1.8	1.8	1.8	2.1	0.2	1.3	2.0	1.3	3.0	1.3	2.1	-	-	0.2	8.2	22.8
4. Grade 10 (Sophomore)	1.2	1.1	1.4	1.5	0.3	0.9	1.8	1.0	1.2	1.2	1.2	-	-	1.0	5.0	17.5
5. Grade 11 (Junior)	1.4	1.9	1.0	1.7	0.5	1.1	1.5	1.3	1.8	1.6	1.2	-	-	2.3	5.8	-
6. Grade 12 (Senior)	0.5	0.7	0.4	0.6	0.2	0.7	0.5	0.4	0.6	0.7	0.4	-	-	1.0	1.4	20.0
Item 5680 Subject A01g N	3086	1475	1566	2383	396	699	889	1009	489	1683	1159	1220	796	377	602	22

The next questions are about your experiences in school.

*=less than .05 per cent.

QUESTIONNAIRE FORM 1 1983	TOTAL	SEX		RACE		REGION				4YR COLLEGE PLANS		ILLICIT DRUG USE: LIFETIME				
		M	F	White	Black	NE	NC	S	W	Yes	No	None	Marijuana Only	Few Pills	More Pills	Any Heroin
N (Weighted No. of Cases):	3448	1611	1667	2555	435	814	974	1118	541	1798	1246	1269	848	428	746	30
% of Weighted Total:	100.0	46.7	48.3	74.1	12.6	23.6	28.3	32.4	15.7	52.2	36.1	36.8	24.6	12.4	21.6	.9

D001: Some people like school very much. Others don't. How do you feel about going to school?

	TOTAL	M	F	White	Black	NE	NC	S	W	Yes	No	None	Mar. Only	Few Pills	More Pills	Any Her.
5. I like school very much	13.6	12.1	15.0	12.1	22.5	10.3	11.4	16.8	15.5	16.2	10.2	17.8	12.8	10.5	8.1	14.1
4. I like school quite a lot	32.0	30.3	33.7	32.3	30.8	28.0	32.7	32.3	35.4	37.7	24.7	36.8	32.3	31.6	23.0	29.0
3. I like school some	41.1	43.4	38.8	41.3	38.7	45.3	42.2	39.4	36.9	37.3	46.8	37.0	43.5	42.3	45.0	33.5
2. I don't like school very much	9.7	10.0	9.6	10.6	5.4	12.3	9.4	8.5	9.3	7.0	12.5	6.5	8.6	12.2	16.2	7.6
1. I don't like school at all	3.6	4.2	2.9	3.7	2.6	4.1	4.3	3.1	2.8	1.8	5.8	2.0	2.8	3.4	7.6	15.9
Item 7630　Subject B01,Q08　N	3080	1459	1575	2393	391	662	909	1007	502	1749	1192	1204	768	381	621	23

D002: How often do you feel that the school work you are assigned is meaningful and important?

	TOTAL	M	F	White	Black	NE	NC	S	W	Yes	No	None	Mar. Only	Few Pills	More Pills	Any Her.
5. Almost always	14.8	12.0	17.1	12.1	28.0	13.6	11.9	17.1	16.7	16.0	13.1	18.7	13.6	13.1	7.8	30.9
4. Often	25.6	25.1	26.3	25.5	27.9	22.7	26.1	27.5	25.0	29.0	21.3	29.9	24.0	24.8	19.8	18.5
3. Sometimes	41.3	40.8	41.6	43.1	32.8	41.1	44.9	38.7	40.1	41.7	41.3	38.5	46.3	43.1	41.4	28.5
2. Seldom	15.8	18.4	13.7	16.8	9.7	19.4	14.6	14.7	15.8	12.5	20.0	11.2	14.8	16.9	25.4	22.2
1. Never	2.5	3.7	1.3	2.4	1.5	3.2	2.5	2.0	2.4	0.8	4.4	1.7	1.3	2.1	5.6	-
Item 5700　Subject B01　N	3067	1452	1571	2383	392	662	906	1001	498	1744	1186	1201	767	376	617	23

D003: How interesting are most of your courses to you?

	TOTAL	M	F	White	Black	NE	NC	S	W	Yes	No	None	Mar. Only	Few Pills	More Pills	Any Her.
5. Very exciting and stimulating	4.2	3.2	5.1	3.0	9.0	2.2	2.6	6.0	6.1	4.1	4.3	5.4	3.7	2.2	3.2	5.6
4. Quite interesting	30.6	29.3	31.9	29.7	36.5	27.6	31.4	33.6	27.0	34.4	25.6	37.9	28.3	25.4	22.0	35.8
3. Fairly interesting	45.4	44.9	45.5	46.1	43.0	45.1	46.8	42.5	48.9	44.7	46.7	41.7	49.6	51.8	44.1	31.8
2. Slightly dull	15.6	16.8	14.7	16.5	9.5	20.3	14.6	13.7	14.9	14.4	16.9	11.9	14.4	16.5	23.8	16.2
1. Very dull	4.3	5.8	2.8	4.7	2.1	4.8	4.7	4.1	3.2	2.5	6.6	3.1	4.0	4.2	6.9	10.6
Item 5710　Subject B01　N	3060	1446	1569	2379	388	659	905	997	498	1741	1185	1199	762	379	617	23

D004: How important do you think the things you are learning in school are going to be for your later life?

	TOTAL	M	F	White	Black	NE	NC	S	W	Yes	No	None	Mar. Only	Few Pills	More Pills	Any Her.
5. Very important	21.0	20.1	21.7	18.0	32.2	16.5	18.0	26.1	22.3	22.1	19.0	24.3	21.1	18.8	14.7	25.1
4. Quite important	29.3	28.1	30.3	29.3	31.9	27.4	31.8	29.2	27.4	31.8	26.4	33.5	28.4	30.7	22.8	25.3
3. Fairly important	29.7	29.5	29.8	31.5	23.5	29.5	30.4	28.7	30.8	30.3	29.5	27.6	30.2	27.9	34.2	19.5
2. Slightly important	17.2	19.0	16.0	18.4	11.1	23.2	17.9	13.4	16.0	14.6	20.3	12.8	18.0	20.1	23.3	22.7
1. Not at all important	2.7	3.3	2.1	2.8	1.2	3.3	2.0	2.6	3.5	1.2	4.9	1.9	2.2	2.5	4.9	7.5
Item 5720　Subject B01　N	3049	1440	1564	2372	383	650	907	995	497	1735	1182	1196	759	378	613	23

D005: How much competition for grades is there among students at your school?

	TOTAL	M	F	White	Black	NE	NC	S	W	Yes	No	None	Mar. Only	Few Pills	More Pills	Any Her.
1. None	5.9	5.8	6.1	5.8	4.6	6.7	5.0	5.6	7.4	4.1	8.0	5.0	4.6	6.4	8.6	17.8
2. A little	21.3	24.3	18.5	21.4	18.0	20.7	20.4	20.2	25.8	17.6	26.6	18.7	22.8	22.4	25.1	8.3
3. Some	34.8	36.2	33.5	36.3	30.1	34.8	36.2	33.2	35.6	33.0	37.6	34.0	34.0	36.0	35.5	42.0
4. Quite a bit	28.3	26.4	30.2	27.8	30.2	29.5	28.2	29.1	25.2	33.3	21.2	30.4	28.8	26.7	24.8	26.8
5. A great deal	9.7	7.3	11.7	8.6	17.1	8.3	10.2	12.0	6.0	11.9	6.6	11.9	9.8	8.5	6.0	5.1
Item 5730　Subject B04　N	3029	1430	1555	2365	382	647	898	991	492	1725	1174	1186	757	370	614	23

D006: How do you think most of the students in your classes would feel if you cheated on a test?

	TOTAL	M	F	White	Black	NE	NC	S	W	Yes	No	None	Mar. Only	Few Pills	More Pills	Any Her.
1. They would like it very much	2.0	2.5	1.5	1.5	3.1	2.1	1.5	2.5	1.8	1.4	2.9	1.8	2.5	1.4	1.1	27.0
2. They would like it	2.2	2.5	1.9	1.9	3.7	2.2	2.1	2.2	2.3	2.1	2.3	1.4	1.8	1.9	4.1	-
3. They would not care	79.7	81.7	78.4	81.0	75.5	81.3	79.4	79.2	79.5	78.1	82.2	75.0	80.8	85.2	85.3	64.6
4. They would dislike it	12.5	10.3	14.4	12.9	10.3	10.8	14.5	11.4	13.5	14.7	9.3	16.1	12.3	10.1	7.9	8.4
5. They would dislike it very much	3.5	2.9	3.7	2.7	7.4	3.6	2.4	4.7	2.8	3.7	3.3	5.6	2.5	1.3	1.5	-
Item 5740　Subject B04　N	3027	1433	1550	2362	376	643	902	989	493	1719	1174	1187	753	373	611	23

QUESTIONNAIRE FORM 1 1983	TOTAL	SEX		RACE		REGION				4YR COLLEGE PLANS		ILLICIT DRUG USE: LIFETIME				
		M	F	White	Black	NE	NC	S	W	Yes	No	None	Mari-juana Only	Few Pills	More Pills	Any Her-oin
N (Weighted No. of Cases):	3448	1611	1667	2555	435	814	974	1118	541	1798	1246	1269	848	428	746	30
% of Weighted Total:	100.0	46.7	48.3	74.1	12.6	23.6	28.3	32.4	15.7	52.2	36.1	36.8	24.6	12.4	21.6	.9

D007: How do you think most of the students in your classes would feel if you intentionally did things to make your teachers angry?

	TOTAL	M	F	White	Black	NE	NC	S	W	Yes	No	None	Mar. Only	Few Pills	More Pills	Heroin
1. They would like it very much	4.2	6.0	2.5	3.6	6.6	4.4	3.8	5.4	2.5	3.4	5.4	4.4	4.5	3.6	4.3	8.8
2. They would like it	10.2	13.6	7.3	10.6	7.6	12.8	9.6	9.2	9.8	10.4	10.3	10.3	9.3	9.2	10.8	10.8
3. They would not care	42.9	43.9	41.8	42.6	45.7	45.7	45.1	41.2	38.6	39.7	46.7	38.0	47.1	47.0	46.2	49.7
4. They would dislike it	36.0	32.0	39.8	37.5	29.2	30.6	36.6	36.4	41.5	39.5	31.6	38.9	33.8	34.9	33.9	23.0
5. They would dislike it very much	6.7	4.4	8.6	5.7	10.8	6.5	5.0	7.7	7.7	7.1	6.0	8.5	5.3	5.3	4.9	7.7
Item 5750 Subject B04 N	3007	1422	1541	2351	372	637	903	980	487	1706	1168	1182	747	370	605	23

D008: How often do you find that your friends encourage you to do things which your teachers wouldn't like?

	TOTAL	M	F	White	Black	NE	NC	S	W	Yes	No	None	Mar. Only	Few Pills	More Pills	Heroin
1. Never	37.4	25.3	48.6	34.3	49.5	40.1	36.3	35.4	40.1	35.6	38.8	39.5	37.5	36.7	32.2	26.6
2. Seldom	35.3	37.2	33.9	37.6	25.7	29.1	36.8	37.2	36.6	38.0	32.5	35.9	35.4	35.2	35.0	40.3
3. Sometimes	19.4	26.2	12.9	20.9	13.5	22.1	20.1	18.1	17.2	19.6	19.3	16.8	19.6	22.6	23.3	23.5
4. Often	6.3	9.1	3.6	5.8	8.9	6.8	5.6	7.4	4.8	5.7	7.4	6.1	5.8	4.8	8.1	9.7
5. Almost always	1.6	2.2	1.0	1.5	2.4	1.9	1.1	1.9	1.3	1.1	2.0	1.7	1.6	0.7	1.4	-
Item 5760 Subject B04 N	3010	1422	1543	2350	371	638	899	982	490	1713	1168	1184	747	373	606	23

D009: Have you ever been in a work-study program–that is, a program where you work on a job as part of your schooling?

	TOTAL	M	F	White	Black	NE	NC	S	W	Yes	No	None	Mar. Only	Few Pills	More Pills	Heroin
1. No, not ever	75.6	78.1	73.5	78.6	67.3	82.5	78.9	68.8	74.7	82.5	67.2	80.2	75.7	73.0	70.5	52.6
2. Yes, for a half year or less	8.4	6.9	9.8	7.0	11.8	4.9	7.1	9.2	13.6	6.5	10.2	6.1	8.6	10.7	10.3	19.8
3. Yes, for about a year	10.4	9.9	11.0	9.9	11.3	6.1	9.8	14.6	8.7	7.3	14.5	8.4	12.1	10.0	11.5	21.4
4. Yes, for about two years	3.8	3.4	3.9	3.4	5.4	2.9	2.6	6.1	2.1	2.5	5.4	3.4	2.7	4.6	5.1	6.2
5. Yes, for more than two years	1.8	1.8	1.9	1.0	4.3	3.6	1.6	1.3	0.9	1.2	2.8	1.9	1.0	1.7	2.6	-
Item 5770 Subject B02,C01 N	3005	1421	1539	2349	372	633	900	983	490	1710	1166	1186	743	370	603	23

D010: How many times this school year have you seen a counselor individually?

	TOTAL	M	F	White	Black	NE	NC	S	W	Yes	No	None	Mar. Only	Few Pills	More Pills	Heroin
1. No times	17.1	16.7	16.9	17.8	14.7	15.6	16.8	20.8	12.4	13.6	21.8	17.2	17.9	18.5	14.0	32.7
2. 1 time	14.7	14.7	14.8	15.7	11.2	15.7	15.5	14.6	12.0	12.2	18.1	14.8	16.1	14.9	14.9	21.3
3. 2 times	19.8	20.5	19.4	20.6	16.9	22.2	20.0	19.2	17.7	18.6	21.8	20.8	17.3	19.1	21.5	3.6
4. 3 or 4 times	27.1	28.1	26.2	26.8	28.0	24.3	27.3	26.5	31.4	28.6	24.8	25.8	28.2	30.3	27.1	19.6
5. 5 - 7 times	12.0	11.8	12.3	11.2	14.1	12.9	11.2	10.5	15.1	15.0	8.4	13.1	11.5	12.1	10.8	10.2
6. 8 - 10 times	4.4	3.8	4.8	3.6	6.4	4.3	3.7	4.0	6.4	5.6	2.6	3.6	3.8	4.8	5.6	7.8
7. 11 or more times	5.0	4.4	5.6	4.3	8.8	5.1	5.5	4.3	5.0	6.4	2.6	4.7	5.2	4.0	6.0	4.7
Item 5780 Subject B05 N	3001	1423	1534	2346	371	633	898	980	491	1706	1167	1182	743	369	604	23

D011: How many times this school year have you seen a counselor as a part of a group of other students?

	TOTAL	M	F	White	Black	NE	NC	S	W	Yes	No	None	Mar. Only	Few Pills	More Pills	Heroin
1. No times	52.9	52.3	53.4	54.1	44.4	51.3	53.4	51.4	56.7	49.7	56.8	49.7	53.5	54.4	56.3	52.9
2. 1 time	15.9	16.5	15.4	16.7	13.8	18.1	16.2	15.9	12.7	15.2	17.4	17.3	11.9	18.5	17.1	21.7
3. 2 times	13.6	13.7	13.6	12.7	17.1	12.4	13.2	14.5	14.4	14.3	12.5	13.6	16.9	9.6	11.8	9.7
4. 3 or 4 times	12.6	12.5	12.7	12.1	16.5	11.9	13.4	12.9	11.5	14.4	10.0	14.0	12.3	13.4	10.4	5.6
5. 5 - 7 times	3.0	2.9	2.9	2.7	5.4	3.5	2.6	3.3	2.4	3.7	2.2	3.4	2.9	2.9	2.6	2.6
6. 8 - 10 times	0.8	0.8	0.8	0.7	1.5	1.4	0.2	1.0	0.6	0.8	0.6	0.4	1.4	0.5	0.7	7.5
7. 11 or more times	1.2	1.2	1.3	1.0	1.3	1.4	1.1	1.0	1.7	1.8	0.5	1.5	1.0	0.8	1.1	-
Item 5790 Subject B05 N	2995	1417	1532	2339	369	631	896	978	490	1707	1163	1180	742	371	601	23

D012: Would you have preferred to see a counselor more or less often than you have during the past year?

	TOTAL	M	F	White	Black	NE	NC	S	W	Yes	No	None	Mar. Only	Few Pills	More Pills	Heroin
5. Much more often	7.9	6.8	8.7	5.7	16.4	9.9	5.2	9.6	7.4	8.5	7.4	7.0	8.6	9.3	6.4	40.8
4. A little more often	25.4	26.2	24.6	24.5	31.7	24.1	22.7	27.8	26.9	26.8	23.4	26.0	25.9	25.7	22.7	22.1
3. About as often	50.3	49.6	51.4	53.4	35.3	48.6	53.6	46.7	53.3	53.7	46.4	52.8	51.0	49.2	48.0	19.1
2. A little less often	6.6	6.0	7.2	6.7	8.2	6.5	6.7	7.1	5.6	4.9	8.8	6.1	5.4	6.1	9.1	7.0
1. Much less often	9.8	11.4	8.1	9.7	8.5	10.8	11.9	8.8	6.8	6.1	14.0	8.1	9.2	9.7	13.8	10.9
Item 5800 Subject B05 N	2957	1397	1516	2308	368	618	890	966	483	1685	1148	1165	736	361	596	20

QUESTIONNAIRE FORM 1 1983	TOTAL	SEX		RACE		REGION				4YR COLLEGE PLANS		ILLICIT DRUG USE: LIFETIME				
		M	F	White	Black	NE	NC	S	W	Yes	No	None	Mari-juana Only	Few Pills	More Pills	Any Her-oin
N (Weighted No. of Cases):	3448	1611	1667	2555	435	814	974	1118	541	1798	1246	1269	848	428	746	30
% of Weighted Total:	100.0	46.7	48.3	74.1	12.6	23.6	28.3	32.4	15.7	52.2	36.1	36.8	24.6	12.4	21.6	.9

D013: How helpful have your sessions with a counselor been to you?

	TOTAL	M	F	White	Black	NE	NC	S	W	Yes	No	None	Mari-juana Only	Few Pills	More Pills	Any Her-oin
5. Extremely helpful	12.1	11.8	12.1	9.2	25.8	10.2	8.7	15.4	13.9	13.0	10.6	13.2	12.6	10.9	9.7	-
4. Quite helpful	24.2	23.4	25.3	23.6	27.8	20.3	24.8	24.1	28.0	26.1	21.4	25.0	24.4	22.0	22.9	25.7
3. Somewhat helpful	22.2	23.2	21.6	23.0	18.2	22.5	23.5	18.6	26.5	23.7	20.5	22.9	21.6	22.5	22.1	11.3
2. A little helpful	20.1	19.0	21.1	20.7	15.6	22.3	19.9	19.7	18.5	19.5	21.1	20.6	18.1	21.3	21.6	29.1
1. Not at all helpful	9.9	10.9	9.0	10.6	4.6	13.8	9.6	9.5	6.2	8.1	11.5	7.0	10.9	11.9	13.1	19.4
8. Did not see a counselor this year	11.6	11.7	10.9	12.9	8.0	10.9	13.4	12.7	7.0	9.6	14.9	11.3	12.5	11.4	10.7	14.5
Item 5810 Subject B05 N	2987	1412	1529	2330	372	624	899	979	485	1687	1153	1174	744	372	596	21

D014: Would you have preferred more or less of each of the following types of counseling in the last year?

D014A: Choosing what courses to take

	TOTAL	M	F	White	Black	NE	NC	S	W	Yes	No	None	Mari-juana Only	Few Pills	More Pills	Any Her-oin
5. Much more	20.7	19.0	21.9	17.8	32.5	18.9	18.3	23.3	22.3	18.9	23.0	20.2	20.8	20.9	21.0	42.0
4. A little more	25.0	26.1	24.5	25.5	23.7	24.4	24.8	25.0	26.4	26.9	22.9	25.3	24.7	23.3	27.6	25.3
3. About right	46.3	45.9	46.7	49.2	35.1	47.0	49.2	43.4	45.7	48.4	43.2	47.6	47.5	48.6	40.5	20.3
2. A little less	2.9	3.4	2.5	2.6	4.5	3.5	2.7	2.9	2.7	2.6	3.4	2.3	3.5	1.3	3.8	6.0
1. Much less	5.1	5.7	4.3	5.0	4.2	6.2	5.1	5.4	2.9	3.3	7.5	4.5	3.6	6.0	7.2	6.4
Item 5811 Subject B05 N	2927	1384	1498	2290	361	608	887	955	478	1661	1130	1163	734	357	580	20

D014B: Discussing problems with course work

	TOTAL	M	F	White	Black	NE	NC	S	W	Yes	No	None	Mari-juana Only	Few Pills	More Pills	Any Her-oin
5. Much more	13.0	11.5	14.0	9.5	29.6	14.8	9.9	15.8	11.1	11.4	14.9	10.9	14.4	13.1	14.4	39.3
4. A little more	24.2	24.1	24.5	23.0	27.0	26.4	21.5	22.5	29.4	25.0	22.3	23.0	26.1	23.6	24.6	32.5
3. About right	50.4	50.5	50.5	55.0	32.8	46.0	55.5	48.3	50.4	54.6	45.3	53.8	50.2	49.5	45.4	28.1
2. A little less	4.6	5.6	3.9	4.6	4.7	3.9	4.9	5.6	3.1	3.8	6.1	4.6	4.1	5.7	3.9	-
1. Much less	7.8	8.4	7.2	7.9	5.8	8.8	8.2	7.7	6.0	5.2	11.3	7.7	5.2	8.1	11.8	-
Item 5812 Subject B05 N	2893	1373	1476	2265	357	602	876	940	474	1639	1119	1139	727	354	579	20

D014C: Discussing any trouble you've gotten into

	TOTAL	M	F	White	Black	NE	NC	S	W	Yes	No	None	Mari-juana Only	Few Pills	More Pills	Any Her-oin
5. Much more	7.9	7.6	7.7	5.4	17.8	9.5	4.6	9.6	8.2	5.9	9.7	6.3	8.1	8.9	7.8	31.7
4. A little more	11.9	13.8	10.2	10.4	17.0	11.4	9.6	12.7	15.0	11.0	13.1	10.0	14.2	11.0	12.7	5.9
3. About right	58.7	57.6	59.9	63.5	39.7	55.8	63.1	55.3	60.6	65.9	50.0	63.2	58.8	58.6	51.2	46.7
2. A little less	5.4	6.2	4.7	4.5	8.1	4.8	5.1	6.1	5.3	3.8	7.3	4.6	4.9	6.0	6.6	8.4
1. Much less	16.2	14.8	17.5	16.2	17.4	18.5	17.5	16.3	10.9	13.4	20.0	15.8	14.0	15.5	21.8	7.4
Item 5813 Subject B05 N	2809	1347	1420	2197	346	581	856	914	458	1585	1091	1096	707	349	565	18

D014D: Discussing military plans

	TOTAL	M	F	White	Black	NE	NC	S	W	Yes	No	None	Mari-juana Only	Few Pills	More Pills	Any Her-oin
5. Much more	5.6	6.8	4.0	3.7	14.4	5.7	3.6	8.2	3.7	3.6	7.1	5.9	6.6	5.1	2.7	28.1
4. A little more	8.4	12.3	4.8	7.1	14.9	11.1	6.9	9.3	5.7	7.0	10.4	8.7	8.3	8.4	7.0	17.7
3. About right	44.6	41.9	47.4	48.9	24.4	41.1	48.5	40.8	49.7	50.8	37.3	49.0	43.6	45.1	39.4	21.5
2. A little less	6.5	8.1	5.1	6.4	5.7	6.2	7.4	5.4	7.4	6.1	7.1	5.6	6.7	8.7	6.1	5.3
1. Much less	35.0	30.9	38.7	33.9	40.7	35.8	33.6	36.3	33.6	32.5	38.2	30.8	34.7	32.7	44.9	27.5
Item 5814 Subject B05 N	2752	1328	1385	2158	341	567	842	898	444	1549	1076	1071	691	340	560	20

D014E: Discussing education or training plans

	TOTAL	M	F	White	Black	NE	NC	S	W	Yes	No	None	Mari-juana Only	Few Pills	More Pills	Any Her-oin
5. Much more	21.3	18.9	22.9	17.7	38.6	19.6	19.1	24.1	22.2	23.4	18.0	21.7	23.2	21.4	16.5	38.1
4. A little more	32.7	31.8	34.0	33.8	28.0	31.0	33.8	31.7	34.9	35.7	28.4	33.6	31.4	35.9	31.3	29.0
3. About right	34.9	37.1	33.1	37.5	24.4	36.3	37.0	31.7	35.6	34.1	36.5	35.2	35.6	33.9	34.7	17.8
2. A little less	3.4	4.0	2.9	3.1	3.6	3.1	3.0	4.7	2.0	2.5	4.9	3.1	2.7	2.6	5.4	-
1. Much less	7.6	8.2	7.1	7.8	5.4	10.0	7.0	7.8	5.3	4.4	12.1	6.3	7.1	6.1	12.0	15.0
Item 5815 Subject B05 N	2871	1361	1469	2251	354	591	867	936	477	1627	1110	1131	716	353	576	20

D014F: Discussing career plans or job choice

	TOTAL	M	F	White	Black	NE	NC	S	W	Yes	No	None	Mari-juana Only	Few Pills	More Pills	Any Her-oin
5. Much more	27.8	24.7	30.2	24.1	45.1	26.4	24.0	31.9	28.3	29.7	24.3	28.6	29.6	28.8	21.7	47.6
4. A little more	33.1	32.7	34.1	34.7	25.9	32.6	35.6	31.4	32.3	34.9	31.3	32.7	32.7	33.9	34.4	25.7
3. About right	30.7	33.1	28.3	32.8	22.5	31.1	32.1	27.9	32.9	30.6	30.9	31.7	30.4	28.6	31.1	20.7
2. A little less	2.4	3.1	1.7	2.0	2.8	1.0	2.6	2.7	3.1	1.5	3.5	1.9	2.3	2.0	3.1	6.0
1. Much less	6.1	6.4	5.8	6.3	3.7	9.0	5.5	6.1	3.4	3.4	10.0	5.0	4.9	6.6	9.7	-
Item 5816 Subject B05 N	2869	1362	1464	2243	354	592	869	938	471	1625	1112	1132	717	351	576	20

QUESTIONNAIRE FORM 1 1983	TOTAL	SEX		RACE		REGION				4YR COLLEGE PLANS		ILLICIT DRUG USE: LIFETIME				
		M	F	White	Black	NE	NC	S	W	Yes	No	None	Marijuana Only	Few Pills	More Pills	Any Heroin
N (Weighted No. of Cases):	3448	1611	1667	2555	435	814	974	1118	541	1798	1246	1269	848	428	746	30
% of Weighted Total:	100.0	46.7	48.3	74.1	12.6	23.6	28.3	32.4	15.7	52.2	36.1	36.8	24.6	12.4	21.6	.9
D014G: Discussing personal problems																
5. Much more	7.4	6.3	8.2	6.0	11.1	5.1	5.9	9.6	8.4	5.9	8.8	6.0	6.3	9.4	8.8	24.7
4. A little more	9.8	10.3	9.4	9.5	11.7	9.1	9.8	9.2	12.0	9.4	10.3	7.9	11.7	10.2	10.9	23.6
3. About right	53.0	53.2	53.4	57.6	33.4	50.8	56.2	48.7	58.7	59.8	44.5	58.2	53.8	52.7	44.2	29.1
2. A little less	6.3	8.1	4.6	5.2	11.6	5.4	6.1	7.5	5.4	5.0	8.4	6.6	5.8	4.9	5.9	9.1
1. Much less	23.5	22.2	24.5	21.7	32.3	29.5	22.0	25.0	15.6	19.9	28.0	21.3	22.4	22.8	30.2	13.5
Item 5817 Subject B05 N	2787	1340	1405	2177	347	574	846	912	455	1569	1087	1086	700	345	565	19

These last questions concern your health.

D015: During the LAST 30 DAYS, on how many days (if any) did you have the following problems or symptoms?

D015A: Headache																
1. None	20.6	29.4	12.2	18.5	28.6	19.0	18.0	22.3	23.9	19.2	21.8	21.8	21.3	17.7	18.0	20.0
2. One day	21.0	25.0	17.3	19.6	26.4	20.2	19.2	22.6	22.0	21.1	20.9	24.3	17.7	26.3	14.7	15.3
3. Two days	22.1	21.0	23.0	22.4	21.1	22.8	22.0	21.2	23.4	23.0	20.9	24.1	22.5	18.8	19.4	28.5
4. 3 to 5 days	19.8	16.1	23.5	21.2	14.6	21.1	21.2	19.5	16.5	19.9	19.9	15.5	24.6	20.6	23.6	4.6
5. 6 to 9 days	8.5	4.9	12.1	9.6	5.6	9.3	10.8	7.2	6.0	9.1	8.1	7.8	7.1	9.6	11.7	12.8
6. 10 to 19 days	5.0	2.3	7.7	5.6	1.8	4.7	5.1	4.4	6.4	5.0	5.1	4.0	4.3	4.8	7.9	18.9
7. 20+ days	2.9	1.3	4.4	3.1	1.9	2.8	3.8	2.8	1.8	2.7	3.1	2.5	2.4	2.2	4.8	-
Item 21310 Subject Q06 N	2948	1395	1507	2297	367	612	882	968	486	1667	1137	1161	732	365	587	22

D015B: Sore throat or hoarse voice																
1. None	38.0	43.6	32.4	35.5	50.0	35.5	33.3	44.2	37.4	36.9	39.1	42.7	39.5	32.9	29.4	40.6
2. One day	16.1	17.5	14.5	15.7	15.3	15.4	15.9	16.1	17.0	15.3	17.5	16.5	13.4	17.0	19.0	9.2
3. Two days	16.3	15.7	16.7	16.9	14.0	21.7	15.7	13.6	15.8	16.5	15.8	14.6	18.1	19.2	16.3	5.5
4. 3 to 5 days	18.3	15.1	21.6	19.5	13.8	16.2	20.8	16.1	20.6	18.8	17.7	15.9	19.2	19.9	18.8	22.2
5. 6 to 9 days	7.4	5.5	9.4	8.0	4.8	7.6	8.8	6.5	6.4	8.3	6.2	6.8	5.3	8.8	10.6	16.3
6. 10 to 19 days	3.2	1.9	4.5	3.6	1.7	2.9	4.6	2.5	2.3	3.5	2.9	2.5	3.7	1.8	5.1	-
7. 20+ days	0.8	0.6	0.9	0.8	0.4	0.8	0.9	0.8	0.5	0.8	0.8	0.9	0.6	0.4	0.8	6.2
Item 21320 Subject Q06 N	2943	1395	1501	2298	362	611	884	962	485	1663	1136	1158	731	366	586	22

D015C: Trouble with sinus congestion, runny nose, or sneezing																
1. None	24.9	26.3	23.4	21.6	40.6	26.6	19.5	28.0	26.7	23.6	26.1	26.3	26.7	22.2	20.4	28.4
2. One day	11.5	12.9	10.2	11.4	9.8	13.0	10.2	11.9	11.4	10.6	12.9	12.5	11.3	12.0	10.1	11.7
3. Two days	13.4	13.9	13.0	13.4	12.6	14.6	14.1	12.0	11.7	13.8	13.2	13.1	14.5	15.4	11.0	17.2
4. 3 to 5 days	22.3	21.3	23.3	23.1	20.2	22.6	23.0	20.5	24.5	21.9	23.2	22.0	22.6	21.7	23.3	6.7
5. 6 to 9 days	13.9	13.2	15.0	15.4	6.3	11.9	17.5	12.2	13.5	14.7	12.6	12.7	12.2	16.0	17.6	14.0
6. 10 to 19 days	8.5	7.4	9.5	9.5	5.0	6.8	9.4	8.9	8.2	9.8	7.1	8.7	7.3	9.3	9.7	15.8
7. 20+ days	5.3	4.9	5.7	5.4	5.6	4.4	6.2	5.5	4.1	5.6	4.8	4.7	5.4	3.4	7.9	6.1
Item 21330 Subject Q06 N	2940	1397	1498	2296	362	611	882	964	483	1665	1132	1158	730	366	585	21

D015D: Coughing spells																
1. None	56.5	60.0	53.1	55.0	60.5	57.0	53.0	56.9	61.4	58.4	54.2	61.7	56.9	51.9	48.6	36.6
2. One day	12.1	12.1	11.8	12.2	12.4	13.1	10.7	13.1	11.5	11.4	12.8	12.1	10.9	16.4	11.2	13.4
3. Two days	9.4	9.4	9.6	9.7	9.6	10.3	11.0	8.9	6.6	9.3	9.8	8.9	8.7	11.2	10.0	17.9
4. 3 to 5 days	11.4	9.6	13.1	11.6	10.2	10.7	13.1	10.3	11.4	11.6	11.3	10.1	12.4	9.7	14.0	17.8
5. 6 to 9 days	5.2	5.3	5.2	5.7	3.7	4.0	6.2	5.5	4.5	4.4	6.0	3.7	5.1	6.9	6.7	7.7
6. 10 to 19 days	3.3	2.0	4.6	3.8	1.2	2.5	3.5	3.6	3.2	3.3	3.5	2.4	3.6	3.0	5.5	-
7. 20+ days	2.0	1.5	2.5	2.0	2.3	2.4	2.5	1.7	1.5	1.8	2.4	1.2	2.5	0.8	4.0	6.6
Item 21340 Subject Q06 N	2942	1396	1500	2296	363	610	885	963	485	1661	1138	1158	731	366	585	22

D015E: Chest colds																
1. None	73.2	75.8	70.8	72.6	75.2	70.0	73.1	73.0	77.9	74.1	72.4	78.3	72.8	71.0	66.2	45.0
2. One day	7.4	8.5	6.4	7.4	4.5	7.9	7.1	7.5	7.0	7.0	7.4	6.6	6.7	9.1	8.8	16.5
3. Two days	7.2	7.2	7.2	7.2	8.0	9.8	7.2	6.7	5.0	6.5	8.2	6.0	6.7	7.3	9.3	6.4
4. 3 to 5 days	6.8	4.9	8.7	7.1	7.2	6.6	7.0	7.0	6.5	7.1	6.6	4.6	8.2	7.4	8.2	19.9
5. 6 to 9 days	3.1	2.0	4.2	3.3	3.3	3.1	3.5	3.0	2.6	3.3	2.9	2.6	2.6	3.7	4.7	6.4
6. 10 to 19 days	1.6	0.9	2.2	1.7	1.0	2.3	1.8	1.5	0.4	1.4	1.9	1.4	2.2	0.8	1.8	2.8
7. 20+ days	0.7	0.7	0.6	0.6	0.7	0.3	0.3	1.2	0.6	0.5	0.6	0.4	0.8	0.6	0.9	3.0
Item 21350 Subject Q06 N	2933	1388	1499	2287	363	611	882	959	481	1656	1133	1153	732	363	585	20

QUESTIONNAIRE FORM 1 1983	TOTAL	SEX		RACE		REGION				4YR COLLEGE PLANS		ILLICIT DRUG USE: LIFETIME				
		M	F	White	Black	NE	NC	S	W	Yes	No	None	Mari-juana Only	Few Pills	More Pills	Any Her-oin
N (Weighted No. of Cases):	3448	1611	1667	2555	435	814	974	1118	541	1798	1246	1269	848	428	746	30
% of Weighted Total:	100.0	46.7	48.3	74.1	12.6	23.6	28.3	32.4	15.7	52.2	36.1	36.8	24.6	12.4	21.6	.9
D015F: Coughing up phlegm or blood																
1. None	83.5	82.4	84.5	81.9	91.9	85.1	78.7	86.3	85.1	82.1	85.8	87.8	85.2	81.6	74.6	63.4
2. One day	3.2	4.3	2.2	3.3	1.9	3.2	4.0	2.6	2.7	3.9	2.2	2.6	3.2	3.6	3.4	11.4
3. Two days	3.8	4.2	3.6	4.3	1.4	4.0	3.9	3.5	4.1	4.5	2.8	3.3	2.8	4.3	5.8	12.1
4. 3 to 5 days	4.5	4.7	4.4	4.9	2.3	3.8	6.9	3.1	3.9	3.9	5.5	2.8	4.0	6.2	7.6	6.1
5. 6 to 9 days	2.5	2.6	2.4	2.7	1.5	1.7	3.8	2.1	1.8	2.8	1.9	1.4	2.8	3.4	3.5	-
6. 10 to 19 days	1.4	0.9	1.7	1.7	-	0.7	1.8	1.4	1.3	1.5	1.1	1.1	0.8	0.8	2.8	4.3
7. 20+ days	1.1	0.9	1.2	1.2	0.9	1.5	1.0	1.1	1.1	1.2	0.8	0.9	1.2	0.2	2.3	2.7
Item 21360　Subject Q06　N	2933	1389	1498	2289	362	610	883	959	481	1653	1137	1156	730	361	584	22
D015G: Shortness of breath when you were not exercising																
1. None	85.2	89.3	81.4	85.2	85.1	85.4	83.0	85.3	88.8	87.6	82.7	90.5	87.7	84.2	73.6	46.4
2. One day	5.0	4.4	5.7	5.2	5.1	4.8	6.5	4.2	4.1	4.3	6.0	3.5	4.2	4.3	8.6	18.6
3. Two days	4.0	3.4	4.7	3.9	4.7	3.3	4.9	4.6	2.1	3.4	4.7	2.7	3.1	5.0	6.3	24.3
4. 3 to 5 days	2.6	1.1	3.9	2.3	3.1	3.0	2.0	3.3	1.8	2.1	3.1	1.6	1.8	3.4	5.0	6.9
5. 6 to 9 days	1.4	0.7	1.9	1.4	0.5	1.5	1.5	1.5	0.7	1.3	1.3	0.6	1.3	1.3	3.0	1.8
6. 10 to 19 days	0.8	0.4	1.3	1.0	-	0.7	1.4	0.5	0.8	0.6	1.1	0.5	0.8	0.9	1.6	2.0
7. 20+ days	1.0	0.6	1.1	0.8	1.6	1.3	0.7	0.6	1.7	0.8	1.1	0.5	1.1	0.9	1.9	-
Item 21370　Subject Q06　N	2936	1390	1500	2292	364	610	885	960	481	1655	1138	1157	731	362	584	22
D015H: Wheezing or gasping																
1. None	89.8	90.5	89.1	89.8	90.6	88.0	90.2	90.3	90.1	91.1	88.7	93.8	91.4	88.1	81.8	61.1
2. One day	4.2	4.5	3.8	4.1	3.9	5.3	4.1	3.5	4.1	4.1	4.0	2.7	3.3	4.4	7.1	20.9
3. Two days	2.5	2.0	2.9	2.6	2.0	3.0	2.5	2.2	2.4	2.1	3.0	1.8	1.7	2.3	4.8	1.8
4. 3 to 5 days	1.6	1.6	1.7	1.8	0.9	2.1	1.3	2.2	0.7	1.2	2.2	0.8	1.3	2.0	3.1	16.3
5. 6 to 9 days	0.7	0.5	0.9	0.7	1.1	0.7	0.8	0.6	0.7	0.7	0.5	0.5	1.0	1.1	0.7	-
6. 10 to 19 days	0.6	0.3	0.9	0.7	-	0.8	0.8	0.5	0.3	0.4	0.9	0.1	0.5	1.4	1.4	-
7. 20+ days	0.6	0.5	0.7	0.4	1.5	0.1	0.4	0.6	1.7	0.5	0.7	0.3	0.8	0.7	1.1	-
Item 21380　Subject Q06　N	2918	1383	1489	2280	360	603	884	955	476	1645	1130	1154	723	359	581	22
D015I: Trouble remembering new things																
1. None	75.5	78.7	72.9	76.2	73.6	74.2	76.5	76.0	74.0	75.1	76.6	81.2	77.7	68.7	66.7	46.7
2. One day	8.0	8.1	7.7	7.4	10.8	10.0	6.2	7.4	10.3	8.8	6.9	6.7	6.7	9.8	10.4	16.9
3. Two days	6.2	4.4	7.7	6.1	6.3	6.1	6.0	6.7	5.8	6.4	5.5	4.6	6.4	10.1	7.0	3.3
4. 3 to 5 days	5.2	4.7	5.6	5.1	4.5	5.0	5.5	4.7	5.6	5.0	5.5	4.3	4.8	6.4	6.4	9.3
5. 6 to 9 days	2.0	1.8	2.2	2.2	1.3	1.8	2.6	2.0	1.3	1.7	2.4	1.2	1.9	1.9	3.3	19.0
6. 10 to 19 days	1.5	1.1	1.9	1.4	1.7	1.3	1.6	1.5	1.6	1.4	1.6	1.0	0.7	1.1	3.9	4.9
7. 20+ days	1.6	1.1	1.8	1.5	1.9	1.5	1.7	1.6	1.4	1.6	1.5	1.0	1.9	2.0	2.3	-
Item 21390　Subject Q06　N	2923	1383	1492	2288	360	608	884	954	477	1648	1132	1155	728	358	581	22
D015J: Difficulty thinking or concentrating																
1. None	54.3	62.0	47.1	53.9	61.5	54.4	53.5	57.0	50.3	52.0	57.3	54.9	57.4	53.6	49.5	36.9
2. One day	13.6	12.7	14.5	13.5	13.2	13.5	14.0	13.1	13.9	13.7	13.8	13.0	13.1	16.1	14.3	8.4
3. Two days	12.5	11.3	13.7	12.6	10.5	13.1	11.8	12.1	14.1	13.3	11.4	12.9	12.3	13.3	11.7	16.0
4. 3 to 5 days	10.6	8.2	13.0	10.5	7.6	10.2	10.3	10.0	13.0	11.6	9.0	11.3	9.6	8.8	11.3	19.3
5. 6 to 9 days	4.2	3.0	5.4	4.4	3.1	3.2	5.7	3.8	3.5	4.2	4.2	3.9	3.3	4.3	5.7	14.2
6. 10 to 19 days	2.3	1.3	3.4	2.6	2.0	2.3	2.5	2.5	2.0	2.3	2.5	1.8	2.1	2.8	3.7	5.2
7. 20+ days	2.4	1.5	3.0	2.5	1.9	3.3	2.2	1.6	3.2	2.9	1.8	2.2	2.3	1.2	3.8	-
Item 21400　Subject Q06　N	2923	1382	1493	2284	360	605	884	955	479	1649	1130	1153	728	358	583	20
D015K: Trouble learning new things																
1. None	71.7	75.3	68.6	72.9	72.3	70.8	71.2	73.6	69.9	71.0	72.8	72.8	75.3	67.2	69.6	44.9
2. One day	10.4	9.4	11.2	9.3	11.9	11.1	9.1	10.4	11.9	10.6	10.0	9.8	9.0	14.2	10.1	23.4
3. Two days	8.2	6.5	9.6	8.3	6.9	9.0	8.9	6.8	8.4	9.1	7.0	9.2	6.1	9.3	7.1	27.7
4. 3 to 5 days	6.1	5.0	6.9	5.5	6.4	5.8	6.8	5.2	6.8	5.7	6.2	5.2	6.3	5.6	7.0	4.0
5. 6 to 9 days	1.7	1.6	1.9	1.8	1.4	1.5	2.0	1.7	1.6	1.8	1.8	1.7	1.7	1.8	2.0	-
6. 10 to 19 days	1.1	1.4	0.7	1.2	0.3	0.7	1.1	1.3	0.9	0.9	1.1	0.7	0.9	1.0	2.3	-
7. 20+ days	0.9	0.6	1.0	1.0	0.8	1.0	0.9	1.0	0.6	0.8	1.0	0.5	0.7	0.9	2.1	-
Item 21410　Subject Q06　N	2924	1384	1493	2285	363	604	882	958	480	1654	1126	1155	727	359	582	20

QUESTIONNAIRE FORM 1 1983	TOTAL	SEX		RACE		REGION				4YR COLLEGE PLANS		ILLICIT DRUG USE: LIFETIME				
		M	F	White	Black	NE	NC	S	W	Yes	No	None	Mari- juana Only	Few Pills	More Pills	Any Her- oin
N (Weighted No. of Cases):	3448	1611	1667	2555	435	814	974	1118	541	1798	1246	1269	848	428	746	30
% of Weighted Total:	100.0	46.7	48.3	74.1	12.6	23.6	28.3	32.4	15.7	52.2	36.1	36.8	24.6	12.4	21.6	.9
D015L: Trouble sleeping																
1. None	43.4	48.2	38.4	40.4	57.6	45.9	37.5	45.3	47.6	42.5	44.2	46.4	42.0	39.3	39.7	41.1
2. One day	15.0	15.5	14.5	15.2	13.3	13.6	16.7	15.3	13.1	15.4	14.9	17.2	14.1	15.6	12.2	24.2
3. Two days	15.0	13.5	16.9	15.8	11.3	17.7	15.5	13.2	14.4	15.8	14.1	14.9	16.2	15.2	14.1	5.4
4. 3 to 5 days	13.7	12.9	14.6	14.9	8.0	13.1	15.5	12.2	13.9	14.0	13.5	11.9	14.4	16.8	15.3	11.6
5. 6 to 9 days	6.0	5.0	7.0	6.5	3.7	5.6	6.3	6.1	5.9	5.9	6.4	4.9	5.8	6.9	8.2	2.7
6. 10 to 19 days	4.0	2.9	5.1	4.2	3.7	2.5	5.0	4.3	3.7	3.8	4.0	2.5	4.1	4.3	6.5	11.8
7. 20+ days	2.8	2.0	3.5	3.0	2.5	1.6	3.5	3.6	1.3	2.5	3.0	2.2	3.4	2.0	4.0	3.3
Item 21420　Subject Q06　N	2919	1382	1491	2283	358	605	877	957	479	1647	1129	1150	724	361	583	22
D015M: Trouble getting started in the morning																
1. None	34.0	38.1	29.8	31.2	47.1	34.9	30.8	38.3	30.0	31.4	36.6	38.4	34.0	28.1	26.9	38.2
2. One day	9.4	9.0	9.8	8.8	10.5	9.9	8.3	10.1	9.4	9.1	10.0	9.0	9.5	12.7	7.8	6.1
3. Two days	12.0	11.8	12.3	12.0	11.8	11.5	11.7	11.4	14.4	12.8	10.6	12.3	12.3	13.0	10.6	11.3
4. 3 to 5 days	14.5	13.3	15.5	15.8	8.8	13.3	15.6	13.4	15.8	15.4	13.5	13.7	15.1	16.8	14.4	10.1
5. 6 to 9 days	9.1	8.3	10.1	9.4	7.5	10.2	8.9	8.6	9.2	10.2	7.9	8.8	8.2	9.1	11.0	2.8
6. 10 to 19 days	7.4	7.2	7.7	8.5	3.5	6.9	9.9	5.7	7.0	7.7	7.7	6.3	7.4	7.3	9.7	23.2
7. 20+ days	13.6	12.4	14.8	14.1	10.8	13.4	14.7	12.5	14.2	13.5	13.7	11.5	13.6	12.9	19.7	8.2
Item 21430　Subject Q06　N	2920	1375	1497	2280	361	606	880	957	477	1649	1127	1149	727	359	583	22
D015N: Stayed home most or all of a day because you were not feeling well																
1. None	61.0	68.8	53.6	60.3	62.9	56.0	62.7	62.6	61.1	61.8	59.8	67.5	60.1	61.3	49.1	54.1
2. One day	17.0	14.0	19.8	17.7	16.0	19.7	15.2	16.3	18.1	17.6	16.4	15.8	17.2	16.7	18.7	21.1
3. Two days	12.8	10.5	14.9	13.3	11.2	13.8	12.9	12.6	11.7	12.4	13.7	11.0	12.4	11.7	18.0	4.9
4. 3 to 5 days	6.5	4.9	8.2	6.6	5.5	7.8	6.7	5.9	5.8	6.3	6.7	4.4	8.2	6.6	8.9	13.0
5. 6 to 9 days	1.4	0.8	2.1	1.2	1.8	2.1	1.7	0.9	1.2	1.3	1.6	0.9	1.5	1.8	2.4	-
6. 10 to 19 days	0.9	0.7	1.1	0.8	1.5	-	0.6	1.2	1.9	0.5	1.3	0.3	0.3	1.5	1.9	6.9
7. 20+ days	0.4	0.3	0.4	0.2	1.1	0.6	0.1	0.5	0.2	0.1	0.6	0.1	0.2	0.5	1.1	-
Item 21440　Subject Q06　N	2935	1390	1499	2291	365	610	884	960	480	1658	1134	1156	730	363	584	22
D016: In the LAST 12 MONTHS, how many times (if any) have you seen a doctor or other professional for each of the following?																
D016A: For a routine physical check-up																
1. None	47.9	48.4	47.8	48.7	42.7	38.7	48.6	51.0	51.9	43.4	54.9	49.9	46.4	43.4	49.3	25.7
2. Once	37.8	38.0	37.6	38.8	32.3	43.5	37.6	34.5	37.5	41.9	31.8	37.6	37.5	42.3	35.0	52.0
3. Twice	10.6	10.2	10.6	9.4	16.8	13.4	9.2	10.8	9.4	11.3	9.7	8.3	12.8	11.5	12.3	8.4
4. 3 to 5 times	2.9	2.6	3.2	2.6	5.6	3.3	3.9	2.7	0.9	2.7	2.7	3.4	2.5	2.4	2.4	14.0
5. 6 to 9 times	0.2	0.3	0.1	0.1	0.4	-	0.2	0.3	0.1	0.2	-	0.1	-	0.2	0.4	-
6. 10+ times	0.7	0.6	0.7	0.4	2.2	1.1	0.5	0.7	0.3	0.5	0.9	0.7	0.9	0.2	0.6	-
Item 21450　Subject Q06　N	2913	1380	1487	2275	359	603	881	950	478	1649	1122	1157	720	360	574	22
D016B: For an injury suffered in a fight, assault, or auto accident																
1. None	91.7	89.3	94.2	91.9	93.3	90.0	92.5	92.7	90.2	92.5	90.8	94.9	90.9	89.7	88.0	70.0
2. Once	5.0	6.5	3.5	5.0	4.1	6.0	4.9	4.2	5.5	4.7	5.6	3.3	5.6	6.9	6.4	14.2
3. Twice	2.0	2.5	1.3	2.0	1.4	2.6	1.7	1.9	2.0	2.0	1.8	0.8	1.6	3.0	4.0	11.1
4. 3 to 5 times	0.8	1.1	0.5	0.7	0.8	0.8	0.4	0.8	1.4	0.6	1.0	0.6	1.1	0.4	1.0	4.7
5. 6 to 9 times	0.2	0.3	0.1	0.1	-	0.5	0.1	-	0.2	0.1	0.2	*	0.4	-	0.3	-
6. 10+ times	0.4	0.4	0.4	0.3	0.4	0.1	0.3	0.4	0.8	0.1	0.6	0.4	0.4	-	0.3	-
Item 21460　Subject Q06　N	2891	1370	1478	2264	352	592	879	941	479	1635	1116	1146	716	360	568	22
D016C: For any other accidental injury																
1. None	81.3	75.4	86.7	79.6	90.4	77.9	80.7	84.7	79.7	78.8	84.7	82.7	79.2	78.2	83.4	58.5
2. Once	9.8	12.4	7.4	10.5	5.5	12.1	9.4	8.7	10.0	10.9	8.6	9.7	10.7	10.6	8.7	5.3
3. Twice	4.5	6.2	3.1	5.2	1.7	5.2	5.4	3.2	4.7	4.7	4.2	3.5	5.2	7.2	4.2	11.1
4. 3 to 5 times	2.8	3.9	1.8	3.0	1.3	2.7	3.5	2.1	3.0	3.3	2.1	2.9	3.2	1.9	2.1	25.1
5. 6 to 9 times	0.9	1.1	0.6	1.0	0.4	1.2	0.8	0.6	1.4	1.3	0.4	0.7	1.0	1.7	1.0	-
6. 10+ times	0.6	0.9	0.4	0.6	0.8	0.9	0.2	0.6	1.1	1.0	0.1	0.4	0.6	0.4	0.6	-
Item 21470　Subject Q06　N	2889	1368	1478	2263	350	593	879	936	480	1635	1113	1149	716	360	565	22

*=less than .05 per cent.

QUESTIONNAIRE FORM 1 1983	TOTAL	SEX		RACE		REGION				4YR COLLEGE PLANS		ILLICIT DRUG USE: LIFETIME				
		M	F	White	Black	NE	NC	S	W	Yes	No	None	Mari- juana Only	Few Pills	More Pills	Any Her- oin
N (Weighted No. of Cases):	3448	1611	1667	2555	435	814	974	1118	541	1798	1246	1269	848	428	746	30
% of Weighted Total:	100.0	46.7	48.3	74.1	12.6	23.6	28.3	32.4	15.7	52.2	36.1	36.8	24.6	12.4	21.6	.9

D016D: For some physical illness or symptom

1. None	62.3	69.6	55.7	60.2	71.8	64.9	61.7	63.1	58.9	59.9	66.4	65.9	61.9	57.0	57.4	59.5
2. Once	18.2	17.0	19.1	18.9	13.5	17.1	18.9	17.6	19.4	18.8	17.2	17.2	19.7	19.2	17.7	29.1
3. Twice	11.0	8.0	13.7	11.6	9.4	11.7	9.3	11.1	13.4	12.0	9.4	9.3	11.3	13.3	13.5	2.4
4. 3 to 5 times	5.6	3.4	7.6	6.2	3.3	3.8	7.3	5.1	5.5	5.8	5.0	4.9	3.9	8.1	8.1	5.7
5. 6 to 9 times	1.3	0.5	2.0	1.4	0.7	0.9	1.4	1.4	1.2	1.5	0.9	1.0	1.5	1.2	1.7	3.2
6. 10+ times	1.6	1.5	1.7	1.7	1.2	1.6	1.4	1.8	1.6	2.0	1.1	1.8	1.7	1.3	1.5	-
Item 21480 Subject Q06 N	2884	1366	1477	2262	351	592	878	941	473	1634	1111	1146	715	359	564	22

D016E: For some emotional or psychological problem or symptom

1. None	96.2	97.3	95.5	96.9	94.5	95.6	95.6	97.1	96.5	96.2	96.6	97.7	97.5	94.4	93.6	81.6
2. Once	1.4	1.3	1.5	1.2	2.2	2.1	1.8	1.0	1.0	1.5	1.2	0.7	1.1	2.6	2.4	5.7
3. Twice	0.8	0.7	0.8	0.6	1.3	0.7	1.1	0.8	0.3	0.7	0.8	0.6	0.4	1.1	1.3	5.2
4. 3 to 5 times	0.5	0.2	0.8	0.5	0.9	-	0.9	0.5	0.7	0.4	0.8	0.5	0.5	0.7	0.6	-
5. 6 to 9 times	0.2	-	0.5	0.2	-	0.4	0.1	0.1	0.5	0.2	0.2	-	0.3	0.1	0.8	-
6. 10+ times	0.8	0.5	0.8	0.6	1.1	1.2	0.6	0.6	1.1	1.1	0.3	0.5	0.4	1.0	1.3	7.4
Item 21490 Subject Q06 N	2884	1368	1472	2257	351	590	876	940	478	1637	1110	1147	713	357	566	22

D017: In the LAST 12 MONTHS, how many times (if any) have you spent one or more nights in the hospital . . .

D017A: Because of an injury

1. None	94.8	92.9	96.6	95.3	91.8	93.5	95.1	94.5	96.5	94.4	95.5	96.1	94.2	96.7	92.5	79.8
2. Once	3.0	4.2	2.0	2.9	4.3	4.1	3.0	3.2	1.5	3.6	2.3	2.3	3.3	3.0	4.1	7.7
3. Twice	1.0	1.4	0.6	1.0	1.2	1.6	1.0	1.1	0.4	0.8	1.3	0.5	1.3	0.3	1.8	7.8
4. 3 to 5 times	0.7	1.0	0.5	0.4	2.0	0.4	0.6	0.7	1.4	0.6	0.6	0.5	1.2	-	1.0	4.7
5. 6 to 9 times	0.2	0.3	0.2	0.2	0.7	0.4	0.2	0.4	-	0.3	0.2	0.3	-	0.1	0.4	-
6. 10+ times	0.2	0.3	0.1	0.2	-	0.2	0.2	0.1	0.2	0.3	*	0.3	0.1	-	0.2	-
Item 21500 Subject Q06 N	2885	1373	1467	2262	350	596	872	942	475	1637	1110	1143	713	359	571	22

D017B: Because of some physical illness

1. None	94.1	94.1	94.1	94.5	90.4	93.6	94.0	93.5	95.8	94.1	94.4	95.4	93.0	93.2	93.6	75.5
2. Once	3.2	3.5	2.8	3.2	4.0	3.1	3.3	3.8	1.9	3.2	3.4	2.1	4.0	5.7	2.6	14.3
3. Twice	1.2	1.3	0.9	1.0	2.1	1.8	0.9	1.2	0.9	1.0	1.1	1.0	1.7	0.8	1.1	3.7
4. 3 to 5 times	1.0	0.6	1.4	0.7	2.1	1.1	0.7	1.1	1.1	1.0	0.6	0.4	1.3	-	1.9	4.7
5. 6 to 9 times	0.3	0.3	0.3	0.2	0.9	0.2	0.6	0.1	0.1	0.2	0.4	0.4	-	0.3	0.4	-
6. 10+ times	0.4	0.2	0.5	0.3	0.4	0.2	0.5	0.3	0.2	0.5	0.1	0.6	0.1	-	0.4	1.7
Item 21510 Subject Q06 N	2883	1369	1469	2261	347	592	873	940	477	1635	1109	1143	715	357	568	22

D018: Overall, relative to other people your age, do you think your physical health over the past year has been . . .

1. Much poorer than average	2.3	2.0	2.4	1.9	2.6	2.4	1.5	2.9	2.7	1.4	3.2	1.9	2.4	2.3	2.8	5.8
2. Somewhat poorer than average	9.1	5.1	12.6	9.1	9.2	10.2	9.1	8.7	8.3	8.8	9.4	7.5	7.8	11.3	13.2	3.1
3. About average	36.6	31.9	41.0	36.1	39.4	36.3	33.9	38.1	39.1	33.3	41.2	33.1	35.8	40.1	41.4	58.4
4. Somewhat better than average	30.0	33.0	27.1	31.5	25.3	32.2	32.8	26.5	28.7	31.7	27.6	31.8	30.3	27.3	28.0	23.4
5. Much better than average	22.0	27.9	16.8	21.4	23.4	18.9	22.7	23.8	21.2	24.8	18.6	25.7	23.6	18.9	14.6	9.2
Item 21520 Subject Q06 N	2886	1357	1484	2271	345	594	877	937	477	1641	1106	1144	717	356	573	19

*=less than .05 per cent.

QUESTIONNAIRE FORM 2 1983	TOTAL	SEX		RACE		REGION				4YR COLLEGE PLANS		ILLICIT DRUG USE: LIFETIME				
		M	F	White	Black	NE	NC	S	W	Yes	No	None	Marijuana Only	Few Pills	More Pills	Any Heroin
N (Weighted No. of Cases):	3435	1671	1641	2610	419	829	979	1077	550	1848	1335	1281	705	472	851	47
% of Weighted Total:	100.0	48.6	47.8	76.0	12.2	24.1	28.5	31.4	16.0	53.8	38.9	37.3	20.5	13.7	24.8	1.4

A01: Taking all things together, how would you say things are these days–would you say you're very happy, pretty happy, or not too happy these days?

	TOTAL	M	F	White	Black	NE	NC	S	W	Yes	No	None	Marijuana Only	Few Pills	More Pills	Any Heroin
3. Very happy	17.3	15.0	19.7	18.7	8.5	18.1	15.2	16.5	21.1	20.1	14.4	18.7	18.7	15.5	15.2	11.6
2. Pretty happy	69.3	72.0	67.0	70.1	72.1	69.4	70.5	70.4	65.1	69.2	70.0	69.2	67.8	74.0	69.1	67.2
1. Not too happy	13.4	13.0	13.3	11.2	19.5	12.5	14.3	13.1	13.8	10.6	15.6	12.1	13.5	10.5	15.6	21.2
Item 1190 Subject P01,Q01 N	3356	1629	1617	2563	410	801	959	1057	539	1819	1296	1254	688	463	831	46

A02: The next questions ask about the kinds of things you might do. How often do you do each of the following?

A02A: Watch TV

	TOTAL	M	F	White	Black	NE	NC	S	W	Yes	No	None	Marijuana Only	Few Pills	More Pills	Any Heroin
5. Almost everyday	75.1	77.1	73.1	74.9	79.8	72.1	75.9	79.6	69.3	74.6	75.4	78.7	75.1	73.7	71.5	59.5
4. At least once a week	21.5	19.5	23.6	21.5	18.3	23.9	20.9	18.7	24.7	22.1	20.9	18.8	22.4	23.3	23.7	31.1
3. Once or twice a month	2.5	2.3	2.6	2.7	0.6	2.9	2.6	1.4	3.8	2.7	2.2	1.8	1.8	2.5	3.6	7.9
2. A few times a year	0.6	0.6	0.6	0.6	1.0	0.6	0.4	0.2	1.7	0.4	0.9	0.6	0.3	0.3	0.9	-
1. Never	0.3	0.5	0.1	0.2	0.3	0.5	0.2	0.2	0.5	0.1	0.6	0.1	0.4	0.2	0.3	1.5
Item 5820 Subject C07 N	3421	1664	1635	2601	415	825	974	1072	550	1843	1327	1274	701	468	851	47

A02B: Go to movies

	TOTAL	M	F	White	Black	NE	NC	S	W	Yes	No	None	Marijuana Only	Few Pills	More Pills	Any Heroin
5. Almost everyday	0.2	0.4	-	0.1	0.1	0.2	0.4	0.1	0.1	0.2	0.2	0.2	0.2	0.3	0.1	1.5
4. At least once a week	10.5	10.7	10.1	9.6	12.8	10.7	9.5	11.5	10.0	10.0	11.4	10.3	12.2	12.1	8.4	3.6
3. Once or twice a month	56.0	55.9	56.9	58.6	44.4	52.1	57.4	55.8	59.8	58.0	54.3	56.2	58.5	54.7	56.2	54.0
2. A few times a year	31.3	30.9	31.4	30.3	38.6	34.7	31.3	30.4	28.0	30.2	32.1	30.9	27.4	31.8	33.8	39.0
1. Never	2.0	2.1	1.6	1.4	4.1	2.2	1.4	2.3	2.2	1.5	1.9	2.4	1.6	1.1	1.5	1.9
Item 5830 Subject C07 N	3417	1664	1631	2600	412	823	973	1072	549	1838	1327	1275	700	467	850	47

A02C: Attend art shows, musical performances, or theater plays

	TOTAL	M	F	White	Black	NE	NC	S	W	Yes	No	None	Marijuana Only	Few Pills	More Pills	Any Heroin
5. Almost everyday	0.3	0.6	0.1	0.3	0.5	0.5	0.1	0.2	0.7	0.4	0.3	0.1	0.4	0.9	0.3	-
4. At least once a week	1.0	1.3	0.7	0.8	1.4	0.6	1.0	1.3	0.8	0.9	1.2	0.8	0.6	0.8	1.4	2.1
3. Once or twice a month	8.1	7.8	8.3	7.7	8.8	8.8	7.0	6.7	11.9	11.0	4.6	7.3	7.3	9.2	9.1	13.1
2. A few times a year	56.8	53.1	61.0	58.8	53.5	56.2	59.0	55.0	57.4	63.9	48.3	58.1	54.3	60.0	55.6	64.0
1. Never	33.8	37.2	29.8	32.4	35.8	33.9	32.8	36.8	29.2	23.9	45.6	33.6	37.4	29.0	33.6	20.9
Item 5840 Subject C07 N	3422	1662	1637	2602	416	825	978	1072	548	1844	1326	1275	703	471	846	47

A02D: Ride around in a car (or motorcycle) just for fun

	TOTAL	M	F	White	Black	NE	NC	S	W	Yes	No	None	Marijuana Only	Few Pills	More Pills	Any Heroin
5. Almost everyday	33.9	37.7	29.6	33.3	34.0	30.9	33.8	36.5	33.4	26.9	42.3	23.9	34.4	35.7	45.9	66.2
4. At least once a week	35.5	36.6	35.5	36.5	34.5	34.1	36.5	37.6	32.0	37.8	33.2	34.0	37.8	39.3	34.2	26.0
3. Once or twice a month	14.9	13.4	16.4	16.3	11.8	16.3	15.3	13.0	15.8	16.9	13.4	17.6	15.9	12.8	12.0	6.9
2. A few times a year	8.7	6.8	10.4	8.5	7.5	9.9	7.7	7.4	11.0	10.4	5.9	13.8	7.5	5.5	4.6	0.9
1. Never	7.0	5.6	8.2	5.5	12.3	8.9	6.6	5.5	7.8	8.0	5.1	10.6	4.4	6.8	3.3	-
Item 5850 Subject C07 N	3431	1668	1641	2608	418	827	978	1075	550	1845	1334	1280	704	471	851	47

A02E: Participate in community affairs or volunteer work

	TOTAL	M	F	White	Black	NE	NC	S	W	Yes	No	None	Marijuana Only	Few Pills	More Pills	Any Heroin
5. Almost everyday	2.3	2.2	2.4	1.7	3.9	3.2	1.3	2.2	2.8	2.5	1.8	3.1	1.8	1.9	1.3	3.4
4. At least once a week	6.5	5.3	7.6	6.6	6.4	5.8	5.7	7.8	6.7	7.9	4.8	8.5	4.4	7.3	5.2	6.3
3. Once or twice a month	13.1	12.1	14.3	12.9	15.1	10.8	14.7	12.7	14.6	14.9	10.7	15.5	11.4	14.3	10.4	6.4
2. A few times a year	46.7	45.9	48.0	48.9	40.6	43.7	48.6	48.1	45.0	49.7	43.9	48.5	48.3	48.2	42.4	44.5
1. Never	31.4	34.5	27.6	29.9	33.9	36.5	29.7	29.3	30.8	25.0	38.9	24.4	34.1	28.3	40.7	39.5
Item 5860 Subject C07,O02 N	3414	1661	1632	2597	417	826	975	1074	539	1837	1327	1275	703	467	844	47

A02F: Play a musical instrument or sing

	TOTAL	M	F	White	Black	NE	NC	S	W	Yes	No	None	Marijuana Only	Few Pills	More Pills	Any Heroin
5. Almost everyday	28.2	24.0	32.6	28.0	33.9	23.9	30.4	28.6	29.8	31.9	23.3	32.9	24.8	25.1	26.4	32.7
4. At least once a week	9.6	9.2	10.3	9.2	12.5	6.6	8.8	12.5	9.9	11.4	7.9	11.2	9.1	9.3	7.5	14.8
3. Once or twice a month	5.5	4.4	6.7	5.4	6.4	5.6	4.7	6.0	5.9	6.0	4.9	6.1	5.0	4.4	5.8	2.9
2. A few times a year	12.3	12.7	12.1	12.2	9.6	13.6	11.7	10.7	14.8	13.1	11.1	12.4	11.3	14.5	12.4	7.4
1. Never	44.4	49.7	38.3	45.2	37.6	50.3	44.4	42.2	39.6	37.6	52.8	37.4	49.8	46.6	47.8	42.2
Item 5870 Subject C07 N	3415	1663	1630	2599	413	822	977	1070	546	1837	1328	1273	701	468	848	47

QUESTIONNAIRE FORM 2 1983	TOTAL	SEX		RACE		REGION				4YR COLLEGE PLANS		ILLICIT DRUG USE: LIFETIME				
		M	F	White	Black	NE	NC	S	W	Yes	No	None	Mari- juana Only	Few Pills	More Pills	Any Her- oin
N (Weighted No. of Cases):	3435	1671	1641	2610	419	829	979	1077	550	1848	1335	1281	705	472	851	47
% of Weighted Total:	100.0	48.6	47.8	76.0	12.2	24.1	28.5	31.4	16.0	53.8	38.9	37.3	20.5	13.7	24.8	1.4

A02G: Do creative writing

5. Almost everyday	4.7	3.3	6.1	4.2	6.4	5.4	5.0	3.4	5.9	5.1	4.4	4.2	3.4	5.6	5.9	6.8
4. At least once a week	12.3	10.7	13.7	12.3	11.7	12.0	11.6	12.1	14.0	14.9	9.1	13.9	9.9	12.5	12.1	17.0
3. Once or twice a month	17.2	15.4	19.3	17.5	15.8	18.4	15.3	16.9	19.3	21.1	12.0	19.0	15.7	16.0	16.9	17.1
2. A few times a year	29.1	28.0	30.3	29.5	28.0	28.3	28.2	29.7	30.8	31.0	27.5	29.9	30.4	30.1	26.6	32.0
1. Never	36.7	42.6	30.7	36.5	38.2	35.9	39.9	37.9	29.9	27.9	47.0	33.0	40.6	35.7	38.6	27.2
Item 5880 Subject C07 N	3413	1663	1628	2596	413	821	976	1071	545	1836	1327	1270	701	469	848	47

A02H: Actively participate in sports, athletics or exercising

5. Almost everyday	45.8	55.8	35.9	45.5	47.1	45.3	45.6	43.3	52.0	52.6	36.9	48.5	49.1	46.8	39.3	42.6
4. At least once a week	24.9	22.2	27.5	25.7	19.7	27.5	24.8	24.1	22.8	23.7	25.7	22.2	23.6	26.1	28.8	35.0
3. Once or twice a month	13.0	9.6	16.4	13.3	13.3	10.9	13.1	15.4	11.7	12.1	14.7	12.8	11.3	12.8	15.6	8.3
2. A few times a year	11.0	8.4	13.7	10.7	12.1	11.0	11.9	10.4	10.3	8.5	14.4	10.9	10.4	9.9	12.0	10.2
1. Never	5.3	3.9	6.5	4.8	7.8	5.3	4.7	6.9	3.2	3.1	8.3	5.7	5.6	4.5	4.3	3.9
Item 5890 Subject C07 N	3418	1663	1634	2604	414	823	977	1069	549	1841	1327	1277	704	470	846	47

A02I: Do art or craft work

5. Almost everyday	11.6	12.6	10.4	11.1	11.5	11.3	11.8	10.3	14.4	9.2	14.5	11.2	11.5	10.1	12.8	16.6
4. At least once a week	9.4	8.6	10.0	9.5	6.4	8.1	10.2	9.4	9.7	10.3	7.7	10.4	7.0	7.4	10.7	6.8
3. Once or twice a month	18.5	16.1	21.2	19.3	13.1	17.1	19.3	16.1	23.9	20.2	17.0	18.8	18.6	19.2	18.4	17.1
2. A few times a year	30.7	31.5	29.8	31.7	27.2	29.5	31.4	29.4	33.7	32.6	28.5	30.7	30.3	34.5	29.6	29.4
1. Never	29.8	31.2	28.6	28.3	41.8	33.9	27.3	34.8	18.3	27.7	32.3	28.9	32.6	28.8	28.6	30.1
Item 5900 Subject C07 N	3415	1664	1632	2601	413	818	975	1073	549	1841	1329	1276	699	468	847	47

A02J: Work around the house, yard, garden, car, etc.

5. Almost everyday	41.8	33.8	49.5	38.7	57.0	36.7	44.3	43.0	42.4	37.3	47.6	43.2	41.0	41.0	39.7	36.2
4. At least once a week	37.7	43.0	32.3	40.5	25.8	37.1	37.0	38.6	38.2	40.3	34.2	36.7	39.7	34.4	40.5	32.7
3. Once or twice a month	13.8	16.2	11.7	14.8	9.7	15.9	12.4	12.7	15.5	15.4	11.9	13.3	12.7	17.7	13.6	17.7
2. A few times a year	5.2	5.4	5.1	5.1	4.3	7.8	5.5	4.0	3.2	5.8	4.6	5.7	5.1	4.6	4.8	7.3
1. Never	1.5	1.6	1.4	0.9	3.2	2.5	0.8	1.7	0.7	1.3	1.6	1.1	1.5	2.4	1.3	6.0
Item 5910 Subject C07 N	3431	1670	1641	2609	418	828	978	1076	549	1848	1333	1281	705	471	850	47

A02K: Get together with friends, informally

5. Almost everyday	46.8	49.9	43.5	46.2	51.5	50.7	44.1	44.6	50.0	46.6	46.0	38.4	48.2	45.7	58.3	52.7
4. At least once a week	40.7	40.0	41.5	42.2	36.3	38.3	42.7	42.1	38.0	41.9	39.9	42.9	42.7	42.9	35.6	30.8
3. Once or twice a month	9.2	7.4	11.0	9.1	8.2	8.5	9.9	9.6	8.3	8.5	10.3	13.4	7.5	9.5	4.0	7.7
2. A few times a year	2.3	1.6	3.1	1.8	2.4	1.4	2.3	2.6	3.1	1.9	2.8	3.7	1.3	1.7	1.5	4.2
1. Never	1.0	1.1	0.9	0.8	1.5	1.0	1.0	1.1	0.7	1.0	1.1	1.6	0.3	0.2	0.7	4.6
Item 5920 Subject C07,M04 N	3412	1662	1630	2600	410	823	974	1066	549	1838	1325	1274	699	466	848	47

A02L: Go shopping or window-shopping

5. Almost everyday	3.2	1.8	4.5	2.2	8.4	5.6	1.6	3.4	2.4	3.0	2.8	3.3	3.3	3.4	2.7	3.2
4. At least once a week	36.2	23.5	49.7	34.8	45.9	40.3	34.2	36.3	33.3	36.8	37.7	38.8	35.0	35.7	34.7	25.8
3. Once or twice a month	44.3	46.9	41.6	46.1	34.2	39.9	47.4	43.7	46.5	46.0	41.6	43.9	44.0	46.2	43.2	49.3
2. A few times a year	12.3	20.2	3.9	12.8	9.1	10.1	12.9	11.9	15.4	11.7	12.3	10.9	14.3	12.2	13.1	13.5
1. Never	4.0	7.6	0.2	4.0	2.5	4.1	3.9	4.7	2.4	2.5	5.6	3.1	3.5	2.4	6.3	8.2
Item 5930 Subject C07,F01 N	3421	1663	1637	2603	415	826	975	1069	550	1840	1332	1274	704	470	848	47

A02M: Spend at least an hour of leisure time alone

5. Almost everyday	43.7	44.0	43.5	42.7	51.0	47.4	44.8	43.7	36.2	45.7	41.5	42.4	43.0	44.8	45.7	42.5
4. At least once a week	34.2	32.8	36.4	36.0	27.7	30.8	34.8	33.7	39.4	35.6	32.3	34.9	33.4	35.1	34.6	34.2
3. Once or twice a month	11.8	11.4	11.9	12.0	9.1	10.7	12.0	11.2	14.0	11.0	12.4	12.5	12.0	9.7	11.8	11.4
2. A few times a year	6.3	7.7	4.3	5.7	6.7	7.2	4.9	6.2	7.5	4.6	8.2	6.4	7.8	5.6	4.5	11.9
1. Never	4.0	4.1	3.9	3.6	5.6	3.9	3.4	5.2	3.0	3.0	5.5	3.8	3.9	4.8	3.5	-
Item 5940 Subject C07 N	3422	1662	1640	2603	417	826	976	1072	548	1842	1332	1278	702	468	851	47

QUESTIONNAIRE FORM 2 1983	TOTAL	SEX		RACE		REGION				4YR COLLEGE PLANS		ILLICIT DRUG USE: LIFETIME				
		M	F	White	Black	NE	NC	S	W	Yes	No	None	Mari- juana Only	Few Pills	More Pills	Any Her- oin
N (Weighted No. of Cases):	3435	1671	1641	2610	419	829	979	1077	550	1848	1335	1281	705	472	851	47
% of Weighted Total:	100.0	48.6	47.8	76.0	12.2	24.1	28.5	31.4	16.0	53.8	38.9	37.3	20.5	13.7	24.8	1.4
A02N: Read books, magazines, or newspapers																
5. Almost everyday	54.6	55.3	54.5	55.6	54.7	56.9	58.1	49.9	54.4	60.6	47.9	56.5	56.3	53.9	51.8	57.6
4. At least once a week	28.7	27.9	29.6	27.8	30.0	28.1	27.1	31.0	28.0	27.3	29.9	28.7	26.5	31.7	28.6	25.9
3. Once or twice a month	10.8	10.1	11.1	10.9	9.5	9.5	10.4	11.5	12.1	9.1	12.6	10.0	10.9	9.5	12.4	8.6
2. A few times a year	4.4	4.9	3.7	4.4	4.4	4.5	3.5	5.3	3.9	2.4	7.1	3.5	4.9	3.7	5.4	5.5
1. Never	1.5	1.8	1.1	1.4	1.4	1.0	1.0	2.2	1.6	0.6	2.5	1.2	1.4	1.3	1.9	2.4
Item 5950　Subject C07　　N	3422	1662	1639	2607	411	822	977	1074	550	1846	1328	1277	701	471	849	47
A02O: Go to taverns, bars or nightclubs																
5. Almost everyday	2.2	3.8	0.6	2.4	1.1	3.4	1.8	2.0	1.4	1.0	3.8	1.1	1.5	1.5	4.6	5.5
4. At least once a week	14.6	17.9	11.1	14.8	16.2	18.5	12.3	18.0	6.1	12.7	17.0	7.9	13.0	14.7	25.3	31.2
3. Once or twice a month	19.0	19.4	17.9	19.3	15.1	20.7	19.6	19.6	14.1	20.0	17.3	13.1	19.6	23.5	24.1	38.2
2. A few times a year	21.5	21.2	22.0	22.6	16.8	22.0	24.3	20.3	18.5	22.8	20.1	18.1	24.7	27.3	21.6	11.2
1. Never	42.7	37.7	48.4	40.9	50.8	35.5	42.0	40.1	60.0	43.5	41.8	59.8	41.3	33.0	24.3	14.0
Item 5960　Subject C07　　N	3421	1664	1638	2602	418	822	975	1075	549	1842	1331	1279	701	468	849	47
A02P: Go to parties or other social affairs																
5. Almost everyday	3.2	4.4	1.8	3.2	3.0	3.6	2.8	3.2	3.4	1.8	4.9	1.0	2.3	3.3	7.0	7.6
4. At least once a week	34.4	37.8	30.9	35.7	28.5	39.7	37.1	30.1	30.1	35.1	33.0	21.5	36.6	35.4	49.9	64.1
3. Once or twice a month	37.7	36.1	39.8	38.1	38.2	35.4	37.5	37.7	41.8	40.9	34.5	41.0	39.1	39.7	32.3	16.5
2. A few times a year	21.3	18.5	23.8	20.3	24.4	18.9	19.4	25.3	20.2	20.0	22.9	30.8	19.2	18.8	10.0	11.8
1. Never	3.4	3.2	3.6	2.7	5.9	2.3	3.2	3.8	4.4	2.2	4.7	5.6	2.9	2.8	0.8	-
Item 5970　Subject C07　　N	3431	1668	1641	2608	418	828	976	1076	550	1848	1333	1281	705	471	850	47
A03: How much do you agree or disagree with each of the following statements?																
A03A: In the United States, we put too much emphasis on making profits and not enough on human well-being																
1. Disagree	6.1	8.3	3.4	6.0	5.0	6.6	4.7	6.3	7.6	5.4	6.5	6.6	5.6	6.2	4.9	8.6
2. Mostly disagree	10.1	12.6	7.7	10.9	7.1	8.7	10.6	9.1	13.4	12.2	7.1	9.3	11.0	9.9	11.5	4.1
3. Neither	17.0	19.4	14.8	18.3	10.1	13.9	19.7	15.4	19.8	16.3	18.6	17.7	15.3	16.9	17.4	23.5
4. Mostly agree	41.7	35.9	48.2	43.2	33.4	42.7	41.8	41.7	39.8	43.0	40.9	42.7	40.9	42.6	41.4	26.3
5. Agree	25.1	23.8	25.9	21.6	44.5	28.0	23.3	27.5	19.4	23.1	26.9	23.7	27.3	24.4	24.8	37.4
Item 5990　Subject F03,O03　　N	3397	1654	1625	2596	411	820	971	1066	540	1836	1320	1272	694	467	844	47
A03B: People are too much concerned with material things these days																
1. Disagree	4.5	5.5	3.3	3.9	6.3	4.8	4.2	4.5	4.7	4.1	4.9	4.2	3.6	4.4	5.0	10.1
2. Mostly disagree	6.9	8.8	4.6	7.7	3.6	6.6	8.1	4.7	9.3	6.7	6.4	5.9	8.4	6.7	7.0	5.5
3. Neither	12.1	15.5	8.3	12.6	7.4	10.6	12.8	11.2	14.6	11.1	13.6	11.4	13.9	11.3	12.3	15.4
4. Mostly agree	38.4	37.0	40.7	39.9	34.3	36.6	41.1	37.8	37.4	39.7	37.1	40.4	37.0	35.7	39.9	29.5
5. Agree	38.2	33.2	43.0	35.9	48.5	41.4	33.8	41.8	34.0	38.5	38.0	38.1	37.1	41.8	35.8	39.4
Item 6000　Subject F02　　N	3397	1652	1631	2592	412	821	971	1067	538	1835	1320	1275	693	469	840	47
A03C: Since it helps the economy to grow, people should be encouraged to buy more																
1. Disagree	19.6	17.3	21.7	17.2	32.6	21.9	15.8	21.6	19.2	17.1	21.4	18.5	22.9	18.4	18.5	22.5
2. Mostly disagree	22.0	18.4	25.8	22.7	19.4	20.1	23.3	22.1	22.5	22.6	22.2	23.9	20.1	20.8	23.1	9.5
3. Neither	28.8	27.1	30.8	30.2	22.8	28.6	29.1	29.0	27.9	30.0	28.3	28.8	29.4	28.1	29.1	35.7
4. Mostly agree	19.6	23.5	15.8	20.4	15.0	19.8	20.3	17.1	23.3	21.0	17.4	19.8	17.2	22.1	19.4	22.8
5. Agree	9.9	13.7	5.9	9.4	10.3	9.6	11.4	10.2	7.1	9.3	10.7	9.0	10.4	10.6	9.9	9.5
Item 6010　Subject F02　　N	3395	1651	1627	2590	411	819	970	1068	539	1828	1323	1273	691	470	840	47

QUESTIONNAIRE FORM 2 1983	TOTAL	SEX		RACE		REGION				4YR COLLEGE PLANS		ILLICIT DRUG USE: LIFETIME				
		M	F	White	Black	NE	NC	S	W	Yes	No	None	Mari-juana Only	Few Pills	More Pills	Any Her-oin
N (Weighted No. of Cases):	3435	1671	1641	2610	419	829	979	1077	550	1848	1335	1281	705	472	851	47
% of Weighted Total:	100.0	48.6	47.8	76.0	12.2	24.1	28.5	31.4	16.0	53.8	38.9	37.3	20.5	13.7	24.8	1.4

A03D: There is nothing wrong with advertising that gets people to buy things they don't really need

1. Disagree	35.7	32.9	38.7	35.9	38.8	38.2	35.2	35.2	33.8	35.4	36.1	33.5	38.0	35.1	37.2	37.0
2. Mostly disagree	24.7	24.2	25.3	25.9	16.0	22.1	24.8	25.2	27.3	25.6	23.6	26.6	23.6	24.2	23.3	24.1
3. Neither	13.9	14.5	13.5	15.2	9.8	12.3	16.6	13.4	12.4	14.4	13.7	14.8	12.7	12.0	14.1	24.1
4. Mostly agree	14.3	15.6	13.1	14.3	13.8	13.4	15.6	13.5	15.1	14.1	14.4	14.2	13.9	17.0	14.3	4.1
5. Agree	11.4	12.7	9.5	8.8	21.7	14.1	7.8	12.6	11.4	10.5	12.3	10.9	11.8	11.7	11.2	10.7
Item 6020 Subject F02 N	3405	1655	1632	2597	414	820	973	1074	539	1838	1325	1279	697	467	842	47

A03E: There will probably be more shortages in the future, so Americans will have to learn how to be happy with fewer "things"

1. Disagree	8.3	10.2	6.4	7.6	11.3	10.4	8.8	7.1	6.7	8.3	8.1	7.2	10.6	8.1	8.1	9.8
2. Mostly disagree	9.6	11.1	8.3	9.6	8.2	9.8	10.2	8.6	10.1	10.1	8.4	10.7	7.2	7.4	11.3	3.4
3. Neither	14.4	14.6	14.3	15.8	8.2	15.0	13.8	13.4	16.8	14.5	14.8	13.6	14.3	16.1	15.8	10.5
4. Mostly agree	29.8	28.0	31.3	31.2	25.1	26.7	31.2	29.4	33.1	31.7	27.9	31.5	28.8	27.6	29.1	33.0
5. Agree	37.8	36.1	39.7	35.9	47.3	38.2	36.0	41.5	33.3	35.5	40.7	37.1	39.1	40.7	35.7	43.2
Item 6030 Subject F02 N	3411	1655	1638	2600	414	825	973	1072	540	1839	1328	1279	697	469	845	47

A04: Below are several ways that people have used to protest about serious social issues. How much do you approve or disapprove of these actions?

A04A: Signing petitions

4. Strongly approve	24.3	24.5	24.4	25.9	16.6	22.2	26.2	21.2	30.2	28.6	19.7	24.7	20.6	25.5	27.2	16.5
3. Approve	46.8	46.5	47.9	49.0	41.3	47.4	45.9	47.1	46.6	49.2	45.0	48.1	49.3	44.8	45.7	31.5
2. Disapprove	2.3	3.1	1.3	2.2	2.3	2.5	2.2	2.4	1.7	1.6	2.9	2.3	2.6	2.2	1.8	3.4
1. Strongly disapprove	0.8	1.0	0.5	0.5	1.3	1.1	0.8	0.8	0.5	0.6	0.9	0.5	1.0	1.4	0.7	-
8. Don't know, or it depends	25.9	25.0	25.8	22.3	38.5	26.9	24.8	28.5	21.0	19.9	31.6	24.5	26.6	26.1	24.6	48.6
Item 6040 Subject I02 N	3394	1646	1633	2591	414	822	967	1065	539	1835	1319	1270	696	469	841	47

A04B: Boycotting certain products or stores

4. Strongly approve	14.1	17.3	10.9	14.2	14.3	16.0	14.7	11.9	14.8	17.6	9.9	12.9	15.7	15.8	14.2	11.8
3. Approve	33.8	36.9	31.2	34.9	31.8	36.7	35.3	30.5	33.5	35.2	32.6	35.3	34.4	30.2	35.1	26.3
2. Disapprove	14.4	13.7	14.7	14.0	14.4	11.9	13.9	16.2	15.4	13.6	15.5	13.6	14.2	15.9	14.1	9.5
1. Strongly disapprove	3.6	4.7	2.4	3.3	5.6	3.0	3.2	4.2	4.0	3.1	3.9	4.0	3.6	2.6	2.7	6.3
8. Don't know, or it depends	34.0	27.3	40.8	33.7	34.0	32.4	32.8	37.2	32.2	30.5	38.1	34.2	32.0	35.5	34.0	46.1
Item 6050 Subject I02 N	3395	1652	1628	2595	413	820	969	1068	537	1835	1320	1273	694	467	843	47

A04C: Lawful demonstrations

4. Strongly approve	17.1	19.5	14.5	17.6	15.0	17.1	18.4	15.6	17.6	21.5	12.5	15.6	18.5	16.9	18.9	12.2
3. Approve	46.3	46.1	46.7	48.0	42.7	43.9	48.8	45.8	46.2	46.5	46.5	47.6	44.4	45.6	47.7	37.9
2. Disapprove	9.5	10.1	8.6	9.0	10.0	10.2	8.3	10.0	9.8	7.8	11.6	8.3	8.7	12.8	8.7	23.3
1. Strongly disapprove	3.3	4.2	2.3	3.0	4.9	1.7	3.3	4.4	3.3	2.8	3.8	3.7	3.3	2.9	2.7	1.5
8. Don't know, or it depends	23.9	20.1	27.8	22.4	27.4	27.1	21.2	24.2	23.1	21.5	25.6	24.7	25.1	21.8	21.9	25.1
Item 6060 Subject I02 N	3370	1642	1615	2582	405	807	966	1061	536	1819	1316	1259	689	465	840	47

A04D: Occupying buildings or factories

4. Strongly approve	5.1	5.7	4.4	4.7	7.0	6.1	5.0	4.7	4.8	4.2	6.4	3.9	5.1	6.3	6.2	12.1
3. Approve	21.1	20.6	20.7	18.8	28.8	22.9	20.9	20.9	19.4	18.2	24.4	19.2	22.1	21.9	21.5	23.7
2. Disapprove	26.6	29.4	24.2	29.4	16.3	24.6	26.7	26.9	29.2	29.1	24.3	28.6	25.5	24.6	27.1	9.9
1. Strongly disapprove	10.6	14.2	7.1	10.6	10.1	9.0	10.5	11.0	12.7	13.7	6.3	13.0	11.1	10.9	7.2	9.8
8. Don't know, or it depends	36.5	30.1	43.7	36.5	37.9	37.5	36.9	36.5	33.9	34.8	38.6	35.4	36.3	36.3	37.9	44.4
Item 6070 Subject I02 N	3364	1642	1610	2582	402	811	962	1058	533	1820	1308	1258	687	465	837	46

A04E: Wildcat strikes

4. Strongly approve	2.3	3.2	1.2	2.3	3.3	3.6	2.2	2.0	1.3	1.9	2.8	1.3	2.8	2.7	3.1	4.4
3. Approve	11.1	13.9	8.1	10.9	11.0	11.5	11.4	10.8	10.2	10.2	12.4	9.0	10.3	13.4	13.0	17.6
2. Disapprove	31.4	33.1	29.8	33.6	23.8	29.6	30.9	32.2	33.8	32.1	30.7	31.4	30.5	29.9	34.0	32.0
1. Strongly disapprove	16.8	19.0	14.8	17.1	15.1	15.8	16.3	18.4	16.1	19.4	13.9	19.3	19.8	14.4	12.2	16.7
8. Don't know, or it depends	38.4	30.8	46.1	36.2	46.8	39.5	39.3	36.5	38.5	36.4	40.3	39.0	36.8	39.5	37.7	29.2
Item 6080 Subject I02 N	3366	1642	1612	2577	408	810	965	1059	532	1824	1305	1260	689	462	837	47

QUESTIONNAIRE FORM 2 1983	TOTAL	SEX		RACE		REGION				4YR COLLEGE PLANS		ILLICIT DRUG USE: LIFETIME				
		M	F	White	Black	NE	NC	S	W	Yes	No	None	Marijuana Only	Few Pills	More Pills	Any Heroin
N (Weighted No. of Cases):	3435	1671	1641	2610	419	829	979	1077	550	1848	1335	1281	705	472	851	47
% of Weighted Total:	100.0	48.6	47.8	76.0	12.2	24.1	28.5	31.4	16.0	53.8	38.9	37.3	20.5	13.7	24.8	1.4
A04F: Blocking traffic																
4. Strongly approve	1.9	2.3	1.4	1.5	3.4	2.6	1.6	1.9	1.2	1.4	2.4	1.1	1.5	2.1	2.7	11.3
3. Approve	3.8	4.6	3.0	3.0	6.0	4.3	2.8	3.9	4.7	3.9	3.8	4.1	3.4	2.8	4.4	5.0
2. Disapprove	39.0	36.0	41.9	39.7	39.3	41.1	39.4	36.6	40.1	39.6	38.5	39.8	37.8	41.4	38.6	33.9
1. Strongly disapprove	44.1	45.0	43.3	45.7	34.8	40.8	43.5	47.6	43.3	45.3	42.3	44.3	46.8	44.9	41.6	33.5
8. Don't know, or it depends	11.1	12.1	10.4	10.0	16.5	11.1	12.7	10.0	10.7	9.8	13.1	10.7	10.5	8.8	12.7	16.2
Item 6090 Subject I02 N	3390	1643	1633	2590	412	818	969	1065	539	1831	1322	1273	691	464	844	47
A04G: Damaging things																
4. Strongly approve	2.9	3.1	2.6	2.3	4.5	3.0	3.5	2.8	1.7	2.4	3.5	2.6	2.0	3.3	3.1	17.1
3. Approve	2.0	2.5	1.3	1.2	4.3	3.9	1.0	1.3	2.2	1.5	2.3	1.9	1.7	1.4	2.3	7.4
2. Disapprove	19.9	22.1	17.4	18.8	25.2	22.6	17.4	20.0	19.7	18.0	21.0	16.9	17.7	23.3	24.4	19.8
1. Strongly disapprove	69.6	64.7	74.9	72.7	58.2	64.2	72.0	71.0	70.9	73.5	66.5	73.8	72.6	67.8	63.1	51.5
8. Don't know, or it depends	5.6	7.6	3.8	5.0	7.8	6.2	6.1	4.9	5.4	4.6	6.8	4.8	6.0	4.3	7.0	4.2
Item 6100 Subject I02 N	3398	1649	1634	2599	412	816	971	1071	539	1838	1322	1277	693	468	841	46
A04H: Personal violence																
4. Strongly approve	3.2	3.7	2.6	2.7	4.8	3.6	3.7	3.2	1.5	2.5	3.8	2.5	2.2	3.8	4.4	8.9
3. Approve	2.9	4.3	1.5	2.3	5.6	4.8	2.6	2.2	2.1	1.8	4.1	2.5	3.6	1.5	3.8	3.7
2. Disapprove	17.7	20.6	14.9	16.5	23.9	20.9	16.6	16.5	17.3	16.9	17.9	15.3	15.9	21.5	20.1	23.5
1. Strongly disapprove	68.2	60.3	76.2	71.7	53.6	62.7	69.7	69.7	70.7	73.2	63.3	73.9	71.2	65.1	61.5	44.3
8. Don't know, or it depends	8.0	11.1	4.8	6.7	12.0	7.9	7.4	8.3	8.3	5.6	10.9	5.7	7.1	8.2	10.2	19.5
Item 6110 Subject I02 N	3403	1653	1635	2601	415	819	974	1071	539	1840	1323	1277	693	469	845	46
A05: Do you think that you would prefer having a mate for most of your life, or would you prefer not having a mate?																
5. Definitely prefer to have a mate	59.3	54.2	64.8	61.4	50.4	59.3	60.9	58.4	58.1	59.7	59.4	61.4	59.9	51.9	60.0	59.8
4. Probably prefer to have a mate	26.7	28.5	25.1	27.2	27.0	25.6	26.7	25.9	29.8	27.6	26.3	25.3	26.0	29.8	28.0	26.1
3. Not sure	10.7	13.5	7.3	8.3	19.5	11.3	9.5	12.2	9.0	9.8	11.0	10.5	11.2	14.4	7.9	10.1
2. Probably prefer not to have a mate	2.6	3.1	2.0	2.4	2.5	2.9	2.3	2.7	2.5	2.3	2.5	2.0	2.6	2.1	3.8	-
1. Definitely prefer not to have a mate	0.7	0.6	0.8	0.6	0.5	0.9	0.6	0.7	0.5	0.6	0.9	0.7	0.3	1.7	0.3	3.9
Item 6120 Subject D01 N	3424	1664	1640	2606	418	824	976	1076	549	1842	1332	1280	705	469	847	47
A06: Which do you think you are most likely to choose in the long run?																
3. Getting married	77.2	73.2	81.7	80.8	64.9	75.1	80.5	76.0	76.8	81.0	73.7	79.3	78.5	75.3	75.0	81.3
2. I have no idea	16.3	19.8	12.2	13.8	23.5	17.9	13.6	16.2	18.6	13.6	18.5	15.6	15.0	17.2	17.1	14.5
1. Not getting married	5.4	6.4	4.4	4.3	10.9	6.6	4.9	5.7	3.8	4.8	5.9	4.2	5.2	6.5	6.5	3.0
8. Am already married	1.1	0.5	1.7	1.1	0.7	0.4	0.9	2.0	0.9	0.7	1.8	0.8	1.3	1.0	1.4	1.2
Item 6130 Subject D01 N	3366	1629	1622	2569	408	818	961	1053	534	1823	1301	1253	692	464	835	47
A07: If you did get married (or are married) . . .																
A07A: How likely do you think it is that you would stay married to the same person for life?																
5. Very likely	61.6	55.5	68.4	63.3	55.7	60.9	62.3	62.2	59.8	63.9	60.2	69.9	62.1	60.3	50.5	59.2
4. Fairly likely	23.1	27.5	18.7	24.3	18.9	21.6	26.7	21.3	22.4	23.7	22.3	19.2	22.5	24.6	29.2	18.8
3. Uncertain	12.9	14.1	11.0	10.2	23.1	14.9	9.3	13.6	14.9	10.1	15.1	9.5	14.0	11.7	16.5	12.4
2. Fairly unlikely	1.4	1.4	1.3	1.3	1.2	1.7	0.7	1.3	2.7	1.4	1.4	0.6	0.9	1.7	2.6	5.2
1. Very unlikely	1.1	1.5	0.6	1.0	1.1	1.0	1.1	1.6	0.1	0.9	1.1	0.9	0.5	1.7	1.2	4.3
Item 6140 Subject D01 N	3261	1574	1572	2482	404	762	932	1048	520	1748	1273	1223	666	447	813	42
A07B: How likely is it that you would want to have children?																
5. Very likely	62.0	59.6	64.9	63.5	58.8	62.9	63.2	60.7	60.9	64.5	59.0	63.2	65.0	60.5	60.4	50.8
4. Fairly likely	19.3	22.0	16.5	19.2	17.8	17.5	18.2	21.0	20.9	20.2	18.4	19.9	18.5	19.6	18.7	20.3
3. Uncertain	11.9	13.0	10.4	11.3	12.5	11.9	11.9	11.8	12.1	10.2	13.5	11.9	10.2	12.4	12.7	10.6
2. Fairly unlikely	2.3	1.7	3.0	2.2	3.2	2.9	2.4	1.8	2.5	2.2	2.9	1.8	2.5	2.2	2.8	4.8
1. Very unlikely	2.8	2.5	3.3	2.6	3.5	3.1	3.0	2.5	2.9	2.1	3.8	2.5	2.2	3.3	3.2	6.2
8. Already have child(ren)	1.6	1.2	1.9	1.1	4.2	1.7	1.4	2.2	0.8	0.9	2.5	0.7	1.6	2.0	2.2	7.3
Item 6150 Subject D02 N	3281	1586	1578	2492	406	769	933	1053	526	1764	1276	1231	675	451	810	43

QUESTIONNAIRE FORM 2 1983	TOTAL	SEX		RACE		REGION				4YR COLLEGE PLANS		ILLICIT DRUG USE: LIFETIME				
		M	F	White	Black	NE	NC	S	W	Yes	No	None	Mari-juana Only	Few Pills	More Pills	Any Her-oin
N (Weighted No. of Cases):	3435	1671	1641	2610	419	829	979	1077	550	1848	1335	1281	705	472	851	47
% of Weighted Total:	100.0	48.6	47.8	76.0	12.2	24.1	28.5	31.4	16.0	53.8	38.9	37.3	20.5	13.7	24.8	1.4

The questions in the next column ask you to imagine different kinds of married life that you might have. We want you to think about different ways you might share responsibilities for working, taking care of the home, and taking care of children. Please indicate how acceptable for you each of the different arrangements would be.

A08: Imagine you are married and have no children–how would you feel about each of the following working arrangements?

A08A: Husband works full-time, wife doesn't work

	TOTAL	M	F	White	Black	NE	NC	S	W	Yes	No	None	Mari-juana Only	Few Pills	More Pills	Any Her-oin
1. Not at all acceptable	26.0	14.6	37.6	22.8	41.7	32.8	21.0	26.2	24.3	27.7	23.9	24.1	29.4	24.6	26.5	27.7
2. Somewhat acceptable	32.9	31.0	35.4	33.8	31.5	31.4	34.5	32.3	33.2	32.8	32.7	32.9	29.8	36.4	34.2	25.3
3. Acceptable	33.1	43.4	22.1	35.6	19.1	30.1	35.9	33.3	32.3	31.5	36.2	34.9	32.9	31.7	31.7	31.7
4. Desirable	8.0	10.9	5.0	7.9	7.7	5.7	8.6	8.2	10.2	8.1	7.2	8.1	7.8	7.3	7.7	15.3
Item 6160 Subject C05,D04 N	3409	1657	1636	2598	416	818	972	1072	547	1836	1329	1275	703	468	845	45

A08B: Husband works full-time, wife works about half-time

	TOTAL	M	F	White	Black	NE	NC	S	W	Yes	No	None	Mari-juana Only	Few Pills	More Pills	Any Her-oin
1. Not at all acceptable	3.7	3.1	4.3	2.6	7.4	3.8	2.3	4.5	4.7	3.4	4.1	3.3	3.6	3.9	3.6	7.7
2. Somewhat acceptable	22.1	18.2	25.8	19.8	32.5	26.6	17.4	24.9	18.2	22.5	21.2	21.7	23.4	22.0	22.0	17.2
3. Acceptable	57.5	62.5	53.1	59.7	50.3	55.2	61.9	56.5	55.1	57.5	57.4	58.2	56.7	56.4	57.0	67.0
4. Desirable	16.6	16.2	16.9	17.9	9.8	14.3	18.3	14.2	22.0	16.6	17.3	16.7	16.2	17.7	17.4	8.2
Item 6170 Subject C05,D04 N	3412	1658	1637	2600	415	819	973	1072	548	1835	1331	1275	705	468	844	45

A08C: Both work full-time

	TOTAL	M	F	White	Black	NE	NC	S	W	Yes	No	None	Mari-juana Only	Few Pills	More Pills	Any Her-oin
1. Not at all acceptable	12.6	16.5	8.3	11.9	14.3	11.9	12.5	13.7	11.6	10.6	14.7	12.3	11.4	11.9	13.6	17.9
2. Somewhat acceptable	19.9	24.7	15.2	21.2	11.5	16.4	21.7	19.1	23.6	18.7	21.1	20.3	18.5	21.0	19.5	18.7
3. Acceptable	45.4	40.1	50.6	44.5	53.5	50.6	43.1	46.7	39.2	46.0	45.2	47.1	49.1	44.2	41.4	41.8
4. Desirable	22.1	18.6	25.9	22.4	20.7	21.0	22.7	20.5	25.6	24.7	19.0	20.3	21.0	22.9	25.4	21.7
Item 6180 Subject C05,D04 N	3404	1652	1636	2598	412	816	969	1071	548	1833	1326	1274	702	467	844	45

A08D: Both work about half-time

	TOTAL	M	F	White	Black	NE	NC	S	W	Yes	No	None	Mari-juana Only	Few Pills	More Pills	Any Her-oin
1. Not at all acceptable	40.5	43.7	37.5	39.3	48.9	41.6	36.0	47.4	33.6	39.1	42.6	40.4	41.7	40.6	39.8	42.9
2. Somewhat acceptable	32.8	30.4	35.1	34.0	25.4	29.5	37.4	30.8	33.1	33.2	32.7	33.8	31.6	32.0	32.5	29.1
3. Acceptable	19.0	17.7	20.2	19.3	18.2	19.8	20.9	15.3	21.8	20.1	17.3	19.8	19.9	19.0	17.7	14.9
4. Desirable	7.7	8.2	7.2	7.4	7.6	9.2	5.7	6.5	11.4	7.6	7.5	6.0	6.8	8.3	10.0	13.2
Item 6190 Subject C05,D04 N	3376	1638	1622	2575	407	807	963	1062	544	1822	1310	1265	697	463	834	44

A08E: Husband works about half-time, wife works full-time

	TOTAL	M	F	White	Black	NE	NC	S	W	Yes	No	None	Mari-juana Only	Few Pills	More Pills	Any Her-oin
1. Not at all acceptable	54.3	60.2	48.1	53.3	60.3	55.0	45.9	62.6	51.8	51.3	58.0	53.2	53.5	51.5	57.4	56.9
2. Somewhat acceptable	28.1	22.8	33.6	29.3	22.0	26.8	33.9	23.4	29.1	30.3	25.5	29.3	27.4	32.4	25.2	18.0
3. Acceptable	14.6	13.1	16.3	15.1	14.2	15.4	17.6	11.0	14.8	16.1	12.8	15.0	16.2	12.5	14.5	16.0
4. Desirable	3.0	3.9	2.0	2.3	3.5	2.8	2.6	2.9	4.3	2.3	3.6	2.6	2.9	3.6	2.9	9.2
Item 6200 Subject C05,D04 N	3400	1650	1634	2593	413	814	972	1068	546	1830	1327	1273	700	466	842	45

A08F: Husband doesn't work, wife works full-time

	TOTAL	M	F	White	Black	NE	NC	S	W	Yes	No	None	Mari-juana Only	Few Pills	More Pills	Any Her-oin
1. Not at all acceptable	80.3	81.8	78.9	80.0	82.8	80.3	77.2	83.4	79.7	80.0	80.5	79.1	81.4	81.3	80.5	80.1
2. Somewhat acceptable	11.4	8.2	15.0	12.9	7.1	10.5	14.8	9.2	11.2	12.0	10.7	13.4	10.0	12.0	10.1	5.9
3. Acceptable	5.2	5.5	4.8	4.9	6.0	6.5	5.6	4.2	4.5	5.5	5.0	5.0	5.9	3.0	5.8	4.3
4. Desirable	3.1	4.5	1.3	2.3	4.2	2.8	2.4	3.1	4.6	2.4	3.8	2.4	2.8	3.7	3.6	9.8
Item 6210 Subject C05,D04 N	3393	1648	1630	2590	411	815	966	1067	546	1830	1320	1267	700	466	842	44

A09: Imagine you are married and have one or more pre-school children. How would you feel about each of the following working arrangements?

QUESTIONNAIRE FORM 2 1983	TOTAL	SEX		RACE		REGION				4YR COLLEGE PLANS		ILLICIT DRUG USE: LIFETIME				
		M	F	White	Black	NE	NC	S	W	Yes	No	None	Mari-juana Only	Few Pills	More Pills	Any Her-oin
N (Weighted No. of Cases):	3435	1671	1641	2610	419	829	979	1077	550	1848	1335	1281	705	472	851	47
% of Weighted Total:	100.0	48.6	47.8	76.0	12.2	24.1	28.5	31.4	16.0	53.8	38.9	37.3	20.5	13.7	24.8	1.4

A09A: Husband works full-time, wife doesn't work

1. Not at all acceptable	9.5	7.5	11.6	6.5	23.9	10.3	6.2	12.7	7.7	9.0	9.4	8.1	9.1	10.4	10.2	12.6
2. Somewhat acceptable	17.1	12.5	21.8	15.2	26.3	15.1	15.9	18.9	18.8	16.9	17.4	17.2	17.2	19.6	16.3	3.6
3. Acceptable	38.2	38.8	37.6	37.9	38.7	41.8	38.8	37.8	32.5	37.1	39.6	37.1	39.2	39.5	38.3	41.5
4. Desirable	35.2	41.3	29.0	40.4	11.1	32.8	39.1	30.6	41.0	37.1	33.6	37.5	34.5	30.5	35.2	42.3
Item 6220 Subject C05,D04 N	3409	1656	1637	2601	415	820	972	1071	547	1837	1331	1275	703	468	844	47

A09B: Husband works full-time, wife works about half-time

1. Not at all acceptable	8.3	10.9	5.4	8.4	7.8	10.5	7.9	6.2	9.6	6.9	9.9	8.2	8.9	7.3	7.8	11.5
2. Somewhat acceptable	24.6	26.8	22.4	24.2	28.0	25.0	23.9	25.9	23.0	24.4	25.0	23.8	23.6	25.5	25.7	28.6
3. Acceptable	53.6	50.6	56.7	53.6	51.5	52.2	54.2	55.1	51.8	53.9	53.2	55.9	54.1	50.4	52.3	53.6
4. Desirable	13.5	11.7	15.5	13.8	12.8	12.3	14.1	12.8	15.6	14.8	11.9	12.1	13.5	16.8	14.1	6.2
Item 6230 Subject C05,D04 N	3411	1657	1636	2601	416	820	973	1071	547	1838	1330	1275	703	468	845	47

A09C: Both work full-time

1. Not at all acceptable	57.7	62.3	53.0	61.3	40.3	61.8	59.6	51.0	60.9	58.8	56.4	58.9	57.2	53.9	59.3	68.6
2. Somewhat acceptable	22.1	18.4	26.1	22.6	19.7	20.2	23.5	24.0	18.6	21.6	23.9	22.9	20.3	20.9	22.9	17.9
3. Acceptable	14.1	13.1	14.7	11.5	27.4	11.5	11.5	18.1	14.6	14.0	13.1	13.2	17.2	16.0	11.1	3.4
4. Desirable	6.2	6.2	6.2	4.6	12.5	6.5	5.4	7.0	5.9	5.6	6.6	5.0	5.3	9.2	6.6	10.0
Item 6240 Subject C05,D04 N	3396	1652	1628	2594	409	817	969	1064	546	1827	1325	1270	699	466	843	46

A09D: Both work about half-time

1. Not at all acceptable	40.6	43.3	38.0	39.2	47.4	42.7	34.9	46.3	36.2	37.1	45.0	40.4	40.3	38.1	42.7	41.6
2. Somewhat acceptable	34.7	33.1	36.0	36.3	26.0	30.3	39.4	32.6	37.3	36.6	32.1	35.8	35.2	35.1	32.4	31.1
3. Acceptable	18.8	17.3	20.4	19.3	19.2	20.2	20.6	15.9	19.2	20.4	17.2	19.6	19.2	18.6	17.8	18.7
4. Desirable	5.9	6.3	5.6	5.2	7.4	6.7	5.2	5.1	7.3	5.9	5.6	4.2	5.3	8.2	7.0	8.6
Item 6250 Subject C05,D04 N	3387	1648	1627	2588	407	810	966	1065	545	1823	1326	1269	698	465	840	47

A09E: Husband works about half-time, wife works full-time

1. Not at all acceptable	61.6	66.1	57.8	62.6	59.6	61.4	55.7	68.0	59.8	59.0	65.8	60.8	62.5	57.6	65.1	59.7
2. Somewhat acceptable	24.8	20.6	28.9	25.0	23.6	23.9	27.9	21.4	27.0	26.4	22.4	26.5	22.1	28.2	22.4	22.1
3. Acceptable	10.8	10.7	10.6	10.1	12.9	11.5	13.3	8.1	10.7	11.8	8.9	10.2	12.6	10.4	10.0	13.2
4. Desirable	2.9	2.6	2.8	2.2	3.9	3.2	3.2	2.5	2.5	2.9	2.8	2.5	2.8	3.8	2.5	5.0
Item 6260 Subject C05,D04 N	3404	1651	1636	2597	414	817	970	1071	546	1834	1328	1274	699	468	844	47

A09F: Husband doesn't work, wife works full-time

1. Not at all acceptable	74.5	76.1	73.3	73.7	79.4	74.1	68.1	79.9	76.0	73.4	76.0	74.5	72.5	74.5	76.2	74.4
2. Somewhat acceptable	13.3	10.7	16.0	13.7	10.6	12.9	15.1	11.2	14.7	14.4	12.4	14.1	13.2	14.4	12.2	3.9
3. Acceptable	8.4	9.0	7.8	9.3	5.6	8.9	13.0	5.6	5.1	8.8	8.0	8.2	10.0	6.9	8.3	12.2
4. Desirable	3.8	4.2	2.9	3.3	4.4	4.1	3.8	3.3	4.3	3.4	3.6	3.2	4.4	4.2	3.4	9.5
Item 6270 Subject C05,D04 N	3397	1648	1632	2593	412	814	968	1069	546	1831	1326	1272	697	466	843	47

A10: Imagine you are married and have one or more pre-school children. Imagine also that the husband is working full-time and the wife does not have a job outside the home. How would you feel about each of these arrangements for the day-to-day care of the child(ren)?

A10A: Wife does all child care

1. Not at all acceptable	32.7	28.2	38.2	33.7	30.9	34.0	34.7	30.8	31.1	35.9	29.1	32.9	33.9	30.7	32.3	41.1
2. Somewhat acceptable	29.0	29.0	28.4	28.6	29.4	31.7	29.0	25.1	32.6	27.0	31.5	29.3	28.4	32.1	27.8	22.8
3. Acceptable	28.0	29.3	26.5	27.3	32.3	25.0	27.8	31.8	25.2	27.8	27.1	28.3	29.1	27.0	27.2	25.3
4. Desirable	10.3	13.4	6.9	10.4	7.5	9.4	8.6	12.3	11.0	9.3	12.2	9.6	8.6	10.2	12.7	10.7
Item 6280 Subject D04 N	3408	1657	1634	2596	416	823	969	1070	545	1834	1329	1274	704	468	843	47

QUESTIONNAIRE FORM 2 1983	TOTAL	SEX		RACE		REGION				4YR COLLEGE PLANS		ILLICIT DRUG USE: LIFETIME				
		M	F	White	Black	NE	NC	S	W	Yes	No	None	Marijuana Only	Few Pills	More Pills	Any Heroin
N (Weighted No. of Cases):	3435	1671	1641	2610	419	829	979	1077	550	1848	1335	1281	705	472	851	47
% of Weighted Total:	100.0	48.6	47.8	76.0	12.2	24.1	28.5	31.4	16.0	53.8	38.9	37.3	20.5	13.7	24.8	1.4
A10B: Wife does most of it																
1. Not at all acceptable	9.4	9.5	9.5	8.2	17.0	9.6	9.4	9.7	8.8	9.2	9.4	10.0	9.5	9.4	8.6	10.5
2. Somewhat acceptable	31.7	30.3	33.1	29.9	34.2	33.0	28.9	32.8	32.5	29.4	33.9	29.1	34.5	31.8	31.8	35.5
3. Acceptable	44.5	44.5	43.9	45.8	40.9	45.8	47.0	42.7	41.6	45.0	44.3	45.5	43.9	44.4	44.6	47.0
4. Desirable	14.4	15.6	13.5	16.0	7.9	11.6	14.7	14.8	17.1	16.4	12.5	15.5	12.1	14.3	15.1	7.0
Item 6290 Subject D04 N	3407	1654	1636	2598	414	821	969	1071	546	1835	1330	1276	703	468	843	47
A10C: Both do it equally																
1. Not at all acceptable	4.8	6.0	3.6	4.1	9.3	4.3	3.8	6.2	4.4	3.8	5.2	3.9	3.8	4.1	7.2	2.7
2. Somewhat acceptable	17.2	19.0	15.4	16.5	15.6	16.7	16.2	15.8	22.6	18.0	16.3	15.6	15.3	20.6	18.9	28.0
3. Acceptable	39.6	41.7	37.2	38.6	47.8	43.7	38.2	42.3	30.6	37.3	43.2	39.4	43.7	41.7	35.2	28.4
4. Desirable	38.4	33.4	43.8	40.8	27.2	35.4	41.7	35.7	42.4	40.9	35.2	41.0	37.2	33.6	38.7	40.8
Item 6300 Subject D04 N	3405	1654	1635	2594	416	821	969	1070	545	1835	1330	1275	702	467	842	47
A10D: Husband does most of it																
1. Not at all acceptable	49.1	47.3	51.1	49.2	48.3	48.5	49.2	49.1	49.9	49.3	49.1	47.7	48.9	49.7	51.3	48.1
2. Somewhat acceptable	37.1	38.3	35.9	38.8	29.9	37.6	38.3	36.7	35.0	37.3	37.2	37.9	36.4	38.2	35.7	40.2
3. Acceptable	10.7	11.4	9.7	10.1	14.4	9.9	10.9	10.4	12.3	10.6	10.4	11.4	11.2	9.8	10.0	4.6
4. Desirable	3.1	2.9	3.2	1.9	7.4	3.9	1.7	3.8	2.8	2.8	3.2	3.0	3.5	2.2	3.0	7.1
Item 6310 Subject D04 N	3397	1650	1632	2591	415	817	967	1069	544	1832	1325	1273	701	467	841	46
A10E: Husband does all of it																
1. Not at all acceptable	85.8	84.3	87.9	88.5	76.2	84.3	87.0	86.4	85.1	86.7	85.5	86.2	86.4	86.5	85.3	85.0
2. Somewhat acceptable	8.8	10.2	7.2	7.8	11.1	9.7	8.2	8.2	9.8	8.8	8.8	8.5	7.8	9.2	9.6	10.7
3. Acceptable	3.0	3.1	2.6	2.5	4.9	3.2	3.3	2.6	2.7	2.8	3.1	3.5	2.9	2.0	2.5	2.9
4. Desirable	2.4	2.4	2.2	1.2	7.8	2.8	1.5	2.8	2.4	1.8	2.6	1.8	2.8	2.3	2.6	1.3
Item 6320 Subject D04 N	3404	1653	1635	2596	416	820	969	1070	545	1833	1330	1275	701	467	844	47

The next section of this questionnaire is about government and public affairs.

A11: Some people think about what's going on in government very often, and others are not that interested. How much of an interest do you take in government and current events?

	TOTAL	M	F	White	Black	NE	NC	S	W	Yes	No	None	Marijuana Only	Few Pills	More Pills	Any Heroin
1. No interest at all	4.5	4.9	4.3	4.1	6.7	7.6	4.1	3.1	3.6	2.3	7.8	3.0	4.9	3.4	6.5	7.8
2. Very little interest	18.2	13.9	22.6	17.5	22.1	19.5	17.6	17.8	18.0	13.0	25.1	16.9	20.1	16.5	18.9	18.9
3. Some interest	47.8	43.4	52.4	47.6	48.3	49.4	47.7	48.5	44.2	48.6	46.5	48.3	48.7	51.2	45.2	45.5
4. A lot of interest	21.5	26.0	16.5	23.0	15.0	15.7	22.9	22.9	25.4	25.7	15.8	24.7	16.2	20.1	23.0	13.7
5. A very great interest	7.9	11.8	4.2	7.9	7.9	7.8	7.7	7.7	8.9	10.4	4.9	7.1	10.1	8.8	6.3	14.1
Item 6330 Subject H01,Q08 N	3413	1658	1638	2599	417	821	972	1073	548	1839	1332	1277	705	467	845	47

A12: Do you think some of the people running the government are crooked or dishonest?

	TOTAL	M	F	White	Black	NE	NC	S	W	Yes	No	None	Marijuana Only	Few Pills	More Pills	Any Heroin
1. Most of them are crooked or dishonest	11.2	12.8	9.7	10.1	16.1	14.2	9.1	12.3	8.4	8.2	14.8	9.7	11.2	9.6	13.9	14.5
2. Quite a few are	32.7	33.0	33.0	32.0	38.1	32.5	33.0	35.3	27.3	33.0	32.2	34.0	31.3	30.0	32.8	39.3
3. Some are	50.3	48.1	52.0	52.2	41.7	49.2	52.1	47.1	54.9	53.6	46.8	49.9	52.2	53.1	48.4	46.2
4. Hardly any are	5.1	5.4	4.8	5.2	3.2	3.7	5.0	4.7	8.5	4.9	5.2	5.7	4.8	6.4	4.3	-
5. None at all are crooked or dishonest	0.7	0.7	0.6	0.5	0.9	0.5	0.8	0.6	1.0	0.3	0.9	0.8	0.4	0.9	0.5	-
Item 6340 Subject H04,K01 N	3409	1658	1635	2598	416	819	971	1071	547	1839	1328	1276	703	468	843	47

A13: Do you think the government wastes much of the money we pay in taxes?

	TOTAL	M	F	White	Black	NE	NC	S	W	Yes	No	None	Marijuana Only	Few Pills	More Pills	Any Heroin
1. Nearly all tax money is wasted	7.3	8.4	6.1	6.6	9.3	8.0	6.7	7.8	6.2	5.2	10.0	7.6	7.4	4.8	6.8	20.5
2. A lot of tax money is wasted	49.1	48.7	50.0	50.5	45.2	52.4	50.8	46.5	46.1	48.7	49.6	46.4	51.2	52.0	50.0	46.5
3. Some tax money is wasted	36.5	35.6	37.1	35.6	37.6	33.5	35.5	38.0	39.5	38.7	33.3	38.0	34.8	36.6	36.7	25.9
4. A little tax money wasted	6.6	6.6	6.6	6.8	7.3	6.0	6.5	6.8	7.5	7.0	6.3	7.3	6.5	6.2	6.0	7.0
5. No tax money is wasted	0.6	0.7	0.3	0.5	0.5	0.1	0.5	0.8	0.7	0.4	0.7	0.7	0.2	0.5	0.6	-
Item 6350 Subject H04,K01 N	3405	1656	1636	2594	417	818	971	1070	546	1836	1329	1275	704	468	842	47

QUESTIONNAIRE FORM 2 1983	TOTAL	SEX		RACE		REGION				4YR COLLEGE PLANS		ILLICIT DRUG USE: LIFETIME				
		M	F	White	Black	NE	NC	S	W	Yes	No	None	Mari-juana Only	Few Pills	More Pills	Any Her-oin
N (Weighted No. of Cases):	3435	1671	1641	2610	419	829	979	1077	550	1848	1335	1281	705	472	851	47
% of Weighted Total:	100.0	48.6	47.8	76.0	12.2	24.1	28.5	31.4	16.0	53.8	38.9	37.3	20.5	13.7	24.8	1.4

A14: How much of the time do you think you can trust the government in Washington to do what is right?

	TOTAL	M	F	White	Black	NE	NC	S	W	Yes	No	None	Mari-juana Only	Few Pills	More Pills	Any Her-oin
1. Almost always	6.9	8.2	5.7	7.5	4.3	6.3	7.0	6.8	8.2	7.9	5.5	9.5	5.8	5.9	4.8	0.9
2. Often	34.2	38.0	30.4	37.2	20.9	32.7	35.8	30.6	41.0	38.7	28.6	33.9	35.7	34.4	35.2	21.0
3. Sometimes	44.5	39.5	49.6	44.7	40.0	45.1	44.6	46.8	38.7	41.3	49.3	42.9	42.2	47.1	47.0	53.8
4. Seldom	12.5	12.0	12.9	9.3	30.6	13.8	10.6	14.4	10.1	11.0	13.7	12.1	13.4	11.7	11.2	20.5
5. Never	1.9	2.4	1.5	1.2	4.2	2.2	2.1	1.4	2.2	1.2	2.9	1.6	2.9	0.9	1.8	3.8
Item 6360　Subject H04,K01　N	3403	1652	1637	2595	414	819	972	1068	545	1836	1326	1271	705	467	844	47

A15: Do you feel that the people running the government are smart people who usually know what they are doing?

	TOTAL	M	F	White	Black	NE	NC	S	W	Yes	No	None	Mari-juana Only	Few Pills	More Pills	Any Her-oin
1. They almost always know what they are doing	10.2	12.0	8.4	10.1	7.3	10.1	9.6	9.3	13.1	10.2	9.7	10.2	11.5	7.6	10.9	4.0
2. They usually know what they are doing	52.6	55.1	50.0	55.1	42.4	49.4	53.4	52.5	56.2	54.7	50.3	52.7	51.4	52.0	54.2	48.5
3. They sometimes know what they are doing	30.4	25.1	35.6	28.9	38.7	33.1	30.2	30.4	26.5	29.7	31.3	30.5	30.8	33.2	27.7	37.9
4. They seldom know what they are doing	5.9	6.5	5.5	5.2	10.4	6.6	5.8	7.1	2.9	4.8	7.4	5.6	5.0	7.3	6.3	6.3
5. They never know what they are doing	0.9	1.4	0.4	0.7	1.2	0.8	1.0	0.7	1.3	0.6	1.2	1.0	1.2	-	0.8	3.4
Item 6370　Subject H04,K01　N	3408	1657	1638	2597	417	819	972	1072	545	1839	1330	1276	702	469	845	47

A16: Would you say the government is pretty much run for a few big interests looking out for themselves, or is it run for the benefit of all the people?

	TOTAL	M	F	White	Black	NE	NC	S	W	Yes	No	None	Mari-juana Only	Few Pills	More Pills	Any Her-oin
1. Nearly always run for a few big interests	8.4	9.8	6.6	7.7	10.9	8.9	7.5	8.7	8.7	7.0	10.6	6.7	6.9	11.4	9.9	12.1
2. Usually run for a few big interests	22.3	23.3	21.6	21.4	25.2	24.1	21.1	22.7	20.8	22.1	22.1	21.5	22.9	22.7	22.7	19.7
3. Run some for the big interests, some for the people	49.2	44.4	54.1	49.9	45.8	50.7	49.0	48.4	48.7	48.5	50.4	47.6	49.9	49.6	49.9	60.9
4. Usually run for the benefit of all the people	17.0	18.5	15.2	17.7	14.7	14.0	18.4	17.0	18.9	19.2	13.9	20.0	16.5	14.2	15.6	4.8
5. Nearly always run for the benefit of all the people	3.2	3.9	2.5	3.3	3.4	2.2	4.1	3.2	2.8	3.2	3.1	4.2	3.8	2.1	1.9	2.4
Item 6380　Subject H04,K01　N	3393	1655	1629	2592	417	811	971	1068	543	1833	1325	1270	697	468	844	47

A17: Have you ever done, or do you plan to do, the following things?

A17A: Vote in a public election

	TOTAL	M	F	White	Black	NE	NC	S	W	Yes	No	None	Mari-juana Only	Few Pills	More Pills	Any Her-oin
1. I probably won't do this	3.8	3.3	4.1	2.8	7.4	6.1	2.8	3.4	3.1	2.9	4.9	4.0	4.3	2.5	3.7	7.0
2. Don't know	8.3	8.1	8.1	6.3	12.6	10.3	6.2	7.7	10.1	4.2	12.5	7.2	8.0	9.8	8.7	12.8
3. I probably will do this	82.4	80.9	84.5	84.7	76.6	80.0	82.9	83.7	82.7	87.2	77.0	82.7	83.3	82.2	82.7	70.6
4. I have already done this	5.5	7.6	3.3	6.2	3.5	3.6	8.1	5.2	4.2	5.6	5.6	6.1	4.5	5.6	4.9	9.6
Item 6390　Subject H05,I02　N	3412	1661	1638	2601	417	821	974	1071	547	1841	1332	1280	703	469	845	47

A17B: Write to public officials

	TOTAL	M	F	White	Black	NE	NC	S	W	Yes	No	None	Mari-juana Only	Few Pills	More Pills	Any Her-oin
1. I probably won't do this	22.8	21.0	24.9	21.4	30.1	23.7	24.6	20.8	22.3	16.1	31.6	19.9	25.6	20.4	24.8	38.3
2. Don't know	45.5	43.9	46.7	45.7	45.1	44.4	43.7	48.2	45.2	45.0	45.2	49.0	42.7	46.8	41.9	36.0
3. I probably will do this	20.8	23.5	18.0	20.5	21.3	18.6	20.9	21.2	23.2	25.3	15.2	20.7	21.5	21.3	21.2	10.4
4. I have already done this	10.9	11.7	10.4	12.4	3.6	13.4	10.8	9.9	9.3	13.5	8.1	10.4	10.2	11.5	12.2	15.3
Item 6400　Subject H05,I02　N	3408	1658	1638	2599	417	819	973	1070	546	1839	1331	1277	703	469	844	47

A17C: Give money to a political candidate or cause

	TOTAL	M	F	White	Black	NE	NC	S	W	Yes	No	None	Mari-juana Only	Few Pills	More Pills	Any Her-oin
1. I probably won't do this	39.7	42.6	36.4	39.2	42.7	42.3	42.0	35.2	40.2	33.9	47.5	36.5	41.8	35.8	44.0	50.2
2. Don't know	40.2	36.2	44.3	40.5	37.9	40.0	38.1	42.1	40.4	42.1	36.5	43.0	38.9	39.7	37.9	28.8
3. I probably will do this	17.0	17.2	17.2	16.9	18.4	14.5	16.9	19.2	16.7	20.8	12.9	18.6	15.7	20.4	14.5	14.4
4. I have already done this	3.1	4.0	2.1	3.4	1.0	3.3	3.0	3.4	2.7	3.2	3.1	1.8	3.6	4.2	3.6	6.7
Item 6410　Subject H05,I02　N	3409	1660	1637	2601	416	820	972	1071	546	1839	1331	1279	702	468	845	47

QUESTIONNAIRE FORM 2 1983	TOTAL	SEX		RACE		REGION				4YR COLLEGE PLANS		ILLICIT DRUG USE: LIFETIME				
		M	F	White	Black	NE	NC	S	W	Yes	No	None	Mari-juana Only	Few Pills	More Pills	Any Heroin
N (Weighted No. of Cases):	3435	1671	1641	2610	419	829	979	1077	550	1848	1335	1281	705	472	851	47
% of Weighted Total:	100.0	48.6	47.8	76.0	12.2	24.1	28.5	31.4	16.0	53.8	38.9	37.3	20.5	13.7	24.8	1.4
A17D: Work in a political campaign																
1. I probably won't do this	47.6	48.8	46.6	48.4	44.4	53.3	47.6	42.9	48.2	39.4	58.3	45.9	48.6	46.7	50.1	51.3
2. Don't know	36.9	36.4	37.0	35.8	39.8	32.1	37.8	38.8	38.6	40.2	32.2	38.1	37.3	35.2	35.3	29.0
3. I probably will do this	8.9	7.5	10.1	8.5	11.3	8.5	7.7	10.7	7.9	11.9	4.9	9.7	9.5	9.7	7.0	6.1
4. I have already done this	6.7	7.2	6.3	7.4	4.5	6.0	6.9	7.7	5.2	8.4	4.6	6.2	4.6	8.5	7.6	13.5
Item 6420　Subject H05,I02　N	3402	1657	1635	2594	417	817	968	1071	546	1838	1328	1278	700	467	845	46
A17E: Participate in a lawful demonstration																
1. I probably won't do this	36.7	34.9	38.6	36.7	36.4	35.0	35.5	38.6	37.3	30.9	44.4	38.3	39.1	32.7	33.6	47.9
2. Don't know	45.4	45.3	45.6	45.5	46.2	44.0	46.9	45.7	44.4	47.7	41.8	46.5	44.8	43.8	46.0	25.4
3. I probably will do this	15.3	16.8	13.7	15.0	16.5	17.1	15.5	14.0	15.1	18.7	11.4	13.5	14.2	20.2	16.6	19.7
4. I have already done this	2.6	3.0	2.1	2.8	1.0	3.8	2.1	1.8	3.1	2.7	2.5	1.7	1.9	3.3	3.8	7.0
Item 6430　Subject H05,I02　N	3405	1656	1637	2600	416	819	972	1070	545	1837	1329	1275	703	468	845	46
A17F: Boycott certain products or stores																
1. I probably won't do this	38.6	34.3	42.7	38.9	40.7	35.5	37.8	42.4	37.0	33.9	44.7	39.6	41.5	34.7	36.7	40.6
2. Don't know	43.5	44.8	42.1	43.3	42.6	41.8	44.3	44.7	42.0	44.8	41.1	44.0	40.5	44.2	44.3	43.9
3. I probably will do this	13.4	15.4	11.6	12.9	14.2	18.1	12.4	9.9	15.1	15.8	10.8	13.3	13.3	15.8	12.7	11.8
4. I have already done this	4.6	5.5	3.6	5.0	2.5	4.6	5.6	3.0	6.0	5.5	3.3	3.0	4.7	5.3	6.3	3.7
Item 6440　Subject H05,I02　N	3407	1657	1637	2599	414	821	972	1068	546	1839	1330	1277	703	467	845	47
A18: How much do you agree or disagree with each of the following statements?																
A18A: The U.S. should begin a gradual program of disarming whether other countries do or not																
1. Disagree	40.3	54.6	26.0	42.8	30.5	36.7	43.3	42.7	35.6	40.9	39.2	39.1	42.3	39.6	40.2	52.1
2. Mostly disagree	18.5	18.4	18.8	19.0	15.7	17.4	19.4	18.1	19.1	20.2	16.5	20.2	14.9	17.9	20.7	6.9
3. Neither	20.4	11.8	29.0	18.8	27.3	17.2	21.0	21.9	20.9	18.5	23.0	20.6	21.6	18.3	19.4	26.7
4. Mostly agree	12.5	8.4	16.9	11.9	14.6	15.3	9.8	10.9	16.0	12.4	13.1	12.0	11.9	15.5	12.1	11.8
5. Agree	8.4	6.8	9.3	7.6	12.0	13.4	6.5	6.4	8.3	8.0	8.2	8.1	9.3	8.8	7.6	2.4
Item 6450　Subject H02,L03　N	3387	1650	1628	2590	412	811	969	1065	543	1831	1322	1274	693	467	842	47
A18B: There may be times when the U.S. should go to war to protect the rights of other countries																
1. Disagree	24.4	23.3	26.0	23.8	32.9	29.0	24.1	23.0	20.7	22.4	27.1	21.8	25.4	22.1	28.7	19.0
2. Mostly disagree	24.0	22.8	25.3	24.6	22.1	24.5	23.8	22.9	26.0	25.6	22.2	24.0	25.8	23.7	23.8	20.1
3. Neither	16.9	16.2	17.5	17.4	11.4	16.2	18.1	15.9	17.6	15.6	18.9	16.5	14.6	17.6	17.7	36.0
4. Mostly agree	21.1	21.0	21.5	21.7	16.5	17.5	21.0	23.7	21.9	23.5	18.5	24.0	18.5	22.1	19.2	12.8
5. Agree	13.6	16.8	9.8	12.6	17.1	12.8	13.0	14.5	13.8	12.9	13.3	13.7	15.7	14.6	10.6	12.0
Item 5690　Subject H02,L03　N	3393	1654	1631	2592	412	814	972	1065	543	1830	1325	1278	696	467	841	47
A18C: The U.S. should be willing to go to war to protect its own economic interests																
1. Disagree	10.2	10.2	10.1	9.0	14.7	12.7	9.1	8.6	11.4	9.4	10.9	9.5	11.8	9.1	9.4	15.0
2. Mostly disagree	13.1	10.7	15.9	13.9	8.4	14.7	14.7	9.4	15.3	15.0	11.6	13.6	13.7	12.3	13.1	12.4
3. Neither	20.3	18.6	21.9	20.8	16.7	22.1	18.9	18.7	23.5	19.5	20.1	21.1	19.8	18.2	20.6	29.9
4. Mostly agree	29.5	30.6	28.4	30.8	25.2	27.1	32.1	30.2	27.2	30.5	29.0	29.7	27.7	32.1	29.9	21.8
5. Agree	26.9	30.0	23.6	25.5	35.1	23.4	25.2	33.1	22.7	25.7	28.5	26.1	27.0	28.3	27.0	21.0
Item 6460　Subject H02,L03　N	3392	1652	1631	2593	412	813	972	1064	544	1830	1326	1274	700	467	839	47
A18D: The only good reason for the U.S. to go to war is to defend against an attack on our own country																
1. Disagree	7.3	9.2	5.3	7.1	8.6	8.0	7.7	7.0	6.4	7.6	7.5	8.0	7.8	6.1	6.5	8.0
2. Mostly disagree	10.6	12.1	9.1	11.1	9.0	7.2	11.9	11.7	11.1	12.2	8.7	11.3	8.1	12.0	10.5	9.0
3. Neither	8.6	7.7	9.1	8.9	6.2	7.4	9.5	8.7	8.6	8.0	8.5	8.4	9.9	7.6	8.2	16.7
4. Mostly agree	30.6	29.4	31.7	31.3	24.9	29.5	32.8	30.2	29.2	32.2	29.4	31.3	31.3	34.1	27.7	29.4
5. Agree	42.9	41.5	44.8	41.6	51.2	47.8	38.2	42.4	44.7	40.0	45.9	40.9	42.9	40.2	47.1	36.8
Item 6470　Subject H02,L03　N	3384	1650	1625	2588	408	814	967	1058	545	1826	1324	1273	698	465	836	47

QUESTIONNAIRE FORM 2 1983	TOTAL	SEX		RACE		REGION				4YR COLLEGE PLANS		ILLICIT DRUG USE: LIFETIME				
		M	F	White	Black	NE	NC	S	W	Yes	No	None	Marijuana Only	Few Pills	More Pills	Any Heroin
N (Weighted No. of Cases):	3435	1671	1641	2610	419	829	979	1077	550	1848	1335	1281	705	472	851	47
% of Weighted Total:	100.0	48.6	47.8	76.0	12.2	24.1	28.5	31.4	16.0	53.8	38.9	37.3	20.5	13.7	24.8	1.4

A18E: The U.S. does not need to have greater military power than the Soviet Union

1. Disagree	35.4	40.2	31.1	34.8	42.8	32.3	33.3	43.9	27.2	32.7	38.9	32.9	39.2	33.8	36.1	44.5
2. Mostly disagree	25.1	25.2	25.6	24.9	24.8	25.9	24.7	25.1	25.0	26.7	23.4	25.9	24.9	26.2	24.8	14.2
3. Neither	18.0	14.1	21.6	18.0	16.5	16.2	20.9	16.2	19.1	18.0	18.4	19.1	15.4	18.6	17.4	28.8
4. Mostly agree	11.6	11.3	11.9	12.2	9.8	14.0	12.0	8.6	13.4	12.0	11.2	12.5	10.7	11.7	11.5	7.6
5. Agree	9.8	9.2	9.8	10.2	6.1	11.6	9.1	6.3	15.3	10.6	8.1	9.6	9.8	9.8	10.1	4.9
Item 6480 Subject H02,L03 N	3378	1647	1623	2587	410	813	964	1061	540	1823	1320	1264	700	468	838	46

A18F: The U.S. ought to have much more military power than any other nation in the world

1. Disagree	15.2	15.3	14.5	15.7	12.9	17.9	15.8	10.1	20.2	17.6	11.8	15.2	14.6	14.6	16.2	11.5
2. Mostly disagree	18.9	18.4	19.8	20.1	11.9	20.4	21.5	14.0	21.3	21.3	15.7	22.2	15.7	18.0	17.4	11.9
3. Neither	25.5	22.1	29.0	26.2	21.2	25.6	25.8	26.6	22.8	25.0	26.5	25.7	27.1	25.1	24.4	31.4
4. Mostly agree	19.1	19.5	19.0	18.5	22.2	15.5	19.5	23.0	16.1	18.2	20.2	17.5	19.8	23.0	18.5	16.1
5. Agree	21.3	24.8	17.7	19.5	31.8	20.7	17.4	26.3	19.6	18.0	25.8	19.3	22.8	19.2	23.4	29.0
Item 6490 Subject H02,L03 N	3390	1653	1629	2594	411	815	969	1062	545	1830	1326	1275	700	467	838	47

A18G: Our present foreign policy is based on our own narrow economic and power interests

1. Disagree	5.3	6.9	3.6	4.9	6.3	7.1	3.6	5.3	5.8	4.8	5.6	6.2	3.6	5.3	5.0	3.9
2. Mostly disagree	9.9	11.0	8.9	10.0	9.6	8.4	9.8	9.9	12.3	11.8	8.1	10.2	12.4	9.2	8.0	11.5
3. Neither	45.1	39.6	50.6	46.5	38.6	44.5	46.6	44.1	45.3	43.2	47.6	42.6	47.0	41.3	49.7	37.6
4. Mostly agree	26.8	27.7	26.4	27.2	29.0	24.4	29.2	28.1	23.8	28.2	25.3	29.4	26.0	28.1	23.2	31.2
5. Agree	12.9	14.7	10.5	11.5	16.5	15.6	10.7	12.7	12.9	12.0	13.4	11.5	11.1	16.1	14.1	15.8
Item 6500 Subject H02,L03 N	3327	1624	1595	2542	403	803	952	1040	532	1806	1294	1251	681	457	828	47

A18H: Servicemen should obey orders without question

1. Disagree	13.1	12.2	13.9	11.4	22.2	17.2	12.3	10.6	13.4	13.4	12.9	14.0	14.4	8.7	12.9	11.4
2. Mostly disagree	18.0	15.2	21.1	18.0	15.7	18.1	18.9	16.2	19.6	20.1	15.5	18.5	17.9	19.6	17.2	10.9
3. Neither	21.7	19.0	24.4	21.8	19.5	22.0	23.4	20.6	20.6	19.1	24.2	22.0	25.0	17.3	21.1	23.5
4. Mostly agree	30.1	31.2	29.0	31.6	23.3	26.2	29.5	33.6	29.8	31.6	28.4	29.1	28.9	35.9	29.8	23.0
5. Agree	17.1	22.4	11.6	17.3	19.3	16.4	16.0	18.9	16.7	15.7	19.0	16.2	13.7	18.6	19.0	31.3
Item 6510 Subject L03 N	3386	1651	1627	2590	413	813	970	1065	539	1830	1322	1273	696	468	840	47

A19: This section deals with activities which may be against the rules or against the law. We hope you will answer all of these questions. However, if you find a question which you cannot answer honestly, we would prefer that you leave it blank. Remember, your answers will never be connected with your name. During the LAST 12 MONTHS, how often have you...

A19A: Argued or had a fight with either of your parents

1. Not at all	11.3	13.3	8.8	7.1	32.0	10.9	6.7	16.1	10.8	10.6	11.1	14.1	12.5	9.3	6.8	9.0
2. Once	11.0	11.2	10.4	8.9	19.0	10.7	9.6	11.2	13.3	10.7	11.1	13.3	11.3	10.8	7.1	4.5
3. Twice	11.6	10.7	12.5	12.4	7.5	12.2	12.3	9.5	13.6	12.5	11.1	14.2	12.1	10.5	8.7	3.4
4. 3 or 4 times	24.4	26.2	22.9	25.6	16.4	24.5	24.3	25.2	22.7	23.7	25.2	22.8	23.8	28.9	24.8	25.2
5. 5 or more times	41.8	38.6	45.3	46.0	25.1	41.7	47.1	38.0	39.6	42.5	41.5	35.7	40.4	40.5	52.7	57.8
Item 6520 Subject M03,S01 N	3395	1658	1630	2596	413	818	970	1063	544	1833	1329	1272	700	467	849	47

A19B: Hit an instructor or supervisor

1. Not at all	96.6	94.6	98.7	96.9	97.2	95.7	96.3	97.6	96.6	97.8	95.0	97.8	99.0	96.4	94.1	77.7
2. Once	1.9	2.9	0.7	1.6	1.9	2.1	1.9	1.1	2.8	1.5	2.6	1.2	0.5	2.2	3.5	6.2
3. Twice	0.7	1.1	0.4	0.8	0.5	0.8	0.9	0.8	0.4	0.3	1.3	0.5	0.3	0.6	1.5	2.1
4. 3 or 4 times	0.5	0.9	0.1	0.3	0.4	1.0	0.4	0.3	0.1	0.3	0.7	0.4	0.1	0.5	0.2	10.2
5. 5 or more times	0.3	0.5	0.1	0.3	-	0.5	0.5	0.2	0.1	0.2	0.4	0.1	0.2	0.2	0.7	3.7
Item 6530 Subject M02,S01 N	3404	1662	1633	2602	414	820	974	1066	544	1837	1331	1277	703	468	847	47

QUESTIONNAIRE FORM 2 1983	TOTAL	SEX		RACE		REGION				4YR COLLEGE PLANS		ILLICIT DRUG USE: LIFETIME				
		M	F	White	Black	NE	NC	S	W	Yes	No	None	Mari- juana Only	Few Pills	More Pills	Any Her- oin
N (Weighted No. of Cases):	3435	1671	1641	2610	419	829	979	1077	550	1848	1335	1281	705	472	851	47
% of Weighted Total:	100.0	48.6	47.8	76.0	12.2	24.1	28.5	31.4	16.0	53.8	38.9	37.3	20.5	13.7	24.8	1.4
A19C: Gotten into a serious fight in school or at work																
1. Not at all	82.4	75.3	89.6	82.3	82.5	79.9	82.9	83.7	82.7	85.9	78.0	88.8	82.2	84.1	73.0	53.9
2. Once	10.7	14.0	7.2	10.4	12.0	12.0	9.0	11.0	11.0	8.8	12.9	7.3	12.9	9.6	14.5	15.1
3. Twice	3.4	5.1	1.6	3.8	1.9	3.6	4.1	2.7	3.6	2.6	4.6	2.3	2.7	2.9	5.7	9.9
4. 3 or 4 times	2.6	4.1	1.3	2.8	3.1	3.2	3.0	2.1	2.1	2.2	3.4	1.2	2.0	2.9	4.9	11.8
5. 5 or more times	0.9	1.4	0.4	0.7	0.5	1.3	1.1	0.4	0.6	0.5	1.1	0.4	0.2	0.5	2.0	9.3
Item 6540 Subject B07,C01,S01 N	3404	1663	1633	2603	413	820	972	1067	544	1838	1330	1275	703	469	849	47
A19D: Taken part in a fight where a group of your friends were against another group																
1. Not at all	82.1	78.5	86.1	82.2	85.9	77.8	80.9	84.0	87.3	84.7	78.5	88.7	82.5	84.8	71.7	50.1
2. Once	10.1	11.1	9.0	10.0	7.0	11.6	10.6	9.4	8.5	8.8	12.0	6.7	10.5	9.7	14.6	24.3
3. Twice	4.2	5.3	3.1	4.0	4.1	5.1	4.7	3.8	2.6	3.5	5.2	2.7	3.3	3.9	7.3	4.0
4. 3 or 4 times	2.2	3.0	1.3	2.6	1.5	3.2	3.0	1.5	0.9	2.1	2.3	1.4	2.2	0.9	3.9	12.8
5. 5 or more times	1.3	2.2	0.5	1.2	1.5	2.3	0.8	1.4	0.7	0.8	2.0	0.6	1.4	0.6	2.5	8.8
Item 6550 Subject S01 N	3401	1660	1633	2599	414	820	969	1069	543	1838	1328	1276	699	469	849	46
A19E: Hurt someone badly enough to need bandages or a doctor																
1. Not at all	88.9	81.4	96.7	89.1	88.3	88.2	88.7	89.0	90.0	90.9	86.8	93.5	91.6	91.0	80.1	61.3
2. Once	7.2	11.7	2.5	7.0	7.9	7.0	7.3	7.3	7.5	6.3	8.3	4.8	5.6	7.1	11.4	21.8
3. Twice	1.7	2.9	0.5	1.8	1.5	1.8	1.8	1.6	1.5	1.5	1.8	0.7	1.2	1.7	3.7	2.6
4. 3 or 4 times	1.3	2.5	*	1.2	1.8	1.6	1.3	1.4	0.6	0.7	1.9	0.7	1.1	0.1	2.8	5.6
5. 5 or more times	0.9	1.5	0.2	0.8	0.5	1.4	0.9	0.8	0.5	0.6	1.3	0.4	0.5	-	2.1	8.7
Item 6560 Subject S01 N	3402	1662	1633	2601	414	818	972	1067	545	1837	1331	1276	702	468	848	47
A19F: Used a knife or gun or some other thing (like a club) to get something from a person																
1. Not at all	97.0	95.2	99.0	97.9	94.9	96.8	97.9	96.0	97.8	98.6	95.5	98.5	97.8	97.6	95.1	79.6
2. Once	1.5	2.2	0.7	1.0	3.3	1.9	0.8	1.7	1.8	1.0	1.9	0.7	1.4	1.5	2.3	6.6
3. Twice	0.6	1.0	0.2	0.5	0.7	0.4	0.6	1.0	0.4	0.3	1.0	0.4	0.3	0.4	1.3	3.1
4. 3 or 4 times	0.3	0.6	-	0.2	0.5	0.5	0.4	0.2	-	0.1	0.5	0.3	0.4	0.2	0.1	3.5
5. 5 or more times	0.6	1.0	0.1	0.4	0.5	0.5	0.3	1.1	*	*	1.1	0.1	0.1	0.3	1.1	7.3
Item 6570 Subject S01 N	3402	1661	1634	2601	414	816	974	1068	545	1837	1330	1277	702	469	846	47
A19G: Taken something not belonging to you worth under $50																
1. Not at all	69.3	61.5	77.2	67.2	80.0	68.1	63.7	75.8	68.3	68.2	71.2	79.6	69.4	69.6	54.1	50.1
2. Once	14.8	16.6	13.3	15.4	11.1	16.3	15.9	13.2	13.9	16.4	12.8	11.9	15.1	17.6	18.1	10.7
3. Twice	6.6	8.8	4.3	7.4	3.7	5.6	8.6	4.7	8.6	6.7	6.4	3.9	5.7	6.9	11.4	9.3
4. 3 or 4 times	4.6	6.3	2.9	5.0	2.5	5.7	6.5	2.6	3.7	4.6	4.6	2.8	4.2	2.7	7.9	20.9
5. 5 or more times	4.6	6.8	2.3	4.9	2.7	4.3	5.4	3.6	5.5	4.1	4.9	1.8	5.6	3.2	8.5	8.9
Item 6580 Subject S01 N	3388	1650	1631	2589	415	812	971	1064	541	1834	1319	1276	697	468	842	47
A19H: Taken something not belonging to you worth over $50																
1. Not at all	93.6	89.9	97.8	94.3	92.7	91.8	94.3	94.4	93.2	95.0	92.5	98.1	94.8	93.9	87.3	68.5
2. Once	3.5	5.7	1.0	3.2	4.0	3.6	4.0	3.2	2.9	2.4	4.3	1.0	2.6	4.1	6.9	14.2
3. Twice	1.3	2.0	0.5	1.1	0.9	1.7	0.6	1.1	2.2	1.1	1.6	0.5	1.3	0.6	2.6	2.7
4. 3 or 4 times	0.9	1.3	0.4	0.7	1.7	1.5	0.8	0.3	1.6	0.9	0.7	0.3	0.9	0.9	1.6	7.4
5. 5 or more times	0.8	1.1	0.2	0.7	0.7	1.4	0.2	1.0	0.1	0.7	0.9	0.1	0.5	0.5	1.6	7.2
Item 6590 Subject S01 N	3390	1652	1633	2594	414	817	971	1066	537	1836	1323	1276	698	466	845	47
A19I: Taken something from a store without paying for it																
1. Not at all	73.9	68.4	79.5	73.7	75.8	70.2	71.7	79.2	72.9	76.6	71.6	86.5	71.9	74.7	57.0	44.5
2. Once	12.7	13.9	11.9	12.7	13.9	13.0	13.5	11.3	13.8	12.0	13.9	7.8	15.4	13.7	17.3	19.4
3. Twice	5.2	6.7	3.4	5.4	4.3	4.9	7.2	4.3	3.8	4.6	5.5	2.4	4.9	4.9	9.8	9.4
4. 3 or 4 times	4.2	5.6	2.6	4.4	2.7	7.1	3.8	1.9	4.7	3.0	5.0	1.8	3.7	3.3	8.4	12.8
5. 5 or more times	4.0	5.3	2.6	3.9	3.3	4.8	3.8	3.3	4.8	3.8	4.1	1.5	4.2	3.5	7.5	13.9
Item 6600 Subject S01 N	3392	1656	1629	2595	414	813	971	1065	543	1829	1329	1272	700	467	845	47

*=less than .05 per cent.

QUESTIONNAIRE FORM 2 1983	TOTAL	SEX		RACE		REGION				4YR COLLEGE PLANS		ILLICIT DRUG USE: LIFETIME				
		M	F	White	Black	NE	NC	S	W	Yes	No	None	Marijuana Only	Few Pills	More Pills	Any Heroin
N (Weighted No. of Cases):	3435	1671	1641	2610	419	829	979	1077	550	1848	1335	1281	705	472	851	47
% of Weighted Total:	100.0	48.6	47.8	76.0	12.2	24.1	28.5	31.4	16.0	53.8	38.9	37.3	20.5	13.7	24.8	1.4

A19J: Taken a car that didn't belong to someone in your family without permission of the owner

	TOTAL	M	F	White	Black	NE	NC	S	W	Yes	No	None	Mari-juana Only	Few Pills	More Pills	Any Heroin
1. Not at all	94.5	92.3	97.0	94.8	95.6	92.4	94.3	95.5	95.9	95.9	93.4	98.1	95.1	93.8	89.8	74.1
2. Once	3.1	3.9	2.3	3.1	3.0	4.9	3.2	2.4	1.9	3.0	3.1	1.1	2.5	4.9	5.7	7.0
3. Twice	1.1	1.6	0.5	1.1	0.4	1.1	1.3	0.8	1.1	0.7	1.3	0.4	0.8	0.7	2.7	1.5
4. 3 or 4 times	0.6	1.1	0.1	0.6	0.5	0.5	0.8	0.7	0.1	0.2	1.0	-	0.6	0.2	1.3	8.1
5. 5 or more times	0.7	1.1	0.1	0.4	0.6	1.0	0.4	0.5	1.0	0.2	1.1	0.4	0.9	0.4	0.5	9.3
Item 6610 Subject S01 N	3402	1661	1634	2602	414	818	974	1067	544	1837	1330	1277	703	469	847	47

A19K: Taken part of a car without permission of the owner

	TOTAL	M	F	White	Black	NE	NC	S	W	Yes	No	None	Mari-juana Only	Few Pills	More Pills	Any Heroin
1. Not at all	94.3	90.9	98.0	94.3	94.8	92.9	94.1	95.4	94.8	95.9	92.6	98.3	93.6	96.0	89.3	70.0
2. Once	2.9	4.7	1.2	3.1	2.1	3.3	3.2	2.4	2.8	2.2	4.1	0.6	2.9	2.3	6.0	13.8
3. Twice	1.5	2.2	0.6	1.3	1.8	1.8	1.5	1.1	1.6	0.9	2.0	0.6	2.1	1.1	2.3	7.5
4. 3 or 4 times	0.7	1.1	0.2	0.7	0.6	1.1	0.6	0.6	0.5	0.6	0.6	0.2	1.1	0.4	1.2	4.0
5. 5 or more times	0.6	1.1	*	0.5	0.7	0.8	0.6	0.5	0.4	0.3	0.7	0.3	0.2	0.3	1.2	4.7
Item 6620 Subject S01 N	3394	1657	1630	2594	414	815	968	1066	545	1831	1328	1276	700	466	845	47

A19L: Gone into some house or building when you weren't supposed to be there

	TOTAL	M	F	White	Black	NE	NC	S	W	Yes	No	None	Mari-juana Only	Few Pills	More Pills	Any Heroin
1. Not at all	76.6	69.3	84.2	75.3	83.1	73.2	76.1	79.9	76.4	76.7	77.7	84.1	79.7	74.2	65.6	47.1
2. Once	11.5	13.6	9.1	11.8	10.0	11.5	11.2	11.4	12.1	11.9	10.4	8.8	8.8	17.1	14.0	22.5
3. Twice	6.8	9.5	4.2	7.9	2.7	9.8	6.5	4.4	7.7	6.9	6.4	4.7	6.4	5.0	11.2	10.4
4. 3 or 4 times	3.0	4.5	1.6	3.1	2.7	3.3	4.0	2.0	2.9	2.4	3.6	1.6	3.3	2.0	4.9	11.1
5. 5 or more times	2.1	3.1	0.9	1.9	1.5	2.3	2.3	2.4	1.0	2.0	2.0	0.7	1.9	1.6	4.3	8.9
Item 6630 Subject S01 N	3394	1657	1630	2594	414	815	971	1064	543	1830	1329	1273	701	468	845	47

A19M: Set fire to someone's property on purpose

	TOTAL	M	F	White	Black	NE	NC	S	W	Yes	No	None	Mari-juana Only	Few Pills	More Pills	Any Heroin
1. Not at all	98.7	97.7	99.9	99.1	98.2	97.9	98.7	99.1	99.6	99.3	98.2	99.7	99.0	99.2	97.7	89.2
2. Once	0.7	1.2	0.1	0.5	1.2	0.6	1.1	0.6	0.4	0.4	0.9	0.2	0.9	0.5	1.3	-
3. Twice	0.2	0.4	-	0.1	0.6	0.6	-	0.2	-	0.1	0.3	0.1	0.1	0.2	0.3	3.6
4. 3 or 4 times	0.1	0.3	-	0.1	-	0.3	0.2	0.1	-	0.1	0.2	-	-	0.1	0.2	2.5
5. 5 or more times	0.2	0.4	*	0.2	-	0.5	0.1	0.2	-	0.1	0.3	0.1	-	-	0.5	4.8
Item 6640 Subject S01 N	3398	1656	1634	2598	415	814	973	1067	545	1837	1327	1276	703	468	844	46

A19N: Damaged school property on purpose

	TOTAL	M	F	White	Black	NE	NC	S	W	Yes	No	None	Mari-juana Only	Few Pills	More Pills	Any Heroin
1. Not at all	85.9	78.5	93.3	85.3	89.3	84.0	82.2	89.9	87.7	88.2	83.1	92.4	87.1	85.7	76.2	64.9
2. Once	7.0	9.9	4.2	7.4	6.6	7.3	8.4	5.3	7.4	6.3	8.3	5.2	6.4	7.9	9.8	11.0
3. Twice	3.2	4.8	1.6	3.5	1.5	4.0	4.3	2.2	1.7	2.6	3.6	1.4	3.0	3.2	5.7	6.2
4. 3 or 4 times	2.3	4.1	0.5	2.5	1.3	2.4	3.4	1.4	2.0	1.6	3.0	0.2	2.4	2.0	5.2	7.0
5. 5 or more times	1.6	2.7	0.5	1.3	1.3	2.3	1.8	1.1	1.2	1.3	2.1	0.7	1.0	1.2	3.0	11.0
Item 6650 Subject B07,S01 N	3387	1653	1628	2594	410	811	971	1065	540	1830	1324	1270	698	468	845	46

A19O: Damaged property at work on purpose

	TOTAL	M	F	White	Black	NE	NC	S	W	Yes	No	None	Mari-juana Only	Few Pills	More Pills	Any Heroin
1. Not at all	94.5	90.1	98.9	94.5	95.6	92.2	94.7	95.8	95.2	95.1	93.8	97.2	93.5	96.2	90.6	90.1
2. Once	2.6	4.3	0.8	2.3	2.7	3.6	2.1	2.1	2.8	2.2	2.8	1.8	3.3	1.6	3.6	3.5
3. Twice	1.4	2.6	0.3	1.5	0.9	1.9	2.1	0.9	0.5	1.1	1.9	0.4	1.5	0.7	3.5	1.7
4. 3 or 4 times	0.9	1.8	-	0.9	0.8	1.3	0.8	0.4	1.1	1.0	0.7	0.3	1.2	0.8	1.2	2.5
5. 5 or more times	0.6	1.2	*	0.7	0.1	0.9	0.4	0.7	0.4	0.6	0.7	0.2	0.5	0.7	1.2	2.2
Item 6660 Subject C01,S01 N	3395	1654	1634	2595	414	816	971	1067	542	1835	1327	1276	700	469	845	47

A19P: Gotten into trouble with police because of something you did

	TOTAL	M	F	White	Black	NE	NC	S	W	Yes	No	None	Mari-juana Only	Few Pills	More Pills	Any Heroin
1. Not at all	78.7	69.6	88.5	77.1	89.9	79.9	73.1	83.2	77.9	81.2	76.5	89.8	80.0	78.8	62.6	40.5
2. Once	13.8	18.1	9.0	15.1	5.7	12.1	17.1	11.6	14.6	12.9	14.3	8.3	14.7	15.0	20.7	15.0
3. Twice	4.5	7.4	1.3	4.6	2.6	4.6	5.9	3.3	4.3	3.6	5.2	1.4	3.3	4.9	9.2	18.2
4. 3 or 4 times	2.1	3.0	1.0	2.2	1.3	1.8	3.1	1.3	2.2	1.5	2.7	0.5	1.6	0.7	5.2	10.7
5. 5 or more times	1.0	1.8	0.2	1.0	0.5	1.6	0.9	0.6	1.0	0.7	1.4	*	0.4	0.6	2.3	15.6
Item 6670 Subject S01 N	3395	1655	1633	2597	413	817	971	1065	543	1832	1330	1275	703	466	846	47

*=less than .05 per cent.

QUESTIONNAIRE FORM 2 1983	TOTAL	SEX		RACE		REGION				4YR COLLEGE PLANS		ILLICIT DRUG USE: LIFETIME				
		M	F	White	Black	NE	NC	S	W	Yes	No	None	Mari- juana Only	Few Pills	More Pills	Any Her- oin
N (Weighted No. of Cases):	3435	1671	1641	2610	419	829	979	1077	550	1848	1335	1281	705	472	851	47
% of Weighted Total:	100.0	48.6	47.8	76.0	12.2	24.1	28.5	31.4	16.0	53.8	38.9	37.3	20.5	13.7	24.8	1.4

A20: The next questions are about some things which may have happened TO YOU. During the LAST 12 MONTHS, how often...

A20A: Has something of yours (worth under $50) been stolen?

1. Not at all	52.4	47.9	56.8	52.2	51.9	51.5	51.9	56.3	47.0	49.0	56.9	56.0	53.7	50.2	46.4	44.4
2. Once	27.2	27.3	27.1	27.5	25.0	28.8	26.4	24.6	31.4	28.8	25.4	28.0	25.3	28.1	28.2	19.6
3. Twice	12.2	14.4	10.1	12.2	13.1	11.5	13.4	10.9	13.7	13.1	11.0	9.1	13.9	13.7	14.3	20.1
4. 3 or 4 times	6.4	8.1	4.6	6.5	6.8	6.0	6.6	6.5	6.5	7.2	5.2	5.5	5.3	5.9	8.9	12.0
5. 5 or more times	1.8	2.2	1.4	1.5	3.1	2.2	1.8	1.7	1.4	1.9	1.5	1.4	1.8	2.1	2.2	3.9
Item 6680 Subject S03 N	3398	1657	1634	2598	415	819	972	1066	542	1832	1330	1273	702	466	848	47

A20B: Has something of yours (worth over $50) been stolen?

1. Not at all	83.7	79.8	88.0	85.3	78.1	84.8	86.5	81.4	81.6	83.0	84.9	88.4	83.3	81.6	79.0	59.0
2. Once	12.2	14.9	9.5	11.1	15.0	11.6	9.8	13.3	15.6	12.6	11.7	8.9	14.0	12.1	15.4	24.3
3. Twice	2.9	3.5	2.0	2.4	5.2	2.7	1.9	4.2	2.3	3.2	2.4	2.2	1.6	4.7	4.0	6.1
4. 3 or 4 times	0.9	1.4	0.3	0.9	1.0	0.6	1.4	0.9	0.4	1.0	0.7	0.3	0.7	1.0	1.3	10.7
5. 5 or more times	0.3	0.4	0.2	0.2	0.6	0.5	0.4	0.2	0.2	0.2	0.3	0.2	0.4	0.5	0.3	-
Item 6690 Subject S03 N	3397	1656	1635	2597	415	818	973	1066	541	1834	1328	1275	703	466	846	46

A20C: Has someone deliberately damaged your property (your car, clothing, etc.)?

1. Not at all	66.9	58.1	76.1	66.0	71.3	71.9	66.2	65.4	63.6	67.7	65.6	71.3	65.1	65.7	62.5	62.5
2. Once	19.9	24.9	14.9	20.7	16.0	16.7	18.4	21.4	24.7	19.1	21.7	18.1	21.2	20.3	21.1	23.2
3. Twice	8.8	11.6	6.0	9.1	7.4	7.8	9.7	9.9	6.7	9.0	8.6	6.9	10.0	10.4	10.4	8.5
4. 3 or 4 times	3.1	4.2	1.9	3.1	3.3	2.4	4.1	2.2	4.1	3.2	2.8	2.9	2.3	2.8	4.1	5.8
5. 5 or more times	1.2	1.3	1.1	1.1	2.0	1.1	1.6	1.0	0.9	1.0	1.2	0.7	1.4	0.7	1.8	-
Item 6700 Subject S03 N	3400	1658	1635	2598	414	817	973	1066	545	1836	1330	1274	702	469	847	47

A20D: Has someone injured you with a weapon (like a knife, gun, or club)?

1. Not at all	94.8	92.2	97.8	95.3	93.2	93.5	95.0	94.8	96.5	95.9	93.8	97.8	96.5	94.7	91.1	70.6
2. Once	3.2	4.8	1.2	2.8	4.4	3.8	3.0	3.4	2.2	2.8	3.1	1.5	2.2	4.4	4.6	15.5
3. Twice	1.3	1.9	0.8	1.3	1.4	2.4	1.1	0.9	0.9	0.8	2.3	0.5	0.7	0.5	2.9	8.6
4. 3 or 4 times	0.4	0.6	0.2	0.3	0.5	0.1	0.6	0.4	0.3	0.4	0.3	0.1	0.2	0.3	0.7	3.2
5. 5 or more times	0.3	0.6	0.1	0.2	0.5	0.2	0.4	0.5	0.1	0.2	0.5	0.1	0.3	-	0.7	2.1
Item 6710 Subject S03 N	3399	1657	1634	2597	414	817	972	1066	544	1835	1329	1273	702	469	848	47

A20E: Has someone threatened you with a weapon, but not actually injured you?

1. Not at all	82.7	77.1	89.4	84.1	76.5	82.7	84.1	79.9	85.6	84.2	82.3	89.9	83.9	81.0	73.4	57.1
2. Once	10.8	14.0	7.5	10.2	15.1	10.8	9.5	12.9	9.4	10.7	10.1	6.3	11.1	14.3	15.5	13.6
3. Twice	3.2	4.2	2.0	2.9	4.7	3.5	3.1	3.6	2.4	2.6	3.9	2.0	2.6	3.6	5.1	9.9
4. 3 or 4 times	1.9	2.8	0.6	1.8	1.5	1.9	2.0	1.7	1.9	1.3	2.2	0.9	1.0	0.6	3.4	17.9
5. 5 or more times	1.4	1.9	0.6	1.0	2.2	1.1	1.2	2.0	0.8	1.2	1.5	0.9	1.5	0.5	2.6	1.5
Item 6720 Subject S03 N	3401	1661	1634	2600	415	819	973	1066	544	1837	1330	1274	703	469	848	46

A20F: Has someone injured you on purpose without using a weapon?

1. Not at all	83.6	82.5	85.3	83.0	86.1	83.2	82.3	84.4	84.9	85.0	81.1	89.7	85.7	82.7	75.1	61.1
2. Once	9.5	10.6	8.2	9.9	8.2	9.7	10.2	9.4	8.2	7.9	12.3	6.0	9.2	11.4	13.1	19.3
3. Twice	3.8	3.6	3.8	3.9	3.6	5.3	3.6	2.9	3.9	3.8	3.9	2.4	3.0	3.1	6.6	13.7
4. 3 or 4 times	1.7	2.1	1.4	1.8	1.0	0.8	2.0	2.0	1.9	2.1	1.3	0.9	1.2	1.6	3.3	6.0
5. 5 or more times	1.3	1.2	1.3	1.3	1.1	1.0	1.9	1.2	1.1	1.3	1.4	1.0	1.0	1.2	1.9	-
Item 6730 Subject S03 N	3398	1658	1633	2596	414	815	972	1066	544	1835	1328	1274	701	467	848	47

QUESTIONNAIRE FORM 2 1983	TOTAL	SEX		RACE		REGION				4YR COLLEGE PLANS		ILLICIT DRUG USE: LIFETIME				
		M	F	White	Black	NE	NC	S	W	Yes	No	None	Mari-juana Only	Few Pills	More Pills	Any Her-oin
N (Weighted No. of Cases):	3435	1671	1641	2610	419	829	979	1077	550	1848	1335	1281	705	472	851	47
% of Weighted Total:	100.0	48.6	47.8	76.0	12.2	24.1	28.5	31.4	16.0	53.8	38.9	37.3	20.5	13.7	24.8	1.4
A20G: Has an unarmed person threatened you with injury, but not actually injured you?																
1. Not at all	70.8	63.4	78.6	70.2	71.8	70.7	69.0	71.2	73.1	72.9	68.7	78.2	71.4	67.8	61.1	56.9
2. Once	14.5	17.1	12.0	14.6	17.5	14.8	14.0	15.4	13.3	13.5	15.7	12.4	13.4	18.6	17.0	5.2
3. Twice	5.4	7.5	3.4	5.5	4.5	5.2	6.7	4.4	5.1	5.1	5.6	3.7	5.3	8.6	5.7	16.4
4. 3 or 4 times	4.2	5.1	3.1	4.5	1.9	4.8	4.7	3.9	3.0	3.2	5.5	2.7	4.0	2.8	7.3	11.1
5. 5 or more times	5.1	7.0	2.9	5.1	4.3	4.4	5.6	5.1	5.4	5.4	4.5	3.0	5.9	2.2	9.0	10.4
Item 6740 Subject S03 N	3396	1655	1635	2596	414	817	971	1064	544	1833	1328	1272	701	468	847	47
A21: The following questions concern cigarettes, alcohol, and a number of other drugs. How difficult do you think it would be for you to get each of the following types of drugs, if you wanted some?																
A21A: Marijuana (pot, grass)																
1. Probably impossible	6.7	4.9	8.0	4.5	16.1	4.9	4.2	10.0	7.2	5.7	7.4	13.6	2.9	4.2	0.7	-
2. Very difficult	2.2	1.8	2.5	1.7	2.5	1.2	2.1	2.8	2.4	2.5	1.7	3.9	1.3	1.8	0.3	2.2
3. Fairly difficult	4.9	5.4	4.7	4.8	3.7	3.5	5.3	5.1	6.1	4.9	5.1	7.5	3.3	4.5	2.6	-
4. Fairly easy	29.4	28.6	30.7	31.0	24.6	28.1	31.3	29.2	28.2	30.2	29.5	35.2	32.4	29.7	20.2	11.5
5. Very easy	56.8	59.3	54.1	57.9	53.1	62.3	57.0	52.8	56.2	56.7	56.3	39.8	60.1	59.9	76.1	86.3
Item 6750 Subject A03a N	3385	1654	1623	2590	411	816	967	1062	540	1830	1323	1260	703	466	850	47
A21B: LSD																
1. Probably impossible	21.9	19.9	23.3	16.9	44.8	20.1	16.2	29.0	21.0	19.1	24.7	25.5	24.0	22.8	14.5	5.9
2. Very difficult	18.7	19.9	17.6	18.7	18.0	20.2	17.0	17.3	22.4	19.8	17.5	17.4	23.8	17.3	17.5	7.9
3. Fairly difficult	28.5	27.9	29.5	31.6	16.2	29.5	33.6	23.6	27.3	30.7	26.8	28.6	28.8	30.7	27.9	21.1
4. Fairly easy	24.1	24.6	24.0	26.0	14.5	23.6	25.3	23.4	24.3	24.4	24.0	23.5	18.3	24.0	30.2	34.4
5. Very easy	6.7	7.7	5.6	6.8	6.5	6.6	7.9	6.7	5.0	6.1	7.1	5.0	5.1	5.2	9.8	30.8
Item 6760 Subject A03a N	3356	1641	1609	2568	404	811	960	1049	536	1812	1314	1250	693	463	844	47
A21C: Some other psychedelic (mescaline, peyote, psilocybin, PCP, etc.)																
1. Probably impossible	25.8	23.7	27.3	21.2	46.4	22.6	20.8	33.0	25.9	22.8	28.9	31.1	31.2	26.0	13.5	6.5
2. Very difficult	22.1	21.8	22.3	23.2	18.8	21.2	23.3	20.1	25.0	23.3	20.5	21.1	21.1	22.9	20.4	—
3. Fairly difficult	25.5	25.8	25.6	27.6	14.5	25.1	28.0	23.2	25.9	26.6	24.9	23.7	22.6	25.9	31.6	13.1
4. Fairly easy	19.9	20.6	19.7	21.7	11.5	21.6	21.6	18.3	17.6	20.5	19.4	19.0	16.1	22.1	22.5	38.6
5. Very easy	6.7	8.2	5.1	6.2	8.8	9.5	6.3	5.4	5.5	6.8	6.3	5.1	6.2	4.8	9.6	21.4
Item 6770 Subject A03a N	3328	1629	1594	2550	400	805	952	1039	532	1793	1308	1238	689	457	841	47
A21D: Amphetamines (uppers, pep pills, bennies, speed)																
1. Probably impossible	11.7	10.4	12.7	7.2	33.0	10.4	7.5	16.4	12.2	10.4	12.7	18.5	12.7	8.0	2.8	-
2. Very difficult	7.4	8.0	6.9	6.6	9.4	7.3	7.4	6.6	8.8	7.9	6.8	10.9	7.9	6.0	1.9	4.3
3. Fairly difficult	12.4	12.7	12.3	12.7	13.3	13.5	12.4	12.1	11.2	13.1	11.7	16.3	13.3	11.3	7.2	2.1
4. Fairly easy	36.0	35.9	36.0	38.2	24.9	37.6	35.1	33.0	41.1	37.5	34.9	35.9	37.0	37.8	35.5	34.9
5. Very easy	32.5	33.1	32.0	35.2	19.4	31.2	37.6	31.9	26.7	31.1	33.9	18.5	29.0	36.8	52.5	58.7
Item 6780 Subject A03a N	3369	1648	1614	2579	407	813	963	1055	538	1820	1320	1255	697	464	849	47
A21E: Barbiturates (downers, goofballs, reds, yellows, etc.)																
1. Probably impossible	15.7	14.2	16.9	10.8	40.3	15.2	11.8	20.4	14.5	13.2	17.9	21.1	18.6	12.4	6.6	-
2. Very difficult	12.2	12.9	11.5	11.6	14.3	11.4	11.6	11.0	16.9	12.3	11.9	14.8	13.0	12.6	8.0	7.8
3. Fairly difficult	19.6	19.6	19.6	21.5	12.6	20.1	20.8	17.4	20.7	20.0	19.9	18.3	19.5	21.0	21.6	12.3
4. Fairly easy	32.2	31.9	32.8	34.9	18.3	34.4	33.6	28.1	34.2	35.5	28.8	31.9	31.1	33.3	33.7	33.4
5. Very easy	20.3	21.4	19.2	21.2	14.5	18.9	22.2	23.1	13.7	18.9	21.4	13.8	17.9	20.7	30.1	46.5
Item 6790 Subject A03a N	3353	1642	1607	2570	403	810	957	1048	538	1808	1317	1247	695	460	849	47
A21F: Tranquilizers																
1. Probably impossible	14.3	13.5	14.7	9.5	37.8	14.0	11.3	17.8	13.4	11.9	16.4	18.7	15.4	11.9	7.6	1.3
2. Very difficult	11.1	12.4	9.6	10.2	11.5	11.9	11.5	9.1	13.2	10.1	12.0	10.6	12.0	11.1	11.0	13.1
3. Fairly difficult	19.3	20.3	18.3	20.2	15.0	21.6	18.5	16.5	22.9	19.8	18.4	18.1	20.0	18.7	21.6	5.3
4. Fairly easy	30.2	30.0	31.0	32.9	21.1	30.1	33.7	27.8	28.8	31.0	30.3	30.4	28.6	30.2	32.4	28.2
5. Very easy	25.1	23.7	26.4	27.2	14.6	22.5	24.9	28.8	21.8	27.2	22.8	22.1	24.0	28.1	27.5	52.1
Item 6800 Subject A03a N	3359	1643	1609	2569	407	814	957	1050	539	1815	1315	1251	697	461	846	47

QUESTIONNAIRE FORM 2 1983	TOTAL	SEX		RACE		REGION				4YR COLLEGE PLANS		ILLICIT DRUG USE: LIFETIME				
		M	F	White	Black	NE	NC	S	W	Yes	No	None	Mari-juana Only	Few Pills	More Pills	Any Her-oin
N (Weighted No. of Cases):	3435	1671	1641	2610	419	829	979	1077	550	1848	1335	1281	705	472	851	47
% of Weighted Total:	100.0	48.6	47.8	76.0	12.2	24.1	28.5	31.4	16.0	53.8	38.9	37.3	20.5	13.7	24.8	1.4
A21G: Cocaine																
1. Probably impossible	18.2	16.4	19.7	15.1	32.3	14.0	16.1	25.6	13.8	16.4	20.2	27.5	19.1	14.1	6.2	1.9
2. Very difficult	15.5	17.0	14.2	16.3	8.2	11.6	19.6	14.3	16.6	16.5	14.9	17.8	18.0	14.2	10.6	9.5
3. Fairly difficult	23.2	24.0	22.4	25.7	15.2	23.5	28.4	21.7	16.4	22.4	24.3	22.7	23.0	27.8	22.9	14.3
4. Fairly easy	26.9	26.0	28.4	28.1	22.9	27.3	26.2	25.8	29.9	28.9	24.9	23.4	24.7	28.5	33.5	31.6
5. Very easy	16.2	16.6	15.2	14.7	21.4	23.6	9.7	12.6	23.3	15.8	15.7	8.5	15.2	15.5	26.9	42.7
Item 6810 Subject A03a N	3351	1639	1604	2562	405	811	954	1048	538	1802	1320	1244	697	459	847	46
A21H: Heroin (smack, horse)																
1. Probably impossible	32.6	31.5	33.0	29.4	47.3	32.4	29.7	36.8	30.0	29.4	36.0	34.0	33.4	32.4	30.6	9.2
2. Very difficult	23.9	25.8	22.1	25.9	14.2	23.6	26.2	20.4	27.4	25.8	22.2	21.7	25.3	24.0	26.7	17.5
3. Fairly difficult	24.2	23.5	25.1	26.3	14.1	22.9	26.3	22.9	24.9	25.0	23.0	23.7	21.2	26.4	26.2	38.3
4. Fairly easy	13.6	12.9	14.7	13.5	14.7	12.6	14.1	14.1	13.4	14.4	13.1	16.2	12.7	11.4	12.0	13.1
5. Very easy	5.7	6.3	5.0	5.0	9.7	8.6	3.8	5.8	4.3	5.4	5.6	4.5	7.4	5.8	4.6	22.0
Item 6820 Subject A03a N	3343	1635	1602	2554	405	806	952	1048	538	1800	1316	1244	695	457	843	47
A21I: Some other narcotic (methadone, opium, codeine, paregoric, etc.)																
1. Probably impossible	25.5	23.9	26.9	21.4	44.6	24.2	22.5	31.8	20.9	22.0	29.4	30.6	30.9	24.7	14.2	8.6
2. Very difficult	20.0	20.8	18.7	20.2	16.9	20.5	19.6	17.9	24.2	21.5	18.5	18.7	23.5	20.6	19.0	19.6
3. Fairly difficult	24.4	24.6	24.7	27.4	11.5	24.3	28.6	21.5	23.0	25.3	23.3	25.1	20.3	23.0	27.8	25.1
4. Fairly easy	19.6	19.8	19.8	20.5	17.8	21.5	18.3	20.0	18.3	20.9	18.8	18.3	15.6	21.3	24.1	17.8
5. Very easy	10.4	11.0	9.9	10.4	9.2	9.5	11.1	8.9	13.7	10.4	10.1	7.2	9.7	10.5	14.9	28.8
Item 6830 Subject A03a N	3351	1640	1604	2564	404	811	953	1049	538	1803	1318	1247	694	460	846	47

This section asks for your views and feelings about a number of different things.

D01: How satisfied are you with your life as a whole these days?	TOTAL	M	F	White	Black	NE	NC	S	W	Yes	No	None	Mari-juana Only	Few Pills	More Pills	Any Her-oin
1. Completely dissatisfied	2.9	3.3	2.6	2.5	4.6	2.6	3.5	2.7	2.7	2.5	3.3	2.5	3.0	1.1	4.2	8.2
2. Quite dissatisfied	9.6	9.8	9.3	9.3	10.5	9.2	9.7	9.2	11.0	10.8	7.6	8.8	11.6	8.3	9.5	7.9
3. Somewhat dissatisfied	11.0	11.3	10.9	9.7	18.4	10.9	10.1	11.8	11.3	10.7	11.9	10.3	10.8	10.3	12.8	6.5
4. Neither, or mixed feelings	13.0	13.1	12.9	12.7	13.8	12.6	14.0	12.6	12.6	10.7	15.8	11.2	11.8	12.6	16.4	33.8
5. Somewhat satisfied	23.1	24.0	22.4	24.5	18.6	23.9	25.2	22.0	20.1	22.4	24.3	22.1	22.6	27.2	23.6	9.6
6. Quite satisfied	34.6	33.3	35.5	35.9	26.2	34.7	33.0	34.9	37.0	38.1	29.9	37.8	34.6	36.5	29.5	28.0
7. Completely satisfied	5.7	5.2	6.4	5.4	7.9	6.1	4.5	6.7	5.3	4.8	7.2	7.3	5.6	3.9	4.0	6.0
Item 6840 Subject P01,Q01 N	3205	1553	1582	2507	381	737	945	1011	512	1804	1288	1229	666	448	773	42

D02: These next questions ask you to guess how well you might do in several different situations. How good do you think you would be...

D02A: As a husband or wife?	TOTAL	M	F	White	Black	NE	NC	S	W	Yes	No	None	Mari-juana Only	Few Pills	More Pills	Any Her-oin
1. Poor	1.1	1.5	0.6	0.8	1.1	1.1	1.2	1.0	0.9	0.7	1.2	0.8	0.6	0.7	1.8	2.0
2. Not so good	1.4	1.4	0.9	1.6	0.9	1.6	1.2	0.9	2.4	1.4	1.5	0.6	1.0	1.3	2.9	3.7
3. Fairly good	9.8	10.7	8.7	9.5	10.8	7.9	9.7	10.6	11.0	8.2	11.6	9.2	10.0	12.5	9.4	7.2
4. Good	34.2	37.2	31.7	35.2	28.1	32.7	35.7	32.3	37.1	36.0	31.9	36.2	32.3	33.8	32.2	39.8
5. Very good	49.9	44.8	54.7	49.6	55.4	52.8	48.0	51.2	46.4	50.8	48.8	49.2	51.7	49.8	50.0	41.6
8. Don't know	3.8	4.3	3.1	3.4	3.7	3.8	4.3	3.9	2.2	2.8	4.9	4.0	4.3	1.9	3.8	5.7
Item 6850 Subject D01,Q01 N	3191	1541	1580	2497	379	730	943	1010	509	1797	1281	1222	662	450	771	40

D02B: As a parent?	TOTAL	M	F	White	Black	NE	NC	S	W	Yes	No	None	Mari-juana Only	Few Pills	More Pills	Any Her-oin
1. Poor	1.4	1.3	1.4	1.2	1.7	1.4	1.9	0.7	1.8	0.7	2.1	0.9	0.5	1.3	2.6	2.3
2. Not so good	2.4	1.6	3.2	2.6	1.8	2.3	1.8	2.5	3.6	2.4	2.5	1.8	2.7	1.7	3.5	3.7
3. Fairly good	9.3	10.8	7.6	9.8	5.0	6.7	11.1	8.6	11.2	8.3	10.9	10.2	7.8	8.7	9.4	16.8
4. Good	33.2	36.4	30.4	35.2	22.0	31.1	37.0	32.2	31.4	35.2	31.2	35.0	29.7	34.2	33.2	35.2
5. Very good	48.9	44.2	53.3	46.5	64.4	54.5	42.5	50.9	48.5	49.1	47.8	47.8	54.4	49.5	45.9	35.9
8. Don't know	4.8	5.6	4.0	4.7	5.1	4.1	5.7	5.1	3.6	4.2	5.5	4.4	4.8	4.7	5.4	6.1
Item 6860 Subject D02,Q01 N	3182	1533	1579	2493	377	727	940	1008	507	1793	1277	1217	662	449	769	40

QUESTIONNAIRE FORM 2 1983	TOTAL	SEX		RACE		REGION				4YR COLLEGE PLANS		ILLICIT DRUG USE: LIFETIME				
		M	F	White	Black	NE	NC	S	W	Yes	No	None	Mari- juana Only	Few Pills	More Pills	Any Her- oin
N (Weighted No. of Cases):	3435	1671	1641	2610	419	829	979	1077	550	1848	1335	1281	705	472	851	47
% of Weighted Total:	100.0	48.6	47.8	76.0	12.2	24.1	28.5	31.4	16.0	53.8	38.9	37.3	20.5	13.7	24.8	1.4
D02C: As a worker on a job?																
1. Poor	0.3	0.6	*	0.2	0.7	0.4	0.4	0.2	0.3	0.2	0.5	0.2	-	-	0.5	3.2
2. Not so good	0.3	0.2	0.4	0.3	-	0.1	0.3	0.4	0.5	0.4	0.2	0.3	0.2	0.2	0.4	-
3. Fairly good	4.3	4.1	4.1	4.3	2.3	3.3	5.0	4.3	4.2	3.5	5.3	3.8	3.6	4.1	5.5	12.9
4. Good	30.6	29.7	31.6	32.3	19.8	29.1	31.8	31.7	28.4	30.5	31.1	31.3	29.2	32.2	30.6	21.1
5. Very good	63.2	64.2	62.4	61.7	75.8	65.9	61.0	62.0	65.8	64.6	60.9	63.2	65.6	62.5	62.0	60.0
8. Don't know	1.3	1.2	1.4	1.1	1.3	1.3	1.6	1.3	0.8	0.9	2.0	1.2	1.5	1.0	1.0	2.9
Item 6870 Subject C03,Q01 N	3182	1533	1580	2491	377	726	942	1008	506	1791	1280	1218	662	449	767	40
D03: Some people think a lot about the so- cial problems of the nation and the world, and about how they might be solved. Others spend little time thinking about these issues. How much do you think about such things?																
1. Never	4.8	5.6	4.1	4.0	9.4	6.1	4.4	4.6	4.1	2.8	7.8	3.4	7.0	4.0	4.8	6.6
2. Seldom	22.5	20.8	24.5	22.1	23.0	23.9	22.0	21.0	24.2	19.9	26.0	20.3	24.7	22.2	23.8	17.6
3. Sometimes	49.2	48.8	49.1	50.8	41.8	48.4	49.6	50.1	47.6	49.3	48.6	52.7	44.4	49.8	47.9	46.8
4. Quite often	18.9	18.8	19.0	18.7	19.6	16.8	19.6	19.5	19.2	22.0	14.5	19.5	18.7	19.8	18.0	23.8
5. A great deal	4.7	6.0	3.3	4.4	6.2	4.8	4.4	4.8	4.9	6.0	3.0	4.1	5.2	4.3	5.6	5.2
Item 6880 Subject J,Q08 N	3169	1531	1569	2484	375	721	938	1002	508	1786	1274	1213	656	450	764	42
D04: Now we'd like you to make some ratings of how honest and moral the people are who run the following organizations. To what extent are there problems of dishonesty and immoral- ity in the leadership of...																
D04A: Large corporations?																
1. Not at all	2.4	2.9	1.8	1.5	7.6	2.9	2.0	3.1	1.2	1.7	3.5	2.3	3.0	2.0	1.5	12.6
2. Slight	15.6	16.6	14.6	15.2	18.6	14.2	14.9	17.0	16.2	14.2	17.7	15.2	15.3	17.5	15.7	8.2
3. Moderate	35.1	36.4	33.7	37.6	25.7	35.0	36.9	33.7	34.5	37.1	32.9	37.8	33.6	35.4	31.2	48.4
4. Considerable	24.1	24.4	24.0	24.8	19.9	23.7	23.5	24.7	24.4	27.0	19.5	24.0	23.4	26.2	25.0	11.5
5. Great	7.0	7.8	6.3	6.4	7.6	7.8	7.4	6.2	6.7	7.4	6.6	7.0	5.8	5.5	9.1	-
8. No opinion	15.8	12.0	19.6	14.5	20.6	16.5	15.3	15.3	17.0	12.6	19.8	13.6	19.0	13.4	17.5	19.4
Item 6890 Subject K01 N	3111	1506	1539	2447	361	702	928	977	503	1754	1251	1198	645	435	750	41
D04B: Major labor unions?																
1. Not at all	3.0	3.1	2.5	2.2	6.4	4.3	2.0	3.1	2.5	2.5	3.7	3.1	2.7	3.0	2.4	9.1
2. Slight	15.2	15.9	14.9	15.0	18.8	16.8	14.8	15.7	12.8	14.4	17.2	15.2	14.2	16.6	15.9	7.3
3. Moderate	33.1	32.8	33.0	34.5	27.0	28.9	33.1	33.9	37.5	34.3	31.3	34.7	31.8	33.5	32.1	34.7
4. Considerable	21.6	23.4	19.8	22.6	18.0	21.4	23.6	21.1	19.1	23.1	18.9	22.2	21.0	22.8	20.3	25.1
5. Great	7.8	10.9	4.9	8.1	5.3	8.2	8.7	7.2	6.7	9.3	5.6	7.2	9.5	8.0	7.0	6.6
8. No opinion	19.3	13.8	24.9	17.6	24.5	20.3	17.7	19.0	21.4	16.3	23.3	17.6	20.9	16.0	22.3	17.2
Item 6900 Subject K01 N	3097	1498	1533	2437	362	700	928	973	496	1751	1242	1192	644	433	746	41
D04C: The nation's colleges and universities?																
1. Not at all	6.9	7.0	6.8	6.8	8.8	8.9	6.1	5.7	7.7	6.7	7.3	7.1	7.9	6.4	5.5	15.6
2. Slight	33.4	33.7	33.4	36.2	22.1	32.8	37.7	32.2	28.8	37.4	27.9	35.7	31.1	30.3	33.9	34.3
3. Moderate	25.8	27.0	24.3	26.5	23.7	24.5	24.9	27.3	26.1	26.4	24.7	27.0	25.1	27.5	23.8	19.5
4. Considerable	13.3	12.6	13.7	12.1	17.2	12.8	13.6	12.4	15.2	13.8	12.4	12.7	13.8	14.4	13.6	9.6
5. Great	5.1	6.1	4.2	4.4	9.1	5.2	3.3	6.1	6.4	5.0	5.6	5.2	5.8	5.5	4.5	-
8. No opinion	15.5	13.5	17.6	14.1	19.2	15.8	14.4	16.2	15.7	10.7	22.0	12.3	16.3	16.0	18.7	21.0
Item 6910 Subject B10,K01 N	3093	1500	1526	2436	358	698	928	969	497	1745	1240	1192	639	432	747	41
D04D: The nation's public schools?																
1. Not at all	7.0	6.5	7.4	6.9	7.9	9.4	6.4	6.3	6.0	6.7	6.9	7.3	6.0	7.1	6.5	11.2
2. Slight	31.8	32.5	31.2	33.9	23.5	30.7	35.5	28.8	32.3	33.9	29.5	34.9	31.3	30.0	29.6	25.7
3. Moderate	26.8	27.8	25.3	26.7	25.3	27.1	24.6	27.7	28.4	27.3	25.4	26.2	26.1	26.4	28.0	30.0
4. Considerable	15.6	14.2	17.3	15.1	19.7	14.4	15.8	17.3	13.7	16.6	14.7	16.3	16.9	17.4	12.9	7.1
5. Great	7.7	8.1	7.3	6.5	15.0	6.8	7.2	9.2	7.1	7.3	8.4	6.7	7.5	7.8	9.4	6.6
8. No opinion	11.1	10.9	11.5	10.9	8.6	11.6	10.4	10.7	12.5	8.2	15.1	8.6	12.2	11.2	13.5	19.3
Item 6920 Subject B10,K01 N	3074	1484	1522	2424	355	694	919	966	494	1735	1237	1189	636	429	737	41

*=less than .05 per cent.

QUESTIONNAIRE FORM 2 1983	TOTAL	SEX		RACE		REGION				4YR COLLEGE PLANS		ILLICIT DRUG USE: LIFETIME				
		M	F	White	Black	NE	NC	S	W	Yes	No	None	Mari-juana Only	Few Pills	More Pills	Any Her-oin
N (Weighted No. of Cases):	3435	1671	1641	2610	419	829	979	1077	550	1848	1335	1281	705	472	851	47
% of Weighted Total:	100.0	48.6	47.8	76.0	12.2	24.1	28.5	31.4	16.0	53.8	38.9	37.3	20.5	13.7	24.8	1.4
D04E: Churches and religious organizations?																
1. Not at all	17.5	16.4	18.6	18.8	9.8	19.0	18.7	15.9	16.4	17.5	17.9	18.0	15.1	17.3	19.2	19.5
2. Slight	33.7	35.6	32.3	35.8	28.3	34.6	34.8	32.8	32.5	36.8	29.4	36.0	31.3	33.3	33.2	22.4
3. Moderate	14.6	14.6	14.0	14.3	15.3	11.8	16.5	15.0	14.0	15.7	12.9	14.5	17.3	14.6	11.9	22.2
4. Considerable	11.0	11.2	10.9	10.3	15.8	11.4	10.7	11.5	10.4	11.7	10.1	10.2	12.0	10.7	12.1	4.1
5. Great	9.7	10.5	9.1	8.4	16.3	7.9	7.6	11.8	12.1	9.0	10.8	10.7	8.1	10.3	8.9	13.7
8. No opinion	13.4	11.7	15.2	12.4	14.5	15.3	11.7	13.0	14.6	9.4	18.9	10.6	16.1	13.8	14.6	18.2
Item 6930 Subject G,K01 N	3089	1496	1525	2432	362	695	925	973	496	1740	1242	1191	639	432	744	40
D04F: The national news media (TV, maga-zines, news services)?																
1. Not at all	3.4	3.8	2.8	3.0	4.9	2.6	3.4	3.7	3.4	2.7	4.3	3.1	4.1	2.8	3.0	10.5
2. Slight	19.1	19.4	19.0	19.0	21.4	17.9	21.3	19.2	16.5	18.3	20.4	19.3	19.6	19.9	18.4	6.9
3. Moderate	29.6	31.0	28.0	31.5	20.2	28.6	32.8	28.9	26.4	33.4	23.9	31.8	27.2	30.8	27.8	35.6
4. Considerable	24.4	23.5	25.6	24.6	24.3	25.8	22.9	23.5	27.0	25.4	23.1	24.7	24.1	26.5	23.8	14.6
5. Great	12.6	12.4	12.8	11.6	15.9	13.6	10.3	12.8	14.7	12.5	12.6	11.6	11.7	12.9	14.2	14.3
8. No opinion	10.9	9.9	11.9	10.2	13.4	11.5	9.2	11.8	12.0	7.6	15.6	9.4	13.3	7.1	12.8	18.2
Item 6940 Subject K01 N	3084	1494	1524	2424	362	693	921	973	497	1740	1238	1189	634	432	747	41
D04G: The Presidency and the administration?																
1. Not at all	4.5	4.9	4.1	3.7	8.9	4.6	3.7	5.5	3.9	4.2	5.2	5.2	4.7	3.8	3.7	6.4
2. Slight	20.9	23.2	18.7	21.8	17.8	19.5	22.5	21.2	19.3	23.0	17.6	23.9	19.1	18.3	18.9	17.4
3. Moderate	29.3	28.6	29.9	31.2	21.8	28.3	31.0	27.9	30.6	31.5	26.3	30.1	27.1	32.6	28.5	35.4
4. Considerable	20.8	21.0	20.8	20.5	21.6	21.4	20.7	19.1	23.2	22.2	19.0	19.4	19.9	23.8	21.9	17.5
5. Great	10.2	10.6	9.8	9.5	14.6	11.6	9.3	10.3	9.9	9.2	11.8	8.9	11.0	10.2	12.2	3.6
8. No opinion	14.2	11.6	16.7	13.3	15.3	14.6	12.8	15.9	13.1	10.0	20.1	12.4	18.1	11.3	14.7	19.7
Item 6950 Subject H04,K01 N	3080	1489	1524	2424	361	692	922	970	496	1739	1234	1190	637	426	744	41
D04H: Congress–that is, the U.S. Senate and House of Representatives?																
1. Not at all	3.4	4.0	2.8	2.5	8.0	3.3	3.2	4.0	2.8	2.9	4.3	3.8	4.1	2.4	2.6	5.4
2. Slight	18.8	20.4	17.5	19.3	17.6	19.4	18.6	18.4	19.4	19.9	17.2	19.7	18.1	19.1	18.2	18.0
3. Moderate	30.0	28.8	30.5	31.0	24.9	28.0	33.0	28.3	30.2	32.7	26.0	32.8	28.7	30.3	26.4	36.6
4. Considerable	21.9	23.7	20.4	22.6	17.8	22.1	22.8	20.2	23.3	23.8	19.6	21.7	20.1	22.9	23.6	13.4
5. Great	9.6	11.1	8.5	9.4	11.9	9.5	8.7	11.4	8.1	8.4	10.9	8.5	9.4	10.2	11.7	3.9
8. No opinion	16.3	12.0	20.3	15.1	19.8	17.8	13.9	17.6	16.3	12.3	21.9	13.5	19.7	15.1	17.5	22.7
Item 6960 Subject H04,K01 N	3075	1491	1517	2416	360	688	921	967	499	1735	1233	1186	637	426	743	41
D04I: The U.S. Supreme Court?																
1. Not at all	13.1	14.9	11.7	13.5	10.8	13.2	12.3	13.7	13.6	13.9	12.3	13.4	13.4	12.5	13.4	14.4
2. Slight	26.1	29.4	22.7	27.7	20.3	23.6	28.9	25.7	25.1	29.2	21.0	27.3	25.0	27.7	25.0	18.8
3. Moderate	23.8	21.9	25.5	24.9	18.7	26.2	26.2	20.1	23.3	24.1	23.7	25.0	22.8	23.4	22.8	38.6
4. Considerable	12.0	11.4	12.5	10.6	18.4	13.5	10.6	11.6	13.3	11.8	12.1	12.7	9.7	12.4	12.6	4.0
5. Great	7.1	8.5	6.1	6.4	9.9	5.0	6.3	8.9	8.2	6.8	7.9	6.6	8.4	7.0	6.8	4.6
8. No opinion	17.8	14.0	21.5	16.8	21.8	18.4	15.6	20.1	16.5	14.1	23.0	15.1	20.6	16.9	19.4	19.5
Item 6970 Subject H04,K01 N	3062	1485	1510	2409	355	691	919	953	500	1734	1222	1181	631	426	742	40
D04J: All the courts and the justice system in general?																
1. Not at all	5.7	6.0	5.5	5.3	7.2	6.6	4.7	6.1	5.7	5.0	6.8	6.3	5.5	5.7	4.9	12.8
2. Slight	26.0	27.6	24.7	27.8	20.1	22.9	28.9	25.1	26.8	27.5	24.1	27.6	27.4	25.1	23.5	22.1
3. Moderate	29.9	30.2	29.4	30.8	23.1	32.6	30.7	27.1	30.0	32.1	26.3	31.2	27.4	28.4	30.6	35.4
4. Considerable	14.3	14.2	14.2	14.2	16.3	13.6	14.2	14.8	14.7	15.3	13.3	12.9	13.5	17.8	15.9	7.3
5. Great	7.4	8.8	6.2	6.4	12.0	5.8	6.1	9.1	8.6	6.8	8.1	7.3	7.7	6.3	7.3	9.7
8. No opinion	16.6	13.2	20.0	15.5	21.2	18.6	15.3	17.8	14.2	13.3	21.4	14.7	18.4	16.7	17.7	12.7
Item 6980 Subject H04,K01 N	3076	1490	1519	2419	359	688	921	968	498	1738	1230	1187	638	426	742	41

QUESTIONNAIRE FORM 2 1983	TOTAL	SEX		RACE		REGION				4YR COLLEGE PLANS		ILLICIT DRUG USE: LIFETIME				
		M	F	White	Black	NE	NC	S	W	Yes	No	None	Marijuana Only	Few Pills	More Pills	Any Heroin
N (Weighted No. of Cases):	3435	1671	1641	2610	419	829	979	1077	550	1848	1335	1281	705	472	851	47
% of Weighted Total:	100.0	48.6	47.8	76.0	12.2	24.1	28.5	31.4	16.0	53.8	38.9	37.3	20.5	13.7	24.8	1.4
D04K: The police and other law enforcement agencies?																
1. Not at all	4.5	4.6	4.0	3.9	8.1	4.5	4.1	4.3	5.4	3.3	5.8	4.9	5.1	3.0	3.7	9.1
2. Slight	23.4	23.0	23.9	24.4	16.4	24.7	23.7	21.3	25.0	24.2	22.8	25.4	21.0	26.7	21.4	10.0
3. Moderate	31.0	31.1	30.6	32.8	23.2	29.6	33.3	30.7	29.0	34.0	26.6	33.5	31.7	30.8	26.9	29.1
4. Considerable	20.1	20.3	19.8	20.1	20.5	20.6	19.3	20.6	19.9	21.1	19.0	17.2	19.9	23.4	22.9	20.2
5. Great	10.2	11.7	8.9	8.6	18.5	8.8	9.4	12.0	10.1	9.4	10.9	9.1	9.0	7.5	14.1	13.6
8. No opinion	10.9	9.2	12.7	10.3	13.3	11.8	10.3	11.1	10.5	8.0	14.9	9.9	13.2	8.5	10.9	18.0
Item 6990 Subject K01 N	3078	1490	1521	2424	360	691	922	968	497	1737	1235	1188	638	425	744	41
D04L: The U.S. military?																
1. Not at all	7.8	7.7	7.8	7.3	10.2	8.6	7.0	7.8	8.0	6.8	9.0	6.8	9.4	5.5	8.8	12.4
2. Slight	26.6	27.8	25.6	28.7	21.2	26.5	26.5	27.1	26.0	27.3	25.4	28.9	21.6	29.0	26.5	17.5
3. Moderate	25.4	26.0	24.4	26.9	16.5	23.2	30.5	24.3	21.2	28.6	21.3	27.8	23.8	23.9	24.5	18.1
4. Considerable	13.3	15.1	11.5	12.7	15.2	13.8	12.9	11.8	16.3	14.8	11.4	13.1	13.0	13.9	13.7	19.9
5. Great	7.4	9.6	5.3	5.9	13.9	7.0	5.7	8.1	9.5	6.7	8.2	6.7	8.4	10.1	5.9	11.2
8. No opinion	19.6	13.8	25.3	18.3	23.0	20.9	17.5	20.9	19.0	15.9	24.7	16.6	23.8	17.6	20.5	20.8
Item 7000 Subject K01,L04 N	3075	1489	1519	2420	359	690	921	964	499	1737	1231	1185	638	425	744	41
D05: How much do you agree or disagree with each of the following statements?																
D05A: There is too much competition in this society																
1. Disagree	10.0	15.2	4.9	10.6	10.1	7.5	11.2	10.1	10.9	12.0	6.4	10.8	10.8	8.1	9.1	11.1
2. Mostly disagree	13.8	16.5	11.1	14.8	10.3	13.1	15.3	13.0	13.8	15.6	11.3	14.6	14.8	13.0	12.7	6.2
3. Neither	23.3	26.7	20.0	24.2	20.1	21.2	23.3	25.4	21.7	22.2	24.9	23.3	21.3	21.1	26.7	21.9
4. Mostly agree	34.4	27.0	41.9	34.4	32.3	32.5	36.0	33.2	36.2	33.2	36.3	33.7	36.5	35.8	32.2	46.0
5. Agree	18.6	14.7	22.0	16.0	27.3	25.6	14.2	18.3	17.3	17.0	21.1	17.6	16.6	22.1	19.3	14.8
Item 7010 Subject Q08 N	3095	1484	1543	2430	360	692	920	983	500	1757	1232	1199	637	432	744	41
D05B: Too many young people are sloppy about their grooming and clothing, and just don't care how they look																
1. Disagree	15.7	17.4	14.3	15.7	17.3	18.0	17.1	13.3	15.1	15.9	15.3	14.2	14.6	15.9	18.4	24.0
2. Mostly disagree	29.3	27.5	30.9	30.9	19.5	29.2	32.5	25.6	31.0	31.0	26.7	28.8	29.0	28.9	31.6	24.0
3. Neither	21.2	24.5	17.7	21.4	19.1	21.0	22.1	18.7	24.4	21.0	21.8	19.8	24.0	16.8	22.4	30.7
4. Mostly agree	21.9	19.2	24.4	22.3	22.4	19.9	18.3	27.8	19.5	22.2	21.5	24.3	20.5	24.4	18.8	12.4
5. Agree	11.9	11.4	12.7	9.8	21.7	11.9	10.1	14.6	10.1	9.9	14.7	12.9	11.9	14.0	8.9	8.9
Item 7020 Subject Q08 N	3103	1493	1542	2437	361	696	922	985	500	1761	1236	1199	639	436	747	40
D05C: There is too much hard rock music on the radio these days																
1. Disagree	42.3	46.9	38.0	46.0	28.4	46.8	46.3	38.7	36.0	38.6	47.4	28.5	45.7	44.2	60.2	58.4
2. Mostly disagree	21.5	20.4	22.2	22.8	16.4	20.2	22.1	21.4	22.2	24.1	18.4	22.3	21.8	23.5	18.5	24.5
3. Neither	18.0	16.3	19.6	16.7	23.9	19.3	16.6	18.2	18.5	19.0	16.3	23.9	18.9	15.5	9.9	17.1
4. Mostly agree	9.4	8.7	10.1	8.1	12.8	6.6	8.4	10.8	12.4	9.4	9.1	13.4	7.2	7.9	6.2	-
5. Agree	8.8	7.7	10.1	6.3	18.6	7.1	6.5	10.9	10.9	8.9	8.8	12.0	6.3	8.9	5.2	-
Item 7030 Subject Q08 N	3099	1490	1541	2434	360	695	924	983	497	1761	1232	1198	637	435	747	40
D05D: People should do their own thing, even if other people think it's strange																
1. Disagree	2.7	3.7	1.7	2.0	6.8	3.4	2.7	2.4	2.7	2.4	3.3	2.8	3.1	1.4	2.4	6.8
2. Mostly disagree	5.1	5.9	4.2	5.3	4.2	3.7	6.0	5.0	5.5	4.8	5.2	5.9	5.2	4.9	3.8	8.9
3. Neither	11.8	12.4	11.2	11.6	8.6	10.6	10.5	12.5	14.3	11.6	11.5	13.8	12.7	10.3	8.6	17.0
4. Mostly agree	37.4	36.3	38.3	39.2	27.6	35.6	39.6	37.2	36.4	40.5	33.2	39.5	37.3	37.5	35.3	36.9
5. Agree	43.0	41.7	44.6	41.9	52.8	46.7	41.2	42.9	41.1	40.8	46.7	38.0	41.7	45.9	49.9	30.4
Item 7040 Subject Q08 N	3084	1475	1541	2421	361	693	917	976	497	1745	1233	1190	629	435	744	41

QUESTIONNAIRE FORM 2 1983	TOTAL	SEX		RACE		REGION				4YR COLLEGE PLANS		ILLICIT DRUG USE: LIFETIME				
		M	F	White	Black	NE	NC	S	W	Yes	No	None	Marijuana Only	Few Pills	More Pills	Any Heroin
N (Weighted No. of Cases):	3435	1671	1641	2610	419	829	979	1077	550	1848	1335	1281	705	472	851	47
% of Weighted Total:	100.0	48.6	47.8	76.0	12.2	24.1	28.5	31.4	16.0	53.8	38.9	37.3	20.5	13.7	24.8	1.4
D05E: I get a real kick out of doing things that are a little dangerous																
1. Disagree	23.0	13.2	32.6	19.6	40.9	20.9	20.0	28.9	20.1	22.4	24.1	31.6	19.7	20.3	13.2	20.6
2. Mostly disagree	19.8	17.3	22.3	20.2	19.5	18.2	18.9	20.5	22.6	21.5	17.9	23.2	22.6	16.3	14.8	2.8
3. Neither	26.3	27.0	25.6	28.1	15.2	27.6	27.7	24.0	26.8	26.8	24.7	25.0	29.4	25.0	26.7	30.4
4. Mostly agree	20.2	27.2	13.3	21.5	13.1	20.2	22.3	17.4	21.7	20.0	20.5	13.7	19.2	27.2	27.7	27.2
5. Agree	10.6	15.2	6.2	10.6	11.2	13.1	11.1	9.3	8.8	9.2	12.8	6.5	9.2	11.1	17.5	18.9
Item 7050 Subject Q04 N	3078	1470	1540	2418	361	694	916	975	493	1743	1229	1190	625	435	744	41
D05F: I like to test myself every now and then by doing something a little risky																
1. Disagree	21.5	11.9	30.5	18.9	35.6	19.7	19.4	26.9	17.0	20.4	23.3	29.1	20.0	17.7	13.4	12.7
2. Mostly disagree	16.5	15.3	17.9	17.2	14.0	17.2	15.4	16.4	17.7	17.7	15.2	18.8	17.7	14.3	13.1	11.2
3. Neither	21.4	20.3	22.2	22.2	15.9	21.2	21.5	20.0	24.2	21.8	20.3	22.0	21.7	18.6	21.5	19.4
4. Mostly agree	26.7	32.7	20.9	27.9	19.4	25.6	28.2	24.8	29.2	27.5	25.0	20.7	28.2	35.6	30.8	28.3
5. Agree	14.0	19.7	8.5	13.8	15.0	16.3	15.6	12.0	11.8	12.6	16.1	9.5	12.5	13.8	21.3	28.4
Item 7060 Subject Q04 N	3070	1466	1537	2412	360	693	913	972	492	1737	1228	1186	625	434	743	41
D06: How many of your friends would you estimate . . .																
D06A: Smoke cigarettes?																
1. None	13.0	14.1	11.9	12.0	16.6	8.3	13.5	11.9	21.3	15.5	9.5	19.8	10.7	11.4	5.0	8.9
2. A few	36.3	36.5	36.6	36.6	34.2	33.8	33.7	37.8	41.8	39.1	32.1	45.3	38.6	36.0	21.6	20.1
3. Some	28.3	28.7	27.8	28.8	26.2	30.2	29.4	30.0	20.0	29.4	27.1	24.6	29.4	33.0	31.4	15.0
4. Most	20.4	18.9	21.7	21.0	18.4	24.3	22.0	18.5	15.9	15.1	27.9	9.7	18.3	18.1	39.0	52.0
5. All	2.0	1.8	2.0	1.5	4.6	3.4	1.5	1.9	1.0	1.0	3.4	0.6	3.0	1.4	2.9	4.0
Item 7070 Subject A02a N	3095	1488	1538	2428	365	693	926	981	495	1746	1241	1194	635	434	747	43
D06B: Smoke marijuana (pot, grass) or hashish?																
1. None	19.7	18.3	21.2	20.4	13.0	11.9	22.4	22.1	20.9	22.1	16.5	38.2	10.4	11.3	3.4	9.5
2. A few	33.6	33.6	34.1	34.2	32.2	32.1	33.3	36.2	31.1	35.0	30.8	39.9	40.2	35.1	19.0	11.7
3. Some	25.0	25.5	24.1	25.2	24.7	25.8	25.1	24.4	24.9	24.8	25.2	16.6	31.4	32.1	28.7	25.9
4. Most	17.6	17.8	17.5	17.3	20.1	24.1	16.7	13.2	19.1	15.2	21.7	4.8	14.4	17.9	40.0	30.8
5. All	4.1	4.8	3.1	2.9	10.0	6.2	2.5	4.0	4.1	3.0	5.8	0.4	3.7	3.6	8.9	22.1
Item 7080 Subject A02a N	3092	1487	1538	2425	364	694	924	977	496	1742	1239	1190	635	435	747	43
D06C: Take LSD?																
1. None	76.0	73.5	78.7	74.9	85.7	72.7	73.9	80.1	76.1	79.1	71.1	86.6	85.9	73.0	55.0	18.2
2. A few	17.5	19.5	15.2	18.3	9.0	19.9	17.2	15.1	19.5	17.1	18.5	11.0	11.5	21.8	29.4	47.9
3. Some	5.2	5.2	5.2	5.4	4.1	5.7	7.0	3.8	3.6	3.3	7.8	1.9	2.6	4.9	12.1	16.2
4. Most	1.1	1.3	0.9	1.2	0.9	1.5	1.5	0.7	0.4	0.4	2.0	0.3	*	0.4	2.9	15.1
5. All	0.3	0.5	0.1	0.2	0.3	0.3	0.3	0.2	0.3	0.1	0.5	0.2	-	-	0.7	2.7
Item 7090 Subject A02a N	3064	1474	1524	2404	361	686	916	973	489	1730	1226	1181	629	429	740	43
D06D: Take other psychedelics (mescaline, peyote, PCP, etc.)?																
1. None	77.9	76.7	79.4	77.0	84.9	72.9	75.6	82.7	80.0	81.0	73.4	88.3	86.8	74.5	58.8	18.6
2. A few	17.1	18.0	16.1	18.1	9.2	20.9	18.1	14.4	15.4	15.7	19.3	10.3	12.1	19.8	29.6	47.2
3. Some	3.4	3.6	3.2	3.5	3.2	4.3	4.4	1.8	3.1	2.4	4.7	0.8	1.0	4.8	8.1	13.3
4. Most	1.2	1.1	1.1	1.0	1.7	1.6	1.3	0.9	1.0	0.8	1.9	0.5	*	1.0	2.8	14.7
5. All	0.4	0.6	0.2	0.3	1.0	0.2	0.5	0.2	0.5	0.2	0.7	0.2	-	-	0.6	6.2
Item 7100 Subject A02a N	3075	1477	1529	2413	361	688	919	974	494	1734	1231	1182	631	434	743	43
D06E: Take amphetamines (uppers, pep pills, bennies, speed)?																
1. None	53.9	53.9	53.7	51.0	73.0	51.3	50.3	58.9	54.6	57.7	47.9	75.2	65.5	43.6	17.7	20.2
2. A few	28.3	29.6	27.3	29.8	15.9	33.1	28.6	25.3	26.8	29.0	27.3	20.5	28.0	39.3	34.3	33.0
3. Some	12.8	12.1	13.5	13.7	8.2	11.0	14.2	11.8	14.5	10.2	16.8	3.4	6.1	12.9	33.1	17.6
4. Most	4.1	3.2	4.7	4.6	1.6	4.0	5.4	3.1	3.6	2.5	6.5	0.6	0.4	3.9	11.6	24.8
5. All	1.0	1.2	0.9	0.9	1.3	0.6	1.6	0.9	0.5	0.6	1.5	0.2	-	0.3	3.2	4.4
Item 7110 Subject A02a N	3067	1477	1525	2411	360	687	921	973	486	1731	1226	1182	626	433	740	43

*=less than .05 per cent.

QUESTIONNAIRE FORM 2 1983	TOTAL	SEX		RACE		REGION				4YR COLLEGE PLANS		ILLICIT DRUG USE: LIFETIME				
		M	F	White	Black	NE	NC	S	W	Yes	No	None	Mari- juana Only	Few Pills	More Pills	Any Her- oin
N (Weighted No. of Cases):	3435	1671	1641	2610	419	829	979	1077	550	1848	1335	1281	705	472	851	47
% of Weighted Total:	100.0	48.6	47.8	76.0	12.2	24.1	28.5	31.4	16.0	53.8	38.9	37.3	20.5	13.7	24.8	1.4
D06F: Take quaaludes (quads, methaqualone)?																
1. None	70.3	67.4	73.2	68.4	84.5	68.7	70.5	69.5	73.6	73.6	65.2	84.3	80.3	67.7	42.7	24.2
2. A few	20.7	23.7	17.7	22.2	9.6	22.3	19.7	21.3	19.3	20.4	21.5	13.0	16.6	25.4	33.4	39.3
3. Some	6.4	5.5	7.2	6.7	3.8	6.6	6.4	6.3	6.4	4.5	9.3	1.9	2.7	5.5	16.7	18.5
4. Most	2.1	2.7	1.6	2.4	1.2	1.9	2.9	2.3	0.6	1.3	3.4	0.6	0.4	1.3	6.0	12.3
5. All	0.5	0.8	0.2	0.4	0.9	0.4	0.5	0.6	*	0.3	0.6	0.1	-	-	1.1	5.6
Item 7120 Subject A02a N	3065	1474	1525	2406	360	685	915	974	492	1729	1227	1180	626	433	740	43
D06G: Take barbiturates (downers, goofballs, reds, yellows, etc.)?																
1. None	71.7	70.7	72.8	70.8	81.5	70.2	68.8	74.0	74.9	75.4	66.5	82.9	81.1	69.5	49.1	26.4
2. A few	21.2	22.4	20.1	22.2	11.2	23.2	23.3	18.8	19.3	19.9	23.0	14.6	16.3	24.8	33.7	38.7
3. Some	5.3	4.6	5.9	5.4	4.3	4.8	5.7	5.5	4.7	3.7	7.7	1.8	2.0	5.1	12.7	23.4
4. Most	1.3	1.7	1.1	1.2	2.8	1.2	1.6	1.4	1.1	0.9	2.0	0.6	0.5	0.6	3.4	4.8
5. All	0.4	0.7	0.2	0.4	0.3	0.6	0.6	0.4	*	0.1	0.8	0.2	-	-	1.2	6.6
Item 7130 Subject A02a N	3066	1475	1523	2408	360	681	917	976	491	1728	1228	1180	628	433	739	43
D06H: Take tranquilizers?																
1. None	73.3	72.2	74.4	72.1	83.1	72.0	72.7	74.0	74.9	76.0	69.1	82.3	82.3	70.1	54.9	29.3
2. A few	21.2	22.8	19.5	22.4	11.1	21.7	20.7	21.2	21.6	20.0	23.0	15.5	16.1	24.4	32.3	42.0
3. Some	4.2	3.5	4.9	4.3	3.7	5.2	4.7	3.8	2.8	3.3	5.6	1.4	1.2	4.8	10.2	20.1
4. Most	0.8	0.8	0.9	0.8	1.1	0.8	1.6	0.4	0.4	0.4	1.5	0.6	0.4	0.6	1.5	3.0
5. All	0.4	0.7	0.2	0.4	1.0	0.4	0.4	0.5	0.3	0.2	0.7	0.2	-	0.1	1.1	5.6
Item 7140 Subject A02a N	3065	1473	1524	2408	358	683	915	974	492	1729	1227	1180	628	434	738	43
D06I: Take cocaine?																
1. None	62.4	61.1	64.0	63.6	62.4	50.5	70.8	69.7	48.9	65.2	58.2	82.5	69.8	54.8	31.2	14.5
2. A few	23.3	24.9	21.6	22.5	22.6	28.7	18.8	21.7	27.3	22.9	23.8	13.7	24.2	30.7	32.8	31.3
3. Some	9.2	9.3	8.9	8.9	8.6	12.4	7.6	5.6	15.0	7.4	12.0	3.1	5.2	11.8	19.5	32.7
4. Most	4.0	3.3	4.7	3.9	4.8	6.8	1.8	2.4	7.6	3.7	4.5	0.4	0.6	2.7	13.0	14.4
5. All	1.1	1.3	0.9	1.0	1.6	1.7	1.1	0.6	1.2	0.8	1.5	0.2	0.3	-	3.5	7.1
Item 7150 Subject A02a N	3061	1469	1524	2400	361	683	912	972	493	1728	1225	1176	629	434	736	43
D06J: Take heroin (smack, horse)?																
1. None	88.0	87.9	88.3	88.5	86.7	85.1	88.5	88.7	89.5	90.1	84.9	91.0	91.6	86.5	84.4	30.5
2. A few	9.3	9.8	8.7	9.3	7.6	10.8	8.8	9.1	8.3	8.0	11.2	7.3	6.7	9.6	13.0	32.6
3. Some	2.0	1.4	2.3	1.6	3.5	2.8	2.0	1.8	1.6	1.5	2.7	1.0	1.3	3.6	1.5	30.3
4. Most	0.5	0.4	0.6	0.4	1.4	0.8	0.5	0.2	0.6	0.3	0.8	0.4	0.2	0.3	0.8	2.2
5. All	0.3	0.5	0.1	0.2	0.8	0.5	0.3	0.2	-	0.2	0.4	0.2	0.3	-	0.2	4.4
Item 7160 Subject A02a N	3053	1462	1523	2402	354	680	913	968	492	1719	1225	1177	626	433	731	43
D06K: Take other narcotics (methadone, opium, codeine, paregoric, etc.)?																
1. None	79.2	77.6	81.0	78.4	86.8	78.6	76.3	82.9	78.2	82.2	74.8	88.6	88.8	77.4	58.8	49.0
2. A few	15.1	17.0	13.0	16.0	7.6	16.1	16.8	12.2	16.4	13.4	17.5	9.7	9.3	18.2	26.8	19.4
3. Some	4.3	3.9	4.6	4.4	2.6	3.2	5.6	3.6	4.5	3.5	5.5	1.4	1.6	3.8	10.5	22.0
4. Most	1.1	0.9	1.3	0.9	2.1	1.8	0.9	0.8	0.9	0.8	1.5	0.3	0.3	0.6	3.2	5.6
5. All	0.3	0.6	0.1	0.3	0.9	0.3	0.5	0.4	0.1	0.1	0.6	0.2	*	-	0.7	4.0
Item 7170 Subject A02a N	3054	1465	1522	2402	353	677	910	973	494	1724	1222	1174	626	433	736	43
D06L: Use inhalants (sniffing glue, aerosols, laughing gas, etc.)?																
1. None	83.9	82.7	85.0	83.4	87.5	83.7	83.7	85.3	81.5	85.1	81.5	87.4	87.8	82.2	77.0	64.5
2. A few	12.9	14.1	11.7	13.8	8.0	13.1	12.7	11.7	15.6	12.3	14.5	10.6	10.7	14.2	17.3	21.7
3. Some	2.1	1.6	2.5	2.1	0.7	2.2	2.3	1.8	2.1	1.7	2.5	1.1	0.5	2.9	4.1	7.5
4. Most	0.7	0.9	0.5	0.4	2.9	0.6	0.6	0.8	0.8	0.7	0.7	0.5	0.7	0.3	1.1	1.0
5. All	0.4	0.7	0.2	0.3	0.9	0.4	0.6	0.5	0.1	0.2	0.8	0.3	0.2	0.4	0.5	5.4
Item 7180 Subject A02a N	3048	1460	1522	2395	356	676	910	970	492	1724	1216	1173	621	434	737	43

*=less than .05 per cent.

QUESTIONNAIRE FORM 2 1983	TOTAL	SEX		RACE		REGION				4YR COLLEGE PLANS		ILLICIT DRUG USE: LIFETIME				
		M	F	White	Black	NE	NC	S	W	Yes	No	None	Mari-juana Only	Few Pills	More Pills	Any Her-oin
N (Weighted No. of Cases):	3435	1671	1641	2610	419	829	979	1077	550	1848	1335	1281	705	472	851	47
% of Weighted Total:	100.0	48.6	47.8	76.0	12.2	24.1	28.5	31.4	16.0	53.8	38.9	37.3	20.5	13.7	24.8	1.4

D06M: Drink alcoholic beverages (liquor, beer, wine)?

1. None	4.5	5.6	3.4	2.8	10.9	3.2	3.4	5.6	6.0	4.7	3.7	7.3	4.0	3.2	0.4	5.3
2. A few	10.1	8.3	11.7	8.4	16.4	8.1	9.3	10.3	13.6	10.2	9.6	16.9	7.8	7.2	3.2	-
3. Some	16.5	13.5	19.6	14.7	26.7	13.9	14.4	20.3	16.2	16.9	16.1	25.4	14.9	12.5	6.5	5.9
4. Most	43.1	45.5	41.1	46.1	29.0	39.3	43.8	44.2	44.4	44.7	40.6	39.2	46.3	49.0	44.4	27.4
5. All	25.9	27.1	24.3	27.9	16.9	35.5	29.1	19.5	19.8	23.6	29.9	11.1	27.1	28.0	45.5	61.3
Item 7190 Subject A02a N	3053	1462	1524	2398	354	674	913	971	495	1725	1221	1178	624	432	735	41

D06N: Get drunk at least once a week?

1. None	16.1	15.2	16.8	13.2	28.3	12.6	15.5	16.0	21.9	18.0	13.0	25.7	14.7	12.0	4.5	7.5
2. A few	26.2	22.4	30.0	25.4	28.3	24.7	22.4	27.1	33.5	27.6	24.2	32.5	26.9	22.8	18.3	6.6
3. Some	26.8	27.6	26.0	28.7	18.5	25.4	29.0	27.9	22.6	26.8	27.1	26.5	27.0	29.0	26.6	25.2
4. Most	21.3	23.6	19.2	23.1	14.2	22.5	22.9	21.0	17.2	20.4	22.3	11.8	23.4	25.8	32.0	22.7
5. All	9.7	11.3	7.9	9.6	10.7	14.8	10.2	8.0	4.9	7.2	13.4	3.4	8.0	10.4	18.5	37.9
Item 7200 Subject A02a N	3063	1470	1526	2405	358	680	915	978	490	1732	1223	1181	625	434	738	43

Lately there has been increased attention paid to two types of drugs: PCP and amyl or butyl nitrite.

E01: How many of your friends would you estimate . . .

E01A: Take PCP (angel dust, crystal, peace pill, killer weed, supergrass, crystal cyclone)?

1. None	85.8	86.6	84.9	85.9	87.0	82.7	85.7	87.6	86.6	89.1	80.9	91.6	91.7	85.4	73.6	51.9
2. A few	11.2	10.6	11.9	11.6	8.3	13.7	11.6	9.7	9.9	9.0	14.6	7.1	6.9	12.0	20.1	28.7
3. Some	2.0	1.6	2.3	1.7	2.6	2.1	1.9	1.6	2.5	1.2	2.9	0.8	1.3	1.5	4.5	5.7
4. Most	0.7	0.7	0.7	0.6	1.2	0.9	0.6	0.5	0.7	0.5	1.0	0.2	0.1	0.6	1.3	9.2
5. All	0.4	0.5	0.2	0.2	0.8	0.6	0.1	0.5	0.3	0.2	0.6	0.3	-	0.4	0.4	4.6
Item 7201 Subject A02a N	3023	1444	1513	2384	350	667	904	964	489	1717	1201	1177	616	424	727	41

E01B: Take amyl or butyl nitrites (poppers, snappers, Locker Room, Vaporole, Rush, Kick, Bullet)?

1. None	85.5	84.7	86.3	84.8	90.7	84.4	85.4	85.9	86.2	87.7	82.0	92.7	91.7	83.5	71.9	47.9
2. A few	11.2	11.3	11.1	12.3	4.4	12.7	10.7	10.4	11.9	10.0	13.2	6.3	7.2	14.1	20.3	23.6
3. Some	2.6	3.1	2.2	2.4	4.2	2.1	3.2	2.9	1.6	2.0	3.6	0.9	1.0	1.9	6.5	17.5
4. Most	0.5	0.6	0.3	0.4	0.7	0.4	0.5	0.7	0.1	0.2	0.9	-	0.1	0.5	1.2	4.5
5. All	0.2	0.3	0.1	0.2	-	0.3	0.2	0.1	0.2	*	0.3	0.1	-	-	0.2	6.5
Item 7202 Subject A02a N	2998	1428	1503	2368	345	660	901	953	484	1704	1188	1164	613	420	724	39

E02: On how many occasions (if any) have you used PCP (angel dust, crystal, peace pill, killer weed, supergrass, crystal cyclone)?

E02A: . . . in your lifetime?

1. 0 occasions	94.4	93.1	95.8	94.0	96.7	94.0	93.8	95.7	93.9	96.5	91.2	99.7	98.6	96.6	83.6	48.5
2. 1-2	3.8	4.8	3.0	4.4	1.5	4.5	4.6	2.5	4.0	2.4	6.1	0.2	1.4	2.8	11.4	22.3
3. 3-5	0.5	0.7	0.4	0.5	0.8	0.4	0.6	0.6	0.5	0.2	1.0	-	-	-	1.5	13.1
4. 6-9	0.3	0.4	0.2	0.3	0.4	0.3	0.3	0.2	0.6	0.3	0.3	-	-	-	0.9	4.9
5. 10-19	0.4	0.4	0.2	0.4	0.1	0.4	0.5	0.4	0.1	0.3	0.6	-	0.1	0.3	1.4	-
6. 20-39	0.2	0.2	-	0.1	0.4	0.1	-	0.2	0.4	0.1	0.2	-	-	-	0.5	2.5
7. 40 or more	0.3	0.4	0.3	0.4	0.2	0.3	0.2	0.4	0.6	0.2	0.6	0.1	-	0.4	0.6	8.7
Item 1181 Subject A01a N	3010	1435	1510	2379	345	657	902	962	488	1707	1198	1172	618	421	725	42

E02B: . . . during the last 12 months?

1. 0 occasions	97.4	96.8	98.1	97.4	98.0	96.8	97.4	98.1	96.9	98.6	95.6	100.0	99.5	99.1	92.2	63.9
2. 1-2	1.5	1.9	1.0	1.6	0.8	1.8	1.9	0.7	1.7	0.6	2.8	-	0.4	0.3	4.3	22.7
3. 3-5	0.3	0.4	0.2	0.2	0.3	0.6	0.1	0.3	0.2	0.2	0.4	-	-	-	1.0	3.9
4. 6-9	0.3	0.3	0.3	0.3	0.3	0.5	0.3	0.2	0.1	0.2	0.3	-	-	0.2	0.9	2.5
5. 10-19	0.3	0.2	0.2	0.3	0.4	0.2	0.1	0.4	0.7	0.3	0.4	-	0.1	-	1.1	2.5
6. 20-39	0.1	0.1	-	0.1	-	0.1	-	-	0.2	-	0.1	-	-	-	0.2	-
7. 40 or more	0.2	0.2	0.1	0.2	0.2	-	0.2	0.3	0.2	0.1	0.3	-	-	0.4	0.2	4.4
Item 1182 Subject A01b N	3006	1429	1512	2375	345	658	898	962	487	1708	1192	1172	618	422	721	42

*=less than .05 per cent.

QUESTIONNAIRE FORM 2 1983	TOTAL	SEX		RACE		REGION				4YR COLLEGE PLANS		ILLICIT DRUG USE: LIFETIME				
		M	F	White	Black	NE	NC	S	W	Yes	No	None	Mari-juana Only	Few Pills	More Pills	Any Her-oin
N (Weighted No. of Cases):	3435	1671	1641	2610	419	829	979	1077	550	1848	1335	1281	705	472	851	47
% of Weighted Total:	100.0	48.6	47.8	76.0	12.2	24.1	28.5	31.4	16.0	53.8	38.9	37.3	20.5	13.7	24.8	1.4

E02C: . . . during the last 30 days?

1. 0 occasions	98.7	98.5	99.1	98.8	98.9	98.8	98.6	99.0	98.5	99.3	97.9	100.0	99.9	99.6	95.9	85.1
2. 1-2	0.8	0.9	0.6	0.8	0.3	0.8	1.1	0.4	0.6	0.4	1.3	-	0.1	-	2.4	10.4
3. 3-5	0.1	0.1	0.1	*	0.5	0.2	*	0.1	-	0.1	-	-	-	-	0.3	-
4. 6-9	0.2	0.2	*	0.1	0.4	0.2	0.1	0.1	0.4	0.1	0.2	-	-	-	0.8	-
5. 10-19	0.1	0.2	*	0.2	-	-	-	0.3	0.3	0.1	0.2	-	-	-	0.4	2.8
6. 20-39	*	0.1	-	*	-	-	-	0.1	*	-	0.1	-	-	-	*	1.7
7. 40 or more	0.1	-	0.1	0.1	-	-	0.2	-	0.1	-	0.2	-	-	0.4	0.1	-
Item 1183 Subject A01c N	3007	1430	1512	2376	345	658	900	962	487	1710	1192	1172	618	423	721	42

E03: On how many occasions (if any) have you used amyl or butyl nitrites (poppers, snappers, Locker Room, Vaporole, Rush, Kick, Bullet)?

E03A: . . . in your lifetime?

1. 0 occasions	91.6	88.1	94.8	91.2	93.2	91.6	91.4	91.0	93.1	92.8	89.5	99.5	96.4	92.8	75.4	53.1
2. 1-2	4.8	6.6	3.2	5.0	4.4	5.0	5.0	4.8	4.3	4.2	6.2	0.1	3.0	4.3	14.2	14.7
3. 3-5	1.6	2.4	0.9	1.8	0.4	1.1	2.2	1.4	1.4	1.4	1.8	0.3	0.2	1.1	4.7	12.4
4. 6-9	1.0	1.2	0.9	1.1	1.1	0.9	0.5	1.7	0.9	0.9	1.3	*	-	0.5	3.8	2.1
5. 10-19	0.4	0.8	0.1	0.4	0.9	0.8	0.2	0.3	0.2	0.5	0.3	-	0.3	0.3	1.0	2.8
6. 20-39	0.2	0.3	-	0.2	-	0.1	0.1	0.3	-	0.1	0.2	-	0.1	0.4	0.3	1.9
7. 40 or more	0.4	0.6	0.2	0.4	-	0.5	0.6	0.4	-	0.1	0.8	0.1	-	0.6	0.6	13.0
Item 1184 Subject A01a N	2982	1419	1499	2358	345	648	894	956	484	1699	1178	1166	614	419	714	36

E03B: . . . during the last 12 months?

1. 0 occasions	96.4	95.1	97.6	96.2	97.1	95.9	97.0	95.7	97.0	96.7	95.7	99.7	99.2	96.9	89.4	68.0
2. 1-2	2.3	3.3	1.5	2.5	2.5	2.5	1.8	3.0	1.9	2.2	2.6	0.2	0.5	1.7	7.0	18.7
3. 3-5	0.7	0.7	0.7	0.7	0.5	1.1	0.3	0.6	1.0	0.7	0.7	-	0.3	0.3	2.1	8.2
4. 6-9	0.2	0.4	0.1	0.2	-	0.3	0.5	*	0.1	0.2	0.2	*	-	0.2	0.7	-
5. 10-19	0.1	0.2	-	0.1	-	-	0.1	0.2	-	-	0.2	-	-	-	0.2	2.0
6. 20-39	0.1	0.3	-	0.1	-	-	-	0.4	-	0.1	0.2	-	-	0.6	-	3.2
7. 40 or more	0.2	0.1	0.2	0.2	-	0.2	0.3	*	-	*	0.4	-	-	0.4	0.5	-
Item 1185 Subject A01b N	2979	1416	1499	2357	344	647	894	955	483	1698	1177	1165	614	420	712	36

E03C: . . . during the last 30 days?

1. 0 occasions	98.6	97.8	99.5	98.6	98.7	98.9	98.7	98.0	99.4	99.2	97.7	99.9	99.9	98.2	96.4	84.9
2. 1-2	0.8	1.3	0.2	0.7	1.3	0.5	0.7	1.2	0.6	0.4	1.3	*	0.1	0.7	2.0	11.9
3. 3-5	0.1	0.3	-	0.2	-	0.1	-	0.4	-	0.2	0.1	-	-	0.5	0.3	-
4. 6-9	0.2	0.4	*	0.3	-	0.3	0.3	0.1	-	0.1	0.4	*	-	-	0.8	-
5. 10-19	*	-	0.1	0.1	-	0.1	-	*	-	*	0.1	-	-	-	0.2	-
6. 20-39	0.1	0.2	-	*	-	-	-	0.2	-	-	0.2	-	-	0.2	-	3.2
7. 40 or more	0.1	0.1	0.1	0.1	-	0.1	0.3	-	-	-	0.3	-	-	0.4	0.3	-
Item 1186 Subject A01c N	2981	1419	1499	2359	344	648	895	955	483	1698	1179	1165	614	421	713	36

E04: When (if ever) did you FIRST do each of the following things?

E04A: Try PCP

8. Never	96.1	95.1	96.9	95.7	97.8	95.9	95.7	96.8	95.8	97.1	94.4	99.9	99.9	98.2	87.7	49.7
1. Grade 6 or below	0.3	0.3	0.1	0.3	-	0.2	0.3	0.3	0.1	0.1	0.5	0.1	-	0.2	0.5	6.0
2. Grade 7 or 8	0.7	1.0	0.4	0.7	0.6	0.5	0.7	0.4	1.4	0.6	0.7	-	-	0.6	2.1	6.9
3. Grade 9 (Freshman)	1.0	1.1	1.1	1.1	1.2	0.9	1.4	0.7	1.3	0.7	1.6	-	-	0.1	3.4	15.0
4. Grade 10 (Sophomore)	0.8	1.3	0.4	1.0	-	0.9	1.1	0.6	0.5	0.4	1.4	-	-	0.2	2.7	11.3
5. Grade 11 (Junior)	0.8	0.8	0.8	0.9	0.4	1.3	0.5	0.9	0.3	0.7	1.0	-	-	0.7	2.3	7.5
6. Grade 12 (Senior)	0.4	0.4	0.3	0.4	-	0.2	0.3	0.4	0.6	0.4	0.3	-	0.1	-	1.3	3.6
Item 5686 Subject A01g N	2912	1379	1472	2306	332	633	875	935	470	1670	1139	1160	599	407	671	41

E04B: Try amyl or butyl nitrites

8. Never	94.0	91.8	96.0	93.4	96.4	94.3	93.9	93.2	95.3	94.6	92.9	99.6	98.0	95.0	81.5	57.3
1. Grade 6 or below	0.5	0.6	0.3	0.4	0.6	0.4	0.6	0.4	0.4	0.3	0.8	0.2	-	0.1	1.3	6.9
2. Grade 7 or 8	1.1	1.8	0.4	1.1	1.3	2.0	0.5	1.3	0.2	1.2	1.0	-	1.0	0.3	3.1	9.2
3. Grade 9 (Freshman)	1.6	2.1	1.1	1.9	0.1	1.3	2.5	1.2	1.0	1.2	2.1	0.1	0.4	0.4	5.8	8.7
4. Grade 10 (Sophomore)	0.9	1.2	0.6	1.1	-	0.7	0.8	1.1	0.8	1.2	0.5	-	0.1	1.4	2.5	9.7
5. Grade 11 (Junior)	1.4	1.5	1.3	1.5	0.9	0.9	1.4	1.8	1.0	1.1	1.9	0.1	0.2	1.6	4.3	8.3
6. Grade 12 (Senior)	0.7	0.9	0.3	0.6	0.6	0.4	0.3	0.9	1.2	0.5	0.8	0.1	0.3	1.3	1.5	-
Item 5687 Subject A01g N	2881	1349	1470	2287	327	628	859	923	472	1653	1127	1158	598	406	650	35

*=less than .05 per cent.

QUESTIONNAIRE FORM 2 1983	TOTAL	SEX		RACE		REGION				4YR COLLEGE PLANS		ILLICIT DRUG USE: LIFETIME				
		M	F	White	Black	NE	NC	S	W	Yes	No	None	Mari-juana Only	Few Pills	More Pills	Any Her-oin
N (Weighted No. of Cases):	3435	1671	1641	2610	419	829	979	1077	550	1848	1335	1281	705	472	851	47
% of Weighted Total:	100.0	48.6	47.8	76.0	12.2	24.1	28.5	31.4	16.0	53.8	38.9	37.3	20.5	13.7	24.8	1.4
E05: What is your best guess about whether your parents think you drink alcoholic beverages (beer, wine, liquor)?																
1. They feel sure I don't drink	26.1	20.5	31.4	22.9	39.8	20.5	22.0	31.7	30.0	28.1	22.6	49.2	11.6	16.3	7.1	5.2
2. They think I probably don't drink	12.6	12.4	13.0	12.8	14.1	14.2	12.2	12.9	10.7	13.5	10.9	13.1	18.3	13.8	6.1	9.6
3. I don't know, or they differ in whether they think I do	9.2	8.7	9.8	8.9	10.4	10.0	10.5	8.5	7.3	9.6	9.3	8.3	11.3	10.8	7.9	11.9
4. They think I probably drink	16.5	17.8	15.2	16.8	16.4	17.5	16.5	15.3	17.6	16.2	16.7	11.1	20.3	18.2	21.2	22.8
5. They feel sure (or know) that I drink	35.6	40.6	30.6	38.6	19.3	37.9	38.9	31.5	34.4	32.6	40.5	18.3	38.5	41.0	57.7	50.5
Item 7510 Subject A09a N	2969	1408	1495	2348	350	649	887	958	475	1689	1178	1155	609	414	713	41
E06: What's your best guess about whether your parents think you smoke marijuana?																
1. They feel sure I don't	69.0	64.4	73.9	69.7	61.7	65.2	68.6	72.4	68.0	73.4	62.5	94.2	65.1	63.9	35.7	41.7
2. They think I probably don't	12.3	13.1	11.0	12.3	13.8	13.7	12.2	11.3	12.4	11.7	13.0	3.0	18.4	16.0	20.1	7.7
3. I don't know, or they differ in whether they think I do	7.0	8.3	5.9	7.2	7.0	7.5	7.7	6.3	6.6	6.0	8.5	1.2	9.2	7.5	13.7	16.3
4. They think I probably do	5.4	5.9	4.4	4.7	9.3	7.0	4.5	5.0	5.6	4.7	6.5	0.5	4.2	7.2	12.3	21.2
5. They feel sure (or know) that I do	6.4	8.2	4.8	6.2	8.2	6.7	7.1	5.0	7.3	4.1	9.5	1.0	3.1	5.3	18.3	13.1
Item 7520 Subject A09a N	2955	1404	1485	2338	346	647	884	948	475	1682	1170	1149	608	411	709	40
E07: Within the past three months, how often have you . . .																
E07A: Had arguments or quarrels with your parents or other older relatives?																
1. Not at all	17.9	21.4	14.5	14.2	35.9	16.3	15.4	20.9	18.7	17.2	18.3	20.8	18.7	15.3	13.3	16.3
2. Once or twice	46.8	46.7	46.9	47.7	39.3	46.4	44.2	47.9	50.2	46.0	48.1	49.1	46.5	49.3	42.9	38.2
3. Every month	14.0	13.5	14.3	15.3	9.8	14.2	14.7	13.4	13.3	15.7	11.9	12.0	14.0	15.1	16.7	12.3
4. Every week	14.8	14.0	15.7	16.4	9.3	16.6	17.3	12.0	13.6	15.3	14.0	12.9	16.9	13.4	17.1	20.0
5. Almost daily	6.5	4.3	8.7	6.3	5.8	6.6	8.5	5.8	4.2	5.8	7.7	5.2	4.0	6.8	9.9	13.2
Item 19530 Subject M03,Q09 N	2962	1410	1487	2342	346	647	888	949	478	1681	1176	1149	606	415	712	41
E07B: Had arguments or quarrels with people in positions of authority?																
1. Not at all	58.4	48.7	67.7	56.5	66.4	52.0	57.1	63.3	59.8	57.4	61.2	66.2	59.9	57.6	45.3	47.9
2. Once or twice	31.9	37.6	26.5	33.4	24.8	35.0	31.9	30.3	31.0	32.4	29.6	27.6	29.4	35.5	39.6	30.6
3. Every month	5.5	8.0	3.1	5.9	3.1	7.3	5.6	3.7	6.4	6.0	4.9	3.9	6.5	4.1	7.9	10.9
4. Every week	3.0	4.6	1.6	3.3	3.0	4.3	4.0	1.5	2.4	3.0	3.0	1.7	3.2	2.0	5.4	5.8
5. Almost daily	1.2	1.2	1.1	1.0	2.7	1.4	1.4	1.2	0.5	1.1	1.3	0.6	1.1	0.8	1.8	4.8
Item 19540 Subject Q09 N	2964	1411	1490	2342	348	647	888	951	478	1684	1176	1152	605	416	711	41
E07C: Been mad enough to feel like smashing something, but I didn't?																
1. Not at all	24.1	21.1	26.5	21.6	34.5	22.8	22.1	25.8	26.4	23.8	24.5	27.8	25.4	25.0	16.5	18.6
2. Once or twice	46.2	43.2	49.4	46.5	44.1	45.9	43.4	48.8	46.5	47.3	44.7	49.5	45.6	46.1	41.9	40.1
3. Every month	13.8	17.0	10.9	15.5	5.4	12.9	15.6	11.8	15.7	13.9	13.3	11.5	14.6	11.2	18.8	8.6
4. Every week	11.6	14.2	9.3	12.6	8.4	14.1	13.9	9.3	8.6	11.2	12.6	8.5	10.8	13.0	16.7	14.9
5. Almost daily	4.3	4.6	3.9	3.8	7.5	4.3	5.1	4.3	2.9	3.8	4.9	2.7	3.7	4.7	6.1	17.8
Item 19550 Subject Q09 N	2956	1408	1486	2341	344	647	886	948	475	1680	1173	1151	605	415	709	37
E07D: Been mad enough so you actually did smash something?																
1. Not at all	72.2	61.4	82.5	71.4	77.2	66.7	70.8	75.6	75.5	75.4	67.5	82.1	72.9	70.2	58.4	37.3
2. Once or twice	20.5	26.7	14.5	21.2	16.8	24.8	20.0	18.2	20.0	18.7	23.4	13.8	19.0	24.6	30.2	27.6
3. Every month	4.5	7.1	1.8	4.8	1.6	4.6	6.5	3.3	3.0	3.7	5.3	2.3	4.4	3.5	7.5	20.3
4. Every week	2.1	3.8	0.5	1.7	4.0	3.0	1.7	2.3	1.2	1.8	2.5	1.4	3.2	0.7	2.6	6.7
5. Almost daily	0.8	1.0	0.6	0.8	0.4	0.9	1.0	0.7	0.4	0.4	1.3	0.3	0.5	0.9	1.3	8.1
Item 19560 Subject Q09 N	2955	1407	1485	2336	344	643	885	951	476	1684	1168	1150	604	414	709	38

QUESTIONNAIRE FORM 2 1983	TOTAL	SEX		RACE		REGION				4YR COLLEGE PLANS		ILLICIT DRUG USE: LIFETIME				
		M	F	White	Black	NE	NC	S	W	Yes	No	None	Marijuana Only	Few Pills	More Pills	Any Heroin
N (Weighted No. of Cases):	3435	1671	1641	2610	419	829	979	1077	550	1848	1335	1281	705	472	851	47
% of Weighted Total:	100.0	48.6	47.8	76.0	12.2	24.1	28.5	31.4	16.0	53.8	38.9	37.3	20.5	13.7	24.8	1.4
E07E: Felt like getting into a fist fight with someone, but didn't?																
1. Not at all	44.7	32.0	56.5	44.2	43.7	41.2	44.1	45.4	49.2	46.7	41.7	54.2	43.8	42.8	32.0	22.5
2. Once or twice	40.1	46.1	34.6	40.9	40.1	42.9	37.5	42.2	36.7	39.3	42.0	35.6	40.1	44.9	44.9	44.5
3. Every month	7.4	11.0	4.1	7.9	4.3	7.2	9.4	5.6	7.6	7.2	7.3	4.7	8.1	6.4	11.2	20.2
4. Every week	5.2	7.9	2.7	4.9	5.8	6.1	6.5	3.7	4.2	4.8	5.6	3.7	5.0	4.0	8.4	6.1
5. Almost daily	2.6	3.0	2.2	2.1	6.2	2.5	2.4	3.0	2.3	2.1	3.4	1.8	3.0	1.8	3.5	6.7
Item 19570 Subject Q09 N	2956	1407	1487	2339	344	644	885	948	478	1683	1170	1152	603	416	709	38
E07F: Actually got into a fight and hit somebody?																
1. Not at all	83.4	77.0	89.7	83.9	80.7	82.0	81.8	83.9	87.5	86.4	79.2	90.3	84.6	86.0	71.6	49.3
2. Once or twice	13.7	19.0	8.6	13.3	15.4	14.3	15.0	13.4	11.4	11.4	17.0	8.2	13.1	12.2	23.0	37.3
3. Every month	1.6	2.2	1.1	1.8	1.2	1.9	2.5	1.2	0.6	1.4	2.1	1.0	0.9	0.2	3.9	7.5
4. Every week	0.7	1.1	0.3	0.5	1.9	1.2	0.3	0.8	0.4	0.5	0.9	0.3	0.7	0.9	0.7	4.9
5. Almost daily	0.5	0.7	0.3	0.4	0.9	0.6	0.5	0.7	0.1	0.3	0.9	0.2	0.7	0.7	0.8	1.1
Item 19580 Subject Q09 N	2955	1406	1486	2336	345	643	885	949	478	1680	1171	1152	605	415	707	38
The next questions are about military service.																
E08: Do you favor or oppose a military draft at the present time?																
1. Strongly oppose	21.4	23.8	18.8	21.5	23.1	23.2	20.9	20.8	21.1	20.9	23.1	19.1	21.7	22.2	24.1	21.5
2. Mostly oppose	19.2	18.5	19.7	19.7	16.5	23.2	21.0	16.0	21.0	20.8	16.8	17.6	19.9	20.6	19.7	31.2
3. No opinion, or mixed	40.8	34.3	47.5	39.9	44.6	40.2	39.6	43.0	39.5	40.0	42.2	41.4	40.3	39.9	41.8	29.2
4. Mostly favor	12.4	13.5	11.2	12.5	9.6	10.8	13.4	12.7	11.9	12.8	11.6	15.0	11.3	11.9	9.3	7.5
5. Strongly favor	6.2	9.8	2.8	6.3	6.2	5.7	5.1	7.5	6.6	5.6	6.3	6.9	6.8	5.4	5.0	10.6
Item 21060 Subject L02 N	2924	1408	1458	2312	344	639	879	942	464	1671	1146	1139	603	411	693	38
E09: Do you think any military draft in the U.S. should include women as well as men?																
1. No	29.1	17.9	39.9	28.8	34.3	26.8	27.1	31.9	30.0	29.9	28.4	31.8	25.7	30.1	26.5	29.1
2. Uncertain	33.6	28.5	39.1	33.4	36.7	33.5	33.8	32.9	35.0	32.2	35.3	35.2	36.7	31.4	30.5	35.2
3. Yes	37.3	53.7	21.0	37.8	29.0	39.7	39.0	35.2	35.0	37.9	36.3	33.0	37.6	38.5	43.1	35.7
Item 21070 Subject L02 N	2918	1403	1456	2303	346	637	873	940	467	1667	1144	1134	599	411	695	38
One idea for getting more high school graduates to serve in the military is to offer them a paid college education after three years of service in the armed forces. During the three years of military duty their pay would be fairly low, but afterward the government would pay their tuition plus $300 a month living expenses for up to four academic years.																
E10: Do you think it would be a good idea for the U.S. to have such a program of paid college in return for military service?																
1. Definitely not	2.2	2.4	2.0	2.0	3.7	2.4	2.2	2.5	1.6	1.9	2.7	2.1	1.7	1.8	3.1	2.8
2. Probably not	4.1	5.2	3.1	3.8	5.9	4.8	4.3	2.8	5.3	3.9	4.5	3.4	6.1	5.1	2.7	14.3
3. No opinion or uncertain	18.1	16.1	19.8	17.5	22.1	17.6	17.7	18.8	17.9	13.7	24.6	17.8	18.6	15.9	18.3	24.1
4. Yes, probably	30.3	28.7	31.6	31.6	27.1	30.5	30.3	30.0	30.5	30.7	30.5	32.0	28.6	30.1	29.3	23.5
5. Yes, definitely	45.3	47.6	43.6	45.2	41.2	44.6	45.5	45.9	44.7	49.8	37.7	44.7	45.1	47.2	46.7	35.3
Item 21080 Subject L02 N	2897	1393	1445	2291	340	632	865	936	463	1658	1136	1130	594	406	688	37
E11: If paid college in return for military service were available NOW, how likely is it that you would sign up for such a plan?																
1. Definitely would not	27.7	20.7	34.7	28.7	25.2	29.9	27.0	26.4	28.6	27.3	29.2	32.5	24.0	26.0	25.0	18.0
2. Probably would not	40.5	41.4	39.8	42.7	28.8	41.3	44.0	38.8	36.2	41.3	39.1	39.5	41.7	43.3	40.1	37.5
3. Probably would	25.1	28.0	21.8	22.8	33.4	23.3	22.5	26.5	29.2	24.2	26.3	21.2	28.2	23.0	28.8	30.4
4. Definitely would	6.7	9.9	3.7	5.8	12.5	5.5	6.4	8.2	5.9	7.2	5.4	6.8	6.1	7.6	6.1	14.0
Item 21090 Subject L02 N	2882	1385	1438	2280	336	629	857	934	463	1648	1131	1125	593	401	685	37

QUESTIONNAIRE FORM 2 1983	TOTAL	SEX		RACE		REGION				4YR COLLEGE PLANS		ILLICIT DRUG USE: LIFETIME				
		M	F	White	Black	NE	NC	S	W	Yes	No	None	Mari- juana Only	Few Pills	More Pills	Any Her- oin
N (Weighted No. of Cases):	3435	1671	1641	2610	419	829	979	1077	550	1848	1335	1281	705	472	851	47
% of Weighted Total:	100.0	48.6	47.8	76.0	12.2	24.1	28.5	31.4	16.0	53.8	38.9	37.3	20.5	13.7	24.8	1.4

E12: Some people like school very much. Others don't. How do you feel about going to school?

	TOTAL	M	F	White	Black	NE	NC	S	W	Yes	No	None	Mari.	Few	More	Any
5. I like school very much	13.9	13.6	14.0	11.9	24.8	11.1	12.1	15.7	17.4	16.5	9.6	17.8	12.4	14.9	7.5	10.5
4. I like school quite a lot	29.5	26.7	32.6	30.1	28.8	24.2	33.6	29.7	28.7	34.2	23.7	34.2	30.8	28.1	23.6	7.8
3. I like school some	39.5	41.0	37.9	39.5	37.4	42.1	37.2	40.5	38.5	37.4	42.9	38.1	41.9	40.5	39.4	44.4
2. I don't like school very much	11.8	12.4	11.2	13.0	6.0	15.5	11.3	10.1	10.8	8.8	15.6	7.6	10.1	13.1	19.1	13.3
1. I don't like school at all	5.3	6.4	4.3	5.5	3.0	7.0	5.8	4.0	4.5	3.1	8.3	2.4	4.7	3.4	10.5	23.9
Item 7630 Subject B01,Q08 N	2929	1395	1470	2319	340	636	875	951	467	1673	1150	1142	596	409	701	38

E13: About how many hours do you spend in an average week on all your homework including both in school and out of school?

	TOTAL	M	F	White	Black	NE	NC	S	W	Yes	No	None	Mari.	Few	More	Any
1. 0 hours	7.3	9.1	5.3	6.9	7.8	9.1	6.0	7.6	6.6	4.0	11.7	4.9	6.9	6.8	11.5	14.8
2. 1-4 hours	41.9	44.0	39.9	41.1	44.8	45.2	36.1	44.3	43.0	36.0	49.8	37.7	44.3	45.2	44.9	32.6
3. 5-9 hours	24.3	23.4	25.2	24.3	25.2	24.0	26.1	23.2	23.3	27.1	20.4	26.3	25.1	21.6	22.0	25.3
4. 10-14 hours	13.0	11.1	14.7	13.0	12.4	13.1	14.5	11.7	12.4	16.7	8.0	15.7	10.8	12.8	10.6	14.4
5. 15-19 hours	5.1	4.4	5.7	5.6	3.3	4.2	6.7	4.3	5.1	6.5	3.4	5.7	5.6	5.9	2.9	4.0
6. 20-24 hours	4.1	3.6	4.6	4.5	2.3	1.7	4.8	4.7	5.0	4.7	3.3	4.3	3.3	3.5	4.9	6.0
7. 25 or more hours	4.4	4.3	4.6	4.5	4.1	2.8	5.8	4.1	4.5	5.0	3.4	5.4	4.1	4.2	3.3	2.9
Item 7640 Subject B01 N	2913	1393	1460	2312	338	631	868	950	464	1663	1145	1139	594	405	699	36

E14: In general, how much say or influence do you feel each of the following has on HOW YOUR SCHOOL IS RUN?

E14A: The principal

	TOTAL	M	F	White	Black	NE	NC	S	W	Yes	No	None	Mari.	Few	More	Any
1. Little or no influence	11.5	13.5	9.4	10.3	15.6	12.6	10.3	12.2	10.8	9.0	14.4	10.0	12.3	8.5	14.0	23.8
2. Some influence	14.0	13.2	14.6	14.0	12.1	13.6	15.9	11.4	16.2	12.2	17.0	13.7	12.0	15.1	15.7	9.1
3. Moderate influence	14.3	14.6	13.9	14.1	12.6	14.2	14.6	12.5	17.4	12.5	16.2	11.7	18.0	16.7	14.4	15.9
4. Considerable influence	23.2	24.3	22.5	24.9	16.0	20.2	24.6	24.2	22.6	24.9	21.7	25.2	20.0	26.9	20.6	22.9
5. A great deal of influence	37.0	34.3	39.5	36.7	43.6	39.4	34.6	39.7	33.1	41.4	30.7	39.4	37.7	32.7	35.3	28.3
Item 7650 Subject B10 N	2879	1379	1444	2296	332	621	863	934	461	1644	1133	1120	588	403	695	35

E14B: The teachers

	TOTAL	M	F	White	Black	NE	NC	S	W	Yes	No	None	Mari.	Few	More	Any
1. Little or no influence	8.4	11.1	5.8	8.2	9.1	9.2	8.7	8.2	7.0	6.0	11.2	7.7	7.8	8.2	10.0	16.1
2. Some influence	20.5	20.5	20.4	19.9	22.0	21.5	19.6	20.4	21.2	19.5	22.2	18.9	22.7	19.3	21.6	28.0
3. Moderate influence	31.4	31.5	31.2	33.3	21.1	32.6	32.3	29.4	32.0	32.0	31.2	29.2	33.4	31.7	33.2	27.0
4. Considerable influence	28.7	27.2	30.6	28.8	30.9	24.8	30.3	29.7	29.2	31.5	24.6	32.4	28.2	28.0	24.4	23.5
5. A great deal of influence	11.0	9.8	12.1	9.8	16.9	11.9	9.2	12.3	10.6	11.0	10.8	11.7	8.0	12.6	10.9	5.4
Item 7660 Subject B10 N	2874	1376	1441	2292	329	619	866	930	460	1640	1134	1122	586	402	693	34

E14C: The students

	TOTAL	M	F	White	Black	NE	NC	S	W	Yes	No	None	Mari.	Few	More	Any
1. Little or no influence	30.1	32.7	27.7	31.7	25.2	34.0	31.3	28.3	26.1	29.8	31.0	27.5	30.3	27.8	34.9	45.9
2. Some influence	28.8	29.7	27.8	29.1	26.4	29.3	29.9	28.3	26.8	30.4	26.4	29.5	28.0	28.7	28.7	23.8
3. Moderate influence	19.2	17.6	20.9	18.7	20.5	16.5	17.7	20.2	23.8	19.5	18.4	21.3	20.1	21.9	14.0	10.0
4. Considerable influence	12.0	10.5	13.3	11.6	13.8	9.3	13.3	12.0	13.5	11.2	13.5	12.5	12.9	10.9	11.6	6.7
5. A great deal of influence	9.9	9.5	10.3	8.9	14.1	10.9	7.8	11.2	9.8	9.1	10.7	9.2	8.8	10.6	10.9	13.6
Item 7670 Subject B10 N	2867	1372	1438	2288	326	615	865	929	459	1637	1130	1115	585	402	692	34

E14D: Parents of students

	TOTAL	M	F	White	Black	NE	NC	S	W	Yes	No	None	Mari.	Few	More	Any
1. Little or no influence	21.8	24.8	18.6	21.9	21.0	23.8	22.8	20.7	19.2	19.8	25.0	19.6	21.2	21.0	25.6	36.5
2. Some influence	33.4	31.1	35.8	35.4	24.8	36.5	34.5	31.4	31.3	33.8	32.6	30.8	37.1	33.1	35.3	40.1
3. Moderate influence	20.5	19.3	21.9	21.7	17.6	17.2	22.5	20.7	20.4	20.7	20.3	21.8	20.5	20.6	19.2	5.2
4. Considerable influence	14.8	15.5	14.0	13.8	16.2	13.8	13.8	14.4	19.0	15.6	13.4	17.2	13.1	13.9	12.6	11.5
5. A great deal of influence	9.5	9.4	9.8	7.3	20.5	8.7	6.4	12.6	10.1	10.1	8.6	10.6	8.0	11.4	7.3	6.7
Item 7680 Subject B10 N	2873	1373	1441	2290	328	616	866	931	460	1641	1132	1119	586	402	694	34

E15: Have you had any drug education courses or lectures in school?

	TOTAL	M	F	White	Black	NE	NC	S	W	Yes	No	None	Mari.	Few	More	Any
1. No–GO TO Q.E19	25.6	27.7	23.7	25.1	28.3	21.7	28.8	27.2	21.7	24.1	28.3	27.4	25.8	26.5	20.7	32.0
2. No, and I wish I had– GO TO Q.E19	4.3	4.3	4.3	4.1	5.0	4.9	3.5	5.2	2.9	3.4	5.5	4.4	2.9	5.4	4.2	5.2
3. Yes	70.1	68.0	72.0	70.8	66.7	73.5	67.7	67.5	75.4	72.5	66.2	68.3	71.4	68.2	75.1	62.8
Item 7690 Subject A10a N	2719	1274	1390	2204	277	585	818	874	443	1574	1052	1074	551	372	658	34

QUESTIONNAIRE FORM 2 1983	TOTAL	SEX		RACE		REGION				4YR COLLEGE PLANS		ILLICIT DRUG USE: LIFETIME				
		M	F	White	Black	NE	NC	S	W	Yes	No	None	Mari- juana Only	Few Pills	More Pills	Any Her- oin
N (Weighted No. of Cases):	3435	1671	1641	2610	419	829	979	1077	550	1848	1335	1281	705	472	851	47
% of Weighted Total:	100.0	48.6	47.8	76.0	12.2	24.1	28.5	31.4	16.0	53.8	38.9	37.3	20.5	13.7	24.8	1.4
E16: Would you say that the information about drugs that you received in school classes or programs has . . .																
1. Made you less interested in trying drugs	54.7	47.1	61.7	52.3	72.1	49.1	53.2	61.9	51.7	54.0	55.8	70.7	60.2	49.3	30.8	13.8
2. Not changed your interest in trying drugs	42.5	48.7	37.1	45.3	25.0	48.3	44.3	35.2	45.0	44.2	39.6	28.1	37.3	48.6	63.5	81.6
3. Made you more interested in trying drugs	2.8	4.3	1.2	2.5	2.9	2.6	2.5	2.9	3.3	1.8	4.6	1.1	2.6	2.2	5.7	4.6
Item 7840 Subject A10a N★	1921	882	1001	1571	184	434	555	593	339	1148	706	736	401	256	496	21
E17: How many of the following drug education experiences have you had in high school? (Mark all that apply.)																
A. A special course about drugs	21.4	24.7	18.8	20.9	23.9	27.2	17.0	21.5	20.9	22.0	20.9	20.3	22.7	18.8	22.7	31.8
B. Films, lectures, or discussions in one of my regular courses	77.1	75.0	79.3	77.3	75.3	74.1	77.8	74.6	84.2	78.3	76.1	78.3	74.6	77.7	77.9	56.1
C. Films or lectures, outside of my regular courses	23.9	25.3	22.5	24.8	19.2	18.5	27.5	26.8	19.6	26.6	19.5	25.4	24.7	21.3	22.9	20.1
D. Special discussions ("rap" groups) about drugs	21.2	20.8	22.1	21.3	25.1	19.0	22.7	22.8	19.1	20.9	20.7	20.8	19.7	16.5	25.5	22.9
Item 7850-7880 Subject A10a N★	1897	862	998	1554	181	424	549	588	335	1137	695	727	394	254	490	21
E18: Overall, how valuable were the experiences to you?																
1. Little or no value	18.5	22.6	15.3	18.7	16.4	18.6	19.4	17.7	18.2	18.4	18.9	16.9	15.5	16.0	23.9	32.1
2. Some value	43.0	43.1	42.5	45.5	26.5	50.4	43.2	34.3	48.1	45.3	38.8	40.0	41.5	48.3	45.3	49.9
3. Considerable value	23.7	21.2	25.8	23.3	24.8	19.5	24.5	27.0	21.9	23.4	24.7	24.6	25.0	24.6	21.6	11.8
4. Great value	14.9	13.0	16.4	12.4	32.2	11.5	12.9	21.0	11.8	12.9	17.6	18.5	18.0	11.1	9.3	6.2
Item 7890 Subject A10a N★	1907	871	997	1562	181	431	552	588	335	1140	700	727	397	256	494	21
E19: Some people have suggested that there be standard tests of high school skills in arithmetic, reading, and writing. What do you think about each of the following possible uses of such a test?																
E19A: Any student age 16 or older who can pass such a test should be given a high school diploma and be allowed to leave high school early																
1. Disagree	37.0	36.0	38.1	37.3	38.2	37.7	38.5	38.5	30.4	40.2	32.3	39.8	38.6	38.2	32.1	20.3
2. Mostly disagree	22.6	20.9	24.1	23.8	17.8	21.1	23.5	21.9	23.9	24.7	19.7	24.8	18.0	22.7	22.8	14.9
3. Neither	15.4	16.4	14.5	15.6	12.4	13.5	17.1	14.6	16.5	13.7	17.2	14.1	17.8	12.4	17.4	14.0
4. Mostly agree	13.8	12.6	14.9	13.1	17.8	14.6	12.4	13.7	15.7	13.4	14.8	12.2	13.4	16.8	15.0	19.3
5. Agree	11.2	14.2	8.5	10.2	13.8	13.1	8.6	11.2	13.6	8.0	15.9	9.0	12.2	9.9	12.7	31.5
Item 7900 Subject B08 N	2836	1348	1428	2268	318	599	861	918	458	1620	1115	1113	573	396	679	36
E19B: Any student age 14 or older who can pass such a test should be given a high school diploma and be allowed to leave high school early																
1. Disagree	62.7	58.9	67.0	64.6	56.0	62.1	63.5	64.1	59.0	65.2	59.9	63.7	61.7	63.4	62.9	42.6
2. Mostly disagree	20.1	20.5	19.6	19.7	19.2	21.6	19.1	18.7	23.1	19.7	20.2	19.8	21.3	18.7	20.7	17.5
3. Neither	9.9	12.4	7.3	9.6	10.1	9.3	10.8	9.1	10.7	8.8	10.8	9.5	10.4	10.5	9.3	15.8
4. Mostly agree	4.1	3.9	4.0	3.3	9.2	2.7	4.1	5.0	4.1	3.7	4.8	3.5	4.3	5.6	4.0	6.3
5. Agree	3.2	4.2	2.2	2.8	5.6	4.2	2.5	3.1	3.1	2.6	4.2	3.4	2.3	1.8	3.1	17.8
Item 7910 Subject B08 N	2833	1345	1428	2265	317	601	859	917	456	1616	1115	1114	570	395	679	36

★=excludes respondents for whom question was inappropriate.

QUESTIONNAIRE FORM 2 1983	TOTAL	SEX		RACE		REGION				4YR COLLEGE PLANS		ILLICIT DRUG USE: LIFETIME				
		M	F	White	Black	NE	NC	S	W	Yes	No	None	Mari-juana Only	Few Pills	More Pills	Any Her-oin
N (Weighted No. of Cases):	3435	1671	1641	2610	419	829	979	1077	550	1848	1335	1281	705	472	851	47
% of Weighted Total:	100.0	48.6	47.8	76.0	12.2	24.1	28.5	31.4	16.0	53.8	38.9	37.3	20.5	13.7	24.8	1.4

E19C: Before any student (no matter what age) is given a high school diploma, he or she should have to pass such a standard test

1. Disagree	22.7	25.1	20.9	23.3	18.3	26.5	21.9	21.8	21.0	20.5	26.2	21.3	24.1	20.4	25.4	24.6
2. Mostly disagree	9.6	9.6	9.4	9.6	10.4	8.9	10.7	10.2	6.9	8.6	10.5	10.0	10.0	7.6	9.7	3.5
3. Neither	15.3	15.3	14.7	15.4	12.6	15.3	16.7	14.2	14.7	13.9	16.4	14.5	16.0	13.5	16.3	16.6
4. Mostly agree	21.4	21.0	21.7	21.2	24.0	19.1	21.9	23.0	20.0	23.8	18.3	21.2	21.0	24.6	20.5	19.4
5. Agree	31.1	29.0	33.4	30.5	34.6	30.2	28.7	30.8	37.4	33.2	28.5	33.0	28.9	33.9	28.0	35.9
Item 7920 Subject B08 N	*2822*	*1334*	*1428*	*2261*	*315*	*595*	*854*	*917*	*456*	*1611*	*1109*	*1112*	*565*	*393*	*680*	*36*

E20: How often do you . . .

E20A: Eat breakfast?

1. Never	8.5	7.0	9.8	8.2	7.7	10.7	6.4	8.7	9.1	7.5	10.4	6.0	8.2	9.0	11.2	23.4
2. Seldom	27.5	23.7	31.1	25.9	33.6	27.6	29.6	25.8	26.8	24.4	31.6	22.6	27.3	29.5	33.5	35.2
3. Sometimes	17.4	15.9	18.4	16.2	22.8	16.6	14.7	19.5	19.5	18.0	16.4	18.9	16.1	15.8	17.4	7.5
4. Most days	10.5	10.2	11.1	11.1	8.3	10.6	10.4	11.1	9.6	10.0	10.9	10.2	9.3	13.3	11.0	-
5. Nearly every day	11.5	11.8	11.6	12.1	10.3	10.6	12.1	11.3	11.9	12.8	9.9	12.6	12.8	10.2	10.0	9.3
6. Every day	24.6	31.4	18.1	26.6	17.3	23.9	26.8	23.7	23.0	27.3	20.9	29.7	26.3	22.2	17.0	24.6
Item 20740 Subject Q06 N	*2875*	*1365*	*1445*	*2287*	*325*	*610*	*866*	*935*	*465*	*1639*	*1130*	*1119*	*584*	*403*	*689*	*38*

E20B: Eat at least some green vegetables?

1. Never	3.4	3.7	3.1	2.6	5.3	4.0	3.1	3.1	3.7	2.4	4.7	3.1	3.3	2.3	4.0	9.8
2. Seldom	8.5	7.3	9.7	7.4	12.9	9.7	7.4	9.3	7.2	6.9	10.3	7.3	8.5	8.9	9.5	13.7
3. Sometimes	21.2	19.3	22.8	20.1	25.8	22.2	24.1	18.9	18.9	19.3	23.9	19.5	22.3	19.8	23.5	21.0
4. Most days	23.9	23.3	24.7	24.6	19.9	22.9	23.3	25.1	23.8	24.1	23.5	21.0	25.1	28.3	24.8	30.6
5. Nearly every day	23.2	23.3	23.1	23.7	21.7	22.3	22.8	22.7	25.8	25.9	19.6	27.1	20.8	20.7	21.2	9.9
6. Every day	20.0	23.1	16.7	21.5	14.4	19.0	19.3	20.9	20.6	21.4	18.0	21.9	20.0	19.9	17.0	15.0
Item 20750 Subject Q06 N	*2860*	*1356*	*1439*	*2275*	*322*	*608*	*863*	*927*	*462*	*1633*	*1123*	*1115*	*578*	*402*	*686*	*38*

E20C: Eat at least some fruit?

1. Never	1.8	2.3	1.4	1.5	2.8	2.2	1.5	2.4	0.8	1.2	2.7	1.3	1.5	1.9	2.1	9.5
2. Seldom	7.7	6.4	9.0	7.3	10.6	8.0	8.2	8.2	5.1	6.0	10.0	7.2	6.6	7.6	8.9	17.9
3. Sometimes	26.3	24.2	28.2	26.4	26.3	24.5	27.8	29.1	20.4	23.5	30.5	24.4	26.0	26.6	29.6	13.0
4. Most days	24.5	25.3	23.8	24.1	23.0	22.7	25.0	25.6	23.8	25.3	22.7	23.1	27.1	25.2	24.7	25.2
5. Nearly every day	21.2	20.8	21.4	21.6	22.2	22.8	19.2	19.5	26.1	23.1	19.3	23.6	19.7	20.1	19.4	17.7
6. Every day	18.5	21.0	16.1	19.1	15.1	19.8	18.4	15.2	23.7	20.9	14.8	20.3	19.1	18.5	15.3	16.7
Item 20760 Subject Q06 N	*2853*	*1352*	*1436*	*2271*	*324*	*607*	*861*	*926*	*458*	*1628*	*1122*	*1114*	*578*	*398*	*684*	*38*

E20D: Exercise vigorously (jogging, swimming, calisthenics, or any other active sports)?

1. Never	3.5	2.6	4.3	2.5	7.3	4.5	3.1	4.2	1.6	2.3	5.1	3.2	3.1	3.7	3.3	3.3
2. Seldom	12.1	8.1	16.0	12.2	12.9	13.9	11.5	12.7	9.8	8.9	16.9	12.1	11.8	11.5	12.6	15.6
3. Sometimes	27.4	21.0	33.6	27.5	25.3	28.2	29.1	25.8	26.4	26.1	29.4	26.2	26.9	26.9	30.9	26.2
4. Most days	18.2	18.8	17.5	18.8	15.6	17.4	17.1	17.9	22.1	18.8	17.9	16.3	19.6	18.7	20.4	14.8
5. Nearly every day	17.1	20.6	13.9	17.3	17.4	15.2	17.1	19.7	14.2	19.4	13.3	17.7	16.2	16.7	16.9	13.0
6. Every day	21.7	28.9	14.6	21.8	21.5	20.9	22.2	19.7	25.8	24.5	17.4	24.5	22.4	22.5	16.0	27.1
Item 20770 Subject Q06 N	*2865*	*1360*	*1441*	*2278*	*325*	*609*	*865*	*929*	*463*	*1635*	*1126*	*1119*	*580*	*401*	*686*	*38*

E20E: Get at least seven hours of sleep?

1. Never	2.1	2.5	1.8	1.8	2.3	2.2	2.0	2.0	2.6	1.5	2.9	1.7	1.3	2.0	3.1	4.7
2. Seldom	10.0	8.7	11.2	9.4	13.7	11.2	8.7	11.4	8.0	9.7	10.5	8.2	9.2	9.9	13.6	16.9
3. Sometimes	17.5	15.4	19.3	17.6	15.6	19.8	18.3	15.8	16.4	15.9	19.9	13.9	14.0	22.1	22.8	27.0
4. Most days	23.9	23.7	24.4	24.5	18.6	20.1	26.5	22.3	27.3	24.2	23.5	23.4	25.1	20.9	26.2	16.4
5. Nearly every day	24.5	25.2	23.7	25.8	19.9	23.4	23.8	26.1	24.0	26.6	21.8	28.7	25.4	24.0	18.1	18.2
6. Every day	22.0	24.6	19.6	20.9	29.8	23.3	20.7	22.4	21.8	22.1	21.4	24.2	25.0	21.0	16.1	16.8
Item 20780 Subject Q06 N	*2861*	*1357*	*1442*	*2276*	*324*	*607*	*865*	*927*	*461*	*1633*	*1124*	*1118*	*579*	*401*	*684*	*38*

QUESTIONNAIRE FORM 2 1983	TOTAL	SEX		RACE		REGION				4YR COLLEGE PLANS		ILLICIT DRUG USE: LIFETIME				
		M	F	White	Black	NE	NC	S	W	Yes	No	None	Mari-juana Only	Few Pills	More Pills	Any Her-oin
N (Weighted No. of Cases):	3435	1671	1641	2610	419	829	979	1077	550	1848	1335	1281	705	472	851	47
% of Weighted Total:	100.0	48.6	47.8	76.0	12.2	24.1	28.5	31.4	16.0	53.8	38.9	37.3	20.5	13.7	24.8	1.4
E20F: Get less sleep than you think you should?																
1. Never	9.3	8.5	10.0	7.5	19.6	11.3	8.5	9.4	7.8	7.4	12.3	10.3	10.3	7.8	7.3	10.2
2. Seldom	19.8	20.0	19.1	19.4	18.9	17.7	20.3	19.7	21.7	18.9	20.5	21.1	21.5	18.6	16.9	13.4
3. Sometimes	30.6	28.7	32.6	30.9	28.3	28.0	33.8	29.2	30.7	31.5	29.5	32.2	30.5	29.5	29.5	16.8
4. Most days	15.7	15.9	15.3	16.5	12.7	17.6	14.1	15.8	16.1	16.7	14.1	13.8	17.8	16.2	16.2	16.7
5. Nearly every day	13.4	14.0	12.8	14.2	8.5	13.5	12.5	13.3	14.9	14.1	12.3	12.8	8.6	16.3	16.8	23.8
6. Every day	11.3	12.8	10.1	11.5	12.1	11.9	10.8	12.7	8.9	11.3	11.2	9.8	11.2	11.6	13.2	19.0
Item 20790 Subject Q06 N	2858	1356	1439	2276	322	606	864	928	461	1632	1123	1116	580	400	684	38

QUESTIONNAIRE FORM 3 1983	TOTAL	SEX		RACE		REGION				4YR COLLEGE PLANS		ILLICIT DRUG USE: LIFETIME				
		M	F	White	Black	NE	NC	S	W	Yes	No	None	Mari- juana Only	Few Pills	More Pills	Any Her- oin
N (Weighted No. of Cases):	3382	1575	1660	2571	403	828	931	1081	541	1837	1322	1173	701	469	926	37
% of Weighted Total:	100.0	46.6	49.1	76.0	11.9	24.5	27.5	32.0	16.0	54.3	39.1	34.7	20.7	13.9	27.4	1.1

A01: Taking all things together, how would you say things are these days-would you say you're very happy, pretty happy, or not too happy these days?

3. Very happy	18.5	16.7	20.0	20.5	10.1	18.0	18.1	18.5	19.9	18.9	17.9	22.0	18.9	17.0	14.3	13.2
2. Pretty happy	67.6	68.9	66.9	69.0	62.8	65.8	69.6	67.7	66.8	68.2	67.4	63.8	66.6	70.1	71.7	82.8
1. Not too happy	13.9	14.4	13.1	10.5	27.1	16.2	12.3	13.8	13.3	12.8	14.7	14.2	14.5	12.9	13.9	4.0
Item 1190 Subject P01,Q01 N	3369	1569	1657	2565	402	826	930	1079	533	1833	1318	1169	701	467	923	36

A02: Some people think a lot about the social problems of the nation and the world, and about how they might be solved. Others spend little time thinking about these issues. How much do you think about such things?

1. Never	2.0	2.3	1.5	1.8	1.8	2.0	1.4	2.2	2.4	1.0	2.9	1.2	1.5	2.3	2.6	11.7
2. Seldom	15.6	16.5	14.7	16.3	13.4	16.4	16.3	14.1	16.2	13.6	18.2	15.0	15.8	14.5	16.4	20.2
3. Sometimes	51.1	47.2	55.0	52.7	47.0	51.3	54.6	49.6	47.7	49.9	53.6	51.6	51.8	52.7	49.5	42.6
4. Quite often	25.6	27.3	24.3	24.4	29.8	24.7	23.5	27.7	26.4	28.9	21.0	24.4	24.7	27.5	27.4	23.6
5. A great deal	5.7	6.7	4.5	4.7	8.0	5.6	4.2	6.4	7.3	6.7	4.2	7.8	6.2	3.0	4.0	2.0
Item 6880 Subject J,Q08 N	3372	1569	1659	2568	401	826	931	1079	536	1834	1319	1172	700	467	923	36

A03: The next questions ask your opinions about a number of different topics. How much do you agree or disagree with each statement below?

A03A: Men and women should be paid the same money if they do the same work

1. Disagree	2.4	3.6	1.0	1.9	4.1	2.0	2.4	2.1	3.6	2.0	2.5	2.2	3.8	1.4	1.6	6.5
2. Mostly disagree	1.6	2.7	0.5	1.6	1.8	1.4	1.8	1.8	1.2	1.3	1.8	1.1	1.3	1.3	1.9	10.1
3. Neither	2.0	3.4	0.7	2.2	0.5	1.7	2.2	2.2	1.7	1.7	2.1	2.3	2.2	1.3	1.8	-
4. Mostly agree	14.6	20.6	9.0	14.3	15.6	14.3	12.9	16.0	15.3	13.7	15.2	14.0	14.8	14.4	15.1	19.8
5. Agree	79.4	69.7	88.8	80.0	78.0	80.6	80.8	77.8	78.1	81.3	78.4	80.4	77.8	81.7	79.6	63.6
Item 7930 Subject D06 N	3377	1573	1660	2571	403	828	931	1080	537	1835	1322	1171	701	469	926	37

A03B: Women should be considered as seriously as men for jobs as executives or politicians

1. Disagree	4.6	7.9	1.0	4.4	3.6	3.7	3.5	5.7	5.5	3.6	4.8	5.0	5.0	3.8	3.1	18.0
2. Mostly disagree	4.0	6.7	1.4	4.2	2.7	3.0	3.4	4.9	5.0	3.6	4.4	3.7	4.1	4.2	3.6	11.6
3. Neither	4.6	7.6	1.2	4.5	3.5	3.8	5.2	4.7	4.4	4.2	4.6	4.2	4.5	3.2	5.7	5.9
4. Mostly agree	22.6	29.5	16.0	22.6	22.1	20.5	23.7	23.4	22.7	21.5	24.3	22.6	22.2	22.2	22.5	25.9
5. Agree	64.2	48.4	80.4	64.4	68.2	69.1	64.1	61.3	62.4	67.0	61.9	64.4	64.2	66.6	65.1	38.6
Item 7940 Subject D06,H02 N	3373	1574	1656	2570	401	826	931	1078	538	1835	1319	1171	701	469	923	37

A03C: A woman should have exactly the same job opportunities as a man

1. Disagree	7.8	11.5	3.2	7.1	8.6	6.8	7.0	8.9	8.4	5.1	9.6	7.6	8.0	8.1	5.8	27.9
2. Mostly disagree	5.8	8.7	2.9	6.1	4.4	5.3	5.6	6.5	5.8	6.6	5.1	5.1	6.9	4.8	6.5	8.5
3. Neither	5.6	7.7	3.6	5.7	4.5	4.9	6.4	5.7	5.0	4.9	6.3	4.7	5.9	3.7	7.3	5.4
4. Mostly agree	29.6	32.1	27.3	30.7	21.1	28.9	30.0	27.7	34.0	29.6	30.4	30.7	28.7	28.1	30.6	21.3
5. Agree	51.2	39.9	63.0	50.4	61.5	54.0	51.1	51.3	46.8	53.8	48.6	51.9	50.5	55.4	49.7	36.8
Item 7950 Subject D06 N	3358	1564	1652	2559	398	825	929	1074	530	1828	1315	1164	696	467	923	37

A03D: A woman should have exactly the same educational opportunities as a man

1. Disagree	1.2	1.9	0.4	0.8	1.5	0.9	2.0	0.8	1.2	0.9	1.1	1.5	0.4	0.8	1.2	6.7
2. Mostly disagree	0.7	1.1	0.4	0.7	1.4	0.4	1.0	0.6	1.0	0.6	0.9	1.3	0.1	0.7	0.3	1.2
3. Neither	1.4	1.8	0.9	1.2	1.2	1.4	1.5	1.3	1.6	0.8	1.9	1.1	1.7	1.6	1.2	2.0
4. Mostly agree	8.8	10.4	6.8	7.8	10.3	8.3	7.6	9.4	10.4	7.7	9.3	8.6	9.4	7.4	8.3	13.0
5. Agree	87.9	84.7	91.6	89.4	85.6	89.0	87.9	88.0	85.8	90.0	86.7	87.5	88.4	89.5	89.0	77.2
Item 7960 Subject D06 N	3360	1568	1649	2559	400	824	927	1072	537	1825	1318	1166	696	469	922	36

QUESTIONNAIRE FORM 3 1983	TOTAL	SEX		RACE		REGION				4YR COLLEGE PLANS		ILLICIT DRUG USE: LIFETIME				
		M	F	White	Black	NE	NC	S	W	Yes	No	None	Mari- juana Only	Few Pills	More Pills	Any Her- oin
N (Weighted No. of Cases):	3382	1575	1660	2571	403	828	931	1081	541	1837	1322	1173	701	469	926	37
% of Weighted Total:	100.0	46.6	49.1	76.0	11.9	24.5	27.5	32.0	16.0	54.3	39.1	34.7	20.7	13.9	27.4	1.1
A03E: It is usually better for everyone involved if the man is the achiever outside the home and the woman takes care of the home and family																
1. Disagree	27.1	14.9	39.0	24.8	38.0	32.1	25.5	25.5	25.4	28.3	25.5	27.3	25.6	26.2	28.1	35.1
2. Mostly disagree	17.6	15.1	20.0	18.3	15.5	19.5	15.9	17.0	18.8	18.9	16.0	16.7	18.4	18.0	18.9	9.6
3. Neither	16.9	20.2	14.2	17.5	12.8	15.5	18.3	15.6	18.8	18.9	14.5	16.0	15.6	19.7	17.5	14.1
4. Mostly agree	21.4	24.5	18.2	22.5	17.8	20.4	22.5	21.2	21.4	20.3	22.8	21.9	22.0	21.1	20.9	18.8
5. Agree	17.0	25.3	8.6	17.0	15.9	12.4	17.7	20.7	15.7	13.6	21.3	18.1	18.4	15.0	14.6	22.4
Item 7970 Subject D05 N	3367	1568	1655	2565	401	826	928	1076	537	1834	1315	1169	699	469	922	37
A03F: A preschool child is likely to suffer if the mother works																
1. Disagree	17.7	11.4	23.3	14.1	33.8	19.4	17.0	18.4	14.7	15.7	19.2	17.4	16.9	17.4	17.6	16.7
2. Mostly disagree	18.2	13.0	23.4	18.6	19.8	17.6	18.4	17.7	19.5	19.6	16.5	15.5	18.0	21.8	20.4	10.4
3. Neither	13.6	14.3	13.4	14.1	10.2	14.0	12.9	13.0	15.6	15.8	11.1	13.2	16.5	13.7	11.9	21.4
4. Mostly agree	24.7	26.0	23.8	26.6	18.4	25.0	25.2	24.3	24.0	25.6	24.4	27.6	22.2	21.9	25.0	26.1
5. Agree	25.9	35.2	16.0	26.6	17.8	24.0	26.5	26.6	26.2	23.3	28.7	26.4	26.4	25.3	25.2	25.4
Item 7980 Subject D05 N	3349	1558	1647	2550	401	821	921	1068	538	1823	1308	1164	697	462	919	35
A03G: A working mother can establish just as warm and secure a relationship with her children as a mother who does not work																
1. Disagree	14.3	20.0	8.1	14.6	8.7	14.5	14.6	14.6	13.0	12.0	16.6	15.5	14.6	12.7	13.4	16.9
2. Mostly disagree	17.7	23.4	12.2	19.9	9.4	16.8	20.4	15.7	18.6	17.8	18.3	18.9	17.7	14.7	18.1	18.4
3. Neither	9.7	12.6	7.2	10.6	4.5	7.9	11.7	8.5	11.2	9.9	9.7	10.4	7.6	9.7	10.4	9.9
4. Mostly agree	25.2	21.8	28.2	26.1	21.0	24.7	24.2	25.6	26.5	27.1	22.4	25.0	25.0	24.3	25.4	29.1
5. Agree	33.1	22.1	44.3	28.8	56.4	36.1	29.1	35.6	30.6	33.2	33.0	30.3	35.1	38.7	32.6	25.6
Item 7990 Subject D05 N	3370	1571	1657	2567	402	826	931	1076	537	1835	1317	1169	700	469	924	37
A04: The next questions are about pollution and the environment. How much do you agree or disagree with each statement below?																
A04A: Pollution of most types has increased in the U.S. in the last ten years																
1. Disagree	3.1	4.7	1.3	2.8	3.5	3.2	3.2	2.7	3.6	2.8	3.0	2.1	3.4	3.2	3.3	7.4
2. Mostly disagree	5.4	7.6	3.4	5.5	5.2	4.1	7.9	4.4	5.0	6.3	4.0	5.8	5.6	4.1	5.0	6.6
3. Neither	8.1	8.0	8.4	8.2	8.1	6.9	10.7	7.0	8.0	8.0	8.1	7.8	8.0	6.2	9.7	9.9
4. Mostly agree	28.2	24.7	31.5	29.5	26.4	28.7	29.3	28.3	25.7	27.7	29.3	27.2	28.9	29.3	28.1	25.5
5. Agree	55.1	55.0	55.5	53.9	56.8	57.1	49.0	57.6	57.8	55.1	55.6	57.1	54.1	57.2	53.7	50.5
Item 8000 Subject F04 N	3362	1567	1653	2565	398	820	931	1075	536	1831	1314	1170	694	465	925	37
A04B: Government should take steps to deal with our environmental problems, even if it means that most of us pay higher prices or taxes																
1. Disagree	9.9	11.3	8.1	8.0	16.6	9.0	8.7	11.5	10.2	6.7	14.0	8.9	8.7	9.8	11.1	20.8
2. Mostly disagree	10.0	9.7	10.2	9.0	13.7	11.9	11.1	8.4	8.4	9.0	11.0	8.2	10.9	11.7	10.6	17.1
3. Neither	17.5	13.9	21.8	19.0	9.7	16.5	20.5	15.5	17.6	17.0	18.5	17.0	17.1	16.7	18.6	21.7
4. Mostly agree	36.4	35.2	37.3	38.1	31.0	35.5	34.9	37.4	38.4	38.7	34.7	37.5	33.9	36.4	38.4	25.5
5. Agree	26.2	29.9	22.5	25.9	29.1	27.1	24.6	27.2	25.5	28.7	21.7	28.5	29.4	25.5	21.2	15.0
Item 8010 Subject F04,H02 N	3357	1568	1648	2559	398	822	929	1074	534	1828	1313	1166	694	467	923	37
A04C: I would prefer to pay more money for things that will last a long time, rather than have them cost less and break sooner																
1. Disagree	1.1	1.4	0.6	0.8	1.3	1.1	1.0	0.8	1.4	0.7	1.2	1.2	0.8	0.9	0.6	9.5
2. Mostly disagree	1.3	1.3	1.2	0.9	1.8	1.0	2.1	0.9	1.4	0.8	1.9	1.1	1.1	1.0	1.5	7.0
3. Neither	3.5	4.1	2.9	3.3	2.4	3.8	3.3	3.8	3.0	3.0	4.0	2.6	2.7	4.8	4.3	4.9
4. Mostly agree	20.7	20.4	21.4	21.9	16.6	19.3	22.4	18.4	24.3	22.2	19.7	21.2	21.7	20.5	20.7	5.6
5. Agree	73.4	72.8	73.9	73.1	77.9	74.8	71.3	76.0	69.9	73.3	73.2	73.9	73.7	72.8	72.8	73.0
Item 8020 Subject F01 N	3364	1567	1654	2563	399	826	930	1070	537	1833	1314	1171	696	466	922	37

QUESTIONNAIRE FORM 3 1983	TOTAL	SEX		RACE		REGION				4YR COLLEGE PLANS		ILLICIT DRUG USE: LIFETIME				
		M	F	White	Black	NE	NC	S	W	Yes	No	None	Mari-juana Only	Few Pills	More Pills	Any Her-oin
N (Weighted No. of Cases):	3382	1575	1660	2571	403	828	931	1081	541	1837	1322	1173	701	469	926	37
% of Weighted Total:	100.0	46.6	49.1	76.0	11.9	24.5	27.5	32.0	16.0	54.3	39.1	34.7	20.7	13.9	27.4	1.1
A04D: I would probably be willing to use a bicycle or mass transit (if available) rather than a car to get to work																
1. Disagree	30.0	31.1	28.6	27.5	43.3	32.0	25.9	34.2	25.6	25.6	34.6	25.8	30.3	34.0	31.3	58.1
2. Mostly disagree	18.3	18.2	18.5	19.0	15.9	18.3	16.8	20.1	17.5	18.5	17.9	18.3	20.4	19.5	17.2	6.7
3. Neither	11.1	13.5	9.0	12.1	8.0	11.8	11.6	10.6	10.2	11.9	10.6	10.8	11.2	9.1	12.6	10.9
4. Mostly agree	22.3	19.9	25.0	23.6	17.0	22.0	27.6	17.5	23.3	24.3	20.1	22.1	20.0	22.7	24.2	13.3
5. Agree	18.3	17.3	18.9	17.8	15.8	16.0	18.2	17.6	23.4	19.6	16.8	22.9	18.1	14.8	14.8	11.0
Item 8030　Subject F07　　N	3364	1569	1652	2562	398	824	928	1075	537	1832	1313	1171	693	468	924	37
A04E: I would be willing to eat less meat and more grains and vegetables, if it would help provide food for starving people																
1. Disagree	10.8	16.6	5.0	11.3	9.8	11.2	11.0	9.8	11.7	10.5	10.6	8.4	11.7	10.5	12.1	27.0
2. Mostly disagree	8.1	11.1	5.2	8.2	5.2	8.0	8.7	7.7	7.8	7.9	7.8	7.8	8.4	6.9	8.9	4.6
3. Neither	13.6	17.8	10.3	14.6	10.9	13.9	14.3	12.1	15.3	14.2	13.2	14.5	16.2	11.4	11.2	25.5
4. Mostly agree	29.6	29.2	29.9	30.1	29.7	32.8	30.2	28.4	26.1	30.4	29.3	30.9	29.6	30.3	28.8	19.1
5. Agree	37.9	25.3	49.6	35.8	44.4	34.2	35.8	42.0	39.1	37.0	39.1	38.4	34.0	40.9	39.0	23.8
Item 8040　Subject F03,O03　　N	3361	1564	1655	2562	400	823	930	1072	536	1831	1313	1170	695	468	921	37
A05: In the following list you will find some statements about leisure time and work. Please show whether you agree or disagree with each statement.																
A05A: I like the kind of work you can forget about after the work day is over																
1. Disagree	14.6	15.2	14.1	12.4	25.9	15.8	14.4	14.6	12.9	15.6	12.3	17.4	15.2	13.6	10.4	11.9
2. Mostly disagree	15.0	15.3	14.7	15.6	14.4	15.2	16.9	12.9	15.6	16.7	12.8	16.0	14.1	15.9	14.6	15.4
3. Neither	13.9	13.6	14.4	14.8	8.4	15.1	15.5	10.8	15.2	16.3	11.1	13.3	15.6	13.9	13.0	25.6
4. Mostly agree	23.0	21.0	25.0	23.8	18.9	21.9	22.2	23.9	24.2	22.9	23.6	23.3	21.6	22.4	24.9	9.7
5. Agree	33.6	35.0	31.9	33.4	32.4	32.1	31.0	37.7	32.0	28.6	40.1	30.1	33.6	34.2	37.1	37.4
Item 8050　Subject C04　　N	3367	1573	1652	2564	401	825	931	1073	537	1832	1318	1167	700	468	924	37
A05B: To me, work is nothing more than making a living																
1. Disagree	43.3	40.2	46.7	44.2	37.2	40.1	44.0	43.1	47.4	46.4	40.3	48.6	43.0	41.6	39.3	29.9
2. Mostly disagree	27.1	25.3	29.7	30.3	16.8	29.6	29.4	24.2	25.3	28.8	25.0	25.6	24.6	30.4	30.5	21.9
3. Neither	8.2	9.7	7.2	9.0	5.3	8.2	8.5	7.8	8.9	7.5	8.9	7.2	8.1	7.7	10.1	10.5
4. Mostly agree	10.4	12.8	7.7	9.3	15.0	9.9	9.6	11.9	9.2	9.3	12.1	10.4	10.2	9.7	10.4	12.2
5. Agree	10.9	12.0	8.8	7.3	25.7	12.1	8.6	13.0	9.1	8.0	13.7	8.3	14.1	10.6	9.8	25.5
Item 8060　Subject C06　　N	3368	1573	1654	2568	402	825	931	1077	535	1833	1319	1167	700	468	925	37
A05C: I expect my work to be a very central part of my life																
1. Disagree	4.6	4.2	4.7	3.8	3.4	6.7	3.6	3.9	4.5	4.3	5.1	5.1	4.4	4.3	4.0	2.4
2. Mostly disagree	7.9	6.9	8.8	8.8	3.8	7.7	8.2	7.8	8.0	7.5	8.7	8.4	6.2	10.3	7.7	5.6
3. Neither	13.5	13.5	13.6	14.2	7.6	13.4	13.6	12.5	15.1	12.8	14.7	11.9	13.9	13.7	14.5	18.1
4. Mostly agree	35.4	35.6	35.5	37.2	30.0	35.4	37.9	33.9	34.2	37.5	32.3	36.7	33.7	33.2	37.2	34.9
5. Agree	38.6	39.8	37.5	35.9	55.2	36.9	36.7	41.9	38.2	37.9	39.2	37.8	41.8	38.5	36.6	39.0
Item 8070　Subject C06　　N	3364	1571	1653	2564	401	824	931	1073	536	1831	1316	1168	700	468	922	37
A05D: I want to do my best in my job, even if this sometimes means working overtime																
1. Disagree	2.0	2.0	2.0	1.7	3.1	2.6	2.1	1.6	2.0	2.0	2.0	1.4	2.3	1.7	2.6	6.7
2. Mostly disagree	2.3	2.4	2.2	2.2	2.8	2.7	2.4	2.4	1.6	2.4	2.2	2.6	2.0	2.5	2.0	3.7
3. Neither	3.3	4.5	2.1	3.5	2.9	3.6	3.8	2.2	4.3	3.4	3.1	2.6	3.3	3.8	3.8	5.5
4. Mostly agree	28.9	29.4	28.4	30.4	22.9	30.2	29.0	27.5	29.7	29.9	27.8	27.8	25.7	31.0	31.8	35.5
5. Agree	63.4	61.6	65.3	62.2	68.3	60.9	62.7	66.3	62.4	62.3	64.8	65.5	66.8	60.9	59.8	48.6
Item 8080　Subject C06　　N	3364	1572	1652	2562	402	826	924	1078	537	1833	1315	1170	697	468	922	37

QUESTIONNAIRE FORM 3 1983	TOTAL	SEX		RACE		REGION				4YR COLLEGE PLANS		ILLICIT DRUG USE: LIFETIME				
		M	F	White	Black	NE	NC	S	W	Yes	No	None	Mari- juana Only	Few Pills	More Pills	Any Her- oin
N (Weighted No. of Cases):	3382	1575	1660	2571	403	828	931	1081	541	1837	1322	1173	701	469	926	37
% of Weighted Total:	100.0	46.6	49.1	76.0	11.9	24.5	27.5	32.0	16.0	54.3	39.1	34.7	20.7	13.9	27.4	1.1
A05E: I would like to stay in the same job for most of my adult life																
1. Disagree	13.9	13.7	13.9	12.0	20.9	16.7	11.7	13.9	13.4	12.2	15.4	12.8	15.3	13.6	14.3	13.3
2. Mostly disagree	11.9	10.7	12.6	12.0	11.1	13.3	11.6	10.9	12.2	11.8	11.8	10.4	11.5	14.7	12.8	8.5
3. Neither	15.8	16.7	14.9	17.4	9.9	16.2	16.7	13.9	17.6	17.0	14.8	15.6	15.2	14.3	16.9	30.5
4. Mostly agree	25.3	24.4	26.0	25.1	27.4	24.2	25.9	24.8	26.9	26.0	24.5	27.4	26.6	23.6	22.8	18.3
5. Agree	33.1	34.5	32.5	33.5	30.7	29.6	34.1	36.6	29.8	32.9	33.5	33.7	31.4	33.8	33.1	29.4
Item 8090 Subject C03　　N	3360	1568	1650	2558	400	823	930	1071	536	1828	1314	1168	697	466	922	37
A06: If you were to get enough money to live as comfortably as you'd like for the rest of your life, would you want to work?																
1. I would want to work	77.0	75.3	79.1	76.1	81.5	76.0	79.9	74.5	78.5	78.2	76.3	80.6	75.4	76.5	74.4	75.4
2. I would not want to work	23.0	24.7	20.9	23.9	18.5	24.0	20.1	25.5	21.5	21.8	23.7	19.4	24.6	23.5	25.6	24.6
Item 8100 Subject C06　　N	3303	1532	1637	2532	388	805	921	1054	522	1817	1281	1150	684	463	905	36
The next questions are about living or working with people of different races. Please rate each of the statements below using the following terms:																
Not at all acceptable: I'd avoid this if I possibly could.																
Somewhat acceptable: I could live with this, but not be happy about it.																
Acceptable: This would be O.K., or I'd be neutral about this.																
Desirable: I'd really like this.																
A07: How would you feel about . . .																
A07A: Having close personal friends of another race?																
1. Not at all acceptable	2.9	3.7	1.9	3.2	1.2	2.2	3.5	3.3	2.0	2.4	3.3	2.5	2.1	3.1	3.4	13.2
2. Somewhat acceptable	6.0	7.0	4.7	6.4	3.9	5.9	5.2	7.8	4.2	4.4	8.0	6.2	5.5	6.3	6.3	9.6
3. Acceptable	56.9	60.8	53.9	60.3	47.7	59.3	59.3	54.7	53.7	55.6	58.5	54.6	58.7	57.4	58.4	51.7
4. Desirable	34.2	28.5	39.5	30.1	47.3	32.6	32.0	34.2	40.1	37.5	30.2	36.7	33.8	33.3	32.0	25.4
Item 8110 Subject N01　　N	3364	1569	1653	2566	398	825	927	1075	538	1829	1318	1166	698	469	924	37
A07B: Having a job with a supervisor of a different race?																
1. Not at all acceptable	3.0	4.0	1.7	3.6	0.7	2.0	4.3	3.4	1.6	2.8	3.1	2.8	2.8	3.5	3.0	13.1
2. Somewhat acceptable	8.9	10.6	6.9	9.2	7.9	7.9	8.2	11.4	6.6	7.4	10.9	8.0	8.2	9.9	9.4	19.4
3. Acceptable	70.6	72.7	69.4	72.6	66.0	72.9	72.8	68.2	67.9	71.3	69.7	70.8	70.9	68.3	71.8	59.3
4. Desirable	17.5	12.7	21.9	14.7	25.5	17.2	14.6	17.0	23.9	18.5	16.3	18.4	18.2	18.2	15.9	8.2
Item 8120 Subject C05,N01　　N	3363	1571	1651	2566	396	823	926	1076	538	1830	1317	1169	697	468	923	37
A07C: Having a family of a different race (but same level of education and income) move next door to you?																
1. Not at all acceptable	5.8	7.3	3.7	6.6	2.2	4.6	5.6	7.5	4.4	4.9	6.4	5.4	5.9	5.5	6.2	8.7
2. Somewhat acceptable	10.6	12.2	8.8	11.8	6.3	9.4	11.5	13.5	5.2	9.1	12.2	9.1	10.6	9.1	12.9	12.5
3. Acceptable	58.9	59.9	58.6	60.3	55.8	63.9	60.2	56.5	53.9	59.2	58.6	58.6	57.6	62.3	59.3	51.9
4. Desirable	24.7	20.6	28.8	21.3	35.8	22.2	22.6	22.5	36.6	26.8	22.7	26.9	25.9	23.2	21.6	26.8
Item 8130 Subject N01　　N	3359	1568	1651	2564	396	822	925	1076	536	1825	1318	1168	697	466	922	37
A07D: Having your (future) children's friends be all of your race?																
1. Not at all acceptable	17.5	15.8	19.1	15.4	25.4	17.1	13.9	19.9	19.3	18.6	15.8	18.3	18.5	16.2	16.3	18.1
2. Somewhat acceptable	20.7	21.4	19.8	20.1	21.4	23.0	17.3	20.4	23.4	22.1	19.4	21.2	21.3	19.5	20.7	9.4
3. Acceptable	43.2	42.2	44.2	44.7	38.0	42.6	49.7	38.0	43.0	42.5	44.5	42.3	41.7	41.7	46.0	40.3
4. Desirable	18.7	20.6	16.9	19.8	15.2	17.3	19.0	21.7	14.2	16.9	20.3	18.2	18.5	22.6	17.1	32.2
Item 8140 Subject N01　　N	3333	1565	1633	2551	391	816	924	1064	528	1812	1307	1159	691	466	914	35

QUESTIONNAIRE FORM 3 1983	TOTAL	SEX		RACE		REGION				4YR COLLEGE PLANS		ILLICIT DRUG USE: LIFETIME				
		M	F	White	Black	NE	NC	S	W	Yes	No	None	Mari-juana Only	Few Pills	More Pills	Any Her-oin
N (Weighted No. of Cases):	3382	1575	1660	2571	403	828	931	1081	541	1837	1322	1173	701	469	926	37
% of Weighted Total:	100.0	46.6	49.1	76.0	11.9	24.5	27.5	32.0	16.0	54.3	39.1	34.7	20.7	13.9	27.4	1.1
A07E: Having some of your (future) children's friends be of other races?																
1. Not at all acceptable	3.4	4.6	1.8	3.5	2.3	3.3	3.8	3.9	1.7	2.7	3.5	2.8	2.6	3.0	3.6	13.4
2. Somewhat acceptable	8.6	9.2	7.3	8.6	6.9	6.7	8.3	10.9	7.5	6.7	11.0	8.1	9.3	8.3	8.3	14.6
3. Acceptable	53.0	56.5	50.5	55.5	46.6	54.8	56.5	51.4	47.7	50.6	56.4	51.0	53.5	52.1	56.5	50.8
4. Desirable	35.0	29.8	40.4	32.3	44.2	35.2	31.4	33.8	43.1	40.0	29.1	38.1	34.6	36.6	31.7	21.2
Item 8150 Subject N01 N	3352	1563	1650	2561	393	817	927	1069	538	1825	1313	1165	692	468	922	37
A08: How would you feel about having a job where . . .																
A08A: . . . all the employees are of your race?																
1. Not at all acceptable	8.2	6.5	9.5	5.2	21.4	8.8	4.7	10.5	8.7	8.9	7.2	9.2	9.5	7.2	5.6	17.6
2. Somewhat acceptable	13.6	13.7	13.5	10.1	28.1	15.5	9.9	14.0	16.1	13.6	13.1	12.1	16.5	16.9	11.2	7.7
3. Acceptable	53.7	53.3	54.6	57.5	38.3	53.1	59.0	47.9	57.0	56.0	51.2	56.6	49.5	51.1	55.8	42.3
4. Desirable	24.5	26.5	22.4	27.2	12.2	22.6	26.4	27.5	18.2	21.5	28.6	22.1	24.6	24.9	27.4	32.4
Item 8160 Subject C05,N01 N	3348	1563	1646	2561	389	817	925	1072	534	1827	1309	1169	689	469	920	37
A08B: . . . some employees are of a different race?																
1. Not at all acceptable	1.3	1.9	0.9	1.4	0.3	1.0	1.6	1.5	1.2	0.8	1.9	1.1	0.5	1.6	1.6	14.4
2. Somewhat acceptable	4.9	5.9	3.6	5.1	4.6	4.8	5.4	5.5	3.3	3.9	6.3	4.5	5.2	4.9	5.3	11.0
3. Acceptable	66.1	70.6	62.5	69.9	53.2	66.5	69.2	64.8	62.8	66.5	65.5	65.7	66.2	63.9	68.0	61.5
4. Desirable	27.6	21.5	33.0	23.7	41.9	27.8	23.9	28.3	32.7	28.8	26.3	28.7	28.1	29.6	25.0	13.1
Item 8170 Subject C05,N01 N	3358	1565	1653	2566	392	820	928	1072	538	1830	1315	1170	694	468	924	37
A08C: . . . most employees are of a different race?																
1. Not at all acceptable	12.5	14.5	10.2	14.6	3.9	10.4	14.0	15.4	7.2	12.1	13.2	11.1	10.7	14.8	14.5	22.2
2. Somewhat acceptable	33.5	33.3	34.0	36.9	25.0	36.4	32.9	34.7	27.6	33.9	33.1	34.2	32.8	31.2	35.2	22.6
3. Acceptable	45.1	44.6	45.6	43.6	51.3	42.8	46.8	41.7	52.7	45.7	44.9	45.8	46.3	46.9	42.2	42.7
4. Desirable	8.9	7.6	10.1	4.9	19.8	10.3	6.3	8.2	12.5	8.3	8.7	8.9	10.2	7.0	8.1	12.5
Item 8180 Subject C05,N01 N	3348	1562	1646	2560	391	817	924	1073	534	1827	1311	1167	691	468	921	37
A09: How would you feel about living in an area where . . .																
A09A: . . . all the neighbors are of your race?																
1. Not at all acceptable	4.8	3.8	5.8	2.5	14.2	5.5	1.9	5.8	6.5	5.3	4.0	5.5	5.9	4.9	2.7	6.5
2. Somewhat acceptable	9.3	8.9	9.6	6.5	19.6	10.1	7.6	8.6	12.6	9.5	9.0	8.7	9.5	11.8	8.3	5.9
3. Acceptable	49.7	49.8	49.7	50.4	46.2	52.3	52.1	43.5	54.2	51.6	47.3	51.8	49.5	48.4	48.4	37.4
4. Desirable	36.2	37.4	35.0	40.6	19.9	32.2	38.4	42.1	26.8	33.5	39.8	34.0	35.1	34.8	40.6	50.1
Item 8190 Subject N01 N	3352	1564	1647	2564	392	817	926	1075	535	1827	1311	1168	692	468	921	36
A09B: . . . some of the neighbors are of other races?																
1. Not at all acceptable	2.6	3.1	1.8	2.8	0.7	2.3	2.4	3.9	1.0	2.2	3.0	2.2	1.9	2.7	3.3	8.7
2. Somewhat acceptable	8.5	9.4	7.2	8.5	7.7	6.5	9.1	10.4	6.4	7.5	9.1	8.2	8.5	9.3	7.7	12.5
3. Acceptable	66.8	70.1	64.0	69.8	57.0	68.7	69.5	65.3	62.3	67.5	66.2	66.2	65.6	65.2	69.6	67.9
4. Desirable	22.1	17.4	27.0	18.9	34.5	22.5	19.0	20.3	30.4	22.8	21.8	23.4	24.1	22.7	19.3	10.9
Item 8200 Subject N01 N	3356	1564	1652	2563	394	820	927	1072	537	1827	1315	1167	696	469	923	37
A09C: . . . most of the neighbors are of other races?																
1. Not at all acceptable	21.5	23.7	19.0	25.0	8.6	21.0	20.9	26.3	13.9	21.1	22.2	19.6	19.3	24.2	24.9	25.1
2. Somewhat acceptable	35.3	34.3	36.7	38.7	25.0	35.6	37.0	36.4	29.9	36.5	33.6	34.7	33.6	34.4	38.5	31.1
3. Acceptable	36.6	36.2	37.0	33.1	49.1	34.3	38.9	30.9	47.4	36.3	37.9	39.7	37.2	36.9	31.8	40.5
4. Desirable	6.6	5.7	7.3	3.2	17.2	9.1	3.3	6.4	8.8	6.0	6.3	6.0	9.9	4.6	4.8	3.3
Item 8210 Subject N01 N	3349	1563	1646	2557	392	818	926	1070	536	1826	1309	1168	690	469	920	37
A10: How would you feel about having your (future) children go to schools where . . .																

QUESTIONNAIRE FORM 3 1983	TOTAL	SEX		RACE		REGION				4YR COLLEGE PLANS		ILLICIT DRUG USE: LIFETIME				
		M	F	White	Black	NE	NC	S	W	Yes	No	None	Marijuana Only	Few Pills	More Pills	Any Heroin
N (Weighted No. of Cases):	3382	1575	1660	2571	403	828	931	1081	541	1837	1322	1173	701	469	926	37
% of Weighted Total:	100.0	46.6	49.1	76.0	11.9	24.5	27.5	32.0	16.0	54.3	39.1	34.7	20.7	13.9	27.4	1.1

A10A: ... all the children are of your race?

	TOTAL	M	F	White	Black	NE	NC	S	W	Yes	No	None	Marijuana Only	Few Pills	More Pills	Any Heroin
1. Not at all acceptable	9.8	8.6	11.0	6.3	25.3	10.6	5.5	11.7	12.0	10.7	8.0	10.9	9.8	9.4	8.3	8.4
2. Somewhat acceptable	12.0	10.8	12.7	9.2	20.4	12.1	9.3	12.5	15.2	13.0	10.9	11.6	13.4	14.4	9.7	15.7
3. Acceptable	46.3	47.5	45.4	48.3	40.5	49.1	48.7	40.6	49.3	47.6	44.9	47.6	44.7	43.0	48.1	27.0
4. Desirable	32.0	33.1	30.8	36.3	13.7	28.3	36.5	35.1	23.5	28.8	36.2	29.9	32.0	33.2	33.8	48.9
Item 8220 Subject B03,N01 N	3352	1566	1648	2563	394	821	923	1073	535	1827	1310	1167	693	468	920	37

A10B: ... some of the children are of other races?

	TOTAL	M	F	White	Black	NE	NC	S	W	Yes	No	None	Marijuana Only	Few Pills	More Pills	Any Heroin
1. Not at all acceptable	1.7	2.2	1.0	1.7	0.5	1.5	2.0	1.9	1.0	1.1	2.1	1.4	1.0	2.6	1.4	12.5
2. Somewhat acceptable	5.9	6.3	4.7	5.6	6.1	5.5	5.0	7.0	6.1	4.7	7.3	6.1	4.0	7.6	5.3	10.1
3. Acceptable	62.9	67.8	59.1	65.4	55.6	62.5	68.3	61.3	57.5	62.2	64.3	60.4	63.5	60.1	67.6	68.3
4. Desirable	29.5	23.7	35.1	27.3	37.8	30.5	24.6	29.9	35.4	31.9	26.3	32.1	31.5	29.6	25.7	9.2
Item 8230 Subject B03,N01 N	3358	1568	1653	2565	395	822	925	1073	538	1828	1317	1167	696	469	923	37

A10C: ... most of the children are of other races?

	TOTAL	M	F	White	Black	NE	NC	S	W	Yes	No	None	Marijuana Only	Few Pills	More Pills	Any Heroin
1. Not at all acceptable	24.2	26.7	21.2	28.2	10.1	22.7	23.4	30.5	15.1	23.6	24.8	22.8	20.0	26.0	28.3	30.7
2. Somewhat acceptable	35.9	35.4	37.3	39.5	28.1	38.7	37.3	34.0	33.3	37.3	34.7	35.0	37.8	36.3	36.7	34.0
3. Acceptable	32.7	31.6	33.8	28.9	43.5	30.5	34.7	28.3	41.2	32.0	34.3	34.5	33.5	31.5	30.1	29.6
4. Desirable	7.2	6.3	7.7	3.5	18.3	8.1	4.6	7.2	10.4	7.1	6.2	7.7	8.7	6.2	4.9	5.7
Item 8240 Subject B03,N01 N	3345	1561	1647	2557	391	820	924	1069	532	1825	1305	1165	690	469	919	37

A11: What race are your close friends?

	TOTAL	M	F	White	Black	NE	NC	S	W	Yes	No	None	Marijuana Only	Few Pills	More Pills	Any Heroin
1. All my race	34.5	32.2	36.7	39.3	21.1	33.1	48.3	30.0	21.9	33.0	36.5	35.9	31.3	30.9	37.9	27.9
2. Almost all my race	30.0	31.8	28.2	33.4	20.9	31.4	30.5	29.1	28.6	31.3	28.3	29.7	32.0	32.2	27.9	34.2
3. Mostly my race	20.4	21.9	19.7	20.0	24.4	18.5	13.6	24.4	26.6	21.5	19.2	18.6	19.9	21.5	22.8	16.9
4. About half my race	9.3	8.8	9.3	5.7	18.8	8.9	4.7	12.2	12.0	8.2	10.9	8.7	10.7	10.0	8.1	11.4
5. Mostly other race(s)	3.6	3.6	3.6	1.1	7.7	4.7	1.7	2.8	6.6	3.3	3.3	4.3	4.4	3.4	1.7	7.3
6. Almost all other race(s)	2.3	1.7	2.5	0.5	7.1	3.3	1.2	1.4	4.3	2.6	1.7	2.9	1.7	1.9	1.6	2.4
Item 8250 Subject N03 N	3336	1553	1646	2549	392	820	921	1065	530	1818	1307	1166	690	466	912	37

A12: What race are the people in your neighborhood?

	TOTAL	M	F	White	Black	NE	NC	S	W	Yes	No	None	Marijuana Only	Few Pills	More Pills	Any Heroin
1. All my race	49.9	50.3	49.5	56.3	35.8	45.7	67.1	49.2	27.9	48.7	51.7	52.3	49.1	47.1	49.6	52.0
2. Almost all my race	25.2	24.6	25.9	27.8	18.6	27.5	19.8	26.0	29.7	27.7	22.4	23.1	23.8	27.6	28.6	13.2
3. Mostly my race	11.3	12.1	10.7	10.8	12.7	11.1	6.5	12.0	18.2	10.6	12.2	10.1	11.2	12.6	11.9	17.0
4. About half my race	6.4	5.9	6.8	3.4	16.3	7.1	4.0	7.1	8.3	5.3	7.5	5.9	8.1	6.0	5.8	5.3
5. Mostly other race(s)	3.5	3.8	3.2	0.9	10.0	4.0	1.3	3.0	7.8	3.3	3.3	3.5	4.9	3.2	2.2	6.0
6. Almost all other race(s)	3.7	3.3	3.9	0.8	6.7	4.6	1.4	2.7	8.1	4.4	2.9	5.1	3.0	3.5	2.0	6.5
Item 8260 Subject N03 N	3338	1555	1645	2550	392	821	921	1063	532	1813	1311	1163	692	466	916	37

A13: What race were the students in the elementary school where you spent the most time?

	TOTAL	M	F	White	Black	NE	NC	S	W	Yes	No	None	Marijuana Only	Few Pills	More Pills	Any Heroin
1. All my race	34.1	32.9	35.3	38.6	18.9	33.0	56.0	23.8	18.3	34.3	33.9	36.4	33.5	31.1	34.1	27.2
2. Almost all my race	29.6	31.6	27.8	33.2	18.0	33.1	25.7	27.5	35.1	30.0	29.4	28.6	30.3	28.4	30.5	40.3
3. Mostly my race	14.2	13.9	14.3	14.5	13.0	13.7	8.2	18.0	18.1	14.7	13.9	12.8	12.7	18.7	14.8	10.4
4. About half my race	13.3	12.9	13.7	10.6	29.2	11.0	6.2	21.2	13.2	12.3	14.3	12.7	13.4	13.0	14.1	7.4
5. Mostly other race(s)	5.1	5.3	4.7	2.0	13.3	4.2	1.9	7.1	8.2	5.1	5.1	5.1	5.3	5.3	4.7	3.5
6. Almost all other race(s)	3.7	3.3	4.1	1.1	7.6	5.0	2.0	2.4	7.2	3.6	3.4	4.3	4.7	3.6	1.8	11.2
Item 8270 Subject B03,N03 N	3330	1553	1646	2549	393	815	922	1066	527	1813	1308	1159	691	467	912	37

A14: What race are the students in your present school (if you are in school)?

	TOTAL	M	F	White	Black	NE	NC	S	W	Yes	No	None	Marijuana Only	Few Pills	More Pills	Any Heroin
1. All my race	13.1	14.4	12.1	15.6	4.1	7.5	31.6	5.8	4.6	13.0	13.6	14.5	11.6	11.4	13.8	16.2
2. Almost all my race	31.6	33.1	30.5	37.0	15.6	42.3	37.7	21.6	24.5	32.6	30.5	30.6	31.9	31.4	33.1	30.6
3. Mostly my race	23.5	24.4	22.5	25.8	16.6	24.9	16.2	24.8	31.4	24.5	22.7	21.4	25.5	26.1	23.8	25.5
4. About half my race	20.5	18.5	22.4	17.1	35.8	10.8	9.9	36.4	22.1	19.1	22.6	20.0	20.0	19.6	21.9	11.5
5. Mostly other race(s)	7.1	6.2	7.9	3.4	17.3	8.2	2.1	8.8	10.9	7.4	6.1	8.2	7.4	7.0	5.0	10.9
6. Almost all other race(s)	4.1	3.4	4.6	1.1	10.6	6.3	2.6	2.7	6.4	3.4	4.6	5.3	3.7	4.5	2.5	5.2
Item 8280 Subject B03,N03 N	3325	1553	1641	2546	392	814	919	1066	526	1810	1306	1158	690	466	911	37

QUESTIONNAIRE FORM 3 1983	TOTAL	SEX		RACE		REGION				4YR COLLEGE PLANS		ILLICIT DRUG USE: LIFETIME				
		M	F	White	Black	NE	NC	S	W	Yes	No	None	Mari-juana Only	Few Pills	More Pills	Any Her-oin
N (Weighted No. of Cases):	3382	1575	1660	2571	403	828	931	1081	541	1837	1322	1173	701	469	926	37
% of Weighted Total:	100.0	46.6	49.1	76.0	11.9	24.5	27.5	32.0	16.0	54.3	39.1	34.7	20.7	13.9	27.4	1.1

A15: What race are the people that you work with on your job (if you have a job)?

1. All my race	44.8	44.8	45.2	53.3	8.9	42.0	63.6	33.4	37.5	42.8	48.8	47.7	41.9	41.7	46.2	47.7
2. Almost all my race	20.8	21.3	20.3	23.4	11.2	24.6	17.3	21.7	19.5	22.3	19.2	21.0	19.0	17.9	24.1	13.9
3. Mostly my race	12.5	13.0	12.1	13.0	11.8	12.7	8.2	15.7	13.7	13.9	11.1	10.3	13.7	17.3	11.5	13.3
4. About half my race	10.5	9.7	11.0	7.6	27.4	7.5	5.4	17.6	10.6	9.8	10.7	9.3	11.3	11.2	10.4	10.9
5. Mostly other race(s)	6.6	6.5	6.7	2.0	26.7	6.4	2.8	9.3	8.5	6.2	6.6	5.3	8.8	7.2	5.3	7.8
6. Almost all other race(s)	4.8	4.7	4.8	0.8	14.0	6.8	2.7	2.4	10.1	5.1	3.7	6.4	5.4	4.6	2.7	6.5
Item 8290　Subject N03　　N	2712	1302	1296	2121	271	666	771	835	440	1453	1082	884	569	397	774	33

A16: How often do you do things (like having a conversation, eating together, playing sports) with people of other races?

1. Not at all	11.8	10.7	13.0	13.3	4.7	9.4	20.9	8.4	6.5	9.3	14.9	11.9	10.6	10.0	13.8	19.0
2. A little	30.9	31.2	30.3	34.6	22.0	33.8	34.5	28.5	24.9	30.4	31.8	30.9	32.8	29.9	30.0	22.0
3. Some	36.3	37.2	35.4	35.9	38.3	34.8	31.8	39.4	40.3	36.3	35.9	36.5	34.1	37.3	37.4	31.7
4. A lot	21.0	20.9	21.3	16.1	35.0	22.0	12.9	23.7	28.3	24.0	17.5	20.7	22.5	22.7	18.9	27.3
Item 8300　Subject N03　　N	3341	1558	1647	2551	395	819	924	1063	534	1817	1312	1164	691	468	917	37

A17: Generally, how do you feel about the experiences you have had with people of other races?

5. Very good	24.1	19.1	29.2	21.9	31.1	22.5	25.2	20.6	31.8	27.6	20.1	28.4	25.0	22.4	19.4	19.1
4. Mostly good	41.1	40.3	42.0	42.4	38.1	41.4	42.0	41.3	38.5	41.9	41.0	41.0	40.6	45.5	40.0	30.4
3. Mixed	31.6	35.9	27.4	32.2	29.4	33.5	29.5	34.3	26.6	28.1	35.4	27.9	31.3	29.6	36.7	37.8
2. Mostly bad	2.3	3.1	1.2	2.5	1.3	1.6	2.2	3.0	1.9	1.9	2.6	2.3	2.4	1.3	2.5	6.7
1. Very bad	1.0	1.5	0.2	0.9	-	1.0	1.1	0.8	1.1	0.5	0.8	0.4	0.6	1.1	1.5	6.0
Item 8310　Subject N03　　N	3331	1556	1640	2542	394	818	918	1061	533	1812	1307	1160	690	468	913	37

A18: The next questions are about some of your own plans. Are you married or engaged?

1. Married–SKIP TO Q.A20	0.7	0.3	1.0	0.5	-	0.8	0.8	0.7	0.5	0.3	1.4	0.5	0.5	1.1	1.0	1.6
2. Engaged	8.2	5.3	11.1	7.9	8.8	6.8	7.9	10.1	7.3	5.0	12.7	6.5	7.3	10.7	9.3	19.3
3. Neither	91.0	94.4	87.9	91.6	91.2	92.4	91.3	89.2	92.2	94.6	85.9	93.0	92.2	88.2	89.8	79.1
Item 8320　Subject D01,R01　　N	3094	1424	1553	2420	325	755	862	978	498	1727	1185	1080	633	441	859	34

A19: If it were just up to you, what would be the ideal time for you to get married?

1. Within the next year or so	7.5	3.5	11.5	7.5	6.3	6.5	8.9	8.3	5.2	3.2	13.4	5.7	6.5	8.6	9.9	12.3
2. Two or three years from now	19.1	13.7	23.6	20.4	13.7	14.8	21.0	21.8	16.8	12.4	28.9	18.9	16.7	18.0	21.5	17.8
3. Four or five years from now	32.5	31.9	33.1	34.3	25.4	29.4	37.0	32.5	29.6	36.1	28.8	35.3	33.6	30.4	29.9	12.8
4. Over five years from now	35.8	45.2	27.5	34.6	41.4	43.5	29.4	31.4	44.1	44.5	23.3	36.1	37.7	37.5	33.4	44.8
5. I don't want to marry	5.0	5.7	4.3	3.4	13.2	5.8	3.8	5.9	4.3	3.9	5.6	4.0	5.5	5.5	5.3	12.3
Item 8330　Subject D01　　N★	3179	1484	1578	2463	363	776	885	1007	512	1767	1218	1112	657	448	874	34

A20: Have you thought at all about whether you'd like to have children or how many you'd like to have?

3. I've thought about it a lot	40.0	26.9	52.7	39.1	49.1	40.3	39.1	42.0	37.2	37.7	43.2	39.0	38.9	41.9	41.1	31.7
2. I've thought about it a little	49.8	57.4	43.0	51.4	40.3	50.3	50.6	48.0	51.5	53.0	45.8	49.9	51.1	51.5	49.0	36.7
1. I haven't thought about it at all	10.1	15.7	4.3	9.6	10.5	9.4	10.3	10.0	11.4	9.3	11.0	11.1	10.0	6.7	9.9	31.6
Item 8340　Subject D02　　N	3250	1525	1596	2493	385	793	899	1042	516	1780	1275	1126	676	457	895	37

A21: All things considered, if you could have exactly the number of children you want, what number would you choose to have?

1. None	3.6	3.2	3.9	3.4	2.8	2.9	3.6	4.1	3.4	3.5	3.6	3.0	3.2	2.8	4.8	8.4
2. One	5.7	4.8	6.1	4.8	12.6	6.5	5.0	6.8	3.4	5.1	5.7	4.7	5.9	5.4	6.2	11.2
3. Two	46.6	46.9	46.4	47.5	43.7	40.4	44.3	52.9	47.5	44.4	49.9	41.7	47.2	50.2	50.9	48.7
4. Three	20.9	21.2	20.2	20.5	21.7	21.2	22.8	19.7	19.3	21.3	20.2	22.4	24.2	18.5	17.7	12.5
5. Four	10.3	8.6	12.0	10.3	11.3	11.4	11.3	8.6	10.2	11.6	9.1	12.7	7.8	10.6	9.1	6.6
6. Five	2.5	2.2	2.9	2.6	1.3	3.9	2.1	1.2	3.8	3.1	2.0	3.0	2.3	3.3	2.0	-
7. Six or more	2.4	2.3	2.6	2.3	2.2	3.5	1.8	1.5	3.4	2.4	2.0	3.0	2.1	1.7	2.2	2.6
8. Don't know	8.1	10.7	6.0	8.5	4.5	10.1	9.1	5.2	9.0	8.5	7.6	9.5	7.3	7.7	7.0	10.1
Item 8350　Subject D02　　N	3322	1555	1637	2540	394	815	918	1063	525	1808	1306	1154	694	466	909	36

★=excludes respondents for whom question was inappropriate.

QUESTIONNAIRE FORM 3 1983	TOTAL	SEX		RACE		REGION				4YR COLLEGE PLANS		ILLICIT DRUG USE: LIFETIME				
		M	F	White	Black	NE	NC	S	W	Yes	No	None	Mari- juana Only	Few Pills	More Pills	Any Her- oin
N (Weighted No. of Cases):	3382	1575	1660	2571	403	828	931	1081	541	1837	1322	1173	701	469	926	37
% of Weighted Total:	100.0	46.6	49.1	76.0	11.9	24.5	27.5	32.0	16.0	54.3	39.1	34.7	20.7	13.9	27.4	1.1

A22: If the "population explosion" were NOT a problem, would you choose to have a larger number of children?

4. Yes, I'm sure I would want more	6.7	6.0	7.6	6.3	4.0	8.8	7.4	4.8	6.1	6.4	6.6	7.4	5.7	8.4	5.4	5.8
3. I probably would want more	12.5	11.9	12.7	12.5	11.9	13.5	12.8	12.1	11.4	12.3	13.6	13.5	11.2	13.3	12.4	2.6
2. I probably would not want more	33.8	33.8	33.9	34.5	32.9	31.7	35.7	33.1	35.3	35.0	31.8	32.5	37.8	36.3	31.2	35.2
1. I'm sure I would not want more	30.3	28.1	32.3	30.0	36.8	25.3	27.8	35.9	31.5	30.2	31.2	28.3	29.7	28.7	34.8	32.7
8. Don't know, no idea	16.6	20.3	13.4	16.6	14.4	20.7	16.3	14.2	15.7	16.1	16.8	18.4	15.6	13.3	16.4	23.7
Item 8360 Subject D02,E01 N	3350	1570	1647	2562	397	819	926	1072	533	1825	1315	1165	696	467	924	37

A23: If it were just up to you, how soon after getting married would you want to have your first child?

1. I don't want to have children (or get married)	4.4	4.1	4.5	4.1	5.2	3.3	4.4	5.1	4.5	3.8	5.1	3.7	4.3	4.3	5.1	8.4
2. I wouldn't wait at all	5.0	7.3	2.6	4.4	7.0	4.7	5.4	4.1	6.4	4.2	5.7	5.1	4.5	4.5	4.5	11.6
3. I would wait one year	26.7	29.2	24.1	25.8	30.9	28.8	25.9	26.9	24.8	25.6	27.3	27.6	28.1	28.5	23.5	25.3
4. I would wait two years	31.1	26.3	36.5	32.3	27.6	31.2	33.0	30.1	29.9	33.8	28.8	33.3	27.8	32.5	31.3	19.3
5. I would wait three years	14.0	12.0	15.8	14.7	10.1	12.7	14.5	14.2	14.8	14.1	14.2	13.0	13.9	14.5	16.0	10.5
6. I would wait four or five years	7.9	6.1	9.2	8.5	5.1	6.0	7.8	10.1	6.5	8.7	6.9	7.1	7.9	7.6	8.9	8.2
7. I would wait more than five years	2.0	1.9	2.1	2.1	1.2	2.0	1.8	2.1	1.9	2.0	2.1	1.8	2.6	2.3	1.5	-
8. Don't know, or already have a child	8.9	13.1	5.1	8.3	12.9	11.4	7.3	7.3	11.1	8.0	10.0	8.3	10.8	5.9	9.3	16.7
Item 8370 Subject D02 N	3313	1551	1632	2534	393	809	916	1058	529	1807	1304	1156	693	464	903	36

A24: Now we'd like you to make some ratings of how good or bad a job you feel each of the following organizations is doing for the country as a whole. For each one, mark the circle that best describes how you feel.

How good or bad a job is being done for the country as a whole by...

A24A: Large corporations?

1. Very poor	2.7	4.1	1.4	2.7	2.0	2.6	2.7	2.2	4.0	2.5	3.1	2.6	3.9	1.6	2.6	2.0
2. Poor	9.6	12.4	7.1	10.6	6.9	8.7	12.2	6.6	12.4	9.7	9.5	8.0	10.5	11.3	10.2	14.3
3. Fair	33.6	35.5	31.8	33.2	32.4	30.9	35.8	34.8	31.4	33.6	33.6	33.7	35.2	32.0	33.6	27.0
4. Good	31.1	29.6	32.5	32.7	27.5	33.0	29.8	31.5	29.8	32.3	29.7	32.4	29.6	30.5	31.0	29.7
5. Very good	7.6	7.4	7.9	6.8	12.4	7.7	6.9	9.4	4.9	7.5	7.6	8.5	6.5	7.7	6.9	13.3
8. No opinion	15.4	11.0	19.3	13.8	18.8	17.0	12.7	15.5	17.5	14.4	16.5	14.8	14.2	16.9	15.8	13.7
Item 8380 Subject K02 N	3332	1564	1637	2551	393	811	924	1065	532	1824	1309	1164	693	467	915	37

A24B: Major labor unions?

1. Very poor	5.2	7.3	2.9	5.8	1.3	3.6	5.9	6.1	4.6	6.0	4.1	5.3	5.1	4.8	5.7	6.1
2. Poor	14.6	18.7	10.5	15.3	9.3	14.8	15.7	12.9	15.5	15.6	13.0	15.7	15.8	12.5	13.2	13.2
3. Fair	32.7	33.3	32.3	32.9	34.0	29.9	34.5	35.6	27.9	32.5	33.7	32.4	33.5	35.0	31.0	27.6
4. Good	25.5	24.5	26.8	25.2	27.0	28.2	24.1	23.0	28.7	26.1	24.4	22.3	26.0	28.9	27.0	40.6
5. Very good	4.5	4.6	4.2	3.7	7.2	5.2	4.5	3.7	5.0	4.1	5.0	5.2	4.6	3.3	4.6	-
8. No opinion	17.5	11.6	23.3	17.0	21.2	18.3	15.2	18.6	18.2	15.7	19.8	19.1	14.9	15.6	18.5	12.5
Item 8390 Subject K02 N	3317	1559	1628	2544	390	804	923	1057	532	1817	1303	1162	685	467	910	36

A24C: The nation's colleges and universities?

1. Very poor	1.2	1.4	0.5	0.7	1.1	0.8	1.6	1.3	0.9	0.4	1.6	0.7	1.4	0.6	1.4	9.5
2. Poor	2.5	3.0	2.1	2.2	3.5	3.2	2.6	2.1	1.8	1.8	3.3	2.5	3.1	1.5	2.3	2.0
3. Fair	16.8	17.7	15.6	15.3	24.9	17.7	16.2	17.5	14.9	14.9	18.9	17.3	17.4	14.6	16.3	23.2
4. Good	41.7	41.7	42.5	43.4	35.9	40.3	43.2	40.8	42.9	43.6	40.6	41.6	43.1	42.1	41.4	37.6
5. Very good	33.1	32.1	34.2	34.0	28.4	32.0	32.1	34.5	33.7	36.5	28.7	33.2	32.1	37.3	32.3	19.7
8. No opinion	4.8	4.1	5.1	4.3	6.1	6.0	4.4	3.7	5.9	2.7	6.9	4.6	2.8	3.7	6.3	8.0
Item 8400 Subject B10,K02 N	3329	1564	1634	2551	394	809	923	1065	532	1824	1306	1165	693	461	917	37

QUESTIONNAIRE FORM 3 1983	TOTAL	SEX		RACE		REGION				4YR COLLEGE PLANS		ILLICIT DRUG USE: LIFETIME				
		M	F	White	Black	NE	NC	S	W	Yes	No	None	Mari-juana Only	Few Pills	More Pills	Any Her-oin
N (Weighted No. of Cases):	3382	1575	1660	2571	403	828	931	1081	541	1837	1322	1173	701	469	926	37
% of Weighted Total:	100.0	46.6	49.1	76.0	11.9	24.5	27.5	32.0	16.0	54.3	39.1	34.7	20.7	13.9	27.4	1.1

A24D: The nation's public schools?

1. Very poor	4.3	5.5	2.5	3.9	3.4	4.7	4.9	3.6	3.9	3.9	4.6	3.9	5.4	3.5	4.2	7.0
2. Poor	14.7	16.2	13.5	15.2	7.1	16.4	15.1	10.3	19.9	16.6	12.2	14.5	13.5	13.5	16.4	18.6
3. Fair	33.4	32.7	34.3	33.6	38.1	36.0	31.4	33.6	32.2	34.1	32.2	32.7	30.7	37.7	34.9	21.5
4. Good	32.4	30.6	34.4	33.0	32.6	29.4	33.6	34.6	30.7	32.4	32.7	33.9	33.8	29.6	31.4	20.5
5. Very good	11.9	11.3	12.4	11.2	15.1	8.8	12.1	14.8	10.4	10.8	13.5	11.9	13.5	12.9	9.8	15.4
8. No opinion	3.3	3.7	2.9	3.0	3.7	4.5	2.8	3.1	2.9	2.2	4.8	3.1	3.2	2.7	3.3	16.9
Item 8410 Subject B10,K02 N	3327	1563	1633	2551	388	811	918	1065	532	1821	1308	1163	688	465	918	37

A24E: Churches and religious organizations?

1. Very poor	2.1	3.3	0.9	2.1	1.3	1.6	1.2	2.4	3.9	2.0	2.3	2.0	2.5	1.2	2.4	2.6
2. Poor	5.5	6.3	4.7	5.3	4.7	6.6	5.9	3.8	6.5	5.8	4.9	5.0	5.5	5.0	5.7	19.7
3. Fair	24.2	25.0	23.6	24.9	18.2	26.7	25.7	20.7	25.2	24.0	24.0	22.7	25.0	24.0	26.2	20.3
4. Good	36.0	34.3	38.1	37.1	35.8	35.7	35.7	39.4	30.6	37.0	36.2	38.7	34.2	35.6	35.2	20.4
5. Very good	20.6	19.0	21.7	19.6	27.8	15.6	20.9	25.9	17.0	20.7	19.7	21.9	20.6	22.3	17.4	25.0
8. No opinion	11.5	12.0	11.1	11.0	12.2	13.9	10.7	7.9	16.8	10.4	12.9	9.8	12.2	11.8	13.1	12.1
Item 8420 Subject G,K02 N	3333	1564	1638	2556	391	811	925	1063	533	1823	1311	1163	693	467	918	37

A24F: The national news media (TV, magazines, news services)?

1. Very poor	3.1	4.4	1.9	3.2	1.6	2.4	2.7	3.6	4.1	3.1	3.1	2.7	3.8	3.7	2.9	2.4
2. Poor	7.6	9.0	6.1	8.2	4.4	7.5	7.3	7.7	7.8	9.3	5.4	8.4	7.3	7.2	6.9	7.5
3. Fair	26.1	25.8	26.8	26.9	22.8	28.9	27.8	23.0	25.0	27.2	25.4	25.1	27.3	26.6	26.3	23.5
4. Good	36.1	35.9	36.3	36.8	31.2	34.8	38.8	34.8	35.8	36.3	35.6	35.3	37.0	37.0	36.6	19.3
5. Very good	22.1	21.0	23.0	20.3	33.7	22.1	18.3	25.7	21.7	20.8	23.4	23.7	20.3	21.0	22.0	26.7
8. No opinion	5.0	4.0	5.9	4.6	6.4	4.3	5.1	5.3	5.6	3.2	7.1	4.8	4.2	4.5	5.3	20.6
Item 8430 Subject K02 N	3331	1563	1636	2554	391	809	926	1062	533	1822	1309	1160	693	467	918	37

A24G: The President and his administration?

1. Very poor	12.6	12.0	13.0	9.3	29.5	14.6	13.0	12.1	9.6	11.7	13.3	8.9	16.0	14.5	13.2	22.0
2. Poor	16.4	15.9	16.8	16.6	15.9	19.9	16.7	14.7	14.1	15.9	16.9	14.7	16.5	16.6	18.6	15.5
3. Fair	31.2	31.1	31.5	33.0	24.1	33.4	32.9	29.6	28.4	32.4	30.3	30.7	32.1	32.9	30.7	36.2
4. Good	22.8	25.1	20.9	25.6	8.4	17.7	23.7	23.5	27.8	24.5	20.7	26.4	20.0	23.5	20.9	10.2
5. Very good	8.3	9.7	7.1	9.4	3.4	6.1	7.2	10.4	9.5	8.8	7.8	11.1	7.8	6.4	5.9	6.7
8. No opinion	8.7	6.3	10.7	7.8	11.0	8.4	6.6	9.7	10.6	6.8	11.0	8.3	7.6	6.2	10.8	9.4
Item 8440 Subject H04,K02 N	3335	1565	1639	2557	392	810	926	1066	533	1823	1311	1164	693	467	918	37

A24H: Congress–that is, the U.S. Senate and House of Representatives?

1. Very poor	6.6	7.7	5.1	5.6	9.7	6.5	7.4	6.8	4.7	6.2	6.8	5.0	7.1	8.7	6.6	20.1
2. Poor	13.9	15.2	12.6	13.5	15.1	16.2	14.2	12.1	13.4	14.2	12.2	13.4	15.8	15.8	12.2	10.2
3. Fair	40.2	41.6	39.1	41.2	39.6	38.7	43.3	40.4	36.6	40.3	41.1	39.7	40.1	41.0	40.1	43.3
4. Good	20.0	20.9	19.4	21.5	13.0	18.2	19.0	21.0	22.1	22.1	17.4	21.9	20.3	18.7	18.7	13.0
5. Very good	3.2	2.7	3.6	2.9	3.0	2.3	2.9	4.0	3.5	3.1	3.6	3.8	3.2	2.6	2.8	1.5
8. No opinion	16.3	11.9	20.2	15.3	19.7	18.1	13.2	15.7	19.8	14.1	18.9	16.2	13.4	13.2	19.7	11.8
Item 8450 Subject H04,K02 N	3326	1563	1632	2551	392	808	922	1064	532	1820	1307	1158	693	465	915	37

A24I: The U.S. Supreme Court?

1. Very poor	3.8	3.9	3.6	3.3	3.7	4.3	4.4	3.2	3.3	3.3	4.1	3.0	4.3	4.7	3.7	12.3
2. Poor	6.7	7.3	6.2	6.6	6.0	7.3	6.8	6.4	6.1	6.2	6.9	6.3	6.1	8.1	6.6	8.0
3. Fair	32.5	30.8	33.5	32.7	35.9	31.8	34.9	33.5	27.5	32.2	33.6	34.1	29.2	33.1	32.6	33.8
4. Good	28.8	31.5	26.8	30.5	21.4	26.8	30.3	27.2	32.1	31.2	25.7	27.2	30.2	28.0	30.7	20.2
5. Very good	7.6	9.3	5.9	7.3	9.4	5.9	6.6	9.6	8.1	8.4	6.6	8.5	10.0	7.0	4.9	4.6
8. No opinion	20.6	17.2	24.1	19.6	23.6	23.9	17.0	20.2	22.7	18.6	23.1	20.9	20.2	19.1	21.6	21.1
Item 8460 Subject H04,K02 N	3320	1561	1631	2546	390	809	920	1058	533	1819	1302	1157	692	465	914	37

A24J: All the courts and the justice system in general?

1. Very poor	7.5	8.9	5.8	6.8	5.1	9.8	6.4	6.5	7.8	7.2	6.9	5.6	6.7	9.2	8.7	25.1
2. Poor	16.9	18.6	15.2	18.0	10.8	19.4	15.1	16.5	17.1	17.2	16.1	16.7	15.5	18.8	17.2	17.8
3. Fair	36.6	35.6	37.6	36.8	42.2	37.8	36.4	37.9	32.2	37.6	36.1	37.3	38.3	36.3	34.9	33.6
4. Good	21.9	21.5	22.7	23.1	15.9	17.2	24.7	21.4	25.4	23.2	20.9	21.9	22.7	19.9	23.1	9.7
5. Very good	3.8	3.9	3.7	3.2	7.6	2.9	3.4	5.1	3.5	3.5	4.3	3.8	3.9	5.5	2.7	3.4
8. No opinion	13.3	11.5	15.0	12.1	18.4	12.9	13.9	12.6	14.1	11.3	15.8	14.7	12.8	10.3	13.4	10.3
Item 8470 Subject H04,K02 N	3328	1564	1633	2550	393	811	922	1065	531	1818	1310	1163	693	464	915	37

QUESTIONNAIRE FORM 3 1983	TOTAL	SEX		RACE		REGION				4YR COLLEGE PLANS		ILLICIT DRUG USE: LIFETIME				
		M	F	White	Black	NE	NC	S	W	Yes	No	None	Marijuana Only	Few Pills	More Pills	Any Heroin
N (Weighted No. of Cases):	3382	1575	1660	2571	403	828	931	1081	541	1837	1322	1173	701	469	926	37
% of Weighted Total:	100.0	46.6	49.1	76.0	11.9	24.5	27.5	32.0	16.0	54.3	39.1	34.7	20.7	13.9	27.4	1.1

A24K: The police and other law enforcement agencies?

	TOTAL	M	F	White	Black	NE	NC	S	W	Yes	No	None	Mari-juana Only	Few Pills	More Pills	Any Heroin
1. Very poor	6.0	7.5	4.4	4.9	9.7	8.2	5.8	4.9	5.0	5.2	6.4	3.6	5.2	7.5	7.7	24.5
2. Poor	13.4	13.5	13.3	13.1	15.7	14.1	12.5	14.9	11.1	12.7	14.1	12.2	13.5	16.1	13.4	18.8
3. Fair	38.2	37.7	38.9	38.9	38.3	38.4	40.7	37.0	35.7	39.7	36.6	36.2	39.1	40.3	39.0	38.8
4. Good	30.2	30.3	30.3	31.8	21.5	27.1	30.3	30.4	34.3	32.2	27.9	35.3	30.5	24.3	27.5	5.6
5. Very good	7.2	6.6	7.5	6.9	8.3	6.5	5.6	8.6	8.4	6.7	8.2	7.1	7.5	8.4	6.9	2.0
8. No opinion	5.0	4.3	5.6	4.3	6.5	5.7	5.1	4.2	5.5	3.5	6.8	5.6	4.1	3.5	5.4	10.3
Item 8480 Subject K02 N	3331	1562	1638	2555	390	808	926	1064	533	1821	1311	1164	693	464	918	37

A24L: The U.S. military?

	TOTAL	M	F	White	Black	NE	NC	S	W	Yes	No	None	Mari-juana Only	Few Pills	More Pills	Any Heroin
1. Very poor	3.2	4.6	2.0	2.9	2.1	3.0	3.8	1.9	5.1	3.7	2.6	2.9	3.3	2.3	3.8	12.3
2. Poor	4.7	5.3	4.0	5.1	2.3	4.3	4.3	4.7	5.8	5.4	3.8	4.1	4.1	5.5	5.2	11.7
3. Fair	23.5	22.7	24.9	23.4	21.2	26.4	25.5	20.1	22.4	24.8	21.7	25.3	23.7	21.7	22.7	15.2
4. Good	36.7	37.6	35.3	37.7	33.4	36.1	36.8	39.1	32.9	38.0	35.2	35.5	38.9	40.9	35.1	27.3
5. Very good	19.6	20.6	18.4	18.8	29.2	15.4	18.1	24.2	19.2	15.6	24.5	19.5	19.0	18.0	20.2	21.1
8. No opinion	12.3	9.2	15.4	12.1	11.7	14.8	11.6	9.9	14.7	12.5	12.1	12.6	11.0	11.6	13.0	12.3
Item 8490 Subject K02,L04 N	3327	1563	1633	2553	392	808	924	1062	532	1820	1308	1158	692	467	917	37

A25: All things considered, do you think the armed services presently have too much or too little influence on the way this country is run?

	TOTAL	M	F	White	Black	NE	NC	S	W	Yes	No	None	Mari-juana Only	Few Pills	More Pills	Any Heroin
1. Far too little	3.6	4.2	2.6	3.5	3.2	2.5	3.1	4.8	3.9	2.6	4.6	3.4	3.3	3.2	3.8	10.0
2. Too little	17.5	16.9	18.1	17.0	18.8	18.5	15.3	21.2	12.1	16.5	17.8	17.1	18.3	20.7	15.6	16.3
3. About right	61.6	60.6	62.7	63.0	56.3	59.1	62.1	62.7	62.4	60.7	64.1	62.5	60.1	59.9	63.0	63.0
4. Too much	13.7	13.6	14.0	13.4	16.5	15.5	17.1	8.9	15.0	16.0	10.5	12.6	14.5	13.8	14.8	10.7
5. Far too much	3.6	4.7	2.6	3.1	5.2	4.4	2.4	2.5	6.6	4.2	3.0	4.5	3.8	2.4	2.9	-
Item 8500 Subject K03,L04 N	3285	1543	1613	2516	391	794	910	1057	524	1796	1291	1140	689	460	902	37

A26: Do you think the U.S. spends too much or too little on the armed services?

	TOTAL	M	F	White	Black	NE	NC	S	W	Yes	No	None	Mari-juana Only	Few Pills	More Pills	Any Heroin
1. Far too little	6.1	8.7	3.2	6.2	4.3	3.8	4.2	10.2	4.7	5.4	7.2	5.9	6.0	6.2	5.9	12.6
2. Too little	21.6	25.3	17.6	22.1	20.7	17.6	19.5	27.4	19.7	21.8	21.6	21.0	22.1	21.0	21.4	40.9
3. About right	38.5	34.0	43.2	39.0	36.1	37.6	37.9	39.6	39.0	34.5	42.8	39.2	35.9	40.8	39.4	19.0
4. Too much	24.4	22.0	27.0	23.9	30.7	28.3	29.5	18.2	22.0	27.0	21.1	25.7	26.0	25.7	21.9	10.1
5. Far too much	9.4	9.9	9.0	8.7	8.1	12.7	8.9	4.6	14.6	11.3	7.4	8.3	10.0	6.3	11.4	17.4
Item 8510 Subject K03,L04 N	3293	1554	1610	2520	392	795	916	1054	528	1800	1295	1143	692	457	909	37

A27: Next are some questions which ask about your experiences and attitudes concerning particular drugs. First we want your answers about some drugs that can be bought at a drugstore without a doctor's prescription–sometimes called over-the-counter or non-prescription drugs.

DURING THE LAST 12 MONTHS, on how many occasions have you...

A27A: . . . used non-prescription drugs which are supposed to relieve pain (such as aspirin, Anacin, Bufferin, or Excedrin)?

	TOTAL	M	F	White	Black	NE	NC	S	W	Yes	No	None	Mari-juana Only	Few Pills	More Pills	Any Heroin
1. 0 occasions	9.4	11.0	7.5	6.2	24.0	9.8	7.6	11.2	8.4	7.8	11.2	12.6	8.1	7.8	6.9	8.1
2. 1-2	19.2	22.1	15.4	16.7	25.4	20.9	17.0	17.6	23.7	17.6	20.3	23.2	20.7	16.6	13.3	9.3
3. 3-5	17.1	19.1	15.4	16.8	18.8	16.9	14.3	19.0	18.6	16.8	17.7	18.8	17.0	19.8	13.5	30.2
4. 6-9	14.1	14.8	13.8	15.2	10.9	14.6	16.1	12.6	13.2	14.7	13.6	14.5	12.9	16.2	14.1	6.8
5. 10-19	16.5	14.9	18.9	18.7	9.0	16.2	16.1	18.0	14.6	18.1	14.4	14.5	18.8	15.9	18.5	6.7
6. 20-39	11.1	8.6	13.8	12.8	6.0	9.6	14.2	10.9	8.3	12.4	10.5	8.4	11.9	13.5	13.4	7.3
7. 40 or more	12.5	9.7	15.3	13.4	5.9	12.0	14.6	10.6	13.2	12.6	12.2	8.0	10.5	10.2	20.3	31.6
Item 8520 Subject A01b N	3331	1562	1640	2557	397	810	926	1065	529	1820	1309	1167	699	464	915	37

QUESTIONNAIRE FORM 3 1983	TOTAL	SEX		RACE		REGION				4YR COLLEGE PLANS		ILLICIT DRUG USE: LIFETIME				
		M	F	White	Black	NE	NC	S	W	Yes	No	None	Mari-juana Only	Few Pills	More Pills	Any Her-oin
N (Weighted No. of Cases):	3382	1575	1660	2571	403	828	931	1081	541	1837	1322	1173	701	469	926	37
% of Weighted Total:	100.0	46.6	49.1	76.0	11.9	24.5	27.5	32.0	16.0	54.3	39.1	34.7	20.7	13.9	27.4	1.1

A27B: ... used non-prescription drugs that are supposed to help people get to sleep (such as Sleep-Eze, Sominex, or Nytol)?

1. 0 occasions	89.9	90.4	90.1	89.9	91.5	91.5	89.7	89.4	88.7	90.8	88.5	94.5	93.0	86.8	84.4	65.2
2. 1-2	5.5	5.3	5.5	5.9	2.6	3.7	6.3	5.1	7.3	5.8	5.3	3.9	3.3	8.7	7.3	5.4
3. 3-5	2.0	2.0	2.0	2.0	1.7	2.7	1.4	1.9	2.2	1.6	2.9	0.5	1.3	3.0	3.6	7.3
4. 6-9	1.2	1.1	1.0	1.0	1.7	0.4	1.0	2.1	0.8	1.0	1.3	0.5	0.8	1.1	2.0	10.1
5. 10-19	0.7	0.5	1.0	0.7	1.2	0.8	1.0	0.7	0.3	0.5	0.9	0.3	0.4	0.2	1.7	4.8
6. 20-39	0.1	0.2	*	0.1	0.1	0.1	-	0.2	0.2	0.1	0.1	-	-	0.1	0.3	-
7. 40 or more	0.7	0.6	0.5	0.3	1.2	0.9	0.5	0.6	0.6	0.2	1.0	0.3	1.3	-	0.7	7.2
Item 8530 Subject A01b N	3327	1554	1644	2555	395	806	924	1065	532	1821	1306	1168	698	462	912	37

A27C: ... used non-prescription drugs that are supposed to help people stay awake (such as No-Doz, Wake, or Vivarin)?

1. 0 occasions	86.4	84.9	88.3	85.3	94.5	91.7	83.6	86.2	83.8	88.3	83.8	95.2	92.3	88.8	71.2	51.8
2. 1-2	5.8	7.2	4.6	6.4	2.2	3.2	7.2	5.9	7.0	5.8	6.0	2.7	4.3	7.3	10.0	10.2
3. 3-5	2.3	2.5	1.8	2.4	1.0	1.8	2.3	2.5	2.9	2.1	2.7	0.3	1.4	2.1	5.1	11.7
4. 6-9	1.5	1.6	1.4	1.8	0.3	1.0	1.9	1.5	1.7	1.3	1.8	0.7	1.0	0.5	3.5	1.3
5. 10-19	1.6	1.9	1.2	1.6	0.5	0.5	2.5	1.2	2.2	1.3	2.0	0.5	0.2	0.9	4.2	1.6
6. 20-39	0.9	0.6	1.3	1.1	0.4	0.7	1.2	0.9	0.8	0.4	1.5	-	-	-	3.0	4.1
7. 40 or more	1.5	1.3	1.5	1.3	1.2	1.1	1.3	1.8	1.6	0.8	2.3	0.5	0.9	0.4	3.0	19.3
Item 8540 Subject A01b N	3328	1555	1644	2553	395	808	925	1063	532	1822	1306	1167	696	463	916	37

A27D: ... used non-prescription drugs that are supposed to calm people down–keep them from being nervous or in a bad mood (such as Cope, Compoz, Devarex, or Miles Nervine)?

1. 0 occasions	94.6	94.6	95.0	95.1	93.7	96.1	95.1	93.3	94.2	96.3	92.7	98.0	97.8	93.7	90.0	66.0
2. 1-2	2.5	2.5	2.5	2.5	2.6	2.7	1.8	3.0	2.4	2.2	3.0	1.0	0.3	4.4	4.8	10.4
3. 3-5	0.7	0.9	0.5	0.5	1.4	0.4	0.6	0.8	1.1	0.3	1.1	0.2	0.2	0.9	1.0	5.0
4. 6-9	0.7	0.6	0.5	0.6	0.9	0.1	0.7	1.2	0.4	0.5	0.9	0.2	0.4	0.4	1.1	13.8
5. 10-19	0.5	0.6	0.5	0.6	0.3	0.1	0.4	0.8	1.0	0.3	0.8	0.2	0.4	-	1.4	-
6. 20-39	0.3	0.2	0.3	0.3	0.4	0.4	0.5	0.1	-	-	0.6	-	0.2	-	0.7	-
7. 40 or more	0.7	0.6	0.7	0.4	0.7	0.3	0.9	0.8	0.9	0.4	0.9	0.4	0.6	0.6	0.9	4.8
Item 8550 Subject A01b N	3328	1558	1644	2556	396	809	922	1064	534	1823	1307	1169	697	463	915	37

A28: Individuals differ in whether or not they disapprove of people doing certain things. Do YOU disapprove of people (who are 18 or older) doing each of the following?

A28A: Smoking one or more packs of cigarettes per day

1. Don't disapprove	29.2	28.0	29.8	30.5	22.0	30.0	34.3	28.0	21.4	23.6	36.4	15.6	28.4	26.0	47.4	56.5
2. Disapprove	36.8	35.8	38.2	37.2	37.9	39.8	34.6	36.5	36.9	38.2	35.3	39.3	39.0	41.6	30.4	27.2
3. Strongly disapprove	34.0	36.2	32.0	32.3	40.1	30.2	31.2	35.5	41.7	38.2	28.3	45.0	32.6	32.4	22.2	16.3
Item 8560 Subject A11a N	3341	1567	1648	2558	401	817	922	1069	533	1828	1314	1170	699	466	919	37

A28B: Trying marijuana (pot, grass) once or twice

1. Don't disapprove	53.7	55.7	52.2	56.0	51.0	63.2	54.8	45.6	53.9	51.9	55.0	19.2	64.6	64.2	83.1	80.3
2. Disapprove	22.1	22.2	22.1	21.7	23.5	20.2	21.9	24.0	21.3	24.2	19.7	31.7	22.3	19.6	11.5	15.3
3. Strongly disapprove	24.2	22.2	25.7	22.4	25.6	16.5	23.3	30.5	24.8	23.9	25.3	49.1	13.1	16.2	5.4	4.4
Item 8570 Subject A11a N	3336	1565	1646	2556	399	811	922	1070	533	1824	1312	1169	695	466	920	37

A28C: Smoking marijuana occasionally

1. Don't disapprove	39.3	41.2	37.4	40.9	37.0	47.4	39.7	32.7	39.4	35.8	42.3	8.8	41.7	44.1	72.0	73.8
2. Disapprove	24.9	25.3	25.0	25.0	26.8	24.8	24.7	25.0	24.9	26.8	22.7	26.6	31.4	29.5	15.9	16.9
3. Strongly disapprove	35.9	33.5	37.6	34.1	36.2	27.8	35.5	42.3	35.7	37.3	34.9	64.6	26.9	26.4	12.2	9.2
Item 8580 Subject A11a N	3332	1562	1644	2551	399	813	921	1068	530	1821	1310	1166	693	467	919	37

*=less than .05 per cent.

MONITORING THE FUTURE

QUESTIONNAIRE FORM 3 1983	TOTAL	SEX		RACE		REGION				4YR COLLEGE PLANS		ILLICIT DRUG USE: LIFETIME				
		M	F	White	Black	NE	NC	S	W	Yes	No	None	Mari-juana Only	Few Pills	More Pills	Any Her-oin
N (Weighted No. of Cases):	3382	1575	1660	2571	403	828	931	1081	541	1837	1322	1173	701	469	926	37
% of Weighted Total:	100.0	46.6	49.1	76.0	11.9	24.5	27.5	32.0	16.0	54.3	39.1	34.7	20.7	13.9	27.4	1.1
A28D: Smoking marijuana regularly																
1. Don't disapprove	17.5	20.7	14.1	17.1	17.0	19.7	18.4	15.6	16.6	13.2	22.0	2.9	12.8	15.9	37.9	70.2
2. Disapprove	27.2	28.2	26.7	27.7	30.1	32.2	26.2	23.9	28.2	26.7	27.6	16.1	34.6	32.8	33.3	16.4
3. Strongly disapprove	55.2	51.1	59.2	55.2	52.9	48.2	55.4	60.5	55.1	60.1	50.5	81.0	52.6	51.3	28.8	13.4
Item 8590 Subject A11a N	3323	1558	1639	2547	395	808	921	1063	530	1820	1307	1169	692	462	915	37
A28E: Trying LSD once or twice																
1. Don't disapprove	10.9	13.2	8.4	11.2	7.8	11.6	12.3	8.6	12.2	10.1	11.4	3.3	5.7	9.8	23.1	56.9
2. Disapprove	19.3	18.7	19.9	19.8	16.0	22.9	20.0	15.7	20.0	18.3	20.2	14.5	21.2	19.3	24.1	22.8
3. Strongly disapprove	69.7	68.1	71.7	68.9	76.2	65.5	67.7	75.6	67.8	71.6	68.3	82.1	73.2	71.0	52.8	20.3
Item 8600 Subject A11a N	3335	1559	1650	2553	401	814	919	1068	534	1825	1310	1166	698	466	918	37
A28F: Taking LSD regularly																
1. Don't disapprove	3.0	4.2	1.7	2.7	2.8	2.6	3.5	3.1	2.9	2.1	3.7	2.0	2.2	2.8	3.8	35.3
2. Disapprove	11.0	11.9	9.9	10.3	13.2	12.5	11.6	9.3	11.4	9.7	12.5	6.2	10.0	9.4	17.3	38.9
3. Strongly disapprove	85.9	83.9	88.4	87.1	84.0	84.9	84.9	87.6	85.7	88.2	83.8	91.8	87.8	87.7	78.8	25.8
Item 8610 Subject A11a N	3329	1559	1647	2551	400	814	917	1069	530	1819	1310	1167	699	464	913	37
A28G: Trying heroin (smack, horse) once or twice																
1. Don't disapprove	5.7	6.5	4.8	4.7	6.3	6.1	6.3	4.8	5.8	4.9	6.6	2.8	4.5	5.6	8.3	56.4
2. Disapprove	15.6	15.9	15.4	15.6	16.0	17.9	16.3	13.1	16.0	14.7	16.5	11.6	17.2	17.2	18.6	16.3
3. Strongly disapprove	78.7	77.5	79.8	79.6	77.7	76.0	77.4	82.1	78.2	80.4	76.9	85.7	78.3	77.3	73.1	27.4
Item 8620 Subject A11a N	3336	1561	1650	2555	400	814	920	1069	533	1825	1312	1168	697	464	921	37
A28H: Taking heroin occasionally																
1. Don't disapprove	3.1	4.0	2.1	2.4	4.2	3.1	3.1	3.3	2.9	2.5	3.6	2.0	2.3	2.5	4.0	39.2
2. Disapprove	10.9	10.3	11.0	9.9	15.1	11.8	10.7	11.3	9.1	9.2	12.8	7.3	11.3	10.6	13.4	45.0
3. Strongly disapprove	86.0	85.7	86.9	87.7	80.7	85.1	86.3	85.5	88.0	88.3	83.6	90.7	86.4	86.9	82.5	15.8
Item 8630 Subject A11a N	3340	1564	1649	2558	401	815	921	1070	534	1827	1312	1169	698	466	920	37
A28I: Taking heroin regularly																
1. Don't disapprove	2.3	3.2	1.3	1.8	3.5	2.1	2.2	2.8	2.0	1.7	2.7	1.6	1.9	2.0	2.7	24.5
2. Disapprove	7.7	7.9	7.3	6.8	11.4	7.9	7.6	7.9	6.9	5.7	10.3	5.8	7.3	7.2	9.2	39.5
3. Strongly disapprove	90.0	89.0	91.4	91.4	85.0	90.0	90.2	89.3	91.1	92.6	86.9	92.6	90.8	90.8	88.2	36.0
Item 8640 Subject A11a N	3321	1560	1635	2545	396	808	916	1066	531	1821	1302	1165	690	461	918	37
A28J: Trying a barbiturate (downer, goofball, red, yellow, etc.) once or twice																
1. Don't disapprove	16.9	17.8	15.7	17.9	10.1	17.8	18.4	15.3	16.2	14.3	19.6	4.5	8.5	13.8	38.4	79.7
2. Disapprove	23.7	24.5	23.1	24.6	19.0	27.2	24.3	19.9	24.8	23.8	24.0	16.0	25.0	31.2	29.5	8.8
3. Strongly disapprove	59.4	57.7	61.2	57.5	70.9	55.0	57.3	64.8	59.0	61.9	56.4	79.5	66.5	55.1	32.1	11.5
Item 8650 Subject A11a N	3337	1564	1647	2556	400	814	920	1070	533	1827	1311	1168	699	466	919	37
A28K: Taking barbiturates regularly																
1. Don't disapprove	4.9	5.7	3.7	4.7	3.9	5.0	5.5	5.0	3.6	3.3	6.7	1.8	2.4	3.6	9.9	42.0
2. Disapprove	22.0	23.5	20.4	21.5	22.3	23.9	22.2	21.4	19.6	19.2	24.9	12.6	19.5	20.8	35.8	34.0
3. Strongly disapprove	73.1	70.8	75.8	73.8	73.8	71.2	72.3	73.5	76.9	77.5	68.4	85.6	78.1	75.5	54.4	24.0
Item 8660 Subject A11a N	3327	1560	1642	2554	397	808	918	1069	532	1822	1310	1165	692	465	919	37
A28L: Trying an amphetamine (upper, pep pill, bennie, speed) once or twice																
1. Don't disapprove	27.7	28.7	26.4	29.8	15.0	30.0	31.0	23.9	26.2	24.4	31.2	5.5	14.5	25.0	65.6	83.2
2. Disapprove	24.2	25.1	23.6	24.4	24.3	26.0	24.9	21.3	25.8	24.9	23.6	20.2	29.1	35.2	20.1	11.8
3. Strongly disapprove	48.1	46.2	50.0	45.7	60.8	44.0	44.1	54.8	48.0	50.7	45.2	74.3	56.4	39.8	14.3	5.0
Item 8670 Subject A11a N	3328	1564	1641	2556	396	810	920	1067	531	1820	1311	1165	694	465	920	37

QUESTIONNAIRE FORM 3 1983	TOTAL	SEX		RACE		REGION				4YR COLLEGE PLANS		ILLICIT DRUG USE: LIFETIME				
		M	F	White	Black	NE	NC	S	W	Yes	No	None	Mari-juana Only	Few Pills	More Pills	Any Her-oin
N (Weighted No. of Cases):	3382	1575	1660	2571	403	828	931	1081	541	1837	1322	1173	701	469	926	37
% of Weighted Total:	100.0	46.6	49.1	76.0	11.9	24.5	27.5	32.0	16.0	54.3	39.1	34.7	20.7	13.9	27.4	1.1
A28M: Taking amphetamines regularly																
1. Don't disapprove	7.4	8.2	6.5	7.3	5.4	7.7	8.6	6.8	6.2	5.0	10.5	2.1	2.3	4.6	17.9	45.3
2. Disapprove	22.0	23.5	20.4	22.1	19.0	23.3	22.2	21.2	21.1	19.4	24.6	10.9	18.4	22.0	38.2	37.1
3. Strongly disapprove	70.6	68.3	73.1	70.6	75.7	69.0	69.2	72.0	72.6	75.5	64.9	87.0	79.3	73.4	43.9	17.6
Item 8680 Subject A11a N	3317	1555	1638	2547	395	805	918	1065	529	1817	1304	1162	691	464	914	37
A28N: Trying cocaine once or twice																
1. Don't disapprove	23.0	26.2	19.3	23.3	18.8	29.1	20.9	17.3	28.8	21.8	23.9	4.3	13.7	23.0	51.5	83.2
2. Disapprove	18.4	19.2	18.1	18.6	18.7	21.3	17.3	16.2	20.6	17.7	18.9	15.6	21.7	24.3	16.8	5.3
3. Strongly disapprove	58.5	54.6	62.6	58.0	62.5	49.6	61.8	66.4	50.7	60.5	57.2	80.1	64.7	52.7	31.7	11.5
Item 8690 Subject A11a N	3325	1560	1641	2553	397	810	919	1066	530	1819	1308	1165	694	464	916	37
A28O: Taking cocaine regularly																
1. Don't disapprove	6.8	8.9	4.5	6.4	5.9	7.2	7.2	5.8	7.7	4.8	8.9	1.7	2.8	3.8	15.8	53.8
2. Disapprove	16.0	16.6	15.0	15.5	18.2	20.6	14.7	12.9	17.4	14.9	17.3	7.7	14.1	16.2	27.1	33.6
3. Strongly disapprove	77.2	74.4	80.5	78.2	75.9	72.1	78.1	81.3	74.9	80.2	73.8	90.6	83.1	80.1	57.0	12.6
Item 8700 Subject A11a N	3302	1552	1628	2542	387	802	915	1056	529	1810	1297	1159	682	461	916	37
A28P: Trying one or two drinks of an alcoholic beverage (beer, wine, liquor)																
1. Don't disapprove	81.6	83.4	80.6	85.3	69.0	84.9	88.7	75.5	76.5	82.2	81.2	66.4	87.2	85.4	94.9	93.1
2. Disapprove	11.5	9.3	13.1	9.6	17.6	8.7	7.3	15.8	14.2	11.1	11.8	20.7	6.7	11.5	3.7	4.9
3. Strongly disapprove	6.9	7.3	6.3	5.1	13.4	6.3	4.0	8.7	9.2	6.7	6.9	12.9	6.1	3.1	1.4	1.9
Item 8710 Subject A11a N	3326	1560	1641	2554	395	809	921	1068	528	1820	1309	1164	693	465	918	37
A28Q: Taking one or two drinks nearly every day																
1. Don't disapprove	31.1	37.0	24.7	33.4	16.6	33.3	35.5	28.7	24.8	27.4	35.7	18.8	30.7	29.2	46.0	67.8
2. Disapprove	40.3	38.9	42.4	41.3	41.9	37.2	43.6	39.5	41.1	41.6	38.8	41.3	41.8	41.5	38.7	18.6
3. Strongly disapprove	28.6	24.1	32.9	25.3	41.5	29.5	20.9	31.8	34.1	31.0	25.6	39.9	27.4	29.3	15.2	13.6
Item 8720 Subject A11a N	3312	1553	1637	2542	395	809	910	1065	527	1815	1301	1158	691	462	915	37
A28R: Taking four or five drinks nearly every day																
1. Don't disapprove	10.0	13.0	6.4	10.4	6.7	9.6	11.2	10.0	8.2	6.3	14.1	4.5	10.1	8.5	15.3	50.4
2. Disapprove	27.2	31.0	23.0	29.0	19.4	26.9	30.8	26.8	22.4	25.6	28.6	21.3	28.9	24.9	34.5	24.3
3. Strongly disapprove	62.8	55.9	70.5	60.7	73.9	63.5	58.0	63.2	69.4	68.1	57.3	74.2	61.0	66.6	50.2	25.2
Item 8730 Subject A11a N	3318	1556	1639	2550	394	809	916	1063	530	1819	1305	1164	691	461	915	37
A28S: Having five or more drinks once or twice each weekend																
1. Don't disapprove	43.4	51.8	35.3	47.6	21.9	44.4	49.7	39.7	38.4	40.3	47.2	22.7	45.7	44.1	65.4	84.0
2. Disapprove	24.9	21.5	28.0	25.4	26.1	26.1	25.8	23.9	23.7	25.8	24.2	27.2	26.8	27.0	20.0	12.6
3. Strongly disapprove	31.7	26.8	36.7	27.0	52.0	29.5	24.5	36.4	37.9	33.9	28.6	50.1	27.5	28.8	14.5	3.4
Item 8740 Subject A11a N	3324	1560	1639	2554	394	808	919	1066	531	1818	1310	1161	693	464	919	37
A29: During the LAST 12 MONTHS, how often have you been around people who were taking each of the following to get high or for "kicks"?																
A29A: Marijuana (pot, grass) or hashish																
1. Not at all	23.8	21.1	26.3	23.6	22.3	18.6	25.0	26.3	24.7	25.1	22.1	46.9	15.8	14.7	5.7	10.9
2. Once or twice	24.1	25.1	22.7	23.8	26.4	22.1	22.3	28.2	22.4	24.4	24.0	31.4	30.1	25.2	10.9	2.0
3. Occasionally	25.9	26.0	26.1	26.8	25.6	26.5	26.4	24.7	26.4	28.2	23.2	16.0	33.0	34.1	29.2	15.8
4. Often	26.1	27.8	24.9	25.7	25.7	32.9	26.2	20.8	26.5	22.3	30.7	5.7	21.2	26.0	54.3	71.3
Item 20590 Subject A02b N	3334	1562	1647	2559	396	810	924	1066	534	1825	1310	1166	698	467	917	36

QUESTIONNAIRE FORM 3 1983	TOTAL	SEX		RACE		REGION				4YR COLLEGE PLANS		ILLICIT DRUG USE: LIFETIME				
		M	F	White	Black	NE	NC	S	W	Yes	No	None	Marijuana Only	Few Pills	More Pills	Any Heroin
N (Weighted No. of Cases):	3382	1575	1660	2571	403	828	931	1081	541	1837	1322	1173	701	469	926	37
% of Weighted Total:	100.0	46.6	49.1	76.0	11.9	24.5	27.5	32.0	16.0	54.3	39.1	34.7	20.7	13.9	27.4	1.1

A29B: LSD

1. Not at all	86.2	85.9	86.6	85.2	95.4	84.9	84.4	89.1	85.4	87.1	85.1	94.5	92.0	89.8	71.4	27.5
2. Once or twice	8.8	8.1	9.2	9.5	3.4	9.1	10.8	6.3	10.0	8.5	9.4	4.5	5.7	6.3	17.0	33.4
3. Occasionally	3.7	4.2	3.2	4.2	0.9	4.8	3.5	3.1	3.2	3.6	3.6	0.6	1.5	3.2	9.2	13.7
4. Often	1.4	1.8	1.0	1.1	0.3	1.2	1.3	1.5	1.3	0.8	2.0	0.4	0.7	0.7	2.4	25.4
Item 20600 Subject A02b N	3286	1534	1632	2530	388	803	909	1049	526	1804	1289	1149	692	458	906	35

A29C: Other psychedelics (mescaline, peyote, PCP, etc.)

1. Not at all	86.9	86.3	87.4	86.4	92.4	80.5	86.3	91.6	88.0	88.2	85.7	95.7	91.8	87.9	73.0	40.9
2. Once or twice	8.6	9.1	8.3	9.1	5.1	12.6	8.9	5.4	8.8	8.2	8.9	3.4	6.1	9.6	16.2	28.1
3. Occasionally	3.3	3.2	3.5	3.5	1.9	6.2	3.0	1.8	2.6	3.2	3.5	0.7	1.1	1.7	8.8	14.2
4. Often	1.1	1.4	0.9	1.0	0.6	0.7	1.7	1.2	0.6	0.4	1.9	0.2	0.9	0.8	2.0	16.8
Item 20610 Subject A02b N	3317	1557	1638	2553	393	803	922	1060	532	1815	1308	1158	697	463	917	36

A29D: Amphetamines (uppers, pep pills, bennies, speed)

1. Not at all	53.9	53.9	54.0	49.4	78.1	54.1	48.3	57.4	56.1	57.2	49.0	79.7	68.5	42.1	17.1	9.9
2. Once or twice	21.4	22.0	20.9	22.7	14.9	22.1	21.5	20.6	21.8	22.1	20.4	14.7	21.9	36.8	22.3	12.9
3. Occasionally	14.7	14.6	14.6	16.6	4.6	14.3	18.7	12.0	13.7	13.0	17.6	4.7	6.9	15.3	32.9	23.4
4. Often	10.1	9.4	10.5	11.3	2.4	9.6	11.5	10.1	8.5	7.7	13.0	1.0	2.7	5.9	27.7	53.8
Item 20620 Subject A02b N	3324	1557	1644	2556	393	806	922	1064	532	1819	1309	1162	698	465	917	36

A29E: Barbiturates (downers, goofballs, reds, yellows, etc.)

1. Not at all	77.5	76.4	78.6	75.7	89.0	77.7	75.3	78.3	79.6	79.8	74.3	90.7	86.6	79.9	55.0	16.5
2. Once or twice	13.3	14.2	12.4	14.5	7.5	12.8	15.3	11.9	13.5	13.4	13.5	7.1	10.1	14.0	22.8	28.3
3. Occasionally	6.2	6.2	6.2	6.9	2.4	7.0	6.3	6.2	4.6	4.9	8.1	1.9	2.1	4.8	15.0	18.6
4. Often	3.0	3.2	2.8	2.9	1.0	2.5	3.1	3.6	2.3	2.0	4.1	0.3	1.2	1.2	7.2	36.5
Item 20630 Subject A02b N	3316	1554	1640	2550	393	803	920	1063	531	1817	1304	1160	696	463	915	36

A29F: Tranquilizers (Librium, Valium, Miltown)

1. Not at all	76.5	76.6	76.6	74.4	90.6	73.2	77.4	76.8	79.2	76.9	75.5	86.7	85.1	74.4	59.2	41.8
2. Once or twice	14.4	14.0	14.8	15.9	6.9	16.3	14.9	12.9	14.0	16.0	13.1	10.5	10.4	18.2	20.6	12.6
3. Occasionally	6.1	6.4	5.7	6.8	2.3	6.9	5.2	6.7	5.3	5.0	7.5	2.3	3.0	5.1	13.1	32.9
4. Often	2.9	3.1	2.9	2.9	0.2	3.6	2.5	3.6	1.6	2.1	3.8	0.5	1.5	2.2	7.1	12.8
Item 20640 Subject A02b N	3312	1551	1638	2547	390	799	920	1062	531	1814	1304	1160	695	463	912	36

A29G: Cocaine ("coke")

1. Not at all	66.7	65.1	67.9	67.0	68.8	55.0	73.3	75.1	56.0	68.3	65.2	86.2	76.5	60.4	39.5	13.9
2. Once or twice	18.7	20.4	17.6	18.6	20.3	22.4	17.7	14.7	22.9	19.3	17.8	10.7	17.8	28.0	25.2	10.6
3. Occasionally	9.4	8.9	9.9	9.3	8.5	14.9	6.2	6.7	11.8	8.8	9.7	2.4	4.1	8.5	22.3	21.8
4. Often	5.2	5.6	4.6	5.2	2.3	7.6	2.8	3.4	9.3	3.5	7.4	0.8	1.6	3.0	13.0	53.7
Item 20650 Subject A02b N	3321	1555	1643	2554	392	806	922	1061	531	1817	1308	1161	696	465	916	36

A29H: Heroin (smack, horse)

1. Not at all	94.9	95.6	94.3	95.3	95.8	94.2	95.0	95.0	95.2	95.8	93.7	96.7	96.3	96.4	93.4	29.4
2. Once or twice	3.6	2.8	4.1	3.6	3.0	3.6	3.7	3.5	3.4	3.2	4.1	2.6	1.7	2.3	5.0	43.7
3. Occasionally	0.9	1.0	0.8	0.7	0.9	1.4	1.0	0.7	0.4	0.6	1.4	0.3	0.9	0.6	1.1	16.7
4. Often	0.7	0.6	0.8	0.4	0.3	0.9	0.2	0.8	1.0	0.4	0.9	0.3	1.0	0.6	0.5	10.3
Item 20660 Subject A02b N	3307	1547	1638	2544	390	800	914	1060	532	1807	1304	1157	696	458	913	36

A29I: Other narcotics (methadone, opium, codeine, paregoric, etc.)

1. Not at all	82.7	82.6	83.2	81.8	90.7	81.7	83.7	84.7	78.5	83.9	81.0	92.2	90.9	81.5	66.9	27.7
2. Once or twice	12.0	11.8	12.1	12.7	7.8	13.2	12.2	9.4	15.0	11.4	12.9	6.3	6.7	14.4	21.7	22.0
3. Occasionally	3.1	3.2	2.9	3.5	1.1	3.6	1.9	3.6	3.6	3.1	3.4	0.9	1.3	3.7	6.4	23.3
4. Often	2.2	2.4	1.8	2.0	0.5	1.4	2.2	2.3	3.0	1.6	2.7	0.5	1.1	0.4	5.0	27.0
Item 20670 Subject A02b N	3316	1555	1640	2552	391	802	922	1062	531	1815	1307	1160	696	464	915	36

QUESTIONNAIRE FORM 3 1983	TOTAL	SEX		RACE		REGION				4YR COLLEGE PLANS		ILLICIT DRUG USE: LIFETIME				
		M	F	White	Black	NE	NC	S	W	Yes	No	None	Mari-juana Only	Few Pills	More Pills	Any Her-oin
N (Weighted No. of Cases):	3382	1575	1660	2571	403	828	931	1081	541	1837	1322	1173	701	469	926	37
% of Weighted Total:	100.0	46.6	49.1	76.0	11.9	24.5	27.5	32.0	16.0	54.3	39.1	34.7	20.7	13.9	27.4	1.1

A29J: Alcoholic beverages (beer, wine, liquor)

	TOTAL	M	F	White	Black	NE	NC	S	W	Yes	No	None	Mari-juana Only	Few Pills	More Pills	Any Heroin
1. Not at all	6.0	4.4	7.0	4.9	8.9	7.0	4.2	5.7	8.0	5.9	5.8	13.0	4.2	1.4	0.4	-
2. Once or twice	9.8	8.5	11.1	7.3	19.8	9.1	8.4	11.3	10.3	9.4	10.4	16.7	9.0	8.0	2.7	3.5
3. Occasionally	24.0	24.0	24.0	23.5	31.5	22.7	22.8	27.2	21.7	24.9	22.2	32.8	26.0	25.9	11.3	4.2
4. Often	60.2	63.1	57.9	64.3	39.8	61.2	64.5	55.9	60.0	59.7	61.6	37.5	60.7	64.7	85.6	92.2
Item 20680 Subject A02b N	3331	1561	1646	2557	396	811	922	1063	534	1823	1311	1165	699	467	917	36

This section asks for your views and feelings about a number of different things.

D01: How satisfied are you with your life as a whole these days?

	TOTAL	M	F	White	Black	NE	NC	S	W	Yes	No	None	Mari-juana Only	Few Pills	More Pills	Any Heroin
1. Completely dissatisfied	1.9	2.2	1.4	1.4	2.9	1.8	2.0	2.0	1.2	1.5	2.2	2.1	1.6	1.2	1.7	7.8
2. Quite dissatisfied	8.9	7.8	9.7	8.7	9.7	11.3	8.1	8.2	8.3	9.4	8.1	10.0	8.3	8.4	8.4	4.5
3. Somewhat dissatisfied	11.5	10.6	12.5	10.9	15.5	13.7	11.1	9.9	12.2	10.7	12.5	9.1	9.4	13.1	14.7	18.0
4. Neither, or mixed feelings	12.4	12.2	12.8	11.3	15.0	11.3	11.0	13.8	13.9	11.1	14.2	12.0	11.6	12.8	13.2	13.9
5. Somewhat satisfied	27.5	28.8	26.5	28.3	26.7	26.3	30.5	26.5	26.0	28.3	27.2	24.1	28.5	30.0	30.3	26.5
6. Quite satisfied	32.5	33.1	31.8	34.7	21.7	31.2	32.0	33.7	32.5	34.2	29.9	35.8	35.6	30.2	27.6	28.7
7. Completely satisfied	5.3	5.2	5.4	4.8	8.5	4.3	5.1	5.9	5.8	4.7	5.8	7.0	5.0	4.3	4.0	0.7
Item 6840 Subject P01,Q01 N	3173	1481	1604	2494	362	747	896	1018	512	1799	1277	1124	659	451	870	34

D02: These questions are about your health during the last MONTH.

D02A: Have you been bothered by shortness of breath when you were not exercising or working hard?

	TOTAL	M	F	White	Black	NE	NC	S	W	Yes	No	None	Mari-juana Only	Few Pills	More Pills	Any Heroin
1. Never	73.0	78.4	68.5	73.5	71.3	68.6	74.1	73.6	76.5	76.1	68.8	78.7	76.6	75.3	62.6	56.8
2. Seldom	17.0	13.9	19.7	17.2	16.0	19.8	16.0	15.8	16.8	15.1	19.8	13.2	16.4	17.6	21.7	20.5
3. Sometimes	8.5	6.3	10.2	7.9	9.8	9.5	8.7	9.3	5.2	7.4	9.7	6.8	6.3	6.1	13.2	13.2
4. Often	1.5	1.3	1.6	1.4	2.8	2.1	1.2	1.3	1.5	1.4	1.7	1.2	0.7	0.9	2.5	9.4
Item 8850 Subject Q06 N	3178	1480	1608	2495	361	745	901	1017	516	1799	1283	1125	659	452	873	34

D02B: Have you been bothered by your heart beating hard?

	TOTAL	M	F	White	Black	NE	NC	S	W	Yes	No	None	Mari-juana Only	Few Pills	More Pills	Any Heroin
1. Never	74.7	78.1	71.7	74.7	74.4	73.8	74.1	73.4	79.3	75.5	73.2	79.7	77.8	75.4	65.8	72.6
2. Seldom	16.2	14.6	17.8	16.5	14.9	16.0	16.9	17.0	13.7	16.0	16.6	13.5	16.2	17.0	19.8	6.5
3. Sometimes	7.7	6.1	9.0	7.8	7.6	8.2	7.3	8.6	6.0	7.3	8.5	6.0	5.2	6.7	12.1	14.6
4. Often	1.4	1.3	1.5	1.0	3.2	2.0	1.7	0.9	1.0	1.2	1.7	0.8	0.8	0.9	2.3	6.2
Item 8860 Subject Q06 N	3167	1475	1601	2489	358	739	900	1015	513	1794	1278	1124	657	450	870	33

D02C: Have you had spells of dizziness?

	TOTAL	M	F	White	Black	NE	NC	S	W	Yes	No	None	Mari-juana Only	Few Pills	More Pills	Any Heroin
1. Never	61.0	72.5	50.3	60.5	61.8	63.0	58.8	59.6	64.5	60.3	61.7	61.9	70.1	60.9	52.6	65.5
2. Seldom	24.1	19.4	28.2	24.8	23.3	21.6	27.2	24.3	21.7	25.4	22.3	24.5	20.9	26.3	25.2	18.7
3. Sometimes	12.3	7.0	17.5	12.4	12.0	12.6	11.1	14.2	10.3	11.7	13.2	11.3	7.9	11.0	17.6	13.7
4. Often	2.7	1.1	3.9	2.4	2.9	2.9	3.0	1.9	3.5	2.6	2.9	2.3	1.1	1.8	4.6	2.1
Item 8870 Subject Q06 N	3159	1472	1597	2488	352	738	898	1009	514	1790	1275	1118	655	449	871	34

D02D: Have your hands trembled enough to bother you?

	TOTAL	M	F	White	Black	NE	NC	S	W	Yes	No	None	Mari-juana Only	Few Pills	More Pills	Any Heroin
1. Never	79.3	85.8	73.5	78.2	83.8	79.8	77.6	79.1	81.9	80.0	77.9	83.6	83.0	80.8	70.2	75.2
2. Seldom	12.8	9.5	15.6	13.8	9.0	13.2	13.7	13.4	9.3	12.9	13.2	10.3	12.4	13.7	16.0	6.3
3. Sometimes	6.5	3.5	9.2	6.5	5.5	6.2	7.4	5.9	6.6	6.0	6.9	5.1	4.3	3.5	11.4	10.2
4. Often	1.4	1.1	1.7	1.5	1.7	0.8	1.3	1.6	2.3	1.1	2.0	1.0	0.2	2.0	2.4	8.2
Item 8880 Subject Q06 N	3166	1476	1600	2487	358	739	896	1015	516	1793	1278	1120	657	451	871	34

D02E: Have you been troubled by your hands sweating so that they felt damp and clammy?

	TOTAL	M	F	White	Black	NE	NC	S	W	Yes	No	None	Mari-juana Only	Few Pills	More Pills	Any Heroin
1. Never	68.9	73.1	65.3	68.1	73.9	70.6	65.5	69.1	71.6	70.0	67.3	71.1	73.2	71.4	61.1	75.9
2. Seldom	19.6	16.9	21.9	20.7	16.7	18.3	21.4	19.6	18.5	19.8	19.2	19.3	17.4	18.0	23.1	13.5
3. Sometimes	8.5	7.1	9.8	8.5	7.5	8.2	10.1	8.5	6.0	7.9	9.4	7.4	7.1	7.9	11.1	8.6
4. Often	3.0	2.9	3.1	2.7	1.9	2.9	2.9	2.8	3.9	2.3	4.1	2.2	2.2	2.7	4.7	2.1
Item 8890 Subject Q06 N	3169	1476	1602	2492	358	740	900	1014	515	1795	1279	1123	655	452	871	34

QUESTIONNAIRE FORM 3 1983	TOTAL	SEX		RACE		REGION				4YR COLLEGE PLANS		ILLICIT DRUG USE: LIFETIME				
		M	F	White	Black	NE	NC	S	W	Yes	No	None	Mari-juana Only	Few Pills	More Pills	Any Her-oin
N (Weighted No. of Cases):	3382	1575	1660	2571	403	828	931	1081	541	1837	1322	1173	701	469	926	37
% of Weighted Total:	100.0	46.6	49.1	76.0	11.9	24.5	27.5	32.0	16.0	54.3	39.1	34.7	20.7	13.9	27.4	1.1

D02F: Have there been times when you couldn't take care of things because you just couldn't get going?

	TOTAL	M	F	White	Black	NE	NC	S	W	Yes	No	None	Mari-juana Only	Few Pills	More Pills	Any Her-oin
1. Never	51.7	59.1	44.9	50.3	53.2	50.6	50.5	51.3	56.1	51.3	52.0	56.3	54.9	51.3	42.6	65.2
2. Seldom	28.3	25.8	30.1	30.4	22.3	27.1	28.8	29.7	26.7	29.5	26.7	27.7	28.3	30.1	29.4	15.7
3. Sometimes	16.0	12.4	19.7	15.7	18.1	18.1	16.0	15.6	13.9	15.2	17.1	12.9	13.7	15.2	22.1	13.6
4. Often	4.0	2.7	5.3	3.6	6.4	4.3	4.7	3.4	3.3	4.0	4.2	3.1	3.2	3.4	5.9	5.5
Item 8900 Subject Q06 N	3165	1477	1600	2491	356	739	901	1012	514	1792	1279	1122	657	450	871	34

D03: At any time during the LAST 12 MONTHS, have you felt in your own mind that you should REDUCE or STOP your use of . . .

D03A: Alcohol?

	TOTAL	M	F	White	Black	NE	NC	S	W	Yes	No	None	Mari-juana Only	Few Pills	More Pills	Any Her-oin
1. Yes	34.9	39.2	31.2	35.3	33.1	31.1	33.7	39.1	34.7	35.5	34.3	24.8	40.7	43.9	38.3	21.9
2. No	52.7	49.9	55.2	55.1	38.0	59.4	56.5	44.8	50.6	51.5	53.7	45.8	52.3	51.8	59.7	78.1
8. Haven't used in last 12 months	12.5	10.8	13.6	9.6	28.9	9.5	9.8	16.2	14.7	12.9	12.1	29.4	7.0	4.2	2.0	-
Item 8910 Subject A01i N	2758	1318	1359	2245	262	657	811	841	449	1560	1111	894	585	381	839	31

D03B: Cigarettes?

	TOTAL	M	F	White	Black	NE	NC	S	W	Yes	No	None	Mari-juana Only	Few Pills	More Pills	Any Her-oin
1. Yes	24.0	21.5	26.1	24.5	19.9	28.6	25.0	23.9	15.9	19.4	30.2	6.7	21.7	26.9	46.1	35.3
2. No	14.8	12.3	16.8	14.6	14.3	14.2	15.1	13.4	17.8	12.3	18.1	8.0	16.0	15.1	20.8	29.4
8. Haven't used in last 12 months	61.2	66.2	57.1	60.9	65.8	57.2	59.9	62.7	66.3	68.3	51.7	85.3	62.4	58.1	33.1	35.3
Item 8920 Subject A01i N	3084	1429	1561	2443	333	721	893	974	496	1748	1240	1076	646	434	860	33

D03C: Marijuana?

	TOTAL	M	F	White	Black	NE	NC	S	W	Yes	No	None	Mari-juana Only	Few Pills	More Pills	Any Her-oin
1. Yes	20.0	23.4	17.4	20.1	20.9	23.5	18.2	17.1	23.7	17.4	23.2	-	26.7	25.2	38.8	22.8
2. No	21.5	22.0	20.6	21.5	22.4	25.3	22.3	18.1	21.2	19.2	24.7	-	27.5	25.0	41.4	72.2
8. Haven't used in last 12 months	58.5	54.6	62.0	58.4	56.8	51.2	59.5	64.8	55.1	63.5	52.0	100.0	45.8	49.8	19.8	5.0
Item 8930 Subject A01i N	2744	1276	1395	2205	277	648	804	852	439	1586	1070	1011	523	373	779	28

D03D: Psychedelics (LSD, etc.)?

	TOTAL	M	F	White	Black	NE	NC	S	W	Yes	No	None	Mari-juana Only	Few Pills	More Pills	Any Her-oin
1. Yes	2.4	3.1	1.8	2.6	0.6	4.3	2.4	1.0	2.1	1.8	3.3	-	-	0.7	7.8	23.7
2. No	2.0	1.7	1.7	1.8	0.9	2.2	1.5	1.9	2.8	1.2	2.8	-	0.1	-	5.6	42.7
8. Haven't used in last 12 months	95.7	95.2	96.5	95.6	98.5	93.6	96.1	97.1	95.0	97.0	93.9	100.0	99.9	99.3	86.6	33.6
Item 8940 Subject A01i N	2764	1274	1411	2224	285	646	807	872	438	1612	1066	1010	589	389	727	23

D03E: Amphetamines (uppers)?

	TOTAL	M	F	White	Black	NE	NC	S	W	Yes	No	None	Mari-juana Only	Few Pills	More Pills	Any Her-oin
1. Yes	8.0	8.2	7.9	9.0	1.8	7.1	9.8	7.9	6.6	6.8	9.7	-	-	5.0	31.2	34.1
2. No	8.5	7.5	9.1	9.2	1.8	8.9	9.2	6.8	10.0	6.2	11.9	*	0.3	3.9	32.1	54.8
8. Haven't used in last 12 months	83.5	84.3	83.0	81.8	96.3	84.0	81.0	85.3	83.4	87.0	78.4	100.0	99.7	91.1	36.7	11.2
Item 8950 Subject A01i N	2549	1213	1266	2039	268	599	725	822	402	1493	977	1011	588	324	577	25

D03F: Tranquilizers?

	TOTAL	M	F	White	Black	NE	NC	S	W	Yes	No	None	Mari-juana Only	Few Pills	More Pills	Any Her-oin
1. Yes	1.3	1.4	1.2	1.3	1.3	1.2	1.4	1.5	0.7	1.1	1.5	-	0.2	0.1	4.3	15.5
2. No	3.0	2.9	2.8	3.1	0.7	1.7	3.7	3.5	2.6	2.3	4.1	*	0.3	0.7	9.8	32.7
8. Haven't used in last 12 months	95.7	95.8	96.0	95.6	98.1	97.2	94.9	95.0	96.8	96.5	94.4	100.0	99.6	99.2	85.9	51.8
Item 9005 Subject A01i N	2713	1242	1392	2184	277	636	804	851	422	1593	1041	1010	590	377	689	23

D03G: Barbiturates/Quaaludes (downers)?

	TOTAL	M	F	White	Black	NE	NC	S	W	Yes	No	None	Mari-juana Only	Few Pills	More Pills	Any Her-oin
1. Yes	2.3	3.5	1.3	2.5	0.8	2.0	1.9	3.2	1.8	1.4	3.5	-	-	0.1	8.2	18.5
2. No	3.2	3.0	3.0	3.4	0.4	2.0	3.4	3.8	3.3	2.1	5.0	*	0.1	0.3	9.6	54.7
8. Haven't used in last 12 months	94.5	93.5	95.7	94.2	98.8	96.0	94.6	93.0	95.0	96.6	91.5	100.0	99.9	99.7	82.2	26.8
Item 8970 Subject A01i N	2744	1271	1394	2206	279	635	816	860	433	1596	1064	1009	588	377	721	23

D03H: Cocaine?

	TOTAL	M	F	White	Black	NE	NC	S	W	Yes	No	None	Mari-juana Only	Few Pills	More Pills	Any Her-oin
1. Yes	3.3	3.8	3.0	3.2	3.5	5.3	2.0	1.7	6.0	2.7	4.1	-	-	4.3	9.3	19.4
2. No	7.0	8.3	5.7	7.1	4.5	10.8	4.7	3.9	12.2	5.6	9.0	-	-	3.7	21.2	59.6
8. Haven't used in last 12 months	89.6	87.9	91.2	89.8	92.0	83.8	93.3	94.4	81.8	91.7	86.8	100.0	100.0	92.0	69.4	21.1
Item 8980 Subject A01i N	2787	1282	1427	2252	275	647	832	871	436	1617	1083	1007	588	379	759	29

*=less than .05 per cent.

QUESTIONNAIRE FORM 3 1983	TOTAL	SEX		RACE		REGION				4YR COLLEGE PLANS		ILLICIT DRUG USE: LIFETIME				
		M	F	White	Black	NE	NC	S	W	Yes	No	None	Mari-juana Only	Few Pills	More Pills	Any Her-oin
N (Weighted No. of Cases):	3382	1575	1660	2571	403	828	931	1081	541	1837	1322	1173	701	469	926	37
% of Weighted Total:	100.0	46.6	49.1	76.0	11.9	24.5	27.5	32.0	16.0	54.3	39.1	34.7	20.7	13.9	27.4	1.1
D03I: Heroin?																
1. Yes	0.2	0.4	-	0.1	-	0.2	0.2	0.3	-	0.2	0.2	-	-	-	0.2	14.2
2. No	0.5	0.5	0.3	0.4	0.8	0.3	0.4	0.7	0.7	0.1	1.1	*	-	-	0.1	43.6
8. Haven't used in last 12 months	99.3	99.1	99.7	99.4	99.2	99.5	99.5	99.0	99.3	99.7	98.7	100.0	100.0	100.0	99.8	42.2
Item 8990 Subject A01i N	2823	1306	1438	2286	281	654	840	887	442	1636	1103	1009	588	392	783	27
D03J: Other narcotics?																
1. Yes	0.9	1.5	0.4	0.8	1.1	0.9	0.4	1.3	1.1	0.7	1.3	-	-	-	2.7	25.3
2. No	2.1	1.8	2.0	2.1	0.8	2.3	2.0	1.6	3.0	1.2	3.5	*	-	1.0	5.6	50.9
8. Haven't used in last 12 months	97.0	96.7	97.6	97.1	98.1	96.9	97.6	97.1	96.0	98.1	95.2	100.0	100.0	99.0	91.7	23.8
Item 9000 Subject A01i N	2707	1245	1387	2182	278	622	815	851	419	1578	1048	1009	585	383	684	23
D04: How likely is it that you will use marijuana in the next 12 months?																
1. Definitely will-GO TO Q.D05	11.6	12.7	10.2	11.9	8.7	13.7	11.9	10.2	10.5	9.8	14.5	1.9	8.3	9.8	28.3	51.5
2. Probably will-GO TO Q.D05	13.9	14.7	13.1	14.5	11.2	17.3	13.8	10.8	15.1	12.1	16.1	0.9	18.0	18.1	27.1	16.9
3. Probably will not	19.4	20.4	18.6	19.3	21.7	21.8	20.9	16.1	19.5	20.3	17.9	11.6	29.7	22.7	20.8	17.6
4. Definitely will not	55.2	52.2	58.1	54.3	58.4	47.2	53.3	62.9	55.0	57.8	51.4	85.6	44.0	49.5	23.9	14.0
Item 9010 Subject A01b N	2865	1316	1466	2280	297	660	836	899	469	1664	1123	1082	597	399	738	24

Here are some reasons people give for not using marijuana, or for stopping use. If you have never used marijuana, or if you have stopped using it, please tell us which reasons are true for you. (Mark all that apply.)

	TOTAL	M	F	White	Black	NE	NC	S	W	Yes	No	None	Mari-juana Only	Few Pills	More Pills	Any Her-oin
A. Concerned about possible psychological damage	67.2	65.6	68.9	68.6	62.9	66.4	66.0	69.9	64.9	70.5	62.4	75.3	59.5	61.7	59.9	33.0
B. Concerned about possible physical damage	65.8	65.2	66.5	67.4	62.1	65.1	64.3	69.3	62.1	68.7	61.7	73.6	61.6	58.3	56.1	67.2
C. Concerned about getting arrested	40.2	44.5	36.7	40.8	39.8	35.5	40.6	44.3	37.3	39.8	40.1	41.1	37.8	39.4	41.8	44.2
D. Concerned about becoming addicted to marijuana	41.8	42.5	41.3	40.7	46.7	39.4	41.7	45.9	37.0	40.0	44.9	48.6	36.9	37.9	31.7	54.0
E. It's against my beliefs	52.7	51.3	53.9	55.0	37.8	47.0	51.1	54.3	59.7	56.4	46.5	68.4	38.0	46.2	31.0	8.5
F. Concerned about loss of energy or ambition	36.4	38.9	34.0	35.2	40.4	38.0	32.8	36.8	40.2	37.5	34.1	37.9	33.6	37.3	36.1	11.3
G. Concerned about possible loss of control of myself	49.4	46.6	51.5	49.7	46.7	47.9	47.2	52.2	49.7	52.1	45.2	55.8	44.0	44.2	44.0	-
H. It might lead to stronger drugs	49.2	51.5	47.1	48.3	51.7	48.5	47.7	53.6	43.4	46.7	52.6	53.7	48.5	45.6	39.8	19.8
I. Not enjoyable, I didn't like it	35.4	35.5	34.8	35.0	38.6	38.2	31.0	35.3	40.0	33.3	38.7	24.2	53.1	39.3	43.6	24.3
J. My parents would disapprove	57.5	55.6	59.6	58.4	54.1	55.3	58.1	58.6	57.1	57.4	57.4	60.1	57.7	55.8	51.7	-
K. My husband/wife (or boyfriend/ girlfriend) would disapprove	30.6	29.6	31.4	32.2	23.7	24.6	35.6	31.3	27.9	28.1	34.8	31.2	28.1	34.3	28.7	22.5
L. I don't like being with the people who use it	40.6	39.7	41.4	41.0	33.3	35.2	38.3	43.0	46.9	43.2	36.9	51.5	32.7	36.8	21.8	22.5
M. My friends don't use it	34.7	33.0	36.4	37.9	17.9	31.5	35.5	35.5	35.8	37.5	30.6	43.3	29.1	29.2	21.5	22.5
N. I might have a bad trip	21.8	20.9	22.0	21.0	26.1	21.2	20.1	23.0	23.2	20.5	24.0	22.8	20.2	19.2	24.2	21.7
O. Too expensive	25.4	29.7	21.4	26.7	22.1	19.1	30.7	24.6	25.7	25.1	26.6	22.6	27.3	25.5	31.1	33.0
P. Not available	5.9	5.8	5.7	6.0	5.4	5.8	5.3	6.5	5.7	6.3	5.2	6.2	6.5	5.9	3.5	21.7
Q. Don't feel like getting high	59.6	55.6	63.2	59.6	55.5	58.4	59.8	55.8	68.2	58.8	61.2	61.5	56.2	56.7	62.5	8.5
Item 9020-9180 Subject A06a N ★	2059	903	1103	1616	230	436	596	691	337	1248	756	994	429	291	319	6

D05A: Has your use of alcohol ever caused any of the following problems for you?

Responses to this set of questions are not included because of complexities in the presentation and interpretation of the data.

Item 9190-9350   Subject A07b   N

---

*=less than .05 per cent.   ★=excludes respondents for whom question was inappropriate.

QUESTIONNAIRE FORM 3 1983	TOTAL	SEX		RACE		REGION				4YR COLLEGE PLANS		ILLICIT DRUG USE: LIFETIME				
		M	F	White	Black	NE	NC	S	W	Yes	No	None	Mari-juana Only	Few Pills	More Pills	Any Her-oin
N (Weighted No. of Cases):	3382	1575	1660	2571	403	828	931	1081	541	1837	1322	1173	701	469	926	37
% of Weighted Total:	100.0	46.6	49.1	76.0	11.9	24.5	27.5	32.0	16.0	54.3	39.1	34.7	20.7	13.9	27.4	1.1

D05M: Has your use of marijuana ever caused any of the following problems for you? (Mark all that apply.)

Responses to this set of questions are not included because of complexities in the presentation and interpretation of the data.

Item 9360-9520   Subject A07b   N

D05O: Has your use of other drugs ever caused any of the following problems for you? (Mark all that apply.)

Responses to this set of questions are not included because of complexities in the presentation and interpretation of the data.

Item 9530-9690   Subject A07b   N

E01: Do you agree or disagree that most efforts to prevent (or clean up) pollution . . .

E01A: . . . are just too expensive

	TOTAL	M	F	White	Black	NE	NC	S	W	Yes	No	None	Mari-juana Only	Few Pills	More Pills	Any Her-oin
1. Disagree	22.0	24.9	19.5	20.6	29.8	23.6	18.8	22.4	24.9	22.8	20.6	21.9	24.2	20.5	20.8	25.9
2. Mostly disagree	22.6	20.8	24.7	24.5	15.0	25.7	21.6	21.2	22.9	26.0	18.4	24.5	20.2	22.1	23.4	7.1
3. Neither	33.8	32.5	35.3	35.1	28.2	29.8	37.5	35.2	29.8	33.0	35.2	32.0	33.9	34.9	35.1	38.7
4. Mostly agree	15.2	15.1	15.0	15.0	16.1	14.8	17.0	13.7	15.6	13.4	17.4	15.1	15.3	16.2	14.9	12.0
5. Agree	6.4	6.7	5.6	4.8	10.9	6.0	5.2	7.5	6.8	4.8	8.4	6.5	6.3	6.3	5.8	16.2
Item 9700 Subject F04 N	2968	1383	1500	2354	324	676	865	946	481	1718	1158	1062	622	419	804	29

E01B: . . . cost more jobs than it's worth

	TOTAL	M	F	White	Black	NE	NC	S	W	Yes	No	None	Mari-juana Only	Few Pills	More Pills	Any Her-oin
1. Disagree	25.7	29.0	22.6	25.6	26.7	27.5	23.5	24.6	29.4	27.6	22.5	26.0	28.7	22.6	24.8	24.0
2. Mostly disagree	27.5	28.1	27.8	30.0	18.0	29.5	28.8	25.6	26.1	29.6	24.6	27.7	24.2	31.9	28.0	17.2
3. Neither	30.5	27.6	33.3	31.1	26.5	29.6	34.1	30.4	25.7	29.8	31.9	30.7	31.0	26.9	31.3	44.3
4. Mostly agree	11.4	11.0	11.1	9.7	18.7	9.5	9.6	12.7	14.9	9.4	14.6	10.4	11.5	12.5	12.0	9.6
5. Agree	4.9	4.3	5.1	3.5	10.1	3.9	4.1	6.8	3.9	3.7	6.4	5.2	4.5	6.1	4.0	4.9
Item 9710 Subject F04 N	2948	1373	1488	2340	319	671	861	937	478	1709	1148	1054	619	418	796	29

E01C: . . . are proposed by people who usually don't know what they are talking about

	TOTAL	M	F	White	Black	NE	NC	S	W	Yes	No	None	Mari-juana Only	Few Pills	More Pills	Any Her-oin
1. Disagree	17.4	19.0	15.9	17.2	19.2	19.6	17.3	15.8	17.5	20.4	13.1	17.7	20.1	17.0	15.0	18.9
2. Mostly disagree	23.8	23.8	24.4	24.6	20.5	24.4	23.0	23.2	25.8	25.7	21.3	25.1	25.6	22.1	22.9	4.7
3. Neither	33.7	31.4	36.0	34.4	32.3	33.9	34.6	32.9	33.6	31.9	36.2	32.7	30.2	35.0	36.6	39.4
4. Mostly agree	16.2	16.0	16.2	15.9	17.5	13.0	16.7	18.7	15.0	15.3	17.9	16.1	15.3	17.8	16.4	16.2
5. Agree	8.8	9.6	7.6	7.8	10.5	9.1	8.3	9.4	8.1	6.7	11.5	8.4	8.8	8.2	9.1	20.8
Item 9720 Subject F04 N	2915	1349	1478	2320	311	663	851	925	476	1697	1129	1045	612	413	785	29

E01D: . . . will not be enough anyhow

	TOTAL	M	F	White	Black	NE	NC	S	W	Yes	No	None	Mari-juana Only	Few Pills	More Pills	Any Her-oin
1. Disagree	19.0	21.2	17.0	18.8	22.1	22.2	15.8	18.1	21.7	21.0	15.9	20.3	20.6	16.9	16.7	26.4
2. Mostly disagree	22.4	21.6	23.8	23.5	15.6	23.0	22.3	21.8	23.1	25.0	18.5	25.5	20.1	23.1	20.8	1.9
3. Neither	32.9	32.9	33.0	33.4	30.9	30.9	34.5	33.5	31.7	30.0	37.6	28.6	35.4	33.4	35.4	46.2
4. Mostly agree	18.1	17.8	18.3	17.8	20.3	15.3	20.8	17.7	18.1	18.2	18.1	19.5	15.8	18.4	18.8	11.3
5. Agree	7.5	6.5	7.9	6.5	11.1	8.5	6.6	8.8	5.5	5.7	9.8	6.2	8.2	8.2	8.3	14.2
Item 9730 Subject F04 N	2889	1345	1456	2302	306	655	852	920	463	1678	1121	1039	602	410	778	29

QUESTIONNAIRE FORM 3 1983	TOTAL	SEX		RACE		REGION				4YR COLLEGE PLANS		ILLICIT DRUG USE: LIFETIME				
		M	F	White	Black	NE	NC	S	W	Yes	No	None	Marijuana Only	Few Pills	More Pills	Any Heroin
N (Weighted No. of Cases):	3382	1575	1660	2571	403	828	931	1081	541	1837	1322	1173	701	469	926	37
% of Weighted Total:	100.0	46.6	49.1	76.0	11.9	24.5	27.5	32.0	16.0	54.3	39.1	34.7	20.7	13.9	27.4	1.1

E01E: ... are useless because this society won't last long enough for such efforts to do any good

	TOTAL	M	F	White	Black	NE	NC	S	W	Yes	No	None	Mari.	Few	More	Any Her.
1. Disagree	37.2	39.6	35.8	39.2	26.6	36.5	36.5	35.3	43.1	42.4	29.0	41.2	38.3	33.9	33.8	23.3
2. Mostly disagree	21.5	21.3	22.0	21.9	19.0	23.2	21.0	20.5	21.8	23.3	19.2	19.8	20.5	29.3	20.5	16.6
3. Neither	27.0	25.3	28.2	26.9	28.2	26.6	28.2	28.5	22.4	22.7	33.5	25.5	26.8	22.1	31.0	32.1
4. Mostly agree	8.6	8.6	8.2	7.6	13.7	7.8	9.7	8.1	8.6	7.1	11.0	7.9	8.7	7.9	9.7	9.5
5. Agree	5.8	5.2	5.8	4.4	12.5	5.8	4.7	7.6	4.1	4.5	7.4	5.5	5.7	6.8	5.0	18.5
Item 9740 Subject F04 N	2897	1347	1464	2307	310	657	853	919	467	1686	1125	1039	610	408	780	29

E02: There has been talk about shortages of energy, food, and raw materials in this country. Do you think that in the coming years we will have plenty to meet our needs, a sufficient amount, or will we have to consume less?

	TOTAL	M	F	White	Black	NE	NC	S	W	Yes	No	None	Mari.	Few	More	Any Her.
1. Plenty to meet our needs	14.9	21.5	8.9	15.5	13.6	10.4	14.1	18.3	16.3	13.5	16.6	14.4	14.8	17.1	14.1	24.9
2. A sufficient amount	51.8	51.7	51.5	52.0	51.8	52.9	52.5	53.6	45.4	50.5	54.1	50.4	52.8	51.5	53.0	53.9
3. Will have to consume less	33.3	26.9	39.6	32.5	34.5	36.7	33.4	28.1	38.4	36.0	29.3	35.2	32.4	31.4	32.9	21.2
Item 9750 Subject F05 N	2810	1295	1438	2255	294	633	836	885	456	1641	1083	1016	585	398	765	24

E03: The questions in this section deal with population problems. How much do you agree or disagree with each statement?

E03A: Our government should help other countries to control their population

	TOTAL	M	F	White	Black	NE	NC	S	W	Yes	No	None	Mari.	Few	More	Any Her.
1. Disagree	25.1	28.2	21.9	24.9	28.4	25.3	25.9	24.1	25.0	22.4	29.0	23.2	25.8	22.8	27.3	46.9
2. Mostly disagree	18.2	18.4	18.4	19.1	16.9	17.9	18.5	18.3	18.1	18.9	17.1	19.4	16.0	18.4	18.9	14.0
3. Neither	23.6	21.0	26.4	24.1	19.4	24.7	24.3	22.9	21.9	25.2	20.9	24.7	23.3	23.8	22.7	20.0
4. Mostly agree	20.8	19.4	22.0	20.9	20.0	21.4	20.2	20.1	22.8	22.7	18.8	20.4	21.1	22.0	20.7	14.0
5. Agree	12.3	12.9	11.3	11.0	15.3	10.7	11.1	14.6	12.2	10.8	14.1	12.4	13.8	13.0	10.4	5.1
Item 9760 Subject E01,H02 N	2917	1353	1474	2321	311	658	862	921	475	1680	1144	1041	610	410	798	28

E03B: Governments should avoid making policy about population and let the individual decide

	TOTAL	M	F	White	Black	NE	NC	S	W	Yes	No	None	Mari.	Few	More	Any Her.
1. Disagree	12.0	14.4	9.4	10.9	16.9	11.6	10.3	13.7	12.2	11.5	12.5	11.8	13.7	9.9	11.7	17.4
2. Mostly disagree	20.2	21.1	19.4	21.4	12.8	19.6	21.2	18.9	21.5	20.6	19.7	20.0	20.8	21.9	18.9	17.1
3. Neither	26.8	25.8	27.9	27.7	20.5	27.1	27.4	27.0	24.7	27.5	25.6	23.7	27.6	26.1	30.1	37.9
4. Mostly agree	25.2	23.5	26.6	25.4	26.0	25.6	25.7	24.0	26.0	25.4	25.7	26.3	23.6	23.9	26.2	16.3
5. Agree	15.9	15.2	16.8	14.6	23.8	16.1	15.4	16.4	15.5	15.1	16.5	18.3	14.2	18.2	13.2	11.3
Item 9770 Subject E01,H02 N	2905	1344	1471	2311	310	654	857	920	475	1674	1138	1040	603	409	796	27

E03C: I feel strongly enough about preventing overpopulation that I'd be willing to limit my family to two children

	TOTAL	M	F	White	Black	NE	NC	S	W	Yes	No	None	Mari.	Few	More	Any Her.
1. Disagree	16.1	17.0	15.7	15.1	22.8	21.2	14.3	14.0	16.1	15.5	16.4	17.1	17.3	14.8	14.0	21.9
2. Mostly disagree	13.5	12.3	14.5	13.8	10.5	14.6	14.4	11.1	14.6	14.6	11.7	14.8	13.3	15.0	11.4	17.1
3. Neither	23.1	24.1	22.6	23.6	20.2	24.7	23.5	23.5	19.3	23.3	22.9	23.2	21.8	18.7	26.1	22.9
4. Mostly agree	20.3	20.2	20.0	20.3	20.2	19.0	21.5	20.1	20.7	21.1	19.6	20.1	20.4	20.6	21.0	4.8
5. Agree	27.0	26.5	27.2	27.2	26.3	20.5	26.2	31.3	29.3	25.5	29.3	24.8	27.2	31.0	27.5	33.4
Item 9780 Subject E01 N	2894	1338	1467	2304	307	653	853	914	473	1663	1139	1036	598	409	794	29

E03D: To prevent overpopulation, I might decide not to have any children of my own

	TOTAL	M	F	White	Black	NE	NC	S	W	Yes	No	None	Mari.	Few	More	Any Her.
1. Disagree	53.1	48.6	57.7	53.8	51.8	55.7	51.4	53.6	52.0	52.8	53.5	53.2	53.7	54.3	52.0	48.2
2. Mostly disagree	18.1	20.2	16.6	18.1	17.6	17.9	18.2	18.1	18.5	19.1	16.7	19.4	18.8	17.1	16.9	22.7
3. Neither	15.4	18.1	12.5	15.6	13.8	14.8	16.8	15.0	14.0	14.4	16.6	14.5	13.5	14.7	17.7	27.0
4. Mostly agree	5.8	6.1	5.1	5.4	7.4	6.6	5.3	5.8	5.8	5.4	6.5	4.8	5.1	6.6	7.3	2.1
5. Agree	7.5	6.9	8.0	7.0	9.4	5.0	8.4	7.5	9.6	8.2	6.7	8.1	8.9	7.3	6.0	-
Item 9790 Subject E01 N	2875	1333	1453	2290	303	646	851	907	471	1656	1130	1025	597	406	790	27

	TOTAL	SEX		RACE		REGION				4YR COLLEGE PLANS		ILLICIT DRUG USE: LIFETIME				
QUESTIONNAIRE FORM 3 1983		M	F	White	Black	NE	NC	S	W	Yes	No	None	Mari- juana Only	Few Pills	More Pills	Any Her- oin
N (Weighted No. of Cases):	3382	1575	1660	2571	403	828	931	1081	541	1837	1322	1173	701	469	926	37
% of Weighted Total:	100.0	46.6	49.1	76.0	11.9	24.5	27.5	32.0	16.0	54.3	39.1	34.7	20.7	13.9	27.4	1.1

E03E: High schools should offer instruction in birth control methods

1. Disagree	6.7	7.6	5.6	6.7	5.5	7.0	6.1	6.4	7.7	5.9	8.0	8.5	5.8	7.3	4.6	2.7
2. Mostly disagree	4.2	4.4	3.8	4.1	5.0	5.8	4.0	2.9	4.8	4.3	4.3	5.2	3.8	2.9	3.1	11.4
3. Neither	13.8	16.2	11.5	14.2	11.7	11.1	18.0	13.4	10.8	12.9	15.2	15.3	13.0	12.6	12.6	20.7
4. Mostly agree	24.0	26.2	22.3	24.6	20.0	24.5	26.2	23.8	19.6	23.4	24.6	26.7	23.4	21.0	22.9	13.7
5. Agree	51.3	45.6	56.7	50.4	57.8	51.7	45.6	53.4	57.1	53.5	48.0	44.2	54.0	56.2	56.9	51.6
Item 9800 Subject E02 N	2881	1334	1457	2292	308	649	851	909	471	1662	1127	1029	596	405	793	27

E03F: I personally consider most methods of birth control to be immoral

1. Disagree	44.2	39.9	48.3	46.2	37.1	47.4	41.2	43.5	46.4	45.7	41.6	36.3	43.6	43.0	55.9	35.7
2. Mostly disagree	19.2	20.9	18.2	20.2	15.2	18.0	20.6	18.6	19.2	20.8	16.5	20.3	20.6	20.7	15.8	21.3
3. Neither	22.4	25.0	20.1	21.2	23.8	19.5	24.3	23.0	21.7	20.3	25.9	26.0	20.7	20.8	19.3	30.0
4. Mostly agree	7.2	8.2	5.8	6.0	14.2	6.5	6.7	8.2	6.9	6.6	8.4	8.7	7.6	7.2	5.1	2.6
5. Agree	7.2	6.1	7.7	6.4	9.8	8.6	7.2	6.7	5.9	6.6	7.6	8.7	7.5	8.4	3.9	10.4
Item 9810 Subject E02 N	2861	1329	1443	2279	304	643	845	907	466	1652	1119	1022	592	405	786	27

E03G: The government should make birth control information and services available without cost to anyone who wants them

1. Disagree	7.2	6.9	7.3	7.4	5.5	9.5	6.6	6.2	7.0	6.8	7.8	8.5	5.4	8.9	5.4	8.2
2. Mostly disagree	7.6	7.9	7.3	8.3	4.6	7.4	9.4	6.3	7.1	7.8	7.3	8.7	6.1	8.5	6.8	10.7
3. Neither	15.1	17.6	12.9	15.7	10.8	14.1	16.1	15.8	13.5	14.5	15.7	18.3	11.7	13.4	14.0	20.8
4. Mostly agree	25.9	27.4	24.8	26.5	22.7	25.2	28.1	25.6	23.3	26.1	25.8	28.0	28.1	24.1	23.1	15.4
5. Agree	44.2	40.1	47.7	42.0	56.4	43.8	39.8	46.2	49.1	44.8	43.4	36.5	48.7	45.0	50.8	44.9
Item 9820 Subject E02,H02 N	2875	1332	1453	2287	307	643	853	910	469	1658	1127	1028	597	403	788	29

E04: Did you have a unit on sex education when you were in high school?

1. No, and I'm glad I didn't	8.3	9.9	7.0	8.7	5.4	4.1	8.8	10.8	8.5	7.5	9.2	10.8	7.0	7.1	6.6	9.5
2. No, and I wish I had	23.6	22.6	24.5	23.0	27.5	19.8	23.4	30.0	16.8	22.3	25.4	24.5	22.6	21.7	24.3	17.0
3. Yes, and it was very worthwhile	28.3	24.4	31.5	26.4	39.4	30.7	27.2	28.0	27.5	26.4	30.8	26.7	31.1	30.7	27.0	23.8
4. Yes, and it was somewhat worthwhile	30.9	33.0	29.4	32.4	24.3	37.3	30.6	23.9	36.3	34.8	26.0	31.3	32.1	30.2	30.6	22.7
5. Yes, but it was not worthwhile at all	8.8	10.1	7.6	9.6	3.3	8.1	9.9	7.3	10.8	9.0	8.5	6.7	7.2	10.2	11.5	27.0
Item 9860 Subject B01,E02 N	2868	1312	1471	2273	309	654	847	902	465	1659	1121	1029	599	396	789	27

E05: Did you ever study about birth control methods in high school?

1. No, and I'm glad I didn't	11.7	14.9	9.1	12.1	8.3	8.6	11.5	13.0	14.0	10.5	13.4	16.7	9.6	11.9	6.9	18.7
2. No, and I wish I had	31.8	30.7	32.9	32.3	28.7	30.5	33.5	34.8	24.7	30.0	34.3	29.5	31.1	31.7	35.4	17.2
3. Yes, and it was very worthwhile	27.4	21.9	31.7	24.7	42.0	25.2	25.8	30.0	28.4	26.9	28.3	26.1	31.2	28.2	25.5	29.5
4. Yes, and it was somewhat worthwhile	23.9	26.2	22.2	25.4	17.7	29.6	24.6	17.8	26.2	27.5	18.8	23.7	23.1	22.0	25.8	22.9
5. Yes, but it was not worthwhile at all	5.2	6.3	4.1	5.6	3.3	6.1	4.5	4.5	6.7	5.1	5.3	3.9	5.0	6.2	6.4	11.7
Item 9870 Subject B01,E02 N	2842	1295	1462	2252	307	648	840	892	463	1639	1114	1015	594	397	783	27

E06: How important is each of the following for being looked up to or having high status in your school?

E06A: Coming from the right family

1. No importance	14.8	17.2	12.9	13.5	19.8	17.6	14.2	11.8	18.3	12.0	18.4	15.1	16.3	13.1	14.5	19.6
2. Little importance	19.8	21.2	18.7	20.7	14.7	18.7	18.5	19.4	23.7	22.9	15.5	21.1	19.6	20.6	18.3	12.4
3. Moderate importance	30.5	28.5	33.0	33.4	18.2	30.1	33.1	30.0	27.4	32.7	27.4	29.2	28.9	30.8	33.2	39.0
4. Great importance	18.2	17.7	18.6	17.7	20.8	17.6	17.9	18.3	19.7	18.2	18.5	18.3	17.3	20.0	18.4	7.4
5. Very great importance	16.6	15.5	16.9	14.7	26.5	15.3	16.4	20.6	11.0	14.1	20.3	16.4	18.0	15.5	15.7	21.5
Item 13580 Subject B04 N	2848	1313	1449	2259	309	638	844	905	461	1642	1115	1034	587	391	779	28

QUESTIONNAIRE FORM 3 1983	TOTAL	SEX		RACE		REGION				4YR COLLEGE PLANS		ILLICIT DRUG USE: LIFETIME				
		M	F	White	Black	NE	NC	S	W	Yes	No	None	Marijuana Only	Few Pills	More Pills	Any Heroin
N (Weighted No. of Cases):	3382	1575	1660	2571	403	828	931	1081	541	1837	1322	1173	701	469	926	37
% of Weighted Total:	100.0	46.6	49.1	76.0	11.9	24.5	27.5	32.0	16.0	54.3	39.1	34.7	20.7	13.9	27.4	1.1

E06B: Being a leader in student activities

1. No importance	11.0	11.5	10.3	9.9	13.4	13.6	10.7	9.9	10.3	5.5	18.2	9.4	11.2	7.5	14.0	21.0
2. Little importance	15.0	14.4	15.4	15.1	13.9	17.5	14.6	13.1	15.8	14.0	16.7	12.8	15.4	18.5	15.5	21.8
3. Moderate importance	33.3	35.0	32.0	35.0	26.7	36.0	33.9	29.9	35.1	35.6	30.3	33.6	33.7	35.2	32.1	27.8
4. Great importance	26.4	27.0	26.1	27.2	22.7	21.9	27.5	28.5	26.6	29.2	22.7	28.0	26.7	25.6	25.1	19.3
5. Very great importance	14.3	12.1	16.1	12.8	23.3	11.0	13.3	18.6	12.2	15.7	12.2	16.2	13.1	13.3	13.2	10.1
Item 13590 Subject B04,M05 N	2839	1311	1443	2257	305	640	844	893	462	1641	1108	1028	585	390	779	28

E06C: Having a nice car

1. No importance	15.9	14.0	17.8	14.0	23.6	21.5	13.5	14.3	15.8	13.8	19.2	17.0	18.5	13.7	14.0	6.8
2. Little importance	24.0	21.9	26.0	24.4	20.2	26.7	24.6	20.6	25.5	26.3	21.0	25.9	23.3	24.3	22.3	26.5
3. Moderate importance	31.9	33.4	30.8	34.3	24.8	28.5	32.6	33.6	32.1	34.2	28.6	33.1	30.4	32.8	31.3	26.7
4. Great importance	17.0	19.8	14.3	16.7	18.5	14.4	16.9	18.5	17.8	17.1	16.2	14.5	18.3	17.1	19.5	3.8
5. Very great importance	11.2	10.9	11.1	10.7	13.0	8.9	12.3	13.0	8.8	8.5	15.0	9.5	9.5	12.1	12.9	36.2
Item 13600 Subject B04,F01 N	2842	1309	1446	2255	308	637	842	902	460	1641	1110	1029	584	392	779	28

E06D: Getting good grades

1. No importance	4.7	5.8	3.8	4.8	2.8	5.7	4.3	4.2	5.0	2.2	7.7	4.3	5.2	3.6	5.4	8.3
2. Little importance	11.4	13.0	10.3	12.5	4.6	8.7	12.6	11.5	12.9	11.2	11.7	9.5	11.4	12.1	13.3	26.4
3. Moderate importance	34.6	33.8	36.0	38.6	16.8	35.2	37.1	32.2	33.9	35.7	33.6	33.1	35.0	34.8	36.8	25.4
4. Great importance	28.1	28.3	27.4	27.5	30.0	27.6	27.8	27.9	29.8	30.2	25.5	29.1	27.6	26.2	28.5	28.1
5. Very great importance	21.1	19.1	22.6	16.7	45.8	22.8	18.1	24.2	18.4	20.6	21.5	24.1	20.8	23.2	16.0	11.8
Item 13610 Subject B04 N	2839	1309	1445	2254	309	638	843	900	459	1639	1111	1028	585	391	777	27

E06E: Being a good athlete

1. No importance	9.8	7.6	11.9	8.7	15.5	10.4	9.4	10.5	8.2	5.6	15.6	8.0	11.2	7.6	11.6	24.1
2. Little importance	12.7	10.9	13.9	12.2	14.7	16.1	12.1	12.1	10.1	10.2	16.3	10.7	13.0	15.0	14.1	10.4
3. Moderate importance	29.2	30.4	27.8	30.2	24.6	30.9	29.0	28.5	28.5	30.2	28.0	28.2	28.2	29.2	31.4	18.1
4. Great importance	27.8	30.1	26.6	29.1	21.6	25.7	28.5	26.6	31.6	31.9	21.8	31.9	27.9	26.3	23.6	12.6
5. Very great importance	20.6	21.0	19.8	20.0	23.5	16.9	21.0	22.2	21.6	22.2	18.3	21.1	19.7	21.9	19.2	34.8
Item 13620 Subject B04 N	2831	1301	1445	2248	308	639	836	900	456	1642	1100	1028	579	389	778	28

E06F: Knowing a lot about intellectual matters

1. No importance	12.8	12.4	13.3	13.0	10.4	13.2	15.5	10.1	12.6	9.3	17.4	10.5	14.5	9.4	15.9	25.0
2. Little importance	25.5	23.8	27.6	27.1	19.1	26.8	26.2	24.0	25.5	26.6	24.2	24.9	23.6	26.3	27.4	33.8
3. Moderate importance	36.9	37.6	36.0	39.4	24.3	37.0	37.7	35.5	37.6	38.5	34.5	38.3	36.2	39.7	35.0	20.6
4. Great importance	16.6	17.4	15.9	14.7	24.9	16.3	13.7	19.5	16.9	17.5	15.6	17.9	16.7	16.5	15.5	9.0
5. Very great importance	8.2	8.7	7.1	5.8	21.3	6.7	6.8	10.9	7.4	8.1	8.4	8.3	9.0	8.1	6.2	11.7
Item 13630 Subject B04 N	2830	1307	1438	2254	304	637	840	896	457	1634	1107	1024	585	390	772	28

E06G: Planning to go to college

1. No importance	12.3	12.5	11.9	11.3	14.3	13.0	12.8	12.2	10.3	6.7	20.2	10.2	14.1	10.7	14.2	22.2
2. Little importance	16.2	17.9	14.1	17.8	8.6	11.0	19.0	16.2	18.1	14.3	18.7	16.5	15.9	16.1	15.9	23.1
3. Moderate importance	31.2	31.7	31.2	33.2	22.2	34.1	29.2	29.9	33.4	30.7	32.1	32.0	29.2	28.6	32.8	38.5
4. Great importance	21.5	20.9	22.0	22.2	17.7	24.4	21.4	20.1	20.3	25.9	15.2	20.9	22.7	24.2	20.6	13.5
5. Very great importance	18.9	17.0	20.8	15.4	37.1	17.5	17.6	21.7	17.9	22.3	13.8	20.5	18.1	20.4	16.6	2.6
Item 13640 Subject B04 N	2842	1310	1446	2256	310	639	841	903	459	1639	1113	1030	586	392	777	28

E07: How about using drugs (other than marijuana or alcohol)–does that cause a student to be looked up to or looked down on?

E07A: Among the majority of students in my school, such drug use is . . .

1. Looked down on a lot	23.6	26.0	22.0	24.1	22.1	19.1	26.6	25.2	21.4	25.6	21.1	29.9	22.6	23.1	16.8	16.4
2. Looked down on some	23.9	22.9	24.5	25.6	16.4	21.9	25.0	24.5	23.7	25.9	20.9	27.7	22.6	20.4	22.3	16.6
3. Neither, or mixed	43.2	42.2	44.1	42.2	46.6	46.7	41.4	41.5	44.7	40.0	47.6	34.4	46.1	47.3	50.7	40.3
4. Looked up to some	7.1	7.6	6.4	6.7	9.8	7.9	6.0	7.0	8.4	6.7	7.8	5.9	6.6	7.8	8.2	23.3
5. Looked up to a lot	2.2	1.3	3.1	1.5	5.0	4.4	1.0	1.9	1.8	1.7	2.6	2.2	2.1	1.5	2.0	3.4
Item 13650 Subject A12b N	2824	1305	1435	2239	304	628	840	895	461	1630	1106	1009	588	391	780	28

QUESTIONNAIRE FORM 3 1983	TOTAL	SEX		RACE		REGION				4YR COLLEGE PLANS		ILLICIT DRUG USE: LIFETIME				
		M	F	White	Black	NE	NC	S	W	Yes	No	None	Marijuana Only	Few Pills	More Pills	Any Heroin
N (Weighted No. of Cases):	3382	1575	1660	2571	403	828	931	1081	541	1837	1322	1173	701	469	926	37
% of Weighted Total:	100.0	46.6	49.1	76.0	11.9	24.5	27.5	32.0	16.0	54.3	39.1	34.7	20.7	13.9	27.4	1.1

E07B: Among my own group of friends, such drug use is . . .

1. Looked down on a lot	38.3	38.5	38.6	40.1	30.6	33.2	39.4	38.9	42.1	44.1	30.9	60.4	39.6	31.6	13.8	10.0
2. Looked down on some	18.3	16.6	19.4	17.9	22.2	16.6	17.1	20.7	18.0	20.3	15.3	16.1	20.1	22.8	18.0	4.6
3. Neither, or mixed	34.0	34.9	33.4	33.4	36.5	41.4	33.7	31.6	29.1	27.9	42.1	20.2	32.9	36.9	49.9	53.7
4. Looked up to some	7.6	8.0	7.0	7.3	7.7	6.4	8.6	6.5	9.6	6.8	8.3	2.7	6.6	7.7	14.2	19.6
5. Looked up to a lot	1.8	2.0	1.6	1.4	2.9	2.4	1.2	2.3	1.2	0.8	3.4	0.6	0.9	1.0	4.0	12.2
Item 13660 Subject A12b N	2821	1303	1434	2239	303	625	840	895	461	1628	1104	1009	585	391	780	28

E07C: My own feelings about such drug use is that . . .

1. I look down on it a lot	51.5	50.9	52.9	52.3	49.4	49.2	51.5	52.1	53.5	56.0	45.5	78.0	51.5	41.7	23.8	5.1
2. I look down on it some	17.4	16.9	17.6	17.5	21.2	16.6	16.7	19.2	16.4	18.5	15.6	11.7	19.7	23.1	20.8	6.5
3. Neither, or mixed	27.1	27.4	26.4	26.5	26.4	30.2	28.0	24.6	26.3	22.7	33.4	9.5	27.0	33.8	45.5	56.6
4. I look up to it some	3.1	3.8	2.4	3.0	2.3	3.7	2.8	3.3	2.4	2.4	4.1	0.5	1.5	1.0	7.7	29.3
5. I look up to it a lot	0.8	1.1	0.6	0.8	0.7	0.3	1.0	0.8	1.4	0.4	1.4	0.3	0.3	0.4	2.2	2.5
Item 13670 Subject A11c N	2817	1301	1433	2235	304	627	839	892	460	1630	1098	1011	586	391	774	28

E08: The next questions are about some things which may have happened TO YOU while you were at school (inside or outside or in a schoolbus).

During the LAST 12 MONTHS, how often ...

E08A: Has something of yours (worth under $50) been stolen?

1. Not at all	63.7	60.7	66.7	63.1	64.8	67.5	62.5	62.8	62.3	62.1	66.1	69.7	63.4	57.7	59.3	69.6
2. Once	25.5	27.2	23.6	26.3	24.5	22.3	26.9	26.5	25.1	26.3	24.3	22.2	27.4	30.1	26.7	9.8
3. Twice	7.2	7.5	7.1	7.2	7.4	7.3	6.7	7.5	7.4	7.9	6.1	5.8	6.0	9.2	8.7	13.6
4. 3 or 4 times	2.8	3.3	2.1	2.5	2.3	2.2	3.0	2.4	4.0	3.0	2.3	1.9	2.4	2.3	3.9	
5. 5 or more times	0.9	1.3	0.6	0.8	1.0	0.7	1.0	0.8	1.2	0.6	1.2	0.4	0.9	0.8	1.4	7.0
Item 9871 Subject B07,S03 N	2858	1322	1450	2263	308	635	845	915	464	1643	1122	1029	588	397	784	28

E08B: Has something of yours (worth over $50) been stolen?

1. Not at all	88.0	86.5	90.3	89.4	81.1	89.6	89.4	86.4	86.6	88.3	88.1	92.7	89.5	83.9	84.2	70.0
2. Once	8.7	9.8	7.3	8.3	13.1	6.9	8.3	10.1	9.5	8.8	8.6	5.2	8.0	12.0	12.3	8.7
3. Twice	2.2	2.8	1.5	1.7	3.5	2.2	1.8	2.1	3.3	2.0	2.4	1.5	1.4	3.2	2.5	18.9
4. 3 or 4 times	0.7	0.8	0.7	0.4	1.7	0.8	0.3	1.2	0.5	0.7	0.8	0.5	0.6	0.7	0.9	2.5
5. 5 or more times	0.2	0.2	0.2	0.1	0.6	0.5	0.2	0.2	0.1	0.3	0.1	0.1	0.5	0.3	0.2	-
Item 9872 Subject B07,S03 N	2856	1319	1449	2262	304	633	844	911	468	1640	1121	1030	586	396	783	28

E08C: Has someone deliberately damaged your property (your car, clothing, etc.)?

1. Not at all	74.5	67.2	81.7	75.0	76.9	74.6	75.0	73.8	75.2	74.3	74.8	80.1	71.9	71.4	71.7	62.1
2. Once	17.9	23.1	13.1	18.1	14.6	16.8	18.9	18.6	16.2	17.2	19.0	14.0	20.0	22.4	18.9	27.3
3. Twice	5.3	6.7	3.8	5.1	5.0	5.7	4.6	5.3	5.9	5.6	4.8	3.9	5.4	4.1	7.6	2.0
4. 3 or 4 times	1.6	1.9	1.0	1.2	3.2	1.8	1.0	1.7	2.2	2.2	0.6	1.3	2.0	1.2	1.5	3.1
5. 5 or more times	0.7	1.1	0.4	0.6	0.3	1.1	0.5	0.7	0.6	0.6	0.8	0.7	0.7	0.8	0.3	5.4
Item 9873 Subject B07,S03 N	2848	1319	1442	2259	303	633	842	912	462	1637	1117	1027	588	394	780	28

E08D: Has someone injured you with a weapon (like a knife, gun, or club)?

1. Not at all	95.1	92.9	97.6	95.7	94.4	93.9	96.8	94.0	95.8	96.1	93.9	96.7	96.7	95.2	92.1	89.4
2. Once	3.1	4.3	1.5	2.8	3.2	3.3	1.9	3.9	3.3	2.6	3.8	2.1	1.9	2.7	5.5	2.0
3. Twice	1.3	2.0	0.5	1.1	1.6	1.9	0.7	1.6	0.8	1.0	1.7	0.7	0.6	1.3	2.0	6.0
4. 3 or 4 times	0.3	0.4	0.2	0.2	0.7	0.5	0.5	0.2	-	0.2	0.3	0.1	0.5	0.6	0.3	-
5. 5 or more times	0.3	0.4	0.1	0.2	0.1	0.4	0.2	0.4	*	0.2	0.3	0.4	0.3	0.2	-	2.5
Item 9874 Subject B07,S03 N	2852	1320	1445	2259	304	632	844	911	464	1637	1120	1029	586	394	783	28

*=less than .05 per cent.

QUESTIONNAIRE FORM 3 1983	TOTAL	SEX		RACE		REGION				4YR COLLEGE PLANS		ILLICIT DRUG USE: LIFETIME				
		M	F	White	Black	NE	NC	S	W	Yes	No	None	Mari-juana Only	Few Pills	More Pills	Any Her-oin
N (Weighted No. of Cases):	3382	1575	1660	2571	403	828	931	1081	541	1837	1322	1173	701	469	926	37
% of Weighted Total:	100.0	46.6	49.1	76.0	11.9	24.5	27.5	32.0	16.0	54.3	39.1	34.7	20.7	13.9	27.4	1.1
E08E: Has someone threatened you with a weapon, but not actually injured you?																
1. Not at all	87.0	82.8	91.8	88.1	85.2	85.0	89.7	84.5	89.8	88.9	84.7	90.6	87.9	87.8	82.1	69.5
2. Once	8.9	11.2	5.7	8.0	10.2	11.2	6.9	9.9	7.2	7.3	10.8	6.6	8.9	7.9	11.7	19.4
3. Twice	2.4	3.4	1.6	2.4	3.3	1.8	1.6	3.7	2.3	2.3	2.7	1.3	1.8	2.9	4.0	6.1
4. 3 or 4 times	0.8	1.4	0.2	0.8	0.9	1.0	0.7	0.9	0.4	0.8	0.7	0.7	0.7	0.2	1.1	2.5
5. 5 or more times	0.9	1.2	0.7	0.8	0.4	0.9	1.2	1.0	0.3	0.7	1.0	0.7	0.8	1.1	1.1	2.5
Item 9875 Subject B07,S03 N	2845	1315	1444	2254	303	631	842	908	464	1634	1117	1026	585	394	779	28
E08F: Has someone injured you on purpose without using a weapon?																
1. Not at all	86.0	83.0	89.0	86.6	86.8	85.1	86.3	86.0	86.5	87.5	84.1	89.1	89.5	83.0	81.5	79.5
2. Once	9.1	10.8	7.3	8.5	8.8	9.7	8.8	8.8	9.6	8.5	9.8	8.0	7.0	11.3	10.5	12.6
3. Twice	2.5	3.1	2.1	2.6	3.3	2.7	2.2	2.7	2.5	2.2	3.0	1.0	1.7	3.2	4.9	2.9
4. 3 or 4 times	1.1	1.4	0.8	1.1	0.7	1.8	1.0	1.1	0.6	0.8	1.5	0.9	0.8	0.4	1.9	2.5
5. 5 or more times	1.2	1.7	0.8	1.2	0.4	0.8	1.6	1.4	0.7	0.9	1.5	0.9	1.1	2.0	1.2	2.5
Item 9876 Subject B07,S03 N	2840	1314	1440	2254	302	629	840	908	463	1633	1114	1025	585	391	779	28
E08G: Has an unarmed person threatened you with injury, but not actually injured you?																
1. Not at all	75.7	68.6	82.3	76.1	75.5	74.5	74.5	76.3	78.1	76.3	75.1	82.3	76.7	73.0	68.0	66.9
2. Once	13.1	14.9	11.0	12.7	13.9	14.9	14.0	11.7	11.7	13.3	12.6	9.0	14.2	17.2	15.8	15.4
3. Twice	5.3	7.3	3.5	5.4	4.9	5.6	5.3	5.5	4.5	4.9	6.1	3.9	4.5	5.0	7.9	6.6
4. 3 or 4 times	3.1	4.3	1.9	2.8	3.6	2.5	2.8	3.8	3.0	2.8	3.4	2.4	2.8	3.0	4.1	3.1
5. 5 or more times	2.9	4.7	1.3	3.0	2.1	2.4	3.4	2.7	2.7	2.8	2.9	2.5	1.9	1.8	4.2	8.0
Item 9877 Subject B07,S03 N	2837	1308	1443	2253	303	630	839	910	459	1634	1109	1026	585	392	776	28
E09: Looking toward the future, how important would it be for you to have each of the following things?																
E09A: At least one car																
1. Not important	2.8	3.5	2.0	2.2	4.0	2.1	2.9	2.5	4.0	2.4	3.4	2.6	3.4	2.3	1.9	17.1
2. Somewhat important	16.4	15.9	17.1	14.7	24.3	19.1	13.6	16.1	18.7	17.1	15.0	18.7	18.9	14.8	11.9	19.3
3. Quite important	37.6	37.9	37.2	38.4	34.0	40.2	39.2	36.9	32.4	39.4	34.9	40.8	36.0	37.8	35.7	14.2
4. Extremely important	43.2	42.7	43.7	44.7	37.7	38.6	44.4	44.5	45.0	41.1	46.7	38.0	41.7	45.1	50.6	49.3
Item 13835 Subject F01 N	2820	1303	1436	2235	304	627	838	897	457	1622	1105	1020	578	394	767	28
E09B: At least two cars																
1. Not important	46.5	38.6	54.7	45.1	53.8	53.5	45.5	41.7	48.4	46.3	46.9	47.6	50.1	47.1	42.3	37.1
2. Somewhat important	31.7	34.0	28.9	33.1	25.5	31.9	34.3	31.8	26.5	31.7	31.9	32.9	28.5	31.4	33.5	31.9
3. Quite important	15.0	18.2	11.8	15.5	10.9	11.3	13.2	17.6	18.0	16.2	12.8	13.1	16.7	14.6	16.2	8.8
4. Extremely important	6.8	9.1	4.6	6.3	9.7	3.2	7.0	8.8	7.1	5.8	8.5	6.4	4.7	6.8	8.1	22.2
Item 13840 Subject F01 N	2816	1297	1437	2229	305	623	837	899	457	1620	1103	1019	575	396	766	28
E09C: A large (full-sized) car																
1. Not important	66.8	57.5	75.6	67.7	62.2	68.9	67.2	63.7	69.7	66.4	67.1	66.1	67.5	66.2	67.6	71.7
2. Somewhat important	20.9	25.6	16.4	21.4	18.3	19.6	20.4	22.4	20.5	22.2	19.0	20.3	21.5	22.8	20.9	7.1
3. Quite important	7.3	10.3	4.6	7.1	8.4	7.3	7.2	8.3	5.5	7.2	7.6	8.6	6.8	5.3	6.5	15.3
4. Extremely important	5.0	6.6	3.4	3.8	11.2	4.3	5.2	5.6	4.3	4.2	6.4	5.0	4.2	5.7	5.0	5.8
Item 13850 Subject F01 N	2794	1289	1425	2218	304	622	825	893	453	1610	1091	1007	578	391	760	28
E09D: A new car every two or three years																
1. Not important	67.2	59.7	74.9	66.9	66.8	72.6	65.7	62.3	72.3	66.1	68.9	70.1	68.9	61.3	65.6	61.4
2. Somewhat important	19.6	23.7	15.5	20.8	15.2	18.0	20.2	21.2	17.3	19.9	19.2	18.7	18.3	23.1	20.3	13.2
3. Quite important	8.0	10.3	5.9	7.7	9.4	5.7	8.1	10.0	7.3	9.1	6.3	6.9	8.7	10.3	7.3	10.9
4. Extremely important	5.2	6.3	3.7	4.6	8.7	3.7	6.0	6.5	3.0	4.9	5.6	4.4	4.1	5.2	6.8	14.5
Item 13860 Subject F01 N	2794	1294	1420	2217	302	621	833	889	451	1603	1098	1010	570	390	763	28

QUESTIONNAIRE FORM 3 1983	TOTAL	SEX		RACE		REGION				4YR COLLEGE PLANS		ILLICIT DRUG USE: LIFETIME				
		M	F	White	Black	NE	NC	S	W	Yes	No	None	Mari- juana Only	Few Pills	More Pills	Any Her- oin
N (Weighted No. of Cases):	3382	1575	1660	2571	403	828	931	1081	541	1837	1322	1173	701	469	926	37
% of Weighted Total:	100.0	46.6	49.1	76.0	11.9	24.5	27.5	32.0	16.0	54.3	39.1	34.7	20.7	13.9	27.4	1.1

E09E: Clothes in the latest style

1. Not important	15.8	21.4	10.8	16.1	7.5	14.7	17.3	11.9	22.3	14.2	17.7	17.0	14.7	12.3	16.4	19.5
2. Somewhat important	38.0	37.5	38.5	38.6	32.2	36.3	40.0	37.1	38.4	37.4	39.3	42.3	36.3	35.8	35.3	32.9
3. Quite important	29.7	29.6	29.8	30.9	29.5	31.6	29.9	30.3	25.5	31.8	27.1	26.6	33.2	30.4	31.5	24.7
4. Extremely important	16.5	11.5	20.9	14.4	30.8	17.5	12.8	20.7	13.9	16.6	15.9	14.1	15.8	21.4	16.7	23.0
Item 13870 Subject F01 N	2796	1291	1424	2215	305	621	834	889	452	1609	1096	1010	579	391	756	28

E09F: A house of my own (instead of an apartment or condominium)

1. Not important	15.2	12.9	17.6	15.1	16.5	14.2	16.5	14.6	15.5	14.2	16.1	12.0	16.7	13.1	18.6	21.1
2. Somewhat important	24.6	22.7	25.6	26.0	19.0	25.1	26.6	21.6	26.0	24.6	24.4	26.6	23.1	24.8	22.8	33.1
3. Quite important	29.0	31.1	27.6	29.5	23.9	32.3	27.7	28.7	27.6	29.8	28.4	29.4	30.1	28.8	28.5	25.0
4. Extremely important	31.2	33.3	29.2	29.3	40.7	28.5	29.3	35.1	30.9	31.3	31.0	32.0	30.1	33.2	30.1	20.9
Item 13880 Subject F01 N	2808	1298	1431	2225	305	620	836	897	455	1612	1103	1018	573	394	764	28

E09G: Lots of space around my house, a big yard

1. Not important	14.2	13.0	15.5	13.4	18.4	11.2	15.8	15.0	13.9	12.4	16.8	10.9	15.9	12.7	17.4	29.8
2. Somewhat important	29.7	27.4	31.4	30.2	28.6	31.1	30.7	27.8	29.9	30.9	28.3	30.8	29.7	30.2	28.3	31.7
3. Quite important	30.4	32.4	28.6	31.1	26.1	32.7	28.4	30.7	30.6	31.3	29.0	30.7	31.4	29.3	30.1	22.1
4. Extremely important	25.6	27.2	24.5	25.3	26.9	25.1	25.1	26.4	25.5	25.4	25.9	27.6	23.1	27.8	24.2	16.5
Item 13890 Subject F01 N	2796	1290	1426	2214	304	616	834	891	455	1609	1095	1010	571	392	764	28

E09H: A well-kept garden and lawn

1. Not important	12.0	13.3	10.4	11.2	15.9	11.3	11.4	13.5	11.2	11.0	13.2	9.2	15.0	9.4	13.5	34.1
2. Somewhat important	32.8	31.7	33.7	33.6	26.2	38.0	34.3	28.6	31.3	32.6	33.0	34.4	30.6	33.0	33.0	18.8
3. Quite important	32.5	32.6	32.6	33.3	31.5	31.1	31.8	34.1	32.3	34.0	30.7	31.7	32.0	35.1	33.0	18.1
4. Extremely important	22.7	22.3	23.2	22.0	26.3	19.7	22.5	23.8	25.2	22.4	23.1	24.7	22.4	22.5	20.5	29.0
Item 13900 Subject F01 N	2789	1290	1419	2211	299	613	834	887	454	1600	1094	1009	567	391	762	28

E09I: Major labor-saving appliances (washer, drier, dishwasher, etc.)

1. Not important	8.7	8.4	8.8	8.0	10.3	9.3	9.7	6.9	9.9	7.1	10.9	7.7	9.3	7.2	9.6	22.3
2. Somewhat important	29.1	30.7	27.5	29.6	28.8	30.8	30.3	27.8	27.2	29.6	28.2	30.2	29.7	29.0	27.6	21.3
3. Quite important	36.7	39.6	34.5	38.1	27.9	37.3	36.5	35.8	38.2	37.3	36.6	36.7	36.5	40.0	36.2	25.2
4. Extremely important	25.4	21.3	29.3	24.3	33.0	22.7	23.6	29.5	24.6	26.0	24.3	25.4	24.5	23.9	26.6	31.2
Item 13910 Subject F01 N	2802	1295	1426	2217	306	616	836	894	456	1608	1101	1012	571	393	766	28

E09J: A high-quality stereo

1. Not important	14.4	9.9	18.9	14.0	16.8	12.7	15.7	15.0	13.3	13.8	15.3	19.2	14.4	11.0	9.9	11.7
2. Somewhat important	32.7	27.5	37.8	32.5	34.4	37.9	30.4	32.9	29.5	33.2	31.8	36.9	34.8	34.2	25.7	14.6
3. Quite important	29.0	31.1	26.9	30.2	24.5	26.0	29.9	29.7	30.1	29.9	28.0	26.3	29.2	31.6	31.3	32.1
4. Extremely important	23.9	31.5	16.4	23.2	24.3	23.5	24.0	22.4	27.1	23.1	24.9	17.6	21.6	23.1	33.0	41.5
Item 13920 Subject F01 N	2799	1295	1423	2217	304	614	836	892	458	1605	1098	1009	570	393	767	28

E09K: A vacation house

1. Not important	58.3	53.2	64.1	59.4	57.5	55.1	60.8	58.5	57.6	57.4	59.6	62.9	60.4	53.5	53.6	54.2
2. Somewhat important	25.5	29.0	21.7	25.6	21.6	28.9	25.4	24.2	23.7	26.6	23.9	21.5	24.5	28.2	30.3	10.7
3. Quite important	8.3	9.0	7.4	8.0	9.8	7.4	7.3	8.9	10.2	8.3	8.1	8.6	8.7	8.6	7.3	13.0
4. Extremely important	7.9	8.8	6.8	7.0	11.1	8.6	6.5	8.5	8.5	7.7	8.4	7.1	6.3	9.8	8.7	22.2
Item 13930 Subject F01 N	2786	1292	1416	2208	304	613	833	887	452	1607	1087	1010	568	389	758	28

E09L: A motor-powered, recreational vehicle (powerboat, snowmobile)

1. Not important	52.2	38.8	65.1	49.9	68.5	55.8	49.2	53.7	49.6	54.8	48.9	57.5	53.8	48.8	46.8	30.7
2. Somewhat important	26.0	30.4	22.4	27.6	16.5	26.3	27.2	26.0	23.1	25.0	27.0	23.4	27.9	28.2	27.1	13.1
3. Quite important	12.7	17.4	7.5	13.7	6.3	11.1	13.6	10.9	16.8	12.0	13.3	12.3	10.9	13.2	13.8	18.8
4. Extremely important	9.2	13.3	4.9	8.8	8.7	6.8	9.9	9.4	10.5	8.2	10.7	6.8	7.4	9.8	12.3	37.3
Item 13940 Subject F01 N	2797	1294	1423	2216	305	616	837	893	451	1606	1097	1010	572	391	763	28

QUESTIONNAIRE FORM 3 1983	TOTAL	SEX M	SEX F	RACE White	RACE Black	REGION NE	REGION NC	REGION S	REGION W	4YR COLLEGE PLANS Yes	4YR COLLEGE PLANS No	None	Mari- juana Only	Few Pills	More Pills	Any Her- oin
N (Weighted No. of Cases):	3382	1575	1660	2571	403	828	931	1081	541	1837	1322	1173	701	469	926	37
% of Weighted Total:	100.0	46.6	49.1	76.0	11.9	24.5	27.5	32.0	16.0	54.3	39.1	34.7	20.7	13.9	27.4	1.1

E10: When (if ever) did you FIRST do each of the following things? Don't count anything you took because a doctor told you to.

E10A: Smoke cigarettes on a daily basis

	TOTAL	M	F	White	Black	NE	NC	S	W	Yes	No	None	Mari.	Few	More	Heroin
8. Never	65.7	72.2	60.5	64.1	80.8	61.1	59.9	67.9	78.6	75.2	52.0	90.4	66.9	60.4	36.0	38.8
1. Grade 6 or below	5.3	4.4	5.6	5.5	2.7	4.9	7.6	4.6	2.7	3.5	8.0	0.7	3.4	6.5	11.2	28.5
2. Grade 7 or 8	9.5	7.8	10.9	10.3	4.4	12.7	8.7	9.8	5.9	6.9	13.4	3.3	7.3	10.3	18.8	17.4
3. Grade 9 (Freshman)	6.8	4.9	8.3	7.1	2.3	9.3	7.8	5.7	3.7	4.9	9.7	1.6	8.8	5.3	13.1	2.9
4. Grade 10 (Sophomore)	5.1	4.4	5.9	5.4	2.8	4.9	6.9	3.9	4.7	3.5	6.9	1.1	5.3	8.1	8.3	7.1
5. Grade 11 (Junior)	4.4	3.2	5.6	4.6	1.6	4.0	5.5	4.3	3.0	3.5	5.6	1.3	4.5	4.3	8.7	-
6. Grade 12 (Senior)	3.2	3.1	3.3	3.1	5.4	3.1	3.6	3.8	1.5	2.5	4.4	1.6	3.8	5.1	3.9	5.2
Item 5570 Subject A01g N	2498	1147	1278	1996	267	539	757	806	396	1459	957	919	488	339	700	24

E10B: Try an alcoholic beverage - more than just a few sips

	TOTAL	M	F	White	Black	NE	NC	S	W	Yes	No	None	Mari.	Few	More	Heroin
8. Never	7.8	7.8	7.5	5.6	15.9	4.9	5.4	10.2	11.5	7.7	8.2	19.9	1.3	2.7	0.4	2.9
1. Grade 6 or below	9.0	11.3	7.0	9.0	6.3	8.0	10.6	8.1	9.3	8.3	9.5	6.0	8.1	6.5	13.5	31.5
2. Grade 7 or 8	21.1	24.7	17.9	22.3	13.2	25.4	23.4	16.2	20.3	20.6	22.3	9.5	24.2	23.6	31.1	33.5
3. Grade 9 (Freshman)	25.5	24.5	26.6	27.2	18.7	28.0	27.5	25.1	19.3	24.1	27.6	17.3	28.0	29.3	31.8	15.7
4. Grade 10 (Sophomore)	18.3	16.1	20.2	19.1	16.2	15.8	18.7	19.3	18.8	19.4	16.1	19.1	22.4	23.1	12.4	10.6
5. Grade 11 (Junior)	12.0	11.0	13.1	11.9	14.2	12.4	10.1	12.3	14.4	13.5	10.2	18.6	9.5	9.6	8.1	-
6. Grade 12 (Senior)	6.3	4.7	7.6	4.8	15.5	5.4	4.3	8.8	6.4	6.4	6.1	9.6	6.5	5.1	2.7	5.8
Item 5580 Subject A01g N	2532	1170	1294	2035	252	568	767	790	406	1450	1001	852	530	364	732	25

E10C: Try marijuana or hashish

	TOTAL	M	F	White	Black	NE	NC	S	W	Yes	No	None	Mari.	Few	More	Heroin
8. Never	44.2	42.5	46.1	43.5	45.8	36.2	44.7	49.3	44.2	49.1	37.6	100.0	0.5	26.7	9.5	7.9
1. Grade 6 or below	3.1	4.2	1.9	2.5	4.1	2.8	3.2	2.5	4.6	2.3	4.2	-	3.9	2.7	5.5	33.7
2. Grade 7 or 8	14.5	16.5	12.9	15.4	10.0	18.0	16.2	10.5	14.7	14.0	15.4	-	18.7	16.2	30.1	22.3
3. Grade 9 (Freshman)	16.0	16.7	15.4	16.1	15.1	18.1	15.4	15.4	15.3	14.4	18.1	-	25.4	22.3	28.1	12.5
4. Grade 10 (Sophomore)	10.6	10.0	11.4	11.1	10.6	12.5	10.9	9.9	9.1	9.2	12.7	-	20.4	15.8	15.4	15.3
5. Grade 11 (Junior)	7.0	6.3	7.2	6.7	8.3	6.9	5.9	8.0	7.3	6.6	7.5	-	17.7	10.4	7.2	8.3
6. Grade 12 (Senior)	4.5	3.8	5.1	4.6	6.1	5.6	3.8	4.4	4.8	4.4	4.6	-	13.3	5.7	4.2	-
Item 5590 Subject A01g N	2626	1209	1343	2107	263	575	791	827	433	1529	1014	979	502	368	726	27

E10D: Try LSD

	TOTAL	M	F	White	Black	NE	NC	S	W	Yes	No	None	Mari.	Few	More	Heroin
8. Never	93.9	93.5	94.3	93.3	98.8	93.7	91.9	95.1	95.5	95.2	91.7	100.0	100.0	98.4	80.4	23.6
1. Grade 6 or below	0.1	0.1	-	0.1	-	0.3	-	-	-	-	0.1	-	-	-	-	8.1
2. Grade 7 or 8	0.5	0.4	0.6	0.5	0.4	0.2	1.0	0.3	0.5	0.4	0.8	-	-	0.3	1.0	25.1
3. Grade 9 (Freshman)	1.2	1.1	1.2	1.3	-	0.7	1.6	1.1	1.1	0.7	1.9	-	-	-	4.0	12.7
4. Grade 10 (Sophomore)	1.3	1.6	0.9	1.3	0.4	1.0	2.0	1.2	0.6	1.3	1.4	-	-	0.5	4.3	8.9
5. Grade 11 (Junior)	2.2	2.4	2.1	2.5	0.4	2.7	2.9	1.6	1.4	1.6	3.1	-	-	0.5	7.3	21.6
6. Grade 12 (Senior)	0.9	0.8	0.8	1.0	-	1.4	0.6	0.8	0.9	0.8	0.9	-	-	0.4	3.1	-
Item 5600 Subject A01g N	2695	1242	1379	2141	295	589	803	863	441	1575	1037	997	561	372	712	24

E10E: Try any psychedelic other than LSD

	TOTAL	M	F	White	Black	NE	NC	S	W	Yes	No	None	Mari.	Few	More	Heroin
8. Never	96.8	96.3	97.5	96.6	99.6	95.5	96.7	98.0	96.4	97.4	96.0	100.0	100.0	98.3	90.1	37.6
1. Grade 6 or below	0.1	0.1	0.1	0.1	-	0.5	-	-	-	0.1	0.2	-	-	-	0.2	7.8
2. Grade 7 or 8	0.5	0.4	0.4	0.5	-	0.3	0.7	0.3	0.5	0.6	0.3	-	-	0.6	1.3	6.3
3. Grade 9 (Freshman)	0.8	0.9	0.7	0.8	0.4	0.8	1.5	0.4	0.3	0.1	1.9	-	-	-	2.2	30.8
4. Grade 10 (Sophomore)	0.6	0.6	0.4	0.4	-	1.2	0.5	0.3	0.4	0.5	0.4	-	-	0.4	1.8	5.2
5. Grade 11 (Junior)	0.7	0.9	0.6	0.9	-	0.8	0.2	0.6	1.4	0.7	0.7	-	-	-	2.5	7.7
6. Grade 12 (Senior)	0.6	0.8	0.4	0.7	-	0.9	0.4	0.4	0.9	0.7	0.5	-	-	0.7	1.9	4.5
Item 5610 Subject A01g N	2643	1219	1348	2092	290	575	780	856	432	1548	1009	996	563	376	660	20

E10F: Try amphetamines

	TOTAL	M	F	White	Black	NE	NC	S	W	Yes	No	None	Mari.	Few	More	Heroin
8. Never	79.9	82.7	77.3	76.7	95.3	78.8	77.1	81.5	83.2	83.6	74.1	99.9	99.9	69.6	18.1	17.6
1. Grade 6 or below	0.4	0.2	0.6	0.4	-	0.4	0.5	0.4	0.2	0.2	0.8	-	-	-	1.5	8.4
2. Grade 7 or 8	2.3	2.5	2.1	2.5	-	1.7	3.5	1.8	2.0	1.3	4.1	-	-	0.2	9.9	27.7
3. Grade 9 (Freshman)	4.2	3.9	4.5	5.0	1.3	5.7	5.1	3.1	2.8	3.3	5.3	-	-	3.9	18.5	14.2
4. Grade 10 (Sophomore)	6.2	4.8	7.3	7.1	1.1	5.9	7.1	6.2	4.8	5.3	7.8	0.1	0.1	6.4	26.7	19.4
5. Grade 11 (Junior)	4.2	3.7	4.5	4.9	1.2	5.4	4.3	3.8	2.9	3.6	5.0	-	-	8.1	17.1	-
6. Grade 12 (Senior)	2.8	2.1	3.7	3.4	1.0	2.1	2.4	3.2	4.0	2.8	2.9	-	-	11.8	8.2	12.7
Item 5620 Subject A01g N	2260	1083	1120	1781	267	506	654	737	363	1349	834	992	557	206	453	24

QUESTIONNAIRE FORM 3 1983	TOTAL	SEX		RACE		REGION				4YR COLLEGE PLANS		ILLICIT DRUG USE: LIFETIME				
		M	F	White	Black	NE	NC	S	W	Yes	No	None	Mari- juana Only	Few Pills	More Pills	Any Her- oin
N (Weighted No. of Cases):	3382	1575	1660	2571	403	828	931	1081	541	1837	1322	1173	701	469	926	37
% of Weighted Total:	100.0	46.6	49.1	76.0	11.9	24.5	27.5	32.0	16.0	54.3	39.1	34.7	20.7	13.9	27.4	1.1

E10G: Try quaaludes

8. Never	92.3	92.0	92.7	91.1	99.4	92.2	92.4	90.8	95.3	94.6	89.1	100.0	100.0	96.9	74.9	36.1
1. Grade 6 or below	0.1	0.1	0.1	0.1	-	0.1	-	0.2	-	0.1	0.1	-	-	-	0.2	3.3
2. Grade 7 or 8	0.9	0.9	0.8	0.9	-	0.9	1.0	1.0	0.6	0.5	1.3	-	-	0.1	2.5	19.7
3. Grade 9 (Freshman)	2.0	1.9	1.9	2.4	-	2.0	2.0	2.3	1.6	1.3	3.0	-	-	0.8	7.1	5.2
4. Grade 10 (Sophomore)	2.1	1.9	2.4	2.5	0.6	2.0	2.2	2.6	1.1	1.4	3.3	-	-	1.1	6.6	22.4
5. Grade 11 (Junior)	1.7	2.2	1.3	2.0	-	1.6	1.8	1.9	1.2	1.5	2.0	-	-	0.8	5.9	-
6. Grade 12 (Senior)	0.9	1.0	0.9	1.1	-	1.3	0.6	1.3	0.2	0.5	1.1	-	-	0.3	2.9	13.4
Item 5630　Subject A01g　N	2697	1239	1385	2140	290	597	817	847	437	1560	1047	996	560	375	712	25

E10H: Try barbiturates

8. Never	94.3	94.2	94.6	93.9	99.3	94.4	94.1	94.1	95.3	96.1	91.6	100.0	100.0	98.3	79.6	43.2
1. Grade 6 or below	0.1	0.2	*	0.1	-	0.1	-	0.2	-	*	0.2	-	-	-	0.3	3.9
2. Grade 7 or 8	0.8	0.8	0.8	0.8	-	0.6	1.1	0.5	0.7	0.6	1.1	-	-	-	2.3	20.3
3. Grade 9 (Freshman)	1.8	1.7	1.7	2.0	0.3	3.0	1.6	1.4	1.1	1.1	2.7	-	-	0.4	6.5	18.1
4. Grade 10 (Sophomore)	1.5	1.3	1.7	1.7	0.4	0.8	1.2	2.5	1.1	1.1	2.3	-	-	0.3	5.7	10.3
5. Grade 11 (Junior)	1.1	1.4	0.7	1.0	-	0.4	1.6	0.8	1.6	0.5	2.0	*	-	0.2	4.1	4.2
6. Grade 12 (Senior)	0.4	0.4	0.5	0.4	-	0.7	0.4	0.4	0.2	0.6	0.1	-	-	0.8	1.3	-
Item 5640　Subject A01g　N	2593	1195	1330	2049	290	579	779	813	423	1524	983	995	561	360	627	21

E10I: Try tranquilizers

8. Never	93.2	93.5	93.0	92.3	98.6	94.5	92.9	91.8	94.8	94.8	91.1	100.0	100.0	95.9	76.0	47.2
1. Grade 6 or below	0.2	0.2	0.3	0.2	-	0.2	0.2	0.4	-	0.2	0.2	-	-	0.1	0.7	3.8
2. Grade 7 or 8	1.2	1.3	1.1	1.4	-	1.0	1.4	1.4	0.9	0.7	2.1	-	-	-	3.9	34.7
3. Grade 9 (Freshman)	1.5	1.4	1.6	1.7	0.3	1.1	1.4	1.9	1.6	1.2	1.9	-	-	1.5	5.5	-
4. Grade 10 (Sophomore)	1.6	1.9	1.5	1.8	0.9	1.1	2.0	2.0	1.0	1.2	2.4	-	-	0.8	5.8	14.3
5. Grade 11 (Junior)	1.2	1.0	1.4	1.5	0.3	1.2	1.2	1.4	1.2	0.8	1.9	-	-	0.9	4.7	-
6. Grade 12 (Senior)	0.9	0.7	1.1	1.2	-	1.0	0.9	1.0	0.6	1.0	0.4	-	-	0.8	3.4	-
Item 5650　Subject A01g　N	2546	1161	1314	2024	278	570	764	807	405	1487	970	993	561	325	617	22

E10J: Try cocaine

8. Never	85.7	84.1	87.4	85.5	89.4	79.8	89.9	90.0	77.8	88.6	81.6	100.0	100.0	81.7	59.0	18.0
1. Grade 6 or below	0.2	0.3	0.2	0.1	0.6	0.4	-	0.2	0.3	0.1	0.4	-	-	0.4	0.5	3.4
2. Grade 7 or 8	0.7	1.0	0.5	0.7	1.0	0.8	0.4	1.1	0.5	0.6	0.9	-	-	0.8	1.8	12.7
3. Grade 9 (Freshman)	1.7	1.7	1.4	1.5	1.4	2.1	1.2	1.6	2.1	1.3	2.1	-	-	0.3	4.8	31.8
4. Grade 10 (Sophomore)	3.0	3.3	2.9	3.5	0.2	3.6	2.8	2.0	4.7	2.2	4.4	-	-	2.8	9.5	14.1
5. Grade 11 (Junior)	4.6	5.2	4.3	4.6	4.4	9.0	3.5	2.6	4.9	4.0	5.8	-	-	6.6	13.3	20.1
6. Grade 12 (Senior)	4.0	4.6	3.4	4.0	3.1	4.3	2.2	2.5	9.7	3.2	4.8	-	-	7.4	11.0	-
Item 5660　Subject A01g　N	2693	1239	1380	2139	285	592	816	851	435	1563	1040	993	557	375	715	24

E10K: Try heroin

8. Never	99.6	99.6	99.7	99.7	99.2	99.6	99.6	99.6	99.7	99.7	99.4	100.0	100.0	100.0	100.0	-
1. Grade 6 or below	0.1	0.1	-	*	-	0.1	0.1	-	-	0.1	0.1	-	-	-	-	16.4
2. Grade 7 or 8	*	-	*	*	-	-	-	-	0.1	*	-	-	-	-	-	4.9
3. Grade 9 (Freshman)	*	-	0.1	-	0.4	-	-	0.1	-	-	0.1	-	-	-	-	11.0
4. Grade 10 (Sophomore)	*	*	-	*	-	-	0.1	-	-	-	0.1	-	-	-	-	5.1
5. Grade 11 (Junior)	0.2	0.2	0.2	0.1	0.4	0.2	0.2	0.1	0.2	0.2	0.2	-	-	-	-	46.3
6. Grade 12 (Senior)	0.1	0.1	-	0.1	-	0.1	-	0.1	-	-	0.1	-	-	-	-	16.2
Item 5670　Subject A01g　N	2725	1259	1391	2167	294	603	818	861	442	1587	1047	995	560	386	746	10

E10L: Try any narcotic other than heroin

8. Never	97.6	97.3	97.9	97.4	99.0	97.9	98.3	97.1	96.9	97.9	97.0	100.0	100.0	98.0	92.9	44.9
1. Grade 6 or below	*	0.1	-	0.1	-	0.1	-	0.1	-	*	0.1	-	-	-	0.1	4.1
2. Grade 7 or 8	0.2	0.1	0.3	0.3	-	0.4	0.2	0.1	0.1	0.2	0.2	-	-	-	0.8	2.5
3. Grade 9 (Freshman)	0.5	0.5	0.5	0.6	0.4	0.7	0.4	0.7	0.1	0.4	0.7	-	-	0.5	1.1	24.1
4. Grade 10 (Sophomore)	0.5	0.5	0.5	0.6	-	0.1	0.3	0.7	0.8	0.4	0.6	-	-	0.4	1.7	2.7
5. Grade 11 (Junior)	0.7	0.9	0.6	0.7	0.4	0.4	0.5	0.8	1.2	0.6	0.9	-	-	0.2	2.2	18.1
6. Grade 12 (Senior)	0.4	0.6	0.3	0.4	0.2	0.3	0.4	0.5	0.7	0.4	0.5	-	-	1.0	1.2	3.5
Item 5680　Subject A01g　N	2565	1172	1320	2021	286	569	775	812	410	1505	976	994	559	361	601	20

*=less than .05 per cent.

QUESTIONNAIRE FORM 3 1983	TOTAL	SEX		RACE		REGION				4YR COLLEGE PLANS		ILLICIT DRUG USE: LIFETIME				
		M	F	White	Black	NE	NC	S	W	Yes	No	None	Mari- juana Only	Few Pills	More Pills	Any Her- oin
N (Weighted No. of Cases):	3382	1575	1660	2571	403	828	931	1081	541	1837	1322	1173	701	469	926	37
% of Weighted Total:	100.0	46.6	49.1	76.0	11.9	24.5	27.5	32.0	16.0	54.3	39.1	34.7	20.7	13.9	27.4	1.1

E10M: Try inhalants

	TOTAL	M	F	White	Black	NE	NC	S	W	Yes	No	None	Mari-juana Only	Few Pills	More Pills	Any Heroin
8. Never	92.2	90.5	94.0	91.7	96.3	92.6	91.5	93.5	90.3	92.4	92.0	98.7	96.7	87.7	81.9	72.2
1. Grade 6 or below	1.4	1.3	1.3	1.4	1.1	1.7	1.6	0.7	2.1	1.2	1.5	0.5	0.9	2.8	1.8	16.1
2. Grade 7 or 8	1.9	2.3	1.4	1.9	1.3	1.7	1.7	1.6	3.1	1.7	2.1	0.1	1.1	2.8	4.7	5.8
3. Grade 9 (Freshman)	1.4	2.1	0.8	1.7	0.3	1.8	1.2	1.1	1.7	1.4	1.4	0.2	0.3	1.9	3.9	-
4. Grade 10 (Sophomore)	1.0	1.0	1.0	1.1	0.5	1.0	1.5	0.9	0.1	1.1	0.9	0.1	0.5	1.2	2.6	-
5. Grade 11 (Junior)	1.1	1.5	0.9	1.2	0.3	0.5	1.1	1.2	1.9	1.1	1.2	0.2	0.1	1.8	3.0	-
6. Grade 12 (Senior)	1.0	1.3	0.6	1.1	0.3	0.7	1.4	1.0	0.8	1.1	0.9	0.2	0.4	1.8	2.2	6.0
Item 5685 Subject A01g N	2551	1155	1327	2023	279	567	762	808	414	1489	979	976	518	348	660	21

QUESTIONNAIRE FORM 4 1983	TOTAL	SEX		RACE		REGION				4YR COLLEGE PLANS		ILLICIT DRUG USE: LIFETIME				
		M	F	White	Black	NE	NC	S	W	Yes	No	None	Mari- juana Only	Few Pills	More Pills	Any Her- oin
N (Weighted No. of Cases):	3344	1610	1630	2556	406	793	949	1075	527	1733	1355	1233	699	455	814	51
% of Weighted Total:	100.0	48.1	48.8	76.4	12.1	23.7	28.4	32.2	15.8	51.8	40.5	36.9	20.9	13.6	24.3	1.5

A01: Taking all things together, how would you say things are these days-would you say you're very happy, pretty happy, or not too happy these days?

	TOTAL	M	F	White	Black	NE	NC	S	W	Yes	No	None	Mari- juana Only	Few Pills	More Pills	Any Her- oin
3. Very happy	15.6	13.5	17.6	17.0	8.9	14.5	13.5	15.0	22.3	17.8	13.0	16.1	15.0	15.0	16.0	9.9
2. Pretty happy	69.6	71.1	68.4	70.7	69.5	68.7	72.4	71.2	62.4	70.1	70.8	71.2	68.0	70.3	69.3	64.6
1. Not too happy	14.8	15.4	13.9	12.3	21.7	16.8	14.1	13.8	15.4	12.1	16.3	12.7	17.0	14.6	14.8	25.5
Item 1190 Subject P01,Q01 N	3334	1605	1626	2549	405	789	947	1073	524	1731	1349	1232	698	453	809	51

A02: Looking ahead to the next five years, do you think that things in this country will get better or worse?

	TOTAL	M	F	White	Black	NE	NC	S	W	Yes	No	None	Mari- juana Only	Few Pills	More Pills	Any Her- oin
1. Get much better	4.1	6.0	2.0	3.9	3.0	1.2	5.0	4.9	5.2	5.0	3.0	4.6	3.8	4.5	3.2	0.4
2. Get somewhat better	41.6	46.4	37.2	42.5	38.6	38.8	42.6	42.7	41.8	43.0	40.5	40.9	44.2	39.7	42.0	42.8
3. Stay about the same	24.3	22.1	26.9	26.3	17.5	27.2	25.4	21.9	23.0	24.6	24.9	25.7	23.9	27.1	22.0	11.1
4. Get somewhat worse	25.2	21.8	28.3	23.4	33.5	27.5	21.9	26.9	24.3	23.4	26.3	23.8	25.0	26.1	26.8	29.6
5. Get much worse	4.8	3.8	5.6	4.0	7.3	5.3	5.2	3.6	5.6	4.1	5.3	4.9	3.1	2.7	5.9	16.1
Item 9940 Subject I01 N	3336	1604	1629	2554	406	791	949	1074	522	1732	1352	1231	699	455	809	51

A03: Looking ahead to the next five years, do you think that things in the rest of the world will get better or worse?

	TOTAL	M	F	White	Black	NE	NC	S	W	Yes	No	None	Mari- juana Only	Few Pills	More Pills	Any Her- oin
1. Get much better	1.4	1.7	1.1	1.1	2.1	0.5	1.4	2.2	1.2	1.5	1.2	1.5	1.8	1.5	1.0	-
2. Get somewhat better	21.0	21.6	20.2	19.4	25.9	19.6	22.0	20.3	22.7	20.5	20.9	21.6	20.9	19.9	19.3	23.1
3. Stay about the same	31.7	32.1	31.3	33.3	28.2	33.5	31.9	32.2	27.5	33.2	29.9	30.6	35.9	29.8	31.7	18.5
4. Get somewhat worse	37.9	36.0	40.0	39.4	32.2	37.9	36.7	37.6	40.8	37.4	39.2	38.1	35.4	43.9	38.6	38.9
5. Get much worse	8.0	8.6	7.3	6.8	11.6	8.4	8.0	7.8	7.9	7.4	8.9	8.3	5.9	4.8	9.4	19.5
Item 9950 Subject I01 N	3323	1602	1619	2541	406	784	946	1071	522	1728	1343	1224	693	453	810	51

A04: How do you think your own life will go in the next five years–do you think it will get better or worse?

	TOTAL	M	F	White	Black	NE	NC	S	W	Yes	No	None	Mari- juana Only	Few Pills	More Pills	Any Her- oin
1. Get much better	41.9	40.3	43.3	40.8	51.3	41.5	37.6	43.0	48.0	44.5	37.9	39.8	42.5	40.3	45.5	33.1
2. Get somewhat better	47.3	47.1	47.7	48.0	44.1	48.5	49.4	46.8	43.0	46.1	49.6	49.7	46.2	46.0	45.5	47.2
3. Stay about the same	9.1	10.5	7.6	9.5	3.8	7.5	11.4	9.3	6.8	8.2	10.3	9.0	10.3	11.2	7.2	14.7
4. Get somewhat worse	1.3	1.7	1.0	1.4	0.6	1.8	1.2	0.6	2.2	1.1	1.5	1.5	1.0	1.5	1.3	-
5. Get much worse	0.4	0.3	0.5	0.3	0.3	0.7	0.4	0.3	-	0.1	0.7	0.1	-	1.0	0.5	5.1
Item 9960 Subject I01 N	3328	1601	1624	2552	404	790	948	1071	519	1729	1352	1228	694	453	809	51

A05: Some people think a lot about the social problems of the nation and the world, and about how they might be solved. Others spend little time thinking about these issues. How much do you think about such things?

	TOTAL	M	F	White	Black	NE	NC	S	W	Yes	No	None	Mari- juana Only	Few Pills	More Pills	Any Her- oin
1. Never	2.6	3.2	2.0	2.1	2.2	3.1	2.7	1.4	4.2	1.2	4.0	2.0	2.5	1.9	3.6	9.6
2. Seldom	19.8	19.0	20.4	20.7	16.9	20.5	21.9	18.7	17.1	16.9	22.8	17.5	19.2	23.3	21.1	19.5
3. Sometimes	49.7	47.7	51.6	51.3	44.9	51.0	50.5	49.8	45.9	49.2	51.6	49.9	53.6	45.9	49.4	43.5
4. Quite often	23.8	25.5	22.3	22.5	29.1	21.2	21.6	25.2	28.7	27.6	19.3	25.4	21.7	25.3	22.3	25.0
5. A great deal	4.1	4.6	3.6	3.4	6.8	4.3	3.2	4.9	4.0	5.1	2.2	5.2	3.0	3.7	3.7	2.3
Item 6880 Subject J,Q08 N	3338	1607	1629	2556	404	791	949	1074	525	1733	1352	1232	699	455	812	50

A06: These questions are about pollution and the environment. Please mark the circle that shows how much you agree or disagree with each statement below.

A06A: In general, pollution has increased in the U.S. in the last ten years

	TOTAL	M	F	White	Black	NE	NC	S	W	Yes	No	None	Mari- juana Only	Few Pills	More Pills	Any Her- oin
1. Disagree	4.4	5.8	3.0	3.8	7.0	4.1	3.9	5.0	4.4	3.4	5.5	4.6	4.0	3.7	4.6	4.3
2. Mostly disagree	6.8	7.5	6.0	7.2	6.8	7.1	7.7	6.8	4.7	7.4	6.3	6.4	6.8	8.3	6.0	9.2
3. Neither	6.5	7.0	5.7	6.5	6.2	5.7	8.9	6.3	3.9	7.4	5.5	7.1	6.9	4.5	6.8	-
4. Mostly agree	33.0	29.0	36.8	33.8	30.2	30.8	32.3	35.6	32.1	32.6	33.5	31.3	29.8	40.6	33.7	29.8
5. Agree	49.3	50.7	48.6	48.7	49.7	52.3	47.1	46.3	54.9	49.3	49.2	50.6	52.4	43.0	48.9	56.7
Item 9970 Subject F04 N	3328	1603	1625	2549	406	788	943	1073	524	1728	1351	1230	698	454	807	51

QUESTIONNAIRE FORM 4 1983	TOTAL	SEX		RACE		REGION				4YR COLLEGE PLANS		ILLICIT DRUG USE: LIFETIME				
		M	F	White	Black	NE	NC	S	W	Yes	No	None	Mari-juana Only	Few Pills	More Pills	Any Her-oin
N (Weighted No. of Cases):	3344	1610	1630	2556	406	793	949	1075	527	1733	1355	1233	699	455	814	51
% of Weighted Total:	100.0	48.1	48.8	76.4	12.1	23.7	28.4	32.2	15.8	51.8	40.5	36.9	20.9	13.6	24.3	1.5
A06B: The dangers of pollution are not really as great as government, the media, and environmental groups would like us to believe																
1. Disagree	38.1	38.6	38.1	37.7	41.9	41.9	39.7	34.7	36.3	41.4	34.2	41.3	35.5	33.4	38.9	34.2
2. Mostly disagree	27.6	25.2	30.3	30.4	18.0	22.7	30.3	28.5	28.3	30.5	25.3	26.9	28.5	33.7	25.9	23.6
3. Neither	10.5	10.7	10.0	10.3	7.8	10.5	9.8	11.4	10.0	8.2	13.1	9.6	9.3	12.3	10.7	14.0
4. Mostly agree	14.3	14.9	13.0	13.4	15.6	13.9	13.1	14.7	16.1	12.7	15.6	13.6	15.2	12.1	14.9	10.8
5. Agree	9.5	10.7	8.5	8.2	16.7	11.0	7.1	10.8	9.2	7.2	11.9	8.5	11.5	8.5	9.6	17.5
Item 9980 Subject F04 N	3313	1592	1623	2543	399	778	945	1067	522	1723	1345	1223	691	453	808	51
A06C: America needs growth to survive, and that is going to require some increase in pollution																
1. Disagree	35.1	36.6	34.4	35.1	35.5	39.1	32.7	35.4	32.4	36.8	33.7	38.1	34.5	30.7	33.7	40.1
2. Mostly disagree	21.8	19.9	23.5	23.3	15.7	19.5	25.6	20.1	21.7	23.5	20.8	20.6	20.7	22.8	24.4	18.4
3. Neither	12.4	12.8	11.9	12.7	10.4	10.3	13.9	12.4	12.8	12.7	12.0	11.8	12.2	12.8	13.0	12.8
4. Mostly agree	19.0	18.9	18.9	19.4	16.9	19.3	18.2	18.0	21.8	16.7	20.6	17.6	19.6	22.4	19.1	11.0
5. Agree	11.8	11.8	11.3	9.5	21.5	11.8	9.6	14.2	11.3	10.2	12.9	11.8	12.9	11.3	9.8	17.7
Item 9990 Subject F04 N	3316	1596	1622	2541	403	781	944	1069	523	1726	1347	1229	694	452	804	51
A06D: People will have to change their buying habits and way of life to correct our environmental problems																
1. Disagree	14.0	16.1	11.8	12.7	18.7	17.1	12.6	13.7	12.2	13.2	15.0	13.7	15.7	11.3	14.4	14.5
2. Mostly disagree	13.2	14.7	12.0	12.9	14.5	12.2	13.5	13.2	13.9	12.6	13.8	13.7	13.7	12.8	12.5	12.6
3. Neither	15.1	15.2	14.9	16.1	10.1	16.2	15.7	14.1	14.5	14.6	16.5	12.7	16.3	15.0	17.2	16.6
4. Mostly agree	30.0	26.5	33.4	31.5	24.9	28.6	33.1	29.4	28.0	32.1	27.7	30.5	27.6	33.9	30.5	23.4
5. Agree	27.7	27.6	27.9	26.9	31.7	25.9	25.0	29.6	31.4	27.5	26.9	29.4	26.8	27.0	25.5	32.9
Item 10000 Subject F04 N	3311	1591	1620	2536	404	780	942	1068	521	1720	1341	1219	694	452	809	51
A06E: Government should take action to solve our environmental problems even if it means that some of the products we now use would have to be changed or banned																
1. Disagree	4.8	5.9	3.5	4.3	7.2	5.2	3.9	5.3	4.7	3.6	5.6	3.7	5.2	4.5	5.5	8.6
2. Mostly disagree	6.8	7.5	5.9	6.6	7.9	5.3	6.4	7.8	7.3	6.2	7.4	6.2	6.4	7.8	6.4	11.6
3. Neither	11.3	12.3	9.8	11.1	10.3	9.6	11.8	10.9	13.7	10.5	12.1	12.4	8.9	10.9	11.2	15.0
4. Mostly agree	35.8	33.0	38.5	37.7	27.9	33.0	39.5	34.5	36.0	37.3	34.6	35.7	36.7	36.6	35.5	33.1
5. Agree	41.4	41.3	42.2	40.3	46.7	46.9	38.4	41.6	38.3	42.5	40.2	42.1	42.7	40.2	41.5	31.8
Item 10010 Subject F04,H02 N	3316	1593	1623	2544	398	781	944	1068	522	1725	1345	1229	690	453	808	50
A06F: Government should place higher taxes on products which cause pollution in their manufacture or disposal, so that companies will be encouraged to find better ways to produce them																
1. Disagree	15.7	15.5	15.7	14.6	18.6	16.9	13.5	16.8	15.8	12.5	19.3	16.5	16.2	14.4	14.2	9.2
2. Mostly disagree	12.9	13.4	12.4	12.7	15.1	14.0	14.4	13.6	12.7	10.7	13.2	10.7	12.1	16.5	15.1	6.5
3. Neither	13.1	12.5	13.2	14.0	9.9	11.7	14.3	13.2	12.7	12.3	13.2	13.6	13.4	13.6	12.6	14.1
4. Mostly agree	27.2	26.1	29.0	28.4	21.9	25.4	28.2	27.1	28.3	30.3	24.5	26.5	28.3	26.9	27.8	32.2
5. Agree	31.1	32.5	29.7	30.3	34.5	35.6	29.7	29.3	30.5	31.9	29.8	32.7	30.0	28.6	30.4	38.0
Item 10020 Subject F04,H02 N	3320	1602	1618	2542	404	786	943	1068	522	1723	1350	1226	693	454	809	50
A06G: I wish that government would ban throw-away bottles and beverage cans																
1. Disagree	28.1	27.5	28.8	28.3	31.6	27.5	26.7	30.2	27.5	27.2	29.4	28.2	24.9	29.0	29.9	23.3
2. Mostly disagree	14.2	14.5	14.1	14.6	13.5	13.3	16.8	13.4	12.6	15.7	12.7	13.4	16.1	15.6	13.2	11.0
3. Neither	23.0	20.6	25.2	23.2	20.3	23.9	20.4	23.5	25.1	23.5	22.4	23.0	22.4	25.5	21.6	24.9
4. Mostly agree	15.0	15.0	15.1	14.8	14.1	14.0	17.4	13.7	15.1	14.2	15.8	14.9	16.0	13.2	15.6	22.6
5. Agree	19.6	22.5	16.9	19.0	20.5	21.4	18.6	19.2	19.6	19.4	19.7	20.5	20.5	16.8	19.7	18.3
Item 10030 Subject F04,H02 N	3314	1597	1618	2540	401	781	942	1069	522	1723	1344	1222	695	452	807	50

QUESTIONNAIRE FORM 4 1983	TOTAL	SEX		RACE		REGION				4YR COLLEGE PLANS		ILLICIT DRUG USE: LIFETIME				
		M	F	White	Black	NE	NC	S	W	Yes	No	None	Mari- juana Only	Few Pills	More Pills	Any Her- oin
N (Weighted No. of Cases):	3344	1610	1630	2556	406	793	949	1075	527	1733	1355	1233	699	455	814	51
% of Weighted Total:	100.0	48.1	48.8	76.4	12.1	23.7	28.4	32.2	15.8	51.8	40.5	36.9	20.9	13.6	24.3	1.5
A06H: T.V. commercials stimulate people to buy a lot of things they don't really need																
1. Disagree	5.2	6.6	3.8	4.8	6.9	5.2	4.1	5.6	6.6	5.9	4.3	6.1	3.5	5.2	5.2	9.1
2. Mostly disagree	6.5	7.5	5.5	6.5	6.0	6.3	5.5	7.3	7.3	6.8	6.0	5.6	7.6	6.5	6.9	4.9
3. Neither	6.1	7.0	4.7	6.5	3.4	4.9	7.0	5.9	6.5	6.8	5.4	5.7	7.5	3.5	6.3	6.6
4. Mostly agree	27.2	28.1	26.3	28.1	21.6	24.6	28.6	27.3	28.5	27.1	26.7	26.8	26.1	29.1	28.6	21.4
5. Agree	54.9	50.7	59.7	54.2	62.1	59.0	54.8	53.9	51.1	53.4	57.6	55.8	55.3	55.8	53.0	58.0
Item 10040 Subject F02 N	3315	1594	1623	2539	404	787	942	1066	521	1724	1345	1223	695	454	805	50
A06I: T.V. commercials do a lot of good by showing new products that we might not know about otherwise																
1. Disagree	7.3	7.6	7.1	7.4	6.9	8.6	7.8	5.5	8.2	7.3	7.2	6.9	5.6	6.3	9.9	8.2
2. Mostly disagree	10.9	11.1	10.5	11.5	4.3	11.8	12.3	8.3	11.9	11.5	9.9	9.9	11.2	10.4	11.4	10.5
3. Neither	14.7	15.1	14.2	15.6	8.1	14.1	15.6	11.8	20.0	15.7	13.6	13.8	13.9	14.3	16.8	21.0
4. Mostly agree	35.0	32.1	38.4	37.1	29.8	33.1	34.2	36.3	36.2	36.9	33.1	34.7	35.8	39.4	34.2	35.5
5. Agree	32.2	34.2	29.8	28.3	50.9	32.4	30.0	38.1	23.6	28.7	36.2	34.7	33.4	29.6	27.7	24.8
Item 10050 Subject F02 N	3320	1598	1623	2541	404	783	944	1069	524	1728	1343	1226	694	452	809	50
A06J: My family and I often buy things we don't really need; we could get along with much less																
1. Disagree	15.0	14.9	15.1	12.4	28.5	17.4	12.1	16.2	14.1	13.0	17.3	17.2	13.7	11.3	14.5	14.7
2. Mostly disagree	14.7	15.4	14.0	14.6	12.9	15.2	15.2	13.1	16.1	15.7	13.6	15.1	14.9	12.1	15.2	14.5
3. Neither	11.7	13.3	9.8	11.8	10.5	12.4	9.4	12.0	14.1	11.8	11.3	11.6	13.5	12.0	9.6	9.2
4. Mostly agree	27.3	27.7	27.1	29.0	19.0	27.3	30.6	24.7	26.8	28.6	25.8	27.9	26.7	28.0	28.4	13.9
5. Agree	31.3	28.8	34.0	32.2	29.2	27.7	32.6	33.9	29.0	30.9	32.1	28.2	31.1	36.6	32.4	47.6
Item 10060 Subject F01 N	3317	1596	1622	2538	404	782	943	1068	525	1727	1343	1227	694	452	807	50
A06K: By the year 2000, engineers and scientists will probably have invented devices that will solve our pollution problems																
1. Disagree	12.4	13.4	11.5	12.2	14.3	15.2	12.5	9.6	13.7	12.7	12.0	13.9	11.8	12.2	10.8	14.6
2. Mostly disagree	17.1	18.2	16.3	17.9	13.4	16.8	16.6	16.8	18.8	17.7	16.4	15.2	15.9	15.7	20.9	22.4
3. Neither	23.3	21.1	25.5	24.3	17.5	22.2	24.1	21.6	27.2	21.9	24.4	23.7	23.6	22.3	23.8	23.4
4. Mostly agree	31.3	30.3	31.7	32.0	26.7	27.8	34.6	32.4	28.1	34.7	28.2	32.1	31.2	33.3	29.9	24.6
5. Agree	15.9	16.9	14.9	13.6	28.1	18.0	12.1	19.6	12.3	13.1	19.0	15.0	17.4	16.5	14.6	15.1
Item 10070 Subject F04 N	3324	1598	1629	2548	404	787	943	1070	524	1726	1348	1228	697	453	808	50
A07: In your own actions–the things you buy and the things you do–how much of an effort do you make to conserve energy and protect the environment?																
1. None	5.3	5.3	5.4	4.9	8.5	5.8	5.6	5.2	4.4	4.5	6.2	4.0	4.6	6.3	6.0	22.3
2. A little	27.0	26.7	27.2	27.6	26.3	26.4	26.8	29.7	22.7	27.0	27.1	21.6	33.1	29.4	28.9	28.2
3. Some	53.7	53.6	54.1	54.8	48.5	55.1	55.5	51.3	53.6	54.1	53.8	58.4	50.9	50.9	52.6	24.0
4. Quite a bit	13.9	14.5	13.3	12.7	16.7	12.7	12.1	13.7	19.3	14.4	12.9	16.0	11.4	13.3	12.4	25.4
Item 10080 Subject F04 N	3173	1493	1588	2450	375	758	900	1020	496	1665	1278	1186	670	429	760	48
The next questions are about work.																
A08: Different people may look for different things in their work. Below is a list of some of these things. Please read each one, then indicate how important this thing is for you.																
A08A: A job where you can see the results of what you do																
1. Not important	1.1	2.0	0.2	1.0	-	1.1	1.3	0.5	1.7	0.8	1.3	0.7	1.0	1.2	1.3	5.0
2. A little important	5.8	7.1	4.7	5.8	6.0	5.9	6.1	5.3	6.0	5.0	6.1	5.3	5.6	7.3	5.3	6.4
3. Pretty important	35.7	37.2	34.4	37.7	24.2	32.5	42.1	32.3	36.1	35.4	36.9	35.2	36.5	36.7	35.9	29.4
4. Very important	57.4	53.7	60.7	55.5	69.9	60.5	50.5	61.9	56.1	58.8	55.7	58.8	56.9	54.8	57.6	59.1
Item 10090 Subject C04 N	3324	1601	1625	2544	404	783	944	1072	525	1728	1347	1228	699	454	805	51

QUESTIONNAIRE FORM 4 1983	TOTAL	SEX M	SEX F	RACE White	RACE Black	REGION NE	REGION NC	REGION S	REGION W	4YR COLLEGE PLANS Yes	4YR COLLEGE PLANS No	ILLICIT DRUG USE: LIFETIME None	Marijuana Only	Few Pills	More Pills	Any Heroin
N (Weighted No. of Cases):	3344	1610	1630	2556	406	793	949	1075	527	1733	1355	1233	699	455	814	51
% of Weighted Total:	100.0	48.1	48.8	76.4	12.1	23.7	28.4	32.2	15.8	51.8	40.5	36.9	20.9	13.6	24.3	1.5
A08B: A job that has high status and prestige																
1. Not important	7.4	7.6	7.4	8.0	2.9	5.1	8.6	7.3	8.6	6.8	8.0	8.9	5.1	4.5	9.0	6.8
2. A little important	25.8	24.5	27.2	27.8	14.0	24.9	28.5	23.4	26.8	24.6	27.3	28.7	24.4	25.3	23.6	18.3
3. Pretty important	38.6	38.9	38.2	39.1	37.0	40.0	37.7	37.5	40.1	39.8	37.5	35.8	38.7	42.3	41.1	38.6
4. Very important	28.3	29.1	27.2	25.2	46.1	30.1	25.1	31.7	24.5	28.8	27.2	26.5	31.8	27.9	26.3	36.3
Item 10100 Subject C04 N	3302	1593	1615	2532	401	773	939	1070	520	1726	1333	1221	690	454	801	51
A08C: A job which is interesting to do																
1. Not important	0.3	0.4	0.2	0.2	1.0	0.4	-	0.6	0.2	0.3	0.3	-	0.8	-	0.2	3.8
2. A little important	1.4	1.6	1.1	0.8	3.1	1.5	1.1	1.6	1.5	0.9	2.0	1.7	1.6	0.9	0.7	3.9
3. Pretty important	11.4	12.4	10.0	10.8	13.0	11.2	11.9	11.9	9.4	8.4	13.3	10.5	11.0	11.6	12.0	10.4
4. Very important	86.9	85.6	88.7	88.2	82.9	87.0	87.0	85.9	88.8	90.4	84.4	87.9	86.6	87.5	87.2	82.0
Item 10110 Subject C04 N	3302	1588	1616	2525	402	777	938	1064	522	1717	1339	1219	692	452	803	50
A08D: A job where the chances for advancement and promotion are good																
1. Not important	1.2	1.5	0.9	1.3	0.8	1.0	1.5	1.1	1.0	1.2	1.2	1.0	1.0	1.0	1.5	5.8
2. A little important	7.0	6.8	7.4	6.9	4.0	7.0	7.9	5.0	9.6	6.4	7.7	8.4	7.3	4.2	6.1	5.1
3. Pretty important	26.6	26.7	26.8	27.6	19.2	26.1	28.7	24.4	28.0	26.4	26.7	28.2	26.5	26.4	24.9	23.0
4. Very important	65.2	65.0	65.0	64.1	76.0	65.9	61.9	69.5	61.3	66.0	64.4	62.3	65.2	68.4	67.5	66.1
Item 10120 Subject C04 N	3323	1600	1625	2543	404	783	942	1073	524	1727	1348	1228	699	451	805	51
A08E: A job that gives you an opportunity to be directly helpful to others																
1. Not important	2.8	4.5	1.0	2.9	1.3	3.2	3.2	2.0	3.1	2.0	3.7	2.3	2.7	2.0	3.9	7.2
2. A little important	14.4	20.1	8.3	15.1	10.0	12.1	15.5	14.7	14.9	12.8	15.5	12.1	14.0	16.6	16.4	15.8
3. Pretty important	35.3	38.8	32.0	36.5	30.5	33.6	36.2	35.3	36.2	36.1	35.4	34.1	37.5	35.1	34.8	51.8
4. Very important	47.6	36.5	58.7	45.6	58.2	51.1	45.1	48.0	45.7	49.1	45.4	51.5	45.7	46.3	45.0	25.3
Item 10130 Subject C04,O01 N	3313	1592	1624	2536	402	780	945	1066	522	1720	1344	1221	695	453	804	51
A08F: A job which provides you with a chance to earn a good deal of money																
1. Not important	1.6	1.7	1.5	1.6	1.2	0.9	1.8	1.5	2.3	1.8	1.0	1.9	1.3	0.8	1.5	5.8
2. A little important	7.0	5.2	8.9	7.7	2.8	7.2	9.3	4.5	7.8	8.0	5.8	9.7	6.1	3.8	6.0	1.2
3. Pretty important	35.2	32.6	38.4	38.9	20.8	36.4	39.0	31.5	34.0	37.4	34.2	37.6	35.7	37.9	32.4	16.9
4. Very important	56.2	60.5	51.2	51.8	75.1	55.5	49.8	62.4	55.8	52.8	59.0	50.8	56.8	57.4	60.2	76.1
Item 10140 Subject C04,F01 N	3325	1600	1627	2546	404	784	943	1073	525	1728	1348	1228	698	454	807	51
A08G: A job where you have the chance to be creative																
1. Not important	6.4	8.4	4.6	6.8	3.7	6.1	8.0	5.9	4.9	5.3	8.1	6.6	7.3	6.2	5.5	5.0
2. A little important	22.7	24.2	20.9	22.7	20.1	21.5	25.3	21.1	24.1	21.9	24.1	22.7	23.7	21.7	23.2	15.3
3. Pretty important	35.0	32.8	37.3	35.8	35.9	34.0	34.1	36.7	34.6	33.9	35.7	33.1	36.3	35.8	35.9	41.4
4. Very important	35.9	34.6	37.2	34.6	40.3	38.3	32.6	36.2	37.6	38.9	32.2	37.5	32.7	36.3	35.5	38.2
Item 10150 Subject C04 N	3311	1595	1621	2540	398	782	941	1066	523	1719	1344	1223	695	451	803	51
A08H: A job where the skills you learn will not go out of date																
1. Not important	3.6	4.6	2.6	3.6	3.2	3.1	3.9	3.5	4.1	4.0	3.1	4.4	2.4	4.0	2.7	8.4
2. A little important	10.3	10.0	10.8	10.9	9.0	10.3	10.3	10.3	10.0	10.9	9.7	9.6	10.2	11.6	11.7	1.8
3. Pretty important	30.2	30.3	30.1	32.0	23.0	31.9	32.7	26.0	31.9	31.0	30.1	30.2	32.1	32.9	28.1	18.6
4. Very important	55.9	55.1	56.4	53.6	64.7	54.6	53.1	60.2	53.9	54.1	57.0	55.9	55.3	51.4	57.6	71.2
Item 10160 Subject C04 N	3312	1592	1622	2533	404	780	940	1068	523	1718	1344	1222	697	453	801	51
A08I: A job that gives you a chance to make friends																
1. Not important	2.1	2.3	1.9	1.6	4.3	2.5	1.4	2.3	2.4	2.2	2.0	2.3	1.5	2.3	1.7	10.4
2. A little important	10.7	12.6	8.9	9.7	15.9	9.1	11.4	11.5	10.4	10.1	11.7	8.6	12.2	10.7	11.8	7.2
3. Pretty important	36.7	41.2	31.9	37.1	34.1	38.1	37.8	35.2	35.8	35.7	37.7	35.9	36.9	36.9	38.6	43.4
4. Very important	50.4	43.9	57.4	51.6	45.8	50.3	49.3	51.0	51.4	52.0	48.6	53.2	49.4	50.1	47.9	39.0
Item 10170 Subject C04,M04 N	3318	1596	1624	2543	400	782	942	1070	524	1727	1343	1223	697	453	805	51

QUESTIONNAIRE FORM 4 1983	TOTAL	SEX		RACE		REGION				4YR COLLEGE PLANS		ILLICIT DRUG USE: LIFETIME				
		M	F	White	Black	NE	NC	S	W	Yes	No	None	Mari- juana Only	Few Pills	More Pills	Any Her- oin
N (Weighted No. of Cases):	3344	1610	1630	2556	406	793	949	1075	527	1733	1355	1233	699	455	814	51
% of Weighted Total:	100.0	48.1	48.8	76.4	12.1	23.7	28.4	32.2	15.8	51.8	40.5	36.9	20.9	13.6	24.3	1.5
A08J: A job which uses your skills and abilities—lets you do the things you can do best																
1. Not important	0.5	0.9	0.1	0.5	0.6	1.1	0.1	0.6	0.3	0.4	0.5	0.4	0.8	0.5	0.2	3.8
2. A little important	3.5	4.3	2.5	3.6	1.1	3.0	3.2	3.8	4.2	2.3	5.1	3.2	3.2	2.1	4.8	3.4
3. Pretty important	23.9	25.5	22.4	24.1	22.7	22.0	25.6	24.6	22.5	23.2	25.3	23.2	24.3	22.2	24.6	31.8
4. Very important	72.1	69.2	74.9	71.8	75.6	74.0	71.2	71.1	72.9	74.1	69.1	73.2	71.8	75.2	70.4	61.0
Item 10180 Subject C04　N	3318	1598	1622	2540	403	782	943	1070	522	1726	1344	1226	699	453	801	49
A08K: A job that is worthwhile to society																
1. Not important	3.7	5.4	2.0	3.3	4.2	3.7	4.0	3.2	3.9	3.1	4.3	3.5	3.8	2.8	3.9	11.0
2. A little important	13.6	15.4	11.9	14.1	11.7	14.5	14.1	12.3	14.3	11.8	15.7	12.6	13.6	12.3	15.7	16.9
3. Pretty important	38.3	40.5	35.5	39.1	36.4	36.0	41.7	36.7	38.7	37.0	39.3	36.0	39.4	40.9	39.2	35.0
4. Very important	44.4	38.7	50.7	43.5	47.7	45.7	40.3	47.8	43.0	48.1	40.7	47.9	43.1	43.9	41.2	37.2
Item 10190 Subject C04,O01　N	3303	1592	1614	2529	401	777	939	1069	518	1720	1335	1217	696	452	799	51
A08L: A job where you have more than two weeks vacation																
1. Not important	22.2	20.0	24.9	23.0	20.9	19.9	26.6	22.1	18.0	21.6	24.4	21.8	22.3	21.6	23.8	22.7
2. A little important	35.2	32.2	38.7	35.9	36.3	37.2	33.8	35.1	35.0	36.8	34.0	34.9	36.3	37.7	35.7	22.9
3. Pretty important	25.0	26.5	23.3	24.8	23.7	25.6	25.5	23.7	25.7	25.2	24.4	27.7	23.2	24.5	21.6	27.6
4. Very important	17.5	21.4	13.0	16.2	19.0	17.2	14.0	19.0	21.3	16.5	17.2	15.6	18.1	16.1	18.9	26.9
Item 10200 Subject C04　N	3320	1598	1624	2540	404	782	943	1072	523	1725	1346	1227	697	454	803	51
A08M: A job where you get a chance to partic- ipate in decision making																
1. Not important	4.2	5.7	2.7	4.3	3.2	3.3	4.7	3.9	5.4	2.7	6.3	4.5	3.6	3.7	4.8	6.3
2. A little important	21.7	21.5	22.4	23.2	17.9	19.8	24.1	22.3	19.4	18.0	27.1	22.3	22.4	20.9	21.0	24.4
3. Pretty important	45.0	43.1	46.5	45.3	42.4	45.4	45.5	43.3	46.8	46.6	42.2	43.4	46.0	45.4	46.9	41.4
4. Very important	29.0	29.7	28.4	27.2	36.5	31.5	25.6	30.6	28.4	32.6	24.4	29.8	28.0	30.0	27.4	27.9
Item 10210 Subject C04　N	3313	1597	1621	2535	404	783	942	1068	520	1720	1347	1222	699	451	803	51
A08N: A job which leaves a lot of time for other things in your life																
1. Not important	3.0	2.5	3.4	2.8	4.5	2.7	2.6	2.8	4.2	3.3	2.6	2.6	3.2	3.3	3.0	3.7
2. A little important	19.2	17.9	20.6	19.9	15.4	18.7	20.7	18.2	19.0	18.4	20.6	19.0	19.6	17.1	21.6	10.9
3. Pretty important	42.3	38.8	45.9	43.3	37.2	40.9	45.2	40.2	43.5	44.4	40.0	42.5	39.0	50.2	40.1	50.8
4. Very important	35.5	40.7	30.1	34.1	42.9	37.7	31.4	38.7	33.2	34.0	36.8	35.8	38.3	29.4	35.4	34.7
Item 10220 Subject C04　N	3316	1593	1625	2537	404	782	941	1069	524	1724	1344	1226	696	450	804	51
A08O: A job which allows you to establish roots in a community and not have to move from place to place																
1. Not important	10.5	11.3	9.8	10.5	10.4	12.7	10.0	8.8	11.5	11.1	9.8	8.7	10.5	12.3	12.7	14.8
2. A little important	18.4	17.5	19.4	18.5	18.4	18.8	18.6	18.1	18.0	20.6	15.6	17.7	14.8	19.1	20.8	21.2
3. Pretty important	32.1	31.3	32.9	32.2	30.6	31.6	33.1	31.5	32.2	32.4	32.3	31.9	30.9	32.7	33.3	25.1
4. Very important	39.0	39.9	37.9	38.8	40.5	37.0	38.3	41.6	38.3	35.8	42.2	41.8	43.8	35.9	33.1	38.9
Item 10230 Subject C04　N	3323	1600	1625	2544	403	783	944	1072	524	1728	1346	1226	699	454	805	51
A08P: A job which leaves you mostly free of supervision by others																
1. Not important	8.6	8.4	8.5	8.1	11.3	9.9	6.5	9.3	8.7	8.5	8.4	8.6	8.3	8.9	8.1	5.8
2. A little important	28.9	26.6	31.3	29.4	27.1	27.3	33.3	28.4	24.6	29.2	29.0	29.4	29.4	31.4	27.3	19.0
3. Pretty important	38.3	37.2	39.3	39.0	35.1	38.4	37.3	37.1	42.5	39.5	37.2	39.6	37.9	39.9	37.1	33.0
4. Very important	24.2	27.8	20.8	23.5	26.6	24.5	22.9	25.2	24.2	22.8	25.5	22.4	24.4	19.9	27.5	42.2
Item 10240 Subject C04　N	3320	1596	1626	2544	403	783	942	1072	523	1725	1347	1226	698	453	805	51

QUESTIONNAIRE FORM 4 1983	TOTAL	SEX		RACE		REGION				4YR COLLEGE PLANS		ILLICIT DRUG USE: LIFETIME				
		M	F	White	Black	NE	NC	S	W	Yes	No	None	Marijuana Only	Few Pills	More Pills	Any Heroin
N (Weighted No. of Cases):	3344	1610	1630	2556	406	793	949	1075	527	1733	1355	1233	699	455	814	51
% of Weighted Total:	100.0	48.1	48.8	76.4	12.1	23.7	28.4	32.2	15.8	51.8	40.5	36.9	20.9	13.6	24.3	1.5
A08Q: A job that offers a reasonably predictable, secure future																
1. Not important	1.2	1.5	0.9	1.3	0.8	0.8	2.2	0.8	0.9	0.9	1.3	1.0	1.1	1.3	1.4	2.7
2. A little important	4.5	5.2	3.9	4.6	3.5	5.7	3.8	3.8	5.7	4.2	4.9	3.7	4.5	3.9	5.3	16.5
3. Pretty important	29.0	29.8	28.4	30.5	18.3	27.6	31.0	26.0	33.7	29.0	30.1	29.4	27.3	31.5	28.9	23.2
4. Very important	65.2	63.6	66.9	63.6	77.3	65.9	63.0	69.5	59.6	66.0	63.6	66.0	67.1	63.3	64.4	57.6
Item 10250 Subject C04 N	3315	1595	1622	2540	402	783	939	1070	524	1723	1344	1223	697	454	803	51
A08R: A job where you can learn new things, learn new skills																
1. Not important	1.3	2.0	0.6	1.4	0.6	1.2	1.3	1.4	1.1	1.4	0.8	0.8	1.5	0.8	1.6	5.6
2. A little important	10.8	12.6	9.1	11.9	5.0	11.5	12.8	8.8	10.1	12.0	9.3	10.1	11.5	11.3	10.8	17.7
3. Pretty important	41.8	42.5	41.1	44.3	34.8	39.8	46.2	41.0	38.9	41.8	43.6	41.7	41.3	42.2	44.2	37.9
4. Very important	46.1	42.9	49.3	42.4	59.7	47.5	39.8	48.9	49.9	44.8	46.3	47.4	45.6	45.6	43.3	38.8
Item 10260 Subject B02,C04 N	3319	1596	1625	2541	402	783	943	1070	523	1726	1345	1226	696	454	803	51
A08S: A job where you do not have to pretend to be a type of person that you are not																
1. Not important	4.6	5.5	3.8	3.9	7.8	5.8	2.8	5.0	5.5	3.5	5.5	3.6	5.5	4.7	4.6	10.8
2. A little important	5.9	8.5	3.3	5.7	6.3	5.3	7.3	5.2	5.8	5.1	6.4	5.6	5.1	5.2	6.8	4.9
3. Pretty important	18.7	22.1	15.1	19.1	17.4	19.0	20.3	17.2	18.3	18.1	19.7	17.3	20.3	22.2	17.2	17.3
4. Very important	70.8	63.9	77.8	71.3	68.6	69.9	69.6	72.7	70.4	73.3	68.4	73.5	69.0	67.9	71.4	66.9
Item 10270 Subject C04 N	3307	1590	1620	2532	401	779	941	1064	523	1718	1341	1221	697	452	799	50
A08T: A job that most people look up to and respect																
1. Not important	4.5	5.9	3.2	4.4	3.9	4.0	4.7	4.4	4.7	3.8	5.1	3.6	3.7	3.8	6.7	11.6
2. A little important	17.5	17.7	17.5	18.2	11.8	14.6	21.9	14.2	20.7	16.5	19.4	18.0	16.3	14.8	19.7	16.4
3. Pretty important	39.0	40.4	37.8	40.7	36.1	41.6	39.2	37.7	37.4	40.7	37.7	38.0	42.0	42.3	37.5	27.1
4. Very important	39.0	36.0	41.4	36.7	48.3	39.7	34.2	43.7	37.1	39.1	37.7	40.4	38.1	39.0	36.1	44.9
Item 10280 Subject C04 N	3315	1597	1621	2539	402	780	943	1070	523	1725	1342	1221	697	454	804	51
A08U: A job that permits contact with a lot of people																
1. Not important	7.5	10.6	4.3	7.5	8.3	7.0	7.3	8.9	5.9	6.7	8.4	7.2	7.5	7.0	7.8	13.5
2. A little important	24.4	28.6	20.0	24.2	25.3	24.3	25.6	23.0	25.0	20.8	28.4	24.8	24.3	22.7	25.1	21.4
3. Pretty important	35.3	35.0	35.6	35.2	37.4	33.2	35.4	36.2	36.2	35.6	34.9	34.4	37.4	37.5	34.4	24.1
4. Very important	32.9	25.8	40.1	33.0	29.1	35.4	31.7	31.9	33.0	36.9	28.3	33.5	30.8	32.8	32.7	41.1
Item 10290 Subject C04,M05 N	3311	1592	1621	2537	399	781	941	1066	523	1718	1345	1221	697	452	802	51
A08V: A job with an easy pace that lets you work slowly																
1. Not important	28.8	30.2	27.7	30.0	28.8	28.3	29.6	28.7	28.4	31.2	26.7	27.6	28.5	28.8	32.5	27.6
2. A little important	38.6	35.4	41.6	39.2	34.9	38.8	39.7	36.6	40.6	39.8	36.8	37.8	40.3	39.0	39.7	23.9
3. Pretty important	23.3	23.5	23.1	22.5	23.9	25.2	21.6	24.2	21.9	20.9	26.1	25.7	22.9	24.2	18.5	31.1
4. Very important	9.2	10.9	7.6	8.2	12.4	7.7	9.0	10.5	9.1	8.0	10.3	9.0	8.3	8.1	9.3	17.4
Item 10300 Subject C04 N	3315	1593	1626	2542	401	783	941	1068	524	1723	1345	1222	697	454	804	51
A08W: A job where most problems are quite difficult and challenging																
1. Not important	16.1	14.5	17.7	16.5	14.2	16.5	17.7	16.2	12.2	12.0	20.7	17.2	13.8	14.7	16.8	21.9
2. A little important	34.5	32.5	36.6	36.1	30.2	29.6	37.9	34.9	34.8	33.6	37.0	33.4	34.9	34.1	36.8	29.2
3. Pretty important	36.1	38.3	33.9	35.6	35.4	40.2	32.5	35.1	38.7	40.2	30.6	36.5	38.1	37.4	34.0	35.6
4. Very important	13.3	14.7	11.8	11.8	20.2	13.7	11.8	13.8	14.3	14.2	11.6	12.9	13.2	13.8	12.4	13.3
Item 10310 Subject C04 N	3312	1593	1621	2537	399	781	941	1066	524	1725	1342	1223	696	454	803	49

QUESTIONNAIRE FORM 4 1983	TOTAL	SEX		RACE		REGION				4YR COLLEGE PLANS		ILLICIT DRUG USE: LIFETIME				
		M	F	White	Black	NE	NC	S	W	Yes	No	None	Mari-juana Only	Few Pills	More Pills	Any Her-oin
N (Weighted No. of Cases):	3344	1610	1630	2556	406	793	949	1075	527	1733	1355	1233	699	455	814	51
% of Weighted Total:	100.0	48.1	48.8	76.4	12.1	23.7	28.4	32.2	15.8	51.8	40.5	36.9	20.9	13.6	24.3	1.5

A09: What kind of work do you think you will be doing when you are 30 years old? Mark the one that comes closest to what you expect to be doing.

	TOTAL	M	F	White	Black	NE	NC	S	W	Yes	No	None	Mari-juana Only	Few Pills	More Pills	Any Her-oin
01. Laborer (car washer, sanitary worker, farm laborer)	0.4	0.8	-	0.5	-	0.7	0.7	-	0.3	0.1	0.8	0.2	-	0.7	1.0	
02. Service worker (cook, waiter, barber, janitor, gas station attendant, practical nurse, beautician)	3.0	1.3	4.7	3.0	3.1	2.8	3.5	2.7	2.7	0.9	5.5	2.1	3.0	5.8	2.5	6.9
03. Operative or semi-skilled worker (garage worker, taxicab, bus or truck driver, assembly line worker, welder)	2.7	4.9	0.3	2.3	1.5	1.8	4.0	2.5	2.2	0.4	5.7	2.2	1.5	3.5	3.4	7.5
04. Sales clerk in a retail store (shoe salesperson, department store clerk, drug store clerk)	1.4	0.6	2.2	1.2	2.8	1.6	0.7	2.0	0.9	0.4	2.7	1.6	0.1	2.0	1.5	
05. Clerical or office worker (bank teller, bookkeeper, secretary, typist, postal clerk or carrier, ticket agent)	10.7	1.3	19.8	10.1	13.1	11.8	9.4	10.7	11.4	5.9	17.2	11.2	9.9	12.7	10.2	4.4
06. Protective service (police officer, fireman, detective)	2.6	4.0	1.2	2.7	3.1	3.1	1.5	3.0	3.2	1.8	3.6	2.5	2.3	1.9	3.3	6.6
07. Military service	4.5	7.5	1.4	3.6	9.4	3.5	3.0	8.2	1.4	2.9	6.2	3.6	5.7	3.8	4.8	3.9
08. Craftsman or skilled worker (carpenter, electrician, brick layer, mechanic, machinist, tool and die maker, telephone installer)	8.4	15.9	0.9	8.5	6.4	5.4	10.0	9.4	7.7	2.5	15.3	7.0	9.7	5.8	9.9	13.9
09. Farm owner, farm manager	1.6	2.6	0.5	1.8	-	0.5	3.3	0.9	1.3	0.5	3.0	2.4	0.7	0.9	1.5	-
10. Owner of small business (restaurant owner, shop owner)	5.9	6.8	4.6	5.8	3.5	5.4	6.2	5.5	6.6	5.6	6.5	4.4	6.0	3.1	9.3	12.6
11. Sales representative (insurance agent, real estate broker, bond salesman)	1.1	1.5	0.7	1.1	0.4	0.6	1.0	1.1	1.9	1.5	0.6	0.9	1.1	2.0	1.0	
12. Manager or administrator (office manager, sales manager, school administrator, government official)	7.3	7.0	7.7	7.2	9.3	8.9	7.4	6.9	5.9	9.9	3.9	7.1	9.4	7.4	6.8	-
13. Professional without doctoral degree (registered nurse, librarian, engineer, architect, social worker, technician, accountant, actor, artist, musician)	29.0	25.8	32.7	29.6	30.3	31.6	28.8	26.6	30.3	39.0	16.8	30.3	29.5	28.0	26.7	27.6
14. Professional with doctoral degree or equivalent (lawyer, physician, dentist, scientist, college professor)	12.9	13.2	12.8	13.1	12.5	14.3	10.3	12.6	16.2	21.8	2.0	14.6	14.0	14.4	10.0	4.9
15. Full-time homemaker or housewife	2.8	*	5.7	3.4	-	2.1	3.3	3.1	2.6	1.8	4.4	3.1	2.8	3.2	1.9	8.1
16. Don't know-GO TO Q.A13	5.7	6.7	4.9	6.0	4.6	5.7	6.8	4.9	5.2	5.1	5.9	6.9	4.1	4.7	6.1	3.7
Item 10320 Subject C03 N	3119	1501	1543	2429	354	724	897	999	499	1660	1256	1161	663	430	754	43

A10: How likely do you think it is that you will actually get to do this kind of work?

	TOTAL	M	F	White	Black	NE	NC	S	W	Yes	No	None	Mari-juana Only	Few Pills	More Pills	Any Her-oin
1. Not very likely	1.3	1.3	1.2	1.0	2.3	0.7	1.8	1.2	1.4	0.9	1.9	1.5	1.2	1.3	0.8	-
2. Somewhat likely	7.2	7.9	6.3	6.5	7.8	6.3	9.5	6.4	6.4	6.2	8.0	6.8	7.1	6.2	7.2	9.7
3. Fairly likely	23.5	24.6	22.0	23.4	26.0	25.2	23.8	22.2	22.7	23.0	22.1	23.9	21.3	27.5	22.0	20.1
4. Very likely	42.5	40.9	44.6	43.8	39.6	43.1	39.0	44.2	44.6	47.0	38.3	42.4	46.3	40.1	42.7	44.2
5. Certain	17.5	16.6	18.6	16.8	20.3	18.6	16.2	17.6	17.7	19.1	16.4	18.2	19.0	15.6	16.4	16.4
6. I already do this kind of work	8.0	8.7	7.4	8.4	4.1	6.1	9.8	8.4	7.1	3.9	13.3	7.0	5.1	9.3	10.8	9.7
Item 10330 Subject C03 N★	3045	1448	1510	2331	375	714	860	988	482	1606	1227	1117	658	417	728	46

A11: How certain are you that this kind of work is a good choice for you?

	TOTAL	M	F	White	Black	NE	NC	S	W	Yes	No	None	Mari-juana Only	Few Pills	More Pills	Any Her-oin
1. Not at all certain	2.6	2.7	2.4	2.4	2.5	3.0	3.3	2.5	1.1	2.7	2.6	2.6	2.8	2.4	2.5	1.2
2. Somewhat certain	7.3	8.2	6.4	7.1	8.8	7.0	9.1	7.1	5.0	6.1	9.1	6.7	7.5	7.0	8.1	9.4
3. Fairly certain	29.8	28.7	31.2	31.5	23.3	29.6	29.0	30.4	30.6	30.6	27.8	30.1	30.4	31.0	28.8	29.1
4. Very certain	41.4	41.0	41.8	41.6	43.6	41.8	41.4	40.6	42.5	42.8	40.5	40.6	41.9	42.5	41.2	50.7
5. Completely certain	18.8	19.5	18.2	17.5	21.9	18.6	17.2	19.5	20.8	17.9	19.9	19.9	17.5	17.1	19.4	9.6
Item 10340 Subject C03 N★	3066	1466	1513	2346	376	717	867	994	488	1611	1237	1124	657	422	736	47

*=less than .05 per cent.   ★=excludes respondents for whom question was inappropriate.

QUESTIONNAIRE FORM 4 1983	TOTAL	SEX		RACE		REGION				4YR COLLEGE PLANS		ILLICIT DRUG USE: LIFETIME				
		M	F	White	Black	NE	NC	S	W	Yes	No	None	Mari-juana Only	Few Pills	More Pills	Any Her-oin
N (Weighted No. of Cases):	3344	1610	1630	2556	406	793	949	1075	527	1733	1355	1233	699	455	814	51
% of Weighted Total:	100.0	48.1	48.8	76.4	12.1	23.7	28.4	32.2	15.8	51.8	40.5	36.9	20.9	13.6	24.3	1.5
A12: How satisfying do you think this kind of work will be for you?																
1. Not very satisfying	0.8	0.9	0.6	0.5	1.4	0.9	0.5	1.0	0.4	0.5	1.1	0.5	1.1	0.2	1.0	5.0
2. Somewhat satisfying	5.4	5.1	5.3	5.1	5.0	6.7	5.7	5.2	3.1	3.0	7.7	4.5	5.5	6.1	5.9	1.2
3. Quite satisfying	25.8	27.4	24.0	25.6	25.4	26.7	25.6	27.0	22.2	23.3	27.4	25.8	25.6	29.3	23.2	29.0
4. Very satisfying	42.5	42.9	42.6	42.9	44.3	41.5	44.3	40.6	44.4	44.4	41.4	41.3	45.1	42.9	42.8	36.8
5. Extremely satisfying	25.6	23.7	27.5	26.0	23.9	24.2	23.9	26.1	29.8	28.9	22.5	28.0	22.7	21.5	27.2	28.0
Item 10350　Subject C03,P02　　N★	3064	1465	1512	2344	376	717	867	992	488	1612	1235	1123	657	422	736	47
A13: To what extent do you think the things listed below will prevent you from getting the kind of work you would like to have?																
A13A: Your religion																
1. Not at all	90.3	89.2	92.0	93.0	81.7	92.0	90.4	89.8	88.5	91.4	89.3	88.5	92.9	91.5	92.1	85.0
2. Somewhat	4.0	4.7	3.2	3.2	5.2	4.0	3.9	3.9	4.3	3.8	4.3	5.1	2.7	4.5	2.9	3.9
3. A lot	1.6	1.9	1.1	0.6	4.6	1.4	1.6	1.8	1.7	1.4	1.8	2.4	1.1	0.4	0.9	7.5
8. Don't know	4.1	4.2	3.8	3.2	8.5	2.6	4.2	4.5	5.4	3.4	4.6	4.0	3.4	3.6	4.1	3.6
Item 10360　Subject C03,G　　N	3184	1536	1558	2456	383	754	908	1023	498	1671	1294	1175	674	436	774	49
A13B: Your sex																
1. Not at all	76.5	87.5	65.6	77.2	70.6	73.1	77.0	77.7	78.0	75.1	78.7	77.1	77.6	75.2	75.9	73.9
2. Somewhat	17.1	7.5	26.8	17.1	19.6	19.7	17.4	15.4	16.1	18.5	14.6	17.1	16.1	18.0	17.5	14.2
3. A lot	4.0	3.4	4.5	3.5	5.8	4.0	3.9	4.4	3.3	3.6	4.5	4.1	3.1	3.9	4.4	6.8
8. Don't know	2.5	1.6	3.1	2.1	4.0	3.2	1.7	2.5	2.7	2.8	2.2	1.8	3.3	2.9	2.2	5.2
Item 10370　Subject C03,D06　　N	3183	1536	1559	2455	383	753	905	1025	500	1671	1293	1175	674	435	775	49
A13C: Your race																
1. Not at all	82.6	82.3	83.7	92.5	36.1	80.7	87.7	79.1	83.4	82.9	84.0	82.7	80.4	82.7	87.5	72.4
2. Somewhat	10.4	9.8	10.9	4.2	39.7	11.7	6.2	13.5	9.6	11.2	8.4	10.8	13.1	11.3	6.3	11.0
3. A lot	3.8	4.5	2.8	1.9	14.3	4.9	3.7	3.3	3.0	3.6	3.7	3.3	3.2	2.7	4.4	8.2
8. Don't know	3.2	3.5	2.7	1.4	9.9	2.7	2.3	4.1	4.0	2.4	3.8	3.2	3.4	3.3	1.8	8.4
Item 10380　Subject C03,N02　　N	3180	1536	1555	2452	383	752	905	1024	499	1673	1288	1176	675	436	771	48
A13D: Your family background																
1. Not at all	86.3	85.0	88.1	88.6	76.5	87.4	86.5	86.2	84.6	87.8	85.6	87.4	87.6	85.5	86.4	69.2
2. Somewhat	7.6	7.6	7.5	7.0	10.4	5.8	8.3	7.5	9.1	7.3	7.1	7.0	7.4	6.8	8.4	16.0
3. A lot	2.8	3.5	1.8	2.2	4.7	3.9	2.3	1.8	4.1	2.5	2.9	2.4	2.2	3.3	2.7	8.8
8. Don't know	3.3	3.9	2.6	2.3	8.4	2.9	2.9	4.5	2.3	2.5	4.3	3.2	2.8	4.4	2.5	5.9
Item 10390　Subject C03　　N	3186	1538	1559	2456	384	754	906	1025	500	1672	1294	1176	675	436	776	50
A13E: Your political views																
1. Not at all	81.6	81.8	81.6	85.1	66.9	79.0	83.9	80.9	82.6	83.4	80.0	81.8	81.8	82.7	82.8	73.0
2. Somewhat	8.7	9.2	8.2	7.4	14.3	10.6	7.2	9.3	7.5	8.7	8.7	8.9	8.2	9.5	8.0	9.3
3. A lot	1.5	1.7	1.4	1.2	2.7	1.4	1.6	1.8	1.2	1.4	1.9	1.9	1.1	1.1	1.4	6.9
8. Don't know	8.2	7.3	8.8	6.3	16.1	9.1	7.2	8.1	8.7	6.5	9.4	7.5	8.9	6.8	7.8	10.8
Item 10400　Subject C03,H01　　N	3184	1536	1558	2453	384	753	906	1026	499	1672	1293	1177	675	436	773	49
A13F: Your education																
1. Not at all	48.4	47.4	49.6	48.3	48.9	52.3	44.4	49.7	47.0	54.0	42.6	50.5	49.0	46.4	46.6	46.7
2. Somewhat	23.7	23.3	23.8	24.1	24.6	22.6	25.4	22.1	25.4	18.1	29.5	21.8	23.1	24.6	25.9	25.7
3. A lot	25.0	26.5	23.6	24.9	22.9	21.4	28.0	24.9	25.1	25.7	24.3	24.8	24.8	27.4	24.0	23.8
8. Don't know	3.0	2.9	2.9	2.7	3.7	3.8	2.2	3.3	2.6	2.1	3.6	2.9	3.0	1.6	3.6	3.8
Item 10410　Subject B09,C03　　N	3192	1544	1561	2458	387	753	910	1027	502	1674	1298	1176	676	438	779	49
A13G: Lack of vocational training																
1. Not at all	50.9	51.5	51.2	51.4	50.8	53.6	47.2	54.3	46.7	55.5	46.5	50.2	53.2	47.5	52.7	56.2
2. Somewhat	26.8	25.8	27.2	27.6	21.9	23.7	30.1	24.4	30.2	24.0	30.0	26.3	26.6	32.0	25.3	14.7
3. A lot	14.1	14.8	13.3	13.5	16.5	13.4	15.4	12.3	16.6	11.3	17.2	14.3	12.5	13.5	14.5	19.1
8. Don't know	8.2	7.9	8.2	7.4	10.8	9.3	7.3	8.9	6.5	9.2	6.2	9.1	7.8	6.9	7.5	10.0
Item 10420　Subject C03　　N	3184	1539	1554	2450	387	756	905	1021	502	1666	1291	1173	675	436	777	49

QUESTIONNAIRE FORM 4 1983	TOTAL	SEX		RACE		REGION				4YR COLLEGE PLANS		ILLICIT DRUG USE: LIFETIME				
		M	F	White	Black	NE	NC	S	W	Yes	No	None	Mari-juana Only	Few Pills	More Pills	Any Her-oin
N (Weighted No. of Cases):	3344	1610	1630	2556	406	793	949	1075	527	1733	1355	1233	699	455	814	51
% of Weighted Total:	100.0	48.1	48.8	76.4	12.1	23.7	28.4	32.2	15.8	51.8	40.5	36.9	20.9	13.6	24.3	1.5
A13H: Lack of ability																
1. Not at all	58.4	60.3	56.7	58.1	61.6	62.1	54.6	59.0	58.2	58.7	58.2	57.1	57.8	54.0	63.1	60.9
2. Somewhat	16.1	15.0	17.0	16.6	12.9	14.2	18.9	15.5	14.9	15.3	16.8	16.5	16.3	18.7	13.9	14.9
3. A lot	22.1	22.0	22.2	22.0	22.2	20.6	22.6	21.9	24.1	22.4	21.9	22.2	22.7	24.2	20.6	24.2
8. Don't know	3.4	2.7	4.1	3.4	3.4	3.1	3.9	3.6	2.8	3.5	3.2	4.1	3.2	3.1	2.4	-
Item 10430 Subject C03 N	3182	1538	1556	2453	384	752	907	1023	500	1670	1294	1175	675	435	775	49
A13I: Not knowing the right people																
1. Not at all	45.0	42.3	48.2	46.0	37.2	42.7	43.9	45.8	48.8	43.4	48.1	45.3	44.7	44.6	45.4	47.5
2. Somewhat	38.9	40.5	37.3	39.7	38.7	40.3	40.7	37.0	37.0	40.9	36.1	40.3	39.6	39.6	36.2	27.2
3. A lot	8.8	10.4	7.1	8.4	10.2	8.1	8.6	10.0	7.9	8.9	8.6	7.6	7.3	8.3	12.2	14.2
8. Don't know	7.3	6.8	7.4	5.9	13.8	8.9	6.7	7.1	6.4	6.9	7.2	6.8	8.4	7.4	6.1	11.2
Item 10440 Subject C03 N	3185	1539	1557	2453	385	751	908	1025	500	1671	1297	1175	674	435	779	49
A13J: Not wanting to work hard																
1. Not at all	61.7	60.5	62.9	61.6	62.4	64.9	59.8	61.4	60.6	61.6	61.8	59.3	63.5	59.3	65.0	65.0
2. Somewhat	9.4	10.1	8.6	9.1	10.2	9.3	9.3	9.4	9.7	9.7	8.7	9.9	8.7	11.3	8.1	7.2
3. A lot	26.7	26.8	26.6	27.3	23.5	23.8	28.3	26.6	28.4	26.7	27.0	28.3	24.6	27.4	26.1	23.6
8. Don't know	2.2	2.5	1.9	1.9	3.8	2.0	2.5	2.6	1.3	2.0	2.5	2.5	3.2	2.0	0.8	4.1
Item 10450 Subject C03,Q07 N	3179	1536	1555	2450	383	754	902	1024	499	1669	1291	1173	673	435	775	49
A13K: Not wanting to conform																
1. Not at all	51.8	50.7	53.1	51.9	51.6	54.9	49.6	51.1	52.6	50.5	53.1	52.1	55.3	50.4	49.9	52.0
2. Somewhat	21.8	22.5	20.7	22.6	17.1	19.5	25.8	20.2	21.3	24.3	18.3	22.0	21.1	23.7	20.9	13.9
3. A lot	15.1	15.8	14.6	14.8	17.1	12.8	13.9	17.5	15.8	16.0	15.1	16.0	12.2	15.2	16.5	15.5
8. Don't know	11.3	11.1	11.6	10.7	14.2	12.8	10.7	11.2	10.3	9.3	13.5	10.0	11.4	10.8	12.6	18.7
Item 10460 Subject C03,Q08 N	3154	1531	1539	2436	379	747	899	1014	493	1663	1283	1169	668	431	767	49
A14: If you were to get enough money to live as comfortably as you'd like for the rest of your life, would you want to work?																
1. I would want to work	78.9	76.8	81.2	78.8	79.5	81.1	78.6	76.0	82.4	80.7	77.0	82.1	78.6	79.1	74.5	63.7
2. I would not want to work	21.1	23.2	18.8	21.2	20.5	18.9	21.4	24.0	17.6	19.3	23.0	17.9	21.4	20.9	25.5	36.3
Item 8100 Subject C06 N	3309	1596	1622	2539	405	779	941	1067	522	1721	1347	1222	697	453	805	51
A15: How much do you agree or disagree with each statement below?																
A15A: One sees so few good or happy marriages that one questions it as a way of life																
1. Disagree	30.0	29.1	31.8	32.0	24.7	29.0	30.2	29.9	31.5	33.2	27.1	36.4	29.4	24.2	25.7	30.5
2. Mostly disagree	19.2	18.1	20.3	21.2	9.9	18.2	23.9	16.3	18.6	22.4	15.9	20.5	19.7	18.3	18.7	15.3
3. Neither	18.9	23.4	14.6	18.5	18.9	17.5	18.4	18.8	21.9	16.1	22.7	16.4	20.2	21.3	20.2	16.7
4. Mostly agree	19.1	17.9	19.9	18.0	21.7	20.3	18.0	20.4	16.6	17.8	19.5	15.7	19.0	21.1	22.5	20.1
5. Agree	12.7	11.5	13.5	10.3	24.8	14.9	9.5	14.5	11.5	10.5	14.8	11.0	11.7	15.1	12.9	17.4
Item 10470 Subject D03 N	3282	1585	1612	2529	400	768	933	1063	518	1717	1340	1217	693	450	797	50
A15B: It is usually a good idea for a couple to live together before getting married in order to find out whether they really get along																
1. Disagree	26.9	19.9	34.5	28.1	23.8	21.6	28.2	29.5	27.1	29.5	24.5	39.4	24.5	21.1	15.3	5.0
2. Mostly disagree	14.7	14.4	15.2	15.6	9.9	16.6	14.7	13.6	14.3	17.2	11.9	16.4	13.9	15.7	12.1	13.1
3. Neither	15.5	16.9	13.7	16.6	10.5	15.7	15.7	15.2	15.2	16.7	14.8	13.6	19.7	15.4	15.6	10.0
4. Mostly agree	20.3	21.8	18.6	20.6	20.2	18.8	21.2	21.0	19.4	17.9	22.9	16.1	19.2	26.7	23.9	27.2
5. Agree	22.6	27.1	18.0	19.2	35.7	27.3	20.2	20.7	23.9	18.6	26.0	14.6	22.7	21.1	33.2	44.8
Item 10480 Subject D03 N	3312	1598	1626	2544	403	776	941	1071	523	1728	1347	1227	697	454	803	51

QUESTIONNAIRE FORM 4 1983	TOTAL	SEX		RACE		REGION				4YR COLLEGE PLANS		ILLICIT DRUG USE: LIFETIME				
		M	F	White	Black	NE	NC	S	W	Yes	No	None	Mari- juana Only	Few Pills	More Pills	Any Her- oin
N (Weighted No. of Cases):	3344	1610	1630	2556	406	793	949	1075	527	1733	1355	1233	699	455	814	51
% of Weighted Total:	100.0	48.1	48.8	76.4	12.1	23.7	28.4	32.2	15.8	51.8	40.5	36.9	20.9	13.6	24.3	1.5
A15C: Having a close intimate relationship with only one partner is too restrictive for the average person																
1. Disagree	40.0	33.7	46.8	41.9	33.5	38.6	39.9	39.5	43.5	41.6	39.7	44.7	38.7	39.5	36.7	21.7
2. Mostly disagree	24.2	23.5	24.7	25.8	18.3	26.1	26.7	21.3	22.5	25.3	22.7	22.2	26.2	25.2	25.8	15.6
3. Neither	13.3	15.4	11.0	13.1	10.9	12.0	12.7	13.7	15.5	11.7	14.8	12.4	13.7	15.1	13.5	10.2
4. Mostly agree	14.2	16.7	11.7	12.6	21.2	13.6	14.3	15.6	11.9	14.1	14.3	13.2	13.7	12.6	15.5	27.8
5. Agree	8.3	10.6	5.8	6.7	16.1	9.7	6.4	9.7	6.6	7.2	8.5	7.6	7.7	7.7	8.5	24.6
Item 10490 Subject D03 N	3296	1585	1622	2536	401	774	939	1068	516	1724	1341	1218	694	453	799	51
A15D: Having a job takes away from a woman's relationship with her husband																
1. Disagree	46.2	37.2	55.9	45.7	57.0	48.7	42.8	47.8	45.3	49.0	43.3	45.5	48.6	45.4	46.3	47.3
2. Mostly disagree	27.6	28.1	26.9	27.9	22.1	26.8	28.5	25.4	32.0	28.5	26.9	28.0	26.7	29.4	26.8	18.9
3. Neither	12.7	15.5	9.4	13.0	8.3	11.5	13.5	13.8	11.1	11.3	14.3	12.5	11.9	13.6	13.0	15.5
4. Mostly agree	9.3	12.9	5.8	9.5	8.0	8.4	10.9	9.6	7.0	8.2	10.2	10.1	8.4	9.6	9.1	3.8
5. Agree	4.1	6.2	1.9	3.8	4.5	4.6	4.2	3.4	4.6	3.0	5.2	3.9	4.4	2.1	4.7	14.4
Item 10500 Subject D05 N	3306	1593	1623	2543	402	776	941	1068	520	1726	1344	1225	697	454	800	50
A15E: Having a job gives a wife more of a chance to develop herself as a person																
1. Disagree	3.6	5.0	2.4	3.4	3.4	3.3	3.6	3.2	5.1	2.8	4.7	3.1	3.3	2.9	5.0	7.2
2. Mostly disagree	3.1	4.1	2.0	3.0	2.7	2.2	4.4	2.5	3.2	2.0	4.3	2.8	3.1	2.5	3.9	1.4
3. Neither	8.3	12.5	3.8	8.6	5.9	5.0	10.3	8.4	9.2	6.9	9.8	7.6	8.9	6.1	9.6	11.6
4. Mostly agree	30.4	36.5	24.2	31.3	22.5	27.8	33.1	30.3	29.4	30.4	30.5	30.9	29.5	31.2	29.1	39.9
5. Agree	54.6	41.8	67.7	53.7	65.6	61.7	48.6	55.5	53.2	57.9	50.7	55.6	55.2	57.3	52.4	39.9
Item 10510 Subject D05 N	3303	1590	1625	2539	403	777	941	1064	521	1726	1343	1220	697	452	803	51
A15F: Being a father and raising children is one of the most fulfilling experiences a man can have																
1. Disagree	4.4	5.6	3.3	3.8	6.8	2.5	5.5	4.7	4.7	3.8	5.1	3.4	3.7	3.7	6.3	13.9
2. Mostly disagree	5.1	6.0	4.1	5.2	3.7	4.2	5.4	4.7	6.8	4.7	5.5	5.5	3.5	5.1	5.2	17.0
3. Neither	19.2	16.7	22.1	20.7	9.6	18.7	19.6	18.5	20.9	18.6	19.1	17.1	18.0	20.1	23.4	13.5
4. Mostly agree	32.5	31.6	33.2	32.5	33.4	32.6	33.3	31.6	32.6	33.8	32.0	32.7	31.2	37.7	31.8	23.1
5. Agree	38.8	40.3	37.3	37.7	46.6	42.0	36.2	40.5	35.0	39.1	38.3	41.3	43.6	33.5	33.2	32.6
Item 10520 Subject D05 N	3271	1592	1592	2506	401	771	929	1052	518	1705	1333	1211	692	445	792	51
A15G: Most mothers should spend more time with their children than they do now																
1. Disagree	5.4	4.8	6.3	5.3	5.8	7.1	4.2	5.4	4.9	4.8	6.1	5.2	4.9	5.6	6.4	2.2
2. Mostly disagree	9.5	10.2	9.0	10.6	5.8	12.8	11.3	6.2	8.6	10.6	8.7	7.5	10.3	13.8	10.1	8.6
3. Neither	25.7	29.7	21.9	27.6	15.7	26.5	30.2	22.2	23.4	28.8	22.2	25.4	26.1	23.2	28.3	24.6
4. Mostly agree	31.4	30.0	33.0	32.1	27.4	30.6	30.9	31.8	32.9	31.5	31.4	31.0	33.3	30.8	30.5	27.0
5. Agree	27.9	25.3	29.9	24.4	45.3	23.0	23.4	34.4	30.1	24.4	31.7	30.9	25.4	26.6	24.8	37.5
Item 10530 Subject D05 N	3300	1589	1624	2534	402	774	939	1068	519	1720	1344	1220	696	450	801	51
A15H: If a wife works, her husband should take a greater part in housework and child-care																
1. Disagree	5.6	7.0	4.3	4.9	6.6	7.0	4.5	4.9	7.0	4.7	6.6	5.4	4.5	5.5	5.6	13.8
2. Mostly disagree	6.6	6.6	6.6	6.3	6.7	6.7	6.2	6.8	6.6	6.0	7.2	4.7	7.6	7.9	7.9	4.9
3. Neither	14.3	15.9	12.9	14.7	10.4	12.3	15.1	13.9	16.9	12.8	16.2	15.3	14.8	14.5	11.6	22.8
4. Mostly agree	35.0	36.4	33.5	36.1	28.5	34.5	39.1	32.1	34.2	35.0	34.7	34.9	34.7	37.3	36.5	27.0
5. Agree	38.5	34.1	42.7	37.9	47.7	39.4	35.2	42.2	35.3	41.5	35.3	39.7	38.4	34.8	38.3	31.5
Item 10540 Subject D05 N	3305	1592	1625	2535	403	776	941	1065	522	1723	1345	1221	695	452	804	51

QUESTIONNAIRE FORM 4 1983	TOTAL	SEX		RACE		REGION				4YR COLLEGE PLANS		ILLICIT DRUG USE: LIFETIME				
		M	F	White	Black	NE	NC	S	W	Yes	No	None	Mari-juana Only	Few Pills	More Pills	Any Her-oin
N (Weighted No. of Cases):	3344	1610	1630	2556	406	793	949	1075	527	1733	1355	1233	699	455	814	51
% of Weighted Total:	100.0	48.1	48.8	76.4	12.1	23.7	28.4	32.2	15.8	51.8	40.5	36.9	20.9	13.6	24.3	1.5

A16: How much TV do you estimate you watch on an average weekday?

1. None	2.9	2.2	3.6	3.0	1.2	3.5	3.0	1.8	4.4	3.4	2.5	3.3	2.8	1.9	3.4	2.7
2. Half-hour or less	10.7	11.3	10.5	11.8	4.3	10.2	10.3	9.8	14.1	12.1	8.7	9.5	10.7	10.4	13.4	6.0
3. About one hour	19.9	20.8	19.1	21.5	9.6	20.3	21.9	16.3	22.9	23.0	16.2	18.0	20.2	22.5	22.2	14.8
4. About two hours	21.5	22.0	20.7	22.0	18.5	21.7	22.4	19.3	23.9	23.0	19.6	21.4	23.4	21.3	20.3	19.6
5. About three hours	19.3	19.0	19.5	18.9	20.8	20.1	17.2	20.9	18.4	17.1	22.2	20.5	18.8	18.3	17.6	22.3
6. About four hours	13.0	13.3	12.3	11.8	18.3	10.6	12.9	16.3	10.0	11.4	14.7	14.5	12.6	10.5	12.0	22.4
7. Five hours or more	12.8	11.3	14.2	11.0	27.3	13.6	12.3	15.8	6.3	10.0	16.0	12.8	11.5	15.1	11.1	12.3
Item 10550 Subject C07 N	3306	1589	1627	2539	400	777	940	1069	519	1722	1343	1224	694	453	803	51

A17: In the past year, how many books have you read just because you wanted to–that is, without their being assigned?

1. None	19.0	26.9	10.8	19.6	14.2	16.3	21.9	20.2	15.5	15.4	23.3	16.3	19.7	17.4	23.1	23.0
2. One	13.9	15.0	12.7	14.0	11.5	14.1	13.6	13.4	15.3	12.3	15.3	13.2	14.7	17.0	13.0	15.0
3. Two to five	38.4	36.8	40.5	37.3	45.3	41.9	35.6	39.3	36.5	39.9	36.8	38.4	41.3	38.2	36.2	36.5
4. Six to ten	12.1	9.6	14.4	11.9	15.0	13.5	11.8	11.2	12.5	13.3	10.2	12.7	11.5	13.7	10.8	6.5
5. Ten or more	16.5	11.8	21.5	17.2	14.1	14.2	17.1	16.0	20.1	19.1	14.3	19.4	12.8	13.7	17.0	19.0
Item 10560 Subject C07 N	3317	1604	1628	2551	404	781	944	1068	524	1729	1354	1232	697	453	807	51

A18: Some people think about what's going on in government very often, and others are not that interested. How much of an interest do you take in government and current events?

1. No interest at all	4.0	4.0	3.6	3.6	4.6	4.9	5.5	2.3	3.6	2.7	5.2	3.2	3.2	4.2	4.7	14.2
2. Very little interest	20.0	15.7	24.4	19.2	21.7	20.4	21.1	17.9	21.8	14.6	25.9	18.5	21.4	20.2	21.9	5.0
3. Some interest	48.6	45.4	51.7	50.4	45.7	49.7	47.0	51.7	43.5	49.0	48.4	47.7	49.5	48.3	49.5	47.5
4. A lot of interest	20.3	25.0	16.0	20.3	19.2	18.3	20.2	20.4	23.2	24.6	15.5	22.7	20.4	19.7	17.6	20.5
5. A very great interest	7.1	10.0	4.3	6.5	8.8	6.7	6.3	7.7	7.9	9.0	5.0	7.9	5.6	7.7	6.4	12.8
Item 6330 Subject H01,Q08 N	3312	1601	1624	2547	401	777	944	1067	524	1728	1351	1232	693	453	807	51

A19: Some people think that there ought to be changes in the amount of influence and power that certain organizations have in our society. Do you think the following organizations should have more influence, less influence, or about the same amount of influence as they have now?

A19A: Large corporations?

1. Much less	6.1	7.5	4.9	6.8	1.6	6.8	5.5	5.3	7.5	6.8	5.6	5.8	5.4	5.6	7.3	6.0
2. Less	29.4	31.4	27.8	31.9	19.4	32.0	30.9	25.0	31.6	34.1	24.0	30.7	30.9	28.4	28.0	30.7
3. Same as now	36.9	35.5	38.6	37.7	31.2	31.7	38.1	40.1	35.9	36.4	38.3	36.4	36.2	40.0	37.1	28.7
4. More	10.5	10.7	10.2	8.9	19.1	11.9	7.7	12.1	10.4	8.0	13.4	10.4	10.0	10.7	10.4	13.1
5. Much more	3.4	4.0	2.6	1.9	10.2	4.0	2.8	4.4	1.5	2.9	3.6	3.3	4.2	2.6	2.8	5.8
8. No opinion	13.7	11.0	15.9	12.8	18.5	13.7	14.9	13.0	13.0	11.8	15.2	13.4	13.4	12.7	14.4	15.6
Item 10570 Subject K03 N	3278	1593	1601	2525	399	763	938	1061	516	1714	1339	1218	688	451	799	49

A19B: Major labor unions?

1. Much less	8.6	12.2	5.3	9.8	3.2	6.3	10.7	8.6	8.3	10.2	7.3	10.5	7.7	6.1	8.1	10.2
2. Less	22.6	25.0	20.5	25.9	9.3	23.3	25.2	20.0	21.9	25.0	20.1	24.6	21.1	23.3	21.2	17.3
3. Same as now	29.7	29.0	30.4	30.4	26.1	28.4	29.7	29.2	32.7	28.9	31.7	27.8	32.7	29.6	30.2	26.7
4. More	19.1	16.0	21.9	16.9	25.9	23.1	16.9	17.8	19.7	17.1	20.8	16.7	20.7	21.0	20.0	11.6
5. Much more	6.3	6.9	5.5	3.9	18.1	6.0	3.6	9.9	4.4	5.9	6.4	6.2	6.3	6.3	5.3	21.3
8. No opinion	13.7	11.0	16.3	13.2	17.4	12.9	13.9	14.4	13.0	12.9	13.7	14.2	11.5	13.7	15.2	12.9
Item 10580 Subject K03 N	3282	1593	1605	2529	398	764	940	1060	517	1717	1340	1222	689	450	799	49

A19C: Churches and religious organizations?

1. Much less	5.6	7.5	3.6	5.9	2.7	5.7	5.6	4.3	7.8	5.2	6.3	3.8	4.6	6.4	8.2	13.1
2. Less	9.6	11.4	8.1	10.3	4.0	10.0	9.7	7.6	12.8	10.8	8.4	8.4	9.8	12.2	9.6	9.7
3. Same as now	33.7	34.2	33.7	36.0	21.7	35.5	37.6	27.0	37.6	36.4	30.9	30.0	38.1	34.8	35.5	32.6
4. More	23.5	22.2	24.8	24.0	23.9	23.4	23.5	25.8	18.8	22.9	24.9	25.4	23.7	20.5	23.1	19.9
5. Much more	17.7	14.6	20.5	14.6	36.3	14.5	14.3	25.5	12.7	17.2	18.3	23.0	16.0	15.3	12.4	7.8
8. No opinion	9.9	10.1	9.4	9.1	11.4	10.9	9.3	9.7	10.3	7.5	11.2	9.4	7.8	10.8	11.3	16.8
Item 10590 Subject G,K03 N	3279	1592	1603	2529	396	761	940	1061	517	1716	1341	1219	688	451	799	50

QUESTIONNAIRE FORM 4 1983	TOTAL	SEX		RACE		REGION				4YR COLLEGE PLANS		ILLICIT DRUG USE: LIFETIME				
		M	F	White	Black	NE	NC	S	W	Yes	No	None	Mari-juana Only	Few Pills	More Pills	Any Her-oin
N (Weighted No. of Cases):	3344	1610	1630	2556	406	793	949	1075	527	1733	1355	1233	699	455	814	51
% of Weighted Total:	100.0	48.1	48.8	76.4	12.1	23.7	28.4	32.2	15.8	51.8	40.5	36.9	20.9	13.6	24.3	1.5

A19D: The national news media (TV, magazines, news services)?

1. Much less	8.3	9.3	7.5	9.2	3.8	7.9	9.2	7.4	8.9	7.7	9.4	8.4	8.2	7.2	9.1	7.5
2. Less	24.7	23.5	26.5	26.4	16.7	27.2	23.4	24.7	23.4	27.7	21.9	25.3	23.6	24.5	26.5	17.2
3. Same as now	42.6	43.1	42.2	44.1	36.4	41.0	45.6	41.1	42.5	44.4	40.6	44.6	43.1	41.1	41.5	38.0
4. More	12.6	12.7	12.4	11.2	19.6	13.1	12.9	11.9	12.9	11.3	13.9	11.4	13.0	14.9	11.5	16.6
5. Much more	5.2	5.3	4.9	3.4	14.2	4.7	3.4	7.3	5.1	4.4	5.9	4.8	5.5	5.4	5.2	7.4
8. No opinion	6.5	6.1	6.5	5.6	9.3	6.1	5.4	7.6	7.1	4.5	8.4	5.5	6.6	6.8	6.3	13.3
Item 10600 Subject K03 N	3280	1591	1605	2530	397	764	941	1059	517	1716	1342	1220	687	451	800	50

A19E: The Presidency and the administration?

1. Much less	4.2	3.8	4.7	3.2	10.5	5.3	4.1	4.0	3.2	3.8	4.7	4.0	4.1	3.6	4.6	9.6
2. Less	11.7	11.4	11.9	10.6	16.0	13.7	11.3	10.2	12.5	10.3	13.4	8.4	13.6	11.6	14.1	18.4
3. Same as now	39.4	37.6	41.5	41.5	30.6	39.6	41.5	38.0	38.0	41.3	37.8	41.7	41.1	40.8	36.2	18.6
4. More	21.1	24.2	17.9	23.0	12.6	17.5	22.1	22.6	21.3	24.0	18.0	23.2	18.7	21.0	20.5	22.1
5. Much more	11.7	12.8	10.8	10.9	13.8	12.1	9.7	12.4	13.4	12.0	11.1	11.8	10.6	12.6	11.8	11.3
8. No opinion	11.9	10.3	13.2	10.7	16.5	11.7	11.2	12.8	11.6	8.6	14.9	10.9	11.9	10.4	12.7	19.9
Item 10610 Subject H04,K03 N	3276	1590	1603	2524	398	761	937	1062	517	1715	1340	1222	685	449	798	50

A19F: The Congress–that is, the U.S. Senate and House of Representatives?

1. Much less	2.8	3.0	2.7	2.4	6.0	2.4	2.7	3.3	2.8	2.6	3.1	2.6	2.7	1.9	3.4	7.6
2. Less	11.3	12.7	9.8	11.1	11.8	12.6	12.4	9.9	10.0	10.3	12.7	8.7	12.5	12.1	13.0	16.6
3. Same as now	41.7	42.2	41.2	43.6	34.1	40.1	41.3	43.7	40.3	43.2	40.3	43.6	45.1	41.4	38.0	15.2
4. More	21.5	20.8	22.7	22.3	18.2	22.8	20.8	20.9	22.2	24.2	18.5	22.7	17.5	22.0	23.0	24.5
5. Much more	8.4	9.5	7.3	7.0	14.5	8.5	6.9	8.6	10.6	8.4	8.4	8.2	8.7	9.6	7.8	7.3
8. No opinion	14.3	11.8	16.3	13.6	15.5	13.6	15.7	13.5	14.1	11.3	17.1	14.3	13.5	12.9	14.9	28.7
Item 10620 Subject H04,K03 N	3276	1589	1604	2526	399	762	938	1062	515	1714	1340	1221	688	449	797	50

A19G: The U.S. Supreme Court?

1. Much less	1.6	2.1	1.0	1.4	2.8	1.3	1.6	1.7	2.0	1.3	1.9	1.2	1.9	1.7	1.4	3.3
2. Less	5.6	6.4	4.5	5.4	6.9	6.0	5.6	5.6	4.9	4.7	6.6	5.4	5.4	6.1	5.2	10.7
3. Same as now	43.7	44.5	43.4	45.8	33.8	42.4	45.1	42.2	46.0	46.7	40.4	43.6	45.9	42.8	44.9	19.2
4. More	24.6	23.7	25.5	24.9	24.6	24.9	25.8	23.6	23.9	25.7	23.6	27.0	21.8	23.5	24.1	28.7
5. Much more	11.6	12.5	10.6	10.1	17.8	12.6	8.2	14.1	11.0	11.6	11.3	11.3	11.9	13.9	10.1	16.5
8. No opinion	13.0	10.8	15.0	12.5	14.0	12.7	13.7	12.9	12.2	9.9	16.1	11.5	13.0	12.0	14.3	21.6
Item 10630 Subject H04,K03 N	3261	1584	1595	2513	396	758	932	1056	515	1706	1334	1214	685	447	793	50

A19H: All the courts and the justice system in general?

1. Much less	1.5	1.9	1.1	1.3	2.4	1.0	1.9	1.5	1.6	1.3	1.7	1.0	1.6	1.4	1.7	7.9
2. Less	5.5	7.1	3.8	5.4	5.6	4.5	7.6	4.9	4.6	4.8	6.9	4.4	4.8	6.5	6.5	14.3
3. Same as now	40.8	43.3	38.6	42.1	34.3	38.3	43.9	39.8	41.1	42.8	39.1	38.4	47.6	38.5	40.1	28.5
4. More	29.1	25.5	32.8	29.4	29.4	29.7	26.7	29.9	30.8	30.3	28.1	32.0	26.7	30.5	26.9	20.2
5. Much more	11.3	12.0	10.5	10.3	15.0	15.3	7.7	12.1	10.3	11.7	10.3	13.1	8.8	12.6	10.1	14.4
8. No opinion	11.8	10.2	13.2	11.4	13.4	11.2	12.2	11.9	11.6	9.1	14.0	11.0	10.5	10.5	14.6	14.7
Item 10640 Subject H04,K03 N	3273	1588	1604	2525	397	762	937	1058	516	1712	1340	1219	689	446	800	50

A19I: The police and other law enforcement agencies?

1. Much less	2.2	3.0	1.4	2.0	2.9	2.4	1.8	2.4	2.3	1.8	2.7	1.4	2.1	2.0	3.3	10.4
2. Less	7.2	9.3	5.0	6.8	8.4	6.7	8.6	6.4	7.1	6.8	7.3	3.9	8.7	8.0	10.3	6.0
3. Same as now	29.1	32.2	26.0	30.5	22.6	29.2	32.2	25.7	30.3	31.9	25.9	26.0	31.9	30.9	30.9	25.6
4. More	33.1	30.3	36.2	34.3	26.3	30.7	33.9	32.8	35.6	33.9	33.5	38.2	30.0	32.7	28.9	27.1
5. Much more	20.9	18.8	23.0	19.7	28.5	24.0	15.6	24.8	17.8	19.6	22.0	23.9	19.1	20.7	18.1	16.7
8. No opinion	7.5	6.4	8.4	6.7	11.4	7.1	7.9	7.9	6.9	6.0	8.8	6.6	8.2	5.7	8.4	14.2
Item 10650 Subject K03 N	3272	1589	1600	2522	400	762	939	1061	511	1714	1340	1220	686	449	795	50

QUESTIONNAIRE FORM 4 1983	TOTAL	SEX		RACE		REGION				4YR COLLEGE PLANS		ILLICIT DRUG USE: LIFETIME				
		M	F	White	Black	NE	NC	S	W	Yes	No	None	Mari-juana Only	Few Pills	More Pills	Any Her-oin
N (Weighted No. of Cases):	3344	1610	1630	2556	406	793	949	1075	527	1733	1355	1233	699	455	814	51
% of Weighted Total:	100.0	48.1	48.8	76.4	12.1	23.7	28.4	32.2	15.8	51.8	40.5	36.9	20.9	13.6	24.3	1.5

A19J: The U.S. military?

1. Much less	3.8	5.1	2.6	3.6	3.2	4.7	3.1	2.4	6.5	3.9	3.8	3.6	5.0	2.6	3.0	14.5
2. Less	8.0	8.5	7.4	8.0	9.3	8.1	9.5	5.9	9.1	8.3	7.0	8.5	8.8	7.5	6.5	6.5
3. Same as now	37.4	36.2	38.8	39.0	30.8	38.8	40.3	33.9	37.2	39.2	36.2	37.1	40.8	38.2	37.0	18.6
4. More	24.0	24.7	23.7	24.4	23.0	22.9	24.4	25.6	21.6	25.3	22.9	24.8	20.4	25.3	25.3	15.3
5. Much more	15.8	17.4	13.5	14.6	20.6	14.9	11.4	21.2	14.1	14.0	17.3	14.5	16.0	17.0	15.6	31.3
8. No opinion	11.0	8.0	13.9	10.4	13.2	10.6	11.3	10.9	11.5	9.3	12.7	11.5	9.0	9.5	12.6	13.8
Item 10660 Subject K03,L04 N	3275	1589	1604	2524	401	764	939	1059	513	1714	1342	1221	689	449	796	50

The next questions ask your views about drugs.

A20: Do you think that people (who are 18 or older) should be prohibited by law from doing each of the following?

A20A: Smoking marijuana (pot, grass) in private

1. No	46.9	49.0	45.1	46.0	53.0	53.0	44.3	43.0	50.2	43.7	50.4	26.9	47.8	51.1	72.3	70.0
2. Not sure	15.3	14.0	16.5	15.4	15.3	14.2	15.9	16.4	13.9	15.0	15.8	16.0	17.0	21.7	9.9	11.4
3. Yes	37.8	37.0	38.5	38.6	31.7	32.8	39.8	40.7	35.9	41.3	33.8	57.1	35.2	27.2	17.8	18.5
Item 10780 Subject A13a N	3315	1603	1627	2551	402	783	943	1066	524	1728	1352	1229	694	454	809	51

A20B: Smoking marijuana in public places

1. No	16.3	19.3	12.9	14.6	21.9	17.9	15.6	16.9	14.0	11.1	21.9	11.9	13.1	17.5	21.9	45.5
2. Not sure	10.2	11.1	9.2	10.6	7.1	10.1	10.7	8.9	11.8	8.2	12.2	4.1	10.5	9.9	18.3	18.0
3. Yes	73.6	69.6	77.9	74.7	71.0	72.0	73.8	74.2	74.2	80.7	65.8	84.0	76.4	72.6	59.8	36.5
Item 10790 Subject A13a N	3314	1601	1628	2549	403	783	942	1066	523	1727	1351	1230	693	454	809	51

A20C: Taking LSD in private

1. No	22.5	25.7	19.2	20.1	33.5	24.2	22.1	22.0	21.6	18.0	26.2	15.7	20.7	23.9	29.8	55.1
2. Not sure	10.8	11.1	10.4	9.7	16.4	11.5	10.1	11.6	9.6	9.6	12.4	10.6	8.5	11.3	12.9	7.3
3. Yes	66.7	63.2	70.5	70.2	50.1	64.3	67.8	66.4	68.8	72.4	61.4	73.7	70.8	64.8	57.3	37.6
Item 10800 Subject A13a N	3308	1597	1627	2550	401	780	941	1064	523	1726	1348	1229	694	453	805	51

A20D: Taking LSD in public places

1. No	13.9	17.0	10.4	11.8	21.0	14.3	13.3	15.2	11.6	9.2	18.3	11.3	13.2	14.9	15.2	24.4
2. Not sure	3.3	4.5	2.1	2.9	3.7	3.1	4.1	2.5	4.0	2.0	4.5	2.5	1.4	1.4	6.0	19.0
3. Yes	82.8	78.5	87.5	85.2	75.2	82.5	82.6	82.2	84.4	88.8	77.2	86.2	85.4	83.7	78.8	56.5
Item 10810 Subject A13a N	3301	1595	1622	2540	401	782	937	1059	523	1721	1345	1227	691	450	806	49

A20E: Taking amphetamines (uppers) or barbiturates (downers) in private

1. No	31.4	34.2	28.9	30.9	36.0	34.7	29.9	31.0	30.3	25.9	36.5	20.0	26.7	33.0	49.4	62.8
2. Not sure	15.8	15.5	16.1	14.8	18.9	16.2	15.6	15.1	16.8	15.5	16.1	14.3	14.8	18.1	17.5	17.2
3. Yes	52.8	50.3	54.9	54.4	45.1	49.2	54.5	53.9	52.9	58.6	47.4	65.7	58.5	49.0	33.1	20.0
Item 10820 Subject A13a N	3309	1599	1626	2547	401	782	940	1064	523	1727	1348	1228	692	453	809	51

A20F: Taking amphetamines or barbiturates in public places

1. No	16.2	18.6	13.6	14.9	20.3	15.9	17.0	16.4	14.9	10.9	21.5	11.7	13.0	16.7	23.6	30.9
2. Not sure	7.1	8.2	5.9	6.8	6.3	7.4	7.0	6.8	7.3	6.2	7.9	4.0	4.8	6.8	12.5	20.5
3. Yes	76.7	73.2	80.5	78.3	73.5	76.6	76.0	76.8	77.9	82.9	70.6	84.4	82.3	76.5	63.9	48.5
Item 10830 Subject A13a N	3306	1596	1625	2548	398	782	942	1061	521	1727	1344	1228	691	452	808	50

A20G: Taking heroin (smack, horse) in private

1. No	21.4	24.3	18.4	18.6	33.6	25.4	18.8	21.3	20.1	16.5	25.6	16.0	21.3	23.1	25.8	41.7
2. Not sure	8.9	9.0	8.9	8.1	13.9	8.2	8.4	10.5	7.7	8.0	10.1	8.7	6.1	10.4	10.2	10.7
3. Yes	69.7	66.7	72.8	73.3	52.5	66.4	72.8	68.1	72.1	75.6	64.3	75.3	72.6	66.5	64.0	47.6
Item 10840 Subject A13a N	3299	1597	1617	2541	399	775	939	1064	522	1721	1344	1221	692	451	808	51

QUESTIONNAIRE FORM 4 1983	TOTAL	SEX		RACE		REGION				4YR COLLEGE PLANS		ILLICIT DRUG USE: LIFETIME				
		M	F	White	Black	NE	NC	S	W	Yes	No	None	Mari- juana Only	Few Pills	More Pills	Any Her- oin
N (Weighted No. of Cases):	3344	1610	1630	2556	406	793	949	1075	527	1733	1355	1233	699	455	814	51
% of Weighted Total:	100.0	48.1	48.8	76.4	12.1	23.7	28.4	32.2	15.8	51.8	40.5	36.9	20.9	13.6	24.3	1.5
A20H: Taking heroin in public places																
1. No	13.2	15.5	10.5	11.2	21.1	13.8	12.5	14.6	11.0	8.4	17.9	11.1	13.0	14.1	13.8	23.9
2. Not sure	3.1	4.3	2.0	2.8	3.6	2.4	3.5	3.4	2.8	1.8	4.4	2.1	1.7	2.0	5.8	10.0
3. Yes	83.7	80.2	87.6	86.0	75.3	83.8	84.0	82.0	86.2	89.8	77.7	86.8	85.3	83.9	80.4	66.1
Item 10850 Subject A13a N	3301	1593	1623	2544	400	780	939	1061	521	1723	1344	1224	694	452	803	51
A20I: Getting drunk in private																
1. No	65.8	67.1	64.7	68.0	59.6	68.7	66.5	63.2	65.4	66.5	65.6	52.0	70.3	71.4	80.2	73.4
2. Not sure	14.3	12.5	16.3	13.9	15.1	12.2	14.3	16.3	13.5	15.5	12.9	21.6	11.9	11.8	6.8	8.1
3. Yes	19.9	20.5	19.0	18.2	25.3	19.2	19.1	20.5	21.0	18.1	21.5	26.3	17.8	16.8	13.0	18.5
Item 10860 Subject A13a N	3310	1598	1627	2545	402	782	940	1065	524	1724	1351	1227	691	454	809	51
A20J: Getting drunk in public places																
1. No	27.5	29.8	25.3	27.6	27.2	31.8	28.1	26.3	22.3	23.9	31.6	18.7	26.3	32.1	38.5	36.9
2. Not sure	20.3	20.9	19.7	23.4	7.0	17.8	25.4	18.0	19.5	18.9	22.2	16.6	22.6	23.0	22.9	23.7
3. Yes	52.2	49.3	55.0	49.0	65.8	50.4	46.5	55.6	58.2	57.1	46.3	64.7	51.1	44.9	38.7	39.4
Item 10870 Subject A13a N	3310	1600	1625	2548	400	782	942	1062	523	1724	1350	1226	694	454	808	51
A20K: Smoking tobacco in certain specified public places																
1. No	44.0	42.5	45.8	45.2	38.0	46.2	45.3	42.7	40.8	41.6	46.6	34.2	45.0	42.7	58.4	51.0
2. Not sure	15.6	15.5	15.5	14.8	18.8	12.2	16.7	18.5	12.6	13.6	18.4	18.8	13.8	15.2	11.7	14.0
3. Yes	40.5	41.9	38.7	39.9	43.3	41.6	38.0	38.8	46.6	44.8	34.9	47.0	41.2	42.1	29.9	35.0
Item 10760 Subject A13a N	3310	1599	1627	2547	402	783	941	1064	522	1726	1350	1228	693	453	808	51
A21: In particular, there has been a great deal of public debate about whether marijuana use should be legal. Which of the following policies would you favor?																
1. Using marijuana should be entirely legal	18.9	23.1	14.7	19.4	15.8	20.0	18.2	17.2	22.2	16.4	21.1	6.3	15.0	18.8	38.8	57.9
2. It should be a minor violation –like a parking ticket– but not a crime	26.3	24.9	27.5	25.1	33.2	28.8	25.6	24.6	27.5	26.7	25.2	15.9	33.7	36.8	31.0	15.0
3. It should be a crime	36.7	34.6	39.2	38.2	28.7	31.3	39.9	40.1	31.9	39.9	34.4	60.5	31.5	23.4	14.6	16.9
4. Don't know	18.1	17.3	18.6	17.3	22.3	19.9	16.3	18.2	18.4	17.0	19.3	17.3	19.8	21.0	15.7	10.2
Item 10880 Subject A13b N	3301	1594	1622	2543	398	779	942	1058	523	1724	1346	1227	692	450	809	50
A22: If it were legal for people to USE marijuana, should it also be legal to SELL marijuana?																
1. No	27.4	25.7	29.1	27.0	26.7	25.2	28.1	29.0	25.9	26.9	28.1	41.7	21.0	23.9	13.7	15.2
2. Yes, but only to adults	47.6	50.5	44.7	48.3	47.9	48.0	45.2	47.5	51.3	48.7	46.0	35.4	51.4	52.5	60.1	49.6
3. Yes, to anyone	10.5	11.6	9.2	9.8	11.5	10.2	11.2	10.1	10.4	10.6	10.3	9.3	9.8	8.7	12.3	24.0
4. Don't know	14.6	12.1	17.0	14.9	13.8	16.6	15.4	13.3	12.4	13.7	15.6	13.6	17.8	14.9	13.8	11.3
Item 10890 Subject A13b N	3300	1594	1623	2544	398	782	941	1057	521	1724	1347	1228	694	452	806	50
A23: If marijuana were legal to use and legally available, which of the following would you be most likely to do?																
1. Not use it, even if it were legal and available	60.1	55.7	64.5	60.6	55.1	55.0	61.1	62.7	60.5	62.8	57.4	90.7	54.7	50.6	26.6	14.0
2. Try it	7.2	7.4	7.1	7.0	9.9	6.8	6.7	8.1	6.8	8.0	5.6	4.4	11.5	11.1	5.6	4.6
3. Use it about as often as I do now	19.8	22.1	17.5	20.4	17.0	23.5	20.8	15.3	21.5	18.4	21.8	0.5	18.9	22.4	48.3	33.7
4. Use it more often than I do now	4.9	6.3	3.6	5.0	4.2	4.5	6.3	4.1	4.9	4.2	5.9	0.4	3.4	6.5	10.2	40.7
5. Use it less than I do now	1.5	2.0	1.0	1.1	3.7	2.4	0.9	1.7	1.2	1.4	1.8	0.2	2.8	1.0	2.6	1.2
6. Don't know	6.4	6.4	6.4	5.9	10.2	7.7	4.2	8.1	5.1	5.1	7.6	3.8	8.7	8.4	6.7	5.8
Item 10900 Subject A13b N	3296	1594	1623	2543	396	779	941	1055	522	1726	1347	1226	693	453	809	50

This section asks for your views and feelings about a number of different things.

QUESTIONNAIRE FORM 4 1983	TOTAL	SEX		RACE		REGION				4YR COLLEGE PLANS		ILLICIT DRUG USE: LIFETIME				
		M	F	White	Black	NE	NC	S	W	Yes	No	None	Mari- juana Only	Few Pills	More Pills	Any Her- oin
N (Weighted No. of Cases):	3344	1610	1630	2556	406	793	949	1075	527	1733	1355	1233	699	455	814	51
% of Weighted Total:	100.0	48.1	48.8	76.4	12.1	23.7	28.4	32.2	15.8	51.8	40.5	36.9	20.9	13.6	24.3	1.5

D01: How satisfied are you with your life as a whole these days?

1. Completely dissatisfied	2.0	2.0	1.9	1.7	3.5	2.3	1.7	2.5	1.3	1.8	2.4	1.8	1.8	2.2	1.9	6.1
2. Quite dissatisfied	8.5	7.8	8.9	8.2	7.0	8.3	8.1	8.1	10.1	8.7	7.7	8.0	8.5	7.6	9.7	8.9
3. Somewhat dissatisfied	10.5	10.0	10.7	10.2	10.8	10.8	10.7	10.7	9.5	9.6	11.2	9.1	10.6	10.2	12.3	26.7
4. Neither, or mixed feelings	14.0	14.6	13.2	13.5	13.5	15.1	13.7	14.7	11.8	12.1	16.7	13.9	12.9	14.2	15.7	8.3
5. Somewhat satisfied	26.6	28.2	25.3	26.9	27.9	24.6	27.0	27.1	27.8	25.4	28.3	23.4	25.6	32.8	28.3	27.9
6. Quite satisfied	33.3	32.3	35.1	35.2	30.1	34.9	33.7	32.0	33.2	37.1	29.4	38.2	34.4	30.4	28.0	19.3
7. Completely satisfied	4.9	5.1	4.9	4.2	7.1	4.0	4.9	4.9	6.4	5.4	4.3	5.6	6.2	2.7	4.1	2.8
Item 6840 Subject P01,Q01 N	3111	1486	1574	2448	360	705	911	1005	489	1696	1315	1174	645	432	763	45

D02: FOR THOSE WHO HAVE A JOB: All things considered, how satisfied are you with your present job?

1. Completely dissatisfied	4.4	5.2	3.6	4.0	7.9	3.6	3.9	5.4	4.4	4.0	4.6	4.1	5.7	3.4	4.0	11.8
2. Quite dissatisfied	9.6	10.4	9.0	9.7	6.7	10.4	9.7	7.8	12.0	10.1	9.1	9.1	10.9	7.3	11.0	7.1
3. Somewhat dissatisfied	13.2	12.4	13.6	12.8	17.6	12.7	15.0	11.8	13.2	13.7	12.4	10.5	14.5	13.6	15.7	14.5
4. Neither, or mixed feelings	14.4	15.2	13.2	14.1	13.2	17.1	12.9	13.7	14.7	14.5	14.1	13.4	15.9	16.4	13.8	10.0
5. Somewhat satisfied	26.9	28.0	25.9	27.3	29.1	24.7	28.6	28.1	24.4	26.4	28.0	27.3	24.3	29.3	26.3	22.1
6. Quite satisfied	24.6	22.4	27.3	25.2	23.8	24.9	23.9	26.8	21.4	25.7	23.8	27.0	24.2	22.9	23.3	16.1
7. Completely satisfied	6.9	6.4	7.3	6.9	4.6	6.6	6.0	6.4	9.8	5.5	8.1	8.6	4.6	7.0	5.9	18.3
Item 10910 Subject C01,P02 N★	1944	982	931	1605	157	435	577	612	321	1059	820	685	402	283	524	27

D03A: Which best describes your recent employment experience?

1. I have a paid job now.	62.3	63.0	61.9	64.8	44.6	61.0	63.1	61.3	64.5	62.3	61.9	58.0	64.7	65.5	66.5	46.7
2. No paid job now, but I had one during the past 3 months.	8.2	9.4	7.0	8.0	9.2	8.5	7.9	8.4	8.2	7.6	8.9	6.8	9.6	6.2	9.4	21.4
3. No paid job in the past 3 months –GO TO QUESTION D10	21.0	21.5	20.1	19.9	28.0	22.4	21.4	20.0	20.0	21.9	20.3	22.0	19.4	22.7	19.5	23.0
4. Never had a paid job–GO TO QUESTION D10	8.5	6.1	11.0	7.3	18.2	8.0	7.6	10.2	7.4	8.1	8.8	13.1	6.2	5.6	4.6	9.0
Item 21530 Subject C01 N	2767	1342	1381	2231	290	618	824	893	432	1529	1151	1042	564	382	700	43

The next questions are about your present or most recent paid job. (If you presently hold more than one paid job, answer for the more important one.)

D03B: On the average, how many hours per week do (did) you work on this particular job?

1. 5 or less hours	8.7	8.0	9.6	7.7	15.7	7.5	8.3	8.2	12.3	8.5	9.2	11.2	7.4	11.9	4.5	8.9
2. 6 to 10 hours	12.8	12.8	12.4	12.2	16.4	13.5	11.7	11.9	15.9	13.8	11.5	16.4	13.2	10.4	10.1	6.6
3. 11 to 15 hours	14.9	12.9	17.1	15.2	14.9	15.2	15.7	12.3	18.3	17.5	11.3	15.7	14.1	14.2	15.5	11.5
4. 16 to 20 hours	24.7	21.6	27.7	25.2	19.4	30.7	26.3	21.4	20.0	25.9	23.6	23.8	29.0	24.0	22.8	27.0
5. 21 to 25 hours	17.7	17.9	17.3	18.0	15.2	19.0	15.8	18.9	16.6	16.5	19.0	14.3	19.2	17.7	21.3	10.0
6. 26 to 30 hours	9.6	10.9	8.3	9.8	9.0	7.7	8.7	12.0	9.1	8.5	11.5	8.8	7.9	10.6	10.6	20.8
7. 31 to 35 hours	5.1	6.8	3.5	5.5	4.2	2.4	6.0	7.0	3.4	4.0	6.2	3.8	4.4	5.8	6.3	9.0
8. 36 or more hours	6.5	9.0	4.0	6.6	5.3	4.0	7.5	8.3	4.3	5.3	7.7	6.0	4.7	5.5	8.9	6.2
Item 21540 Subject C01 N★	2109	1042	1035	1727	183	467	619	688	335	1151	892	731	447	298	568	36

D04: About how old is (was) your supervisor?

1. Age 20 or younger	3.1	3.9	2.1	2.6	5.3	2.1	2.5	3.9	3.9	2.8	3.5	2.6	4.2	2.7	3.2	4.0
2. 21 to 25	15.1	13.9	16.5	15.4	14.0	16.9	17.2	13.4	12.4	13.6	16.2	13.1	14.0	12.3	20.6	11.7
3. 26 to 30	22.9	21.9	23.5	22.0	31.4	21.4	21.9	23.7	25.0	23.5	22.3	21.6	25.3	18.8	23.9	17.8
4. 31 or older	58.9	60.3	57.9	60.0	49.3	59.6	58.4	59.0	58.6	60.1	58.0	62.7	56.5	66.2	52.3	66.5
Item 21550 Subject C01,M02 N★	2102	1042	1030	1716	184	466	615	687	335	1146	888	728	453	296	568	31

★=excludes respondents for whom question was inappropriate.

QUESTIONNAIRE FORM 4 1983	TOTAL	SEX		RACE		REGION				4YR COLLEGE PLANS		ILLICIT DRUG USE: LIFETIME				
		M	F	White	Black	NE	NC	S	W	Yes	No	None	Mari-juana Only	Few Pills	More Pills	Any Her-oin
N (Weighted No. of Cases):	3344	1610	1630	2556	406	793	949	1075	527	1733	1355	1233	699	455	814	51
% of Weighted Total:	100.0	48.1	48.8	76.4	12.1	23.7	28.4	32.2	15.8	51.8	40.5	36.9	20.9	13.6	24.3	1.5

D05: How many of the other workers are within 2 or 3 years of your own age?

1. None	21.6	19.7	23.7	21.1	23.4	16.7	21.8	24.3	22.8	19.1	25.4	25.4	21.7	22.1	16.6	13.9
2. A few	28.8	30.5	27.4	28.4	30.6	33.7	27.4	26.9	28.5	28.2	29.6	30.9	27.6	29.2	27.8	18.9
3. About half	14.5	13.8	14.8	15.1	14.1	14.6	13.4	17.3	10.7	15.6	12.5	13.6	12.7	11.5	16.9	34.9
4. Most	13.6	14.2	13.1	13.4	13.3	14.9	14.4	12.9	11.9	14.4	13.0	10.3	16.8	13.8	15.4	11.4
5. Nearly all	15.2	15.0	15.4	15.5	14.3	15.4	15.4	13.6	18.0	15.8	14.3	13.8	14.8	17.4	16.4	17.4
6. All	6.2	6.7	5.7	6.5	4.3	4.7	7.6	5.0	8.0	6.9	5.3	6.0	6.5	5.9	6.8	3.5
Item 21560 Subject C01 N★	2088	1034	1023	1710	179	464	608	680	336	1143	878	728	445	291	566	31

D06: To what extent does (did) this job . . .

D06A: Use your skills and abilities–let you do the things you do best?

1. Not at all	21.1	23.5	18.7	21.1	18.9	25.6	22.4	17.4	19.8	22.6	19.1	20.4	22.6	19.0	22.4	19.4
2. A little	28.5	26.8	29.9	29.0	26.7	27.5	29.0	27.6	30.8	29.4	27.9	26.3	31.1	29.9	28.7	28.8
3. Some extent	24.8	23.8	25.6	25.0	26.3	21.9	25.5	27.4	22.1	24.3	26.0	26.0	22.4	27.4	23.0	26.6
4. Considerable extent	14.7	13.2	16.2	14.6	15.8	13.0	12.9	16.3	16.9	14.5	14.4	14.1	15.7	14.9	14.5	13.9
5. A great extent	11.0	12.7	9.5	10.3	12.2	11.9	10.2	11.3	10.4	9.2	12.6	13.1	8.2	8.7	11.4	11.4
Item 21570 Subject C01 N★	2099	1037	1031	1718	181	467	612	689	331	1149	883	736	439	296	568	32

D06B: Teach you new skills that will be useful in your future work?

1. Not at all	23.6	25.5	21.2	23.6	17.8	25.9	25.5	20.6	23.3	24.5	22.5	22.5	25.8	17.3	25.9	37.0
2. A little	25.4	25.9	25.2	25.9	21.9	28.2	26.7	24.1	21.7	25.7	25.6	24.2	25.3	28.8	25.7	13.0
3. Some extent	20.9	19.4	22.0	20.6	25.8	20.3	19.5	20.3	25.3	22.0	19.6	21.4	23.4	17.4	19.2	42.3
4. Considerable extent	15.9	15.4	16.8	16.5	14.2	11.7	15.5	18.5	17.2	16.0	15.6	15.4	13.4	21.7	16.0	7.7
5. A great extent	14.2	13.8	14.9	13.4	20.3	13.9	12.7	16.5	12.6	11.8	16.7	16.5	12.1	14.9	13.2	-
Item 21580 Subject C01 N★	2093	1032	1029	1714	181	465	612	686	330	1149	876	733	441	294	566	31

D06C: Make good use of special skills you learned in technical, vocational, business, or professional studies?

1. Not at all	55.2	55.1	55.1	56.5	44.2	63.4	57.0	47.7	55.8	58.8	51.6	53.6	58.4	53.7	55.9	49.6
2. A little	16.3	17.8	14.7	16.1	15.9	13.4	16.7	18.0	16.4	16.0	16.5	15.6	15.3	19.6	15.8	30.0
3. Some extent	12.5	13.1	12.0	12.8	15.6	8.7	13.5	14.9	11.2	11.0	14.2	11.7	12.7	13.6	13.1	12.5
4. Considerable extent	8.3	8.3	8.5	7.9	9.8	7.0	7.5	9.9	8.4	7.5	9.3	9.4	7.6	7.7	7.5	5.6
5. A great extent	7.6	5.6	9.7	6.7	14.5	7.5	5.3	9.5	8.2	6.7	8.5	9.7	6.0	5.4	7.7	2.3
Item 21590 Subject C01 N★	2081	1027	1022	1705	177	464	608	680	328	1140	873	726	438	290	567	31

D06D: Let you get to know people with social backgrounds very different from yours?

1. Not at all	19.8	20.5	19.3	20.0	16.6	22.4	24.1	14.5	19.5	18.2	21.8	21.3	20.0	18.9	17.9	25.8
2. A little	21.2	22.3	19.6	21.1	20.0	16.9	22.5	23.0	21.1	20.9	21.8	20.3	24.0	20.6	21.7	10.7
3. Some extent	22.6	24.0	21.0	23.0	19.7	22.6	21.1	23.1	24.0	22.5	22.7	20.9	23.2	20.8	24.1	40.6
4. Considerable extent	19.1	19.8	18.6	19.5	19.9	21.4	17.9	18.9	18.2	19.9	18.5	20.0	18.2	22.9	17.6	14.5
5. A great extent	17.3	13.4	21.4	16.5	23.9	16.8	14.4	20.4	17.2	18.6	15.3	17.5	14.6	16.8	18.7	8.4
Item 21600 Subject C01,M05 N★	2081	1028	1022	1705	178	463	610	681	328	1139	874	727	437	293	566	31

D06E: Let you get to know people over age 30?

1. Not at all	11.7	12.4	11.2	10.8	15.8	12.6	13.0	8.9	14.2	10.8	12.6	12.0	10.6	12.6	11.7	12.0
2. A little	17.5	19.3	15.5	17.7	15.4	16.6	19.1	17.6	15.5	17.3	18.2	16.7	18.0	15.9	19.9	6.9
3. Some extent	22.1	24.6	18.9	21.8	25.4	21.0	21.9	22.9	22.2	22.0	22.8	19.9	25.1	21.4	21.0	39.2
4. Considerable extent	22.6	21.5	24.3	23.8	17.2	20.5	22.0	25.7	20.4	23.7	21.3	25.8	20.3	24.0	20.2	22.9
5. A great extent	26.1	22.2	30.1	25.8	26.2	29.3	24.1	25.0	27.6	26.2	25.1	25.6	26.0	26.0	27.1	19.0
Item 21610 Subject C01,M02 N★	2074	1024	1020	1701	176	463	608	677	326	1138	869	723	436	292	564	31

D06F: Cause you stress and tension?

1. Not at all	25.5	29.0	21.8	24.6	31.1	24.2	25.2	26.3	26.3	25.1	26.4	26.2	26.2	23.7	24.1	36.0
2. A little	33.6	31.8	35.6	34.8	28.4	32.8	32.5	32.6	39.2	32.6	34.9	34.3	33.5	34.6	33.0	28.8
3. Some extent	21.5	21.2	21.7	21.8	17.6	22.4	23.9	20.7	17.2	22.9	19.5	21.6	22.2	22.7	20.3	16.7
4. Considerable extent	11.4	10.2	12.9	11.5	12.8	11.4	12.5	11.6	9.3	12.6	10.3	11.1	11.0	12.0	12.4	11.6
5. A great extent	7.9	7.9	8.1	7.3	10.0	9.2	5.9	8.8	7.9	6.8	8.8	6.8	7.1	7.0	10.3	6.9
Item 21620 Subject C01 N★	2075	1024	1020	1702	175	459	609	680	327	1136	871	725	435	291	567	31

★=excludes respondents for whom question was inappropriate.

QUESTIONNAIRE FORM 4 1983	TOTAL	SEX		RACE		REGION				4YR COLLEGE PLANS		ILLICIT DRUG USE: LIFETIME				
		M	F	White	Black	NE	NC	S	W	Yes	No	None	Mari-juana Only	Few Pills	More Pills	Any Her-oin
N (Weighted No. of Cases):	3344	1610	1630	2556	406	793	949	1075	527	1733	1355	1233	699	455	814	51
% of Weighted Total:	100.0	48.1	48.8	76.4	12.1	23.7	28.4	32.2	15.8	51.8	40.5	36.9	20.9	13.6	24.3	1.5
D06G: Interfere with your education?																
1. Not at all	51.0	50.1	52.0	51.2	51.8	49.7	52.1	50.6	51.4	47.8	55.1	53.5	50.1	49.2	49.2	50.4
2. A little	27.7	26.6	28.8	28.2	25.0	29.2	25.8	27.3	29.9	29.9	24.8	26.8	28.0	26.3	29.6	24.8
3. Some extent	13.3	14.4	12.1	13.0	15.2	11.5	13.6	14.9	11.8	13.9	12.8	12.4	13.4	16.4	12.6	15.4
4. Considerable extent	4.6	5.3	3.8	4.4	4.1	5.2	5.1	3.6	4.7	4.7	4.5	4.4	4.2	5.1	4.7	4.1
5. A great extent	3.5	3.6	3.3	3.2	3.8	4.4	3.4	3.6	2.2	3.6	2.8	2.9	4.3	3.0	3.9	5.5
Item 21630 Subject C01 N★	2069	1018	1019	1700	172	459	604	678	327	1136	866	721	435	290	567	29
D06H: Interfere with your social life?																
1. Not at all	29.4	27.3	31.4	26.4	42.8	29.0	26.4	29.2	35.8	26.0	33.0	34.0	29.1	28.8	24.9	22.4
2. A little	31.1	31.5	30.9	32.2	28.4	28.9	32.8	32.4	28.5	32.2	30.4	29.9	32.2	32.4	31.5	30.8
3. Some extent	19.5	19.7	19.3	20.5	13.9	21.2	20.9	17.6	18.4	21.2	17.8	17.0	21.6	17.7	20.6	29.6
4. Considerable extent	10.7	11.8	9.5	11.7	5.0	11.4	10.7	10.2	10.8	12.1	9.1	10.5	9.2	12.6	11.8	9.9
5. A great extent	9.2	9.8	8.8	9.1	9.8	9.4	9.1	10.6	6.4	8.6	9.7	8.6	8.1	8.6	11.2	7.3
Item 21640 Subject C01 N★	2065	1012	1021	1692	174	460	603	676	326	1136	862	720	436	288	563	31
D06I: Interfere with your family life?																
1. Not at all	51.1	48.7	53.8	49.0	64.6	53.1	49.1	51.3	51.9	49.4	53.1	50.9	54.3	52.7	47.5	55.0
2. A little	24.7	25.2	24.4	26.6	17.2	24.5	26.5	22.7	26.0	25.2	24.6	23.5	23.2	25.0	27.9	23.3
3. Some extent	14.5	15.2	13.5	14.8	9.1	13.3	14.8	14.8	14.9	15.7	13.0	15.0	14.6	14.2	14.2	4.4
4. Considerable extent	5.8	6.7	4.9	5.9	3.8	4.8	5.5	7.0	5.7	6.5	5.2	7.3	3.7	5.5	6.0	9.9
5. A great extent	3.8	4.1	3.4	3.7	5.2	4.2	4.2	4.3	1.5	3.2	4.1	3.3	4.2	2.7	4.4	7.4
Item 21650 Subject C01 N★	2070	1022	1017	1696	177	462	607	675	327	1139	864	718	438	292	565	31
D07: To what extent is (was) this job . . .																
D07A: An interesting job to do?																
1. Not at all	16.7	19.3	14.0	17.0	14.5	20.3	17.5	13.8	16.4	18.3	14.8	14.0	20.4	12.7	18.1	39.1
2. A little	24.1	25.6	22.7	23.7	22.6	20.5	25.7	23.2	27.8	23.7	25.6	23.7	23.4	25.1	25.8	14.4
3. Some extent	26.1	23.1	28.7	26.1	28.3	27.4	25.7	27.7	21.9	26.5	25.2	25.8	24.5	30.4	25.6	25.5
4. Considerable extent	18.0	17.5	18.4	18.5	14.9	15.8	18.6	17.5	20.6	18.8	16.8	19.4	16.8	20.5	16.1	14.6
5. A great extent	15.2	14.4	16.1	14.7	19.7	16.0	12.5	17.8	13.4	12.7	17.6	17.0	14.9	11.2	14.4	6.3
Item 21660 Subject C01 N★	2067	1019	1017	1695	175	460	608	674	326	1136	863	720	434	292	564	31
D07B: A job you COULD be happy doing for most of your life?																
1. Not at all	62.3	61.0	63.9	63.2	62.2	66.5	62.1	58.3	65.1	70.1	52.8	59.6	66.3	61.8	64.5	50.7
2. A little	12.2	10.8	13.5	12.3	8.9	10.2	11.2	14.2	13.0	11.0	13.7	12.1	8.9	14.1	13.4	13.8
3. Some extent	10.8	13.3	8.2	10.3	11.5	8.9	10.6	12.2	11.4	9.3	12.9	12.3	11.1	10.6	8.7	19.7
4. Considerable extent	8.1	7.0	9.1	8.2	5.2	6.1	10.2	8.9	5.0	5.2	11.6	8.8	7.1	7.7	7.8	12.9
5. A great extent	6.5	7.8	5.4	6.0	12.3	8.2	6.0	6.4	5.6	4.5	8.9	7.2	6.6	5.9	5.6	3.0
Item 21670 Subject C01 N★	2061	1014	1017	1693	175	455	608	672	326	1135	859	719	435	290	561	31
D07C: The type of work you EXPECT to be doing for most of your life?																
1. Not at all	71.0	68.1	74.0	71.9	68.4	76.6	69.7	66.4	75.2	79.1	61.9	69.8	72.8	70.3	73.0	50.6
2. A little	10.5	12.0	8.9	10.5	9.1	7.6	11.4	10.8	12.1	8.7	12.1	10.0	10.3	12.7	9.8	20.0
3. Some extent	6.9	7.7	6.1	6.7	6.5	5.4	7.2	8.6	5.2	5.0	9.3	7.4	7.1	5.2	6.2	16.2
4. Considerable extent	5.7	5.9	5.5	5.5	6.2	4.4	6.3	6.9	4.1	3.9	8.1	6.1	4.9	6.1	5.8	6.5
5. A great extent	5.8	6.3	5.5	5.3	9.8	6.0	5.4	7.3	3.4	3.3	8.6	6.7	4.9	5.6	5.2	6.6
Item 21680 Subject C01 N★	2059	1014	1015	1695	173	455	604	674	326	1133	859	719	434	290	561	31
D07D: A good stepping-stone toward the kind of work you want in the long run?																
1. Not at all	53.4	54.8	51.8	53.5	55.4	58.6	53.4	50.9	51.3	57.4	48.1	51.4	58.0	53.6	52.9	48.1
2. A little	17.8	17.5	18.1	18.0	16.0	18.9	16.0	17.0	21.6	18.4	17.8	18.1	14.0	16.0	21.0	23.1
3. Some extent	9.4	9.2	9.6	8.9	10.3	7.3	9.1	9.7	12.5	8.5	9.8	8.8	10.9	10.5	7.8	10.6
4. Considerable extent	8.6	8.4	8.7	8.5	8.0	6.1	11.0	10.0	4.4	6.8	11.0	8.7	7.4	11.6	8.0	7.9
5. A great extent	10.8	10.1	11.8	11.0	10.4	9.1	10.6	12.3	10.3	8.8	13.3	12.9	9.7	8.4	10.2	10.4
Item 21690 Subject C01 N★	2059	1013	1015	1693	173	456	606	672	325	1135	857	715	435	292	562	31

★=excludes respondents for whom question was inappropriate.

QUESTIONNAIRE FORM 4 1983	TOTAL	SEX		RACE		REGION				4YR COLLEGE PLANS		ILLICIT DRUG USE: LIFETIME				
		M	F	White	Black	NE	NC	S	W	Yes	No	None	Marijuana Only	Few Pills	More Pills	Any Heroin
N (Weighted No. of Cases):	3344	1610	1630	2556	406	793	949	1075	527	1733	1355	1233	699	455	814	51
% of Weighted Total:	100.0	48.1	48.8	76.4	12.1	23.7	28.4	32.2	15.8	51.8	40.5	36.9	20.9	13.6	24.3	1.5

D07E: The kind of work people do just for the money?

	TOTAL	M	F	White	Black	NE	NC	S	W	Yes	No	None	Marijuana Only	Few Pills	More Pills	Any Heroin
1. Not at all	20.6	17.9	23.4	21.3	20.9	19.9	19.1	22.9	19.6	19.8	21.8	22.9	17.6	19.0	21.0	33.5
2. A little	17.6	18.0	17.4	18.0	12.1	14.0	18.4	19.1	18.3	15.4	21.3	18.4	18.1	16.7	16.8	12.8
3. Some extent	20.0	20.1	19.6	19.7	20.0	18.1	20.2	21.2	19.8	18.5	22.4	19.2	18.8	24.5	19.4	19.9
4. Considerable extent	16.8	16.9	16.7	16.5	16.6	20.3	17.0	14.6	16.2	18.2	14.2	17.2	17.5	17.7	15.7	7.1
5. A great extent	24.9	27.1	22.7	24.4	30.4	27.7	25.3	22.2	26.0	28.0	20.4	22.3	28.0	22.1	27.1	26.8
Item 21700 Subject C01 N★	2052	1011	1011	1686	173	452	603	670	326	1132	855	718	431	291	556	31

D08: To what extent did any high school teacher or counselor help you get this job?

	TOTAL	M	F	White	Black	NE	NC	S	W	Yes	No	None	Marijuana Only	Few Pills	More Pills	Any Heroin
1. Not at all	78.0	79.3	77.0	80.9	55.5	82.4	78.1	73.9	80.4	82.2	73.7	76.6	79.2	77.1	80.1	81.6
2. A little	4.4	5.4	3.4	3.5	8.7	3.4	3.7	5.0	5.8	3.3	5.7	4.8	4.1	4.9	3.6	5.6
3. Some extent	4.6	4.7	4.4	4.2	8.3	3.7	5.0	5.6	3.2	4.0	5.3	5.2	5.2	4.0	3.0	4.9
4. Considerable extent	4.8	4.1	5.4	4.6	6.4	4.1	4.1	5.7	5.0	3.3	6.1	4.7	3.3	6.2	5.1	4.4
5. A great extent	8.2	6.6	9.9	6.8	21.2	6.4	9.1	9.8	5.6	7.1	9.1	8.6	8.2	7.8	8.3	3.5
Item 21710 Subject C01,M02 N★	2014	993	992	1657	172	440	593	661	319	1108	843	700	425	290	545	31

D09: Is (was) this job part of a work-study program?

	TOTAL	M	F	White	Black	NE	NC	S	W	Yes	No	None	Marijuana Only	Few Pills	More Pills	Any Heroin
1. Yes	18.9	15.2	22.7	16.6	36.7	13.1	19.0	25.3	13.8	13.9	24.4	18.2	17.3	21.9	19.5	16.3
2. No	81.1	84.8	77.3	83.4	63.3	86.9	81.0	74.7	86.2	86.1	75.6	81.8	82.7	78.1	80.5	83.7
Item 21720 Subject C01 N★	2015	975	1011	1672	161	448	595	653	319	1115	839	695	427	288	553	29

D10: People have different opinions about world problems. How much do you agree or disagree with each of the following statements?

D10A: I feel that I can do very little to change the way the world is today

	TOTAL	M	F	White	Black	NE	NC	S	W	Yes	No	None	Marijuana Only	Few Pills	More Pills	Any Heroin
1. Disagree	8.6	9.0	8.0	7.1	15.4	9.6	6.1	10.3	8.0	9.7	7.3	9.1	9.5	6.1	7.4	8.2
2. Mostly disagree	20.1	17.5	22.7	21.0	16.6	19.5	18.3	22.0	20.6	25.0	14.0	21.6	20.2	19.6	18.7	10.4
3. Neither	24.2	27.1	21.6	24.1	23.8	22.4	25.0	24.2	25.5	21.3	27.9	23.7	24.9	22.8	25.4	19.7
4. Mostly agree	28.5	26.9	30.3	30.6	19.5	28.5	30.3	26.7	29.0	29.6	27.1	27.8	28.1	32.0	28.6	25.9
5. Agree	18.5	19.5	17.4	17.2	24.7	20.0	20.3	16.7	16.9	14.4	23.8	17.6	17.2	19.4	19.9	35.8
Item 10920 Subject I02,J N	2958	1406	1501	2354	329	660	876	959	462	1627	1237	1123	608	410	733	40

D10B: It does little good to clean up air and water pollution because this society will not last long enough for it to matter

	TOTAL	M	F	White	Black	NE	NC	S	W	Yes	No	None	Marijuana Only	Few Pills	More Pills	Any Heroin
1. Disagree	43.9	44.3	44.1	44.9	37.8	46.5	44.5	39.9	47.6	49.2	37.2	47.2	44.0	42.6	40.9	27.0
2. Mostly disagree	27.4	26.6	28.1	29.4	20.1	26.8	27.0	28.9	25.9	28.3	26.7	26.4	28.9	30.7	26.9	17.7
3. Neither	15.9	15.8	15.7	15.2	17.7	15.7	16.8	15.8	14.6	13.4	18.9	12.8	14.6	16.8	20.8	15.4
4. Mostly agree	6.9	7.2	6.5	5.8	12.6	4.8	6.8	8.6	6.6	5.2	9.1	7.0	7.0	6.4	5.8	22.6
5. Agree	5.9	6.1	5.6	4.7	11.8	6.2	5.0	6.8	5.3	3.9	8.0	6.6	5.5	3.6	5.6	17.3
Item 10930 Subject F05,J N	2936	1398	1488	2341	325	650	875	950	461	1614	1228	1111	603	411	728	40

D10C: When things get tough enough, we'll put our minds to it and find a technological solution

	TOTAL	M	F	White	Black	NE	NC	S	W	Yes	No	None	Marijuana Only	Few Pills	More Pills	Any Heroin
1. Disagree	5.6	5.0	6.1	4.9	9.0	6.4	4.1	5.6	7.6	5.4	5.7	5.9	3.9	6.1	5.6	11.5
2. Mostly disagree	10.6	9.6	11.5	10.7	9.5	11.3	11.4	9.5	10.2	9.5	11.8	10.7	10.8	12.0	9.9	6.0
3. Neither	21.9	19.9	23.7	22.0	15.8	20.9	22.8	20.2	25.1	19.7	24.8	21.3	21.0	20.6	23.7	30.6
4. Mostly agree	39.1	39.0	39.5	41.3	30.8	36.8	40.9	40.6	35.7	41.3	37.1	35.9	40.6	40.3	43.1	33.5
5. Agree	22.8	26.4	19.2	21.1	34.9	24.6	20.8	24.1	21.4	24.1	20.7	26.3	23.7	21.1	17.7	18.4
Item 10940 Subject I01,J N	2916	1390	1476	2323	325	644	868	947	457	1606	1216	1108	595	406	723	40

★=excludes respondents for whom question was inappropriate.

QUESTIONNAIRE FORM 4 1983	TOTAL	SEX		RACE		REGION				4YR COLLEGE PLANS		ILLICIT DRUG USE: LIFETIME				
		M	F	White	Black	NE	NC	S	W	Yes	No	None	Marijuana Only	Few Pills	More Pills	Any Heroin
N (Weighted No. of Cases):	3344	1610	1630	2556	406	793	949	1075	527	1733	1355	1233	699	455	814	51
% of Weighted Total:	100.0	48.1	48.8	76.4	12.1	23.7	28.4	32.2	15.8	51.8	40.5	36.9	20.9	13.6	24.3	1.5

D10D: When I think about all the terrible things that have been happening, it is hard for me to hold out much hope for the world

1. Disagree	17.7	20.6	14.8	17.4	19.7	19.2	16.8	18.0	16.7	19.3	15.5	19.0	19.2	16.4	15.1	8.4
2. Mostly disagree	27.2	27.0	27.5	29.8	14.9	25.6	31.2	23.3	29.8	31.8	21.9	28.5	28.0	25.5	25.7	19.4
3. Neither	26.9	27.0	26.7	27.5	23.3	25.4	26.9	27.9	26.9	23.8	30.9	24.5	25.6	31.4	29.8	24.0
4. Mostly agree	19.7	17.2	22.1	18.4	25.8	20.4	19.1	20.8	17.3	18.6	21.2	19.4	19.4	18.2	20.9	27.4
5. Agree	8.6	8.3	8.8	7.0	16.3	9.3	6.1	10.0	9.3	6.5	10.5	8.5	7.9	8.4	8.5	20.8
Item 10950 Subject J N	2913	1388	1475	2321	323	641	870	945	457	1606	1214	1106	596	406	722	40

D10E: I often wonder if there is any real purpose to my life in light of the world situation

1. Disagree	26.5	26.6	26.4	27.0	29.2	29.3	24.7	24.4	30.1	29.9	22.1	29.8	30.3	21.7	21.5	24.1
2. Mostly disagree	23.1	22.0	24.3	24.1	17.5	22.8	26.1	21.4	21.1	26.7	19.0	22.2	22.6	27.1	22.7	23.8
3. Neither	26.5	27.7	25.3	26.6	22.0	22.9	26.4	27.4	29.6	22.3	32.0	25.4	24.0	24.5	32.2	15.8
4. Mostly agree	15.4	14.6	16.0	15.0	16.2	15.3	16.0	16.9	11.1	13.7	17.2	14.4	16.8	16.4	14.1	20.7
5. Agree	8.6	9.1	8.1	7.3	15.1	9.6	6.8	9.8	8.2	7.4	9.7	8.2	6.4	10.3	9.4	15.6
Item 10960 Subject J N	2894	1380	1464	2305	320	634	864	940	456	1598	1204	1099	589	404	719	40

D10F: My guess is that this country will be caught up in a major world upheaval in the next 10 years

1. Disagree	12.2	14.1	10.5	12.4	14.4	13.3	13.1	11.6	10.3	12.0	12.4	13.4	12.2	11.5	10.9	7.9
2. Mostly disagree	15.5	17.3	13.9	16.5	12.0	14.9	16.6	16.3	12.9	18.1	12.2	16.7	17.2	18.3	11.8	7.3
3. Neither	33.9	31.2	36.4	34.2	29.4	34.8	32.6	33.3	36.4	32.4	36.1	33.6	32.7	35.2	34.9	31.5
4. Mostly agree	24.8	23.4	26.1	24.8	25.4	22.8	25.7	26.0	23.3	25.2	24.6	22.8	25.4	24.1	27.2	30.2
5. Agree	13.6	14.0	13.1	12.1	18.7	14.1	12.0	12.9	17.1	12.3	14.7	13.5	12.4	10.8	15.2	23.1
Item 10970 Subject J N	2890	1382	1459	2304	320	636	864	936	454	1596	1204	1094	593	405	716	40

D10G: Nuclear or biological annihilation will probably be the fate of all mankind, within my lifetime

1. Disagree	17.7	20.7	15.0	18.3	16.0	19.0	18.8	16.5	16.5	20.5	14.5	20.0	18.3	15.2	15.9	9.5
2. Mostly disagree	17.8	19.0	16.5	19.3	13.7	17.7	18.7	16.7	18.8	20.7	14.5	18.5	20.4	19.3	14.7	11.6
3. Neither	33.4	31.4	35.3	33.4	29.6	33.3	31.1	34.1	36.3	30.9	36.0	32.7	31.4	34.1	35.5	28.4
4. Mostly agree	19.4	16.9	21.9	18.7	23.3	18.7	21.3	20.1	15.4	17.8	22.0	18.7	17.7	21.1	20.0	30.2
5. Agree	11.6	12.0	11.3	10.3	17.4	11.4	10.1	12.6	13.0	10.2	13.0	10.1	12.4	10.3	14.0	20.3
Item 10980 Subject J N	2876	1379	1448	2292	318	630	857	935	453	1588	1198	1094	588	397	714	40

D10H: The human race has come through tough times before, and will do so again

1. Disagree	4.2	5.3	3.2	3.5	5.5	3.5	4.7	4.0	4.6	2.6	5.9	3.9	4.2	4.2	3.9	12.1
2. Mostly disagree	6.1	7.3	5.0	5.5	7.7	5.6	5.2	6.9	7.1	5.6	6.4	6.3	5.0	7.5	5.7	7.6
3. Neither	20.6	21.1	20.3	20.3	19.8	19.9	22.2	19.4	21.3	17.9	24.3	20.4	20.3	18.8	21.8	22.3
4. Mostly agree	37.9	34.7	41.1	40.1	31.3	39.9	38.6	37.7	34.0	39.6	36.5	37.8	37.4	40.6	38.4	28.5
5. Agree	31.2	31.6	30.5	30.6	35.8	31.2	29.3	32.0	33.0	34.3	26.9	31.6	33.1	28.8	30.2	29.5
Item 10990 Subject J N	2898	1383	1466	2310	320	633	869	940	456	1599	1206	1102	591	404	718	40

The next questions are about alcohol use–this time asking separately about beer, wine, and hard liquor.

D11: On how many occasions (if any) have you had a beer to drink . . .

D11A: . . . in your lifetime?

1. 0 occasions	10.9	8.3	13.4	9.1	20.8	8.1	8.3	13.1	15.4	11.7	9.7	23.0	3.9	5.4	1.9	3.9
2. 1-2	10.2	7.5	12.7	9.2	12.4	8.0	9.0	12.5	10.9	11.2	9.3	18.2	7.3	6.8	2.7	6.0
3. 3-5	7.7	6.2	9.1	6.7	15.9	5.8	6.9	9.2	9.0	7.1	8.2	12.2	6.9	5.1	3.4	6.7
4. 6-9	6.2	5.6	6.7	6.1	8.9	6.8	5.5	7.2	5.0	5.8	6.6	7.3	9.1	4.4	3.6	2.6
5. 10-19	10.7	8.8	12.4	10.2	14.8	12.0	10.1	10.6	9.9	11.3	10.3	11.1	13.0	16.2	5.3	10.0
6. 20-39	13.5	13.9	13.1	14.3	8.4	16.7	13.5	12.3	11.2	13.4	13.2	11.2	14.0	18.4	13.5	8.0
7. 40 or more	40.9	49.7	32.5	44.4	18.7	42.7	46.8	35.1	38.5	39.6	42.6	17.0	45.8	43.6	69.6	62.9
Item 11000 Subject A01a N	2793	1321	1424	2274	285	614	849	886	444	1544	1162	1044	571	403	701	36

QUESTIONNAIRE FORM 4 1983	TOTAL	SEX		RACE		REGION				4YR COLLEGE PLANS		ILLICIT DRUG USE: LIFETIME				
		M	F	White	Black	NE	NC	S	W	Yes	No	None	Mari- juana Only	Few Pills	More Pills	Any Her- oin
N (Weighted No. of Cases):	3344	1610	1630	2556	406	793	949	1075	527	1733	1355	1233	699	455	814	51
% of Weighted Total:	100.0	48.1	48.8	76.4	12.1	23.7	28.4	32.2	15.8	51.8	40.5	36.9	20.9	13.6	24.3	1.5
D11B: . . . during the last 12 months?																
1. 0 occasions	21.6	16.8	26.4	18.8	38.6	14.7	18.5	26.7	26.9	22.5	20.6	39.3	13.6	13.2	7.4	10.6
2. 1-2	12.3	9.3	14.9	11.6	14.4	12.4	10.7	12.6	14.4	12.0	12.3	17.5	11.5	11.5	5.7	6.7
3. 3-5	10.4	9.5	11.2	9.9	15.6	10.1	10.2	11.1	9.6	9.9	11.4	11.3	12.8	10.3	7.0	16.5
4. 6-9	9.6	9.8	9.4	9.3	11.2	12.2	8.4	8.8	9.7	9.3	9.5	8.6	10.5	14.5	7.4	9.0
5. 10-19	13.7	13.6	13.8	14.7	8.0	18.6	15.2	11.1	9.3	14.1	12.9	10.4	15.6	15.1	16.5	5.7
6. 20-39	14.2	15.2	13.1	15.3	7.1	16.8	14.3	12.9	12.6	15.3	13.1	6.6	19.0	19.3	18.8	10.3
7. 40 or more	18.3	26.0	11.2	20.4	5.1	15.1	22.7	16.7	17.5	16.8	20.2	6.3	17.1	16.0	37.3	41.1
Item 11010 Subject A01b N	2754	1306	1404	2250	279	607	835	873	438	1531	1136	1030	558	399	698	35
D11C: . . . during the last 30 days?																
1. 0 occasions	38.3	30.3	46.0	34.7	58.1	31.7	33.4	43.5	46.2	38.9	37.6	59.6	31.1	31.2	17.2	27.9
2. 1-2	16.8	16.5	16.9	16.9	17.7	16.9	18.3	15.7	16.0	17.1	16.6	18.5	17.6	18.3	13.4	14.0
3. 3-5	16.4	17.1	15.1	16.9	12.7	22.0	15.4	14.5	14.2	17.5	14.6	11.6	20.1	20.7	18.5	3.9
4. 6-9	11.9	13.5	10.7	13.1	6.2	15.9	12.9	9.7	8.7	11.9	12.0	5.5	15.6	14.8	16.6	10.5
5. 10-19	10.5	12.8	8.6	11.8	3.6	8.9	12.3	10.7	9.0	9.7	12.0	3.6	9.4	10.4	20.8	28.2
6. 20-39	3.2	4.6	1.9	3.3	0.7	2.7	4.3	2.6	3.1	2.5	3.9	0.8	3.5	3.4	6.2	8.8
7. 40 or more	3.0	5.2	0.8	3.2	0.9	2.0	3.4	3.3	2.8	2.4	3.3	0.3	2.6	1.3	7.4	6.6
Item 11020 Subject A01c N	2758	1309	1404	2251	278	605	841	871	441	1530	1140	1029	556	400	704	33
D12: Think back over the LAST TWO WEEKS. How many times have you had five or more 12-ounce cans of beer (or the equivalent) in a row?																
1. None	61.9	50.2	72.6	59.1	80.1	62.1	54.9	64.9	68.7	65.7	56.9	81.2	59.5	60.1	37.0	35.5
2. Once	10.4	12.5	8.4	11.1	6.8	10.2	11.0	10.2	9.8	11.2	9.3	7.2	12.6	12.6	12.5	6.6
3. Twice	10.0	11.8	8.2	10.8	6.3	11.3	10.7	9.7	7.4	9.2	11.3	6.5	12.4	10.4	12.9	6.6
4. Three to five times	11.1	15.1	7.4	12.0	3.5	10.2	14.7	9.1	9.6	9.7	13.0	3.6	10.8	13.4	21.3	20.4
5. Six to nine times	4.4	6.8	2.3	4.8	3.0	3.8	5.9	4.3	2.4	2.8	6.2	0.7	2.8	2.0	11.4	24.6
6. Ten or more times	2.3	3.6	1.1	2.2	0.3	2.5	2.7	1.8	2.2	1.5	3.3	0.9	1.8	1.6	4.9	6.3
Item 11030 Subject A01d N	2731	1279	1405	2235	275	590	835	869	437	1528	1118	1032	557	393	682	32
D13: On how many occasions (if any) have you had wine to drink . . .																
D13A: . . . in your lifetime?																
1. 0 occasions	12.3	13.3	11.5	10.2	23.1	6.9	11.0	15.7	15.6	11.1	13.7	22.3	6.0	7.1	5.5	5.7
2. 1-2	16.8	17.6	15.9	15.9	19.7	12.4	16.1	19.5	18.5	16.1	17.0	22.9	16.8	14.4	9.1	9.7
3. 3-5	16.4	15.7	17.1	16.9	12.2	14.2	16.3	18.4	15.7	14.8	18.5	17.7	16.9	19.0	13.1	9.3
4. 6-9	15.3	15.2	15.5	15.7	14.5	15.6	15.8	15.4	14.0	16.4	14.4	14.3	15.3	19.8	15.2	7.2
5. 10-19	17.0	17.7	16.4	17.8	15.8	21.0	17.9	14.8	14.5	18.7	15.2	13.1	20.9	20.5	18.3	10.2
6. 20-39	10.9	10.4	11.5	11.7	8.6	14.9	10.2	8.7	11.5	12.1	9.5	5.4	12.8	10.5	17.2	28.1
7. 40 or more	11.2	10.1	12.1	11.7	6.1	15.0	12.8	7.5	10.3	10.7	11.7	4.3	11.4	8.8	21.5	29.8
Item 11040 Subject A01a N	2799	1330	1421	2273	285	602	860	889	448	1542	1170	1035	580	403	706	37
D13B: . . . during the last 12 months?																
1. 0 occasions	31.2	33.4	29.4	28.7	43.9	19.9	29.9	38.0	35.5	27.6	35.4	43.8	25.1	24.8	20.7	21.5
2. 1-2	25.9	25.7	25.9	26.1	22.6	25.1	27.0	24.5	27.6	26.4	25.1	28.3	28.8	28.1	19.9	8.7
3. 3-5	17.2	18.1	16.5	18.2	15.2	19.0	17.9	16.5	14.6	18.4	16.1	14.9	18.3	23.0	17.4	10.8
4. 6-9	11.3	10.7	11.7	11.7	9.6	14.6	10.9	11.2	7.7	12.6	9.8	6.9	11.8	12.4	16.7	18.8
5. 10-19	8.3	7.2	9.3	9.1	4.2	12.1	8.1	5.9	8.1	9.2	6.9	3.8	9.9	6.9	13.6	20.7
6. 20-39	3.5	2.5	4.2	3.4	2.9	4.9	3.9	1.9	3.7	3.4	3.5	1.3	3.8	3.9	5.6	7.6
7. 40 or more	2.7	2.3	3.0	2.8	1.6	4.4	2.3	1.9	2.7	2.4	3.1	1.0	2.3	1.0	6.1	11.9
Item 11050 Subject A01b N	2754	1307	1402	2247	277	591	849	872	443	1523	1149	1012	572	398	699	37
D13C: . . . during the last 30 days?																
1. 0 occasions	64.0	66.2	62.3	62.8	72.5	54.0	64.0	69.1	67.6	62.8	65.6	74.6	60.0	62.1	54.5	29.4
2. 1-2	22.2	21.5	23.1	23.3	16.6	24.4	24.1	19.0	21.7	23.2	21.5	18.1	22.8	27.0	24.7	37.5
3. 3-5	8.4	8.3	8.1	8.6	7.1	12.5	6.9	8.9	4.8	9.1	7.4	5.0	11.6	6.9	11.6	6.1
4. 6-9	2.9	1.9	3.8	2.8	3.3	5.4	2.3	1.8	3.1	2.9	2.7	1.0	3.0	2.9	4.8	14.8
5. 10-19	1.6	1.3	2.0	1.7	0.4	2.4	1.9	0.8	1.9	1.7	1.6	0.8	1.8	1.0	2.8	11.0
6. 20-39	0.3	0.2	0.4	0.2	-	0.4	0.3	0.3	0.1	0.2	0.4	*	0.2	0.1	0.8	-
7. 40 or more	0.5	0.6	0.3	0.5	-	0.8	0.6	0.1	0.8	0.2	0.8	0.4	0.6	-	0.9	1.3
Item 11060 Subject A01c N	2753	1306	1401	2247	276	591	850	870	442	1521	1151	1012	573	399	699	36

*=less than .05 per cent.

QUESTIONNAIRE FORM 4 1983	TOTAL	SEX		RACE		REGION				4YR COLLEGE PLANS		ILLICIT DRUG USE: LIFETIME				
		M	F	White	Black	NE	NC	S	W	Yes	No	None	Mari-juana Only	Few Pills	More Pills	Any Her-oin
N (Weighted No. of Cases):	3344	1610	1630	2556	406	793	949	1075	527	1733	1355	1233	699	455	814	51
% of Weighted Total:	100.0	48.1	48.8	76.4	12.1	23.7	28.4	32.2	15.8	51.8	40.5	36.9	20.9	13.6	24.3	1.5

D14: Think back over the LAST TWO WEEKS. How many times have you had five or more 4-ounce glasses of wine in a row (or the equivalent, which is about three-fourths of a bottle)?

	TOTAL	M	F	White	Black	NE	NC	S	W	Yes	No	None	Mari-juana Only	Few Pills	More Pills	Any Heroin
1. None	85.7	85.6	86.1	85.8	87.9	80.9	86.4	87.5	86.9	86.8	84.3	93.0	86.6	83.2	76.8	60.6
2. Once	8.3	8.4	8.4	8.8	5.1	10.2	8.3	6.1	10.1	8.5	8.4	4.3	8.5	12.0	11.5	16.8
3. Twice	2.9	2.9	2.5	2.7	3.6	4.7	1.8	3.8	0.4	2.8	3.0	1.8	2.1	3.3	4.6	2.6
4. Three to five times	1.8	1.9	1.7	1.7	2.5	2.2	1.5	1.9	1.6	1.6	1.7	0.4	2.0	0.3	4.2	10.1
5. Six to nine times	0.8	0.6	0.8	0.5	0.9	1.3	1.1	0.5	0.1	0.3	1.3	0.2	0.3	1.2	1.7	2.9
6. Ten or more times	0.6	0.7	0.5	0.7	-	0.7	0.8	0.1	1.0	0.1	1.2	0.3	0.4	0.1	1.2	7.1
Item 11070　Subject A01d　　N	2715	1280	1388	2213	274	579	847	854	435	1512	1121	1023	552	398	677	33

These next questions are about hard liquor. (Hard liquor includes whiskey, Scotch, bourbon, gin, vodka, rum, etc., or mixed drinks made with liquor.)

D15: On how many occasions (if any) have you had liquor to drink . . .

D15A: . . . in your lifetime?

	TOTAL	M	F	White	Black	NE	NC	S	W	Yes	No	None	Mari-juana Only	Few Pills	More Pills	Any Heroin
1. 0 occasions	16.2	15.3	17.0	12.1	40.1	14.5	11.7	19.8	19.9	17.3	14.5	32.6	8.7	8.8	2.3	8.5
2. 1-2	10.8	11.6	10.1	10.2	13.6	7.5	10.0	13.4	11.2	11.1	10.7	17.3	9.2	9.0	3.1	13.7
3. 3-5	12.7	11.8	13.6	12.6	12.0	14.6	12.5	12.7	10.3	12.8	12.0	13.9	14.9	16.4	7.1	-
4. 6-9	12.2	11.0	13.2	12.6	10.8	14.1	11.0	11.2	13.7	13.2	11.3	11.9	12.9	17.9	9.2	1.6
5. 10-19	16.3	15.7	16.5	17.7	9.2	18.1	18.3	13.9	14.9	15.5	17.4	11.7	22.9	17.0	17.9	5.5
6. 20-39	12.8	12.3	13.2	13.9	7.4	12.7	13.7	11.6	13.3	12.5	13.3	6.9	14.3	15.4	18.2	27.0
7. 40 or more	19.2	22.2	16.3	20.9	6.9	18.5	22.7	17.4	16.7	17.6	20.7	5.7	17.0	15.5	42.3	43.8
Item 11080　Subject A01a　　N	2776	1317	1410	2250	290	593	852	893	438	1534	1155	1035	579	394	694	38

D15B: . . . during the last 12 months?

	TOTAL	M	F	White	Black	NE	NC	S	W	Yes	No	None	Mari-juana Only	Few Pills	More Pills	Any Heroin
1. 0 occasions	28.0	27.4	28.8	23.7	51.6	23.7	22.5	33.4	33.5	27.9	27.9	47.2	21.0	20.7	9.1	18.9
2. 1-2	19.4	19.7	19.2	19.4	20.6	18.4	20.9	18.6	19.3	20.7	18.3	22.8	21.4	20.7	11.8	13.8
3. 3-5	15.2	13.4	16.8	16.4	8.3	19.0	14.8	12.9	15.5	14.9	15.1	12.6	17.1	20.9	14.5	1.5
4. 6-9	13.3	13.8	12.6	14.4	7.7	14.5	14.7	11.8	11.9	12.8	14.2	9.3	15.9	14.8	17.1	8.1
5. 10-19	11.7	12.3	11.1	12.7	7.5	12.7	12.2	11.5	10.1	11.6	12.0	4.9	12.9	12.9	19.9	23.8
6. 20-39	7.0	6.8	7.3	7.8	1.2	6.5	8.6	6.0	6.7	7.4	6.4	1.8	8.1	5.8	14.6	12.1
7. 40 or more	5.4	6.6	4.3	5.6	3.2	5.2	6.4	5.8	2.9	4.8	6.1	1.4	3.6	4.0	13.0	21.8
Item 11090　Subject A01b　　N	2747	1307	1393	2229	287	587	842	884	434	1521	1141	1031	569	387	690	36

D15C: . . . during the last 30 days?

	TOTAL	M	F	White	Black	NE	NC	S	W	Yes	No	None	Mari-juana Only	Few Pills	More Pills	Any Heroin
1. 0 occasions	53.7	51.2	56.3	50.8	70.6	49.2	49.5	56.7	61.6	54.7	52.6	73.0	51.0	50.1	29.7	24.9
2. 1-2	22.6	24.3	21.1	23.8	17.6	24.7	24.6	19.9	21.5	21.8	23.5	17.1	24.8	26.0	27.9	18.7
3. 3-5	12.6	12.3	12.4	13.6	5.6	17.5	11.2	11.3	11.1	13.0	11.9	6.7	14.5	14.1	18.6	15.1
4. 6-9	6.1	6.5	5.7	6.6	3.2	4.5	7.5	7.3	3.0	6.4	5.6	2.1	5.0	7.3	11.6	19.4
5. 10-19	3.4	3.3	3.4	3.4	2.2	3.3	5.3	2.3	1.6	2.5	4.6	0.8	3.0	1.6	8.1	10.6
6. 20-39	0.7	0.9	0.6	0.7	0.3	0.4	0.8	0.9	0.7	0.6	0.7	-	0.7	0.6	1.8	3.1
7. 40 or more	1.0	1.5	0.5	1.0	0.5	0.4	1.0	1.6	0.6	0.8	1.1	0.3	1.1	0.4	2.0	8.1
Item 11100　Subject A01c　　N	2746	1307	1391	2228	287	589	840	885	432	1517	1142	1030	570	387	687	38

D16: Think back over the LAST TWO WEEKS. How many times have you had five or more mixed drinks or shot-glasses of hard liquor in a row?

	TOTAL	M	F	White	Black	NE	NC	S	W	Yes	No	None	Mari-juana Only	Few Pills	More Pills	Any Heroin
1. None	78.0	73.6	82.2	77.0	86.1	75.3	76.0	79.3	83.0	80.8	74.3	91.3	78.4	78.5	58.8	41.9
2. Once	9.7	11.4	8.0	10.2	6.5	10.2	10.5	9.1	8.9	8.8	11.3	5.5	11.4	9.3	14.7	11.4
3. Twice	5.4	6.9	4.1	5.9	2.9	7.0	4.5	5.5	5.1	4.7	6.5	1.7	4.7	7.2	10.2	21.6
4. Three to five times	4.2	4.9	3.7	4.4	2.4	4.7	5.7	3.8	1.3	3.9	4.5	1.0	3.8	3.8	9.3	13.3
5. Six to nine times	1.3	1.7	1.0	1.3	1.7	1.8	1.3	1.4	0.7	1.1	1.4	-	0.7	0.8	3.9	7.3
6. Ten or more times	1.3	1.5	1.1	1.3	0.4	0.9	2.0	0.9	1.1	0.7	2.0	0.5	1.0	0.3	3.0	4.6
Item 11110　Subject A01d　　N	2683	1264	1372	2176	285	576	822	857	429	1499	1102	1021	558	373	664	37

These next questions ask for your opinions about the military services in the United States.

E01: To what extent do you think the following opportunities are available to people who work in the military services?

QUESTIONNAIRE FORM 4 1983	TOTAL	SEX		RACE		REGION				4YR COLLEGE PLANS		ILLICIT DRUG USE: LIFETIME				
		M	F	White	Black	NE	NC	S	W	Yes	No	None	Marijuana Only	Few Pills	More Pills	Any Heroin
N (Weighted No. of Cases):	3344	1610	1630	2556	406	793	949	1075	527	1733	1355	1233	699	455	814	51
% of Weighted Total:	100.0	48.1	48.8	76.4	12.1	23.7	28.4	32.2	15.8	51.8	40.5	36.9	20.9	13.6	24.3	1.5

E01A: A chance to get ahead

	TOTAL	M	F	White	Black	NE	NC	S	W	Yes	No	None	Mar.Only	Few	More	Any Her
1. To a very little extent	7.3	10.6	4.4	6.9	8.6	7.9	5.9	8.2	7.6	7.5	6.9	8.1	7.7	7.2	5.4	14.9
2. To a little extent	11.3	13.9	8.9	11.0	9.3	9.1	12.8	10.2	13.6	11.6	11.1	9.6	11.6	11.5	12.6	23.2
3. To some extent	42.1	40.3	44.1	43.6	33.7	40.5	47.2	38.6	41.5	43.9	40.2	44.8	41.6	43.1	38.7	34.7
4. To a great extent	24.7	21.6	27.4	24.9	27.4	28.3	21.5	26.0	23.4	25.4	23.5	23.6	26.4	26.5	25.2	16.3
5. To a very great extent	14.6	13.7	15.3	13.6	21.0	14.1	12.7	17.0	13.8	11.6	18.4	13.8	12.7	11.7	18.2	10.9
Item 11120 Subject L04 N	2804	1333	1420	2235	307	595	859	906	445	1546	1168	1068	575	389	689	39

E01B: A chance to get more education

	TOTAL	M	F	White	Black	NE	NC	S	W	Yes	No	None	Mar.Only	Few	More	Any Her
1. To a very little extent	3.8	5.2	2.3	3.4	3.7	4.0	3.4	3.7	4.1	3.9	3.4	4.3	4.5	1.6	3.3	4.9
2. To a little extent	8.6	10.3	6.8	8.6	8.0	7.9	8.6	8.8	9.1	9.3	7.9	9.1	7.9	8.4	8.5	11.6
3. To some extent	28.5	30.3	27.1	28.9	21.1	28.0	30.5	25.8	30.9	30.4	26.1	30.4	29.2	26.9	26.5	27.1
4. To a great extent	37.0	34.1	39.6	37.9	36.4	36.5	37.1	37.4	36.9	37.7	36.6	35.1	36.0	43.0	37.4	46.3
5. To a very great extent	22.1	20.1	24.1	21.2	30.8	23.6	20.4	24.3	19.0	18.7	26.0	21.0	22.3	20.0	24.3	10.0
Item 11130 Subject B10,L04 N	2798	1327	1419	2232	306	594	857	904	443	1544	1165	1069	576	387	685	38

E01C: A chance to advance to a more responsible position

	TOTAL	M	F	White	Black	NE	NC	S	W	Yes	No	None	Mar.Only	Few	More	Any Her
1. To a very little extent	3.9	6.0	1.9	3.6	4.0	4.7	3.7	3.6	3.8	3.9	3.6	4.7	4.1	1.2	3.8	7.8
2. To a little extent	8.1	10.8	5.7	8.5	6.2	7.1	8.2	8.6	8.4	7.4	8.8	7.7	9.7	8.3	7.1	20.4
3. To some extent	28.0	28.6	27.9	28.0	25.3	26.6	29.6	26.1	30.5	30.3	25.2	28.2	27.8	26.7	28.9	23.3
4. To a great extent	39.6	36.3	42.0	40.1	37.9	41.5	40.6	38.1	38.3	40.5	39.1	40.5	38.3	44.4	37.1	31.7
5. To a very great extent	20.3	18.2	22.4	19.8	26.6	20.1	17.8	23.6	18.9	17.8	23.3	18.8	20.1	19.4	23.1	16.8
Item 11140 Subject L04 N	2794	1324	1418	2228	307	593	856	904	442	1541	1163	1064	576	387	684	39

E01D: A chance to have a personally more fulfilling job

	TOTAL	M	F	White	Black	NE	NC	S	W	Yes	No	None	Mar.Only	Few	More	Any Her
1. To a very little extent	6.7	9.0	4.5	6.9	5.6	5.8	8.0	6.4	6.2	7.5	5.5	6.8	6.9	4.7	7.0	17.7
2. To a little extent	11.0	12.6	9.5	11.0	10.5	11.0	11.5	10.0	12.2	12.5	9.4	10.7	11.6	12.0	11.4	7.1
3. To some extent	33.9	32.9	35.2	35.2	25.3	34.5	34.6	31.5	36.7	36.1	31.6	34.9	34.2	35.2	31.7	29.3
4. To a great extent	31.9	30.4	33.3	31.7	34.4	33.0	31.3	32.6	30.4	30.6	33.3	31.0	31.8	33.9	32.7	33.0
5. To a very great extent	16.4	15.1	17.6	15.2	24.2	15.7	14.5	19.5	14.5	13.3	20.2	16.5	15.5	14.3	17.2	12.9
Item 11150 Subject C05,L04 N	2790	1322	1415	2223	307	591	854	905	440	1537	1163	1059	575	387	686	39

E01E: A chance to get their ideas heard

	TOTAL	M	F	White	Black	NE	NC	S	W	Yes	No	None	Mar.Only	Few	More	Any Her
1. To a very little extent	16.4	22.5	10.8	17.8	9.8	16.8	17.6	14.1	18.2	19.3	12.6	16.3	19.4	11.4	17.1	25.2
2. To a little extent	22.2	22.0	22.6	23.3	15.9	20.6	23.2	20.8	25.5	25.2	18.9	21.8	21.1	26.0	22.5	15.0
3. To some extent	35.7	31.7	39.7	35.7	35.5	36.8	37.4	33.6	35.4	34.3	38.2	36.5	34.6	37.8	35.0	36.5
4. To a great extent	16.4	14.5	17.8	15.7	22.3	18.2	14.8	19.3	11.1	13.4	19.7	16.7	16.0	16.0	15.5	14.6
5. To a very great extent	9.3	9.3	9.1	7.6	16.5	7.6	7.1	12.1	9.8	7.8	10.7	8.8	8.9	8.8	9.9	8.7
Item 11160 Subject L04 N	2790	1322	1416	2227	306	590	855	904	441	1538	1164	1060	574	387	687	38

E02: To what extent is it likely that a person in the military can get things changed and set right if he is being treated unjustly by a superior?

	TOTAL	M	F	White	Black	NE	NC	S	W	Yes	No	None	Mar.Only	Few	More	Any Her
1. To a very little extent	21.6	25.1	18.4	22.5	15.5	22.7	25.0	18.7	19.6	24.0	18.6	20.0	20.6	23.1	23.9	39.6
2. To a little extent	28.9	28.4	29.4	29.9	24.3	28.1	28.9	28.9	30.0	31.9	25.4	30.6	30.5	29.4	25.7	14.2
3. To some extent	35.6	31.7	39.7	35.5	36.3	38.9	34.3	33.8	37.5	33.2	38.3	37.0	34.7	33.3	35.7	29.3
4. To a great extent	10.5	11.5	9.7	9.8	16.0	8.2	9.3	13.7	9.7	7.8	14.1	8.8	11.7	10.6	11.7	15.7
5. To a very great extent	3.3	3.4	2.9	2.3	7.9	2.1	2.4	4.9	3.2	3.0	3.6	3.5	2.5	3.6	3.0	1.2
Item 11170 Subject L04 N	2743	1307	1385	2194	296	578	844	884	436	1512	1145	1044	564	385	671	38

E03: To what extent do you think there is any discrimination against women who are in the armed services?

	TOTAL	M	F	White	Black	NE	NC	S	W	Yes	No	None	Mar.Only	Few	More	Any Her
1. To a very little extent	15.0	17.7	12.4	13.9	21.2	16.0	13.6	17.3	11.9	12.4	18.3	14.5	14.7	12.3	17.7	20.8
2. To a little extent	27.9	28.6	27.2	29.4	19.7	27.1	30.7	26.4	26.4	26.6	29.4	26.7	27.8	33.6	26.5	32.2
3. To some extent	38.7	38.4	39.4	39.4	35.1	38.1	40.1	36.3	42.0	41.5	35.6	41.3	39.2	34.7	37.8	22.5
4. To a great extent	12.6	9.7	15.3	12.5	14.7	13.4	11.9	13.3	11.7	13.5	11.4	11.7	11.8	15.2	13.1	11.2
5. To a very great extent	5.7	5.7	5.7	4.9	9.3	5.5	3.7	6.7	8.0	6.0	5.3	5.8	6.5	4.2	4.9	13.2
Item 11180 Subject D06,L04 N	2743	1302	1389	2194	296	577	842	889	435	1513	1142	1044	563	383	670	40

QUESTIONNAIRE FORM 4 1983	TOTAL	SEX		RACE		REGION				4YR COLLEGE PLANS		ILLICIT DRUG USE: LIFETIME				
		M	F	White	Black	NE	NC	S	W	Yes	No	None	Mari-juana Only	Few Pills	More Pills	Any Her-oin
N (Weighted No. of Cases):	3344	1610	1630	2556	406	793	949	1075	527	1733	1355	1233	699	455	814	51
% of Weighted Total:	100.0	48.1	48.8	76.4	12.1	23.7	28.4	32.2	15.8	51.8	40.5	36.9	20.9	13.6	24.3	1.5

E04: To what extent do you think there is any discrimination against black people who are in the armed services?

	TOTAL	M	F	White	Black	NE	NC	S	W	Yes	No	None	Mari-juana Only	Few Pills	More Pills	Any Her-oin
1. To a very little extent	30.8	34.3	27.2	31.3	27.8	28.9	29.6	33.0	31.3	29.0	32.5	31.7	31.1	28.6	31.6	27.7
2. To a little extent	29.6	28.3	30.8	31.1	23.2	31.0	30.2	28.8	28.0	30.5	28.7	29.3	29.7	33.2	27.5	36.4
3. To some extent	29.8	27.4	32.3	29.8	26.2	29.6	31.6	26.5	33.0	30.2	29.7	30.5	28.5	27.7	31.3	23.8
4. To a great extent	6.4	5.9	6.9	5.4	13.6	7.5	5.6	7.6	4.4	7.1	5.7	6.3	6.3	7.9	5.8	2.5
5. To a very great extent	3.4	4.1	2.8	2.3	9.3	3.0	3.1	4.2	3.2	3.2	3.4	2.3	4.4	2.6	3.8	9.7
Item 11190 Subject L04,N02 N	2723	1294	1377	2180	292	568	839	880	435	1504	1134	1036	557	379	670	38

E05: Do you personally feel that you would receive more just and fair treatment as a civilian or as a member of the military service?

	TOTAL	M	F	White	Black	NE	NC	S	W	Yes	No	None	Mari-juana Only	Few Pills	More Pills	Any Her-oin
1. Much more fair in the military service	6.6	7.5	5.4	5.5	12.7	5.6	5.8	8.6	5.4	4.7	9.3	6.9	6.6	6.1	4.4	21.5
2. More fair in the military service	12.6	13.1	12.1	12.2	17.0	16.4	11.9	12.3	9.6	12.2	13.6	11.1	11.2	15.1	14.9	15.3
3. About the same	42.3	38.5	45.9	42.9	40.5	44.1	44.8	41.0	37.8	41.6	42.5	42.8	42.8	42.8	41.8	25.4
4. More fair as a civilian	14.1	15.8	12.5	15.0	6.8	11.8	14.2	14.1	17.1	15.5	12.5	14.2	14.1	12.7	14.7	16.3
5. Much more fair as a civilian	11.2	15.0	7.7	11.8	6.1	7.8	12.7	10.2	14.5	13.1	8.5	11.1	12.4	10.2	11.6	8.4
6. Question not appropriate for me	13.2	10.1	16.4	12.6	17.0	14.3	10.5	13.8	15.5	12.9	13.7	14.0	12.9	13.0	12.6	13.0
Item 11200 Subject L04 N	2725	1300	1374	2186	291	570	838	885	432	1505	1132	1035	556	383	672	39

E06: If YOU felt that it was necessary for the U.S. to fight in some future war, how likely is it that you would volunteer for military service in that war?

	TOTAL	M	F	White	Black	NE	NC	S	W	Yes	No	None	Mari-juana Only	Few Pills	More Pills	Any Her-oin
1. I'm sure that I would volunteer	14.5	23.0	6.5	14.7	9.3	14.5	13.3	16.1	13.5	12.1	17.5	14.5	15.4	14.2	13.0	12.2
2. I would very likely volunteer	7.4	9.9	5.1	7.9	6.5	7.9	5.2	9.6	6.2	8.4	5.5	6.7	7.5	6.9	8.8	1.8
3. I would probably volunteer	18.6	22.3	14.9	19.1	12.5	18.1	18.5	19.1	18.4	19.5	17.3	17.3	17.0	19.4	21.2	21.0
4. I would probably NOT volunteer	17.3	15.9	18.2	17.1	17.9	16.6	19.7	16.6	15.2	18.7	16.0	20.1	15.8	17.9	14.5	10.2
5. I would very likely NOT volunteer	6.7	3.4	9.5	7.1	5.9	7.0	5.7	7.0	7.5	7.5	5.5	6.3	5.1	10.1	6.7	12.9
6. I would definitely NOT volunteer	13.7	9.6	17.8	13.0	23.1	14.4	14.2	12.9	13.3	14.0	13.4	15.0	16.8	11.7	10.8	15.9
7. In my opinion, there is no such thing as a "necessary" war	21.9	15.9	28.0	21.2	24.7	21.5	23.4	18.7	25.9	19.8	24.8	20.3	22.4	19.8	25.0	26.1
Item 11220 Subject L03 N	2710	1287	1372	2177	287	565	836	877	431	1498	1123	1030	549	382	669	39

E07: How closely do your ideas agree with your PARENTS' ideas about . . .

Our ideas are . . .

E07A: What you should do with your life.

	TOTAL	M	F	White	Black	NE	NC	S	W	Yes	No	None	Mari-juana Only	Few Pills	More Pills	Any Her-oin
1. Very similar	29.7	29.2	30.2	29.4	33.7	30.3	28.9	30.1	29.6	34.2	23.6	33.6	31.8	25.1	25.4	25.6
2. Mostly similar	44.0	44.0	44.2	45.6	35.2	45.4	43.2	41.0	49.6	46.7	40.7	45.0	45.3	46.8	41.2	21.2
3. Mostly different	11.5	10.9	12.0	11.8	8.8	11.7	12.2	11.0	10.7	9.2	14.7	9.5	10.3	11.6	21.6	21.6
4. Very different	7.5	6.9	8.0	6.3	13.1	6.9	7.8	9.3	3.9	4.8	10.7	5.3	5.3	6.3	11.7	20.3
8. Don't know	7.4	9.0	5.6	6.9	9.2	5.7	8.0	8.6	6.1	5.1	10.3	6.5	7.3	10.3	6.2	11.2
Item 11230 Subject M03 N	2771	1298	1423	2221	295	574	859	891	447	1538	1146	1049	572	389	680	38

E07B: What you do in your leisure time

	TOTAL	M	F	White	Black	NE	NC	S	W	Yes	No	None	Mari-juana Only	Few Pills	More Pills	Any Her-oin
1. Very similar	10.7	9.9	11.2	9.9	13.6	9.4	9.6	12.5	10.6	9.9	11.4	13.8	9.3	7.9	8.2	12.3
2. Mostly similar	34.4	32.3	36.7	35.7	28.7	33.2	35.9	33.2	35.6	38.0	29.4	40.9	36.1	34.7	25.3	12.2
3. Mostly different	26.6	26.6	26.3	26.7	24.6	26.6	25.5	25.4	31.3	27.4	26.3	25.0	25.8	35.3	24.8	21.1
4. Very different	22.2	23.5	21.3	22.4	23.4	25.0	22.3	22.7	17.6	19.7	25.4	15.2	21.2	16.9	35.9	40.9
8. Don't know	6.1	7.7	4.4	5.3	9.8	5.8	6.7	6.2	4.9	4.9	7.5	5.2	7.7	5.2	5.8	13.5
Item 11240 Subject C08,M03 N	2766	1299	1417	2223	292	576	856	888	446	1534	1147	1049	568	387	680	38

E07C: How you dress–what clothes you wear

	TOTAL	M	F	White	Black	NE	NC	S	W	Yes	No	None	Mari-juana Only	Few Pills	More Pills	Any Her-oin
1. Very similar	26.8	23.6	30.1	26.9	28.8	28.1	24.7	27.3	28.5	28.3	25.7	27.2	29.0	25.4	26.2	20.4
2. Mostly similar	42.1	41.1	43.1	44.4	30.1	41.7	43.9	40.1	43.2	44.8	38.4	45.8	42.0	42.4	38.8	15.4
3. Mostly different	15.1	16.4	13.6	15.0	15.2	14.1	15.0	15.9	15.4	15.1	15.1	14.4	14.6	14.6	16.0	18.1
4. Very different	11.6	13.4	9.8	9.9	17.8	12.0	11.3	12.4	9.9	8.3	15.8	8.6	9.5	14.0	14.5	39.2
8. Don't know	4.3	5.4	3.3	3.8	8.2	4.1	5.1	4.3	3.0	3.5	5.1	4.0	4.9	3.6	4.5	7.0
Item 11250 Subject M03 N	2760	1292	1418	2213	295	574	855	885	446	1535	1138	1046	570	385	677	40

QUESTIONNAIRE FORM 4 1983	TOTAL	SEX		RACE		REGION				4YR COLLEGE PLANS		ILLICIT DRUG USE: LIFETIME				
		M	F	White	Black	NE	NC	S	W	Yes	No	None	Mari- juana Only	Few Pills	More Pills	Any Her- oin
N (Weighted No. of Cases):	3344	1610	1630	2556	406	793	949	1075	527	1733	1355	1233	699	455	814	51
% of Weighted Total:	100.0	48.1	48.8	76.4	12.1	23.7	28.4	32.2	15.8	51.8	40.5	36.9	20.9	13.6	24.3	1.5

E07D: How you spend your money

	TOTAL	M	F	White	Black	NE	NC	S	W	Yes	No	None	Mari- juana Only	Few Pills	More Pills	Any Her- oin
1. Very similar	13.1	10.1	15.6	12.1	20.1	12.3	12.6	13.2	14.8	12.2	14.3	15.7	12.5	11.1	10.1	9.8
2. Mostly similar	33.2	29.6	36.7	35.1	18.9	32.0	36.1	29.5	36.6	38.7	26.5	39.3	33.4	29.6	27.0	22.1
3. Mostly different	24.8	27.1	22.5	25.6	21.8	23.2	24.0	26.8	24.5	25.7	24.3	23.3	24.9	30.8	24.7	16.3
4. Very different	24.8	29.0	21.3	23.6	32.1	28.6	22.3	26.7	21.1	20.3	29.8	18.5	24.0	24.7	34.1	45.2
8. Don't know	4.1	4.3	3.8	3.5	7.1	4.0	5.0	3.8	3.0	3.1	5.1	3.2	5.2	3.8	4.1	6.7
Item 11260 Subject M03 N	2760	1292	1417	2215	293	573	854	888	444	1535	1140	1048	570	387	674	38

E07E: What things are O.K. to do when you are on a date

	TOTAL	M	F	White	Black	NE	NC	S	W	Yes	No	None	Mari- juana Only	Few Pills	More Pills	Any Her- oin
1. Very similar	17.6	13.8	21.5	16.8	22.0	15.5	16.2	19.3	19.7	17.8	17.1	22.4	13.7	14.7	15.0	19.3
2. Mostly similar	31.2	29.2	32.9	32.9	23.5	26.9	32.1	32.4	32.7	34.1	28.0	33.7	31.5	30.9	28.6	12.4
3. Mostly different	15.5	15.0	15.9	16.0	13.4	17.8	15.6	14.2	14.9	16.3	14.8	13.8	17.0	20.7	13.5	25.7
4. Very different	21.5	23.7	19.8	21.2	22.4	23.9	21.2	21.2	19.8	19.1	24.2	14.6	23.6	19.6	31.4	29.3
8. Don't know	14.1	18.3	10.0	13.2	18.7	16.0	14.9	12.8	12.8	12.7	15.9	15.6	14.2	14.2	11.5	13.3
Item 11270 Subject M03 N	2761	1293	1418	2216	292	571	856	887	446	1535	1142	1048	570	387	676	37

E07F: Whether it is O.K. to drink

	TOTAL	M	F	White	Black	NE	NC	S	W	Yes	No	None	Mari- juana Only	Few Pills	More Pills	Any Her- oin
1. Very similar	24.3	23.3	25.4	22.8	30.2	19.4	22.6	27.3	28.0	26.1	21.7	36.1	17.0	21.4	14.2	13.2
2. Mostly similar	34.2	34.0	34.6	36.3	21.4	34.4	36.9	31.3	34.9	35.5	33.2	31.3	36.1	40.4	35.3	27.2
3. Mostly different	18.0	18.9	16.9	19.0	13.2	18.1	21.4	15.3	16.6	18.3	17.9	12.8	21.1	20.0	22.3	17.1
4. Very different	18.2	18.1	18.3	18.4	21.0	22.7	15.3	19.5	15.3	16.2	20.4	13.7	20.8	14.8	23.8	40.1
8. Don't know	5.3	5.6	4.7	3.5	14.2	5.4	3.9	6.5	5.2	3.9	6.9	6.1	5.0	3.5	4.5	2.4
Item 11280 Subject M03 N	2780	1308	1421	2225	300	584	859	887	449	1537	1148	1055	576	383	683	39

E07G: Whether it is O.K. to use marijuana

	TOTAL	M	F	White	Black	NE	NC	S	W	Yes	No	None	Mari- juana Only	Few Pills	More Pills	Any Her- oin
1. Very similar	46.7	44.2	49.3	48.0	36.8	41.0	49.3	49.6	43.6	52.0	40.0	74.2	39.5	37.7	16.8	15.5
2. Mostly similar	13.0	11.7	14.1	13.4	12.4	11.9	12.1	13.0	16.4	14.3	11.7	10.3	15.2	15.8	15.1	5.1
3. Mostly different	8.9	8.5	9.1	9.0	8.3	9.9	7.3	7.7	12.6	9.0	8.9	3.0	10.9	10.1	15.3	17.5
4. Very different	23.7	26.2	21.6	23.6	26.9	28.4	24.3	21.8	20.5	18.9	29.3	5.9	26.8	26.5	45.8	51.2
8. Don't know	7.6	9.3	5.9	6.0	15.6	8.8	7.0	7.9	6.9	5.8	10.1	6.5	7.6	9.9	7.1	10.7
Item 11290 Subject M03 N	2769	1299	1418	2218	298	584	857	880	448	1533	1142	1048	572	382	682	39

E07H: Whether it is O.K. to use other drugs

	TOTAL	M	F	White	Black	NE	NC	S	W	Yes	No	None	Mari- juana Only	Few Pills	More Pills	Any Her- oin
1. Very similar	57.5	55.0	60.4	60.1	44.0	54.0	60.7	58.2	54.8	64.2	49.6	79.4	58.7	52.5	29.2	10.7
2. Mostly similar	11.2	10.2	12.0	11.7	8.5	12.8	8.9	10.8	14.4	12.0	10.7	8.1	13.7	14.3	13.2	-
3. Mostly different	4.6	5.6	3.7	4.8	3.2	3.6	4.9	3.9	6.4	4.3	5.0	1.5	4.0	5.2	9.3	10.3
4. Very different	19.3	20.5	18.0	18.1	27.1	21.3	19.3	19.1	17.0	14.4	24.4	5.0	16.2	18.6	41.0	71.4
8. Don't know	7.3	8.7	5.9	5.3	17.2	8.2	6.1	8.0	7.4	5.0	10.3	6.0	7.3	9.3	7.3	7.5
Item 11300 Subject M03 N	2754	1292	1412	2211	294	580	853	873	448	1525	1137	1043	569	379	682	38

E07I: What values are important in life

	TOTAL	M	F	White	Black	NE	NC	S	W	Yes	No	None	Mari- juana Only	Few Pills	More Pills	Any Her- oin
1. Very similar	38.1	37.5	39.1	37.7	42.4	38.2	35.1	40.7	38.6	41.3	34.1	45.1	39.3	35.9	29.6	10.8
2. Mostly similar	39.5	39.2	39.6	41.9	27.5	41.6	41.7	36.5	38.7	41.4	37.4	37.7	40.2	46.1	38.6	38.3
3. Mostly different	10.6	10.6	10.5	10.2	8.9	9.9	11.2	9.7	12.0	9.1	12.4	9.4	8.3	8.2	14.7	25.2
4. Very different	6.3	6.2	6.3	5.7	10.8	5.2	6.6	7.0	5.5	4.1	9.1	3.2	5.1	5.1	11.5	16.7
8. Don't know	5.5	6.5	4.5	4.5	10.4	5.1	5.5	6.1	5.2	4.2	7.0	4.6	7.1	4.7	5.5	9.0
Item 11310 Subject M03 N	2756	1295	1409	2207	295	580	852	878	447	1522	1139	1044	569	379	680	39

E07J: The value of education

	TOTAL	M	F	White	Black	NE	NC	S	W	Yes	No	None	Mari- juana Only	Few Pills	More Pills	Any Her- oin
1. Very similar	56.7	55.7	57.6	56.2	61.3	57.6	52.4	59.2	59.0	65.9	44.4	63.6	58.8	52.4	47.9	44.5
2. Mostly similar	31.6	30.8	32.5	33.6	21.4	32.0	34.5	28.0	32.5	27.9	37.1	27.5	31.5	37.7	35.2	30.5
3. Mostly different	5.7	6.1	5.3	5.6	3.9	5.7	7.5	4.9	3.6	3.2	9.3	4.2	5.4	4.3	8.0	15.9
4. Very different	3.8	4.6	3.0	3.1	8.6	3.2	3.3	5.3	2.8	1.7	5.8	2.9	2.4	3.1	6.0	6.7
8. Don't know	2.2	2.8	1.6	1.4	4.8	1.5	2.3	2.6	2.2	1.2	3.4	1.8	1.9	2.6	2.9	2.4
Item 11320 Subject B09,M03 N	2762	1297	1412	2212	296	582	855	880	445	1529	1139	1047	572	380	679	39

QUESTIONNAIRE FORM 4 1983	TOTAL	SEX		RACE		REGION				4YR COLLEGE PLANS		ILLICIT DRUG USE: LIFETIME				
		M	F	White	Black	NE	NC	S	W	Yes	No	None	Mari- juana Only	Few Pills	More Pills	Any Her- oin
N (Weighted No. of Cases):	3344	1610	1630	2556	406	793	949	1075	527	1733	1355	1233	699	455	814	51
% of Weighted Total:	100.0	48.1	48.8	76.4	12.1	23.7	28.4	32.2	15.8	51.8	40.5	36.9	20.9	13.6	24.3	1.5
E07K: What are appropriate roles for women																
1. Very similar	29.5	22.5	36.0	29.2	32.8	29.5	25.6	31.8	32.6	33.3	23.8	34.0	29.5	27.3	25.0	14.6
2. Mostly similar	39.3	40.7	38.1	41.7	25.7	39.4	41.2	37.5	39.1	40.5	38.9	38.2	38.9	44.6	38.9	37.4
3. Mostly different	11.0	11.8	10.0	10.7	11.5	11.1	11.9	10.9	9.3	10.1	11.7	10.1	10.0	12.8	11.9	15.8
4. Very different	6.2	6.4	6.2	5.6	8.3	6.2	5.4	7.6	5.1	4.7	8.4	4.9	4.9	3.2	9.9	16.9
8. Don't know	14.0	18.6	9.7	12.8	21.7	13.8	16.0	12.2	13.9	11.4	17.2	12.8	16.7	12.1	14.3	15.3
Item 11330　Subject D05,M03 N	*2751*	*1294*	*1405*	*2203*	*295*	*580*	*851*	*879*	*441*	*1524*	*1132*	*1039*	*569*	*378*	*681*	*39*
E07L: Conservation and pollution issues																
1. Very similar	22.7	21.6	23.7	22.3	21.7	22.8	21.6	23.1	23.8	24.5	19.9	27.8	21.3	18.7	18.0	16.0
2. Mostly similar	30.3	33.5	27.7	32.6	17.7	30.1	30.5	28.7	33.4	32.6	28.0	30.6	31.2	35.7	27.1	32.6
3. Mostly different	7.3	9.0	5.6	6.9	10.3	7.5	6.9	7.4	8.0	5.9	8.7	6.5	6.0	6.9	8.8	11.2
4. Very different	3.9	3.7	4.0	3.2	8.6	3.9	3.3	4.8	3.4	2.8	5.4	3.0	3.1	2.9	5.9	13.8
8. Don't know	35.7	32.2	38.9	35.0	41.8	35.7	37.7	36.0	31.3	34.2	38.0	32.1	38.4	35.8	40.2	26.3
Item 11340　Subject F04,M03 N	*2747*	*1290*	*1405*	*2203*	*292*	*572*	*851*	*879*	*445*	*1518*	*1136*	*1044*	*569*	*375*	*676*	*38*
E07M: Racial issues																
1. Very similar	28.8	27.5	30.0	26.6	42.0	30.8	22.5	32.8	30.7	32.7	23.4	31.1	31.3	28.5	23.2	20.4
2. Mostly similar	32.0	33.2	31.1	33.5	25.6	32.9	31.6	32.2	31.3	33.1	30.9	34.5	27.9	33.9	31.5	29.2
3. Mostly different	10.8	9.5	11.8	11.1	7.7	11.5	12.0	8.2	12.5	11.3	9.9	10.2	10.3	11.9	10.4	14.7
4. Very different	5.9	6.7	5.2	5.8	6.8	6.8	5.9	6.2	4.3	4.7	7.4	4.5	5.1	5.2	9.0	8.8
8. Don't know	22.4	23.0	21.8	23.0	17.9	18.0	28.0	20.6	21.2	18.2	28.4	19.7	25.4	20.5	25.9	27.0
Item 11350　Subject M03,N02 N	*2740*	*1290*	*1399*	*2198*	*293*	*573*	*849*	*878*	*440*	*1516*	*1132*	*1037*	*567*	*377*	*677*	*39*
E07N: Religion																
1. Very similar	40.7	39.1	42.5	39.3	48.9	39.6	38.6	45.4	36.6	44.0	36.8	48.9	38.8	36.9	32.3	33.8
2. Mostly similar	31.5	31.9	31.1	33.1	23.3	33.1	34.4	27.9	31.1	32.6	30.7	29.9	33.5	36.8	31.1	15.4
3. Mostly different	9.1	8.9	9.0	9.7	5.2	8.3	10.0	7.8	10.8	8.3	10.2	7.5	9.1	9.6	11.0	10.6
4. Very different	7.3	7.2	7.5	7.0	9.4	8.4	6.0	7.7	7.4	6.8	7.4	4.5	6.0	6.9	11.6	18.2
8. Don't know	11.5	12.9	9.9	10.9	13.3	10.5	10.9	11.3	14.2	8.3	14.9	9.1	12.5	9.8	14.1	22.0
Item 11360　Subject G,M03 N	*2747*	*1290*	*1404*	*2199*	*295*	*573*	*851*	*879*	*443*	*1518*	*1136*	*1038*	*569*	*377*	*678*	*39*
E07O: Politics																
1. Very similar	18.9	20.1	17.9	17.8	23.1	19.7	16.8	20.8	18.3	20.7	16.2	22.5	21.2	17.1	12.2	12.5
2. Mostly similar	30.1	30.7	29.7	32.3	23.4	28.8	30.7	30.2	30.7	33.0	26.9	30.8	28.0	33.7	30.7	28.9
3. Mostly different	8.8	10.3	7.5	9.2	5.5	9.4	8.5	8.0	10.1	8.8	8.7	8.0	8.5	6.8	10.0	18.1
4. Very different	5.9	7.3	4.5	5.0	9.4	5.6	5.8	6.2	6.0	4.2	7.7	4.3	5.1	6.1	8.1	13.2
8. Don't know	36.3	31.6	40.5	35.7	38.7	36.5	38.3	34.9	34.9	33.2	40.5	34.4	37.1	36.3	39.1	27.3
Item 11370　Subject H01,M03 N	*2746*	*1288*	*1404*	*2199*	*294*	*572*	*851*	*879*	*443*	*1518*	*1135*	*1043*	*567*	*376*	*676*	*39*
E08: How do you think your CLOSE FRIENDS feel (or would feel) about YOU doing each of the following things?																
E08A: Smoking one or more packs of ciga- rettes per day																
1. Not disapprove	27.8	27.7	28.2	28.5	25.0	33.5	30.3	27.3	16.6	21.7	35.2	17.0	25.4	26.7	44.7	59.8
2. Disapprove	34.8	35.3	33.6	34.7	33.3	33.2	35.8	36.3	32.1	35.9	34.8	35.0	37.7	39.9	30.7	18.4
3. Strongly disapprove	37.4	37.0	38.2	36.9	41.7	33.3	33.9	36.4	51.3	42.5	30.1	48.0	37.0	33.3	24.6	21.8
Item 11470　Subject A12b N	*2722*	*1280*	*1388*	*2179*	*293*	*563*	*843*	*880*	*435*	*1502*	*1123*	*1024*	*565*	*376*	*672*	*39*
E08B: Trying marijuana (pot, grass) once or twice																
1. Not disapprove	48.0	49.0	46.8	49.0	42.4	55.4	47.7	40.5	54.2	46.9	49.4	19.1	57.3	56.6	77.6	83.6
2. Disapprove	24.2	24.8	23.9	23.7	29.6	25.7	22.6	27.6	18.4	25.2	22.8	31.5	26.5	24.0	13.3	1.9
3. Strongly disapprove	27.8	26.2	29.3	27.3	28.0	18.9	29.7	31.8	27.4	27.9	27.8	49.5	16.2	19.4	9.1	14.5
Item 11480　Subject A12b N	*2715*	*1275*	*1388*	*2171*	*294*	*561*	*840*	*880*	*435*	*1500*	*1119*	*1022*	*565*	*373*	*671*	*39*

QUESTIONNAIRE FORM 4 1983	TOTAL	SEX		RACE		REGION				4YR COLLEGE PLANS		ILLICIT DRUG USE: LIFETIME				
		M	F	White	Black	NE	NC	S	W	Yes	No	None	Mari- juana Only	Few Pills	More Pills	Any Her- oin
N (Weighted No. of Cases):	3344	1610	1630	2556	406	793	949	1075	527	1733	1355	1233	699	455	814	51
% of Weighted Total:	100.0	48.1	48.8	76.4	12.1	23.7	28.4	32.2	15.8	51.8	40.5	36.9	20.9	13.6	24.3	1.5
E08C: Smoking marijuana occasionally																
1. Not disapprove	40.1	42.3	37.9	40.4	38.2	48.0	38.9	34.5	43.6	37.3	43.4	14.1	45.7	44.9	70.0	83.5
2. Disapprove	26.0	25.2	26.6	25.2	31.5	28.6	25.5	26.7	22.1	28.1	23.9	28.3	31.4	29.7	17.4	5.1
3. Strongly disapprove	33.9	32.5	35.6	34.4	30.4	23.3	35.6	38.8	34.3	34.5	32.7	57.6	22.9	25.5	12.6	11.4
Item 11490 Subject A12b N	2713	1275	1387	2174	291	561	841	877	434	1499	1121	1022	563	373	673	38
E08D: Smoking marijuana regularly																
1. Not disapprove	22.4	26.5	18.2	21.7	23.7	24.5	24.4	20.1	20.5	17.6	28.2	6.9	18.1	18.4	48.0	70.3
2. Disapprove	28.9	29.2	28.9	28.6	32.6	33.7	26.6	28.0	28.9	30.0	27.8	23.8	35.2	36.5	28.1	15.6
3. Strongly disapprove	48.7	44.3	53.0	49.7	43.8	41.8	49.0	51.9	50.6	52.4	44.1	69.3	46.7	45.0	23.9	14.1
Item 11500 Subject A12b N	2698	1263	1382	2162	290	559	837	870	432	1493	1111	1017	561	369	670	39
E08E: Trying LSD once or twice																
1. Not disapprove	12.2	14.9	9.3	12.4	9.3	11.4	13.9	11.2	12.0	10.7	14.1	5.5	7.1	10.5	24.5	50.9
2. Disapprove	23.3	23.2	23.0	22.8	26.7	26.9	23.5	22.7	19.4	22.1	24.8	20.8	22.8	27.1	25.6	24.8
3. Strongly disapprove	64.5	61.9	67.7	64.8	64.0	61.7	62.7	66.2	68.6	67.2	61.1	73.7	70.1	62.4	49.9	24.3
Item 11510 Subject A12b N	2697	1262	1383	2163	288	559	838	872	429	1495	1113	1017	559	369	671	39
E08F: Trying an amphetamine (upper, pep pill, bennie, speed) once or twice																
1. Not disapprove	23.2	24.4	21.7	24.5	14.8	22.0	26.1	20.0	25.3	21.5	25.3	7.5	14.0	23.4	51.9	67.6
2. Disapprove	25.1	25.6	24.7	25.1	24.6	29.4	25.5	25.3	18.1	24.8	25.1	26.6	23.5	27.4	23.7	18.1
3. Strongly disapprove	51.8	50.0	53.6	50.4	60.6	48.6	48.3	54.7	56.6	53.7	49.7	65.9	62.5	49.2	24.3	14.2
Item 11520 Subject A12b N	2700	1266	1382	2165	287	559	838	873	430	1496	1112	1019	561	370	669	39
E08G: Taking one or two drinks nearly every day																
1. Not disapprove	28.3	36.9	20.1	29.0	21.9	28.3	31.9	28.6	20.8	23.8	33.9	19.8	28.1	24.8	41.0	68.9
2. Disapprove	36.0	34.0	37.4	36.4	33.3	35.8	37.4	35.2	35.0	38.0	34.1	35.4	35.6	42.0	35.2	24.3
3. Strongly disapprove	35.8	29.1	42.5	34.6	44.8	35.9	30.7	36.2	44.2	38.2	32.0	44.8	36.2	33.2	23.8	6.7
Item 11530 Subject A12b N	2702	1268	1383	2166	292	561	835	874	432	1495	1113	1019	562	370	668	39
E08H: Taking four or five drinks nearly every day																
1. Not disapprove	14.0	20.5	7.8	13.8	10.3	11.7	17.9	13.5	10.4	10.5	18.8	9.3	10.5	13.1	22.4	40.3
2. Disapprove	29.8	31.8	28.1	30.2	29.9	32.2	30.4	31.1	22.6	28.0	31.8	25.7	31.9	31.5	33.3	31.5
3. Strongly disapprove	56.2	47.7	64.2	56.0	59.8	56.1	51.7	55.4	67.0	61.5	49.4	65.0	57.6	55.3	44.3	28.2
Item 11540 Subject A12b N	2703	1268	1383	2165	291	559	838	874	432	1498	1113	1022	561	370	668	39
E08I: Having five or more drinks once or twice each weekend																
1. Not disapprove	49.4	56.7	42.4	54.0	22.4	51.0	56.4	45.1	42.7	46.3	53.5	33.2	50.6	51.0	71.2	73.6
2. Disapprove	22.2	19.0	24.8	20.6	30.3	24.0	20.4	22.7	22.1	24.5	19.6	24.7	24.4	26.4	14.7	18.2
3. Strongly disapprove	28.4	24.3	32.8	25.4	47.3	25.0	23.3	32.1	35.2	29.2	26.8	42.0	25.1	22.5	14.1	8.1
Item 11550 Subject A12b N	2703	1272	1380	2164	293	559	836	877	431	1497	1112	1019	562	370	671	39
E09: In some communities parents who are particularly concerned with drug or alcohol abuse among young people have formed groups of concerned parents to deal with these problems. In these groups parents try to become more informed and sometimes to set some common guidelines for young peoples' behavior. In general, what do you think of the idea of having parents get together in groups such as these?																
1. A bad idea	6.4	10.5	2.5	5.7	9.5	6.3	6.7	6.6	5.3	5.6	7.4	4.4	7.8	6.7	7.6	7.9
2. More bad than good	7.1	8.7	5.5	7.3	6.3	6.2	5.7	9.0	7.3	7.2	6.4	4.6	6.8	6.6	11.4	3.9
3. Don't know or can't say	30.7	33.4	28.3	31.7	24.0	31.8	35.2	25.9	30.3	27.1	34.9	23.8	31.9	36.6	35.3	49.9
4. More good than bad	23.3	19.8	26.4	24.9	21.0	23.2	24.5	23.1	21.3	25.6	20.8	24.1	23.5	25.0	22.8	7.7
5. A good idea	32.5	27.5	37.2	30.5	39.2	32.5	27.9	35.4	35.7	34.6	30.4	43.1	30.1	25.1	22.9	30.6
Item 21730 Subject A16a N	2669	1248	1370	2135	295	548	829	863	428	1482	1094	1016	554	368	648	40

QUESTIONNAIRE FORM 4 1983	TOTAL	SEX		RACE		REGION				4YR COLLEGE PLANS		ILLICIT DRUG USE: LIFETIME				
		M	F	White	Black	NE	NC	S	W	Yes	No	None	Mari- juana Only	Few Pills	More Pills	Any Her- oin
N (Weighted No. of Cases):	3344	1610	1630	2556	406	793	949	1075	527	1733	1355	1233	699	455	814	51
% of Weighted Total:	100.0	48.1	48.8	76.4	12.1	23.7	28.4	32.2	15.8	51.8	40.5	36.9	20.9	13.6	24.3	1.5
E10: To the best of your knowledge, how many of your close friends have parents who are involved in such parent groups?																
1. None	73.0	69.2	77.2	75.1	63.2	69.3	74.8	71.4	77.3	72.6	74.4	76.5	73.5	73.9	68.4	60.5
2. A few	18.8	21.5	16.2	17.9	23.4	21.7	17.2	19.9	16.1	19.7	17.8	16.8	17.0	17.7	23.5	25.9
3. Some	7.3	8.3	6.0	6.3	12.2	8.2	7.1	7.4	6.6	7.2	6.8	5.7	8.3	7.7	7.9	11.8
4. Most or all	0.9	1.0	0.7	0.7	1.2	0.8	1.0	1.3	-	0.6	1.1	0.9	1.2	0.7	0.3	1.8
Item 21740 Subject A16a N	2656	1244	1361	2126	290	544	824	859	427	1474	1091	1013	548	364	648	40
E11: Has either (or both) of your own parents been involved in such a group?																
1. No–GO TO QUESTION E14.	92.8	90.9	94.9	94.2	85.9	93.2	93.8	91.3	93.7	93.2	93.4	94.1	92.5	93.1	91.9	81.5
2. Yes, in the past, but not now	4.9	6.5	3.2	3.9	9.9	5.0	3.4	6.5	4.3	4.3	4.9	4.3	4.6	4.8	5.3	10.2
3. Yes, now	2.3	2.6	1.9	1.9	4.2	1.9	2.8	2.2	2.0	2.5	1.7	1.5	2.9	2.1	2.8	8.3
Item 21750 Subject A16a N	2595	1209	1337	2087	273	535	805	835	420	1445	1062	1000	539	348	630	39
E12: Has the involvement of your parent(s) in such a group had any impact on your own feelings about drug or alcohol use?																
1. Made me much less likely to use drugs or alcohol	25.2	21.9	27.6	20.6	34.4	17.3	27.8	27.3	26.2	23.9	25.4	40.6	21.4	22.9	10.9	11.2
2. Made me somewhat less likely to use drugs or alcohol	12.7	12.0	13.5	12.3	16.4	18.6	13.4	11.6	5.7	12.2	11.3	10.0	16.0	14.5	8.2	24.6
3. No impact either way	56.5	60.4	53.5	61.1	43.9	58.1	54.6	52.8	68.1	60.4	54.4	45.2	59.2	56.9	72.8	38.6
4. Made me somewhat more likely to use drugs or alcohol	3.1	2.8	3.1	3.6	1.5	5.0	2.1	3.9	-	1.8	4.8	0.8	3.4	2.7	4.1	25.6
5. Made me much more likely to use drugs or alcohol	2.5	2.9	2.3	2.4	3.8	1.1	2.1	4.4	-	1.7	4.1	3.4	-	3.0	4.0	-
Item 21760 Subject A16a N★	297	176	105	181	72	62	75	118	41	154	117	96	66	42	73	8
E13: What about your relationship with your parents? Has their involvement in the parent group made your relationship better or worse?																
1. Much worse	8.9	12.5	0.9	6.8	8.1	3.8	8.7	9.1	15.9	11.0	6.2	10.4	5.6	4.1	10.1	27.3
2. Somewhat worse	9.6	8.7	11.5	8.4	9.9	7.7	10.4	10.7	7.8	9.0	9.2	9.5	9.3	11.5	6.7	21.1
3. No effect, don't know	50.4	48.8	55.1	57.2	46.3	56.8	52.0	48.8	42.8	52.4	51.6	46.6	59.6	37.7	54.5	41.6
4. Somewhat better	13.9	12.7	14.8	14.2	14.2	17.0	9.7	18.2	4.3	12.1	11.6	9.2	17.8	19.5	13.5	10.0
5. Much better	17.3	17.4	17.7	13.4	21.5	14.7	19.1	13.2	29.1	15.5	21.5	24.2	7.7	27.3	15.1	-
Item 21770 Subject A16a N★	287	166	106	171	69	60	70	116	42	147	116	95	62	42	68	8
E14: In some communities young people themselves have formed groups aimed at avoiding drug use, such as Youth for Drug-Free Alternatives. How many of your close friends have been members of such a group?																
1. None	87.5	85.4	90.4	89.2	84.2	89.1	87.1	86.2	88.8	88.8	86.9	90.5	89.2	85.8	83.6	74.5
2. A few	8.6	9.5	7.3	7.9	7.9	7.1	8.2	9.8	9.0	8.1	9.1	7.0	7.2	9.7	11.8	13.8
3. Some	3.1	4.2	2.0	2.3	7.3	2.8	3.6	3.4	1.7	2.8	3.1	2.0	3.3	4.1	3.4	9.9
4. Most or all	0.8	0.9	0.3	0.6	0.6	1.0	1.0	0.6	0.5	0.4	1.0	0.5	0.4	0.4	1.2	1.8
Item 21780 Subject A16a N	2651	1240	1359	2122	291	545	820	856	430	1470	1090	1008	552	367	644	40
E15: Have you ever participated in such a group?																
3. Yes, now	1.6	1.7	1.2	1.4	2.2	2.0	1.7	1.3	1.8	1.6	1.6	1.5	1.1	1.7	1.8	2.6
2. Yes, in the past, but not now	3.3	3.7	2.6	2.5	6.4	2.0	3.3	4.4	2.7	2.8	3.4	2.6	2.1	2.3	4.8	14.5
1. No	95.1	94.6	96.2	96.1	91.5	96.1	95.0	94.4	95.6	95.7	94.9	95.8	96.8	96.0	93.4	82.9
Item 21790 Subject A16a N	2597	1215	1332	2084	280	535	811	834	417	1446	1063	996	540	358	630	36

★=excludes respondents for whom question was inappropriate.

QUESTIONNAIRE FORM 5 1983	TOTAL	SEX		RACE		REGION				4YR COLLEGE PLANS		ILLICIT DRUG USE: LIFETIME				
		M	F	White	Black	NE	NC	S	W	Yes	No	None	Mari-juana Only	Few Pills	More Pills	Any Her-oin
N (Weighted No. of Cases):	3339	1608	1628	2513	404	793	950	1082	514	1846	1297	1125	646	492	970	42
% of Weighted Total:	100.0	48.2	48.8	75.3	12.1	23.8	28.5	32.4	15.4	55.3	38.8	33.7	19.3	14.7	29.0	1.2

A01: Taking all things together, how would you say things are these days–would you say you're very happy, pretty happy, or not too happy these days?

3. Very happy	15.9	13.9	18.2	17.4	11.1	16.0	13.9	17.5	16.4	18.4	13.3	19.4	16.8	14.1	12.6	11.7
2. Pretty happy	68.1	69.5	66.7	70.0	63.8	67.1	71.4	67.1	65.3	68.0	69.1	66.5	67.7	70.0	70.1	67.4
1. Not too happy	16.0	16.7	15.1	12.5	25.2	16.9	14.7	15.3	18.2	13.6	17.6	14.1	15.5	16.0	17.3	20.8
Item 1190 Subject P01,Q01 N	3329	1604	1624	2507	404	793	945	1082	509	1841	1294	1121	645	490	969	42

A02: Some people think a lot about the social problems of the nation and the world, and about how they might be solved. Others spend little time thinking about these issues. How much do you think about such things?

1. Never	1.4	1.3	1.4	1.3	0.8	2.3	1.6	0.7	1.0	0.8	2.1	1.0	0.7	1.3	2.2	2.8
2. Seldom	16.1	16.7	15.7	16.5	13.1	18.9	17.2	13.7	15.0	13.6	19.8	15.6	13.8	16.8	17.7	16.8
3. Sometimes	52.9	50.4	55.4	54.3	50.5	54.7	52.7	53.6	49.3	51.4	54.0	52.2	56.1	51.4	52.4	56.8
4. Quite often	25.3	27.0	23.6	24.7	28.2	21.1	24.0	27.0	30.9	29.4	20.5	26.6	25.8	26.5	23.4	17.6
5. A great deal	4.2	4.6	3.9	3.3	7.5	3.0	4.5	5.0	3.7	4.8	3.5	4.6	3.6	4.1	4.3	6.0
Item 6880 Subject J,Q08 N	3332	1604	1628	2512	403	792	948	1081	511	1844	1294	1124	646	491	968	42

A03: Of all the problems facing the nation today, how often do you worry about each of the following?

A03A: Chance of nuclear war

1. Never	9.8	9.2	10.5	8.7	15.3	10.4	9.5	10.2	8.8	7.3	13.2	11.1	9.1	8.6	9.0	13.8
2. Seldom	23.6	23.4	24.2	23.9	23.0	25.0	24.4	23.1	20.7	22.9	24.8	23.9	23.6	22.9	22.9	28.1
3. Sometimes	41.1	40.0	42.1	42.1	34.9	41.8	42.1	38.9	43.0	42.8	38.6	41.0	42.4	41.0	40.9	34.7
4. Often	25.5	27.5	23.2	25.3	26.8	22.7	24.0	27.9	27.5	27.0	23.4	24.0	25.0	27.5	27.2	23.5
Item 11660 Subject J N	3327	1603	1624	2511	403	790	946	1079	512	1845	1291	1123	642	492	967	42

A03B: Population growth

1. Never	26.2	28.4	24.3	27.3	22.4	31.1	28.1	22.2	23.5	25.8	27.4	26.0	29.1	23.2	26.3	26.5
2. Seldom	42.3	44.2	40.5	43.5	40.1	43.0	43.3	44.3	35.5	43.9	40.5	42.5	41.1	43.3	43.5	39.5
3. Sometimes	24.2	21.3	26.8	23.6	24.1	21.0	23.7	24.5	29.5	23.5	24.3	24.7	23.6	24.8	23.0	24.8
4. Often	7.3	6.1	8.5	5.6	13.4	4.9	5.0	9.0	11.5	6.9	7.8	6.8	6.2	8.7	7.2	9.2
Item 11670 Subject E01,J N	3324	1604	1619	2511	403	788	946	1077	512	1844	1289	1119	642	492	967	42

A03C: Crime and violence

1. Never	1.6	2.5	0.7	1.4	1.7	1.7	1.8	1.8	1.0	1.0	2.3	1.3	2.0	2.0	1.6	1.7
2. Seldom	13.0	18.8	7.0	14.1	6.7	9.4	18.3	11.7	11.5	13.1	13.3	12.5	11.9	13.7	13.4	23.7
3. Sometimes	40.3	45.1	35.9	43.3	24.5	40.4	41.0	37.7	44.1	40.7	40.1	38.5	39.7	40.0	43.4	39.5
4. Often	45.1	33.5	56.5	41.2	67.1	48.6	38.9	48.8	43.5	45.2	44.3	47.7	46.5	44.3	41.5	35.1
Item 11680 Subject J N	3320	1599	1622	2508	400	791	942	1076	511	1841	1287	1119	642	490	966	42

A03D: Pollution

1. Never	11.1	12.0	10.3	10.6	16.1	10.4	10.7	13.0	8.7	9.3	13.8	11.1	12.8	11.6	9.9	13.3
2. Seldom	36.0	35.4	36.5	36.6	35.5	36.7	36.3	36.0	34.3	37.9	34.0	36.8	34.3	34.5	37.5	30.4
3. Sometimes	37.2	36.5	37.3	37.5	35.8	35.9	38.6	36.9	37.1	36.4	37.2	36.5	39.0	37.2	35.8	38.3
4. Often	15.8	16.0	15.9	15.3	12.6	17.0	14.4	14.1	19.9	16.5	15.1	15.6	13.9	16.7	16.8	17.9
Item 11690 Subject F04,J N	3316	1600	1617	2505	399	785	946	1076	509	1842	1285	1119	641	491	964	41

A03E: Energy shortages

1. Never	12.8	12.1	13.8	12.4	16.0	13.3	12.6	12.7	12.9	11.6	14.6	11.7	13.4	11.2	14.2	20.9
2. Seldom	37.2	36.9	37.4	38.5	34.9	40.3	35.8	34.8	40.2	37.4	36.9	36.7	37.8	35.9	38.5	34.1
3. Sometimes	36.6	36.4	36.8	36.5	34.6	35.4	37.6	37.3	35.2	38.4	33.7	38.1	36.1	35.8	35.5	34.0
4. Often	13.3	14.7	11.9	12.6	14.6	11.1	13.9	15.3	11.7	12.6	14.8	13.5	12.7	17.0	11.7	11.1
Item 11700 Subject F05,J N	3320	1601	1618	2510	398	787	943	1077	512	1842	1289	1121	639	492	965	42

QUESTIONNAIRE FORM 5 1983	TOTAL	SEX		RACE		REGION				4YR COLLEGE PLANS		ILLICIT DRUG USE: LIFETIME				
		M	F	White	Black	NE	NC	S	W	Yes	No	None	Mari- juana Only	Few Pills	More Pills	Any Her- oin
N (Weighted No. of Cases):	3339	1608	1628	2513	404	793	950	1082	514	1846	1297	1125	646	492	970	42
% of Weighted Total:	100.0	48.2	48.8	75.3	12.1	23.8	28.5	32.4	15.4	55.3	38.8	33.7	19.3	14.7	29.0	1.2

A03F: Race relations

1. Never	19.8	20.3	19.6	22.2	9.1	22.6	20.5	16.6	20.8	16.6	24.3	19.0	16.8	24.8	20.5	16.7
2. Seldom	34.8	38.9	30.1	38.3	16.9	30.1	38.6	32.7	39.1	34.6	34.2	34.5	31.4	32.6	37.3	48.1
3. Sometimes	28.1	25.3	30.5	28.2	30.9	29.7	27.6	29.7	23.1	30.0	26.0	29.0	30.6	26.3	26.8	28.1
4. Often	17.4	15.5	19.8	11.4	43.0	17.6	13.3	21.0	17.0	18.8	15.4	17.5	21.2	16.3	15.4	7.2
Item 11710 Subject J,N02 N	3308	1597	1611	2501	399	788	940	1071	509	1835	1285	1117	640	488	961	42

A03G: Hunger and poverty

1. Never	9.2	14.2	4.1	9.9	6.8	10.2	9.2	8.1	9.7	8.3	10.8	9.5	8.8	7.0	10.1	18.1
2. Seldom	31.7	39.3	23.5	34.5	20.2	30.1	36.1	29.2	31.7	32.3	31.0	30.8	31.8	31.0	33.5	18.1
3. Sometimes	38.6	34.2	43.4	38.8	39.5	40.3	37.1	38.7	38.2	38.9	38.1	36.8	41.2	39.4	38.6	35.7
4. Often	20.5	12.2	28.9	16.8	33.5	19.4	17.6	24.0	20.3	20.6	20.1	22.8	18.2	22.5	17.8	28.1
Item 11720 Subject F03,J N	3318	1602	1616	2506	401	789	945	1075	509	1841	1288	1120	639	490	967	41

A03H: Using open land for housing or industry

1. Never	37.5	35.6	39.6	37.3	45.5	38.9	36.7	39.6	32.5	37.4	38.5	37.1	37.9	38.0	38.2	31.8
2. Seldom	30.6	30.2	30.8	30.4	28.3	32.0	32.4	28.3	29.7	31.3	29.7	29.9	31.5	29.6	31.0	32.7
3. Sometimes	20.1	21.9	18.3	19.9	17.7	18.1	19.9	20.4	23.2	20.2	19.6	22.3	20.1	20.1	17.6	19.3
4. Often	11.8	12.3	11.2	12.3	8.5	11.0	11.0	11.7	14.7	11.0	12.1	10.7	10.5	12.3	13.1	16.2
Item 11730 Subject F05,J N	3325	1604	1621	2510	403	789	946	1078	512	1843	1292	1121	641	492	968	42

A03I: Urban decay

1. Never	43.0	39.5	46.3	43.4	46.2	40.4	43.2	46.9	38.0	39.7	48.1	44.1	41.2	44.9	42.8	36.4
2. Seldom	37.5	39.8	35.3	38.1	31.9	37.6	39.1	35.0	40.0	39.0	35.0	36.9	39.1	34.3	38.4	35.7
3. Sometimes	14.7	15.1	14.5	14.1	16.3	15.3	12.5	14.6	17.9	15.5	13.1	14.6	14.4	16.2	13.8	22.0
4. Often	4.8	5.6	4.0	4.4	5.6	6.6	5.3	3.5	4.0	5.8	3.8	4.4	5.3	4.7	5.0	5.9
Item 11740 Subject J N	3298	1594	1604	2496	394	784	939	1071	505	1833	1280	1113	635	488	959	42

A03J: Economic problems

1. Never	5.6	5.7	5.4	5.3	5.8	8.2	4.6	4.4	5.7	4.4	7.4	5.3	5.5	4.9	6.2	9.7
2. Seldom	21.0	20.3	21.9	21.5	18.5	23.1	19.9	19.5	22.8	18.8	23.5	20.7	19.9	19.4	22.1	22.6
3. Sometimes	42.6	42.6	42.3	42.2	45.2	41.7	42.9	43.4	41.8	43.2	42.2	41.5	46.0	42.3	41.6	44.5
4. Often	30.9	31.4	30.4	31.1	30.5	26.9	32.6	32.8	29.7	33.7	27.0	32.5	28.5	33.3	30.1	23.2
Item 11750 Subject J N	3319	1601	1618	2511	399	790	944	1074	512	1838	1291	1118	641	490	968	42

A03K: Drug abuse

1. Never	9.3	14.0	4.4	9.4	8.9	8.8	10.7	8.9	8.2	9.1	9.3	9.2	7.0	8.0	10.7	23.7
2. Seldom	21.9	28.1	15.7	22.8	15.2	18.7	25.3	20.1	24.6	21.3	22.7	19.8	23.1	22.0	24.2	11.8
3. Sometimes	37.1	34.9	39.4	38.9	34.5	38.3	38.5	34.5	38.5	37.6	36.3	37.2	40.2	37.2	36.7	22.1
4. Often	31.6	22.9	40.5	28.9	41.4	34.1	25.4	36.5	28.7	31.9	31.6	33.9	29.7	32.8	28.4	42.5
Item 11760 Subject J N	3325	1602	1623	2512	403	789	946	1079	511	1844	1292	1122	643	489	968	42

A04: How well do you think your experiences and training (at home, school, work, etc.) have prepared you to be a good...

A04A: Husband or wife

1. Poorly	1.9	2.2	1.4	1.6	1.5	2.9	1.1	1.5	2.9	1.8	2.0	1.8	2.0	1.4	2.1	5.5
2. Not so well	4.5	6.0	3.0	4.1	4.0	4.5	4.7	3.8	5.3	3.9	5.3	3.0	3.8	5.3	6.0	3.6
3. Fairly well	22.0	26.9	16.8	22.6	19.7	23.4	23.4	20.1	21.3	21.6	22.8	19.4	22.9	23.0	23.4	31.5
4. Well	42.2	43.2	41.5	43.1	35.0	40.6	44.8	41.2	42.1	39.6	46.2	42.8	42.3	42.0	41.9	33.6
5. Very well	29.3	21.7	37.4	28.6	39.8	28.6	25.9	33.3	28.4	33.1	23.8	32.9	28.9	28.3	26.6	25.8
Item 11770 Subject D01 N	3230	1559	1578	2452	386	760	920	1047	502	1810	1243	1091	626	472	942	40

A04B: Parent

1. Poorly	1.9	2.5	1.2	2.0	0.8	2.1	1.8	1.8	2.1	1.6	2.4	1.4	2.1	1.8	2.1	10.9
2. Not so well	6.1	8.0	3.9	6.0	5.1	5.1	7.8	5.1	6.5	5.7	6.4	5.1	5.0	7.4	7.2	2.8
3. Fairly well	21.4	26.2	16.6	22.6	12.0	20.5	22.4	20.6	22.9	19.2	24.7	19.2	20.0	20.4	25.2	33.0
4. Well	37.4	37.4	37.5	39.3	28.6	35.7	39.2	36.3	38.7	36.7	38.8	36.4	37.7	38.6	38.3	21.9
5. Very well	33.2	26.0	40.8	30.1	53.4	36.7	28.8	36.1	29.7	36.8	27.7	38.0	35.2	31.7	27.1	31.3
Item 11780 Subject D02 N	3256	1563	1600	2464	393	767	933	1049	508	1817	1260	1098	628	477	954	40

QUESTIONNAIRE FORM 5 1983	TOTAL	SEX		RACE		REGION				4YR COLLEGE PLANS		ILLICIT DRUG USE: LIFETIME				
		M	F	White	Black	NE	NC	S	W	Yes	No	None	Marijuana Only	Few Pills	More Pills	Any Heroin
N (Weighted No. of Cases):	3339	1608	1628	2513	404	793	950	1082	514	1846	1297	1125	646	492	970	42
% of Weighted Total:	100.0	48.2	48.8	75.3	12.1	23.8	28.5	32.4	15.4	55.3	38.8	33.7	19.3	14.7	29.0	1.2

A04C: Worker on a job

1. Poorly	1.0	1.3	0.5	1.0	1.0	1.3	0.6	0.9	1.3	0.7	1.2	1.3	0.9	0.8	0.6	3.9
2. Not so well	2.1	2.4	1.7	1.8	2.3	1.8	2.6	1.8	2.2	2.3	1.7	1.8	2.6	1.6	2.1	12.5
3. Fairly well	13.4	13.9	13.0	13.6	9.7	14.8	15.2	10.7	13.6	14.0	12.7	13.1	11.4	12.2	15.8	4.6
4. Well	37.9	38.2	37.6	40.1	26.7	34.6	41.6	36.3	39.4	35.6	41.9	36.8	35.4	42.8	37.8	43.4
5. Very well	45.7	44.2	47.3	43.5	60.4	47.5	40.0	50.2	43.5	47.5	42.5	47.1	49.7	42.6	43.7	35.7
Item 11790 Subject C01 N	3304	1593	1612	2496	398	782	943	1070	510	1839	1277	1112	640	487	965	40

A05: Apart from the particular kind of work you want to do, how would you rate each of the following settings as a place to work?

A05A: Working in a large corporation

1. Not at all acceptable	4.2	4.2	4.1	4.2	2.8	3.4	5.1	4.1	4.0	3.4	5.4	4.3	3.6	4.0	4.4	9.2
2. Somewhat acceptable	21.3	22.2	20.4	22.1	13.6	21.8	18.8	20.5	27.3	17.6	25.8	21.5	19.2	21.4	22.4	19.8
3. Acceptable	47.7	47.4	47.7	47.6	45.7	46.0	51.3	46.7	45.7	47.6	47.5	46.7	50.3	47.3	47.2	46.6
4. Desirable	26.8	26.2	27.7	26.2	37.9	28.8	24.8	28.7	23.1	31.5	21.2	27.5	26.9	27.2	26.0	24.5
Item 11800 Subject C05 N	3316	1596	1620	2507	401	787	943	1077	509	1836	1292	1115	642	490	967	42

A05B: Working in a small business

1. Not at all acceptable	3.5	3.3	3.9	2.8	6.6	4.5	3.5	3.5	2.2	3.0	4.2	4.0	2.4	3.7	3.6	1.5
2. Somewhat acceptable	23.0	22.9	22.9	21.3	27.1	21.7	22.6	24.1	23.5	23.6	21.3	21.1	24.2	26.6	22.3	36.5
3. Acceptable	54.3	53.4	54.9	54.4	53.4	56.5	54.2	52.3	55.1	54.1	54.7	54.3	55.1	51.7	54.5	48.4
4. Desirable	19.2	20.5	18.3	21.5	12.9	17.3	19.7	20.1	19.1	19.3	19.8	20.6	18.3	18.0	19.5	13.6
Item 11810 Subject C05 N	3315	1595	1620	2508	398	787	944	1075	509	1835	1292	1115	639	491	967	42

A05C: Working in a government agency

1. Not at all acceptable	19.3	18.5	19.4	19.9	13.8	17.0	21.7	18.2	20.7	13.8	26.5	17.0	15.9	21.4	22.9	21.9
2. Somewhat acceptable	32.6	34.1	31.8	34.8	20.3	32.5	34.9	29.9	34.3	33.7	31.8	33.8	32.0	32.0	31.9	29.9
3. Acceptable	30.7	29.1	32.6	30.5	34.0	31.1	29.0	31.6	31.4	34.9	24.7	32.0	33.6	31.3	27.6	25.0
4. Desirable	17.4	18.3	16.1	14.9	31.9	19.4	14.4	20.3	13.6	17.5	17.0	17.2	18.5	15.4	17.6	23.2
Item 11820 Subject C05,H05 N	3308	1591	1616	2503	398	787	940	1073	508	1830	1291	1109	639	491	966	42

A05D: Working in the military service

1. Not at all acceptable	43.5	37.6	49.5	45.1	34.1	47.2	44.1	37.8	48.8	46.4	40.3	41.6	40.0	45.5	47.7	39.7
2. Somewhat acceptable	28.1	28.0	27.9	29.1	21.1	26.9	31.5	26.5	27.0	29.9	25.4	30.6	26.4	26.4	27.4	26.8
3. Acceptable	17.5	20.0	15.1	16.2	25.8	15.1	14.9	21.9	16.3	14.9	20.8	17.9	18.9	15.7	16.7	14.9
4. Desirable	10.9	14.4	7.5	9.5	19.1	10.8	9.5	13.7	7.8	8.8	13.5	9.9	14.7	12.4	8.2	18.5
Item 11830 Subject C05,L04 N	3309	1594	1615	2506	398	787	941	1073	509	1835	1287	1113	640	489	965	42

A05E: Working in a school or university

1. Not at all acceptable	25.2	31.0	19.2	25.7	19.6	27.3	25.9	25.1	20.7	18.5	34.6	21.2	26.2	24.4	29.2	28.9
2. Somewhat acceptable	34.4	34.9	34.1	34.6	35.5	34.1	34.4	33.7	36.1	34.0	34.8	33.7	34.6	35.9	33.5	42.9
3. Acceptable	29.2	26.1	32.4	28.9	33.6	27.9	29.7	29.3	30.0	33.1	24.0	32.3	28.9	26.7	27.9	19.3
4. Desirable	11.3	8.1	14.3	10.8	11.4	10.7	10.0	11.9	13.2	14.4	6.5	12.8	10.4	13.0	9.4	9.0
Item 11840 Subject B10,C05 N	3315	1596	1618	2505	398	788	943	1077	507	1836	1289	1117	640	489	965	42

A05F: Working in a police department or police agency

1. Not at all acceptable	28.9	28.7	29.2	27.9	32.8	27.9	27.8	31.0	28.1	29.6	27.4	29.0	25.6	28.1	31.4	24.9
2. Somewhat acceptable	33.4	32.7	34.3	34.3	31.2	32.7	33.9	33.3	34.0	34.4	32.1	35.6	33.1	34.2	31.1	38.5
3. Acceptable	26.5	26.4	26.4	27.1	23.8	28.1	27.6	25.7	24.1	26.0	27.4	25.6	28.2	26.8	26.6	22.2
4. Desirable	11.2	12.2	10.1	10.6	12.2	11.4	10.8	10.1	13.7	10.0	13.2	9.8	13.1	10.9	11.0	14.4
Item 11850 Subject C05 N	3313	1596	1617	2507	396	786	943	1074	509	1836	1290	1111	640	491	968	42

A05G: Working in a social service organization

1. Not at all acceptable	23.1	32.9	13.4	23.8	14.9	25.6	21.2	22.7	23.8	20.4	26.7	22.2	21.7	24.1	24.8	27.4
2. Somewhat acceptable	36.5	42.0	30.4	37.4	32.7	34.9	36.1	38.0	36.2	36.8	35.8	36.8	40.7	35.9	33.6	46.1
3. Acceptable	28.0	20.7	35.4	26.4	38.1	27.5	29.1	27.0	28.9	29.1	26.5	28.4	28.4	26.2	27.8	23.2
4. Desirable	12.4	4.4	20.8	12.4	14.3	12.0	13.6	12.2	11.0	13.7	11.0	12.6	9.2	13.8	13.7	3.3
Item 11860 Subject C05,O01 N	3302	1590	1612	2501	394	783	941	1071	507	1828	1288	1110	638	488	963	42

QUESTIONNAIRE FORM 5 1983	TOTAL	SEX		RACE		REGION				4YR COLLEGE PLANS		ILLICIT DRUG USE: LIFETIME				
		M	F	White	Black	NE	NC	S	W	Yes	No	None	Marijuana Only	Few Pills	More Pills	Any Heroin
N (Weighted No. of Cases):	3339	1608	1628	2513	404	793	950	1082	514	1846	1297	1125	646	492	970	42
% of Weighted Total:	100.0	48.2	48.8	75.3	12.1	23.8	28.5	32.4	15.4	55.3	38.8	33.7	19.3	14.7	29.0	1.2
A05H: Working with a small group of partners																
1. Not at all acceptable	9.5	9.6	9.5	9.0	11.7	11.6	8.8	9.6	7.7	7.5	11.8	9.7	8.5	11.0	8.8	12.1
2. Somewhat acceptable	27.4	24.6	30.1	26.4	33.6	29.2	24.0	30.0	25.2	26.6	27.9	26.0	29.3	27.2	27.2	34.8
3. Acceptable	43.6	47.2	40.2	44.3	39.3	42.7	46.3	40.9	45.8	44.5	42.3	45.4	42.9	44.5	42.5	31.0
4. Desirable	19.5	18.6	20.2	20.3	15.4	16.5	21.0	19.5	21.2	21.3	18.0	18.8	19.3	17.3	21.5	22.1
Item 11870 Subject C05 N	3311	1593	1619	2505	398	787	945	1072	507	1836	1290	1115	640	489	964	42
A05I: Working on your own (self-employed)																
1. Not at all acceptable	8.3	5.9	10.7	8.4	7.8	8.8	8.9	7.9	7.3	7.7	9.3	8.8	8.0	8.7	7.5	8.4
2. Somewhat acceptable	16.0	12.8	19.3	15.5	16.9	17.2	15.5	14.7	17.9	15.6	17.1	16.5	17.1	15.4	15.0	16.8
3. Acceptable	31.5	32.5	30.2	31.3	31.1	32.4	31.1	32.3	29.0	32.8	29.1	33.0	33.1	33.3	27.4	29.8
4. Desirable	44.2	48.7	39.8	44.8	44.2	41.7	44.6	45.0	45.8	43.8	44.6	41.7	41.8	42.6	50.1	45.0
Item 11880 Subject C05 N	3316	1596	1620	2509	398	787	945	1075	509	1837	1291	1116	640	491	967	42
A06: If you were to get enough money to live as comfortably as you'd like for the rest of your life, would you want to work?																
1. I would want to work	81.4	79.9	82.8	80.4	84.7	81.1	81.6	81.0	82.2	82.4	80.5	83.3	82.0	82.2	78.5	80.0
2. I would not want to work	18.6	20.1	17.2	19.6	15.3	18.9	18.4	19.0	17.8	17.6	19.5	16.7	18.0	17.8	21.5	20.0
Item 8100 Subject C06 N	3285	1572	1616	2485	391	777	938	1063	506	1822	1278	1106	635	485	958	41
A07: The next questions are about race relations. How much have you gotten to know people of other races...																
A07A: In school?																
1. Not at all	7.4	8.3	6.3	8.5	2.1	7.3	14.7	3.2	3.1	7.6	7.2	7.7	6.2	5.0	9.0	9.6
2. A little	20.3	21.7	19.1	22.9	10.2	19.5	27.8	14.3	20.1	19.1	22.0	18.7	21.2	22.2	21.0	26.1
3. Some	30.9	30.9	30.9	32.2	25.2	34.8	27.9	28.9	34.7	31.5	30.2	30.2	33.7	30.7	30.6	21.6
4. A lot	38.2	35.0	41.5	32.9	60.5	36.8	23.1	51.4	40.7	38.7	37.4	39.4	36.4	39.8	36.9	27.3
8. Does not apply to me	3.2	4.1	2.2	3.5	1.9	1.7	6.6	2.1	1.5	3.1	3.3	4.0	2.5	2.3	2.6	15.6
Item 11890 Subject B03,N03 N	3328	1603	1626	2512	403	790	946	1079	513	1843	1293	1123	643	492	968	41
A07B: In your neighborhood?																
1. Not at all	35.3	34.7	36.1	40.0	18.2	36.1	43.2	31.5	27.4	37.0	33.6	34.3	34.0	32.4	39.6	34.7
2. A little	22.0	21.8	22.3	22.1	21.6	21.9	18.6	22.8	26.6	21.8	22.8	23.0	23.6	22.3	20.0	20.8
3. Some	17.6	16.6	18.7	15.5	22.3	17.6	12.8	17.7	26.5	16.8	18.6	16.9	17.4	17.8	18.2	19.4
4. A lot	13.5	14.3	12.6	9.1	30.9	16.1	8.7	15.8	13.5	12.2	14.6	12.8	13.5	14.9	12.4	16.7
8. Does not apply to me	11.6	12.6	10.4	13.4	6.9	8.3	16.7	12.1	6.0	12.2	10.4	13.0	11.4	12.6	9.9	8.5
Item 11900 Subject N03 N	3318	1600	1620	2507	402	786	944	1076	512	1838	1292	1118	642	491	966	41
A07C: In church?																
1. Not at all	37.5	38.8	36.5	41.1	25.6	42.8	42.0	33.9	28.8	37.4	38.9	32.5	37.4	38.9	43.1	44.6
2. A little	20.8	20.6	20.8	20.2	19.5	20.4	21.2	20.6	21.0	21.0	20.4	21.8	23.1	19.2	18.4	19.3
3. Some	13.6	10.7	16.2	12.7	17.1	11.4	10.8	15.8	17.3	14.0	12.8	15.7	12.0	14.8	11.3	3.4
4. A lot	9.0	8.1	9.7	5.5	24.0	7.8	5.5	11.7	11.3	8.4	9.1	11.6	10.1	9.2	5.1	8.3
8. Does not apply to me	19.2	21.8	16.8	20.5	13.8	17.6	20.6	18.0	21.6	19.1	18.9	18.3	17.4	17.9	22.2	24.4
Item 11910 Subject G,N03 N	3307	1596	1614	2495	399	784	942	1073	508	1831	1288	1116	641	489	961	41
A07D: On sports teams?																
1. Not at all	18.5	14.0	23.2	20.1	9.8	21.2	22.3	13.8	17.2	16.3	21.5	18.0	14.6	17.3	22.1	21.1
2. A little	16.2	16.7	15.7	16.7	14.9	15.4	19.5	14.0	15.7	17.5	15.1	15.5	15.7	18.6	16.2	16.9
3. Some	22.2	24.5	19.8	23.2	16.5	23.3	21.4	21.3	24.2	22.1	22.5	20.7	26.3	20.6	22.3	8.9
4. A lot	24.8	30.7	19.1	21.0	41.5	21.8	17.3	32.4	27.4	26.5	21.6	25.3	28.3	25.6	21.5	26.9
8. Does not apply to me	18.3	14.2	22.3	19.0	17.2	18.3	19.4	18.5	15.5	17.6	19.3	20.4	15.1	17.9	17.9	26.2
Item 11920 Subject N03 N	3318	1600	1622	2507	400	785	945	1076	512	1837	1293	1120	641	491	966	41

QUESTIONNAIRE FORM 5 1983	TOTAL	SEX		RACE		REGION				4YR COLLEGE PLANS		ILLICIT DRUG USE: LIFETIME				
		M	F	White	Black	NE	NC	S	W	Yes	No	None	Marijuana Only	Few Pills	More Pills	Any Heroin
N (Weighted No. of Cases):	3339	1608	1628	2513	404	793	950	1082	514	1846	1297	1125	646	492	970	42
% of Weighted Total:	100.0	48.2	48.8	75.3	12.1	23.8	28.5	32.4	15.4	55.3	38.8	33.7	19.3	14.7	29.0	1.2
A07E: In clubs?																
1. Not at all	26.0	27.8	24.4	28.6	12.1	27.9	34.7	18.7	22.4	23.5	29.9	24.6	24.7	24.4	29.4	20.0
2. A little	19.4	19.2	19.6	20.3	15.6	20.2	19.2	19.2	18.9	21.5	17.0	18.7	20.7	18.1	20.0	22.3
3. Some	20.9	19.2	22.6	20.6	23.3	18.4	14.8	26.5	24.0	21.9	19.5	21.2	20.6	24.0	19.7	24.8
4. A lot	14.8	13.0	16.5	11.1	31.2	12.3	8.5	21.5	16.1	15.9	12.7	17.5	14.6	16.6	10.5	8.1
8. Does not apply to me	18.9	20.7	16.9	19.4	17.8	21.2	22.8	14.0	18.7	17.3	20.8	17.9	19.4	17.0	20.4	24.7
Item 11930 Subject N03 N	3313	1596	1619	2505	398	786	945	1074	508	1834	1290	1119	639	488	965	41
A07F: On a job?																
1. Not at all	17.4	18.6	16.5	20.0	5.7	18.1	25.4	11.4	14.2	16.7	18.6	17.5	20.4	16.7	16.3	12.4
2. A little	14.2	14.1	14.2	15.8	7.0	13.6	15.4	12.5	16.2	13.1	15.4	13.2	11.7	12.9	17.9	6.5
3. Some	21.8	21.8	21.5	22.3	17.9	22.0	17.4	23.1	26.9	21.8	21.6	21.7	21.5	24.7	20.8	21.2
4. A lot	31.4	31.3	31.4	25.9	53.3	34.1	21.2	38.9	30.0	32.3	29.9	28.5	33.0	31.4	32.9	32.6
8. Does not apply to me	15.3	14.3	16.3	16.0	16.1	12.1	20.5	14.2	12.7	16.0	14.6	19.1	13.4	14.3	12.1	27.3
Item 11940 Subject C01,N03 N	3313	1598	1618	2504	399	788	942	1072	511	1836	1288	1113	641	491	967	41
A08: Thinking about the country as a whole, would you say relations between white people and black people have been getting better, getting worse, or staying pretty much the same?																
1. Better	20.6	20.9	20.8	21.4	13.5	18.2	16.7	22.3	28.0	22.0	19.4	21.0	18.9	22.6	21.2	6.8
2. A little better	46.6	45.5	47.3	46.5	51.6	48.7	47.4	43.6	47.9	49.1	43.0	47.5	51.2	46.2	43.0	54.6
3. Same	24.4	25.9	23.0	23.9	24.0	24.2	27.5	24.2	19.4	21.9	27.4	23.1	22.4	24.1	26.4	30.1
4. A little worse	6.1	5.6	6.6	6.1	7.2	6.6	5.9	6.9	3.6	5.8	6.3	6.5	5.5	4.5	6.8	7.9
5. Worse	2.3	2.2	2.4	2.0	3.7	2.2	2.4	2.9	1.1	1.2	3.9	2.0	2.1	2.7	2.7	0.5
Item 11950 Subject N02 N	3330	1605	1625	2511	403	790	946	1082	512	1842	1295	1125	645	491	967	41
The next questions are about driving.																
A09: Do you have a driver's license?																
1. Yes	86.4	91.9	81.0	91.0	59.8	75.3	93.2	88.1	87.4	87.7	85.7	85.3	83.9	88.7	88.2	98.1
2. No, but I soon will– GO TO Q.A13	11.1	7.0	15.2	7.5	32.5	19.8	5.8	9.9	10.4	10.5	11.3	12.5	13.1	8.8	9.4	-
3. No–GO TO Q.A13	2.5	1.0	3.9	1.4	7.7	4.9	1.0	2.1	2.3	1.8	3.1	2.3	3.0	2.5	2.3	1.9
Item 11960 Subject F07 N	3207	1554	1565	2473	360	751	929	1036	491	1803	1223	1071	619	475	950	38
A10: Do you own a car?																
1. Yes	48.9	57.4	38.5	49.7	28.4	34.4	44.5	59.5	54.8	44.1	55.5	44.3	49.1	52.1	52.0	63.5
2. No, but I expect to own one in another year or two	32.4	27.9	37.6	30.8	52.9	40.1	34.0	27.4	29.9	30.6	35.4	29.0	31.1	33.2	36.0	32.6
3. No	18.7	14.6	23.9	19.5	18.7	25.6	21.6	13.2	15.3	25.3	9.2	26.7	19.9	14.6	12.0	3.9
Item 11970 Subject F07 N★	2773	1429	1267	2252	215	565	868	911	429	1582	1048	915	517	422	840	37
A11: Are you able to use someone else's car when you want to?																
1. Yes, whenever I wish	30.7	29.2	32.5	31.2	25.9	22.8	30.6	34.7	33.0	33.7	27.6	30.0	31.1	30.6	30.9	39.5
2. Yes, most of the time	45.9	44.6	47.5	47.4	43.9	52.0	48.3	41.7	41.8	46.9	44.1	48.1	44.2	47.4	44.9	36.3
3. Sometimes	15.8	18.2	12.9	14.4	20.3	15.8	15.0	15.8	17.5	13.7	18.1	15.2	16.9	14.2	16.5	11.0
4. Rarely	5.2	5.2	5.1	4.9	6.9	6.3	4.0	5.5	5.3	3.6	7.1	3.7	6.4	5.7	5.4	4.5
5. Never	2.4	2.8	2.0	2.1	3.0	3.1	1.9	2.3	2.3	2.0	3.0	3.0	1.4	2.1	2.2	8.7
Item 11980 Subject F07 N★	2770	1427	1267	2249	215	565	864	912	429	1578	1049	912	518	421	840	37
A12: Do you make an effort to cut down on driving, in order to save gasoline?																
1. Not at all	16.7	20.1	12.3	16.6	14.5	20.6	15.3	17.0	13.9	15.4	18.2	14.2	15.4	17.6	18.6	26.9
2. Not very much	32.5	32.1	33.4	33.5	30.4	33.1	31.1	31.5	36.6	35.1	29.5	30.2	34.2	34.4	34.1	28.8
3. Yes, to some extent	40.4	38.0	43.2	40.2	38.9	34.5	43.1	41.3	40.9	39.9	40.9	43.4	41.1	38.6	38.2	30.8
4. Yes, quite a bit	7.1	7.1	7.2	6.8	10.1	8.5	7.4	7.1	4.7	7.1	7.1	8.4	6.7	6.8	6.3	8.4
8. Don't know	3.2	2.6	3.9	2.8	6.1	3.3	3.2	3.0	3.8	2.5	4.4	3.7	2.6	2.7	2.9	5.2
Item 11990 Subject F07 N★	2770	1427	1266	2251	214	565	865	911	429	1578	1049	912	518	422	839	37

★=excludes respondents for whom question was inappropriate.

QUESTIONNAIRE FORM 5 1983	TOTAL	SEX		RACE		REGION				4YR COLLEGE PLANS		ILLICIT DRUG USE: LIFETIME				
		M	F	White	Black	NE	NC	S	W	Yes	No	None	Marijuana Only	Few Pills	More Pills	Any Heroin
N (Weighted No. of Cases):	3339	1608	1628	2513	404	793	950	1082	514	1846	1297	1125	646	492	970	42
% of Weighted Total:	100.0	48.2	48.8	75.3	12.1	23.8	28.5	32.4	15.4	55.3	38.8	33.7	19.3	14.7	29.0	1.2

A13: Do you make an effort to cut down on the amount of electricity you use in order to save energy?

	TOTAL	M	F	White	Black	NE	NC	S	W	Yes	No	None	Marijuana Only	Few Pills	More Pills	Any Heroin
1. Not at all	7.6	9.5	5.9	7.8	5.4	8.7	7.8	7.1	6.3	7.1	8.5	7.2	7.6	6.5	8.6	13.0
2. Not very much	26.0	26.6	25.2	28.1	19.4	26.2	26.9	26.1	23.9	27.7	23.5	23.8	25.9	29.4	27.7	13.1
3. Yes, to some extent	46.3	45.1	47.1	46.1	47.1	47.2	47.3	43.4	49.2	46.3	46.3	46.8	47.0	46.6	44.4	44.0
4. Yes, quite a bit	17.8	16.7	19.2	16.3	24.8	15.7	16.5	20.5	17.8	17.4	18.3	19.3	17.9	16.0	16.8	25.2
8. Don't know	2.3	2.0	2.7	1.7	3.4	2.2	1.6	2.8	2.9	1.5	3.5	2.9	1.6	1.5	2.6	4.7
Item 12000 Subject F05 N	3328	1603	1627	2508	403	792	946	1078	512	1844	1291	1124	643	490	968	41

A14: In the house or apartment where you live, is an effort made to reduce heat during the winter, in order to save energy?

	TOTAL	M	F	White	Black	NE	NC	S	W	Yes	No	None	Marijuana Only	Few Pills	More Pills	Any Heroin
1. Not at all	4.3	4.9	3.6	3.6	6.7	4.3	2.6	5.0	5.9	3.4	5.4	4.2	3.9	3.5	5.2	3.4
2. Not very much	13.6	13.5	13.4	12.0	19.4	13.1	11.8	15.6	13.6	12.9	14.6	12.6	14.9	14.1	13.3	15.2
3. Yes, to some extent	37.8	38.5	37.1	37.9	41.4	35.6	37.8	39.8	37.3	38.2	36.6	38.8	38.9	37.3	36.3	44.6
4. Yes, quite a bit	41.4	40.8	42.5	44.4	27.5	44.6	45.3	36.8	39.1	43.4	39.4	41.1	39.1	43.0	43.1	36.7
8. Don't know	2.8	2.2	3.5	2.0	5.1	2.4	2.5	2.7	4.2	2.0	4.0	3.3	3.3	2.2	2.1	-
Item 12010 Subject F05 N	3330	1604	1627	2510	403	791	947	1078	513	1844	1292	1123	645	490	969	41

A15: How do you feel about each of the following?

A15A: How much do you enjoy shopping for things like clothes, records, sporting goods, and books?

	TOTAL	M	F	White	Black	NE	NC	S	W	Yes	No	None	Marijuana Only	Few Pills	More Pills	Any Heroin
1. Not at all	1.3	2.2	0.3	1.2	0.4	1.0	2.0	1.2	0.9	0.9	1.6	1.2	1.5	1.3	1.0	1.7
2. Not very much	9.5	15.2	3.6	10.2	4.7	8.4	12.2	8.2	8.7	8.9	10.0	10.5	7.9	10.6	8.4	17.4
3. Pretty much	31.6	45.3	17.7	33.7	21.2	30.4	33.5	31.2	30.8	31.2	32.4	32.2	34.1	29.3	31.2	25.8
4. Very much	57.6	37.3	78.4	54.9	73.7	60.2	52.3	59.4	59.6	59.0	56.1	56.1	56.5	58.8	59.4	55.2
Item 12020 Subject F01 N	3328	1602	1627	2510	401	791	947	1076	514	1844	1291	1123	645	490	969	41

A15B: How much do you care about having the latest fashion in your clothes, records, leisure activities, and so on?

	TOTAL	M	F	White	Black	NE	NC	S	W	Yes	No	None	Marijuana Only	Few Pills	More Pills	Any Heroin
1. Not at all	6.0	8.4	3.3	6.3	1.6	7.0	6.4	5.0	5.9	4.5	7.2	6.3	4.7	5.6	6.3	14.0
2. Not very much	25.9	32.1	20.0	27.7	13.4	25.1	32.9	19.3	28.3	25.7	27.0	29.0	23.5	22.3	26.7	26.7
3. Pretty much	38.4	36.1	40.9	38.9	35.2	36.1	36.6	39.9	41.8	38.8	38.5	39.2	36.8	38.3	38.7	37.9
4. Very much	29.7	23.4	35.8	27.0	49.8	31.7	24.1	35.7	24.1	31.1	27.2	25.5	34.9	33.9	28.3	21.4
Item 12030 Subject F01 N	3326	1602	1625	2509	402	790	946	1078	511	1841	1293	1124	643	490	968	41

A15C: How much do you care about whether your family has most of the things your friends and neighbors have?

	TOTAL	M	F	White	Black	NE	NC	S	W	Yes	No	None	Marijuana Only	Few Pills	More Pills	Any Heroin
1. Not at all	24.1	23.7	24.2	22.3	29.4	26.7	23.8	21.5	26.3	21.8	26.4	22.4	27.2	21.4	25.7	21.2
2. Not very much	47.3	48.0	47.5	48.2	47.8	45.9	48.1	47.5	47.7	49.0	46.7	50.6	47.2	47.5	43.4	56.2
3. Pretty much	21.4	21.9	20.7	22.7	14.8	21.2	21.2	21.6	21.8	22.0	20.3	20.5	18.7	24.2	23.2	17.2
4. Very much	7.1	6.4	7.6	6.8	8.1	6.2	6.9	9.3	4.2	7.1	6.7	6.6	6.9	6.9	7.7	5.3
Item 12040 Subject F01 N	3323	1599	1625	2509	401	790	946	1078	509	1841	1290	1123	643	488	968	41

A16: When you are older, do you expect to own more possessions than your parents do now, or about the same, or less?

I expect to own . . .

	TOTAL	M	F	White	Black	NE	NC	S	W	Yes	No	None	Marijuana Only	Few Pills	More Pills	Any Heroin
1. Much less than my parents	1.7	1.7	1.8	1.3	1.6	1.9	1.6	1.1	2.8	1.0	2.5	1.7	1.3	1.8	1.6	4.3
2. Somewhat less than my parents	7.2	7.1	7.2	7.0	5.7	7.3	7.8	6.7	7.4	5.4	9.2	6.8	6.7	6.6	8.6	2.2
3. About as much as my parents	35.5	32.3	38.5	37.3	28.0	33.3	38.3	36.3	32.2	31.8	40.6	37.9	31.4	35.6	35.0	34.5
4. Somewhat more than my parents	39.3	39.1	40.3	39.6	42.8	41.5	37.8	39.6	38.4	42.1	36.1	39.3	42.7	40.3	37.3	40.8
5. Much more than my parents	16.2	19.8	12.2	14.7	21.9	16.0	14.6	16.3	19.3	19.6	11.6	14.2	17.9	15.6	17.5	18.2
Item 12050 Subject F01 N	3326	1602	1626	2508	402	789	946	1078	513	1842	1291	1124	645	489	966	41

QUESTIONNAIRE FORM 5 1983	TOTAL	SEX		RACE		REGION				4YR COLLEGE PLANS		ILLICIT DRUG USE: LIFETIME				
		M	F	White	Black	NE	NC	S	W	Yes	No	None	Mari- juana Only	Few Pills	More Pills	Any Her- oin
N (Weighted No. of Cases):	3339	1608	1628	2513	404	793	950	1082	514	1846	1297	1125	646	492	970	42
% of Weighted Total:	100.0	48.2	48.8	75.3	12.1	23.8	28.5	32.4	15.4	55.3	38.8	33.7	19.3	14.7	29.0	1.2

A17: Compared with your parents, what is the smallest amount that you could be content or satisfied to own?

The least I could be content to own is . . .

	TOTAL	M	F	White	Black	NE	NC	S	W	Yes	No	None	Mari- juana Only	Few Pills	More Pills	Any Her- oin
1. Much less than my parents	9.5	8.8	10.2	10.3	5.0	8.3	10.7	7.7	12.7	8.6	10.7	8.7	7.6	7.5	12.8	7.0
2. Somewhat less than my parents	29.5	27.5	31.8	33.1	16.4	28.7	31.3	29.9	26.8	30.5	28.2	31.6	28.7	28.0	29.4	38.7
3. About as much as my parents	44.2	45.4	43.5	43.7	46.1	44.2	44.0	44.9	43.5	43.8	46.2	43.9	45.4	47.7	42.3	33.2
4. Somewhat more than my parents	13.5	14.2	12.1	10.7	24.7	15.6	11.4	14.4	12.0	13.5	12.3	12.7	13.3	14.3	13.0	18.0
5. Much more than my parents	3.3	4.0	2.4	2.2	7.8	3.2	2.6	3.1	5.1	3.5	2.6	3.1	5.0	2.5	2.5	3.1
Item 12060 Subject F01 N	3303	1586	1619	2495	397	781	937	1073	512	1832	1282	1113	640	487	960	41

A18: These next questions ask your opinions about a number of different topics. How much do you agree or disagree with each statement below?

A18A: We ought to worry about our own country and let the rest of the world take care of itself

	TOTAL	M	F	White	Black	NE	NC	S	W	Yes	No	None	Mari- juana Only	Few Pills	More Pills	Any Her- oin
1. Disagree	20.5	20.0	21.3	18.2	27.7	20.6	18.4	22.2	20.7	21.3	19.0	20.5	22.3	21.6	18.5	18.8
2. Mostly disagree	23.7	23.1	24.5	25.4	17.4	24.6	24.4	21.6	25.4	27.4	18.0	25.5	24.1	24.7	21.6	22.0
3. Neither	12.5	11.2	13.4	12.7	10.3	11.5	13.4	10.8	16.0	12.8	12.6	12.5	12.2	12.7	12.3	16.2
4. Mostly agree	28.7	29.2	27.9	29.7	27.3	29.8	28.4	29.0	26.8	27.2	30.8	27.4	28.9	28.4	30.2	12.7
5. Agree	14.6	16.4	12.8	14.0	17.3	13.6	15.4	16.5	11.1	11.3	19.7	14.1	12.4	12.7	17.4	30.3
Item 12070 Subject O03 N	3330	1605	1626	2511	402	791	947	1079	513	1844	1293	1122	645	492	969	42

A18B: It would be better if we all felt more like citizens of the world than of any particular country

	TOTAL	M	F	White	Black	NE	NC	S	W	Yes	No	None	Mari- juana Only	Few Pills	More Pills	Any Her- oin
1. Disagree	11.9	14.3	9.3	12.4	9.1	11.6	11.7	12.7	10.7	11.7	12.7	10.5	11.1	11.5	13.9	28.0
2. Mostly disagree	12.6	13.5	12.1	13.6	6.4	11.4	13.9	12.1	13.1	13.6	11.4	13.3	14.0	12.9	11.4	2.2
3. Neither	20.8	20.2	21.6	22.1	14.6	22.3	20.6	20.6	19.4	20.5	21.4	19.9	18.5	19.1	24.5	17.3
4. Mostly agree	28.4	25.9	30.4	28.3	32.0	25.4	30.0	27.3	32.3	27.7	28.2	31.2	26.4	29.0	25.6	30.3
5. Agree	26.3	26.1	26.6	23.6	37.9	29.3	23.9	27.3	24.4	26.4	26.2	25.1	30.0	27.6	24.6	22.3
Item 12080 Subject O03 N	3320	1604	1621	2508	402	787	946	1078	510	1840	1293	1120	643	489	969	42

A18C: I find it hard to be sympathetic toward starving people in foreign lands, when there is so much trouble in our own country

	TOTAL	M	F	White	Black	NE	NC	S	W	Yes	No	None	Mari- juana Only	Few Pills	More Pills	Any Her- oin
1. Disagree	35.4	24.3	47.5	34.2	44.2	35.3	35.9	35.7	33.9	37.1	33.5	36.8	34.8	35.4	35.6	16.3
2. Mostly disagree	24.4	23.1	25.2	26.4	17.2	25.3	25.3	23.3	23.5	26.8	21.3	24.1	26.0	28.6	21.8	28.7
3. Neither	12.8	16.7	8.5	13.2	9.2	12.4	12.7	12.5	14.5	12.4	13.0	12.3	13.0	10.5	13.6	14.9
4. Mostly agree	16.2	21.5	11.0	16.3	14.5	16.5	16.6	15.2	17.3	14.2	18.6	17.3	13.8	14.2	17.7	15.2
5. Agree	11.2	14.4	7.6	10.0	14.9	10.5	9.5	13.3	10.8	9.6	13.5	9.5	12.5	11.2	11.3	24.8
Item 12090 Subject F03,O03 N	3326	1604	1625	2509	401	786	948	1079	513	1842	1294	1120	645	492	969	42

A18D: Maybe some minority groups do get unfair treatment, but that's no business of mine

	TOTAL	M	F	White	Black	NE	NC	S	W	Yes	No	None	Mari- juana Only	Few Pills	More Pills	Any Her- oin
1. Disagree	40.1	31.6	49.3	36.6	56.0	44.0	36.7	37.8	45.2	45.9	32.3	42.2	42.3	39.0	37.0	36.1
2. Mostly disagree	30.6	31.8	29.8	33.1	21.1	29.3	32.0	30.8	29.6	32.5	27.2	30.5	32.1	33.5	30.1	14.8
3. Neither	17.6	20.7	14.0	19.2	9.7	16.0	19.8	17.8	15.4	14.2	22.9	16.5	14.5	16.3	21.1	13.5
4. Mostly agree	7.0	9.5	4.3	6.5	7.0	5.4	7.1	8.7	6.0	5.2	9.4	6.2	8.2	6.0	6.7	20.9
5. Agree	4.7	6.4	2.6	4.5	6.3	5.3	4.4	5.0	3.8	2.2	8.2	4.7	2.9	5.3	5.1	14.7
Item 12100 Subject N02,O03 N	3310	1598	1616	2500	400	782	947	1070	511	1836	1285	1116	644	489	963	42

A18E: I get very upset when I see other people treated unfairly

	TOTAL	M	F	White	Black	NE	NC	S	W	Yes	No	None	Mari- juana Only	Few Pills	More Pills	Any Her- oin
1. Disagree	3.1	3.2	3.0	3.1	3.0	3.7	2.5	2.5	4.2	3.3	2.7	3.0	1.8	4.4	3.1	5.6
2. Mostly disagree	4.4	5.3	3.1	4.1	3.7	4.9	4.0	4.7	3.8	4.0	5.0	3.1	4.1	5.1	5.2	9.1
3. Neither	8.7	13.4	3.8	9.3	5.1	8.2	9.9	8.3	7.9	6.6	11.1	7.5	7.8	7.7	10.8	16.5
4. Mostly agree	34.1	39.3	29.1	36.7	25.9	32.4	37.8	32.5	33.1	34.6	33.4	32.2	35.4	34.4	35.7	27.2
5. Agree	49.7	38.8	61.0	46.8	62.3	50.7	45.7	52.0	51.0	51.6	47.8	54.2	50.9	48.4	45.2	41.6
Item 12110 Subject O03 N	3322	1603	1623	2509	399	788	948	1075	511	1839	1294	1122	642	490	969	42

QUESTIONNAIRE FORM 5 1983	TOTAL	SEX		RACE		REGION				4YR COLLEGE PLANS		ILLICIT DRUG USE: LIFETIME				
		M	F	White	Black	NE	NC	S	W	Yes	No	None	Mari-juana Only	Few Pills	More Pills	Any Her-oin
N (Weighted No. of Cases):	3339	1608	1628	2513	404	793	950	1082	514	1846	1297	1125	646	492	970	42
% of Weighted Total:	100.0	48.2	48.8	75.3	12.1	23.8	28.5	32.4	15.4	55.3	38.8	33.7	19.3	14.7	29.0	1.2
A18F: I would agree to a good plan to make a better life for the poor, even if it cost me money																
1. Disagree	7.9	10.7	5.0	8.0	7.5	9.1	8.2	6.7	8.4	6.1	10.3	8.1	6.0	7.9	9.3	7.6
2. Mostly disagree	10.1	12.3	7.6	11.1	6.8	10.2	8.9	10.6	11.5	9.9	10.2	8.3	10.9	10.0	11.6	14.2
3. Neither	24.4	28.8	19.8	26.2	14.5	23.1	26.5	23.7	23.8	22.3	26.8	21.9	22.7	25.4	27.9	31.2
4. Mostly agree	36.7	31.7	42.6	37.3	37.1	33.6	39.0	37.0	36.5	40.4	32.9	37.9	38.9	36.2	34.7	29.1
5. Agree	20.9	16.5	25.0	17.3	34.2	23.9	17.5	22.1	19.8	21.2	19.8	23.8	21.5	20.4	16.5	17.8
Item 12120　Subject O03　　N	3311	1595	1621	2501	399	783	948	1072	508	1837	1285	1117	645	488	962	42
A18G: It's not really my problem if others are in trouble and need help																
1. Disagree	39.0	31.2	46.8	36.9	51.5	40.8	38.0	39.5	37.1	41.9	34.6	42.5	40.4	36.6	35.8	32.3
2. Mostly disagree	34.5	35.6	34.0	37.1	25.5	32.4	36.8	33.7	35.0	36.2	32.7	33.1	35.9	36.7	34.5	36.0
3. Neither	14.6	17.5	11.4	15.0	9.2	13.6	14.3	14.0	17.6	12.5	18.2	13.4	12.2	14.0	17.8	13.9
4. Mostly agree	8.6	11.4	5.7	8.2	9.3	8.9	8.4	8.9	7.7	7.4	9.5	8.3	7.8	8.6	8.8	11.3
5. Agree	3.4	4.3	2.2	2.7	4.5	4.3	2.5	3.9	2.5	1.9	5.0	2.7	3.7	4.2	3.1	6.5
Item 12130　Subject O03　　N	3320	1596	1624	2503	402	786	948	1077	508	1837	1292	1119	644	488	967	42
A18H: Americans could change their eating habits to provide more food for the hungry people in other parts of the world, and at the same time be healthier themselves																
1. Disagree	10.0	14.4	5.8	10.1	9.4	10.2	9.9	10.9	8.0	9.1	10.9	9.1	10.7	8.1	10.9	23.6
2. Mostly disagree	11.3	14.3	8.0	11.2	12.8	10.3	12.1	10.9	12.1	11.0	12.0	9.4	11.0	12.0	13.4	12.9
3. Neither	18.6	21.3	15.9	18.7	18.2	19.3	17.6	17.3	22.1	18.0	19.0	18.0	19.8	18.2	18.1	21.1
4. Mostly agree	28.7	26.5	30.8	29.6	28.4	26.6	31.1	29.6	25.5	29.0	29.2	30.3	28.7	30.1	26.6	22.4
5. Agree	31.4	23.5	39.5	30.5	31.2	33.5	29.4	31.3	32.3	32.9	28.9	33.2	29.8	31.6	31.0	20.0
Item 12140　Subject F03,O03　　N	3317	1599	1620	2503	398	786	948	1072	511	1838	1288	1120	644	492	964	42
A18I: My family and I often buy things we really don't need; we could get along with much less																
1. Disagree	14.6	16.2	13.0	12.2	27.9	17.7	12.5	13.7	15.7	12.4	16.0	13.1	18.2	10.9	15.6	13.7
2. Mostly disagree	16.4	17.7	15.0	16.1	16.7	18.9	16.6	15.8	13.7	15.6	17.6	16.1	18.1	16.4	15.3	24.9
3. Neither	15.5	17.5	13.4	16.2	12.3	16.8	15.7	14.0	16.4	15.8	14.9	16.5	15.0	18.2	13.3	17.0
4. Mostly agree	29.4	29.1	29.9	31.4	22.3	25.4	30.7	30.7	30.6	29.8	29.8	31.0	26.3	30.8	28.8	33.6
5. Agree	24.0	19.4	28.8	24.2	20.9	21.2	24.5	25.8	23.5	26.4	21.7	23.2	22.4	23.7	27.0	10.8
Item 10060　Subject F01　　N	3317	1601	1620	2507	398	783	945	1078	511	1842	1287	1120	641	490	967	42
A18J: Most people will have fuller and happier lives if they choose legal marriage rather than staying single, or just living with someone																
1. Disagree	20.9	18.4	23.6	20.2	24.0	28.3	19.1	17.1	21.2	18.5	24.1	14.3	23.0	18.3	28.7	24.7
2. Mostly disagree	15.1	15.8	14.3	15.0	15.4	16.3	15.5	13.5	15.8	14.8	15.5	11.6	16.1	16.3	17.5	29.1
3. Neither	26.5	26.8	26.0	26.9	27.5	26.1	28.9	25.6	24.6	26.7	25.9	27.3	26.1	27.8	24.4	28.9
4. Mostly agree	16.0	17.8	14.0	16.5	13.8	13.4	18.0	18.1	11.7	16.4	15.4	19.6	16.7	15.1	12.1	6.6
5. Agree	21.5	21.2	22.0	21.4	19.3	15.9	18.5	25.7	26.8	23.7	19.0	27.2	18.1	22.5	17.2	10.7
Item 12150　Subject D03　　N	3321	1600	1624	2502	402	787	946	1078	511	1838	1293	1119	644	491	967	42
A18K: Parents should encourage just as much independence in their daughters as in their sons																
1. Disagree	4.9	7.8	1.9	4.2	6.0	3.3	5.3	6.0	4.4	4.0	5.8	3.8	6.1	7.5	4.1	6.9
2. Mostly disagree	6.1	9.6	2.7	5.9	7.0	6.0	5.7	6.6	6.3	5.8	6.9	6.0	8.1	5.6	4.8	10.7
3. Neither	9.6	15.1	4.0	9.8	6.8	9.0	11.3	8.6	9.4	9.6	9.2	9.7	7.6	6.9	12.0	13.7
4. Mostly agree	23.9	29.2	18.6	23.7	23.5	23.3	23.6	24.3	24.6	23.4	24.4	25.4	22.6	25.4	21.5	33.3
5. Agree	55.4	38.2	72.8	56.3	56.7	58.3	54.2	54.4	55.3	57.2	53.7	55.0	55.6	54.6	57.6	35.5
Item 12160　Subject D05　　N	3326	1603	1625	2511	401	788	948	1078	512	1843	1294	1123	644	492	967	42

QUESTIONNAIRE FORM 5 1983	TOTAL	SEX		RACE		REGION				4YR COLLEGE PLANS		ILLICIT DRUG USE: LIFETIME				
		M	F	White	Black	NE	NC	S	W	Yes	No	None	Mari-juana Only	Few Pills	More Pills	Any Her-oin
N (Weighted No. of Cases):	3339	1608	1628	2513	404	793	950	1082	514	1846	1297	1125	646	492	970	42
% of Weighted Total:	100.0	48.2	48.8	75.3	12.1	23.8	28.5	32.4	15.4	55.3	38.8	33.7	19.3	14.7	29.0	1.2

A18L: Being a mother and raising children is one of the most fulfilling experiences a woman can have

1. Disagree	4.9	3.0	6.5	4.9	3.8	6.2	4.2	4.6	5.0	4.3	5.6	4.1	4.0	3.5	7.0	11.0
2. Mostly disagree	7.1	5.4	8.5	7.5	6.4	7.6	7.9	6.1	6.6	7.6	6.1	6.3	5.9	4.9	9.4	9.9
3. Neither	28.5	42.6	15.0	31.4	16.5	29.7	32.6	24.7	26.8	29.9	26.2	26.7	29.4	25.1	31.9	32.8
4. Mostly agree	25.2	22.1	28.3	24.8	25.2	24.0	25.6	25.0	26.7	25.8	24.7	24.6	25.8	28.4	23.9	16.2
5. Agree	34.4	26.9	41.7	31.4	48.2	32.5	29.7	39.6	34.9	32.4	37.4	38.3	34.9	38.1	27.8	30.0
Item 12170 Subject D05 N	3261	1551	1618	2458	396	773	934	1051	504	1809	1264	1096	632	484	953	41

A18M: Most fathers should spend more time with their children than they do now

1. Disagree	1.5	1.7	1.3	1.3	1.1	2.0	0.9	2.0	0.9	0.9	2.3	1.3	1.8	1.6	1.4	6.4
2. Mostly disagree	2.5	3.0	2.1	2.9	1.0	3.2	2.9	2.1	1.5	2.4	2.8	2.3	1.6	3.3	3.1	0.9
3. Neither	14.6	16.5	12.9	15.8	10.3	16.2	14.7	12.2	17.3	15.5	13.1	15.0	15.3	9.7	16.8	14.8
4. Mostly agree	35.8	39.2	32.3	37.8	27.3	33.7	39.6	33.1	38.1	36.4	35.5	33.2	35.9	39.4	36.6	43.2
5. Agree	45.5	39.6	51.5	42.1	60.4	44.9	41.8	50.6	42.2	44.7	46.4	48.2	45.4	46.0	42.1	34.7
Item 12180 Subject D05 N	3321	1602	1622	2505	400	787	948	1075	511	1839	1294	1120	644	491	967	42

A18N: The husband should make all the important decisions in the family

1. Disagree	39.6	22.0	57.2	40.4	47.0	46.9	38.4	35.5	39.1	42.2	35.8	40.1	38.8	36.3	42.2	29.5
2. Mostly disagree	20.1	20.4	20.2	19.6	23.2	18.5	22.5	20.1	18.1	20.7	19.6	19.5	22.6	21.8	18.7	10.8
3. Neither	17.2	24.8	9.4	18.0	11.3	16.8	16.8	17.4	17.9	16.3	18.6	18.0	14.3	18.3	16.6	28.3
4. Mostly agree	13.9	18.1	9.4	13.5	12.4	10.6	13.4	15.7	16.3	12.4	15.6	13.9	13.1	13.2	14.1	23.1
5. Agree	9.2	14.6	3.8	8.6	6.1	7.3	9.0	11.2	8.6	8.2	10.5	8.5	11.2	10.3	8.4	8.3
Item 12190 Subject D05 N	3324	1604	1623	2507	402	787	947	1079	511	1841	1293	1123	643	489	969	42

A19: Some people think about what's going on in government very often, and others are not that interested. How much of an interest do you take in government and current events?

1. No interest at all	4.3	4.3	4.0	3.9	3.6	7.4	4.0	3.1	2.8	1.9	7.4	4.1	4.2	3.3	4.7	10.6
2. Very little interest	18.6	14.4	23.1	18.3	18.3	20.7	17.2	17.8	19.6	16.0	22.5	16.6	19.0	16.3	22.1	12.8
3. Some interest	47.8	43.8	51.9	48.3	48.3	48.1	51.3	46.8	42.9	46.6	49.5	47.7	47.3	50.5	47.2	38.6
4. A lot of interest	21.9	27.4	16.4	22.2	20.5	18.2	19.7	23.7	27.6	25.6	16.7	22.5	23.5	21.7	20.2	24.7
5. A very great interest	7.5	10.1	4.6	7.4	9.3	5.6	7.9	8.6	7.1	9.8	3.8	9.1	6.1	8.2	5.9	13.3
Item 6330 Subject H01,Q08 N	3313	1593	1623	2503	398	785	944	1072	512	1835	1287	1119	644	488	964	41

A20: If you have at least an average income in the future, how likely is it that you will contribute money to the following organizations? If you have already contributed, mark the last circle only. Are you likely to contribute to...

A20A: The United Fund or other community charities?

1. Definitely not	4.5	6.2	2.7	4.3	5.2	5.5	4.8	3.4	4.6	3.2	5.8	4.7	2.6	5.3	5.0	3.7
2. Probably not	17.9	21.6	14.3	18.8	11.4	18.3	17.2	16.2	22.1	15.7	20.4	17.7	14.4	17.8	20.5	19.4
3. Don't know	43.8	44.7	43.3	44.3	41.4	43.7	45.9	39.9	48.0	43.3	44.7	42.8	47.9	39.1	44.1	41.9
4. Probably will	23.5	19.0	27.3	22.7	28.5	22.9	23.1	27.2	16.8	25.5	21.2	24.9	23.9	27.2	20.0	18.8
5. Definitely will	3.0	2.8	3.3	2.4	6.8	2.5	2.3	4.4	2.3	3.1	2.8	3.1	3.9	3.6	2.0	5.1
6. Already have	7.4	5.8	9.0	7.6	6.6	7.2	6.7	8.8	6.1	9.2	5.0	6.8	7.4	7.0	8.4	11.1
Item 12200 Subject O02 N	3282	1580	1607	2491	396	777	941	1062	502	1824	1277	1109	638	488	953	40

A20B: International relief organizations (CARE, UNICEF, etc.)?

1. Definitely not	4.2	6.6	1.6	4.3	2.8	3.8	4.1	3.9	5.8	3.2	5.7	4.4	2.2	4.5	5.2	3.7
2. Probably not	15.7	20.5	11.1	17.0	9.3	14.3	16.9	14.4	18.2	13.9	18.2	13.7	14.7	15.0	18.6	32.1
3. Don't know	31.2	34.0	28.4	32.0	27.2	28.2	34.1	29.9	33.0	31.0	31.1	31.6	34.6	27.7	30.0	26.6
4. Probably will	32.3	27.8	36.8	31.1	41.6	32.3	32.1	33.7	29.7	33.6	30.3	33.4	31.5	35.5	29.9	23.4
5. Definitely will	7.4	4.7	10.0	5.2	14.3	9.9	3.6	9.7	5.9	7.5	7.1	8.5	8.2	7.5	5.9	7.1
6. Already have	9.2	6.5	12.1	10.4	4.8	11.6	9.1	8.4	7.4	10.8	7.5	8.4	8.9	10.0	10.4	7.1
Item 12210 Subject O02 N	3279	1580	1604	2492	393	774	941	1063	501	1821	1277	1106	636	487	955	40

QUESTIONNAIRE FORM 5 1983	TOTAL	SEX		RACE		REGION				4YR COLLEGE PLANS		ILLICIT DRUG USE: LIFETIME				
		M	F	White	Black	NE	NC	S	W	Yes	No	None	Mari-juana Only	Few Pills	More Pills	Any Her-oin
N (Weighted No. of Cases):	3339	1608	1628	2513	404	793	950	1082	514	1846	1297	1125	646	492	970	42
% of Weighted Total:	100.0	48.2	48.8	75.3	12.1	23.8	28.5	32.4	15.4	55.3	38.8	33.7	19.3	14.7	29.0	1.2

A20C: Minority group organizations (NAACP, SCLC, etc.)?

1. Definitely not	11.0	14.8	7.2	12.4	3.8	11.8	10.5	11.6	9.2	10.3	11.9	9.5	9.5	12.2	13.0	16.1
2. Probably not	28.3	30.7	25.9	33.0	6.8	24.0	31.0	28.3	29.5	28.0	28.9	28.6	23.9	27.5	31.0	38.9
3. Don't know	39.4	35.6	43.7	42.3	21.5	36.2	43.4	35.9	44.5	39.3	40.4	39.7	40.8	38.5	38.8	34.3
4. Probably will	14.9	13.9	15.6	11.0	32.1	17.8	12.9	14.9	14.5	15.5	13.7	15.8	15.0	15.6	13.6	3.5
5. Definitely will	5.2	3.9	6.1	0.8	30.0	8.0	1.8	7.8	1.8	5.6	3.9	5.4	9.0	4.3	2.6	7.2
6. Already have	1.2	1.0	1.6	0.5	5.8	2.2	0.5	1.6	0.4	1.4	1.2	0.9	1.8	2.0	1.0	-
Item 12220 Subject N02,O02 N	3270	1573	1603	2486	393	772	940	1057	502	1813	1277	1103	634	485	952	40

A20D: Church or religious organizations?

1. Definitely not	5.5	7.1	3.8	5.8	2.5	5.9	5.5	3.8	8.7	5.0	6.1	4.9	3.1	4.4	8.4	10.7
2. Probably not	8.2	7.2	8.9	8.6	4.9	9.8	7.2	5.5	13.0	7.2	9.2	6.8	6.5	9.9	9.8	11.6
3. Don't know	13.5	14.9	12.0	12.9	11.9	14.7	12.9	11.1	17.5	10.9	15.9	11.6	14.0	9.0	17.3	19.1
4. Probably will	24.7	27.8	21.5	24.3	26.7	25.5	25.8	24.1	22.6	23.0	27.4	20.5	30.0	28.1	24.0	16.0
5. Definitely will	15.6	15.9	15.5	14.5	25.1	15.3	13.4	20.4	9.6	17.5	13.0	18.2	16.6	17.4	11.3	9.4
6. Already have	32.6	27.1	38.2	33.9	28.8	28.8	35.2	35.0	28.6	36.4	28.5	37.8	29.8	31.2	29.3	33.1
Item 12230 Subject G,O02 N	3282	1580	1606	2492	395	773	941	1065	503	1824	1277	1109	637	488	954	40

A20E: Political parties or organizations?

1. Definitely not	18.6	19.7	17.5	17.6	22.0	22.1	17.4	17.4	17.9	16.1	22.2	17.2	17.6	19.8	20.6	18.3
2. Probably not	29.1	27.7	30.6	30.4	22.9	30.6	30.8	26.4	29.5	28.8	29.2	31.2	27.6	26.4	28.8	33.1
3. Don't know	32.3	31.0	33.2	31.2	36.1	30.1	34.3	32.6	31.1	31.4	33.8	32.6	31.4	32.9	32.1	26.6
4. Probably will	14.5	15.0	13.9	15.3	14.3	12.3	12.9	17.9	13.3	16.9	11.1	13.7	17.5	14.3	13.5	11.3
5. Definitely will	2.7	2.9	2.5	2.8	1.8	2.0	2.1	2.5	5.2	3.6	1.6	2.8	3.2	3.1	2.1	5.8
6. Already have	2.8	3.7	2.2	2.6	2.9	2.8	2.4	3.2	2.9	3.2	2.2	2.5	2.8	3.5	2.9	4.9
Item 12240 Subject H05,O02 N	3273	1578	1600	2485	395	769	938	1062	504	1819	1274	1107	637	485	950	40

A20F: Citizen lobbies (Common Cause, Public Citizen, etc.)?

1. Definitely not	10.6	13.5	7.8	10.5	10.2	12.3	10.2	10.2	9.6	9.1	12.8	10.6	11.2	9.2	11.0	15.5
2. Probably not	25.1	25.3	24.9	26.8	17.0	23.2	28.1	23.6	25.9	25.9	24.4	25.8	22.0	25.2	26.8	27.0
3. Don't know	46.2	42.7	49.7	46.5	47.8	45.9	45.0	46.7	47.8	46.9	44.9	45.7	48.5	46.7	45.1	24.9
4. Probably will	14.3	14.3	14.3	13.3	16.9	15.2	13.6	14.3	14.3	14.2	14.4	14.2	14.1	15.5	13.9	20.8
5. Definitely will	2.8	3.3	2.2	2.2	5.4	1.9	2.3	4.1	1.9	3.0	2.4	2.7	3.5	2.2	2.2	9.3
6. Already have	1.0	0.9	1.1	0.7	2.8	1.4	0.9	1.1	0.4	0.9	1.1	1.0	0.7	1.2	1.0	2.4
Item 12250 Subject H05,I02,O02 N	3280	1578	1607	2490	396	774	942	1058	505	1825	1274	1108	637	487	953	40

A20G: Charities to help fight diseases (Cancer, Heart Disease, etc.)?

1. Definitely not	1.8	2.8	0.7	1.6	2.4	1.8	1.6	1.9	1.7	1.1	2.7	1.9	1.3	1.8	1.9	-
2. Probably not	3.1	4.9	1.2	3.3	1.8	2.5	3.0	2.6	5.3	2.5	4.1	2.2	2.6	3.7	3.9	6.4
3. Don't know	12.0	14.6	9.0	11.7	11.4	10.3	13.6	10.7	14.5	10.1	13.7	10.2	13.0	12.5	12.9	13.3
4. Probably will	40.2	43.0	37.3	40.7	36.8	40.6	40.7	38.9	41.3	41.0	39.1	41.2	42.6	42.1	37.1	31.7
5. Definitely will	25.6	22.0	29.5	24.1	34.6	26.6	23.6	27.3	24.5	25.7	25.5	28.1	23.9	23.9	25.1	21.8
6. Already have	17.3	12.6	22.3	18.6	12.9	18.2	17.5	18.7	12.8	19.7	14.9	16.4	16.9	16.1	19.1	26.9
Item 12260 Subject O02 N	3282	1580	1607	2493	393	773	941	1062	506	1824	1277	1106	639	487	956	40

A20H: Organizations concerned with population problems (Planned Parenthood, ZPG, etc.)?

1. Definitely not	8.9	12.0	5.7	9.0	7.6	9.6	8.7	8.9	8.2	8.6	9.3	9.4	8.4	8.2	9.4	3.4
2. Probably not	21.5	25.5	17.7	23.8	11.8	21.0	22.8	22.5	17.7	22.6	20.7	24.5	21.8	17.1	19.6	23.6
3. Don't know	41.2	42.1	40.3	42.0	38.9	37.9	44.2	40.7	41.7	41.2	40.2	43.0	39.9	44.1	38.9	38.3
4. Probably will	19.3	15.0	23.7	17.5	26.6	22.5	16.1	18.2	22.5	19.1	19.9	17.6	22.8	19.0	19.2	21.9
5. Definitely will	7.6	4.4	10.5	6.3	13.7	6.9	7.1	8.6	7.7	7.2	8.1	4.9	6.7	9.1	10.3	7.4
6. Already have	1.5	1.0	2.1	1.4	1.5	2.1	1.1	1.2	2.2	1.2	1.7	0.6	0.4	2.4	2.6	5.4
Item 12270 Subject E01,O02 N	3285	1581	1609	2494	396	774	942	1064	505	1827	1277	1110	639	488	954	40

QUESTIONNAIRE FORM 5 1983	TOTAL	SEX		RACE		REGION				4YR COLLEGE PLANS		ILLICIT DRUG USE: LIFETIME				
		M	F	White	Black	NE	NC	S	W	Yes	No	None	Marijuana Only	Few Pills	More Pills	Any Heroin
N (Weighted No. of Cases):	3339	1608	1628	2513	404	793	950	1082	514	1846	1297	1125	646	492	970	42
% of Weighted Total:	100.0	48.2	48.8	75.3	12.1	23.8	28.5	32.4	15.4	55.3	38.8	33.7	19.3	14.7	29.0	1.2

A20I: Organizations concerned with environmental problems (Sierra Club, Friends of Earth, etc.)?

	TOTAL	M	F	White	Black	NE	NC	S	W	Yes	No	None	Mar. Only	Few Pills	More Pills	Any Heroin
1. Definitely not	9.3	11.1	7.5	9.5	8.9	10.4	8.3	9.9	8.4	7.9	11.5	8.7	10.7	7.7	10.1	12.9
2. Probably not	22.6	21.9	23.6	23.7	19.3	22.8	23.4	22.2	21.4	22.9	22.7	23.1	20.1	22.5	23.6	27.0
3. Don't know	39.4	34.5	44.6	38.3	45.1	35.1	44.3	39.2	37.7	38.4	40.7	40.8	40.0	38.4	37.5	34.9
4. Probably will	18.8	21.3	16.0	18.9	17.6	20.9	17.0	18.9	19.0	20.4	16.8	18.9	19.9	20.7	17.5	14.0
5. Definitely will	7.8	8.8	6.7	7.5	6.8	8.4	6.1	7.7	10.1	8.0	6.9	7.1	7.5	8.7	8.6	3.4
6. Already have	2.1	2.4	1.5	2.0	2.3	2.6	1.0	2.1	3.4	2.4	1.4	1.5	1.8	2.0	2.8	7.9
Item 12280 Subject F04,O02 N	3287	1584	1608	2494	399	773	942	1066	505	1830	1277	1112	639	488	956	40

Now we have a different kind of question.

A21: How satisfied are you with your life as a whole these days?

	TOTAL	M	F	White	Black	NE	NC	S	W	Yes	No	None	Mar. Only	Few Pills	More Pills	Any Heroin
1. Completely dissatisfied	1.9	1.9	2.0	1.8	1.8	1.7	1.3	1.7	3.7	1.9	2.1	2.1	1.6	1.7	1.9	4.7
2. Quite dissatisfied	6.8	7.3	6.2	6.9	7.3	6.8	6.5	6.7	7.4	7.4	5.9	7.2	5.4	6.7	7.4	-
3. Somewhat dissatisfied	9.5	10.2	8.7	9.2	11.7	9.5	11.1	8.2	9.1	8.1	11.0	7.0	9.9	9.2	12.1	15.6
4. Neither, or mixed feelings	15.1	13.7	16.8	13.9	14.8	16.0	15.6	15.5	12.1	13.5	17.1	12.1	14.0	17.3	17.2	11.5
5. Somewhat satisfied	25.8	25.7	25.6	25.8	26.2	25.6	24.8	26.4	26.6	24.3	27.6	25.1	26.6	27.7	25.4	30.9
6. Quite satisfied	34.9	34.8	35.1	36.8	31.8	35.4	34.5	35.5	33.7	38.8	30.7	38.3	36.4	32.9	31.7	25.3
7. Completely satisfied	6.0	6.4	5.6	5.7	6.4	4.9	6.2	6.0	7.4	6.0	5.7	8.2	6.0	4.5	4.3	12.0
Item 6840 Subject P01,Q01 N	3298	1590	1613	2498	391	777	945	1068	507	1833	1283	1118	641	487	961	40

A22: These questions are about whether you think women are discriminated against in each of the following areas. To what extent are women discriminated against...

A22A: In getting a college education?

	TOTAL	M	F	White	Black	NE	NC	S	W	Yes	No	None	Mar. Only	Few Pills	More Pills	Any Heroin
1. Not at all	45.2	54.0	36.9	46.3	40.2	45.5	45.1	46.5	42.0	45.0	44.6	43.8	47.1	45.8	45.4	44.2
2. Very little	32.5	26.2	39.2	35.1	27.2	32.9	33.5	30.8	33.6	36.1	29.0	32.5	32.9	34.5	32.6	20.3
3. Some	10.9	8.2	13.4	10.2	13.2	10.9	12.2	10.2	9.8	11.0	10.5	11.8	9.6	9.9	10.9	13.2
4. A good deal	2.5	2.2	2.7	1.9	3.7	2.4	2.3	2.7	2.5	1.9	3.1	2.9	2.4	1.5	2.2	4.4
5. A great deal	1.5	1.3	1.3	0.7	4.2	1.2	1.2	1.9	1.9	0.9	2.0	1.7	1.7	1.9	0.7	6.0
8. Don't know	7.4	8.1	6.5	5.8	11.6	7.1	5.7	7.9	10.3	5.0	10.7	7.3	6.4	6.5	8.1	11.9
Item 12290 Subject D06 N	3300	1592	1613	2495	398	782	943	1069	506	1835	1283	1118	638	488	964	42

A22B: In gaining positions of leadership over men and women?

	TOTAL	M	F	White	Black	NE	NC	S	W	Yes	No	None	Mar. Only	Few Pills	More Pills	Any Heroin
1. Not at all	5.6	8.5	2.3	5.5	6.5	5.9	5.1	6.4	4.1	5.2	5.8	4.9	5.6	6.9	5.3	10.6
2. Very little	12.1	16.3	8.1	12.1	9.5	11.0	10.8	12.1	16.4	11.3	13.2	11.3	13.2	12.4	12.1	20.7
3. Some	36.6	37.2	36.3	39.2	26.8	33.5	39.1	36.1	38.0	37.9	36.0	37.9	36.0	37.7	35.6	45.1
4. A good deal	26.5	22.7	30.7	27.2	26.6	29.0	26.6	25.6	24.6	27.9	25.1	26.2	26.4	26.4	27.5	9.3
5. A great deal	14.4	9.7	18.8	12.3	23.6	16.8	14.0	14.3	11.9	14.4	14.2	14.6	14.3	12.8	14.7	7.8
8. Don't know	4.7	5.5	3.8	3.7	6.9	3.8	4.4	5.4	5.0	3.3	6.8	5.1	4.4	3.8	4.8	6.5
Item 12300 Subject D06 N	3300	1592	1612	2498	396	780	945	1069	507	1837	1283	1118	640	488	963	42

A22C: In obtaining executive positions in business?

	TOTAL	M	F	White	Black	NE	NC	S	W	Yes	No	None	Mar. Only	Few Pills	More Pills	Any Heroin
1. Not at all	7.6	10.5	4.6	6.9	10.9	9.5	7.2	7.9	4.6	6.1	9.4	6.5	8.0	8.7	7.5	7.8
2. Very little	13.7	14.3	13.0	14.3	9.5	15.9	12.2	11.8	16.9	12.8	15.1	14.3	12.4	12.9	13.9	27.8
3. Some	34.5	35.2	33.5	35.8	28.3	31.9	35.8	33.3	39.0	34.5	34.5	33.3	38.6	35.1	33.6	22.2
4. A good deal	24.9	24.0	26.4	25.8	21.7	24.4	26.4	25.7	24.0	26.9	21.9	25.0	22.7	25.3	25.9	29.4
5. A great deal	13.2	9.6	16.8	11.8	19.7	14.4	13.7	13.9	8.9	14.2	11.8	13.9	13.3	11.4	13.5	7.2
8. Don't know	6.2	6.4	5.7	5.5	9.9	6.0	4.7	7.5	6.5	5.5	7.3	6.9	5.1	6.6	5.6	5.7
Item 12310 Subject D06 N	3295	1593	1608	2493	398	781	938	1070	507	1836	1279	1118	640	488	959	42

A22D: In obtaining top jobs in the professions?

	TOTAL	M	F	White	Black	NE	NC	S	W	Yes	No	None	Mar. Only	Few Pills	More Pills	Any Heroin
1. Not at all	9.0	11.6	6.3	8.3	10.9	9.6	8.2	10.0	7.5	7.7	10.0	7.9	8.1	10.6	9.4	13.1
2. Very little	18.0	18.9	17.1	19.3	11.9	21.0	18.2	15.2	18.8	17.7	18.7	17.2	17.5	22.6	16.3	30.7
3. Some	32.5	33.0	32.0	34.0	26.6	30.8	31.4	32.7	37.1	34.2	30.3	32.5	35.5	27.8	34.4	25.9
4. A good deal	22.1	21.3	23.3	23.0	19.3	20.4	25.2	21.3	20.3	24.1	19.7	23.7	18.4	22.2	22.4	21.4
5. A great deal	12.4	8.7	16.1	9.9	23.1	13.1	11.5	13.9	9.8	11.7	13.1	12.0	15.2	10.9	11.8	7.8
8. Don't know	6.0	6.4	5.3	5.5	8.3	5.2	5.4	6.9	6.5	4.6	8.1	6.7	5.4	5.9	5.8	1.2
Item 12320 Subject D06 N	3299	1591	1612	2497	397	781	943	1068	507	1835	1283	1119	640	486	963	42

QUESTIONNAIRE FORM 5 1983	TOTAL	SEX		RACE		REGION				4YR COLLEGE PLANS		ILLICIT DRUG USE: LIFETIME				
		M	F	White	Black	NE	NC	S	W	Yes	No	None	Marijuana Only	Few Pills	More Pills	Any Heroin
N (Weighted No. of Cases):	3339	1608	1628	2513	404	793	950	1082	514	1846	1297	1125	646	492	970	42
% of Weighted Total:	100.0	48.2	48.8	75.3	12.1	23.8	28.5	32.4	15.4	55.3	38.8	33.7	19.3	14.7	29.0	1.2

A22E: In getting skilled labor jobs?

1. Not at all	9.2	11.0	7.4	8.6	10.5	8.2	8.6	9.7	10.7	7.9	10.7	9.2	7.3	11.1	9.5	2.0
2. Very little	19.5	21.6	17.4	20.3	16.1	21.8	19.8	17.6	19.3	19.7	19.1	20.0	23.2	18.9	16.6	28.4
3. Some	31.8	32.0	31.6	33.5	22.1	32.2	33.1	29.8	32.6	32.1	31.9	30.4	28.7	34.4	34.0	36.8
4. A good deal	19.6	18.1	21.3	19.2	22.6	20.2	21.3	20.2	14.3	20.0	19.0	18.2	22.7	18.0	20.2	16.9
5. A great deal	9.4	7.6	10.8	8.3	16.2	8.1	8.4	11.2	9.5	9.6	8.9	9.3	9.4	9.9	8.8	13.6
8. Don't know	10.6	9.7	11.5	10.2	12.5	9.5	8.8	11.5	13.6	10.6	10.4	12.9	8.7	7.7	10.9	2.3
Item 12330 Subject D06 N	3292	1585	1612	2490	398	778	941	1068	504	1831	1280	1115	638	483	964	42

A22F: In getting elected to political office?

1. Not at all	5.3	7.5	2.9	4.9	7.3	5.6	5.1	6.0	3.9	4.4	6.1	5.2	5.3	6.3	4.6	10.6
2. Very little	11.4	14.7	8.2	12.1	7.7	10.6	11.7	11.1	12.9	11.4	11.5	12.1	11.2	11.6	10.0	14.2
3. Some	23.1	25.9	20.6	23.9	18.5	22.2	27.1	20.0	23.6	23.9	22.3	22.5	23.9	22.0	24.4	22.6
4. A good deal	26.3	25.6	27.4	27.9	21.2	27.7	26.3	24.7	27.8	27.6	25.3	26.7	25.5	26.6	26.8	20.0
5. A great deal	27.7	19.6	35.8	25.8	37.0	29.4	23.8	30.8	26.1	28.3	26.7	27.0	28.0	29.3	27.9	30.1
8. Don't know	6.1	6.8	5.0	5.3	8.3	4.5	6.0	7.4	5.7	4.4	8.2	6.5	6.1	4.2	6.3	2.5
Item 12340 Subject D06,H02 N	3299	1593	1610	2494	398	780	945	1068	507	1837	1281	1117	639	488	962	42

A22G: In getting equal pay for equal work?

1. Not at all	14.1	19.9	8.3	13.3	16.3	13.5	12.7	15.9	13.6	14.0	13.8	13.3	15.2	14.9	13.1	21.9
2. Very little	20.1	23.4	17.3	22.1	13.6	19.9	20.7	20.3	19.0	21.1	18.8	19.4	20.4	19.7	21.6	14.2
3. Some	24.6	24.7	24.3	25.6	20.1	27.9	23.6	23.7	23.5	25.3	23.2	25.2	25.4	23.9	24.3	24.7
4. A good deal	18.0	15.3	20.8	18.7	17.0	17.9	18.7	16.1	20.4	18.3	18.0	19.0	17.0	20.4	16.8	4.4
5. A great deal	18.1	11.1	24.8	16.0	25.4	17.6	19.2	17.8	17.3	17.2	19.7	17.8	18.4	17.3	17.6	30.2
8. Don't know	5.2	5.6	4.6	4.4	7.5	3.1	5.2	6.2	6.3	4.1	6.5	5.4	3.6	3.8	6.7	4.6
Item 12350 Subject D06 N	3298	1592	1611	2494	398	778	945	1068	507	1835	1282	1116	640	488	962	42

A23: The next questions ask for your opinions on the effects of using certain drugs and other substances. First, how much do you think people risk harming themselves (physically or in other ways), if they...

A23A: Smoke one or more packs of cigarettes per day

1. No risk	1.6	1.9	1.2	0.7	3.4	1.8	1.6	1.7	1.1	1.0	2.2	2.1	1.4	0.7	1.3	2.3
2. Slight risk	7.0	8.0	6.1	6.6	4.9	7.5	8.3	6.7	4.8	4.7	10.6	6.4	4.8	8.3	8.2	19.2
3. Moderate risk	28.8	28.7	28.5	30.3	24.9	29.6	31.1	28.7	23.3	26.3	32.0	25.2	24.7	33.7	33.7	35.6
4. Great risk	61.2	59.5	63.4	61.4	63.3	61.0	58.0	60.6	68.7	66.8	53.5	64.5	67.7	55.8	56.3	37.9
5. Can't say, drug unfamiliar	1.4	1.9	0.8	1.0	3.5	0.2	1.0	2.3	2.1	1.2	1.8	1.8	1.4	1.6	0.5	5.0
Item 12360 Subject A14a N	3305	1594	1614	2494	399	782	943	1072	508	1836	1286	1122	639	487	963	42

A23B: Try marijuana (pot, grass) once or twice

1. No risk	38.2	40.7	35.9	38.8	33.2	45.4	40.9	29.4	40.3	37.5	38.6	14.5	46.0	39.3	59.8	51.4
2. Slight risk	34.4	32.6	36.3	36.1	30.4	32.7	36.4	34.9	31.7	35.6	33.6	36.9	36.4	39.1	28.2	22.0
3. Moderate risk	11.9	11.2	12.8	11.6	14.4	10.3	10.4	13.4	13.0	12.4	11.1	19.2	8.4	9.1	7.6	12.3
4. Great risk	12.7	12.0	13.0	11.1	17.8	9.2	10.1	17.8	12.0	12.3	12.5	23.7	7.9	10.4	3.7	8.7
5. Can't say, drug unfamiliar	2.9	3.5	2.1	2.4	4.2	2.4	2.2	3.8	2.9	2.2	4.2	5.7	1.2	2.1	0.7	5.6
Item 12370 Subject A14a N	3295	1591	1610	2491	396	778	945	1068	505	1831	1284	1116	636	487	962	42

A23C: Smoke marijuana occasionally

1. No risk	11.3	13.9	8.6	10.8	10.2	12.4	10.9	10.3	12.2	9.6	13.1	3.2	10.8	8.9	21.5	23.2
2. Slight risk	28.9	29.1	28.9	29.9	26.2	32.7	33.0	22.2	29.5	29.2	27.7	12.5	34.1	32.3	42.7	36.8
3. Moderate risk	36.5	34.3	39.1	38.0	35.4	35.1	37.8	37.5	34.1	38.5	35.1	42.8	37.2	41.4	27.3	23.4
4. Great risk	20.6	19.5	21.5	18.9	24.4	17.5	16.1	26.1	22.2	20.7	20.1	36.3	16.3	15.8	7.6	11.0
5. Can't say, drug unfamiliar	2.7	3.3	1.9	2.4	3.7	2.3	2.1	3.8	2.0	1.9	3.9	5.2	1.6	1.6	0.9	5.6
Item 12380 Subject A14a N	3292	1590	1607	2492	393	778	943	1067	503	1831	1279	1115	637	485	962	42

QUESTIONNAIRE FORM 5 1983	TOTAL	SEX		RACE		REGION				4YR COLLEGE PLANS		ILLICIT DRUG USE: LIFETIME				
		M	F	White	Black	NE	NC	S	W	Yes	No	None	Marijuana Only	Few Pills	More Pills	Any Heroin
N (Weighted No. of Cases):	3339	1608	1628	2513	404	793	950	1082	514	1846	1297	1125	646	492	970	42
% of Weighted Total:	100.0	48.2	48.8	75.3	12.1	23.8	28.5	32.4	15.4	55.3	38.8	33.7	19.3	14.7	29.0	1.2
A23D: Smoke marijuana regularly																
1. No risk	3.2	4.6	1.6	2.4	3.9	2.0	3.3	4.1	3.0	1.8	4.9	2.0	2.5	0.9	5.9	7.3
2. Slight risk	9.0	10.5	7.3	8.6	8.5	10.5	8.5	7.8	10.3	8.3	9.3	2.0	8.3	9.5	17.2	17.4
3. Moderate risk	22.2	23.8	20.6	22.5	21.5	24.9	24.9	17.5	22.8	21.7	23.1	9.7	24.6	21.6	35.1	32.4
4. Great risk	62.8	57.6	68.4	64.0	61.8	60.3	61.1	66.7	61.7	65.9	58.8	80.7	63.4	66.3	40.8	39.6
5. Can't say, drug unfamiliar	2.8	3.4	2.0	2.5	3.3	2.3	2.2	3.9	2.3	2.2	3.8	5.6	1.2	1.6	1.0	3.3
Item 12390 Subject A14a N	3290	1586	1609	2491	396	776	944	1068	502	1829	1280	1117	634	484	962	42
A23E: Try LSD once or twice																
1. No risk	4.0	5.1	2.9	3.3	5.2	4.6	3.3	3.5	5.2	3.9	4.1	2.5	2.5	2.7	7.0	8.9
2. Slight risk	15.2	15.3	15.4	16.0	9.5	16.4	19.5	12.3	11.7	14.9	15.9	10.8	13.3	15.3	20.6	44.5
3. Moderate risk	25.3	23.6	27.2	27.0	17.6	26.0	28.0	23.2	23.9	25.9	24.7	24.7	24.8	26.8	26.8	11.5
4. Great risk	44.7	44.7	44.8	45.0	50.0	42.4	39.0	48.8	49.9	47.0	41.3	50.9	46.0	45.9	37.1	28.7
5. Can't say, drug unfamiliar	10.8	11.3	9.7	8.7	17.6	10.6	10.2	12.3	9.3	8.4	13.9	11.1	13.4	9.4	8.5	6.4
Item 12400 Subject A14a N	3295	1591	1609	2495	397	776	943	1071	505	1832	1283	1121	636	487	960	42
A23F: Take LSD regularly																
1. No risk	1.5	1.8	1.0	0.5	4.1	1.5	0.7	2.1	1.7	1.1	1.6	2.3	0.5	0.7	1.4	6.0
2. Slight risk	0.8	1.1	0.5	0.9	0.4	1.0	1.1	0.8	0.3	0.6	1.0	*	0.5	1.0	1.7	4.9
3. Moderate risk	4.1	4.3	3.9	3.8	4.3	3.8	5.2	3.5	4.1	3.7	4.6	2.3	3.2	3.8	6.1	30.7
4. Great risk	83.2	81.7	85.5	86.7	74.3	83.8	83.4	81.4	85.6	86.8	79.2	84.9	83.5	85.2	82.1	58.4
5. Can't say, drug unfamiliar	10.3	11.1	9.1	8.0	17.9	9.9	9.6	12.2	8.4	7.8	13.6	10.5	12.3	9.3	8.7	-
Item 12410 Subject A14a N	3291	1587	1609	2495	398	778	940	1071	503	1831	1279	1118	637	484	960	42
A23G: Try heroin (smack, horse) once or twice																
1. No risk	2.3	2.9	1.7	1.5	4.6	2.9	1.7	2.5	2.0	2.2	2.4	1.8	2.0	2.0	3.2	4.4
2. Slight risk	10.3	9.3	11.2	10.4	8.2	12.0	12.8	8.8	6.1	10.3	10.1	10.5	9.2	11.5	9.7	21.1
3. Moderate risk	24.2	21.7	27.5	26.1	19.3	25.9	26.3	21.7	23.0	24.8	24.2	24.4	23.1	24.5	24.8	28.0
4. Great risk	50.8	53.6	48.1	51.7	49.4	47.2	47.3	53.2	57.9	52.4	48.5	50.8	51.6	50.7	51.1	42.5
5. Can't say, drug unfamiliar	12.4	12.6	11.4	10.3	18.5	11.9	11.8	13.7	11.0	10.3	14.7	12.5	14.1	11.4	11.1	4.0
Item 12420 Subject A14a N	3295	1591	1608	2494	396	777	944	1069	505	1833	1281	1120	636	486	961	42
A23H: Take heroin occasionally																
1. No risk	1.3	1.5	0.9	0.4	3.7	1.1	0.9	2.0	0.9	1.0	1.6	1.6	0.6	1.0	1.1	11.8
2. Slight risk	1.7	1.9	1.4	1.5	0.7	2.2	2.5	0.9	1.1	1.4	1.8	0.9	1.7	1.1	2.7	1.7
3. Moderate risk	14.0	11.6	16.5	14.0	16.1	15.4	14.5	14.2	10.2	13.7	14.6	14.9	12.7	16.5	11.9	31.7
4. Great risk	71.8	73.1	71.0	74.7	62.3	71.2	71.4	69.8	77.5	74.4	68.8	72.0	71.9	69.9	73.7	54.7
5. Can't say, drug unfamiliar	11.3	11.8	10.3	9.4	17.2	10.1	10.7	13.1	10.3	9.6	13.3	10.6	13.1	11.5	10.5	-
Item 12430 Subject A14a N	3294	1588	1610	2493	397	778	942	1071	504	1833	1279	1118	637	484	963	42
A23I: Take heroin regularly																
1. No risk	1.1	1.4	0.8	0.3	3.3	1.0	0.4	1.9	1.0	0.8	1.4	1.6	0.5	0.5	1.0	6.5
2. Slight risk	0.4	0.2	0.5	0.2	1.3	0.7	0.3	0.6	-	0.3	0.5	0.6	0.2	0.6	0.1	6.8
3. Moderate risk	1.6	1.5	1.7	0.9	2.2	1.7	2.1	1.6	0.4	1.6	1.7	1.1	2.1	1.0	2.1	1.2
4. Great risk	86.1	85.4	87.3	89.6	76.3	87.2	86.6	83.7	88.2	88.2	83.6	86.3	85.2	87.0	86.7	85.6
5. Can't say, drug unfamiliar	10.8	11.5	9.7	8.9	16.9	9.4	10.6	12.3	10.4	9.1	12.8	10.3	12.0	10.8	10.1	-
Item 12440 Subject A14a N	3277	1583	1598	2484	390	779	938	1060	500	1827	1271	1109	634	486	957	42
A23J: Try barbiturates (downers, goofballs, reds, yellows, etc.) once or twice																
1. No risk	9.5	11.4	7.8	10.1	4.1	10.1	11.4	7.5	9.4	8.7	10.2	3.5	4.6	7.9	20.4	20.5
2. Slight risk	24.6	24.5	24.4	26.8	14.7	24.7	29.2	21.6	22.2	23.0	26.6	17.9	23.1	26.9	32.0	34.2
3. Moderate risk	28.4	26.3	31.3	30.0	24.5	31.0	28.1	26.0	29.9	31.1	25.7	28.6	28.3	32.8	27.2	21.9
4. Great risk	27.0	27.5	25.9	25.4	34.3	23.9	23.1	32.1	28.2	27.8	25.6	37.7	30.5	23.1	13.9	17.8
5. Can't say, drug unfamiliar	10.5	10.2	10.6	7.7	22.4	10.4	8.2	12.8	10.2	9.5	12.0	12.3	13.6	9.3	6.5	5.6
Item 12450 Subject A14a N	3297	1590	1612	2495	397	779	944	1071	505	1834	1282	1120	637	487	962	42

*=less than .05 per cent.

QUESTIONNAIRE FORM 5 1983	TOTAL	SEX		RACE		REGION				4YR COLLEGE PLANS		ILLICIT DRUG USE: LIFETIME				
		M	F	White	Black	NE	NC	S	W	Yes	No	None	Mari- juana Only	Few Pills	More Pills	Any Her- oin
N (Weighted No. of Cases):	3339	1608	1628	2513	404	793	950	1082	514	1846	1297	1125	646	492	970	42
% of Weighted Total:	100.0	48.2	48.8	75.3	12.1	23.8	28.5	32.4	15.4	55.3	38.8	33.7	19.3	14.7	29.0	1.2
A23K: Take barbiturates regularly																
1. No risk	1.4	1.8	1.0	0.6	3.0	1.6	0.6	2.2	1.1	1.0	1.8	2.0	0.5	1.0	1.5	2.3
2. Slight risk	4.3	5.1	3.5	4.5	2.6	3.9	5.5	3.7	3.9	3.0	5.6	1.1	1.1	3.7	9.6	24.2
3. Moderate risk	16.3	18.7	13.7	17.5	8.2	16.6	19.8	13.6	15.3	13.2	20.5	8.1	13.3	17.2	27.5	22.0
4. Great risk	67.7	63.8	72.2	69.8	64.5	67.6	65.9	68.3	69.9	73.6	60.4	76.6	72.1	68.9	55.2	46.1
5. Can't say, drug unfamiliar	10.3	10.6	9.6	7.6	21.7	10.3	8.2	12.3	9.7	9.1	11.8	12.1	13.0	9.2	6.3	5.4
Item 12460 Subject A14a N	3295	1590	1610	2494	396	778	943	1070	505	1833	1281	1120	637	486	959	42
A23L: Try amphetamines (uppers, pep pills, bennies, speed) once or twice																
1. No risk	14.4	16.6	12.3	15.7	5.9	16.5	15.7	11.3	15.1	13.0	15.7	4.6	5.8	11.9	32.0	36.1
2. Slight risk	26.3	26.7	25.9	28.4	16.7	23.8	32.1	23.8	24.6	25.3	28.5	16.8	27.8	30.4	35.0	29.0
3. Moderate risk	26.9	23.9	30.2	27.2	29.0	29.9	24.6	27.1	26.2	28.4	24.4	32.4	30.4	31.4	19.7	19.0
4. Great risk	24.7	25.0	24.2	23.0	32.4	22.8	21.5	28.4	25.7	26.3	22.5	35.8	30.4	19.5	10.6	10.0
5. Can't say, drug unfamiliar	7.8	7.8	7.3	5.7	16.0	7.1	6.1	9.4	8.3	6.9	8.9	10.4	10.5	6.8	2.6	5.9
Item 12470 Subject A14a N	3293	1589	1609	2492	398	777	941	1070	504	1835	1276	1120	637	484	959	42
A23M: Take amphetamines regularly																
1. No risk	2.0	2.3	1.6	1.4	3.3	2.1	1.4	3.0	1.1	1.2	2.8	2.4	0.5	1.0	3.1	0.9
2. Slight risk	7.3	8.7	5.9	7.7	3.8	7.0	9.0	6.0	7.4	5.5	9.3	0.9	2.3	6.8	17.2	34.3
3. Moderate risk	17.8	21.4	14.0	18.9	10.1	18.0	20.7	15.4	17.0	15.1	21.9	8.8	15.7	18.1	29.5	17.6
4. Great risk	64.8	59.2	71.0	66.1	64.9	65.1	62.5	65.7	66.4	70.9	56.8	77.9	70.3	66.2	46.8	41.6
5. Can't say, drug unfamiliar	8.1	8.5	7.6	5.9	18.0	7.7	6.4	10.0	8.1	7.3	9.2	10.0	11.3	7.8	3.4	5.6
Item 12480 Subject A14a N	3292	1587	1610	2493	396	779	941	1068	505	1832	1279	1115	637	486	963	42
A23N: Try cocaine once or twice																
1. No risk	12.6	15.7	9.8	12.6	9.5	15.1	11.8	8.5	19.2	12.5	12.1	2.9	4.8	10.4	29.5	35.3
2. Slight risk	22.3	22.7	21.9	23.0	18.3	27.8	22.3	18.6	21.9	20.4	24.3	14.2	22.1	21.7	31.6	41.7
3. Moderate risk	25.0	21.5	28.6	25.4	26.6	24.9	26.2	25.1	22.3	26.6	23.7	28.8	26.2	29.8	18.5	8.8
4. Great risk	33.0	32.6	33.4	32.9	34.7	27.0	33.1	38.8	29.6	34.9	30.8	45.8	37.8	31.8	16.2	8.8
5. Can't say, drug unfamiliar	7.1	7.5	6.3	6.0	10.8	5.1	6.6	8.9	7.0	5.6	9.1	8.2	9.1	6.2	4.2	5.4
Item 12490 Subject A14a N	3287	1589	1603	2490	394	774	944	1066	504	1830	1277	1116	636	487	958	42
A23O: Take cocaine regularly																
1. No risk	2.2	2.9	1.3	1.5	3.9	2.0	1.2	2.7	3.1	1.5	2.8	2.1	0.5	1.5	3.4	4.0
2. Slight risk	4.2	5.2	3.2	3.9	3.9	5.1	3.6	3.5	5.5	4.3	4.1	0.3	0.8	1.9	11.3	29.3
3. Moderate risk	12.4	15.0	10.1	12.6	10.1	14.4	14.1	8.5	14.3	10.8	14.1	4.8	8.8	11.3	23.6	27.4
4. Great risk	74.3	69.3	79.4	76.2	71.9	73.3	74.9	76.1	70.6	78.0	70.1	84.6	81.3	78.9	57.5	36.1
5. Can't say, drug unfamiliar	7.0	7.6	6.0	5.8	10.9	5.3	6.2	9.2	6.4	5.4	9.0	8.2	8.7	6.4	4.3	3.3
Item 12500 Subject A14a N	3284	1584	1606	2489	393	778	941	1063	503	1829	1275	1116	636	485	959	42
A23P: Try one or two drinks of an alcoholic beverage (beer, wine, liquor)																
1. No risk	55.6	60.3	51.8	58.9	40.8	62.5	59.9	48.4	52.2	55.8	55.3	38.8	59.0	59.1	71.7	68.5
2. Slight risk	32.5	29.1	35.8	32.0	37.2	27.2	32.0	37.1	31.6	33.0	32.9	41.6	31.8	32.2	22.6	20.0
3. Moderate risk	6.7	4.8	8.2	5.2	11.9	6.0	4.6	7.6	9.5	6.4	6.3	9.8	6.2	5.6	3.9	2.6
4. Great risk	4.2	4.5	3.6	3.0	7.7	3.3	2.9	5.3	5.2	4.0	4.1	7.7	2.4	2.7	1.4	3.3
5. Can't say, drug unfamiliar	1.1	1.3	0.6	0.8	2.5	0.9	0.6	1.5	1.5	0.8	1.4	2.1	0.6	0.5	0.3	5.6
Item 12510 Subject A14a N	3290	1585	1610	2493	397	776	942	1070	501	1833	1278	1119	635	485	961	42
A23Q: Take one or two drinks nearly every day																
1. No risk	9.4	12.4	6.2	9.4	8.1	10.1	9.4	10.1	7.0	7.8	11.8	6.0	8.7	5.8	15.3	20.5
2. Slight risk	27.8	31.3	24.8	29.1	20.6	29.3	32.1	24.4	24.7	25.5	30.4	24.9	28.9	31.3	29.6	17.1
3. Moderate risk	40.1	37.3	42.9	40.2	42.1	39.4	38.8	42.0	39.5	42.6	37.7	41.0	42.5	42.0	35.8	52.5
4. Great risk	21.6	17.8	25.3	20.6	26.3	20.7	19.0	21.7	27.3	23.3	18.7	26.2	19.0	20.1	19.1	4.3
5. Can't say, drug unfamiliar	1.1	1.3	0.7	0.7	2.8	0.4	0.8	1.7	1.5	0.8	1.5	1.8	1.0	0.7	0.3	5.6
Item 12520 Subject A14a N	3287	1590	1604	2490	396	776	940	1070	501	1832	1278	1117	636	487	960	42

QUESTIONNAIRE FORM 5 1983	TOTAL	SEX		RACE		REGION				4YR COLLEGE PLANS		ILLICIT DRUG USE: LIFETIME				
		M	F	White	Black	NE	NC	S	W	Yes	No	None	Mari-juana Only	Few Pills	More Pills	Any Heroin
N (Weighted No. of Cases):	3339	1608	1628	2513	404	793	950	1082	514	1846	1297	1125	646	492	970	42
% of Weighted Total:	100.0	48.2	48.8	75.3	12.1	23.8	28.5	32.4	15.4	55.3	38.8	33.7	19.3	14.7	29.0	1.2

A23R: Take four or five drinks nearly every day

1. No risk	2.6	3.6	1.5	1.9	4.7	2.5	1.3	4.0	2.4	1.6	4.0	2.7	2.1	1.7	2.9	9.4
2. Slight risk	6.6	8.8	4.3	6.9	3.9	6.1	8.8	6.4	3.7	5.3	8.3	3.7	4.9	6.4	10.9	12.9
3. Moderate risk	22.8	26.7	19.0	23.9	16.8	26.0	25.5	20.4	18.1	20.0	26.3	21.1	20.9	25.5	25.1	16.9
4. Great risk	66.8	59.6	74.5	66.6	71.8	65.0	63.7	67.3	74.3	72.1	60.0	70.8	70.8	65.9	60.8	55.2
5. Can't say, drug unfamiliar	1.1	1.4	0.8	0.8	2.8	0.5	0.6	1.8	1.5	1.0	1.4	1.7	1.3	0.4	0.3	5.6
Item 12530 Subject A14a N	3290	1587	1610	2495	393	779	942	1065	505	1830	1281	1117	637	486	962	42

A23S: Have five or more drinks once or twice each weekend

1. No risk	10.4	14.3	6.1	9.9	9.2	12.4	11.1	9.6	7.3	8.8	12.0	4.7	10.6	9.4	16.3	28.0
2. Slight risk	17.5	20.5	14.5	19.3	9.3	19.2	19.8	15.1	15.5	17.8	17.2	11.5	18.0	20.8	22.5	21.3
3. Moderate risk	32.1	31.5	33.0	33.7	22.4	34.5	33.8	29.6	30.5	32.3	31.3	29.6	33.8	33.1	33.9	34.1
4. Great risk	38.6	32.0	45.5	36.0	56.1	32.4	34.4	43.9	44.9	39.9	37.8	51.9	36.4	35.8	26.6	11.0
5. Can't say, drug unfamiliar	1.4	1.7	0.9	1.1	3.0	1.5	0.8	1.8	1.7	1.2	1.7	2.3	1.2	0.8	0.7	5.6
Item 12540 Subject A14a N	3296	1590	1612	2496	397	779	942	1070	505	1834	1282	1120	637	487	962	42

This section asks for your views and feelings about a number of different things.

D01: Do you agree or disagree with each of the following?

D01A: I take a positive attitude toward myself

1. Disagree	1.4	0.9	1.8	1.2	2.8	2.0	0.6	1.5	1.6	1.5	1.2	1.4	1.9	0.7	1.1	-
2. Mostly disagree	6.3	4.0	8.3	6.3	5.4	6.6	7.4	5.1	6.3	5.9	7.1	6.0	5.1	6.8	6.9	3.0
3. Neither	6.7	6.3	7.2	7.2	3.3	6.7	7.9	5.5	6.6	5.7	7.8	4.8	5.2	7.2	9.4	6.6
4. Mostly agree	48.6	49.0	48.4	51.1	27.8	47.7	48.8	47.6	51.3	47.3	50.2	46.9	48.7	48.7	50.9	54.8
5. Agree	37.1	39.9	34.2	34.1	60.7	36.9	35.4	40.2	34.1	39.7	33.7	40.9	39.1	36.6	31.7	35.5
Item 12550 Subject Q01 N	3158	1519	1577	2435	365	728	912	1027	491	1811	1255	1084	600	468	929	39

D01B: Good luck is more important than hard work for success

1. Disagree	37.8	33.6	41.7	37.6	44.0	36.4	38.3	39.0	36.4	38.7	37.0	41.4	37.3	35.8	35.6	30.7
2. Mostly disagree	37.4	37.6	37.6	39.2	27.0	39.4	38.0	33.8	40.7	38.4	35.7	35.3	40.8	37.7	38.4	26.9
3. Neither	15.5	17.4	13.3	15.7	11.8	15.6	15.2	15.6	15.5	15.4	15.5	14.2	14.0	14.9	18.0	21.6
4. Mostly agree	6.3	7.2	5.3	5.6	8.2	6.1	5.2	8.2	4.6	5.3	7.7	6.1	5.7	8.9	5.2	8.6
5. Agree	3.1	4.1	2.0	1.9	9.0	2.5	3.2	3.4	2.7	2.3	4.1	2.9	2.2	2.7	2.8	12.2
Item 12560 Subject Q02 N	3156	1516	1575	2432	364	725	912	1027	491	1810	1256	1081	599	470	927	39

D01C: I feel I am a person of worth, on an equal plane with others

1. Disagree	1.0	1.1	0.8	0.8	1.8	1.5	0.9	0.9	0.7	0.8	1.3	1.1	0.8	0.9	1.0	1.7
2. Mostly disagree	4.0	3.5	4.3	3.8	3.9	5.2	4.8	2.5	3.7	3.5	4.6	3.8	2.7	3.8	5.1	-
3. Neither	9.4	9.3	9.4	9.9	6.2	8.4	9.9	8.9	11.1	8.0	11.2	7.7	8.9	8.5	11.1	26.9
4. Mostly agree	39.1	39.0	39.5	40.6	27.9	38.5	40.8	37.2	40.9	36.8	42.2	36.7	40.8	39.3	41.7	30.0
5. Agree	46.5	47.1	45.9	44.9	60.2	46.5	43.7	50.5	43.6	51.0	40.7	50.7	46.8	47.6	41.2	41.3
Item 12570 Subject Q01 N	3142	1513	1565	2424	361	725	907	1021	489	1809	1244	1077	597	466	922	39

D01D: I am able to do things as well as most other people

1. Disagree	0.9	0.7	1.0	0.6	1.4	1.2	0.8	0.8	0.7	0.7	1.0	1.0	0.8	1.0	0.7	-
2. Mostly disagree	1.7	1.5	1.9	1.6	1.1	2.1	1.3	1.7	2.1	1.2	2.6	1.8	1.2	1.5	2.1	2.5
3. Neither	5.5	5.5	5.2	5.9	3.9	5.4	6.1	4.6	6.1	4.6	6.7	4.6	4.2	5.6	7.1	5.8
4. Mostly agree	44.5	40.8	48.0	46.2	29.9	43.8	45.8	44.3	43.5	42.1	47.5	41.8	42.8	45.5	48.2	46.0
5. Agree	47.4	51.5	43.9	45.7	63.7	47.5	46.0	48.6	47.5	51.4	42.1	50.8	50.9	46.3	41.8	45.7
Item 12580 Subject Q01 N	3137	1509	1566	2424	358	725	904	1019	490	1806	1243	1072	597	465	925	39

QUESTIONNAIRE FORM 5 1983	TOTAL	SEX		RACE		REGION				4YR COLLEGE PLANS		ILLICIT DRUG USE: LIFETIME				
		M	F	White	Black	NE	NC	S	W	Yes	No	None	Mari- juana Only	Few Pills	More Pills	Any Her- oin
N (Weighted No. of Cases):	3339	1608	1628	2513	404	793	950	1082	514	1846	1297	1125	646	492	970	42
% of Weighted Total:	100.0	48.2	48.8	75.3	12.1	23.8	28.5	32.4	15.4	55.3	38.8	33.7	19.3	14.7	29.0	1.2

D01E: Every time I try to get ahead, something or somebody stops me

1. Disagree	17.6	15.5	19.5	16.8	24.3	17.5	14.7	18.8	20.4	20.5	13.8	19.2	20.6	18.3	13.6	17.1
2. Mostly disagree	32.7	31.6	34.0	35.2	24.5	36.2	32.5	28.8	35.7	36.7	26.9	34.1	35.4	32.1	30.9	15.8
3. Neither	25.2	26.2	24.3	26.0	17.9	23.1	27.8	24.7	24.5	23.3	27.7	25.2	22.8	23.3	27.7	28.7
4. Mostly agree	17.4	18.6	15.9	16.4	19.8	17.1	18.0	18.5	14.3	14.2	21.7	14.0	15.6	19.6	20.7	22.5
5. Agree	7.2	8.0	6.3	5.6	13.6	6.1	6.9	9.2	5.0	5.3	9.8	7.5	5.6	6.7	7.1	15.9
Item 12590 Subject Q02 N	3140	1511	1566	2420	361	724	908	1020	488	1808	1243	1078	595	466	923	39

D01F: Planning only makes a person unhappy since plans hardly ever work out anyway

1. Disagree	30.1	27.8	32.3	30.5	35.0	27.1	30.1	30.4	34.1	33.5	25.4	35.2	31.5	28.0	25.5	23.4
2. Mostly disagree	33.2	32.8	34.1	35.1	24.4	32.0	34.2	33.1	33.5	36.1	29.2	32.7	33.5	36.5	33.3	9.5
3. Neither	16.1	17.1	14.9	16.1	13.0	18.0	16.1	14.9	15.5	15.2	17.1	15.3	14.2	14.6	18.3	23.0
4. Mostly agree	14.3	15.0	13.4	13.6	13.9	15.8	14.9	14.4	10.8	10.9	19.3	11.7	13.7	15.2	16.5	27.8
5. Agree	6.3	7.3	5.4	4.6	13.8	7.1	4.7	7.2	6.1	4.4	9.0	5.0	7.1	5.7	6.3	16.2
Item 12600 Subject Q02 N	3142	1509	1570	2424	360	726	908	1019	488	1806	1248	1077	597	467	924	39

D01G: People who accept their condition in life are happier than those who try to change things

1. Disagree	19.3	18.8	19.8	19.1	25.0	19.4	17.2	20.5	20.6	23.2	14.0	19.4	21.2	19.6	18.4	9.5
2. Mostly disagree	23.6	25.7	22.0	24.9	19.0	23.9	26.9	20.4	24.0	26.5	18.8	25.0	22.1	21.8	24.7	17.0
3. Neither	21.2	21.5	20.7	21.6	15.7	20.6	21.9	18.6	26.1	20.4	22.1	20.8	21.0	18.3	22.9	27.3
4. Mostly agree	22.2	21.0	23.4	22.8	18.1	23.8	21.5	23.8	17.8	19.0	27.2	21.2	19.9	25.9	22.5	31.8
5. Agree	13.6	13.1	14.1	11.6	22.1	12.3	12.5	16.7	11.5	10.9	17.8	13.6	15.8	14.5	11.4	14.5
Item 12610 Subject Q02 N	3138	1505	1571	2422	359	725	906	1018	489	1805	1245	1077	595	465	924	39

D01H: On the whole, I'm satisfied with myself

1. Disagree	2.7	2.5	3.0	2.3	5.7	3.7	2.0	2.4	2.8	2.5	2.9	2.3	3.6	1.3	3.3	1.2
2. Mostly disagree	6.6	6.2	6.9	6.5	6.8	5.8	7.4	5.8	7.9	6.3	7.0	4.9	4.9	7.5	8.9	8.0
3. Neither	8.7	9.1	8.2	9.0	5.8	7.3	11.4	7.4	8.5	7.3	10.4	7.3	6.4	7.2	12.0	6.6
4. Mostly agree	41.9	40.6	43.3	43.2	31.8	41.6	42.4	40.7	43.6	42.6	40.9	38.8	46.0	43.5	42.6	45.1
5. Agree	40.1	41.6	38.6	39.1	50.0	41.6	36.7	43.6	37.3	41.3	38.7	46.8	39.1	40.5	33.2	39.1
Item 12620 Subject P01,Q01 N	3132	1503	1566	2422	358	722	906	1017	487	1806	1238	1076	593	464	922	39

D01I: People like me don't have much of a chance to be successful in life

1. Disagree	58.2	55.5	60.6	58.3	65.7	58.3	55.6	59.0	61.0	63.4	50.9	62.2	60.2	55.1	54.9	37.2
2. Mostly disagree	26.4	27.2	26.0	27.8	16.6	25.5	30.4	25.5	22.4	25.8	27.5	23.5	26.9	28.2	29.6	14.9
3. Neither	9.0	9.8	8.1	8.6	7.6	9.0	8.4	7.9	12.5	6.6	12.1	8.2	6.7	9.7	9.4	31.7
4. Mostly agree	4.4	5.2	3.5	3.9	6.0	4.8	4.2	4.8	3.2	3.0	6.2	3.9	3.8	5.7	4.5	8.5
5. Agree	2.1	2.3	1.8	1.3	4.1	2.4	1.4	2.9	1.0	1.2	3.3	2.2	2.4	1.3	1.6	7.7
Item 12630 Subject Q02 N	3132	1501	1569	2421	358	722	906	1019	485	1801	1244	1073	594	466	922	39

D01J: When I make plans, I am almost certain that I can make them work

1. Disagree	2.3	1.8	2.7	1.9	3.7	2.5	2.4	2.4	1.3	1.5	3.5	2.1	2.9	1.6	2.6	-
2. Mostly disagree	5.2	4.4	6.0	4.9	4.4	5.0	3.8	5.9	6.6	4.0	6.7	4.3	4.9	1.6	4.0	11.3
3. Neither	15.7	16.8	14.5	16.3	13.1	15.7	17.6	12.9	18.1	14.3	17.5	15.4	13.2	15.9	17.1	15.8
4. Mostly agree	48.3	48.1	49.0	50.4	34.0	50.1	49.8	46.9	45.8	50.1	46.5	48.1	47.1	53.5	47.8	38.5
5. Agree	28.6	28.9	27.9	26.4	44.8	26.7	26.5	32.0	28.2	30.1	25.8	30.1	32.0	24.3	26.0	34.5
Item 12640 Subject Q02 N	3136	1506	1567	2419	359	724	907	1016	489	1807	1241	1076	596	465	921	39

D01K: A lot of times I feel lonely

1. Disagree	15.8	16.8	14.7	14.6	25.3	19.5	12.9	16.1	15.3	16.3	15.3	16.6	18.2	12.9	14.7	23.4
2. Mostly disagree	29.6	28.4	30.6	32.4	17.4	26.6	32.5	26.1	35.3	32.3	25.1	30.7	30.2	31.5	27.0	33.3
3. Neither	18.1	21.6	14.7	19.4	11.6	17.0	20.9	16.6	17.8	17.3	19.4	15.6	18.2	17.4	21.6	12.8
4. Mostly agree	23.8	21.9	25.6	23.2	22.7	24.2	21.9	26.4	21.0	22.4	25.6	24.1	20.3	26.8	24.3	18.1
5. Agree	12.8	11.3	14.4	10.4	23.0	12.7	11.8	14.8	10.6	11.7	14.6	13.1	13.1	11.5	12.4	12.4
Item 12650 Subject Q03 N	3115	1493	1562	2404	352	713	900	1009	493	1784	1231	1070	599	460	911	36

QUESTIONNAIRE FORM 5 1983	TOTAL	SEX		RACE		REGION				4YR COLLEGE PLANS		ILLICIT DRUG USE: LIFETIME				
		M	F	White	Black	NE	NC	S	W	Yes	No	None	Mari-juana Only	Few Pills	More Pills	Any Her-oin
N (Weighted No. of Cases):	3339	1608	1628	2513	404	793	950	1082	514	1846	1297	1125	646	492	970	42
% of Weighted Total:	100.0	48.2	48.8	75.3	12.1	23.8	28.5	32.4	15.4	55.3	38.8	33.7	19.3	14.7	29.0	1.2
D01L: I feel I do not have much to be proud of																
1. Disagree	44.9	42.9	46.3	44.6	55.2	46.9	39.7	49.2	42.8	49.3	38.8	50.1	45.4	42.8	39.8	41.8
2. Mostly disagree	31.7	33.0	30.8	34.4	18.3	31.2	34.8	28.5	32.9	31.7	31.7	29.5	31.0	34.6	34.6	22.7
3. Neither	9.6	9.9	9.5	9.5	9.2	8.4	11.7	8.5	9.9	7.7	12.2	8.3	10.5	8.4	11.1	14.6
4. Mostly agree	10.1	11.2	9.0	8.7	11.9	9.4	10.0	10.6	10.1	8.3	12.5	9.0	8.7	11.8	10.0	18.6
5. Agree	3.7	3.0	4.5	2.9	5.4	4.0	3.8	3.2	4.3	2.9	4.7	3.1	4.4	2.5	4.5	2.4
Item 12660 Subject Q01 N	3104	1486	1557	2396	350	708	900	1004	491	1778	1228	1066	599	458	906	36
D01M: There is always someone I can turn to if I need help																
1. Disagree	3.0	3.3	2.7	2.4	4.0	3.2	2.4	3.1	3.8	3.1	2.9	2.9	2.4	2.7	2.9	10.5
2. Mostly disagree	5.2	6.2	4.2	5.1	5.0	5.3	5.5	4.8	5.5	5.2	5.5	4.8	5.0	5.2	6.0	5.4
3. Neither	6.5	9.0	4.1	6.4	4.6	7.2	6.7	5.2	7.9	7.1	5.6	6.9	5.4	6.7	6.4	13.4
4. Mostly agree	28.7	32.1	26.1	29.7	21.2	27.7	32.4	26.8	27.7	27.7	30.6	25.4	30.4	28.1	32.3	25.6
5. Agree	56.5	49.4	62.9	56.5	65.3	56.6	53.0	60.2	55.1	56.9	55.4	60.0	56.8	57.3	52.4	45.2
Item 12670 Subject Q03 N	3088	1480	1548	2390	347	707	892	1000	489	1767	1223	1060	593	455	906	36
D01N: Sometimes I think that I am no good at all																
1. Disagree	32.6	35.0	30.0	30.1	52.8	35.4	25.6	37.9	30.9	34.5	29.6	36.2	34.1	31.4	28.9	22.7
2. Mostly disagree	25.9	27.2	24.9	27.8	16.9	24.8	27.3	23.8	29.5	27.1	24.8	26.2	26.5	27.5	24.5	34.8
3. Neither	16.5	16.7	16.3	17.4	9.7	16.3	19.6	13.7	17.0	15.8	17.0	15.2	14.2	17.3	19.4	13.4
4. Mostly agree	15.4	13.5	17.5	15.9	11.1	14.6	18.2	14.4	13.7	14.7	16.5	13.7	14.0	15.7	18.0	18.6
5. Agree	9.4	7.6	11.3	8.8	9.5	8.9	9.3	10.2	8.9	7.9	12.0	8.7	11.1	8.1	9.2	10.5
Item 12680 Subject Q01 N	3091	1479	1552	2392	346	705	896	999	491	1771	1222	1061	595	459	904	36
D01O: I often feel left out of things																
1. Disagree	20.4	21.5	19.0	18.4	31.9	23.8	14.7	21.5	23.7	20.7	19.6	20.3	22.8	18.9	19.6	15.5
2. Mostly disagree	27.5	27.1	28.4	29.9	16.9	27.1	29.1	26.3	27.4	28.5	25.9	27.3	26.0	30.0	28.2	22.7
3. Neither	18.4	20.3	16.6	19.1	14.7	16.6	21.6	16.6	19.0	18.9	18.0	18.1	16.9	15.8	21.4	26.8
4. Mostly agree	23.1	21.4	24.6	23.7	20.2	22.1	24.4	23.8	20.8	22.8	23.7	22.9	23.6	24.4	22.0	25.6
5. Agree	10.6	9.7	11.5	9.0	16.4	10.4	10.2	11.7	9.2	9.1	12.8	11.4	10.7	11.0	8.8	9.4
Item 12690 Subject Q03 N	3083	1479	1543	2384	346	704	892	998	489	1766	1219	1059	596	455	901	34
D01P: I believe a person is master of his/her own fate																
1. Disagree	4.1	3.4	4.9	3.7	5.7	3.7	3.7	5.1	3.5	4.6	3.3	4.8	3.2	4.1	3.6	5.2
2. Mostly disagree	5.6	4.6	6.6	5.5	5.5	5.3	4.5	7.6	3.5	4.9	6.4	4.8	6.3	5.2	5.7	15.3
3. Neither	18.5	16.8	20.1	19.0	14.2	21.2	18.1	15.5	21.7	18.3	18.7	18.7	17.1	18.9	19.7	11.1
4. Mostly agree	35.9	36.0	36.1	38.6	22.7	36.6	39.4	33.5	33.7	36.8	35.1	35.5	36.5	35.3	37.2	25.3
5. Agree	35.9	39.4	32.3	33.2	51.9	33.3	34.3	38.3	37.7	35.4	36.5	36.2	36.9	36.5	33.8	43.0
Item 12700 Subject Q02 N	3079	1475	1546	2382	348	699	896	997	488	1765	1218	1063	592	452	900	36
D01Q: There is usually someone I can talk to, if I need to																
1. Disagree	2.1	2.5	1.6	1.6	2.9	1.7	1.6	2.3	3.5	2.2	2.0	1.5	1.4	2.6	2.6	6.7
2. Mostly disagree	4.6	5.5	3.9	4.5	3.7	4.0	4.8	4.5	5.0	5.1	3.7	4.1	4.5	4.4	5.5	3.3
3. Neither	5.5	7.7	3.1	5.3	5.0	4.7	6.0	5.0	6.5	5.3	5.8	5.3	4.8	4.2	6.4	7.8
4. Mostly agree	27.4	31.9	23.5	28.0	22.0	29.1	28.8	25.5	26.4	25.4	30.5	26.1	29.3	27.8	27.7	34.5
5. Agree	60.4	52.4	67.9	60.6	66.5	60.4	58.9	62.6	58.6	62.1	57.9	63.1	60.0	61.0	57.8	47.8
Item 12710 Subject Q03 N	3075	1471	1545	2381	344	698	897	995	485	1763	1216	1059	592	453	899	36
D01R: I feel that I can't do anything right																
1. Disagree	45.6	48.2	43.3	45.1	56.0	47.4	44.6	46.1	44.0	50.4	39.4	48.9	50.4	42.0	41.4	32.6
2. Mostly disagree	29.1	27.6	30.6	31.2	18.5	30.9	29.6	28.0	27.7	29.6	27.6	29.7	26.7	28.7	30.9	27.5
3. Neither	13.1	13.2	12.8	13.4	6.1	11.0	15.3	11.3	15.6	10.9	16.6	11.1	9.5	16.1	15.7	17.2
4. Mostly agree	8.4	7.6	9.2	7.3	11.6	6.7	8.5	9.7	8.2	6.3	11.5	7.2	10.0	9.3	8.1	7.7
5. Agree	3.8	3.3	4.2	3.0	7.8	4.1	1.9	4.9	4.5	2.8	4.9	3.1	3.5	3.9	3.9	14.9
Item 12720 Subject Q01 N	3069	1467	1544	2374	346	694	893	996	486	1757	1216	1057	592	451	897	36

QUESTIONNAIRE FORM 5 1983	TOTAL	SEX		RACE		REGION				4YR COLLEGE PLANS		ILLICIT DRUG USE: LIFETIME				
		M	F	White	Black	NE	NC	S	W	Yes	No	None	Mari-juana Only	Few Pills	More Pills	Any Her-oin
N (Weighted No. of Cases):	3339	1608	1628	2513	404	793	950	1082	514	1846	1297	1125	646	492	970	42
% of Weighted Total:	100.0	48.2	48.8	75.3	12.1	23.8	28.5	32.4	15.4	55.3	38.8	33.7	19.3	14.7	29.0	1.2
D01S: I often wish I had more good friends																
1. Disagree	16.5	15.4	17.8	16.6	17.7	21.0	14.9	15.8	14.6	17.9	14.5	17.6	16.8	14.8	16.0	9.8
2. Mostly disagree	15.7	13.2	18.1	16.9	12.7	18.3	17.0	12.9	15.4	16.6	14.2	15.3	16.3	15.8	16.0	21.8
3. Neither	18.5	20.8	16.4	19.5	14.3	18.1	22.1	15.1	19.7	17.2	20.4	16.6	16.6	19.3	21.3	34.3
4. Mostly agree	26.9	29.8	24.2	27.1	23.3	23.5	24.5	31.5	27.1	26.6	27.7	26.9	27.1	27.7	26.5	22.2
5. Agree	22.3	20.8	23.6	19.9	31.9	19.1	21.6	24.7	23.2	21.7	23.3	23.5	23.1	22.4	20.1	11.8
Item 12730 Subject Q03 N	3062	1466	1537	2369	346	697	893	990	483	1752	1214	1057	591	448	894	36
D01T: Planning ahead makes things turn out better																
1. Disagree	3.8	3.3	4.2	2.9	7.8	5.7	2.7	4.1	2.3	2.9	4.9	3.2	4.6	2.9	4.0	4.3
2. Mostly disagree	6.9	6.4	7.5	6.7	7.4	9.7	6.4	6.1	5.4	6.1	8.1	5.3	7.6	6.5	8.6	5.4
3. Neither	19.0	19.5	18.7	19.0	17.3	19.6	20.2	17.1	19.8	16.7	21.9	18.0	19.3	17.0	20.7	28.8
4. Mostly agree	40.2	40.4	40.0	43.0	26.6	38.4	42.3	39.0	41.3	43.0	36.9	39.6	40.0	41.3	41.0	38.0
5. Agree	30.2	30.3	29.7	28.4	40.9	26.5	28.5	33.8	31.2	31.2	28.2	33.9	28.6	32.3	25.8	23.4
Item 12740 Subject Q02 N	3058	1468	1531	2368	342	692	892	990	485	1748	1215	1049	586	453	897	36
D01U: I feel that my life is not very useful																
1. Disagree	51.2	50.3	52.0	51.2	62.3	53.0	48.9	53.9	47.3	55.3	45.2	56.1	52.9	52.0	44.6	37.0
2. Mostly disagree	28.0	29.2	27.0	29.5	16.6	25.6	30.0	26.1	31.5	28.9	26.8	26.2	29.2	26.6	30.8	27.5
3. Neither	12.0	12.1	12.0	11.7	8.7	11.1	13.8	10.5	13.2	9.7	15.7	10.3	9.3	12.8	14.7	14.9
4. Mostly agree	6.3	6.0	6.6	5.7	6.7	7.8	5.4	6.4	5.9	4.4	8.9	4.5	5.6	7.9	7.4	19.2
5. Agree	2.5	2.5	2.4	1.9	5.8	2.6	2.0	3.0	2.0	1.7	3.3	2.8	3.1	0.8	2.5	1.4
Item 12750 Subject Q01 N	3054	1464	1533	2366	341	688	895	988	483	1747	1211	1049	585	452	895	36
D01V: I usually have a few friends around that I can get together with																
1. Disagree	3.9	3.5	4.1	3.6	5.7	3.2	2.3	4.7	6.3	4.0	3.9	3.7	4.4	2.9	3.7	8.3
2. Mostly disagree	5.2	4.0	6.4	4.9	7.9	6.6	5.8	3.8	5.4	5.2	5.1	6.5	5.4	3.5	4.7	6.7
3. Neither	6.7	7.5	5.8	6.6	5.6	6.4	6.1	7.3	6.9	5.2	9.0	6.9	5.7	7.4	6.3	10.7
4. Mostly agree	37.1	37.1	37.3	37.0	34.4	34.5	38.0	38.7	36.2	36.7	37.9	36.7	34.5	37.7	39.0	44.2
5. Agree	47.0	47.8	46.4	48.0	46.4	49.3	47.8	45.6	45.3	48.8	44.2	46.2	50.0	48.4	46.2	30.1
Item 12760 Subject Q03 N	3061	1465	1538	2371	342	690	894	991	486	1751	1214	1053	588	453	895	36
D01W: I am eager to leave home and live on my own–independent from my parents																
1. Disagree	8.0	7.8	8.2	6.8	11.1	9.1	6.4	8.5	8.4	7.7	8.3	10.9	8.3	7.3	4.7	5.8
2. Mostly disagree	11.4	12.8	9.9	11.6	9.2	11.8	9.9	10.9	14.7	11.0	11.3	14.9	13.0	10.6	7.1	8.3
3. Neither	20.1	21.8	17.7	20.8	16.8	20.2	22.4	18.7	18.3	20.7	19.4	21.2	21.2	17.2	19.1	26.6
4. Mostly agree	29.7	28.3	31.5	30.5	28.6	28.6	30.1	30.1	29.8	30.7	28.5	28.7	31.9	30.5	29.4	29.8
5. Agree	30.8	29.3	32.7	30.3	34.3	30.3	31.2	31.8	28.8	29.9	32.6	24.3	25.6	34.4	39.7	29.5
Item 13950 Subject I03,Q01 N	3056	1463	1534	2367	341	691	894	985	486	1750	1210	1051	586	451	896	36
D01X: I feel hesitant about taking a full-time job and becoming part of the "adult world"																
1. Disagree	34.1	35.4	32.9	33.2	42.7	33.5	33.0	35.2	34.9	32.9	36.5	31.5	34.9	32.6	38.0	26.3
2. Mostly disagree	22.8	23.0	22.9	23.6	18.9	23.1	22.4	22.0	24.9	24.0	20.3	22.8	23.2	23.3	23.0	13.3
3. Neither	14.1	15.4	12.7	14.1	11.2	14.7	15.5	12.6	13.9	14.1	14.3	15.6	14.4	11.0	13.7	14.8
4. Mostly agree	18.9	18.2	19.7	19.4	16.5	18.6	19.0	20.5	15.8	18.6	19.7	19.8	18.2	22.0	16.3	30.0
5. Agree	10.0	7.9	11.8	9.7	10.8	10.0	10.2	9.6	10.5	10.5	9.2	10.3	9.3	11.1	9.0	15.7
Item 13960 Subject I03,Q01 N	3054	1460	1537	2364	342	690	891	990	484	1748	1211	1050	588	453	894	36

The next two questions ask your views about different lifestyles that have been in the news lately.

QUESTIONNAIRE FORM 5 1983	TOTAL	SEX		RACE		REGION				4YR COLLEGE PLANS		ILLICIT DRUG USE: LIFETIME				
		M	F	White	Black	NE	NC	S	W	Yes	No	None	Mari-juana Only	Few Pills	More Pills	Any Her-oin
N (Weighted No. of Cases):	3339	1608	1628	2513	404	793	950	1082	514	1846	1297	1125	646	492	970	42
% of Weighted Total:	100.0	48.2	48.8	75.3	12.1	23.8	28.5	32.4	15.4	55.3	38.8	33.7	19.3	14.7	29.0	1.2

D02: A man and a woman who live together without being married are . . . (Mark ONE circle.)

	TOTAL	M	F	White	Black	NE	NC	S	W	Yes	No	None	Mari-juana Only	Few Pills	More Pills	Any Her-oin
1. Experimenting with a worthwhile alternative lifestyle	23.4	22.5	23.8	22.9	26.1	26.2	23.2	19.5	27.4	22.4	25.3	17.9	26.2	22.3	28.5	19.8
2. Doing their own thing and not affecting anyone else	51.3	53.9	48.9	52.3	44.1	57.7	52.6	47.8	47.0	49.7	53.2	42.5	52.2	56.7	58.3	58.8
3. Living in a way that could be destructive to society	8.1	9.0	7.1	7.6	12.6	5.2	10.1	9.1	6.5	8.8	7.5	10.4	8.8	7.4	4.8	9.2
4. Violating a basic principle of human morality	17.2	14.5	20.1	17.3	17.3	10.9	14.1	23.6	19.1	19.1	14.0	29.2	12.8	13.6	8.4	12.1
8. None of the above	-	-	-	-	-	-	-	-	-	-	-	-	-	-	-	-
Item 12770 Subject D03 N	2784	1333	1400	2173	300	623	815	901	445	1598	1097	929	545	419	824	35

D03: A man and a woman who decide to have and raise a child out of wedlock are . . .

	TOTAL	M	F	White	Black	NE	NC	S	W	Yes	No	None	Mari-juana Only	Few Pills	More Pills	Any Her-oin
1. Experimenting with a worthwhile alternative lifestyle	8.4	8.7	7.9	6.7	13.2	9.7	8.0	7.8	8.3	7.0	10.1	5.8	10.6	9.4	8.6	23.4
2. Doing their own thing and not affecting anyone else	34.5	35.8	33.0	32.5	41.5	41.7	32.7	30.4	36.1	32.3	37.6	26.3	35.5	34.8	43.5	38.9
3. Living in a way that could be destructive to society	23.1	22.9	23.5	24.1	22.6	22.3	25.0	21.5	24.2	25.1	20.5	22.1	23.7	22.1	23.6	32.7
4. Violating a basic principle of human morality	34.0	32.6	35.7	36.7	22.6	26.4	34.3	40.3	31.4	35.7	31.9	45.9	30.2	33.6	24.3	5.0
8. None of the above	-	-	-	-	-	-	-	-	-	-	-	-	-	-	-	-
Item 12775 Subject D03 N	2603	1266	1286	2033	289	580	772	842	409	1502	1021	880	503	394	763	33

D04: These next questions ask how you feel about your present financial situation and your future financial security.

D04A: I feel that I have enough money to get along pretty well

	TOTAL	M	F	White	Black	NE	NC	S	W	Yes	No	None	Mari-juana Only	Few Pills	More Pills	Any Her-oin
1. Never	11.8	11.2	12.4	9.5	19.9	10.4	11.5	11.7	14.2	9.1	16.1	11.7	10.9	11.5	12.5	5.8
2. Seldom	19.9	18.3	21.5	19.9	21.4	21.5	21.0	18.6	18.6	18.3	22.1	18.9	16.9	24.3	20.9	22.7
3. Sometimes	35.6	35.8	35.4	35.9	35.2	35.3	33.3	38.1	35.3	34.3	37.3	34.7	39.1	35.0	35.0	39.9
4. Often	23.6	25.2	22.1	24.9	16.9	24.3	26.8	21.2	21.7	27.7	17.6	25.4	24.6	21.6	22.3	15.1
5. Always	9.0	9.5	8.5	9.9	6.7	8.4	7.4	10.3	10.3	10.6	7.0	9.3	8.6	7.7	9.4	16.5
Item 12990 Subject C02 N	3004	1435	1513	2333	335	669	884	973	478	1725	1187	1033	574	448	879	35

D04B: I get very concerned about how I am going to be able to pay my next bills

	TOTAL	M	F	White	Black	NE	NC	S	W	Yes	No	None	Mari-juana Only	Few Pills	More Pills	Any Her-oin
1. Never	24.6	22.4	26.8	23.2	35.0	25.9	22.4	25.1	26.1	26.2	22.3	28.8	24.1	23.5	21.1	18.2
2. Seldom	26.8	28.8	24.9	28.5	18.7	24.7	27.2	26.6	29.4	28.5	24.3	26.3	29.0	25.8	27.4	17.1
3. Sometimes	26.5	26.2	26.8	27.2	27.2	25.6	28.3	27.1	23.4	26.4	27.4	24.2	25.5	28.0	28.6	29.4
4. Often	15.4	16.3	14.6	14.7	12.5	16.7	15.0	15.2	15.1	13.3	18.1	13.7	16.0	16.9	15.7	30.0
5. Always	6.6	6.3	6.8	6.3	6.6	7.2	7.1	5.9	6.1	5.6	7.9	7.0	5.3	5.8	7.2	5.3
Item 13000 Subject C02 N	2977	1423	1501	2310	333	662	876	964	476	1706	1181	1020	573	443	873	34

D04C: I worry whether I will have any job at all in a few months

	TOTAL	M	F	White	Black	NE	NC	S	W	Yes	No	None	Mari-juana Only	Few Pills	More Pills	Any Her-oin
1. Never	32.0	32.5	31.6	33.4	32.1	33.1	29.2	32.4	34.9	35.3	27.2	34.0	31.4	31.5	31.0	22.4
2. Seldom	22.0	24.5	19.4	22.5	17.3	19.8	22.1	24.0	20.6	24.2	19.4	20.7	24.0	19.5	23.6	18.6
3. Sometimes	20.9	19.8	22.0	20.6	20.0	23.2	21.6	19.1	20.0	19.9	21.5	21.6	20.0	22.6	19.5	29.4
4. Often	15.7	14.9	16.4	15.5	17.3	15.0	16.7	15.3	15.5	13.8	18.8	14.9	15.0	16.5	16.6	11.4
5. Always	9.4	8.2	10.5	8.0	13.3	8.8	10.5	9.2	9.0	6.9	13.1	8.9	9.6	9.8	9.3	18.3
Item 13010 Subject C02 N	2965	1422	1488	2305	331	663	867	961	475	1697	1178	1019	570	437	869	35

D04D: I feel sure that I could go out and get a new job (with decent pay) whenever I want one

	TOTAL	M	F	White	Black	NE	NC	S	W	Yes	No	None	Mari-juana Only	Few Pills	More Pills	Any Her-oin
1. Never	14.0	13.0	14.8	11.9	22.0	14.8	16.4	13.0	10.8	10.2	19.2	14.3	11.0	15.6	14.6	18.6
2. Seldom	26.7	23.9	29.6	27.7	24.5	24.6	29.6	25.9	25.7	25.0	29.3	25.5	23.8	28.0	29.4	25.8
3. Sometimes	34.3	33.6	35.2	35.1	31.5	36.0	33.5	34.7	32.9	36.3	31.8	35.1	36.7	34.1	32.2	30.8
4. Often	17.2	20.2	14.4	17.7	13.8	17.7	14.5	17.6	20.6	19.3	14.1	17.9	20.5	14.8	15.6	14.8
5. Always	7.7	9.3	6.1	7.6	8.2	6.9	6.1	8.7	10.0	9.3	5.6	7.1	8.0	7.4	8.2	10.1
Item 13020 Subject C02 N	2970	1425	1490	2309	333	664	871	960	475	1703	1177	1020	572	437	873	34

	TOTAL	SEX		RACE		REGION				4YR COLLEGE PLANS		ILLICIT DRUG USE: LIFETIME				
QUESTIONNAIRE FORM 5 1983		M	F	White	Black	NE	NC	S	W	Yes	No	None	Mari- juana Only	Few Pills	More Pills	Any Her- oin
N (Weighted No. of Cases):	3339	1608	1628	2513	404	793	950	1082	514	1846	1297	1125	646	492	970	42
% of Weighted Total:	100.0	48.2	48.8	75.3	12.1	23.8	28.5	32.4	15.4	55.3	38.8	33.7	19.3	14.7	29.0	1.2

FOR THOSE WHO HAVE A JOB:

D04E: I feel sure I that can keep working steadily with my present employer as long as I want to

1. Never	6.0	7.0	4.9	5.1	11.0	5.8	6.1	5.8	6.6	5.2	7.2	6.8	5.6	4.7	6.0	2.1
2. Seldom	7.7	8.4	6.9	7.2	9.1	5.5	8.5	7.9	9.2	6.2	9.8	8.2	6.4	8.5	7.6	12.5
3. Sometimes	15.4	16.8	13.4	14.3	22.4	15.3	17.2	14.7	13.3	12.4	20.0	13.7	14.1	20.1	15.6	25.6
4. Often	25.5	22.8	28.9	26.1	21.8	28.7	24.9	24.9	23.3	26.9	23.1	26.3	27.5	23.6	24.7	11.2
5. Always	45.3	45.0	45.9	47.3	35.8	44.7	43.3	46.6	47.6	49.3	39.9	45.0	46.4	43.1	46.1	48.5
Item 13030 Subject C02 N★	1892	976	877	1501	185	442	567	591	292	1075	769	614	364	277	603	18

D04F: I worry about getting fired or laid-off from my job

1. Never	52.4	50.1	55.5	54.2	51.0	52.0	50.4	53.5	54.7	55.7	48.4	56.4	55.2	45.3	50.1	41.6
2. Seldom	25.4	24.3	26.2	25.8	22.1	28.6	23.9	25.4	23.4	27.0	23.0	22.4	24.7	30.1	26.8	33.6
3. Sometimes	12.7	14.9	10.2	11.8	16.9	12.8	13.2	12.1	12.5	10.6	15.5	11.2	11.7	14.6	14.1	8.4
4. Often	5.8	6.5	5.0	5.5	4.9	4.3	8.0	5.1	5.0	3.9	8.4	6.5	3.7	6.4	5.8	8.1
5. Always	3.7	4.2	3.2	2.7	5.1	2.2	4.6	3.8	4.3	2.8	4.6	3.5	4.7	3.6	3.2	8.3
Item 13040 Subject C02 N★	1881	967	875	1492	185	439	559	592	291	1068	768	605	363	277	600	18

D05: Please think about all the money you earned during the past year, including last summer.

About how much of your past year's earnings have gone into:

D05A: Savings for your future education

1. None	50.8	48.5	52.8	49.7	51.8	42.0	47.6	56.6	56.8	41.8	63.6	45.1	46.0	53.4	57.9	66.7
2. A little	21.2	23.4	19.1	21.1	20.8	23.2	21.1	19.8	21.4	23.0	19.1	21.5	23.4	20.1	20.5	11.1
3. Some	10.6	10.7	10.4	11.1	10.6	13.5	10.8	9.3	8.9	12.8	7.1	11.3	11.9	11.8	8.7	8.0
4. About half	7.5	6.8	8.0	7.6	6.9	8.1	9.0	5.9	6.8	9.4	4.6	8.9	7.3	6.3	6.8	6.9
5. Most	5.2	6.2	4.4	5.7	3.5	6.5	6.8	3.6	3.7	7.2	2.5	5.9	7.9	4.8	2.7	4.5
6. Almost all	3.6	3.3	4.1	3.8	3.3	5.5	3.8	3.3	1.5	4.8	1.9	5.8	2.7	3.6	1.8	2.8
7. All	1.1	1.2	1.1	0.9	3.2	1.2	0.9	1.4	0.9	1.0	1.2	1.5	0.8	-	1.5	-
Item 20830 Subject C02 N	2844	1371	1421	2243	293	623	837	921	463	1648	1112	986	534	426	838	33

D05B: Savings or payments for a car or car expenses

1. None	47.4	37.2	57.7	45.3	63.0	52.2	45.5	45.9	47.5	52.2	41.6	53.4	48.1	45.9	41.1	43.1
2. A little	17.7	19.8	15.6	18.1	13.5	14.1	20.4	17.6	17.9	18.1	17.3	16.6	12.4	19.3	21.3	22.8
3. Some	14.1	16.2	11.9	14.4	10.2	13.8	13.1	15.0	14.7	13.0	15.1	10.9	17.2	15.0	15.0	22.9
4. About half	8.9	11.6	6.1	9.7	3.1	7.2	9.9	9.1	8.8	6.6	12.4	7.0	8.5	9.9	11.1	5.5
5. Most	6.9	9.4	4.3	7.5	3.9	6.4	6.5	7.4	7.0	6.6	7.1	6.6	8.6	5.5	6.7	2.7
6. Almost all	3.8	4.6	2.9	3.8	4.0	4.9	3.5	3.7	2.8	2.6	5.1	3.3	4.4	3.8	3.8	3.1
7. All	1.3	1.2	1.4	1.1	2.2	1.4	1.1	1.3	1.4	1.0	1.5	2.1	0.9	0.6	0.9	-
Item 20840 Subject C02 N	2828	1359	1418	2229	291	617	833	914	463	1641	1103	984	525	426	837	30

D05C: Other savings for long-range purposes

1. None	47.5	45.8	48.8	47.0	48.8	43.0	48.7	48.8	48.8	47.9	48.1	45.0	46.2	48.0	50.6	48.0
2. A little	23.6	25.3	22.0	24.3	19.9	24.1	24.4	22.8	22.9	24.4	21.8	24.9	26.2	20.9	22.6	7.9
3. Some	13.5	13.7	13.2	13.7	13.4	14.0	12.5	13.6	14.3	12.7	14.7	12.1	13.2	15.7	13.6	29.5
4. About half	6.5	6.8	6.2	6.3	6.5	8.2	5.8	5.8	6.6	6.1	6.9	6.4	6.9	6.1	6.2	8.1
5. Most	4.6	4.0	5.2	4.6	5.1	5.8	4.2	5.1	2.9	4.4	4.7	4.9	4.3	5.8	4.1	5.1
6. Almost all	3.3	3.1	3.5	3.2	3.6	3.9	3.8	2.7	2.6	3.4	2.9	5.0	2.5	2.6	2.2	-
7. All	1.1	1.3	0.9	0.9	2.8	1.1	0.5	1.2	1.9	1.1	0.9	1.8	0.7	0.8	0.8	1.5
Item 20850 Subject C02 N	2820	1355	1413	2222	290	613	831	913	462	1635	1102	978	529	421	834	32

★=excludes respondents for whom question was inappropriate.

QUESTIONNAIRE FORM 5 1983	TOTAL	SEX		RACE		REGION				4YR COLLEGE PLANS		ILLICIT DRUG USE: LIFETIME				
		M	F	White	Black	NE	NC	S	W	Yes	No	None	Mari-juana Only	Few Pills	More Pills	Any Her-oin
N (Weighted No. of Cases):	3339	1608	1628	2513	404	793	950	1082	514	1846	1297	1125	646	492	970	42
% of Weighted Total:	100.0	48.2	48.8	75.3	12.1	23.8	28.5	32.4	15.4	55.3	38.8	33.7	19.3	14.7	29.0	1.2

D05D: Spending on your own needs and activities – things such as clothing, stereo, TV, records, other possessions, movies, eating out, other recreation, hobbies, gifts for others, and other personal expenses

	TOTAL	M	F	White	Black	NE	NC	S	W	Yes	No	None	Mar.	Few	More	Her.
1. None	6.0	6.7	5.0	4.0	12.6	6.0	4.8	7.3	5.8	4.1	8.7	7.8	6.0	5.4	4.3	3.7
2. A little	18.9	21.3	16.7	20.0	16.3	20.0	17.6	19.4	19.0	21.0	16.2	22.0	19.6	19.1	14.9	20.4
3. Some	18.3	19.7	16.9	19.3	12.6	17.5	19.4	16.9	19.7	17.8	19.1	18.7	18.3	17.0	18.2	23.4
4. About half	17.8	18.3	17.0	17.8	15.0	18.2	19.8	15.4	18.3	17.3	18.6	15.7	18.3	17.6	20.5	6.7
5. Most	17.2	17.2	17.4	17.1	18.6	16.8	18.5	17.3	15.2	18.5	15.6	17.7	15.6	19.0	16.8	11.4
6. Almost all	13.6	9.7	17.5	13.7	13.7	14.0	13.1	13.8	13.5	13.6	13.2	10.6	13.8	15.6	15.7	21.0
7. All	8.2	7.1	9.4	8.0	11.2	7.5	6.8	10.0	8.4	7.8	8.7	7.5	8.4	6.3	9.8	13.3
Item 20860 Subject C02 N	2820	1352	1417	2223	291	609	833	916	461	1638	1102	979	527	421	836	31

D05E: Helping to pay family living expenses (groceries, housing, etc.)

	TOTAL	M	F	White	Black	NE	NC	S	W	Yes	No	None	Mar.	Few	More	Her.
1. None	56.2	56.2	56.2	61.5	32.5	55.0	61.8	52.4	55.3	60.8	50.4	56.9	56.6	56.2	56.1	42.4
2. A little	24.6	26.7	22.5	24.0	24.9	22.9	24.6	25.5	25.0	23.3	26.1	23.2	25.6	25.3	25.2	24.2
3. Some	9.0	8.1	10.2	7.3	19.3	12.2	6.7	9.0	9.3	7.7	11.1	8.7	8.7	8.3	10.1	4.8
4. About half	4.4	5.0	3.8	3.5	9.5	4.7	3.7	4.6	4.9	4.0	4.9	4.2	4.8	4.4	4.4	5.6
5. Most	2.8	1.9	3.7	1.9	6.6	3.4	1.2	4.0	2.7	2.2	3.7	3.5	1.9	3.2	2.3	6.0
6. Almost all	2.0	1.4	2.5	1.1	5.2	1.4	1.1	3.1	2.3	1.4	2.8	2.4	1.8	2.1	1.3	6.7
7. All	0.9	0.7	1.1	0.7	2.0	0.5	0.9	1.4	0.6	0.7	1.0	1.2	0.6	0.5	0.6	10.2
Item 20870 Subject C02 N	2815	1349	1415	2214	294	609	831	915	461	1635	1098	979	526	419	833	31

The next questions ask about characteristics which some people associate with the use of particular drugs. First, we want to know what you think.

E01: Do YOU think that people who smoke marijuana several times a week tend to be . . .

E01A: More creative than average

	TOTAL	M	F	White	Black	NE	NC	S	W	Yes	No	None	Mar.	Few	More	Her.
1. No	63.3	62.3	64.6	65.8	53.6	64.8	61.6	63.4	64.1	67.5	57.4	70.6	67.0	62.2	53.7	48.8
2. Yes	13.8	16.6	11.1	12.9	15.9	13.4	15.6	13.2	12.3	11.4	17.2	6.8	10.7	14.8	22.6	36.5
3. Not sure, no opinion	22.9	21.0	24.3	21.3	30.5	21.8	22.7	23.4	23.6	21.2	25.4	22.7	22.3	23.0	23.7	14.7
Item 13060 Subject A11c N	2939	1402	1484	2287	328	641	868	955	475	1688	1161	1022	556	436	855	35

E01B: Less sensible than average

	TOTAL	M	F	White	Black	NE	NC	S	W	Yes	No	None	Mar.	Few	More	Her.
1. No	23.9	26.9	21.0	22.9	24.3	25.6	22.3	24.4	23.5	21.6	26.6	12.6	23.1	24.1	37.0	57.1
2. Yes	59.1	56.4	61.9	62.1	47.8	57.6	62.6	58.3	56.2	62.7	54.5	69.3	60.1	59.6	47.1	25.2
3. Not sure, no opinion	17.1	16.7	17.1	14.9	27.9	16.8	15.1	17.4	20.3	15.8	18.9	18.1	16.8	16.3	15.8	17.7
Item 13070 Subject A11c N	2936	1403	1481	2288	326	641	867	954	474	1688	1159	1019	554	435	858	35

E01C: More interesting people than average

	TOTAL	M	F	White	Black	NE	NC	S	W	Yes	No	None	Mar.	Few	More	Her.
1. No	66.5	64.1	69.1	69.3	52.9	67.8	67.5	65.9	64.0	70.1	61.8	74.8	65.7	70.1	56.4	45.0
2. Yes	14.9	17.8	12.0	13.5	21.5	14.2	13.0	16.0	16.9	12.2	18.4	6.8	16.7	13.9	23.5	24.3
3. Not sure, no opinion	18.7	18.0	18.9	17.2	25.6	17.9	19.5	18.1	19.1	17.7	19.7	18.4	17.5	16.0	20.1	30.6
Item 13080 Subject A11c N	2932	1404	1477	2283	327	640	866	953	473	1687	1159	1019	554	434	857	35

E01D: Less hard-working than average

	TOTAL	M	F	White	Black	NE	NC	S	W	Yes	No	None	Mar.	Few	More	Her.
1. No	25.7	27.2	24.3	25.2	28.0	31.3	24.3	24.2	23.5	22.4	30.0	13.6	26.1	27.1	38.2	33.0
2. Yes	57.1	55.9	58.5	59.4	44.9	51.8	58.5	57.2	61.6	60.2	53.0	65.0	56.2	59.3	48.3	50.8
3. Not sure, no opinion	17.2	16.9	17.2	15.4	27.1	16.9	17.3	18.6	14.8	17.4	17.0	21.4	17.7	13.6	13.5	16.2
Item 13090 Subject A11c N	2931	1403	1476	2285	326	637	864	956	474	1690	1153	1015	554	434	857	35

E01E: More independent than average

	TOTAL	M	F	White	Black	NE	NC	S	W	Yes	No	None	Mar.	Few	More	Her.
1. No	53.1	48.8	57.3	54.9	46.7	52.4	50.3	54.1	57.0	54.3	51.4	55.9	51.7	57.1	49.6	46.2
2. Yes	26.5	32.7	20.7	27.0	21.9	29.2	29.1	24.2	22.6	25.6	27.6	21.0	26.0	24.9	33.2	38.0
3. Not sure, no opinion	20.5	18.6	22.0	18.1	31.3	18.4	20.6	21.7	20.4	20.1	21.0	23.1	22.2	18.0	17.2	15.9
Item 13100 Subject A11c N	2926	1401	1474	2277	327	639	863	950	473	1688	1151	1016	553	434	853	35

QUESTIONNAIRE FORM 5 1983	TOTAL	SEX		RACE		REGION				4YR COLLEGE PLANS		ILLICIT DRUG USE: LIFETIME				
		M	F	White	Black	NE	NC	S	W	Yes	No	None	Mari-juana Only	Few Pills	More Pills	Any Her-oin
N (Weighted No. of Cases):	3339	1608	1628	2513	404	793	950	1082	514	1846	1297	1125	646	492	970	42
% of Weighted Total:	100.0	48.2	48.8	75.3	12.1	23.8	28.5	32.4	15.4	55.3	38.8	33.7	19.3	14.7	29.0	1.2
E01F: More emotionally unstable than average																
1. No	23.5	27.6	19.6	23.5	21.7	26.6	24.3	21.7	21.4	21.0	27.2	13.9	22.7	20.9	36.4	35.3
2. Yes	58.3	53.3	63.5	60.4	50.6	53.7	60.0	58.7	60.5	61.4	54.0	66.4	56.4	62.3	48.5	55.7
3. Not sure, no opinion	18.2	19.0	16.9	16.0	27.7	19.7	15.7	19.6	18.1	17.6	18.9	19.7	21.0	16.8	15.0	9.0
Item 13110 Subject A11c N	2924	1400	1472	2277	326	638	863	950	473	1686	1149	1015	552	432	855	35
E01G: More concerned about other people than average																
1. No	71.2	70.6	72.3	74.1	57.0	67.1	75.4	71.3	68.9	73.5	67.9	75.0	73.5	72.8	65.3	70.9
2. Yes	8.5	9.9	7.1	8.0	9.9	11.1	7.7	7.5	8.7	7.1	11.0	4.4	7.1	8.8	13.7	13.9
3. Not sure, no opinion	20.3	19.5	20.6	17.8	33.0	21.8	16.9	21.2	22.4	19.4	21.1	20.6	19.4	18.4	21.0	15.3
Item 13120 Subject A11c N	2923	1402	1469	2276	324	637	862	950	473	1684	1150	1014	555	430	855	35
E01H: More weak-willed than average																
1. No	25.2	27.4	23.0	25.5	25.6	28.6	24.6	24.5	23.4	23.7	27.3	14.2	26.6	24.3	36.9	55.4
2. Yes	53.4	52.0	55.1	54.8	44.8	48.9	56.1	54.2	52.8	55.8	50.4	63.3	49.5	54.9	44.5	27.0
3. Not sure, no opinion	21.4	20.5	22.0	19.7	29.6	22.5	19.3	21.3	23.8	20.5	22.3	22.4	24.0	20.8	18.6	17.6
Item 13130 Subject A11c N	2919	1398	1470	2273	324	634	863	952	470	1684	1147	1015	555	431	848	35
E01I: More criminal than average																
1. No	26.9	28.7	25.5	27.3	24.6	27.0	25.0	26.2	31.7	26.1	28.1	13.9	25.4	28.7	41.6	58.2
2. Yes	51.9	51.6	52.2	53.0	45.3	49.6	55.2	53.4	45.8	53.2	50.9	62.6	52.1	53.1	39.1	27.5
3. Not sure, no opinion	21.2	19.7	22.3	19.8	30.1	23.3	19.8	20.4	22.5	20.8	21.0	23.5	22.5	18.2	19.2	14.3
Item 13140 Subject A11c N	2922	1398	1473	2276	325	637	863	951	471	1682	1152	1014	553	431	854	35

Next we want to ask you how you think most of the people you know would answer the same questions.

E02: Do you think that MOST OF THE PEOPLE YOU KNOW feel that individuals who smoke marijuana several times a week tend to be . . .

	TOTAL	M	F	White	Black	NE	NC	S	W	Yes	No	None	Mari-juana Only	Few Pills	More Pills	Any Her-oin
E02A: More creative than average																
1. No	59.7	57.6	62.0	62.8	43.8	60.0	61.6	57.4	60.5	63.7	54.2	63.8	60.4	60.4	55.2	42.9
2. Yes	18.6	20.1	17.4	17.8	22.5	19.7	17.7	19.5	17.0	16.0	22.6	14.3	17.3	18.5	23.6	49.5
3. Not sure, no opinion	21.7	22.3	20.6	19.5	33.7	20.4	20.7	23.1	22.5	20.4	23.2	21.9	22.3	21.1	21.2	7.5
Item 13190 Subject A12c N	2875	1379	1445	2240	318	623	855	935	461	1656	1130	1003	546	422	834	35
E02B: Less sensible than average																
1. No	26.5	27.2	25.9	26.2	25.9	29.3	27.6	24.1	25.5	24.5	28.6	20.4	26.7	25.0	33.8	54.4
2. Yes	55.5	53.7	57.6	57.7	47.1	53.6	55.7	56.6	55.4	58.9	51.2	60.9	55.2	57.3	49.4	32.3
3. Not sure, no opinion	18.0	19.1	16.5	16.1	27.0	17.0	16.7	19.3	19.1	16.5	20.2	18.7	18.1	17.7	16.8	13.3
Item 13200 Subject A12c N	2871	1378	1443	2238	316	621	854	932	464	1655	1129	1001	545	422	835	34
E02C: More interesting people than average																
1. No	58.0	55.9	60.5	61.1	43.1	58.3	60.6	55.7	57.6	60.9	54.4	62.7	58.8	61.8	51.2	37.4
2. Yes	21.4	22.6	20.5	20.1	26.4	20.7	19.3	23.2	22.6	19.6	23.7	16.9	22.1	18.2	27.2	50.5
3. Not sure, no opinion	20.5	21.6	18.9	18.8	30.4	21.0	20.1	21.0	19.8	19.5	22.0	20.5	19.1	19.9	21.6	12.1
Item 13210 Subject A12c N	2862	1372	1441	2232	316	618	851	931	462	1652	1125	1000	542	420	832	34
E02D: Less hard-working than average																
1. No	25.8	24.6	26.9	25.1	28.9	28.7	24.2	25.4	25.5	23.1	29.0	20.0	25.5	24.9	33.0	38.8
2. Yes	55.5	55.2	56.2	57.9	44.1	53.5	58.4	54.4	54.9	58.9	50.8	59.1	56.0	59.6	50.0	41.9
3. Not sure, no opinion	18.8	20.3	16.9	17.0	27.0	17.8	17.4	20.2	19.7	18.0	20.2	20.9	18.6	15.5	17.1	19.3
Item 13220 Subject A12c N	2858	1372	1437	2228	315	616	851	929	462	1649	1122	997	544	417	832	34

QUESTIONNAIRE FORM 5 1983	TOTAL	SEX		RACE		REGION				4YR COLLEGE PLANS		ILLICIT DRUG USE: LIFETIME				
		M	F	White	Black	NE	NC	S	W	Yes	No	None	Marijuana Only	Few Pills	More Pills	Any Heroin
N (Weighted No. of Cases):	3339	1608	1628	2513	404	793	950	1082	514	1846	1297	1125	646	492	970	42
% of Weighted Total:	100.0	48.2	48.8	75.3	12.1	23.8	28.5	32.4	15.4	55.3	38.8	33.7	19.3	14.7	29.0	1.2
E02E: More independent than average																
1. No	49.9	45.9	54.2	51.0	42.9	48.4	49.1	51.0	51.1	50.3	49.2	51.4	51.4	50.9	47.4	50.8
2. Yes	27.8	31.4	24.5	28.5	25.9	30.3	29.7	26.0	24.8	28.0	27.5	24.7	27.6	27.6	31.5	41.5
3. Not sure, no opinion	22.3	22.7	21.3	20.5	31.3	21.3	21.1	23.0	24.1	21.7	23.3	24.0	21.1	21.4	21.0	7.7
Item 13230 Subject A12c N	2852	1364	1438	2229	313	618	847	925	462	1643	1123	997	538	418	831	34
E02F: More emotionally unstable than average																
1. No	25.7	27.7	23.7	25.2	28.3	28.5	24.4	26.3	23.0	24.0	28.1	19.3	28.0	23.3	32.7	51.0
2. Yes	53.8	49.9	58.2	56.2	42.0	51.3	56.3	52.5	55.2	56.6	49.7	60.2	50.7	57.1	47.9	32.9
3. Not sure, no opinion	20.5	22.5	18.1	18.7	29.7	20.2	19.3	21.2	21.8	19.4	22.2	20.5	21.3	19.7	19.4	16.2
Item 13240 Subject A12c N	2849	1365	1433	2225	313	615	850	923	460	1643	1119	998	542	414	827	34
E02G: More concerned about other people than average																
1. No	65.7	64.0	67.8	69.1	50.8	64.9	67.6	66.0	62.7	69.3	61.0	68.5	65.1	67.3	62.2	73.1
2. Yes	11.5	12.7	10.2	10.1	15.9	12.4	9.7	11.4	13.5	9.3	14.8	7.7	13.6	11.5	14.2	19.2
3. Not sure, no opinion	22.8	23.3	22.0	20.8	33.3	22.7	22.7	22.6	23.8	21.4	24.2	23.8	21.3	21.2	23.6	7.7
Item 13250 Subject A12c N	2846	1365	1431	2223	314	613	850	923	461	1642	1118	995	543	414	826	34
E02H: More weak-willed than average																
1. No	26.5	25.8	27.1	26.5	26.2	30.1	25.0	25.4	26.4	25.3	27.6	20.0	28.7	25.4	32.2	50.2
2. Yes	50.7	50.6	50.9	52.4	41.4	47.0	53.4	51.9	48.1	53.9	46.7	56.8	48.2	52.6	45.0	39.3
3. Not sure, no opinion	22.9	23.6	22.0	21.1	32.4	22.9	21.6	22.7	25.6	20.8	25.7	23.2	23.1	22.0	22.8	10.5
Item 13260 Subject A12c N	2842	1367	1424	2217	316	610	850	924	458	1641	1117	994	543	412	825	34
E02I: More criminal than average																
1. No	26.7	25.6	27.6	26.3	28.6	27.2	24.8	26.8	29.5	24.9	29.1	20.0	26.4	28.1	34.2	42.5
2. Yes	51.9	53.0	51.5	53.6	43.2	49.8	55.7	51.7	48.3	54.8	48.3	57.5	52.5	52.3	44.6	42.4
3. Not sure, no opinion	21.3	21.4	20.9	20.1	28.2	22.9	19.5	21.5	22.3	20.4	22.6	22.5	21.1	19.6	21.1	15.0
Item 13270 Subject A12c N	2846	1365	1430	2223	316	615	848	923	461	1640	1119	998	540	413	826	35

The next questions are similar, but ask about illegal drugs other than marijuana–like psychedelics, barbiturates, narcotics, and amphetamines.

E03: Do YOU think that people who use illegal drugs (other than marijuana) several times a week tend to be . . .

	TOTAL	M	F	White	Black	NE	NC	S	W	Yes	No	None	Marijuana Only	Few Pills	More Pills	Any Heroin
E03A: More creative than average																
1. No	68.0	66.1	69.6	70.2	57.7	68.7	66.8	67.6	69.8	71.4	62.9	72.7	69.4	70.1	61.7	49.3
2. Yes	11.1	12.4	10.0	10.5	12.7	11.5	11.8	11.2	9.1	8.7	14.6	6.9	8.4	12.4	16.3	26.3
3. Not sure, no opinion	20.9	21.5	20.4	19.3	29.6	19.8	21.4	21.2	21.1	19.8	22.4	20.4	22.2	17.4	22.0	24.5
Item 13330 Subject A11c N	2795	1331	1416	2186	309	599	838	905	453	1611	1099	985	525	405	815	33
E03B: Less sensible than average																
1. No	14.0	15.7	12.0	12.5	21.2	14.8	13.4	14.4	13.3	12.1	16.3	9.1	12.7	18.7	17.9	34.6
2. Yes	68.2	64.8	71.8	71.8	51.9	68.1	70.2	66.8	67.1	72.0	63.0	74.2	67.2	66.5	64.1	41.5
3. Not sure, no opinion	17.8	19.4	16.2	15.7	26.9	17.1	16.3	18.8	19.5	15.9	20.7	16.6	20.1	14.8	18.0	23.9
Item 13340 Subject A11c N	2789	1331	1410	2183	310	595	836	904	454	1606	1100	986	523	404	814	32
E03C: More interesting people than average																
1. No	70.0	66.9	72.9	73.0	54.1	69.7	70.7	69.3	70.3	73.9	64.2	74.7	69.4	73.2	64.4	51.2
2. Yes	9.7	10.7	8.7	8.8	13.9	10.8	9.4	10.4	7.7	7.8	12.6	5.9	8.4	10.5	14.4	25.1
3. Not sure, no opinion	20.3	22.3	18.3	18.1	32.0	19.5	20.0	20.3	22.0	18.2	23.2	19.4	22.2	16.4	21.2	23.8
Item 13350 Subject A11c N	2788	1326	1414	2180	308	598	834	901	455	1607	1097	981	525	403	817	30

QUESTIONNAIRE FORM 5 1983	TOTAL	SEX		RACE		REGION				4YR COLLEGE PLANS		ILLICIT DRUG USE: LIFETIME				
		M	F	White	Black	NE	NC	S	W	Yes	No	None	Mari- juana Only	Few Pills	More Pills	Any Her- oin
N (Weighted No. of Cases):	3339	1608	1628	2513	404	793	950	1082	514	1846	1297	1125	646	492	970	42
% of Weighted Total:	100.0	48.2	48.8	75.3	12.1	23.8	28.5	32.4	15.4	55.3	38.8	33.7	19.3	14.7	29.0	1.2

E03D: Less hard-working than average

1. No	16.8	16.9	16.5	15.7	21.1	18.3	15.7	16.2	17.9	14.6	19.7	11.3	15.3	18.2	22.7	39.8
2. Yes	62.9	62.1	63.9	65.7	49.4	61.0	64.8	63.8	60.2	66.6	57.5	69.9	62.5	64.2	55.5	50.3
3. Not sure, no opinion	20.3	21.0	19.6	18.6	29.5	20.7	19.4	20.0	21.9	18.7	22.8	18.8	22.2	17.6	21.9	9.9
Item 13360 Subject A11c N	2786	1328	1411	2180	306	594	836	903	453	1604	1098	982	522	403	816	32

E03E: More independent than average

1. No	55.9	51.7	59.8	57.8	48.5	55.8	54.6	56.6	57.1	57.5	53.9	58.6	53.5	59.2	54.3	42.5
2. Yes	21.3	25.0	18.1	21.2	19.2	22.3	23.5	20.8	17.1	20.8	22.1	19.2	20.9	21.1	23.0	36.7
3. Not sure, no opinion	22.7	23.4	22.1	21.0	32.3	21.8	21.8	22.6	25.8	21.7	24.1	22.2	25.6	19.7	22.7	20.8
Item 13370 Subject A11c N	2783	1328	1408	2177	309	596	834	901	453	1604	1096	979	521	404	817	31

E03F: More emotionally unstable than average

1. No	13.3	15.5	10.9	12.2	20.4	12.8	14.4	13.5	11.7	11.2	16.1	9.9	13.7	12.4	17.2	26.4
2. Yes	67.4	62.6	72.5	70.8	52.6	67.7	68.0	67.2	66.6	72.6	60.1	73.1	64.2	70.3	62.3	57.3
3. Not sure, no opinion	19.2	21.9	16.6	17.1	27.0	19.5	17.6	19.3	21.7	16.2	23.7	17.0	22.2	17.3	20.5	16.3
Item 13380 Subject A11c N	2784	1327	1409	2180	307	594	833	904	453	1605	1096	982	523	402	815	31

E03G: More concerned about other people than average

1. No	71.8	69.3	74.4	75.0	56.6	71.5	75.3	70.4	68.8	75.8	66.2	76.5	69.8	73.3	68.0	74.8
2. Yes	6.9	8.3	5.5	6.0	11.5	6.4	5.9	8.3	6.9	5.7	8.9	4.9	7.5	9.1	7.8	5.8
3. Not sure, no opinion	21.2	22.4	20.1	19.0	31.8	22.1	18.8	21.4	24.3	18.6	25.0	18.7	22.7	17.7	24.2	19.4
Item 13390 Subject A11c N	2785	1327	1410	2178	307	597	835	900	453	1607	1095	980	524	401	818	31

E03H: More weak-willed than average

1. No	15.4	15.7	15.0	14.9	17.6	17.9	14.8	15.7	13.0	13.4	18.5	11.6	13.9	15.5	20.0	32.9
2. Yes	63.2	62.4	64.1	65.5	53.6	60.3	66.3	63.1	61.2	67.6	56.7	69.7	62.9	65.0	56.1	44.6
3. Not sure, no opinion	21.4	21.9	20.9	19.6	28.8	21.8	19.0	21.2	25.8	19.0	24.8	18.7	23.3	19.5	23.9	22.5
Item 13400 Subject A11c N	2780	1328	1406	2176	306	595	834	901	450	1605	1092	980	521	403	814	31

E03I: More criminal than average

1. No	15.6	16.0	15.2	15.4	17.0	13.8	15.5	16.3	16.8	14.2	17.9	10.5	14.6	18.3	20.8	28.4
2. Yes	63.1	62.3	63.8	64.9	53.6	62.9	66.2	63.3	57.1	66.4	58.1	69.7	62.5	63.8	55.4	58.8
3. Not sure, no opinion	21.3	21.7	21.0	19.6	29.4	23.3	18.2	20.4	26.1	19.4	23.9	19.8	22.9	17.9	23.8	12.8
Item 13410 Subject A11c N	2784	1330	1407	2180	305	592	839	899	454	1608	1092	979	524	404	815	31

E04: Do you think that MOST OF THE PEOPLE YOU KNOW feel that individuals who use illegal drugs (other than marijuana) several times a week tend to be . . .

E04A: More creative than average

1. No	62.1	60.2	63.9	64.8	49.4	62.1	62.9	61.8	61.1	66.4	55.9	64.6	64.0	63.3	58.1	53.6
2. Yes	13.5	13.9	13.3	12.7	19.3	14.8	13.9	12.9	12.5	11.1	17.3	11.3	12.3	15.6	16.0	15.5
3. Not sure, no opinion	24.4	25.9	22.8	22.5	31.4	23.1	23.2	25.3	26.4	22.4	26.8	24.0	23.8	21.1	25.9	30.9
Item 13490 Subject A12c N	2764	1318	1398	2164	302	593	833	892	447	1591	1088	972	518	401	810	31

E04B: Less sensible than average

1. No	16.0	17.2	14.7	14.9	21.2	17.9	13.6	16.0	17.7	14.6	18.2	14.8	14.1	15.3	18.3	39.6
2. Yes	62.7	60.3	65.5	65.9	48.9	61.1	67.6	60.5	59.9	66.3	57.4	65.5	63.8	64.7	59.0	39.3
3. Not sure, no opinion	21.3	22.5	19.8	19.2	29.9	20.9	18.8	23.4	22.4	19.1	24.4	19.7	22.2	19.9	22.7	21.1
Item 13500 Subject A12c N	2759	1318	1395	2161	301	592	831	891	446	1592	1085	971	518	401	808	31

E04C: More interesting people than average

1. No	62.6	61.0	64.6	65.5	47.5	62.5	65.4	60.8	61.2	66.2	57.8	65.3	62.7	64.3	60.1	42.1
2. Yes	13.7	13.5	13.9	12.8	20.4	14.8	11.8	14.6	14.2	12.6	15.5	12.6	12.8	12.9	15.5	27.5
3. Not sure, no opinion	23.6	25.5	21.5	21.7	32.1	22.6	22.8	24.6	24.5	21.2	26.8	22.1	24.6	22.8	24.4	30.4
Item 13510 Subject A12c N	2758	1314	1398	2161	300	593	832	887	446	1590	1085	972	517	398	809	31

QUESTIONNAIRE FORM 5 1983	TOTAL	SEX		RACE		REGION				4YR COLLEGE PLANS		ILLICIT DRUG USE: LIFETIME				
		M	F	White	Black	NE	NC	S	W	Yes	No	None	Marijuana Only	Few Pills	More Pills	Any Heroin
N (Weighted No. of Cases):	3339	1608	1628	2513	404	793	950	1082	514	1846	1297	1125	646	492	970	42
% of Weighted Total:	100.0	48.2	48.8	75.3	12.1	23.8	28.5	32.4	15.4	55.3	38.8	33.7	19.3	14.7	29.0	1.2

E04D: Less hard-working than average

1. No	17.7	17.4	17.9	17.3	18.2	20.1	15.8	16.8	20.3	15.6	20.6	15.5	15.8	17.2	21.3	36.7
2. Yes	58.9	58.4	59.8	61.4	48.3	56.8	62.6	58.1	56.1	63.0	52.8	62.6	59.9	62.8	53.2	46.4
3. Not sure, no opinion	23.4	24.2	22.3	21.2	33.5	23.2	21.7	25.1	23.7	21.4	26.5	21.9	24.3	20.0	25.5	16.9
Item 13520 Subject A12c N	2761	1318	1396	2161	302	590	831	893	447	1590	1087	970	520	400	809	31

E04E: More independent than average

1. No	50.7	47.1	54.4	52.1	46.3	50.3	48.1	52.8	51.9	52.3	48.4	51.5	52.0	55.9	47.7	39.8
2. Yes	23.8	27.1	20.8	23.7	22.3	25.4	26.0	21.5	21.9	23.3	24.6	23.9	21.6	21.2	25.5	45.0
3. Not sure, no opinion	25.5	25.8	24.9	24.1	31.4	24.3	25.9	25.6	26.2	24.4	27.0	24.6	26.4	22.9	26.8	15.2
Item 13530 Subject A12c N	2756	1313	1395	2159	299	590	828	891	447	1590	1084	970	516	401	807	31

E04F: More emotionally unstable than average

1. No	15.6	17.3	13.9	15.0	19.8	17.1	14.9	15.7	14.7	14.0	17.4	15.7	15.2	13.9	16.0	34.6
2. Yes	62.0	58.2	66.0	64.6	49.5	62.0	62.9	60.1	63.8	66.3	55.8	64.9	60.9	64.7	59.3	45.3
3. Not sure, no opinion	22.4	24.5	20.1	20.3	30.7	20.9	22.2	24.1	21.6	19.7	26.8	19.4	23.9	21.4	24.7	20.0
Item 13540 Subject A12c N	2756	1312	1396	2158	300	590	831	889	445	1591	1083	972	516	401	804	31

E04G: More concerned about other people than average

1. No	66.7	64.6	69.3	69.8	53.4	65.5	70.0	65.8	64.3	70.9	60.6	69.9	65.5	68.4	63.5	66.7
2. Yes	8.7	9.7	7.7	7.7	14.0	10.3	6.6	9.1	9.5	7.4	10.6	7.9	8.6	11.0	8.5	13.2
3. Not sure, no opinion	24.6	25.7	22.9	22.5	32.6	24.2	23.4	25.1	26.2	21.7	28.8	22.2	26.0	20.5	28.0	20.1
Item 13550 Subject A12c N	2758	1316	1394	2159	302	593	830	889	445	1588	1087	970	518	401	806	32

E04H: More weak-willed than average

1. No	16.8	16.2	17.3	16.5	17.9	18.9	15.4	16.5	17.0	16.0	17.9	14.9	15.1	16.4	19.5	33.1
2. Yes	59.0	58.8	59.7	61.1	51.4	56.2	61.7	58.8	58.1	62.4	54.1	63.1	60.2	61.2	53.7	47.3
3. Not sure, no opinion	24.2	25.1	23.0	22.4	30.7	24.9	22.9	24.7	24.9	21.6	28.0	22.0	24.7	22.4	26.8	19.6
Item 13560 Subject A12c N	2755	1314	1393	2158	300	591	831	889	443	1588	1084	971	517	401	803	32

E04I: More criminal than average

1. No	16.2	15.4	17.1	16.2	19.7	17.7	14.5	16.0	17.4	15.1	17.8	14.1	15.6	17.0	18.1	31.8
2. Yes	59.8	60.0	60.0	61.5	49.7	57.7	62.9	60.2	56.1	63.2	55.0	64.1	60.5	62.1	53.8	43.8
3. Not sure, no opinion	24.0	24.6	22.9	22.3	30.6	24.7	22.5	23.7	26.5	21.8	27.2	21.8	23.9	20.9	28.1	24.4
Item 13570 Subject A12c N	2753	1314	1391	2158	298	588	831	887	446	1589	1082	968	517	401	805	31

The next few questions ask how YOU view cigarette smoking.

E05: In my opinion, when a guy my age is smoking a cigarette, it makes him look . . .

E05A: Cool, calm, in-control

1. Disagree	58.6	59.3	58.5	60.6	52.9	53.6	52.2	63.2	68.3	61.2	55.3	72.7	59.6	52.5	45.4	36.0
2. Mostly disagree	14.1	14.1	14.2	14.4	11.3	12.2	18.5	12.3	12.0	15.1	13.0	10.6	15.9	20.8	13.5	27.1
3. Neither	19.7	18.4	20.6	19.5	18.9	24.3	22.2	17.5	13.4	17.5	22.5	11.7	16.1	19.4	31.2	28.8
4. Mostly agree	5.2	5.2	5.0	3.9	9.2	7.1	5.3	3.9	4.9	4.3	6.2	3.4	6.5	5.0	6.8	4.0
5. Agree	2.3	3.0	1.8	1.5	7.7	2.8	1.7	3.1	1.3	1.9	3.0	1.6	1.9	2.5	3.1	4.1
Item 20880 Subject A11c N	2802	1341	1408	2196	300	599	847	902	454	1607	1104	978	523	421	812	33

E05B: Insecure

1. Disagree	14.6	14.3	15.1	13.6	18.6	14.9	14.4	16.4	11.1	11.8	19.1	9.5	16.7	12.8	20.7	15.2
2. Mostly disagree	9.8	10.8	8.9	8.8	13.4	11.3	10.0	9.6	8.0	7.9	12.8	7.4	10.7	12.6	11.2	7.6
3. Neither	31.2	29.6	32.3	31.1	32.2	34.7	34.2	27.7	28.1	29.8	32.1	24.7	31.5	31.3	38.6	23.8
4. Mostly agree	22.5	22.8	22.4	24.2	13.3	18.9	23.9	22.8	23.8	26.3	17.4	24.9	22.8	23.1	18.4	38.9
5. Agree	21.9	22.5	21.2	22.3	22.5	20.2	17.5	23.4	29.0	24.2	18.6	33.5	18.2	20.3	11.1	14.6
Item 20890 Subject A11c N	2792	1341	1398	2189	301	593	846	899	454	1605	1098	977	522	421	806	33

QUESTIONNAIRE FORM 5 1983	TOTAL	SEX		RACE		REGION				4YR COLLEGE PLANS		ILLICIT DRUG USE: LIFETIME				
		M	F	White	Black	NE	NC	S	W	Yes	No	None	Mari-juana Only	Few Pills	More Pills	Any Her-oin
N (Weighted No. of Cases):	3339	1608	1628	2513	404	793	950	1082	514	1846	1297	1125	646	492	970	42
% of Weighted Total:	100.0	48.2	48.8	75.3	12.1	23.8	28.5	32.4	15.4	55.3	38.8	33.7	19.3	14.7	29.0	1.2
E05C: Rugged, tough, independent																
1. Disagree	49.7	50.8	49.0	51.8	44.3	47.8	41.7	54.9	56.7	51.0	48.2	59.3	49.0	48.2	40.5	34.2
2. Mostly disagree	16.2	15.9	16.7	16.5	14.6	15.3	19.3	15.3	13.5	17.4	14.6	14.2	17.6	20.0	15.2	27.9
3. Neither	22.5	22.9	21.7	22.0	22.8	24.8	25.7	19.5	19.9	20.7	24.8	16.2	20.7	20.8	31.9	28.7
4. Mostly agree	8.0	7.2	8.7	7.1	11.1	7.6	9.7	7.2	7.0	8.0	8.2	7.3	8.1	7.7	9.3	3.8
5. Agree	3.5	3.2	4.0	2.6	7.3	4.4	3.7	3.1	2.9	2.9	4.2	3.0	4.6	3.2	3.1	5.4
Item 20900　Subject A11c　　N	2788	1338	1397	2186	300	589	842	902	456	1598	1102	974	519	419	809	33
E05D: Conforming																
1. Disagree	27.3	27.6	26.9	26.0	31.7	27.0	22.4	31.9	28.0	24.8	31.6	30.2	27.1	26.4	24.5	23.0
2. Mostly disagree	9.5	10.0	9.1	9.6	10.1	9.6	9.4	10.2	8.3	8.5	10.9	7.2	9.9	14.2	9.3	14.6
3. Neither	38.9	37.4	39.9	38.6	39.0	39.5	43.7	36.2	34.4	35.3	42.8	35.4	37.2	35.8	45.1	45.3
4. Mostly agree	13.9	14.3	13.7	14.6	9.6	12.9	14.9	12.3	16.6	17.6	9.1	13.1	16.0	15.7	13.3	7.1
5. Agree	10.4	10.6	10.5	11.2	9.5	11.1	9.7	9.5	12.8	13.8	5.6	14.1	9.9	7.8	7.7	10.1
Item 20910　Subject A11c　　N	2746	1326	1368	2156	292	587	833	885	441	1581	1079	953	514	414	801	33
E05E: Mature, sophisticated																
1. Disagree	56.5	56.5	57.1	58.2	52.5	54.4	49.9	59.6	65.6	59.7	52.9	69.9	55.4	52.3	44.5	37.4
2. Mostly disagree	16.7	17.7	15.7	17.0	12.5	14.3	21.6	15.4	13.3	16.6	16.7	13.5	18.4	20.9	17.3	14.1
3. Neither	20.3	18.3	21.5	20.2	21.4	22.5	23.4	18.5	14.9	17.8	23.0	11.8	17.1	20.6	31.5	34.4
4. Mostly agree	4.4	5.2	3.6	3.3	7.7	5.7	3.7	4.1	4.8	4.1	4.9	3.4	6.5	3.6	4.6	10.0
5. Agree	2.1	2.2	2.0	1.3	6.0	3.0	1.5	2.4	1.4	1.8	2.6	1.4	2.6	2.5	2.1	4.1
Item 20920　Subject A11c　　N	2768	1330	1387	2176	295	590	836	890	451	1593	1094	968	512	419	804	33
E05F: Like he's TRYING to appear mature and sophisticated																
1. Disagree	13.5	13.1	13.9	12.7	16.0	15.6	12.9	14.2	10.6	10.0	17.7	10.4	13.9	12.4	17.8	6.6
2. Mostly disagree	6.2	7.3	5.3	5.6	8.6	7.1	6.6	5.9	5.1	5.7	7.2	3.7	6.3	7.2	8.5	13.3
3. Neither	17.9	17.2	18.0	18.2	12.5	18.8	21.3	14.4	17.3	15.9	20.2	10.7	15.2	19.2	27.1	26.4
4. Mostly agree	22.1	22.1	22.0	22.4	19.7	20.1	23.8	21.7	22.0	23.6	20.2	23.0	27.5	20.9	18.4	18.1
5. Agree	40.3	40.4	40.8	41.0	43.2	38.3	35.4	43.8	44.9	44.7	34.7	52.1	37.1	40.3	28.3	35.6
Item 20930　Subject A11c　　N	2783	1336	1396	2187	298	592	839	899	453	1596	1101	977	512	419	810	31
E06: In my opinion, when a girl my age is smoking a cigarette, it makes her look . . .																
E06A: Cool, calm, in-control																
1. Disagree	64.5	65.4	64.0	66.2	60.5	57.3	59.9	70.1	71.7	68.2	60.0	78.2	66.5	60.5	50.3	30.8
2. Mostly disagree	12.7	13.4	12.1	12.7	9.7	14.0	15.7	9.9	10.8	12.0	13.6	8.9	13.3	14.4	15.4	27.2
3. Neither	16.8	14.8	18.3	16.6	16.8	20.5	18.8	14.2	13.5	14.5	19.5	8.8	14.5	17.2	27.2	32.5
4. Mostly agree	3.8	4.0	3.7	2.9	7.5	5.4	4.2	2.9	2.7	3.3	4.4	2.5	3.7	4.3	5.0	4.2
5. Agree	2.2	2.3	1.9	1.6	5.5	2.8	1.5	2.9	1.4	2.0	2.5	1.7	2.0	3.6	2.1	5.3
Item 20940　Subject A11c　　N	2756	1309	1399	2169	293	587	839	882	448	1590	1083	968	514	410	800	33
E06B: Insecure																
1. Disagree	15.8	16.0	15.5	14.0	22.9	14.7	15.4	18.8	11.9	12.6	20.0	11.0	17.0	17.2	19.9	2.5
2. Mostly disagree	8.8	9.6	8.0	8.0	12.2	10.5	8.9	7.7	8.3	7.1	11.6	6.0	8.8	10.9	10.4	23.5
3. Neither	25.5	24.1	26.8	25.3	27.1	28.3	27.0	22.8	24.6	23.0	28.4	19.6	26.5	23.0	33.3	33.4
4. Mostly agree	19.7	19.3	20.2	21.0	11.2	20.1	21.4	18.9	17.5	22.2	16.1	20.7	19.5	19.9	18.6	24.3
5. Agree	30.2	31.0	29.5	31.7	26.6	26.4	27.3	31.7	37.7	35.0	23.9	42.7	28.2	28.9	17.8	16.3
Item 20950　Subject A11c　　N	2761	1315	1398	2173	294	585	840	887	448	1591	1087	970	516	411	799	33
E06C: Independent and liberated																
1. Disagree	52.3	53.2	51.6	53.7	50.0	48.0	47.6	57.2	57.0	54.4	49.2	64.4	51.1	51.9	40.3	28.5
2. Mostly disagree	15.3	15.3	15.4	14.7	14.2	14.8	16.5	14.8	14.8	15.7	15.1	13.4	18.5	15.9	14.5	29.7
3. Neither	19.9	18.2	21.2	20.2	19.7	24.4	21.7	16.8	16.9	18.0	22.4	13.5	16.2	19.3	30.2	23.0
4. Mostly agree	9.2	9.7	8.9	8.7	9.9	8.8	11.7	7.2	9.0	9.1	9.7	5.9	11.0	8.6	12.6	8.4
5. Agree	3.3	3.5	2.8	2.7	6.3	4.0	2.6	4.0	2.3	2.8	3.6	2.9	3.2	4.3	2.4	10.4
Item 20960　Subject A11c　　N	2743	1305	1389	2161	292	578	841	881	443	1580	1084	957	515	409	797	33

QUESTIONNAIRE FORM 5 1983	TOTAL	SEX		RACE		REGION				4YR COLLEGE PLANS		ILLICIT DRUG USE: LIFETIME				
		M	F	White	Black	NE	NC	S	W	Yes	No	None	Mari- juana Only	Few Pills	More Pills	Any Her- oin
N (Weighted No. of Cases):	3339	1608	1628	2513	404	793	950	1082	514	1846	1297	1125	646	492	970	42
% of Weighted Total:	100.0	48.2	48.8	75.3	12.1	23.8	28.5	32.4	15.4	55.3	38.8	33.7	19.3	14.7	29.0	1.2
E06D: Conforming																
1. Disagree	31.1	31.3	30.8	29.1	39.3	29.3	28.4	35.7	29.7	27.8	36.2	33.9	31.2	30.7	28.0	20.8
2. Mostly disagree	10.4	11.0	9.7	10.0	11.4	11.7	9.9	10.0	10.6	9.9	11.3	8.5	10.7	14.5	10.4	13.3
3. Neither	33.0	30.8	34.9	33.4	30.6	33.2	37.4	30.0	30.6	30.1	36.7	28.0	32.7	30.6	39.9	50.8
4. Mostly agree	12.1	12.8	11.7	12.7	8.4	11.9	12.1	10.9	14.5	14.2	9.0	12.1	11.8	12.0	12.7	5.1
5. Agree	13.3	14.1	13.0	14.9	10.2	13.9	12.2	13.5	14.6	18.0	6.8	17.4	13.6	12.3	9.1	10.1
Item 20970 Subject A11c N	2717	1296	1374	2140	290	575	834	872	436	1571	1070	943	511	405	795	33
E06E: Mature, sophisticated																
1. Disagree	60.0	60.8	59.7	62.1	54.4	55.2	57.7	62.9	64.9	64.4	54.1	73.7	59.3	59.3	46.0	26.0
2. Mostly disagree	14.4	14.5	14.4	14.5	11.2	15.2	17.0	13.1	10.9	13.0	16.5	12.1	15.4	14.2	15.8	28.5
3. Neither	18.0	16.3	19.2	17.8	18.6	21.6	19.0	15.9	15.8	16.5	19.5	9.3	15.8	18.8	29.5	25.4
4. Mostly agree	5.0	5.8	4.4	3.8	9.0	4.8	4.6	5.2	5.5	4.1	6.4	3.2	6.1	4.8	6.3	8.9
5. Agree	2.6	2.7	2.3	1.8	6.9	3.0	1.7	2.9	3.0	2.0	3.4	1.6	3.3	2.9	2.5	11.3
Item 20980 Subject A11c N	2740	1299	1393	2160	291	580	837	879	444	1584	1075	962	511	407	796	33
E06F: Like she's TRYING to appear mature and sophisticated																
1. Disagree	14.2	13.8	14.2	12.6	19.3	13.8	14.1	15.8	11.4	11.3	17.9	12.4	15.2	13.3	15.5	13.8
2. Mostly disagree	5.6	6.5	4.5	5.0	7.8	6.3	5.7	5.4	4.8	4.3	7.6	3.2	6.0	7.8	6.9	4.3
3. Neither	15.9	15.8	15.9	16.3	13.0	18.7	18.4	12.6	14.0	14.2	17.9	8.2	13.9	16.3	25.7	30.4
4. Mostly agree	20.1	20.1	20.0	20.1	17.9	19.7	22.5	18.1	20.2	20.4	19.1	19.6	23.8	17.5	20.1	19.7
5. Agree	44.2	43.7	45.2	46.0	42.1	41.5	39.3	48.0	49.7	49.8	37.5	56.6	41.1	45.0	31.8	31.7
Item 20990 Subject A11c N	2744	1297	1396	2163	291	580	841	877	445	1582	1082	963	510	408	796	33
E07: Do you agree or disagree..																
E07A: Smokers know how to enjoy life more than nonsmokers																
1. Disagree	72.1	67.7	76.7	73.8	67.7	69.0	68.5	75.5	75.8	76.1	67.5	82.6	74.6	68.1	60.6	56.7
2. Mostly disagree	10.7	12.5	9.2	10.4	8.8	12.6	12.1	7.5	12.0	10.0	11.9	7.5	8.5	12.0	15.4	14.9
3. Neither	13.6	15.3	11.6	13.1	15.5	15.0	15.5	12.7	9.9	11.3	15.8	6.7	14.0	16.1	20.3	13.2
4. Mostly agree	1.8	2.3	1.2	1.5	3.5	1.9	1.9	1.9	1.1	1.2	2.4	1.8	1.1	2.2	1.6	7.8
5. Agree	1.8	2.3	1.3	1.2	4.6	1.4	1.9	2.3	1.2	1.3	2.5	1.5	1.8	1.5	2.1	7.4
Item 21000 Subject A11c N	2784	1322	1411	2184	299	589	840	903	452	1601	1098	974	516	417	810	33
E07B: I prefer to date people who don't smoke																
1. Disagree	8.9	6.9	10.5	8.2	10.7	10.1	10.2	7.9	7.0	6.4	12.6	4.1	11.0	11.0	12.1	5.5
2. Mostly disagree	5.0	5.3	4.7	4.8	5.8	5.2	6.1	4.0	4.4	3.9	6.5	2.0	3.7	8.1	7.7	9.5
3. Neither	17.3	16.6	17.8	17.0	18.3	21.6	18.3	16.7	11.0	13.9	22.0	9.2	18.3	13.4	27.1	37.6
4. Mostly agree	10.9	10.9	11.1	10.7	9.5	12.1	12.1	9.3	10.5	11.0	10.5	9.5	9.5	11.6	13.7	7.6
5. Agree	57.9	60.3	55.8	59.3	55.7	51.0	53.2	62.0	67.1	64.8	48.5	75.2	57.5	55.9	39.4	39.8
Item 21010 Subject A11c N	2770	1314	1404	2175	297	587	836	896	451	1597	1088	968	514	416	808	32
E07C: The harmful effects of cigarettes have been exaggerated																
1. Disagree	45.6	43.8	47.9	47.7	41.2	45.9	42.3	44.1	54.7	49.8	40.9	55.9	46.4	42.6	35.8	24.9
2. Mostly disagree	19.3	17.8	20.6	20.5	12.7	19.4	22.2	17.8	16.4	21.1	16.4	18.3	18.4	18.2	21.5	33.9
3. Neither	17.7	18.7	16.0	17.1	19.3	17.0	19.1	18.4	14.4	14.9	21.2	13.1	19.2	19.1	20.6	27.7
4. Mostly agree	9.8	11.3	8.6	9.1	9.7	10.1	9.8	10.4	8.4	8.8	11.1	5.8	9.1	13.2	13.6	5.9
5. Agree	7.6	8.4	6.9	5.7	17.1	7.6	6.6	9.3	6.1	5.4	10.4	6.9	6.9	6.8	8.5	7.6
Item 21020 Subject A11c N	2769	1317	1399	2176	298	586	837	897	450	1597	1089	972	511	415	805	32
E07D: I think that becoming a smoker reflects poor judgment																
1. Disagree	10.8	9.4	12.1	10.2	13.4	14.8	8.2	12.2	7.8	8.7	13.5	7.6	12.2	10.9	13.6	15.5
2. Mostly disagree	8.5	9.4	7.7	8.4	6.9	8.3	9.2	7.9	8.3	7.8	9.5	6.3	8.0	11.4	9.7	17.3
3. Neither	21.7	20.7	22.4	21.6	21.7	25.3	22.5	19.8	19.1	19.3	24.7	15.1	20.3	19.8	30.9	27.0
4. Mostly agree	17.5	17.2	17.8	17.7	13.6	13.5	22.4	14.9	18.8	19.3	15.2	17.8	19.6	15.3	17.2	16.9
5. Agree	41.5	43.4	39.9	42.1	44.3	38.0	37.7	45.2	46.1	44.9	37.2	53.2	39.9	42.6	28.5	23.2
Item 21030 Subject A11c N	2759	1313	1393	2166	295	584	836	889	450	1593	1084	968	511	415	800	32

QUESTIONNAIRE FORM 5 1983	TOTAL	SEX		RACE		REGION				4YR COLLEGE PLANS		ILLICIT DRUG USE: LIFETIME				
		M	F	White	Black	NE	NC	S	W	Yes	No	None	Marijuana Only	Few Pills	More Pills	Any Heroin
N (Weighted No. of Cases):	3339	1608	1628	2513	404	793	950	1082	514	1846	1297	1125	646	492	970	42
% of Weighted Total:	100.0	48.2	48.8	75.3	12.1	23.8	28.5	32.4	15.4	55.3	38.8	33.7	19.3	14.7	29.0	1.2

E07E: I personally don't mind being around people who are smoking

1. Disagree	34.6	34.4	34.7	34.9	35.4	32.6	29.0	37.6	41.4	37.3	31.5	47.9	33.2	33.6	21.1	19.1
2. Mostly disagree	15.7	16.1	15.3	16.2	13.2	14.2	18.1	14.1	16.4	18.2	11.8	17.2	14.1	13.0	16.9	5.3
3. Neither	13.2	14.9	11.1	12.6	15.9	11.9	14.9	12.8	12.8	12.3	14.4	12.0	14.6	11.1	13.9	12.0
4. Mostly agree	16.7	17.0	16.6	17.1	13.7	18.2	17.3	16.0	15.3	16.3	17.6	12.7	18.6	19.9	19.0	26.0
5. Agree	19.8	17.6	22.2	19.1	21.7	23.2	20.7	19.5	14.1	15.9	24.7	10.1	19.6	22.4	29.1	37.7
Item 21040 Subject A11c N	2762	1313	1400	2170	296	585	835	895	448	1590	1086	971	510	412	803	32

E07F: Smoking is a dirty habit

1. Disagree	9.9	10.0	9.7	8.8	13.4	10.9	10.3	10.8	6.2	8.0	12.5	7.1	10.3	10.9	12.2	20.1
2. Mostly disagree	7.0	7.1	6.8	6.6	7.7	9.6	5.1	7.3	6.4	7.2	6.5	5.2	6.8	7.8	8.8	13.9
3. Neither	15.9	17.1	14.5	15.3	20.4	17.2	18.0	13.9	14.1	13.9	18.0	12.1	16.8	13.9	20.3	20.2
4. Mostly agree	16.8	17.6	16.2	17.7	8.4	15.7	19.4	14.8	17.3	17.8	15.5	14.8	16.5	18.7	18.4	13.7
5. Agree	50.5	48.1	52.9	51.6	50.1	46.7	47.2	53.2	56.0	53.1	47.5	60.8	49.7	48.7	40.2	32.2
Item 21050 Subject A11c N	2764	1315	1398	2170	297	585	836	893	450	1593	1086	970	511	414	802	32

E08: The next question is about soft drinks which contain caffeine. These include cola drinks like Coca-Cola, Pepsi-Cola, Diet-Pepsi, Tab, Dr. Pepper, etc. They also include Mountain Dew, Mr. Pibb, and Mello Yello. About how many 12-ounce cans or bottles (or the equivalent) of these do you drink per day, on the average?

1. None	9.3	8.6	10.0	8.6	11.7	13.1	7.0	7.9	11.5	9.9	9.0	12.3	9.6	7.0	6.9	6.4
2. Less than one a day	27.4	28.2	26.7	27.8	26.6	31.9	27.6	22.3	31.4	30.9	22.1	31.4	29.0	23.0	24.2	19.3
3. About one	25.0	25.3	25.0	25.5	23.9	24.6	25.6	24.4	25.6	25.6	23.3	26.6	24.6	27.1	23.1	10.3
4. About two	20.6	19.9	21.0	20.7	20.9	16.2	21.5	24.3	17.1	18.0	24.4	15.1	21.3	25.4	23.9	37.7
5. About three	9.8	9.7	9.8	10.3	6.8	7.9	10.8	10.5	8.8	8.5	11.6	8.7	8.1	10.7	11.9	8.9
6. About four	4.9	4.8	4.9	4.6	4.9	3.1	5.2	6.4	3.8	4.3	6.1	3.6	4.9	4.8	6.3	8.5
7. About five to six	1.7	1.8	1.7	1.5	1.6	1.9	1.6	1.9	1.2	1.5	2.1	1.6	1.3	1.3	2.0	-
8. Seven or more	1.3	1.7	1.0	0.9	3.5	1.4	0.6	2.3	0.5	1.2	1.5	0.7	1.3	0.8	1.8	8.9
Item 21130 Subject A01d N	2475	1194	1238	1960	259	524	760	790	401	1443	955	881	459	365	711	30

E09: About how many 12-ounce cans or bottles (or the equivalent) of OTHER soft drinks do you drink per day, on the average–such things as 7-Up, Sprite, root beer, carbonated orange or grape drinks, etc.?

1. None	21.1	19.1	23.2	22.4	12.1	21.8	21.4	20.4	20.6	21.8	20.0	21.7	20.6	19.7	22.4	9.8
2. Less than one a day	36.1	37.1	35.0	37.8	30.5	36.5	39.6	32.2	36.7	39.8	30.6	39.2	36.1	32.8	34.2	30.7
3. About one	21.6	21.1	22.1	21.3	23.7	21.8	20.1	21.8	23.4	20.7	22.5	22.5	21.6	21.9	20.4	15.0
4. About two	12.6	13.1	12.2	11.1	19.1	11.9	11.7	14.6	11.2	10.1	16.7	8.7	13.6	15.1	14.9	20.5
5. About three	4.4	4.6	4.3	3.7	5.5	4.2	3.7	4.9	5.1	3.6	5.5	4.0	3.5	5.0	4.7	12.2
6. About four	2.6	2.5	2.4	2.2	5.3	2.6	2.5	3.2	1.8	2.8	2.4	1.9	3.5	4.0	2.1	4.8
7. About five to six	0.7	1.1	0.3	0.8	0.6	0.1	0.7	1.0	0.7	0.5	1.0	1.1	0.2	0.3	0.5	-
8. Seven or more	1.0	1.4	0.6	0.6	3.3	1.1	0.2	1.8	0.5	0.6	1.4	0.8	1.1	1.4	0.7	7.0
Item 21140 Subject A01d N	2732	1297	1388	2152	296	577	828	883	444	1574	1080	960	507	407	794	31

E10: About how many cups of coffee (or glasses of iced coffee) do you drink per day on the average? Do NOT include decaffeinated coffees such as Sanka or Brim. (NOTE: If you use a mug that would hold two regular coffee-cups, for instance, count that as two cups.)

1. None	64.1	61.9	66.8	64.2	68.6	59.3	65.0	65.0	66.9	64.9	63.3	72.9	63.8	58.0	56.9	47.8
2. Less than one a day	14.5	14.9	14.3	14.8	12.7	16.5	13.8	13.4	15.4	15.1	13.2	12.0	16.0	17.2	15.4	21.0
3. About one	9.3	10.2	8.3	9.0	10.8	10.7	9.8	9.8	5.6	9.1	9.5	7.2	10.7	8.2	11.5	9.4
4. About two	5.5	5.7	5.1	5.5	4.4	6.2	4.6	5.9	5.5	5.1	6.1	3.7	4.5	8.0	6.7	13.0
5. About three	2.8	3.2	2.4	2.8	1.6	2.6	2.8	3.2	2.2	2.6	3.1	1.9	1.6	5.1	3.5	2.2
6. About four	2.3	2.3	2.2	2.3	0.5	3.4	1.9	1.2	3.7	1.9	2.8	1.5	2.1	2.2	3.6	-
7. About five to six	0.7	0.7	0.8	0.8	-	0.8	1.1	0.5	0.1	0.6	1.0	0.4	0.6	0.7	1.1	2.2
8. Seven or more	0.8	1.2	0.2	0.6	1.5	0.4	0.9	1.1	0.6	0.7	1.0	0.4	0.7	0.7	1.2	4.3
Item 21150 Subject A01d N	2725	1295	1382	2144	294	577	826	881	442	1571	1074	958	503	408	792	32

QUESTIONNAIRE FORM 5 1983	TOTAL	SEX		RACE		REGION				4YR COLLEGE PLANS		ILLICIT DRUG USE: LIFETIME				
		M	F	White	Black	NE	NC	S	W	Yes	No	None	Mari-juana Only	Few Pills	More Pills	Any Her-oin
N (Weighted No. of Cases):	3339	1608	1628	2513	404	793	950	1082	514	1846	1297	1125	646	492	970	42
% of Weighted Total:	100.0	48.2	48.8	75.3	12.1	23.8	28.5	32.4	15.4	55.3	38.8	33.7	19.3	14.7	29.0	1.2
E11: About how many cups of tea (or glasses of iced tea) do you drink per day on the average? Do not include decaffeinated teas.																
1. None	43.8	46.7	40.9	43.4	44.6	40.0	52.5	32.4	54.9	43.5	44.3	46.3	43.9	42.3	42.2	27.5
2. Less than one a day	21.3	20.2	22.4	21.2	23.0	26.8	20.5	18.4	21.6	22.7	19.7	19.6	20.8	20.4	24.0	35.7
3. About one	12.5	11.0	14.0	12.1	12.2	13.1	9.4	15.8	11.1	13.4	10.9	12.2	12.6	11.6	13.0	17.1
4. About two	9.6	9.0	10.2	9.7	11.1	8.3	7.2	14.4	5.9	8.8	10.7	10.0	10.8	12.0	7.1	8.4
5. About three	6.5	6.3	6.6	7.0	3.9	6.0	5.0	9.9	2.9	5.8	7.2	6.5	5.9	8.2	6.0	-
6. About four	3.6	3.7	3.4	3.8	3.5	3.1	2.7	5.6	1.8	2.9	4.7	3.0	3.4	4.0	4.1	3.0
7. About five to six	1.3	1.4	1.3	1.5	0.6	1.9	1.1	1.1	1.4	1.5	0.9	1.5	1.0	1.1	1.4	3.9
8. Seven or more	1.4	1.7	1.2	1.4	1.1	0.7	1.5	2.3	0.5	1.3	1.7	1.0	1.5	0.4	2.2	4.3
Item 21160 Subject A01d N	2719	1290	1382	2140	295	572	822	880	444	1567	1072	955	504	408	788	32
E12: About how many cups (or glasses) of DE-CAFFEINATED coffee or tea do you drink per day on the average?																
1. None	83.5	83.5	83.8	85.9	76.4	79.8	86.6	84.4	81.0	85.1	81.8	85.6	82.4	79.6	83.7	79.0
2. Less than one a day	8.5	9.0	8.1	7.5	12.8	11.5	7.2	7.0	10.2	8.0	9.1	7.4	9.3	10.1	8.7	9.9
3. About one	3.6	3.0	4.1	3.1	5.1	5.4	2.5	3.4	3.6	3.3	3.9	2.8	3.8	4.7	3.9	2.2
4. About two	1.9	1.7	2.0	1.6	3.9	1.8	1.9	1.7	2.3	1.5	2.2	2.0	1.9	1.8	1.8	1.4
5. About three	1.1	1.2	0.9	0.9	-	0.5	0.9	1.3	1.6	1.0	1.2	0.5	1.6	2.8	0.8	-
6. About four	0.7	0.7	0.6	0.6	0.2	0.4	0.6	0.9	0.8	0.6	0.9	0.8	0.2	0.8	0.8	3.1
7. About five to six	0.3	0.2	0.4	0.2	0.5	0.3	0.1	0.4	0.4	0.2	0.4	0.5	0.4	-	0.1	-
8. Seven or more	0.4	0.7	0.1	0.2	1.1	0.2	0.1	0.9	0.1	0.4	0.5	0.4	0.5	0.2	0.3	4.4
Item 21170 Subject A01d N	2703	1280	1376	2127	292	569	817	873	442	1555	1068	953	501	403	783	31
E13: If you had ever used marijuana or hashish, do you think that you would have said so in this questionnaire?																
1. No	5.1	6.6	3.7	3.8	10.8	4.4	4.5	7.3	2.8	4.0	6.9	6.8	4.0	7.5	1.9	4.7
2. Not sure	6.1	7.0	5.2	5.6	7.4	5.6	5.2	6.5	7.5	6.4	5.7	11.0	4.3	2.3	3.0	11.3
3. Yes	59.1	57.5	60.6	59.5	59.1	55.3	58.3	63.7	56.3	61.2	56.0	78.7	49.4	60.5	42.3	34.0
4. I did say so	29.8	29.0	30.6	31.1	22.6	34.7	32.0	22.6	33.4	28.4	31.3	3.5	42.3	29.7	52.7	50.0
Item 20800 Subject A15a N	2675	1263	1366	2108	290	563	812	857	442	1540	1055	928	493	406	785	32
E14: If you had ever used amphetamines (without a doctor's orders), do you think that you would have said so in this questionnaire?																
1. No	7.1	8.5	5.6	4.7	17.2	6.2	5.9	10.0	5.0	6.0	9.2	7.1	9.1	9.1	4.2	11.6
2. Not sure	7.6	8.7	6.4	7.1	9.6	8.5	7.0	7.0	8.6	8.1	6.9	12.4	6.9	4.8	3.9	6.0
3. Yes	67.3	65.2	69.6	68.8	66.3	65.6	66.0	69.3	67.7	69.7	63.6	76.9	77.2	70.0	50.3	25.3
4. I did say so	18.0	17.5	18.3	19.4	6.9	19.7	21.1	13.7	18.8	16.3	20.3	3.7	6.7	16.1	41.7	57.1
Item 20810 Subject A15a N	2673	1264	1362	2108	290	563	810	858	442	1541	1051	929	492	405	783	32
E15: If you had ever used heroin, do you think that you would have said so in this questionnaire?																
1. No	9.5	11.7	7.2	7.2	17.5	8.5	8.9	11.4	8.0	7.4	12.6	8.1	10.5	10.4	9.5	7.8
2. Not sure	10.3	12.0	8.8	10.2	11.2	12.0	9.5	9.2	11.7	11.4	8.9	14.7	8.2	7.8	8.0	6.5
3. Yes	71.8	68.5	75.6	75.0	64.3	71.1	73.2	72.2	69.8	74.2	68.5	73.2	75.0	72.6	70.4	21.7
4. I did say so	8.4	7.9	8.4	7.6	7.1	8.4	8.4	7.2	10.6	7.0	10.0	3.9	6.3	9.1	12.1	64.0
Item 20820 Subject A15a N	2676	1266	1364	2110	290	561	811	862	443	1542	1054	930	492	405	785	32

Cross-Time Index of Questionnaire Items, 1975-1983

Introduction to the Indexing Conventions

Beginning with the 1982 volume, the cross-time index of question locations is organized first by subject area (see Table 3 for complete listing). Within each subject area, questions are listed in numerical sequence according to item reference number, which is the unique numerical identifier assigned to each question in the study.

The Question Index may be used in two major ways:

1. **Locating a Question Across Years.** Having located a question of interest in the Descriptive Results section, the reader may determine in what other years that same question has appeared by simply looking it up by subject area and item reference number. The Index will show all years in which that item has appeared and also show its location each year (by questionnaire form, section, and item number). All items will retain their unique reference numbers in future years as well, and thus may be located in exactly the same way in subsequent volumes in this series.

EXAMPLE: A reader interested in a particular item about the nation needing more long-range planning would note that it has been classified under subject area I01 ("Expectations concerning social change") and that it has been assigned item reference number 1200. The index entry for item 1200 shows that this item has appeared in Section A of questionnaire Form 1 in all annual surveys in the series. Its question number was 4A in 1975 and 2A thereafter.

2. **Locating Questions by Subject Area.** Given an interest in some particular subject area, one can quickly scan the Index to locate all questions dealing with that area. Table 3 lists all the subject areas into which items are classified, along with the alphanumeric code assigned to each area.

EXAMPLE: A reader interested in items dealing with religion should first locate the relevant code in Table 3: Code G, "Religion." The second step is to scan that section of the item index, noting for every item its item reference number and page location in this volume. The reader may or may not find the abbreviated description of the item (given in the third column of the index and further described below) helpful in deciding whether to look up a particular item in the Descriptive Results section. Some of these descriptions are rather clear as to their meaning, but others are less so.

Definition of the Column Headings

The definitions of column headings, and the conventions used for the entries in each column, are given below under the numbers indicated in the following key.

①**Item Reference Number.** A unique identification number is assigned to each question for the duration of this research and reporting series. It appears below that question in the Descriptive Results section, as well as in this index and the indices of all other volumes in this series.

②**Page Location.** The second column of the Question Index gives the page number of the present volume on which a verbatim statement of the question may be found along with this year's descriptive results.

③**Item Description (Abbreviated).** This is a brief mnemonic description — up to 16 characters in length — that attempts to characterize the content of the question. Originally developed for question identification on OSIRIS computer files, it may in many cases allow one to determine the relevance of the question to one's own interest and thus reduce the number of irrelevant questions that must be looked up in the Descriptive Results section.

④ **Questionnaire Location by Year.** An entry is provided for every year in which an item appeared in one of the study's questionnaire forms. The six (or fewer) characters comprising the entry indicate the form in which the question appeared, the section of that form, and the question number. Take as an example the questionnaire location 1A004A. This location code indicates that the question appeared in Form 1, Section A, and was labeled as Question 4a.

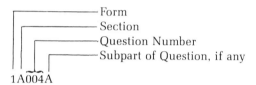

Occasionally an entry will be enclosed in parentheses. This indicates that there was a change (usually minor) in the wording of the question and/or the answer alternatives in subsequent years.

A form number (ranging from 1 to 5) is usually shown in the first character location. However, two substitute characters will replace the form number at times:

+ A plus sign indicates that the item appeared in all five forms that year and that it appeared in the same location on all forms.

* An asterisk indicates that the item appeared in four forms (Forms 2 through 5) and in the same location on all forms.

⑤ **Subject Area.** Table 3 shows the subject content areas that have been distinguished here and gives the alphanumeric code assigned to each of them. Every question item in the index has been classified into (and listed under) one or more of the subject areas, and the index (beginning with the 1982 volume) has been organized by subject area.

Figure 2

Guide to Cross-Time Index

①	②	③	④								

Item Refer- ence Number	Page Loc. in this Volume	ITEM DESCRIPTION (ABBREVIATED)	QUESTIONNAIRE LOCATION BY YEAR (FORM, SECTION, AND QUESTION NUMBER)								
			1975	1976	1977	1978	1979	1980	1981	1982	1983

⑤ — **A01a: DRUGS. Number of uses in lifetime**

760	41	EVR SMK CIG,REGL	1A018 *B01	+B001	+B001	+B001	+B001	+B001	+B001	+B001	+B001
790	25	EVER DRINK	1A026 *B03	*B03	*B03	*B03	*B03	*B03	*B03	*B03	*B03
810	42	#X DRNK/LIFETIME	1A028A	1B007A	1B007A	1B007A	1B007A	1B007A	1B007A	1B007A	1B007A
	25		*B04A	*B04A	*B04A	*B04A	*B04A	*B04A	*B04A	*B04A	*B04A
860		#XMJ+HS/LIFETIME	1A044A								
	26		*B07A	*B07A	*B07A	*B07A	*B07A	*B07A	*B07A	*B07A	*B07A
890	51	#X LSD/LIFETIME	1A057A	1B029A	1B029A	1B029A	1B029A	1B029A	1B029A	1B033A	1B033A
	27		*B08A	*B08A	*B08A	*B08A	*B08A	*B08A	*B08A	*B08A	*B08A
920	54	#X PSYD/LIFETIME	1A071A	1B038A	1B038A	1B038A	1B038A	1B038A	1B038A	1B042A	1B042A
	27		*B09A	*B09A	*B09A	*B09A	*B09A	*B09A	*B09A	*B09A	*B09A
950	71	#X COKE/LIFETIME	1A144A	1B076A	1B076A	1B076A	1B076A	1B076A	1B076A	1B083A	1B083A
	28		*B10A	*B10A	*B10A	*B10A	*B10A	*B10A	*B10A	*B10A	*B10A
980	57	#X AMPH/LIFETIME	1A087A	1B043A	1B043A	1B043A	1B043A	1B043A	1B043A	1B050A	1B050A
	29		*B11A	*B11A	*B11A	*B11A	*B11A	*B11A	*B11A	*B11A	*B11A
1010	61	#X QUAD/LIFETIME	1A102A	1B053A	1B053A	1B053A	1B053A	1B053A	1B053A	1B060A	1B060A
	30		*B12A	*B12A	*B12A	*B12A	*B12A	*B12A	*B12A	*B12A	*B12A
1040	62	#X BRBT/LIFETIME	1A116A	1B057A	1B057A	1B057A	1B057A	1B057A	1B057A	1B064A	1B064A
	30		*B13A	*B13A	*B13A	*B13A	*B13A	*B13A	*B13A	*B13A	*B13A
1070	67	#X TRQL/LIFETIME	1A131A	1B067A	1B067A	1B067A	1B067A	1B067A	1B067A	1B074A	1B074A
	31		*B14A	*B14A	*B14A	*B14A	*B14A	*B14A	*B14A	*B14A	*B14A
1100	75	#X "H"/LIFETIME	1A158A	1B085A	1B085A	1B085A	1B085A	1B085A	1B085A	1B092A	1B092A
	31		*B15A	*B15A	*B15A	*B15A	*B15A	*B15A	*B15A	*B15A	*B15A
1130	76	#X NARC/LIFETIME	1A173A	1B095A	1B095A	1B095A	1B095A	1B095A	1B095A	1B094A	1B094A
	32		*B16A	*B16A	*B16A	*B16A	*B16A	*B16A	*B16A	*B16A	*B16A
1160	32	#X INHL/LIFETIME		*B17A	*B17A	*B17A	*B17A	*B17A	*B17A	*B17A	*B17A
1181	111	#X PCP/LIFETIME							⁻²⁰A	2E02A	2E02A
1184	112	#X PPRS/LIFETIME								⁻E03A	2E03A
2040	46	#X HASH/LIFETIM		1B018A							1B018A
2070	47	#X MARJ/LIFETIME		1B⁰							⁻⁰19A
11000	164	#X BEER/LIFETIME									
11040	165	#X WINE/LIFETIME									
11080	166	#X LIQR/LIFETIME									
21180	50	MJ/HSH EVR DLY									
⁻¹²²⁰	55	#X DIETPIL									

Table 3

Subject Area Key
(Referenced by letter in the Question Index)

A. **Drugs.** Drug use and related attitudes and beliefs, drug availabilty and exposure, surrounding conditions and social meaning of drug use. Views of significant others regarding drugs.

A01   Use of Drugs
        A01a — . . . in lifetime
        A01b — . . . in the last 12 months
        A01c — . . . in the last 30 days
        A01d —Quantity used
        A01e —How high? (How often?)
        A01f —How long high?
        A01g —Incidence of first use
        A01h —Use with other drugs
        A01i —Try to stop?
        A01j — . . . on doctor's orders?
        A01k —Bad trip?
        A01l —Kinds of drugs

A02   Exposure to Drug Use
        A02a —Friends' use of drugs
        A02b —Exposure to users

A03   Availability of Drugs

A04   Expected Future Use

A05   Conditions of Use
        A05a —Alone
        A05b —With others
        A05c —Settings
        A05d —Mode of drug administration

A06   Reasons for Use, Abstention, and Stopping

A07   Problems with Drugs

A08   Sources of Help regarding Drugs

A09   Parental Awareness of Use

A10   Drug Education

A11   Own Attitudes regarding Drugs and Drug Users
        A11a —For adults
        A11b —For own children
        A11c —Perception of drug users

A12   Others' Attitudes regarding Drugs and Drug Users

        A12a —Parents
        A12b —Friends
        A12c —Students in school
        A12d —Perception of Drug Users

A13   Legal Issues regarding Drugs
        A13a —Preferred legality for adults
        A13b —Own response to legalization
        A13c —Knowledge of marijuana laws

A14   Risk of Drug Harm
        A14a —To self
        A14b —To others

B. **Education.**

B01   High school: scholastic status, objectives, experiences

B02   Combining work and school: attitudes, experiences

B03   Interracial contact at school

B04   Student norms

B05   Counseling

B06   Absenteeism and truancy

B07   Delinquency and victimization at school

B08   Opinions regarding competency testing

B09   Post high school: status, plans, characteristics

B10   Attitudes regarding educational institutions

C. **Work and Leisure.**

C01   Present or recent work experience

C02   Income sources; financial security

C03   Vocational plans, aspiration, expectations

C04   Preferences regarding job characteristics

Table 3 (continued)

C05 Desirability of different working arrangements and settings

C06 Work ethic/success orientation

C07 Leisure time: extent, activities

C08 Attitudes toward leisure time

D. **Sex Roles and Family.**

D01 Dating and marriage: status, attitudes, expectations

D02 Parenthood: status, attitudes, expectations

D03 Values surrounding marriage and family

D04 Preferences regarding marital/familial arrangements

D05 Sex role attitudes

D06 Opinions regarding sex discrimination

E. **Population Concerns.**

E01 Overpopulation

E02 Birth control

F. **Conservation, Materialism, Equity, etc.**

F01 Personal materialism

F02 Societal materialism and advertising

F03 Concern with world hunger and poverty

F04 Ecological concerns

F05 Concern with conservation of resources

F06 Preferences regarding dwelling type and urbanicity

F07 Driving and use of mass transit

G. **Religion.** **Religious preferences, activities, views.**

H. **Politics.**

H01 Political interest and preferences

H02 Attitudes toward governmental policies and practices

H03 Views about the role of citizens in government. (See also I02: Attitudes regarding activism)

H04 Confidence in government

H05 Voting, political activism

I. **Social Change.**

I01 Expectations concerning societal change

I02 Attitudes regarding activism

I03 Reactions to personal and social change

J. **Social Problems. Interest and concerns.**

K. **Major Social Institutions**

K01 Trust (See also C05: Institutions as work settings)

K02 Satisfaction with performance

K03 Preferred influence

L. **Military.**

L01 Plans for military service

L02 Attitudes toward a draft

L03 Views about the use of military force

L04 Attitudes toward the military as an institution and occupation

M. **Interpersonal Relationships.**

M01 Dating

M02 Cross-age relationships with adults outside the family (See also B05)

M03 Agreement/disagreement with parents

Table 3 (continued)

M04 Friendships (See also Q03: Loneliness)

M05 Community at large

N. Race Relations.

N01 Preferred interracial contact

N02 Attitudes about discrimination

N03 Actual interracial contacts

O. Concern for Others.

O01 Attitudes regarding social service, charitable activism

O02 Involvement in community, altruistic activities

O03 Concern with the problems of others

P. Happiness.

P01 Happiness; satisfaction with life and self

P02 Satisfaction with specific life domains

Q. Other Personality Variables.

Q01 Attitudes about self, self-esteem

Q02 Locus of control

Q03 Loneliness

Q04 Risk taking

Q05 Trust in others

Q06 Health habits and symptoms

Q07 Importance placed on various life goals

Q08 Social, political, cultural orientation

Q09 Hostility

R. Background

R01 Age, sex, race, and marital status

R02 Family characteristics

R03 Living arrangements and household characteristics

S. Deviance and Victimization

S01 Delinquent behaviors

S02 Driving violations and accidents

S03 Victimization experiences

Item Reference Number	Page Loc. in this Volume	ITEM DESCRIPTION (ABBREVIATED)	QUESTIONNAIRE LOCATION BY YEAR (FORM, SECTION, AND QUESTION NUMBER)								
			1975	1976	1977	1978	1979	1980	1981	1982	1983

A01a: DRUGS. Number of uses in lifetime

Item Reference Number	Page Loc. in this Volume	ITEM DESCRIPTION (ABBREVIATED)	1975	1976	1977	1978	1979	1980	1981	1982	1983
760	41	EVR SMK CIG,REGL	1A018 *B01	+B001	+B001	+B001	+B001	+B001	+B001	+B001	+B001
790	25	EVER DRINK	1A026 *B03	*B03	*B03	*B03	*B03	*B03	*B03	*B03	*B03
810	42	#X DRNK/LIFETIME	1A028A	1B007A	1B007A	1B007A	1B007A	1B007A	1B007A	1B007A	1B007A
	25		*B04A	*B04A	*B04A	*B04A	*B04A	*B04A	*B04A	*B04A	*B04A
860		#XMJ+HS/LIFETIME	1A044A								
	26		*B07A	*B07A	*B07A	*B07A	*B07A	*B07A	*B07A	*B07A	*B07A
890	51	#X LSD/LIFETIME	1A057A	1B029A	1B029A	1B029A	1B029A	1B029A	1B029A	1B033A	1B033A
	27		*B08A	*B08A	*B08A	*B08A	*B08A	*B08A	*B08A	*B08A	*B08A
920	54	#X PSYD/LIFETIME	1A071A	1B038A	1B038A	1B038A	1B038A	1B038A	1B038A	1B042A	1B042A
	27		*B09A	*B09A	*B09A	*B09A	*B09A	*B09A	*B09A	*B09A	*B09A
950	71	#X COKE/LIFETIME	1A144A	1B076A	1B076A	1B076A	1B076A	1B076A	1B076A	1B083A	1B083A
	28		*B10A	*B10A	*B10A	*B10A	*B10A	*B10A	*B10A	*B10A	*B10A
980	57	#X AMPH/LIFETIME	1A087A	1B043A	1B043A	1B043A	1B043A	1B043A	1B043A	1B050A	1B050A
	29		*B11A	*B11A	*B11A	*B11A	*B11A	*B11A	*B11A	*B11A	*B11A
1010	61	#X QUAD/LIFETIME	1A102A	1B053A	1B053A	1B053A	1B053A	1B053A	1B053A	1B060A	1B060A
	30		*B12A	*B12A	*B12A	*B12A	*B12A	*B12A	*B12A	*B12A	*B12A
1040	62	#X BRBT/LIFETIME	1A116A	1B057A	1B057A	1B057A	1B057A	1B057A	1B057A	1B064A	1B064A
	30		*B13A	*B13A	*B13A	*B13A	*B13A	*B13A	*B13A	*B13A	*B13A
1070	67	#X TRQL/LIFETIME	1A131A	1B067A	1B067A	1B067A	1B067A	1B067A	1B067A	1B074A	1B074A
	31		*B14A	*B14A	*B14A	*B14A	*B14A	*B14A	*B14A	*B14A	*B14A
1100	75	#X "H"/LIFETIME	1A158A	1B085A	1B085A	1B085A	1B085A	1B085A	1B085A	1B092A	1B092A
	31		*B15A	*B15A	*B15A	*B15A	*B15A	*B15A	*B15A	*B15A	*B15A
1130	76	#X NARC/LIFETIME	1A173A	1B095A	1B095A	1B095A	1B095A	1B095A	1B095A	1B094A	1B094A
	32		*B16A	*B16A	*B16A	*B16A	*B16A	*B16A	*B16A	*B16A	*B16A
1160	32	#X INHL/LIFETIME		*B17A	*B17A	*B17A	*B17A	*B17A	*B17A	*B17A	*B17A
1181	111	#X PCP/LIFETIME					2E02A	2E02A	2E02A	2E02A	2E02A
1184	112	#X PPRS/LIFETIME					2E03A	2E03A	2E03A	2E03A	2E03A
2040	46	#X HASH/LIFETIM		1B018A	1B018A	1B018A	1B018A	1B018A	1B018A	1B018A	1B018A
2070	47	#X MARJ/LIFETIME		1B019A	1B019A	1B019A	1B019A	1B019A	1B019A	1B019A	1B019A
11000	164	#X BEER/LIFETIME		4D04A	4D04A	4D04A	4D04A	4D04A	4D04A	4D11A	4D11A
11040	165	#X WINE/LIFETIME		4D06A	4D06A	4D06A	4D06A	4D06A	4D06A	4D13A	4D13A
11080	166	#X LIQR/LIFETIME		4D08A	4D08A	4D08A	4D08A	4D08A	4D08A	4D15A	4D15A
21180	50	MJ/HSH EVR DLY								1B028	1B028
21220	55	#X DIETPILL/LFT								1B046A	1B046A
21250	56	#X STA-AWAK/LFT								1B047A	1B047A
21280	56	#X LOOKALIK/LFT								1B048A	1B048A

A01b: DRUGS. Number of uses in last 12 months

Item Reference Number	Page Loc. in this Volume	ITEM DESCRIPTION (ABBREVIATED)	1975	1976	1977	1978	1979	1980	1981	1982	1983
820	43	#X DRNK/LAST12MO	1A028B	1B007B	1B007B	1B007B	1B007B	1B007B	1B007B	1B007B	1B007B
	25		*B04B	*B04B	*B04B	*B04B	*B04B	*B04B	*B04B	*B04B	*B04B
870		#XMJ+HS/LAST12MO	1A044B								
	26		*B07B	*B07B	*B07B	*B07B	*B07B	*B07B	*B07B	*B07B	*B07B
900	51	#X LSD/LAST 12MO	1A057B	1B029B	1B029B	1B029B	1B029B	1B029B	1B029B	1B033B	1B033B
	27		*B08B	*B08B	*B08B	*B08B	*B08B	*B08B	*B08B	*B08B	*B08B
930	54	#X PSYD/LAST12MO	1A071B	1B038B	1B038B	1B038B	1B038B	1B038B	1B038B	1B042B	1B042B
	27		*B09B	*B09B	*B09B	*B09B	*B09B	*B09B	*B09B	*B09B	*B09B
960	71	#X COKE/LAST12MO	1A144B	1B076B	1B076B	1B076B	1B076B	1B076B	1B076B	1B083B	1B083B
	28		*B10B	*B10B	*B10B	*B10B	*B10B	*B10B	*B10B	*B10B	*B10B
990	57	#X AMPH/LAST12MO	1A087B	1B043B	1B043B	1B043B	1B043B	1B043B	1B043B	1B050B	1B050B
	29		*B11B	*B11B	*B11B	*B11B	*B11B	*B11B	*B11B	*B11B	*B11B
1020	61	#X QUAD/LAST12MO	1A102B	1B053B	1B053B	1B053B	1B053B	1B053B	1B053B	1B060B	1B060B
	30		*B12B	*B12B	*B12B	*B12B	*B12B	*B12B	*B12B	*B12B	*B12B
1050	63	#X BRBT/LAST12MO	1A116B	1B057B	1B057B	1B057B	1B057B	1B057B	1B057B	1B064B	1B064B
	30		*B13B	*B13B	*B13B	*B13B	*B13B	*B13B	*B13B	*B13B	*B13B
1080	67	#X TRQL/LAST12MO	1A131B	1B067B	1B067B	1B067B	1B067B	1B067B	1B067B	1B074B	1B074B
	31		*B14B	*B14B	*B14B	*B14B	*B14B	*B14B	*B14B	*B14B	*B14B
1110	75	#X "H"/LAST 12MO	1A158B	1B085B	1B085B	1B085B	1B085B	1B085B	1B085B	1B092B	1B092B
	31		*B15B	*B15B	*B15B	*B15B	*B15B	*B15B	*B15B	*B15B	*B15B
1140	76	#X NARC/LAST12MO	1A173B	1B095B	1B095B	1B095B	1B095B	1B095B	1B095B	1B094B	1B094B
	32	(continued)	*B16B	*B16B	*B16B	*B16B	*B16B	*B16B	*B16B	*B16B	*B16B

Item Reference Number	Page Loc. in this Volume	ITEM DESCRIPTION (ABBREVIATED)	QUESTIONNAIRE LOCATION BY YEAR (FORM, SECTION, AND QUESTION NUMBER)								
			1975	1976	1977	1978	1979	1980	1981	1982	1983

A01b: DRUGS. Number of uses in last 12 months (continued)

Item Reference Number	Page Loc.	ITEM DESCRIPTION	1975	1976	1977	1978	1979	1980	1981	1982	1983
1170	33	#X INHL/LAST12MO		*B17B	*B17B	*B17B	*B17B	*B17B	*B17B	*B17B	*B17B
1182	111	#X PCP/LAST12MO					2E02B	2E02B	2E02B	2E02B	2E02B
1185	112	#X PPRS/LAST12MO					2E03B	2E03B	2E03B	2E03B	2E03B
2050	46	#X HASH/LAST12M		1B018B	1B018B	1B018B	1B018B	1B018B	1B018B	1B018B	1B018B
2080	47	#X MARJ/LAST12MO		1B019B	1B019B	1B019B	1B019B	1B019B	1B019B	1B019B	1B019B
8520	128	12MO,#OCC PAINRF	3A48A	3A27A	3A27A	3A27A	3A27A	3A27A	3A27A	3A27A	3A27A
8530	129	12MO,#OCC SLP PL	3A48B	3A27B	3A27B	3A27B	3A27B	3A27B	3A27B	3A27B	3A27B
8540	129	12MO,#OCC AWK PL	3A48C	3A27C	3A27C	3A27C	3A27C	3A27C	3A27C	3A27C	3A27C
8550	129	12MO,#OCC CALM P	3A48D	3A27D	3A27D	3A27D	3A27D	3A27D	3A27D	3A27D	3A27D
9010	135	NXT 12MOS USE MJ			3D04	3D04	3D04	3D04	3D04	3D04	3D04
11010	165	#X BEER/LAST12MO		4D04B	4D04B	4D04B	4D04B	4D04B	4D04B	4D11B	4D11B
11050	165	#X WINE/LAST12MO		4D06B	4D06B	4D06B	4D06B	4D06B	4D06B	4D13B	4D13B
11090	166	#X LIQR/LAST12MO		4D08B	4D08B	4D08B	4D08B	4D08B	4D08B	4D15B	4D15B
21230	55	#X DIETPILL/12M								1B046B	1B046B
21260	56	#X STA-AWAK/12M								1B047B	1B047B
21290	57	#X LOOKALIK/12M								1B048B	1B048B

A01c: DRUGS. Number of uses in last 30 days

Item Reference Number	Page Loc.	ITEM DESCRIPTION	1975	1976	1977	1978	1979	1980	1981	1982	1983
780	42	#CIGS SMKD/30DAY	1A020	1B003	1B003	1B003	1B003	1B003	1B003	1B003	1B003
	25		*B02	*B02	*B02	*B02	*B02	*B02	*B02	*B02	*B02
830	43	#X DRNK/LAST30DA	1A028C	1B007C	1B007C	1B007C	1B007C	1B007C	1B007C	1B007C	1B007C
	25		*B04C	*B04C	*B04C	*B04C	*B04C	*B04C	*B04C	*B04C	*B04C
880		#XMJ+HS/LAST30DA	1A044C								
	27		*B07C	*B07C	*B07C	*B07C	*B07C	*B07C	*B07C	*B07C	*B07C
910	51	#X LSD/LAST 30DA	1A057C	1B029C	1B029C	1B029C	1B029C	1B029C	1B029C	1B033C	1B033C
	27		*B08C	*B08C	*B08C	*B08C	*B08C	*B08C	*B08C	*B08C	*B08C
940	54	#X PSYD/LAST30DA	1A071C	1B038C	1B038C	1B038C	1B038C	1B038C	1B038C	1B042C	1B042C
	28		*B09C	*B09C	*B09C	*B09C	*B09C	*B09C	*B09C	*B09C	*B09C
970	71	#X COKE/LAST30DA	1A144C	1B076C	1B076C	1B076C	1B076C	1B076C	1B076C	1B083C	1B083C
	28		*B10C	*B10C	*B10C	*B10C	*B10C	*B10C	*B10C	*B10C	*B10C
1000	58	#X AMPH/LAST30DA	1A087C	1B043C	1B043C	1B043C	1B043C	1B043C	1B043C	1B050C	1B050C
	29		*B11C	*B11C	*B11C	*B11C	*B11C	*B11C	*B11C	*B11C	*B11C
1030	61	#X QUAD/LAST30DA	1A102C	1B053C	1B053C	1B053C	1B053C	1B053C	1B053C	1B060C	1B060C
	30		*B12C	*B12C	*B12C	*B12C	*B12C	*B12C	*B12C	*B12C	*B12C
1060	63	#X BRBT/LAST30DA	1A116C	1B057C	1B057C	1B057C	1B057C	1B057C	1B057C	1B064C	1B064C
	30		*B13C	*B13C	*B13C	*B13C	*B13C	*B13C	*B13C	*B13C	*B13C
1090	67	#X TRQL/LAST30DA	1A131C	1B067C	1B067C	1B067C	1B067C	1B067C	1B067C	1B074C	1B074C
	31		*B14C	*B14C	*B14C	*B14C	*B14C	*B14C	*B14C	*B14C	*B14C
1120	75	#X "H"/LAST 30DA	1A158C	1B085C	1B085C	1B085C	1B085C	1B085C	1B085C	1B092C	1B092C
	32		*B15C	*B15C	*B15C	*B15C	*B15C	*B15C	*B15C	*B15C	*B15C
1150	76	#X NARC/LAST30DA	1A173C	1B095C	1B095C	1B095C	1B095C	1B095C	1B095C	1B094C	1B094C
	32		*B16C	*B16C	*B16C	*B16C	*B16C	*B16C	*B16C	*B16C	*B16C
1180	33	#X INHL/LAST30DA		*B17C	*B17C	*B17C	*B17C	*B17C	*B17C	*B17C	*B17C
1183	112	#X PCP/LAST30DA					2E02C	2E02C	2E02C	2E02C	2E02C
1186	112	#X PPRS/LAST30DA					2E03C	2E03C	2E03C	2E03C	2E03C
2060	46	#X HASH/LAST30D		1B018C	1B018C	1B018C	1B018C	1B018C	1B018C	1B018C	1B018C
2090	47	#X MARJ/LAST30DA		1B019C	1B019C	1B019C	1B019C	1B019C	1B019C	1B019C	1B019C
11020	165	#X BEER/LAST30DA		4D04C	4D04C	4D04C	4D04C	4D04C	4D04C	4D11C	4D11C
11060	165	#X WINE/LAST30DA		4D06C	4D06C	4D06C	4D06C	4D06C	4D06C	4D13C	4D13C
11100	166	#X LIQR/LAST30DA		4D08C	4D08C	4D08C	4D08C	4D08C	4D08C	4D15C	4D15C
21240	55	#X DIETPILL/30D								1B046C	1B046C
21270	56	#X STA-AWAK/30D								1B047C	1B047C
21300	57	#X LOOKALIK/30D								1B048C	1B048C

A01d: DRUGS. Quantity used

Item Reference Number	Page Loc.	ITEM DESCRIPTION	1975	1976	1977	1978	1979	1980	1981	1982	1983
850	45	5+DRK ROW/LST 2W	1A035	1B012	1B012	1B012	1B012	1B012	1B012	1B012	1B012
	26		*B06	*B06	*B06	*B06	*B06	*B06	*B06	*B06	*B06
1990	45	#X/2W,3-4 DR RW	1A036	1B013	1B013	1B013	1B013	1B013	1B013	1B013	1B013
2000	45	#X/2WK,2 DRK RW	1A037	1B014	1B014	1B014	1B014	1B014	1B014	1B014	1B014
2010	46	#X/2WK,JST 1DRK	1A038	1B015	1B015	1B015	1B015	1B015	1B015	1B015	1B015
2360	49	JOINT/DA LST MO		1B025	1B025	1B025	1B025	1B025	1B025	1B025	1B025
		(continued)									

Item Reference Number	Page Loc. in this Volume	Item Description (Abbreviated)	QUESTIONNAIRE LOCATION BY YEAR (FORM, SECTION, AND QUESTION NUMBER)								
			1975	1976	1977	1978	1979	1980	1981	1982	1983

A01d: DRUGS. Quantity used (continued)

Item Reference Number	Page Loc. in this Volume	Item Description (Abbreviated)	1975	1976	1977	1978	1979	1980	1981	1982	1983
2370	49	OZS.MJ LST MO/6		1B026	1B026	1B026	1B026	1B026	1B026	1B026	1B026
11030	165	5+BR/LST2WK,10+X		4D05	4D05	4D05	4D05	4D05	4D05	4D12	4D12
11070	166	#X 20OZ+ WN/2 WK		4D07	4D07	4D07	4D07	4D07	4D07	4D14	4D14
11110	166	#X 5+LIQ/LST 2WK		4D09	4D09	4D09	4D09	4D09	4D09	4D16	4D16
21100		#CANS COLA/DAY							5E10		
21110		#CUPS COFFEE/DAY							5E11		
21120		#CUPS TEA/DAY							5E12		
21130	200	#12OZ CAF DRK/DA								5E08	5E08
21140	200	#12OZ OTH DRK/DA								5E09	5E09
21150	200	#CUPS COFFEE/DA								5E10	5E10
21160	201	#CUPS OF TEA/DAY								5E11	5E11
21170	201	#CUPS DECAFF/DAY								5E12	5E12
21210	50	#X DAILY MJ/LFT								1B031	1B031

A01e: DRUGS. How high, how often high

Item Reference Number	Page Loc. in this Volume	Item Description (Abbreviated)	1975	1976	1977	1978	1979	1980	1981	1982	1983
840	26	#X DRK ENF FL HI	*B05	*B05	*B05	*B05	*B05	*B05	*B05	*B05	*B05
1970	45	#X DRK ENF FL 4	1A033	1B010	1B010	1B010	1B010	1B010	1B010	1B010	1B010
2340	49	MJ/HSH,VRY HIGH	1A050	1B023	1B023	1B023	1B023	1B023	1B023	1B023	1B023
2650	53	LSD,GET VERY HI	1A063	1B033	1B033	1B033	1B033	1B033	1B033	1B037	1B037
2700	54	PSYD,GT VERY HI	1A077	1B039	1B039	1B039	1B039	1B039	1B039	1B043	1B043
3100	60	AMPH,GT VERY HI	1A093	1B047	1B047	1B047	1B047	1B047	1B047	1B054	1B054
3260	62	QUAD GT VERY HI	1A108	1B054	1B054	1B054	1B054	1B054	1B054	1B061	1B061
3590	65	BARB,GT VERY HI	1A122	1B061	1B061	1B061	1B061	1B061	1B061	1B068	1B068
4050	70	TRNQ,GT VERY HI	1A137	1B071	1B071	1B071	1B071	1B071	1B071	1B078	1B078
4520	74	COK,GET VERY HI	1A150	1B080	1B080	1B080	1B080	1B080	1B080	1B087	1B087
4930		HER,GT VERY HI	1A164	1B089	1B089	1B089	1B089	1B089	1B089		
5380	80	NARC,GT VERY HI	1A179	1B099	1B099	1B099	1B099	1B099	1B099	1B098	1B098

A01f: DRUGS. How long high

Item Reference Number	Page Loc. in this Volume	Item Description (Abbreviated)	1975	1976	1977	1978	1979	1980	1981	1982	1983
1980	45	DRK AL,HI24+HR	1A034	1B011	1B011	1B011	1B011	1B011	1B011	1B011	1B011
2350	49	MJ/HSH,HI 24+HR	1A051	1B024	1B024	1B024	1B024	1B024	1B024	1B024	1B024
2660	53	LSD,HIGH 24+ HR	1A064	1B034	1B034	1B034	1B034	1B034	1B034	1B038	1B038
2710	55	PSYD,HI 24+ HRS	1A078	1B040	1B040	1B040	1B040	1B040	1B040	1B044	1B044
3110	60	AMPH,HI 24+ HRS	1A094	1B048	1B048	1B048	1B048	1B048	1B048	1B055	1B055
3270	62	QUAD,HI 24+ HRS	1A109	1B055	1B055	1B055	1B055	1B055	1B055	1B062	1B062
3600	66	BARB,HI 24+ HRS	1A123	1B062	1B062	1B062	1B062	1B062	1B062	1B069	1B069
4060	70	TRNQ,HI 24+ HRS	1A138	1B072	1B072	1B072	1B072	1B072	1B072	1B079	1B079
4530	74	COK,HIGH 24+ HR	1A151	1B081	1B081	1B081	1B081	1B081	1B081	1B088	1B088
4940		HER,HI 24+ HRS	1A165	1B090	1B090	1B090	1B090	1B090	1B090		
5390	80	NARC,HI 24+ HRS	1A180	1B100	1B100	1B100	1B100	1B100	1B100	1B099	1B099

A01g: DRUGS. Incidence of first use

Item Reference Number	Page Loc. in this Volume	Item Description (Abbreviated)	1975	1976	1977	1978	1979	1980	1981	1982	1983
1680	41	SMK CIG DLY/12G	1A019	1B002	(1B002)	1B002	1B002	1B002	1B002	1B002	1B002
5570	81	GR 1ST SMOK DLY	1A019	1B105A	1B105A	1B105A	1B105A	1B105A	1B105A	1B104A	1B104A
	143				3E12A	3E12A	3E12A	3E12A	3E12A	3E10A	3E10A
5580	81	GR 1ST TRY ALC	1A027	1B105B	1B105B	1B105B	1B105B	1B105B	1B105B	1B104B	1B104B
	143				3E12B	3E12B	3E12B	3E12B	3E12B	3E10B	3E10B
5590	81	GR 1ST TRY MJ	1A043	1B105C	1B105C	1B105C	1B105C	1B105C	1B105C	1B104C	1B104C
	143				3E12C	3E12C	3E12C	3E12C	3E12C	3E10C	3E10C
5600	81	GR 1ST TRY LSD	1A056	1B105D	1B105D	1B105D	1B105D	1B105D	1B105D	1B104D	1B104D
	143				3E12D	3E12D	3E12D	3E12D	3E12D	3E10D	3E10D
5610	81	GR 1ST TRY PSY	1A070	1B105E	1B105E	1B105E	1B105E	1B105E	1B105E	1B104E	1B104E
	143				3E12E	3E12E	3E12E	3E12E	3E12E	3E10E	3E10E
5620	81	GR 1ST TRY AMP	1A086	1B105F	1B105F	1B105F	1B105F	1B105F	1B105F	1B104F	1B104F
	143				3E12F	3E12F	3E12F	3E12F	3E12F	3E10F	3E10F
5630	82	GR 1ST TRY QUA	1A101	1B105G	1B105G	1B105G	1B105G	1B105G	1B105G	1B104G	1B104G
	144				3E12G	3E12G	3E12G	3E12G	3E12G	3E10G	3E10G
5640	82	GR 1ST TRY BRB	1A115	1B105H	1B105H	1B105H	1B105H	1B105H	1B105H	1B104H	1B104H
	144				3E12H	3E12H	3E12H	3E12H	3E12H	3E10H	3E10H
5650	82	GR 1ST TRY TRN	1A130	1B105I	1B105I	1B105I	1B105I	1B105I	1B105I	1B104I	1B104I

(continued)

Item Reference Number	Page Loc. in this Volume	ITEM DESCRIPTION (ABBREVIATED)	QUESTIONNAIRE LOCATION BY YEAR (FORM, SECTION, AND QUESTION NUMBER)								
			1975	1976	1977	1978	1979	1980	1981	1982	1983

A01g: DRUGS. Incidence of first use (continued)

Item Reference Number	Page Loc.	ITEM DESCRIPTION	1975	1976	1977	1978	1979	1980	1981	1982	1983
5660	144 / 82	GR 1ST TRY COK	1A143	1B105J	3E12I / 1B105J	3E12I / 1B105J	3E12I / 1B105J	3E12I / 1B105J	3E12I / 1B105J	3E10I / 1B104J	3E10I / 1B104J
5670	82 / 144	GR 1ST TRY HER	1A157	1B105K	3E12J / 1B105K / 3E12K	3E12J / 1B105K / 3E12K	3E12J / 1B105K / 3E12K	3E12J / 1B105K / 3E12K	3E12J / 1B105K / 3E12K	3E10J / 1B104K / 3E10K	3E10J / 1B104K / 3E10K
5680	82 / 144	GR 1ST TRY NRC	1A172	1B105L	1B105L / 3E12L	1B105L / 3E12L	1B105L / 3E12L	1B105L / 3E12L	1B105L / 3E12L	1B104L / 3E10L	1B104L / 3E10L
5685	145	GR 1ST TRY INHAL				3E12M	3E12M	3E12M	3E12M	3E10M	3E10M
5686	112	GR 1ST TRY PCP						2E04A	2E04A	2E04A	2E04A
5687	112	GR 1ST TRY PPRS						2E04B	2E04B	2E04B	2E04B
21190	50	GR 1ST DAILY MJ								1B029	1B029
21200	50	RECENT DAILY MJ								1B030	1B030

A01h: DRUGS. Use with other drugs

Item Reference Number	Page Loc.	ITEM DESCRIPTION	1975	1976	1977	1978	1979	1980	1981	1982	1983
2500	52	#X OVL LSD+ ALC		1B031A	1B031A	1B031A	1B031A	1B031A	1B031A	1B035A	1B035A
2510	53	#X OVL LSD+ MJ		1B031B	1B031B	1B031B	1B031B	1B031B	1B031B	1B035B	1B035B
2900	59	#X OVL AMPH+ALC		1B045A	1B045A	1B045A	1B045A	1B045A	1B045A	1B052A	1B052A
2910	59	#X OVL AMPH+MJ		1B045B	1B045B	1B045B	1B045B	1B045B	1B045B	1B052B	1B052B
2920	59	#X OVL AMPH+LSD		1B045C	1B045C	1B045C	1B045C	1B045C	1B045C	1B052C	1B052C
2930	60	#X OVL AMPH+PSY		1B045D	1B045D	1B045D	1B045D	1B045D	1B045D	1B052D	1B052D
3390	64	#X OVL BARB+ALC		1B059A	1B059A	1B059A	1B059A	1B059A	1B059A	1B066A	1B066A
3400	64	#X OVL BARB+MJ		1B059B	1B059B	1B059B	1B059B	1B059B	1B059B	1B066B	1B066B
3410	65	#X OVL BARB+LSD		1B059C	1B059C	1B059C	1B059C	1B059C	1B059C	1B066C	1B066C
3420	65	#X OVL BARB+PSY		1B059D	1B059D	1B059D	1B059D	1B059D	1B059D	1B066D	1B066D
3430	65	#X OVL BARB+AMP		1B059E	1B059E	1B059E	1B059E	1B059E	1B059E	1B066E	1B066E
3440	65	#X OVL BARB+QUA		1B059F	1B059F	1B059F	1B059F	1B059F	1B059F	1B066F	1B066F
3840	69	#X OVL TRQL+ALC		1B069A	1B069A	1B069A	1B069A	1B069A	1B069A	1B076A	1B076A
3850	69	#X OVL TRQL+MJ		1B069B	1B069B	1B069B	1B069B	1B069B	1B069B	1B076B	1B076B
3860	69	#X OVL TRQL+LSD		1B069C	1B069C	1B069C	1B069C	1B069C	1B069C	1B076C	1B076C
3870	69	#X OVL TRQL+PSY		1B069D	1B069D	1B069D	1B069D	1B069D	1B069D	1B076D	1B076D
3880	69	#X OVL TRQL+AMP		1B069E	1B069E	1B069E	1B069E	1B069E	1B069E	1B076E	1B076E
3890	69	#X OVL TRQL+QUA		1B069F	1B069F	1B069F	1B069F	1B069F	1B069F	1B076F	1B076F
3900	69	#X OVL TRQL+BRB		1B069G	1B069G	1B069G	1B069G	1B069G	1B069G	1B076G	1B076G
4290	73	#X OVL COKE+ALC		1B078A	1B078A	1B078A	1B078A	1B078A	1B078A	1B085A	1B085A
4300	73	#X OVL COKE+MJ		1B078B	1B078B	1B078B	1B078B	1B078B	1B078B	1B085B	1B085B
4310	73	#X OVL COKE+LSD		1B078C	1B078C	1B078C	1B078C	1B078C	1B078C	1B085C	1B085C
4320	73	#X OVL COKE+PSY		1B078D	1B078D	1B078D	1B078D	1B078D	1B078D	1B085D	1B085D
4330	73	#X OVL COKE+AMP		1B078E	1B078E	1B078E	1B078E	1B078E	1B078E	1B085E	1B085E
4340	73	#X OVL COKE+QUA		1B078F	1B078F	1B078F	1B078F	1B078F	1B078F	1B085F	1B085F
4350	74	#X OVL COKE+BRB		1B078G	1B078G	1B078G	1B078G	1B078G	1B078G	1B085G	1B085G
4360	74	#X OVL COKE+TRN		1B078H	1B078H	1B078H	1B078H	1B078H	1B078H	1B085H	1B085H
4710		#X OVL HER +ALC		1B087A	1B087A	1B087A	1B087A	1B087A	1B087A		
4720		#X OVL HER +MJ		1B087B	1B087B	1B087B	1B087B	1B087B	1B087B		
4730		#X OVL HER +LSD		1B087C	1B087C	1B087C	1B087C	1B087C	1B087C		
4740		#X OVL HER +PSY		1B087D	1B087D	1B087D	1B087D	1B087D	1B087D		
4750		#X OVL HER +AMP		1B087E	1B087E	1B087E	1B087E	1B087E	1B087E		
4760		#X OVL HER +QUA		1B087F	1B087F	1B087F	1B087F	1B087F	1B087F		
4770		#X OVL HER +BRB		1B087G	1B087G	1B087G	1B087G	1B087G	1B087G		
4780		#X OVL HER +TRN		1B087H	1B087H	1B087H	1B087H	1B087H	1B087H		
4790		#X OVL HER +COK		1B087I	1B087I	1B087I	1B087I	1B087I	1B087I		
5130	78	#X OVL NARC+ALC		1B097A	1B097A	1B097A	1B097A	1B097A	1B097A	1B096A	1B096A
5140	78	#X OVL NARC+MJ		1B097B	1B097B	1B097B	1B097B	1B097B	1B097B	1B096B	1B096B
5150	78	#X OVL NARC+LSD		1B097C	1B097C	1B097C	1B097C	1B097C	1B097C	1B096C	1B096C
5160	78	#X OVL NARC+PSY		1B097D	1B097D	1B097D	1B097D	1B097D	1B097D	1B096D	1B096D
5170	78	#X OVL NARC+AMP		1B097E	1B097E	1B097E	1B097E	1B097E	1B097E	1B096E	1B096E
5180	78	#X OVL NARC+QUA		1B097F	1B097F	1B097F	1B097F	1B097F	1B097F	1B096F	1B096F
5190	79	#X OVL NARC+BRB		1B097G	1B097G	1B097G	1B097G	1B097G	1B097G	1B096G	1B096G
5200	79	#X OVL NARC+TRN		1B097H	1B097H	1B097H	1B097H	1B097H	1B097H	1B096H	1B096H
5210	79	#X OVL NARC+COK		1B097I	1B097I	1B097I	1B097I	1B097I	1B097I	1B096I	1B096I
5220	79	#X OVL NARC+HER		1B097J	1B097J	1B097J	1B097J	1B097J	1B097J	1B096J	1B096J

Item Reference Number	Page Loc. in this Volume	ITEM DESCRIPTION (ABBREVIATED)	QUESTIONNAIRE LOCATION BY YEAR (FORM, SECTION, AND QUESTION NUMBER)								
			1975	1976	1977	1978	1979	1980	1981	1982	1983

A01i: DRUGS. Tried to stop

Item Reference Number	Page Loc. in this Volume	ITEM DESCRIPTION (ABBREVIATED)	1975	1976	1977	1978	1979	1980	1981	1982	1983
1690	42	*TRY STP SMK&FL	1A021	1B004	1B004	1B004	1B004	1B004	1B004	1B004	1B004
1700	42	*WNT STP SMK NW	1A022	1B005	1B005	1B005	1B005	1B005	1B005	1B005	1B005
2020	46	*TRY STP ALC&FL	1A039	1B016	1B016	1B016	1B016	1B016	1B016	1B016	1B016
2380	50	*TRY STP MJ &FL	1A052	1B027	1B027	1B027	1B027	1B027	1B027	1B027	1B027
2680	53	*TRY STP LSD&FL	1A066	1B036	1B036	1B036	1B036	1B036	1B036	1B040	1B040
3240	61	*TRY STP AMP&FL	1A096	1B051	1B051	1B051	1B051	1B051	1B051	1B058	1B058
3710	66	TRY STP BARB&FL	1A125	1B064	1B064	1B064	1B064	1B064	1B064	1B071	1B071
4170	70	*TRY STP TRQ&FL	1A139	1B074	1B074	1B074	1B074	1B074	1B074	1B081	1B081
4540	74	*TRY STP COK&FL	1A152	1B082	1B082	1B082	1B082	1B082	1B082	1B089	1B089
4950		TRY STP HER& FL	1A166	1B091	1B091	1B091	1B091	1B091	1B091		
5500	80	TRY STP NARC&FL	1A182	1B102	1B102	1B102	1B102	1B102	1B102	1B101	1B101
8910	134	12MO REDUCE ALCL		3D03A	3D03A	3D03A	3D03A	3D03A	3D03A	3D03A	3D03A
8920	134	12MO REDUCE CIG		3D03B	3D03B	3D03B	3D03B	3D03B	3D03B	3D03B	3D03B
8930	134	12MO REDUCE MARJ		3D03C	3D03C	3D03C	3D03C	3D03C	3D03C	3D03C	3D03C
8940	134	12MO REDUCE PSYC		3D03D	3D03D	3D03D	3D03D	3D03D	3D03D	3D03D	3D03D
8950	134	12MO REDUCE AMPH		3D03E	3D03E	3D03E	3D03E	3D03E	3D03E	3D03E	3D03E
8960		12MO REDUCE QUAL		3D03F	3D03F	3D03F					
8970	134	12MO REDUCE BARB		3D03G	3D03G	(3D03G)	3D03G	3D03G	3D03G	3D03G	3D03G
8980	134	12MO REDUCE COKE		3D03H	3D03H	3D03H	3D03H	3D03H	3D03H	3D03H	3D03H
8990	135	12MO REDUCE HRN		3D03I	3D03I	3D03I	3D03I	3D03I	3D03I	3D03I	3D03I
9000	135	12MO REDUCE NARC		3D03J	3D03J	3D03J	3D03J	3D03J	3D03J	3D03J	3D03J
9005	134	12MO REDUCE TRQL					3D03F	3D03F	3D03F	3D03F	3D03F

A01j: DRUGS. Use on doctor's orders

Item Reference Number	Page Loc. in this Volume	ITEM DESCRIPTION (ABBREVIATED)	1975	1976	1977	1978	1979	1980	1981	1982	1983
2790	57	DR TOLD TK AMPH	1A085	1B042	1B042	1B042	1B042	1B042	1B042	1B049	1B049
3280	62	DR TOLD TK BARB	1A114	1B056	1B056	1B056	1B056	1B056	1B056	1B063	1B063
3730	66	DR TOLD TK TRNQ	1A129	1B066	1B066	1B066	1B066	1B066	1B066	1B073	1B073
5020	76	DR TOLD TK NARC	1A171	1B094	1B094	1B094	1B094	1B094	1B094	1B093	1B093

A01k: DRUGS. Bad trip

Item Reference Number	Page Loc. in this Volume	ITEM DESCRIPTION (ABBREVIATED)	1975	1976	1977	1978	1979	1980	1981	1982	1983
2670	53	1+ BAD TRIP LSD	1A065	1B035	1B035	1B035	1B035	1B035	1B035	1B039	1B039

A01l: DRUGS. Specific kinds of drugs

Item Reference Number	Page Loc. in this Volume	ITEM DESCRIPTION (ABBREVIATED)	1975	1976	1977	1978	1979	1980	1981	1982	1983
2720	55	TKN YR,MESCALIN	1A079A	1B041A	1B041A	1B041A	1B041A	1B041A	1B041A	1B045A	1B045A
2730	55	TKN YR,PEYOTE	1A079B	1B041B	1B041B	1B041B	1B041B	1B041B	1B041B	1B045B	1B045B
2740	55	TKN YR,PSILOCYB	1A079C	1B041C	1B041C	1B041C	1B041C	1B041C	1B041C	1B045C	1B045C
2750	55	TKN YR,PCP		1B041D	1B041D	1B041D	1B041D	1B041D	1B041D	1B045D	1B045D
2760	55	TKN YR,CNCT THC	1A079D	1B041E	1B041E	1B041E	1B041E	1B041E	1B041E	1B045E	1B045E
2770	55	TKN YR,OTH PSYD	1A079E	1B041F	1B041F	1B041F	1B041F	1B041F	1B041F	1B045F	1B045F
2780	55	TKN YR,DK NAME	1A079F	1B041G	1B041G	1B041G	1B041G	1B041G	1B041G	1B045G	1B045G
3120	60	TKN YR,BENZDRIN	1A095A	1B049A	1B049A	1B049A	1B049A	1B049A	1B049A	1B056A	1B056A
3130	60	TKN YR,DEXEDRIN	1A095B	1B049B	1B049B	1B049B	1B049B	1B049B	1B049B	1B056B	1B056B
3140	60	TKN YR,METHDRIN	1A095C	1B049C	1B049C	1B049C	1B049C	1B049C	1B049C	1B056C	1B056C
3150	60	TKN YR,RITALIN	1A095D	1B049D	1B049D	1B049D	1B049D	1B049D	1B049D	1B056D	1B056D
3160	60	TKN YR,PRELUDIN	1A095E	1B049E	1B049E	1B049E	1B049E	1B049E	1B049E	1B056E	1B056E
3170	60	TKN YR,DEXAMYL	1A095F	1B049F	1B049F	1B049F	1B049F	1B049F	1B049F	1B056F	1B056F
3180	60	TKN YR,METHAMPH	1A095G	1B049G	1B049G	1B049G	1B049G	1B049G	1B049G	1B056G	1B056G
3190	60	TKN YR,OTH AMPH	1A095H	1B049H	1B049H	1B049H	1B049H	1B049H	1B049H	1B056H	1B056H
3200	60	TKN YR,DNT KN N	1A095I	1B049I	1B049I	1B049I	1B049I	1B049I	1B049I	1B056I	1B056I
3610	66	TKN YR,PHNOBARB	1A124A	1B063A	1B063A	1B063A	1B063A	1B063A	1B063A	1B070A	1B070A
3620	66	TKN YR,SECONAL	1A124B	1B063B	1B063B	1B063B	1B063B	1B063B	1B063B	1B070B	1B070B
3630	66	TKN YR,TUINAL	1A124C	1B063C	1B063C	1B063C	1B063C	1B063C	1B063C	1B070C	1B070C
3640	66	TKN YR,NEMBUTAL	1A124D	1B063D	1B063D	1B063D	1B063D	1B063D	1B063D	1B070D	1B070D
3650	66	TKN YR,LUMINAL	1A124E	1B063E	1B063E	1B063E	1B063E	1B063E	1B063E	1B070E	1B070E
3660	66	TKN YR,DESBUTAL	1A124F	1B063F	1B063F	1B063F	1B063F	1B063F	1B063F	1B070F	1B070F
3670	66	TKN YR,AMYTAL	1A124G	1B063G	1B063G	1B063G	1B063G	1B063G	1B063G	1B070G	1B070G
3680	66	TKN YR,ADRNOCAL	1A124H	1B063H	1B063H	1B063H	1B063H	1B063H	1B063H	1B070H	1B070H
3690	66	TKN YR,OTH BRBT	1A124I	1B063I	1B063I	1B063I	1B063I	1B063I	1B063I	1B070I	1B070I
3700	66	TKN YR,DNT KNOW	1A124J	1B063J	1B063J	1B063J	1B063J	1B063J	1B063J	1B070J	1B070J
4070	70	TKN YR,LIBRIUM		1B073A	1B073A	1B073A	1B073A	1B073A	1B073A	1B080A	1B080A

(continued)

Item Reference Number	Page Loc. in this Volume	ITEM DESCRIPTION (ABBREVIATED)	QUESTIONNAIRE LOCATION BY YEAR (FORM, SECTION, AND QUESTION NUMBER)								
			1975	1976	1977	1978	1979	1980	1981	1982	1983

A01I: DRUGS. Specific kinds of drugs (continued)

Item Reference Number	Page Loc. in this Volume	ITEM DESCRIPTION (ABBREVIATED)	1975	1976	1977	1978	1979	1980	1981	1982	1983
4080	70	TKN YR,VALIUM		1B073B	1B073B	1B073B	1B073B	1B073B	1B073B	1B080B	1B080B
4090	70	TKN YR,MILTOWN		1B073C	1B073C	1B073C	1B073C	1B073C	1B073C	1B080C	1B080C
4100	70	TKN YR,EQUANIL		1B073D	1B073D	1B073D	1B073D	1B073D	1B073D	1B080D	1B080D
4110	70	TKN YR,MEPRBMTE		1B073E	1B073E	1B073E	1B073E	1B073E	1B073E	1B080E	1B080E
4120	70	TKN YR,SERAX		1B073F	1B073F	1B073F	1B073F	1B073F	1B073F	1B080E	1B080F
4130	70	TKN YR,ATARAX		1B073G	1B073G	1B073G	1B073G	1B073G	1B073G	1B080G	1B080G
4140	70	TKN YR,TRANXENE		1B073H	1B073H	1B073H	1B073H	1B073H	1B073H	1B080H	1B080H
4150	70	TKN YR,VISTARIL		1B073I	1B073I	1B073I	1B073I	1B073I	1B073I	1B080I	1B080I
4160	70	TKN YR,DNT KNW		1B073J	1B073J	1B073J	1B073J	1B073J	1B073J	1B080J	1B080J
5400	80	NARC TKN MTHDNE	1A181A	1B101A	1B101A	1B101A	1B101A	1B101A	1B101A	1B100A	1B100A
5410	80	NARC TKN OPIUM	1A181B	1B101B	1B101B	1B101B	1B101B	1B101B	1B101B	1B100B	1B100B
5420	80	NARC TKN MRPHNE	1A181C	1B101C	1B101C	1B101C	1B101C	1B101C	1B101C	1B100C	1B100C
5430	80	NARC TKN CODEIN	1A181D	1B101D	1B101D	1B101D	1B101D	1B101D	1B101D	1B100D	1B100D
5440	80	NARC TKN DEMROL	1A181E	1B101E	1B101E	1B101E	1B101E	1B101E	1B101E	1B100E	1B100E
5450	80	NARC TKN PARGRC	1A181F	1B101F	1B101F	1B101F	1B101F	1B101F	1B101F	1B100F	1B100F
5460	80	NARC TKN TALWIN	1A181G	1B101G	1B101G	1B101G	1B101G	1B101G	1B101G	1B100G	1B100G
5470	80	NARC TKN LDANUM	1A181H	1B101H	1B101H	1B101H	1B101H	1B101H	1B101H	1B100H	1B100H
5480	80	NARC TKN OTHER	1A181I	1B101I	1B101I	1B101I	1B101I	1B101I	1B101I	1B100I	1B100I
5490	80	NARC TKN DNT KN	1A181J	1B101J	1B101J	1B101J	1B101J	1B101J	1B101J	1B100J	1B100J

A02a: DRUGS. Friends' use

Item Reference Number	Page Loc. in this Volume	ITEM DESCRIPTION (ABBREVIATED)	1975	1976	1977	1978	1979	1980	1981	1982	1983
7070	109	ALL FRD SMK CIGS	2A41A	2D06A	2D06A	2D06A	2D06A	2D06A	2D06A	2D06A	2D06A
7080	109	ALL FRD SMK MARJ	2A41B	2D06B	2D06B	2D06B	2D06B	2D06B	2D06B	2D06B	2D06B
7090	109	ALL FRD TAKE LSD	2A41C	2D06C	2D06C	2D06C	2D06C	2D06C	2D06C	2D06C	2D06C
7100	109	ALL FRD TK PSYDL	2A41D	2D06D	2D06D	2D06D	2D06D	2D06D	2D06D	2D06D	2D06D
7110	109	ALL FRD TK AMPH	2A41E	2D06E	2D06E	2D06E	2D06E	2D06E	2D06E	2D06E	2D06E
7120	110	ALL FRD TK QUALD	2A41F	2D06F	2D06F	2D06F	2D06F	2D06F	2D06F	2D06F	2D06F
7130	110	ALL FRD TK BARBT	2A41G	2D06G	2D06G	2D06G	2D06G	2D06G	2D06G	2D06G	2D06G
7140	110	ALL FRD TK TRNQL	2A41H	2D06H	2D06H	2D06H	2D06H	2D06H	2D06H	2D06H	2D06H
7150	110	ALL FRD TK COKE	2A41I	2D06I	2D06I	2D06I	2D06I	2D06I	2D06I	2D06I	2D06I
7160	110	ALL FRD TK HERON	2A41J	2D06J	2D06J	2D06J	2D06J	2D06J	2D06J	2D06J	2D06J
7170	110	ALL FRD TK NARC	2A41K	2D06K	2D06K	2D06K	2D06K	2D06K	2D06K	2D06K	2D06K
7180	110	ALL FRD TK INHL	2A41L	2D06L	2D06L	2D06L	2D06L	2D06L	2D06L	2D06L	2D06L
7190	111	ALL FRD DRK ALCL	2A41M	2D06M	2D06M	2D06M	2D06M	2D06M	2D06M	2D06M	2D06M
7200	111	ALL FRD GT DRUNK	2A41N	2D06N	2D06N	2D06N	2D06N	2D06N	2D06N	2D06N	2D06N
7201	111	# FRNDS TAKE PCP					2E01A	2E01A	2E01A	2E01A	2E01A
7202	111	# FRNDS TK PPRS					2E01B	2E01B	2E01B	2E01B	2E01B

A02b: DRUGS. Exposure to users

Item Reference Number	Page Loc. in this Volume	ITEM DESCRIPTION (ABBREVIATED)	1975	1976	1977	1978	1979	1980	1981	1982	1983
8750		OFT W PL TK MARJ	3A55A	5E07A	5E08A	5E08A					
8760		OFT W PL TK LSD	3A55B	5E07B	5E08B	5E08B					
8770		OFT W PL TK PSYC	3A55C	5E07C	5E08C	5E08C					
8780		OFT W PL TK QUAL		5E07D	5E08D	5E08D					
8790		OFT W PL TK BARB	3A55E	5E07E	5E08E	5E08E					
8800		OFT W PL TK TRQL	3A55F	5E07F	5E08F	5E08F					
8810		OFT W PL TK COKE	3A55G	5E07G	5E08G	5E08G					
8820		OFT W PL TK HRN	3A55H	5E07H	5E08H	5E08H					
8830		OFT W PL TK NARC	3A55I	5E07I	5E08I	5E08I					
8835		OFT W PL TK INHL		5E07J	5E08J	5E08J					
8840		OFT W PL TK ALCL	3A55K	5E07K	5E08K	5E08K					
20590	131	12MO NR OTH MARJ		3A29A	3A29A	3A29A	3A29A	3A29A	3A29A	3A29A	3A29A
20600	132	12MO NR OTH LSD		3A29B	3A29B	3A29B	3A29B	3A29B	3A29B	3A29B	3A29B
20610	132	12MO NR OTH PSYC		3A29C	3A29C	3A29C	3A29C	3A29C	3A29C	3A29C	3A29C
20620	132	12MO NR OTH AMPH		3A29D	3A29D	3A29D	3A29D	3A29D	3A29D	3A29D	3A29D
20630	132	12MO NR OTH BARB		3A29E	3A29E	3A29E	3A29E	3A29E	3A29E	3A29E	3A29E
20640	132	12MO NR OTH TRQL		3A29F	3A29F	3A29F	3A29F	3A29F	3A29F	3A29F	3A29F
20650	132	12MO NR OTH COKE		3A29G	3A29G	3A29G	3A29G	3A29G	3A29G	3A29G	3A29G
20660	132	12MO NR OTH HRN		3A29H	3A29H	3A29H	3A29H	3A29H	3A29H	3A29H	3A29H
20670	132	12MO NR OTH NARC		3A29I	3A29I	3A29I	3A29I	3A29I	3A29I	3A29I	3A29I
20680	133	12MO NR OTH ALCL		3A29J	3A29J	3A29J	3A29J	3A29J	3A29J	3A29J	3A29J

Item Reference Number	Page Loc. in this Volume	ITEM DESCRIPTION (ABBREVIATED)	QUESTIONNAIRE LOCATION BY YEAR (FORM, SECTION, AND QUESTION NUMBER)								
			1975	1976	1977	1978	1979	1980	1981	1982	1983

A03a: DRUGS. Availability

Item Reference Number	Page Loc. in this Volume	ITEM DESCRIPTION (ABBREVIATED)	1975	1976	1977	1978	1979	1980	1981	1982	1983
6750	104	EASY GT MARIJUAN	2A40A	2A21A	2A21A	2A21A	2A21A	2A21A	2A21A	2A21A	2A21A
6760	104	EASY GT LSD	2A40B	2A21B	2A21B	2A21B	2A21B	2A21B	2A21B	2A21B	2A21B
6770	104	EASY GT PSYDELIC	2A40C	2A21C	2A21C	2A21C	2A21C	2A21C	2A21C	2A21C	2A21C
6780	104	EASY GT AMPHTMNS	2A40D	2A21D	2A21D	2A21D	2A21D	2A21D	2A21D	2A21D	2A21D
6790	104	EASY GT BBTUATES	2A40F	2A21E	2A21E	2A21E	2A21E	2A21E	2A21E	2A21E	2A21E
6800	104	EASY GT TRANQLIZ	2A40G	2A21F	2A21F	2A21F	2A21F	2A21F	2A21F	2A21F	2A21F
6810	105	EASY GT COCAINE	2A40H	2A21G	2A21G	2A21G	2A21G	2A21G	2A21G	2A21G	2A21G
6820	105	EASY GT HEROIN	2A40I	2A21H	2A21H	2A21H	2A21H	2A21H	2A21H	2A21H	2A21H
6830	105	EASY GT NARCOTIC	2A40J	2A21I	2A21I	2A21I	2A21I	2A21I	2A21I	2A21I	2A21I

A04a: DRUGS. Expected future use

Item Reference Number	Page Loc. in this Volume	ITEM DESCRIPTION (ABBREVIATED)	1975	1976	1977	1978	1979	1980	1981	1982	1983
1710	42	NO SMK IN 5 YR	1A023	1B006	1B006	1B006	1B006	1B006	1B006	1B006	1B006
2030	46	NO ALC IN 5 YR	1A040	1B017	1B017	1B017	1B017	1B017	1B017	1B017	1B017
2390	50	NO MJ/HSH IN5YR	1A053	1B028	1B028	1B028	1B028	1B028	1B028	1B032	1B032
2690	54	NO LSD IN 5 YRS	1A067	1B037	1B037	1B037	1B037	1B037	1B037	1B041	1B041
3250	61	NO AMPH IN 5YR	1A097	1B052	1B052	1B052	1B052	1B052	1B052	1B059	1B059
3720	66	NO BARB IN5YR	1A126	1B065	1B065	1B065	1B065	1B065	1B065	1B072	1B072
4180	71	NO TRNQ IN 5YR	1A140	1B075	1B075	1B075	1B075	1B075	1B075	1B082	1B082
4600	75	NO COKE IN 5YR	1A154	1B084	1B084	1B084	1B084	1B084	1B084	1B091	1B091
5010		NO HER IN 5 YR	1A168	1B093	1B093	1B093	1B093	1B093	1B093		
5560	80	NO NARC IN 5YR	1A184	1B104	1B104	1B104	1B104	1B104	1B104	1B103	1B103

A05a: DRUGS. Use alone

Item Reference Number	Page Loc. in this Volume	ITEM DESCRIPTION (ABBREVIATED)	1975	1976	1977	1978	1979	1980	1981	1982	1983
1720	43	#X/YR ALC ALONE		1B008A	1B008A	1B008A	1B008A	1B008A	1B008A	1B008A	1B008A
2100	47	#X/YR MJ ALONE	1A045	1B020A	1B020A	1B020A	1B020A	1B020A	1B020A	1B020A	1B020A
2400	51	#X/YR LSD ALONE		1B030A	1B030A	1B030A	1B030A	1B030A	1B030A	1B034A	1B034A
2800	58	#X/YR AMPH ALNE		1B044A	1B044A	1B044A	1B044A	1B044A	1B044A	1B051A	1B051A
3290	63	#X/YR BRBT ALNE		1B058A	1B058A	1B058A	1B058A	1B058A	1B058A	1B065A	1B065A
3740	67	#X/YR TRQL ALNE		1B068A	1B068A	1B068A	1B068A	1B068A	1B068A	1B075A	1B075A
4190	71	#X/YR COKE ALNE		1B077A	1B077A	1B077A	1B077A	1B077A	1B077A	1B084A	1B084A
4610		#X/YR HER ALONE		1B086A	1B086A	1B086A	1B086A	1B086A	1B086A		
5030	76	#X/YR NARC ALNE		1B096A	1B096A	1B096A	1B096A	1B096A	1B096A	1B095A	1B095A

A05b: DRUGS. Use with others

Item Reference Number	Page Loc. in this Volume	ITEM DESCRIPTION (ABBREVIATED)	1975	1976	1977	1978	1979	1980	1981	1982	1983
1730	43	#X/YR ALC-2 PPL		1B008B	1B008B	1B008B	1B008B	1B008B	1B008B	1B008B	1B008B
1750	43	#X/YR ALC-DT/SP		1B008D	1B008D	1B008D	1B008D	1B008D	1B008D	1B008D	1B008D
1760	44	#X/YR ALC-ADLTS		1B008E	1B008E	1B008E	1B008E	1B008E	1B008E	1B008E	1B008E
2110	47	#X/YR MJ-2 PPL		1B020B	1B020B	1B020B	1B020B	1B020B	1B020B	1B020B	1B020B
2130	48	#X/YR MJ-DT/SP		1B020D	1B020D	1B020D	1B020D	1B020D	1B020D	1B020D	1B020D
2140	48	#X/YR MJ-ADLTS		1B020E	1B020E	1B020E	1B020E	1B020E	1B020E	1B020E	1B020E
2410	51	#X/YR LSD-2 PPL		1B030B	1B030B	1B030B	1B030B	1B030B	1B030B	1B034B	1B034B
2430	52	#X/YR LSD-DT/SP		1B030D	1B030D	1B030D	1B030D	1B030D	1B030D	1B034D	1B034D
2440	52	#X/YR LSD-ADLTS		1B030E	1B030E	1B030E	1B030E	1B030E	1B030E	1B034E	1B034E
2810	58	#X/YR AMPH-2PPL		1B044B	1B044B	1B044B	1B044B	1B044B	1B044B	1B051B	1B051B
2830	58	#X/YR AMPH-DT/S		1B044D	1B044D	1B044D	1B044D	1B044D	1B044D	1B051D	1B051D
2840	58	#X/YR AMPH-ADLT		1B044E	1B044E	1B044E	1B044E	1B044E	1B044E	1B051E	1B051E
3300	63	#X/YR BRBT-2PPL		1B058B	1B058B	1B058B	1B058B	1B058B	1B058B	1B065B	1B065B
3320	63	#X/YR BRBT-DT/S		1B058D	1B058D	1B058D	1B058D	1B058D	1B058D	1B065D	1B065D
3330	64	#X/YR BRBT-ADLT		1B058E	1B058E	1B058E	1B058E	1B058E	1B058E	1B065E	1B065E
3750	67	#X/YR TRQL-2PPL		1B068B	1B068B	1B068B	1B068B	1B068B	1B068B	1B075B	1B075B
3770	68	#X/YR TRQL-DT/S		1B068D	1B068D	1B068D	1B068D	1B068D	1B068D	1B075D	1B075D
3780	68	#X/YR TRQL-ADLT		1B068E	1B068E	1B068E	1B068E	1B068E	1B068E	1B075E	1B075E
4200	72	#X/YR COKE-2PPL		1B077B	1B077B	1B077B	1B077B	1B077B	1B077B	1B084B	1B084B
4220	72	#X/YR COKE-DT/S		1B077D	1B077D	1B077D	1B077D	1B077D	1B077D	1B084D	1B084D
4230	72	#X/YR COKE-ADLT		1B077E	1B077E	1B077E	1B077E	1B077E	1B077E	1B084E	1B084E
4620		#X/YR HER-2 PPL		1B086B	1B086B	1B086B	1B086B	1B086B	1B086B		
4640		#X/YR HER-DA/SP		1B086D	1B086D	1B086D	1B086D	1B086D	1B086D		
4650		#X/YR HER-ADULT		1B086E	1B086E	1B086E	1B086E	1B086E	1B086E		
5040	77	#X/YR NARC-2PPL		1B096B	1B096B	1B096B	1B096B	1B096B	1B096B	1B095B	1B095B
5060	77	#X/YR NARC-DT/S		1B096D	1B096D	1B096D	1B096D	1B096D	1B096D	1B095D	1B095D
5070	77	#X/YR NARC-ADLT		1B096E	1B096E	1B096E	1B096E	1B096E	1B096E	1B095E	1B095E

Item Reference Number	Page Loc. in this Volume	ITEM DESCRIPTION (ABBREVIATED)	QUESTIONNAIRE LOCATION BY YEAR (FORM, SECTION, AND QUESTION NUMBER)								
			1975	1976	1977	1978	1979	1980	1981	1982	1983

A05c: DRUGS. Settings of use

Item Reference Number	Page Loc.	ITEM DESCRIPTION	1975	1976	1977	1978	1979	1980	1981	1982	1983
1740	43	#X/YR ALC@PARTY		1B008C	1B008C	1B008C	1B008C	1B008C	1B008C	1B008C	1B008C
1770	44	#X/YR ALC-DATIM		1B008F	1B008F	1B008F	1B008F	1B008F	1B008F	1B008F	1B008F
1780	44	#X/YR ALC@HOME		1B008G	1B008G	1B008G	1B008G	1B008G	1B008G	1B008G	1B008G
1790	44	#X/YR ALC@SCHL		1B008H	1B008H	1B008H	1B008H	1B008H	1B008H	1B008H	1B008H
1810	44	#X/YR ALCIN CAR		1B008I	1B008I	1B008I	1B008I	1B008I	1B008I	1B008I	1B008I
2120	47	#X/YR MJ@PARTY		1B020C	1B020C	1B020C	1B020C	1B020C	1B020C	1B020C	1B020C
2150	48	#X/YR MJ-DATIME		1B020F	1B020F	1B020F	1B020F	1B020F	1B020F	1B020F	1B020F
2160	48	#X/YR MJ@HOME		1B020G	1B020G	1B020G	1B020G	1B020G	1B020G	1B020G	1B020G
2170	48	#X/YR MJ@SCHL		1B020H	1B020H	1B020H	1B020H	1B020H	1B020H	1B020H	1B020H
2190	48	#X/YR MJIN CAR		1B020I	1B020I	1B020I	1B020I	1B020I	1B020I	1B020I	1B020I
2420	51	#X/YR LSD@PARTY		1B030C	1B030C	1B030C	1B030C	1B030C	1B030C	1B034C	1B034C
2450	52	#X/YR LSD-DATIM		1B030F	1B030F	1B030F	1B030F	1B030F	1B030F	1B034F	1B034F
2460	52	#X/YR LSD@HOME		1B030G	1B030G	1B030G	1B030G	1B030G	1B030G	1B034G	1B034G
2470	52	#X/YR LSD@SCHL		1B030H	1B030H	1B030H	1B030H	1B030H	1B030H	1B034H	1B034H
2490	52	#X/YR LSDIN CAR		1B030I	1B030I	1B030I	1B030I	1B030I	1B030I	1B034I	1B034I
2820	58	#X/YR AMPH@PRTY		1B044C	1B044C	1B044C	1B044C	1B044C	1B044C	1B051C	1B051C
2850	59	#X/YR AMPH-DATM		1B044F	1B044F	1B044F	1B044F	1B044F	1B044F	1B051F	1B051F
2860	59	#X/YR AMPH@HOME		1B044G	1B044G	1B044G	1B044G	1B044G	1B044G	1B051G	1B051G
2880	59	#X/YR AMPH@SCHL		1B044H	1B044H	1B044H	1B044H	1B044H	1B044H	1B051H	1B051H
2890	59	#X/YR AMPH@CAR		1B044I	1B044I	1B044I	1B044I	1B044I	1B044I	1B051I	1B051I
3310	63	#X/YR BRBT@PRTY		1B058C	1B058C	1B058C	1B058C	1B058C	1B058C	1B065C	1B065C
3340	64	#X/YR BRBT-DATM		1B058F	1B058F	1B058F	1B058F	1B058F	1B058F	1B065F	1B065F
3350	64	#X/YR BRBT@HOME		1B058G	1B058G	1B058G	1B058G	1B058G	1B058G	1B065G	1B065G
3360	64	#X/YR BRBT@SCHL		1B058H	1B058H	1B058H	1B058H	1B058H	1B058H	1B065H	1B065H
3380	64	#X/YR BRBT@CAR		1B058I	1B058I	1B058I	1B058I	1B058I	1B058I	1B065I	1B065I
3760	68	#X/YR TRQL@PRTY		1B068C	1B068C	1B068C	1B068C	1B068C	1B068C	1B075C	1B075C
3790	68	#X/YR TRQL-DATM		1B068F	1B068F	1B068F	1B068F	1B068F	1B068F	1B075F	1B075F
3800	68	#X/YR TRQL@HOME		1B068G	1B068G	1B068G	1B068G	1B068G	1B068G	1B075G	1B075G
3810	68	#X/YR TRQL@SCHL		1B068H	1B068H	1B068H	1B068H	1B068H	1B068H	1B075H	1B075H
3830	68	#X/YR TRQL@CAR		1B068I	1B068I	1B068I	1B068I	1B068I	1B068I	1B075I	1B075I
4210	72	#X/YR COKE@PRTY		1B077C	1B077C	1B077C	1B077C	1B077C	1B077C	1B084C	1B084C
4240	72	#X/YR COKE-DATM		1B077F	1B077F	1B077F	1B077F	1B077F	1B077F	1B084F	1B084F
4250	72	#X/YR COKE@HOME		1B077G	1B077G	1B077G	1B077G	1B077G	1B077G	1B084G	1B084G
4260	72	#X/YR COKE@SCHL		1B077H	1B077H	1B077H	1B077H	1B077H	1B077H	1B084H	1B084H
4280	73	#X/YR COKE@CAR		1B077I	1B077I	1B077I	1B077I	1B077I	1B077I	1B084I	1B084I
4630		#X/YR HER@PARTY		1B086C	1B086C	1B086C	1B086C	1B086C	1B086C		
4660		#X/YR HER-DATIM		1B086F	1B086F	1B086F	1B086F	1B086F	1B086F		
4670		#X/YR HER@HOME		1B086G	1B086G	1B086G	1B086G	1B086G	1B086G		
4680		#X/YR HER@SCHL		1B086H	1B086H	1B086H	1B086H	1B086H	1B086H		
4700		#X/YR HER@CAR		1B086I	1B086I	1B086I	1B086I	1B086I	1B086I		
5050	77	#X/YR NARC@PRTY		1B096C	1B096C	1B096C	1B096C	1B096C	1B096C	1B095C	1B095C
5080	77	#X/YR NARC-DATM		1B096F	1B096F	1B096F	1B096F	1B096F	1B096F	1B095F	1B095F
5090	77	#X/YR NARC@HOME		1B096G	1B096G	1B096G	1B096G	1B096G	1B096G	1B095G	1B095G
5100	77	#X/YR NARC@SCHL		1B096H	1B096H	1B096H	1B096H	1B096H	1B096H	1B095H	1B095H
5120	78	#X/YR NARC @CAR		1B096I	1B096I	1B096I	1B096I	1B096I	1B096I	1B095I	1B095I

A05d: DRUGS. Mode of administration

Item Reference Number	Page Loc.	ITEM DESCRIPTION	1975	1976	1977	1978	1979	1980	1981	1982	1983
3210	61	MTHD AMPH-MOUTH		1B050A	1B050A	1B050A	1B050A	1B050A	1B050A	1B057A	1B057A
3220	61	MTHD AMPH-INJCT		1B050B	1B050B	1B050B	1B050B	1B050B	1B050B	1B057B	1B057B
3230	61	MTHD AMPH-OTHER		1B050C	1B050C	1B050C	1B050C	1B050C	1B050C	1B057C	1B057C
4550	75	MTHD COKE SNORT	1A153A	1B083A	1B083A	1B083A	1B083A	1B083A	1B083A	1B090A	1B090A
4560	75	MTHD COKE-SMOKE	1A153B	1B083B	1B083B	1B083B	1B083B	1B083B	1B083B	1B090B	1B090B
4570	75	MTHD COKE-INJCT	1A153C	1B083C	1B083C	1B083C	1B083C	1B083C	1B083C	1B090C	1B090C
4580	75	MTHD COKE-MOUTH	1A153D	1B083D	1B083D	1B083D	1B083D	1B083D	1B083D	1B090D	1B090D
4590	75	MTHD COKE-OTHER	1A153E	1B083E	1B083E	1B083E	1B083E	1B083E	1B083E	1B090E	1B090E
4960		METHD HRN SNORT	1A167A	1B092A	1B092A	1B092A	1B092A	1B092A	1B092A		
4970		METHD HRN-SMOKE	1A167B	1B092B	1B092B	1B092B	1B092B	1B092B	1B092B		
4980		METHD HRN-INJCT	1A167C	1B092C	1B092C	1B092C	1B092C	1B092C	1B092C		
4990		METHD HRN-MOUTH	1A167D	1B092D	1B092D	1B092D	1B092D	1B092D	1B092D		
5000		METHD HRN-OTHER	1A167E	1B092E	1B092E	1B092E	1B092E	1B092E	1B092E		
5510	80	METH NARC SNORT	1A183A	1B103A	1B103A	1B103A	1B103A	1B103A	1B103A	1B102A	1B102A
5520	80	METH NARC SMOKE	1A183B	1B103B	1B103B	1B103B	1B103B	1B103B	1B103B	1B102B	1B102B
		(continued)									

Item Reference Number	Page Loc. in this Volume	ITEM DESCRIPTION (ABBREVIATED)	QUESTIONNAIRE LOCATION BY YEAR (FORM, SECTION, AND QUESTION NUMBER)								
			1975	1976	1977	1978	1979	1980	1981	1982	1983

A05d: DRUGS. Mode of administration *(continued)*

5530	80	METH NARC INJCT	1A183C	1B103C	1B103C	1B103C	1B103C	1B103C	1B103C	1B102C	1B102C
5540	80	METH NARC MOUTH	1A183D	1B103D	1B103D	1B103D	1B103D	1B103D	1B103D	1B102D	1B102D
5550	80	METH NARC OTHER	1A183E	1B103E	1B103E	1B103E	1B103E	1B103E	1B103E	1B102E	1B102E

A06a: DRUGS. Reasons for use, abstention, and stopping

1820	44	ALC EXPERIMENT		1B009A	1B009A	1B009A	1B009A	1B009A	1B009A	1B009A	1B009A
1830	44	ALC RELAX	1A032A	1B009B	1B009B	1B009B	1B009B	1B009B	1B009B	1B009B	1B009B
1840	44	ALC GET HIGH	1A032B	1B009C	1B009C	1B009C	1B009C	1B009C	1B009C	1B009C	1B009C
1850	44	ALC SEEK INSGHT	1A032C	1B009D	1B009D	1B009D	1B009D	1B009D	1B009D	1B009D	1B009D
1860	44	ALC GD TM FRNDS	1A032D	1B009E	1B009E	1B009E	1B009E	1B009E	1B009E	1B009E	1B009E
1870	44	ALC FIT IN GRP	1A032E	1B009F	1B009F	1B009F	1B009F	1B009F	1B009F	1B009F	1B009F
1880	44	ALC GET AWY PRB	1A032F	1B009G	1B009G	1B009G	1B009G	1B009G	1B009G	1B009G	1B009G
1890	44	ALC BOREDOM	1A032G	1B009H	1B009H	1B009H	1B009H	1B009H	1B009H	1B009H	1B009H
1900	44	ALC ANGR&FRSTRN	1A032H	1B009I	1B009I	1B009I	1B009I	1B009I	1B009I	1B009I	1B009I
1910	44	ALC GT THRU DAY	1A032J	1B009J	1B009J	1B009J	1B009J	1B009J	1B009J	1B009J	1B009J
1920	44	ALC INCRS EF DR	1A032K	1B009K	1B009K	1B009K	1B009K	1B009K	1B009K	1B009K	1B009K
1930	44	ALC DECRS EF DR	1A032L	1B009L	1B009L	1B009L	1B009L	1B009L	1B009L	1B009L	1B009L
1940	44	ALC GET SLEEP		1B009M	1B009M	1B009M	1B009M	1B009M	1B009M	1B009M	1B009M
1950	44	ALC TASTES GOOD	1A032N	1B009N	1B009N	1B009N	1B009N	1B009N	1B009N	1B009N	1B009N
1960	44	ALC I AM HOOKED	1A032M	1B009O	1B009O	1B009O	1B009O	1B009O	1B009O	1B009O	1B009O
2200	48	#X OVL MJ+ ALC		1B021	1B021	1B021	1B021	1B021	1B021	1B021	1B021
2210	49	MJ EXPERIMENT	1A049A	1B022A	1B022A	1B022A	1B022A	1B022A	1B022A	1B022A	1B022A
2220	49	MJ RELAX	1A049B	1B022B	1B022B	1B022B	1B022B	1B022B	1B022B	1B022B	1B022B
2230	49	MJ GET HIGH	1A049C	1B022C	1B022C	1B022C	1B022C	1B022C	1B022C	1B022C	1B022C
2240	49	MJ SEEK INSIGHT	1A049D	1B022D	1B022D	1B022D	1B022D	1B022D	1B022D	1B022D	1B022D
2250	49	MJ GD TM FRNDS	1A049E	1B022E	1B022E	1B022E	1B022E	1B022E	1B022E	1B022E	1B022E
2260	49	MJ FIT IN GRP	1A049F	1B022F	1B022F	1B022F	1B022F	1B022F	1B022F	1B022F	1B022F
2270	49	MJ GET AWY PRB	1A049G	1B022G	1B022G	1B022G	1B022G	1B022G	1B022G	1B022G	1B022G
2280	49	MJ BOREDOM	1A049H	1B022H	1B022H	1B022H	1B022H	1B022H	1B022H	1B022H	1B022H
2290	49	MJ ANGR&FRUSTRN	1A049I	1B022I	1B022I	1B022I	1B022I	1B022I	1B022I	1B022I	1B022I
2300	49	MJ GET THRU DAY	1A049K	1B022J	1B022J	1B022J	1B022J	1B022J	1B022J	1B022J	1B022J
2310	49	MJ INCRS EF DRG	1A049L	1B022K	1B022K	1B022K	1B022K	1B022K	1B022K	1B022K	1B022K
2320	49	MJ DECRS EF DRG	1A049M	1B022L	1B022L	1B022L	1B022L	1B022L	1B022L	1B022L	1B022L
2330	49	MJ I AM HOOKED		1B022M	1B022M	1B022M	1B022M	1B022M	1B022M	1B022M	1B022M
2520	53	LSD EXPERIMENT	1A062A	1B032A	1B032A	1B032A	1B032A	1B032A	1B032A	1B036A	1B036A
2530	53	LSD RELAX	1A062B	1B032B	1B032B	1B032B	1B032B	1B032B	1B032B	1B036B	1B036B
2540	53	LSD GET HIGH	1A062C	1B032C	1B032C	1B032C	1B032C	1B032C	1B032C	1B036C	1B036C
2550	53	LSD SEEK INSGHT	1A062D	1B032D	1B032D	1B032D	1B032D	1B032D	1B032D	1B036D	1B036D
2560	53	LSD GD TM FRNDS	1A062E	1B032E	1B032E	1B032E	1B032E	1B032E	1B032E	1B036E	1B036E
2570	53	LSD FIT IN GRP	1A062F	1B032F	1B032F	1B032F	1B032F	1B032F	1B032F	1B036F	1B036F
2580	53	LSD GT AWY PRB	1A062G	1B032G	1B032G	1B032G	1B032G	1B032G	1B032G	1B036G	1B036G
2590	53	LSD BOREDOM	1A062H	1B032H	1B032H	1B032H	1B032H	1B032H	1B032H	1B036H	1B036H
2600	53	LSD ANGR&FRSTRN	1A062I	1B032I	1B032I	1B032I	1B032I	1B032I	1B032I	1B036I	1B036I
2610	53	LSD GT THRU DAY	1A062K	1B032J	1B032J	1B032J	1B032J	1B032J	1B032J	1B036J	1B036J
2620	53	LSD INCRS EF DR	1A062L	1B032K	1B032K	1B032K	1B032K	1B032K	1B032K	1B036K	1B036K
2630	53	LSD DCRS EF DRG	1A062M	1B032L	1B032L	1B032L	1B032L	1B032L	1B032L	1B036L	1B036L
2640	53	LSD I AM HOOKED		1B032M	1B032M	1B032M	1B032M	1B032M	1B032M	1B036M	1B036M
2940	60	AMPH EXPERIMENT	1A092A	1B046A	1B046A	1B046A	1B046A	1B046A	1B046A	1B053A	1B053A
2950	60	AMPH RELAX	1A092B	1B046B	1B046B	1B046B	1B046B	1B046B	1B046B	1B053B	1B053B
2960	60	AMPH GET HIGH	1A092C	1B046C	1B046C	1B046C	1B046C	1B046C	1B046C	1B053C	1B053C
2970	60	AMPH SK INSIGHT	1A092D	1B046D	1B046D	1B046D	1B046D	1B046D	1B046D	1B053D	1B053D
2980	60	AMPH GD TM FRND	1A092E	1B046E	1B046E	1B046E	1B046E	1B046E	1B046E	1B053E	1B053E
2990	60	AMPH FIT IN GRP	1A092F	1B046F	1B046F	1B046F	1B046F	1B046F	1B046F	1B053F	1B053F
3000	60	AMPH GT AWY PRB	1A092G	1B046G	1B046G	1B046G	1B046G	1B046G	1B046G	1B053G	1B053G
3010	60	AMPH BOREDOM	1A092H	1B046H	1B046H	1B046H	1B046H	1B046H	1B046H	1B053H	1B053H
3020	60	AMPH ANGR&FRSTN	1A092I	1B046I	1B046I	1B046I	1B046I	1B046I	1B046I	1B053I	1B053I
3030	60	AMPH GT THRU DA	1A092K	1B046J	1B046J	1B046J	1B046J	1B046J	1B046J	1B053J	1B053J
3040	60	AMPH INCR EF DR	1A092L	1B046K	1B046K	1B046K	1B046K	1B046K	1B046K	1B053K	1B053K
3050	60	AMPH DCRS EF DR	1A092M	1B046L	1B046L	1B046L	1B046L	1B046L	1B046L	1B053L	1B053L
3060	60	AMPH STAY AWAKE	1A092N	1B046M	1B046M	1B046M	1B046M	1B046M	1B046M	1B053M	1B053M
3070	60	AMPH GET>ENERGY	1A092O	1B046N	1B046N	1B046N	1B046N	1B046N	1B046N	1B053N	1B053N
3080	60	AMPH LOSE WGHT	1A092P	1B046O	1B046O	1B046O	1B046O	1B046O	1B046O	1B053O	1B053O
		(continued)									

Item Reference Number	Page Loc. in this Volume	ITEM DESCRIPTION (ABBREVIATED)	QUESTIONNAIRE LOCATION BY YEAR (FORM, SECTION, AND QUESTION NUMBER)								
			1975	1976	1977	1978	1979	1980	1981	1982	1983

A06a: DRUGS. Reasons for use, abstention, and stopping *(continued)*

Item Reference Number	Page Loc.	ITEM DESCRIPTION	1975	1976	1977	1978	1979	1980	1981	1982	1983
3090	60	AMPH I AM HOOKD	1A092Q	1B046P	1B046P	1B046P	1B046P	1B046P	1B046P	1B053P	1B053P
3450	65	BARB EXPERIMENT	1A121A	1B060A	1B060A	1B060A	1B060A	1B060A	1B060A	1B067A	1B067A
3460	65	BARB RELAX	1A121B	1B060B	1B060B	1B060B	1B060B	1B060B	1B060B	1B067B	1B067B
3470	65	BARB GET HIGH	1A121C	1B060C	1B060C	1B060C	1B060C	1B060C	1B060C	1B067C	1B067C
3480	65	BARB SK INSIGHT	1A121D	1B060D	1B060D	1B060D	1B060D	1B060D	1B060D	1B067D	1B067D
3490	65	BARB GD TM FRND	1A121E	1B060E	1B060E	1B060E	1B060E	1B060E	1B060E	1B067E	1B067E
3500	65	BARB FIT IN GRP	1A121F	1B060F	1B060F	1B060F	1B060F	1B060F	1B060F	1B067F	1B067F
3510	65	BARB GT AWY PRB	1A121G	1B060G	1B060G	1B060G	1B060G	1B060G	1B060G	1B067G	1B067G
3520	65	BARB BOREDOM	1A121H	1B060H	1B060H	1B060H	1B060H	1B060H	1B060H	1B067H	1B067H
3530	65	BARB ANGR&FRSTN	1A121I	1B060I	1B060I	1B060I	1B060I	1B060I	1B060I	1B067I	1B067I
3540	65	BARB GT THRU DA	1A121K	1B060J	1B060J	1B060J	1B060J	1B060J	1B060J	1B067J	1B067J
3550	65	BARB INCR EF DR	1A121L	1B060K	1B060K	1B060K	1B060K	1B060K	1B060K	1B067K	1B067K
3560	65	BARB DCRS EF DR	1A121M	1B060L	1B060L	1B060L	1B060L	1B060L	1B060L	1B067L	1B067L
3570	65	BARB GET SLEEP	1A121N	1B060M	1B060M	1B060M	1B060M	1B060M	1B060M	1B067M	1B067M
3575	65	BARB RLV PHYS PN				1B060N	1B060N	1B060N	1B060N	1B067N	1B067N
3580	65	BARB I AM HOOKD	1A121O	1B060N	1B060N	1B060O	1B060O	1B060O	1B060O	1B067O	1B067O
3910	70	TRNQ EXPERIMENT	1A136A	1B070A	1B070A	1B070A	1B070A	1B070A	1B070A	1B077A	1B077A
3920	70	TRNQ RELAX	1A136B	1B070B	1B070B	1B070B	1B070B	1B070B	1B070B	1B077B	1B077B
3930	70	TRNQ GET HIGH	1A136C	1B070C	1B070C	1B070C	1B070C	1B070C	1B070C	1B077C	1B077C
3940	70	TRNQ SK INSIGHT	1A136D	1B070D	1B070D	1B070D	1B070D	1B070D	1B070D	1B077D	1B077D
3950	70	TRNQ GD TM FRND	1A136E	1B070E	1B070E	1B070E	1B070E	1B070E	1B070E	1B077E	1B077E
3960	70	TRNQ FIT IN GRP	1A136F	1B070F	1B070F	1B070F	1B070F	1B070F	1B070F	1B077F	1B077F
3970	70	TRNQ GT AWY PRB	1A136G	1B070G	1B070G	1B070G	1B070G	1B070G	1B070G	1B077G	1B077G
3980	70	TRNQ BOREDOM	1A136H	1B070H	1B070H	1B070H	1B070H	1B070H	1B070H	1B077H	1B077H
3990	70	TRNQ ANGR&FRSTN	1A136I	1B070I	1B070I	1B070I	1B070I	1B070I	1B070I	1B077I	1B077I
4000	70	TRNQ GT THRU DA	1A136K	1B070J	1B070J	1B070J	1B070J	1B070J	1B070J	1B077J	1B077J
4010	70	TRNQ INCR EF DR	1A136L	1B070K	1B070K	1B070K	1B070K	1B070K	1B070K	1B077K	1B077K
4020	70	TRNQ DCRS EF DR	1A136M	1B070L	1B070L	1B070L	1B070L	1B070L	1B070L	1B077L	1B077L
4030	70	TRNQ GET SLEEP	1A136N	1B070M	1B070M	1B070M	1B070M	1B070M	1B070M	1B077M	1B077M
4035	70	TRNQ RLV PHYS PN				1B070N	1B070N	1B070N	1B070N	1B077N	1B077N
4040	70	TRNQ I AM HOOKD	1A136O	1B070N	1B070N	1B070O	1B070O	1B070O	1B070O	1B077O	1B077O
4370	74	COKE EXPERIMENT	1A149A	1B079A	1B079A	1B079A	1B079A	1B079A	1B079A	1B086A	1B086A
4380	74	COKE RELAX	1A149B	1B079B	1B079B	1B079B	1B079B	1B079B	1B079B	1B086B	1B086B
4390	74	COKE GET HIGH	1A149C	1B079C	1B079C	1B079C	1B079C	1B079C	1B079C	1B086C	1B086C
4400	74	COKE SK INSIGHT	1A149D	1B079D	1B079D	1B079D	1B079D	1B079D	1B079D	1B086D	1B086D
4410	74	COKE GD TM FRND	1A149E	1B079E	1B079E	1B079E	1B079E	1B079E	1B079E	1B086E	1B086E
4420	74	COKE FIT IN GRP	1A149F	1B079F	1B079F	1B079F	1B079F	1B079F	1B079F	1B086F	1B086F
4430	74	COKE GT AWY PRB	1A149G	1B079G	1B079G	1B079G	1B079G	1B079G	1B079G	1B086G	1B086G
4440	74	COKE BOREDOM	1A149H	1B079H	1B079H	1B079H	1B079H	1B079H	1B079H	1B086H	1B086H
4450	74	COKE ANGR&FRSTN	1A149I	1B079I	1B079I	1B079I	1B079I	1B079I	1B079I	1B086I	1B086I
4460	74	COKE GT THRU DA	1A149K	1B079J	1B079J	1B079J	1B079J	1B079J	1B079J	1B086J	1B086J
4470	74	COKE INCR EF DR	1A149L	1B079K	1B079K	1B079K	1B079K	1B079K	1B079K	1B086K	1B086K
4480	74	COKE DCRS EF DR	1A149M	1B079L	1B079L	1B079L	1B079L	1B079L	1B079L	1B086L	1B086L
4490	74	COKE STAY AWAKE		1B079M	1B079M	1B079M	1B079M	1B079M	1B079M	1B086M	1B086M
4500	74	COKE GET>ENERGY	1A149N	1B079N	1B079N	1B079N	1B079N	1B079N	1B079N	1B086N	1B086N
4510	74	COKE I AM HOOKD	1A149O	1B079O	1B079O	1B079O	1B079O	1B079O	1B079O	1B086O	1B086O
4800		HERIN EXPERMENT	1A163A	1B088A	1B088A	1B088A	1B088A	1B088A	1B088A		
4810		HERIN RELAX	1A163B	1B088B	1B088B	1B088B	1B088B	1B088B	1B088B		
4820		HERIN GET HIGH	1A163C	1B088C	1B088C	1B088C	1B088C	1B088C	1B088C		
4830		HERIN SK INSIGT	1A163D	1B088D	1B088D	1B088D	1B088D	1B088D	1B088D		
4840		HERIN GD TM FRN	1A163E	1B088E	1B088E	1B088E	1B088E	1B088E	1B088E		
4850		HERIN FT IN GRP	1A163F	1B088F	1B088F	1B088F	1B088F	1B088F	1B088F		
4860		HERIN GT AWY PB	1A163G	1B088G	1B088G	1B088G	1B088G	1B088G	1B088G		
4870		HERIN BOREDOM	1A163H	1B088H	1B088H	1B088H	1B088H	1B088H	1B088H		
4880		HERIN ANGR&FRST	1A163I	1B088I	1B088I	1B088I	1B088I	1B088I	1B088I		
4890		HERIN GT THR DA	1A163K	1B088J	1B088J	1B088J	1B088J	1B088J	1B088J		
4900		HERIN INC EF DG	1A163L	1B088K	1B088K	1B088K	1B088K	1B088K	1B088K		
4910		HERIN DEC EF DG	1A163M	1B088L	1B088L	1B088L	1B088L	1B088L	1B088L		
4920		HERIN I AM HOOK	1A163N	1B088M	1B088M	1B088M	1B088M	1B088M	1B088M		
5230	79	NARC EXPERIMENT	1A178A	1B098A	1B098A	1B098A	1B098A	1B098A	1B098A	1B097A	1B097A
5240	79	NARC RELAX	1A178B	1B098B	1B098B	1B098B	1B098B	1B098B	1B098B	1B097B	1B097B
5250	79	NARC GET HIGH	1A178C	1B098C	1B098C	1B098C	1B098C	1B098C	1B098C	1B097C	1B097C
5260	79	NARC SK INSIGTS	1A178D	1B098D	1B098D	1B098D	1B098D	1B098D	1B098D	1B097D	1B097D
		(continued)									

Item Reference Number	Page Loc. in this Volume	ITEM DESCRIPTION (ABBREVIATED)	QUESTIONNAIRE LOCATION BY YEAR (FORM, SECTION, AND QUESTION NUMBER)								
			1975	1976	1977	1978	1979	1980	1981	1982	1983

A06a: DRUGS. Reasons for use, abstention, and stopping (continued)

			1975	1976	1977	1978	1979	1980	1981	1982	1983
5270	79	NARC GD TM FRND	1A178E	1B098E	1B098E	1B098E	1B098E	1B098E	1B098E	1B097E	1B097E
5280	79	NARC FIT IN GRP	1A178F	1B098F	1B098F	1B098F	1B098F	1B098F	1B098F	1B097F	1B097F
5290	79	NARC GT AWY PBM	1A178G	1B098G	1B098G	1B098G	1B098G	1B098G	1B098G	1B097G	1B097G
5300	79	NARC BOREDOM	1A178H	1B098H	1B098H	1B098H	1B098H	1B098H	1B098H	1B097H	1B097H
5310	79	NARC ANGR&FRSTN	1A178I	1B098I	1B098I	1B098I	1B098I	1B098I	1B098I	1B097I	1B097I
5320	79	NARC GT THRU DA	1A178K	1B098J	1B098J	1B098J	1B098J	1B098J	1B098J	1B097J	1B097J
5330	79	NARC INC EF DG	1A178L	1B098K	1B098K	1B098K	1B098K	1B098K	1B098K	1B097K	1B097K
5340	79	NARC DEC EF DG	1A178M	1B098L	1B098L	1B098L	1B098L	1B098L	1B098L	1B097L	1B097L
5350	79	NARC GET SLEEP		1B098M	1B098M	1B098M	1B098M	1B098M	1B098M	1B097M	1B097M
5360	79	NARC SBST HERIN	1A178O	1B098N	1B098N	1B098N	1B098N	1B098N	1B098N	1B097N	1B097N
5363	79	NARC RLV PHYS PN				1B098O	1B098O	1B098O	1B098O	1B097O	1B097O
5366	79	NARC RLV COUGHNG				1B098P	1B098P	1B098P	1B098P	1B097P	1B097P
5370	79	NARC I AM HOOKD	1A178N	1B098O	1B098O	1B098Q	1B098Q	1B098Q	1B098Q	1B097Q	1B097Q
9020	135	CNCRN PSYCH DAMG		(3D04A)	3D04A	3D04A	3D04A	3D04A	3D04A	3D04A	3D04A
9030	135	CNCRN PHYSCL DMG		(3D04B)	3D04B	3D04B	3D04B	3D04B	3D04B	3D04B	3D04B
9040	135	CNCRN GT ARRSTD		(3D04C)	3D04C	3D04C	3D04C	3D04C	3D04C	3D04C	3D04C
9050	135	CNCRN BECOM ADCT		(3D04D)	3D04D	3D04D	3D04D	3D04D	3D04D	3D04D	3D04D
9060	135	AGST MY BELIEFS		(3D04E)	3D04E	3D04E	3D04E	3D04E	3D04E	3D04E	3D04E
9070	135	CNCRN LEGY&AMBTN		(3D04F)	3D04F	3D04F	3D04F	3D04F	3D04F	3D04F	3D04F
9080	135	CNCRN LOSS CNTRL		(3D04G)	3D04G	3D04G	3D04G	3D04G	3D04G	3D04G	3D04G
9090	135	MJ ->STRNGR DRGS		(3D04H)	3D04H	3D04H	3D04H	3D04H	3D04H	3D04H	3D04H
9100	135	MJ NOT ENJOYABLE		(3D04I)	3D04I	3D04I	3D04I	3D04I	3D04I	3D04I	3D04I
9110	135	PRNTS DISAPPROVE		(3D04J)	3D04J	3D04J	3D04J	3D04J	3D04J	3D04J	3D04J
9120	135	HS/WF DISAPPROVE		(3D04K)	3D04K	3D04K	3D04K	3D04K	3D04K	3D04K	3D04K
9130	135	DONT LIKE USERS		(3D04L)	3D04L	3D04L	3D04L	3D04L	3D04L	3D04L	3D04L
9140	135	FRNDS DNT USE IT		(3D04M)	3D04M	3D04M	3D04M	3D04M	3D04M	3D04M	3D04M
9150	135	PSSBLY BAD TRIP		(3D04N)	3D04N	3D04N	3D04N	3D04N	3D04N	3D04N	3D04N
9160	135	TOO EXPENSIVE			3D04O	3D04O	3D04O	3D04O	3D04O	3D04O	3D04O
9170	135	NOT AVAILABLE			3D04P	3D04P	3D04P	3D04P	3D04P	3D04P	3D04P
9180	135	NOT WNT GET HIGH			3D04Q	3D04Q	3D04Q	3D04Q	3D04Q	3D04Q	3D04Q

A07a: DRUGS. Tickets, accidents after use

			1975	1976	1977	1978	1979	1980	1981	1982	1983
650	22	#X/12MO R TCKTD		+C28	+C28	+C28	+C28	+C28	+C28	+C28	+C28
660	22	#TCKTS AFT DRNK		+C29A	+C29A	+C29A	+C29A	+C29A	+C29A	+C29A	+C29A
670	22	#TCKTS AFT MARJ		+C29B	+C29B	+C29B	+C29B	+C29B	+C29B	+C29B	+C29B
680	22	#TCKTS AFT OTDG		+C29C	+C29C	+C29C	+C29C	+C29C	+C29C	+C29C	+C29C
690	23	#ACCIDNTS/12 MO		+C30	+C30	+C30	+C30	+C30	+C30	+C30	+C30
700	23	#ACDTS AFT DRNK		+C31A	+C31A	+C31A	+C31A	+C31A	+C31A	+C31A	+C31A
710	23	#ACDTS AFT MARJ		+C31B	+C31B	+C31B	+C31B	+C31B	+C31B	+C31B	+C31B
720	23	#ACDTS AFT OTDG		+C31C	+C31C	+C31C	+C31C	+C31C	+C31C	+C31C	+C31C

A07b: DRUGS. Problems after use

			1975	1976	1977	1978	1979	1980	1981	1982	1983
9190	135	AL CS BEHV REGRT		3D05A	3D05A	3D05A	3D05A	3D05A	3D05A	3D05A	3D05A
9200	135	AL HURT REL PRNT		3D05A	3D05A	3D05A	3D05A	3D05A	3D05A	3D05A	3D05A
9210	135	AL HURT REL SPSE		3D05A	3D05A	3D05A	3D05A	3D05A	3D05A	3D05A	3D05A
9220	135	AL HURT REL FRND		3D05A	3D05A	3D05A	3D05A	3D05A	3D05A	3D05A	3D05A
9230	135	AL HURT REL TCHR		3D05A	3D05A	3D05A	3D05A	3D05A	3D05A	3D05A	3D05A
9240	135	AL INV PL BD INF		3D05A	3D05A	3D05A	3D05A	3D05A	3D05A	3D05A	3D05A
9250	135	AL HURT PERF JOB		3D05A	3D05A	3D05A	3D05A	3D05A	3D05A	3D05A	3D05A
9260	135	AL CAUS <INTERSTD		3D05A	3D05A	3D05A	3D05A	3D05A	3D05A	3D05A	3D05A
9270	135	AL CS <STABL EMTN		3D05A	3D05A	3D05A	3D05A	3D05A	3D05A	3D05A	3D05A
9280	135	AL CS HAV <ENERGY		3D05A	3D05A	3D05A	3D05A	3D05A	3D05A	3D05A	3D05A
9290	135	AL INTF THNK CLR		3D05A	3D05A	3D05A	3D05A	3D05A	3D05A	3D05A	3D05A
9300	135	AL BD PSYCH EFCT		3D05A	3D05A	3D05A	3D05A	3D05A	3D05A	3D05A	3D05A
9310	135	AL CS HEALTH BAD		3D05A	3D05A	3D05A	3D05A	3D05A	3D05A	3D05A	3D05A
9320	135	AL CS DRIV UNSAF		3D05A	3D05A	3D05A	3D05A	3D05A	3D05A	3D05A	3D05A
9330	135	AL GT TRBL W POL		3D05A	3D05A	3D05A	3D05A	3D05A	3D05A	3D05A	3D05A
9340	135	AL CS NO PROBLEM			3D05A	3D05A	3D05A	3D05A	3D05A	3D05A	3D05A
9350	135	AL NEVER USED DG			3D05A	3D05A	3D05A	3D05A	3D05A	3D05A	3D05A
9360	136	MJ CS BEHV REGRT		3D05M	3D05M	3D05M	3D05M	3D05M	3D05M	3D05M	3D05M
9370	136	MJ HURT REL PRNT		3D05M	3D05M	3D05M	3D05M	3D05M	3D05M	3D05M	3D05M
		(continued)									

Item Reference Number	Page Loc. in this Volume	ITEM DESCRIPTION (ABBREVIATED)	QUESTIONNAIRE LOCATION BY YEAR (FORM, SECTION, AND QUESTION NUMBER)								
			1975	1976	1977	1978	1979	1980	1981	1982	1983

A07b: DRUGS. Problems after use (continued)

Item Reference Number	Page Loc. in this Volume	ITEM DESCRIPTION (ABBREVIATED)	1975	1976	1977	1978	1979	1980	1981	1982	1983
9380	136	MJ HURT REL SPSE		3D05M	3D05M	3D05M	3D05M	3D05M	3D05M	3D05M	3D05M
9390	136	MJ HURT REL FRND		3D05M	3D05M	3D05M	3D05M	3D05M	3D05M	3D05M	3D05M
9400	136	MJ HURT REL TCHR		3D05M	3D05M	3D05M	3D05M	3D05M	3D05M	3D05M	3D05M
9410	136	MJ INV PL BD INF		3D05M	3D05M	3D05M	3D05M	3D05M	3D05M	3D05M	3D05M
9420	136	MJ HURT PERF JOB		3D05M	3D05M	3D05M	3D05M	3D05M	3D05M	3D05M	3D05M
9430	136	MJ CAUS <INTERSTD		3D05M	3D05M	3D05M	3D05M	3D05M	3D05M	3D05M	3D05M
9440	136	MJ CS <STABL EMTN		3D05M	3D05M	3D05M	3D05M	3D05M	3D05M	3D05M	3D05M
9450	136	MJ CS HAV <ENERGY		3D05M	3D05M	3D05M	3D05M	3D05M	3D05M	3D05M	3D05M
9460	136	MJ INTF THNK CLR		3D05M	3D05M	3D05M	3D05M	3D05M	3D05M	3D05M	3D05M
9470	136	MJ BD PSYCH EFCT		3D05M	3D05M	3D05M	3D05M	3D05M	3D05M	3D05M	3D05M
9480	136	MJ CS HEALTH BAD		3D05M	3D05M	3D05M	3D05M	3D05M	3D05M	3D05M	3D05M
9490	136	MJ CS DRIV UNSAF		3D05M	3D05M	3D05M	3D05M	3D05M	3D05M	3D05M	3D05M
9500	136	MJ GT TRBL W POL		3D05M	3D05M	3D05M	3D05M	3D05M	3D05M	3D05M	3D05M
9510	136	MJ CS NO PROBLEM			3D05M	3D05M	3D05M	3D05M	3D05M	3D05M	3D05M
9520	136	MJ NEVER USED DG			3D05M	3D05M	3D05M	3D05M	3D05M	3D05M	3D05M
9530	136	OT CS BEHV REGRT		3D05O	3D05O	3D05O	3D05O	3D05O	3D05O	3D05O	3D05O
9540	136	OT HURT REL PRNT		3D05O	3D05O	3D05O	3D05O	3D05O	3D05O	3D05O	3D05O
9550	136	OT HURT REL SPSE		3D05O	3D05O	3D05O	3D05O	3D05O	3D05O	3D05O	3D05O
9560	136	OT HURT REL FRND		3D05O	3D05O	3D05O	3D05O	3D05O	3D05O	3D05O	3D05O
9570	136	OT HURT REL TCHR		3D05O	3D05O	3D05O	3D05O	3D05O	3D05O	3D05O	3D05O
9580	136	OT INV PL BD INF		3D05O	3D05O	3D05O	3D05O	3D05O	3D05O	3D05O	3D05O
9590	136	OT HURT PERF JOB		3D05O	3D05O	3D05O	3D05O	3D05O	3D05O	3D05O	3D05O
9600	136	OT CAUS <INTERSTD		3D05O	3D05O	3D05O	3D05O	3D05O	3D05O	3D05O	3D05O
9610	136	OT CS <STABL EMTN		3D05O	3D05O	3D05O	3D05O	3D05O	3D05O	3D05O	3D05O
9620	136	OT CS HAV <ENERGY		3D05O	3D05O	3D05O	3D05O	3D05O	3D05O	3D05O	3D05O
9630	136	OT INTF THNK CLR		3D05O	3D05O	3D05O	3D05O	3D05O	3D05O	3D05O	3D05O
9640	136	OT BD PSYCH EFCT		3D05O	3D05O	3D05O	3D05O	3D05O	3D05O	3D05O	3D05O
9650	136	OT CS HEALTH BAD		3D05O	3D05O	3D05O	3D05O	3D05O	3D05O	3D05O	3D05O
9660	136	OT CS DRIV UNSAF		3D05O	3D05O	3D05O	3D05O	3D05O	3D05O	3D05O	3D05O
9670	136	OT GT TRBL W POL		3D05O	3D05O	3D05O	3D05O	3D05O	3D05O	3D05O	3D05O
9680	136	OT CS NO PROBLEM			3D05O	3D05O	3D05O	3D05O	3D05O	3D05O	3D05O
9690	136	OT NEVER USED DG			3D05O	3D05O	3D05O	3D05O	3D05O	3D05O	3D05O

A08a: DRUGS. Sources of help

Item Reference Number	Page Loc. in this Volume	ITEM DESCRIPTION (ABBREVIATED)	1975	1976	1977	1978	1979	1980	1981	1982	1983
7540		TRN FA/MO DRG HP			2E05A		2E07A				
7550		TRN SR/BR DRG HP			2E05B		2E07B				
7560		TRN RLTVS DRG HP			2E05C		2E07C				
7570		TRN FRND DRG HP			2E05D		2E07D				
7580		TRN DOCTR DRG HP			2E05E		2E07E				
7590		TRN CLINC DRG HP			2E05F		2E07F				
7600		TRN CNSLR DRG HP			2E05G		2E07G				
7610		TRN TCHR DRG HP			2E05H		2E07H				
7620		TRN MNSTR DRG HP			2E05I		2E07I				

A09a: DRUGS. Parental awareness of use

Item Reference Number	Page Loc. in this Volume	ITEM DESCRIPTION (ABBREVIATED)	1975	1976	1977	1978	1979	1980	1981	1982	1983
7510	113	PRNT THK U DRINK			2E02	2E01	2E04	2E05	2E05	2E05	2E05
7520	113	PRNT THK U SM MJ			2E03	2E02	2E05	2E06	2E06	2E06	2E06
7530		PRNT THK USE DRG			2E04	2E03	2E06	2E07	2E07		

A10a: DRUGS. Education

Item Reference Number	Page Loc. in this Volume	ITEM DESCRIPTION (ABBREVIATED)	1975	1976	1977	1978	1979	1980	1981	1982	1983
7690	115	HAD DRUG EDUCATN		2E05	2E09	2E09	2E11	2E12	2E12	2E15	2E15
7840	116	DG ED,>DG INTRST		2E06	2E10	2E10	2E12	2E13	2E13	2E16	2E16
7850	116	DG ED,SPC COURSE		2E07A	2E11A	2E11A	2E13A	2E14A	2E14A	2E17A	2E17A
7860	116	DG ED,IN REG CRS		2E07B	2E11B	2E11B	2E13B	2E14B	2E14B	2E17B	2E17B
7870	116	DG ED,NT REG CRS		2E07C	2E11C	2E11C	2E13C	2E14C	2E14C	2E17C	2E17C
7880	116	DG ED,SPC DISCUS		2E07D	2E11D	2E11D	2E13D	2E14D	2E14D	2E17D	2E17D
7890	116	DG ED,GRT VALUE		2E08	2E12	2E12	2E14	2E15	2E15	2E18	2E18

Item Reference Number	Page Loc. in this Volume	ITEM DESCRIPTION (ABBREVIATED)	1975	1976	1977	1978	1979	1980	1981	1982	1983

A11a: DRUGS. Own attitudes about use by adults

Item Reference Number	Page Loc. in this Volume	ITEM DESCRIPTION (ABBREVIATED)	1975	1976	1977	1978	1979	1980	1981	1982	1983
8560	129	DAP SMK 1PCK CIG	(3A53A)	3A28A	3A28A	3A28A	3A28A	3A28A	3A28A	3A28A	3A28A
8570	129	DAP TRY MRJ 1-2T	(3A53B)	3A28B	3A28B	3A28B	3A28B	3A28B	3A28B	3A28B	3A28B
8580	129	DAP SMK MRJ OCCS	(3A53C)	3A28C	3A28C	3A28C	3A28C	3A28C	3A28C	3A28C	3A28C
8590	130	DAP SMK MRJ REGL	(3A53D)	3A28D	3A28D	3A28D	3A28D	3A28D	3A28D	3A28D	3A28D
8600	130	DAP TRY LSD 1-2T	(3A53E)	3A28E	3A28E	3A28E	3A28E	3A28E	3A28E	3A28E	3A28E
8610	130	DAP TKG LSD REGL	(3A53F)	3A28F	3A28F	3A28F	3A28F	3A28F	3A28F	3A28F	3A28F
8620	130	DAP TRY HRN 1-2T	(3A53G)	3A28G	3A28G	3A28G	3A28G	3A28G	3A28G	3A28G	3A28G
8630	130	DAP TKG HRN OCCS	(3A53H)	3A28H	3A28H	3A28H	3A28H	3A28H	3A28H	3A28H	3A28H
8640	130	DAP TKG HRN REGL	(3A53I)	3A28I	3A28I	3A28I	3A28I	3A28I	3A28I	3A28I	3A28I
8650	130	DAP TRY BRB 1-2T	(3A53J)	3A28J	3A28J	3A28J	3A28J	3A28J	3A28J	3A28J	3A28J
8660	130	DAP TKG BRB REGL	(3A53K)	3A28K	3A28K	3A28K	3A28K	3A28K	3A28K	3A28K	3A28K
8670	130	DAP TRY AMP 1-2T	(3A53L)	3A28L	3A28L	3A28L	3A28L	3A28L	3A28L	3A28L	3A28L
8680	131	DAP TKG AMP REGL	(3A53M)	3A28M	3A28M	3A28M	3A28M	3A28M	3A28M	3A28M	3A28M
8690	131	DAP TRY COC 1-2T	(3A53N)	3A28N	3A28N	3A28N	3A28N	3A28N	3A28N	3A28N	3A28N
8700	131	DAP TKG COC REGL	(3A53O)	3A28O	3A28O	3A28O	3A28O	3A28O	3A28O	3A28O	3A28O
8710	131	DAP TRY DRK ALCL	(3A53P)	3A28P	3A28P	3A28P	3A28P	3A28P	3A28P	3A28P	3A28P
8720	131	DAP 1-2 DRK/DAY	(3A53Q)	3A28Q	3A28Q	3A28Q	3A28Q	3A28Q	3A28Q	3A28Q	3A28Q
8730	131	DAP 4-5 DRK/DAY	(3A53R)	3A28R	3A28R	3A28R	3A28R	3A28R	3A28R	3A28R	3A28R
8740	131	DAP 5+ DRK WKNDS	(3A53S)	3A28S	3A28S	3A28S	3A28S	3A28S	3A28S	3A28S	3A28S

A11b: DRUGS. Own attitudes about use by own children

Item Reference Number	Page Loc. in this Volume	ITEM DESCRIPTION (ABBREVIATED)	1975	1976	1977	1978	1979	1980	1981	1982	1983
7210		FBD CHLD CIG RGL			2E01A						
7220		FBD CHLD MJ OCCS			2E01B						
7230		FBD CHLD MJ RGLY			2E01C						
7240		FBD CHLD LSD OCC			2E01D						
7250		FBD CHLD AMPH OC			2E01E						
7260		FBD CHLD BARB OC			2E01F						
7270		FBD CHLD COKE OC			2E01G						
7280		FBD CHLD HRN OCC			2E01H						
7290		FBD CHLD DRNK OC			2E01I						
7300		FBD CHLD DRNK RG			2E01J						
7310		FBD CHLD DRUNKOC			2E01K						

A11c: DRUGS. Own perceptions of users

Item Reference Number	Page Loc. in this Volume	ITEM DESCRIPTION (ABBREVIATED)	1975	1976	1977	1978	1979	1980	1981	1982	1983
13060	193	I/MJ USR,>CREATV			5E01A	5E01A	5E01A	5E01A	5E01A	5E01A	5E01A
13070	193	I/MJ USR,<SENSBL			5E01B	5E01B	5E01B	5E01B	5E01B	5E01B	5E01B
13080	193	I/MJ USR,>INTRST			5E01C	5E01C	5E01C	5E01C	5E01C	5E01C	5E01C
13090	193	I/MJ USR,<HRDWKG			5E01D	5E01D	5E01D	5E01D	5E01D	5E01D	5E01D
13100	193	I/MJ USR,>INDPND			5E01E	5E01E	5E01E	5E01E	5E01E	5E01E	5E01E
13110	194	I/MJ USR,>UNSTBL			5E01F	5E01F	5E01F	5E01F	5E01F	5E01F	5E01F
13120	194	I/MJ USR,>CNCRND			5E01G	5E01G	5E01G	5E01G	5E01G	5E01G	5E01G
13130	194	I/MJ USR,>WKWLD			5E01H	5E01H	5E01H	5E01H	5E01H	5E01H	5E01H
13140	194	I/MJ USR,>CRMNL			5E01I	5E01I	5E01I	5E01I	5E01I		
13330	195	I/DG USR,>CREATV			5E03A	5E03A		5E03A		5E03A	5E03A
13340	195	I/DG USR,<SENSBL			5E03B	5E03B		5E03B		5E03B	5E03B
13350	195	I/DG USR,>INTRST			5E03C	5E03C		5E03C		5E03C	5E03C
13360	196	I/DG USR,<HRDWKG			5E03D	5E03D		5E03D		5E03D	5E03D
13370	196	I/DG USR,>INDPND			5E03E	5E03E		5E03E		5E03E	5E03E
13380	196	I/DG USR,>UNSTBL			5E03F	5E03F		5E03F		5E03F	5E03F
13390	196	I/DG USR,>CNCRND			5E03G	5E03G		5E03G		5E03G	5E03G
13400	196	I/DG USR,>WKWLD			5E03H	5E03H		5E03H		5E03H	5E03H
13410	196	I/DG USR,>CRMNL			5E03I	5E03I		5E03I		5E03I	5E03I
13670	140	DRG USE+,MY FLGS			5E07C	5E07C	5E05C	5E07C		3E07C	3E07C
20880	197	GUY SMK COOL							5E03A	5E05A	5E05A
20890	197	GUY SMK INSECURE							5E03B	5E05B	5E05B
20900	198	GUY SMK INDPNDNT							5E03C	5E05C	5E05C
20910	198	GUY SMK CONFORMG							5E03D	5E05D	5E05D
20920	198	GUY SMK MATURE							5E03E	5E05E	5E05E
20930	198	GUY SM TRY MATUR							5E03F	5E05F	5E05F
20940	198	GIRL SMK COOL							5E04A	5E06A	5E06A
20950	198	GRL SMK INSECURE							5E04B	5E06B	5E06B

(continued)

Item Reference Number	Page Loc. in this Volume	ITEM DESCRIPTION (ABBREVIATED)	QUESTIONNAIRE LOCATION BY YEAR (FORM, SECTION, AND QUESTION NUMBER)								
			1975	1976	1977	1978	1979	1980	1981	1982	1983

A11c: DRUGS. Own perceptions of users (continued)

Item Ref	Page	Description	1975	1976	1977	1978	1979	1980	1981	1982	1983
20960	198	GRL SMK INDPNDNT							5E04C	5E06C	5E06C
20970	199	GRL SMK CONFORMG							5E04D	5E06D	5E06D
20980	199	GRL SMK MATURE							5E04E	5E06E	5E06E
20990	199	GRL SM TRY MATUR							5E04F	5E06F	5E06F
21000	199	SMKRS ENJOY LIFE							5E05A	5E07A	5E07A
21010	199	PRFR DATE N-SMKR							5E05B	5E07B	5E07B
21020	199	HARMFUL CIG EXAG							5E05C	5E07C	5E07C
21030	199	SMKR POOR JDGMNT							5E05D	5E07D	5E07D
21040	200	DONT MIND SMOKNG							5E05E	5E07E	5E07E
21050	200	SMKG DIRTY HABIT							5E05F	5E07F	5E07F

A12a: DRUGS. Parents' attitudes about use

Item Ref	Page	Description	1975	1976	1977	1978	1979	1980	1981	1982	1983
11380		PRNT DAP CIGS	4A35A	4E09A	4E09A	4E08A	4E08A				
11390		PRNT DAP TRY MRJ	4A35B	4E09B	4E09B	4E08B	4E08B				
11400		PRNT DAP MJ OCC	4A35C	4E09C	4E09C	4E08C	4E08C				
11410		PRNT DAP MJ REG	4A35D	4E09D	4E09D	4E08D	4E08D				
11420		PRNT DAP TRY LSD	4A35E	4E09E	4E09E	4E08E	4E08E				
11430		PRNT DAP TRY AMP	4A35F	4E09F	4E09F	4E08F	4E08F				
11440		PRNT DAP 1-2DR/D	4A35G	4E09G	4E09G	4E08G	4E08G				
11450		PRNT DAP 4-5DR/D	4A35H	4E09H	4E09H	4E08H	4E08H				
11460		PRNT DAP 5+DR/WE	4A35I	4E09I	4E09I	4E08I	4E08I				

A12b: DRUGS. Friends' and students' attitudes about use

Item Ref	Page	Description	1975	1976	1977	1978	1979	1980	1981	1982	1983
11470	170	FRD DAP CIGS			4E10A		4E09A	4E08A	4E08A	4E08A	4E08A
11480	170	FRD DAP TRY MARJ			4E10B		4E09B	4E08B	4E08B	4E08B	4E08B
11490	171	FRD DAP MJ OCC			4E10C		4E09C	4E08C	4E08C	4E08C	4E08C
11500	171	FRD DAP MJ REG			4E10D		4E09D	4E08D	4E08D	4E08D	4E08D
11510	171	FRD DAP TRY LSD			4E10E		4E09E	4E08E	4E08E	4E08E	4E08E
11520	171	FRD DAP TRY AMP			4E10F		4E09F	4E08F	4E08F	4E08F	4E08F
11530	171	FRD DAP 1-2DR/DA			4E10G		4E09G	4E08G	4E08G	4E08G	4E08G
11540	171	FRD DAP 4-5DR/DA			4E10H		4E09H	4E08H	4E08H	4E08H	4E08H
11550	171	FRD DAP 5+DR/WKD			4E10I		4E09I	4E08I	4E08I	4E08I	4E08I
13650	139	DRG USE+,MAJ STD		5E06A	5E07A	5E07A	5E05A	5E07A		3E07A	3E07A
13660	140	DRG USE+,MY FRND		5E06B	5E07B	5E07B	5E05B	5E07B		3E07B	3E07B

A12c: DRUGS. Others' perceptions of users

Item Ref	Page	Description	1975	1976	1977	1978	1979	1980	1981	1982	1983
12780		PSN TKG MJ/AMBTS		5D02A							
12790		PSN TKG MJ/-SOCL		5D02B							
12800		PSN TKG MJ/CNFMG		5D02C							
12810		PSN TKG MJ/CRMNL		5D02D							
12820		PSN TKG MJ/-STBL		5D02E							
12830		PSN TKG MJ/INTRS		5D02F							
12840		PSN TKG MJ/RBLS		5D02G							
12850		PSN TKG MJ/SNSBL		5D02H							
12860		PSN TKG MJ/SX PR		5D02I							
12870		PSN TKG MJ/WKWLD		5D02J							
12890		PSN TKG DG/AMBTS		5D03A							
12900		PSN TKG DG/-SOCL		5D03B							
12910		PSN TKG DG/CNFMG		5D03C							
12920		PSN TKG DG/CRMNL		5D03D							
12930		PSN TKG DG/-STBL		5D03E							
12940		PSN TKG DG/INTRS		5D03F							
12950		PSN TKG DG/RBLS		5D03G							
12960		PSN TKG DG/SNSBL		5D03H							
12970		PSN TKG DG/SX PR		5D03I							
12980		PSN TKG DG/WKWLD		5D03J							
13190	194	PPL/MJUSR>CREATV			5E02A	5E02A		5E02A	5E02A	5E02A	5E02A
13200	194	PPL/MJUSR<SENSBL			5E02B	5E02B		5E02B	5E02B	5E02B	5E02B
13210	194	PPL/MJUSR>INTRST			5E02C	5E02C		5E02C	5E02C	5E02C	5E02C
13220	194	PPL/MJUSR<HRDWKG			5E02D	5E02D		5E02D	5E02D	5E02D	5E02D

(continued)

Item Reference Number	Page Loc. in this Volume	ITEM DESCRIPTION (ABBREVIATED)	QUESTIONNAIRE LOCATION BY YEAR (FORM, SECTION, AND QUESTION NUMBER)								
			1975	1976	1977	1978	1979	1980	1981	1982	1983

A12c: DRUGS. Others' perceptions of users (continued)

13230	195	PPL/MJUSR>INDPND			5E02E	5E02E		5E02E	5E02E	5E02E	5E02E
13240	195	PPL/MJUSR>UNSTBL			5E02F	5E02F		5E02F	5E02F	5E02F	5E02F
13250	195	PPL/MJUSR>CNCRND			5E02G	5E02G		5E02G	5E02G	5E02G	5E02G
13260	195	PPL/MJUSR>WKWLD			5E02H	5E02H		5E02H	5E02H	5E02H	5E02H
13270	195	PPL/MJUSR>CRMNL			5E02I	5E02I		5E02I	5E02I	5E02I	5E02I
13490	196	PPL/DGUSR>CREATV			5E04A	5E04A		5E04A		5E04A	5E04A
13500	196	PPL/DGUSR<SENSBL			5E04B	5E04B		5E04B		5E04B	5E04B
13510	196	PPL/DGUSR>INTRST			5E04C	5E04C		5E04C		5E04C	5E04C
13520	197	PPL/DGUSR<HRDWKG			5E04D	5E04D		5E04D		5E04D	5E04D
13530	197	PPL/DGUSR>INDPND			5E04E	5E04E		5E04E		5E04E	5E04E
13540	197	PPL/DGUSR>UNSTBL			5E04F	5E04F		5E04F		5E04F	5E04F
13550	197	PPL/DGUSR>CNCRND			5E04G	5E04G		5E04G		5E04G	5E04G
13560	197	PPL/DGUSR>WKWLD			5E04H	5E04H		5E04H		5E04H	5E04H
13570	197	PPL/DGUSR>CRMNL			5E04I	5E04I		5E04I		5E04I	5E04I

A13a: DRUGS. Preferred legality for adults

10760	159	LAW 4 SMK TOBPUB			4A20K	4A20K	4A20K	4A20K	4A20K	4A20K	4A20K
10770		ILGL AD SMK CIG		4A20A							
10780	158	ILGL AD MRJ PRIV		4A20B	4A20A	4A20A	4A20A	4A20A	4A20A	4A20A	4A20A
10790	158	ILGL AD MRJ PUBL		4A20C	4A20B	4A20B	4A20B	4A20B	4A20B	4A20B	4A20B
10800	158	ILGL AD LSD PRIV		4A20D	4A20C	4A20C	4A20C	4A20C	4A20C	4A20C	4A20C
10810	158	ILGL AD LSD PUBL		4A20E	4A20D	4A20D	4A20D	4A20D	4A20D	4A20D	4A20D
10820	158	ILGL AD AMP PRIV		4A20F	4A20E	4A20E	4A20E	4A20E	4A20E	4A20E	4A20E
10830	158	ILGL AD AMP PUBL		4A20G	4A20F	4A20F	4A20F	4A20F	4A20F	4A20F	4A20F
10840	158	ILGL AD HRN PRIV		4A20H	4A20G	4A20G	4A20G	4A20G	4A20G	4A20G	4A20G
10850	159	ILGL AD HRN PUBL		4A20I	4A20H	4A20H	4A20H	4A20H	4A20H	4A20H	4A20H
10860	159	ILGL AD DRNK PRV		4A20J	4A20I	4A20I	4A20I	4A20I	4A20I	4A20I	4A20I
10870	159	ILGL AD DRNK PBL		4A20K	4A20J	4A20J	4A20J	4A20J	4A20J	4A20J	4A20J

A13b: DRUGS. Own response to legalization

10880	159	CRIME 2 USE MARJ	4A32	4A21	4A21	4A21	4A21	4A21	4A21	4A21	4A21
10890	159	LEGAL 2 SELL MRJ	4A33	4A22	4A22	4A22	4A22	4A22	4A22	4A22	4A22
10900	159	USE<MJ IF LEGAL	4A34	4A23	4A23	4A23	4A23	4A23	4A23	4A23	4A23

A13c: DRUGS. Knowledge of marijuana laws

13050		R'S STATE LAW/MJ		5D04	5D05	5D05	5D05	5D05			

A14a: DRUGS. Risk of harm to self

12360	184	RSK OF CIG1+PK/D	5A41A	5A23A	5A23A	5A23A	5A23A	5A23A	5A23A	5A23A	5A23A
12370	184	RSK OF MJ 1-2 X	5A41B	5A23B	5A23B	5A23B	5A23B	5A23B	5A23B	5A23B	5A23B
12380	184	RSK OF MJ OCSNLY	5A41C	5A23C	5A23C	5A23C	5A23C	5A23C	5A23C	5A23C	5A23C
12390	185	RSK OF MJ REGLY	5A41D	5A23D	5A23D	5A23D	5A23D	5A23D	5A23D	5A23D	5A23D
12400	185	RSK OF LSD 1-2 X	5A41E	5A23E	5A23E	5A23E	5A23E	5A23E	5A23E	5A23E	5A23E
12410	185	RSK OF LSD REGLY	5A41F	5A23F	5A23F	5A23F	5A23F	5A23F	5A23F	5A23F	5A23F
12420	185	RSK OF 'H' 1-2 X	5A41G	5A23G	5A23G	5A23G	5A23G	5A23G	5A23G	5A23G	5A23G
12430	185	RSK OF 'H' OCSNL	5A41H	5A23H	5A23H	5A23H	5A23H	5A23H	5A23H	5A23H	5A23H
12440	185	RSK OF 'H' REGLY	5A41I	5A23I	5A23I	5A23I	5A23I	5A23I	5A23I	5A23I	5A23I
12450	185	RSK OF BARB 1-2X	5A41J	5A23J	5A23J	5A23J	5A23J	5A23J	5A23J	5A23J	5A23J
12460	186	RSK OF BARB REGY	5A41K	5A23K	5A23K	5A23K	5A23K	5A23K	5A23K	5A23K	5A23K
12470	186	RSK OF AMPH 1-2X	5A41L	5A23L	5A23L	5A23L	5A23L	5A23L	5A23L	5A23L	5A23L
12480	186	RSK OF AMPH REG	5A41M	5A23M	5A23M	5A23M	5A23M	5A23M	5A23M	5A23M	5A23M
12490	186	RSK OF COKE 1-2X	5A41N	5A23N	5A23N	5A23N	5A23N	5A23N	5A23N	5A23N	5A23N
12500	186	RSK OF COKE REG	5A41O	5A23O	5A23O	5A23O	5A23O	5A23O	5A23O	5A23O	5A23O
12510	186	RSK OF 1-2 DRINK	5A41P	5A23P	5A23P	5A23P	5A23P	5A23P	5A23P	5A23P	5A23P
12520	186	RSK OF 1-2 DR/DA	5A41Q	5A23Q	5A23Q	5A23Q	5A23Q	5A23Q	5A23Q	5A23Q	5A23Q
12530	187	RSK OF 4-5 DR/DA	5A41R	5A23R	5A23R	5A23R	5A23R	5A23R	5A23R	5A23R	5A23R
12540	187	RSK OF 5+DR/WKND	5A41S	5A23S	5A23S	5A23S	5A23S	5A23S	5A23S	5A23S	5A23S

Item Reference Number	Page Loc. in this Volume	ITEM DESCRIPTION (ABBREVIATED)	QUESTIONNAIRE LOCATION BY YEAR (FORM, SECTION, AND QUESTION NUMBER)								
			1975	1976	1977	1978	1979	1980	1981	1982	1983

A14b: DRUGS. Risk of harm to others

Item Reference Number	Page Loc. in this Volume	ITEM DESCRIPTION (ABBREVIATED)	1975	1976	1977	1978	1979	1980	1981	1982	1983
7320		RSK/OT CIG1+PK/D		2E01A							
7330		RSK/OT MJ 1-2 X		2E01B							
7340		RSK/OT MJ OCSNLY		2E01C							
7350		RSK/OT MJ REGLY		2E01D							
7360		RSK/OT LSD 1-2 X		2E01E							
7370		RSK/OT LSD REGLY		2E01F							
7380		RSK/OT 'H' 1-2 X		2E01G							
7390		RSK/OT 'H' OCSNL		2E01H							
7400		RSK/OT 'H' REGLY		2E01I							
7410		RSK/OT BARB 1-2X		2E01J							
7420		RSK/OT BARB REGY		2E01K							
7430		RSK/OT AMPH 1-2X		2E01L							
7440		RSK/OT AMPH REG		2E01M							
7450		RSK/OT COKE 1-2X		2E01N							
7460		RSK/OT COKE REG		2E01O							
7470		RSK/OT 1-2 DRINK		2E01P							
7480		RSK/OT 1-2 DR/DA		2E01Q							
7490		RSK/OT 4-5 DR/DA		2E01R							
7500		RSK/OT 5+DR/WKND		2E01S							

A15a: DRUGS. Admitting use in questionnaire

Item Reference Number	Page Loc. in this Volume	ITEM DESCRIPTION (ABBREVIATED)	1975	1976	1977	1978	1979	1980	1981	1982	1983
20800	201	WLD ADMT USE MJ					5E09	5E09	5E14	5E13	5E13
20810	201	WLD ADMT USE AMP					5E10	5E10	5E15	5E14	5E14
20820	201	WLD ADMT USE HER					5E11	5E11	5E16	5E15	5E15

A16a: DRUGS. Parent groups

Item Reference Number	Page Loc. in this Volume	ITEM DESCRIPTION (ABBREVIATED)	1975	1976	1977	1978	1979	1980	1981	1982	1983
21730	171	IDEA PARENTS GRP									4E09
21740	172	#FRNDS PRNTS GRP									4E10
21750	172	OWN PRNTS IN GRP									4E11
21760	172	GP IMPCT OWN FLG									4E12
21770	172	GP CHG RELP PRNT									4E13
21780	172	#FRNDS ANTIDG GP									4E14
21790	172	EVR IN ANTIDG GP									4E15

B01: EDUCATION. High school: scholastic status, objectives, experiences

Item Reference Number	Page Loc. in this Volume	ITEM DESCRIPTION (ABBREVIATED)	1975	1976	1977	1978	1979	1980	1981	1982	1983
390	18	WHEN R XPCT GRAD		+C14	+C14	+C14	+C14	+C14	+C14	+C14	+C14
400	18	R'S HS PROGRAM		+C15	+C15	+C15	+C15	+C15	+C15	+C15	+C15
410	19	RT SF SCH AB>AVG		+C16	+C16	+C16	+C16	+C16	+C16	+C16	+C16
420	19	RT SF INTELL>AVG		+C17	+C17	+C17	+C17	+C17	+C17	+C17	+C17
470	20	R HS GRADE/D=1		+C20	+C20	+C20	+C20	+C20	+C20	+C20	+C20
1310	36	SAT EDUC EXPRNCS	1A009E	1A006E	1A006E	1A006E	1A006E	1A006E	1A006E	1A006E	1A006E
1660	41	GO SCH ENJY XPR	1A013I	1A011I	1A011I	1A011I	1A011I	1A011I	1A011I	1A011I	1A011I
1670	41	DO WL SC IMP/JB	1A013H	1A011J	1A011J	1A011J	1A011J	1A011J	1A011J	1A011J	1A011J
5700	83	*SC WRK NVR MNG		1D002	1D002	1D002	1D002	1D002	1D002	1D002	1D002
5710	83	*MST COUR V DUL		1D003	1D003	1D003	1D003	1D003	1D003	1D003	1D003
5720	83	*LRN SCH NT IMP		1D004	1D004	1D004	1D004	1D004	1D004	1D004	1D004
7630	83	R LIKES SCHOOL		1D001	1D001	1D001	1D001	1D001	1D001	1D001	1D001
	115			2E02	2E06	2E06	2E08	2E09	2E09	2E12	2E12
				3E08	3E07	3E07	3E07	3E07	3E07		
				4E10	5E05	5E05	5E03	5E05			
				5E04							
7640	115	HRS/WK SPND HMWK		2E03	2E07	2E07	2E09	2E10	2E10	2E13	2E13
9860	138	HAD SEX ED IN HS		3E09	3E08	3E08	3E08	3E08	3E08	3E04	3E04
9870	138	STUDY BC IN HS		3E10	3E09	3E09	3E09	3E09	3E09	3E05	3E05

B02: EDUCATION. Combining work and school: attitudes, experiences

Item Reference Number	Page Loc. in this Volume	ITEM DESCRIPTION (ABBREVIATED)	1975	1976	1977	1978	1979	1980	1981	1982	1983
5770	84	R IN WK-STDY PG		1D009	1D009	1D009	1D009	1D009	1D009	1D009	1D009
10260	151	JOB IMPC LRNING	4A08R	4A08R	4A08R	4A08R	4A08R	4A08R	4A08R	4A08R	4A08R

Item Reference Number	Page Loc. in this Volume	ITEM DESCRIPTION (ABBREVIATED)	QUESTIONNAIRE LOCATION BY YEAR (FORM, SECTION, AND QUESTION NUMBER)								
			1975	1976	1977	1978	1979	1980	1981	1982	1983

B03: EDUCATION. Interracial contact at school

Item Reference Number	Page Loc.	ITEM DESCRIPTION	1975	1976	1977	1978	1979	1980	1981	1982	1983
8220	124	DES AL CHL SM RC	3A19L	3A10A	3A10A	3A10A	3A10A	3A10A	3A10A	3A10A	3A10A
8230	124	DES SM CHL OT RC	3A19M	3A10B	3A10B	3A10B	3A10B	3A10B	3A10B	3A10B	3A10B
8240	124	DES MS CHL OT RC	3A19N	3A10C	3A10C	3A10C	3A10C	3A10C	3A10C	3A10C	3A10C
8270	124	ELEMSCH AL OT RC	3A21	3A13	3A13	3A13	3A13	3A13	3A13	3A13	3A13
8280	124	HISCH AL OT RC	3A20	3A14	3A14	3A14	3A14	3A14	3A14	3A14	3A14
11890	176	RCL CNTCT SCHOOL		5A07A	5A07A	5A07A	5A07A	5A07A	5A07A	5A07A	5A07A

B04: EDUCATION. Student norms

Item Reference Number	Page Loc.	ITEM DESCRIPTION	1975	1976	1977	1978	1979	1980	1981	1982	1983
5730	83	LOT CMPTN GRADE		1D005	1D005	1D005	1D005	1D005	1D005	1D005	1D005
5740	83	STDTS DSLK CHTG		1D006	1D006	1D006	1D006	1D006	1D006	1D006	1D006
5750	84	ST -LK PROV TCH		1D007	1D007	1D007	1D007	1D007	1D007	1D007	1D007
5760	84	FRD NCG/TCH -LK		1D008	1D008	1D008	1D008	1D008	1D008	1D008	1D008
13580	138	STS SCH RT FAMLY		5E05A	5E06A	5E06A	5E04A	5E06A		3E06A	3E06A
13590	139	STS SCH LDS STU		5E05B	5E06B	5E06B	5E04B	5E06B		3E06B	3E06B
13600	139	STS SCH NIC CAR		5E05C	5E06C	5E06C	5E04C	5E06C		3E06C	3E06C
13610	139	STS SCH HI GRDE		5E05D	5E06D	5E06D	5E04D	5E06D		3E06D	3E06D
13620	139	STS SCH GD ATHLT		5E05E	5E06E	5E06E	5E04E	5E06E		3E06E	3E06E
13630	139	STS SCH INTLCTL		5E05F	5E06F	5E06F	5E04F	5E06F		3E06F	3E06F
13640	139	STS SCH PLN CLG		5E05G	5E06G	5E06G	5E04G	5E06G		3E06G	3E06G

B05: EDUCATION. Counseling

Item Reference Number	Page Loc.	ITEM DESCRIPTION	1975	1976	1977	1978	1979	1980	1981	1982	1983
5780	84	#X/YR COUNS IND		1D010	1D010	1D010	1D010	1D010	1D010	1D010	1D010
5790	84	#X/YR COUNS GRP		1D011	1D011	1D011	1D011	1D011	1D011	1D011	1D011
5800	84	R LK C COUNS MR		1D012	1D012	1D012	1D012	1D012	1D012	1D012	1D012
5810	85	CSLNG VRY HLPFL		(1D013)	1D013	1D013	1D013	1D013	1D013	1D013	1D013
5811	85	CNSL COURSES					1D014A	1D014A	1D014A	1D014A	1D014A
5812	85	CNSL CL PROB					1D014B	1D014B	1D014B	1D014B	1D014B
5813	85	CNSL TRBL R IN					1D014C	1D014C	1D014C	1D014C	1D014C
5814	85	CNSL MILTRY PLN					1D014D	1D014D	1D014D	1D014D	1D014D
5815	85	CNSL EDUC PLANS					1D014E	1D014E	1D014E	1D014E	1D014E
5816	85	CNSL CAREER PLN					1D014F	1D014F	1D014F	1D014F	1D014F
5817	86	CNSL PRNL PROB					1D014G	1D014G	1D014G	1D014G	1D014G

B06: EDUCATION. Absenteeism and truancy

Item Reference Number	Page Loc.	ITEM DESCRIPTION	1975	1976	1977	1978	1979	1980	1981	1982	1983
430	19	#DA/4W SC MS ILL		+C18A	+C18A	+C18A	+C18A	+C18A	+C18A	+C18A	+C18A
440	19	#DA/4W SC MS CUT		+C18B	+C18B	+C18B	+C18B	+C18B	+C18B	+C18B	+C18B
450	19	#DA/4W SC MS OTH		+C18C	+C18C	+C18C	+C18C	+C18C	+C18C	+C18C	+C18C
460	19	#DA/4W SKP CLASS		+C19	+C19	+C19	+C19	+C19	+C19	+C19	+C19

B07: EDUCATION. Delinquency and victimization at school

Item Reference Number	Page Loc.	ITEM DESCRIPTION	1975	1976	1977	1978	1979	1980	1981	1982	1983
6540	101	FRQ FGT WRK/SCHL	2A39C	2A19C	2A19C	2A19C	2A19C	2A19C	2A19C	2A19C	2A19C
6650	102	FRQ DMG SCH PPTY	2A39N	2A19N	2A19N	2A19N	2A19N	2A19N	2A19N	2A19N	2A19N
9871	140	SM1 SCL ROB <$50		4E11A	3E10A	3E10A	5E06A	5E08A	5E13A	3E08A	3E08A
9872	140	SM1 SCL ROB >$50		4E11B	3E10B	3E10B	5E06B	5E08B	5E13B	3E08B	3E08B
9873	140	SM1 SCL DMG PRTY		4E11C	3E10C	3E10C	5E06C	5E08C	5E13C	3E08C	3E08C
9874	140	SM1 SCL IN U W/W		4E11D	3E10D	3E10D	5E06D	5E08D	5E13D	3E08D	3E08D
9875	141	SM1 SCL TH U W/W		4E11E	3E10E	3E10E	5E06E	5E08E	5E13E	3E08E	3E08E
9876	141	SM1 SCL IN U -WP		4E11F	3E10F	3E10F	5E06F	5E08F	5E13F	3E08F	3E08F
9877	141	SM1 SCL TH U W/I		4E11G	3E10G	3E10G	5E06G	5EO8G	5E13G	3E08G	3E08G

B08: EDUCATION. Opinions regarding competency testing

Item Reference Number	Page Loc.	ITEM DESCRIPTION	1975	1976	1977	1978	1979	1980	1981	1982	1983
7900	116	16YR+,TEST->DIPL			2E13A	(2E13A)	5E07A	2E16A	2E16A	2E19A	2E19A
7910	116	14YR+,TEST->DIPL			2E13B	(2E13B)	5E07B	2E16B	2E16B	2E19B	2E19B
7920	117	ALL STD H.S.TEST			2E13C	(2E13C)	5E07C	2E16C	2E16C	2E19C	2E19C

Item Reference Number	Page Loc. in this Volume	ITEM DESCRIPTION (ABBREVIATED)	QUESTIONNAIRE LOCATION BY YEAR (FORM, SECTION, AND QUESTION NUMBER)								
			1975	1976	1977	1978	1979	1980	1981	1982	1983

B09: EDUCATION. Post high school: status, plans, characteristics

480	20	R WL DO VOC/TEC		+C21A	+C21A	+C21A	+C21A	+C21A	+C21A	+C21A	+C21A
490	20	R WL DO ARMD FC		+C21B	+C21B	+C21B	+C21B	+C21B	+C21B	+C21B	+C21B
500	20	R WL DO 2YR CLG		+C21C	+C21C	+C21C	+C21C	+C21C	+C21C	+C21C	+C21C
510	20	R WL DO 4YR CLG		+C21D	+C21D	+C21D	+C21D	+C21D	+C21D	+C21D	+C21D
520	20	R WL DO GRD/PRF		+C21E	+C21E	+C21E	+C21E	+C21E	+C21E	+C21E	+C21E
530	21	R WNTDO VOC/TEC		+C22A	+C22A	+C22A	+C22A	+C22A	+C22A	+C22A	+C22A
540	21	R WNTDO ARMD FC		+C22B	+C22B	+C22B	+C22B	+C22B	+C22B	+C22B	+C22B
550	21	R WNTDO 2YR CLG		+C22C	+C22C	+C22C	+C22C	+C22C	+C22C	+C22C	+C22C
560	21	R WNTDO 4YR CLG		+C22D	+C22D	+C22D	+C22D	+C22D	+C22D	+C22D	+C22D
570	21	R WNTDO GRD/PRF		+C22E	+C22E	+C22E	+C22E	+C22E	+C22E	+C22E	+C22E
580	21	R WNTDO NONE		+C22F	+C22F	+C22F	+C22F	+C22F	+C22F	+C22F	+C22F
10410	153	JOB OBSTC EDUCTN		4A13F	4A13F	4A13F	4A13F	4A13F	4A13F	4A13F	4A13F
11320	169	P'IDEA OF EDUC	4A27J	4E08J	4E08J	4E07J	4E07J	4E07J	4E07J	4E07J	4E07J

B10: EDUCATION. Attitudes regarding educational institutions

6910	106	DHNSTY COLL&UNIV	2A20C	2D04C	2D04C	2D04C	2D04C	2D04C	2D04C	2D04C	2D04C
6920	106	DHNSTY PBLC SCHL	2A20D	2D04D	2D04D	2D04D	2D04D	2D04D	2D04D	2D04D	2D04D
7650	115	PRCL INFL SCL RN		2E04A	2E08A	2E08A	2E10A	2E11A	2E11A	2E14A	2E14A
7660	115	TCHR INFL SCL RN		2E04B	2E08B	2E08B	2E10B	2E11B	2E11B	2E14B	2E14B
7670	115	STDS INFL SCL RN		2E04C	2E08C	2E08C	2E10C	2E11C	2E11C	2E14C	2E14C
7680	115	PRTS INFL SCL RN		2E04D	2E08D	2E08D	2E10D	2E11D	2E11D	2E14D	2E14D
8400	126	GD JB COLLG&UNIV	3A27C	3A24C	3A24C	3A24C	3A24C	3A24C	3A24C	3A24C	3A24C
8410	127	GD JB PBLC SCHOL	3A27D	3A24D	3A24D	3A24D	3A24D	3A24D	3A24D	3A24D	3A24D
11130	167	MLTRY MORE ED		4E01B	4E01B	4E01B	4E01B	4E01B	4E01B	4E01B	4E01B
11840	175	PLC WRK SCH/UNIV	5A09E	5A05E	5A05E	5A05E	5A05E	5A05E	5A05E	5A05E	5A05E

C01: WORK and LEISURE. Present or recent work experience

590	21	HRS/W WRK SCHYR		+C23	+C23	+C23	+C23	+C23	+C23	+C23	+C23
1270	35	SAT PRESENT JOB	1A009A	1A006A	1A006A	1A006A	1A006A	1A006A	1A006A	1A006A	1A006A
5770	84	R IN WK-STDY PG		1D009	1D009	1D009	1D009	1D009	1D009	1D009	1D009
6540	101	FRQ FGT WRK/SCHL	2A39C	2A19C	2A19C	2A19C	2A19C	2A19C	2A19C	2A19C	2A19C
6660	102	FRQ DMG WK PRPTY	2A39O	2A19O	2A19O	2A19O	2A19O	2A19O	2A19O	2A19O	2A19O
10910	160	CMP SATFD W/JOB		4D02	4D02	4D02	4D02	4D02	4D02	4D02	4D02
11790	175	XPRC MK R GD WKR		5A04C	5A04C	5A04C	5A04C	5A04C	5A04C	5A04C	5A04C
11940	177	RCL CNTCT JOB		5A07F	5A07F	5A07F	5A07F	5A07F	5A07F	5A07F	5A07F
21530	160	RCNT EMPLYMT EXP								4D03A	4D03A
21540	160	JOB-#HRS/WEEK								4D03B	4D03B
21550	160	JOB-SUPERVSR AGE								4D04	4D04
21560	161	JOB-#WKRS OWN AG								4D05	4D05
21570	161	JOB-USE BEST SKL								4D06A	4D06A
21580	161	JOB-TEACH SKILLS								4D06B	4D06B
21590	161	JOB-USE LRND SKL								4D06C	4D06C
21600	161	JOB-DIF SOC BKGD								4D06D	4D06D
21610	161	JOB-OVER AGE 30								4D06E	4D06E
21620	161	JOB->STRESS								4D06F	4D06F
21630	162	JOB-INTRFR W ED								4D06G	4D06G
21640	162	JOB-INTRFR W SOC								4D06H	4D06H
21650	162	JOB-INTRFR W FAM								4D06I	4D06I
21660	162	JOB-INTERESTING								4D07A	4D07A
21670	162	JOB-HAPPY FR LIF								4D07B	4D07B
21680	162	JOB-EXPCT FR LIF								4D07C	4D07C
21690	162	JOB-STEP STONE								4D07D	4D07D
21700	163	JOB-DO JST FOR $								4D07E	4D07E
21710	163	JOB-TCHR HELP GT								4D08	4D08
21720	163	JOB-WORK STUDY								4D09	4D09

C02: WORK and LEISURE. Income sources; financial security

600	21	R$/AVG WEEK JOB		+C24A	+C24A	+C24A	+C24A	+C24A	(+C24A)	+C24A	+C24A
610	21	R$/AVG WEEK OTH		+C24B	+C24B	+C24B	+C24B	+C24B	(+C24B)	+C24B	+C24B
12990	191	I HAVE ENOUGH $		5D04A	5D04A	5D04A	5D04A	5D02A	5D04A	5D04A	

(continued)

Item Reference Number	Page Loc. in this Volume	ITEM DESCRIPTION (ABBREVIATED)	QUESTIONNAIRE LOCATION BY YEAR (FORM, SECTION, AND QUESTION NUMBER)								
			1975	1976	1977	1978	1979	1980	1981	1982	1983

C02: WORK and LEISURE. Income sources; financial security *(continued)*

Item Reference Number	Page Loc. in this Volume	ITEM DESCRIPTION (ABBREVIATED)	1975	1976	1977	1978	1979	1980	1981	1982	1983
13000	191	I LACK $FR BILL				5D04B	5D04B	5D04B	5D02B	5D04B	5D04B
13010	191	I WRY@-FINDG JOB				5D04C	5D04C	5D04C	5D02C	5D04C	5D04C
13020	191	I CAN FIND JOB				5D04D	5D04D	5D04D	5D02D	5D04D	5D04D
13030	192	I CAN KEEP MYJOB				5D04E	5D04E	5D04E	5D02E	5D04E	5D04E
13040	192	I WRY@LOSS MYJOB				5D04F	5D04F	5D04F	5D02F	5D04F	5D04F
20830	192	%$SAVE FUTR EDUC							5D03A	5D05A	5D05A
20840	192	%$SAVE/SPEND CAR							5D03B	5D05B	5D05B
20850	192	%$SAVE OTHER							5D03C	5D05C	5D05C
20860	193	%$SPEND ON SELF							5D03D	5D05D	5D05D
20870	193	%$SPEND HELP FAM							5D03E	5D05E	5D05E

C03: WORK and LEISURE. Vocational plans, aspirations, expectations

Item Reference Number	Page Loc. in this Volume	ITEM DESCRIPTION (ABBREVIATED)	1975	1976	1977	1978	1979	1980	1981	1982	1983
480	20	R WL DO VOC/TEC		+C21A	+C21A	+C21A	+C21A	+C21A	+C21A	+C21A	+C21A
530	21	R WNTDO VOC/TEC		+C22A	+C22A	+C22A	+C22A	+C22A	+C22A	+C22A	+C22A
6870	106	HOW GD AS WORKER	2A19C	2D02C	2D02C	2D02C	2D02C	2D02C	2D02C	2D02C	2D02C
8090	122	SAME JOB MST LIF	3A08I	3A05E	3A05E	3A05E	3A05E	3A05E	3A05E	3A05E	3A05E
10320	152	KIND OF WORK @30	4A09	4A09	4A09	4A09	4A09	4A09	4A09	4A09	4A09
10330	152	R SURE GT THS WK		4A10	4A10	4A10	4A10	4A10	4A10	4A10	4A10
10340	152	R SURE WK GD CHC		4A11	4A11	4A11	4A11	4A11	4A11	4A11	4A11
10350	153	R THNK WK BE SAT		4A12	4A12	4A12	4A12	4A12	4A12	4A12	4A12
10360	153	JOB OBSTC RELGN		4A13A	4A13A	4A13A	4A13A	4A13A	4A13A	4A13A	4A13A
10370	153	JOB OBSTC SEX		4A13B	4A13B	4A13B	4A13B	4A13B	4A13B	4A13B	4A13B
10380	153	JOB OBSTC RACE		4A13C	4A13C	4A13C	4A13C	4A13C	4A13C	4A13C	4A13C
10390	153	JOB OBSTC BKGRND		4A13D	4A13D	4A13D	4A13D	4A13D	4A13D	4A13D	4A13D
10400	153	JOB OBSTC POL VW		4A13E	4A13E	4A13E	4A13E	4A13E	4A13E	4A13E	4A13E
10410	153	JOB OBSTC EDUCTN		4A13F	4A13F	4A13F	4A13F	4A13F	4A13F	4A13F	4A13F
10420	153	JOB OBSTC -VOC T		4A13G	4A13G	4A13G	4A13G	4A13G	4A13G	4A13G	4A13G
10430	154	JOB OBSTC -ABLTY		4A13H	4A13H	4A13H	4A13H	4A13H	4A13H	4A13H	4A13H
10440	154	JOB OBSTC - PULL		4A13I	4A13I	4A13I	4A13I	4A13I	4A13I	4A13I	4A13I
10450	154	JOB OBSTC -WK HD		4A13J	4A13J	4A13J	4A13J	4A13J	4A13J	4A13J	4A13J
10460	154	JOB OBSTC -CONFM		4A13K	4A13K	4A13K	4A13K	4A13K	4A13K	4A13K	4A13K

C04: WORK and LEISURE. Preferences regarding job characteristics

Item Reference Number	Page Loc. in this Volume	ITEM DESCRIPTION (ABBREVIATED)	1975	1976	1977	1978	1979	1980	1981	1982	1983
1460	38	IMP STEADY WORK		1A007F	1A007F	1A007F	1A007F	1A007F	1A007F	1A007F	1A007F
8050	121	LIK WRK CAN FRGT	3A08D	3A05A	3A05A	3A05A	3A05A	3A05A	3A05A	3A05A	3A05A
10090	148	JOB IMPC SE RSLT	4A08A	4A08A	4A08A	4A08A	4A08A	4A08A	4A08A	4A08A	4A08A
10100	149	JOB IMPC STATUS	4A08B	4A08B	4A08B	4A08B	4A08B	4A08B	4A08B	4A08B	4A08B
10110	149	JOB IMPC INTRSTG	4A08C	4A08C	4A08C	4A08C	4A08C	4A08C	4A08C	4A08C	4A08C
10120	149	JOB IMPC ADVNCMT	4A08D	4A08D	4A08D	4A08D	4A08D	4A08D	4A08D	4A08D	4A08D
10130	149	JOB IMPC HLP OTH	4A08E	4A08E	4A08E	4A08E	4A08E	4A08E	4A08E	4A08E	4A08E
10140	149	JOB IMPC EARN $	4A08F	4A08F	4A08F	4A08F	4A08F	4A08F	4A08F	4A08F	4A08F
10150	149	JOB IMPC CREATVY	4A08G	4A08G	4A08G	4A08G	4A08G	4A08G	4A08G	4A08G	4A08G
10160	149	JOB IMPC UTILITY	4A08H	4A08H	4A08H	4A08H	4A08H	4A08H	4A08H	4A08H	4A08H
10170	149	JOB IMPC MK FRND	4A08I	4A08I	4A08I	4A08I	4A08I	4A08I	4A08I	4A08I	4A08I
10180	150	JOB IMPC USE SKL	4A08J	4A08J	4A08J	4A08J	4A08J	4A08J	4A08J	4A08J	4A08J
10190	150	JOB IMPC WRTHWLE	4A08K	4A08K	4A08K	4A08K	4A08K	4A08K	4A08K	4A08K	4A08K
10200	150	JOB IMPC VACATN	4A08L	4A08L	4A08L	4A08L	4A08L	4A08L	4A08L	4A08L	4A08L
10210	150	JOB IMPC MK DCSN	4A08M	4A08M	4A08M	4A08M	4A08M	4A08M	4A08M	4A08M	4A08M
10220	150	JOB IMPC FRE TIM		4A08N	4A08N	4A08N	4A08N	4A08N	4A08N	4A08N	4A08N
10230	150	JOB IMPC NO MVNG	4A08O	4A08O	4A08O	4A08O	4A08O	4A08O	4A08O	4A08O	4A08O
10240	150	JOB IMPC NO SPRV	4A08P	4A08P	4A08P	4A08P	4A08P	4A08P	4A08P	4A08P	4A08P
10250	151	JOB IMPC SECURTY	4A08Q	4A08Q	4A08Q	4A08Q	4A08Q	4A08Q	4A08Q	4A08Q	4A08Q
10260	151	JOB IMPC LRNING	4A08R	4A08R	4A08R	4A08R	4A08R	4A08R	4A08R	4A08R	4A08R
10270	151	JOB IMPC BE SELF	4A08S	4A08S	4A08S	4A08S	4A08S	4A08S	4A08S	4A08S	4A08S
10280	151	JOB IMPC RESPECT	4A08T	4A08T	4A08T	4A08T	4A08T	4A08T	4A08T	4A08T	4A08T
10290	151	JOB IMPC CNTC PL	4A08U	4A08U	4A08U	4A08U	4A08U	4A08U	4A08U	4A08U	4A08U
10300	151	JOB IMPC EZ PACE		4A08V	4A08V	4A08V	4A08V	4A08V	4A08V	4A08V	4A08V
10310	151	JOB IMPC HRD PRB		4A08W	4A08W	4A08W	4A08W	4A08W	4A08W	4A08W	4A08W

Item Reference Number	Page Loc. in this Volume	ITEM DESCRIPTION (ABBREVIATED)	QUESTIONNAIRE LOCATION BY YEAR (FORM, SECTION, AND QUESTION NUMBER)								
			1975	1976	1977	1978	1979	1980	1981	1982	1983

C05: WORK and LEISURE. Desirability of different working arrangements and settings

Item Reference Number	Page Loc. in this Volume	ITEM DESCRIPTION (ABBREVIATED)	1975	1976	1977	1978	1979	1980	1981	1982	1983
6160	95	-CHL,HB WK1.,W=0	2A15A	2A08A	2A08A	2A08A	2A08A	2A08A	2A08A	2A08A	2A08A
6170	95	-CHL,HB WK1.,W.5	2A15B	2A08B	2A08B	2A08B	2A08B	2A08B	2A08B	2A08B	2A08B
6180	95	-CHL,HB&WF WK 1.	2A15C	2A08C	2A08C	2A08C	2A08C	2A08C	2A08C	2A08C	2A08C
6190	95	-CHL,HB&WF WK .5	2A15D	2A08D	2A08D	2A08D	2A08D	2A08D	2A08D	2A08D	2A08D
6200	95	-CHL,W WK 1.,H.5	2A15E	2A08E	2A08E	2A08E	2A08E	2A08E	2A08E	2A08E	2A08E
6210	95	-CHL,W WK 1.,H=0	2A15F	2A08F	2A08F	2A08F	2A08F	2A08F	2A08F	2A08F	2A08F
6220	96	PSCH,HB WK1.,W=0	2A16A	2A09A	2A09A	2A09A	2A09A	2A09A	2A09A	2A09A	2A09A
6230	96	PSCH,HB WK1.,W.5	2A16B	2A09B	2A09B	2A09B	2A09B	2A09B	2A09B	2A09B	2A09B
6240	96	PSCH,HB&WF WK 1.	2A16C	2A09C	2A09C	2A09C	2A09C	2A09C	2A09C	2A09C	2A09C
6250	96	PSCH,HB&WF WK .5	2A16D	2A09D	2A09D	2A09D	2A09D	2A09D	2A09D	2A09D	2A09D
6260	96	PSCH,WF WK1.,H.5	2A16E	2A09E	2A09E	2A09E	2A09E	2A09E	2A09E	2A09E	2A09E
6270	96	PSCH,WF WK1.,H=0	2A16F	2A09F	2A09F	2A09F	2A09F	2A09F	2A09F	2A09F	2A09F
8120	122	DES SUPVR DIF RC	3A19B	3A07B	3A07B	3A07B	3A07B	3A07B	3A07B	3A07B	3A07B
8160	123	DES AL WKS SM RC	3A19F	3A08A	3A08A	3A08A	3A08A	3A08A	3A08A	3A08A	3A08A
8170	123	DES SO WKS DF RC	3A19G	3A08B	3A08B	3A08B	3A08B	3A08B	3A08B	3A08B	3A08B
8180	123	DES MS WKS DF RC	3A19H	3A08C	3A08C	3A08C	3A08C	3A08C	3A08C	3A08C	3A08C
11150	167	MLTRY >FLFLLG JB		4E01D	4E01D	4E01D	4E01D	4E01D	4E01D	4E01D	4E01D
11800	175	PLC WRK LG CORPN	5A09A	5A05A	5A05A	5A05A	5A05A	5A05A	5A05A	5A05A	5A05A
11810	175	PLC WRK SM BSNSS	5A09B	5A05B	5A05B	5A05B	5A05B	5A05B	5A05B	5A05B	5A05B
11820	175	PLC WRK GVT AGCY	5A09C	5A05C	5A05C	5A05C	5A05C	5A05C	5A05C	5A05C	5A05C
11830	175	PLC WRK MLTY SVC	5A09D	5A05D	5A05D	5A05D	5A05D	5A05D	5A05D	5A05D	5A05D
11840	175	PLC WRK SCH/UNIV	5A09E	5A05E	5A05E	5A05E	5A05E	5A05E	5A05E	5A05E	5A05E
11850	175	PLC WRK PLC DEPT	5A09F	5A05F	5A05F	5A05F	5A05F	5A05F	5A05F	5A05F	5A05F
11860	175	PLC WRK SOC SVCS	5A09G	5A05G	5A05G	5A05G	5A05G	5A05G	5A05G	5A05G	5A05G
11870	176	PLC WRK SML GRP	5A09H	5A05H	5A05H	5A05H	5A05H	5A05H	5A05H	5A05H	5A05H
11880	176	PLC WRK SLF EMPL	5A09I	5A05I	5A05I	5A05I	5A05I	5A05I	5A05I	5A05I	5A05I

C06: WORK and LEISURE. Work ethic/success orientation

Item Reference Number	Page Loc. in this Volume	ITEM DESCRIPTION (ABBREVIATED)	1975	1976	1977	1978	1979	1980	1981	1982	1983
1410	37	IMP B SUCCSS WK		1A007A	1A007A	1A007A	1A007A	1A007A	1A007A	1A007A	1A007A
8060	121	WRK=ONLY MK LVNG	3A08E	3A05B	3A05B	3A05B	3A05B	3A05B	3A05B	3A05B	3A05B
8070	121	WRK CNTRL PRT LF	3A08G	3A05C	3A05C	3A05C	3A05C	3A05C	3A05C	3A05C	3A05C
8080	121	OVTM 2DO BST JOB	3A08H	3A05D	3A05D	3A05D	3A05D	3A05D	3A05D	3A05D	3A05D
8100	122	ENUF$,NT WNT WRK	3A10	3A06	3A06	3A06	3A06	3A06	3A06	3A06	3A06
	154		4A09A	4A14	4A14	4A14	4A14	4A14	4A14	4A14	4A14
	176		5A11	5A06	5A06	5A06	5A06	5A06	5A06	5A06	5A06

C07: WORK and LEISURE. Leisure time: extent, activities

Item Reference Number	Page Loc. in this Volume	ITEM DESCRIPTION (ABBREVIATED)	1975	1976	1977	1978	1979	1980	1981	1982	1983
620	21	#X/AV WK GO OUT		+C25	+C25	+C25	+C25	+C25	+C25	+C25	+C25
630	22	#X DATE 3+/WK		+C26	+C26	+C26	+C26	+C26	+C26	+C26	+C26
5820	90	DALY WATCH TV		2A02A	2A02A	2A02A	2A02A	2A02A	2A02A	2A02A	2A02A
5830	90	DALY GO TO MOVIE		2A02B	2A02B	2A02B	2A02B	2A02B	2A02B	2A02B	2A02B
5840	90	DALY ART,MSC,PLA		2A02C	2A02C	2A02C	2A02C	2A02C	2A02C	2A02C	2A02C
5850	90	DALY RIDE FORFUN			2A02D	2A02D	2A02D	2A02D	2A02D	2A02D	2A02D
5860	90	DALY CMNTY AFFRS		2A02E	2A02E	2A02E	2A02E	2A02E	2A02E	2A02E	2A02E
5870	90	DALY PLA MSC,SNG		2A02F	2A02F	2A02F	2A02F	2A02F	2A02F	2A02F	2A02F
5880	91	DALY CREAT WRTNG		2A02G	2A02G	2A02G	2A02G	2A02G	2A02G	2A02G	2A02G
5890	91	DALY ACTV SPORTS		2A02H	2A02H	2A02H	2A02H	2A02H	2A02H	2A02H	2A02H
5900	91	DALY ART/CRAFTS		2A02I	2A02I	2A02I	2A02I	2A02I	2A02I	2A02I	2A02I
5910	91	DALY WRK HSE,CAR		2A02J	2A02J	2A02J	2A02J	2A02J	2A02J	2A02J	2A02J
5920	91	DALY VIST W/FRDS		2A02K	2A02K	2A02K	2A02K	2A02K	2A02K	2A02K	2A02K
5930	91	DALY GO SHOPPING		2A02L	2A02L	2A02L	2A02L	2A02L	2A02L	2A02L	2A02L
5940	91	DALY ALONE LEISR		(2A02M)	2A02M	2A02M	2A02M	2A02M	2A02M	2A02M	2A02M
5950	92	DALY READ BK,MAG		2A02N	2A02N	2A02N	2A02N	2A02N	2A02N	2A02N	2A02N
5960	92	DALY GO TO BARS		2A02O	2A02O	2A02O	2A02O	2A02O	2A02O	2A02O	2A02O
5970	92	DALY GO TO PARTY		2A02P	2A02P	2A02P	2A02P	2A02P	2A02P	2A02P	2A02P
5980		DALY GO CHURCH		2A02D							
10550	156	#HRS TV/DAY/5+		4A16	4A16	4A16	4A16	4A16	4A16	4A16	4A16
10560	156	#BKS LAST YR/10+		4A17	4A17	4A17	4A17	4A17	4A17	4A17	4A17

Item Reference Number	Page Loc. in this Volume	ITEM DESCRIPTION (ABBREVIATED)	QUESTIONNAIRE LOCATION BY YEAR (FORM, SECTION, AND QUESTION NUMBER)								
			1975	1976	1977	1978	1979	1980	1981	1982	1983

C08: WORK and LEISURE. Attitudes toward leisure time

Item Reference Number	Page Loc.	ITEM DESCRIPTION	1975	1976	1977	1978	1979	1980	1981	1982	1983
1370	37	SAT SPD LEISR	1A009K	1A006K	1A006K	1A006K	1A006K	1A006K	1A006K	1A006K	1A006K
1440	38	IMP TM RCRN&HBY		1A007D	1A007D	1A007D	1A007D	1A007D	1A007D	1A007D	1A007D
9880		DK DO W LEISR TM			3E11A		3E11A	3E11A	3E11A		
9890		TM QUIK/LEIS HRS			3E11B		3E11B	3E11B	3E11B		
9900		WASTE LEIS TIME			3E11C		3E11C	3E11C	3E11C		
9910		ENUF TIME FR THG			3E11D		3E11D	3E11D	3E11D		
11240	168	P'IDEA OF LSR TM	4A27B	4E08B	4E08B	4E07B	4E07B	4E07B	4E07B	4E07B	4E07B

D01: SEX ROLES and FAMILY. Dating and marriage: status, attitudes, expectations

Item Reference Number	Page Loc.	ITEM DESCRIPTION	1975	1976	1977	1978	1979	1980	1981	1982	1983
60	16	R NOT MARRIED		+C06	+C06	+C06	+C06	+C06	+C06	+C06	+C06
6120	94	DFNTLY PRFR MATE	2A10	2A05	2A05	2A05	2A05	2A05	2A05	2A05	2A05
6130	94	THINK WILL MARRY	2A11	2A06	2A06	2A06	2A06	2A06	2A06	2A06	2A06
6140	94	LIKLY STAY MARRD	2A12A	2A07A	2A07A	2A07A	2A07A	2A07A	2A07A	2A07A	2A07A
6850	105	HOW GD AS SPOUSE	2A19A	2D02A	2D02A	2D02A	2D02A	2D02A	2D02A	2D02A	2D02A
8320	125	MARRD OR ENGAGED	3A41	3A18	3A18	3A18	3A18	3A18	3A18	3A18	3A18
8330	125	WHN WANT GT MARR	3A42	3A19	3A19	3A19	3A19	3A19	3A19	3A19	3A19
11770	174	XPRC MK R GD SPS		5A04A	5A04A	5A04A	5A04A	5A04A	5A04A	5A04A	5A04A

D02: SEX ROLES and FAMILY. Parenthood: status, attitudes, expectations

Item Reference Number	Page Loc.	ITEM DESCRIPTION	1975	1976	1977	1978	1979	1980	1981	1982	1983
6150	94	LIKLY HAVE KIDS	2A12B	2A07B	2A07B	2A07B	2A07B	2A07B	2A07B	2A07B	2A07B
6860	105	HOW GD AS PARENT	2A19B	2D02B	2D02B	2D02B	2D02B	2D02B	2D02B	2D02B	2D02B
8340	125	THGT LOT HAV CHL	3A43	3A20	3A20	3A20	3A20	3A20	3A20	3A20	3A20
8350	125	# CHLDN WANT(6+)	3A44	3A21	3A21	3A21	3A21	3A21	3A21	3A21	3A21
8360	126	IF -POP, MR CHLD	3A45	3A22	3A22	3A22	3A22	3A22	3A22	3A22	3A22
8370	126	WHN 1ST CHL(5+Y)	3A46	3A23	3A23	3A23	3A23	3A23	3A23	3A23	3A23
11780	174	XPRC MK R GD PRT		5A04B	5A04B	5A04B	5A04B	5A04B	5A04B	5A04B	5A04B

D03: SEX ROLES and FAMILY. Values surrounding marriage and family

Item Reference Number	Page Loc.	ITEM DESCRIPTION	1975	1976	1977	1978	1979	1980	1981	1982	1983
1420	38	IMP GD MRRG&FAM		1A007B	1A007B	1A007B	1A007B	1A007B	1A007B	1A007B	1A007B
10470	154	FEW GD MAR, ? IT	4A11A	4A15A	4A15A	4A15A	4A15A	4A15A	4A15A	4A15A	4A15A
10480	154	GD LIV TG BF MRG	4A11B	4A15B	4A15B	4A15B	4A15B	4A15B	4A15B	4A15B	4A15B
10490	155	1 PRTNR=RSTRCTVE	4A11C	4A15C	4A15C	4A15C	4A15C	4A15C	4A15C	4A15C	4A15C
12150	180	FULLR LVS IF MRY	5A12A	5A18J	5A18J	5A18J	5A18J	5A18J	5A18J	5A18J	5A18J
12770	191	LV TGTH=BD MRLTY		5D05	5D02	5D02	5D02	5D02		5D02	5D02
12775	191	FAM-MAR=BD MRLTY		5D06	5D03	5D03	5D03	5D03		5D03	5D03

D04: SEX ROLES and FAMILY. Preferences regarding marital/familial arrangements

Item Reference Number	Page Loc.	ITEM DESCRIPTION	1975	1976	1977	1978	1979	1980	1981	1982	1983
6160	95	-CHL,HB WK1.,W=0	2A15A	2A08A	2A08A	2A08A	2A08A	2A08A	2A08A	2A08A	2A08A
6170	95	-CHL,HB WK1.,W.5	2A15B	2A08B	2A08B	2A08B	2A08B	2A08B	2A08B	2A08B	2A08B
6180	95	-CHL,HB&WF WK 1.	2A15C	2A08C	2A08C	2A08C	2A08C	2A08C	2A08C	2A08C	2A08C
6190	95	-CHL,HB&WF WK .5	2A15D	2A08D	2A08D	2A08D	2A08D	2A08D	2A08D	2A08D	2A08D
6200	95	-CHL,W WK 1.,H.5	2A15E	2A08E	2A08E	2A08E	2A08E	2A08E	2A08E	2A08E	2A08E
6210	95	-CHL,W WK 1.,H=0	2A15F	2A08F	2A08F	2A08F	2A08F	2A08F	2A08F	2A08F	2A08F
6220	96	PSCH,HB WK1.,W=0	2A16A	2A09A	2A09A	2A09A	2A09A	2A09A	2A09A	2A09A	2A09A
6230	96	PSCH,HB WK1.,W.5	2A16B	2A09B	2A09B	2A09B	2A09B	2A09B	2A09B	2A09B	2A09B
6240	96	PSCH,HB&WF WK 1.	2A16C	2A09C	2A09C	2A09C	2A09C	2A09C	2A09C	2A09C	2A09C
6250	96	PSCH,HB&WF WK .5	2A16D	2A09D	2A09D	2A09D	2A09D	2A09D	2A09D	2A09D	2A09D
6260	96	PSCH,WF WK1.,H.5	2A16E	2A09E	2A09E	2A09E	2A09E	2A09E	2A09E	2A09E	2A09E
6270	96	PSCH,WF WK1.,H=0	2A16F	2A09F	2A09F	2A09F	2A09F	2A09F	2A09F	2A09F	2A09F
6280	96	H WK,W -WK,W CCR	2A17A	2A10A	2A10A	2A10A	2A10A	2A10A	2A10A	2A10A	2A10A
6290	97	H WK,W -WK,W>CCR	2A17B	2A10B	2A10B	2A10B	2A10B	2A10B	2A10B	2A10B	2A10B
6300	97	H WK,W -WK,=CHCR	2A17C	2A10C	2A10C	2A10C	2A10C	2A10C	2A10C	2A10C	2A10C
6310	97	H WK,W -WK,H>CCR	2A17D	2A10D	2A10D	2A10D	2A10D	2A10D	2A10D	2A10D	2A10D
6320	97	H WK,W -WK,H CCR	2A17E	2A10E	2A10E	2A10E	2A10E	2A10E	2A10E	2A10E	2A10E
11560		H&W WK,WF AL HWK			4E11A	4E10A	4E10A	4E10A	4E10A		
11570		H&W WK,WF MS HWK			4E11B	4E10B	4E10B	4E10B	4E10B		
11580		H&W WK,DO = HWRK			4E11C	4E10C	4E10C	4E10C	4E10C		
11590		H&W WK,HB MS HWK			4E11D	4E10D	4E10D	4E10D	4E10D		
11600		H&W WK,HB AL HWK			4E11E	4E10E	4E10E	4E10E	4E10E		
		(continued)									

Item Refer- ence Number	Page Loc. in this Volume	ITEM DESCRIPTION (ABBREVIATED)	QUESTIONNAIRE LOCATION BY YEAR (FORM, SECTION, AND QUESTION NUMBER)								
			1975	1976	1977	1978	1979	1980	1981	1982	1983

D04: SEX ROLES and FAMILY. Preferences regarding marital/familial arrangements (continued)

Item Ref	Page	Desc	1975	1976	1977	1978	1979	1980	1981	1982	1983
11610		H&W WK+CH,W CHCR			4E12A	4E11A	4E11A	4E11A	4E11A		
11620		H&W WK+CH,W>CHCR			4E12B	4E11B	4E11B	4E11B	4E11B		
11630		H&W WK+CH,=CHCAR			4E12C	4E11C	4E11C	4E11C	4E11C		
11640		H&W WK+CH,H>CHCR			4E12D	4E11D	4E11D	4E11D	4E11D		
11650		H&W WK+CH,H CHCR			4E12E	4E11E	4E11E	4E11E	4E11E		
13150		FAM+REL GD/CHILD		5E01A							
13160		FAM+REL GD/PARNT		5E01B							
13170		FAM+REL GD/GRPNT		5E01C							
13180		FAM+REL,R LIK/PT		5E01D							
13280		FAM+CPL GD/CHILD		5E02A							
13290		FAM+CPL GD/PARNT		5E02B							
13300		FAM+CPL GD/CPLS		5E02C							
13310		FAM+CPL,LIK/PRNT		5E02D							
13320		FAM+CPL,LIK/-CHD		5E02E							
13420		CPL+OTH +CHD MAR		5E03A							
13430		CPL+OTH +CHD DVC		5E03B							
13440		CPL+OTH +MAR CPL		5E03C							
13450		CPL+OTH +DIV PRT		5E03D							
13460		CPL+OTH +UNMARRD		5E03E							
13470		CPL+OTH,LK,MR PT		5E03F							
13480		CPL+OTH,LK,DVC P		5E03G							

D05: SEX ROLES and FAMILY. Sex role attitudes

Item Ref	Page	Desc	1975	1976	1977	1978	1979	1980	1981	1982	1983
7970	120	MN=ACHV/WMN=HOME	3A17H	3A03E	3A03E	3A03E	3A03E	3A03E	3A03E	3A03E	3A03E
7980	120	CHL SUFF W WK MO	3A17I	3A03F	3A03F	3A03F	3A03F	3A03F	3A03F	3A03F	3A03F
7990	120	WK MO AS WRM REL	3A17J	3A03G	3A03G	3A03G	3A03G	3A03G	3A03G	3A03G	3A03G
10500	155	JB INTFR REL HBD	4A11E	4A15D	4A15D	4A15D	4A15D	4A15D	4A15D	4A15D	4A15D
10510	155	JB DVLP WF PERSN	4A11G	4A15E	4A15E	4A15E	4A15E	4A15E	4A15E	4A15E	4A15E
10520	155	RS CHLD + FR MAN	4A11H	4A15F	4A15F	4A15F	4A15F	4A15F	4A15F	4A15F	4A15F
10530	155	MO SH B W CHL>TM	4A11I	4A15G	4A15G	4A15G	4A15G	4A15G	4A15G	4A15G	4A15G
10540	155	WF WK,HBD SHD>HW	4A11K	4A15H	4A15H	4A15H	4A15H	4A15H	4A15H	4A15H	4A15H
11330	170	P'IDEA OF SX RLS	4A27K	4E08K	4E08K	4E07K	4E07K	4E07K	4E07K	4E07K	4E07K
12160	180	ENCRG=INDP DT/SN	5A12B	5A18K	5A18K	5A18K	5A18K	5A18K	5A18K	5A18K	5A18K
12170	181	BNG MOTH V FULFL	5A12D	5A18L	5A18L	5A18L	5A18L	5A18L	5A18L	5A18L	5A18L
12180	181	FTHR>TIME W CHLD	5A12G	5A18M	5A18M	5A18M	5A18M	5A18M	5A18M	5A18M	5A18M
12190	181	HSB MAK IMP DCSN	5A12H	5A18N	5A18N	5A18N	5A18N	5A18N	5A18N	5A18N	5A18N

D06: SEX ROLES and FAMILY. Opinions regarding sex discrimination

Item Ref	Page	Desc	1975	1976	1977	1978	1979	1980	1981	1982	1983
7930	119	MEN&WOMN/=$,=WRK	3A17A	3A03A	3A03A	3A03A	3A03A	3A03A	3A03A	3A03A	3A03A
7940	119	CNSDR WMN/HI JOB	3A17B	3A03B	3A03B	3A03B	3A03B	3A03B	3A03B	3A03B	3A03B
7950	119	WMN SHD =JOB OPP	3A17C	3A03C	3A03C	3A03C	3A03C	3A03C	3A03C	3A03C	3A03C
7960	119	WMN SHD =ED OPP	3A17D	3A03D	3A03D	3A03D	3A03D	3A03D	3A03D	3A03D	3A03D
10370	153	JOB OBSTC SEX		4A13B	4A13B	4A13B	4A13B	4A13B	4A13B	4A13B	4A13B
11180	167	MLTRY DSCRM WOMN		4E03	4E03	4E03	4E03	4E03	4E03	4E03	4E03
12290	183	DSCM WN COLLG ED	5A21A	5A22A	5A22A	5A22A	5A22A	5A22A	5A22A	5A22A	5A22A
12300	183	DSCM WN LDRSHP	5A21B	5A22B	5A22B	5A22B	5A22B	5A22B	5A22B	5A22B	5A22B
12310	183	DSCM WN EXEC/BSN	5A21C	5A22C	5A22C	5A22C	5A22C	5A22C	5A22C	5A22C	5A22C
12320	183	DSCM WN TOP/PRFN	5A21D	5A22D	5A22D	5A22D	5A22D	5A22D	5A22D	5A22D	5A22D
12330	184	DSCM WN SKL LABR	5A21E	5A22E	5A22E	5A22E	5A22E	5A22E	5A22E	5A22E	5A22E
12340	184	DSCM WN PLTCL OF	5A21F	5A22F	5A22F	5A22F	5A22F	5A22F	5A22F	5A22F	5A22F
12350	184	DSCM WN =PAY =WK	5A21G	5A22G	5A22G	5A22G	5A22G	5A22G	5A22G	5A22G	5A22G

E01: POPULATION CONCERNS. Overpopulation

Item Ref	Page	Desc	1975	1976	1977	1978	1979	1980	1981	1982	1983
8360	126	IF -POP, MR CHLD	3A45	3A22	3A22	3A22	3A22	3A22	3A22	3A22	3A22
9760	137	GOV HP PRB POPL	3A32N	3E04A	3E04A	3E04A	3E04A	3E04A	3E04A	3E03A	3E03A
9770	137	GOV NO POP PLCY	3A32A	3E04B	3E04B	3E04B	3E04B	3E04B	3E04B	3E03B	3E03B
9780	137	STR OVPOP,LMT FM	3A32B	3E04C	3E04C	3E04C	3E04C	3E04C	3E04C	3E03C	3E03C
9790	137	PRV OVPOP,NO CHL	3A32C	3E04D	3E04D	3E04D	3E04D	3E04D	3E04D	3E03D	3E03D
9830		US POP SZ LRGER	3A34	3E06	3E05	3E05	3E05	3E05	3E05		
9840		GVNG FOOD O CNTY	3A33	3E05							
		(continued)									

Item Reference Number	Page Loc. in this Volume	ITEM DESCRIPTION (ABBREVIATED)	QUESTIONNAIRE LOCATION BY YEAR (FORM, SECTION, AND QUESTION NUMBER)								
			1975	1976	1977	1978	1979	1980	1981	1982	1983

E01: POPULATION CONCERNS. Overpopulation (continued)

Item Reference Number	Page Loc.	ITEM DESCRIPTION	1975	1976	1977	1978	1979	1980	1981	1982	1983
9850		WRLD POP SZ LRGR	3A35	3E07	3E06	3E06	3E06	3E06	3E06		
11670	173	WR/NT POP GROWTH	5A04B	5A03B	5A03B	5A03B	5A03B	5A03B	5A03B	5A03B	5A03B
12270	182	CTB TO POP PRBMS	5A20H	5A20H	5A20H	5A20H	5A20H	5A20H	5A20H	5A20H	5A20H

E02: POPULATION CONCERNS. Birth control

Item Reference Number	Page Loc.	ITEM DESCRIPTION	1975	1976	1977	1978	1979	1980	1981	1982	1983
9800	138	HISCH INS BRTH C	3A32E	3E04E	3E04E	3E04E	3E04E	3E04E	3E04E	3E03E	3E03E
9810	138	BRTH CNT IMMORAL	3A32I	3E04F	3E04F	3E04F	3E04F	3E04F	3E04F	3E03F	3E03F
9820	138	GOV BRTHC NO CST	3A32M	3E04G	3E04G	3E04G	3E04G	3E04G	3E04G	3E03G	3E03G
9860	138	HAD SEX ED IN HS		3E09	3E08	3E08	3E08	3E08	3E08	3E04	3E04
9870	138	STUDY BC IN HS		3E10	3E09	3E09	3E09	3E09	3E09	3E05	3E05

F01: CONSERVATION, MATERIALISM, EQUITY, ETC. Personal materialism

Item Reference Number	Page Loc.	ITEM DESCRIPTION	1975	1976	1977	1978	1979	1980	1981	1982	1983
1350	36	SAT STD OF LVG	1A009I	1A006I	1A006I	1A006I	1A006I	1A006I	1A006I	1A006I	1A006I
1430	38	IMP LOTS OF $		1A007C	1A007C	1A007C	1A007C	1A007C	1A007C	1A007C	1A007C
5930	91	DALY GO SHOPPING		2A02L	2A02L	2A02L	2A02L	2A02L	2A02L	2A02L	2A02L
7700		NOW OWN HAIR DRY		2E09A							
7710		NOW OWN WT/S SKI		2E09B							
7720		NOW OWN CAMERA		2E09C							
7730		NOW OWN WATCH		2E09D							
7740		NOW OWN HKG BKPK		2E09E							
7750		NOW OWN CK RADIO		2E09F							
7760		NOW OWN EL SHAVR		2E09G							
7770		NOW OWN TENIS RQ		2E09H							
7780		NOW OWN TV SET		2E09I							
7790		NOW OWN BICYCLE		2E09J							
7800		NOW OWN CAR		2E09K							
7810		NOW OWN TAPE REC		2E09L							
7820		NOW OWN ELT CALC		2E09M							
7830		NOW OWN BT/SNMBL		2E09N							
8020	120	MR$FR LASTG THG	3A31E	3A04C	3A04C	3A04C	3A04C	3A04C	3A04C	3A04C	3A04C
10060	148	FAM BUYS THG -ND	4A22L	4A06J	4A06J	4A06J	4A06J	4A06J	4A06J	4A06J	4A06J
	180			5A18I	5A18I	5A18I	5A18I	5A18I	5A18I	5A18I	5A18I
10140	149	JOB IMPC EARN $	4A08F	4A08F	4A08F	4A08F	4A08F	4A08F	4A08F	4A08F	4A08F
12020	178	ENJOY SHOPPING	5A35A	5A15A	5A15A	5A15A	5A15A	5A15A	5A15A	5A15A	5A15A
12030	178	CARE LATST FASHN	5A35B	5A15B	5A15B	5A15B	5A15B	5A15B	5A15B	5A15B	5A15B
12040	178	CR FAM HV NBR HV	5A35C	5A15C	5A15C	5A15C	5A15C	5A15C	5A15C	5A15C	5A15C
12050	178	XPCT 2 OWN>PRNTS	5A36	5A16	5A16	5A16	5A16	5A16	5A16	5A16	5A16
12060	179	LST CNT OWN>PRNT	5A37	5A17	5A17	5A17	5A17	5A17	5A17	5A17	5A17
13600	139	STS SCH NIC CAR		5E05C	5E06C	5E06C	5E04C	5E06C		3E06C	3E06C
13700		BY SOON HAIR DRY		2E10A							
13710		BY SOON WT/S SKI		2E10B							
13720		BY SOON CAMERA		2E10C							
13730		BY SOON WATCH		2E10D							
13740		BY SOON HKG BKPK		2E10E							
13750		BY SOON CK RADIO		2E10F							
13760		BY SOON EL SHAVR		2E10G							
13770		BY SOON TENIS RQ		2E10H							
13780		BY SOON TV SET		2E10I							
13790		BY SOON BICYCLE		2E10J							
13800		BY SOON CAR		2E10K							
13810		BY SOON TAPE REC		2E10L							
13820		BY SOON ELT CALC		2E10M							
13830		BY SOON BT/SNMBL		2E10N							
13835	141	IMP HAV 1 CAR		3E12A		3E11A	3E10A	3E10A	3E10A	3E09A	3E09A
13840	141	IMP HAV 2 CARS		3E12B		3E11B	3E10B	3E10B	3E10B	3E09B	3E09B
13850	141	IMP HAV LARG CAR		3E12C		3E11C	3E10C	3E10C	3E10C	3E09C	3E09C
13860	141	IMP HAV NW CR OF		3E12D		3E11D	3E10D	3E10D	3E10D	3E09D	3E09D
13870	142	IMP HAV NW CLTHS		3E12E		3E11E	3E10E	3E10E	3E10E	3E09E	3E09E
13880	142	IMP HAV OWN HSE		3E12F		3E11F	3E10F	3E10F	3E10F	3E09F	3E09F
13890	142	IMP HAV BIG YARD		3E12G		3E11G	3E10G	3E10G	3E10G	3E09G	3E09G
13900	142	IMP HAV NEAT LWN		3E12H		3E11H	3E10H	3E10H	3E10H	3E09H	3E09H
		(continued)									

Item Reference Number	Page Loc. in this Volume	ITEM DESCRIPTION (ABBREVIATED)	QUESTIONNAIRE LOCATION BY YEAR (FORM, SECTION, AND QUESTION NUMBER)								
			1975	1976	1977	1978	1979	1980	1981	1982	1983

F01: CONSERVATION, MATERIALISM, EQUITY, ETC. Personal materialism *(continued)*

Item Reference Number	Page Loc. in this Volume	ITEM DESCRIPTION (ABBREVIATED)	1975	1976	1977	1978	1979	1980	1981	1982	1983
13910	142	IMP HAV APPLINCS		3E12I		3E11I	3E10I	3E10I	3E10I	3E09I	3E09I
13920	142	IMP HAV G STEREO		3E12J		3E11J	3E10J	3E10J	3E10J	3E09J	3E09J
13930	142	IMP HAV VAC HSE		3E12K		3E11K	3E10K	3E10K	3E10K	3E09K	3E09K
13940	142	IMP HAV REC VEH		3E12L		3E11L	3E10L	3E10L	3E10L	3E09L	3E09L

F02: CONSERVATION, MATERIALISM, EQUITY, ETC. Societal materialism and advertising

Item Reference Number	Page Loc. in this Volume	ITEM DESCRIPTION (ABBREVIATED)	1975	1976	1977	1978	1979	1980	1981	1982	1983
6000	92	2MUCH CNCRN MTRL	2A23K	2A03B	2A03B	2A03B	2A03B	2A03B	2A03B	2A03B	2A03B
6010	92	ENCOURG PPL BUY>	2A23L	2A03C	2A03C	2A03C	2A03C	2A03C	2A03C	2A03C	2A03C
6020	93	-WRNG ADVERTISNG	2A23M	2A03D	2A03D	2A03D	2A03D	2A03D	2A03D	2A03D	2A03D
6030	93	MOR SHORTGS FUTR	2A23N	2A03E	2A03E	2A03E	2A03E	2A03E	2A03E	2A03E	2A03E
10040	148	TV COMM CRT NDS	4A22H	4A06H	4A06H	4A06H	4A06H	4A06H	4A06H	4A06H	4A06H
10050	148	TV COMMRCLS GOOD	4A22I	4A06I	4A06I	4A06I	4A06I	4A06I	4A06I	4A06I	4A06I

F03: CONSERVATION, MATERIALISM, EQUITY, ETC. Concern with world hunger and poverty

Item Reference Number	Page Loc. in this Volume	ITEM DESCRIPTION (ABBREVIATED)	1975	1976	1977	1978	1979	1980	1981	1982	1983
5990	92	US 2 MUCH PROFIT	2A23J	2A03A	2A03A	2A03A	2A03A	2A03A	2A03A	2A03A	2A03A
8040	121	EAT DIF->FD STRV	3A31G	3A04E	3A04E	3A04E	3A04E	3A04E	3A04E	3A04E	3A04E
11720	174	WR/NT HNGR&PVRTY	5A04G	5A03G	5A03G	5A03G	5A03G	5A03G	5A03G	5A03G	5A03G
12090	179	-SYMP TWD STARVG	5A19E	5A18C	5A18C	5A18C	5A18C	5A18C	5A18C	5A18C	5A18C
12140	180	RB CHNG ETG HABT		5A18H	5A18H	5A18H	5A18H	5A18H	5A18H	5A18H	5A18H
16440		SAT EAT<BEEF>GRN				2E05B					
19470		EAT<FD,>OWN CITY					5E08A				
19480		EAT<FD,>NRBY STT					5E08B				
19490		EAT<FD,>DIF REGN					5E08C				
19500		EAT<FD,>ASIAN CN					5E08D				

F04: CONSERVATION, MATERIALISM, EQUITY, ETC. Ecological concerns

Item Reference Number	Page Loc. in this Volume	ITEM DESCRIPTION (ABBREVIATED)	1975	1976	1977	1978	1979	1980	1981	1982	1983
1640	41	US NEEDS GROWTH	1A013E	1A011G	1A011G	1A011G	1A011G	1A011G	1A011G	1A011G	1A011G
8000	120	POLLUT INCREASED	3A31A	3A04A	3A04A	3A04A	3A04A	3A04A	3A04A	3A04A	3A04A
8010	120	GOVT DEAL ENV PR	3A31D	3A04B	3A04B	3A04B	3A04B	3A04B	3A04B	3A04B	3A04B
9700	136	PRVNT POL TOO >$		3E02A	3E02A	3E02A	3E02A	3E02A	3E02A	3E01A	3E01A
9710	136	PRVNT POL CST JB		3E02B	3E02B	3E02B	3E02B	3E02B	3E02B	3E01B	3E01B
9720	136	PRVNT POL PPL DK		3E02C	3E02C	3E02C	3E02C	3E02C	3E02C	3E01C	3E01C
9730	136	PRVNT POL -ENUF		3E02D	3E02D	3E02D	3E02D	3E02D	3E02D	3E01D	3E01D
9740	137	PRVNT POL USELSS		3E02E	3E02E	3E02E	3E02E	3E02E	3E02E	3E01E	3E01E
9970	146	PLLTN INCR IN US	4A22A	4A06A	4A06A	4A06A	4A06A	4A06A	4A06A	4A06A	4A06A
9980	147	PLLTN NT SO DANG	4A22B	4A06B	4A06B	4A06B	4A06B	4A06B	4A06B	4A06B	4A06B
9990	147	PLLTN NEC 4 GRTH	4A22C	4A06C	4A06C	4A06C	4A06C	4A06C	4A06C	4A06C	4A06C
10000	147	INDVL RESP 4 ENV	4A22D	4A06D	4A06D	4A06D	4A06D	4A06D	4A06D	4A06D	4A06D
10010	147	GOVT RESP 4 ENV	4A22E	4A06E	4A06E	4A06E	4A06E	4A06E	4A06E	4A06E	4A06E
10020	147	GOVT TAX PLLTRS	4A22F	4A06F	4A06F	4A06F	4A06F	4A06F	4A06F	4A06F	4A06F
10030	147	GOVT BAN DSPSBLE	4A22G	4A06G	4A06G	4A06G	4A06G	4A06G	4A06G	4A06G	4A06G
10070	148	POL SLVD BY 2000	4A22M	4A06K	4A06K	4A06K	4A06K	4A06K	4A06K	4A06K	4A06K
10080	148	R EFRT 2 HLP ENV	4A23	4A07	4A07	4A07	4A07	4A07	4A07	4A07	4A07
11340	170	P'IDEA OF ECLOGY	4A27L	4E08L	4E08L	4E08L	4E07L	4E07L	4E07L	4E07L	4E07L
11690	173	WR/NT POLLUTION	5A04D	5A03D	5A03D	5A03D	5A03D	5A03D	5A03D	5A03D	5A03D
12280	183	CTB TO ENVIR PBM	5A20I	5A20I	5A20I	5A20I	5A20I	5A20I	5A20I	5A20I	5A20I
16450		SAT TAX FR ECLGY					2E05C				

F05: CONSERVATION, MATERIALISM, EQUITY, ETC. Concern with conservation of resources

Item Reference Number	Page Loc. in this Volume	ITEM DESCRIPTION (ABBREVIATED)	1975	1976	1977	1978	1979	1980	1981	1982	1983
9750	137	FUTR,HAV2 CNSUM<		3E03	3E03	3E03	3E03	3E03	3E03	3E02	3E02
10930	163	SOCTY WONT LAST	4A28B	4D03B	4D03B	4D03B	4D03B	4D03B	4D03B	4D10B	4D10B
11700	173	WR/NT ENRGY SHRT	5A04E	5A03E	5A03E	5A03E	5A03E	5A03E	5A03E	5A03E	5A03E
11730	174	WR/NT USE OPN LD	5A04H	5A03H	5A03H	5A03H	5A03H	5A03H	5A03H	5A03H	5A03H
12000	178	R CUT ELECTRICTY		5A13	5A13	5A13	5A13	5A13	5A13	5A13	5A13
12010	178	RDCE HEAT R'S HM		5A14	5A14	5A14	5A14	5A14	5A14	5A14	5A14

Item Reference Number	Page Loc. in this Volume	ITEM DESCRIPTION (ABBREVIATED)	QUESTIONNAIRE LOCATION BY YEAR (FORM, SECTION, AND QUESTION NUMBER)								
			1975	1976	1977	1978	1979	1980	1981	1982	1983

F06: CONSERVATION, MATERIALISM, EQUITY, ETC. Preferences regarding dwelling type and urbanicity

Item Reference Number	Page Loc.	ITEM DESCRIPTION	1975	1976	1977	1978	1979	1980	1981	1982	1983
17860		DESRD LVG RURAL				4E09A		4E09A	4E09A	4E09A	
17870		DESRD LVG SM TWN				4E09B		4E09B	4E09B	4E09B	
17880		DESRD LVG SM CTY				4E09C		4E09C	4E09C	4E09C	
17890		DESRD LVG SUBURB				4E09D		4E09D	4E09D	4E09D	
17900		DESRD LVG LG CTY				4E09E		4E09E	4E09E	4E09E	
17910		DSRD HSG 1 FAMLY				4E09F		4E09F	4E09F	4E09F	
17920		DSRD HSG 2 FAMLY				4E09G		4E09G	4E09G	4E09G	
17930		DSRD HSG CNDMINM				4E09H		4E09H	4E09H	4E09H	
17940		DSRD HSG APT BLD				4E09I		4E09I	4E09I	4E09I	
17950		DSRD HSG HI RISE				4E09J		4E09J	4E09J	4E09J	

F07: CONSERVATION, MATERIALISM, EQUITY, ETC. Driving and use of mass transit

Item Reference Number	Page Loc.	ITEM DESCRIPTION	1975	1976	1977	1978	1979	1980	1981	1982	1983
640	22	DRIVE>200 MI/WK		+C27	+C27	+C27	+C27	+C27	+C27	+C27	+C27
8030	121	USE BYC/MAS TRAN	3A31F	3A04D	3A04D	3A04D	3A04D	3A04D	3A04D	3A04D	3A04D
11960	177	DNT HV DRVR LCNS	5A22	5A09	5A09	5A09	5A09	5A09	5A09	5A09	5A09
11970	177	DONT OWN CAR	5A23	5A10	5A10	5A10	5A10	5A10	5A10	5A10	5A10
11980	177	NEVR USE OTHS CR	5A24	5A11	5A11	5A11	5A11	5A11	5A11	5A11	5A11
11990	177	R CUT DRIVING		5A12	5A12	5A12	5A12	5A12	5A12	5A12	5A12
16430		SAT EVB CAR POOL				2E05A					

G: RELIGION. Religious preferences, activities, views

Item Reference Number	Page Loc.	ITEM DESCRIPTION	1975	1976	1977	1978	1979	1980	1981	1982	1983
360	18	R'S RELGS PRFNC		+C13A	+C13A	+C13A	+C13A	+C13A	(+C13A)	+C13A	+C13A
370	18	R'ATTND REL SVC		+C13B	+C13B	+C13B	+C13B	+C13B	+C13B	+C13B	+C13B
380	18	RLGN IMP R'S LF		+C13C	+C13C	+C13C	+C13C	+C13C	+C13C	+C13C	+C13C
5980		DALY GO CHURCH		2A02D							
6930	107	DHNSTY CHURCHES	2A20E	2D04E	2D04E	2D04E	2D04E	2D04E	2D04E	2D04E	2D04E
8420	127	GD JB CHURCHES	3A27E	3A24E	3A24E	3A24E	3A24E	3A24E	3A24E	3A24E	3A24E
10360	153	JOB OBSTC RELGN		4A13A	4A13A	4A13A	4A13A	4A13A	4A13A	4A13A	4A13A
10590	156	>INFLC CHURCHES	4A14C	4A19C	4A19C	4A19C	4A19C	4A19C	4A19C	4A19C	4A19C
11360	170	P'IDEA OF RLGION	4A27N	4E08N	4E08N	4E07N	4E07N	4E07N	4E07N	4E07N	4E07N
11910	176	RCL CNTCT CHURCH	5A07C	5A07C	5A07C	5A07C	5A07C	5A07C	5A07C	5A07C	5A07C
12230	182	CTB TO RELGS ORG	5A20D	5A20D	5A20D	5A20D	5A20D	5A20D	5A20D	5A20D	5A20D

H01: POLITICS. Political interest and preferences

Item Reference Number	Page Loc.	ITEM DESCRIPTION	1975	1976	1977	1978	1979	1980	1981	1982	1983
340	17	R'S POLTL PRFNC		+C11	+C11	+C11	+C11	+C11	+C11	+C11	+C11
350	18	R'POL BLF RADCL		+C12	+C12	+C12	+C12	+C12	+C12	+C12	+C12
6330	97	INTEREST IN GOVT	2A31	2A11	2A11	2A11	2A11	2A11	2A11	2A11	2A11
	156		4A29	3E01	3E01	3E01	3E01	3E01	3E01	4A18	4A18
	181		5A40	4A18	4A18	4A18	4A18	4A18	4A18	5A19	5A19
				5A19	5A19	5A19	5A19	5A19	5A19		
10400	153	JOB OBSTC POL VW		4A13E	4A13E	4A13E	4A13E	4A13E	4A13E	4A13E	4A13E
11370	170	P'IDEA OF PLTICS	4A27O	4E08O	4E08O	4E07O	4E07O	4E07O	4E07O	4E07O	4E07O

H02: POLITICS. Attitudes toward governmental policies and practices

Item Reference Number	Page Loc.	ITEM DESCRIPTION	1975	1976	1977	1978	1979	1980	1981	1982	1983
1390	37	SAT GOVT OPRTNG		1A006M	1A006M	1A006M	1A006M	1A006M	1A006M	1A006M	1A006M
5690	99	US GO WAR FR OTH	2A38B	2A18B	2A18B	2A18B	2A18B	2A18B	2A18B	2A18B	2A18B
6450	99	US SHD DISARM	2A38A	2A18A	2A18A	2A18A	2A18A	2A18A	2A18A	2A18A	2A18A
6460	99	US WAR PRTCT ECN	2A38C	2A18C	2A18C	2A18C	2A18C	2A18C	2A18C	2A18C	2A18C
6470	99	US ONLY WAR DFNS	2A38D	2A18D	2A18D	2A18D	2A18D	2A18D	2A18D	2A18D	2A18D
6480	100	-US MIL PWR>USSR	2A38E	2A18E	2A18E	2A18E	2A18E	2A18E	2A18E	2A18E	2A18E
6490	100	US NEED>PWR OTHS	2A38F	2A18F	2A18F	2A18F	2A18F	2A18F	2A18F	2A18F	2A18F
6500	100	US FRN PLCY NRRW	2A38G	2A18G	2A18G	2A18G	2A18G	2A18G	2A18G	2A18G	2A18G
7940	119	CNSDR WMN/HI JOB	3A17B	3A03B	3A03B	3A03B	3A03B	3A03B	3A03B	3A03B	3A03B
8010	120	GOVT DEAL ENV PR	3A31D	3A04B	3A04B	3A04B	3A04B	3A04B	3A04B	3A04B	3A04B
9760	137	GOV HP PRB POPL	3A32N	3E04A	3E04A	3E04A	3E04A	3E04A	3E04A	3E03A	3E03A
9770	137	GOV NO POP PLCY	3A32A	3E04B	3E04B	3E04B	3E04B	3E04B	3E04B	3E03B	3E03B
9820	138	GOV BRTHC NO CST	3A32M	3E04G	3E04G	3E04G	3E04G	3E04G	3E04G	3E03G	3E03G
10010	147	GOVT RESP 4 ENV	4A22E	4A06E	4A06E	4A06E	4A06E	4A06E	4A06E	4A06E	4A06E
10020	147	GOVT TAX PLLTRS	4A22F	4A06F	4A06F	4A06F	4A06F	4A06F	4A06F	4A06F	4A06F
		(continued)									

Item Reference Number	Page Loc. in this Volume	ITEM DESCRIPTION (ABBREVIATED)	QUESTIONNAIRE LOCATION BY YEAR (FORM, SECTION, AND QUESTION NUMBER)								
			1975	1976	1977	1978	1979	1980	1981	1982	1983

H02: POLITICS. Attitudes toward governmental policies and practices *(continued)*

10030	147	GOVT BAN DSPSBLE	4A22G	4A06G	4A06G	4A06G	4A06G	4A06G	4A06G	4A06G	4A06G
11210		-MLTRY COUP U.S.		4E06	4E06						
12340	184	DSCM WN PLTCL OF	5A21F	5A22F	5A22F	5A22F	5A22F	5A22F	5A22F	5A22F	5A22F

H03: POLITICS. Views about the role of citizens in government (See also I02: Attitudes regarding activism)

1580	40	-OBY LW=-GD CTZN		1A011A	1A011A	1A011A	1A011A	1A011A	1A011A	1A011A	1A011A
1590	40	GD CTZN ALG GOVT		1A011B	1A011B	1A011B	1A011B	1A011B	1A011B	1A011B	1A011B
1600	40	GD CTZN CHG GOVT	1A013B	1A011C	1A011C	1A011C	1A011C	1A011C	1A011C	1A011C	1A011C
1620	40	CTZN GRP HV EFCT		1A011E	1A011E	1A011E	1A011E	1A011E	1A011E	1A011E	1A011E

H04: POLITICS. Confidence in government

1630	40	OUR SYST ST BS	1A013C	1A011F	1A011F	1A011F	1A011F	1A011F	1A011F	1A011F	1A011F
6340	97	GOVT PPL -DSHNST	2A32	2A12	2A12	2A12	2A12	2A12	2A12	2A12	2A12
6350	97	GOVT DSNT WASTE$	2A33	2A13	2A13	2A13	2A13	2A13	2A13	2A13	2A13
6360	98	NEVER TRUST GOVT	2A34	2A14	2A14	2A14	2A14	2A14	2A14	2A14	2A14
6370	98	GVT PPL DK DOING	2A35	2A15	2A15	2A15	2A15	2A15	2A15	2A15	2A15
6380	98	GOVT RUN FOR PPL	2A36	2A16	2A16	2A16	2A16	2A16	2A16	2A16	2A16
6950	107	DHNSTY PRES&ADMN	2A20G	2D04G	2D04G	2D04G	2D04G	2D04G	2D04G	2D04G	2D04G
6960	107	DHNSTY CONGRESS	2A20H	2D04H	2D04H	2D04H	2D04H	2D04H	2D04H	2D04H	2D04H
6970	107	DHNSTY SUPRM CRT	2A20I	2D04I	2D04I	2D04I	2D04I	2D04I	2D04I	2D04I	2D04I
6980	107	DHNSTY JUSTC SYS	2A20J	2D04J	2D04J	2D04J	2D04J	2D04J	2D04J	2D04J	2D04J
8440	127	GD JB PRES&ADMN	3A27G	3A24G	3A24G	3A24G	3A24G	3A24G	3A24G	3A24G	3A24G
8450	127	GD JB CONGRESS	3A27H	3A24H	3A24H	3A24H	3A24H	3A24H	3A24H	3A24H	3A24H
8460	127	GD JB SUPRM CRT	3A27I	3A24I	3A24I	3A24I	3A24I	3A24I	3A24I	3A24I	3A24I
8470	127	GD JB JUSTC SYST	3A27J	3A24J	3A24J	3A24J	3A24J	3A24J	3A24J	3A24J	3A24J
10610	157	>INFLC PRES&ADMN	4A14E	4A19E	4A19E	4A19E	4A19E	4A19E	4A19E	4A19E	4A19E
10620	157	>INFLC CONGRESS	4A14F	4A19F	4A19F	4A19F	4A19F	4A19F	4A19F	4A19F	4A19F
10630	157	>INFLC SUPRM CRT	4A14G	4A19G	4A19G	4A19G	4A19G	4A19G	4A19G	4A19G	4A19G
10640	157	>INFLC JUSTC SYS	4A14H	4A19H	4A19H	4A19H	4A19H	4A19H	4A19H	4A19H	4A19H

H05: POLITICS. Voting, political activism

1610	40	VOTE->MAJ IMPCT		1A011D	1A011D	1A011D	1A011D	1A011D	1A011D	1A011D	1A011D
6390	98	DO OR PLN VOTE	2A37A	2A17A	2A17A	2A17A	2A17A	2A17A	2A17A	2A17A	2A17A
6400	98	DO OR PLN WRITE	2A37B	2A17B	2A17B	2A17B	2A17B	2A17B	2A17B	2A17B	2A17B
6410	98	DO OR PLN GIVE $	2A37C	2A17C	2A17C	2A17C	2A17C	2A17C	2A17C	2A17C	2A17C
6420	99	DO OR PLN WK CPG	2A37D	2A17D	2A17D	2A17D	2A17D	2A17D	2A17D	2A17D	2A17D
6430	99	DO OR PLN DEMNST	2A37E	2A17E	2A17E	2A17E	2A17E	2A17E	2A17E	2A17E	2A17E
6440	99	DO OR PLN BOYCOT	2A37F	2A17F	2A17F	2A17F	2A17F	2A17F	2A17F	2A17F	2A17F
9920		R WL VOTE IN '76		3E11							
11820	175	PLC WRK GVT AGCY	5A09C	5A05C	5A05C	5A05C	5A05C	5A05C	5A05C	5A05C	5A05C
12240	182	CTB TO PLTCL PTY	5A20E	5A20E	5A20E	5A20E	5A20E	5A20E	5A20E	5A20E	5A20E
12250	182	CTB TO CTZN LBBY	5A20F	5A20F	5A20F	5A20F	5A20F	5A20F	5A20F	5A20F	5A20F
16340		EFCTV VOTING				2E04C					

I01: SOCIAL CHANGE. Expectations concerning societal change

1200	34	US NEEDS PLANNG	1A004A	1A002A	1A002A	1A002A	1A002A	1A002A	1A002A	1A002A	1A002A
1230	34	X AHEAD TOUGHER	1A004G	1A002D	1A002D	1A002D	1A002D	1A002D	1A002D	1A002D	1A002D
9940	146	FUTR CNTRY WORSE	+A01	4A02	4A02	4A02	4A02	4A02	4A02	4A02	4A02
9950	146	FUTR WORLD WORSE	+A02	4A03	4A03	4A03	4A03	4A03	4A03	4A03	4A03
9960	146	FUTR R LIFE WRSE	+A03	4A04	4A04	4A04	4A04	4A04	4A04	4A04	4A04
10940	163	THG TUF,TCHN SLV	4A28C	4D03C	4D03C	4D03C	4D03C	4D03C	4D03C	4D10C	4D10C

I02: SOCIAL CHANGE. Attitudes regarding activism

1610	40	VOTE->MAJ IMPCT		1A011D	1A011D	1A011D	1A011D	1A011D	1A011D	1A011D	1A011D
1620	40	CTZN GRP HV EFCT		1A011E	1A011E	1A011E	1A011E	1A011E	1A011E	1A011E	1A011E
1650	41	LV THNGS TO GOD	1A004C	1A011H	1A011H	1A011H	1A011H	1A011H	1A011H	1A011H	1A011H
6040	93	APRV PETITIONS	2A21A	2A04A	2A04A	2A04A	2A04A	2A04A	2A04A	2A04A	2A04A
6050	93	APRV BOYCOTT	2A21B	2A04B	2A04B	2A04B	2A04B	2A04B	2A04B	2A04B	2A04B
		(continued)									

Item Reference Number	Page Loc. in this Volume	ITEM DESCRIPTION (ABBREVIATED)	QUESTIONNAIRE LOCATION BY YEAR (FORM, SECTION, AND QUESTION NUMBER)								
			1975	1976	1977	1978	1979	1980	1981	1982	1983

I02: SOCIAL CHANGE. Attitudes regarding activism (continued)

6060	93	APRV LWFL DMSTN	2A21C	2A04C	2A04C	2A04C	2A04C	2A04C	2A04C	2A04C	2A04C
6070	93	APRV OCCUPY BLDG	2A21D	2A04D	2A04D	2A04D	2A04D	2A04D	2A04D	2A04D	2A04D
6080	93	APRV WLDCAT STRK	2A21E	2A04E	2A04E	2A04E	2A04E	2A04E	2A04E	2A04E	2A04E
6090	94	APRV BLK TRAFFIC	2A21F	2A04F	2A04F	2A04F	2A04F	2A04F	2A04F	2A04F	2A04F
6100	94	APRV DAMAG THING	2A21G	2A04G	2A04G	2A04G	2A04G	2A04G	2A04G	2A04G	2A04G
6110	94	APRV PSNL VIOLNC	2A21H	2A04H	2A04H	2A04H	2A04H	2A04H	2A04H	2A04H	2A04H
6390	98	DO OR PLN VOTE	2A37A	2A17A	2A17B	2A17B	2A17B	2A17B	2A17B	2A17B	2A17B
6400	98	DO OR PLN WRITE	2A37B	2A17B	2A17B	2A17B	2A17B	2A17B	2A17B	2A17B	2A17B
6410	98	DO OR PLN GIVE $	2A37C	2A17C	2A17C	2A17C	2A17C	2A17C	2A17C	2A17C	2A17C
6420	99	DO OR PLN WK CPG	2A37D	2A17D	2A17D	2A17D	2A17D	2A17D	2A17D	2A17D	2A17D
6430	99	DO OR PLN DEMNST	2A37E	2A17E	2A17E	2A17E	2A17E	2A17E	2A17E	2A17E	2A17E
6440	99	DO OR PLN BOYCOT	2A37F	2A17F	2A17F	2A17F	2A17F	2A17F	2A17F	2A17F	2A17F
10920	163	I CNT CHNG WORLD	4A28A	4D03A	4D03A	4D03A	4D03A	4D03A	4D03A	4D10A	4D10A
12250	182	CTB TO CTZN LBBY	5A20F	5A20F	5A20F	5A20F	5A20F	5A20F	5A20F	5A20F	5A20F
16320		EFCTV WRIT OFCLS				2E04A					
16330		EFCTV WRK PL CPN				2E04B					
16340		EFCTV VOTING				2E04C					
16350		EFCTV PETITIONS				2E04D					
16360		EFCTV BOYCOTT				2E04E					
16370		EFCTV LWFL DMSTN				2E04F					
16380		EFCTV OCPY BLDGS				2E04G					
16390		EFCTV WLDCT STRK				2E04H					
16400		EFCTV BLK TRAFIC				2E04I					
16410		EFCTV DAMAG THNG				2E04J					
16420		EFCTV PSNL VLNC				2E04K					

I03: SOCIAL CHANGE. Reactions to personal and social change

1210	34	ENJOY FAST PACE	1A004B	1A002B	1A002B	1A002B	1A002B	1A002B	1A002B	1A002B	1A002B
1220	34	THG CHG 2 QUICK	1A004D	1A002C	1A002C	1A002C	1A002C	1A002C	1A002C	1A002C	1A002C
13950	190	EAGR TO LEAV HOM						5D01W	5D01W	5D01W	5D01W
13960	190	HEST PRT ADLT WL						5D01X	5D01X	5D01X	5D01X

J: SOCIAL PROBLEMS. Interest and concerns

1230	34	X AHEAD TOUGHER	1A004G	1A002D	1A002D	1A002D	1A002D	1A002D	1A002D	1A002D	1A002D
6880	106	THK ABT SOC ISSU	*A06	2D03	2D03	2D03	2D03	2D03	2D03	2D03	2D03
	119			3A02	3A02	3A02	3A02	3A02	3A02	3A02	3A02
	146				4A05	4A05	4A05	4A05	4A05	4A05	4A05
	173				5A02	5A02	5A02	5A02	5A02	5A02	5A02
10920	163	I CNT CHNG WORLD	4A28A	4D03A	4D03A	4D03A	4D03A	4D03A	4D03A	4D10A	4D10A
10930	163	SOCTY WONT LAST	4A28B	4D03B	4D03B	4D03B	4D03B	4D03B	4D03B	4D10B	4D10B
10940	163	THG TUF,TCHN SLV	4A28C	4D03C	4D03C	4D03C	4D03C	4D03C	4D03C	4D10C	4D10C
10950	164	NO HOPE 4 WORLD	4A28D	4D03D	4D03D	4D03D	4D03D	4D03D	4D03D	4D10D	4D10D
10960	164	WNDR PURPS 2 LIF	4A28E	4D03E	4D03E	4D03E	4D03E	4D03E	4D03E	4D10E	4D10E
10970	164	WRLD UPHVL 10 YR	4A28F	4D03F	4D03F	4D03F	4D03F	4D03F	4D03F	4D10F	4D10F
10980	164	ANNIHLTN IN LFTM	4A28G	4D03G	4D03G	4D03G	4D03G	4D03G	4D03G	4D10G	4D10G
10990	164	HMN RCE RSILIENT	4A28H	4D03H	4D03H	4D03H	4D03H	4D03H	4D03H	4D10H	4D10H
11660	173	WR/NT NUCLER WAR	5A04A	5A03A	5A03A	5A03A	5A03A	5A03A	5A03A	5A03A	5A03A
11670	173	WR/NT POP GROWTH	5A04B	5A03B	5A03B	5A03B	5A03B	5A03B	5A03B	5A03B	5A03B
11680	173	WR/NT CRIME&VLNC	5A04C	5A03C	5A03C	5A03C	5A03C	5A03C	5A03C	5A03C	5A03C
11690	173	WR/NT POLLUTION	5A04D	5A03D	5A03D	5A03D	5A03D	5A03D	5A03D	5A03D	5A03D
11700	173	WR/NT ENRGY SHRT	5A04E	5A03E	5A03E	5A03E	5A03E	5A03E	5A03E	5A03E	5A03E
11710	174	WR/NT RACE RELTN	5A04F	5A03F	5A03F	5A03F	5A03F	5A03F	5A03F	5A03F	5A03F
11720	174	WR/NT HNGR&PVRTY	5A04G	5A03G	5A03G	5A03G	5A03G	5A03G	5A03G	5A03G	5A03G
11730	174	WR/NT USE OPN LD	5A04H	5A03H	5A03H	5A03H	5A03H	5A03H	5A03H	5A03H	5A03H
11740	174	WR/NT URBN DECAY	5A04I	5A03I	5A03I	5A03I	5A03I	5A03I	5A03I	5A03I	5A03I
11750	174	WR/NT ECON PRBLM	5A04J	5A03J	5A03J	5A03J	5A03J	5A03J	5A03J	5A03J	5A03J
11760	174	WR/NT DRUG ABUSE	5A04K	5A03K	5A03K	5A03K	5A03K	5A03K	5A03K	5A03K	5A03K

Item Refer- ence Number	Page Loc. in this Volume	ITEM DESCRIPTION (ABBREVIATED)	1975	1976	1977	1978	1979	1980	1981	1982	1983
\
> **QUESTIONNAIRE LOCATION BY YEAR (FORM, SECTION, AND QUESTION NUMBER)** ||||||||||||

K01: MAJOR SOCIAL INSTITUTIONS. Trust (See also C05: Institutions as work settings)

Item Ref.	Page	Item Description	1975	1976	1977	1978	1979	1980	1981	1982	1983
6340	97	GOVT PPL -DSHNST	2A32	2A12	2A12	2A12	2A12	2A12	2A12	2A12	2A12
6350	97	GOVT DSNT WASTE$	2A33	2A13	2A13	2A13	2A13	2A13	2A13	2A13	2A13
6360	98	NEVER TRUST GOVT	2A34	2A14	2A14	2A14	2A14	2A14	2A14	2A14	2A14
6370	98	GVT PPL DK DOING	2A35	2A15	2A15	2A15	2A15	2A15	2A15	2A15	2A15
6380	98	GOVT RUN FOR PPL	2A36	2A16	2A16	2A16	2A16	2A16	2A16	2A16	2A16
6890	106	DHNSTY LARG CORP	2A20A	2D04A	2D04A	2D04A	2D04A	2D04A	2D04A	2D04A	2D04A
6900	106	DHNSTY LBR UNION	2A20B	2D04B	2D04B	2D04B	2D04B	2D04B	2D04B	2D04B	2D04B
6910	106	DHNSTY COLL&UNIV	2A20C	2D04C	2D04C	2D04C	2D04C	2D04C	2D04C	2D04C	2D04C
6920	106	DHNSTY PBLC SCHL	2A20D	2D04D	2D04D	2D04D	2D04D	2D04D	2D04D	2D04D	2D04D
6930	107	DHNSTY CHURCHES	2A20E	2D04E	2D04E	2D04E	2D04E	2D04E	2D04E	2D04E	2D04E
6940	107	DHNSTY NEWS MDIA	2A20F	2D04F	2D04F	2D04F	2D04F	2D04F	2D04F	2D04F	2D04F
6950	107	DHNSTY PRES&ADMN	2A20G	2D04G	2D04G	2D04G	2D04G	2D04G	2D04G	2D04G	2D04G
6960	107	DHNSTY CONGRESS	2A20H	2D04H	2D04H	2D04H	2D04H	2D04H	2D04H	2D04H	2D04H
6970	107	DHNSTY SUPRM CRT	2A20I	2D04I	2D04I	2D04I	2D04I	2D04I	2D04I	2D04I	2D04I
6980	107	DHNSTY JUSTC SYS	2A20J	2D04J	2D04J	2D04J	2D04J	2D04J	2D04J	2D04J	2D04J
6990	108	DHNSTY POLICE	2A20K	2D04K	2D04K	2D04K	2D04K	2D04K	2D04K	2D04K	2D04K
7000	108	DHNSTY MILITARY	2A20L	2D04L	2D04L	2D04L	2D04L	2D04L	2D04L	2D04L	2D04L

K02: MAJOR SOCIAL INSTITUTIONS. Satisfaction with performance

Item Ref.	Page	Item Description	1975	1976	1977	1978	1979	1980	1981	1982	1983
1390	37	SAT GOVT OPRTNG		1A006M	1A006M	1A006M	1A006M	1A006M	1A006M	1A006M	1A006M
8380	126	GD JB LARG CORPS	3A27A	3A24A	3A24A	3A24A	3A24A	3A24A	3A24A	3A24A	3A24A
8390	126	GD JB LBR UNIONS	3A27B	3A24B	3A24B	3A24B	3A24B	3A24B	3A24B	3A24B	3A24B
8400	126	GD JB COLLG&UNIV	3A27C	3A24C	3A24C	3A24C	3A24C	3A24C	3A24C	3A24C	3A24C
8410	127	GD JB PBLC SCHOL	3A27D	3A24D	3A24D	3A24D	3A24D	3A24D	3A24D	3A24D	3A24D
8420	127	GD JB CHURCHES	3A27E	3A24E	3A24E	3A24E	3A24E	3A24E	3A24E	3A24E	3A24E
8430	127	GD JB NEWS MEDIA	3A27F	3A24F	3A24F	3A24F	3A24F	3A24F	3A24F	3A24F	3A24F
8440	127	GD JB PRES&ADMIN	3A27G	3A24G	3A24G	3A24G	3A24G	3A24G	3A24G	3A24G	3A24G
8450	127	GD JB CONGRESS	3A27H	3A24H	3A24H	3A24H	3A24H	3A24H	3A24H	3A24H	3A24H
8460	127	GD JB SUPRM CRT	3A27I	3A24I	3A24I	3A24I	3A24I	3A24I	3A24I	3A24I	3A24I
8470	127	GD JB JUSTC SYST	3A27J	3A24J	3A24J	3A24J	3A24J	3A24J	3A24J	3A24J	3A24J
8480	128	GD JB POLICE	3A27K	3A24K	3A24K	3A24K	3A24K	3A24K	3A24K	3A24K	3A24K
8490	128	GD JB MILITARY	3A27L	3A24L	3A24L	3A24L	3A24L	3A24L	3A24L	3A24L	3A24L

K03: MAJOR SOCIAL INSTITUTIONS. Preferred influence

Item Ref.	Page	Item Description	1975	1976	1977	1978	1979	1980	1981	1982	1983
8500	128	MIL TOO MCH INFL	3A28	3A25	3A25	3A25	3A25	3A25	3A25	3A25	3A25
8510	128	US TOO MCH$MILT	3A29	3A26	3A26	3A26	3A26	3A26	3A26	3A26	3A26
10570	156	>INFLC LARG CORP	4A14A	4A19A	4A19A	4A19A	4A19A	4A19A	4A19A	4A19A	4A19A
10580	156	>INFLC LBR UNION	4A14B	4A19B	4A19B	4A19B	4A19B	4A19B	4A19B	4A19B	4A19B
10590	156	>INFLC CHURCHES	4A14C	4A19C	4A19C	4A19C	4A19C	4A19C	4A19C	4A19C	4A19C
10600	157	>INFLC NEWS MDIA	4A14D	4A19D	4A19D	4A19D	4A19D	4A19D	4A19D	4A19D	4A19D
10610	157	>INFLC PRES&ADMN	4A14E	4A19E	4A19E	4A19E	4A19E	4A19E	4A19E	4A19E	4A19E
10620	157	>INFLC CONGRESS	4A14F	4A19F	4A19F	4A19F	4A19F	4A19F	4A19F	4A19F	4A19F
10630	157	>INFLC SUPRM CRT	4A14G	4A19G	4A19G	4A19G	4A19G	4A19G	4A19G	4A19G	4A19G
10640	157	>INFLC JUSTC SYS	4A14H	4A19H	4A19H	4A19H	4A19H	4A19H	4A19H	4A19H	4A19H
10650	157	>INFLC POLICE	4A14I	4A19I	4A19I	4A19I	4A19I	4A19I	4A19I	4A19I	4A19I
10660	158	>INFLC MILITARY	4A14J	4A19J	4A19J	4A19J	4A19J	4A19J	4A19J	4A19J	4A19J

L01: MILITARY. Plans for military service

Item Ref.	Page	Item Description	1975	1976	1977	1978	1979	1980	1981	1982	1983
490	20	R WL DO ARMD FC		+C21B	+C21B	+C21B	+C21B	+C21B	+C21B	+C21B	+C21B
540	21	R WNTDO ARMD FC		+C22B	+C22B	+C22B	+C22B	+C22B	+C22B	+C22B	+C22B
730	23	R'S BRANCH SERV		+C32	+C32	+C32	+C32	+C32	+C32	+C32	+C32
740	23	R XPCTS B OFFCR		+C33	+C33	+C33	+C33	+C33	+C33	+C33	+C33
750	24	R XPCTS MLTR CR		+C34	+C34	+C34	+C34	+C34	+C34	+C34	+C34

L02: MILITARY. Attitudes toward a draft

Item Ref.	Page	Item Description	1975	1976	1977	1978	1979	1980	1981	1982	1983
21060	114	FAVOR MLTY DRAFT							5E06	2E08	2E08
21070	114	DRAFT INCL WOMEN							5E07	2E09	2E09
21080	114	MLTRY PAY CLG GD							5E08	2E10	2E10
21090	114	R WD DO MLTY/CLG							5E09	2E11	2E11

Item Reference Number	Page Loc. in this Volume	ITEM DESCRIPTION (ABBREVIATED)	QUESTIONNAIRE LOCATION BY YEAR (FORM, SECTION, AND QUESTION NUMBER)								
			1975	1976	1977	1978	1979	1980	1981	1982	1983

L03: MILITARY. Views about the use of military force

5690	99	US GO WAR FR OTH	2A38B	2A18B	2A18B	2A18B	2A18B	2A18B	2A18B	2A18B	2A18B
6450	99	US SHD DISARM	2A38A	2A18A	2A18A	2A18A	2A18A	2A18A	2A18A	2A18A	2A18A
6460	99	US WAR PRTCT ECN	2A38C	2A18C	2A18C	2A18C	2A18C	2A18C	2A18C	2A18C	2A18C
6470	99	US ONLY WAR DFNS	2A38D	2A18D	2A18D	2A18D	2A18D	2A18D	2A18D	2A18D	2A18D
6480	100	-US MIL PWR>USSR	2A38E	2A18E	2A18E	2A18E	2A18E	2A18E	2A18E	2A18E	2A18E
6490	100	US NEED>PWR OTHS	2A38F	2A18F	2A18F	2A18F	2A18F	2A18F	2A18F	2A18F	2A18F
6500	100	US FRN PLCY NRRW	2A38G	2A18G	2A18G	2A18G	2A18G	2A18G	2A18G	2A18G	2A18G
6510	100	SRVCMEN SHD OBEY	2A38H	2A18H	2A18H	2A18H	2A18H	2A18H	2A18H	2A18H	2A18H
11210		-MLTRY COUP U.S.		4E06	4E06						
11220	168	NT VOL 4 NEC WAR		4E07	4E07	4E06	4E06	4E06	4E06	4E06	4E06

L04: MILITARY. Attitudes toward the military as an institution and occupation

7000	108	DHNSTY MILITARY	2A20L	2D04L	2D04L	2D04L	2D04L	2D04L	2D04L	2D04L	2D04L
8490	128	GD JB MILITARY	3A27L	3A24L	3A24L	3A24L	3A24L	3A24L	3A24L	3A24L	3A24L
8500	128	MIL TOO MCH INFL	3A28	3A25	3A25	3A25	3A25	3A25	3A25	3A25	3A25
8510	128	US TOO MCH$MILT	3A29	3A26	3A26	3A26	3A26	3A26	3A26	3A26	3A26
10660	158	>INFLC MILITARY	4A14J	4A19J	4A19J	4A19J	4A19J	4A19J	4A19J	4A19J	4A19J
11120	167	MLTRY GET AHEAD		4E01A	4E01A	4E01A	4E01A	4E01A	4E01A	4E01A	4E01A
11130	167	MLTRY MORE ED		4E01B	4E01B	4E01B	4E01B	4E01B	4E01B	4E01B	4E01B
11140	167	MLTRY ADVNC RESP		4E01C	4E01C	4E01C	4E01C	4E01C	4E01C	4E01C	4E01C
11150	167	MLTRY >FLFLLG JB		4E01D	4E01D	4E01D	4E01D	4E01D	4E01D	4E01D	4E01D
11160	167	MLTRY IDEAS HERD		4E01E	4E01E	4E01E	4E01E	4E01E	4E01E	4E01E	4E01E
11170	167	EXTNT MLTRY JSTC		4E02	4E02	4E02	4E02	4E02	4E02	4E02	4E02
11180	167	MLTRY DSCRM WOMN		4E03	4E03	4E03	4E03	4E03	4E03	4E03	4E03
11190	168	MLTRY DSCRM BLKS		4E04	4E04	4E04	4E04	4E04	4E04	4E04	4E04
11200	168	>FAIR MLTRY CVLN		4E05	4E05	4E05	4E05	4E05	4E05	4E05	4E05
11830	175	PLC WRK MLTY SVC	5A09D	5A05D	5A05D	5A05D	5A05D	5A05D	5A05D	5A05D	5A05D

M01: INTERPERSONAL RELATIONSHIPS. Dating

620	21	#X/AV WK GO OUT		+C25	+C25	+C25	+C25	+C25	+C25	+C25	+C25
630	22	#X DATE 3+/WK		+C26	+C26	+C26	+C26	+C26	+C26	+C26	+C26

M02: INTERPERSONAL RELATIONSHIPS. Cross-age relationships with adults outside the family (See also B05)

1240	34	TM SPT ADLT MST	1A006	1A003	1A003	1A003	1A003	1A003	1A003	1A003	1A003
1250	35	LK MR TM ADLT	1A007	1A004	1A004	1A004	1A004	1A004	1A004	1A004	1A004
1260	35	LK MR TM YG CHD	1A008	1A005	1A005	1A005	1A005	1A005	1A005	1A005	1A005
6530	100	FRQ HIT SUPRVISR	2A39B	2A19B	2A19B	2A19B	2A19B	2A19B	2A19B	2A19B	2A19B
21550	160	JOB-SUPERVSR AGE								4D04	4D04
21610	161	JOB-OVER AGE 30								4D06E	4D06E
21710	163	JOB-TCHR HELP GT								4D08	4D08

M03: INTERPERSONAL RELATIONSHIPS. Agreement/disagreement with parents

1330	36	SAT GT ALNG PRNT	1A009G	1A006G	1A006G	1A006G	1A006G	1A006G	1A006G	1A006G	1A006G
1500	39	IMP LIV CLS PRNT		1A007J	1A007J	1A007J	1A007J	1A007J	1A007J	1A007J	1A007J
6520	100	FRQ FIGHT PARNTS	2A39A	2A19A	2A19A	2A19A	2A19A	2A19A	2A19A	2A19A	2A19A
11230	168	P'IDEA OF DO LIF	4A27A	4E08A	4E08A	4E07A	4E07A	4E07A	4E07A	4E07A	4E07A
11240	168	P'IDEA OF LSR TM	4A27B	4E08B	4E08B	4E07B	4E07B	4E07B	4E07B	4E07B	4E07B
11250	168	P'IDEA OF CLTHES	4A27C	4E08C	4E08C	4E07C	4E07C	4E07C	4E07C	4E07C	4E07C
11260	169	P'IDEA OF SPND $	4A27D	4E08D	4E08D	4E07D	4E07D	4E07D	4E07D	4E07D	4E07D
11270	169	P'IDEA OF DATE	4A27E	4E08E	4E08E	4E07E	4E07E	4E07E	4E07E	4E07E	4E07E
11280	169	P'IDEA OF OK DRK	4A27F	4E08F	4E08F	4E07F	4E07F	4E07F	4E07F	4E07F	4E07F
11290	169	P'IDEA OF OK MRJ	4A27G	4E08G	4E08G	4E07G	4E07G	4E07G	4E07G	4E07G	4E07G
11300	169	P'IDEA OF OK DRG	4A27H	4E08H	4E08H	4E07H	4E07H	4E07H	4E07H	4E07H	4E07H
11310	169	P'IDEA OF VALUES	4A27I	4E08I	4E08I	4E07I	4E07I	4E07I	4E07I	4E07I	4E07I
11320	169	P'IDEA OF EDUC	4A27J	4E08J	4E08J	4E07J	4E07J	4E07J	4E07J	4E07J	4E07J
11330	170	P'IDEA OF SX RLS	4A27K	4E08K	4E08K	4E07K	4E07K	4E07K	4E07K	4E07K	4E07K
11340	170	P'IDEA OF ECLOGY	4A27L	4E08L	4E08L	4E07L	4E07L	4E07L	4E07L	4E07L	4E07L
11350	170	P'IDEA OF RCL IS	4A27M	4E08M	4E08M	4E07M	4E07M	4E07M	4E07M	4E07M	4E07M
11360	170	P'IDEA OF RLGION	4A27N	4E08N	4E08N	4E07N	4E07N	4E07N	4E07N	4E07N	4E07N
		(continued)									

Item Reference Number	Page Loc. in this Volume	Item Description (Abbreviated)	Questionnaire Location By Year (Form, Section, and Question Number)								
			1975	1976	1977	1978	1979	1980	1981	1982	1983

M03: INTERPERSONAL RELATIONSHIPS. Agreement/disagreement with parents *(continued)*

Item Reference Number	Page Loc. in this Volume	Item Description (Abbreviated)	1975	1976	1977	1978	1979	1980	1981	1982	1983
11370	170	P'IDEA OF PLTICS	4A27O	4E08O	4E08O	4E07O	4E07O	4E07O	4E07O	4E07O	4E07O
13150		FAM+REL GD/CHILD		5E01A							
13160		FAM+REL GD/PARNT		5E01B							
13170		FAM+REL GD/GRPNT		5E01C							
13180		FAM+REL,R LIK/PT		5E01D							
19530	113	3MO/DLY ARG PRNT						2E08A	2E08A	2E07A	2E07A

M04: INTERPERSONAL RELATIONSHIPS. Friendships (See also Q03: Loneliness)

Item Reference Number	Page Loc. in this Volume	Item Description (Abbreviated)	1975	1976	1977	1978	1979	1980	1981	1982	1983
1320	36	SAT OWN FRIENDS	1A009F	1A006F	1A006F	1A006F	1A006F	1A006F	1A006F	1A006F	1A006F
1450	38	IMP STRG FRDSHP		1A007E	1A007E	1A007E	1A007E	1A007E	1A007E	1A007E	1A007E
5920	91	DALY VIST W/FRDS		2A02K	2A02K	2A02K	2A02K	2A02K	2A02K	2A02K	2A02K
10170	149	JOB IMPC MK FRND	4A08I	4A08I	4A08I	4A08I	4A08I	4A08I	4A08I	4A08I	4A08I

M05: INTERPERSONAL RELATIONSHIPS. Community at large

Item Reference Number	Page Loc. in this Volume	Item Description (Abbreviated)	1975	1976	1977	1978	1979	1980	1981	1982	1983
1480	38	IMP LDR COMUNTY		1A007H	1A007H	1A007H	1A007H	1A007H	1A007H	1A007H	1A007H
10290	151	JOB IMPC CNTC PL	4A08U	4A08U	4A08U	4A08U	4A08U	4A08U	4A08U	4A08U	4A08U
13590	139	STS SCH LDS STU		5E05B	5E06B	5E06B	5E04B	5E06B		3E06B	3E06B
21600	161	JOB-DIF SOC BKGD								4D06D	4D06D
21730	171	IDEA PARENTS GRP									4E09
21740	172	#FRNDS PRNTS GRP									4E10
21750	172	OWN PRNTS IN GRP									4E11
21760	172	GP IMPCT OWN FLG									4E12
21770	172	GP CHG RELP PRNT									4E13
21780	172	#FRNDS ANTIDG GP									4E14
21790	172	EVR IN ANTIDG GP									4E15

N01: RACE RELATIONS. Preferred interracial contact

Item Reference Number	Page Loc. in this Volume	Item Description (Abbreviated)	1975	1976	1977	1978	1979	1980	1981	1982	1983
8110	122	DES FRND OTH RC	3A19A	3A07A	3A07A	3A07A	3A07A	3A07A	3A07A	3A07A	3A07A
8120	122	DES SUPVR DIF RC	3A19B	3A07B	3A07B	3A07B	3A07B	3A07B	3A07B	3A07B	3A07B
8130	122	DES FAM NX DF RC	3A19C	3A07C	3A07C	3A07C	3A07C	3A07C	3A07C	3A07C	3A07C
8140	122	DES CHL FD SM RC	3A19D	3A07D	3A07D	3A07D	3A07D	3A07D	3A07D	3A07D	3A07D
8150	123	DES CHL FD OT RC	3A19E	3A07E	3A07E	3A07E	3A07E	3A07E	3A07E	3A07E	3A07E
8160	123	DES AL WKS SM RC	3A19F	3A08A	3A08A	3A08A	3A08A	3A08A	3A08A	3A08A	3A08A
8170	123	DES SO WKS DF RC	3A19G	3A08B	3A08B	3A08B	3A08B	3A08B	3A08B	3A08B	3A08B
8180	123	DES MS WKS DF RC	3A19H	3A08C	3A08C	3A08C	3A08C	3A08C	3A08C	3A08C	3A08C
8190	123	DES AL NGB SM RC	3A19I	3A09A	3A09A	3A09A	3A09A	3A09A	3A09A	3A09A	3A09A
8200	123	DES SO NGB OT RC	3A19J	3A09B	3A09B	3A09B	3A09B	3A09B	3A09B	3A09B	3A09B
8210	123	DES MS NGB OT RC	3A19K	3A09C	3A09C	3A09C	3A09C	3A09C	3A09C	3A09C	3A09C
8220	124	DES AL CHL SM RC	3A19L	3A10A	3A10A	3A10A	3A10A	3A10A	3A10A	3A10A	3A10A
8230	124	DES SM CHL OT RC	3A19M	3A10B	3A10B	3A10B	3A10B	3A10B	3A10B	3A10B	3A10B
8240	124	DES MS CHL OT RC	3A19N	3A10C	3A10C	3A10C	3A10C	3A10C	3A10C	3A10C	3A10C

N02: RACE RELATIONS. Attitudes about discrimination

Item Reference Number	Page Loc. in this Volume	Item Description (Abbreviated)	1975	1976	1977	1978	1979	1980	1981	1982	1983
1520	39	IMP CRRCT INEQL		1A007L	1A007L	1A007L	1A007L	1A007L	1A007L	1A007L	1A007L
10380	153	JOB OBSTC RACE		4A13C	4A13C	4A13C	4A13C	4A13C	4A13C	4A13C	4A13C
11190	168	MLTRY DSCRM BLKS		4E04	4E04	4E04	4E04	4E04	4E04	4E04	4E04
11350	170	P'IDEA OF RCL IS	4A27M	4E08M	4E08M	4E07M	4E07M	4E07M	4E07M	4E07M	4E07M
11710	174	WR/NT RACE RELTN	5A04F	5A03F	5A03F	5A03F	5A03F	5A03F	5A03F	5A03F	5A03F
11950	177	B/W RLTNS WRSE	5A15	5A08	5A08	5A08	5A08	5A08	5A08	5A08	5A08
12100	179	MNRTY NT MY BSNS	5A19F	5A18D	5A18D	5A18D	5A18D	5A18D	5A18D	5A18D	5A18D
12220	182	CTB TO MNRTY GRP	5A20C	5A20C	5A20C	5A20C	5A20C	5A20C	5A20C	5A20C	5A20C

N03: RACE RELATIONS. Actual interracial contacts

Item Reference Number	Page Loc. in this Volume	Item Description (Abbreviated)	1975	1976	1977	1978	1979	1980	1981	1982	1983
8250	124	FRNDS AL OT RC	3A22	3A11	3A11	3A11	3A11	3A11	3A11	3A11	3A11
8260	124	NGBHD AL OT RC	3A23	3A12	3A12	3A12	3A12	3A12	3A12	3A12	3A12
8270	124	ELEMSCH AL OT RC	3A21	3A13	3A13	3A13	3A13	3A13	3A13	3A13	3A13
8280	124	HISCH AL OT RC	3A20	3A14	3A14	3A14	3A14	3A14	3A14	3A14	3A14
8290	125	WRKRS AL OT RC		3A15	3A15	3A15	3A15	3A15	3A15	3A15	3A15
		(continued)									

Item Reference Number	Page Loc. in this Volume	ITEM DESCRIPTION (ABBREVIATED)	QUESTIONNAIRE LOCATION BY YEAR (FORM, SECTION, AND QUESTION NUMBER)								
			1975	1976	1977	1978	1979	1980	1981	1982	1983

N03: RACE RELATIONS. Actual interracial contacts *(continued)*

Item Reference Number	Page Loc.	ITEM DESCRIPTION	1975	1976	1977	1978	1979	1980	1981	1982	1983
8300	125	DO LOT THG OT RC	3A24	3A16	3A16	3A16	3A16	3A16	3A16	3A16	3A16
8310	125	VRY GD EXP OT RC	3A25	3A17	3A17	3A17	3A17	3A17	3A17	3A17	3A17
11890	176	RCL CNTCT SCHOOL		5A07A	5A07A	5A07A	5A07A	5A07A	5A07A	5A07A	5A07A
11900	176	RCL CNTCT NGHBHD		5A07B	5A07B	5A07B	5A07B	5A07B	5A07B	5A07B	5A07B
11910	176	RCL CNTCT CHURCH		5A07C	5A07C	5A07C	5A07C	5A07C	5A07C	5A07C	5A07C
11920	176	RCL CNTCT SPORTS		5A07D	5A07D	5A07D	5A07D	5A07D	5A07D	5A07D	5A07D
11930	177	RCL CNTCT CLUBS		5A07E	5A07E	5A07E	5A07E	5A07E	5A07E	5A07E	5A07E
11940	177	RCL CNTCT JOB		5A07F	5A07F	5A07F	5A07F	5A07F	5A07F	5A07F	5A07F

O01: CONCERN FOR OTHERS. Attitudes regarding social service, charitable activism

Item Reference Number	Page Loc.	ITEM DESCRIPTION	1975	1976	1977	1978	1979	1980	1981	1982	1983
1470	38	IMP CNTRBTN SOC		1A007G	1A007G	1A007G	1A007G	1A007G	1A007G	1A007G	1A007G
1520	39	IMP CRRCT INEQL		1A007L	1A007L	1A007L	1A007L	1A007L	1A007L	1A007L	1A007L
10130	149	JOB IMPC HLP OTH	4A08E	4A08E	4A08E	4A08E	4A08E	4A08E	4A08E	4A08E	4A08E
10190	150	JOB IMPC WRTHWLE	4A08K	4A08K	4A08K	4A08K	4A08K	4A08K	4A08K	4A08K	4A08K
11860	175	PLC WRK SOC SVCS	5A09G	5A05G	5A05G	5A05G	5A05G	5A05G	5A05G	5A05G	5A05G

O02: CONCERN FOR OTHERS. Involvement in community, altruistic activities

Item Reference Number	Page Loc.	ITEM DESCRIPTION	1975	1976	1977	1978	1979	1980	1981	1982	1983
5860	90	DALY CMNTY AFFRS		2A02E	2A02E	2A02E	2A02E	2A02E	2A02E	2A02E	2A02E
12200	181	CTB TO UNTD FUND	5A20A	5A20A	5A20A	5A20A	5A20A	5A20A	5A20A	5A20A	5A20A
12210	181	CTB TO INTL RELF	5A20B	5A20B	5A20B	5A20B	5A20B	5A20B	5A20B	5A20B	5A20B
12220	182	CTB TO MNRTY GRP	5A20C	5A20C	5A20C	5A20C	5A20C	5A20C	5A20C	5A20C	5A20C
12230	182	CTB TO RELGS ORG	5A20D	5A20D	5A20D	5A20D	5A20D	5A20D	5A20D	5A20D	5A20D
12240	182	CTB TO PLTCL PTY	5A20E	5A20E	5A20E	5A20E	5A20E	5A20E	5A20E	5A20E	5A20E
12250	182	CTB TO CTZN LBBY	5A20F	5A20F	5A20F	5A20F	5A20F	5A20F	5A20F	5A20F	5A20F
12260	182	CTB TO VS DISEAS	5A20G	5A20G	5A20G	5A20G	5A20G	5A20G	5A20G	5A20G	5A20G
12270	182	CTB TO POP PRBMS	5A20H	5A20H	5A20H	5A20H	5A20H	5A20H	5A20H	5A20H	5A20H
12280	183	CTB TO ENVIR PBM	5A20I	5A20I	5A20I	5A20I	5A20I	5A20I	5A20I	5A20I	5A20I

O03: CONCERN FOR OTHERS. Concern with the problems of others

Item Reference Number	Page Loc.	ITEM DESCRIPTION	1975	1976	1977	1978	1979	1980	1981	1982	1983
5990	92	US 2 MUCH PROFIT	2A23J	2A03A	2A03A	2A03A	2A03A	2A03A	2A03A	2A03A	2A03A
8040	121	EAT DIF->FD STRV	3A31G	3A04E	3A04E	3A04E	3A04E	3A04E	3A04E	3A04E	3A04E
9840		GVNG FOOD O CNTY	3A33	3E05							
12070	179	WRRY ABT OW CTRY	5A19A	5A18A	5A18A	5A18A	5A18A	5A18A	5A18A	5A18A	5A18A
12080	179	BTTR IF CTZ WRLD	5A19C	5A18B	5A18B	5A18B	5A18B	5A18B	5A18B	5A18B	5A18B
12090	179	-SYMP TWD STARVG	5A19E	5A18C	5A18C	5A18C	5A18C	5A18C	5A18C	5A18C	5A18C
12100	179	MNRTY NT MY BSNS	5A19F	5A18D	5A18D	5A18D	5A18D	5A18D	5A18D	5A18D	5A18D
12110	179	UPST PL TR -FAIR	5A19G	5A18E	5A18E	5A18E	5A18E	5A18E	5A18E	5A18E	5A18E
12120	180	HELP POOR W MY $	5A19I	5A18F	5A18F	5A18F	5A18F	5A18F	5A18F	5A18F	5A18F
12130	180	-MY PRB OT ND HP	5A19K	5A18G	5A18G	5A18G	5A18G	5A18G	5A18G	5A18G	5A18G
12140	180	RB CHNG ETG HABT		5A18H	5A18H	5A18H	5A18H	5A18H	5A18H	5A18H	5A18H
16430		SAT EVB CAR POOL				2E05A					
16440		SAT EAT <BEEF>GRN				2E05B					
19470		EAT <FD,>OWN CITY					5E08A				
19480		EAT <FD,>NRBY STT					5E08B				
19490		EAT <FD,>DIF REGN					5E08C				
19500		EAT <FD,>ASIAN CN					5E08D				

P01: HAPPINESS. Happiness; satisfaction with life and self

Item Reference Number	Page Loc.	ITEM DESCRIPTION	1975	1976	1977	1978	1979	1980	1981	1982	1983
1190	34	VRY HPY THS DAYS		1A001	1A001	1A001	1A001	1A001	1A001	1A001	1A001
	90			2A01	2A01	2A01	2A01	2A01	2A01	2A01	2A01
	119			3A01	3A01	3A01	3A01	3A01	3A01	3A01	3A01
	146			4A01	4A01	4A01	4A01	4A01	4A01	4A01	4A01
	173			5A01	5A01	5A01	5A01	5A01	5A01	5A01	5A01
1340	36	SAT YOURSELF	1A009H	1A006H	1A006H	1A006H	1A006H	1A006H	1A006H	1A006H	1A006H
1380	37	SAT LIFE AS WHLE	1A009L	1A006L	1A006L	1A006L	1A006L	1A006L	1A006L	1A006L	1A006L
6840	105	CMP SATFD W/LIFE		2D01	2D01	2D01	2D01	2D01	2D01	2D01	2D01
	133			3D01	3D01	3D01	3D01	3D01	3D01	3D01	3D01
	160			4D01	4D01	4D01	4D01	4D01	4D01	4D01	4D01
	183			5A21	5A21	5A21	5A21	5A21	5A21	5A21	5A21
12620	188	SATISFD W MYSELF	5A39H	5D01H	5D01H	5D01H	5D01H	5D01H	5D01H	5D01H	5D01H

Item Reference Number	Page Loc. in this Volume	ITEM DESCRIPTION (ABBREVIATED)	QUESTIONNAIRE LOCATION BY YEAR (FORM, SECTION, AND QUESTION NUMBER)								
			1975	1976	1977	1978	1979	1980	1981	1982	1983

P02: HAPPINESS. Satisfaction with specific life domains

Item Reference Number	Page Loc.	ITEM DESCRIPTION	1975	1976	1977	1978	1979	1980	1981	1982	1983
1270	35	SAT PRESENT JOB	1A009A	1A006A	1A006A	1A006A	1A006A	1A006A	1A006A	1A006A	1A006A
1280	35	SAT NEIGHBORHOD	1A009B	1A006B	1A006B	1A006B	1A006B	1A006B	1A006B	1A006B	1A006B
1290	35	SAT PRSNL SAFTY	1A009C	1A006C	1A006C	1A006C	1A006C	1A006C	1A006C	1A006C	1A006C
1300	36	SAT OWN PROP SF	1A009D	1A006D	1A006D	1A006D	1A006D	1A006D	1A006D	1A006D	1A006D
1310	36	SAT EDUC EXPRNCS	1A009E	1A006E	1A006E	1A006E	1A006E	1A006E	1A006E	1A006E	1A006E
1320	36	SAT OWN FRIENDS	1A009F	1A006F	1A006F	1A006F	1A006F	1A006F	1A006F	1A006F	1A006F
1330	36	SAT GT ALNG PRNT	1A009G	1A006G	1A006G	1A006G	1A006G	1A006G	1A006G	1A006G	1A006G
1350	36	SAT STD OF LVG	1A009I	1A006I	1A006I	1A006I	1A006I	1A006I	1A006I	1A006I	1A006I
1360	37	SAT TIME FR THGS	1A009J	1A006J	1A006J	1A006J	1A006J	1A006J	1A006J	1A006J	1A006J
1370	37	SAT SPD LEISR	1A009K	1A006K	1A006K	1A006K	1A006K	1A006K	1A006K	1A006K	1A006K
1400	37	SAT AMT OF FUN		1A006N	1A006N	1A006N	1A006N	1A006N	1A006N	1A006N	1A006N
10350	153	R THNK WK BE SAT		4A12	4A12	4A12	4A12	4A12	4A12	4A12	4A12
10910	160	CMP SATFD W/JOB		4D02	4D02	4D02	4D02	4D02	4D02	4D02	4D02

Q01: OTHER PERSONALITY VARIABLES. Attitudes about self, self-esteem

Item Reference Number	Page Loc.	ITEM DESCRIPTION	1975	1976	1977	1978	1979	1980	1981	1982	1983
1190	34	VRY HPY THS DAYS		1A001	1A001	1A001	1A001	1A001	1A001	1A001	1A001
	90			2A01	2A01	2A01	2A01	2A01	2A01	2A01	2A01
	119			3A01	3A01	3A01	3A01	3A01	3A01	3A01	3A01
	146			4A01	4A01	4A01	4A01	4A01	4A01	4A01	4A01
	173			5A01	5A01	5A01	5A01	5A01	5A01	5A01	5A01
1340	36	SAT YOURSELF	1A009H	1A006H	1A006H	1A006H	1A006H	1A006H	1A006H	1A006H	1A006H
1400	37	SAT AMT OF FUN		1A006N	1A006N	1A006N	1A006N	1A006N	1A006N	1A006N	1A006N
6840	105	CMP SATFD W/LIFE		2D01	2D01	2D01	2D01	2D01	2D01	2D01	2D01
	133			3D01	3D01	3D01	3D01	3D01	3D01	3D01	3D01
	160			4D01	4D01	4D01	4D01	4D01	4D01	4D01	4D01
	183			5A21	5A21	5A21	5A21	5A21	5A21	5A21	5A21
6850	105	HOW GD AS SPOUSE	2A19A	2D02A	2D02A	2D02A	2D02A	2D02A	2D02A	2D02A	2D02A
6860	105	HOW GD AS PARENT	2A19B	2D02B	2D02B	2D02B	2D02B	2D02B	2D02B	2D02B	2D02B
6870	106	HOW GD AS WORKER	2A19C	2D02C	2D02C	2D02C	2D02C	2D02C	2D02C	2D02C	2D02C
12550	187	POS ATT TWD SELF	5A39A	5D01A	5D01A	5D01A	5D01A	5D01A	5D01A	5D01A	5D01A
12570	187	AM PRSN OF WORTH	5A39C	5D01C	5D01C	5D01C	5D01C	5D01C	5D01C	5D01C	5D01C
12580	187	DO WELL AS OTHRS	5A39D	5D01D	5D01D	5D01D	5D01D	5D01D	5D01D	5D01D	5D01D
12620	188	SATISFD W MYSELF	5A39H	5D01H	5D01H	5D01H	5D01H	5D01H	5D01H	5D01H	5D01H
12660	189	-MUCH TO B PROUD			5D01L	5D01L	5D01L	5D01L	5D01L	5D01L	5D01L
12680	189	I AM NO GOOD			5D01N	5D01N	5D01N	5D01N	5D01N	5D01N	5D01N
12720	189	I DO WRONG THING			5D01R	5D01R	5D01R	5D01R	5D01R	5D01R	5D01R
12750	190	MY LIFE NT USEFL			5D01U	5D01U	5D01U	5D01U	5D01U	5D01U	5D01U
13950	190	EAGR TO LEAV HOM						5D01W	5D01W	5D01W	5D01W
13960	190	HEST PRT ADLT WL						5D01X	5D01X	5D01X	5D01X

Q02: OTHER PERSONALITY VARIABLES. Locus of control

Item Reference Number	Page Loc.	ITEM DESCRIPTION	1975	1976	1977	1978	1979	1980	1981	1982	1983
1210	34	ENJOY FAST PACE	1A004B	1A002B	1A002B	1A002B	1A002B	1A002B	1A002B	1A002B	1A002B
1220	34	THG CHG 2 QUICK	1A004D	1A002C	1A002C	1A002C	1A002C	1A002C	1A002C	1A002C	1A002C
12560	187	LUCK>IMP HRD WRK	5A39B	5D01B	5D01B	5D01B	5D01B	5D01B	5D01B	5D01B	5D01B
12590	188	TRY GT AHD,STOPD	5A39E	5D01E	5D01E	5D01E	5D01E	5D01E	5D01E	5D01E	5D01E
12600	188	PLNNG MKS UNHPPY	5A39F	5D01F	5D01F	5D01F	5D01F	5D01F	5D01F	5D01F	5D01F
12610	188	ACPT LIFE->HAPPR	5A39G	5D01G	5D01G	5D01G	5D01G	5D01G	5D01G	5D01G	5D01G
12630	188	PPL LK ME -CHANC	5A39I	5D01I	5D01I	5D01I	5D01I	5D01I	5D01I	5D01I	5D01I
12640	188	MY PLANS DO WORK			5D01J	5D01J	5D01J	5D01J	5D01J	5D01J	5D01J
12700	189	PPL MASTER FATE			5D01P	5D01P	5D01P	5D01P	5D01P	5D01P	5D01P
12740	190	PLANS->BTR RSLTS			5D01T	5D01T	5D01T	5D01T	5D01T	5D01T	5D01T

Q03: OTHER PERSONALITY VARIABLES. Loneliness

Item Reference Number	Page Loc.	ITEM DESCRIPTION	1975	1976	1977	1978	1979	1980	1981	1982	1983
12650	188	OFTN FEEL LONELY			5D01K	5D01K	5D01K	5D01K	5D01K	5D01K	5D01K
12670	189	ALWYS SM1 HELP R			5D01M	5D01M	5D01M	5D01M	5D01M	5D01M	5D01M
12690	189	OFTN FL LEFT OUT			5D01O	5D01O	5D01O	5D01O	5D01O	5D01O	5D01O
12710	189	USLY SM1 TALK TO			5D01Q	5D01Q	5D01Q	5D01Q	5D01Q	5D01Q	5D01Q
12730	190	OFT WSH MOR FRND			5D01S	5D01S	5D01S	5D01S	5D01S	5D01S	5D01S
12760	190	USLY FRDS BE WTH			5D01V	5D01V	5D01V	5D01V	5D01V	5D01V	5D01V

Item Reference Number	Page Loc. in this Volume	ITEM DESCRIPTION (ABBREVIATED)	QUESTIONNAIRE LOCATION BY YEAR (FORM, SECTION, AND QUESTION NUMBER)								
			1975	1976	1977	1978	1979	1980	1981	1982	1983

Q04: OTHER PERSONALITY VARIABLES. Risk taking

Item Reference Number	Page Loc. in this Volume	ITEM DESCRIPTION (ABBREVIATED)	1975	1976	1977	1978	1979	1980	1981	1982	1983
7050	109	KICK DO DANGR TH		2D05E	2D05E	2D05E	2D05E	2D05E	2D05E	2D05E	2D05E
7060	109	LIKE RISK SOME X		2D05F	2D05F	2D05F	2D05F	2D05F	2D05F	2D05F	2D05F

Q05: OTHER PERSONALITY VARIABLES. Trust in others

Item Reference Number	Page Loc. in this Volume	ITEM DESCRIPTION (ABBREVIATED)	1975	1976	1977	1978	1979	1980	1981	1982	1983
1550	39	PPL CAN B TRSTD	1A010	1A008	1A008	1A008	1A008	1A008	1A008	1A008	1A008
1560	39	PPL TRY B HLPFL	1A011	1A009	1A009	1A009	1A009	1A009	1A009	1A009	1A009
1570	39	PPL TRY BE FAIR	1A012	1A010	1A010	1A010	1A010	1A010	1A010	1A010	1A010

Q06: OTHER PERSONALITY VARIABLES. Health habits and symptoms

Item Reference Number	Page Loc. in this Volume	ITEM DESCRIPTION (ABBREVIATED)	1975	1976	1977	1978	1979	1980	1981	1982	1983
8850	133	OFTN SHRTNS BRTH		(3D02A)	3D02A	3D02A	3D02A	3D02A	3D02A	3D02A	3D02A
8860	133	OFTN HEART BEATG		(3D02B)	3D02B	3D02B	3D02B	3D02B	3D02B	3D02B	3D02B
8870	133	OFTN SPLLS DZZNS		(3D02C)	3D02C	3D02C	3D02C	3D02C	3D02C	3D02C	3D02C
8880	133	OFTN HNDS TRMBLE		(3D02D)	3D02D	3D02D	3D02D	3D02D	3D02D	3D02D	3D02D
8890	133	OFTN HNDS SWEATG		(3D02E)	3D02E	3D02E	3D02E	3D02E	3D02E	3D02E	3D02E
8900	134	OFTN CDNT GT GNG		(3D02F)	3D02F	3D02F	3D02F	3D02F	3D02F	3D02F	3D02F
20690		ATTN TO NUTRITON					2E15A				
20700		MIN CHOLESTEROL					2E15B				
20710		AVOID ADDITIVES					2E15C				
20720		TRY GET EXERCISE					2E15D				
20730		CNTRL OWN HEALTH					2E16				
20740	117	OFTN EAT BRKFST					2E17A	2E17A	2E17A	2E20A	2E20A
20750	117	OFTN EAT GN VEG					2E17B	2E17B	2E17B	2E20B	2E20B
20760	117	OFTN EAT FRUIT					2E17C	2E17C	2E17C	2E20C	2E20C
20770	117	OFTN EXERCISE					2E17D	2E17D	2E17D	2E20D	2E20D
20780	117	OFTN 7HRS SLEEP					2E17E	2E17E	2E17E	2E20E	2E20E
20790	118	OFTN SLEEP <SHLD					2E17F	2E17F	2E17F	2E20F	2E20F
21310	86	#DA HEADACHE								1D015A	1D015A
21320	86	#DA SORE THROAT								1D015B	1D015B
21330	86	#DA SINUS CONG								1D015C	1D015C
21340	86	#DA COUGHING								1D015D	1D015D
21350	86	#DA CHEST COLD								1D015E	1D015E
21360	87	#DA COUGH PHLM								1D015F	1D015F
21370	87	#DA SHORT BRTH								1D015G	1D015G
21380	87	#DA WHEEZING								1D015H	1D015H
21390	87	#DA TRBL REMEM								1D015I	1D015I
21400	87	#DA DFCT THINK								1D015J	1D015J
21410	87	#DA TRBL LEARN								1D015K	1D015K
21420	88	#DA TRBL SLEEP								1D015L	1D015L
21430	88	#DA TRBL START								1D015M	1D015M
21440	88	#DA STAY HOME								1D015N	1D015N
21450	88	#X/12M DOC-CHEK								1D016A	1D016A
21460	88	#X/12M DOC-FGHT								1D016B	1D016B
21470	88	#X/12M DOC-INJ								1D016C	1D016C
21480	89	#X/12M DOC-ILL								1D016D	1D016D
21490	89	#X/12M DOC-PSY								1D016E	1D016E
21500	89	#X/12M HSP-INJ								1D017A	1D017A
21510	89	#X/12M HSP-ILL								1D017B	1D017B
21520	89	RLTV PHY HEALTH								1D018	1D018

Q07: OTHER PERSONALITY VARIABLES. Importance placed on various life goals

Item Reference Number	Page Loc. in this Volume	ITEM DESCRIPTION (ABBREVIATED)	1975	1976	1977	1978	1979	1980	1981	1982	1983
590	21	HRS/W WRK SCHYR		+C23	+C23	+C23	+C23	+C23	+C23	+C23	+C23
1410	37	IMP B SUCCSS WK		1A007A	1A007A	1A007A	1A007A	1A007A	1A007A	1A007A	1A007A
1420	38	IMP GD MRRG&FAM		1A007B	1A007B	1A007B	1A007B	1A007B	1A007B	1A007B	1A007B
1430	38	IMP LOTS OF $		1A007C	1A007C	1A007C	1A007C	1A007C	1A007C	1A007C	1A007C
1440	38	IMP TM RCRN&HBY		1A007D	1A007D	1A007D	1A007D	1A007D	1A007D	1A007D	1A007D
1450	38	IMP STRG FRDSHP		1A007E	1A007E	1A007E	1A007E	1A007E	1A007E	1A007E	1A007E
1460	38	IMP STEADY WORK		1A007F	1A007F	1A007F	1A007F	1A007F	1A007F	1A007F	1A007F
1470	38	IMP CNTRBTN SOC		1A007G	1A007G	1A007G	1A007G	1A007G	1A007G	1A007G	1A007G
1480	38	IMP LDR COMUNTY		1A007H	1A007H	1A007H	1A007H	1A007H	1A007H	1A007H	1A007H
1490	38	IMP CHLD BTR OPP		1A007I	1A007I	1A007I	1A007I	1A007I	1A007I	1A007I	1A007I

(continued)

Item Reference Number	Page Loc. in this Volume	ITEM DESCRIPTION (ABBREVIATED)	QUESTIONNAIRE LOCATION BY YEAR (FORM, SECTION, AND QUESTION NUMBER)								
			1975	1976	1977	1978	1979	1980	1981	1982	1983

Q07: OTHER PERSONALITY VARIABLES. Importance placed on various life goals (continued)

1500	39	IMP LIV CLS PRNT		1A007J	1A007J	1A007J	1A007J	1A007J	1A007J	1A007J	1A007J
1510	39	IMP GT AWY AREA		1A007K	1A007K	1A007K	1A007K	1A007K	1A007K	1A007K	1A007K
1520	39	IMP CRRCT INEQL		1A007L	1A007L	1A007L	1A007L	1A007L	1A007L	1A007L	1A007L
1530	39	IMP NEW XPRNCE		1A007M	1A007M	1A007M	1A007M	1A007M	1A007M	1A007M	1A007M
1540	39	IMP FND PRPS LF		1A007N	1A007N	1A007N	1A007N	1A007N	1A007N	1A007N	1A007N
10450	154	JOB OBSTC -WK HD		4A13J	4A13J	4A13J	4A13J	4A13J	4A13J	4A13J	4A13J

Q08: OTHER PERSONALITY VARIABLES. Social, political, cultural orientation

6330	97	INTEREST IN GOVT	2A31	2A11	2A11	2A11	2A11	2A11	2A11	2A11	2A11
	156		4A29	3E01	3E01	3E01	3E01	3E01	3E01	4A18	4A18
	181		5A40	4A18	4A18	4A18	4A18	4A18	4A18	5A19	5A19
				5A19	5A19	5A19	5A19	5A19	5A19		
6880	106	THK ABT SOC ISSU	*A06	2D03	2D03	2D03	2D03	2D03	2D03	2D03	2D03
	119			3A02	3A02	3A02	3A02	3A02	3A02	3A02	3A02
	146			4A05	4A05	4A05	4A05	4A05	4A05	4A05	4A05
	173			5A02	5A02	5A02	5A02	5A02	5A02	5A02	5A02
7010	108	2MCH COMPTN SCTY	2A23C	2D05A	2D05A	2D05A	2D05A	2D05A	2D05A	2D05A	2D05A
7020	108	2MANY YNG SLOPPY	2A23H	2D05B	2D05B	2D05B	2D05B	2D05B	2D05B	2D05B	2D05B
7030	108	2MUCH HARD ROCK	2A23I	2D05C	2D05C	2D05C	2D05C	2D05C	2D05C	2D05C	2D05C
7040	108	SHD DO OWN THING	2A23A	2D05D	2D05D	2D05D	2D05D	2D05D	2D05D	2D05D	2D05D
7630	83	R LIKES SCHOOL		1D001	1D001	1D001	1D001	1D001	1D001	1D001	1D001
	115			2E02	2E06	2E06	2E08	2E09	2E09	2E12	2E12
				3E08	3E07	3E07	3E07	3E07	3E07		
				4E10	5E05	5E05	5E03	5E05			
				5E04							
10460	154	JOB OBSTC -CONFM		4A13K	4A13K	4A13K	4A13K	4A13K	4A13K	4A13K	4A13K
17570		PPL SHD CONFORM					5E02A				
17580		PPL SHD LV HRMNY					5E02B				
17590		PPL SHD B FRANK					5E02C				
17600		PPL SHD THK FREE					5E02D				
17610		PPL SHD B INDPNT					5E02E				

Q09: OTHER PERSONALITY VARIABLES. Hostility

19530	113	3MO/DLY ARG PRNT						2E08A	2E08A	2E07A	2E07A
19540	113	3MO/DLY ARG AUTH						2E08B	2E08B	2E07B	2E07B
19550	113	3MO/DLY MAD						2E08C	2E08C	2E07C	2E07C
19560	113	3MO/DLY MAD,SMSH						2E08D	2E08D	2E07D	2E07D
19570	114	3MO/DLY WANT FGT						2E08E	2E08E	2E07E	2E07E
19580	114	3MO/DLY DID FGHT						2E08F	2E08F	2E07F	2E07F

R01: BACKGROUND. Age, sex, race, and marital status

10	16	R'S BIRTH YEAR		+C01	+C01	+C01	+C01	+C01	+C01	+C01	+C01
20	16	R'S BIRTH MONTH		+C02	+C02	+C02	+C02	+C02	+C02	+C02	+C02
30	16	R'S SEX		+C03	+C03	+C03	+C03	+C03	+C03	+C03	+C03
40	16	R'S RACE		+C04	+C04	+C04	+C04	+C04	+C04	+C04	+C04
60	16	R NOT MARRIED		+C06	+C06	+C06	+C06	+C06	+C06	+C06	+C06
8320	125	MARRD OR ENGAGED	3A41	3A18	3A18	3A18	3A18	3A18	3A18	3A18	3A18

R02: BACKGROUND. Family characteristics

310	17	FATHR EDUC LEVEL		+C08	+C08	+C08	+C08	+C08	+C08	+C08	+C08
320	17	MOTHR EDUC LEVEL		+C09	+C09	+C09	+C09	+C09	+C09	+C09	+C09
330	17	MOTH PD JB R YNG		+C10	+C10	+C10	+C10	+C10	+C10	+C10	+C10

R03: BACKGROUND. Living arrangements and household characteristics

50	16	R SPD >TIM R-URB		+C05	+C05	+C05	+C05	+C05	+C05	+C05	+C05
80	17	R'S HSHLD ALONE		+C07A	+C07A	+C07A	+C07A	+C07A	+C07A	+C07A	+C07A
90	17	R'S HSHLD FATHER		+C07B	+C07B	+C07B	+C07B	+C07B	+C07B	+C07B	+C07B
100	17	R'S HSHLD MOTHER		+C07C	+C07C	+C07C	+C07C	+C07C	+C07C	+C07C	+C07C
		(continued)									

Item Reference Number	Page Loc. in this Volume	ITEM DESCRIPTION (ABBREVIATED)	QUESTIONNAIRE LOCATION BY YEAR (FORM, SECTION, AND QUESTION NUMBER)								
			1975	1976	1977	1978	1979	1980	1981	1982	1983

R03: BACKGROUND. Living arrangements and household characteristics (continued)

Item Reference Number	Page Loc.	ITEM DESCRIPTION	1975	1976	1977	1978	1979	1980	1981	1982	1983
110	17	R'S HSHLD BR/SR		+C07D	+C07D	+C07D	+C07D	+C07D	+C07D	+C07D	+C07D
120	17	R'S HSHLD GRPRNT		+C07E	+C07E	+C07E	+C07E	+C07E	+C07E	+C07E	+C07E
130	17	R'S HSHLD SPOUSE		+C07F	+C07F	+C07F	+C07F	+C07F	+C07F	+C07F	+C07F
140	17	R'S HSHLD CHLDRN		+C07G	+C07G	+C07G	+C07G	+C07G	+C07G	+C07G	+C07G
150	17	R'S HSHLD RELTVS		+C07H	+C07H	+C07H	+C07H	+C07H	+C07H	+C07H	+C07H
160	17	R'S HSHLD NONRLT		+C07I	+C07I	+C07I	+C07I	+C07I	+C07I	+C07I	+C07I

S01: DEVIANCE AND VICTIMIZATION. Delinquent behaviors

Item Reference Number	Page Loc.	ITEM DESCRIPTION	1975	1976	1977	1978	1979	1980	1981	1982	1983
6520	100	FRQ FIGHT PARNTS	2A39A	2A19A	2A19A	2A19A	2A19A	2A19A	2A19A	2A19A	2A19A
6530	100	FRQ HIT SUPRVISR	2A39B	2A19B	2A19B	2A19B	2A19B	2A19B	2A19B	2A19B	2A19B
6540	101	FRQ FGT WRK/SCHL	2A39C	2A19C	2A19C	2A19C	2A19C	2A19C	2A19C	2A19C	2A19C
6550	101	FRQ GANG FIGHT	2A39D	2A19D	2A19D	2A19D	2A19D	2A19D	2A19D	2A19D	2A19D
6560	101	FRQ HURT SM1 BAD	2A39E	2A19E	2A19E	2A19E	2A19E	2A19E	2A19E	2A19E	2A19E
6570	101	FRQ THREAT WEAPN	2A39F	2A19F	2A19F	2A19F	2A19F	2A19F	2A19F	2A19F	2A19F
6580	101	FRQ STEAL <$50	2A39G	2A19G	2A19G	2A19G	2A19G	2A19G	2A19G	2A19G	2A19G
6590	101	FRQ STEAL >$50	2A39H	2A19H	2A19H	2A19H	2A19H	2A19H	2A19H	2A19H	2A19H
6600	101	FRQ SHOPLIFT	2A39I	2A19I	2A19I	2A19I	2A19I	2A19I	2A19I	2A19I	2A19I
6610	102	FRQ CAR THEFT	2A39J	2A19J	2A19J	2A19J	2A19J	2A19J	2A19J	2A19J	2A19J
6620	102	FRQ STEAL CAR PT	2A39K	2A19K	2A19K	2A19K	2A19K	2A19K	2A19K	2A19K	2A19K
6630	102	FRQ TRESPAS BLDG	2A39L	2A19L	2A19L	2A19L	2A19L	2A19L	2A19L	2A19L	2A19L
6640	102	FRQ ARSON	2A39M	2A19M	2A19M	2A19M	2A19M	2A19M	2A19M	2A19M	2A19M
6650	102	FRQ DMG SCH PPTY	2A39N	2A19N	2A19N	2A19N	2A19N	2A19N	2A19N	2A19N	2A19N
6660	102	FRQ DMG WK PRPTY	2A39O	2A19O	2A19O	2A19O	2A19O	2A19O	2A19O	2A19O	2A19O
6670	102	FRQ TRUBL POLICE	2A39P	2A19P	2A19P	2A19P	2A19P	2A19P	2A19P	2A19P	2A19P

S02: DEVIANCE AND VICTIMIZATION. Driving violations and accidents

Item Reference Number	Page Loc.	ITEM DESCRIPTION	1975	1976	1977	1978	1979	1980	1981	1982	1983
650	22	#X/12MO R TCKTD		+C28	+C28	+C28	+C28	+C28	+C28	+C28	+C28
660	22	#TCKTS AFT DRNK		+C29A	+C29A	+C29A	+C29A	+C29A	+C29A	+C29A	+C29A
670	22	#TCKTS AFT MARJ		+C29B	+C29B	+C29B	+C29B	+C29B	+C29B	+C29B	+C29B
680	22	#TCKTS AFT OTDG		+C29C	+C29C	+C29C	+C29C	+C29C	+C29C	+C29C	+C29C
690	23	#ACCIDNTS/12 MO		+C30	+C30	+C30	+C30	+C30	+C30	+C30	+C30
700	23	#ACDTS AFT DRNK		+C31A	+C31A	+C31A	+C31A	+C31A	+C31A	+C31A	+C31A
710	23	#ACDTS AFT MARJ		+C31B	+C31B	+C31B	+C31B	+C31B	+C31B	+C31B	+C31B
720	23	#ACDTS AFT OTDG		+C31C	+C31C	+C31C	+C31C	+C31C	+C31C	+C31C	+C31C

S03: DEVIANCE AND VICTIMIZATION. Victimization experiences

Item Reference Number	Page Loc.	ITEM DESCRIPTION	1975	1976	1977	1978	1979	1980	1981	1982	1983
6680	103	SM1 ROB YRS <$50		2A20A	2A20A	2A20A	2A20A	2A20A	2A20A	2A20A	2A20A
6690	103	SM1 ROB YRS >$50		2A20B	2A20B	2A20B	2A20B	2A20B	2A20B	2A20B	2A20B
6700	103	SM1 DMG YR PRPTY		2A20C	2A20C	2A20C	2A20C	2A20C	2A20C	2A20C	2A20C
6710	103	SM1 INJR U W/WPN		2A20D	2A20D	2A20D	2A20D	2A20D	2A20D	2A20D	2A20D
6720	103	SM1 THRTN U W/WP		2A20E	2A20E	2A20E	2A20E	2A20E	2A20E	2A20E	2A20E
6730	103	SM1 INJR YU -WPN		2A20F	2A20F	2A20F	2A20F	2A20F	2A20F	2A20F	2A20F
6740	104	SM1 THRT U W/INJ		2A20G	2A20G	2A20G	2A20G	2A20G	2A20G	2A20G	2A20G
9871	140	SM1 SCL ROB <$50		4E11A	3E10A	3E10A	5E06A	5E08A	5E13A	3E08A	3E08A
9872	140	SM1 SCL ROB >$50		4E11B	3E10B	3E10B	5E06B	5E08B	5E13B	3E08B	3E08B
9873	140	SM1 SCL DMG PRTY		4E11C	3E10C	3E10C	5E06C	5E08C	5E13C	3E08C	3E08C
9874	140	SM1 SCL IN U W/W		4E11D	3E10D	3E10D	5E06D	5E08D	5E13D	3E08D	3E08D
9875	141	SM1 SCL TH U W/W		4E11E	3E10E	3E10E	5E06E	5E08E	5E13E	3E08E	3E08E
9876	141	SM1 SCL IN U -WP		4E11F	3E10F	3E10F	5E06F	5E08F	5E13F	3E08F	3E08F
9877	141	SM1 SCL TH U W/I		4E11G	3E10G	3E10G	5E06G	5EO8G	5E13G	3E08G	3E08G

Appendix A
Sampling Error Estimates and Tables

All of the percentages reported in this volume are really *estimates* of the response percentages that would have been obtained if, instead of using a sample survey, we had asked all high schools throughout the United States to participate, and in all schools that agreed to participate we had invited the whole senior class to fill out the questionnaires. The question naturally arises: How accurate are the present percentage estimates based on a limited number of schools and seniors? For any particular percentage resulting from a sample survey we cannot know exactly how much error has resulted from sampling, but we can make reasonably good estimates of "confidence intervals" — ranges within which the "true" population value is very likely to fall. The word "true" in this context is defined quite narrowly; it refers only to the value that would be found if we had set out to survey the total population — all high school seniors in the United States. Thus this concept of "true" population value does *not* take account of biases that might occur due to refusals, distortion of responses, faulty question wording, and other factors. Each of these sources of possible error is discussed in the "Representativeness and Validity" section of the Introduction to this volume. The reader is urged to review this material and take it into account along with the sampling error estimates included in this appendix.

The estimation of confidence intervals in surveys involving complex samples can be a highly complicated combination of statistical science plus informed judgment. It is an area in which there is no single "right answer" or "best approach." We suspect that many of those using this volume will not be especially interested in *how* we have chosen to solve the problems involved in estimating confidence intervals, so long as we provide guidelines that can be applied in a fairly simple and straightforward manner. This appendix is designed to accomplish that. Appendix B provides a more extensive discussion of how we obtained the confidence intervals shown here, and it also provides guidelines for computing specific confidence intervals for a wider range of possible applications than can be covered in the tables provided in this appendix.

A very rough example of a confidence interval can be stated in these terms: For percentages based on the total sample (all five questionnaire forms), the "true" values are rarely more than 1.5 percent higher or lower than the percentage estimates reported in this volume. How rarely? The chances are much lower than 1 in 20. Indeed, many of the percentages reported for the total sample are accurate to within one percent.

Of course, most of the data reported here are based on items included only in one or another of the five questionnaire forms. Since such percentages are based on only one-fifth of the total sample, they are somewhat less accurate. The loss in accuracy is less than might be imagined, however, for reasons spelled out in Appendix B. For present purposes, it is enough to say that percentages based on 3,000 or more seniors responding to one questionnaire form are rarely (less than 1 in 20) farther than 2.4 percent away from the "true" value.

We have thus far provided two very rough illustrations of confidence intervals — a range of ± 1.5 percent for percentages based on the total sample, and a range of ± 2.4 percent for percentages based on the number of seniors responding to one questionnaire form. While these two intervals provide some notion of the overall range of accuracy of the sample, they fall short of our needs in a number of respects. We need to be able to assign confidence intervals for subgroups such as males, females, those who plan to complete college, and so forth, all of which involve smaller numbers of cases and thus some reduction in accuracy. We also need to take account of the fact that, other things equal, confidence intervals grow smaller when one moves from the middle of the scale (percentages near 50 percent) to the extremes (e.g., 4 percent or 96 percent). Further, we need to provide guidelines for evaluating the *difference* between two percentages; for example, we may wish to know whether the difference between male and female percentages in response to a particular question is large enough so that it is not likely to be merely the result of sampling error. Another type of difference of considerable interest is that between percentages from two different years; for example, we may wish to know whether an increase in the percentage of daily marijuana users from one year to the next is large enough to be considered a statistically significant change.

Each of the requirements mentioned above is taken into account in the tables of confidence intervals which follow.

Confidence Intervals for Single Percentages

Table A-1 provides confidence intervals for single percentages that are reasonably good approximations for most *variables* and for most *subgroups* (as well as for the total sample). The table entries slightly underestimate the confidence intervals for regional subgroups and for blacks. These underestimates can be corrected reasonably well by multiplying the entries in Table A-1 by a factor of 1.1 for data based on a single form and by a factor of 1.33 for data based on all five forms. A more serious problem is that the table entries substantially underestimate the confidence intervals for certain variables which tend to be somewhat homogeneous within schools, as well as other factors likely to show clustering according to geographical area or socioeconomic level. A discussion of some of these variables is provided at the end of this appendix.

Table A-1 accommodates various numbers of cases (presented as different columns in the table), and various percentages (presented as different rows in the table). The table entries, when added to and subtracted from the observed percentage, establish the 95 percent confidence interval (calculated as 1.96 sampling errors). Thus, for example, to determine the accuracy of a result of 67.4 percent based on a sample of 1,632 cases, one should first look for the closest values in the table (in this case, about 70 percent and a number of cases approximately equal to 1,500); next determine the values to be added to and subtracted from the observed percentage (in this case the values

would be + 2.8 percent and − 2.9 percent); and then compute the confidence interval around the observed percentage of 67.4 percent (in this case an interval ranging from 64.5 percent to 70.2 percent). This procedure yields an interval such that, for most variables, the chances are 95 in 100 that if all high school seniors in the country had been asked to participate in the survey the resulting percentage would fall within the interval.

Confidence Intervals for Differences between Two Percentages

Table A-2 provides confidence intervals for differences between certain percentages. Specifically, the table can be used for *comparisons* between males and females, between those who do and do not plan to complete four years of college, and between those falling into different categories of the five-level index of drug usage. The above comparisons are appropriate for data from any single year (e.g., male seniors in 1976 compared with female seniors in 1976, or the "marijuana only" seniors in 1977 compared with the "no illicit drugs" seniors in 1977). Table A-2 is also useful in assessing *one-year* trends for any of the above subgroups as well as for the total sample. For example, one may be interested in a confidence interval (or significance level) for the difference between the percentage of female seniors in 1977 who used marijuana and the percentage of female seniors in 1978 who did so. The values in Table A-2 are appropriate for confidence intervals across adjacent years (e.g., 1976 compared with 1977), provided the same subgroup (e.g., females) is being considered both years. The confidence intervals for comparisons across non-adjacent years (e.g., 1976 compared with 1978), are slightly larger.

With appropriate corrections, the entries in Table A-2 can be used for trends covering more than one year and for trends or comparisons involving regional subgroups and blacks. Each of these applications requires some upward adjustment of the table entries; guidelines for such adjustments are provided in the notes accompanying Table A-2.

For information on the derivation of Table A-2 and for guidelines to be used in computing confidence intervals not covered in that table, the reader is referred to Appendix B.

In order to find the appropriate confidence interval in Table A-2, one must first locate that portion of the table which deals with percentage values closest to the two percentages being compared (for example, if one wished to compare a value of 28.1 percent with one of 35.4 percent, the "p = 30 percent or 70 percent" portion of the table would be closest). The next step is to locate the specific table entry which corresponds most closely to the numbers of cases involved in the two percentages being compared (e.g., if those numbers were 1,478 and 1,563 for 28.1 percent and 35.4 percent, the correct table entry would be 3.9 percent). That table entry, when added to and subtracted from the difference between the two percentages, yields the 95 percent confidence interval for the difference. (In the above illustration that would be 7.3 percent ± 3.9 percent or an interval from 3.4 percent to 11.2 percent.) The chances are only 1 in 20 that the "true" difference between two percentages lies outside of this interval.

Another use of Table A-2 is to test whether a difference between two percentages is "statistically significant." If the table entry is smaller than the difference between the two percentages (as is true in the above illustration), then the difference is statistically significant at the 95 percent level (sometimes indicated as p<.05).

Some Cautions

The tables provided here are based on averages of large numbers of sampling errors computed across a wide range of the variables which appear in this volume, as well as across all of the subgroups for which data are reported here. We are confident that the values in the tables are reasonably accurate for most purposes, but we must repeat the caution that the tables slightly underestimate confidence intervals for the following groups and comparisons:

> Blacks
> Regions (Northeast, North Central,
>   South, West)
> Comparisons among regions
> Comparisons across non-adjacent years
>   (e.g., 1976 vs. 1978)

A more important problem is that the tables substantially underestimate the confidence intervals for certain variables that, for various reasons, show greater than average homogeneity within schools. After an extensive, but by no means exhaustive, sampling of the kinds of variables which might show such clustering by school, we can provide the following examples of the kinds of variables for which Tables A-1 and A-2 substantially underestimate the confidence intervals.

Variables Related to Educational Background and Aspirations. The questionnaire items dealing with father's education, mother's education, high school curriculum (college preparatory versus all other), and plans for completing four years of college, all show an appreciable amount of clustering by school. Accordingly, for such variables the confidence intervals provided in the tables should be doubled.

Other items dealing with plans for technical/vocational schooling, a two-year college program, or graduate/professional study, also require adjustment. The confidence intervals in the tables should be multiplied by a factor of 1.5 in order to be applicable to these variables.

It seems clear that the common factor underlying these particular variables is the tendency for family socioeconomic level to be somewhat homogeneous within school districts — some schools serve wealthier populations than others. That makes the form of sampling we use somewhat less efficient for measuring those variables (like those listed above) which are closely associated with family socioeconomic level. Therefore, we urge the reader to treat with caution any variables which are likely to be strongly linked to socioeconomic factors. In the absence of more specific computations of sampling errors, a good rule of thumb for dealing with such variables would be to double the confidence intervals provided in Tables A-1 and A-2.

Variables Related to Geographic Location. Another category of variables which are somewhat homogeneous within schools and school districts consists of those things which reflect differences in region and/or urbanicity. An obvious example is a background question asking where the respondent grew up; the response category "on a farm" shows a very high degree of clustering within schools. One would have to more than double the confidence intervals in the tables to deal with such a measure. Similarly high clustering was found for some responses about religious preference; for example, those whose preference is Baptist are located primarily in the South (and probably heavily in rural areas), whereas those whose preference is Jewish are located primarily in the Northeast (especially in larger cities). The confidence intervals in Tables A-1 and A-2 should be multiplied by a factor as large as 3 in order to be applicable to such variables.

Other variables which show some greater than average homogeneity within schools include such ideologically related dimensions as frequency of attending religious services, importance of religion, and political preference. Still other variables showing high homogeneity, probably because of their association with urbanicity, include driving (percentage who usually do not drive at all), working (percentage with no job), and household composition (percentage with father not living in the home). For each of the variables mentioned in this paragraph, the confidence intervals shown in Tables A-1 and A-2 should be multiplied by a factor of about 1.5.

Variables Involving Use of Alcohol and Marijuana. Extensive work has been done to compute sampling errors and confidence intervals for the drug use measures included in this volume (see Johnston, Bachman, and O'Malley, 1977, 1979, especially Appendix B). Most drug use variables show sampling errors which lie within the range of those provided in Tables A-1 and A-2. Usage levels for alcohol and marijuana, however, show some degree of homogeneity within schools, thus requiring that the table levels be adjusted. For items dealing with alcohol use, the entries in Table A-1 should be multiplied by a factor of 1.6; for items dealing with marijuana use, the correction factor is 1.35.

As noted earlier, this appendix has presented guidelines for using the tables of confidence intervals provided herein. Those readers interested in learning more about the rationale underlying such tables, the procedures used to derive the particular tables presented here, and guidelines for further computations of confidence intervals may consult Appendix B of this volume.

Notes to Table A-1

Caution: The entries in this table systematically underestimate confidence intervals for regional subgroups and for blacks. In order to correct these underestimates, the table entries should be multiplied by a factor of 1.10 for data from a single form and by a factor of 1.33 for data based on five forms. Further cautions and corrections are required for some specific variables which relate to educational background and aspirations, geographic location, and the use of alcohol and marijuana (see discussion in the final sections of Appendix A).

The values in this table, when added to and subtracted from an observed percentage, establish the 95 percent confidence interval around that percentage, incorporating a design effect. Table values were calculated using the following formula (adapted from Hays, 1973, p. 379): ·

$$\text{lower limit} = p - \frac{2N'p + (1.96)^2 - 1.96\sqrt{4N'p\,(1-p) + (1.96)^2}}{2[N' + (1.96)^2]}$$

$$\text{upper limit} = \frac{2N'p + (1.96)^2 + 1.96\sqrt{4N'p\,(1-p) + (1.96)^2}}{2[N' + (1.96)^2]} - p$$

where p = the percentage, and N' is the "effective N," $N' = N/(1.3 + .00015N)$. (See Appendix B for a discussion of the concept of "effective N.")

Table A-1

Confidence Intervals (95% Level) around Percentage Values

Number of Cases

	100	200	300	400	500	700	1000	1500	2000	2500	3000	3500	4000	5000	7000	10000	15000	20000
99%+	0.9	0.8	0.7	0.7	0.6	0.6	0.5	0.5	0.4	0.4	0.4	0.4	0.3	0.3	0.3	0.3	0.3	0.2
−	5.6	3.2	2.4	1.9	1.7	1.3	1.1	0.8	0.7	0.6	0.6	0.6	0.5	0.5	0.4	0.4	0.3	0.3
97%+	2.1	1.8	1.6	1.4	1.3	1.2	1.0	0.9	0.8	0.8	0.7	0.7	0.6	0.6	0.6	0.5	0.5	0.5
−	6.6	4.1	3.2	2.6	2.3	1.9	1.6	1.3	1.1	1.0	0.9	0.9	0.8	0.8	0.7	0.6	0.6	0.5
95%+	3.1	2.5	2.2	2.0	1.8	1.6	1.4	1.2	1.1	1.0	0.9	0.9	0.9	0.8	0.7	0.7	0.6	0.6
−	7.4	4.7	3.7	3.1	2.7	2.3	1.9	1.5	1.4	1.2	1.1	1.1	1.0	0.9	0.8	0.8	0.7	0.7
90%+	4.9	3.8	3.3	2.9	2.7	2.3	2.0	1.7	1.5	1.4	1.3	1.3	1.2	1.1	1.0	0.9	0.9	0.8
−	8.8	5.8	4.6	4.0	3.5	2.9	2.5	2.0	1.8	1.6	1.5	1.4	1.4	1.3	1.1	1.0	0.9	0.9
85%+	6.6	4.8	4.1	3.6	3.3	2.9	2.5	2.1	1.9	1.7	1.6	1.5	1.5	1.4	1.2	1.1	1.0	1.0
−	9.7	6.6	5.3	4.5	4.0	3.4	2.9	2.4	2.1	1.9	1.8	1.7	1.6	1.5	1.3	1.2	1.1	1.1
80%+	7.4	5.6	4.7	4.2	3.8	3.3	2.8	2.4	2.1	2.0	1.8	1.7	1.7	1.5	1.4	1.3	1.2	1.1
−	10.3	7.1	5.7	4.9	4.4	3.7	3.1	2.6	2.3	2.1	2.0	1.8	1.8	1.6	1.5	1.3	1.2	1.2
70%+	9.1	6.8	5.6	5.0	4.5	3.9	3.3	2.8	2.5	2.3	2.1	2.0	1.9	1.8	1.6	1.5	1.4	1.3
−	11.1	7.7	6.3	5.5	4.9	4.2	3.5	2.9	2.6	2.4	2.2	2.1	2.0	1.8	1.7	1.5	1.4	1.3
50%+	11.0	7.9	6.5	5.7	5.1	4.4	3.7	3.1	2.8	2.5	2.4	2.2	2.1	2.0	1.8	1.6	1.5	1.4
−	11.0	7.9	6.5	5.7	5.1	4.4	3.7	3.1	2.8	2.5	2.4	2.2	2.1	2.0	1.8	1.6	1.5	1.4
30%+	11.1	7.7	6.3	5.5	4.9	4.2	3.5	2.9	2.6	2.4	2.2	2.1	2.0	1.8	1.7	1.5	1.4	1.3
−	9.1	6.8	5.6	5.0	4.5	3.9	3.3	2.8	2.5	2.3	2.1	2.0	1.9	1.8	1.6	1.5	1.4	1.3
20%+	10.3	7.1	5.7	4.9	4.4	3.7	3.1	2.6	2.3	2.1	2.0	1.8	1.8	1.6	1.5	1.3	1.2	1.2
−	7.4	5.6	4.7	4.2	3.8	3.3	2.8	2.4	2.1	2.0	1.6	1.7	1.7	1.5	1.4	1.3	1.2	1.1
15%+	9.7	6.6	5.3	4.5	4.0	3.4	2.9	2.4	2.1	1.9	1.8	1.7	1.6	1.5	1.3	1.2	1.1	1.1
−	6.3	4.8	4.1	3.6	3.3	2.9	2.5	2.1	1.9	1.7	1.6	1.5	1.5	1.4	1.2	1.1	1.0	1.0
10%+	8.8	5.8	4.6	4.0	3.5	2.9	2.5	2.0	1.8	1.6	1.5	1.4	1.4	1.3	1.1	1.0	0.9	0.9
−	4.9	3.8	3.3	2.9	2.7	2.3	2.0	1.7	1.5	1.4	1.3	1.3	1.2	1.1	1.0	0.9	0.9	0.8
5%+	7.4	4.7	3.7	3.1	2.7	2.3	1.9	1.5	1.4	1.2	1.1	1.1	1.0	0.9	0.8	0.8	0.7	0.7
−	3.1	2.5	2.2	2.0	1.8	1.6	1.4	1.2	1.1	1.0	0.9	0.9	0.9	0.8	0.7	0.7	0.6	0.6
3%+	6.6	4.1	3.2	2.6	2.3	1.9	1.6	1.3	1.1	1.0	0.9	0.9	0.8	0.8	0.7	0.6	0.6	0.5
−	2.1	1.8	1.6	1.4	1.3	1.2	1.0	0.9	0.8	0.8	0.7	0.7	0.6	0.6	0.6	0.5	0.5	0.5
1%+	5.6	3.2	2.4	1.9	1.7	1.3	1.1	0.8	0.7	0.6	0.6	0.6	0.5	0.5	0.4	0.4	0.3	0.3
−	0.9	0.8	0.7	0.7	0.6	0.6	0.5	0.5	0.4	0.4	0.4	0.4	0.3	0.3	0.3	0.3	0.3	0.2

Notes to Table A-2

The entries in this table (which appear on the next two pages) are appropriate for *comparisons* between (a) males and females, (b) those who do and do not plan four years of college, and (c) those falling into different categories of the five-level index of drug usage. The table entries are also appropriate for *one-year trends* for the total sample and any of the subgroups except region. Most other trends and subgroup comparisons require that the table entries be multiplied by an adjustment factor, given below.

Outline of Steps to Follow (see text of appendix for illustrations)

1. Locate the portion of the table with "p" values closest to the two percentages being compared.

2. Locate the specific entry closest to the weighted Ns for the two percentages.

3. Multiply that entry by any necessary adjustment factor (see below).

4. That table value (or adjusted table value), when added to and subtracted from the difference between the two percentages, yields the 95 percent confidence interval for the difference.

5. Also, if the table value (or adjusted table value) is smaller than the difference between the two percentages, then the difference may be described as "statistically significant at the 95 percent level."

	Adjustment Factor (to be multiplied by table entry)
Adjustment Factors	
For comparisons between blacks and whites	
based on single form data	*
based on five form data	1.25
For comparisons between any two regions	
based on single form data	1.15
based on five form data	1.50
For one-year trends involving any region	
based on single form data	*
based on five form data	1.25
For trends over two or more years involving any region	
based on single form data	*
based on five form data	1.35
For trends over two or more years involving all other groups	
based on single form data	*
based on five form data	1.15

*indicates that no adjustment is necessary for category shown

NOTE: The table entries were calculated using the following formula: $1.96\sqrt{p(1-p)\left[\frac{1}{N'_1}+\frac{1}{N'_2}\right]}$

where $N'_1 = N_1/\text{DEFF}$, and $N'_2 = N_2/\text{DEFF}$, $\text{DEFF} = 1.3 + .000075\left[\frac{N_1 N_2}{N_1 + N_2}\right]$

Table A-2

Confidence Intervals (95% Confidence Level) for Differences Between Two Percentages

p = 1% or 99%

	$N_1 = 100$	200	300	400	500	700	1000	1500	2000	3000	4000	5000	7000	10000	15000	20000
$N_2 = 100$	3.2															
200	2.7	2.2														
300	2.6	2.0	1.8													
400	2.5	1.9	1.7	1.6												
500	2.4	1.9	1.6	1.5	1.4											
700	2.4	1.8	1.6	1.4	1.3	1.2										
1000	2.3	1.7	1.5	1.3	1.2	1.1	1.0									
1500	2.3	1.7	1.4	1.3	1.2	1.0	0.9	0.8								
2000	2.3	1.7	1.4	1.2	1.1	1.0	0.9	0.8	0.7							
3000	2.3	1.6	1.4	1.2	1.1	1.0	0.8	0.7	0.7	0.6						
4000	2.3	1.6	1.4	1.2	1.1	0.9	0.8	0.7	0.7	0.6	0.6					
5000	2.3	1.6	1.3	1.2	1.1	0.9	0.8	0.7	0.6	0.6	0.5	0.5				
7000	2.3	1.6	1.3	1.2	1.1	0.9	0.8	0.7	0.6	0.5	0.5	0.5	0.4			
10000	2.2	1.6	1.3	1.2	1.0	0.9	0.8	0.7	0.6	0.5	0.5	0.5	0.4	0.4		
15000	2.2	1.6	1.3	1.2	1.0	0.9	0.8	0.6	0.6	0.5	0.5	0.4	0.4	0.4	0.4	
20000	2.2	1.6	1.3	1.1	1.0	0.9	0.8	0.6	0.6	0.5	0.5	0.4	0.4	0.4	0.3	0.3

p = 3% or 97%

	$N_1 = 100$	200	300	400	500	700	1000	1500	2000	3000	4000	5000	7000	10000	15000	20000
$N_2 = 100$	5.4															
200	4.7	3.8														
300	4.4	3.5	3.1													
400	4.3	3.3	2.9	2.7												
500	4.2	3.2	2.8	2.6	2.4											
700	4.1	3.1	2.7	2.4	2.3	2.1										
1000	4.0	3.0	2.5	2.3	2.1	1.9	1.8									
1500	4.0	2.9	2.4	2.2	2.0	1.8	1.6	1.5								
2000	3.9	2.9	2.4	2.1	1.9	1.7	1.5	1.4	1.3							
3000	3.9	2.8	2.3	2.1	1.9	1.7	1.5	1.3	1.2	1.1						
4000	3.9	2.8	2.3	2.0	1.9	1.6	1.4	1.2	1.1	1.0	0.9					
5000	3.9	2.8	2.3	2.0	1.8	1.6	1.4	1.2	1.1	1.0	0.9	0.9				
7000	3.9	2.8	2.3	2.0	1.8	1.6	1.4	1.2	1.0	0.9	0.9	0.8	0.8			
10000	3.9	2.8	2.3	2.0	1.8	1.5	1.3	1.1	1.0	0.9	0.8	0.8	0.7	0.7		
15000	3.8	2.7	2.3	2.0	1.8	1.5	1.3	1.1	1.0	0.9	0.8	0.7	0.7	0.6	0.6	
20000	3.8	2.7	2.3	2.0	1.8	1.5	1.3	1.1	1.0	0.9	0.8	0.7	0.7	0.6	0.6	0.6

Table A-2 (continued)

$p = 5\%$ or 95%

$N_1 =$	100	200	300	400	500	700	1000	1500	2000	3000	4000	5000	7000	10000	15000	20000
$N_2 = 100$	6.9															
200	6.0	4.9														
300	5.6	4.5	4.0													
400	5.5	4.3	3.8	3.5												
500	5.4	4.1	3.6	3.3	3.1											
700	5.2	3.9	3.4	3.1	2.9	2.7										
1000	5.1	3.8	3.2	2.9	2.7	2.5	2.2									
1500	5.1	3.7	3.1	2.8	2.6	2.3	2.1	1.9								
2000	5.0	3.6	3.1	2.7	2.5	2.2	2.0	1.7	1.6							
3000	5.0	3.6	3.0	2.6	2.4	2.1	1.9	1.6	1.5	1.4						
4000	5.0	3.6	3.0	2.6	2.4	2.1	1.8	1.6	1.4	1.3	1.2					
5000	4.9	3.6	2.9	2.6	2.3	2.0	1.8	1.5	1.4	1.2	1.2	1.1				
7000	4.9	3.5	2.9	2.6	2.3	2.0	1.7	1.5	1.3	1.2	1.1	1.0	1.0			
10000	4.9	3.5	2.9	2.5	2.3	2.0	1.7	1.4	1.3	1.1	1.1	1.0	0.9	0.9		
15000	4.9	3.5	2.9	2.5	2.3	2.0	1.7	1.4	1.3	1.1	1.0	1.0	0.9	0.8	0.8	
20000	4.9	3.5	2.9	2.5	2.3	1.9	1.7	1.4	1.3	1.1	1.0	0.9	0.9	0.8	0.7	0.7

$p = 10\%$ or 90%

$N_1 =$	100	200	300	400	500	700	1000	1500	2000	3000	4000	5000	7000	10000	15000	20000
$N_1 = 100$	9.5															
200	8.2	6.7														
300	7.8	6.2	5.5													
400	7.5	5.9	5.2	4.8												
500	7.4	5.7	4.9	4.6	4.3											
700	7.2	5.4	4.7	4.3	4.0	3.7										
1000	7.1	5.2	4.5	4.0	3.7	3.4	3.1									
1500	7.0	5.1	4.3	3.8	3.5	3.2	2.8	2.6								
2000	6.9	5.0	4.2	3.7	3.4	3.0	2.7	2.4	2.2							
3000	6.9	4.9	4.1	3.6	3.3	2.9	2.6	2.2	2.1	1.9						
4000	6.8	4.9	4.1	3.6	3.3	2.8	2.5	2.2	2.0	1.8	1.7					
5000	6.8	4.9	4.0	3.6	3.2	2.8	2.4	2.1	1.9	1.7	1.6	1.5				
7000	6.8	4.9	4.0	3.5	3.2	2.8	2.4	2.0	1.8	1.6	1.5	1.4	1.3			
10000	6.8	4.8	4.0	3.5	3.2	2.7	2.3	2.0	1.8	1.6	1.4	1.4	1.3	1.2		
15000	6.8	4.8	4.0	3.5	3.1	2.7	2.3	2.0	1.8	1.5	1.4	1.3	1.2	1.1	1.1	
20000	6.8	4.8	4.0	3.5	3.1	2.7	2.3	1.9	1.7	1.5	1.4	1.3	1.2	1.1	1.0	1.0

Table A-2 (continued)

p = 15% or 85%

	$N_1 = 100$	200	300	400	500	700	1000	1500	2000	3000	4000	5000	7000	10000	15000	20000
$N_2 = 100$	11.3															
200	9.8	8.0														
300	9.3	7.3	6.6													
400	9.0	7.0	6.2	5.7												
500	8.8	6.7	5.9	5.4	5.1											
700	8.6	6.5	5.6	5.1	4.8	4.4										
1000	8.4	6.2	5.3	4.8	4.5	4.0	3.7									
1500	8.3	6.1	5.1	4.6	4.2	3.8	3.4	3.0								
2000	8.2	6.0	5.0	4.5	4.1	3.6	3.2	2.9	2.7							
3000	8.2	5.9	4.9	4.3	3.9	3.5	3.0	2.7	2.5	2.2						
4000	8.1	5.8	4.9	4.3	3.9	3.4	2.9	2.6	2.3	2.1	2.0					
5000	8.1	5.8	4.8	4.2	3.8	3.3	2.9	2.5	2.3	2.0	1.9	1.8				
7000	8.1	5.8	4.8	4.2	3.8	3.3	2.8	2.4	2.2	1.9	1.8	1.7	1.6			
10000	8.1	5.8	4.8	4.2	3.8	3.2	2.8	2.4	2.1	1.9	1.7	1.6	1.5	1.4		
15000	8.1	5.7	4.7	4.1	3.7	3.2	2.7	2.3	2.1	1.8	1.7	1.6	1.4	1.3	1.3	
20000	8.0	5.7	4.7	4.1	3.7	3.2	2.7	2.3	2.1	1.8	1.6	1.5	1.4	1.3	1.2	1.2

p = 20% or 80%

	$N_1 = 100$	200	300	400	500	700	1000	1500	2000	3000	4000	5000	7000	10000	15000	20000
$N_2 = 100$	12.7															
200	11.0	9.0														
300	10.4	8.2	7.4													
400	10.0	7.8	6.9	6.4												
500	9.8	7.5	6.6	6.1	5.7											
700	9.6	7.2	6.2	5.7	5.3	4.9										
1000	9.4	7.0	6.0	5.4	5.0	4.5	4.1									
1500	9.3	6.8	5.7	5.1	4.7	4.2	3.8	3.4								
2000	9.2	6.7	5.6	5.0	4.6	3.6	3.2	3.0								
3000	9.1	6.6	5.5	4.9	4.4	3.9	3.4	3.0	2.8	2.5						
4000	9.1	6.5	5.4	4.8	4.3	3.8	3.3	2.9	2.6	2.4	2.2					
5000	9.1	6.5	5.4	4.7	4.3	3.7	3.2	2.8	2.6	2.3	2.1	2.0				
7000	9.1	6.5	5.4	4.7	4.2	3.7	3.2	2.7	2.5	2.2	2.0	1.9	1.8			
10000	9.0	6.5	5.3	4.7	4.2	3.6	3.1	2.7	2.4	2.1	1.9	1.8	1.7	1.6		
15000	9.0	6.4	5.3	4.6	4.2	3.6	3.1	2.6	2.3	2.0	1.9	1.7	1.6	1.5	1.4	
20000	9.0	6.4	5.3	4.6	4.2	3.6	3.1	2.6	2.3	2.0	1.8	1.7	1.6	1.5	1.4	1.3

Table A-2 (continued)

$N_1 =$ 100	200	300	400	500	700	1000	1500	2000	3000	4000	5000	7000	10000	15000	20000
$N_2 =$ 100 14.5															
200 12.6	10.3														
300 11.9	9.4	8.4													
400 11.5	8.9	7.9	7.3												
500 11.3	8.6	7.6	7.0	6.6							$p = 30\%$ or 70%				
700 11.0	8.3	7.2	6.5	6.1	5.6										
1000 10.8	8.0	6.8	6.2	5.7	5.2	4.7									
1500 10.6	7.8	6.6	5.9	5.4	4.8	4.3	3.9								
2000 10.6	7.7	6.4	5.7	5.2	4.6	4.1	3.7	3.4							
3000 10.5	7.6	6.3	5.6	5.1	4.4	3.9	3.4	3.2	2.9						
4000 10.4	7.5	6.2	5.5	5.0	4.3	3.8	3.3	3.0	2.7	2.5					
5000 10.4	7.5	6.2	5.4	4.9	4.3	3.7	3.2	2.9	2.6	2.4	2.3				
7000 10.4	7.4	6.1	5.4	4.9	4.2	3.6	3.1	2.5	2.3	2.2	2.1				
10000 10.4	7.4	6.1	5.3	4.8	4.2	3.6	3.0	2.7	2.4	2.2	2.1	1.9	1.8		
15000 10.3	7.4	6.1	5.3	4.8	4.1	3.5	3.0	2.7	2.3	2.1	2.0	1.8	1.7	1.6	
20000 10.3	7.4	6.1	5.3	4.8	4.1	3.5	3.0	2.6	2.3	2.1	2.0	1.8	1.7	1.6	1.5

$N_1 =$ 100	200	300	400	500	700	1000	1500	2000	3000	4000	5000	7000	10000	15000	20000
$N_2 =$ 100 15.8															
200 13.7	11.2														
300 13.0	10.3	9.2													
400 12.6	9.8	8.6	8.0												
500 12.3	9.4	8.2	7.6	7.2							$p = 35\%$ or 65%				
700 12.0	9.0	7.8	7.1	6.7	6.1										
1000 11.8	8.7	7.5	6.7	6.2	5.6	5.1									
1500 11.6	8.5	7.2	6.4	5.9	5.3	4.7	4.3								
2000 11.5	8.4	7.0	6.2	5.7	5.1	4.5	4.0	3.7							
3000 11.4	8.2	6.9	6.1	5.5	4.8	4.3	3.7	3.4	3.1						
4000 11.4	8.2	6.8	6.0	5.4	4.7	4.1	3.6	3.3	3.0	2.8					
5000 11.3	8.1	6.7	5.9	5.4	4.7	4.1	3.5	3.2	2.8	2.7	2.5				
7000 11.3	8.1	6.7	5.9	5.3	4.6	4.0	3.4	3.1	2.7	2.5	2.4	2.2			
10000 11.3	8.1	6.7	5.8	5.3	4.5	3.9	3.3	3.0	2.6	2.4	2.3	2.1	2.0		
15000 11.3	8.0	6.6	5.8	5.2	4.5	3.8	3.3	2.9	2.5	2.3	2.2	2.0	1.9	1.8	
20000 11.3	8.0	6.6	5.8	5.2	4.5	3.8	3.2	2.9	2.5	2.3	2.1	2.0	1.8	1.7	1.6

Appendix B
Procedures Used to Derive Design Effects and Sampling Errors

Appendix A provided a very brief and relatively nontechnical explanation of sampling error estimates, accompanied by two tables of confidence intervals which can be used to ascertain the accuracy of most percentages reported in this volume. The present appendix is intended to provide some background concerning the strategy and rationale involved in computing these confidence intervals. It also offers guidance for those wishing to make sampling computations beyond those contained in Appendix A.

This appendix, like the first, is intended to be readable and usable by the nonstatistician. For that reason, we take the time to outline (albeit briefly) a number of relatively elementary factors involved in estimating confidence intervals.

Factors Influencing the Size of Confidence Intervals

The most straightforward types of samples, from a statistical standpoint at least, are simple random samples. In such samples the confidence limits for a proportion are influenced by the size of the sample or subgroups being considered and also by the size of the proportion. For example, the 95 percent confidence interval for a proportion p based on a simple random sample of N cases is approximated by:
$p \pm 1.96 \sqrt{p(1-p)/N}$. In a complex probability sample such as the present one, there are a number of other factors which influence the size of confidence limits. This section lists all of the factors which have been taken into account in calculating confidence intervals for use with the data in this volume, beginning with the most simple factors and then proceeding to the more complex.

Number of Cases (N). Other things equal, the larger a sample (or subgroup within a sample), the smaller or more precise will be the confidence interval for a percentage based on that sample. One of the factors determining the size of the confidence interval is $1/\sqrt{N}$. Thus, for example, if all other things were equal, a sample of 400 would have confidence intervals half as large (or twice as precise) as a sample of 100, because $1/\sqrt{400}$ is half as large as $1/\sqrt{100}$.

Size of Percentage. Other things equal, percentage values around 50 percent have larger confidence intervals than higher or lower percentage values. This is because another of the factors determining the size of the confidence interval is $\sqrt{p(1-p)}$ where p is a proportion ranging from 0 to 1.0 (or, to put it in percentage terms, the factor is $\sqrt{x\%(100-x\%)}$). Thus, for example, a proportion of either .1 or .9 (a percentage of either 10 percent or 90 percent) will have a confidence interval only three-fifths as large as the confidence interval around a proportion of .5 (or 50 percent), because $\sqrt{.1(1-.1)}$ is three-fifths as large as $\sqrt{.5(1-.5)}$.

Design Effects in Complex Samples. Under conditions of simple random sampling, a confidence interval can be determined solely on the basis of the number of cases and the percentage value involved. More complex samples such as the one used in the present study make use of stratification and clustering and often differential weighting of respondent scores, and these all influence sampling error. While stratification tends to heighten the precision of a sample, the effects of clustering and weighting reduce precision (compared with a simple random sample of the same size). Therefore, it is not appropriate to apply the

255

standard, simple random sampling formulas to such complex samples in order to obtain estimates of sampling errors, because they would almost always underestimate the actual sampling errors.

Methods exist for correcting for this underestimation, however. Kish (1965, p. 258) defines a correction term called the design effect (DEFF), where:

$$DEFF = \frac{\text{actual sampling variance}}{\substack{\text{expected sampling variance} \\ \text{from a simple random sample} \\ \text{with same number of elements}}}$$

Thus, if the actual sampling variance in a complex sample is four times as large as the expected sampling variance from a simple random sample with the same number of cases, the DEFF is 4.0. Since confidence intervals are proportionate to the square root of variance, the confidence intervals for such a sample would be twice as large (because the square root of 4 is 2) as the confidence interval for a simple random sample with the same number of cases. A fairly simple and straightforward way of applying the concept of design effect may be to note that an increase in design effect has the same impact on precision as a reduction in the number of cases in a simple random sample. For example, a sample of 16,000 cases with a design effect of 4.0 would have the same degree of precision (the same size confidence intervals around various percentages) as a simple random sample of 4,000.

In principle, every different statistic resulting from a complex sample can have its own design effect, and different statistics in the same sample may have quite different design effects. However, it is not feasible to compute every design effect, nor would it be feasible to report every one. Thus, in practice, design effects are averaged across a number of statistics and these average values are used to estimate the design effects for other statistics based on the same sample. Sometimes a single design effect is applied to all statistics of a given type (e.g., percentages) for a given sample. In the present study, however, a rather extensive exploration of design effects revealed a number of systematic differences. These systematic differences have to do with the particular measures being examined, the subgroups involved, and the question of whether a trend over time is being considered. The most consistent difference involves the number of cases in the group or subgroup for which the design effect is computed.

The Relationship between Subgroup Size and Design Effects. Kish et al. (1976) have observed that design effects tend to be smaller for subgroups than for total samples; moreover, the smaller the subgroup the smaller the design effect is likely to be. The ex-

planation for this widespread phenomenon is that the average number of cases in each sampling cluster is an important factor in determining the size of the design effect, and as subgroup size decreases so does this average number of cases per cluster. This point is illustrated by several subgroups treated in the present volume — males, females, those planning four years of college, and those not planning four years of college. All (or virtually all) of the schools in the sample have both male and female students, as well as some students who plan four years of college and others who do not. Thus, each of these four subgroups is spread more or less evenly across the full number of clusters (schools). Since each of these subgroups includes roughly half of the total sample, the average number of cases per cluster is about half as large as for the total sample, and this leads to a smaller design effect than is found for the total sample. Other subgroups involving different patterns of drug use are also distributed more or less evenly across all clusters and thus are subject to the same phenomenon of smaller design effects because of the smaller number of cases per cluster.

One very important exception to the pattern of smaller design effects for subgroups involves the four geographic region subgroups presented in this volume. These subgroups do not cut across all clusters; instead, regions have been described as "segregated" subgroups, in contrast to the "cross-class" subgroups discussed above. For such segregated subgroups the average number of cases per cluster is about the same as is found in the total sample, and thus the design effects are not lower than those for the total sample (Kish et al., 1976). Another subgroup which is in some respects similar to regional subgroups is the category of blacks. Black respondents are not found equally across high schools throughout the United States. There are, of course, regional differences in proportions of blacks, and these contribute substantially to this lack of equal distribution. In addition, there are patterns of segregation in housing which continue to be reflected in the unequal distribution of blacks in high schools. The net effect of these several factors is that the black subgroup in our sample is "partially segregated" in a sampling sense as well as in the more usual usage of that word. For that reason, the design effects for blacks are somewhat larger than for other subgroups of approximately similar size.

Because the subgroups consisting of blacks and the four regional groups all have larger design effects than other subgroups of the same size, it is necessary to adjust the confidence intervals for these subgroups as indicated in Appendix A. (At a later point in the present appendix we will say more about these adjustment factors.)

One other kind of "subgroup" must be noted in this discussion of the relationship between subgroup size and design effects. One-fifth of the total sample filled out each of the five separate questionnaire forms, and thus the respondents to each of these forms may be viewed as a "cross-class" subgroup of the total sample. The average cluster size for a single form is exactly 20 percent of the average cluster size for the total sample. That means, of course, that the single form samples (which are the basis for the large majority of the data presented in this volume) are distinctly more "efficient" than the sample based on all five forms. Accordingly, single form data have much smaller design effects (as displayed later in this appendix).

Design Effects for Comparisons between Subgroups. We noted above that a number of subgroups treated in this volume can be described as "cross-class" subgroups, meaning that members of the subgroup are distributed more or less evenly across sampling clusters. For these kinds of subgroups, it turns out that *comparisons* are relatively efficient, from a sampling standpoint. The technical explanation for this phenomenon is that there is a higher degree of covariance between such subgroup pairs than would be the case in a comparison of independent subgroups. Now let us offer a fairly nontechnical illustration to indicate why this is so. Suppose that a researcher interested in use of marijuana during the senior year of high school obtained data from five high schools concerning female seniors' marijuana use and data from five other high schools concerning male seniors' marijuana use. Suppose that the percentage values for marijuana use during senior year were as follows:

Female seniors (five schools): 60%, 20%,
   65%, 30%, 50%

Male seniors (five other schools): 40%,
   80%, 25%, 70%, 60%

Even though there is a difference of ten percentage points between males and females (if the five schools in each case are averaged), there is still so much variability among schools that one would not conclude with very much confidence that females in general are less likely than males to use marijuana during the senior year of high school. Suppose, on the other hand, that the researcher had obtained data from a total of only five schools and had obtained data concerning both male and female seniors in each school as follows:

	Females	Males
School A	60%	70%
School B	20%	25%
School C	65%	80%
School D	30%	40%
School E	50%	60%

The same group of percentages, this time based on five pairings of males and females rather than independent observations, are much more strongly suggestive of systematic differences between the sexes.

A process analogous to that illustrated above is involved when "cross-class" subgroups are compared, and the increased accuracy or sampling efficiency is reflected in relatively small sampling errors and design effects.

Design Effects for Trends. Thus far this discussion of factors influencing design effects and confidence intervals has focused only on groups and subgroups within a single year. But one of the central purposes of the Monitoring the Future project is to monitor trends over time; indeed, the study procedures have been standardized across years insofar as possible in order to provide the opportunity for sensitive measurement of change. One of the factors designed to produce an added degree of consistency from one year to the next is the use of each school for two data collections, which means that for any two successive years half of the sample of schools is the same. This, plus the fact that the other half of the school sample in a given year is from the same primary sampling units as the half sample it replaced, means that there is a good deal of consistency in the sampling and clustering of the sample from one year to the next. As a result, when cross-year comparisons are made (say, between 1976 and 1977), the design effects are appreciably smaller (i.e., the efficiency is greater) than if completely independent samples of schools had been drawn each year. In other words, the 1976 and 1977 samples are not independent; on the contrary, there is a considerable degree of covariance between them. A similar level of covariance occurs between any pair of adjacent-year samples (e.g., 1977 and 1978), because about half of the schools in both samples were the same. This covariance, or partial "matching," reduces the design effect for differences observed between adjacent years, compared to what they would have been with totally independent samples.

It follows from the discussion above that a trend over an interval greater than one year (e.g., a comparison between 1976 and 1978 which involves totally non-overlapping school samples) is likely to have a design effect which is larger than that for a comparison between adjacent-year samples.

Variables with Unusually Large Design Effects. Kish et al. (1976) stress the importance of computing sampling errors for many kinds of variables, and they point out that they have found "very wide ranges in values of sampling errors (standard errors and design effects) between diverse variables within the same survey" (p. 21). Our own experience has been that, among most variables, the variation in sampling errors and design effects seems more random than consistent, and thus we are reasonably comfortable with the use of averaging procedures (described below) in order to derive a set of general purpose tables. There are some important exceptions to the above generalization, however. Variables which are likely to be grouped according to geographical area (region and/or urbanicity), as well as variables that may differ systematically from one school to another, show much higher than usual amounts of homogeneity within sample clusters. It follows necessarily that such variables also have much higher than usual design effects. The variables in the Monitoring the Future study which seem most likely to show such high design effects tend to be grouped into the questionnaire segment dealing with background factors and educational aspirations (Section C of all questionnaire forms). These variables were excluded from the process of computing overall design effects and the confidence intervals provided in Tables A-1 and A-2. Appendix A provides a further discussion of some of these variables and offers some suggestions for adjusting the confidence interval tables to deal with them.

Procedures Used in Deriving Design Effects and Tables of Confidence Intervals

Having taken some pains to review the several factors which can influence design effects and confidence intervals, it is now a fairly simple matter for us to summarize the steps followed to compute the tables of confidence intervals shown in Appendix A. We were heavily influenced in this effort by the work of Kish and his colleagues (Kish, 1965; Kish et al., 1976) in two ways. First, we followed their recommendation that sampling errors be computed and averaged across a goodly number of variables and subgroups. Second, we paid particular attention to their observation that design effects tend to be smaller for subgroups than for total samples (a point discussed earlier in this appendix).

Confidence Intervals for Single Percentages. Our procedure was to compute sampling errors and design effects for most of the variables which are common to all five forms (those in the C sections of all questionnaires, and those in the B sections of Forms 2 through 5), and for every twentieth variable in the A, D, and E sections of Forms 2 through 5. (Form 1 was omitted because most of this form is comprised of drug-related items, and such items involve high proportions of missing data because respondents are instructed to skip over many questions which are not applicable to them). Design effects were computed for each of the subgroups reported in this volume, as well as for the total sample. Design effects for each subgroup and for the total were averaged across variables for the C sec-

tion material (all five forms), the B section material (drug use measures, all five forms), and the sampling of variables from the A, D, and E sections (single form data). As noted earlier, the variables which showed unusually high levels of homogeneity within sample clusters were excluded from the C section variables when they were averaged. The 1977 data were used for this analysis. Later replication using 1976 data provided nearly identical values.

The averaging process consisted of taking a mean of the *square roots* of the design effects. Kish and his colleagues (1976) refer to the design effect as DEFF, and to the square root of the design effect as DEFT; thus, $\sqrt{DEFF} = DEFT$. We will find it useful to use this terminology in what follows. The rationale for computing means of DEFT rather than DEFF is that the former value is directly proportionate to the size of confidence intervals. A further reason for doing so is that the values of DEFT approximate a normal distribution much more closely than the values of DEFF, which are skewed upward. (A comparison of mean DEFTs and median DEFTs showed them to be quite similar, something which certainly is not true of mean and median DEFFs).

Bearing in mind that design effects tend to be smaller for subgroups than for total samples, and bearing in mind also that confidence intervals are directly proportionate to DEFT and to $\sqrt{N}$, we plotted the mean DEFT values for the total sample and for all subgroups, in each case relating DEFT to $\sqrt{N}$. The results are shown in Figure B-1. Note that distinctions are made between "cross-class" and "segregated" subgroups, and between mean DEFTs based on five forms and those based on single forms (the $\sqrt{N}$ values for the latter are, of course, much smaller).*

Setting aside the "segregated" subgroups (regions and blacks) for the moment, it is clear that the rest of the mean DEFTs in Figure B-1 show a very clear and consistent pattern: the higher the value $\sqrt{N}$ the higher the mean DEFT. It turns out that these mean DEFT values are very closely approximated by the function DEFT = $\sqrt{1.3 + .00015N}$, as shown by the solid line in the figure. (The function can also be stated as DEFF = 1.3 + .00015N.) The particular parameters in that function were derived empirically, but the basic function (i.e., DEFT = $\sqrt{a + bN}$) was adapted directly from the work of Kish et al. (1976).

Given the above function that fitted the mean DEFT values for the total sample and the "cross-class" subgroups, we returned to the problem of assigning DEFT values for the "segregated" subgroups. The simplest solution was to select two adjustment factors which could be multiplied by the confidence interval values in Table A-1. These adjustment factors are shown by the dashed lines in Figure B-1; they cor-

---

* The five form data consisted of C section material, excluding those variables related to region, urbanicity, and/or socioeconomic level.

Figure B-1
Design Effects for Single Percentages

respond to multiplying the "standard" DEFT (solid line) by a factor of 1.1 for single form data and by a factor of 1.33 for five form data. These adjustments, which were selected on empirical grounds, yield design effects for the "segregated" subgroups which are approximately equal to the design effects for the total sample (treating single form and five form data separately, of course). This is reassuring, since Kish et al. (1976) have reported that "segregated" subgroups can in general be expected to show design effects approximately equivalent to the design effects for the total sample.

After the data in Figure B-1 were plotted and the form of the main function (indicated by the solid line) was determined, DEFT values for drug use measures (material in Section B of all forms) were checked. It was found that the DEFTs for only two drug categories, alcohol and marijuana, exceeded the values indicated by the function; accordingly, adjustment factors were developed for these two drugs (1.6 and 1.35, respectively).

Confidence Intervals for Differences between Two Percentages. Our procedure here was directly parallel to that followed in determining confidence intervals for single percentages. DEFT values for the differences between 1977 and 1976 percentages were computed using virtually the same set of items as used earlier. Also computed were mean DEFT values for comparisons in the same year between subgroups such as males and females, those who did and did not plan to complete four years of college, blacks and whites, pairings of regions, and pairings of drug use groups. It was found that, for any given level of N, the mean DEFT values for subgroup comparisons were quite similar to the mean DEFT values for one-year trends; accordingly, all of these mean DEFTs were included in Figure B-2, which plots mean DEFTs for differences between percentages. In this figure, as in Figure B-1, the strong relationship was evident between mean DEFTs and the numbers of cases in the two groups being compared. This relationship can be very closely approximated by the function DEFT = $\sqrt{1.3 + .000075N}$ (which can also be stated DEFF = 1.3 + .000075N), where N = $2N_1N_2/N_1 + N_2$.

It was expected on grounds of sampling theory that as we found earlier, the function which fit most differences between percentages would not fit differences involving regions and differences involving blacks. In fact, the data indicated that some adjustment is necessary for black-white comparisons using data from all five forms, and also for comparisons as well as trends involving any region. We have not tried to show those adjustments in Figure B-2, but the several values involved are shown in the guidelines to Table A-2.

It was also expected on the grounds of sampling theory that trends across an interval of two or more

years would show somewhat higher values of DEFT than one-year trends. It turned out that this was true only for data from all five forms; data based on one form only did not show significantly higher values. The adjustment factors for trends involving five forms over two or more years are shown in Table A-2.

Use of Weighted Numbers of Cases in Entering Confidence Interval Tables. We should mention in passing that the recommendations for using the tables in Appendix A indicate that *weighted* N values should be used. The computer program which generated our design effect statistics makes use of weights in calculating percentages and actual sampling variances. But in computing the DEFF ratio, defined as the actual sampling variance divided by the expected sampling variance from a simple random sample with the same number of elements, the program makes use of the *unweighted* numbers of cases to determine "the same number of elements." Since the mean weights used in the 1975, 1976, and 1977 data tables are slightly lower than 1.0, this means that when entering the tables in Appendix A with weighted data from those years, one is being very slightly "conservative" (slightly reduced risk of a Type 1 error, slightly increased risk of a Type 2 error). It is important to realize that if one took the trouble to make corrections for this "conservatism," the correction would rarely be as great as multiplying the Table A-1 and Table A-2 entries by a factor of .95; and in the large majority of cases the correction would involve multiplying by a factor of about .98. We find such discrepancies to be trivially small, particularly when compared with what Kish et al. (1976, p. 12) describe as the "heroic simplifications" required in some of the steps leading to general purpose tables of design effects and confidence intervals.

Before the 1978 data tables were produced we had come to realize the advantages in having weighted values which averaged 1.0; accordingly, beginning with the 1978 data, the weighted N values in the tables do approximate the actual numbers of cases quite closely. But it was impractical to redo the 1975 through 1977 data tables to incorporate this refinement. Another alternative would have been to employ slightly different versions of Tables A-1 and A-2, containing slightly different confidence intervals for each of those three years; however, we felt that such an approach could introduce confusion when cross-year comparisons were made. Thus, we opted for the solution which seems to us to be most simple and manageable, even though it involves the slight degree of "conservatism" noted above. For readers who find this solution undesirable, we have included Tables B-1 and B-2, which present weighted and unweighted Ns for the various subgroups for each year. Table B-1 contains Ns for all five forms (except for 1975 which shows Ns for Forms 2 through 5), and Table B-2 con-

Figure B-2
Design Effects for Differences Between Percentages

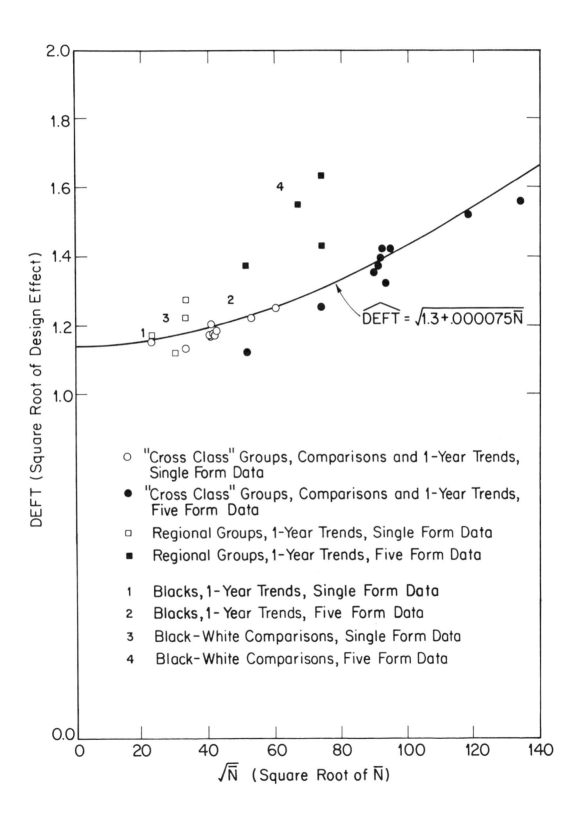

tains approximate Ns for a single form. Thus, readers who wish to avoid the slight "conservatism" (and also to be more precise for subgroups in 1978 and later whose average weight is not exactly 1.0) may determine the unweighted Ns. Some correction for missing data should be made in this case; this can be accomplished by calculating the percentage of missing data (using the weighted Ns from the data table and the weighted N from Table B-1 or B-2) and adjusting the unweighted N accordingly. These adjusted unweighted Ns can then be used in Appendix A.

TABLE B-1

Sample Sizes (Unweighted and Weighted) in Subgroups by Year

Number of Cases

	Class of 1975*		Class of 1976		Class of 1977		Class of 1978		Class of 1979		Class of 1980		Class of 1981		Class of 1982		Class of 1983	
	Unwtd	Wtd	Unwtd	Wtd	Unwtd	Wtd	Unwtd	Wtd	Unwtd	Wtd	Unwtd	Wtd	Unwtd	Wtd	Unwtd	Wtd	Unwtd	Wtd
Total Sample	12627	12108	16678	15138	18436	15830	18924	18916	16662	16662	16524	16524	18267	18267	18348	18348	16947	16947
Sex:																		
Male	5799	5571	7999	7241	8449	7358	8603	8779	7889	7778	7935	7744	8775	8725	8979	8828	8106	8074
Female	6371	6100	7924	7257	9188	7850	9416	9266	8139	8232	7874	8078	8752	8865	8610	8788	8160	8227
Race:																		
White	**	**	12933	11796	13818	12240	14663	14847	13432	13299	12894	12846	13625	13985	13753	13887	12697	12806
Black	**	**	1806	1716	2500	1938	2205	2096	1617	1742	1939	2098	2495	2265	2203	2080	2191	2067
Region:																		
Northeast	3014	2695	4034	3570	4760	3959	4841	4607	3926	4016	4281	3877	4269	4290	4719	4741	4130	4056
North Central	3951	3832	5098	4687	5697	4758	5576	5411	5385	4874	4340	4873	5069	5484	5223	5383	4245	4784
South	3366	3857	4177	4597	4908	4820	5566	6292	4713	5055	4667	5049	5513	5600	5191	5551	5522	5434
West	2296	1724	3369	2284	3071	2294	2941	2605	2638	2717	3236	2726	3416	2893	3215	2672	3050	2673
College Plans:																		
Complete 4 yrs	**	**	7963	6994	8933	7407	9264	8844	8571	8203	9191	8658	10256	9878	9851	9360	9342	9062
None or under 4 yrs	**	**	7179	6877	7764	7048	7857	8413	6715	7063	5995	6578	6486	7008	6971	7507	6214	6555
Illicit Drug Use:																		
None	4329	4400	6532	6091	6672	5878	6400	6595	5426	5654	5322	5591	5954	6148	6157	6328	6001	6082
Marijuana Only	2044	1894	3950	3457	4955	4050	5354	5214	4756	4610	4480	4357	4313	4179	4127	4040	3657	3599
Few Pills	1163	1113	1942	1736	2173	1813	2329	2304	2171	2168	2150	2104	2297	2306	2449	2439	2308	2315
More Pills	2157	1989	3427	2987	3857	3266	3906	3885	3622	3543	3873	3760	4972	4925	4896	4839	4333	4306
Any Heroin	231	216	319	268	321	280	289	302	193	186	186	180	183	189	212	210	210	206

*The number of cases shown for 1975 is based on Forms 2 through 5 only, because the data from Form 1 are intentionally not included in tabulations based on drug and demographic items which appeared in all forms.

**Missing data problems were severe for race and college plans in 1975; accordingly, these data have been excluded from all tables in the 1975 report.

TABLE B-2
Sample Sizes (Unweighted and Weighted) in Subgroups by Year
for Questions on a Single Form*

| | Number of Cases | | | | | | | | | | | | | | | | | |
| | Class of 1975 | | Class of 1976 | | Class of 1977 | | Class of 1978 | | Class of 1979 | | Class of 1980 | | Class of 1981 | | Class of 1982 | | Class of 1983 | |
	Unwtd	Wtd	Unwtd	Wtd	Unwtd	Wtd	Unwtd	Wtd	Unwtd	Wtd	Unwtd	Wtd	Unwtd	Wtd	Unwtd	Wtd	Unwtd	Wtd
Total Sample	3157	3027	3336	3028	3687	3166	3785	3783	3332	3332	3305	3305	3653	3653	3670	3670	3389	3389
Sex:																		
Male	1450	1393	1600	1488	1690	1472	1721	1756	1578	1556	1587	1549	1755	1745	1796	1766	1621	1615
Female	1593	1525	1585	1451	1838	1570	1883	1853	1628	1646	1575	1616	1750	1773	1722	1758	1632	1645
Race:																		
White	**	**	2587	2359	2764	2448	2933	2969	2686	2660	2579	2569	2725	2797	2751	2777	2540	2561
Black	**	**	361	343	500	388	441	419	323	348	388	420	499	453	441	416	438	413
Region:																		
Northeast	754	674	807	714	952	792	968	921	785	803	856	775	854	858	944	948	826	811
North Central	988	958	1020	937	1139	952	1115	1082	1077	975	868	975	1014	1097	1045	1077	849	957
South	842	964	835	919	982	964	1113	1258	943	1011	933	1010	1103	1120	1038	1110	1104	1087
West	574	431	674	457	614	459	588	521	528	543	647	545	683	579	643	534	610	535
College Plans:																		
Complete 4 yrs	**	**	1593	1399	1787	1481	1853	1769	1714	1641	1838	1732	2051	1976	1970	1872	1868	1812
None or under 4 yrs	**	**	1436	1375	1553	1410	1571	1683	1343	1413	1199	1316	1297	1402	1394	1501	1243	1311
Illicit Drug Use																		
None	1082	1100	1306	1218	1334	1176	1280	1319	1085	1131	1064	1118	1191	1230	1231	1266	1200	1216
Marijuana Only	511	474	790	691	991	810	1071	1043	951	922	896	871	863	836	825	808	731	720
Few Pills	291	278	388	347	435	363	466	461	434	434	430	421	459	461	490	488	462	463
More Pills	539	497	685	597	771	653	781	777	724	709	775	752	994	985	979	968	867	861
Any Heroin	58	54	64	54	64	56	58	60	39	37	37	36	37	38	42	42	42	41

*The Ns given here are very close approximations of the N in the given subgroup for any of the five different questionnaire forms used in the year.

**Missing data problems were severe for race and college plans in 1975; accordingly, these data have been excluded from all tables in the 1975 report.

Further Applications of these Design Effects and Sampling Errors

One of the reasons for providing the above review of the factors influencing design effects and confidence intervals, and the procedures used in computing our confidence interval tables, is to provide sufficient background and data to permit the interested reader to go beyond the material provided in Appendix A. In this section we consider two specific extensions, the calculation of levels of "statistical significance" higher than 95 percent and the computation of means and their confidence intervals.

Calculating Confidence Intervals for Higher Levels of Statistical Significance. The entries contained in Tables A-1 and A-2 provide the 95 percent confidence level (also referred to as the .05 level of significance). These entries were computed by multiplying the standard error (square root of sample variance) by a factor of 1.96. The 99 percent confidence interval (.01 level of significance) uses a factor of 2.58 standard errors, and the 99.9 percent confidence interval (.001 level of significance) uses a factor of 3.29 standard errors. To convert the entries in Tables A-1 and A-2 to these higher levels, it is necessary only to multiply the entries by the appropriate constant shown below (keeping in mind that any other adjustments required in the tables must also be applied):

Confidence Interval	Significance Level	Multiply entries in Tables A-1 and A-2 by the following:
99%	.01	2.58/1.96= 1.32
99.9%	.001	3.29/1.96= 1.68

Computing Means and Their Confidence Intervals. Many of the questionnaire items included in this volume have ordinal response scales (e.g., agree, agree mostly, neither, disagree mostly, disagree), and it is often the case that a survey analyst will be willing to treat such scales as if they involved equal intervals. In such cases, means and standard deviations are more "efficient" in their use of information than are dichotomies which yield a single percentage or a pair of percentages (e.g., those who respond "agree" or "agree mostly," versus all others). It is a relatively straightforward matter to compute means and standard deviations for the total sample or any of the subgroups treated in this volume. The problem, then, is to be able to specify confidence intervals for the means, or for the differences between pairs of means. In the case of simple random samples, one needs only the means, standard deviations (or variances), and numbers of cases in order to compute confidence intervals. But in complex samples such as the present one,

it is also necessary to take account of design effects. If an estimate of design effect is available, one of the simplest procedures to follow is to divide the actual numbers of cases by the design effect (thereby "depreciating" the actual number to its equivalent value in simple random sample terms) and then employ the standard statistical procedures which have been developed for application to simple random samples. Thus, for example, if the design effect (DEFF) for a sample of 18,000 were 4.0, then one could divide the 18,000 by 4.0 and the result, 4,500, could be entered as the value of "N" in statistical tables and formulas designed for use with simple random samples. To take another example, if one were comparing means based on two subgroups, each involving about 9,000 cases, and if DEFF (for both subgroups) was 2.0, then one could compute the significance of the difference between the two means as if the N for each group were 4,500 (i.e., 9,000 divided by 2.0).

In short, the strategy involves dividing the actual number of cases by the appropriate DEFF in order to get a "simple random sampling equivalent N" or, more simply, an "effective N" for use in statistical procedures designed for random samples.

Design Effects for Use in Computing "Effective Ns." In order to employ the strategy outlined above, one must have estimates of design effects which are judged to be appropriate for one's purposes. In the case of means based on the percentages reported in this volume, we are confident (based on personal communications with Kish) that it is appropriate to use the same DEFF values as were used in developing Tables A-1 and A-2. For other, more complex statistics, we cannot make the same assertion, although it is generally the case that design effects for such statistics are not larger than those for means and percentages (Kish and Frankel, 1970; Frankel, 1971).

In Table B-3 we provide guidelines for computing DEFF values for single percentages (or means) and for differences between two percentages (or means). For reasons discussed elsewhere in this appendix, we must provide for different (and somewhat higher) DEFFs for "segregated" subgroups (regional subgroups and sometimes also blacks), and for trends over two or more years (in contrast to one-year trends). And in all instances, of course, the DEFF values are very much influenced by the average size of sampling clusters, which is always dependent on the number of cases (N). Accordingly, all of the design effect formulas in Table B-3 require computations which take account of N. (It should also be noted that the formulas in Table B-3 correspond exactly to the values of design effects and adjustment factors used in Tables A-1 and A-2 in Appendix A.)

A Concluding Note. In their very useful paper dealing with sampling errors for fertility surveys, Kish

Table B-3
Guidelines for Computing Design Effects (DEFFs) for Percentages
and Means Derived from Monitoring the Future Samples

DEFINITIONS

$$\text{DEFF (design effect} = \frac{\text{estimated sampling variance}}{\text{expected sampling variance from simple random sample with same number of elements}}$$

N = number of respondents on whom a single percentage or mean is based

$\overline{N} = 2N_1N_2/(N_1 + N_2)$, for use in comparisons of two percentages or means, based on two groups of sizes N_1 and N_2.

DESIGN EFFECT FORMULAS

1. For single percentages or means involving . . .
   a. regional subgroups or blacks
      DEFF for single form data ....$(1.3 + .00015N)(1.21)$
      DEFF for five form data ....$(1.3 + .00015N)(1.78)$

   b. all other subgroups or total sample
      DEFF for single form or five form data ....$1.3 + .00015N$

2. For comparisons between . . .
   a. any two regions
      DEFF for single form data ....$(1.3 + .000075\overline{N})(1.32)$
      DEFF for five form data ....$(1.3 + .000075\overline{N})(2.25)$

   b. blacks and whites
      DEFF for single form data..$1.3 + .000075\overline{N}$
      DEFF for five form data ....$(1.3 + .000075\overline{N})(1.56)$

   c. genders, college plans groups, or any two "drug use" subgroups
      DEFF for single form or five form data ....$1.3 + .000075\overline{N}$

3. For one-year trends involving . . .
   a. any region
      DEFF for single form data..$1.3 + .000075\overline{N}$
      DEFF for five form data ....$(1.3 + .000075\overline{N})(1.56)$
   b. all other subgroups or total sample
      DEFF for single form or five form data ....$1.3 + .000075\overline{N}$

4. For trends over two or more years involving . . .
   a. any region
      DEFF for single form data..$1.3 + .000075\overline{N}$
      DEFF for five form data ....$(1.3 + .000075\overline{N})(1.82)$
   b. all other subgroups or total sample
      DEFF for single form data..$1.3 + .000075\overline{N}$
      DEFF for five form data ....$(1.3 + .000075\overline{N})(1.32)$

et al. (1976) commented that some of the methods they used ". . . emerged after several false starts." They went on to say that the volume and diversity of the data they were dealing with ". . . presented new challenges and opportunities." And they added, "Our methods are subject to further developments and modifications, and we invite participation and suggestions" (p. 10). Our own attempts to apply the methods of Kish and his colleagues to the data reported in this volume have been challenged by the diversity of the data, have involved several false starts, and we hope are subject to further developments and modifications. We invite readers to offer their suggestions, and we also encourage readers to inquire about further work that we and/or others may carry out during the coming months and years.

Appendix C
Questionnaire Covers, Instructions, and Sample Page

monitoring the future

a continuing study of the lifestyles and values of youth

This questionnaire is part of a nationwide study of high school seniors, conducted each year by the University of Michigan's Institute for Social Research. The questions ask your opinions about a number of things — the way things are now and the way you think they ought to be in the future. In a sense, many of your answers on this questionnaire will count as "votes" on a wide range of important issues.

If this study is to be helpful, it is important that you answer each question as thoughtfully and frankly as possible. All your answers will be kept strictly confidential, and will never be seen by anyone who knows you.

This study is completely voluntary. If there is any question that you or your parents would find objectionable for any reason, just leave it blank.

In a few months, we would like to mail each of you a summary of the nationwide results from this study. Also, in about a year we would like to mail another questionnaire to some of you, asking about how your plans have worked out and what's happening in your lives.

In order to include you in these mailings, we ask for your name and address on a special form at the end of this questionnaire. This form is to be torn out and handed in separately. Once the address form and the questionnaire have been separated, there is no way they can be matched again, except by using a special computer tape at the University of Michigan. The only purpose for that tape is to match a follow-up questionnaire with this one.

Other seniors have said that these questionnaires are very interesting and that they enjoy filling them out. We hope you will too. Be sure to read the instructions on the other side of this cover page before you begin to answer. Thank you very much for being an important part of this project.

INSTITUTE FOR SOCIAL RESEARCH
THE UNIVERSITY OF MICHIGAN
ANN ARBOR, MICHIGAN

INSTRUCTIONS

1. This is not a test, so there are no right or wrong answers; we would
    like you to work fairly quickly, so that you can finish.

2. All of the questions should be answered by marking one of the answer spaces.
    If you don't always find an answer that fits exactly, use the one that comes
    closest. If any question does not apply to you, or you are not sure of what it
    means, just leave it blank.

3. Your answers will be read automatically by a machine called an optical mark
    reader. Please follow these instructions carefully:

    • Use only the black lead pencil you have been given.

    • Make heavy black marks inside the circles.   These kinds of markings
                                                          will work: ●   ◖   ⬤

    • Erase cleanly any answer you wish to change.

    • Make no other markings or comments on the   These kinds of markings
      answer pages, since they interfere with the   will NOT work: ⊙   ✸   O
      automatic reading. (If you want to add a
      comment about any question, please use the
      space provided below.)

(THIS SPACE FOR WRITTEN COMMENTS)

WHY YOUR NAME AND ADDRESS?

As we told you earlier, we'd like to send you a summary of the nationwide results of the present study, and in about a year we want to mail a shorter questionnaire to some of you. In order to include you in these follow-ups, we would like to have an address where information will be sure to reach you during the coming year.

HOW IS CONFIDENTIALITY PROTECTED?

- The information on this page will be used ONLY for mailing, and will always be kept separate from your answers. A special Grant of Confidentiality from the U.S. government protects all information gathered in this research project.

- The questionnaire and address pages will be collected separately, sealed immediately in separate envelopes, and sent to two different cities for processing.

- Once a questionnaire and address page have been separated, there is no way they can be matched, except by using a special computer tape at the University of Michigan. That tape contains the two DIFFERENT numbers that appear on the back of this address page and on the back of the questionnaire. These numbers will be used ONLY to match a follow-up questionnaire with this one.

> Before filling out this address page, please separate it from the rest of the questionnaire by FOLDING ALONG THE PERFORATED LINE AND TEARING CAREFULLY.

Please **PRINT** your name and the address where you can most likely be reached during the coming year.

Mr.
Miss
Ms. _____
Mrs.   FIRST NAME   INITIAL   LAST NAME

STREET _____

CITY _____

STATE _____ ZIP _____

TELEPHONE NO.   (   ) — _____
                    AREA

In case we should have trouble getting mail to you, if you move, please **PRINT** the name and address of one other person (with a different address than your own) who will know where to reach you in the future. (Examples of such a person: aunt or uncle, older sister or brother, or close friend.)

Mr.
Miss
Ms. _____
Mrs.   FIRST NAME   INITIAL   LAST NAME

STREET _____

CITY _____

STATE _____ ZIP _____

TELEPHONE NO.   (   ) — _____
                    AREA

THANK YOU AGAIN FOR YOUR HELP

PART A

* **BEFORE BEGINNING BE SURE YOU HAVE READ THE INSTRUCTIONS ON THE COVER.**

1. Taking all things together, how would you say things are these days–would you say you're very happy, pretty happy, or not too happy these days?

   ○ Very happy
   ○ Pretty happy
   ○ Not too happy

2. Some people think a lot about the social problems of the nation and the world, and about how they might be solved. Others spend little time thinking about these issues. How much do you think about such things?

   ① Never
   ② Seldom
   ③ Sometimes
   ④ Quite often
   ⑤ A great deal

3. Of all the problems facing the nation today, how often do you worry about each of the following? (Mark one circle for each line.)

	Never	Seldom	Sometimes	Often
a. Chance of nuclear war	①	②	③	④
b. Population growth	①	②	③	④
c. Crime and violence	①	②	③	④
d. Pollution	①	②	③	④
e. Energy shortages	①	②	③	④
f. Race relations	①	②	③	④
g. Hunger and poverty	①	②	③	④
h. Using open land for housing or industry	①	②	③	④
i. Urban decay	①	②	③	④
j. Economic problems	①	②	③	④
k. Drug abuse	①	②	③	④

4. How well do you think your experiences and training (at home, school, work, etc.) have prepared you to be a good. . .

	Poorly	Not So Well	Fairly Well	Well	Very Well
a. ...husband or wife?	①	②	③	④	⑤
b. ...parent?	①	②	③	④	⑤
c. ...worker on a job?	①	②	③	④	⑤

5. Apart from the particular kind of work you want to do, how would you rate each of the following settings as a place to work? (Mark one circle for each line.)

	Not At All Acceptable	Somewhat Acceptable	Acceptable	Desirable
a. Working in a large corporation	①	②	③	④
b. Working in a small business	①	②	③	④
c. Working in a government agency	①	②	③	④
d. Working in the military service	①	②	③	④
e. Working in a school or university	①	②	③	④
f. Working in a police department or police agency	①	②	③	④
g. Working in a social service organization	①	②	③	④
h. Working with a small group of partners	①	②	③	④
i. Working on your own (self-employed)	①	②	③	④

6. If you were to get enough money to live as comfortably as you'd like for the rest of your life, would you want to work?

   ① I would want to work
   ② I would not want to work

—1—

References

Adelson, J. "What Generation Gap?" *New York Times Magazine.* January 18, 1970, pp. 1–11.

Adelson, J. "Adolescence and the Generation Gap." *Psychology Today*, February 1979, pp. 33–37.

Bachman, J.G., and Johnston, L.D. "The Monitoring the Future Project Design and Procedures," (Occasional Paper #1). Institute for Social Research, The University of Michigan, Ann Arbor, 1978.

Bachman, J.D., and Johnston, L.D. "The Freshmen, 1979." *Psychology Today*, September 1979, pp. 79–87.

Bachman, J.G.; Johnston, L.D.; and O'Malley, P.M. "Smoking, Drinking, and Drug Use Among American High School Students: Correlates and Trends. 1975–1979." *American Journal of Public Health* 71 (1981):59–69.

Bachman, J.G., and O'Malley, P.M. "When Four Months Equal a Year: Inconsistencies in Students' Reports of Drug Use." *Public Opinion Quarterly* 45 (1981):536–548.

Bachman, J.G., and O'Malley, P.M. "Yea-saying, Nay-saying, and Going to Extremes: Are Black-White Differences in Survey Results Due to Response Styles?" *Public Opinion Quarterly*, 48 (1984):409–427.

Bachman, J.G.; O'Malley, P.M.; and Johnston, J. Youth in Transition, Volume VI: *Adolescence to Adulthood — A Study of Change and Stability in the Lives of Young Men.* Ann Arbor: Institute for Social Research, The University of Michigan, 1978.

Dearman, N.B., and Plisko, V.W. *The Condition of Education.* (National Center for Education Statistics). Washington, D.C.: U.S. Government Printing Office, 1982.

Frankel, M.R. *Inference from Survey Samples: An Empirical Investigation.* Ann Arbor: Institute for Social Research, The University of Michigan, 1971.

Hays, W.L. *Statistics for the Social Sciences* (2nd ed.). New York: Holt, Rinehart, & Winston, 1973.

Johnston, L.D. *Drugs and American Youth.* Ann Arbor: Institute for Social Research, The University of Michigan, 1973.

Johnston, L.D.; Bachman, J.G.; and O'Malley, P.M. *Drug Use Among American High School Students, 1975–1977* (National Institute on Drug Abuse). Washington, D.C.: U.S. Government Printing Office, 1977.

Johnston, L.D.; Bachman, J.G.; and O'Malley, P.M. *Drugs and the Class of 1978: Behaviors, Attitudes, and Recent National Trends* (National Institute on Drug Abuse). Washington, D.C.: U.S. Government Printing Office, 1979(a).

Johnston, L.D.; Bachman, J.G.; and O'Malley, P.M. *1979 Highlights: Drugs and the Nation's High School Students, Five Year National Trends* (National Institute on Drug Abuse). Washington, D.C.: U.S. Government Printing Office, 1979(b).

Johnston, L.D.; Bachman, J.G.; and O'Malley, P.M. *Highlights from Student Drug Use in America: 1975–1980* (National Institute on Drug Abuse). Washington, D.C.: U.S. Government Printing Office, 1981.

Johnston, L.D.; Bachman, J.G.; and O'Malley, P.M. *Student Drug Use in America, 1975–1981.* (National Institute on Drug Abuse). Washington, D.C.: U.S. Government Printing Office, 1982.

Johnston, L.D.; Bachman, J.G.; and O'Malley, P.M. *Student Drug Use, Attitudes and Beliefs: National Trends 1975–1982.* (National Institute on Drug Abuse). Washington, D.C.: U.S. Government Printing Office, 1983.

Johnston, L.D.; O'Malley, P.M.; and Bachman, J.G. *Highlights from Drugs and American High School Students, 1975–1983.* (National Institute on Drug Abuse). Washington, D.C.: U.S. Government Printing Office, 1984.

Johnston, L.D.; O'Malley, P.M.; and Eveland, L.K. "Some Preliminary Results from Drugs and American Youth II: A Longitudinal Resurvey." (Interim report to the National Institute on Drug Abuse). Ann Arbor: Institute for Social Research, The University of Michigan, 1975, Mimeograph.

Kish, L. *Survey Sampling.* New York: John Wiley & Sons, 1965.

Kish, L., and Frankel, M.R. "Balanced Repeated Replication for Standard Errors." *Journal of the American Statistical Association* 65 (1970):1071–1094.

Kish, L.; Groves, R.M.; and Krotki, K.P. *Sampling Errors for Fertility Surveys* (Occasional Papers Series No. 17). Voorburg, The Netherlands: International Statistical Institute, 1976.

U.S. Bureau of the Census, *Current Population Reports.* Series P-20, No. 319, School enrollment — social and economic characteristics of students, October 1976. Washington, D.C.: U.S. Government Printing Office, 1978.